Text, Cases & Materials on

PUBLIC LAW &
HUMAN RIGHTS

Second Edition

Cavendish
Publishing
Limited

London • Sydney • Portland, Oregon

Text, Cases & Materials on
PUBLIC LAW &
HUMAN RIGHTS

Second Edition

Helen Fenwick, Professor in Law, University of Durham

Gavin Phillipson, Lecturer in Law, University of Durham

Cavendish
Publishing
Limited

London • Sydney • Portland, Oregon

Second edition first published in Great Britain 2003 by
Cavendish Publishing Limited
This edition reprinted 2006
by Routledge-Cavendish
2 Park Square, Milton Park, Abingdon, Oxon OX14 4RN

Simultaneously published in the USA and Canada
by Routledge-Cavendish
270 Madison Avenue, New York, NY 10016

Routledge-Cavendish is an imprint of the Taylor & Francis Group

© Fenwick, Helen and Phillipson, Gavin   2003
Reprinted   2004
Reprinted   2005
Reprinted   2006

British Library Cataloguing in Publication Data
Fenwick, Helen
Public law and human rights: texts, cases and materials – 2nd ed.
1 Public law – Great Britain
I Title   II Phillipson, Gavin
342.4´1

Library of Congress Cataloguing in Publication Data
Data available

ISBN 1-85941-655-1
ISBN 978-1-85941-655-6

7 9 10 8

Typeset by Phoenix Photosetting, Chatham, Kent
Printed and bound in Great Britain
Biddles Ltd, King's Lynn, Norfolk

To Paul and
to Shazia

The constitution of the United Kingdom is currently one of the most dynamic and controversial areas of law and practice to study and debate: the Blair government was elected on a manifesto promising the most radical and far-reaching package of constitutional reform in the 20th century, and, many would say, since the Great Reform Act of 1832. Much of that programme has now been implemented: devolution to Scotland, Wales and Northern Ireland and London; reform of the House of Lords (although this process has been only partially completed); the introduction of the Freedom of Information Act 2000 and of the Human Rights Act 1998, which incorporates the European Convention on Human Rights into domestic law, giving this country its first real Bill of Rights. The devolution process is still on-going: proposals for English Regional Assemblies have been published, while the Northern Ireland settlement remains suspended and subject to further modification at the time of writing. This book aims to help the reader develop an informed critical insight into this reform programme through both a detailed consideration of the reforms themselves and an exploration of the historical roots and contemporary understandings of the constitutional arrangements in the UK. As this book went to press, the abrupt announcement of proposals to abolish the office of Lord Chancellor and establish a new Supreme Court (see further below) has given powerful proof that the process of radical constitutional reform is far from exhausted.

It is widely recognised that any worthwhile study of this area of law requires perusal of a wide selection of materials lying beyond the law's domain; this is partly because large areas of the British constitution remain regulated, or at least strongly influenced, by conventions and shared understandings. Furthermore, this prevalence of non-legal rules in the constitution means that it is necessary to seek the views of those with first hand knowledge or specialist expertise in the contentious areas: civil servants, MPs, government ministers, Ombudsmen, experts in public administration, as well as judges, barristers and academics. Thus the material in this book includes articles from journals on politics and administration as well as law, and extracts from reports of parliamentary committees as well as from the law reports.

The main aim of the book is to cover the areas that students of public/constitutional and administrative law would normally encounter in their studies; however, it also contains material that would facilitate study or enquiry at other levels. In particular, its strong coverage of the Human Rights Act and that Act's impact on freedom of expression, police powers and public order law would make it useful reading for civil liberties courses, while it has sufficiently in-depth coverage of judicial review to make it a helpful supplementary text on administrative law courses. The depth of coverage of these areas is, we believe, unique in a book of this type. Due to the wide selection of views and expertise which the book presents, it is hoped that it will find a readership beyond students of the law; anyone concerned with our system of government, public administration, constitutionalism or the state of liberty in this country will, we hope, find something of interest to them here.

Books of this type vary considerably in the amount of authorial input they contain. Some are literally just a collection of various materials, with virtually no commentary by the authors. Others contain almost equal amounts of authorial and source material. We have attempted to steer a middle course between these two extremes. In particular, the topics covered are presented in a structured way, with authorial introductions to the different sections, and a clear ordering of the different issues raised. Additionally, fairly extensive commentary is provided, which not only explains basic issues where this is appropriate, but also provides additional insights and information, and in places takes a clear stance in an ongoing debate. Questions designed to provoke a critical and sceptical approach to the existing conventional and legal order are also included. To assist in encouraging such an approach, a variety of critical views are presented. Whilst the predominant ideological thrust of the authorial and source material is firmly within the tradition which Martin Loughlin has labelled 'liberal normativism', a conscious attempt has been made to give some space to the views of republican and functionalist critics of the more familiar liberal and conservative paradigms, especially in Part I.

This first part of the book explores basic concepts and principles of constitutionalism, using a strongly comparative approach, and examines how far the view that the UK is radically out of step with such principles requires modification in the light of the constitutional transformation outlined above. The three key devolution settlements are sketched here, with discussion of the consequent evolution of the UK towards a form of quasi-federalism. The peculiar prominence of constitutional conventions within the UK constitutional order is considered in a separate chapter. The European Convention on Human Rights (ECHR) has already had a considerable impact on the traditionally fuzzy separation of powers between executive and judiciary in the UK (most latterly in *R v Secretary of State for the Home Department ex parte Anderson* [2002] 3 WLR 1800), and the independence of the latter (*Starrs v Ruxton* 2000 SLT 42), and this process is given particular prominence in Chapter 3, as is the continuing evolution of the basic principles of the Rule of Law, also now strongly influenced by the ECHR. Parliamentary sovereignty, including its historical and theoretical background, is examined in Chapter 4; challenges to traditional notions of sovereignty posed by the notion of common law fundamental rights as well as by the Human Rights Act 1998 (HRA), are closely analysed. In particular, the decision in *R v A (No 2)* [2002] 1 AC 45; [2001] Cr App R 21 is given detailed coverage. A separate chapter is devoted to the impact of the European legal order on sovereignty, with particular prominence given to the analysis proffered by Laws LJ in *Thoburn v Sunderland City Council* [2002] CMLR 50.

Part II traces the rapid growth in the power and influence of the supranational European institutions and legal instruments, including the European Convention on Human Rights. Chapter 1 presents a clear exposition of the principles governing implementation of European law in Member States, including analysis of the relevant parts of the treaties, and close consideration of direct and indirect effect, the *Francovich* principle and developments in what has been termed the 'triangular' effect of directives. The reception of these principles by UK courts is given separate consideration, with particular focus on the decision in *Factortame (No 4)* [2000] 1 AC 534. Chapter 2 is devoted to analysis of the ECHR. The chapter considers whether the already significant influence of the Convention on the law of the contracting states may be consolidated and augmented due to its increasingly close relationship with the European Union. The Convention has been of considerable importance as a means of raising human rights standards in the UK. However, it has now assumed much greater significance since it was given further effect in UK law under the Human Rights Act 1998. The significance of this radical change in the protection of human rights in the UK is explored in Part VI Chapter 1 and therefore this chapter should be read alongside that part.

Part III examines the changing role of Parliament, with a strong focus on the on-going process of reform within both Houses. The first chapter on the House of Commons considers its overall role within the context of the party and electoral system. The parliamentary debates of spring 2003 on war with Iraq are used to illustrate the paradox of the largely quiescent chamber that yet retains the potential to act as a powerful check, or even threat, to the government of the day. The first main section then considers its legislative role, and in particular, recent innovations in terms of pre-legislative scrutiny and the time-tabling of Bills. The second section examines the Commons' efforts to scrutinise the executive, with particular reference to the reforms of the Select Committees in 2002, and their growing importance within the Commons. The House of Lords is dealt with in a separate chapter; the peculiar value of its legislative work is illustrated in particular by detailed consideration of its role in amending the Anti-Terrorism, Crime and Security Bill 2001. Around half of the chapter is devoted to consideration of reform of the Lords: analysis of issues arising from the proposals of Wakeham, the Public Administration Select Committee and the Joint Committee on Lords Reform in 2002 and 2003 are placed firmly in a comparative context through extensive consideration of second chambers overseas. Particular emphasis is laid upon the arguments surrounding the composition of the House, the method of appointing any nominated members, and the powers of any new second chamber.

Chapter 3 deals with the issues raised by parliamentary privileges and standards, with particular reference to the important report of the Joint Committee on Parliamentary Privilege (1999) and the on-going input of the Committee on Standards in Public Life. Two key areas are given particular prominence. First, the chapter explores the now highly politicised issue of standards in public life, and the ongoing evolution of standard-setting and enforcement mechanisms, in particular the relaxation of the rules relating to members' interests and conduct agreed by the Commons in May 2002 and the compatibility of procedural aspects of self-regulation with Article 6 ECHR. Secondly, we examine freedom of speech: recent case law in this area, including *Al-Fayed v Hamilton* [2001] AC 395, and the impact of the Defamation Act 1996 are subjected to particularly critical scrutiny.

Part IV, on the Central Executive, Powers and Accountability, commences with a chapter on prerogative powers, in which particular emphasis is placed on recent case law on judicial control of the prerogative and the impact of the HRA. Chapter 2 examines first the system of Cabinet government and collective responsibility, looking in particular at innovations towards a stronger centre of government under Blair and his sidelining of Cabinet; the convention of collective responsibility is also analysed, with reference to the resignations of Robin Cook and Clare Short in 2003. The second part of the chapter looks at the main mechanism for ensuring the accountability of central government: ministerial responsibility. A comprehensive analysis of the 'new' doctrine of ministerial responsibility originally advanced under the Major government is attempted and the extent of the duty not to mislead Parliament is subjected to sustained analysis in the light in particular of the findings of the Scott Enquiry in 1996.

The third chapter in Part IV gives extensive consideration to access to government information. In contrast to nearly all modern democracies, the UK had until recently no freedom of information legislation, whilst the government retained extensive powers to punish those who make unauthorised disclosures of information. The Chapter begins by considering the changing and yet unchanged face of official secrecy in the UK and gives lengthy consideration to the House of Lords' decision in *R v Shayler* [2003] 1 AC 247, since it demonstrates that the inception of the Human Rights Act is unlikely to have much impact on official secrecy despite its impact on freedom of expression. The chapter proceeds to consider the doctrine of public interest immunity, including the impact of the Scott Report, and moves on to the radical change brought about in access to official information by the introduction of the Freedom of Information Act 2000 (FoI Act). The Act, which affords UK citizens, for the first time, a right of access to information held by 'public authorities' is afforded extensive coverage, since it represents, potentially, such an important change in the accountability of the state and public sector bodies. The operation of the voluntary code on access to government information introduced by the Major government of 1992–97, is also considered in some detail since until the FoI Act 2000 comes fully into force in 2005 it represents the main means of obtaining access to official information.

Part V provides an introduction to key areas of administrative law. In Chapter 1, the procedural issues relating to judicial review are subjected to detailed analysis in the light of the introduction of CPR, Part 54, with particular reference to the controversial doctrine of procedural exclusivity and the likely spill-over impact of the HRA on the test for amenability of public bodies to review. Chapter 2 examines the principles of judicial review. All the key principles are covered: particular emphasis is placed upon areas of current controversy and change, including review for error of fact, innovations in the duty to give reasons (eg, *Stefan v GMC* [1999] 1 WLR 1293), the emerging doctrine of substantive legitimate expectation (*ex parte Coughlan* [2002] 2 WLR 622) and developments in the rule against bias driven by Article 6 ECHR, in particular the decision in *Porter v Magill* [2002] AC 357 as well as *Locabail* [2000] 2 WLR 870. A section is devoted to discussion of the possible development of proportionality as a free-standing head of review (*R (on the application of Daly) v Secretary of State for the Home Department* [2001] 2 AC 532). Chapter 3 examines the work and evaluates the effectiveness of the parliamentary and local Ombudsmen; the proposals for reform set out in the recent Cabinet Office paper, *Review of the Public Sector Ombudsmen in England* (2000), are given particular prominence.

Part VI gives extensive consideration to the very significant changes in the protection of human rights that have come about since the first edition of this book was published. The Labour government came to power in 1997 with a manifesto which promised, as part of its radical programme of constitutional change, the introduction of the Human Rights Act 1998 as the means of receiving the ECHR into domestic law. The purpose of Part VI is to examine key aspects of the protection of civil liberties in Britain in the light of the impact of the Human Rights Act. Part VI, Chapter 1 examines the Human Rights Act itself in detail and goes on to give extensive consideration to the early, highly significant decisions on it, including *R v A (No 2)* [2002] 1 AC 45; *Brown v Stott* [2001] 2 All ER 97; *S and W (Children) (Care*

Orders) [2002] 2 AC 291; *Daly* [2001] 2 AC 532; *Donoghue* [2001] 4 All ER 604; *Alconbury* [2001] 2 WLR 1389.

The further three chapters in Part VI cover, respectively, freedom of expression, freedom of protest and assembly, police powers and suspect's rights. The topics chosen within these areas and the emphasis placed on them highlight those issues which are of particular significance at the present time, including increases in police powers, erosion of safeguards for suspects and limitation of the freedom to protest. Prominent decisions in these fields, including *Pro-life Alliance v BBC* [2002] 2 All ER 756; *DPP v Jones* [1999] 2 AC 240; *Ashworth Hospital Authority* [2001] 1 WLR 515, are given extended coverage. The chapters consider in detail the extent to which the Convention rights protected under the Act can be afforded real efficacy in the face of a range of rights-invading laws including those recently created by the Terrorism Act 2000, the Police and Criminal Justice Act 2001 and the Anti-Terrorism, Crime and Security Act 2001. The extensive consideration of the state of the freedoms of expression and assembly in the UK and of suspects' rights seeks to make the argument that at the very beginning of the HRA era the danger of a decrease in state accountability and the creation of merely empty or tokenistic guarantees is apparent.

As this book went to press, in June 2003, came the announcement of the abolition of the historic office of the Lord Chancellor, the removal of the Law Lords from the House of Lords and their establishment in a separate Supreme Court, the establishment of an independent judicial appointments commission, of a new Ministry for Constitutional Affairs and the abolition of the offices of Secretary of State for Scotland and Wales. This startling new package of reforms came too late to be covered by this book but a few comments on them can be made here. Essentially, these reforms are aimed at curing a cluster of anomalies in the UK constitution, which together represent quite serious violations of the separation of powers doctrine: once the reforms are in place, we will no longer have a powerful Cabinet Minister (the Lord Chancellor) sitting in our highest court (the House of Lords); our top judges (the Law Lords) will no longer sit in the second chamber of Parliament; our senior judges will be appointed by a body independent of the executive, instead of by one of the most senior members of it (the Lord Chancellor) and their institutional independence will thereby be significantly enhanced. These reforms should therefore be borne in mind, in particular, when reading Part I Chapter 3, parts of which, by highlighting the above anomalies, provide in effect at least some of the arguments in favour of these reforms. For preliminary comment on the reforms, see A Le Sueur, 'New Labour's next (surprisingly quick) steps in constitutional reform' [2003] PL 368.

We would like to thank our partners and family for their support and encouragement during the writing of this book. Cara Annett and Ruth Massey of Cavendish Publishing have been invariably enthusiastic and shown great patience and flexibility during the book's long evolution. We would also like to thank all owners of copyright material who have given their permission to include such material in this book.

The law is stated as at 1 April 2003 but it has been possible to include some later material.

Helen Fenwick

Gavin Phillipson

1 July 2003

CONTENTS

PART II EUROPEAN LAW & INFLUENCE

PART III PARLIAMENT AND ITS REFORM

TABLE OF CASES

TABLE OF STATUTES

TABLE OF STATUTORY INSTRUMENTS

TABLE OF EUROPEAN LEGISLATION

TABLE OF INTERNATIONAL LEGISLATION

PART I

CONSTITUTIONAL FUNDAMENTALS

CHAPTER I

CONSTITUTIONAL THEORY AND THE BRITISH CONSTITUTION AFTER DEVOLUTION

INTRODUCTION

In Part I, the nature of constitutions in general is considered and the UK constitution is placed in this context. The impact of the Blair government's extensive programme of constitutional reform upon traditional ways of examining the UK's uncodified constitution will also be touched on. These reforms constitute by far the greatest change to the UK constitution in the 20th century. The most important parts of that package are: the incorporation into domestic law of the European Convention on Human Rights (ECHR) (see Part II Chapter 2) by the Human Rights Act 1998 (HRA) (see Part VI Chapter 1); devolution to Scotland, Wales, Northern Ireland (considered in this Chapter) and London (further English devolution in the form of directly elected Regional Assemblies is promised); reform of the House of Lords (of which only stage one – the removal of most of the hereditary peers and the rebalancing of party numbers in the House – has been completed) (see Part III Chapter 2); the Freedom of Information Act 2000.[1] The other chapters in Part I concentrate on five aspects of the British constitution: its unusually heavy reliance on constitutional conventions; the rule of law; the separation of powers; parliamentary sovereignty. To an extent, therefore, this first chapter serves to introduce themes examined in more detail in subsequent chapters.

FUNDAMENTAL IDEAS IN CONSTITUTIONAL THEORY

We might begin by asking what is the basic purpose of a constitution. One influential answer, at least in Western constitutional thought, has been that constitutions are necessary in order to control the power of the state; another strand in that train of thought emphasises the role constitutions play in ensuring that that power derives from a legitimate source. On the one hand, it tells us how power may be used; on the other, from where it should derive. To the first idea may be attributed the notions of the Rule of Law, and the separation of powers, whilst the second is clearly related to the notion of democratic legitimacy. It is clear that there can be a tension between these two basic ideas. The following extract portrays that tension at work in history.

> **Francis Sejersted, 'Democracy and the Rule of Law: some historical experiences of contradictions in the striving for good government', in J Elster and R Slagstad (eds), *Constitutionalism and Democracy* (1988), pp 131–33**
>
> The Rule of Law and democracy correspond to the two different concepts of liberty: the negative, which makes liberty dependent on the curbing of authority; and the positive, which makes it dependent on the exercising of authority. These two concepts of liberty are, according to Isaiah Berlin, 'two profoundly divergent and irreconcilable attitudes to the ends of life'. Each of them

---

1   For a recent account of developments relating to this reform package, see R Hazell, M Russell, J Croft, B Seyd and R Masterman, 'The constitution: rolling out the new settlement' (2001) 54 Parl Aff 190.

have, however, 'an equal right to be classed among the deepest interests of mankind' (1958, pp 51–52) ... Is there really such a contradiction between democracy and the Rule of Law?

Democracy and Rule of Law can be seen as two different means of overcoming the inherent contradiction between state and society. State-building is necessary to society, but also represents a threat. Rule of Law was meant to curb state authority, while democracy was meant to mobilise society in the exercising of state authority. This contradiction between state and society must have been strongly felt in the centuries following the Renaissance. There was a need for peace, order and public security, and it went along with a general distrust of human nature. Man was governed by passions and could not withstand the temptations of power. On the other hand there was a growing belief in the possibility of constructing a state where the power was bound and the passions were kept under control. This was the basis for all the intellectual energy which was put into the constitutionalist philosophy of that time. There were two main trends, the one recommending mixed government which opposed power with power, and the other recommending a Separation of Powers. The fundamental trait the two trends had in common was a purely negative approach to the exercise of power. This rather intense process of ideologisation seems to be important as a driving force behind the 'spontaneous outbreak of constitution-making' in the late 18th and early 19th century in the American states and in Europe. This 'conservative element' is now commonly seen as an important element in the American Revolution. Although the European case is not so clear, it seems as if the general tendency in this time of revolutions was the same, namely to block power rather than to take power. Hannah Arendt has argued that the constitutions were not the result of revolutions. 'Their purpose was to stem the tide of revolution' (1963, p 143). It is certainly true that constitution-making could have this counter-revolutionary appearance. In the American Revolution it seems, however, to have been weak, and this is also the case in Norway. Constitution-making was not a reaction to a revolutionary situation; if anything, it was a revolution in itself, directed against the power of the king and furthered by the openness of the situation. The point is that constitution-making was directed against the power of the state, no matter who held power – a king or a democratically elected assembly.

Notes

1   Carl Schmidt argued that the attack on state power represented by liberal constitutionalism was aimed at securing two principle ends: first, certain guarantees of freedom, that is, as Rune Slagstad puts it,[2] 'freedom from state interference'; secondly, a degree of stability and permanence, achieved by basing the constitution on a written document which is more difficult to amend than normal legislation. It is noteworthy that Schmidt includes in his list of freedoms guaranteed, both negative (civil) liberties and the positive right to 'a minimum of popular participation in the legislative process'.[3] Whilst on the one hand, participation in law-making can protect the participator from the power being exercised, it also gives him the opportunity to wield power, thereby giving him the means both to change his own life and to impact on the lives of others. It does not therefore seem particularly helpful to analyse the right to legislative participation as a negative 'freedom from' state interference. Sejersted's analysis seems to unpack the values underlying liberal constitutionalism more helpfully.

2   If guarantees of freedom and institutionalised stability are, as Schmidt contends, the two hallmarks of Western liberal constitutional theory, it is worth noting as an initial observation that neither of them can be found in the formal structure of the

2   We follow here Slagstad's exposition of Schmidt's thought, in 'Liberal constitutionalism and its critics: Carl Schmidt', in J Elster and R Slagstad (eds), *Democracy and Constitutionalism* (1988). The quotes in the text are at p 104.
3   Quoted *ibid*.

British constitution. While the UK now has the Human Rights Act 1998 (HRA), which gives UK citizens the ability to enforce in national courts the rights set out in the European Convention on Human Rights (ECHR), first of all, legislation which clearly infringes the Convention rights must be upheld as still enforceable and of full effect despite its rights-infringing nature, and secondly, the HRA itself may be repealed by ordinary Act of Parliament at any time (see the last section of this chapter).

3   Constitutions, on the above account, are faced with a fairly Herculean role. To be able to function, they evidently need to be seen as both legitimate and authoritative. How can they lay claim to such attributes?

Harry Calvert, *British Constitutional Law* (1985), pp 4–5, 7, 8, 9, 14–15

So far as is known, the constitution of Al Capone's gang has never been published. Yet it undoubtedly had one. It probably contained little more than the basic rule or norm that 'what Big Al says, goes' and, in exercise of this 'authority', Big Al no doubt authorised lieutenants to issue instructions and to order that double-crossers be rubbed out. The appearances are that the Papa Doc regime in Haiti and Idi Amin's regime in Uganda functioned in much the same way.

They headed regimes which, for a while, and within the confines of the immediately pressing political environment, functioned effectively. Whether the Al Capone gang and the modern nation-state differ in other respects is something we must now consider.

It is tempting to seek to distinguish between 'proper' constitutions and other regimes of organisation. In much the same way that we all know an elephant when we see one without necessarily being able to proffer a very good definition of it, so also do we not all recognise a 'proper' state, 'properly' constituted when we see it? The Capone gang clearly fails; Papa Doc and Idi Amin were mere ephemeral aberrations. If there is such a distinction, however, wherein does it lie?

Suffice it to say for the present, that if the legality of the source of a constitution were the criterion of its validity, it would be a brave man who would assert that the UK has ever had a valid constitution. The modern constitution dates (with a few minor quibbles) from the revolution of 1688. Prior to that, the history of England at least is one of dubious claims to title to the Crown, conquests, schisms and broken treaties all offering extremely unsure ground on which to base a legal title.

. . .

So, legality of source will not serve to distinguish between 'proper' and 'improper' constitutions. Such a criterion condemns the constitutions of most of the world's oldest and most stable societies. What clearly is illustrated is that a regime illegal in its origins may nevertheless, in some mysterious way, come to generate its own legality. In international law, this event may be prompted by 'recognition' which, according to some schools of thought, confers legality whilst, according to others, merely declares a legality deriving otherwise. Within the 'state', and after a coup d'état purporting to establish a new constitution but without any initial basis in legality, the courts sometimes come to acknowledge the new 'validity' and consequent legality and offer a variety of reasons for so doing (see, eg, *The State v Dosso* 1958 SC 533, *re Pakistan*). It will not do, however, to regard such decisions as constituting the legality of the new regime, as opposed merely to accepting it as a pre-existing fact. If we do so, we get into all sorts of logical difficulties – whence comes the authority of the court to constitute? Can it really be the case that a constitution firmly in place nevertheless remains invalid pending the caprice of an application to the courts?

Perhaps the distinction is best sought elsewhere. If we are not to look to the pre-existing legal order for validity, perhaps we should look to another source. It is an established historical fact that the constitutions of many modern states were specifically adopted as constitutions intended and resolved to act as the foundation for the new order. There is a superabundance of such instances. Most of the old Commonwealth countries still have, as their constitutional cases, Acts of the old imperial Parliament – here legality and specific adoption meld. In the case of some newer Commonwealth countries, as in the case of the USA, a new constitution has been promulgated without regard for the pre-existing legal order but in title of some asserted natural right so to do. In some cases, such as that of the Republic of Ireland (formerly the Irish Free State) an old constitution has legitimately spawned a newer one. Even in the case of the UK, it may be possible to conjure such an instance out of the legislation of the revolutionary 'Parliament' of 1688–89 and the later Acts of Union with Scotland and Ireland.

In all cases of specific adoption, it is possible to point to a constitutional instrument of some sort. Whilst this is an extremely common phenomenon, however, it does not seem to be absolutely necessary. A few of the world's acknowledged states boast no such instrument yet it would be hard to deny any constitutional function for them. It is normal to rank the UK amongst them for, in truth, the legislation referred to above hardly amounts to a written constitution as the term is usually understood.

. . .

Lawyers tend to yearn for legal criteria, and constitutional lawyers, or at least some of them, would like to be able to say when a constitution is 'in force'. This may be a practical problem where they have had to decide whether or not to regard a new regime as valid. The insuperable problem is, however, that there is no legal system to which one can refer for such questions. *Ex hypothesi*, the legality of a constitution cannot be found within itself. International law purports to offer criteria but they are inapt for the present purpose. Recognition, by which international law purports to confer or endorse constitutional validity, has frequently been withheld for long periods from 'states' undoubtedly functioning under constitutions of one sort or another. Constitutions are simply facts. As facts, we may well make all sorts of intelligent speculations about their origins, functions and prospects. A constitution may simply develop, or be imposed or adopted. It may regulate state activity in a variety of ways. It always stands to be overthrown; how likely this is depends upon how precariously it is in place.

For one interested in studying the function of rules as regulating political behaviour within a state, the only relevant question is: 'Is a given constitution effective in this respect?' Effectiveness and stability are both greatly enhanced by acquiescence – the more the people (who are the potential rebels) are content with the existing regime, the more likely it is to remain in charge. To the extent that acquiescence is lacking, force is necessary. Recognition by other states may make economic and political life somewhat easier for the regime in question but will have only a marginal effect upon its stability. Little more can be said.

Questions

1   On Calvert's account it appears that, in the last resort, constitutional legitimacy is parasitic upon efficacy and acquiescence. Is it therefore the case that, if the Capone gang had eventually become so powerful that it defeated the US government and its agents and took effective control over the US, the rules governing the gang would (if Capone had so wished) have become its constitution?

2   Does it follow that if, as in the case of the US, it is not possible to derive the legitimacy of the constitution from a pre-existing legal system, it is necessary to fall back immediately upon the criterion of actual effectiveness? Does such a criterion give the citizens of the state concerned any reasons to abide by the provisions of the constitution, other than practical ones?

Note

Calvert concludes that the notion of the applicability of a constitution comes down to the social fact of the obedience of the citizens to the relevant state. But it may then be asked, for what reasons do citizens give their loyalty to a state? In liberal theory, citizens consent to be governed by the (liberal) state because they recognise the justice and fairness of the state's arrangements, which also serve their own rational self-interest;[4] indeed the essence of liberal theory lies in the notion that the state can and must command such allegiance without itself espousing any substantive theory about how citizens should lead their lives or what kinds of goals and activities are most worthwhile.[5] It is the fairness of the state in guaranteeing the equal freedom of citizens to pursue their own conceptions of the good which ensures its citizens' loyalty.[6]

CONSTITUTIONAL VARIETY: CLASSIFICATION AND CONTENT

Constitutions can be classified in a number of ways. One distinction often made is between written and unwritten constitutions. Calvert considers the significance of such a distinction below, together with the 'rigid'/'flexible' division.

Harry Calvert, *British Constitutional Law* (1985), pp 9–12

'Written' and 'unwritten' constitutions are often considered to be of two radically different kinds, and it is customary, in discussing constitutions in general, to labour the distinction between them. Commonly, as is stated below, they have distinctive features, but the essential difference between them is nevertheless formal rather than substantial. Take, for example, the differences between the constitutions of the UK and the USA.

So much of the constitution of the UK as is in writing hardly amounts to a written constitution, for too much is omitted. Consider the question whether our courts may strike down, as invalid, an Act of Parliament, commonly a very important function discharged in, for example, the USA by its Supreme Court. We would search in vain for any formal written statement of the position in this respect so far as the UK's constitution is concerned. Written statement says neither that the courts may, nor that they may not, undertake this task. It is left to the courts themselves, as authors of the common law, to declare that they may not, a position progressively arrived at as a result of slow development over centuries.

We would, however, search the written constitution of the USA equally vainly. It has never been denied that the USA functions under a written constitution, yet the fundamentally important power which the Supreme Court exercises to declare invalid laws which transgress the constitution is nowhere written into it. Rather it derives from what the Supreme Court itself has perceived to be the inherent logic of the constitutional structure of the USA – since the constitution of the USA does impose limitations upon legislative power, the Court is confronted by the necessity to choose between enforcing the superior constitutional, or the inferior law and, as a matter of logic, it does the former. The logic is not actually compelling, for a constitution can, and some constitutions do, vest such a function elsewhere, or even state explicitly that the limitations imposed are for guidance only. The function of judicial review on grounds of constitutionality is a later development of the constitution of the USA which has come to be accepted. It is not part of it.

---

4   See generally John Rawls, *A Theory of Justice* (1973). The statement in the text represents of course only the most simplified indication of Rawls' theory. It is from the hypothetical choices of rational, self-interested men (temporarily deprived of the knowledge of their own abilities, position in life and substantive moral convictions) that, in Rawls' theory, the constitution of a just state is framed.

5   This particular aspect of liberal theory has been emphasised most strongly by Ronald Dworkin: see his 'Taking rights seriously', in *Taking Rights Seriously* (1977) and 'Liberalism', in *A Matter of Principle* (1985). The liberal state does of course impose on its citizens the requirement that they must not infringe each other's liberties.

6   Theorists on the Left postulate more pragmatic reasons for such loyalty, such as the ability of the state to supply the material needs of its citizens, especially the poorest, who might otherwise threaten the existing order: for discussion, see Rodney Barker, 'Obedience, legitimacy and the state', in C Harlow (ed), *Public Law and Politics* (1986), pp 4–9.

If we were to study a sample of written constitutions in their socio- and politico-historical contexts, we might well conclude that a 'written' constitution is, in many cases, if not all, no more than a frame in a film. It will have historical antecedents, often of a customary sort and may, indeed, amount to no more than the codification of pre-existing constitutional practice. Then the written constitution itself will come to function as the substructure on which the later developments, essentially customary in character, are built. It would be pressing the argument too far to argue that there is no difference between a written and an unwritten constitution, for the statement, in written form, of a constitution will often crystallise the then existing state of affairs and a peculiar sanctity may well come to attach to it, inhibiting later customary development to some extent. The difference remains, nevertheless, one of degree rather than of kind. The dustbins of history are full of constitutional instruments, which were denied change, adaptation and development according to customary processes. They became obsolete, were replaced and discarded.

One common feature of written constitutions may offer us a criterion whereby to distinguish between regimes such as that of Al Capone or Papa Doc and others. Written constitutions are commonly 'rigid' or 'semi-rigid' in terms, ie, they are explicitly stated to be unchangeable, or able to be changed only by resort to extraordinary processes of amendment. An amendment may require, for example, to be accepted by popular referendum or by a two-thirds majority in a popular assembly. Although in practice most written constitutions are at least semi-rigid, it is not inherently necessary that they should be so; a written constitution could be, and some are, totally flexible, ie able to be changed by ordinary legislative processes. In this latter case, such a constitution would differ from that of a state such as the UK which is supposed to have an unwritten constitution, only in that at one fleeting moment in history, there would be a constitutional text contained in a single instrument. To say of the constitution of the UK that it is unwritten is, therefore, merely to say that its text is not to be found (and, possibly, never was to be found) in a single document, and that is to say very little of any substantial importance about it . . .

Social change is a part of human history and if an organised society is to survive as such, its constitution must be adaptable and sensitive at least to the great tides of social change. A flexible constitution is, by definition, freely adaptable. Beyond that, however, the danger is of making a virtue of necessity. Because we have a flexible constitution (and perhaps also because in some quarters the myth prevails that there is no mechanism by which we could adopt a rigid constitution if we wanted to), we tend to assume that is a good thing in itself. The danger here is that of mistaking the reasons for the present relatively smooth functioning of the existing constitution. If our flexible constitution is working apparently well, not because of any inherent virtue of its own but merely because at this stage in our history we have no need to rely upon it, we are living in a fool's paradise and are no more secure, in the final analysis, than were the members of Al Capone's gang . . .

Notes

1   As Calvert usefully points out, the distinction between flexible and rigid constitutions is rather more important in practice than between unwritten and written. More useful ways of distinguishing between constitutions lie in the following: whether the executive and legislative sources of power in the country are separate (as in the USA) or fused; whether the constitution is flexible, that is, changeable like ordinary law, or inflexible, requiring special procedures; whether the state is unitary – controlled by one, sovereign legislature – or federal, in which there are separate spheres of power in the state, with the central government being unable to legislate in areas reserved to the regions. John F McEldowney, adopting Professor KC Wheare's classifications[7] (similar to those listed by Calvert), finds that 'it is at once apparent that the UK has a unitary, flexible constitution whose powers are fused'.[8]

---

7   KC Wheare, *Modern Constitutions* (1966), pp 4–8.

2   The *content* of constitutions, and their level of detail, tends to vary greatly as well. The following extract from a well-known work outlines the nature and content of four constitutions: those of the Russian Federation (RF), the United States, France and the Federal Republic of Germany (FRG).

SE Finer, V Bogdanor and B Rudden, *Comparing Constitutions* (1995), Chapter 2 (extracts)

Amendment

The provisions on the means by which a constitution may be amended are of both juridical and political importance, they are themselves an exercise of the constituent power in spelling out how its own creation may be changed; they divide the amending power among people, legislature, and executive, or between a federation and its components; and they may express basic values. The last are revealed in those features stated to be unamendable: the republican form of government in France, and in Germany the basic human rights and the federal structure.

In the USA, amendments require a special majority in Congress followed by ratification by three-quarters of the states. The last amendment dealt with members' salaries and was adopted in 1992; the 'equal rights amendment' has not yet succeeded. The French provisions give the President a certain leeway. The amendment bill must be passed by both Houses, but he or she may then either put it to the people or resubmit it to both Houses of Parliament convened together in one body (called Congress), in which case it requires three-fifths of the votes cast....

. . .

By contrast to this process, and mindful of the Weimar provisions for referendum and initiative (which were alleged to have assisted the rise of Hitler), the German Constitution does not involve the people at all in the amendment procedure, but requires a special majority of each House. A similar method used to be employed to amend the previous Soviet and Russian constitutions. But this proved very easy for a body which, under Party rule, had long been accustomed to enthusiastic unanimity, and the years of *perestroika* saw the enactment of hundreds of amendments in the Union and the Republic constitutions. The new text makes the process much more difficult. Nothing is utterly immune from change, but amendments to the basic state structure, the Bill of Rights, and the amendment provisions themselves can be achieved only through the adoption of an entirely new constitution by a constitutional convention or referendum (art 135). The rest of the constitutional machinery can be changed only with the consent of at least two-thirds of the component members of the Federation (art 136).

. . .

General features

The American constitution is very brief. The founders' determination to limit government, both in range and procedure, explains the design of its first three articles, each devoted to a separate branch of federal power, and all interlocking with a system of checks and balances designed to ensure that neither legislature nor executive acquires undue might.... The brevity of the American text is largely offset by its age, by the accretions of customary procedures in the legislative and executive branches, and of course by the enormous achievements and awesome responsibility of the judicial branch of government.

. . .

The ... fundamental concerns of the Basic Law in the FRG are federalism and democracy, both victims of the unitary centralized state which Germany became after 1933. Consequently the text

8   John F McEldowney, *Public Law* (1994), p 4.

spells out and guarantees two main sets of rights: those of the Federation *vis-à-vis* the Länder and vice versa, and those of the people *vis-à-vis* the state. The essentials of both are, as it were, engraved for ever in provisions whose substance is immutable: according to art 9(3) (the 'perpetuity clause') the principles of art 1 (basic human rights) and art 20 (a democratic and social *federal* state) may not be amended. This is, at least in formal terms, quite different from the position elsewhere: in the UK a parliamentary majority (of votes cast) is sovereign; in the USA and Russia no part of the constitution is declared to be unamendable (although there are procedural safeguards of varying strength); while in France only the republican form of government is immune from alteration (art 89, final paragraph).

. . .

The Russian Constitution was born amid the ruins of the Soviet Union as a political entity, and of communism as a political creed. Just as Western economic institutions have been adapted to a post-socialist context, so the constitution shows traces of Western texts. It begins, of course, with 'We the . . . people', and art 1(1) describes the state as 'democratic, federative, law-governed and republican' – all epithets which echo the German art 20. Art 3 locates sovereignty in the people and – like art 3 of the French text – alludes to its direct expression via referendum . . . The first chapter's sixteen articles spell out the principles of human rights, federalism, the social state, and the separation of powers, enshrine private property of land and other natural resources, and recognize ideological diversity. They end by making the rest of the constitution subject to the principles enunciated in that first chapter.

USA

The American constitution created a federal Union. Secession was neither permitted nor forbidden, but South Carolina's attempt to leave triggered the Civil War of 1861–5. The Congress of the United States was given a list of matters on which it might legislate. The states were told that there were certain things they could not do. Everything else was, according to the Xth Amendment, 'reserved to the States respectively or to the people'. But Congress was given the important powers 'to regulate commerce with foreign nations and among the several states' and to make all laws 'necessary and proper' to carry out its tasks. In this way, the federal competence has grown enormously, although it is worth remembering that a constitutional amendment (the XVIth) was needed in order to permit a federal income tax. The Constitution is declared to be the supreme law of the land and so, in case of conflict, overrides any other federal or state provision. Nonetheless, it should be emhasized that, where the states have jurisdiction, this extends to all branches of government, legislative, executive, and judicial. One result of this is the fifty different versions of the basic areas of criminal and civil law (property, succession, contract, and the like).

FRG

By contrast with the US text, the provisions dealing with the German federal structure are both lengthy and complex. The Länder have general legislative competence, but there is a list of exclusive federal powers, and a longer list of powers in art 74 which are described as 'concurrent' (a better rendering would be 'alternative'). . . . The provisions for the Land exercise of governmental powers and execution of federal laws (arts 30, 83) mean that – unlike the situation in the USA – there are few federal agencies, and no first or second-instance federal courts within the Länder. Although in theory the Länder have the general residual legislative power, federal law is supreme, and the erosion of local competence has provoked much discussion . . .

Russian Federation

. . . Of the many problems facing [Russia], the most intractable is surely the fact that it resembles the Roman Empire in the number and complexity of its ethnic components and in their cultural, linguistic, and social diversity. At the same time a 'Russian problem' stems from the Tsarist legacy, the decades of 'democratic centralism', the Russians' numerical supremacy, and the fact that Russia is the *de facto* heir to the USSR's capital city and much of its capital resources.

... There are twenty-one republics, each with its own constitution and legislature. Broadly speaking, this title is accorded to nations which are fairly numerous in population (such as the six million Tatars in the East of European Russia) and which usually make up a majority of the inhabitants of their traditional territory. The lower status of region is accorded to six areas ranging from Krasnodar in the Caucasus to Khabarovsk in the Far East; then come the numerous provinces, the cities of Moscow and St. Petersburg, and the autonomous districts – a status allocated to smaller nations living within a larger, often non-Russian, group. Each of these components is entitled to send two representatives to the Upper House of the legislature, the Federation Council.

As in the German Basic Law, the RF constitution goes on to list a large number of matters within the exclusive federal jurisdiction, and a number of matters within the joint jurisdiction of the RF and its components (arts 71–2). Everything else is for the latter, but within areas of exclusive or joint jurisdiction, federal law is supreme (art 77) and, under the transitional provisions, the RF constitution itself prevails over any conflicting provisions of the various internal federative treaties signed during 1992. . . .

Governance

The 1789 French Declaration proclaimed that a society which lacked the separation of powers had no constitution at all. All the states dealt with in this book have, to a greater or lesser extent, adopted the principle; the latest convert – after seven decades of denial – is the Russian Federation (art 10). In the United Kingdom, however, the principle refers mainly to the independence of the judiciary. Executive and legislative powers are at least as closely fused today as they were when Bagehot published *The English Constitution* in 1867.

Political parties find no formal mention in the US Constitution. Given the Nazi law of 1933 which permitted only one party in the Third Reich, it is not surprising that they are specifically mentioned in art 21 of the FRG Constitution (and can be ruled unconstitutional). They appear also in the French and Russian texts. . . .

USA

The American Constitution devotes each of its first three articles to a separate branch of government. Legislative powers are vested in a bicameral Congress whose members are elected. The House of Representatives is composed of members apportioned among the states and elected for two years. Each state is represented by two senators, elected for a term of six years, and cannot be deprived of this right without its consent. The Lower House exemplifies the principle of the representation of individuals, the Upper House that of the representation of the geographical units comprising the Federation. The equality of representation in the Senate is, of course, out of all proportion to the size or population of the different states, . . . The Houses are equal in that both must concur to pass any law unlike, for instance, the position in Germany, France, Russia, and the UK where the Upper House may, in certain circumstances be overruled by the Lower.

The executive power is vested in a President, elected (in formal terms by an electoral college) for four years, who may not serve more than two terms. The Vice-President is elected in the same manner but separately. The American (and French and Russian) President can be removed only by impeachment, a process in which the legislature becomes the court. The President selects his or her own cabinet, but presidential appointments require confirmation by the Senate. He or she may veto bills, but can be overruled by special majority of the legislator. Conversely, he or she has to persuade Congress to enact his or her own agenda into legislation.

In short, the main features of the presidential form of government as developed in the USA are the following. The President combines ceremonial status and political power. Legislature and executive are elected separately and for different terms, which means that the President may be of one political party and the majority of the legislature of another. The USA is well accustomed to this while, in the 1980s and 1990s, the French Constitution proved able to withstand the strain of *cohabitation* between a socialist President and a legislative majority of the right. The presidential system gives the chief executive length of tenure and wide control over subordinates. Furthermore, since the US executive is no part of Congress, there is little temptation for the latter to federalize the whole system and to overlook states' rights. The legislature cannot remove the President save by impeachment, in which the Lower House lays the charge and the Upper House tries the case.

RF

The new Russian structure embodies several of these features, but expands the presidency in a number of ways. First, the office does not seem to exercise merely the executive power. Although art 10 recites the traditional triad of separate powers, the following article suggests there are four, for it says that state power is exercised by the President, the Federal Assembly (clearly the legislature), the government (executive), and the courts (judiciary). And art 110 states that executive power is exercised by the government, consisting of its chair, vice-chairs, and ministers. Second, following a tradition going back to the Tsars, the office of the President is given wide power to rule by edict (*ukaz*). Apart from the need to comply with the constitution and with federal legislation, this power seems virtually unlimited (art 90). Third, the President appoints the prime minister (with the consent of the Lower House). Fourth, the President seems to be able to dismiss the government, although the Russian is ambiguous, meaning both resignation and dismissal (arts 83(c), 117(2)). As in the USA, the Russian President may veto legislation, but can then be overriden by special majority (art 107(3)). Finally, the President can dissolve the lower House and call new elections if it thrice rejects his or her candidate for premier (art 111), or if it passes a motion of no confidence in the government (art 117(3)(4)).

FRG

...

Because of its federal structure, Germany has always had a bicameral system. The Bundestag, the Lower House, is elected by popular vote for a four-year term. In contrast to the provisions under both the Empire and Weimar, it can be dissolved only under the very exceptional circumstances of arts 63 and 68. The Upper House (Bundesrat) is selected by neither direct nor indirect elections. It is made up of sixty-eight members nominated by the sixteen Land governments, who are in effect delegants of the government rather than of the people or of the Land legislature. Unlike the US Senate, the number – and voting power – of the members (three, four, or five) depend on the population of the Land they represent.

Legislation is by joint action of both Houses, although – as elsewhere – most bills are introduced by the government. The Bundesrat has an absolute veto in certain cases and can otherwise, in the last resort, merely suspend the passage of legislation. Bills duly passed go to the President for formal signature and counter-signature of the Chancellor.

The office of President, allegedly abused by Hindenburg after 1930, is shorn of authority and preserved only as that of a largely ceremonial Head of State. The President is no longer directly elected by the people, but indirectly by a Federal Convention of members of the Federal and Land legislatures. He or she is not in charge of the armed forces, and has no emergency powers; appoints the federal judges and ministers, but does not select them and ratifies international Treaties, but usually only with the consent of the legislature. Like other Heads of State, the President's duties include the formal assent to federal statutes: but this is valid only on countersignature by the Chancellor.

It is this latter office which carries the real power of Head of Government, and the Chancellor is – in legal terms – rather better protected than the British Prime Minister. The President must appoint to the office the person who obtains a majority of the votes of the members of the Bundestag. Only if no one has such a majority may the President choose whether to appoint the person with a majority of the votes cast or to dissolve the Bundestag. Once installed, the Chancellor nominates and demotes ministers (whose formal appointment and dismissal are for the President) and is well-protected against a 'no confidence' defeat in the legislature. It is not enough for the Bundestag to outvote him; a majority of the members must agree on the alternative Chancellor. Thus 'unnatural' combinations of left and right may defeat a Chancellor but they will not force a resignation as they could in the Weimar Republic. . . .

There is no unlimited power in the executive to dissolve the Bundestag and call an election. On the other hand, the Chancellor may use the 'no confidence' procedure in order to demonstrate ability to govern with authority. If his or her motion for a vote of confidence fails, the President may be asked to dissolve the Lower House; and the only way the Bundestag can stop this is by promptly electing another Chancellor by a majority of its members. This device was used by Willy Brandt after an unsuccessful attempt to oust him in 1972. He put a motion of confidence to the Bundestag, planning to lose it, asked the President to dissolve Parliament, and won the next election. . . .

France

The French system has features of both the presidential and the parliamentary models. . . . The President is far from being merely a titular Head of State. Since 1962 he or she is directly elected by the people, has arbitral powers under art 5, and emergency powers under art 16, and signs the regulations emanating from the executive's very extensive lawmaking powers (arts 37, 13). In association with the government he or she can present bills to the people to enact by referendum, thereby bypassing the parliament, and can dissolve the National Assembly and call new elections. By contrast, the legislature is trammeled. Its power to enact laws is laid down in terms not merely or form but of subject-matter, and (under art 41) the government may block any bill which does not fall within the areas listed in art 34. Much of its internal procedure is now defined in the constitution and this gives the Prime Minister and his or her Cabinet great procedural advantages over the Opposition.

. . .

The judicial branch

When it comes to the judiciary, separation of powers is taken quite seriously, although in England this is obscured by the fact that the Upper House of the legislature has the same name as the highest court, and its Speaker (the Lord Chancellor) is the senior judge. In all the systems here dealt with, judges are independent and irremovable. In Russia this is expressly stated, but is a frail novelty. In the USA and UK it is not stated but is the case.

The only topic which merits brief discussion here is the relation between the constitution, the courts, and the legislature. For almost 200 years the USA has led the way in discussion and practice in this area . . . Art VI provides that the Constitution and federal laws made under it and treaties 'shall be the supreme law of the land' and shall bind state judges: thus the supremacy of federal over state law is clearly stated. But nothing expressly subordinates federal legislation to the federal constitution and art III on the judicial power does not in so many words confer jurisdiction to do this. Nonetheless the Supreme Court assumed such a jurisdiction and in 1803 held that 'an Act of the Legislature repugnant to the Constitution is void' (*Marbury v Madison*) As a result, any court of general jurisdiction seems to have power to declare any statute unconstitutional. . . .

The general continental European pattern is much more recent (dating from the 1920s) and tends to differ from the American model in a number of respects. First, the whole topic is expressly dealt with in the constitutional text. Second, the tribunal given a power of constitutional review is quite separate from the ordinary courts of general jurisdiction. Third, and a consequence of this, its jurisdiction is exclusive: other courts cannot decide issues of constitutionality but must, where such questions need to be settled to dispose of the case in hand, refer them to the Constitutional Court. Fourth, process may be instituted in a number of different ways: by ordinary courts in the manner just described; by ordinary citizens complaining that their individual constitutional rights are being infringed by some legislation; by certain high officials (President, Speaker etc.) seeking, in the absence of any particular dispute, to obtain a general and 'abstract' ruling on the constitutionality of a statute; and occasionally the constitutional tribunal is even given the power to review legislation on its own initiative. Finally, the Court's decision that a particular legislative provision is unconstitutional is itself given the force of law so as to bind all courts and officials. The texts printed in this volume adopt varying versions of these features, and add their own particular extensions or limitations.

The German Constitution sets up a Constitutional Court, the name emphasizing its main function ... One most interesting function is that of ruling on the constitutionality of political parties (art 21(2)), though it can be seised only by legislature or government, and has in fact heard only two such cases: in 1952 the neo-Nazi Socialist Reich Party and in 1956 the Communist Party were held to be unconstitutional. It also handles disputes as to jurisdiction between Federal organs (art 93(1)(1) and between Federal and State organs (arts 93(1)(3), 84(4)). At the request of the government or one-third of the Bundestag members, it may rule on the compatibility of legislation with the constitution – and thus does so in the abstract, in the absence of any litigated case. During ordinary lawsuits, however, a German court which thinks that legislation might be unconstitutional, and needs to know in order to decide the dispute before it, must refer the question to the Constitutional Court (art 100). ... A German court may also ask the Federal Constitutional Court whether a rule of international law directly creates rights for the litigants before it (arts 100(2), 25).

In all these types of proceeding, access to the German Constitutional Court is open only to governmental and parliamentary entities and the courts. But a 1969 amendment incorporated in the Constitution an avenue previously opened by statute (art 93.1(4a) and (4b)) whereby anyone who considers that his constitutional rights have been violated by the state may, after exhausting all other legal remedies, file a complaint directly with the Constitutional Court.

In terms of textual appearance, the basic powers of the Russian Constitutional Court are not dissimilar to those of its German counterpart. In terms of political reality, however, it is difficult to see how, after its humiliation by Mikhail Gorbachev's refusal to obey an injunction to appear, and its unconstitutional but effective suspension by Boris Yeltsin, it can readily gain respect.

Just as the French institutional structure is unique, so is its forum for constitutional review. The body in question is, quite deliberately, not established as, or given the name of, a court: it is the Constitutional Council. Its members sit for only nine years, save for ex-Presidents who are *ex officio* members for life. Three of the appointed members are selected by the President of the Republic, and three each by the Speakers of each House. They are not necessarily trained lawyers, but tend to have held high ministerial or academic office.

This forum is an innovation of the Fifth Republic, and its primary functions may be summed up by saying that the Constitutional Council judges only the Parliament; and the Parliament is judged only by the Constitutional Council. ...

The Constitution allows any bill – before promulgation – to be referred to the Council for an assessment of the bill's conformity with the Constitution (art 61 para. 2), and goes on to enact that a provision declared unconstitutional can be neither promulgated nor implemented. ... The Constitutional Council has held a number of bills to be unconstitutional for contravention of human rights and has become, *de facto* if not *de jure*, a constitutional court.

However, the following points need to be stressed. First, statutes which have been promulgated are, as in the UK, entirely immune from constitutional challenge in any jurisdiction whatever. Second, and following from this, ordinary citizens and ordinary courts may not refer matters to the Council. That power is reserved to the President, the prime minister, the two Speakers, and (since a 1974 amendment) any sixty Deputies or Senators. But this last group is, of course, usually the Opposition which frequently refers Government bills in the hope that it will achieve by a lawsuit what it could not attain by a vote. ...

It may finally be worth pointing out that the American-inspired method of permitting an *ex post facto* declaration of unconstitutionality means that statutes can, many years after their enactment and implementation, be held to be null and void. This is costly. By contrast, the French system operates rather like a check on motor-cars before they leave the factory. It is not perfect, since the occasional defective statute may be promulgated without having been referred to the Council. But it is cheap.

. . .

Human rights

The first ten amendments to the US Constitution commit the Union to a respect for certain basic rights, and the XIVth Amendment subjects the states to the same discipline. The rights in question are usually expressed by a negative: Congress shall make no law abridging the freedom of the press; the right to keep and bear arms shall not be infringed; the right to be secure shall not be violated; no person shall be deprived of life, liberty, or property without due process of law; no fact tried by a jury shall be otherwise re-examined than according to the rule of the common law.

The 1789 French Declaration, although somewhat more rhetorical, covers much the same ground and, as we have seen, operates via the 1958 preamble and the powers of the Constitutional Council to restrict the powers of the legislature. The Bill of Rights is deliberately placed at the very beginning of the German constitution (arts 1–19). The rights are acknowledged to be inviolable and inalienable, directly enforceable, and binding on legislature, executive, and judiciary. Furthermore the provisions which describe them are, as we have seen, entrenched against any amendment of their essentials. They are not all, however, expressed in absolute terms. On the contrary, the text seeks to balance the rights of any given individual against those of others, for instance to prevent their being used 'to offend against the constitutional order or against morality' (art 2(1)). But 'the essential content of a basic right may never be encroached upon' (art 19(2)). The society in which these rights are to be enjoyed is that of a representative democracy with separation of powers, described in art 20 as a democratic, social, and federal state in which all state authority emanates from the people, who exercise it by elections and voting and by specific legislative, executive, and judicial organs. Furthermore, the legislator is bound by the constitution, and the executive and judiciary by the law *stricto sensu* – and by justice.

. . . [The rights] are the standard commitments to freedom of personality, belief, expression, assembly, movement, occupation, and property, and the assertion of a right of privacy, of immunity from unauthorized search and seizure, and of a right to judicial protection against the state, the maxim that 'property imposes duties', the guarantee of trade union rights, the provision that the means of production may be nationalized, and the inclusion of the word 'social' in the constitutional description of the state. The Christian heritage ensured that the preamble mentions God, that freedom may not be used to offend against morality, and that the issue of private, including religious, education is fully covered.

. . . But the Bill of Rights is not, and is not intended to be, a set of merely procedural safeguards of the individual. The German constitution is imbued with a ranked set of values of which the most basic is the principle of human dignity, and comes equipped with a unique mechanism for its own and for their protection. Anyone who abuses his or her constitutional freedoms 'in order to combat the free democratic basic order shall forfeit these basic rights' (art 18), and 'all Germans have the right to resist anyone seeking to abolish the constitutional order' (art 20(4)).

The Russian treatment places the Bill of Rights in its second chapter and declares the rights to be directly effective. The core of the list is similar to that found in the 1936 Stalin and 1977 Brezhnev constitutions, and includes numerous claims on the state – to housing, health care, legal aid, and the like. However, the new era is indicated by several provisions such as those ensuring freedom of entrepreneurial activity, private ownership of land, and the right to one's lawful judge.

. . .

THE EXISTENCE AND NATURE OF THE UK CONSTITUTION

The nature and content of the above constitutions give us a useful basis of comparison with the UK constitution. Perhaps the most remarkable characteristic of the UK's constitution is its almost entirely flexible nature. This is reflected in Jennings' vivid description of it as having 'not been made but ... grown' and may be seen in the rather ad hoc mechanisms which the UK government has for dealing with constitutional change, mechanisms that have received greater attention recently, due to the great outburst of reforming activity since 1997.

The Constitution Committee, *Changing the Constitution: The Process of Constitutional Change*, HL 69 (2001–02) (extracts)

7   The onus for proposing significant measures of constitutional change rests, as with any major change in public policy, with Her Majesty's Government ...

8   ... Each proposal is brought to the relevant Cabinet Committee or Sub-Committee for approval. Major issues of constitutional change in the Parliament of 1997–2001 were dealt with by discrete Cabinet Sub-Committees. The unifying element at ministerial level was the Lord Chancellor – who was 'the personification of joined-up constitutional thinking', in the words of one of our number – who chaired all bar one of the Sub-Committees dealing with particular measures of constitutional reform. The membership of the Sub-Committees differed, though there was some overlap. The unifying element at official level was the Constitution Secretariat within the Cabinet Office. This was set up immediately after the general election in 1997 to work alongside departments with lead responsibility for each element in the programme of constitutional reform. It had the task of servicing the collective decision-making necessary to deliver the Government's objectives and a co-ordinating role in bringing together interested departments and ensuring cohesion across the programme as a whole. The Secretariat was headed by a director and had three teams: a devolution, constitutional reform, and Legal Adviser's team. An adviser on parliamentary procedure was also attached to the Secretariat.

9   Following the 2001 general election, the structure of Government changed and a number of responsibilities for constitutional issues were transferred from the Home Office to the Lord Chancellor's Department (LCD). These included responsibility for freedom of information, data protection, the Human Rights Act 1998 and House of Lords reform, as well as advising on Church/State relations and formal contact between HM Government, the Isle of Man Government and the insular authorities of the Channel Islands. The LCD now resembles to a large degree the Ministries of Justice and Constitutional Affairs to be found in other countries. Responsibilities 'to do with the rights of the citizen and the relationship between the citizen and the state which are human rights, freedom of information, data protection, are now brigaded in one department which is also the Ministry of Justice'.

10   The Lord Chancellor has taken over from the Prime Minister as chairman of the Constitutional Reform Policy Committee of the Cabinet. Within the LCD, responsibility for constitutional issues has been assigned to a junior minister. Responsibility for constitutional issues, however, is not exclusive to the LCD. A number are dealt with by other departments, for example the European Union (Foreign Office) and devolution (the Scottish, Welsh and Northern Ireland Offices). The Secretaries of State for these various departments are normally members of the Constitutional Reform Policy (CRP) Committee of the Cabinet. However, responsibility for regional policy – previously within the remit of one department – is now divided among three. There is a separate Regions and Nations Committee of the Cabinet, chaired by the Deputy Prime Minister, on which the relevant ministers serve ...

41   How effective is Government in formulating its measures of constitutional change? In particular, given the number of measures of constitutional reform brought forward by the Government, how able is it to look at these measures in relation to one another?

43 Professor Hazell welcomed the changes that took place in 2001 ... Lord Butler ... and Professor Hennessy referred to the dismantling of the Constitution Secretariat. Lord Butler thought that the Constitution Secretariat 'worked pretty well'. He felt that, with the major reform agenda of the Government being largely completed, the process had worked itself out, with the responsibilities of the Constitution Secretariat taken over by the Home and Economic Secretariat of the Cabinet Office. Though making clear that he was not trying to be critical of the Government's arrangements, he ... went on to say, 'When there was a bespoke Constitution Secretariat in the Cabinet Office, that obviously brought together a great deal of expertise and they would advise specifically on these issues. That has now been dispersed and the Home and Economic Secretariat will not make such a specialisation of this and so the Government will rely more on people in each department who, I hope, will spot the issues which affect them, and bring those to attention' ...

45 The changes in departmental responsibilities are to be welcomed inasmuch as they give greater coherence to Government at departmental level in dealing with constitutional issues. On the surface, they appear to give greater scope for 'joined-up thinking' on constitutional issues. However, we feel we must enter three caveats. The first is the obvious one that, as not all responsibilities for constitutional affairs reside in the LCD, there still needs to be some mechanism for co-ordination within Government. The second is that the creation of the LCD as a Ministry of Justice and Constitutional Affairs was more by accident than design, resulting in a department that comes new to the culture of dealing with issues as 'constitutional' issues. The third flows from the first two. The dismantling of the Constitution Secretariat has removed an important means of utilising experience in this field and of ensuring that linkages are identified and pursued and a source of dispassionate and well informed advice. The first of these three caveats is, we believe, straightforward and requires no further comment. It is the remaining two that we believe deserve further comment.

46 The evidence presented to us suggested that the transfer of responsibility for a number of constitutional issues to the LCD was the product of a desire to tidy up Government and to free the Home Office to concentrate on such issues as law and order and drug enforcement. 'And', as Lord Butler put it, 'the issues which went to the Lord Chancellor's Department, I think – and I do not want to use a pejorative expression – one might describe as rather a "rag bag". They were not issues transferred there in order to give coherent responsibility for constitutional issues'.

47 We share Professor Hazell's concern at the lack of a culture of dealing with constitutional issues. We recognise that bringing together responsibilities for constitutional issues concerned with the citizen is a necessary but not sufficient condition for creating a coherent and effective ministry for constitutional affairs. We note that the Government decide what constitutes a 'constitutional' issue on a pragmatic basis. We have no objection to adopting a pragmatic approach as such. However, that pragmatic approach does nothing to contribute to a culture of discussing the constitution as a constitution.

48 Professor Hazell pointed out that the LCD's website has a promising button headed 'Constitutional Issues' but when you click on to it and go to the Constitutional Policy Division 'you find a wonderful rag-bag of some of the functions that came over from the Home Office ... I applaud the fact that the Lord Chancellor's Department has become in effect the Ministry of Justice and Constitutional Affairs. For the moment I lament that it has not yet fully recognised that or brought together constitutional affairs within the department in a much better integrated portfolio'.

49 This absence of expertise in dealing with constitutional issues as constitutional issues might not be so serious had the Constitution Secretariat of the Cabinet, which embodied such expertise, remained in existence. We are thus in a situation where there is no developed expertise to ensure co-ordination within the LCD and across Government. To repeat Lord Butler's words, one has to 'rely more on people in each department who, I hope, will spot the

issues which affect them, and bring those to attention'. We note, with some concern, that this is an expression of hope.

50 We are thus in a situation where what may be deemed constitutional responsibilities are drawn together within the department of the Lord Chancellor but without the Lord Chancellor having the same degree of institutional support – from the perspective of expertise in the analysis and co-ordination of constitutional issues – that he had in the previous Parliament. The absence of such support may not be so vital in this Parliament as in the last, in that so much of the Government's constitutional reform agenda has been achieved. However, Professor Hennessy argued that what has been carried through is essentially a beginning of a long process of adjustment. That, he said, was the case with devolution, the Human Rights Act 1998 and the Freedom of Information Act 2000. He also noted the need for a civil service bill, to address the issue of Crown Service. 'It is', he said, 'all very messy and too many ministers with a sigh of relief put it all on one side. The unfinished business is enormous.' He went on to argue that 'there are so many other bits of the constitutional settlement that still have to be played with that to reduce it in that way I think is deeply disappointing. If regional Government is going to be one of the last bits of the architecture to be put into place, we have got exactly the wrong configuration for that'.

Notes

1   The above description and analysis indicate clearly the casual and ad hoc nature of the UK's approach to its 'constitution'. In a delightfully revealing passage in the report, the Lord Chancellor said that:

The Government ... do [sic] not have a definition of the constitution and a pragmatic view is taken as to 'whether any particular proposed measure should be regarded as constitutional' [para 60].

2   These features of the UK constitution are brought out in an essay by Barendt, which is cast in the form of a review of Vernon Bogdanor's *Politics and the Constitution* (1996).

E Barendt, 'Is there a United Kingdom constitution?' (1997) 17(1) OJLS 137–46 (extracts)

...

Bogdanor writes in his first essay, *The Political Constitution*, that the Constitution can be reduced to eight words: What the Queen in Parliament enacts is law. Leaving aside the consequences of accession to the European Community, there are no legal constraints on the legislative supremacy of Parliament. The legislature is controlled by the majority political party and every four or five years the electorate. (But provided the consent of the House of Lords is obtained, governments may lawfully postpone elections.) There are in short, as is well known, no legally enforceable guarantees against tyrannical government, or in other words we have what Lord Hailsham (when in opposition) termed an 'elective dictatorship'.

There is a widespread, though not universal, view that this is profoundly unsatisfactory....

Obviously there is a United Kingdom Constitution in some, if not all, of these senses. As Bogdanor, a political scientist, implies in his Introduction, there is clearly a constitution in the sense of a 'power map', outlining where power lies, explaining how it is exercised and so on. This is the constitution in the descriptive sense. There are also laws and decisions of a constitutional character, that is, rules which would form part of a codified constitution for the United Kingdom if it had one. To give just two straightforward examples, the common law concerning the existence and control of the Crown's prerogative powers, and the provisions in the Bill of Rights 1689 vindicating the (legislative) powers of Parliament, are clearly constitutional in substance. Moreover, these principles are normative. They limit the scope of the executive's power to legislate, as the House of Lords held recently in the *Fire Brigades Union* case, and have required the court to determine what counts as an Act of Parliament. So it will not do to say that the terms *constitution* and *constitutional* are only properly used in the United Kingdom in a descriptive sense.

The complaint that there is no Constitution in the United Kingdom either means that only codified constitutions merit this description, or, more seriously, that in the absence of legally enforceable guarantees protecting the freedom of the citizen (and perhaps an effective separation of powers) it is improper to apply the term to our arrangements. The first charge can be dismissed relatively easily. . . .

Much more serious is the point that a constitutional text without legally enforceable guarantees of citizens' freedoms and a proper balance or separation of powers scarcely merits the description of a *constitution*. In contradistinction to the formal argument discussed in the previous paragraph, this is a point about the necessary content of constitutions. As already mentioned, the rise of written constitutions in the nineteenth century occurred to meet the demand for limits on previously absolute government. The development was inspired by the principle of *constitutionalism*, a principle linked to, but significantly different from, those of liberalism and democracy. Liberalism has clearly been concerned among other things with the province of law, but has little to say about the structure of government and the balance of powers. Democracy with its emphasis on majority rule is on one view fundamentally antithetical to the principal demand of constitutionalism, that the concentration of power in the hands of any institution of government is dangerous and that it should so far as practicable be dispersed. Indeed, the separation of powers in some form is arguably the essence of constitutionalism. However, there are plenty of countries which have constitutions but which do not observe the principles of constitutionalism. One-party States where opposition and the press are systematically repressed may still have a text described as 'the constitution'. Such States have what Giovanni Sartori has termed 'nominal' or 'facade' constitutions; the former are perhaps equivalent to Bogdanor's 'power maps', while the latter pretend to guarantee fundamental freedoms, but behind the facade it is a different story, as it was under the constitutions of the Soviet Union. Sartori argues persuasively that the terms 'constitution' and 'constitutional' should be limited to those arrangements which do observe the principles of constitutionalism: 'real' . . . constitutions. Otherwise we must conclude that a tyrannical government behaves constitutionally when it imprisons (or executes) the opposition, provided only it observes the legal forms.

. . .

How should we characterize the UK Constitution? Is it to be viewed now as a 'facade', a curtain behind which some monstrous political melodrama is enacted? Vernon Bogdanor's essays fully chronicle the respects in which our arrangements fail to satisfy the principles of constitutionalism. Power is concentrated in the hands of the Prime Minister and Cabinet, almost always able through party discipline to secure the passage of its legislative programme. The present [Thatcher] Government has removed competing centres of power by abolishing the GLC and the metropolitan borough councils, and elsewhere has significantly cramped the freedom of local authorities. The financing and organization of the political parties, which in government exercise enormous power and influence, is almost entirely unregulated by law. In the final analysis the courts cannot protect fundamental rights when it is the clear intention of Parliament to remove them or to empower ministers to stop their exercise. . . . This looks like a 'facade' constitution. Moreover, its contours are uncertain, as is inevitable with uncodified and to some extent even unwritten arrangements. (Some (alleged) constitutional conventions are reduced to writing only in the texts of constitutional law books.) Dicey would have disagreed with this assessment. Parliamentary supremacy would not in his view lead to authoritarian government because of the internal and external limits on its exercise, the existence of constitutional conventions, and the rule of law doctrine. Conventions ensure the responsibility of Ministers to Parliament, and through the House of Commons to the electorate, a role also discharged by the internal limit that legislation be politically acceptable (or at least not repugnant) to the majority of the public. The rule of law distinguishes proper legislation, Acts of Parliament, from executive decrees and from resolutions of one House.

While the rule of law, for what it is worth, is guaranteed by the courts, Bogdanor is correct to point out that otherwise the values of constitutionalism are protected politically. The existence, scope, and application of conventions are determined by those bound by them, the politicians themselves. As Bogdanor puts it (at 26) '... the peculiarity of the British constitution is that it lacks an umpire. It is the players themselves, the government of the day, who interpret the way in which the rules are to be applied'. Indeed, the rules are made up as the game is played. Hence, Prime Ministers are free to determine when the principles of Cabinet collective responsibility apply, a freedom exploited by both Wilson and Callaghan to allow for dissent among members of their Governments over membership of the European Community. We can be quite sure that if a General Election produces a hung Parliament, politicians will debate in party political terms the appropriate conventions which 'regulate' the discretion of the Queen to choose her Prime Minister.

It would be unjust to Dicey, however, to suggest that he advocated a constitution which violated the very principles of constitutionalism. When he wrote the *Introduction to the Study of the Law of Constitution* in 1885, the principles of balance between, and dispersal of, powers were much better respected than they are a century later. The Monarch enjoyed considerable political discretion, in particular in her choice of Prime Minister, though this was increasingly circumscribed towards the end of the century by party opinion. The House of Lords had the same right to participate in legislation as the Commons, and during the Ulster crisis of 1913–14 George V even contemplated refusing the Royal Assent. The House of Commons quite frequently denied the government the passage of legislation, and the doctrine of ministerial responsibility ensured the accountability of the executive to an often critical legislature.

There was therefore a balance of powers, albeit only a shadow of that which had characterized, say, the seventeenth and eighteenth century constitutions, and of course it could not be enforced by a constitutional court similar to the Supreme Court of the United States. But it would be wrong to underestimate the significance which many still attached to this balance, not only at the end of the nineteenth century, but in the first decade or so of this. The Preamble to the Parliament Act 1911 refers to the eventual replacement of the House of Lords with a popularly elected Second Chamber, hinting at the possible restoration of the power to veto legislation which the house had lost by that measure. Balfour, then Leader of the Conservative Party, George V, and Sir William Anson, all considered the constitution in abeyance until the full check had been restored; further, they considered that as a consequence in the interim the King might be acting constitutionally if he withheld assent to the Ulster Bill. Since the removal of the House of Lords' veto there has been no constitutional check on the supremacy of the House of Commons, in practice the governing political party and its leaders.

...

From a formal perspective, UK constitutional law is a hotchpotch of statutes, case law, and miscellaneous rules (such as the privileges of the Houses of Parliament) which are, it is said, made intelligible by reference to a number of conventions of uncertain scope and inconsistent application. With regard to its substance, the Constitution fails to guarantee fundamental rights such as freedom of speech and the right to a fair trial, and, as Bagehot observed, it is characterized by the fusion, rather than the separation, of powers. Without doubt it fails the test of the French Declaration of the Rights of Man. Yet it seems unhelpful to withdraw from it the title 'Constitution'.

...

Notes

1   It is, of course, the flexibility of the British constitution that is its most remarkable feature. Within the UK there is no written constitution which has a higher status than the rest of the law. The body of rules relating to the structure, functions and powers of the organs of state, their relationship to one another and to the private citizen, is derived from common law, statute and constitutional conventions. Therefore, the constitution does not impose express limits on what may be done by ordinary legislation in the way that many constitutions do. The legislative competence of the UK Parliament is formally unlimited. The lack of any supreme constitutional law means that no Parliament may bind its successors or be bound

by its predecessors and the courts cannot question the validity of an Act of Parliament. Thus, every aspect of the constitution (with the possible exception of parliamentary sovereignty itself (see below, pp 149–67) is subject to change by ordinary Act of Parliament. O Hood Phillips stresses that such flexibility cannot be directly attributable to the (largely) unwritten nature of the UK constitution, pointing out by way of example that 'the constitution of Singapore is written but entirely flexible'.[9]

2   While this radical subjugation of all other aspects of the constitution, however fundamental, to parliamentary sovereignty leads Barendt to conclude only that the UK has an unsatisfactory constitution, some commentators go further.

FF Ridley, 'There is no British constitution: a dangerous case of the Emperor's clothes' (1988) 41 Parl Aff 340, 342, 359–60

Having a constitution seems to be a matter of self-respect; no state is properly dressed without one. Every democracy except Britain, New Zealand and (with qualifications) Israel seems to have a written constitution, plainly labelled. Not to be left out of the world of constitutional democracies, British writers define constitution in a way which appears to give us one too, even though there is no document to prove it. The argument is that a constitution need not be embodied in a single document or, indeed, wholly written. We say instead that a country's constitution is a body of rules – some laws, some conventions – which regulate its system of government. Such a definition does not, however, bridge the gap between Britain and the rest of the world by providing us with a substitute for a documentary constitution: it simply shifts the ground, by using the word in an entirely different way.

We see this ambiguity in KC Wheare's now classic book on constitutions. 'The word constitution is commonly used in at least two senses in ordinary discussion of political affairs. First of all, it is used to describe the whole system of government, the collection of rules which establish and regulate it. These rules are partly legal and partly non-legal. When we speak of the British constitution, that is the normal, if not the only possible meaning the word has.'

Everywhere save Britain the constitution is defined as a special category of law. British usage dissolves the distinction between constitutional law and other laws because British courts recognise no such distinction. British political scientists, for their part, dissolve the distinction between law and other rules of behaviour because they are not much interested in law: for them, the constitution is practice . . .

Use of the word constitution as the manner in which a policy is organised, the main characteristic of its governmental system is undoubtedly the historic one. By the end of the 18th century, however, the word came to have another meaning. The American War of Independence and the French Revolution marked a turning point after which the new meaning became universal, Britain excepted. It applied to a special form of law embodied as a matter of convenience in a single document. As used elsewhere, it is now a term of law not politics. Constitutions therefore have certain essential characteristics, none of them found in Britain. Without these characteristics, it is impossible to distinguish a constitution from a description of the system of government in a way that is analytically precise. Without them, it is impossible to say that a country has a constitution in the current international sense of the word. More important, lest this be thought a linguistic quibble, without them a system of government lacks the legitimacy a constitution gives and a political system the protection it offers.

The characteristics of a constitution are as follows:

(1) It establishes, or constitutes, the system of government. Thus it is prior to the system of government, not part of it, and its rules cannot be derived from that system.

---

9   O Hood Phillips, *Constitutional and Administrative Law*, 7th edn (1987), p 7.

(2) It therefore involves an authority outside and above the order it establishes. This is the notion of the constituent power ('pouvoir constituant' – because we do not think along these lines, the English translation sounds strange). In democracies that power is attributed to the people, on whose ratification the legitimacy of a constitution depends and, with it, the legitimacy of the governmental system.

(3) It is a form of law superior to other laws – because (i) it originates in an authority higher than the legislature which makes ordinary law and (ii) the authority of the legislature derives from it and is thus bound by it. The principle of hierarchy of law generally (but not always) leads to the possibility of judicial review of ordinary legislation.

(4) It is entrenched – (i) because its purpose is generally to limit the powers of government, but also (ii) again because of its origins in a higher authority outside the system. It can thus only be changed by special procedures, generally (and certainly for major change) requiring reference back to the constituent power.

Ridley then acknowledges his debt to James Bryce's earlier analysis and considers specific aspects of the British 'constitution':

The term British constitution is near meaningless ... It is impossible to isolate parts of the system of government to which the label constitutional may authoritatively be attached. There is no test to discriminate between constitutional and less than constitutional elements since labelling has no defined consequence, unlike countries where constitutions are a higher form of law. If used descriptively, as Wheare and others suggest, it is simply a fancy-dress way of saying the British system of government is at best redundant. More dangerous, those who talk of a British constitution may mislead themselves into thinking that there are parts of the system to which a special sanctity attaches. But in that normative sense the term is equally meaningless. When significant parts of the system are reformed, we have no test to tell us whether the outcome is an improper breach of the constitutional order, a proper amendment, or whether the reformed institutions were not part of the 'constitution' at all. I may be told that this is an academic quibble since our democratic politicians know what is of constitutional significance in our way of government, approach such matters differently from other reforms, and are politically if not legally constrained. That, however, is not the case. Our system of government is being changed, with increasing disregard for tradition, the only unwritten rules to which one might appeal as 'constitutional' principles.

There is cause for concern about the muddled way we think about the British 'constitution'; there is even greater cause for concern about the political consequences of its nature. It is sometimes said that our 'constitution' is now under stress as major changes occur far more rapidly than before in its written and unwritten parts. Is this due to changing ideas about how the British system of government should be organised, widely held, or is it simply that the Government of the day is using its power to change the system in the pursuit of its own political goals? Is the constitutional order evolving or is it under attack? We have moved from consensus to conflict in politics: have we moved in that direction, too, as regards our constitutional order, taking that to mean the broad principles underlying the way government is organised and power exercised? Many old principles no longer command universal agreement and there are well-supported demands for new principles. We have had debates on the entrenchment of rights; on federalism or regional devolution as against the unitary state; on the case for consensus rather than majority as a basis for government; on the relative weight of national versus local mandates and the independence of local government; on the duty of civil servants; on electoral reform with all its implications for the operation of government; on who should define the national interest; on open government and official secrecy; on complementing representative democracy by referenda and other forms of participation – and much else. Political disagreement and disagreement on the proper constitutional order are linked. An ideologically-committed Government, determined to implement its policies, will support different constitutional principles from those who want consensus policy-making; those concerned primarily with individual freedom and the rights of the public will support different principles from those who want strong government – and so on. Since opinion is now deeply divided on so many issues, one can probably no longer talk of the constitutional order as if it were a reflection of public opinion.

Notes

1   Two criticisms may be made of Ridley's analysis. First, due to its insistence that any constitution worth the name must be entrenched, it excludes constitutions, like those of Singapore, which are fully written (in a constitutional document) but entirely flexible. It may therefore be seen to distance academic analysis too far from political reality (though of course Ridley's whole thesis is that the word 'constitution', having been used politically, is in danger of becoming so vague a term as to be practically meaningless). Secondly, he arguably goes too far in alleging that there are no parts of the British constitutional order to which any special sanctity attaches. It is surely not complacent to assert that if (say) a government procured the passing of an Act of Parliament which criminalised the publication of any matter critical of government, it would be universally, and with reason, regarded as having acted unconstitutionally. Similarly, it is clear that an Act of Parliament that blatantly intruded into the legislative competence of the Scottish Parliament without the consent of that body would be unconstitutional in the conventional sense (see p 26, below). A more apt criticism of the present arrangements would be that the normative (conventional) aspects of the constitution would bite only in the most extreme (and therefore unlikely to materialise) cases. In more marginal instances (witness the response to curtailment of the right to silence in 1994),[10] the indeterminacy of the constitutional order prevents such a clear cut verdict.

2   Ridley's argument also rests upon the notion that fundamental attributes of the constitution could all be changed by ordinary Acts of Parliament, which is, after all, the orthodox view. However, this orthodoxy may not be quite as solidly based as when he wrote. First of all, it also arguably requires some revision in the light of the decision in *Factortame* in which the House of Lords held that a statute which contravened EC law should be disapplied (see further Chapter 5 of this part). Moreover, recent articles indicate that members of the judiciary, including a very senior member, no longer accept this viewpoint. Lord Woolf has opined[11] that the courts would not apply an Act of Parliament which purported to remove the power of judicial review from the courts, on the basis that this would represent an intolerable attack upon the Rule of Law, on which the constitution is based. Similarly, Sir John Laws (now a judge in the Court of Appeal) has argued[12] that the constitution, not Parliament, is supreme, and that the 'higher order law' which the constitution represents would inhibit Parliament from successfully assailing fundamental human rights, democratic institutions and the Rule of Law. He acknowledges that 'constitutional theory has perhaps occupied too modest a place here in Britain', but urges that 'though our constitution is unwritten, it can and must be articulated'.[13] The primary mover in the attempt to articulate liberal

---

10   By virtue of ss 34–36 Criminal Justice and Public Order Act 1994. See Part VI Chapter 4, pp 1039–47.
11   See 'Droit public – English style' [1995] PL 57.
12   In 'Law and democracy' [1995] PL 72.
13   Extracts from both these articles appear in Part I Chapter 4, pp 147–49. On the relevance of Britain's membership of the EU to this issue, see Part I Chapter 5.

constitutional principles in the UK's constitution is TRS Allen. See, for example, his *Law, Liberty and Justice: the Legal Foundations of British Constitutionalism* (1993).[14]

3   Whilst the uncodified nature of the British constitution may not necessarily be related to the substantive deficiencies discussed above, this characteristic may be blamed for the *uncertainty* of many constitutional doctrines.

P McAuslan and JF McEldowney, 'Legitimacy and the constitution: the dissonance between theory and practice', in P McAuslan and JF McEldowney (eds), *Law, Legitimacy and the Constitution* (1985), pp 12–15

What makes the issue of the legitimacy of our constitutional arrangements so problematic is the general open-endedness of those arrangements; that is, the difficulty of knowing whether a practice or non-practice is or is not constitutional. The example given above of 'packing' the Appellate Committee of the House of Lords with overt political supporters of the ruling party was put forward as a clear example, yet 50 or 60 years ago it would not have been thought particularly remarkable for a Prime Minister to appoint known supporters of his party to the House of Lords or to do likewise with the office of Chief Justice. Judicial appointments in Scotland are still influenced by political considerations and in Northern Ireland by politico-religious ones. Practices, in other words, change over time and may differ in different parts of the UK.

Even where practices may not differ over time, or place, there may be an inconsistency, a lack of knowledge or a long-standing dispute about them, which could make it equally difficult to argue that following or not following a practice was or was not constitutional or legitimate. Probably the best example of this is the use of the Royal Prerogative, and the extent to which the courts may pass judgment on any particular use. Notwithstanding that the Royal Prerogative as a source of power for the Government antedates Acts of Parliament, has been at the root of a civil war and a revolution in England and has been litigated about on countless major occasions in respect of its use both at home and overseas, its scope is still unclear as is the role of the courts in relation thereto. The use by the Prime Minister of powers under the Royal Prerogative to ban trade unions at the Government Communication Headquarters at Cheltenham in 1983 was contested both for its lawfulness – ie, whether such powers could be used and if so whether they were used correctly – and also for its legitimacy – ie, whether, even if the constitutional power existed, this was a proper and fair use of the power. It can be seen that questions of lawfulness and legitimacy shade into one another here though the answers do not: the lawfulness of the action taken, confirmed by the House of Lords in 1984 [*Council of Civil Service Unions v Minister for the Civil Service* [1984] 3 All ER 935], did not and does not dispose of its legitimacy.

The GCHQ case is valuable for another point. We have pointed out that lawfulness is not to be confused with legitimacy. No more is constitutionality. What the Prime Minister did was not merely lawful; she exercised the constitutional powers of her office in the way in which those powers had always been exercised. That is, the use of the Royal Prerogative as the legal backing for the management of the public service, the principle that a civil servant is a servant of the Crown and holds office at the pleasure of the Crown is one of the best known principles of constitutional law, hallowed by usage and sanctioned by the courts. What is in issue from the perspective of legitimacy is whether the particular use made of that undoubted constitutional power, the manner of its use, and the justification both for the use and manner of use – that considerations of national security required both a banning of trade unions and no consultation with affected officers before the ban was announced – was a fair and reasonable use of power? Did it accord with legitimate expectations of fair and reasonable persons or was it a high-handed exercise of power of a kind more to be expected of an authoritarian Government than one guided by and subscribing to principles of limited government?

---

14   For critical commentary see the review article by I Harden [1996] PL 298.

In considering the issue of legitimacy in relation to our constitutional arrangements and the exercise of governmental power, what has to be done is to examine a range of practices, decisions, actions (and non-practices, decisions and actions), statements and policies which between them can amount to a portrait of power, so that we can form a judgment or an assessment of that power set against the principles of limited government outlined and discussed so far. It is not every failure to comply with law or every constitutional and non-constitutional short cut which adds up to an approach to powers which gives rise to questions of legitimacy. If that were so, there would scarcely be a Government in the last 100 years which could be regarded as legitimate, but it is those uses of power and law which seem to betray or which can only be reasonably explained by a contempt for or at least an impatience with the principles of limited government and a belief that the rightness of the policies to be executed excuse or justify the methods whereby they are executed. If, as we believe to be the case, powers are being so exercised, then the issue of constitutional legitimacy which arises is quite simply: what is the value or use of a constitution based on and designed to ensure the maintenance of a system of limited government if it can, quite lawfully and even constitutionally, be set on one side? Have we not in such circumstances arrived at that 'elective dictatorship' of which Lord Hailsham gave warning in 1977 [the Dimbleby Lecture 1977, expanded in *The Dilemma of Democracy* (1978), especially Chapter 20]:

> It is only now that men and women are beginning to realise that representative institutions are not necessarily guardians of freedom but can themselves become engines of tyranny. They can be manipulated by minorities, taken over by extremists, motivated by the self-interest of organised millions [p 13]....

> All the more unfortunate does this become ... when at least one of the parties believes that the prerogative and rights conferred by electoral victory, however narrow, not merely entitle but compel it to impose on the helpless but unorganised majority irreversible changes for which it never consciously voted and to which most of its members are opposed [p 21].

Lord Hailsham was writing in the context of the Labour Government of 1974–79 which never had a majority in the House of Commons greater than three and for much of the time was in a minority and reliant on the Liberal and other parties to support it. During that period the Government expanded the scope of the Welfare State, conferred significant legal rights on trade unionists and trade unions, nationalised the shipbuilding and aircraft manufacturing industries and attempted to provide for a measure of devolution of power ... to Scotland and Wales. All these matters were spelt out in manifestos in the two elections of 1974 and, in the case of devolution, there was in those elections, in terms of votes cast, an absolute majority for that in those two countries. Nonetheless it could be argued, and was being so by Lord Hailsham, that a Government elected by a clear minority of the voters, albeit with a majority in the House of Commons would be wrong – ie it would not be legitimate – to attempt to bring about 'irreversible changes' to which the majority of the voters are opposed, and to the extent to which those Labour Governments sought to do that, they were abusing the electoral process and not acting in a legitimate manner.

Notes

1   It is important to understand what the authors are arguing at this point. They are *not* saying that they agree with Hailsham's contentions – indeed, later in the same essay, they note that the changes which he identifies as being 'irreversible' were in fact all reversed by the Thatcher administration (at p 16). Rather, they are using Hailsham's attack as an illustration of the way in which the indeterminacy of our constitutional arrangements so often leave the legitimacy of government actions open to question.

2   Contemporary examples of behaviour of uncertain constitutional legitimacy are not hard to find. To take just a few examples, the Conservative Party has been wont to refer to the entire Labour constitutional reform programme as amounting to

'vandalism' of the UK constitution. Persistent concerns focus on the Blair government's centralisation of power within the Prime Minister's Office and the far greater use of unelected 'special advisers', who are specifically partisan, unlike the traditionally 'neutral' Civil Service.[15] There is a fear that the influence of 'special advisers' eclipses that of the Civil Service and even that of ministers, while they themselves remain wholly unaccountable to Parliament.[16] Many saw it as 'unconstitutional' for the Prime Minister himself simply to decide and announce that Prime Ministers questions – a highly symbolic forum of constitutional accountability, perhaps the most famous in the UK constitution – would be changed from a twice to a once-weekly format, without even consulting Parliament, the other political parties or anyone else. The major reorganisation of central government, whereby 'Next Step' agencies, designed to operate at arms-length from government, were set up without legislative discussion in Parliament to assume many of the tasks of government departments, with major implications for government accountability and responsibility, is another example (see further Part IV Chapter 2, at pp 532–44).

3   What all these changes indicate are that, in the UK, the constitution, which in many other countries is policed by a constitutional court, or some other body independent of government, for example the French *Conseil D'Etat*, is in the UK an overtly *political* animal, as apt to be reformed to the convenience of government as social or economic policy. This theme, particularly in relation to the protection and enhancement of democracy, is developed in the first part of this chapter, by David Marquand. First we turn to the most radical recent constitutional change of all in the UK – devolution.

THE IMPACT OF DEVOLUTION ON THE UK CONSTITUTION[17]

This subject would comfortably occupy an entire book; indeed whole works could be devoted to any one of the devolution schemes, in particular the Scottish settlement, which is the most radical, in terms of powers transferred. In what follows, therefore, the discussion is confined to a very broad outline of the devolution schemes and the effect of it on the traditional unitary UK constitution. The schemes of devolution to Wales and Northern Ireland in particular will only be sketched. This is because the

---

15   See the Report of the Public Administration Committee, 'Special advisers: boon or bane', HC 293 (2000–01).

16   The Prime Minister reiterated his view on 16 July 2002 that they should not appear before Select Committees of Parliament in evidence to the Liaison Committee (see p 532). For an example of a Select Committee complaint relating to the refusal of a high profile adviser – Lord Birt – to appear before it, see Part III Chapter 1, pp 326–27.

17   See generally A Tomkins (ed), *Devolution and the British Constitution* (1998); A Ward, 'Devolution, Labour's strange constitutional "design"', in J Jowell and D Oliver (eds), *The Changing Constitution*, 4th edn (2000); C Turpin, *British Government and the Constitution*, 5th edn (2002), pp 230–70; R Brazier, 'The Scottish government' [1998] PL 212; P Craig and M Walters, 'The courts, devolution and judicial review' [1999] PL 274; R Brazier, 'The constitution of the UK' (1999) 58 CLJ 98; J Mitchell, 'New Parliament, new politics in Scotland' (2000) 53 Parl Aff 605; V Bogdanor, 'Devolution – the constitutional aspects', in Cambridge Centre for Public Law, *Constitutional Reform in the United Kingdom: Practice and Principles* (1998); R Reed, 'Devolution and the judiciary', in Cambridge Centre for Public Law, *ibid*; N Burrows, 'Unfinished business: the Scotland Act 1998' (1999) 62(2) MLR 241; M O'Neill, 'Great Britain: from Dicey to devolution' (2000) 53 Parl Aff 70; M Laffin, and A Thomas, 'Designing the National Assembly for Wales' (2000) 53 Parl Aff 557; R Wilford, 'Designing the Northern Ireland Assembly' (2000) 53 Parl Aff 577; A Brown, 'Designing the Scottish Parliament' (2000) 53 Part Aff 542.

Welsh scheme, since it does not involve the establishment of an assembly capable of passing primary legislation, is of less constitutional significance. The Northern Ireland settlement is a very complex and distinctive one. However, at the time of writing, the Northern Ireland Assembly is suspended, and has been for some time; the future of devolution in Northern Ireland is therefore highly uncertain.

We may start with a brief outline of the basic imperative that drove devolution, described below as the principle of subsidiarity.

Lord Bingham of Cornhill, 'The evolving constitution' [2002] I EHRLR I (extracts)

Decisions affecting the life and activities of the citizen should generally speaking be made at the lowest level of government consistent with economy, convenience and the rational conduct of public affairs. This is plainly akin to the European principle of subsidiarity ... I shall call this 'the devolutionary principle' ...

While there is endless scope for argument about the application of this principle – what powers should be devolved and to what level? – I doubt if any rational person would challenge the principle as such. It would be obviously absurd if the central government were to concern itself with (for instance) local refuse collection, and equally absurd ... if (say) foreign policy and defence were not conducted by the central government. So the problem is where to draw the line, or lines. The devolutionary principle as I have expressed it is, I think, the ethical principle which underlies any federal or quasi-federal structure, and it recognises what I take to be a fact of political life: that the further removed from the citizen a government is, the more bureaucratic and out of touch with local problems the citizen tends to perceive it to be. The usual British perception of the not very swollen bureaucracy in Brussels illustrates the point.

It would seem clear that the devolutionary principle provides the rationale of the Government of Wales Act 1998, the Scotland Act 1998 [and] the Northern Ireland Act 1998.

The structure of Great Britain prior to devolution and the movement towards greater subsidiarity

England absorbed Wales into a single state in the 13th century via the Statute of Wales Act 1284 and Wales has been ruled from England ever since, through the office of what became, in 1964, the Secretary of State for Wales. Having also been subject to partial rule from England, Scotland achieved complete independence from England by their victory in the battle of Bannockburn in 1314. Strife between the two nations continued, however, and was finally brought to an end at the beginning of the 18th century with the Treaties of Union 1707, which established full political and economic union.

These treaties made the two countries one, setting up a new parliament, the British Parliament, as the supreme legislative body of the new country. However, it was agreed at that time, and written into the treaties as unchangeable principles, that Scotland should retain its separate legal system; its separate established Church – the Presbyterian Church of Scotland – and its separate education system. While the Westminster Parliament legislated for Scotland, many Bills were 'Scottish' Bills, that is, concerned with Scottish affairs only and there was a Scottish Office and Scottish Secretary of State. Before devolution, the Scottish Office, situated in Edinburgh, administered Scottish affairs. Scotland was allocated a block grant, which the Secretary of State was at liberty to allocate in accordance with what were thought to be local needs and priorities. Scotland thus had quite a high degree of executive devolution and preserved its separate legal system, church and education system.

The perceived problem with this state of affairs was two-fold. First, there was what could be termed a representational or legitimacy problem: the partially separate administration of Scotland could well be controlled by a political party that had been clearly rejected in the polls by the Scottish people. For example, throughout the 1980s and in the 1990s, up until the election of a Labour government in 1997, Scotland was governed, like the rest of the UK, by a Conservative administration. The problem was that Scotland had consistently rejected the Conservative Party at the polls during that period, preferring the Labour Party and, to a lesser extent, the Scottish Nationalist Party. For example, in 1987, the ruling Conservative government won only 10 out of Scotland's 70 seats; in 1992, 12 seats. It was thus seen as an unrepresentative system.

The other problem was that the Scottish Administration was seen as being neither sufficiently accountable nor *locally* accountable. While the Scottish Office was situated in Edinburgh, it was not accountable to any Scottish representative body but to the Westminster Parliament, dominated by English MPs. It arguably received inadequate scrutiny there. As Colin Munro notes,

> The Scottish Office's appearance on the parliamentary question rota once every three weeks was hardly commensurate with the scale of their activities, and more generally it was obvious that the House of Commons had insufficient time for scrutiny of Scottish administration.[18]

Thus, a Constitutional Convention, made up of representatives from the Labour Party, Liberal Democrats, trades union, churches and other small parties was set up. The Convention proposed a Parliament for Scotland that would exercise substantial legislative powers.

Devolution to Scotland: an outline

Upon the victory of the Labour Party in the 1997 General Election, on a manifesto promise to implement devolution to Scotland, the proposal that there should be a Scottish Parliament was put to the Scottish people in a referendum. The proposal was approved by nearly 75% of those who took part, on a reasonable turnout of 63.5% and a second question – whether it should have limited tax-raising powers – was approved by a lower, but still convincing, majority of 63.5%. Thus directly mandated by the people, the devolution scheme, as enshrined in the Scotland Act 1998, whilst formally as repealable as any other statutory scheme, clearly acquired a democratic legitimacy of a kind that gives it a *de facto* entrenched status, a point returned to below.

The Scottish Parliament has at present 129 members (known as MSPs), though this number may fall as a result of boundary changes in future. Each elector has two votes. Seventy-three of the MPs are elected in the same way as members of the Westminster Parliament; that is, each constituency elects the candidate who receives the most votes (the first past the post system). The second vote, for a further 56 MSPs, is cast for a party, rather than an individual candidate, under a proportional system known as the additional member system,[19] based on the current Euro-constituencies. The system is inherently unlikely to produce overall majorities for a single party, and so it has proved: in both elections held since the institution of the new Parliament (in 1999 and 2003), Labour was the largest single party, and formed a coalition with the Liberal

---

18 C Munro, *Studies in Constitutional Law*, 2nd edn (1999), p 39.
19 See further on electoral systems, Part III Chapter 1, pp 263–65.

Democrats, the third largest party (the SNP was the second largest party while the Conservatives were the fourth largest). The Scottish Parliament is elected for fixed terms of four years, though there is provision for exceptional early dissolution if the Parliament resolves by a two-thirds majority that it should be dissolved, or if it is unable to agree upon a new First Minister (following the resignation or removal of the incumbent) within 28 days (s 3(1) Scotland Act).

Competencies of the Scottish Parliament

The first and most important point to make about the Scottish Parliament is that it is, unequivocally, both a limited and subordinate legislature. In terms of its limitations, s 29(1) of the Scotland Act, states: 'An Act of the Scottish Parliament is not law so far as any provision of the Act is outside the legislative competence of the Scottish Parliament.' The Act thus gives judges a full strike-down power over the acts of the new legislature. As Reed remarks, some within Scotland, 'might regard it as ironical, to say the least, that the Scots having voted for self-government by a Scottish Parliament are now to be governed, in a sense, by judges'.[20]

Instead of setting out the specific powers to be passed to Scotland, a different route was taken: those powers not being transferred (known as 'reserved powers') are specified; anything not mentioned is deemed to be transferred. Competence is thus defined negatively: the Scottish Parliament may not legislate on 'reserved matters' (enumerated in Sched 5 to the Act), which thus remain within the exclusive competency of Westminster, the reverse of the position adopted under the abortive Scotland Act 1978. The areas reserved exclusively for Westminster include: UK constitutional issues, including the monarchy, the UK Parliament and the registration and funding of political parties and the Civil Service including the Scottish Civil Service; foreign and defence policy, including immigration and citizenship; the fiscal, economic and monetary system (that is, macro-economic issues, including interest rates and currency); common markets for UK goods and services; employment (including industrial relations) and social security; transport safety and regulation; energy, including the ownership and exploration of oil and gas; miscellaneous matters, including abortion, postal services, equal opportunities and broadcasting regulation.

Powers that are thus devolved to the Scottish Parliament include: all areas of education; local government; land development and environmental regulation; many aspects of transport policy; the Scottish NHS, the legal system (civil and criminal law (save that the Scottish Parliament is bound by both EU law and the ECHR)); agriculture and fisheries; sports, arts and culture. It is important to note that the Scottish Parliament has power to amend or repeal existing Acts of the Westminster Parliament relating to the devolved areas. The devolved areas may be altered by Order in Council (s 30(2) Scotland Act), but the Order must be approved by both the Scottish and UK Parliaments. Devolved areas can also be changed by the Westminster Parliament by primary legislation, although that would require amendment of the Scotland Act itself. The budget that the Scottish Parliament and Scottish Executive dispose of is allocated as a block by the Westminster Parliament. The Scottish Parliament may also raise income tax by 3 p in the pound.

---

20   *Op cit*, p 23.

In relation to acts of the Scottish Parliament, there will obviously, on occasions, be borderline cases, in which it is unclear whether an act of the Scottish Parliament is within its competence as defined under the Scotland Act. In such cases, s 101(2) of the Scotland Act instructs the judges that: 'Such a provision is to be read as narrowly as is required for it to be within competence, if such a reading is possible, and is to have effect accordingly.' In other words, the judges are urged to go as far as is possible, in terms of interpretation, to read *down* an act of the Scottish Parliament to ensure that it remains within its competence rather than striking it down as *ultra vires*. There is no provision in the Scotland Act relating to the interpretation of Westminster legislation that covers the devolved areas; however, Ian Loveland has argued that the courts may well develop a rule of interpretation that Westminster is presumed not to have intended to legislate in the devolved areas unless that intention is made plain in the legislation in question.[21]

The Scottish Parliament is further limited: *per* s 29, it may not legislate contrary to EU law or the ECHR or for the territory of another country and nor may it alter the terms of the Scotland Act itself (with a few minor exceptions). Thus the Scotland Act acts, in effect, as a constitution for Scotland in the orthodox sense of the word, since it is a higher framework of law, unrepealable by the legislature.

Since the Scotland Act gives the UK a new, limited legislature, in effect a constitutionalised, rather than an unconstrained legislature, it was clearly necessary to lay down a procedure for determining instances in which it is alleged that the Scottish Parliament has acted beyond its powers. Such procedures are common in other states, and generally take the form of allowing either pre-legislative challenge (as in France – see pp 14–15) or post-legislative challenge (as in the US – see p 13). The Scotland Act uses both techniques. In terms of pre-legislative challenge, if either a Scots or UK law officer raises an issue over whether a given Bill would be beyond the powers of the Parliament, it may, under s 33, be referred to the Judicial Committee of the Privy Council (JCPC) within 28 days for determination of its *vires*. If the JCPC determines that the Bill is outside the powers of the Scottish Parliament, it cannot be presented for royal assent unamended. The UK government can also, under s 35, block a legislative proposal if in its opinion it affects any reserved matter or would be incompatible with the UK's international obligations or defence or national security.

There is also a complex system for a Bill to be challenged once enacted, under the referral procedure in Sched 6 to the Scotland Act. If a devolution issue (ie an issue as to whether an Act of the Scottish Parliament is outside its powers and so void) arises in an ordinary case, a lower court has a discretion to refer the matter to a higher court for determination. Appeals from the higher courts lie to the JCPC, the rulings of which are made binding in all legal proceedings.

The Scottish Parliament is also, clearly, a subordinate legislature. Not only is it, as Brazier remarks, 'the legal creation of [the Westminster] Parliament' and thus subject to abolition, as the Greater London Council and metropolitan county councils were abolished in the 1980s, it is also not granted *exclusive* powers to legislate even in the areas in which it is competent. Section 28(7) of the Scotland Act states that the grant of legislative powers to the Scottish Parliament 'does not affect the power of the UK Parliament to make law for Scotland'. This, of course, would follow from the orthodox

---

21 I Loveland, *Constitutional Law: A Critical Introduction*, 2nd edn (2000), p 625.

view of parliamentary sovereignty, under which Parliament cannot diminish its own powers;[22] however, the fact that this was so baldly stated in the Scotland Act epitomises the way in which the devolution scheme, whilst on the one hand amounting to what Bogdanor has called 'the most radical constitutional reform this country has seen since the Great Reform Act of 1832',[23] yet cleaves resolutely to the most orthodox of foundational UK constitutional principles.

However, as is characteristic of the UK constitution, political and legal realities do not march alongside each other in the devolution scheme. As Tam Dayell, MP remarked in debate: '[s 28(7)] may conceivably be true in an arcane legal sense, but in the political reality of 1998 it is palpably misleading and about as true as it would be to say that the Queen can veto any legislation'.[24] This is because the whole point of devolution is to pass the power to make policy in the devolved area to the directly elected Parliament with a mandate to carry out its election manifesto. As Bogdanor puts it: 'In practice ... sovereignty is being transferred and Westminster will not be able to recover it, except under pathological circumstances.'[25] In fact, the UK government has explicitly recognised this, in a memorandum of understanding made between itself and the devolved administrations. This states:

> ... the UK Government will normally proceed in accordance with the convention that the UK Parliament would not normally legislate with regard to devolved matters except with the agreement of the devolved legislature.[26]

Devolution, federalism and quasi-federalism

Federalism is a complex concept and there is no universally agreed definition of it.[27] However, a rough definition could include three key elements: first, that there be *exclusive* areas of competence allocated to the federal and state/province legislatures; in those areas, only one body is competent to legislate and its legislation in that area cannot be overridden by the other body. Secondly, there is a written constitution, which defines and limits the jurisdiction of both legislatures, such that neither body can unilaterally abolish the other. Thirdly, there is a court, or courts, with power to review the *vires* of the acts of *both* legislatures to ensure that they remain with their respective competencies. If this definition is applied to Scotland, it is immediately apparent that no federal system has been created. The Scottish Parliament has no *exclusive* areas of jurisdiction, since Westminster remains competent to legislate in all the devolved areas. While the Scotland Act could be seen as a written constitution that defines and limits the jurisdiction of the Scottish Parliament, there is no such instrument in relation to Westminster. Finally, whilst the higher courts may review the *vires* of the Scottish Parliament, this is not possible in relation to the Westminster Parliament, at least under the orthodox interpretation of parliamentary sovereignty. Legally, therefore, the position is clear: the UK has not moved to a federal system.

---

22 See further on this, Chapter 4 of this part, at pp 149–67.
23 *Op cit*, p 9
24 HC Deb vol 305 col 366 (28 January 1998).
25 *Op cit*, p 12.
26 Memorandum of Understanding, Cm 4444 (1999).
27 See, for example, P King, *Federalism and Federation* (1982) and G Sawer, *Modern Federalism* (1976).

However, if one brings constitutional *conventions* into the equation, a rather different picture emerges. If a strong convention grows up to the effect that Westminster will *not* in fact legislate for the devolved areas without the consent of the Scottish Parliament, as stated in the above memorandum, then the first requirement is satisfied in the conventional sense: the Scottish Parliament will legislate for Scottish, devolved matters, Westminster will legislate in the reserved areas only. The constitution governing the new system is clearly the Scotland Act: it cannot be repealed or amended by the Scottish Parliament as a matter of law and, as a matter of political reality, given that it has been democratically entrenched by the referendum approving it, it is safe from unilateral repeal by Westminster. The Scotland Act thus remaining in force, and convention precluding Westminster from legislating in the devolved areas it defines, it could come to act as a constitution for Westminster, in the conventional sense. Finally, the higher courts, as well as being able to review the *vires* of acts of the Scottish Parliament, may well, as discussed above, develop an interpretative presumption that Westminster legislation will not be read as intruding into the devolved areas unless that intention is made plain on the face of the act in question, thus providing a strong interpretative restraint upon the Westminster Parliament. As we will see in Chapter 4 of this part, such interpretative presumptions can, in practice, provide a very high level of protection for constitutional principles, in this case the convention that the Scottish Parliament alone should have the right unilaterally to legislate in the devolved areas.

It is thus possible to argue that while the legal position created by the Scotland Act is clearly *not* federalist, a form of quasi-federalism may grow up, through the strong prohibitive influence of constitutional convention. Certainly, Westminster has not, to date, legislated in the devolved areas without the consent of the Scottish Parliament.[28]

The Scottish Executive in outline

The Scotland Act lays out detailed provisions for the formation of the Scottish Executive. In brief, the First Minister is nominated by the Scottish Parliament within 28 days of an election or vacancy and appointed by the Queen. The First Minister's nominees as Scottish ministers are approved by the Scottish Parliament and appointed by the Queen; his nominees for junior ministers, and the Law Officers (the Solicitor General and Lord Advocate) are likewise approved by the Parliament. All ministers (except the Law Officers) must be members of the Scottish Parliament and may be removed at the discretion of the First Minister. The First Minister and other ministers are recognised in law as the Scottish Executive.

This Scottish government (if it may be so called) is, in law, accountable to the Parliament: ministers *must* appear before the Parliament or its committees to give evidence if summoned, and if the Parliament resolves that the Executive no longer enjoys its confidence, the First Minister and all other ministers *must* resign (Scotland Act, ss 45(2), 47(3)(c), 48(2) and 49(4)(c)). The Executive, like the Scottish Parliament, has all the powers and duties that formerly belonged to the Secretary of State for Scotland; additional powers may be transferred by Order in Council, and may, of course, be granted to the Executive under acts of the Scottish Parliament. The Executive is bound not to act incompatibly with EU law and the ECHR (s 57(2)).

28 See further, on the conventional limitations introduced by the Scotland Act, Chapter 2, pp 65–67.

Relations between the Scottish Executive and the UK government are carried on under principles established in concordats signed between the two.[29] There continues to be a Secretary of State for Scotland, who now takes primary responsibility for managing relations with the Scottish Executive.

Devolution to Wales

The vote in support of Welsh devolution in 1997 was much lower than in Scotland, at a mere 50.3%. The margin of support was thus only 0.3%. Moreover the turnout was low, at 51%. Thus barely a quarter of the Welsh people expressed a positive preference for devolution, perhaps reflecting, as Neil suggests, 'a deep ambivalence about [Welsh] national identity'.[30]

The Welsh assembly has 60 members, elected, like those of the Scottish Parliament, under a system of mixed PR and first past the post. The sharpest contrast with the Scottish Parliament comes in the Assembly's limited powers. First of all, whereas the Scottish Parliament has a sweeping array of powers, defined as being all those which are not expressly retained by Westminster, the Welsh Assembly has only those powers which the Secretary of State for Wales transfers to it by Order in Council under s 22(2) of the Government of Wales Act 1998. More importantly, the Welsh Assembly cannot pass primary legislation. Thus, in essence, the Assembly takes over the role of the Secretary of State for Wales in passing detailed delegated legislation to flesh out policies the broad framework of which are set out in Acts passed by Westminster. Powers passed to the Welsh Assembly – which must, of course, be exercised in conformity with Acts of Parliament – include education and training; local government, the environment, regulation; many aspects of transport policy; housing; the health service, agriculture and fisheries; social services; and sports, arts and culture. The Assembly, like the Scottish Parliament, is bound by EU law and by the ECHR (ss 106 and 107). There are similar arrangements for challenges to the *vires* of acts of the Assembly, both before and after they are passed, as apply to the Scottish Parliament.

One of the principal aims behind the setting up of the Assembly was to correct the democratic deficit in Wales arising from the fact that much of the budget for Wales – around £7 billion annually – was, prior to devolution, dispersed by quangos, in respect of which there was no direct accountability to the people of Wales. The Assembly has power to transfer to itself or to other bodies responsibility for matters previously handled by such quangos.

Devolution to Northern Ireland and the peace process

Historical background

It is impossible to understand the scheme of devolution to Northern Ireland without some awareness of its troubled history. The following is a very brief account. Ireland was conquered by England and ruled by it, as a colony, from the 12th century, though it was for long not entirely subdued. From the 15th century the Irish Parliament accepted laws passed by the English Parliament as law there; any Bills passed by it had to be submitted to the King of England and his Council for approval. Once England

---

29 See further on this, R Rawlings, 'Concordats of the constitution' (2000) 116 LQR 257.
30 *Op cit*, p 8.

became Protestant under Henry VIII a vigorous attempt was made to suppress the Catholic religion in Ireland, involving, amongst other things, Protestant settlers from England and Scotland being handed estates in Northern Ireland during the 17th century. Ireland's Parliament, as well as remaining subordinated to the British Parliament, still excluded Catholic members. In 1800, the country was united with Britain, the Irish Parliament being induced to accept the union by heavy bribery and the promise of Catholic emancipation as a quid pro quo. One hundred Irish members sat in the UK Parliament. A growing Irish Nationalist movement gradually increased its representation to a majority of Irish members in Westminster. Attempts to give Home Rule to Ireland were defeated by strikes and threatened insurrection by Protestants in the north of Ireland, who did not want to be governed by a Catholic country. Following the brutal suppression of the Easter Rising, in 1918 Sinn Fein won all but four of the now 128 seats outside the northern counties but, refusing to sit at Westminster, instead set up the Irish Dail. The attempted repression of this attempt at self-government led to a two-year war with the IRA. An eventual compromise was negotiated whereby Ireland would be partitioned. This prevented all-out civil war but at the cost of the Catholic minority in the six Northern counties being subject to continuing, unwanted government by the UK.

In 1920, partition took place: the South obtained (effective) independence and became the Irish Free State (later the Irish Republic); the six Northern Counties, dominated by Protestants, exercised their option to remain part of the UK as Northern Ireland. The Government of Ireland Act established a devolved system of government for Northern Ireland, giving it its own Parliament (known as Stormont) and Executive, though subject to the supremacy of the Westminster Parliament. Stormont had the power to make laws 'for the peace, order and good government of Northern Ireland'; certain subjects, including defence, foreign policy and so on, were reserved to the UK Parliament. A convention was soon established, and followed, that Westminster would not interfere in the matters devolved to Stormont, which allowed it a substantial degree of autonomy.

The essential problem during the devolved period, which lasted from 1921 to 1972, was that the Unionists held a permanent majority in the Parliament and therefore always formed the government. They also controlled local government. The result was serious discrimination against Catholics in various areas, including housing, education and policing policy, the police service (the RUC) being dominated by Protestants. Eventually, increasing civil disorder forced the UK government to re-impose direct rule, including the despatch of British troops, and the introduction of internment. The powers of Stormont were vested in the Secretary of State for Northern Ireland; legislation for Northern Ireland was introduced by him in the form of Orders in Council under the Northern Ireland (Temporary Provisions Act 1972). However, direct rule did not bring an end to sectarian violence between armed Catholic and Protestant groups; the IRA attacked both British troops in Northern Ireland and targets in England, and killings by the British Army, including most notoriously the Bloody Sunday episode, kept nationalist feelings high. Various attempts up until the mid-1980s to restore devolved government and bring the conflict to an end all failed.

The lead up to the Good Friday Agreement, which eventually achieved a ceasefire and restored devolved governance (albeit temporarily), started with the Anglo-Irish Agreement, negotiated between the UK and Irish governments. It stated that there would be no constitutional change to the position of Northern Ireland without the consent of a majority of the Northern Irish population (something enshrined in UK law but long rejected in principle by the Irish government) and it established closer cooperation between the two governments. In a Joint Declaration (1993), the UK government declared it had 'no selfish, strategic or economic interest' in Northern Ireland remaining part of the UK, moving to a position of neutrality on the province's constitutional position. It looked forward to all-party talks provided that those taking part were committed to peaceful means. Following this, the IRA commenced a ceasefire from 1994. This was broken in 1996 with the Canary Wharf bombing, but resumed in 1997 with the election of a Labour government. The Blair administration reversed the previous policy of refusing to hold substantive talks until the IRA had disarmed, and persuaded the Unionists to engage in talks. Although boycotted by the hard-line DUP, these eventually culminated in the Good Friday Agreement (Cm 3833/1998), which was implemented in the UK by means of the Northern Ireland Act 1998 (NIA).

The Good Friday Agreement and the NIA 1998

The fundamental principles of the Good Friday Agreement were as follows:

- Northern Ireland is to remain part of UK unless and until a majority of its citizens by referendum decide otherwise (s 1).

- The Republic of Ireland agreed to amend its Constitution to abandon its territorial claim to Northern Ireland.

- A power-sharing Assembly and Executive were set up (unlike in a normal democracy where one party, provided it received a sufficient share of the votes, could govern on its own, the agreement was structured in such a way that all the main parties would be guaranteed a share in government, in an attempt to avoid the problems arising under the previous Unionist-dominated Stormont Government).

- A North-South Ministerial Council was established to coordinate relations between the Republic and Ulster. This was highly controversial with the Unionists, as it involved giving the Republic a greater say in Northern Irish affairs, something Unionists have always bitterly resisted. However, the NIA provided that all agreements reached by the Council must be approved by the Assembly.

- A Council of the Isles was established to consider matters of mutual interest to Wales, Scotland, Northern Ireland, England and the Channel Islands.

- All parties were to use their best endeavours to secure decommissioning of paramilitary weapons; a deadline of May 2001 was set for total disarmament of all paramilitary organisations (it was not met).

The Good Friday Agreement was endorsed by referenda in both Northern Ireland and the Republic: in the North by 71.1% on an 81.1% turnout; in the South, by 94% on a 56% turnout.

Under the NIA, the Northern Ireland Assembly was established. The Assembly has 108 members elected by a proportional voting system – the single transferable vote – using multi-member constituencies. It is elected for a four-year term, and its powers are similar those of the Scottish Parliament: the Northern Ireland Assembly may pass primary as well as secondary legislation. However, the NIA, like the Scotland Act, explicitly states that the UK Parliament retains in full its ability to legislate for Northern Ireland (s 5(6) NIA); it can thus legislate in the areas devolved to the Assembly as well as in those excluded from its remit. The Assembly, like the Scottish Parliament and the

Welsh Assembly, may not enact legislation contrary to EU law or the ECHR; an additional restriction upon it, again reflecting Northern Ireland's sectarian history, is that it may not enact legislation that discriminates against any person on grounds of religious or political belief (s 6(2)). The NIA sets out three categories of powers: (1) *transferred matters* are those upon which the Assembly is competent to legislate. They include agriculture and rural development, education, environment, health, social services, culture, training and employment. *Excepted matters* (listed in Sched 2) are those that *cannot* be transferred to the NIA; they are similar to the reserved matters under the Scotland Act and include the main provisions of the NIA itself. The *reserved matters* (in Sched 3) are those that are not within the competence of the NIA but which *may* be transferred to it (by Order in Council approved by both Houses of Parliament, following a resolution passed by the NIA with cross-community support (below) requesting such transfer). They include criminal justice and policing, financial services and markets, firearms and explosives and broadcasting. The Secretary of State may block Assembly legislation that is incompatible with the UK's international obligations, for reasons relating to defence or national security or where it is necessary to do so to protect safety or public order. The Assembly can be dissolved either by a two-thirds majority vote (s 32(1)–(2)) or if the First and/or Deputy Minister resign and no replacement can be agreed in six weeks (s 32(3)).

The procedures that the Assembly must follow in terms of the passage of legislation and the construction of its Executive are designed to prevent one-party domination. Thus, the passage of the annual budget requires cross-community support (s 63); but any 30 members can demand that any vote be made subject to the same requirement (s 42(1)). 'Cross-community support' means either a majority of both Unionists and Nationalists ('parallel consent') or the support of 60% of all members including at least 40% from each side ('weighted majority') (s 4(5)).

There are complex rules governing the formation of the Executive, again designed to ensure power-sharing. The Assembly must elect a First Minister and Deputy Minister by parallel consent and these will represent, respectively, the largest Unionist and Nationalist parties. Other posts in the government are allocated to the parties in proportion to the amount of seats won in the Assembly elections. In the 1998 elections the seats won by the major parties were as follows: UUP 28 (Unionist), SDLP 24 (Nationalist), DUP 20 (Unionist), Sinn Fein 18 (Nationalist). Posts in the government were therefore allocated as follows: UUP 3 (in addition to the First Minister); SDLP 3 (in addition to the Deputy Minister); DUP 2; Sinn Fein 2. A minister or party in the Assembly may be excluded from the Assembly by resolution on grounds, *inter alia*, that the person or party is no longer committed to exclusively democratic and peaceful means (s 30); such a resolution needs cross community support. All ministers must take the pledge set out in Schedule 4, which affirms their 'commitment to non-violence and exclusively peaceful means ... to serve all the people of Northern Ireland equally, and ... to promote equality and prevent discrimination'. The Secretary of State for Northern Ireland can also suspend the Assembly and Executive. This has happened four times: in February 2000, August 2001, September 2001 and October 2002.

The Assembly was suspended on 14 October 2002 by John Reid, the Secretary of State for Northern Ireland, after both Unionist Parties stated that they would withdraw from the power-sharing Executive unless Sinn Fein was excluded from it, something unacceptable to the British government and to the nationalist SDLP. Rather than allowing the collapse of the Executive, the British government decided to suspend it and the Assembly. The Unionist ultimatum came after police found evidence that the IRA were operating a spy ring within Sinn Fein at Stormont. The Assembly remains suspended at the time of writing, because the Unionist Parties refuse to take part in the power-sharing Executive with Sinn Fein until the IRA disarms completely, ceases all its activities and (the position of the more hard-line Unionists) disbands completely. Northern Irish devolution, therefore, unlike Scottish and Welsh devolution, is very far from entrenched. Despite the continuing ceasefire of the major terrorist organisations, a comprehensive agreement between the parties on issues such as disarmament of the IRA, policing and the scaling down of the British military presence appears distant.

English regional devolution and the West Lothian question

The introduction of Scottish devolution has given real force to the so-called 'West Lothian' question. So called because it was originally raised by Tam Dayell, MP for West Lothian, in the 1970s, it arises from the fact that Scottish MPs continue to sit in Westminster, despite the creation of the Scottish Parliament. The objection, in essence, is that Scottish MPs can vote on legislation affecting only England (and Wales) whereas English MPs, because of the Scottish Parliament, can, in practice, no longer vote on a large range of matters affecting only Scotland (those devolved to the Scottish Parliament). The problem would be present in its most acute form if a UK government were to be dependent upon the votes of Scottish MPs to pass legislation that affected only England (for example, legislation relating to the NHS), since, seemingly unfairly, legislation on the Scottish NHS would be passed in the Scottish Parliament, by MSPs only. The problem in this acute form would be most likely to arise under a Labour government , since the Labour Party is historically far stronger in Scotland than the Conservatives (for example in the 1997 election, Labour won 56 of the 71 Scottish seats).

There are three main solutions to this problem. The first, and most radical, would entail the creation of an English Parliament with the same powers over English affairs as that held by the Scottish Parliament over Scotland. The second would be the creation of a convention that Scottish MPs did not vote on matters relating exclusively to England (a legal rule to this effect would be problematic, because it would involve the courts enquiring into proceedings in Parliament to determine the validity of an Act, something they have always refused to do).[31] The problem with this second solution would be that it could lead to what is termed an 'in and out' government: if a government were dependent upon the votes of Scottish and Welsh MPs in order to get its legislation passed (as has occurred in the past in relation to Labour governments), then one could have the position that where Parliament was considering matters affecting the whole of the UK, that government had a comfortable majority, but where exclusively English Bills were being considered, the government was unable to ensure their passage.

In the absence of any real enthusiasm amongst the English for their own Parliament (though this has been supported by the Conservative Party) a compromise solution involves giving the English regions greater autonomy and direct representation through the creation of Regional Assemblies to add to the Assembly

---

31   See on this Chapter 4 of this part, at pp 136–38.

and Lord Mayor set up in London in 1998. While this does not answer the West Lothian question directly, it reduces the asymmetry that devolution has caused, in terms of representative bodies and local accountability. The first government has recently announced such a scheme with referenda to be held on the setting up of such assemblies in the North East, North West and Yorkshire, the areas most enthusiastic for some form of devolved governance.

For reasons of space, and because it is uncertain at this time whether Regional Assemblies will in fact go ahead (the outcome of the proposed referenda is by no means assured) the following extract is reproduced to give a brief indication of the government's proposals.[32]

Office of the Deputy Prime Minister, *Your Region, Your Choice: Revitalising the English Regions:* Summary (2002) (extracts)

What will elected regional assemblies do?

Elected regional assemblies will develop a strategic vision for improving the quality of life in their regions, in particular improving economic performance. They will be responsible for setting priorities, delivering regional strategies and allocating funding. In addition, elected assemblies will have a significant influencing role, including scrutiny powers and making appointments to regional public bodies ('quangos').

Subject to agreeing a small number of key national targets, an assembly will have complete freedom over how to spend the resources at its disposal. There are many areas of policy where a regional dimension could improve both the decision-making process and successful implementation. Among those areas where the regional assembly will have specific responsibilities are:

- economic development
- skills and employment
- housing
- sport, culture and tourism
- transport
- land use and regional planning
- environmental protection, biodiversity and waste
- public health

Delivering in the region

Successful redevelopment of an area depends on an integrated approach that provides jobs, homes, transport links and other facilities.

At present, responsibility for these issues rests with a number of different bodies, including the Regional Development Agency, the Government Office, the regional chamber and the Housing Corporation. This can mean duplication, disagreement and delay. An elected regional assembly will produce integrated strategies covering all these issues. It will have direct responsibility for the Regional Development Agency and influence over other regional agencies and public bodies. It will also have money and other powers to help it implement its strategies.

---

32 For the full proposals, see the *White Paper, Your Region, Your Choice: Revitalising the English Regions*, Cm 5511 (2002).

As well as drawing up – and delivering – regional strategies for each of these individual policy areas, their task will also be to ensure they all fit together effectively so they improve people's living standards and quality of life. This is where we believe elected regional assemblies can have an important new role. They will be able to look at 'cross-cutting' issues such as sustainable development across the region.

Democracy, not bureaucracy

Elected assemblies will provide direct accountability over key regional public bodies ('quangos'). Almost all of their functions will be taken from central government, not from local authorities. By providing stronger scrutiny and improving co-ordination between existing bodies, they should reduce bureaucracy, not add to it.

Even so, in areas that currently have a county and district council, a regional assembly would add a third tier of elected government below the national level. We believe that moving to a single tier of local government would:

- simplify relationships for both local authorities and regional assemblies; and
- make it much clearer to the public who does what.

So in any region where the Government decides that a referendum on an elected assembly should be held, there will first be an independent review of local government structures. The review will recommend the most effective wholly unitary local government structure for the region and will be carried out by the Boundary Committee for England. But restructuring of local government would only take place if the region votes for an elected assembly.

Size and constitution of assemblies

The Government wants elected regional assemblies to be:

- democratic and responsive;
- inclusive and representative;
- small and streamlined;
- effective and efficient.

We envisage assemblies will have between 25 and 35 members. They will have a leader and cabinet of up to six members chosen by – and fully accountable to – the full assembly. It would be the task of the cabinet both to develop policies and, after gaining approval for them from the full assembly, to implement them. Regional assemblies will be based on the existing administrative boundaries used by the Government Offices and Regional Development Agencies.

Stakeholder involvement

The aim of the elected regional assemblies is to improve local decision-making. So they will need to ensure they harness the experience, expertise and commitment of others in their region. We want to see them making full use of all stakeholders – including the business community, trade unions, social and environmental partners, and other elected representatives.

Close working with regional partners should ensure that an assembly's policies are soundly based and have widespread support. Such stakeholder forums (such as the Scottish Civic Forum and similar arrangements in Wales and London) have worked well.

Elections

The voting system for elected regional assemblies will be the Additional Member System (AMS) form of proportional representation (PR). This is the system already used for the Scottish Parliament, the Welsh Assembly and the Greater London Authority. It ensures the overall composition of an assembly would broadly reflect the votes cast for the different parties at the assembly election.

Funding of assemblies

Most of an assembly's money will come through a single Government grant. The assembly will decide how it should use this to address key regional priorities. Based on figures for 2001/02, an assembly in the North East would be responsible for around £350 million. And it would influence decisions on how more than £500 million more is spent by its key partners.

Assemblies will be able to raise additional funds through the council tax. The money will be collected on behalf of the assembly by the local authorities in the region as part of their existing arrangements for collecting council tax. Non-domestic rates will not be affected ... An elected assembly would be allowed to set a higher charge to fund additional spending if it considered this desirable. We will, at least initially, limit this amount through arrangements comparable to the existing local authority capping regime.

Note

It remains to be seen whether the necessary enthusiasm amongst the English regions for these assemblies will be found. The example of the London Mayor and Assembly will be a useful one for voters: Ken Livingstone's administration in London has succeeded in carving out some distinctive policies, most notably, the congestion charge. The establishment of such Assemblies would do something to remedy the glaring asymmetry of the present arrangements, but would clearly leave England and her regions with nothing comparable to the powerful Scottish Parliament and would thus leave the substance of the West Lothian question untouched.

THE POLITICS OF THE UK CONSTITUTION AND ITS REFORM

D Marquand, 'Democracy in Britain' (2000) 10(2) Oxford International Review 2–10 (extracts)

...

The New Labour Revolution

I begin with a brief look at the current scene. The present Government was returned to power on the ticket of a 'democratic renewal'. No one quite knew what this meant, but there was little doubt that it implied a reconstruction of the British state more far-reaching than anything attempted since the First World War. The promise of home rule in Scotland and Wales; of freedom of information; of House of Lords reform and the abolition of the voting rights of the hereditary peers; of an act protecting human rights; and of a referendum on electoral reform heralded, between them, a constitutional revolution. The democratisation of Britain, which had stalled after the 1918 Representation of the People Act, seemed about to move forward again.

...

The old constitution – the constitution under which Amery and Crossman both grew up – is dissolving beneath our eyes. The only question is what will replace it.

To that question the authors of the revolution have no answer. On the contrary, they have reacted to the predictable consequences [Labour] of their own achievement with a mixture of incredulity and indignation. Having created new opportunities for voices in Scotland, Wales, and London, they have expended large quantities of political capital on attempts to make sure that the voices merely echo the orthodoxies of the centre. Having abolished the voting rights of most hereditary peers in the name of democratic legitimacy, they have set their faces against an elected second Chamber that might possess sufficient legitimacy to challenge the executive-dominated House of Commons. Though this is not certain, they also appear to have contrived an overwhelmingly nominated House, scarcely more legitimate than the largely hereditary one it has replaced. Their proposals on freedom of information are a pale shadow of the commitments they made in opposition, while the proposed referendum on electoral reform has receded into a hazy, post-election distance.

The Democratisation of Britain

The most frequent explanation for this mixture of boldness and timidity is that Tony Blair is a control freak. That is psychobabble. He may well be a control freak. But I see no evidence that he is more freakish, or more anxious to exert control, than Gladstone, Salisbury, Lloyd George, Neville Chamberlain or Edward Heath, to mention only a few. Few people get to the top of the greasy pole of politics without a masterful ego and a strong appetite for power. The true origins of what I shall call the Blair paradox lie, I believe, in his inheritance, not in the accidents of personal psychology.

They lie, in the first place, in the long, convoluted and fiercely contested process through which Britain became a democracy in the first place. For the notion that this country is, in some sense, the cradle of democracy is a myth. Democracy came to Britain slowly, haltingly, and late. The best part of a century passed between the great Reform Act of 1832, which increased the size of the electorate from 4.5% to 7.0% of the adult population, and the arrival of manhood suffrage in 1918. Even then, women could not vote until they reached the age of 30. As late as 1945, my own parents had four votes between them – two as ordinary citizens and two as university graduates. The first general election in which every adult citizen had one vote, and no one had more than one, was that of 1950. In a different sphere, it was not until 1911 that the House of Lords lost its veto powers, and not until 1999 that most hereditary peers lost their seats within it.

. . .

The history lived on in the mentalities of leaders and led. New groups were incorporated into the political nation; new men joined the political class. But the old, oligarchic order of the past changed the newcomers as much as they changed it.

. . .

Of course, there were differences between left courtiers and their counterparts on the right. For the right, the British state – even in its new democratic incarnation – was clothed in a mystic patina of custom and memory, from which its authority ultimately derived. Enoch Powell went a little far when he compared the kingship of England to the sacred olive tree of the Athenians, but his approach to the foundations of the political order was not unusual. For the left, the state was a utilitarian engine of social transformation, legitimate because it could deliver the goods.

. . .

. . . By the same token, socialists and social democrats were as zealous in their commitment to the British tradition of autonomous executive power and to the doctrine of absolute parliamentary sovereignty that accompanied and sustained it as any Conservative. In effect, the left made a Faustian bargain with the old order: power within the existing system, in exchange for adherence to its norms.

. . .

. . . The task, most social democrats believed, was to use the existing, now democratic constitution to change society from above. The young Aneurin Bevan saw Parliament as 'a sword, pointed at the heart of property power'. What mattered was to use the sword, not to waste time searching for a better one. . . . Most of the progressive left took it for granted that if the central executive were to complement political citizenship with social citizenship, to promote social justice, it would need all the autonomy it could lay its hands on. And so the court tradition reigned, throughout the inter-war years and well into the post-war period. . . .

. . .

Government by Poop-Poop

Then came the Thatcher revolution – the second crucial element in Blair's inheritance. Mrs Thatcher was to the court tradition what Mr Toad was to motorcars. She drove it so hard that she smashed it up. You might call it government by poop-poop. Westminster absolutism and executive autonomy were essential to her whole project. Without the concentration of power that they made possible, her Governments could not have marginalised the trade unions, curbed the local authorities, privatised most of the nationalised industries or imposed market norms on the remaining public sector. But she and her colleagues ignored the intricacies of the apparatus they used with such enthusiasm. The autonomous executive that Amery extolled had been responsive, not pro-active; permissive, not coercive; discreet, not obtrusive. Concentrated power was always there in reserve, but with the unspoken proviso that it should be kept in reserve for as long as possible. In normal times its motto was 'live and let live'. With that motto and the delicate fabric of practices and understandings that embodied it the Thatcher Governments were soon at war: they had to be if they were to reconstruct a complex civil society, rich in intermediate institutions operating by non-market rules, in the stark image of an 'enterprise culture'. But they were using the forms of American democracy to snuff out its spirit.

They paid a heavy price. Their object was a liberal economy, centred on the rational, calculating, freely choosing consumer. But the constitution through which they tried to attain it derived its authority from unchosen custom, beyond rational criticism. Thatcher herself saw no inconsistency in this. For her, free competition and traditional authority went together. She did not reckon with the social forces that she herself summoned up. Market forces were given freer reign; opportunities were widened; the already enfeebled old elites were further undermined; new men and the occasional new woman clawed their way to the top. But in the process, the mystique that had helped to legitimise the court tradition was stripped away. The hedonistic, tradition-scorning individualism that was fundamental to Thatcherite economics eroded the uncalculating respect for custom that was no less fundamental to its politics. The vulgar, vital, undeferential, bourgeois Britain that Thatcherite economics helped to bring into being became less and less willing to doff its cap to monarchical state. By 1991 a Mori survey found that the proportion of those surveyed who thought the system 'needed a great deal of improvement' or could be improved 'quite a lot' had gone up to 63 per cent, while only 4 per cent thought it 'worked extremely well'. The core executive of ministers and officials at the heart of the state responded by becoming increasingly aggressive and determined to concentrate power in its own hands. For its pains, it became increasingly isolated from, and ever-more suspect to, the society for which it claimed to speak. The more vigorously the Thatcherites' capitalist renaissance roared ahead, the less legitimate became the institutions through which they had procured it.

The Blair Paradox

Against that background, the Blair paradox falls into place. New Labour inherited not so much a constitutional crisis as a constitutional vacuum. Confidence in the political system had plummeted. Accusations of 'sleaze' in high places were rife. In Scotland, the demand for home rule had become irresistible. Blair and his colleagues saw that if they were to fill the constitutional vacuum and stem the drain of legitimacy that had helped to undo their predecessors, they would have to reconstruct the political order on lines appropriate to a modern, post-imperial, late twentieth-century society. The trouble was that they had no coherent answer to the obvious consequential questions: What sort of modern society? What kind of reconstruction, informed by what vision of democracy?

They sought diversity, openness, and the devolution of power. As Blair put it in a 1998 Fabian pamphlet,

> The demand for more democratic self-governance is fed by better educated citizens and the free-flow of information provided by new technology ... We must meet this demand by devolving power ... Devolution and local governance are not just important in themselves: open, vibrant, diverse democratic debate is a laboratory for ideas about how we should meet social needs.

That was the republican vision of Crossman and Tawney in a new guise. But Blair and his colleagues belonged to the Westminster village themselves. Its customs and assumptions were in their blood. If they were unwitting republicans they were also unwitting courtiers. They wished to reform the old order, but they also wished to renew the Faustian bargain that an earlier generation of social democrats had made with it. Like their political ancestors of seventy years before, they wanted to use the powers available to the autonomous executive of the court tradition to re-engineer society from the top – not, any longer, in the name of social ownership, or even social citizenship, but in the no less compelling names of equal opportunity and international competitiveness. Their critics on the left are apt to depict them as hopeless conservatives, seeking to fend off radical change. I don't believe that. I think they are torn between two kinds of radicalism, two visions of modernity and two conceptions of what democratic modernisation might mean – between modernisation as reinvented republicanism and modernisation as state-led adaptation to the pressures of the global market-place; between democracy as self-government and democracy as acquiescence.

That, roughly speaking, is where we are now. The strongest argument for any status quo – if it ain't broke, don't fix it – no longer applies. Manifestly, the old constitution *is* broke, partly by social change, partly by Thatcher, and partly by Blair. But, irrespective of party, Crossman's 'routine politicians' are still in thrall to it. So are the functionaries of Millbank and Smith Square and what is left of the mandarinate of Whitehall. As for ministers, they half-want to disperse power in the interests of modernisation from below, and half-want to concentrate it in the interests of modernisation from above. Plainly, this state of affairs cannot last. Further movement is inevitable. The only questions are: In which direction? And, under what banner?

. . .

[One answer, Marquand suggests, lies in the republican tradition that has been confined to the sidelines of politics for so long . . .] The institutional implications of a republican alternative to populism are undeniably complex, but they are not in any way extraordinary. It would mean following through the logic of the constitutional changes that the Government has already made. There would have to be more spaces for voice; more diffusion of power and responsibility; more and stronger checks and balances to counter the inherent tendency of any central executive to limit voice and concentrate power. Thorny practical issues would have to be resolved. The primordial questions of nationhood and identity – fundamental to all modern states – would be on the table. The relationship between Scotland and Wales on the one hand, and England and the English regions on the other, would have settled. So would the relationship between all of these and a post-imperial Britain, inextricably involved in a proto-federal European Union. The democratic deficits in regional and local governance would have to be overcome. The octopoid 'quango state' whose growth has been one of the most remarkable features of the last thirty years would have to be democratised. The composition and powers of an elected second chamber would have to be determined. The form of a proportional electoral system would have to be determined. The form of a proportional electoral system would have to be decided. But none of these questions is unanswerable. Most of them are in the agenda already, though sometimes without acknowledgement, and equivalent questions have been posed and answered in most of the Member-States of the European Union.

The really intractable problems lie elsewhere. A republican alternative would mean a change of mentality and assumption both among leaders and among led. The old Whig fetish of organic evolution would have to be jettisoned. The questions I listed a moment ago will in any case have to be answered sooner or later. But the piecemeal incrementalism of the Whig tradition is unlikely to produce consistent or coherent answers. A reinvented republicanism must be explicit, and the British (or perhaps I should say the English) have never been comfortable with constitutional explicitness. Even that is only the beginning of the story. The republican argument for democracy is that it is better – morally better, not just pleasanter or more convenient – to be a free citizen, bearing the burdens of freedom, than one of De Tocqueville's 'timid and industrious' sheep. From that it follows that it is better to allow people to make the wrong choices for themselves than to make the right choices for them. For politicians and publics schooled in the court tradition, that proposition runs against the grain. Just before he was executed for his part in the doomed Monmouth rebellion of 1685, Richard Rumbold, the old Leveller, distilled the essence of the republican vision in one of the most memorable sentences in British history: 'I am sure there was no man born, marked of God above another; for no man comes into the world with a saddle on his back, neither any booted and spurred to ride him'. So I pose a further question: is Britain of the twenty-first century at last ready for Rumbold? I wish I knew the answer.

Notes

1 Marquand usefully reminds us that issues of constitutionalism and democracy cannot be discussed as if hermetically sealed from quite another discipline – 'politics'. The final section of this chapter sets out different approaches to the UK constitution in the context of the Labour government's reform programme, a programme whose easy and smooth implementation has depended precisely upon the much-derided flexibility of the UK's constitution.

2 It should be noted at the outset, that, from a formal perspective, the government's reform programme makes no difference to the classification of the UK constitution and indeed to the argument, as advanced by Ridley (above) that the UK does not have a constitution worthy of the name at all. Neither of the two most dramatic changes – devolution, as represented for these purposes by the Scotland Act 1998 and the vesting in UK citizens of a set of basic civil rights enforceable in the national courts via the Human Rights Act 1998 (HRA) – create any 'higher' system of law. Both the Scotland Act and the HRA specifically affirm that they do not affect Parliament's continued ability to reverse the changes they make, either wholly or in part. Thus, the HRA makes no attempt to entrench itself and indeed provides quite specifically that, if the courts find a piece of legislation passed either previously or after the HRA to be incompatible with one or more of the Convention rights, this will not affect the validity or continuing effect of that legislation (ss 3(2) and 6(2) of the HRA). The White Paper on incorporation (Cm 3782) stated quite clearly that the HRA was not intended to detract from the sovereignty of Parliament in any way. Similarly, the White Paper on Scottish devolution (Cm 3658) proclaims that 'The United Kingdom is and will remain sovereign in all matters', and this basic statement of principle is clearly enacted in the legislation – Westminster may still legislate in the devolved areas, and may also repeal or modify the Scotland Act itself. These two pieces of legislation introduce, respectively, substantive, rights-based limitations on governmental power (the HRA) and devolution of that power to a specified region (the Scotland Act) – matters which would in most countries be part of 'higher' constitutional law, subject to change only through extraordinary procedures themselves specified in the constitution. Here, the opposite is provided for – following devolution and after the introduction of a Bill of Rights, Parliament will still, as a matter of law, be able to invade basic rights or the legislative autonomy of Scotland as easily and readily as it may change the rate of income tax.

3 Thus, on one level, the 'no constitution' argument will retain its basic force. But on another level, its applicability to the UK will become more problematic. To take Scotland first, its Parliament and thus its government for most matters will be limited by what will be in effect a written constitution, made up of the Scotland Act itself, the European Convention and European Community law. This is because, as seen above, the Scotland Act provides that acts of the Scottish Parliament or Executive which are outside the powers devolved to it by the Act or which infringe Convention rights or EC law will be *ultra vires*, and further that the courts will have what can only be described as a power of constitutional review, being empowered to strike down legislation of the Scottish Parliament, or acts of its executive on those grounds. Of course, in the areas which are not devolved, the Scots will continue to be governed by the unrestrained Westminster Parliament. But the day-to-day experience of the Scottish people will be to live under a government which, in most areas, will be constrained by a written constitution that will protect basic rights, specify the electoral system and set the basic shape of government. Those entrenched matters will be above and beyond the reach of the Scottish government and Parliament (since they may not alter the Scotland Act itself).

4 In answer to this, it may be said that, since the Westminster Parliament will still have the legal right to legislate in the devolved areas without the consent of the Scottish Executive, or even abolish the devolved institutions entirely, the Scots still have no constitutionally limited government. This is true as a matter of strict law, but it is at this point that purely legal perspectives begin to give a misleading view of the broader issue of constitutionalism. For the fact is that these legal rights are, in reality, probably theoretical only. No one seriously expects either to be exercised: the system would be unworkable if Westminster interfered in the devolved matters, while the outright legislative reversal of devolution has become virtually a political impossibility, not least because the devolution proposals were strongly endorsed by the Scottish electorate in a referendum. The Conservative Party, which bitterly opposed the Labour plans for devolution in the run-up to the 1997 election, has bowed to reality and promised that it will not attempt to reverse devolution. Thus, the day-to-day experience of the Scottish people will be to live under a written constitution for the first time.

5 Moreover, it is clear that the term 'unconstitutional' will start to have a very clear and definite meaning, certainly in relation to the government of Scotland but also in relation to Westminster. In relation to the former, it will mean legislation or administrative decisions which violate the legal constraints on the government of Scotland – there will be no doubt as to that. Legislation on rights-related matters will therefore fall to be discussed, and eventually adjudicated upon, in constitutional terms. As to Westminster, it may readily be anticipated that, as devolution and the new Scottish government become firmly entrenched, a convention will grow up to the effect that the Westminster Parliament will not legislate in the devolved area, much as such a convention developed during the period of the Stormont government of Northern Ireland between 1920 and 1972. As Bogdanor puts it, 'In practice ... sovereignty is being transferred and Westminster will not be able to recover it, except under pathological circumstances.'[33] Of course, legislation intruding into the areas of Scottish competency could not be legally condemned by the constitution, but the terminology of constitutionalism will enter into the competency of Westminster. Furthermore, this constitutional convention will not suffer from the indeterminacy of other more vague conventions, such as the principle of individual and collective responsibility of government to Parliament, an indeterminacy that allows such principles to be manipulated by the government of the day and undercuts the confidence of any attempts to label a given act as clearly 'unconstitutional' (the problem discussed by McAuslan and McEldowney, above). This is because the Scotland Act lays down in considerable detail the reserved powers of Westminster and thus the powers devolved. Devolution will thus become constitutionalised – in a very concrete way as far as Scotland and its government are concerned – and in a conventional but nevertheless real way for the Westminster Parliament.

6 Much the same may be said of the Human Rights Act. We have noted that it is not in any formal way entrenched; nevertheless, for the first time, the rights of UK citizens have been authoritatively identified and stated to be fundamental. Executive actions are unlawful if they infringe such rights – unless primary legislation inescapably mandates or authorises the infringement (s 6(2)). For the first time, statutory construction fully and unequivocally recognises the importance

---

33 Bogdanor (1998), *op cit*, p 12.

of basic rights – courts must read both past and future legislation into conformity with European Convention rights if possible (s 3). Ministers must make a statement when introducing legislation into Parliament stating that it does not infringe Convention rights, or that they believe it does, but that they wish to proceed in any event (s 19). Statements of the latter kind would amount to a declaration that the UK intended quite deliberately to violate its treaty obligations and breach international law and this will inevitably act as a powerful deterrent against the introduction of such legislation. Open infringements of the Convention will therefore become almost inconceivable and inadvertent infringements avoided by the need to scrutinise the Bill prior to making the statement to Parliament. Meanwhile, ambiguously worded legislation which may infringe rights can be dealt with via the interpretative obligation of the courts noted above. Together, depending upon how bullishly the courts set about their interpretative task, this could add up to quite a strong guarantee that legislation will no longer in practice infringe basic rights. All this could of course theoretically be removed, simply by repeal of the HRA. But, as with the Scottish Act, this will be highly unlikely, so that, as with devolution of powers, basic rights will become to an extent constitutionalised.

7   It may therefore be argued that while no higher basic norms are, as a matter of law, being created, the effect of the canvassed reforms may in practice be just that. The basic ability of Parliament to remove so-called 'constitutional' guarantees will still remain, at least as a matter of strict law. However, Ridley's view that the notion of 'constitutionalism' at the normative, conventional level cannot be deployed in the UK will lose much of its force, as certain ideas of devolved power and of basic rights attain an authoritatively declared basis and – as is likely – become ringfenced by strong inhibitory conventions.[34] In that sense, these reforms inject a modest dose of normative constitutionalism into UK government and society while leaving us formally still in search of a constitution.

8   Munro's view is somewhat different; he does not accept that a constitution needs to be either codified or have a special higher order status to be worthy of the name.[35] To him, therefore, the question is not whether the constitutional reforms starting in 1997 represent a change in the basic classification of the UK constitution (they do not), but how they change its character. His conclusion is that the reforms 'are apt to require us to modify our view of the British constitution, which is less monolithic, less centralised and less political then before'. Instancing the growing influence and legal supremacy of European Community law, together with the HRA, devolution, the legal regulation of political parties[36] and the partial codification of the doctrine of ministerial responsibility which followed the Scott Enquiry (see Part IV Chapter 2), he goes on:

In these various ways, the British constitution is becoming considerably more rule-based, rather less 'political' and rather more 'legal'. It will be interesting to see how much further these tendencies are taken, and whether there will be a reaction against them.[37]

9   As Munro observes, the UK constitution is becoming more 'legal' by which he means that questions which would hitherto have been decided by politicians on a

---

34   See further the extract from Elliott's article on this matter in Chapter 2 of this part, at pp 65–67.
35   Munro, *op cit*, pp 1–8.
36   Through the Registration of Political Parties Act 1999.
37   Munro, *op cit*, at p 13.

purely discretionary basis have been placed in the hands of the courts. Thus, the above reforms represent a considerable transfer of power within the UK constitution – from the Westminster Parliament to the Scottish Parliament and Northern Ireland Assembly in the case of devolution, and from the executive to the courts in the case of the HRA.[38] If the argument above as to the operation of the HRA in practice is correct, there is also a *de facto* limitation of Parliament's competency in the area of human rights. The transfer of what may be regarded as essentially 'political' questions – the proper scope of human rights and the point at which they should give way to societal interests – is deeply controversial, as the following extract from a well-known article by John Griffith indicates. The article was written partly in response to proposals for constitutional reform brought forward by Lords Hailsham and Scarman at the end of the 1970s, but its basic contentions are still of relevance today, both to the new constitutional settlement and to the ongoing debate as to whether the UK should adopt a codified and entrenched constitution or at least a Bill of Rights that, unlike the HRA, is protected from repeal in the ordinary way by Parliament.

John Griffith, 'The political constitution' (1979) 42 MLR 1 (extracts)

... As part of the recent movement to reintroduce natural law concepts into the theory and practice of politics, 'the law' has been raised from its proper and useful function as a means towards ends (about which it is possible to have differing opinions) to the level of a general concept. On this view, individual rules of law may be good or bad, but 'the law' is undeniably good and must be upheld or chaos will come again. There is more than a suspicion of sleight of hand here. For nobody, except committed anarchists, suggests that 'the law' should be dispensed with.

The ground is then shifted slightly and what becomes sacred and untouchable is something called the Rule of Law. The Rule of Law is an invaluable concept for those who wish not to change the present set up. A person may be said not to be in favour of the Rule of Law if he is critical of the Queen, the Commissioner of Metropolitan Police, the Speaker of the House of Commons, or Lord Denning. Statutes may be contrary to the Rule of Law (like some, but not all, Indemnity Acts) but the common law, it seems, can never be. Objection to the rules of international law in their application to the UK is wholly excusable on proper occasions. Defiance of regulations and directives emanating from Brussels may often be accounted a positive virtue.

If the Rule of Law means that there should be proper and adequate machinery for dealing with criminal offences and for ensuring that public authorities do not exceed their legal powers, and for insisting that official penalties may not be inflicted save on those who have broken the law, then only an outlaw could dispute its desirability. But when it is extended to mean more than that, it is a fantasy invented by Liberals of the old school in the late 19th century and patented by the Tories to throw a protective sanctity around certain legal and political institutions and principles which they wish to preserve at any cost. Then it is become a new metaphysic, seeming to resolve the doubts of the faithful with an old dogma.

The proposals for a written constitution, for a Bill of Rights, for a House of Lords with greater powers to restrain governmental legislation, for regional assemblies, for a supreme court to monitor all these proposals, are attempts to write laws so as to prevent Her Majesty's Government from exercising powers which hitherto that Government has exercised.

The fundamental political objection is this: that law is not and cannot be a substitute for politics. This is a hard truth, perhaps an unpleasant truth. For centuries political philosophers have sought that society in which government is by laws and not by men. It is an unattainable ideal. Written

---

38   The courts will also have an important role to play in determining the legislative competency of the devolved legislatures: see further, pp 26 *et seq*, above.

constitutions do not achieve it. Nor do Bills of Rights or any other devices. They merely pass political decisions out of the hands of politicians and into the hands of judges or other persons. To require a supreme court to make certain kinds of political decisions does not make those decisions any less political.

I believe firmly that political decisions should be taken by politicians. In a society like ours this means by people who are removable. It is an obvious corollary of this that the responsibility and accountability of our rules should be real and not fictitious. And of course our existing institutions, especially the House of Commons, need strengthening. And we need to force Governments out of secrecy and into the open. So also the freedom of the Press should be enlarged by the amendment of laws which restrict discussion. Governments are too easily able to act in an authoritarian manner. But the remedies are political. It is not by attempting to restrict the legal powers of government that we shall defeat authoritarianism. It is by insisting on open government.

That is why these present proposals by Lord Hailsham, Lord Scarman and others are not only mistaken but positively dangerous. They seem to indicate a way by which potential tyranny can be defeated by the intervention of the law and the intervention of institutional devices. There is no such way. Only political control, politically exercised, can supply the remedy.

The philosophical objection to the new proposals stems from an unease about a formulation based exclusively on rights. I suspect I shall be misunderstood on this. So I had better begin by saying that my distrust of Governments and of the claims made by those in authority is as profound as any man's and more profound than most.

I begin by rejecting the existence of that abstraction called the state ... the state is yet another metaphysic invention to conceal the reality of political power. Secondly, then, I reject the notion that those who hold political power have any moral right or moral authority to do so, however they came to their positions. They are there and they have power. No more. Thirdly, following from what I have said, the power they exercise is not special. It is no different in kind from the power exercised by other groups in the community like the owners or controllers of large accumulations of capital or the leaders of large trade unions. Fourthly, it is misleading to speak of certain rights of the individual as being fundamental in character and inherent in the person of the whole individual. As an individual I make claims on the authorities who control the society in which I live. If I am strong enough – and I shall have to join with others to be so – my claim may be recognised within certain limits. It may even be given legal status. There is a continuous struggle between the rulers and the ruled about the size and shape of these claims and that is what is meant by Curran's statement, that the condition upon which God hath given liberty to man is eternal vigilance although, as you will have gathered, I am not persuaded that we have a divine donor in this respect.

... As an individual I may say that I have certain rights – the right to life being the most fundamental. But those who manage the society in which I live will reply: 'put up your claim and we will look at it; don't ring us, we'll ring you.'

In this political, social sense there are no over-riding human rights; no right to freedom, to trial before conviction, to representation before taxation; no right not to be tortured, not to be summarily executed. Instead there are political claims by individuals and by groups.

One danger of arguing from rights is that the real issues can be evaded. What are truly questions of politics and economics are presented as questions of law.

But paradoxically, arguments advanced avowedly for the protection of human rights are often concealed political propaganda. Those for a written constitution, a Bill of Rights, a supreme court and the rest are attempts to resolve political conflicts in our society in a particular way, to minimise change, to maintain (so far as possible) the existing distribution of political and economic power ...

It seems to me that to call political claims 'inherent rights' is to mythologise and confuse the matter. The struggle is political throughout and moral only in the purely subjective sense that I may think I ought to be granted what I claim. Those in authority may think I ought not to be granted my claim. And there is no logic which says that their view is more based on their self-advancement (rather than, say, the public good) than mine is ...

Similarly with lawmakers, like ministers and judges. They have regard to the political ends they subserve. Partly politicians being rather less homogeneous a group than judges are likely to make decisions more distinguishable then the decisions judges make. And the political ends which Ministers subserve are not identical with those which judges subserve. But it seems to me that to suggest ministers or judges are seeking abstractions like justice or the conscience of the community or whatever is 'nonsense on stilts'. They are political animals pursuing political ends which are far narrower, more limited and more short term, than those abstractions ...

A further advantage in treating what others call rights as political claims is that their acceptance or rejection will be in the hands of politicians rather than judges, and the advantage of that is not that politicians are more likely to come up with the right answer but that, as I have said, they are so much more vulnerable than judges and can be dismissed or at least made to suffer in their reputation ...

Question

When Griffith states that 'A person may be said to be not in favour of the Rule of Law if he is critical of the Queen, the Commissioner of Metropolitan Police, the Speaker of the House of Commons or Lord Denning', is he criticising the substance of the doctrine or its misuse? If he is merely complaining that the doctrine is abused (like most theories), is he saying anything of interest?

Notes

1   Griffith's argument is that questions of rights are political and should be resolved by politicians, who are accountable. The problem with this approach appears to be this: rights are usually rights against government, for example, the right to freedom of information, giving the electorate access to information that may be embarrassing to the government, or the right to life or liberty of the person preventing the British government from using its armed forces to kill known members of the IRA in the absence of an immediate threat. Therefore, governments have a vested interest in eroding rights, in order to increase their freedom of action. If there are no legally entrenched rights, then the only sanction to prevent governments from eroding rights is the fear that this will result in political unpopularity. Unfortunately, at least in the UK, questions of rights are simply not major political issues. For example, the 1992 general election was fought almost entirely on social and economic issues,[39] in particular on taxation, the economy, education and health. The same can be said of the 1997 and 2001 elections. Indeed, certain issues, such as the rights of asylum seekers (to benefits, to work, to fair procedures), appear to 'run' in the electoral struggle for mass public opinion primarily for the Right: political advantage appears to lie in being perceived as 'tough', that is, authoritarian and illiberal on such issues. Much the same may be said of measures to counter crime and, in particular, terrorism. The passage of the draconian Anti-Terrorism, Crime and Security Act 2001, which, along with a raft of other authoritarian measures, gave the Home Secretary the right to detain, without trial, those suspected of being international terrorists and posing a threat to the UK, caused no public outcry, even though it required the UK to derogate from (temporarily opt out of) the right to liberty guaranteed by Article 5 of the European Convention on Human Rights. In this respect, it is worthy of note that the elected House of Commons did virtually

39   For an analysis of the campaigning in that election, see D Kavanagh and B Jones, 'Voting behavior' in B Jones (ed), *Politics UK* (1994), pp 193 *et seq.*

nothing to ameliorate the most illiberal aspects of the Act. Such improvement as was achieved by Parliament was almost entirely the work of the unelected House of Lords.[40] It may be argued that the political accountability on rights issues which, in Griffith's scheme, both argues against 'legalising' rights and supposedly ensures their protection, simply does not exist in practice.

2   Griffith describes both judges and politicians as 'political animals, pursuing political ends'. Whatever the argument about the extent to which judges are affected by their personal political views (and Griffith's thesis, put forward elsewhere,[41] that the judges are strongly influenced by their ingrained conservatism, has been vigorously attacked),[42] Griffith surely fails to make a basic distinction: whilst judges purport to approach a politically contentious legal issue from a standpoint of neutrality, and must therefore at least *be seen* to be unbiased in their assessment, politicians make a profession out of constant, unremitting bias in favour of the policies of the party to which they owe their allegiance. In particular, judges are often required to enforce the provisions of laws which it is clear they do not themselves like; politicians will simply seek to change them.

3   For a contemporary exponent of views in the leftist, republican tradition, see Adam Tomkins' review article of Martin Loughlin's *Sword and Scales* (2000): 'In defence of the political constitution' (2002) 22(1) OJLS 157–75.

FURTHER READING

TRS Allan, *Law Liberty and Justice* (1995)
E Barendt, *An Introduction to Constitutional Law* (1998)
D Beetham, *The Legitimisation of Power* (1991)
A Bradley and K Ewing, *Constitutional and Administrative Law*, 13th edn (2002)
PP Craig, *Public Law and Democracy in the United Kingdom and United States of America*
SE Finer, V Bogdanor and B Rudden, *Comparing Constitutions* (1995)
CJ Friedrich, *Limited Government: A Comparison* (1991)
HLA Hart, *The Concept of Law* (1967)
R Holme and M Elliot, *Time for a New Constitution* (1988)
O Hood Phillips, *Constitutional and Administrative Law*, 8th edn (2001)
IPPR, *The Constitution of the United Kingdom* (1991)
Sir WI Jennings, *The Law and the Constitution*, 5th edn (1959)
M Loughlin, *Public Law and Political Theory* (1992)
A Lyon, *Constitutional History of the United Kingdom* (2003)
P McAuslan, and JF McEldowney (eds), *Law, Legitimacy and the Constitution* (1985) (essays)
G Marshall, *Constitutional Theory*; Marshall and Moodie, *Some Problems of the Constitution* (1971)
R Slagstad, 'Liberal Constitutionalism and its Critics' (and other essays), in J Elster and R Slagstad (eds), *Democracy and Constitutionalism* (1988)
C Turpin, *British Government and the Constitution*, 4th edn (1999)
K Wheare, *Modern Constitutions* (1966)
L Woolf-Phillips, 'A long look at the British Constitution' (1984) 37(4) Parl Aff 385

---

40   On the contrast, see Part III Chapter 1, p 270 (Commons) and Part III Chapter 2, pp 365–72 (Lords, including extracts from the debate on the Bill).
41   *The Politics of the Judiciary*, 3rd edn (1985).
42   K Minogue, 'The biases of the Bench', *TLS*, 6 January 1978, and S Lee, *Judging Judges* (1988).

CHAPTER 2

THE NATURE AND ROLE OF CONSTITUTIONAL CONVENTIONS

INTRODUCTION

It is a characteristic of constitutions in general that they contain some areas which are governed by conventions, rather than by strict law. Conventions may be roughly defined as non-legal, generally agreed rules about how government should be conducted and, in particular, governing the relations between different organs of government. Even where a country has a written constitution, conventions tend to evolve around the various rules. Since the UK has no comprehensive written constitution, it is particularly reliant on conventions, even to govern very important aspects of constitutional behaviour. The rule that the Queen will only exercise her very wide statutory and prerogative powers on and in accordance with the advice of ministers is found in convention alone. It is generally known that, in a formal sense, the Queen appoints the Prime Minister. What is perhaps not generally appreciated is that when, for example, the Labour Party won the general election of 1997, that had no legal effect upon the Government. The UK did not have a Labour government until Tony Blair was appointed Prime Minister by the Queen and asked to form a government. Legally, the Queen can appoint whomsoever she chooses to be Prime Minister; it is only by convention that she must appoint as Prime Minister the person who is best able to command a majority in the House of Commons. The democratic basis of the UK's *government* (that is, the formation of its executive) therefore hangs upon convention, not law. The continuing placing of such heavy reliance on convention in a modern democracy purportedly governed by the Rule of Law is one of the more controversial features of the UK constitution.

It should be noted that individual conventions will be examined in detail in subsequent chapters where relevant. Thus, important conventions concerning relations between the organs of government generally are considered in Chapter 3 of this Part; those specifically governing the relations between the Lords and Commons will be examined in Part III Chapter 2; and the key conventions of individual and collective ministerial responsibility are analysed in Part IV Chapter 2.

THE VARIETY OF CONVENTIONS

Conventions rear their heads in a great many areas of the British constitution. Dicey considers a number of the more prominent examples below.

AV Dicey, *An Introduction to the Study of the Law of the Constitution*, 10th edn (1959), pp 419–21

... In short, by the side of our written law, there has grown up an unwritten or conventional constitution. When an Englishman speaks of the conduct of a public man being constitutional or unconstitutional, he means something wholly different from what he means by conduct being legal or illegal. A famous vote of the House of Commons, passed on the motion of a great statesman, once declared that the then ministers of the Crown did not possess the confidence of the House of Commons, and that their continuance in office was therefore at variance with the spirit of the constitution. The truth of such a position, according to the

traditional principles on which public men have acted for some generations, cannot be disputed; but it would be in vain to seek for any trace of such doctrines in any page of our written law. The proposer of that motion did not mean to charge the existing ministry with any illegal act, with any act which could be made the subject either of a prosecution in a lower court or of impeachment in the High Court of Parliament itself. He did not mean that they, ministers of the Crown, appointed during the pleasure of the Crown, committed any breach of the law of which the law could take cognisance, by retaining possession of their offices till such time as the Crown should think good to dismiss them from those offices. What he meant was that the general course of their policy was one which, to a majority of the House of Commons, did not seem to be wise or beneficial to the nation, and that therefore, according to a conventional code as well understood and as effectual as the written law itself, they were bound to resign offices of which the House of Commons no longer held them to be worthy.'
[Freeman, *Growth of the English Constitution*, 1st edn (1872), pp 109–10.]

The one exception which can be taken to this picture of our conventional constitution is the contrast drawn in it between the 'written law' and the 'unwritten constitution'; the true opposition, as already pointed out, is between laws properly so called, whether written or unwritten, and understandings or practices which, though commonly observed, are not laws in any true sense of that word at all. But this inaccuracy is hardly more than verbal, and we may gladly accept Mr Freeman's words as a starting-point whence to inquire into the nature or common quality of the maxims which make up our body of constitutional morality.

Examples of constitutional understandings

The following are examples of the precepts to which Mr Freeman refers, and belong to the code by which public life in England is (or is supposed to be) governed. 'A Ministry which is outvoted in the House of Commons is in many cases bound to retire from office.' 'A Cabinet, when outvoted on any vital question, may appeal once to the country by means of a dissolution.' 'If an appeal to the electors goes against the Ministry they are bound to retire from office, and have no right to dissolve Parliament a second time.' 'The Cabinet are responsible to Parliament as a body, for the general conduct of affairs.' 'They are further responsible to an extent, not however very definitely fixed, for the appointments made by any of their number, or to speak in more accurate language, made by the Crown under the advice of any member of the Cabinet.' 'The party who for the time being command a majority in the House of Commons, have (in general) a right to have their leaders placed in office.' 'The most influential of these leaders ought (generally speaking) to be the Premier, or head of the Cabinet.' These are precepts referring to the position and formation of the Cabinet. It is, however, easy to find constitutional maxims dealing with other topics. 'Treaties can be made without the necessity for any Act of Parliament; but the Crown, or in reality the ministry representing the Crown, ought not to make any treaty which will not command the approbation of Parliament.' 'The foreign policy of the country, the proclamation of war, and the making of peace ought to be left in the hands of the Crown, or in truth of the Crown's servants. But in foreign as in domestic affairs, the wish of the two Houses of Parliament or (when they differ) of the House of Commons ought to be followed.' 'The action of any ministry would be highly unconstitutional if it should involve the proclamation of war, or the making of peace, in defiance of the wishes of the House.' 'If there is a difference of opinion between the House of Lords and the House of Commons, the House of Lords ought, at some point, not definitely fixed, to give way ...

Note

It is interesting to note that the last of these conventions has been at least partially codified by means of the Parliament Acts 1911–49. Nevertheless, that codification has not hindered the continuing influence of more generalised conventions relating to the relationship between the Lords and Commons (see Part III Chapter 2). Geoffrey Marshall considers whether the variety of conventions is not in fact more rich than Dicey allowed for.

Geoffrey Marshall, *Constitutional Conventions* (1984), pp 3–5

In his Introduction to the Study of the Law of the Constitution AV Dicey picked out a number of rules as being constitutional conventions ... He also mentioned various questions that raise issues of conventional (rather than legal) propriety. What, he asked, are the conventions under which a ministry may dissolve Parliament? May a large number of peers be created for the purpose of overruling the Upper House? On what principle may a Cabinet allow of open questions? These last examples appear to be cases in which it cannot be clearly stated what the conventions are, or cases in which the relevant conventions are conflicting or controversial.

Dicey's discussion implied that the conventions of the constitution relate mainly to the exercise of the Crown's prerogatives and he suggested that their purpose was to ensure that these legal powers, formally in the hands of the Crown, were in practice exercised by ministers in accordance with the principles of responsible and representative government. But though the conventions do provide the framework of cabinet government and political accountability, and often modify rules of law, they spread more widely than Dicey's description suggests. Besides the conventional rules that govern the powers of the Crown there are many other constitutional relationships between governmental persons or institutions that illustrate the existence of rules of a conventional character. Examples are:

- relations between the Cabinet and the Prime Minister
- relations between the Government as a whole and Parliament
- relations between the two Houses of Parliament
- relations between Ministers and the Civil Service
- relations between Ministers and the machinery of justice
- relations between the United Kingdom and the member countries of the Commonwealth.

Many of these relationships are in part governed by law and in part by convention, [for example] the relationships of the member countries of the Commonwealth are in a number of fundamental ways regulated by the statute of Westminster, but in other ways rest upon agreements or conventions (some of which are mentioned in the preamble to the Statute).

Amongst the conventions of the Constitution there are some whose formulation is reasonably precise and specific, and others whose formulation is in more general terms. An example of the first kind is the rule that the Queen must assent to Bills that have received the approval of both Houses. An example of the second kind is that the House of Lords should not obstruct the policy of an elected Government with a majority in the House of Commons. Many conventions fall into the second category. This, perhaps, explains why so many questions of constitutional propriety remain unsettled. Might a British Government ever be dismissed by the Crown (comparably with what happened in Australia in 1975)? Is a Prime Minister entitled to dissolve Parliament and hold a general election whenever she wishes? Can a Government continue in office if its major legislation is defeated in the House of Commons? May a minister blame his civil servants if mistakes are made in the work of his department? The answers to all these questions are uncertain because, in each case, there is a general rule whose limits have not been fully explored; or possibly there may be two rules which are potentially in conflict.

Note

Examples of the uncertainty of many important conventions may be multiplied. To give just one example, Geoffrey Marshall and Graeme Moodie note[1] Ivor Jennings' suggestion that: '... in framing social legislation the appropriate department must consult the appropriate "interest" and ask, "what exactly is the rule?" Must every interest be consulted on every piece of social legislation? At what stage must they be

---

1   *Some Problems of the Constitution*, 5th edn (1971), pp 31–32.

consulted?' As suggested above, great uncertainty also surrounds the conventional limits placed upon the extent to which it is constitutionally proper for the unelected House of Lords repeatedly to reject legislation, or particular provisions of legislation, approved by the Commons. There is one clear convention – the Salisbury Convention – to the effect that the Lords should neither reject nor radically amend legislation which puts into effect pledges made in the governing party's manifesto. But the conventional limitations on their powers in relation to non-manifesto legislation are far less clear (see further Part III Chapter 2).

ATTEMPTS TO DEFINE CONVENTIONS

Colin Munro has noted that Dicey's methodology in dealing with conventions was not 'to offer a definition'. Instead, 'Conventions were illustrated by examples, and negatively defined by the fact that they were not court-enforced'.[2] He considers the success of this method, and its critics, particularly Sir Ivor Jennings.

Colin Munro, *Studies in Constitutional Law*, 2nd edn (1999), pp 61–63, 65–66, 70–71

One technique employed by Jennings was to point to certain kinds of similarity or interaction between laws and conventions. Both sorts of rule rested upon general acquiescence, he suggested, and the major conventions were as firmly fixed and might be stated with almost as much accuracy as principles of common law [*The Law and the Constitution*, 5th edn, pp 72, 117]. The late Professor JDB Mitchell built up further arguments of this sort:

> Conventions cannot be regarded as less important than rules of law. Often the legal rule is the less important. In relation to subject-matter the two types of rule overlap: in form they are often not clearly distinguishable ... very many conventions are capable of being expressed with the precision of a Rule of Law, or of being incorporated into law. Precedent is as operative in the formation of convention as it is in that of law. It cannot be said that a Rule of Law is necessarily more certain than is a convention. It may therefore be asked whether it is right to distinguish law from convention [*Constitutional Law*, 2nd edn (1968), p 34] ...

These statements appear to be of varying acceptability, but are apt to mislead. For example, there seems to be only a small number of conventions in this country whose existence and precise formulation are generally agreed, so that the statements about precision and certainty are very questionable. Sometimes there seems to be force in the assertion that the convention is more important than the law, but it is hard to see how their relative importance can be measured.

Besides, the important point is that none of Mitchell's propositions, even if accurate, would entail the conclusion which he went on to derive from them, that any effort to distinguish laws and conventions is bound to fail. This is readily illustrated by applying some of the comparisons to other bodies of rules:

> *Rules of morality* cannot be regarded as less important than rules of law ... in relation to subject-matter the two types of rule overlap ... Very many *religious edicts* are capable of being expressed with the precision of a Rule of Law, or of being incorporated into law. Precedent is as operative in the formation of *etiquette* as it is in that of law. It cannot be said that a Rule of Law is necessarily more certain than is a *rule of cricket*.

These new statements are just as accurate as the others, to put it no higher. We cannot draw from them the conclusion that the laws are *indistinguishable* from rules of morality, religion, etiquette or cricket. In fact, the explanation of why conventions, and all these, reveal some similarities to laws is simple: they are all rules operating in society, and certain similarities, especially of form, are only to be expected.

A ginger ale, however, is not the same as a whisky, merely because each is amber in colour and liquid in form. The critical question is whether laws may be *differentiated* from conventions. Dicey, who was in no doubt that they might be, also suggested a means:

> The rules which make up constitutional law, as the term is used in England, include two sets of principles or maxims of a totally distinct character. The one set of rules are in the strictest sense 'laws', since they are rules which (whether written or unwritten, whether enacted by statute or derived from the mass of custom, tradition or judge-made maxims known as the common law) are enforced by the courts; these rules constitute 'constitutional law' in the proper sense of that term, and may for the sake of distinction be called collectively 'the law of the constitution'.

> The other set of rules consist of conventions, understandings, habits or practices which, though they may regulate the conduct of ... officials, are not in reality laws at all since they are not enforced by the courts. This portion of constitutional law may, for the sake of distinction, be termed the 'conventions of the constitution', or constitutional morality [Dicey, p 23] ...

Laws and enforcement

...

What many have regarded as a more serious challenge to Dicey's test is posed by areas of law where the jurisdiction of the courts is apparently excluded, perhaps by an explicit provision that a duty may not be enforced in court proceedings or by the provision of an administrative channel as the exclusive remedy. Sometimes there are provisions of written constitutions in other countries which are expressed as non-justiciable, or are interpreted as such [for example, the Directive Principles of State Policy in the Constitution of India, which Article 37 declares not enforceable by any court].

Take the example that Jennings gives, a statutory duty upon local authorities to provide adequate sewers and disposal works, which was, under a statute, only remediable by means of complaint to the Minister of Housing and Local Government. When proceedings were brought in court, the House of Lords held that Parliament had deprived the courts of jurisdiction in that area, and that the complaint to the ministry was the sole means of redress (*Passmore v Oswaldwistle UDC*). The error that Jennings makes is in using the case as evidence that the law concerned was not court-enforced. The case is the best evidence possible that the law was court-enforced. Certainly a statutory duty was not judicially enforced, but that was precisely because the law said it should not be, and the courts obeyed the law and put it into effect. Other such examples may be explained in the same way. When provisions are unsusceptible to judicial enforcement, the correct analysis is either that no obligation is involved, as with some of the ideological pronouncements found in written constitutions, or is that an imperfect obligation has been created. None of this should surprise us. A legal system does not consist only of obligations for breach of which there is redress ...

These points are related to a larger contrast which may be drawn. Rules of law form parts of a system. Included in the system are rules about the rules: these are provisions about entry to, and exit from, the system, and procedures for the determination and application of the rules. We cannot conceive of a single legal rule, in isolation from a system. However, conventions do not form a system. There is no unifying feature which they possess, and no apparatus of secondary rules. They merely evolve in isolation from each other.

Here, incidentally, lies the answer to Jennings's specious argument that laws and conventions are the same because both 'rest essentially upon general acquiescence' [*op cit*, p 117]. That is quite misleading. Conventions rest entirely on acquiescence, but individually. If a supposed convention is not accepted as binding by those to whom it would apply, then there could not be said to be a convention, and this is a test on which each must be separately assessed. Laws do not depend upon acquiescence. Individual laws may be unpopular or widely disobeyed, but it does not mean that they are not laws. No doubt the system as a whole must possess some measure of *de facto* effectiveness for us to recognise it as valid, although it might be stretching language to describe the citizens of any country occupied by enemy forces, or ruled by a brutal dictatorship as 'acquiescing' in the laws which govern them. In any event, is it obvious that the comparison is inapt.

Notes

The distinction Munro draws as to the role which general acquiescence plays in relation to laws on the one hand and conventions on the other is a useful one. Jeremy Waldron has also considered this point, and draws a more general conclusion about the nature of conventions and the British constitution, after (in an earlier section of his essay) describing the appointment of Harold Macmillan's successor as Prime Minister.

Jeremy Waldron, *The Law* (1990), pp 62–67

Constitutional conventions

The term used to describe the sort of customs, practices and understandings that were at stake in the succession to Harold Macmillan is 'conventions'. They are not written rules but 'conventions' of the constitution. Or sometimes we are told helpfully that they are 'conventional' and not 'legal' rules. So what is a 'convention'?

It is important to say first that a convention is not just a regularity in political behaviour; it is not just a prediction of what reliably happens. Every year the Prime Minister moves to Chequers from Downing Street for Christmas. We can predict that she will do this, and we would be surprised if she didn't. But surprise is all that would be occasioned by such an 'irregularity'. We wouldn't criticise the Prime Minister for not spending Christmas at Chequers. We don't see it as a principle or norm to judge her by. It is a regularity we have discerned in Prime Ministerial behaviour, not a standard Prime Ministers are supposed to live up to.

Now constitutional conventions are not like that. They are normative. They are used for saying what ought to be done, and, as we saw, they are used as a basis for criticism if someone's behaviour does not live up to them. We use them to judge behaviour not merely to predict it.

But although they are norms, they would never be enforced by a court: you could never get a judge to declare that a convention ought to be followed as a matter of law, and if someone decided to flout a convention the only remedy would be political not legal. (Either those in possession of political power – the people, the other office-holders, the military perhaps in the last resort – would put up with what had happened or they wouldn't. If they did, the convention would in effect have been changed. If they did not, there would be something akin to a revolution.) Most writers have said that since these are norms but not legal norms, the only conclusion possible is that they are moral norms – norms of political morality. AV Dicey, for example, wrote that conventions 'consisting (as they do) of customs, practices, maxims, or precepts which are not enforced or recognised by the courts, make up a body not of laws, but of *constitutional or political ethics*'. And Geoffrey Marshall says that they 'simply spell out the *moral duties, rights, and powers of office-holders* in relation to the machinery of government'.

But calling them 'moral' or 'ethical' doesn't really help. There are all sorts of different views about 'constitutional or political ethics' and about 'the moral duties, rights, and powers of office-holders'. Pacifists may think that MPs have a moral duty not to authorise expenditure on nuclear weapons. Radical democrats believe that no law should be passed without a referendum. Christian fundamentalists may believe that atheists should not be allowed to hold public office. All these are held by their proponents as moral norms, but I take it none of them would regard their principles as conventions of the constitution. Certainly, we think or we hope that there are moral justifications for the conventions we have. But there is no reason to be confident that they capture the best political morality. It is not their moral justification that makes them conventions of the British constitution. We have got to say something more specific.

Sir Kenneth Wheare once wrote that a convention is 'a rule of behaviour accepted as obligatory by those concerned in the working of the constitution'. That is an interesting definition because it suggests that, in the last resort, these rules have no other basis than the fact that the people involved accept them as standards for their behaviour. They follow them in most cases; they feel guilt or compunction when they don't; they criticise deviations from them by others; and, what's more, everyone knows what is going on when these criticisms are made, for everyone has in mind roughly the same set of standards. They are not merely habits or regularities of behaviour; they enter into people's consciousness and become the subject-matter of reflection and of a sense of obligation. But they are not merely subjective views about morality either. They have a social reality, inasmuch as they capture a way in which people interact, a way in which people make demands on one another, and form attitudes and expectations about a common practice with standards that they are all living up to. They get mentioned in newspapers, in periodicals and in learned treaties. Politicians refer to them when they are evaluating one another's behaviour. They are social facts, not mere abstract principles, because they bind people together into a common form of life.

All this sounds very fragile compared with the robust reality of a statutory law or a written constitution. I have made it sound as though constitutional conventions are rules that pull themselves up by their own boot straps. They are rules because they are accepted as rules by those they bind, and if they weren't accepted by those they bind they wouldn't be rules at all. They have no other validity, no other force, than their common acceptance by the people they govern.

Waldron then goes on to consider the jurisprudential aspect of this question, giving a brief outline of HLA Hart's theory that each system of law is based ultimately upon a supreme rule, which he terms 'The rule of recognition'.[3]

Rules of recognition

In Britain, the rule of recognition says (among other things) that a bill passed (in the appropriate way) by the two Houses of Parliament and assented to by the Queen has the force of law, and prevails over any earlier law or any other rule that conflicts with it. It tells us, in effect, to look at the institutional pedigree of a norm to see if it is a legal rule; look at its date, the process of its enactment and the formalities associated with it, and that is all you need to know about its legal status. Other countries have more complicated rules of recognition; in the United States one has to look not only at how and when the Bill was passed (by both Houses of Congress, and with the President's assent or a fresh majority of two-thirds or more in each house of Congress) but also at its compatibility with the Bill of Rights embodied in the 1787 Constitution. And a full statement of the American rule of recognition would have to include the procedures for amending the constitution as well. Whatever the complexities, Hart's argument is that a legal system needs some such rule of recognition to identify what are to count at any time as its laws.

What gives the rule of recognition its legal force? What makes it the authoritative way of determining what the law is? The question does not really have an answer. It's a bit like asking what makes the US Constitution constitutional. The rule of recognition is just there. It is a social fact about the way people involved in the workings of our society – particularly lawyers, parliamentarians, judges, policemen, and so on – behave, and above all it's a fact about how they think they ought to behave. No doubt, judges and so on have their reasons for thinking they should defer to the edicts of Parliament. Some of them may be democratic reasons; some of them may be reasons of tradition. But their practice of doing so – their practice of deferring to Parliament, their practice of taking this as their standard – is not consecrated by any further authority. Their practice, their readiness to regard themselves as bound by this rule, is what makes our society a legal system; it's the fulcrum or the foundation of the rest. Without some social practice of this kind, there would be no legal system in Britain – that is, no shared sense among officials and people of which rules and commands they should expect to be upheld.

---

3   Hart's theory is set out in *The Concept of Law* (1961).

I brought up positivism and Hart's rule of recognition because I wanted to illustrate a general point about the foundations of political life. There is tradition, there is morality, there is affection, there is charisma, there is ideology, there is mystification, there are lies and – ultimately – there are bayonets and bullets. All of these are important in the analysis of politics, and all of them – including the last two (think of Northern Ireland) – have a part to play in explaining the stability of our political system. But there is also law and there is political order, regulating authority, succession, and the transfer and exercise of power. Law and political order matter an awful lot to us. But in the end they amount to an interlocking system of rules and practices that depend on nothing more concrete and nothing more secure than the readiness of those involved in political life to regulate and judge their own and others' behaviour by certain standards. Hart's theory of the rule of recognition implies that something no more secure than this lies at the foundation of every legal system. What we have said about constitutional conventions indicates that they fall into this category as well. It is the fragile readiness of those involved in political life to order their conduct by certain implicit standards that forms the basis of whatever claim Britain has to be a constitutional regime.

What is different, then, about the British constitution is not that it rests in the last resort on a set of fragile understandings; that is true of every legal and constitutional system. Rather, the distinguishing fact about Britain is that so much of its constitutional law has that status. In other countries, there is a written charter whose authority rests implicitly on such a presupposition. Americans tacitly presuppose the authority of the delegates at the 1787 convention who began their document with 'We the People of the United States ...' when they accept that document is binding. In Britain, however, the whole thing is a structure of tacit presuppositions from start to finish. There is no great charter whose authority is tacitly presupposed. There are just tacit presuppositions. That is the peculiar feature of our political life.

Notes

1   It should be noted that many jurists do not accept that the law can be identified solely by reference to its source, and that a legal system is thus based ultimately on a rule of recognition which identifies that source. The 'Natural Law' school argues that the ascertainment of whether a rule is a law is at bottom a moral exercise, whilst Ronald Dworkin has offered a 'third theory of law', in which interpretation and moral analysis play a key role in the identification of law, which, he argues, may exist before it is declared by any authoritative source.[4]

2   Crucial to the definition of conventions is the manner in which they are treated by the courts. Whilst at one time some commentators believed that 'the law courts can take no notice' of conventions at all, this notion has now been firmly scotched by the courts themselves. The Court of Appeal delivered an important judgment in a case arising out of the publication of the diaries of a former Cabinet Minister; the convention concerned was that of the collective responsibility of the Cabinet.

Attorney General v Jonathan Cape Ltd [1976] QB 752, 764, 770–71

Lord Widgery CJ: ... It has always been assumed by lawyers and, I suspect, by politicians and the Civil Service, that Cabinet proceedings and Cabinet papers are secret, and cannot be publicly disclosed until they have passed into history. It is quite clear that no court will compel the production of Cabinet papers in the course of discovery in an action, and the Attorney General contends that not only will the court refuse to compel the production of such matters, but it will go further and positively forbid the disclosure of such papers and proceedings if publication will be contrary to the public interest.

---

4   See *Taking Rights Seriously* (1977), Chapters 2–4, and for a more thorough exposition of R Dworkin's thesis, *Law's Empire* (1987).

The basis of this contention is the confidential character of these papers and proceedings, derived from the convention of joint Cabinet responsibility whereby any policy decision reached by the Cabinet has to be supported thereafter by all members of the Cabinet whether they approve of it or not, unless they feel compelled to resign. It is contended that Cabinet decisions and papers are confidential for a period to the extent at least that they must not be referred to outside the Cabinet in such a way as to disclose the attitude of individual ministers in the argument which preceded the decision. Thus, there may be no objection to a minister disclosing (or leaking, as It was called) the fact that a Cabinet meeting has taken place, or, indeed, the decision taken, so long as the individual views of ministers are not identified.

There is no doubt that Mr Crossman's manuscripts contain frequent references to individual opinions of Cabinet ministers, and this is not surprising because it was his avowed object to obtain a relaxation of the convention regarding memoirs of ex-ministers ... There have, as far as I know, been no previous attempts in any court to define the extent to which Cabinet proceedings should be treated as secret or confidential, and it is not surprising that different views on this subject are contained in the evidence before me ...

It is convenient next to deal with [the] submission ... that the evidence does not prove the existence of a convention as to collective responsibility, or adequately define a sphere of secrecy. I find overwhelming evidence that the doctrine of joint responsibility is generally understood and practised and equally strong evidence that it is on occasion ignored. The general effect of the evidence is that the doctrine is an established feature of the English form of government, and it follows that some matters leading up to a Cabinet decision may be regarded as confidential. Furthermore, I am persuaded that the nature of the confidence is that spoken for by the Attorney General, namely, that since the confidence is imposed to enable the efficient conduct of the Queen's business, the confidence is owed to the Queen and cannot be released by the members of Cabinet themselves. I have been told that a resigning minister who wishes to make a personal statement in the House, and to disclose matters which are confidential under the doctrine, obtains the consent of the Queen for this purpose. Such consent is obtained through the Prime Minister.

The Cabinet is at the very centre of national affairs, and must be in possession at all times of information which is secret or confidential. Secrets relating to national security may require to be preserved indefinitely. Secrets relating to new taxation proposals may be of the highest importance until Budget day, but public knowledge thereafter. To leak a Cabinet decision a day or so before it is officially announced is an accepted exercise in public relations, but to identify the ministers who voted one way or another is objectionable because it undermines the doctrine of joint responsibility.

It is evident that there cannot be a single rule governing the publication of such a variety of matters. In these actions we are concerned with the publication of diaries at a time when 11 years have expired since the first recorded events. The Attorney General must show (a) that such publication would be a breach of confidence; (b) that the public interest requires that the publication be restrained; and (c) that there are no other facts of the public interest contradictory of and more compelling than that relied upon. Moreover, the court, when asked to restrain such a publication, must closely examine the extent to which relief is necessary to ensure that restrictions are not imposed beyond the strict requirement of public need.

Applying those principles to the present case, what do we find? In my judgment, the Attorney General has made out his claim that the expression of individual opinions by Cabinet ministers in the course of Cabinet discussion are matters of confidence, the publication of which can be restrained by the court when this is clearly necessary in the public interest.

The maintenance of the doctrine of joint responsibility within the Cabinet is in the public interest, and the application of that doctrine might be prejudiced by premature disclosure of the views of individual Ministers ...

In the present case there is nothing in Mr Crossman's work to suggest that he did not support the doctrine of joint Cabinet responsibility. The question for the court is whether it is shown that publication now might damage the doctrine notwithstanding that much of the action is up to 10 years old and three general elections have been held meanwhile. So far as the Attorney General relies in his argument on the disclosure of individual ministerial opinions, he has not satisfied me that publication would in any way inhibit free and open discussion in Cabinet hereafter.

Notes

1 The Court of Appeal thus found that the convention in question could support an argument (based on breach of confidence) for legal restraint of publication, though, in the event, the action failed on the ground that, due to the lapse of time, the material had lost its confidential quality. The case is not the only example of conventions being taken into account by the courts. For example, in *Liversidge v Anderson* [1942] AC 206, HL and *Carltona Ltd v Commissioner of Works* [1943] 2 All ER 560 the courts supported the refusal to review the grounds on which executive discretionary powers had been exercised on the basis that a minister is responsible to Parliament for the exercise of his power.

2 In 1982, the Supreme Court of Canada had to consider a convention of the utmost importance, namely the understanding that the Senate and House of Commons of Canada would not seek to amend the constitution of Canada in such a way as to affect either the legislative role or the status of the provincial legislatures without first obtaining the consent of all Canada's provinces to such a change. The federal government of Canada was seeking to make quite important changes to the federal system of Canada and had only obtained the assent of a small number of the provinces; a declaration was sought from the court to the effect that it would be unlawful for such changes to be made without seeking the consent of all the provinces. It was argued that the convention of obtaining such consent, which no one disputed, had 'crystallised' into a (constitutional) law. The court rejected this argument, finding that failure to obtain the necessary consents would not render any subsequent amendment unlawful. It was, however, prepared to say that 'the agreement of the Provinces of Canada, no views being expressed as to its quantification, is constitutionally required' and that acting without such consents 'would be unconstitutional in the conventional sense'.

3 What therefore happened in this case was that a court made a non-binding finding as to what action a particular convention required, thereby giving it at least a degree of justiciability, and greatly increasing the likelihood that the conventional rule, once authoritatively declared, would be followed. Although the Canadian government would, strictly speaking, have been free to ignore this judgment, it clearly did not wish to act in a way which the Supreme Court had described as 'unconstitutional' and therefore entered into negotiations with the provinces, eventually obtaining the consent of nine out of 10 of them to its plans.

4 A more systematic attempt to define conventions has been attempted by Sir Ivor Jennings. His analysis is considered by Marshall and Moodie below.

G Marshall and GC Moodie, *Some Problems of the Constitution*, 5th edn (1971), pp 28–33

Sir Ivor Jennings's account of conventions [in *The Law and the Constitution*, 3rd edn, Chapter 3] is more convincing, but it is not entirely free from obscurity. His criteria for deciding whether a particular convention exists are these:

> First, what are the precedents; secondly, did the actors in the precedents believe that they were bound by a rule; and thirdly, is there a reason for the rule? A single precedent with a

good reason may be enough to establish the rule. A whole string of precedents without such a reason will be of no avail, unless it is perfectly certain that the persons concerned regarded them as bound by it [*ibid*, p 131].

For a convention to exist and operate the actors must obviously be aware of it and, in particular, of its obligatory character (even if in fact they conform to it for reasons other than self-conscious virtue). This awareness of obligation is a necessary characteristic of a convention, but it is a sure guide only if this obligation is felt very generally among those who work the constitution, ie among the authorities. Its absence may be conclusive, but not its presence. In and of itself it is not and cannot be a sufficient test: the actors may be divided in their opinions or they may be mistaken about their obligations ...

4 Precedents

How then are reasons for conventional rules related to precedents? In the English legal system all cases decided in the highest courts of the judicial hierarchy are precedents, in the sense that these decisions are binding upon all other courts in all other similar cases. In this manner, judicial decisions, or precedents, may be said to establish rules of law. Where conventions are concerned, however, it seems that not even a series of similar precedent actions will always suffice to establish a conventional rule – if indeed it ever suffices. A distinction has therefore been drawn by Sir Ivor Jennings between precedents which do, and those which do not, establish a rule, ie between 'normative' and 'simple' precedents [Jennings, *Cabinet Government*, 2nd edn, p 7]. But in both legal and ordinary English we tend to use the word 'precedent' to refer to instances which, for some reason other than the fact of occurrence itself, are deemed to be relevant, desirable, or acceptable models for future action. Sir Ivor remarks at one point of the 'agreement to differ' amongst ministers in 1932: 'No harm was done by the precedent of 1932 provided that it is not regarded as a precedent' [*ibid*, 3rd edn, p 281]. A 'simple' precedent, in other words, could hardly be distinguished from no precedent at all ...

The instance of 1924 is an instructive one. It is justifiable to query the opinion that King George V established a new rule (that the Prime Minister should always be a Member of the House of Commons) when he appointed Mr Baldwin instead of Lord Curzon. On the other hand, there now seems to exist a widespread view that a Prime Minister should not belong to a Chamber in which one party has little representation and in which few major debates or decisions occur. For some such reason, the King's action in 1924 may now be referred to as a precedent. But this reason would have existed whether or not there had existed a noble alternative to Mr Baldwin.

5 Obedience to conventions

Neither a general feeling of obligation among the authorities, nor precedents, therefore, suffice either to establish a rule or conclusively to demonstrate its existence and precise content.

The first part of the answer is contained in Jennings's suggestion that 'conventions are obeyed because of the political difficulties which follow if they are not' [*ibid*, p 129]. To complete the answer one must inquire what sort of political difficulties they are, for it is clear that political difficulties can arise from many actions which involve no breach of a convention. A Government runs into 'political difficulties' whenever it displeases some section of the community, whether it be by raising rents or refusing to issue a stamp commemorating the birth of Robert Burns, but it cannot seriously be claimed that either decision is in any sense 'unconstitutional'. Nevertheless it is by examining the effects of a breach of conventions that the reason for their existence is to be found. If a UK Government had, before 1931, legislated for a 'dominion', or had, since then, introduced legislation affecting the status of the Crown, without obtaining the consent of the countries concerned, it is likely that one or more members of the Commonwealth might have severed their connections with it; or, at least, that Commonwealth ties would have been imperilled. The serious breach in the conventions limiting the power of the House of Lords which occurred in 1909 resulted directly in the passing of the Parliament Act of 1911, just as Roosevelt's re-election for a third and fourth term led to the adoption of the 22nd Amendment to the American

Constitution which makes a third term legally impermissible ... These examples indicate that the conventions describe the way in which certain legal powers must be exercised if the powers are to be tolerated by those affected. The monarch's legal powers to rule, the House of Lords' legal powers to reject a bill passed by the Commons, the legal power of the UK Parliament to pass imperial legislation – all these powers are or were retained only for so long as they are exercised (or not exercised) in accordance with the conventions which have been established. Their potential abolition constitutes the 'political difficulties' which would probably follow upon a breach in the conventions of the constitution.

From this view of the nature of conventions it follows that a crucial question must always be whether or not a particular class of action is likely to destroy respect for the established distribution of authority.

Such an account of the relationship between law and convention bears a resemblance to that put forward by Dicey, but it differs therefrom in an important respect. According to Dicey, a breach in a convention involved the probability of a consequential breach of the law. But the truth is rather that a breach of a convention is likely to induce a change in the law or even in the whole constitutional structure. In this relationship, it may be suggested, is to be found the 'reason' for the conventions, stated in its most general form.

Notes

1   Joseph Jaconelli has recently re-considered Jennings' proposed tests.[5] He criticises the first requirement, that of precedent, noting that it may in practice amount to little more than 'a selective exercise in constitutional history'[6] and that it is not clear how 'history – in some cases ... quite distant history [can] tell us what course of conduct *is required* of [the relevant person]'.[7] He also criticises Jennings for failing to provide any indication of what will count as a 'good' reason for a given alleged convention, when there may be strong reasons both for and against its continuance.[8]

2   As the authors note, of obvious relevance to this debate are the reasons which may be given for the obedience of this affected by them to conventions, an issue considered by Marshall below.

Geoffrey Marshall, *Constitutional Conventions* (1984), pp 5–8

In the opening chapter of the *Law of the Constitution* Dicey, in discussing 'the rules that belong to the conventions of the Constitution', remarks that 'some of these maxims are never violated and are universally admitted to be inviolable. Others on the other hand have nothing but a slight amount of custom in their favour and are of disputable validity' [*Law of the Constitution*, 10th edn, p 26]. Confusingly, he goes on to explain this difference as one that rests upon the distinction between rules that bring their violators into conflict with the law of the land, and rules 'that may be violated without any other consequence than that of exposing the Minister or other person by whom they were broken to blame or unpopularity' [*ibid*]. This does not chime very easily with the thesis that the reason for obedience to all conventions is that breach of the conventions leads more or less directly to a breach of law. Dicey has often been criticised for holding this view, but it seems clear that he did not hold it in relation to all conventions. Indeed, it seems an explanation confined to a single contingency, namely the possibility that a Government might try to remain in office and raise taxes after losing the confidence of the House of Commons. But Dicey mentions a number of examples in which no illegal consequences would follow a breach of conventional

---

5   J Jaconelli, 'The nature of constitutional convention' [1999] LS 24.
6   *Ibid*, p 28.
7   *Ibid*, p 29.
8   *Ibid*.

principles. A Government that persuaded the House of Commons to suspend the Habeas Corpus Acts after one reading, or induced the House to alter the rules as to the number of times a Bill should be read would not, he said, come into conflict with the law of the land. Nor indeed would the House of Lords if it rejected a series of Bills passed by the Commons.

Some who have criticised Dicey's supposed explanation for obedience to conventions have suggested alternative reasons. Sir Ivor Jennings argued, for example, that conventions are obeyed 'because of the political difficulties which follow if they are not' [*The Law and the Constitution*, 5th edn, p 134]. Others have suggested that they are obeyed not because of the probability of a consequential breach of law, but because disregard of convention is likely to induce a change in the law or in the constitutional structure. But it could be objected that, in the case of many infringements of convention, legal or structural change would be an unlikely outcome. It may be more illuminating first to remember that widespread breach of political (as of linguistic) convention may itself sometimes lead to a change of convention, and secondly that conventions are not always obeyed. So, although we can sensibly ask what the uses or purposes of conventions are, it may be unnecessary to ask why they are obeyed when they are obeyed, since we pick out and identify as conventions precisely those rules that are generally obeyed and generally thought to be obligatory. Those who obey moral or other non-legal rules they believe to be obligatory, characteristically do it because of their belief that they are obligatory, or else from some motive of prudence or expected advantage. Those who disobey them do so because they do not regard them as obligatory, or wish to evade them, or wish to change them. In other words we do not need any special or characteristic explanation for obedience to the rules of governmental morality. Whatever we know about compliance with moral rules generally, will suffice.

Note

If the reason that conventions are obeyed is simply that they are thought obligatory by those affected by them, then it appears that the more important question is, what purposes do conventions serve? Whilst answers to this question have been touched on (Dicey – to avoid a breach of the law; Jennings – to avoid political difficulty), these are too general answers as they would also serve as plausible explanations for a great deal of human behaviour. Can more specific purposes for conventions be elucidated?

THE ROLE OF CONVENTIONS

The role of conventions was considered by the Supreme Court of Canada in the case mentioned above.

Reference re Amendment of the Constitution of Canada (1982) 125 DLR (3d) 1

... The main purpose of constitutional conventions is to ensure that the legal framework of the constitution will be operated in accordance with the prevailing constitutional values or principles of the period. For example, the constitutional value which is the pivot of the conventions stated above and relating to responsible government is the democratic principle: the powers of the state must be exercised in accordance with the wishes of the electorate; and the constitutional value or principle which anchors the conventions regulating the relationship between the members of the Commonwealth is the independence of the former British colonies.

Being based on custom and precedent, constitutional conventions are usually unwritten rules. Some of them, however, may be reduced to writing and expressed in the proceedings and documents of imperial conferences, or in the preamble of statutes such as the Statute of Westminster 1931, or in the proceedings and documents of federal-provincial conferences. They are often referred to and recognised in statements made by members of governments.

Perhaps the main reason why convention rules cannot be enforced by the courts is that they are generally in conflict with the legal rules which they postulate, and the courts are bound to enforce the legal rules. The conflict is not of a type which would entail the commission of any illegality. It results from the fact that legal rules create wide powers, discretions and rights which conventions prescribe should be exercised only in a certain limited manner, if at all.

[An] example will illustrate this point. As a matter of law, the Queen, or the Governor General or the Lieutenant Governor could refuse assent to every Bill passed by both Houses of Parliament or by a legislative assembly as the case may be. But by convention they cannot of their own motion refuse to assent to any such Bill on any ground, for instance, because they disapprove of the policy of the Bill. We have here a conflict between a legal rule which creates a complete discretion and a conventional rule which completely neutralises it. But conventions, like laws, are sometimes violated. And if this particular convention were violated and assent were improperly withheld, the courts would be bound to enforce the law, not the convention. They would refuse to recognise the validity of a vetoed bill. This is what happened in *Gallant v The King* (1949) 2 DLR 425 ... a case in keeping with the classic case of *Stockdale v Hansard* (1839) 9 Ad and El, 112 ER 1112, where the English Court of Queen's Bench held that only the Queen and both Houses of Parliament could make or unmake laws. The Lieutenant-Governor who had withheld assent in *Gallant* apparently did so towards the end of his term of office. Had it been otherwise, it is not inconceivable that his withholding of assent might have produced a political crisis leading to his removal from office, which shows that if the remedy for a breach of a convention does not lie with the courts, still the breach is not necessarily without a remedy. The remedy lies with some other institutions of Government; furthermore, it is not a formal remedy and it may be administered with less certainty or regularity than it would be by a court.

It should be borne in mind, however, that, while they are not laws, some conventions may be more important than some laws. Their importance depends on that of the value or principle which they are meant to safeguard. Also, they form an integral part of the constitution and of the constitutional system ...

That is why it is perfectly appropriate to say that to violate a convention is to do something which is unconstitutional, although it entails no direct legal consequence. But the words 'constitutional' and 'unconstitutional' may also be used in a strict legal sense, for instance with respect to a statute which is found *ultra vires* or unconstitutional. The foregoing may perhaps be summarised in an equation: constitutional conventions plus constitutional law equal the total constitution of the country.

Questions

1   Is it not rather a paradoxical state of affairs for any nation that prides itself on upholding the Rule of Law that 'important parts of [its] constitution' which 'may be more important than some laws' may be violated with 'no direct legal consequences'?

2   The court found that the basic purpose of conventions is 'to ensure the legal framework of the Constitution in accordance with the prevailing constitutional values or principles of the period'. No doubt responsiveness to changing views as to what political morality demands is desirable. But take the case of a minister whose department bungles the implementation of a new policy in such a way that there is room for doubt as to whether the policy or its implementation are at fault.[9] The minister claims that the convention of ministerial responsibility has now developed in such a way that it only requires ministerial resignation if it is

---

9   The responsibility of the then Home Secretary Michael Howard for the problems in the Prison Service revealed by the Learmont Report in October 1995 is a case in point. See further Part IV Chapter 2, pp 549–50.

conclusively shown that policy, rather than its implementation, is to blame. Is it necessary that the person who would suffer through the imposition of a conventional rule upon them must be the person who also decides what that rule is?[10] Can flexibility be achieved without allowing people to be judges in their own cause in this way?

Notes

1   Marshall and Moodie note the prevalence of conventions in all constitutions and link this with what they see as their role.

> ... No general Rule of Law is self-applying, but must be applied according to the terms of additional rules. These additional rules may be concerned with the interpretation of the general rule, or with the exact circumstances in which it should apply, about either of which uncertainty may exist, and the greater the generality the greater will the uncertainty tend to be. Many constitutions include a large number of additional legal rules to clarify the meaning and application of their main provisions, but in a changing world it is rarely possible to eradicate or prevent all doubts on these points by enactment or even by adjudication. The result often is to leave significant degree of discretion to those exercising the rights or wielding the powers legally conferred, defined, or permitted. As Dicey pointed out, it is to regulate the use of such discretionary power that conventions develop [*op cit*, pp 426–29].

> The definition of 'conventions' may thus be amplified by saying that their purpose is to define the use of constitutional discretion. To put this in slightly different words, it may be said that conventions are non-legal rules regulating the way in which legal rules shall be applied.[11] ...

2   In an illuminating article published recently, Elliott offers a contemporary example of the effect of conventions upon the most important legal rule in the UK constitution: the sovereignty of Parliament. He argues that one effect of the Labour government's radical programme of constitutional reform has been to widen the gap still further between the strict legal doctrine of parliamentary sovereignty, under which its powers are unlimited, and the political reality: it is, for example, inconceivable that Westminster would in reality simply abolish the Scottish Parliament (at least without the clear consent of the Scottish people). His suggestion is that constitutional conventions form a way of bridging the gap between legal theory and political reality, and may also come to have an influence on the *law* of the constitution as well.

Mark Elliott, 'Parliamentary sovereignty and new constitutional order: legislative freedom, political reality and convention' [2002] 22(3) LS 340 (extracts)

As regional autonomy and human rights become increasingly embedded within the British constitutional order, so it is to be expected that conventions will emerge – indeed some have already begun to emerge [see below for discussion of the Sewel Convention] concerning the acceptable limitations of legislative action by the Westminster Parliament. In this way, convention comes to bridge the gap between a constitutional theory of unlimited legislative authority, and the reality of a political environment within which regional authority and fundamental rights are regarded as tracing the perimeter of acceptable legislative conduct.

The deployment of convention in this manner is already familiar ... [Elliott cites those restraining the Monarch] and conventions already exist which regulate the exercise of legislative action. [Elliott cites the convention observed by the UK Parliament in not legislating in those areas

---

10   The views of the Prime Minister and other ministers on the content of the convention will also obviously be important. However, since resignation (in the example given in the text) would amount to an admission of responsibility for the errors which have come to light, these other parties also have a clear vested outcome in the decision.

11   Marshall and Moodie, *op cit*, pp 24–25.

devolved to Stormont during the period of devolution to Northern Ireland between 1920 and 1972.] Moreover, as ... conventions ... are inherently flexible, those conventions which emerge need not be static: as devolution becomes better established, conventions prohibiting unilateral legislation may well strengthen and may, in terms of the seriousness with which they are treated by the relevant political actors, harden. Similarly, different conventions may regulate the relationship between Westminster and each of the devolved institutions, reflecting the idea of the devolved institutions, reflecting the idea that the inappropriateness of unilateral interference in devolved matters is ultimately a function of the extent to which political autonomy has become an embedded feature of the region in question.

... Some writers view conventions in purely empirical terms. Hood Phillips, for instance, regards them as 'rules of political practice which are regarded as binding by those to whom they apply, but which are not laws' (Constitutional and Administrative Law (8th ed 2001) p 136). Others, however, recognise that conventions reflect both empirical and normative considerations – thus helping to explain why conventions are both descriptive of past practice and prescriptive of future conduct. These dual ... aspects of convention find clear expression in the so-called Jennings Test, which requires not only that the practice is supported by precedent and that political actors feel bound to respect it, but also that there must be a reason for the practice... [see above – Elliott goes on to note Jaconelli's preferred analysis, seeing conventions as 'rules' in the Hartian[12] sense which attract pressure to conform to them].

In the present context, the 'practice' in question is legislative adherence to the principles of human rights and devolution: and it is submitted that there exists a compelling rationale for such adherence which (on Jennings' approach) supplies the 'reason' to support a convention, or which (applying Jaconelli's model) explains why pressure exists in favour of conforming to the practice. The position is self-evident in relation to human rights. The very classification of rights in such terms indicates their inherent worth and fundamental status: this, in turn, furnishes a strong normative reason for legislative adherence to such values, and also identifies the source of considerable pressure in favour of such practice. Similar conclusions may be drawn in relation to devolution. The normative value to be attached to regional autonomy is context-dependant, rather than (as in the case of human rights) inherent. However, in relation to those parts of the UK to which power has been devolved, the political context ascribes considerable weight to regional autonomy, as evidenced by the popular seal of support provided by the devolution referendums. Consequently ... self-determination [is] regarded as normatively valuable in Scotland, Wales and Northern Ireland, and this in turn supplies a strong reason for a mode of legislative behaviour, on the part of the UK Parliament, which respect the devolution settlement [and] ... strong pressure [for such behaviour] ...

Indeed it is said that that a convention has already emerged concerning the relationship between the UK and Scottish legislatures. In the House of Lords ... Lord Sewel explained that:

... we would expect a convention to be established that Westminster would not normally legislate with regard to devolved matters in Scotland without the consent of the Scottish Parliament. [HL Deb (5th series) col 791 (21 July 1998)].

This approach is acknowledged in the principal concordat – an informal, non-binding agreement – entered into following devolution ... the Memorandum of Understanding [Cm 4444, 1999] [which repeats this undertaking].

... In this manner, constitutional convention serves to connect the disparate positions represented by the orthodoxy of unlimited legislative freedom and the political reality of a constitutional order within which the human rights and devolution schemes trace the perimeter of legislative action which is deemed to be constitutionally proper.

---

12   That is, the sense used by the philosopher HLA Hart: see the *Concept of Law* (1961).

[Elliott then goes on to discuss the way in which the sharp distinction between convention and law is blurred when convention supplies a strong reason for the legal finding in a case.]

Prior to [conventional] rules is a foundation of constitutional principle which justifies and gives rise to them; as we saw earlier, this prescriptive aspect is reflected in Jennings' need for a reason for the rule, and also in Jaconelli's theory of conventions as social rules whose observance is directed by some underlying normative imperative.

If this richer conception of convention is adopted, then the justification for sharply distinguishing it from law, and for regarding it as wholly unenforceable judicially, is placed under a good deal of pressure. The law reports are replete with examples of constitutional principle shaping and determining the content of law. Thus the constitutional principle of access to justice requires strict interpretation of [clauses excluding judicial review; *Anisminic Ltd v Foreign Compensation Commission* [1969] 2 AC 147] and of statutory provisions which confer discretionary power [*ex parte Witham* [1998] QB 575], while the constitutional weight attached to freedom of expression dictates that public authorities may not issue claims for defamation [*Derbyshire County Council v Times Newspapers* [1993] AC 534] and compels narrow interpretation of legislative provisions which appear to threaten it [*ex parte Simms* [2000] AC 115]. In broader terms, the constitutional principle of separation of powers determines the perimeter [*ex parte Fire Brigades Union* [1995] 2 AC 513] and intensity [*ex parte Brind* [1991] 1 AC 696; *Daly* [2001] 2 WLR 1622] of judicial review, while the rule of law clearly influences the development of the law in areas as diverse as *locus standi* [*IRC v National Federation of Self-Employed and Small Businesses Ltd* [1982] AC 617 at 644], contempt of court [*re M* [1994] 1 AC 377 at 425–26], collateral challenge[13] [*Boddington v British Transport Police* [1999] 2 AC 143] and the grounds of judicial review. These examples are given not as situations in which *conventions* have acquired legal recognition, but simply as instances of constitutional principle shaping the content of constitutional *law*.

[Thus] this approach ... simply recognises that expression may be given to constitutional principles in different ways – by institutionalising them conventionally or legally – and that there need be no watertight dividing line between those two methodologies. As circumstances change – for instance as greater normative weight is ascribed to a given value – it may be appropriate and desirable to move from political enforcement of the value (by recognising it as giving rise to a convention) towards legal enforcement. This organic process, whereby the common law recognises and gives legal weight to values which are adjudged to be of sufficient normative importance, is well established; and it would be illogical to exclude a given norm (which has hitherto been reflected by convention) from that process of the acquisition of legal weight simply because of a dogma that rigorously divorces convention and law.

SHOULD CONVENTIONS BE CODIFIED?

The uncertainty surrounding the content and even the existence of certain conventions has led a number of commentators to question whether conventions should now be set down in an authoritative text or even enshrined in law. It is supposed to be an advantage of conventions that they represent a means of bringing about developments in the constitution without the need for formal repeal or amendment of the law. The distinction between strict law and conventions grew up due to the need to effect a quiet erosion of the prerogative powers of the monarch. Such powers could by convention be vested in the Cabinet or Prime Minister, thereby avoiding the need for any formal statutory declaration that this had occurred. Conventions thus allow the constitution to evolve and keep up to date with changing circumstances. However, this

---

13 That is, the ability to raise a defence that a statute is *ultra vires* in other proceedings.

very ease of change has for some time been generating unease amongst commentators. In this respect Johnson provides an important historical perspective. He notes the strong influence of Dicey in this area, as in so many others – 'it was he who gave such a large place to convention and attempted to explain how it operated as indispensable complement to constitutional law proper' – and then goes on:

N Johnson, *In Search of the Constitution* (1980), pp 32–34 (extracts)

But the crucial point is that the power of Victorian constitutional convention was incomparably greater than that of any contemporary convention of the same kind. In saying this I am to some extent doing no more than pointing out how much more seriously our forefathers were committed to the firm observance of a range of moral and political conventions far wider than would be conceivable today. In contrast it is a hallmark of our age that practically every aspect of social life is caught up in a process of change, is open to challenge and has lost the predictability which it once had ... The large place [the Victorians gave] to convention was precisely the result of a belief that it was founded on habits and traditions expressive of the genius of the people which, like the rock of ages, would endure ...

[But] in our present political life ... there is no longer that degree of commitment to particular procedures, that respect of traditional values and habits, nor that breadth of agreement about how political authority should be exercised and for what purposes, which justify the belief that convention alone is a sheet-anchor on which we can rely for the protection of civil rights for the survival of a particular form of government. Flexible and adaptable the Constitution remains, but these are qualities that can be used for different purposes, and increasingly it becomes clear that they serve chiefly to justify the relentless extension of public power and the erosion of such notions as may survive of the limits within which it may properly be exercised. Thus what was a valuable element in the British constitutional tradition, a sign of political wisdom, has been perverted ... Meanwhile, the virtues of trusting to convention are extolled as the vital principle of the Constitution by those whose chief interest it is to maintain just such a state of affairs.

... The chief effect of [the] famous flexibility [of the UK Constitution], of course, has been to spare us some of the conflict which might occur under a more formalized constitutional system when proposals for change are under debate, and thus to deprive us of the stimulus having to argue seriously about the principles on which we claim to be acting ...

Marshall and Moodie go on to consider the specific pros and cons of codifying conventions.

G Marshall and GC Moodie, *Some Problems of the Constitution*, 5th edn (1971), pp 34–36

Dr HV Evatt has argued that the practice of enacting conventions, exemplified in such laws as the Parliament Act and the Statute of Westminster, should be extended into other fields in order to end uncertainty about, for example, the royal power of dissolution [*The King and his Dominion Governors*, 1936 (1967), p 268]. In so far as this would lead to more precise formulation of the rules and the use of the courts to give authoritative decisions about their meaning and application, or to the extent that people are more disposed to obey legal than non-legal rules, the advantages are obvious and important. It is nevertheless argued by some that the disadvantages are of greater significance. Thus the Statute of Westminster was resisted in the House of Lords on the grounds that this country 'never has had a written constitution of any sort or kind, and the consequence has been that it has been possible to adapt, from time to time, the various relationships and authorities between every component part of this state, and without any serious mistake or disaster ... You should avoid as far as possible putting a definition of what the relationships may be into the unyielding form of an Act of Parliament' [Lord Buckmaster, quoted in Wheare, *The Statute of Westminster and Dominion Status* (1949), pp 5–6]. This view is hard to accept. Quite apart from the fact that statutes may be repealed or amended with relative ease by a determined Government, or that what are conventions in one country may exist as laws elsewhere without any disastrous effects, the objection overlooks the fact that new conventions may come to qualify any legal rule. British constitutional history would have been very different were statute-law necessarily a source of 'disastrous rigidity' in the constitution.

It would be equally wrong, however, to overestimate what enactment of the conventions would achieve. Let us try to draw up a 'balance sheet' of what it could and could not do.

1 Obedience to the rules would not become any more enforceable than it is now. There would undoubtedly be occasions when the mere clarification of a rule would ensure constitutional behaviour. The courts, moreover, can do much to secure observance of the law by such means as declarations and injunctions. But there are several limits to the effectiveness of judicial, or even legislative, action in the face of determined opposition to the law by a Government or, for that matter, by any powerful social group. The sanctions behind constitutional law, as well as convention, are a compound of the desire to abide by the rules, to be 'constitutional', and of the political penalties of disobedience. Ultimately, revolution or civil war may be necessary to procure obedience, as has been amply demonstrated by the history of American legislation and adjudication upon the rights of Negro population in the south.

2 In the absence of a sufficient body of judicial decisions, even well-established legal principles may (at any given time) be of uncertain formulation and application; the principle of the sovereignty of Parliament itself is a case in point. However, in the event of an important dispute turning upon the interpretation of a legal rule, the machinery exists for an authoritative decision upon its meaning and precise application.

3 Legislation, as we have noted, would not prevent the growth of new conventions, about which uncertainty may exist.

4 It could not prevent dispute about what the rules ought to be. And it is important to realise that it is this type of dispute which underlies many arguments about (apparently) what the rules are. This was obviously the case, for example, in the argument about the royal power to 'veto' legislation which took place in 1913, or the Commons' debates about the extent of parliamentary privilege in 1958. It would be foolish to expect anything else, for convention may be described as the 'battleground' between conflicting political forces and constitutional beliefs in society. But this is true not only of disputes about conventional rules. It applies also to legal argument. To cite American experience again, it is evident that constitutional debates about racial segregation in education, or the powers of the federal government in the social and economic fields, have been more than mere scholarly disputations about the 'real' meaning of the 14th Amendment or the 'inter-state commerce clause', although this is the way in which they may be presented. Primarily, these debates have been attempts to persuade the Supreme Court Justices of what the documentary constitution ought to mean; and the standing of the court at any period will depend, in part, upon whether its interpretations conflict with the wishes and beliefs of the most powerful forces in society at the time. Conversely, it is at least arguable that the high standing of the British courts owes something to the fact that many of the most important constitutional rules are, at present, of a non-legal character. Another important factor is, of course, that the doctrine of parliamentary supremacy saves the British courts from having to give the last word on legal points. However, it is doubtful whether this would prevent the courts from a loss of prestige if they were constantly called upon to decide (even subject to parliamentary 'reversal') a whole series of constitutional controversies.

5 What has just been said suggests that the attempt to enact conventional rules might itself prove extremely difficult. It is likely that the fiercely disputed Parliament Act of 1911 rather than the Statute of Westminster would prove to be typical of the process. Even if agreement could be reached about what the rules are, it is hard to believe that no attempt would be made to formulate the rule with greater precision, in line with particular views as to what it

should be. It can be argued, with come conviction, that this is in fact what happened with the Parliament Act and with the American 'third-term' amendment. It is, moreover, most unlikely that in fact any attempt will be made to 'codify' the conventions until and unless their precise meaning has become a crucial factor in a constitutional crisis – in which case it might not be of very great significance whether the disputed rule was or was not a law, in that further legislation may anyway be needed to settle the dispute.

6   Enactment of the conventions may nevertheless be important, if once successfully achieved. Just as some course of action desired by a section of the community acquires a significant degree of legitimacy and authority simply by virtue of its acceptance as a convention, so a convention may acquire greater legitimacy and authority by its transformation into law. The exact significance of this 'evaluation' will probably vary with different rules.

Notes

1   It is important to note that in a typically British *ad hoc*, unsystematic way, a widespread codification of conventions regulating government behaviour is in fact occurring. An important example is *The Ministerial Code*, published by the Cabinet Office, which sets out in authoritative form a number of important constitutional principles relating to the conduct of ministers, including crucially the convention of ministerial responsibility, as well as rules relating to ethical conduct in relation to gifts and hospitality. A resolution passed by both Houses of Parliament on the content of ministerial responsibility,[14] which the Code follows, reinforces its authority. Similarly, the *Rules Relating to the Conduct of MPs* sets out in detailed form the standards expected of MPs, the *Civil Service Code* clarifies the duties of civil servants in relation to the provision of information to Parliament, and the government's *Code of Practice on Access to Information*, together with legislation on official secrecy, now provides the definitive account of what information ministers may properly refuse to disclose to Parliament, replacing the previous position in which ministers and their predecessors simply refused to answer questions on the basis of custom. As Dawn Oliver commented in 1997:

The upshot of [all] this ... is that in the last two years or so the number of published codes regulating the conduct of ministers, civil servants, and Members of Parliament has increased substantially and their importance to the discipline of constitutional law is growing, as the shortcomings of unarticulated understandings as mechanisms of control have come to be recognised.[15]

2   One of the more cogent arguments against codification is the loss of prestige that the courts might face if forced to adjudicate on controversial issues of convention. However, this point obviously has far more force in relation to some conventions than others. Clearly, areas such as individual and collective ministerial responsibility should not be handed over to the courts for adjudication (though there is no reason an independent committee, staffed, say, by judges, academics and MPs, should not be given the power to make non-binding findings on whether a particular convention has or has not been breached). For one thing, the latter, and on some occasions the former, are generally in the interest of the government and will therefore be enforced by it, within flexible limits. Additionally, individual ministerial responsibility is clearly at the heart of the notion of parliamentary accountability, and the stuff of everyday political conflict. Other conventions, however, such as those relating to the powers of the monarch to refuse assent to

14   HC Deb cols 1046–47 (19 March 1997); HL Deb cols 1055–62 (20 March 1997).
15   D Oliver, 'The changing constitution in the 1990s' [1997] NILQ 1.

legislation and to dissolve Parliament, or the obligation of a government to resign upon being defeated in a general election, are in a different category. First, both because the situations would rarely arise at all, and because, if they did, the conventional rules would probably be followed, just as they are now, the fear that the courts would be 'constantly called upon to decide ... constitutional controversies' is groundless. Secondly, these conventions are vital to democracy itself; as indicated above it seems absurd to exclude constitutional fundamentals from the Rule of Law.

3   On the question of the role of the courts, it should also be pointed out that conventions could be codified, but the code made non-justiciable. Some clarification would thus be achieved without risking the prestige of the courts. Alternatively, it might be possible to set up an independent committee (staffed, say, by judges, academics and MPs) which could be given the power to make non-binding findings on whether a particular convention has or has not been breached even in contentious areas.

4   Codification would resolve the intolerable situation in which the very existence of some conventions has been in doubt. To give a historical example, in 1708 royal assent was withheld from a Bill of which the monarch in question, Queen Anne, disapproved, whereas in 1829 George IV gave consent to a Bill which he disliked. Sometime during those 100 years the convention in question must have come into being. However, it would be impossible to pinpoint the stage at which this occurred; if, during that time, the question had arisen as to whether withholding royal assent was unconstitutional, no answer would be available to the monarch in question; in effect it would not be available until after he or she had acted.

5   Some conventions, of course, benefit from their indeterminacy. The doctrine of collective Cabinet responsibility provides an example. Under the doctrine, ministers are collectively responsible to Parliament for their actions in governing the country and therefore should be in accord on any major question. A minister should resign if he or she is in disagreement with the policy of the Cabinet on any such question. Examples of such resignation include Sir Thomas Dugdale's in 1954 due to his disagreement with the government as to the disposal of an area of land known as Crichel Down (this resignation is not always cited as an example of policy disagreement, but such appears to have been its basis), and Sir Anthony Eden's resignation in 1938 over Chamberlain's policy towards Mussolini. However, there appears to have been some blurring and weakening of the doctrine dating from the mid-1970s. In 1975 the Labour Cabinet was divided on the question of whether the UK should remain in the Common Market. It was agreed that, in the period before the referendum on the question, Cabinet ministers should be able to express a view at variance with the official view of the government that the UK should remain a member of the Common Market. Some weakening of the convention also appears from the Westland affair which, on the face of it, provides an example of its operation; when Michael Heseltine resigned from the Cabinet in 1986 due to his disagreement with government policy, he specifically stated that he did not do so as a result of his perception of an obligation arising from the convention. When John Major's administration was considering whether to allow a referendum on a single currency, the option of suspending collective Cabinet responsibility during the referendum campaign was canvassed as a legitimate possibility open to the Prime Minister, the 1975 suspension being cited as a precedent.

6   If the convention of collective responsibility were enshrined in a statute, departure from it as in 1975 might have been less readily undertaken, even if the provisions of

the statute were made non-justiciable. In any event it would be difficult, and probably undesirable, to define the convention, as discretion in complying with it may be said to be endemic in it. Political inconvenience would clearly arise, and it might be argued that the democratic process would be endangered if ministers could not at times express their views on exceptionally important issues with some freedom. Therefore, it may be argued that no advantage would be gained by enacting such a statute; such crystallisation of the convention would clearly reduce its value.

7 The only sensible conclusion seems to be that a selective approach towards further codification would be a prerequisite for reform.

FURTHER READING

N Johnston, *In Search of the Constitution* (1977), esp Chapter 3
J Madison, *The Federalist Papers* (1987)
Colin Munro, 'Law and conventions distinguished' (1975) 91 LQR 218
JDB Mitchell, *Constitutional Law,* 2nd edn (1968)
I Jennings, *Cabinet Government*, 3rd edn (1959), esp Chapter 1
G Marshall, *Constitutional Conventions* (1984)
A Heard, *Canadian Constitutional Conventions: The Marriage of Law and Politics* (1991)

CHAPTER 3

THE RULE OF LAW AND THE SEPARATION OF POWERS

INTRODUCTION – THE THEORETICAL BASIS OF THE RULE OF LAW[1]

The Rule of Law is a chameleon-like notion. Used by different people it may mean radically different things. As noted in Chapter 1 of this part, an influential commentator on the Left, John Griffith, objects to the notion being used to denote anything more substantive than a set of basic restraints on the powers of the state, particularly its ability to penalise it citizens.[2] Griffith complains that, contrary to his prescription, the doctrine is sometimes used in a much wider sense to create loyalty towards the status quo. Professor Joseph Raz notes that, in 1959, the International Congress of Jurists came up with a definition of the Rule of Law which effectively made it a shorthand for 'a complete social philosophy', prescribing a full panoply of civil, political, economic and social rights.[3]

However, both of these writers, and indeed the vast majority of commentators dealing with this subject, assume that the notion of the Rule of Law must mean at least that people should be ruled by rules (though even traditionalists have now disclaimed Albert Venn Dicey's notion that the granting of discretionary powers to the executive necessarily infringes the doctrine).[4] But is even this modest assumption justifiable? Frederick Schauer considers that the essence of a system run according to law is the notion that power must be *allocated* according to law. Whether that power must then be exercised according to a set of pre-ordained rules is another question.

Frederick Schauer, *Playing by the Rules: A Philosophical Examination of Rule-Based Decision-Making in Law and in Life* (1991), pp 167–68, 10–11

... the relationship between rules and a 'legal system' is contingent, for decision according to rules is but one among several sorts of decision-making. As a result, although empowering rules create the institutions of dispute resolution and empower certain officials to resolve certain sorts of disputes, disputes could still be resolved largely without reference to mandatory rules imposing substantive constraint on the content of the decisions. Having been empowered to resolve a dispute, the adjudicator would be authorized ... to come to a conclusion as open-endedly as appropriate in the circumstances.

... Consider child custody determinations, in which an open-ended 'best interests of the child' standard, rather than any more constraining set of rules, provides guidance for the decision-maker; the system of equity, no less part of the legal system for embodying flexibility and particularly as its method; the traditional sentencing process, in which the range of factors permissibly relevant to the decision is virtually unlimited; and the increasing use of substantially rule-free arbitration, mediation, and conciliation procedures as adjuncts to or substitutes for formal adjudication. These

---

1   For the basic principles of the doctrine see, in this chapter, 'Principles deriving from the Rule of Law', below at pp 77 *et seq*. This introduction considers the theoretical background to the doctrine.
2   See J Griffith, 'The political constitution' (1979) 42 MLR 15; quoted in Chapter 1.
3   J Raz, 'The Rule of Law and its virtue' (1977) 93 LQR 195; quoted below, p 78.
4   See, for example, RFV Heuston, *Essays in Constitutional Law*, 2nd edn (1964), pp 41–42; quoted below, at p 99.

are but a few among many examples of forms of legal decision-making that, only with difficulty, can be characterised as rule-based. Consequently, I want to start with the assumption that rule-governed decision-making is a subset of legal decision-making rather than being congruent with it.

Note
Schauer's distinction between power-allocating and power-exercising rules is useful in that it forces us to realise that a state – at least one like the UK with no fixed constitutional order – could dispense altogether with the idea of governing according to substantive rules without acting illegally. For example, Parliament could repeal the criminal law in its entirety and substitute for it an Act stating that certain government appointees were to have exclusive power to punish, as they thought fit, such acts as they thought ought to be punished within specified geographical areas allocated to them. Whilst such an Act would violate many of the fundamental doctrines of the Rule of Law as they are commonly understood to be – and be incompatible with various provisions of the European Convention on Human Rights (ECHR)[5] – such an Act would not be 'illegal', since Parliament would be exercising power allocated to it by law. (It is also worth noting that judicial review of decisions made under the Act would still be possible if, for example, an appointee purported to punish a citizen in respect of an act which was not committed in his or her allocated area.) Thus, Schauer's point both helps to clear up some confusion between illegal 'enactments' and ones which violate the principles of the Rule of Law, and also to make it clear that those principles are not the necessary attributes of any state established under law, but rather are contingent and therefore vulnerable to erosion.

THE BASIC IDEA OF THE RULE OF LAW: GOVERNMENT UNDER THE LAW

The basic notion that no one may exercise power unless that power has been granted to him or her by law can also be expressed in the notion of 'government under the law'. Jeremy Waldron explains why this notion has such significant connotations.

Jeremy Waldron, *The Law* (1990), pp 31–32

For many of us, the policeman on patrol is the most visible expression of the power of the British state. He represents an organisation that has the ability to overwhelm any of us with physical force if we resist its demands, and he can call on that force any time he wants ... although the police in Britain are not armed as a matter of course except with truncheons, they do have access to firearms and, as events in Northern Ireland have shown, they can ask political leaders to deploy military force if that is necessary to resist some challenge to their authority. Their potential power, like that of any government official, is enormous, for in the last resort they can call upon all the organised force of the state. And the same is true of other officials as well – from taxation officials to social welfare clerks. They are all the agents of an immensely powerful organisation.

When you put it like that, it is hard to resist the image of one group of people – the organised events of the state – wielding power over another, much larger group of people – the rest of us, relatively powerless in ourselves and abjectly vulnerable to their demands. Some are powerful, some are not. The state is the rule of one group of people by another. And that, of course, is an

---

5 Notably the Article 6 guarantee of an 'independent and impartial tribunal' for the determination of criminal offences (see pp 103 *et seq*), and also the requirement that all legal restrictions upon Convention rights must be 'prescribed by law': see below, the extracts from *Malone v UK* (1985) 7 EHRR 14 and *Hashman and Harrup v UK* (2000) 30 EHRR 241.

affront and an indignity to the people who are in the subordinate position, since it leaves us unfree and evidently unequal.

Ever since Aristotle, political philosophers have tried to mitigate or qualify that image. Politics, they have argued, need not be the arbitrary rule of man over man. Perhaps we can imagine a form of political life in which everyone is a subject and everyone is ruled, not by a person or by any particular group of people, but by a shared set of abstract rules. If I am subject to another person, then I am at the mercy of his whims and passions, his angers and prejudices. But if we are both subject to the law, then the personal factor is taken out of politics. By subjecting everyone to the law, we make ourselves, in a sense, equal again.

Notes

1   Waldron's conclusion, that the Rule of Law renders us 'in a sense equal again', refers to a notion of *formal* equality; it does not of course imply that the content of individual laws could not promote *substantive* inequality. As Jeffrey Jowell puts it, the concern of formal equality

> is not with the content of the law but with its *enforcement and application* alone. As long as laws are applied equally, that is without irrational bias or distinction, then formal equality is complied with. Formal equality does not however prohibit *unequal* laws. It constrains, say, racially-biased enforcement of the law, but it does not inhibit racially discriminatory laws from being enacted [original emphasis].[6]

We will return to this distinction again below.

2   As well as promoting the notion of equality, the Rule of Law has perhaps a still more basic purpose: that of acting as a constraint on government power, a power which, as Waldron remarks, 'has the ability to overwhelm any of us with physical force'.[7] Two questions have been posed from the Left about this aspect of the doctrine. The first is whether the Rule of Law can actually achieve its aim of restraint.[8] The second is whether it is *desirable* that government power should be constrained in this way.

Is it *desirable* to restrain state power through the Rule of Law?

The Marxist historian, EP Thompson, has made the claim that: 'The Rule of Law itself, the imposing of effective inhibitions upon power and the defence of the citizen from power's all intrusive claims, seems to me an unqualified human good.'[9] In a critical response, MJ Horowitz expresses vigorous disagreement:

> I do not see how a man of the Left can describe the Rule of Law as an 'unqualified human good'. It undoubtedly restrains power, but it also prevents power's benevolent exercise. It creates formal equality – a not inconsiderable virtue – but it *promotes* substantive inequality by creating a consciousness that radically separates law from politics, means from ends, processes from outcomes. By promoting procedural justice it enables the shrewd, the calculating, and the wealthy

6   J Jowell, 'The Rule of Law today', in J Jowell and D Oliver (eds), *The Changing Constitution*, 3rd edn (1994), p 76.
7   J Waldron, *The Law* (1990), p 31.
8   This question finds particularly strong expression within the 'Critical Legal Studies' school. See, eg, Michael Tushnet, *Red, White and Blue: A Critical Analysis of Constitutional Law* (1988), pp 46–51.
9   EP Thompson, *Whigs and Hunters* (1975), p 266.

to manipulate its forms to their own advantage. And it ratifies and legitimates an adversarial, competitive, and atomistic conception of human relations.[10]

Question

What kinds of 'benevolent' exercises of power would be restrained by the prohibition of arbitrary, unchecked, unaccountable power, exercised without warning, and under no ascertainable authority?

Note

Jowell considers that Horowitz is simply confused, conflating the 'Rule of Law with the substance of particular laws'; he adds that 'To claim that unjust laws and their rigorous enforcement demonstrate that the Rule of Law is an instrument of oppression is ... [profoundly] misleading'.[11] However, Waldron provides a more qualified and subtle refutation of the 'partisan model' of law which, using his terminology, writers like Horowitz represent.

Jeremy Waldron, *The Law* (1990), pp 21–24

Even if [the] contribution [of the law] to bourgeois dominance is to mystify the people and make them think in terms of a neutral or transcendent order, it has got to give them *some* reason for thinking in that way. The point has been powerfully stated by the historian EP Thompson in response to the claim made by some 'structuralist' Marxists that law is *simply* a devise for mystifying the masses and masking the reality of class dominance:

> People are not as stupid as some structuralist philosophers suppose them to be. They will not be mystified by the first man who puts on a wig. It is inherent in the especial character of law, as a body of rules and procedures, that it shall apply logical criteria with reference to standards of universality and equity. It is true that certain categories of person may be excluded from this logic (as children or slaves), that other categories may be debarred from access to parts of the logic (as women or, for many forms of 18th century law, those without certain kinds of property). All this, and more, is true. But if too much of this is true, then the consequences are plainly counterproductive. Most men have a strong sense of justice, at least with regard to their own interests. If the law is evidently partial and unjust, then it will mask nothing, legitimate nothing, contribute nothing to any class's hegemony. The essential precondition for the effectiveness of law, in its function is ideology, is that it shall display an independence from gross manipulation, and shall seem to be just. It cannot seem to be so without upholding its own logic and criteria; indeed, on occasion, by actually being just. [*Whigs and Hunters* (1977), pp 262–63.]

Two points follow. First, it is always possible for members of the ruling class, and certainly the personnel of the state, to become caught up in their own rhetoric. Thompson notes that a ruling ideology cannot usually be dismissed as mere hypocrisy: 'even rules find a need to legitimise their power, to moralise their functions, to feel themselves to be useful and just'. Moreover if their ideology is something as complex as law, 'a discipline that requires years of exacting study to master', many of its practitioners are bound to become so immersed in its logic that they take seriously and in good faith its substance and its reasoning.

The other point is more subtle but even more important. The ideology of the Rule of Law, legality, and so on can help sustain class power only if it is – considered in itself – a morally appealing set of ideas. We may overlay something nasty with something sweet in order to make the nastiness more palatable, but then the something sweet must really *be* sweet, considered in itself, or else it will contribute nothing to the palatability. Law helps to legitimate class power by presenting it to all

---

10   Horowitz, 'The Rule of Law: an unqualified human good?' (1977) 86 Yale LJ 591.

11   In Jowell and Oliver, *op cit*, p 72.

concerned masked in a form which, if it actually *did* correspond to reality, would be the form of a society that was good and fair and just. The idea of a set of rules that apply the same to everyone, the idea that anyone, whatever her class, may come to an impartial tribunal and ask that justice be done, the idea that force may not be used even by those in authority except in pursuance of a general principle – these ideas may be a misdescription of what actually goes on in modern Britain (or in the England that Thompson was writing about), but they are attractive nevertheless and a society which really did conform to them would be a good society.

If this is true, and if the earlier point is true – that a ruling class must actually submit to the Rule of Law some of the time in order to sustain the general *pretence* of legality – then it seems to follow that law and legality, even if they are instruments of class domination, do also make a positive contribution to society. There is a difference, as Thompson notes, between 'direct unmediated force (arbitrary imprisonment, the employment of troops against the crowd, torture, and all those other conveniences of power with which we are all conversant)' and the Rule of Law, even if both are modes of class domination.

All this points in the direction of an approach to law that may not be cynical to all. If we agree that legality and the Rule of Law are *capable* of modifying class conflict and oppression in desirable ways, then maybe we should think favourably about the concept of a society actually ruled by law, not as a description of our society, but as a social ideal, something to be aimed at. Maybe, as things stand at present, legal rules are used to serve partisan ends. We need to be realistic and clear about what is actually going on. But we also need an ideal or an aspiration for political life – some sense of what it would be for things to be better. For this purpose, even in the midst of its partisan embroilment, the image that law projects is an attractive one.

Note

Waldron thus concludes that we should distinguish between the Rule of Law used as a complacent description of the way in which Western democracies are governed today, in which it may indeed veil political inequality, and the doctrine as an aspiration, as a blueprint for good government.

SPECIFIC PRINCIPLES DERIVING FROM THE RULE OF LAW[12]

The notion that the executive is not above the law is related to the Diceyan notion that the Rule of Law includes the idea that there should be one law for all, governed and government alike. Waldron discusses a practical application of this notion and the principles which may be derived from it, referring to the case of *Pedro v Diss* (1981) in which Pedro was acquitted of assault after physically resisting an unlawful arrest made by Police Constable Diss.

Jeremy Waldron, *The Law* (1990), pp 37–38

[Constable] Diss grabs hold of Pedro, and Pedro punches him in the struggle to free himself. The magistrates say he is guilty of assault. On appeal, the High Court says (in effect): 'No. Unless the arrest is lawful, Pedro is entitled to defend himself against Martin Diss just as if he were any other citizen who tried to grab hold of him. Once they go beyond their specified powers, the police have no special privileges. The ordinary rules of self-defence apply. If it's wrong for me to attack Pedro, it's also wrong for Constable Diss to attack Pedro. The law is the same for everyone.'

This requirement of universality – the idea of 'one law for all' – is a prominent feature of the normative ideal of the Rule of Law. But why is universality a good thing? Why is it desirable that there should be one law for everyone, irrespective of who they are, or their official status?

12 In this section, principles of the liberal conception of the Rule of Law are explored.

One obvious application of universality is that we don't, on the whole, allow personalised laws; we don't have laws that make exceptions for particular people. In medieval England, there used to be things called 'Bills of Attainder', announcing that someone in particular (the Earl of Warwick, or the king's brother for example) was thereby banished from the realm and his estates confiscated. The idea of the Rule of Law is that the state should not use personalised mechanisms of that sort.

Moral philosophers link this requirement of universality with morality and with rationality. They say that if you make a moral judgment about someone or something, your judgment can't be based simply on that person or that incident in particular, or if it is, it's arbitrary. It must be based on some feature of the person or action – something *about* what they did, something that might in principle be true of another person or another situation as well. In other words it must be based on something that can be expressed in a universal proposition. For example, if I want to say, 'It is all right for Diss to defend himself', I must say that because I think self defence is all right in general in that sort of case, not merely because I want to get at Pedro or say something special about Diss. So I must also be prepared to say that it would be all right for Pedro to defend himself in a similar circumstance. Unless I can point to some clearly relevant difference between the two cases, then I must accept that the same reasoning applies to both.

Another way of putting it is that universalisability expresses an important principle of justice: it means dealing even-handedly with people and treating like cases alike. If I am committed to treating like cases alike, then I ought to be able to state my principles in a universal form. If I cannot – that is, if I can't find a way to eliminate references to particular people from my legislation – that is probably a good indication that I am drawing arbitrary distinctions based on bias or self-interest or something of that sort.

Notes

1   There are numerous exceptions to the notion of one law applying equally to all. Members of Parliament enjoy complete civil and criminal immunity in respect of words spoken during 'proceedings in Parliament' by virtue of the Bill of Rights 1688, while judges also enjoy various legal privileges. Diplomatic and consular immunities arise under the Diplomatic Privileges Act 1964 and the Consular Relations Act 1968, and these have been left undisturbed by the State Immunity Act 1978, s 16.

2   Waldron demonstrates how principles of justice (treating like cases alike) can be deduced from the simple notion of the law being addressed to, and applicable to, everybody. These ideas have found perhaps their most prominent proponents in the philosophical writings of Raz and John Rawls.

3   Raz is concerned to pare down the notion of the Rule of Law to what he sees as its logically necessary content (as we noted in the introduction to this chapter), whilst demonstrating that it yet prescribes a number of important principles about the application of coercive force within a legal system. Raz's exposition is followed by an extract from Rawl's *A Theory of Justice* (1972), in which he develops in detail the principles of justice that can be derived from the Rule of Law.

Joseph Raz, 'The Rule of Law and its virtue' (1977) 93 LQR 195–98

FA Hayek has provided one of the clearest and most powerful formulations of the ideal of the Rule of Law: 'stripped of all technicalities this means that government in all its actions is bound by rules fixed and announced beforehand – rules which make it possible to foresee with fair certainty how the authority will use its coercive powers in given circumstances, and to plan one's individual affairs on the basis of this knowledge' [*The Road to Serfdom* (1944), p 54]. At the same time the way he draws certain conclusions from this ideal illustrates one of the two main fallacies in the contemporary treatment of the doctrine of the Rule of Law: the assumption of its overriding importance. My purpose is to analyse the ideal of the Rule of Law in the spirit of Hayek's quoted statement of it and to show why some of the conclusions which he drew from it cannot be thus supported. But first we must be put on our guard against the other common fallacy concerning the Rule of Law.

Not uncommonly when a political ideal captures the imagination of large numbers of people its name becomes a slogan used by supporters of ideals which bear little or no relation to the one it originally designated ... In 1959 the International Congress of Jurists gave official blessing to a similar perversion of the doctrine of the Rule of Law.

> The function of the legislature in a free society under the Rule of Law is to create and maintain the conditions which will uphold the dignity of man as an individual. This dignity requires not only the recognition of his civil and political rights but also the establishment of the social, economic, educational and cultural conditions which are essential to the full development of his personality.

The report goes on to mention or refer to just about every political ideal which has found support in any part of the globe during the post-war years.

If the Rule of Law is the rule of the good law then to explain its nature is to propound a complete social philosophy. But if so, the term lacks any useful function. We have no need to be converted to the Rule of Law just in order to discover that to believe in it is to believe that good should triumph. The Rule of Law is a political ideal which a legal system may lack or may possess to a greater or lesser degree. That much is common ground. It is also to be insisted that the Rule of Law is just one of the virtues which a legal system may possess and by which it is to be judged. It is not to be confused with democracy, justice, equality (before the law or otherwise), human rights of any kind or respect for persons or for the dignity of man. A non-democratic legal system, based on the denial of human rights, on extensive poverty, on racial segregation, sexual inequalities and religious persecution may, in principle, conform to the requirements of the Rule of Law better than any of the legal systems of the more enlightened Western democracies. This does not mean that it will be better than those Western democracies. It will be an immeasurably worse legal system, but it will excel in one respect: in its conformity to the Rule of Law ...

'The Rule of Law' means literally what it says: the rule of the law. Taken in its broadest sense this means that people should obey the law and be ruled by it. But in political and legal theory it has come to be read in a narrower sense, that the government shall be ruled by the law and subject to it. The ideal of the Rule of Law in this sense is often expressed by the phrase 'government by law and not by men'. No sooner does one use these formulae than their obscurity becomes evident. Surely government must be both by law and by men. It is said that the Rule of Law means that all government action must have foundation in law, must be authorised by law. But is not that a tautology? Actions not authorised by law cannot be the actions of the government as a government. They would be without legal effect and often unlawful.

It is true that we can elaborate a political notion which is different from the legal one: government as the location of real power in the society. It is in this sense that one can say that Britain is governed by The City or by the trade unions. In this sense of government it is not a tautology to say that government should be based on law. If the trade union ruling a country breaks an industrial relations law in order to impose its will on the parliament or if the President or the FBI authorise burglaries and conspire to pervert justice they can be said to violate the Rule of Law. But here the Rule of Law is used in its original sense of obedience to law. Powerful people and people in government just like anybody else should obey the law. This is no doubt correct, and yet does it exhaust the meaning of the Rule of Law? There is more to the Rule of Law than the law and order interpretation allows. It means more even than law and order applied to the government. I shall proceed on the assumption that we are concerned with government in the legal sense and with the conception of the Rule of Law which applies to government and to law and is no mere application of the law and order conception.

The problem is that now we are back with our initial puzzle. If government is, by definition, government authorised by law, the Rule of Law seems to amount to an empty tautology, not a political ideal.

The solution to this riddle is in the difference between the professional and the lay sense of law. For the lawyer anything is the law if it meets the conditions of validity laid down in the system's rules of recognition or in other rules of the system [I am, here, following Hart, *The Concept of Law* (1961), pp 97–107]. This includes the constitution, parliamentary legislation, ministerial regulations, policeman's orders, the regulations of limited companies, conditions imposed in trading licences, etc. To the layman the law consists only of a sub-class of these. To him the law is essentially a set of open, general and relatively stable laws. Government by law and not by men is not a tautology if 'law' means general, open and relatively stable law. In fact the danger of this interpretation is that the Rule of Law might set too strict a requirement, one which no legal system can meet and which embodies very little virtue. It is humanly inconceivable that law can consist only of general rules and it is very undesirable that it should. Just as we need government both by laws and by men, so we need both general and particular laws to carry out the jobs for which we need the law.

The doctrine of the Rule of Law does not deny that every legal system should consist of both general, open and stable rules (the popular conception of law) and particular laws (legal orders), an essential tool in the hands of the executive and the judiciary alike. As we shall see, what the doctrine requires is the subjection of particular laws to general, open and stable ones. It is one of the important principles of the doctrine that *the making of particular laws should be guided by open and relatively stable general rules.*

This principle shows how the slogan of the Rule of Law and not of men can be read as a meaningful political ideal. The principle does not, however, exhaust the meaning of the Rule of Law and does not by itself illuminate the reasons for its alleged importance. Let us, therefore, return to the literal sense of the Rule of Law. It has two aspects: (1) that people should be ruled by the law and obey it; and (2) that the law should be such that people will be able to be guided by it. As was noted above, it is with the second aspect that we are concerned: the law must be capable of being obeyed. A person conforms with the law to the extent that he does not break the law. But he obeys the law only if part of his reason for conforming is his knowledge of the law. Therefore, if the law is to be obeyed *it must be capable of guiding the behaviour of its subjects.* It must be such that they can find out what it is and act on it.

This is the basic intuition from which the doctrine of the Rule of Law derives: the law must be capable of guiding the behaviour of its subjects. It is evident that this conception of the Rule of Law is a formal one. It says nothing about how the law is to be made: by tyrants, democratic majorities or any other way. It says nothing about fundamental rights, about equality or justice. It may even be thought that this version of the doctrine is formal to the extent that it is almost devoid of content. This is far from the truth. Most of the requirements which were associated with the Rule of Law before it came to signify all the virtues of the state can be derived from this one basic idea.

Note

This chapter follows Raz's assertion that '[the Rule of Law] is not to be confused with democracy, justice, equality (before the law or otherwise), human rights of any kind or respect for persons or for the dignity of man'; it therefore does not include any consideration of substantive human rights sometimes associated with the Rule of Law.[13]

---

13 The distinction here is between what may be termed formal and substantive conceptions of the Rule of Law; on which see further P Craig [1997] PL 467.

John Rawls, *A Theory of Justice* (1972), pp 236–40

Let us begin with the precept that ought implies can. [Thus] . . . the actions which the rules of law require and forbid should be of a kind which men can reasonably be expected to do and to avoid . . . Laws and commands are accepted as laws and commands only if it is generally believed that they can be obeyed and executed . . .

The Rule of Law also implies the precept that similar cases be treated similarly. Men could not regulate actions by means of rules if this precept were not followed . . . The precept forces [judges] to justify the distinctions that they make between persons by reference to the relevant legal rules and principles. In any particular case, if the rules are at all complicated and call for interpretation, it may be easy to justify an arbitrary decision. But as the number of cases increases, plausible justifications for biased judgments become more difficult to construct. The requirement of consistency holds of course for the interpretation of all rules and for justifications at all levels. Eventually reasoned arguments for discriminatory judgments become harder to formulate and the attempt to do so less persuasive.

The precept that there is no offence without a law (*nulla crimien sine lege*), and the requirements it implies, also follow from the idea of a legal system. This precept demands that laws be known and expressly promulgated, that their meaning be clearly defined, that statutes be general both in statement and intent and not be used as a way of harming particular individuals who may be expressly named (Bills of Attainder), that at least the more severe offences be strictly construed, and that penal laws should not be retroactive to the disadvantage of those to whom they apply. These requirements are implicit in the notion of regulating behaviour by public rules. For if, say, statutes are not clear in what they enjoin and forbid, the citizen does not know how he is to behave. Moreover, while there may be occasional Bills of Attainder and retroactive enactments, these cannot be pervasive or characteristic features of the system, else it must have another purpose. A tyrant might change laws without notice, and punish (if that is the right word) his subjects accordingly, because he takes pleasure in seeing how long it takes them to figure out what the new rules are from observing the penalties he inflicts. But these rules would not be a legal system, since they would not serve to organise social behaviour by providing a basis for legitimate expectations.

Finally, there are those precepts defining the notion of natural justice. These are guidelines intended to preserve the integrity of the judicial process. If laws are directives addressed to rational persons for their guidance, courts must be concerned to apply and to enforce these rules in an appropriate way. A conscientious effort must be made to determine whether an infraction has taken place and to impose the correct penalty. Thus a legal system must make provisions for conducting orderly trials and hearings; it must contain rules of evidence that guarantee rational procedures of inquiry. While there are variations in these procedures, the Rule of Law requires some form of due process: that is, a process reasonably designed to ascertain the truth, in ways consistent with the other ends of the legal system, as to whether a violation has taken place and under what circumstances. For example, judges must be independent and impartial, and no man may judge his own case. Trials must be fair and open, but not prejudiced by public clamour. The precepts of natural justice are to insure that the legal order will be impartially and regularly maintained.

Now the connection of the Rule of Law with liberty is clear enough . . . The various liberties specify things that we may choose to do, if we wish, and in regard to which, when the nature of the liberty makes it appropriate, others have a duty not to interfere. But if the precept of no crime without a law is violated, say by statutes being vague and imprecise, what we are at liberty to do is likewise vague and imprecise. The boundaries of our liberty are uncertain. And to the extent that this is so, liberty is restricted by a reasonable fear of its exercise. The same sort of consequences follow if similar cases are not treated similarly, if the judicial process lacks its essential integrity, if the law does not recognise impossibility of performance as a defence, and so on. The principle of legality has a firm foundation, then, in the agreement of rational persons to establish for themselves the greatest equal liberty. To be confident in the possession and exercise of these freedoms, the citizens of a well-ordered society will normally want the Rule of Law maintained.

Notes

1   Perhaps the most important aspect of the Rule of Law, according to Rawls and Raz, is its freedom promoting nature. In making known in advance and in a clear way what the restrictions on conduct are, the Rule of Law allows people to plan and thus control their own lives.

2   The principles which Rawls 'extracts' from the doctrine of the Rule of Law may be summed up as follows: laws must not require the impossible; like cases must be treated alike; conduct can only be criminalised by law which is both reasonably ascertainable (and therefore non-retroactive) and of sufficient clarity; cases must be tried fairly (therefore by an independent judiciary) and according to due process. To these principles, Raz[14] adds that the making of particular laws should be governed by more general 'open stable and clear rules', that the courts must be easily accessible, and that they must have review power to ensure adherence to the other principles.

3   The remainder of this chapter will seek to ascertain how far these principles find legal expression in the UK.

THE RULE OF LAW IN THE BRITISH CONSTITUTION

The requirement of legal justification for government action

Historically, constitutional lawyers in this country have prided themselves on the UK's adherence to the Rule of Law, as upheld by the judges in a number of famous cases. One of these is *Entick v Carrington* (1765) 19 St Tr 1029, in which agents of the King, acting under a warrant issued by the Secretary of State, broke into the house of Entick, alleged to be the author of seditious writings, and removed certain of his papers. It was found that because the action was justified by no specific legal authority, it was a common trespass, for which the Secretary of State was liable in damages. Lord Camden CJ said:

> By the laws of England, every invasion of private property, be it ever so minute, is a trespass. No man can ever set his foot upon my ground without my licence, but he is liable to an action ... If he admits the fact, he is bound to shew by way of justification, that some positive law has empowered or excused him.

If government is under law, then since the courts are empowered to make the authoritative determination of what the law is, this must mean that the government is in a sense under, and therefore obliged to obey orders of the courts, expressed in the form of injunctions. The normal sanction for failure to obey an order of the court is a finding of contempt of court. Perhaps surprisingly, the question whether ministers of the Crown were obliged to obey court orders, and risked a finding of contempt if they did not, remained undecided in law until the case of *M* in 1993.

14   Raz, *op cit*, pp 199–201.

M v Home Office [1992] 2 WLR 73, 80, CA; In Re M [1993] 3 WLR 433, 437–38 and 465–66, HL

In 1993, M, a citizen of Zaire, sought political asylum in the UK. His application was refused by the Home Office, and leave to apply for judicial review of the Home Office's decision was also refused. Just before his removal, a fresh application for judicial review, alleging new grounds, was made to Garland J in chambers; the judge indicated that he wished M's removal to be delayed pending consideration of the fresh application and understood counsel for the Home Office to have given an undertaking that this would be done. However, M's removal was not delayed, due to various mistakes and breakdowns in communication. Learning of this, Garland J then made an *ex parte* order requiring the Home Secretary to procure M's return to England. The Home Secretary, having taken legal advice, decided that the judge had no jurisdiction to make a mandatory interim injunction against him, as a minister of the Crown. Proceedings were then brought against the Home Secretary, alleging that he had been in contempt of court by virtue of his refusal to obey the *ex parte* order and the failure to comply with the terms of counsel's undertaking. The case was dismissed at first instance, and came to the Court of Appeal.

> **Lord Donaldson of Lymington MR:** ... this is a matter of high constitutional importance. Indeed I would say of the very highest ... The system would be put under intolerable strain and would be likely to break down if a significant number of citizens treated the courts' orders as mere requests which could be complied with or ignored as they thought appropriate. I share [the] confidence [of Counsel for the Home Office] that, in the foreseeable future, governments and ministers will recognise their obligations to their opponents, to the courts and to justice. Where I have somewhat less confidence is in the suggestion that, were it ever otherwise, there would be a heavy political price to pay. There might well be, but I am not sure that there would be if, in particular circumstances, popular opinion was firmly on the side of the government and against the person who had obtained the order. Yet it is precisely in those circumstances that individual citizens should be able to look to the judiciary for protection under the law. I therefore do indeed think that it would be a black day for the Rule of Law and for the liberty of the subject if the first instance judge has correctly interpreted the law. I have reached the firm conclusion that he was mistaken ...

The Court of Appeal found the Home Secretary personally to have been in contempt of court. He appealed to the House of Lords.

> **Lord Templeman:** My Lords, Parliament makes the law, the executive carry the law into effect and the judiciary enforce the law. The expression 'the Crown' has two meanings; namely the monarch and the executive ... The judiciary enforce the law against individuals, against institutions and against the executive. The judges cannot enforce the law against the Crown as monarch because the Crown as monarch can do no wrong but judges enforce the law against the Crown as an executive and against the individuals who from time to time represent the Crown. A litigant complaining of a breach of the law by the executive can sue the Crown as executive bringing his action against the minister who is responsible for the department of state involved, in the present case the Secretary of State for Home Affairs. To enforce the law the courts have power to grant remedies including injunctions against a minister in his official capacity. If the minister has personally broken the law, the litigant can sue the minister, in this case Mr Kenneth Baker, in his personal capacity. For the purpose of enforcing the law against all persons and institutions, including ministers in their official capacity and in their personal capacity, the courts are armed with coercive powers exercisable in proceedings for contempt of court.
>
> ... My Lords, the argument that there is no power to enforce the law by injunction or contempt proceedings against a minister in his official capacity would, if upheld, establish the proposition that the executive obey the law as a matter of grace and not as a matter of necessity, a proposition

which would reverse the result of the Civil War. For the reasons given by noble and learned friend, Lord Woolf, and on principle, I am satisfied that injunctions and contempt proceedings may be brought against the minister in his official capacity and that in the present case the Home Office for which the Secretary of State was responsible was in contempt. I am also satisfied that Mr Baker was, throughout, acting in his official capacity on advice which he was entitled to accept and under a mistaken view as to the law. In these circumstances I do not consider that Mr Baker personally was guilty of contempt. I would therefore dismiss this appeal substituting the Secretary of State for Home Affairs as being the person against whom the finding of contempt was made.

Lord Woolf: ...The Court of Appeal were of the opinion that a finding of contempt could not be made against the Crown, a government department or a minister of the Crown in his official capacity. Although it is to be expected that it will be rare indeed that the circumstances will exist in which such a finding would be justified, I do not believe there is any impediment to a court making such a finding, when it is appropriate to do so, not against the Crown directly, but against a government department or a minister of the Crown in his official capacity.

Nolan LJ, at p 311, [in the Court of Appeal] considered that the fact that proceedings for contempt are 'essentially personal and punitive' meant that it was not open to a court, as a matter of law, to make a finding of contempt against the Home Office or the Home Secretary. While contempt proceedings usually have these characteristics and contempt proceedings against a government department or a minister in an official capacity would not be either personal or punitive (it would clearly not be appropriate to fine or sequest the assets of the Crown or a government department or an officer of the Crown acting in his official capacity), this does not mean that a finding of contempt against a government department or minister would be pointless. The very fact of making such a finding would vindicate the requirements of justice. In addition an order for costs could be made to underline the significance of a contempt. A purpose of the courts' powers to make findings of contempt is to ensure that the orders of the court are obeyed ...

In cases not involving a government department or a minister the ability to *punish* for contempt may be necessary. However, as is reflected in the restrictions on execution against the Crown, the Crown's relationship with the courts does not depend on coercion and in the exceptional situation when a government department's conduct justifies this, a finding of contempt should suffice. In that exceptional situation, the ability of the court to make a finding of contempt is of great importance. It would demonstrate that a government department has interfered with the administration of justice. It will then be for Parliament to determine what should be the consequences of that finding.

... the object of the exercise is not so much to punish an individual as to vindicate the Rule of Law by a finding of contempt. This can be achieved equally by a declaratory finding of the court as to the contempt against the minister as representing the department.

Notes

1 It should be noted that counsel for the Home Secretary explicitly stated in argument that it was not part of his case to contend that the Crown was above the law, indeed, 'he accepted that the Crown has a duty to obey the law as declared by the courts'.

2 As TRS Allan notes,[15] the finding in this decision was of symbolic, rather than practical value, since '[t]he relationship between the courts and the Crown cannot ... ultimately be a matter of coercion (as the current restrictions on execution against the Crown confirm)'. Nevertheless, its symbolic value should not be

---

15 (1994) 53 CLJ 1.

understated: to hold, as Simon Brown J did at first instance, that undertakings given by Crown officers were 'no more than unenforceable assurances', and that coercive orders were unavailable against them, would have driven a coach and horses through the notion of equality before the law.

3   The notion, expressed in both the above cases, that exercises of governmental power, particularly those which impact upon the liberty of the citizen, must have a basis in law, has recently found a powerful reinforcement through the incorporation of the European Convention on Human Rights into UK law through the Human Rights Act 1998 (HRA). The Convention rights are now binding on all public authorities, including courts, which act unlawfully if they act incompatibly with them (s 6(1). 'So far as is it is possible to do so, [all] legislation must be [construed compatibly] with the Convention rights' (s 3(1)), though if any primary legislation cannot be so construed, it remains valid and of full effect – the courts are given no strike-down power. Certain of the Convention rights permit interferences with them in limited circumstances: Article 2 (right to life); Article 5 (right to personal liberty); Article 8 (privacy); Article 9 (freedom of religion); Article 10 (freedom of expression); and Article 11 (freedom of assembly and association). In order for such interferences to be lawful under the Convention, the government must first show that the interference was 'prescribed by' or 'in accordance with' the law, that is, that it had a basis in existing domestic law. In other words, an identifiable legal basis authorising the interference must be shown: mere executive discretion cannot suffice.

4   It was on this basis that the UK was held to be in violation of Article 8 of the European Convention in the case of *Malone v United Kingdom* (1985) 7 EHRR 14. Malone, an antiques dealer, was prosecuted for offences relating to dishonest handling of stolen goods. During the trial it emerged that the applicant's telephone had been tapped by the police acting on the authority of a warrant issued by the Home Secretary. Following his acquittal on the criminal charges, the applicant brought civil proceedings seeking to establish that the tapping of his telephone had been unlawful. He complained also of the practice of metering, whereby the Post Office would make available to the police the record of which numbers had been dialled by the suspect and the time and duration of each call. The extract below concerns only the latter complaint.

Malone v United Kingdom (1985) 7 EHRR 14

... 62. Article 8 provides as follows:

1. Everyone has the right to respect for his private and family life, his home and his correspondence.

2. There shall be no interference by a public authority with the exercise of this right except such as is in accordance with the law ...

B. Metering

[The Court first found that] release of [metering] information to the police without the consent of the subscriber also amounts, in the opinion of the Court, to an interference with a right guaranteed by Article 8 ...

86. In England and Wales, although the police do not have any power, in the absence of a subpoena, to compel the production of records of metering, a practice exists whereby the Post Office do on occasions make and provide such records at the request of the police if the information is essential to police enquiries in relation to serious crime and cannot be obtained from other sources...

87. Section 80 of the Post Office Act 1969 has never been applied so as to 'require' the Post Office, pursuant to a warrant of the Secretary of State, to make available to the police in connection with the investigation of crime information obtained from metering. On the other hand, no rule of domestic law makes it unlawful for the Post Office voluntarily to comply with a request from the police to make and supply records of metering. The practice described above, including the limitative conditions as to when the information may be provided, has been made public in answer to parliamentary questions.

However, on the evidence adduced before the Court, apart from the simple absence of prohibition, there would appear to be no legal rules concerning the scope and manner of exercise of the discretion enjoyed by the public authorities. Consequently, although lawful in terms of domestic law, the interference resulting from the existence of the practice in question was not ' in accordance with the law', within the meaning of Article 8(2).

... 89. There has accordingly been a breach of Article 8 in the applicant's case as regards [the] ... release of records of metering to the police.

Notes

1   As a result of this decision, the UK had to pass the Interception of Communications Act 1985, which gave a statutory basis to the power to tap telephones. This has now been replaced by the Regulation of Investigatory Powers Act 2000.

2   It is ironic that in the unsuccessful *domestic* challenge to the legality of telephone tapping which preceded the challenge at Strasbourg, the judge dismissed Malone's case partly on the basis that, since in the UK everyone is free to do that which the law does not forbid, and there was no positive law forbidding telephone tapping, the government was free to do it; in other words, a basic tenet of the Rule of Law was applied to *defeat* the claim. The judgment on this point arguably missed the basic point that this freedom to do that which the law does not forbid should apply to *citizens*, who have a right to liberty, but not to *government*, which does not have such a general liberty of action, but only duties, a distinction eloquently brought out in the following case by Laws LJ (the facts are not material).

R v Somerset County Council ex p Fewings and Others [1995] I All ER 513, 523

... Public bodies and private persons are both subject to the Rule of Law; nothing could be more elementary. But the principles which govern their relationships with the law are wholly different. For private persons, the rule is that you may do anything you choose which the law does not prohibit. It means that the freedoms of the private citizen are not conditional upon some distinct and affirmative justification for which he must burrow in the law books. Such a notion would be anathema to our English legal traditions. But for public bodies the rule is opposite, and so of another character altogether. *It is that any action to be taken must be justified by positive law.* A public body has no heritage of legal rights which it enjoys for its own sake; at every turn, all of its dealings constitute the fulfilment of duties which it owes to others; indeed, it exists for no other purpose. I would say that a public body enjoys no rights properly so called; it may in various contexts be entitled to insist that this or that procedure be followed, whether by a person affected by its decision or by a superior body having power over it; it may come to court as a judicial review applicant to complain of the decision of some other public authority; it may maintain a private law action to enforce a contract or otherwise protect its property... But in every such instance, and no doubt many others where a public body asserts claims or defences in court, it does so, if it acts in good faith, only to vindicate the better performance of the duties for whose fulfilment it exists. It is in this sense that it has no rights of its own, no axe to grind beyond its public responsibility: a responsibility which defines its purpose and justifies its existence. Under our law, this is true of every public body. The rule is necessary in order to protect the people from arbitrary interference by those set in power over them ...

Laws must be sufficiently clear

That laws must be sufficiently clear is an elementary characteristic that any good legal system should possess: laws that are not sufficiently clear cannot guide conduct. This is of particular importance in relation to criminal law. Doubts have been expressed in this regard on the basis that much criminal law is still derived from common law. As ATH Smith has put it: 'My thesis is that ... English criminal law is inherently offensive to the principle of legality – being a common law system, it is in places highly uncertain.'[16] Once again in this area, this basic principle of the Rule of Law has been bolstered by the incorporation of the European Convention on Human Rights by the Human Rights Act 1998. As noted above, interferences with Convention rights must be 'prescribed by law'. The European Court of Human Rights has found that such 'law' must have certain qualities, a matter which it addressed in a famous passage in *Sunday Times v United Kingdom* (1979) 2 EHRR 245, para 49:

> ... a norm cannot be regarded as a 'law' unless it is formulated with sufficient precision to enable the citizen to regulate his conduct; he must be able, if need be with appropriate advice, to foresee to a degree that is reasonable in all the circumstances, the consequences which a given action may entail ... [However] those consequences need not be attainable with absolute certainty: experience shows this to be unattainable ... whilst certainty is highly desirable, it may bring in its train excessive rigidity and the law must be able to keep pace with changing circumstances. Accordingly many laws are inevitably couched in terms which, to a greater or lesser extent, are vague and whose interpretation and application are questions of practice.

Thus, the requirement that interferences be prescribed by law is not only a *formal* requirement, it says something about the qualities which that law must have. One of the relatively rare cases in which an interference with a Convention right was found to be unlawful on this basis[17] was *Hashman and Harrup v UK* (2000) 30 EHRR 241. The application to the European Court of Human Rights was made by hunt saboteurs, complaining of a violation of their right to freedom of expression. They had blown a horn and engaged in 'halloo-ing' with the intention of disrupting a hunt. They succeeded in drawing some of the hounds away from the hunt, and one was killed when it ran across a road. Following a complaint to the local magistrates, they were bound over to keep the peace and be of good behaviour in the sum of £100 for 12 months under the Justices of the Peace Act 1361. The binding over was based on the finding that their behaviour had been '*contra bonos mores*' ('contrary to a good way of life'). The applicants' argument before the European Commission and then Court of Human Rights was that the convictions, which interfered with their right to freedom of expression under Article 10, could not be said to be prescribed by law, as the relevant domestic law was too vague and unclear to satisfy the requirement (in Article 10(2)) that any interference with the right under Article 10 must be 'prescribed by law'.

Hashman v Harrup v UK (2000) 30 EHRR 241, ECtHR (extracts)

> ... 13. Behaviour *contra bonos mores* has been described as 'conduct which has the property of being wrong rather than right in the judgment of the majority of contemporary fellow citizens' (*per* Lord Justice Glidewell in *Hughes v Holley* (1988) 86 Cr App R 130).

---

16 ATH Smith, 'Comment; 1' [1985] PL 608.
17 The complaint as to telephone tapping (as opposed to metering) in *Malone v UK* was also found to disclose a violation of Article 8 on this basis, since the applicable law, together with government statements explaining its practice in relation to telephone tapping, was found to be so vague and complex as not to fulfil the above requirements.

29. The Government submit that the concepts of breach of the peace and behaviour *contra bonos mores* are sufficiently precise and certain ... With particular reference to the concept of behaviour *contra bonos mores*, the Government accept that the power is broadly defined, but claim that the breadth is necessary to meet the aims of the power, and sufficient to meet the requirements of the Convention. They state that the power to bind over to be of good behaviour gives magistrates a vital tool in controlling anti-social behaviour which has the potential to escalate into criminal conduct. They also note that the breadth of the definition facilitates the administration of justice as social standards alter and public perception of acceptable behaviour changes. They also point to the test under English law of whether a person has acted 'dishonestly' for the purpose of the Theft Acts 1968 and 1978 which is at least in part the standard of ordinary reasonable and honest people (*R v Ghosh* [1982] QB 1053), and to the test for whether a publication is defamatory, namely whether the statement concerned would lower a person in the opinion of right thinking members of society. Finally, the Government submit that on the facts of the case, the applicants should have known that what they had done was *contra bonos mores* and they should have known what they should do to avoid such behaviour in the future: they had acted in a way intended to disrupt the lawful activities of others, and should not have been in any doubt that their behaviour was unlawful and should not be repeated. The Government recall that the Court is concerned with the case before it, rather than abstract concerns about the compatibility of domestic law with the Convention *in abstracto* ...

31. [The Court cited the principles laid down in *Sunday Times* quoted above and went on:] The level of precision required of domestic legislation 'which cannot in any case provide for every eventuality' depends to a considerable degree on the content of the instrument in question, the field it is designed to cover and the number and status of those to whom it is addressed ...

37. The Court first recalls that in its *Steel* judgment, it noted that the expression 'to be of good behaviour' 'was particularly imprecise and offered little guidance to the person bound over as to the type of conduct which would amount to a breach of the order'. Those considerations apply equally in the present case, where the applicants were not charged with any criminal offence, and were found not to have breached the peace.

38. The Court next notes that conduct *contra bonos mores* is defined as behaviour which is 'wrong rather than right in the judgment of the majority of contemporary fellow citizens' (see paragraph 13 above). It cannot agree with the Government that this definition has the same objective element as conduct 'likely to cause annoyance', which was at issue in the case of *Chorherr* (1993) A 266-B. The Court considers that the question of whether conduct is 'likely to cause annoyance' is a question which goes to the very heart of the nature of the conduct proscribed: it is conduct whose likely consequence is the annoyance of others. Similarly, the definition of breach of the peace given in the case of *Percy v Director of Public Prosecutions* (see paragraph 11 above) 'that it includes conduct the natural consequences of which would be to provoke others to violence' also describes behaviour by reference to its effects. Conduct which is 'wrong rather than right in the judgment of the majority of contemporary citizens', by contrast, is conduct which is not described at all, but merely expressed to be 'wrong' in the opinion of a majority of citizens.

39. Nor can the Court agree that the Government's other examples of behaviour which are defined by reference to the standards expected by the majority of contemporary opinion are similar to conduct *contra bonos mores* as in each case cited by the Government, the example given is but one element of a more comprehensive definition of the proscribed behaviour.

40. With specific reference to the facts of the present case, the Court does not accept that it must have been evident to the applicants what they were being ordered not to do for the period of their binding over. Whilst in the case of *Steel and Others* the applicants had been found to have breached the peace, and the Court found that it was apparent that the bind over related to similar behaviour, the present applicants did not breach the peace, and given the lack of precision referred to above, it cannot be said that what they were being bound over not to do must have been apparent to them.

41. The Court thus finds that the order by which the applicants were bound over to keep the peace and not to behave *contra bonos mores* did not comply with the requirement of Article 10(2) of the Convention that it be 'prescribed by law'. . .

43. It follows that there has been a violation of Article 10 of the Convention.

Note
It should be recalled that the requirement of the Convention that law must be sufficiently clear only applies to law which authorises interference with Convention rights.

Law shall not be retrospective

In *Phillips v Eyre* (1870) LR 6 QB 1, 23, the strong presumption of the courts that Parliament does not intend to infringe the Rule of Law by penalising people retrospectively was made clear: '. . . the courts will not ascribe retrospective force to new laws affecting rights unless by express words or necessary implication it appears that such was the intention of the legislature.'

In the criminal sphere, the principle of non-retroactivity has been emphatically reaffirmed by the House of Lords. In *Waddington v Miah* [1974] 1 WLR 377, 378–80, their Lordships made it clear that they would be extremely loath to read any Act of Parliament as having retrospective criminal effect, Lord Reid saying, '. . . it is hardly credible that any government department would promote or that Parliament would pass retrospective criminal legislation'. This interpretative principle has now been bolstered, again by the Human Rights Act, in the field of criminal law. Article 7 of the ECHR states:

1   No one shall be held guilty of any criminal offence on account of any act or omission which did not constitute a criminal offence under national or international law at the time when it was committed. Nor shall a heavier penalty be imposed than the one that was applicable at the time the criminal offence was committed.

2   This article shall not prejudice the trial and punishment of any person for any act or omission which, at the time when it was committed, was criminal according to the general principles of law recognised by civilised nations.

To some, the role of the judges in developing that part of the criminal law which is common law was open to question in the light of the requirements of certainty and non-retrospectivity made by the Rule of Law. Unlike changes made by legislation, which are virtually always framed so as to have only prospective effect, if the effect of a judgment is to change the law, that change will affect the person charged with the offence in question, who, axiomatically, carried out the act in question before the judgment was given.[18] Therefore, any change in the law made by that judgment is necessarily retrospective in effect. As ATH Smith has argued:

. . . being a common law system, [English criminal law] is in places highly uncertain, and . . . is therefore necessarily retrospective in character when the law is judicially developed . . . The enactment of a criminal code would provide a fixed and objective starting point for delineating the permissible restrictions on the right to personal freedom, even if it could not solve all the problems of certainty inherent in a government by laws and men.[19]

18   As ATH Smith argues, *op cit.*
19   *Ibid.*

The case in which this issue raised the greatest concern was the decision in *R v R* [1991] 2 All ER 257, in which the House of Lords effectively abolished the marital rape exemption – holding that husbands could thenceforth be guilty of raping their wives.

R v R [1991] 2 All ER 257 (extracts)

The appellant was convicted of attempted rape; he was married to the victim, but she had left the matrimonial home two days earlier and left him a note saying she intended to petition for divorce. He forced his way into the house at which she was staying, assaulted her and attempted to rape her. He appealed against the decision on the basis that it was well established law that a man could not be guilty of raping his wife.

Lord Keith of Kinkel: Sir Matthew Hale, in his History of the Pleas of the Crown, 1st ed (1736), vol 1, ch 58, p 629, wrote:

> But the husband cannot be guilty of a rape committed by himself upon his lawful wife, or by their mutual matrimonial consent and contract the wife hath given herself up in this kind unto her husband which she cannot retract.

... In the first edition (1822) of Archbold, *Pleading and Evidence in Criminal Cases*, at p 259 it was stated, after a reference to Hale, 'A husband also cannot be guilty of a rape upon his wife'. For over 150 years after the publication of Hale's work there appears to have been no reported case in which judicial consideration was given to his proposition.

It may be taken that the proposition was generally regarded as an accurate statement of the common law of England. The common law is, however, capable of evolving in the light of changing social, economic and cultural developments. Hale's proposition reflected the state of affairs in these respects at the time it was enunciated. Since then the status of women, and particularly of married women, has changed out of all recognition in various ways which are very familiar and upon which it is unnecessary to go into detail. Apart from property matters and the availability of matrimonial remedies, one of the most important changes is that marriage is in modern times regarded as a partnership of equals, and no longer one in which the wife must be the subservient chattel of the husband. Hale's proposition involves that by marriage a wife gives her irrevocable consent to sexual intercourse with her husband under all circumstances and irrespective of the state of her health or how she happens to be feeling at the time. In modern times any reasonable person must regard that conception as quite unacceptable.

In *S v HM Advocate*, 1989 SLT 469, the High Court of Justiciary in Scotland recently considered the supposed marital exemption in rape in that country ... [and] held that the exemption, if it had ever been part of the law of Scotland, was no longer so...

The Lord Justice-General, Lord Emslie, who delivered the judgment of the court [said]:

> ... A live system of law will always have regard to changing circumstances to test the justification for any exception to the application of a general rule. Nowadays it cannot seriously be maintained that by marriage a wife submits herself irrevocably to sexual intercourse in all circumstances. It cannot be affirmed nowadays, whatever the position may have been in earlier centuries, that it is an incident of modern marriage that a wife consents to intercourse in all circumstances, including sexual intercourse obtained only by force. There is no doubt that a wife does not consent to assault upon her person and there is no plausible justification for saying today that she nevertheless is to be taken to consent to intercourse by assault ... The fiction of implied consent has no useful purpose to serve today in the law of rape in Scotland.

I consider the substance of that reasoning to be no less valid in England than in Scotland. On grounds of principle there is now no justification for the marital exemption in rape.

It is now necessary to review how the matter stands in English case law ... In *R v Clarence*, 22 QBD 23 a husband who knew that he suffered from a venereal disease communicated it to his wife through sexual intercourse. He was convicted on charges of unlawfully inflicting grievous bodily harm contrary to section 20 of the Offences against the Person Act 1861 and of assault occasioning actual bodily harm contrary to section 47 of the same Act. The convictions were quashed by a court of 13 judges of Crown Cases Reserved, with four dissents. Consideration was given to Hale's proposition, and it appears to have been accepted as sound by a majority of the judges. However, Wills J said, at p 33, that he was not prepared to assent to the proposition that rape between married persons was impossible. Field J (in whose judgment Charles J concurred) said, at p 57, that he should hesitate before he adopted Hale's proposition, and that he thought there might be many cases in which a wife might lawfully refuse intercourse and in which, if the husband imposed it by violence, he might be held guilty of a crime.

[His Lordship then went on to consider subsequent cases which had whittled down the scope of the exemption; in *Rex v Clarke* [1949] 2 All ER 448 it was held that a husband could be guilty of rape 'in circumstances where justices had made an order providing that the wife should no longer be bound to cohabit with the husband'. In *R v Miller* [1954] 2 QB 282 'the husband was charged with rape of his wife after she had left him and filed a petition for divorce. He was also charged with assault upon her occasioning actual bodily harm'. It was found that he could not be charged with rape because 'the wife cannot refuse her consent', but that he could be charged with assault if he used 'force or violence in the exercise of that right' to intercourse with his wife.]

The next case is *R v O'Brien (Edward)* [1974] 3 All ER 663, where Park J held that a *decree nisi* effectively terminated a marriage and revoked the wife's implied consent to marital intercourse, so that subsequent intercourse by the husband without her consent constituted rape. There was a similar holding by the Criminal Division of the Court of Appeal in *R v Steele* (1976) 65 Cr App R 22 as regards a situation where the spouses were living apart and the husband had given an undertaking to the court not to molest his wife. A decision to the like effect was given by the same court in *R v Roberts* [1986] Crim LR 188, where the spouses had entered into a formal separation agreement. In *R v Sharples* [1990] Crim LR 198, however, it was ruled by Judge Fawcus that a husband could not be convicted of rape upon his wife in circumstances where there was in force a family protection order in her favour and he had had sexual intercourse with her against her will. The order was ... in the terms that 'the respondent shall not use or threaten to use violence against the person of the applicant'...

There should be mentioned next a trio of cases which were concerned with the question whether acts done by a husband preliminary to sexual intercourse with an estranged wife against her will could properly be charged as indecent assaults ... The effect of these decisions appears to be that in general acts which would ordinarily be indecent but which are preliminary to an act of normal sexual intercourse are deemed to be covered by the wife's implied consent to the latter, but that certain acts, such as fellatio, are not to be so deemed. Those cases illustrate the contortions to which judges have found it necessary to resort in face of the fiction of implied consent to sexual intercourse. In all of them lip service, at least, was paid to Hale's proposition. Since then there have been three further decisions by single judges.

[His Lordship considered them; in one, the judge followed the Scottish decision, holding that the marital exemption was no longer good law; his Lordship went on:]

A different view was taken in the other two cases, by reason principally of the terms in which rape is defined in section 1(1) of the Sexual Offences (Amendment) Act 1976, viz:

> For the purposes of section 1 of the Sexual Offences Act 1956 (which relates to rape) a man commits rape if — (a) he has unlawful sexual intercourse with a woman who at the time of the intercourse does not consent to it; and (b) at that time he knows that she does not consent to the intercourse or he is reckless as to whether she consents to it ...

In *R v J (Rape: Marital Exemption)* [1991] 1 All ER 759 a husband was charged with having raped his wife, from whom he was living apart at the time. Rougier J ruled that the charge was bad, holding that the effect of section 1(1)(a) of the Act of 1976 was that the marital exemption embodied in Hale's proposition was preserved, subject to those exceptions established by cases decided before the Act was passed. He took the view that the word 'unlawful' in the subsection meant 'illicit', ie outside marriage, that being the meaning which in R v Chapman [1959] 1 QB 100 it had been held to bear in section 19 of the Sexual Offences Act 1956. Then in R v S (unreported), 15 January 1991, Swinton-Thomas J followed Rougier J in holding that section 1(1) of the Act of 1976 preserved the marital exemption subject to the established common law exceptions. Differing, however, from Rougier J, he took the view that it remained open to judges to define further exceptions. In the case before him the wife had obtained a family protection order in similar terms to that in R v Sharples [1990] Crim LR 198. Differing from Judge Fawcus in that case, Swinton-Thomas J held that the existence of the family protection order created an exception to the marital exemption.

The position then is that that part of Hale's proposition which asserts that a wife cannot retract the consent to sexual intercourse which she gives on marriage has been departed from in a series of decided cases. On grounds of principle there is no good reason why the whole proposition should not be held inapplicable in modern times. The only question is whether section 1(1) of the Act of 1976 presents an insuperable obstacle to that sensible course. The argument is that 'unlawful' in the subsection means outside the bond of marriage. That is not the most natural meaning of the word, which normally describes something which is contrary to some law or enactment or is done without lawful justification or excuse. Certainly in modern times sexual intercourse outside marriage would not ordinarily be described as unlawful. If the subsection proceeds on the basis that a woman on marriage gives a general consent to sexual intercourse, there can never be any question of intercourse with her by her husband being without her consent. There would thus be no point in enacting that only intercourse without consent outside marriage is to constitute rape.

... In my opinion there are no rational grounds for putting the suggested gloss on the word, and it should be treated as being mere surplusage in this enactment ...

I am therefore of the opinion that section 1(1) of the Act of 1976 presents no obstacle to this House declaring that in modern times the supposed marital exemption in rape forms no part of the law of England. The Court of Appeal (Criminal Division) took a similar view. Towards the end of the judgment of that court Lord Lane CJ said, ante, p 611:

> The remaining and no less difficult question is whether, despite that view, this is an area where the court should step aside to leave the matter to the Parliamentary process. This is not the creation of a new offence, it is the removal of a common law fiction which has become anachronistic and offensive and we consider that it is our duty having reached that conclusion to act upon it.

I respectfully agree.

My Lords, for these reasons I would dismiss this appeal.

Notes

1   It may be noted that their Lordships gave remarkably little consideration to the supposedly strong common law principle of non-retroactivity; the paragraph at the end of the judgment quoted from the Court of Appeal amounts to the only implied response to the charge of retrospective law-making.

2   The man convicted applied to the European Court of Human Rights on the grounds that at the time that he had forced intercourse with his wife this was not a criminal offence; that the Law Lords had only decided it was an offence after he committed the act, and that he therefore had been penalised for doing something which was not a crime when he did it. The principle of non-retroactivity, which is upheld by Article 7, ECHR, had therefore been violated. The judgment which

appears below also concerned a man who had been convicted of raping his wife in relation to events which happened before the Court of Appeal judgment in *R v R*, but who was tried after it: the judge followed *R v R* and held that he could be convicted despite being married to the victim.

SW and CW v United Kingdom (1996) 21 EHRR 363 (extracts)

. . .

36. However clearly drafted a legal provision may be, in any system of law, including criminal law, there is an inevitable element of judicial interpretation. There will always be a need for elucidation of doubtful points and for adaptation to changing circumstances. Indeed, in the United Kingdom, as in the other Convention States, the progressive development of the criminal law through judicial law-making is a well entrenched and necessary part of legal tradition. Article 7 of the Convention cannot be read as outlawing the gradual clarification of the rules of criminal liability through judicial interpretation from case to case, provided that the resultant development is consistent with the essence of the offence and could reasonably be foreseen.

37. The applicant maintained that the general common law principle that a husband could not be found guilty of rape upon his wife, albeit subject to certain limitations, was still effective on 18 September 1990, when he committed the acts which gave rise to the rape charge. A succession of court decisions before and also after that date, for instance on 20 November 1990 in *R v J*, had affirmed the general principle of immunity. It was clearly beyond doubt that as at 18 September 1990 no change in the law had been effected, although one was being mooted.

. . .

39. Although the Court of Appeal and the House of Lords did not create a new offence or change the basic ingredients of the offence of rape, they were extending an existing offence to include conduct which until then was excluded by the common law. They could not be said to have adapted the law to a new kind of conduct but rather to a change of social attitudes. To extend the criminal law, solely on such a basis, to conduct which was previously lawful was precisely what Article 7 of the Convention was designed to prevent. Moreover, the applicant stressed, it was impossible to specify with precision when the change in question had occurred. In September 1990, change by judicial interpretation was not foreseen by the Law Commission, which considered that a parliamentary enactment would be necessary.

40. The Government and the [European Human Rights] Commission were of the view that by September 1990 there was significant doubt as to the validity of the alleged marital immunity for rape. This was an area where the law had been subject to progressive development and there were strong indications that still wider interpretation by the courts of the inroads on the immunity was probable. In particular, given the recognition of women's equality of status with men in marriage and outside it and of their autonomy over their own bodies, the adaptation of the ingredients of the offence of rape was reasonably foreseeable, with appropriate legal advice, to the applicant. He was not convicted of conduct which did not constitute a criminal offence at the time when it was committed.

43. The decisions of the Court of Appeal and then the House of Lords did no more than continue a perceptible line of case-law development dismantling the immunity of a husband from prosecution for rape upon his wife . . . There was no doubt under the law as it stood on 18 September 1990 that a husband who forcibly had sexual intercourse with his wife could, in various circumstances, be found guilty of rape. Moreover, there was an evident evolution, which was consistent with the very essence of the offence, of the criminal law through judicial interpretation towards treating such conduct generally as within the scope of the offence of rape. This evolution had reached a stage where judicial recognition of the absence of immunity had become a reasonably foreseeable development of the law (see paragraph 36 above).

44. The essentially debasing character of rape is so manifest that the result of the decisions of the Court of Appeal and the House of Lords – that the applicant could be convicted of attempted rape, irrespective of his relationship with the victim – cannot be said to be at variance with the object and purpose of Article 7 (Art 7) of the Convention, namely to ensure that no one should be subjected to arbitrary prosecution, conviction or punishment (see paragraph 34 above). What is more, the abandonment of the unacceptable idea of a husband being immune against prosecution for rape of his wife was in conformity not only with a civilised concept of marriage but also, and above all, with the fundamental objectives of the Convention, the very essence of which is respect for human dignity and human freedom ...

47. In short, the Court, like the Government and the Commission, finds that the Crown Court's decision that the applicant could not invoke immunity to escape conviction and sentence for rape upon his wife did not give rise to a violation of his rights under Article 7 para I of the Convention.

FOR THESE REASONS, THE COURT UNANIMOUSLY

Holds that there has been no violation of Article 7 para I (Art 7-I) of the Convention.

Notes

1   While it is impossible to feel any sympathy for the men involved in these cases, the decision of the court in this case arguably amounted to a dilution of the Article 7 guarantee. There was clearly a strongly arguable case that what had occurred did indeed amount to retroactive criminalisation. In its *Working Paper 116*, 'Rape within Marriage', 17 September 1990, the Law Commission had reviewed the state of the law in this area and concluded:

2.8 It is generally accepted that, subject to exceptions (considered ... below), a husband cannot be convicted of raping his wife ... Indeed there seems to be no recorded prosecution before 1949 of a husband for raping his wife ...

The defendant was convicted in relation to events which happened in October 1989; if, almost a year *after* that date, the Law Commission, a body of distinguished experts, considered the marital exemption still to be good law, subject to some exceptions, it is hard to see how the defendant, even with advice, could have expected to foresee the change that was coming about.

2   While *R v R* arguably represented a judicial violation of the non-retroactivity principle, a far more straightforward – and less defensible – breach of that principle was seriously contemplated by the Blair administration in October 2001. In response to the terrorist attacks on America on 11 September, the government announced that it would be bringing forward emergency anti-terrorist legislation.[20] There had been a number of attacks carried out in the US and the UK using anthrax spores, which created widespread panic, and a number of hoaxers exploited this, giving false warnings to the police. It was initially announced that the Anti-Terrorism Bill would include a measure that would retrospectively increase the penalty for this kind of hoaxing from six months to seven years. Indeed, ministers went as far as announcing that the increased penalty was in force, from 21 October 2001,[21] and that Parliament would 'later' pass legislation retrospectively making this change. This would clearly have amounted to an open and gross breach of Article 7 ECHR[22] and an unprecedented action as a matter of English law.

20   See HC Deb cols 924–39 (15 October 2001).
21   See 'Anthrax hoax law may breach human rights', *Daily Telegraph*, 22 October 2001.
22   See the view of the Joint Committee on Human Rights, *Second Report*, HL 37, HL 372 (2001–02), para 12.

Ministers, however, showed scant regard for the so called fundamental constitutional principles at stake. For example, Home Office Minister, Lord Rooker, reportedly said:

Just because we are a tolerant, liberal democracy does not mean we are going to have people wrecking that by using the very instruments that mean we are a tolerant and liberal democracy. We have not yet published the new legislation, but we have made it clear that we intend not to be ... [hamstrung by] ... human rights legislation which is clearly being abused – aided and abetted by the legal trade – by suspected terrorists.[23]

The same report described Oliver Letwin, shadow Home Secretary, as 'cautiously supportive'. When the Bill was published, the provision was not included; however, the reason given by ministers was not that the government had decided not, after all, to engage in such a blatant violation of its treaty obligations, but simply that the threat of the increased penalty had already had the effect of deterring would-be hoaxers, so that the government considered the measure no longer necessary. Such a cavalier attitude, displayed by the very government which introduced the Human Rights Act, indicates the remarkable lack of respect for the principles of constitutionalism displayed by the British polity, in which the untrammelled ability of the government of the day to respond to events in whatever way it sees fit appears to be the most valued attribute of the UK constitution.

3   The other principles of the Rule of Law mentioned above were that cases must be tried fairly (therefore by an independent judiciary) and according to due process. The issue of the independence of the judiciary is addressed in the second half of this chapter (pp 103 *et seq*). The detail of the fair trial of cases obviously lies within the realm of criminal (and civil) procedure and therefore outside the scope of this work. However, the general principle of fair procedures as expressed in administrative law are discussed below by Jowell. The notions put forward by Raz, that courts must be easily accessible and have review powers to ensure adherence by other public bodies to the principles of the Rule of Law, are clearly critical and are discussed elsewhere: for the availability of judicial review, and statutory attempts to exclude it, see Part V Chapter 1. For the principles governing the right of access to the courts, see the decision in *R v Lord Chancellor ex p Witham* [1998] QB 575, an extract from which appears in Chapter 4 of this part, at pp 141–42. In brief, the case concerned a challenge to changes to the rules governing court fees. The changes in the rules removed from litigants-in-person in receipt of income support their exemption from payment of such fees and the Lord Chancellor's power exceptionally to reduce or remit fees in cases of financial hardship. The applicant was an unemployed man in receipt of income support who wished to issue proceedings in person for defamation, for which legal aid was not available. Such proceedings have to be brought in the High Court and the fee would, under the new regime, be £500. He could not afford the fee and, by virtue of the changes to the rules, was no longer eligible for waiver. The basis of his argument was that the Lord Chancellor's actions had the effect of denying him access to the courts. His challenge succeeded. The judge remarked:

... the right to a fair trial, which of necessity imports the right of access to the court, is as near to an absolute right as any which I can envisage. It seems to me, from all the authorities to which I have referred, that the common law has clearly given special weight to the citizen's right of access to the courts. It has been described as a constitutional right, though the cases do not explain what

---

23   See 'Anthrax hoax law may breach human rights', *Daily Telegraph*, 22 October 2001.

that means. In this whole argument, nothing to my mind has been shown to displace the proposition that the executive cannot in law abrogate the right of access to justice, unless it is specifically so permitted by Parliament; and this is the meaning of the constitutional right.

General legal protection for the Rule of Law in practice

Jowell discusses, first of all, the way in which the requirement of fair procedure – a key aspect of the Rule of Law, going beyond the fairness of formal trials – is upheld, in terms very reminiscent of Rawls, and then goes on to consider the broader role of judicial review in policing adherence to requirements of legality and non-arbitrariness inherent in the Rule of Law.

Jeffrey Jowell, 'The Rule of Law today', in J Jowell and D Oliver (eds), *The Changing Constitution*, 4th edn (2000), pp 13–19 (extracts)

As we have seen, predetermined rules provide one way of controlling official discretion and achieving fairness for persons affected by public regulation. Procedural techniques provide another. I refer to these in connection with the notion contained in the Rule of Law that no person should be condemned unheard, a procedural protection also expressed in terms such as 'due process' or 'natural justice', the essence of which is the participation of affected persons in decisions affecting their rights or interests. This kind of 'structuring' or 'checking' of discretion attempts, like open rules, to promote fidelity to organisational purpose, both by permitting the persons affected to argue their case and, where a reasoned decision is required, giving, through the process of justification, what Fuller has described as 'formal and institutional expression to the influence of reasoned argument in human affairs' ['Collective bargaining and the arbitrator' (1963) Wisconsin L Rev 1, p 3] ... The process itself does encourage 'purposive decisions' [P Nonet, 'The legitimation of purposive decisions' (1980) Calif L Rev 263], as justification must usually be made by reference to a general rule, standard, or principle. Overt reference to arbitrary or particularistic factors (such as the defendant's race or political views) will be difficult to sustain.

British public administration is deeply infused with the notion that adjudicative mechanisms of one form or another are necessary to provide procedural checks on discretion in order to comply with the Rule of Law. Some are provided through appeals – for example, in planning, from local to central government by means of written representations or a public inquiry. In other cases special tribunals exist to permit appeals from the decisions of a variety of officials upon issues as diverse as the registration of a new variety of rose to compensation for the acquisition of land. Some tribunals and inquiries decide not only rights between the individual and the public organisation, but also questions of policy, such as whether a motorway should be built over a stretch of land. Because of their variety, not all tribunals and inquiries are suited to all the procedural protections obtaining in courts of law, where individual rights are in issue, but the trend, at least since the Franks Committee, is towards more judicialisation ...

The practical application of the Rule of Law

...

The day to day, practical implementation and enforcement of the Rule of Law is through the judicial review of the actions and decision of all officials performing public functions ... There are three principal 'grounds' of judicial review: review for 'illegality', for 'procedural impropriety', and for 'irrationality' (or unreasonableness). The implementation of each of these grounds involves the courts in applying different aspects of the Rule of Law.

Under the ground of illegality the courts act as guardian of Parliament's purpose, and may strike down official decisions which violate that purpose. Even when wide discretionary power is conferred upon an official, the courts are not willing to permit decisions which go outside its 'four corners'. Under the ground of procedural propriety the courts may, even where the statute is silent, supply the 'omission of the legislature' in order to insist that the decision-maker grant a fair hearing to the applicant before depriving him or her of a right, interest or legitimate expectation. The doctrine of legitimate expectation is itself rooted in the notion of legal certainty; the courts require a decision-maker at least to provide the affected person with a hearing before disappointing him of an expectation reasonably induced. At times the promised benefit itself may be required. In either case certainty triumphs over administrative convenience.

It is perhaps more difficult to countenance the application of the Rule of Law in the third ground of judicial review, that of irrationality or unreasonableness, because it raises the question whether the principle governs the substance and not merely the procedure of official action.

To what extent does the Rule of Law touch on the substance, as well as the procedure, of official action? We have seen that laws in practice are not always enforced rigorously, but rather selectively, allowing for personal and other mitigating factors (as with the doctor speeding to the scene of an accident in the early hours of the morning). But suppose the police decide to charge only bearded male drivers with traffic offences and leave the clean-shaven and women drivers alone; or to charge only drivers of a particular race? Suppose an education authority chose to dismiss all teachers with red hair? Would these decisions infringe the Rule of Law on the ground of their substance? Courts in this country interfere with this kind of decision on the ground of its being an abuse of discretion, the term used being 'unreasonableness' in the sense set out in the celebrated *Wednesbury* case [*Associated Provincial Picture Houses v Wednesbury Corporation* [1948] 1 KB 223]. Is this judicial interference ultimately justified on the ground that the offending decision was a breach of substantive Rule of Law? If so justified, judges lay themselves open to accusations of improper interference with the substance of administration, about which they are reputed to know very little.

Those who deny that judges inerfere with the substance of decisions contend that what the courts are doing when interfering with arbitrary, capricious, or oppressive decisions is ensuring that the official action is faithful to the law's purpose, thus achieving the containment of the administration in accordance with an implied legislative scheme. Even if a minister has power to act 'as he thinks fit', it is assumed that the statute conferring that power requires standards that are rationally related to purpose, and that the charging of only bearded drivers could not be related to the purpose of preventing unsafe driving. In practice, however, the legislation frequently has no clear 'purpose' itself, and to pretend otherwise is to adopt a fiction. Parliament often delegates enforcement to ministers, other authorities, or officials precisely in order to allow them to define and elaborate purpose. Implementation is often a process from the bottom up, rather than from the top down. When the Rule of Law allows judicial interference on grounds of 'unreasonableness', 'irrationality', or 'oppressiveness', it does become a substantive doctrine, one that is less easily accepted than the procedural, particularly in a society without a written constitution. Courts therefore tread warily on substantive Rule of Law and seek to exclude (or disguise) policy considerations from the decision. The 'unreasonableness' doctrine itself carefully avoids judicial second-guessing of the administration on the grounds of mere disagreement, and only permits interference if the official decision verges on the outlandish ...

Notes

1   The Human Rights Act 1998, s 6(1) states that 'it is unlawful for a public authority to act in a way which is incompatible with a Convention right' (that is, a right protected by the European Convention on Human Rights, as defined in the HRA itself). This represents a new, substantive, head of illegality, subject to the exceptions laid out in the HRA (see further, Part VI Chapter 1; for the grounds for judicial review, see further Part V Chapter 2). Under both the developing common law of judicial review, and the HRA, the courts now extend their protection beyond acts without lawful authorisation, or undertaken without a fair procedure, or which are plainly irrational. The law now affords protection, through judicial review, for a set of substantive rights – personal liberty, freedom of speech, privacy, and the like (for the Convention articles, see Part II Chapter 2). In this new guise,

judicial review protects not just the Rule of Law (it will do so through the Convention requirement that interferences with Convention rights must be 'prescribed by law') but also a substantive set of civil and political rights.[24]

Dicey, the Rule of Law and discretionary powers

The most influential, though also one of the most controversial, expositions of the importance of the Rule of Law in the British constitutional scheme has been that put forward by Dicey. It is of interest today primarily as a starting point in a debate which has raged ever since over the compatibility of broad discretionary powers with the Rule of Law. In Dicey's view the Rule of Law in the UK could be reduced to three propositions.

AV Dicey, *An Introduction to the Study of the Constitution*, 10th edn (1959), pp 188, 195, 202-03

We mean, in the first place, that no man is punishable or can be lawfully made to suffer in body or goods except for a distinct breach of law established before the ordinary courts of the land. In this sense the Rule of Law is contrasted with every system of government based on the exercise by persons in authority of wide, arbitrary or discretionary powers of constraint ... It means ... the absolute supremacy or predominance of regular law as opposed to the influence of arbitrary power, and excludes the existence of arbitrariness, of prerogative, or even of wide discretionary authority on the part of the government ... a man may with us be punished for a breach of the law, but he can be punished for nothing else.

[Secondly] ... It means ... equality of the law, or the equal subjection of all classes to the ordinary law of the land administered by the ordinary law courts; the 'Rule of Law' in this sense excludes the idea of any exemption of officials or others from the duty of obedience to the law which governs other citizens or from the jurisdiction of the ordinary tribunals ...

[Thirdly] from the general principles of the constitution (as for example the right to personal liberty, or the right of public meeting) are with us the result of judicial decisions determining the rights of private persons in particular cases brought before the courts; whereas under many foreign constitutions the security (such as it is) given to the rights of individuals results, or appears to result, from the general principles of the constitution.

Notes

1   In what follows, the discussion will focus on Dicey's first principle – the resistance to discretionary powers. His second, equality before the law, still, as Heuston points out, has some resonance in that 'the social or political or economic status of an individual is by itself no answer to legal proceedings, civil or criminal ...'[25] but has long been discredited, both as an accurate statement of the position in the UK, and insofar as it amounted to a critique of continental countries, such as France, where the *droit administratif* operated a separate form of justice for officials. As Jowell comments:

In 1928 William Robson wrote his celebrated book *Justice and Administrative Law*, in which he roundly criticised Dicey for his misinterpretation of both the English and French systems on that ground. He pointed out that there were in England 'colossal distinctions' [2nd edn (1947), p 343] between the rights and duties of private individuals and those of the administrative organs or

---

24   See generally, J Jowell, 'Beyond the Rule of Law: towards constitutional judicial review' [2000] PL 671.
25   Heuston, *op cit*, p 44.

government even in Dicey's time. Public authorities possessed special rights and special exemptions and immunities, to the extent that the citizen was deprived of a remedy against the State 'in many cases where he most requires it' [*ibid*, p 345]. Robson also convincingly showed how Dicey had misinterpreted French law, where the *droit administratif* was not intended to exempt public officials from the rigour of private law, but to allow experts in public administration to work out the extent of official liability. Robson also noted the extent of Dicey's misrepresentation that disputes between officials and private individuals in Britain were dealt with by the ordinary courts. He pointed to the growth of special tribunals and inquiries that had grown up to decide these disputes outside the courts, and was in no doubt that a 'vast body of administrative law' existed in England [*ibid*] ...[26]

2   Dicey's third principle, that rights in the UK were the result of ordinary court decisions, is arguably more relevant to a discussion of the UK constitution than the Rule of Law. Heuston notes that Dicey was above all a common law lawyer; he considered the specific guarantees of liberty offered by the common law to be of far more value than generally worded constitutions. In this respect, Dicey was merely finding a different application for the view long held by English jurists that common law was inherently superior to statute, due to its organic and evolutionary nature. Thus, in 1612, Sir John Davies, after describing how a 'custome' of the people on being 'continued without interruption time out of mind ... obtaineth the force of a *Law*', goes on to argue:

And this *Customary Law* is the most perfect and the most excellent, and without comparison the best, to make and preserve a Commonwealth. For the *Written Laws* ... are imposed upon the Subject before any Triall or Probation made, whether the same be fit and agreeable to the nature and disposition of the people, or whether they will be any inconvenience or no ...[27]

However, the value which Dicey places upon common law rights over a Bill of Rights has been doubted, since the obvious correlation is that such rights are vulnerable to gradual erosion by statute. This position has been overtaken following enactment of the Human Rights Act, which for the first time gives UK citizens a general legislative statement of enforceable rights.

3   The applicability of the anti-discretionary element in Dicey's exposition of the Rule of Law to contemporary society is discussed further below, but a few comments are in order here. Heuston, a loyal supporter of Dicey, concedes that his view is no longer applicable in this respect, but attempts to place Dicey's opinion within its historical context.

It has been said that Dicey erred in saying that the doctrine of the Rule of Law 'excludes the existence even of wide discretionary authority on the part of the government'. This is certainly not true today. Modern government, as is well known, cannot be carried on at all without a host of wide discretionary powers, which are granted to the executive by the large number of statutes annually passed by Parliament. But it must be remembered, first of all, the kind of man Dicey was, and secondly, the times in which he wrote. First, Dicey was in politics an old-fashioned Whig. He was also a very typical example of the common lawyer who does not seriously believe in the existence of the Statute Book. To the true common lawyer the law is to be found in the law reports and books of authority. There are indeed statutes, but they can always be looked up if the opportunity arises. The judges, as has been well said, have never entered into the spirit of the Benthamite game and have always treated the statute as an interloper upon the rounded majesty of the common law. Secondly, it must be recalled that Dicey's great work was written in the early 1880s, a period when the *laissez faire* state of the Victorians was only just beginning to give way to

---

26   Jowell, *op cit* (1994), pp 58–62.
27   Sir John Davies, Preface to *Irish Reports* (1612), quoted in M Loughlin, *Public Law and Political Theory* (1992), p 44 (original emphasis).

the welfare state of the modern world. Dicey was an acute, a marvellously acute, judge of public opinion and of the impact upon public opinion of legislative power, but even he hardly foresaw the extent to which statutory powers of government would change the nature of English constitutional law. Today the fundamental problem is that of the control of discretionary powers, and it is indeed a serious criticism of Dicey's doctrine that he suggests that discretionary powers are in some way undesirable or unnecessary.[28]

4   As Heuston notes, Dicey's view was very much a product of its age. The 20th century attack on his model of the Rule of Law, which, in this respect at least, had received some support from Hayek[29] and Dickinson,[30] was two-fold. First of all, on the theoretical level, it was convincingly argued that it answered to an essentially conservative political viewpoint: Dicey's model, it was contended, was related to his ideal model of the state, as a minimalist facilitator of individual transactions and guarantor of individual rights. Dicey rightly foresaw that a government which wished to devise and implement those major schemes of public provision for health, education and welfare to which he was opposed would require the granting to it of broad discretionary powers. His objection to the *type* of powers was therefore in reality rooted in his opposition to the *policies* which could be implemented through them. This argument thus reconstructed Dicey's account of the Rule of Law as rooted in a particular conception of government and pronounced that conception anachronistic and reactionary. As Murray Hunt has put it, 'the Rule of Law was nothing short of the encapsulation of his particular Whig conception of societal ordering, according to which the individual's private rights, of property, personal liberty and freedom of discussion and association, ought to be sacrosanct from interference by the state'.[31]

5   The second part of the attack on this aspect of Dicey's argument was on the more practical level, by which the utility of Dicey's model as a prescription for modern government was subjected to a full-scale onslaught.[32] Discretionary powers, it was said, were a practical necessity if the government was to exercise wide-ranging interventionist powers for the public good. It would in many cases be wholly inappropriate and impracticable for officials attempting to implement complex schemes of social reform catering for the differing needs and circumstances of particular groups or individuals, sometimes on a local level and requiring local knowledge, to be fettered and encumbered by rigid rules of primary legislation. Such rules could only be changed with difficulty and delay, and could not be flexible enough to cater for local needs.[33] It was partly the perceived force of these

---

28   Heuston, *op cit*, pp 41–42.

29   See *The Road to Serfdom* (1944) and *The Constitution of Liberty* (1960).

30   See *Administrative Justice and the Supremacy of Law* (1927).

31   'Constitutionalism and contractualisation', in M Taggart (ed), *The Province of Administrative Law* (1997), p 24. See further BJ Hibbits, 'The politics of principle: Albert Venn Dicey and the Rule of Law' (1994) 23 Anglo-Am LR 1.

32   KC Davis provides one of the most readable summaries of this attack, describing the Diceyan model as 'the extravagant version of the Rule of Law' (*Discretionary Justice* (1971), Chapter 1). Davis based his argument on both simple necessity and on the desirability of individualised justice, which often demands wide-ranging discretionary powers. He observes: 'The Franks Committee-Dickinson-Dicey-Hayek versions of the Rule of Law express an emotion, an aspiration, an ideal but none is based on a down to earth analysis of the practical problems with which modern governments are confronted.'

33   As Davis puts it, 'Discretion is indispensable for individualised justice, for creative justice, for new programs in which no one yet knows how to formulate rules, and for old programs in which some aspects cannot be reduced to rules. Eliminating discretionary power would paralyse governmental processes and would stifle individualised justice' (*ibid*, p 40). See further, R Unger, *Law in Modern Society* (1976).

arguments which paved the way for the proliferation of quasi- and non-legal rules which is such a distinctive feature of modern governance.[34]

Thus the central thrust of the argument against Dicey's view is that the immense complexity of the modern state, the desirability of decentralised decision-making, and the growth in sources of (corporate) economic power which can rival those of the state, all mean that a simplistic application of a rather rusty 19th century conception of the Rule of Law is both ineffective and inappropriate. Jowell considers both the continuing value of the doctrine and the aspects of it which warrant re-examination in contemporary society.

Jeffrey Jowell, 'The Rule of Law today', in J Jowell and D Oliver (eds), *The Changing Constitution*, 4th edn (2000), pp 8–11

Certainty and the Rule of Law

An official possessed of discretion frequently has a choice about how it should be operated: whether to keep it open-textured, maintaining the option of a variety of responses to a given situation, or to confine it by a rule of standard – a process of legalisation. For example, officials administering welfare benefits could provide them on a case-by-case basis according to their conception of need, or they could announce precise levels of benefit for given situations. Similarly, laws against pollution could be enforced by a variable standard whereby the official must be satisfied that the polluter is achieving the 'best practicable means' of abatement. Alternatively, levels of pollution could be specified in advance, based on the colour of smoke emission, or the precise quantities of sulphur dioxide. A policy of promoting safe driving could, similarly, be legalised by a rule specifying speeds of no more than 30mph on given streets.

Now for Dicey, and particularly for Hewart and Hayek, who mistrusted the grant of virtually any official discretion, the virtue of rule-bound conduct was principally that it allowed affected persons to know the rules before being subjected to them ex *post facto*. As a principle of justice, it was felt that no person should be condemned without a presumed knowledge of the rule alleged to have been breached. This assumes a penal law or criminal regulation of one form or another, and is understandable in that context where the lack of rules would involve risky guesses with serious consequences for non-compliance. It is fairer to a person prosecuted for a tax offence to have been made aware of the precise tax required than for the levels to be determined at the discretion of an official.

This argument, however, has a somewhat different compulsion when dealing not with penalties but with regulation involving the allocation of scarce resources. Should an applicant for a university place be entitled, out of fairness, to know the precise grades required for entrance? Should the applicant for welfare benefits be entitled to know the rules about allocations of winter coats? In cases such as these the argument in favour of rules over discretion is an argument less from certainty than from *accountability*. This argument has two facets, the first being a concern to provide a published standard against which to measure the legality of official action and thus to allow *individual redress* against official action that does not accord with the rule or standard. Thus, an announced level of resources to qualify for welfare assistance ought to allow redress to a person who qualifies but is refused assistance. The second facet of accountability refers to the fact that the actual process of making rules and their publication generates *public assessment* of the fidelity of the rule to legislative purpose. Many statutes confer powers on officials to further the policy of the Act in accordance with wide discretion. The power may be to allocate council housing, or to provide for the needy, or to diminish unacceptable pollution of the air or water. The process of devising a points system for housing allocation, benefits for the needy, and acceptable

---

34 For discussion, see I Harden and N Lewis, *The Noble Lie: The British Constitution and the Rule of Law* (1986), esp pp 71–72.

emission levels of pollution thus forces the official into producing a formal operational definition of purpose . . .

The virtues of rules, as we have seen, include their qualities of legality, certainty, consistency, uniformity, congruence to purpose, and accountability loosely so called, all of which play an important part in the control of official discretion and may be seen as concrete manifestations of the Rule of Law. KC Davis, a leading American administrative lawyer, proposes in his book *Discretionary Justice* (1969) three main methods of controlling discretion. First is the 'confining' of discretion through rules akin to the legalisation we have just been discussing. He suggests that, wherever possible, discretion should be shaved down to the minimum compatible with the task to be performed. He proposes two other means of controlling discretion: its 'structuring' through open procedures, like the exacting federal rule-making procedures with which administrative agencies in the US must comply before issuing their regulations (Britain, incidentally, almost entirely lacks these procedures); and the 'checking' of discretion by means of a second look (not necessarily by the courts – internal administrative checks would suffice) . . .

The limits of rules

Looking now a little closer at the arguments above about rules governing administrative action, we should consider whether . . . they . . . are after all wholly beneficial in the way that some constitutional theorists have assumed. Hayek gives an example: 'it does not matter whether we all drive on the left or the right-hand side of the roads so long as we all do the same. The important thing is that the rule enables us to predict other people's behaviour correctly, and this requires that it should apply in all cases – even if in a particular instance we feel it to be unjust' [*The Road to Serfdom* (1943), p 60].

We should start by challenging a central assumption of those in favour of rules, that their principal purpose is to constrain officials straining to escape from their legal shackles in order to indulge in discretion unconfined. Officials are well aware of the benefit of rules to their own efficiency. Rules announce or clarify official policies to affected parties, and thus facilitate obedience. They may also allow routine treatment of cases, thus increasing the speed of decision-making. A zoning system in planning, a list of features of 'substandard' housing, and a list of grades for university admission all allow decisions to be taken more quickly than a system that requires constant reappraisal of each case on its merits. Rules, therefore, reduce the anxiety and conserve the energy needed to reach decisions on a case-by-case basis . . . Despite the fact that rules may promote criticism, they also, in the short run at least, provide a shield behind which officials may hide, pleading consistent and uniform justice in response to criticism that the individual's case is unique.

So here we have the tension: the virtues of rules – their objective, even-handed features – are opposed to other administrative benefits, especially those of flexibility, individual treatment, and responsiveness. The virtue of rules to the administrator (routine treatment) may be a defect to the client with a special case (such as the brilliant applicant for a university place who failed to obtain the required grades because of a family upset or illness just before the examination). The administrator's shield may be seen as an unjustified protection from the client's sword. Officials themselves may consider that the job itself requires flexibility, or genuinely want to help a particular client, but feel unable to do so: hence the classic bureaucratic response, 'I'd like to help you – but there is this rule'.

Our administrative law itself recognises the limits of rule-governed conduct in terms of individual justice in its development of the principle against the 'fettering' of discretion. Where an official has wide discretion – for example, to provide grants to industry or to impose penalties upon overspending local authorities – a rule will often be introduced both to assist in the articulation of the standard and its even-handed application, and also to announce the standard to affected persons. The courts have not objected to the rule itself, but they have objected to its blanket application without giving a person with something new or special to say about his case the opportunity to put his argument to the decision-maker. The principle against the fettering of discretion acknowledges how rules can militate against good and fair public administration.

THE SEPARATION OF POWERS

Reduced to its bare essentials, the doctrine of the separation of powers identifies three main organs of government – the legislature, the executive and the judiciary – and demands first that each should be separate and to an extent independent of each other, and secondly that each organ should be vested with only one main function of government. Thus, as Lord Templeman has put it, 'Parliament makes the law, the executive carry the law into effect and the judiciary enforce the law'.[35] It is immediately apparent that the doctrine is associated with that of the Rule of Law, which is strongly concerned with the manner in which the judiciary can keep the executive and (in the UK only to a very limited extent) the legislature within the bounds of its lawful authority. This issue has been explored above, while the practical means of enforcing such limitations – judicial review – is extensively discussed in Part V Chapters 1 and 2. The other substantial concern of the doctrine is the relationship between the legislature and the executive, which is considered in detail in Parts III and IV. Therefore, what follows will confine itself to a brief discussion of the theoretical basis for the doctrine and its application in the UK. The latter part of the discussion will note the significant ways in which the growing influence of Article 6(1) of the ECHR has bolstered a vital aspect of both the separation of powers and the Rule of Law – the independence of the judiciary, and the functional separation between executive and judiciary. A brief comment will also be made on the overall impact of the HRA on the balance of powers between executive and judiciary.

The classic formulation of the doctrine is Montesquieu's:

> When the legislative and executive powers are united in the same person, or in the same body of magistrates, there can be no liberty ... Again, there is no liberty if the power of judging is not separated from the legislative and executive. If it were joined with the legislative, the life and liberty of the subject would be exposed to arbitrary control; for the judge would then be the legislator. If it were joined to the executive power, the judge might behave with violence and oppression. There would be an end to everything, if the same man, or the same body, whether of the nobles or of the people, were to exercise those three powers, that of enacting laws, that of executing public affairs, and that of trying crimes or individual causes. [Quoted in R Shackleton, 'Montesquieu, Bolingbroke and the separation of powers' (1949) 3 FS.]

Notes
1 As Colin Munro notes,[36] Montesquieu advocated that 'the three agencies of Government should perform their functions separately' but did not make it quite clear what form the separation should take, nor whether a 'complete separation of personnel' for the different agencies was required.
2 The classical or 'strict' version of the theory may be summarised as follows:
   (a) The same people should not belong to more than one of the three main institutions of government; thus, for example, judges should not sit in Parliament.
   (b) One organ of government should not control or interfere with the work of one of the other organs; thus ministers should not be able to interfere with the deciding of individual cases by judges.

---

35 *In Re M* [1993] 3 WLR 433.
36 C Munro, *Studies in Constitutional Law* (1987), p 191.

(c) One organ of government should not be able to exercise the functions of another; thus judges should be only be able to interpret the law, not make new laws.

As appears below, however, a modified version of the theory, known as the 'partial separation theory', has recently gained ground.

3 Apart from doubts as to the applicability of the doctrine to the British constitution (discussed below), considerable doubts have been expressed as to the value and coherence of the doctrine itself. These criticisms are discussed and answered by Eric Barendt who first of all notes the criticisms of Sir Ivor Jennings, namely that 'there are no material differences between the three functions, so the separation principle fails to explain why certain functions should be given to one body rather than another'.[37] He also cites Marshall's arguments,[38] to similar effect, that, on the US version of the theory, judicial review of legislation is appropriate 'to check the legislative and executive branches, [which] would be an unwarrantable violation of ... the pure theory' and concludes that the doctrine 'may be counted little more than a jumbled portmanteau of arguments for policies that should be supported or rejected on other grounds'.[39] In reply, Barendt first argues that Jennings exaggerated the difficulties of distinguishing genuinely different functions of government.[40] He then goes on to defend the doctrine on more fundamental grounds, and considers its wider significance.

E Barendt, 'Separation of powers and constitutional government' [1995] PL 599, 606–07

... the Separation of Powers is not in essence concerned with the allocation of functions as such. Its primary purpose ... is the prevention of the arbitrary government, or tyranny, which may arise from the concentration of power. The allocation of functions between three, or perhaps more, branches of government is only a means to achieve that end. It does not matter, therefore, whether powers are always allocated precisely to the most appropriate institution – although an insensitive allocation would probably produce incompetent government ...

This point is perhaps most clearly appreciated if we consider what has become one of the most complex areas for Separation of Powers analysis: the organisation, and control, of administrative authorities and agencies. These range from bodies which allocate social security and welfare benefits (such as public housing), to regulatory bodies, eg the Independent Television Commission and the Monopolies and Mergers Commission, and finally to supervisory or investigatory officers, such as the Comptroller and Auditor-General and the Parliamentary Commissioner for Administration (PCA). Now it can be asked whether these bodies perform legislative (or rule-making, to use the American term), administrative, or judicial functions. But these are impossible questions to answer. For, in truth many agencies perform at least two, and perhaps all three, functions. This is apparent in the US, where it is common for an independent regulatory agency to engage in rule-making, to formulate and apply policies, and to take individual decisions, often after a formal hearing. Perhaps in the UK the only authorities which consistently discharge all three functions are local authorities, which may make by-laws, formulate planning, highways and housing policies, and decide applications for planning permission which might be characterised as judicial, or at least quasi-judicial, decisions. But certainly many agencies, including Government ministers, exercise a variety of functions, some of which can be characterised as executive and some as judicial.

---

37 E Barendt, 'Separation of powers and constitutional government' [1995] PL 599, 603. Barendt here cites Jennings' *The Law and the Constitution*, 5th edn (1959), App I, pp 281–82 and 303.

38 *Ibid*, pp 603–04. Barendt refers to G Marshall's *Constitutional Theory* (1971), Chapter V.

39 Marshall, *ibid*, p 124; quoted in Barendt, *ibid*, at 604.

40 *Ibid*, 605–06.

Does this phenomenon mean that Separation of Powers analysis should be abandoned as hopeless? It would seem so, if the pure theory is adopted, with its rigid insistence that each function of government is discharged by a separate institution. But the answer may be quite different if we see the principle as essentially concerned with the avoidance of concentrations of power. For, then, questions may be asked about the relationship of the agency to the three traditional branches of government. Does Parliament or the Government have sole right to hire and fire members of the authority and its staff? Does the Government have exclusive power to issue directions or guidance to the agency? If the agency takes judicial or quasi-judicial decisions, how far is it subject to review by the ordinary courts? On this approach there would be a violation of the principle if the executive were entitled, without assent of the legislature, to give detailed directions to an agency, and appoint its members, when that agency takes decisions affecting individual rights and judicial review is (virtually) excluded. That would not be because an executive agency carried out judicial functions, but because it was so structured as to create or reinforce a concentration of power in the hands of the Government.

The partial separation theory

The argument in the previous section has shown that the Separation of Powers should not be explained in terms of a strict distribution of *functions* between the three branches of government, but in terms of a network of rules and principles which ensure that power is not concentrated in the hands of one branch. (In practice the danger now is that the executive has too much power, though it is worth remembering that at other times there was more anxiety about self-aggrandisement of the legislature.) That does not mean that the allocation of functions is wholly irrelevant. I will explain in the next section of this article how, in civil liberties cases, courts may properly insist that general rules be made by the legislature and that the executive does not act without legislative authorisation to deprive individuals of their rights. But the importance of a correct definition and allocation of functions should not be exaggerated. Madison for instance was not troubled by these questions, though nobody has argued so cogently for the Separation of Powers principle.

Outside the context of court rulings in civil liberties cases, the principle is most frequently applied in the architecture of the constitution itself. Powers are allocated to different institutions. The legislature is normally divided into two branches, a procedure recommended by Madison on the ground that otherwise it would be too powerful [*Federalist Papers*, No 51]. Each branch is empowered to check the others by exercising a *partial agency or control* over their acts [*ibid*, No 47]. That is why, for example, in the US constitution the Senate must give its advice and consent to the appointment of ministers, ambassadors and judges, and the President may veto Bills passed by the House of Representatives and the Senate, subject to an override by a two-thirds majority vote in each House. It is not very helpful to ask whether, in the former instance, the Senate is exercising an executive power and whether, in the latter, the President acts as a third branch of the legislature. What is important is that there is a system of checks and balances between institutions which otherwise might exercise excessive power. As Madison put it in *Federalist Paper 51*, the structure of government should be so arranged 'that its several constituent parts may, by their mutual relations, be the means of keeping each other in their proper places'.

The separation of powers in the UK constitution

The denial of the doctrine by aspects of the constitution

Colin Munro, *Studies in Constitutional Law*, 2nd edn (1999), pp 302–04 (extracts)

Two initial observations may be made. The first is that the British constitution, with its long and largely unbroken history, is above all the product of experience and experiment. Its development has been characteristically pragmatic rather than principled, and so it is hardly likely absolutely to conform (or not to conform) to any ideal type. A second and related point is that the outlines of the modern British constitution had already been formed by the late 17th century. Therefore, even if earlier versions of the doctrine may not have been without some effect, Montesquieu's formulation of it in the mid-18th century could only have affected such developments as occurred after that date ... What about the 20th century constitution? Writers on the constitution seem to speak almost with one voice in denying that the Separation of Powers is a feature of the constitution.[41]

Munro goes on to note, however, that the judiciary express a different view.

... the House of Lords, in a case concerning an industrial dispute, felt it necessary to rebuke the Court of Appeal for having strayed beyond its proper constitutional function:

At a time when more and more cases involve the application of legislation which gives effect to policies that are the subject of bitter public and parliamentary controversy, it cannot be too strongly emphasised that the British constitution, though largely underwritten, is firmly based on the Separation of Powers: Parliament makes the laws, the judiciary interpret them. [*Dupont Steels Ltd v Sirs* [1980] 1 All ER 529 at 541.]

Lord Scarman, in his speech in the same case, also remarked that 'the constitution's Separation of Powers, or more accurately functions, must be observed if judicial independence is not to be put at risk' [at 551]. In another case later, an applicant was seeking to determine the prospective validity of a draft Order in Council which had yet to be laid before the Houses of Parliament as required. The Court of Appeal held that there was jurisdiction to entertain such a challenge, although it had to be exercised with great circumspection and due regard to the dangers of encroaching on any functions of Parliament. Sir John Donaldson MR said:

Although the UK has no written constitution, it is a constitutional convention of the highest importance that the legislature and the judicature are separate and independent of one another, subject to certain ultimate rights of Parliament over the judicature which are immaterial for present purposes. It therefore behoves the courts to be ever sensitive to the paramount need to refrain from trespassing on the province of Parliament.

Why, then, is there such a denial of the doctrine in the UK by academic commentators? It becomes apparent, when examining this issue, that the judiciary is concerned mainly with defining the correct relationship between the legislative arm and that of the judiciary, whilst academics speak of the broader picture, including the numerous glaring violations of the strict doctrine at least, which the UK constitution displays when the relationship between legislature and executive is considered. One major problem in trying to apply any strict theory of the separation of powers arises when we come to the relationship between the Cabinet – the most important body in the executive – and the legislature, Parliament. First of all, there is a clear overlap of personnel: the Cabinet is made up almost entirely of Members of Parliament, the legislative body, though it should be noted that there is no legal requirement that government ministers must also be MPs: Lord Carrington, Foreign Secretary in the early 80s, sat of course in the House of Lords, and a number of British Prime Ministers have not been MPs though there is now a clear convention to the effect that the Prime Minister should be a Member of Parliament. Of course, the denial of the doctrine in this arrangement is not unique to the UK. It applies equally to all countries which have parliamentary governments, in which the government is drawn from the legislative body, as opposed to France and the US, where the President is elected entirely separately.

---

41   Munro cites various commentators here, *Studies in Constitutional Law*, 2nd edn (1999), pp 304–05.

Moreover, the UK constitution does show some significant reflection of the doctrine in this area: civil servants, who make up the vast majority of the personnel of the executive, cannot stand as MPs under the House of Commons Disqualification Act 1975; under that Act, judges are also ineligible to stand as MPs, as are members of the armed forces and the police, the enforcement arms of the executive. Furthermore, the number of government ministers eligible to sit in the House of Commons is limited by the Act to 95, limiting the overlap in numbers between government and the Commons.

So there is some overlap of membership. More fatally for the strict doctrine, however, is the fact that, on the whole, one may describe central government's relationship with Parliament not so much one of influence or even interference but of outright control; a matter explored in Part III Chapter 1.

The government cannot of course actually exercise the powers of Parliament: it cannot make primary legislation; only Parliament can do that. However, it can procure the passing of very widely drafted primary legislation, giving ministers power to make regulations in a particular area. The regulations made by ministers under such enabling legislation, known as delegated legislation, are an increasingly important source of laws. In fact, far more pages of delegated legislation are passed each year than primary legislation. The enactment of broad enabling powers by Parliament, which in effect give ministers the power to legislate, may be seen as a significant erosion of parliamentary sovereignty and thus of the doctrine of the separation of powers. This issue is examined further in Part III Chapter 1, but a few brief comments will be made here.

There are three restraints on this potential and partly realised power of ministers to take legislative power for themselves. First of all, there is judicial control: the courts will review delegated legislation in order to ascertain whether it makes a proper use of the power given by the parent Act, for example by purporting to do things it was not authorised to do, or by serving a purpose which the courts find was not the purpose of the original Act.[42] Secondly, there is some parliamentary control over delegated legislation: the Statutory Instruments Act 1946 provides that such legislation must be laid before Parliament before coming into effect, though there is some doubt as to the legal effect of this requirement. The aim is clearly to allow Parliament to see whether the delegated legislation is making a reasonable use of the primary enabling legislation (see further Part III Chapter 1 at pp 291–94). Thirdly, the power to grant ministers effective legislative power is restrained by a generally observed *convention* that delegated legislation may not decide matters of important principle.

This principle is, however, being threatened by the use of what are known as 'Henry VIII clauses', that is, provisions in an Act of Parliament which allow ministers, by order, to revoke parts of primary legislation. An important recent example of such a clause appears in the Human Rights Act 1998. The HRA provides that all legislation, whenever acted, must be interpreted compatibly with Convention rights (s 3(1)); however, it provides that if it is not possible to do this, the higher courts may issue a formal declaration of incompatibility between the legislation itself and the Convention right (s 4). Such a declaration has no legal effect on the legislation, which remains valid and of full effect, but it does trigger a power under s 10 of the Act whereby a minister may by order repeal the offending provision.

---

42   See, eg, *Raymond v Honey* [1983] AC 1.

The Human Rights Act 1998

10.— (1) This section applies if—

   (a) a provision of legislation has been declared under section 4 to be incompatible with a Convention right ... or

   (b) it appears to a Minister of the Crown ... that, having regard to a finding of the European Court of Human Rights ... in proceedings against the United Kingdom, a provision of legislation is incompatible with an obligation of the United Kingdom arising from the Convention.

   (2) If a Minister of the Crown considers that there are compelling reasons for proceeding under this section, he may by order make such amendments to the legislation as he considers necessary to remove the incompatibility.

...

Schedule 2 [which applies to s 10]

1.– (1) A remedial order may—

   (a) contain such incidental, supplemental, consequential or transitional provision as the person making it considers appropriate;

   ...

   (2) The power conferred by sub-paragraph (1)(a) includes—

   (a) power to amend primary legislation (including primary legislation other than that which contains the incompatible provision);

   ...

2. No remedial order may be made unless—

   (a) a draft of the order has been approved by a resolution of each House of Parliament made after the end of the period of 60 days beginning with the day on which the draft was laid; or

   (b) it is declared in the order that it appears to the person making it that, because of the urgency of the matter, it is necessary to make the order without a draft being do approved.

[Urgent orders made without being approved in draft must be approved by a resolution of both Houses within 120 days of being laid before Parliament or they will cease to have effect (Sched 2, para 4(4)).]

Notes

1   This provision therefore allows ministers to use delegated legislation to revoke provisions contained in primary legislation. The fact that the government felt it was necessary to prevent the decision being made by the courts was explained by reference to the importance they attached to parliamentary sovereignty – they thought it undemocratic that the courts, rather than Parliament, should have the last word on such matters.[43] However, it was argued in Parliament that if this was genuinely the case, then it should actually be Parliament that takes the decision to change the legislation, not ministers. The government recognised the force of these arguments to some extent: it introduced an amendment to the effect that, as the Act now provides, the power only exists where there are 'compelling reasons' to act under s 10 and moreover orders made by ministers under s 10 must (except in

---

43 See the White Paper which preceded the Human Rights Act, *Bringing Rights Home*, Cm 3782 (1997).

urgent cases) be positively approved by Parliament before coming into force and even in urgent cases, where they may come into force without so being approved, will lapse within 120 days if not approved. Thus, the paradoxical position is apparent that, even where the doctrine of the separation of powers is departed from, its influence cuts down the gravity of the departure.

The relationship between the judiciary and the executive: the doctrine bolstered

Here, it may first be briefly asked what the effect of the HRA is likely to be on the balance of power between the executive and the judiciary, aside from the effect it may have in bolstering judicial independence (see below). At present, the judiciary acts as a significant, though strictly limited, check upon the executive, through the availability of judicial review. Thus, the judiciary ensures that ministers do not act outside the powers lawfully given to them by Acts of Parliament, or by the accepted government prerogatives; that they do not misuse powers given for one purpose for another; that decisions are taken in a way which is procedurally fair (for example, through ensuring adequate consultation, giving both sides a chance to be heard and ensuring there is no bias in the decision-maker); and that their decisions are not grossly unreasonable.

The effect of the HRA here is clear: s 6(1), which makes it unlawful for a public authority to act in violation of a Convention right, represents a significant shift in power from the executive to the judiciary.[44] This is not, as some on the Right have complained, a clear shift in power from *Parliament* to the judiciary because, under the HRA, there is no power given to judges to strike down primary legislation. However, there is a shift from the *executive* to the judiciary, because for the first time the courts will be able to strike down actions *not* because they were outside the powers used to justify the actions, or did not follow a fair procedure, but on the *substantive* basis that they violated human rights. The freedom of action of the executive – the area of discretion it enjoys – is, as a corollary, substantially curtailed. Prior to the HRA, the judges maintained that it was primarily for the executive to ensure that, in the exercise of their lawful discretion, they did not infringe upon basic rights, or did so no more than was strictly necessary. The judges would intervene only where, on a proper construction of legislation, there was no power to do what had been done (as, say, in *ex p Witham* [1998] QB 575), or where no reasonable person could have considered that the rights violation entailed was justified by the aim pursued by the minister (the *Wednesbury* test). Now, primary responsibility for ensuring the protection of those basic rights enumerated in the ECHR will shift to the judges. This is a significant shift in terms of both function and competency from executive to judiciary.

Turning to the issues of judicial independence and functional separation between the judicial and executive roles, the ECHR has already had an impact. An example of what Professor Robert Stevens refers to as 'the casual British attitude to the separation of powers'[45] was the power of the Home Secretary to set the sentence to be served by juvenile killers.[46] Prior to October 1997, such offenders were detained for an indefinite period, wholly at the discretion of the Home Secretary. Under the Crime (Sentences)

---

44 As the current Lord Chancellor, Lord Irvine, has admitted: Interview, *New Statesman*, 6 December 1996, at p 18 (noted in R Stevens, 'A loss of innocence? Judicial independence and the separation of powers' (1999) 19 OJLS 366, see below).

45 Below, p 124.

46 This arose under s 53(1) of the Children and Young Persons Act 1933.

Act 1997, which came into force on 1 October, the Home Secretary set a 'tariff' – that part of a sentence designed to satisfy the demands of retribution and punishment – and upon its expiry, the prisoner became eligible for release by the Parole Board, and would be released unless it was thought that he or she still constituted a danger to society. In effect, therefore,[47] a sentencing function was being formed by a party politician and powerful member of the Cabinet. The obvious risks attendant upon such a state of affairs – the inability of the Home Secretary, as a politician seeking re-election, to put the impact on government popularity of media-driven populist sentiment out of his mind – were illustrated in *R v Secretary of State for the Home Department ex p Venables and Thompson* [1998] AC 407. The Home Secretary, who had fixed a tariff of 15 years in relation to the child killers of Jamie Bulger (the trial judge had recommended eight years), was found to have acted unlawfully in taking into account a petition, organised by the *Sun* newspaper, which urged that the boys be detained for life. However, that decision left unchallenged the power of the Home Secretary to set the tariff in such cases, even though, as Lord Steyn remarked in the case: 'In fixing a tariff the Home Secretary is carrying out, contrary to the constitutional principle of the separation of powers between the executive and the judiciary, a classic judicial function.'

While a fresh decision on the tariff for this case was awaited from the Home Secretary, a more fundamental challenge – to his power to set such tariffs at all – was launched, this time before the European Court of Human Rights, in reliance upon Article 6(1) of the ECHR, which provides: 'In the determination of his civil rights and obligations or of any criminal charge against him, everyone is entitled to a fair and public hearing within a reasonable time by an independent and impartial tribunal established by law.'

T v United Kingdom; V v United Kingdom (2000) 30 EHRR 121 (extracts)

The applicants alleged, *inter alia*, that the fact that their tariff had been set by the Home Secretary constituted a violation of Article 6, because he could not be considered an 'independent and impartial tribunal'. The Court first of all found, contrary to the submission of the government, that the fixing of the tariff period *did* engage Article 6 and then proceeded:

> Both the applicant and the Commission were of the view that the tariff-fixing procedure had failed to comply with Article 6 § 1 in that the decision-maker was the Home Secretary rather than a court or tribunal independent of the executive. In addition the applicant pointed out that there had been no hearing and no opportunity for him to call psychiatric or other evidence, and that the Home Secretary retained a discretion to decide how much of the material before him he disclosed to the applicant.
>
> The Government submitted that there were adequate safeguards to ensure that the procedure for the setting of the tariff was fair. Thus, the Secretary of State sought the views of the trial judge and the Lord Chief Justice, informed the applicant of the judges' views, and invited him to make representations as to the appropriate length of the tariff. The Secretary of State informed the applicant of the tariff fixed, and gave reasons in support of his decision. It was then open to the applicant to challenge the decision by way of judicial review.

---

47   In setting the sentence, the Home Secretary has regard to the views of the trial judge and also consults with the Lord Chief Justice.

The Court notes that Article 6 § 1 guarantees, *inter alia*, 'a fair ... hearing ... by an independent and impartial tribunal ...'. 'Independent' in this context means independent of the parties to the case and also of the executive (see, amongst many other authorities, the *Ringeisen v Austria* judgment of 16 July 1971, Series A no 13, p 39, § 95). The Home Secretary, who set the applicant's tariff, was clearly not independent of the executive, and it follows that there has been a violation of Article 6 § 1.

Notes

1   The result was that the function of setting tariffs for juveniles passed to the judiciary, in the person of the Lord Chief Justice.

2   This judgment clearly also cast into doubt the compatibility of Article 6(1) with the Home Secretary's continuing power to set the tariff for *adult* life prisoners. This was eventually challenged under the HRA in the following case.

R (on the application of Anderson) v Secretary of State for the Home Department [2002] 3 WLR 1800

In accordance with s 1(1) of the Murder (Abolition of Death Penalty) Act 1965, the trial judge imposed a mandatory sentence of life imprisonment. The trial judge and the Lord Chief Justice recommended a tariff of 15 years to be served by the appellant. Pursuant to his powers under s 29 of the Crime (Sentences) Act 1997, the Home Secretary rejected the judicial advice and fixed the tariff at 20 years. The appellant sought judicial review of the decision of the Home Secretary to increase the judicially recommended tariff and argued that the Home Secretary's role in fixing the tariff was incompatible with Article 6 of the ECHR. The Divisional Court dismissed the application and the Court of Appeal dismissed an appeal. The appellant appealed to the House of Lords.

Lord Bingham   13. I return to the fixing of the convicted murderer's tariff term by the Home Secretary ... The true nature of that procedure must be judged as one of substance, not of form or description. It is what happens in practice that matters: *Van Droogenbroeck v Belgium* (1982) 4 EHRR 443 at 456, para 38. What happens in practice is that, having taken advice from the trial judge, the Lord Chief Justice and departmental officials, the Home Secretary assesses the term of imprisonment which the convicted murderer should serve as punishment for his crime or crimes. That decision defines the period to be served before release on licence is considered. This is a classical sentencing function. It is what, in the case of other crimes, judges and magistrates do every day ...

17. ... in *Stafford v United Kingdom* (Application No 46295/99) May 28, 2002, expressing its conclusions in paras 78–80 of the judgment [the European Court of Human Rights said]:

78 The above developments demonstrate an evolving analysis, in terms of the right to liberty and its underlying values, of the role of the Secretary of State concerning life sentences. The abolition of the death penalty in 1965 and the conferring on the Secretary of State of the power to release convicted murderers represented, at that time, a major and progressive reform. However, with the wider recognition of the need to develop and apply, in relation to mandatory life prisoners, judicial procedures reflecting standards of independence, fairness and openness, the continuing role of the Secretary of State in fixing the tariff and in deciding on a prisoner's release following its expiry, has become increasingly difficult to reconcile with the notion of separation of powers between the executive and the judiciary, a notion which has assumed growing importance in the case-law of the Court ...

20. Mr Fitzgerald's argument for the appellant involved the following steps:

(1) Under Art 6(1) of the Convention a criminal defendant has a right to a fair trial by an independent and impartial tribunal.

(2) The imposition of sentence is part of the trial.

(3) Therefore sentence should be imposed by an independent and impartial tribunal.

(4) The fixing of the tariff of a convicted murderer is legally indistinguishable from the imposition of sentence.

(5) Therefore the tariff should be fixed by an independent and impartial tribunal.

(6) The Home Secretary is not an independent and impartial tribunal.

(7) Therefore the Home Secretary should not fix the tariff of a convicted murderer.

I must review these steps in turn.

21. Step (1) is correct. The right to a fair trial by an independent and impartial tribunal is guaranteed by Art 6(1) of the Convention ... and it is one of the most important rights to which domestic effect was given by the Human Rights Act 1998.

22. Step (2) is also correct. Strasbourg authority supporting the proposition is to be found in *Ringeisen v Austria (No 1)* (1971) 1 EHRR 455 [his Lordship cited other authority] ... It makes good sense that the same procedural protections should apply to the imposition of sentence as to the determination of guilt.

23. Step (3) is a logical consequence of steps (1) and (2). But the point was clearly expressed by the Supreme Court of Ireland in *Deaton v Att-Gen and the Revenue Commissioners* [1963] IR 170 at 182–183:

> There is a clear distinction between the prescription of a fixed penalty and the selection of a penalty for a particular case. The prescription of a fixed penalty is the statement of a general rule, which is one of the characteristics of legislation; this is wholly different from the selection of a penalty to be imposed in a particular case ... The Legislature does not prescribe the penalty to be imposed in an individual citizen's case; it states the general rule, and the application of that rule is for the Courts ... the selection of punishment is an integral part of the administration of justice and, as such, cannot be committed to the hands of the Executive.

24. Examination of the facts has already led me to accept the correctness of step (4) ... The clearest authoritative statement of this proposition is in paragraph 79 of the European Court's judgment in *Stafford*, quoted in paragraph 17 above ... It is clear beyond doubt that the fixing of a convicted murderer's tariff, whether it be for the remainder of his days or for a relatively short time only, involves an assessment of the quantum of punishment he should undergo.

25. If it be assumed that steps (1) to (4) are correct, step (5) necessarily follows from them.

26. The correctness of step (6) was accepted on behalf of the Home Secretary, and rightly so. The European Court has interpreted 'independent' in the context of Art 6(1) of the Convention to mean 'independent of the parties to the case and also of the executive': *V v United Kingdom* (1999) 30 EHRR 121 at 186–187, para 114. Far from being independent of the executive, the Home Secretary and his junior Ministers are important members of it ... Plainly, the Home Secretary is not independent of the executive and is not a tribunal.

27. Step (7) follows logically from the preceding steps and must be accepted. In *R v Secretary of State for the Home Department Ex p Stafford* [1998] 1 WLR 503 at 518 the Court of Appeal expressed concern at the imposition of what was in effect a substantial term of imprisonment by the exercise of executive discretion, which in its view lay uneasily with ordinary concepts of the rule of law. This concern was echoed in the House of Lords ([1999] 2 AC 38 at 51), and again by the European Court (*Stafford v UK*) in para 78 of its judgment quoted in para 17 above. In *Benjamin and Wilson v United Kingdom* (Application No 28212/95) September 26, 2002) the European Court

took a step further: it held that the Home Secretary's role in the release of two 'technical lifers' was objectionable because he was not independent of the executive and he could not save the day by showing that he always acted in accordance with the recommendation of the mental health review tribunal (para 36). The European Court observed (para 36):

> This is not a matter of form but impinges on the fundamental principle of separation of powers and detracts from a necessary guarantee against the possibility of abuse ...

The European Court was right to describe the complete functional separation of the judiciary from the executive as 'fundamental', since the rule of law depends on it.

28. Thus I accept each of Mr Fitzgerald's steps (1)–(7) save that, in the light of *Benjamin and Wilson*, it must now be held that the Home Secretary should play no part in fixing the tariff of a convicted murderer, even if he does no more than confirm what the judges have recommended. To that extent the appeal succeeds.

[The House then went on to find that because the Home Secretary's powers were contained in primary legislation, the only relief that could be granted was the issuing of a declaration of incompatibility under s 4, HRA].

Note

As to the independence of the judiciary, one of the most notorious features of the UK constitution is the position of the Lord Chancellor. As Munro notes, he is often referred to as 'a sort of dangerous one man band'.[48] This is because the Lord Chancellor occupies important positions in all three of the main organs of government. He is entitled to, and does, sit in the Judicial Committee of the House of Lords, the highest court in the UK (although infrequently, only three times in 2002); he is an important Cabinet minister and he is also 'speaker' of the House of Lords and an active participant in debates therein. Moreover, the Lord Chancellor has the formal power to decide which judges hear which cases. Whilst, in practice, this function has been delegated to the senior Law Lord, the Lord Chancellor 'can override the senior Law Lord as his delegate'.[49] His position is, indeed, often seen as a living embodiment of the denial of the doctrine of the separation of powers in the UK constitution. However, a recent decision of the European Court of Human Rights concerning Guernsey, one of the UK's dependent territories, but with a largely independent system of government, indicates that his days, at least as a Law Lord, may well be numbered. The decision was made under Article 6(1) of the European Convention on Human Rights, above.

McGonnell v United Kingdom (2000) 30 EHRR 289 (extracts)

McGonnell, a Guernsey flower grower, was refused planning consent to turn his flower-packing shed into a home. The refusal was based upon a development plan (DDP 6) passed by the Island's legislature (the States of Deliberation), which at that time was, as usual, presided over by the Bailiff of Guernsey. McGonnell's appeal against the refusal of planning consent was heard by the Royal Court, also presided over by the Bailiff.

4. The Bailiff is the senior judge of the Royal Court ... In his judicial capacity, the Bailiff is the professional judge (with the lay Jurats) in the Royal Court, and is *ex officio* President of the Guernsey Court of Appeal. In his non-judicial capacity, the Bailiff is President of the States of Election, of the States of Deliberation, of four States Committees (the Appointments Board, the

---

48   Munro (1999), *op cit*, p 328.
49   JUSTICE, 'The judicial function of the House of Lords' (May 1999), para 33.

Emergency Council, the Legislation Committee and the Rules of Procedure Committee), and he plays a role in communications between the Island Authorities and the Government of the United Kingdom and the Privy Council. Where the Bailiff presides in his non-judicial capacity, he has a casting, but not an original, vote.

5. The applicant pointed to the non-judicial functions of the Bailiff, contending that they gave rise to such close connections between the Bailiff as a judicial officer and the legislative and executive functions of government that the Bailiff no longer had the independence and impartiality required by Article 6. As specific examples, the applicant pointed to three matters which were not referred to before the Commission. They are the facts that the Bailiff is invariably appointed from the office of the Attorney General, that he acts as Lieutenant Governor of the island when that office is vacant, and that the Bailiff who sat in the present case had also presided over the States of Deliberation when DDP 6, the very act which was at issue in the applicant's later case, was adopted.

6. The Government recalled that the Convention does not require compliance with any particular doctrine of separation of powers. They maintained that whilst the Bailiff has a number of positions on the island, they cannot give rise to any legitimate fear in a reasonably well informed inhabitant of Guernsey of a lack of independence or impartiality because the positions do not involve any real involvement in legislative or executive functions. In particular, they underlined that when the Bailiff presides over the States of Deliberation or one of the four States Committees in which he is involved, his involvement is not that of an active member, but rather he is an independent umpire, who ensures that the proceedings run smoothly without taking part or expressing approval or disapproval of the matters under discussion.

7. The Court recalls that it found in its *Findlay v United Kingdom* judgment (judgment of 25 February 1997, *Reports* 1997–I, p. 198, § 73) [(1997) 24 EHRR 221] that:

> in order to establish whether a tribunal can be considered as 'independent', regard must be had, *inter alia*, to the manner of appointment of its members and their term of office, the existence of guarantees against outside pressures and the question whether the body presents an appearance of independence ... As to the question of 'impartiality', there are two aspects to this requirement. First, the tribunal must be subjectively free of personal prejudice or bias. Secondly, it must also be impartial from an objective viewpoint, that is, it must offer sufficient guarantees to exclude any legitimate doubt in this respect ... The concepts of independence and objective impartiality are closely linked ...

8. In the present case, too, the concepts of independence and objective impartiality are closely linked, and the Court will consider them together.

9. The Court first observes that there is no suggestion in the present case that the Bailiff was subjectively prejudiced or biased when he heard the applicant's planning appeal in June 1995 ...

10. The Court can agree with the Government that neither Article 6 nor any other provision of the Convention requires States to comply with any theoretical constitutional concepts as such. The question is always whether, in a given case, the requirements of the Convention are met. The present case does not, therefore, require the application of any particular doctrine of constitutional law to the position in Guernsey: the Court is faced solely with questions of whether the Bailiff had the required 'appearance' of independence, or the required 'objective' impartiality.

11. In this connection, the Court notes that the Bailiff's functions are not limited to judicial matters, but that he is also actively involved in non-judicial functions on the island. The Court does not accept the Government's analysis that when the Bailiff acts in a non-judicial capacity he merely occupies positions rather than exercising functions: even a purely ceremonial constitutional role must be classified as a 'function'. The Court must determine whether the Bailiff's functions in his non-judicial capacity were, or were not, compatible with the requirements of Article 6 as to independence and impartiality.

12. The Court observes that the Bailiff in the present case had personal involvement with the planning matters at the heart of the applicant's case on two occasions. The first occasion was in 1990, when, as Deputy Bailiff, he presided over the States of Deliberation at the adoption of DDP 6. The second occasion was on 6 June 1995, when he presided over the Royal Court in the determination of the applicant's planning appeal . . .

13. . . . With particular respect to his presiding, as Deputy Bailiff, over the States of Deliberation in 1990, the Court considers that any direct involvement in the passage of legislation, or of executive rules, is likely to be sufficient to cast doubt on the judicial impartiality of a person subsequently called on to determine a dispute over whether reasons exist to permit a variation from the wording of the legislation or rules at issue. In the present case, in addition to the chairing role as such, the Deputy Bailiff could exercise a casting vote in the event of even voting . . .

14. The Court thus considers that the mere fact that the Deputy Bailiff presided over the States of Deliberation when DDP 6 was adopted in 1990 is capable of casting doubt on his impartiality when he subsequently determined, as the sole judge of the law in the case, the applicant's planning appeal. The applicant therefore had legitimate grounds for fearing that the Bailiff may have been influenced by his prior participation in the adoption of DDP 6. That doubt in itself, however slight its justification, is sufficient to vitiate the impartiality of the Royal Court, and it is therefore unnecessary for the Court to look into the other aspects of the complaint.

15. It follows that there has been a breach of Article 6 § 1.

Notes

1 Since the Lord Chancellor precisely acts as a judge in the House of Lords and presides over it in its legislative capacity, this judgment, if followed[50] by the UK courts, applying the Convention domestically,[51] would prevent the Lord Chancellor from sitting as a judge on any case involving legislation passed or amended since the Labour Party came to power, or any legislation of the previous government during the passage of which he played an active role as opposition spokesman. The current Lord Chancellor, Lord Irvine, has indicated that he does not intend to give up his role as a Law Lord as a result of the *McGonnell* judgment.[52] However, he has indicated that he will not sit in any case concerning legislation he had been involved with, or in any case in which the government's interests are concerned. This undertaking, if adhered to, will preclude the Lord Chancellor from sitting in any case in the Lords concerning the HRA itself.[53]

2 The Lord Chancellor is not the only senior judge whose position is in question following *McGonnell*. The Law Lords, who make up both the Judicial Committee of the House of Lords and the Judicial Committee of the Privy Council, also sit in the House of Lords in its legislative capacity, and participate in its debates. As Meg Russell and Richard Cornes explain below, on this basis, their adjudication in particular cases may also be open to challenge under Article 6 of the ECHR,[54] particularly if they expressed a strong view in the Lords during the passage of legislation, the interpretation of which was at issue in the case now before them.

---

50 Courts are bound under the HRA to 'have regard' to judgments of the European Court and Commission but they are not instructed to follow them (s 2(1)).

51 As noted above, s 6(1) of the HRA states: 'it is unlawful for a public authority to act in a way which is incompatible with a Convention right'. Courts and tribunals are expressly included within the definition of 'public authority' (s 6(3)).

52 'Irvine defends his dual role', *The Times*, 6 July 1999.

53 See further R Cornes, '*McGonnell v United Kingdom*, the Lord Chancellor and the Law Lords' [2000] PL 166.

54 See further *ibid*.

M Russell and R Cornes, 'The Royal Commission on Reform of the House of Lords: a House for the future?' (2001) 64 MLR 82, 93–94

Sir John Laws [sitting as an *ad hoc* judge in *McGonnell*] said: 'Where there is no question of actual bias, our task under Article 6(1) must be to determine whether the reasonable bystander – a fully informed layman who has no axe to grind – would on objective grounds fear that the Royal Court lacks independence and impartiality'. However, the rest of the Court stated: 'Any direct involvement in the passage of legislation, or of executive rules, is *likely* to be sufficient to cast doubt on the judicial impartiality of a person subsequently called to determine a dispute over whether reasons exist to permit a variation from the wording of the legislation or rules at issue' [para 55]. The earlier case of *Procola v Italy* [(1995) 22 EHRR 193] sets out a much stricter approach to Article 6(1): 'The mere fact that certain persons successively performed these two types of function [the pre-legislative review and hearing an appeal concerning the same legislative instrument] in respect of the same decisions is capable of casting doubt on the institution's structural impartiality' [para 45]. The statement in *Procola* is far closer to requiring a strict separation of powers *per se* (especially the reference to 'structural impartiality'), rather than the case by case consideration indicated in the *McGonnell* case. It is also difficult, if not impossible, to reconcile with Sir John Laws' approach in *McGonnell*.

If Article 6(1) does require a strict separation of powers as *Procola* might suggest, then the Law Lords could not continue to be members of the House of Lords; nor could the Lord Chancellor continue his mixed role. If the less stringent approach to Article 6(1) is applied to the Law Lords' position then a more nuanced approach is required. Broadly, one would have to consider whether each of the various roles a Law Lord may carry out (from simply sitting in the upper house without speaking or voting, through to chairing committees, or actually speaking and voting in debates) might in individual cases amount to a breach of Article 6(1) . . .

Note

In an attempt to minimise problems which may arise in this area, and also with an eye towards the preservation of the general reputation of the judiciary for political independence, the Law Lords, as recommended by the Wakeham Report,[55] have now made a statement of the principles that will guide them in participating in the House of Lords' legislative and scrutinising activities.

HL Deb cols 419–20 (22 June 2000)

Lord Bingham of Cornhill: My Lords ... I should like to make a Statement on Recommendation 59 of the Royal Commission on the Reform of the House of Lords. That recommendation is that:

The Lords of Appeal should set out in writing and publish a statement of the principles which they intend to observe when participating in debates and votes in the second chamber and when considering their eligibility to sit on related cases.

I should tell the House that my noble and learned friends have considered this recommendation and have agreed on the terms of a Statement to give effect to it. I will now read the Statement which has been agreed by all the Lords of Appeal in Ordinary:

General Principles: As full members of the House of Lords the Lords of Appeal in Ordinary have a right to participate in the business of the House. However, mindful of their judicial role, they consider themselves bound by two general principles when deciding whether to participate in a

---

55 *A House for the Future*, Cm 4534, Recommendation 59; available at www.official-documents.co.uk/document/cm45/4534/4534.htm.

particular matter, or to vote: first, the Lords of Appeal in Ordinary do not think it appropriate to engage in matters where there is a strong element of party political controversy; and secondly the Lords of Appeal in Ordinary bear in mind that they might render themselves ineligible to sit judicially if they were to express an opinion on a matter which might later be relevant to an appeal to the House.

The Lords of Appeal in Ordinary will continue to be guided by these broad principles. They stress that it is impossible to frame rules which cover every eventuality. In the end it must be for the judgment of each individual Lord of Appeal to decide how to conduct himself in any particular situation.

Eligibility: In deciding who is eligible to sit on an appeal, the Lords of Appeal agree to be guided by the same principles as apply to all judges. These principles were restated by the Court of Appeal in the case of *Locabail (UK) Ltd v Bayfield Properties Ltd and Others and four other actions* [[2000] 1 All ER 65, CA].[56]

Notes

1   As Russell and Cornes comment:

The statement follows the majority position in *McGonnell* and also adopts the statement of the law in the *Locabail* case [[2000] 1 All ER 65]. With the Law Lords soon being faced with Human Rights Act 1998 and devolution cases it will become increasingly important that they have not been involved in the passage of, for example, a Bill subsequently challenged under the Act or an apparently anodyne piece of Westminster legislation which is subsequently argued to be inconsistent with legislation from a devolved legislature. The only sure way of avoiding an Article 6(1) problem remains the removal of the Law Lords from the legislature ...[57]

2   Stevens considers that the advantages of barring the Law Lords from the legislative second chamber outweigh the disadvantages.[58] He notes first of all the highly significant role that they have played, from time to time, in legislative matters:

In theory the law lords are supposed to speak only on legal matters. That did not deter Lord Sumner in the 1920s from defending General Dyer for his role in the Massacre at Amritsar, nor Lord Carson from opposing the Irish Treaty in 1922. Even closer to the legal, however, Lord Goddard and his successor as Chief Justice, Lord Parker were strong advocates of hanging and flogging in the 40s and 50s. Lord Merriman and other divorce judges held up liberalisation in divorce law and procedure in the following decades. Perhaps the most dramatic political activities by the law lords, however, came in the late 80s as Lord Mackay introduced Green Papers designed to make the courts and the profession more efficient and responsive to the needs of the public, primarily by introducing market reforms. The retired law lords behaved in a remarkable manner during the legislative debates. No less than three – Lords Elwyn-Jones (a former Labour Lord Chancellor), Donaldson, and Lane (then retiring as Lord Chief Justice) – implied that the Conservative Lord Chancellor (Mackay) was guilty of Nazi tendencies – and of course violating the independence of the judiciary. Lord Elwyn-Jones announced judges must be 'felt to be completely independent of the state' and 'there was a danger' of' going down the American path'. ['I well remember that in Nazi Europe and the Fascist countries before the War, the authoritarian regimes' first victims were the independence of the judiciary and the independence of the legal profession', Hansard, HL vol 505 col 1307 (7 April 1989).] Lord Hailsham, the then recently retired Conservative Lord Chancellor, expanded the notion of

---

56   For details of this case, see Part V Chapter 2, pp 774–76.
57   M Russell and R Cornes, 'The Royal Commission on Reform of the House of Lords: a House for the future?' (2001) 64 MLR 82.
58   *Op cit*, pp 398–99.

judicial independence far and wide. He regarded the Green Papers as 'an outrage' [*ibid*, at cols 1333–34]. He defended 'the most upright and most independent legal profession known to man ... the judiciary remains the guardian of the liberties of the people ... The independence of the judiciary depends more upon the independence and integrity of the legal profession than upon any other single factor'.

Stevens goes on to suggest that the arguments in favour of the Lords continuing to sit are outweighed by those to the contrary:

> The advantages are always said to be that the House has the benefit of legal expertise, but it may also – as in the Green Papers debate – have the disadvantage of judicial conservatism appearing to undermine democracy. Legal advice is available in other ways. There are other lawyers in the Lords, while the Commons survives quite happily without the presence of judges, but normally with the law officers (although the Blair administration initially put one in the Lords). The biggest disadvantage, however, is the appearance of judicial partiality – and confusion about the role of judges. When the *Fire Brigade* case [[1995] 2 AC 513] came before the Lords in 1995, a decision which eventually struck down Home Secretary Michael Howard's attempt to make cuts in the Criminal Injuries Compensation Scheme, it was difficult to find five law lords to sit judicially, since so many law lords had already spoken out, legislatively, against the Howard proposals. Rosenberg in *Trial of Strength* (1997) describes 27 January 1997 as the day when, in the morning, the law lords heard the judicial appeal about executive extension of the terms of imprisonment of children convicted of murder, and, in the afternoon, the same law lords were actively engaged in the legislative debates on the government's plan for mandatory and minimum sentences. As support for a totally or partially elected Second Chamber grows, the case for taking the law lords out of such a body becomes progressively stronger.

Note

1   While neither the Royal Commission on Lords Reform,[59] nor the government's White Paper in response[60] called for removal of the Law Lords from the second chamber, a recent report by the Public Administration Committee took a different line:

> 152. ... we were impressed by the very different views expressed by the senior law lord, Lord Bingham, who recently raised the issue of whether it was desirable that the second chamber should address judicial functions at all. He cited the Pinochet case which misled some into thinking that 'the issue had ceased to be a judicial and had become a political one'. He also complained that the operations of the law lords were hampered by the cramped accommodation they were forced to use in the House. He called for the creation of a supreme court with proper facilities.

> 153. We recognise that this will take time to plan and to organise, and that there may be a need for a specific inquiry of the kind envisaged by the Royal Commission. But to concentrate minds, and to set a timescale for the exercise, we recommend that the law lords should leave the second chamber at the next general election but one. That should allow plenty of time to think through the consequences for the legal system, and to make the necessary provision for an independent, properly constituted supreme court.[61]

2   The other major issue that arises in relation to the independence of judges is whether the manner of their appointment and terms of their employment serves to guarantee their impartiality. The UK's arrangements in this respect have recently been found again to fall foul of Article 6, ECHR. In this instance, the finding was made by the Scottish courts[62] applying s 57 of the Scotland Act 1998,

---

59   *A House for the Future*, Cm 4534.
60   *The House of Lords: Completing the Reform*, Cmd 529.
61   Fifth Report, HC 494–i (2001–02).
62   The Appeal Court, the High Court of Justiciary.

which binds all members of the Scottish executive to act compatibly with the Convention rights.

Starrs and Chalmers v Procurator Fiscal, Linlithgow (Starrs v Ruxton) **[2000] SLT 42 (extracts)**

The complainers in this case were on trial for a criminal charge, heard by a temporary sheriff; the prosecution had been brought by a Procurator Fiscal. They raised the point that a trial before such a sheriff did not comply with Article 6, ECHR because the sheriff's manner of appointment meant that he could not be considered an 'independent and impartial tribunal'. When the point was dismissed, they appealed to the High Court.

Lord Reed: ... Temporary sheriffs are a statutory creation. The relevant provisions are contained in section 11 of the Sheriff Courts (Scotland) Act 1971. Section 11(1) ... deals with the appointment of temporary sheriffs principal. Section 11(2) is in the following terms:

Where as regards any sheriffdom—

(a) a sheriff is by reason of illness or otherwise unable to perform his duties as sheriff, or

(b) a vacancy occurs in the office of sheriff, or

(c) for any other reason it appears to the Secretary of State expedient so to do in order to avoid delay in the administration of justice in that sheriffdom, the Secretary of State may appoint a person (to be known as a temporary sheriff) to act as a sheriff for the sheriffdom.

The Solicitor General explained to us that all appointments are made under section 11(2)(c). The words 'for any other reason' ... are construed as conferring a wide discretion on the Secretary of State which can be used, as it has been used, to create a large pool of persons, each appointed to act as a sheriff for every sheriffdom in Scotland, and available to supplement the permanent sheriffs as and when the need arises, to the extent of performing (at present) 25% of the total workload.

Section 11(3) stipulates the formal qualification for appointment as a temporary sheriff, namely qualification as an advocate or solicitor for at least five years. This is a lesser requirement than for appointment on a permanent basis, for which the minimum period is ten years: section 5(1).

Section 11(4) provides: 'The appointment of a temporary sheriff principal or of a temporary sheriff shall subsist until recalled by the Secretary of State.'

The Solicitor General accepted that the effect of this provision is that a temporary sheriff holds office at pleasure ... Section 11(4) can be contrasted with the provisions of section 12, which provide security of tenure to permanent sheriffs. Under section 12, a permanent sheriff can be removed from office only by an order which is subject to annulment in pursuance of a resolution of either House of Parliament. Such an order can only be made on a report by the Lord President and the Lord Justice Clerk to the effect that the sheriff is unfit for office by reason of inability, neglect of duty or misbehaviour. Such a report can only be made following an investigation by the Lord President and the Lord Justice Clerk. ... Temporary sheriffs are expressly excluded from the scope of these provisions: section 12(7).

8. ... The Solicitor General founded particularly on what was said by the Grant Committee [Report of the Grant Committee on the Sheriff Court (Cmnd 3248, 1967)] at paragraph 406:

It was put to us that there might be a pool of advocates, perhaps maintained by the Lord Advocate, who would be available to sit as paid honorary or interim sheriffs-substitute throughout Scotland. The idea was that the pool should be a large one, including most advocates, so that the willingness of a particular individual to act as a paid honorary sheriff-substitute should not be construed as a desire for a permanent appointment as a full-time sheriff-substitute, with possible adverse effects on his private legal practice ...

It appears to me however that the suggestion canvassed in that passage ... bears little resemblance to the current system of appointment of temporary sheriffs. The temporary sheriffs form a pool of persons who have been actually appointed to shrieval office, rather than a pool from whom appointments might be made when occasion arose. Far from the pool existing so as to avoid willingness to act being construed as a desire for a permanent appointment, membership of the pool of temporary sheriffs has increasingly come to be coveted as a step on the road towards a permanent appointment, and on the Lord Advocate's side it has equally come to be seen to some extent as, in effect, a probationary period during which potential candidates for a permanent appointment can be assessed.

In relation to section 11(4), the Solicitor General accepted that this impliedly conferred upon the Secretary of State a power to recall the appointment at will ... It was common ground that section 11(4) in particular provided no security of tenure whatsoever for temporary sheriffs. The issue in dispute, so far as security of tenure was concerned, was whether the degree of protection which in practice existed, as a consequence of the involvement of the Lord Advocate and his independence from the political process, was sufficient to satisfy the requirements of Article 6 of the Convention.

[The consequence of the above arrangements is that] temporary sheriffs held office at pleasure, protected only by the integrity and good sense of the Lord Advocate.

17. I turn next to consider whether the temporary sheriff is an 'independent and impartial tribunal' within the meaning of Article 6 paragraph 1 of the Convention ...

18. In order to establish whether a body can be considered to be 'independent', regard must be had, *inter alia*, to the manner of appointment of its members and their term of office, to the existence of guarantees against outside pressures and to the question whether the body presents an appearance of independence: see, *inter alia*, *Bryan* [(1995) A 335-A, para 37)].

19. [Citing *Campbell and Fell v UK* (1984) A 80, para 79, his Lordship found that the manner of appointment of the temporary sheriffs was not objectionable.]

... 21. Considering next the term of office of temporary sheriffs, the appointment is expressed so as to subsist for twelve months unless previously recalled. On behalf of the appellants, reference was made to Çiraklar [*Çiraklar v Turkey* (2001) 32 EHRR 23, ECHR], where the [European Court of Human Rights] indicated (at para 39) that a term of office which lasted only four years, and could be renewed, was a factor pointing towards a lack of independence. Reference was also made to the *Campbell and Fell* judgment, where the court considered a term of three years to be 'relatively short' but understandable in circumstances where the members of the tribunal in question (a prison board of visitors) were unpaid, and where it might be difficult to find individuals willing and suitable to undertake the task if the period were longer ...

22. A short term of office is not, in my opinion, necessarily objectionable, as the *Dupuis* decision indicates ... Temporary appointments are however apt to create particular problems from the point of view of independence, particularly where the duration of the appointment is not fixed so as to expire upon the completion of a particular task or upon the cessation of a particular state of affairs (such as some emergency or exigency), but is a fixed period of time of relatively short duration. In particular, such a term of office is liable to compromise the judge's independence where the appointment can be renewed, as the European Court of Human Rights recognised in the Çiraklar judgment. The possibility of renewal was also emphasised by the Commission in its Opinion in the same case (at para 46). The same point has also been emphasised in other cases (eg *Incal* [v Turkey (2000) 29 EHRR 449, ECHR]). As is stated in the European Charter on the statute for judges, adopted in Strasbourg in July 1998 under the auspices of the Council of Europe (DAJ/DOC (98) 23) (at para 3.3.):

Clearly, the existence of probationary periods or renewal requirements presents difficulties if not dangers from the angle of the independence and impartiality of the judge in question, who is hoping to be established in post or to have his or her contract renewed.

Other international instruments demonstrate an equal awareness of these dangers. For example, the Universal Declaration on the Independence of Justice, adopted in Montreal in June 1983 by the World Conference on the Independence of Justice (UN DOC.E/CN.4/Subs.2/1985/18/Add.6 Annex IV), provides (at para 2.20):

> The appointment of temporary judges and the appointment of judges for probationary periods is inconsistent with judicial independence. Where such appointments exist, they should be phased out gradually.

The European Charter and the Universal Declaration are not legally binding instruments, but they indicate the way in which international opinion has developed, and the existence of a consensus as to the dangers posed to judicial independence by short renewable periods of appointment. . . . the European Court of Human Rights has regard to international standards in the interpretation of the Convention . . . I also note that the United Kingdom practice of appointing temporary judges appears to be unusual within a European context (see S Shetreet and J Deschenes, *Judicial Independence: The Contemporary Debate* (1985). . .: it appears that in almost all the other systems surveyed the appointment of a temporary judge by the Executive for a period of one year, renewable at the discretion of the Executive, would be regarded as unconstitutional).

23. So far as temporary sheriffs are concerned, the period of one year is in itself much shorter than the periods considered in the *Campbell and Fell*, *Çiraklar* and *Incal* judgments. What to my mind is of critical importance, however, is that renewal is both possible and expected, but is at the discretion of the Executive. In effect, temporary sheriffs have their judicial careers broken up into segments of one year, so as to provide the Executive with the possibility of re-considering their appointment on an annual basis. This has obvious implications for security of tenure: although I will discuss that issue separately, it is inextricably linked to the present issue. It also appears to me to be important that temporary sheriffs may well be potential candidates for a permanent appointment in the event of a vacancy occurring, as is recognised in the notes issued to candidates for appointment as temporary sheriffs. The danger to judicial independence in such circumstances is subtle, but has been well described by Kirby J of the High Court of Australia, speaking extra-judicially, in a paper which was drawn to our attention:

> But what of the lawyer who would welcome a permanent appointment? What of the problem of such a lawyer faced with a decision which might be very upsetting to government, unpopular with the media or disturbing to some powerful body with influence? Anecdotal stories soon spread about the 'form' of acting judges which may harm their chances of permanent appointment in a way that is unjust. Such psychological pressures, however subtle, should not be imposed on decision-makers.

('Independence of the judiciary – basic principles, new challenges', delivered to a Human Rights Institute Conference organised by the International Bar Association on 12 June 1998) . . .

24. Given that temporary sheriffs are very often persons who are hoping for graduation to a permanent appointment, and at the least for the renewal of their temporary appointment, the system of short renewable appointments creates a situation in which the temporary sheriff is liable to have hopes and fears in respect of his treatment by the Executive when his appointment comes up for renewal: in short, a relationship of dependency. This is in my opinion a factor pointing strongly away from 'independence' within the meaning of Article 6 . . .

26. The next matter to be considered is the existence of guarantees against outside pressures. In this regard, counsel for the appellants founded upon a number of factors. They submitted in the first place that the power to recall the appointment of a temporary sheriff, or to decline to renew the appointment, is vested in the Scottish Executive, and in practice is exercised by the Lord Advocate. The temporary sheriff can even be deprived of his appointment in substance by being

informally 'sidelined', without any formal recall or non-renewal, if he incurs the displeasure of officials. The consequence is to make the temporary sheriff entirely dependent upon the Scottish Executive, and in particular upon the Lord Advocate, for the continuation and renewal of his appointment. This, it was submitted, is particularly objectionable when the Scottish Executive, and in practice the Lord Advocate, is also responsible for making the permanent appointments which many temporary sheriffs are hoping to obtain. The objection becomes even more serious when it is appreciated that the Lord Advocate is also responsible for the criminal prosecutions which take place before temporary sheriffs. For the temporary sheriff to occupy a role subordinate to one of the parties to proceedings before him is, it was submitted, inconsistent with judicial independence. Reference was made in that regard to *Sramek* [(1984) Series A No 84], and to *Piersack* [(1982) Series A No 53]. . .

30. In relation to security of tenure, the Solicitor General accepted that a temporary sheriff enjoyed no security of tenure as a matter of law. He submitted however that in practice a temporary sheriff's appointment would not be recalled prior to its expiry ... More generally, a temporary sheriff's appointment would be renewed unless he was regarded as unfit, or was over the age of 65, or had failed to fulfil his 20 day quota. In practice, his security of tenure was protected as a result of the involvement of the Lord Advocate, who was distanced to some extent from the political process.

32. In my opinion, the most important of the three factors relied upon by the appellants is the absence of security of tenure. It was common ground before us that, as a matter of law, a temporary sheriff can be removed from office at any time for any reason. It was also common ground that a temporary sheriff can be appointed on an annual basis and that his allocation to courts, and the renewal of his appointment, are thereafter within the unfettered discretion of the Executive ... In these circumstances, I am prepared to proceed on the basis that a temporary sheriff does not, as a matter of law, enjoy anything which constitutes security of tenure in the normally accepted sense of that term.

33. There can be no doubt as to the importance of security of tenure to judicial independence: it can reasonably be said to be one of the cornerstones of judicial independence ... As Lord Blackburn said in *Mackay and Esslement v Lord Advocate*, 1937 SC 860, 865:

> . . . if the office (being salaried) is judicial, then it is inconsistent with the common law nature of the office that its tenure should be precarious.

... So far as the European Convention is concerned, the importance of security of tenure is equally well recognised. In ... *Zand v Austria* (1978) 15 DR 70, for example, the Commission stated (at para 80):

> . . . according to the principles of the Rule of Law in democratic states which is the common heritage of the European countries, the irremovability of judges during their term of office, whether it be for a limited period of time or for lifetime, is a necessary corollary of their independence from the Administration and thus included in the guarantees of Article 6(1) of the Convention.

The Solicitor General however relied on the following passage in the *Campbell and Fell* judgment (at para 80):

> It is true that the irremovability of judges by the executive during their term of office must in general be considered as a corollary of their independence and thus included in the guarantees of Article 6(1). However, the absence of a formal recognition of this irremovability in the law does not in itself imply lack of independence provided that it is recognised in fact and that the other necessary guarantees are present.

... 34. This passage must in my opinion be read in its context. The *Campbell and Fell* case, as I have mentioned already, was concerned with the members of a board of prison visitors. The court accepted that the members were unpaid, and that their term of service was kept relatively short because it might otherwise be difficult to find individuals willing to take on the position. In these circumstances, there was no objective reason to imagine that the possibility of removal from office would influence the members in the slightest. That being the situation, it is not surprising that the court considered that the possibility of the Home Secretary's requiring the resignation of a member, which would be done 'only in the most exceptional circumstances', could not be regarded as threatening their independence.

38. . . . It is apparent that the system as operated depends on an assessment by the Scottish Executive, or in practice an assessment by the Lord Advocate, of what should be regarded as grounds for removal from office (or as grounds for not renewing the appointment or for deciding not to allocate work to a particular temporary sheriff, which are in substance equivalent to removal from office), and of what general policies should be followed (eg as to retiral age). The practice may alter from time to time, as in fact happened when the age limit of 65 was introduced. I do not doubt that the system has been operated by successive Lords Advocate with integrity and sound judgment, free from political considerations, and with a careful regard to the need to respect judicial independence. That is no doubt why it has operated for so long without occasioning any widespread expression of public concern, although disquiet has on occasion been expressed by members of the judiciary and others in Parliament and in academic or professional contexts. There is however no objective guarantee of security of tenure, such as can be found in section 12 of the 1971 Act; and I regard the absence of such a guarantee as fatal to the compatibility of the present system with Article 6.

39. The Solicitor General emphasised that it is inconceivable that the Lord Advocate would interfere with the performance of judicial functions. I readily accept that; but that is not the point. Judicial independence can be threatened not only by interference by the Executive, but also by a judge's being influenced, consciously or unconsciously, by his hopes and fears as to his possible treatment by the Executive. It is for that reason that a judge must not be dependent on the Executive, however well the Executive may behave: 'independence' connotes the absence of dependence. It also has to be borne in mind that judicial independence exists to protect the integrity of the judiciary and confidence in the administration of justice, and thus society as a whole, in bad times as well as good. The adequacy of judicial independence cannot appropriately be tested on the assumption that the Executive will always behave with appropriate restraint: as the European Court of Human Rights has emphasised in its interpretation of Article 6, it is important that there be 'guarantees' against outside pressures. In short, for the judiciary to be dependent on the Executive flies in the face of the principle of the separation of powers which is central to the requirement of judicial independence in Article 6.

42. . . . I would only add this . . . The effect given to the European Convention by the Scotland Act and the Human Rights Act in particular represents, to my mind, a very important shift in thinking about the constitution. It is fundamental to that shift that human rights are no longer dependent solely on conventions, by which I mean values, customs and practices of the constitution which are not legally enforceable. Although the Convention protects rights which reflect democratic values and underpin democratic institutions, the Convention guarantees the protection of those rights through legal processes, rather than political processes. It is for that reason that Article 6 guarantees access to independent courts. It would be inconsistent with the whole approach of the Convention if the independence of those courts itself rested upon convention rather than law . . .

46. . . . My conclusion is fortified by the requirement under Article 6 that the tribunal must present an appearance of independence. I understand this requirement to mean that the test of independence must include the question whether the tribunal should reasonably be perceived as independent. The importance of that question is that the tribunal must be one which commands public confidence: otherwise, to adopt the words of Le Dain J in [a decision of the Supreme Court of Canada, R v Valente (1985) 34 DLR (4th) 161, at 172], 'the system will not command the respect and acceptance that are essential to its effective operation'. Even if I were mistaken in my conclusion that the necessary objective guarantees of independence were lacking, it seems to me

that the need for the temporary sheriff's appointment to be renewed annually at the discretion of the Executive, and his lack of security of tenure, are in any event factors which could give rise to a reasonable perception of dependence upon the Executive. The necessary appearance of independence is therefore in my opinion absent.

Notes

1 The result of the decision was that temporary sheriffs, who had been hearing about 25% of criminal cases in Scotland, could no longer do so. The Scottish Parliament passed an Act which placed the appointment of temporary sheriffs on a new basis, addressing the concerns as to security of tenure raised in the case.

2 The case raised questions for England and Wales as well. While there is no strict equivalent of the temporary sheriffs in England, the principle established in the case was felt to open the way to challenge the independence of a number of the part-time judiciary appointed by the Lord Chancellor, in particular assistant recorders and part-time judges in certain tribunals. New procedures were put in place in order to ensure that these appointments would have sufficient security of tenure in order to satisfy and be seen to satisfy the test of being 'independent and impartial' as required by Article 6. The essence of the new arrangements was a new five-year appointment, with automatic renewal, subject only to narrow and specified grounds of misbehaviour, incapacity, redundancy and so on. Dismissal would similarly also be possible only on such grounds and a decision to dismiss or not to renew an appointment would be subject to the concurrence of the Lord Chief Justice and would be taken only following an investigation by a judge.[63]

3 As Stevens notes, there is a general, and justified belief, that the judicial arm in the UK is independent of government influence, but such independence is not as robustly protected as is commonly believed.

R Stevens, 'A loss of innocence? Judicial independence and the separation of powers' (1999) 19 OJLS 366 (extracts)

In England the concept of judicial independence, an integral part of the separation of powers, is an inchoate one. One might have thought that, since many of the early ideas about the separation of powers developed in England, the concept of judicial independence might be articulately analysed in the legal literature. Far from it. In modern Britain the concept of the separation of powers is cloudy and the notion of the independence of the judiciary remains primarily a term of constitutional rhetoric. Certainly its penumbra, and perhaps even its core, are vague. No general theory exists, although practically the English have developed surprisingly effective informal systems for the separation of powers; although it should never be forgotten that the system of responsible government is based on a co-mingling of the executive with the legislature. The political culture of the United Kingdom, however, provides protections for the independence of the judiciary, which are missing in the law.

It was these very issues – judicial independence, the significance of judicial views, the role of judges in cases with a significant political element – which were peaking in Britain as the country reached the millennium ... For the previous 40 years, the courts had been directed or the judges had drifted back into those policy areas that they had largely left or been excluded from by the time of the First World War. In the 50s it was competition law, the 60s saw a formalized change to *stare decisis*, the 70s saw the renewed incursion into labour law, the renewal of judicial review of administrative decisions and the arrival of the EU. The 80s confirmed an increasingly creative

---

63 For full details, see the Lord Chancellor's Department web page: www.open.gov.uk/lcd.

approach to the common law while the early 90s provided a much wider approach to statutory interpretation ... [In the late 1990s] ... as *The Economist* warned, with the New Labour Government's constitutional changes, there would be 'a much wider array of cases' coming to the Lords:

> ... many of these will be highly contentious, and will bring the law lords into conflict with politicians ... like all senior judges, they are in effect appointed by the Lord Chancellor, who is the government's senior law officer and sits in the Cabinet, after secret consultations among judges and top lawyers. This is an untenable method of selection for judges who will be ruling on issues of great public and political interest ... by embarking on an ambitious programme of reform, the government has encouraged scrutiny of the murkier corners of the constitution and has raised the profile of judges. Having opened this Pandora's box, it will have to confront, probably sooner rather than later, the muddle at the very heart of the British constitution ['Judging the judges', *The Economist*, 23 January 1999].

The Independence of Individual Judges

It is acceptable, if not entirely accurate, to say that England has independence of the judiciary in the sense of independence of an individual judge. To take what are conventionally seen as the hallmarks of such independence – security of tenure, fiscal independence, impartiality and freedom from executive pressure – at the core, there is little doubt that England qualifies under any reasonable standard of judicial independence with respect to individual judges. Even more than other countries, however, one has to look at the English scene historically, and, at least to some extent, sociologically.

Traditionally, and rightly, we look to the Act of Settlement of 1700 as the basis of the judicial independence – for by that Act judges were not to be dismissed without addresses by both Houses of Parliament ...

... The tenure of English judges since 1714 has been relatively peaceful. The closest that a judge has come to being dismissed after addresses by both Houses was Mr Justice Barrington, an Irish judge, for alleged bribery. Mr Justice Grantham, one of the undistinguished political appointments to the High Court bench by Lord Halsbury, the Conservative Lord Chancellor at the turn of the century, was nearly dismissed after a particularly partisan decision in the Yarmouth By-Election case in the first decade of this century. The most noted recent near example was that of Sir John Donaldson, a High Court judge sitting as the President of the Industrial Relations Court. In December 1973, 187 Labour MPs called for his removal for 'political prejudice and partiality'. The move failed and ... Donaldson ended as Master of the Rolls (President of the Civil Division of the Court of Appeal) ... The fact that there were so few ripples to disturb the peace of judicial independence over 300 years is mainly a tribute to the staid quality of the English judiciary and the political process which has protected it.

... Even so, one ought also to insert a few caveats in the litany of praise for judicial protection and integrity. Even as the English courts became less politically important, politics did enter in. Lord Trevethin (Lawrence LJ) appointed Lord Chief Justice in 1921 to keep the seat warm for Sir Gordon Hewart, was required to sign an undated letter of resignation by that devious Prime Minister, Lloyd George, when the Chief was appointed. When the Coalition Government broke up in 1922, Trevethin read of his resignation in *The Times*. Justice was, however, done. Hewart was not an admired Chief Justice and ultimately he too was dismissed by a telephone call from 10 Downing Street – in 1940 when Churchill, in the darkest days of the Second World War, needed to find a berth for Caldecote, his less than effective Dominions Secretary. In 1928, the first Lord Hailsham asked for Lord Atkinson's resignation as a law lord because the Canadian press said there were too many 'old fogies' in the Privy Council and, as Atkinson reported, 'I was the oldest of the old fogies'. Certainly the introduction of a mandatory retirement age in 1959 helped, but the second Lord Hailsham, Lord Chancellor for Prime Ministers Edward Heath and Margaret Thatcher, had to urge Lord Chief Justice Widgery and Lord Denning on their way ...

Protection from politicians and political winds is, however, significantly by tradition. One must also remember that the vast bulk of the full-time judiciary in England (now some 750, including the backbone of the professional judiciary, some 550 circuit judges) has no protection under the Act of Settlement, although they have protected status under other statutes, and the Lord Chancellor's Department handles dismissals with considerable natural justice [See R Stevens, *The Independence of the Judiciary: The View from the Lord Chancellor's Office* (1993)].

... As already suggested, the English Judges rank high on any international table of objectivity, particularly with respect for individual litigants. In the 20th century London has strengthened its reputation as the centre of commercial litigation primarily because of the judicial reputation for integrity, impartiality and technical competence.

... [However] In recent years, there has been increasing scepticism about judicial impartiality on the part of radical critics [see generally, JAG Griffith, *The Politics of the Judiciary*, 5th edn (1997)]. When the Bar is predominantly white, male, middle aged, Oxbridge, and Public School educated, how can they possibly be impartial, is the cry. There is undoubtedly considerable confusion in the mind of judges (and the public and politicians) about what is meant by impartiality. The bulk of the public and politicians, however, are happy to accept the myth, significantly because there is a strong element of truth in the concept, even if it is not easily defined. It was clearly one of the reasons why judges have been so attractive as Chairs of Commissions or Committees of Enquiry and, more dubiously, Commissions or Committees to rethink delicate political issues. Such judicial work is frowned on in the USA ...

When one looks at the actual operation of the separation of powers, there is a working relationship between the branches of government which surprises Americans. The different branches of government interact constantly. Senior judges and ministers meet regularly to discuss possible sources of conflict; and there are instances of powerful exchanges of view. During the Labour Government of 1945–51, Lord Chancellor Jowitt wrote to Lord Goddard, the Lord Chief Justice whom he had appointed, to the effect that he sincerely hoped 'that the judges will not be lenient to these bandits (who) carry arms (to) shoot at the police'. Conversely, the Attorney-General (Shawcross) wrote to the Chief Justice complaining that the Court of Criminal Appeal had gone too far in restricting questions about how confessions had been obtained. The Chief Justice agreed and said he would raise the complaint with his fellow judges. Americans might well believe these to be examples of the executive inappropriately interfering with the judiciary ... In England such relationships are seen as ensuring the smooth running of the system.

Such relationships exist within the acceptable levels of tolerance of the English concepts of separation of powers. One could argue that they reflect a more flexible – and not necessarily irrational – sense of balance of powers. A more egregious example of executive interference is, however, one of the most recent. In the early 1970s, while the Industrial Relations Court under Sir John Donaldson was resorting to imprisonment to break the strike mentality in England, the Court of Appeal, under Lord Denning, as Master of the Rolls, thought that imprisonment was not an appropriate way to settle industrial disputes. The Conservative Lord Chancellor, Lord Hailsham, direct as ever, was furious. He sent for Denning while he was presiding in the Court of Appeal. Denning refused to adjourn court to wait upon the Head of the Judiciary (and Cabinet member). When they did meet, Hailsham accused Denning of deliberately directing certain cases to his court (he after all assigned cases in the Court of Appeal); Denning insisted he merely applied law to the facts. There was, however, something rather unsatisfactory about the encounter, at least as far as the absence of executive influence over the judiciary is concerned.

Lord Donaldson and Lord Hailsham continued to have encounters that questioned any formal separation of powers. It emerged in 1983 that Lord Donaldson, by then Master of the Rolls, had been consulted by civil servants on 'how the judiciary could play a more constructive role in industrial relations'. Lord Hailsham defended such meetings as normal. Two years later, however, when two judges had commented adversely in a judicial appeal on plans to abolish some forms of judicial review, Lord Hailsham, in a legislative debate, proudly announced that he had received letters of apology from the two judges:

> It is utterly improper in my judgment for a Court of Appeal judge or any other judge speaking on the Bench, to criticise matters passing through Parliament ...

Judicial Independence: The Judges as a Separate Branch of Government

... Another of the issues in judicial independence in England is that the judges are chosen, as they are in most other common law countries although normally with the assistance of a Judicial Appointments Commission, by a politician – basically the Lord Chancellor. While the English like to say that judicial appointments in their country are non-political, or even apolitical (and there are in fact no former MPs currently serving as judges), Europeans find it difficult to comprehend how a system which leaves the final say for choosing most judges with an active politician, the Lord Chancellor, with appointments to the House of Lords and Court of Appeal made by the Prime Minister, can be an apolitical system. Even the House of Commons Select Committee on Home Affairs has described the Prime Minister's involvement in senior judicial appointments as 'nothing short of naked political control' [Judicial Appointments Procedures, Vol 1, 5 June 1996, para 126].

... Yet in a sense the claims of the apolitical nature of the process are true. While the judiciary is chosen primarily from the English Bar, it is possible to argue that success and reputation at the Bar far outweigh other attributes. (Of course whether success as an advocate should be the primary criterion for judicial appointment is a different matter.) Once again political convention provides more support than legal rules might. With a relatively small and cohesive Bar, there is an argument that 'the judges select themselves' as Sir George Coldstream, a former Permanent Secretary to the Lord Chancellor put it. It is also true that the days when politics played an important role in getting on the Bench have effectively gone. Lord Halsbury, at the turn of the century, was the last Lord Chancellor who blatantly appointed political supporters to the High Court Bench; and after the 1920s political service played little role in appointment to the House of Lords and Court of Appeal. Yet Mrs Thatcher rejected Lord Hailsham's report of the judges' preference and appointed Sir John Donaldson to be Master of the Rolls in the 1980s, and it was unlikely that she was unaware of Donaldson's work in the Tory cause in the Industrial Relations Court. Of course, what is political is always difficult to define. We should not forget that during the most radical government in Britain's history (the Attlee Government of 1945–51) Lord Chancellor Jowitt refused to appoint divorced persons to the Bench and, for a significant period, members of the Roman Catholic Church. While this latter was allegedly because they might have difficulty hearing divorce petitions on circuit, the real reason may well have been because he and the Home Secretary ... were vigorously anti-Catholic ...

The Institute for Public Policy Research's recommendation for the choosing of judges was a Judicial Appointments Commission ... heavily dominated by the judges. It is an area in which the English have great difficulty. There is an increasing consensus that allowing one politician in the Cabinet to choose judges is unacceptable ... The problem remains, if the judges are not chosen by the Lord Chancellor, then by whom? The idea of the judges as a self-selecting oligarchy, inherent in the IPPR's draft constitution, was unattractive to the Committee on the Judiciary, established by JUSTICE ... in 1991. In its Report, it proposed a Committee composed of a minority of lawyers (and no more than two judges) and a majority of laymen to advise the Lord Chancellor on appointments [The Judiciary in England and Wales (1993)]. JUSTICE's advice was rejected by Lord Mackay and has now probably been abandoned by Lord Irvine [the current Lord Chancellor].

The English are somewhat reluctant to come to grips with the implications of a judiciary increasingly involved with what, in other societies, would be regarded as political issues. The idea of a Judicial Appointments Commission worries them. Many appear to be especially uncomfortable with any system which would allow judges to be questioned either about their political or personal views or their suitability to be judges. They are offended with the American system of Senatorial review of Presidential judicial appointments, which they associate with the Bork and

Thomas hearings, although the typical hearings before the Senate Judiciary Committee provide a more healthy airing of views. Yet other societies have been forced to think in novel ways when faced with the issue of the democratic deficit involved in allowing un-elected judges to make decisions with serious political implications. In 1948, Israel, which had basically a British legal system, established an apolitical Judicial Selection Committee to chose judges. As the Israeli Supreme Court has moved more actively into the political arena, the Knesset [Israeli Parliament] has demanded representation. (The current composition of the Judicial Selection Committee is three judges, two lawyers, two Cabinet Ministers, and two members of the Knesset.) So too with the German Constitutional Court, another aggrandizing judiciary. It is chosen half by the Bundesrat (the Upper Federal House) and half by the Länder (the state governments). In South Africa, Nelson Mandela argued that the President should choose the members of that country's Constitutional Court – while the African National Congress (ANC) opposed the idea of a Constitutional Court altogether, preferring a Council of State. Eventually the Constitutional Convention plumped for a Constitutional Court, along the lines of the German Constitutional Court. The new South African Constitution provides that judges are nominated by the President from a list produced by the Judicial Service Commission. The Commission then holds hearings in public but makes its decisions, on whether to recommend, in private.

England (and Scotland and Northern Ireland) are likely to move down one of these routes ...

Note

While there is, as yet, no indication of such root and branch reform, since this article was written the Lord Chancellor's Department has implemented a modest change to the appointments system for senior judges. As Stevens indicates, the traditional system was that the senior judiciary in England and Wales were appointed by the Lord Chancellor after a series of confidential 'soundings' of other senior judges and QCs. The Law Lords are appointed by the Prime Minister, on the advice of the Lord Chancellor. There was no independent monitoring of the procedure. This procedure has been subject to a great deal of criticism, both because the Lord Chancellor is a member of the Cabinet, raising questions as to the independence of the procedure, and also because it is widely considered that the system perpetuates the current, unrepresentative make-up of the judiciary: in 2000 there were no black or Asian High Court judges, no black circuit judges, and only 42 women among the 534 full-time judges in England and Wales, 70% of whom were educated at public schools. In 2000, the Lord Chancellor implemented the recommendations of the Peach Report,[64] the key element of which is the creation of an Appointments Commission, which provides independent monitoring of the appointments procedure. It also handles grievances and complaints and provide advice to the Lord Chancellor on the workings of the judicial appointments system and areas where improvements or reviews should be undertaken. The Lord Chancellor has said of the Commission: '[The Commissioners] will be able to investigate every appointment, every piece of paper, every assessment, every opinion, and they will also have the right to attend interview for judicial appointments and meetings where the most senior appointments are discussed.'[65] The reform is conservative and limited: it leaves the actual decisions as to appointments in the hands of the Lord Chancellor, and the basic procedures of the current system untouched. It has thus disappointed those looking for the creation of an independent appointments panel; moreover, the Commission's remit excludes the appointment of the Lord Chief Justice and the Law Lords. However, in providing some independent

---

64 Available on the web: www.lcd.gov.uk/judicial/peach/reportfr.htm.
65 Press Release No 376/00, 24 October 2000.

assessment of the current, closed system, it does at least represent a step in the right direction. See further, Sir Thomas Legg, 'Judges for the New Century' [2001] PL 62.

FURTHER READING

Report of the Committee on Ministers' Powers (Cmnd 4060)

TRS Allan, 'The Rule of Law as the rule of reason: consent and constitutionalism' (1999) 115 LQR 221

N Barber, 'Prelude to the separation of powers' [2001] CLJ 59.

E Barendt, 'Dicey and civil liberties' [1985] PL 596

P Craig, 'Dicey: unitary, self-correcting democracy and public law' (1990) 106 LQR 105

P Craig, 'Formal and substantive conceptions of the Rule of Law: an analytical framework' [1997] PL 467

KC Davis, *Discretionary Justice* (1971)

SA de Smith, 'The separation of powers in new dress' (1966) 12 McGill LJ 491

FA Hayek, *The Road to Serfdom* (1944)

M Loughlin, *Public Law and Political Theory* (1992)

C Munro, 'The separation of powers: not such a myth' [1981] PL 19

A Tomkins, 'Of constitutional spectres' [1999] PL 325.

MJC Vile, *Constitutionalism and the Separation of Powers* (1967)

CHAPTER 4

PARLIAMENTARY SOVEREIGNTY

Three main issues are covered in this chapter: the nature of parliamentary sovereignty; possible legal limitations on sovereignty; and the question of whether Parliament is able in any way to entrench legislation, so as to make it impossible or more difficult for subsequent Parliaments to repeal an Act they have passed. The next chapter will consider the impact of European Community law on the traditional doctrine of parliamentary sovereignty. The main concern will be the extent to which the legislative competence of Parliament has been fettered by the impact of Community law.

THE NATURE OF PARLIAMENTARY SOVEREIGNTY

The basic idea of sovereignty

The notion of 'parliamentary sovereignty' or the 'legislative supremacy of Parliament', as it is sometimes termed, can be seen to have both political and legal aspects. Given that the dominant body in Parliament, the Commons, is democratically elected, the notion can be seen as representing a description of the democratic basis for legislation in the UK. As used by constitutional lawyers, however, it means something much more specific: 'By the legislative supremacy of Parliament is meant that there are no *legal* limitations upon the legislative competence of Parliament.'[1]

As AW Bradley has summed up the doctrine:

> The sovereignty of Parliament describes in formal terms the relationship which exists between the legislature and the courts. As analysed by Dicey, the Queen in Parliament (the legislature) has 'the right to make or unmake any law whatever' and no person or body outside the legislature 'is recognised by the law of England as having a right to override or set aside the legislation of Parliament' [AV Dicey, *An Introduction to the Study of the Law of the Constitution*, 10th edn (1959), p 40]. In other words, there are no legal limits to the legislative authority of Parliament. When that authority is exercised in the form of an Act of Parliament, no court or other body has power to hold such an Act to be void or invalid or in any respect lacking in legal effect.[2]

Notes
1 It will be seen that two distinct notions emerge from the above quotations. The first is the lack of legal, as opposed to conventional or moral, constraints on Parliament. Lord Reid has expressed this idea thus:

> It is often said that it would be unconstitutional for the UK Parliament to do certain things, meaning that the moral, political and other reasons against doing them are so strong that most people would regard it as highly improper if Parliament did these things. But that does not mean that it is beyond the power of Parliament to do such things. If Parliament chose to do any of them the courts would not hold the Act of Parliament invalid.[3]

---

1   AW Bradley and ECS Wade, *Constitutional and Administrative Law*, 11th edn (1993), p 69.
2   AW Bradley, 'The sovereignty of Parliament: in perpetuity?', in J Jowell and D Oliver (eds), *The Changing Constitution*, 3rd edn (1994), p 81.
3   *Madzimbamuto v Lardner-Burke* [1969] 1 AC 645, 723.

The second is the fact that the doctrine, in its orthodox form,[4] apparently pays no heed to the make-up of Parliament, or its internal proceedings. Thus, for example, the doctrine is not concerned with whether the Commons is in fact representative of the electorate[5] or whether the balance of power between the Commons and the Lords is politically acceptable.

2   If it is accepted that there are conventional restraints upon Parliament's powers (the legal and political considerations referred to by Lord Reid) then does this mean that the concept of legislative supremacy is parasitic upon the more general distinction between law and convention already considered in Chapter 3?

The historical background[6]

The historical background to the acquisition by Parliament of legislative supremacy represents something of an irony. During the 17th century, in which the relevant events took place, both parliamentarians and common lawyers were united behind a concern to check and control the prerogative powers of the monarch. As Colin Munro observes:

In alliance, [the parliamentarians and the common lawyers] subordinated the powers of the King, and the means of defeating the Crown's attempts to rule by prerogative was the judge's insistence that the limits of prerogative powers, as part of the common law, are determinable by the courts ... For the common lawyers there was a price to pay, and that was the abandonment of the claim they had sometimes advanced, that Parliament could not legislate in derogation of the principles of the common law. As Lord Reid commented in a case in 1974:

In earlier times many learned lawyers seem to have believed that an Act of Parliament could be disregarded in so far as it was contrary to the law of God or the law of nature or natural justice, but since the supremacy of Parliament was finally demonstrated by the revolution of 1688 any such idea has become obsolete [*British Railways Board v Pickin* [1974] 1 All ER 609 at 614].[7]

Note

The efforts of the common lawyers to contain the prerogative powers of the King reached their high water mark in *The Case of Proclamations*.

The Case of Proclamations (1611) 12 Co Rep 74

The King issued proclamations prohibiting the construction of new homes in London and the production of starch from wheat. When the Commons complained that the prerogative power was abused by such usage, the opinion of Chief Justice Coke was sought:

... it was resolved by the two Chief Justices, Chief Baron, and Baron Altham, upon conference betwixt the Lords of the Privy Council and them, that the King by his proclamation cannot create any offence which was not an offence before, for then he may alter the law of the land by his

---

4   But see the views of TRS Allen below, p 145 and of P Craig, 'Public law, political theory and legal theory' [2000] PL 211.

5   It is a truism that the British electoral system, operating on a first-past-the-post basis, disadvantages smaller parties. One of the most striking, recent examples of this was the 1983 general election, in which the SDP-Liberal alliance gained 25% of the total votes cast but only 3.5% of the seats. At the time of writing, the Liberal Democrats advocate a change to a system of proportional representation, the Labour government may hold a referendum on the subject, whilst the Conservative Party remains opposed to both courses of action.

6   For a superb, detailed survey, see JD Goldsworthy, *The Sovereignty of Parliament: History and Philosophy* (1999).

7   C Munro, *Studies in Constitutional Law* (1987), p 130.

proclamation in a high point; for if he may create an offence where none is, upon that ensues fine and imprisonment: also the law of England is divided into three parts, common law, statute law and custom; but the King's proclamation is none of them: also *malum ant est malum in se, aut prohibitum*, that which is against common law is *malum in se, malum prohibitum* is such an offence as is prohibited by Act of Parliament, and not by proclamation.

Also, it was resolved, that the King hath no prerogative, but that which the law of the land allows him.

Notes

1 When the Crown alleged that the security of the realm was threatened, however, the courts were more compliant: see *The Case of Ship Money* (*Hampden* (1637) 3 St Tr 371) and *The Case of Impositions* (*Bate's case* (1606) 2 St Tr 371). Not only was the use of the prerogative to impose emergency taxation upheld in these decisions, but the courts forbore from making any inquiry as to whether the alleged threat to national security justified the measure proposed, holding such a determination to be the exclusive purview of the Crown.

2 As Munro remarks above, the common lawyers accepted the dominance of statute law as the price for finally achieving decisive control over the royal prerogative. In doing so they appeared to relinquish the idea that the common law would not always bow supinely to the force of statute, regardless of its content.[8] As Goldsworthy puts it: 'The historical evidence demonstrates that for several centuries, at least, all three branches of government in Britain have accepted the doctrine that Parliament has sovereign law-making authority.'[9] But this had not always been the attitude of one branch – the judiciary. In *Dr Bonham's* case (1610) 8 Co Rep 113b, 118a, it was said (*per* Coke LJ): '... when an Act of Parliament is against common right and reason, or repugnant, or impossible to be performed, the common law will control it, and adjudge such Act to be void.' Hobart CJ had said in the same year that: '... even an Act of Parliament, made against natural equity, as to make a man judge in his own case, is void in itself.'[10]

3 The irony of these historical events lies in the fact that the common lawyers abandoned such contentions in order to secure the dominance of Parliament as a safeguard against the threat to liberty poised by royal (that is, executive) absolutism. However, since the executive now substantially controls Parliament, through the party machine, it is Parliament's unlimited law-making capability that now poses one of the main threats to civil liberties in the UK.[11] Sir William Blackstone foresaw this as long ago as 1776, when he remarked that: '... it was a known apophthegm of the great lord treasurer Burleigh, "that England could never be ruined but by a Parliament".'[12]

Traditional doctrine scrutinised

Now that the basic parameters of the traditional doctrine and its historical antecedents have been indicated, the substantive content of the doctrine may be considered more closely. As Bradley indicated above, Dicey's conception of the doctrine has been easily

8 But see the views of Craig, *op cit*.
9 Goldsworthy, *op cit* at p 236.
10 Hobb 85, 97.
11 The classic exposition of the thesis can be found in Lord Hailsham's 1976 Hamlyn Lecture, *Elective Dictatorship*.
12 W Blackstone, *Commentaries on the Laws of England* (1776), Book 1, pp 160–61. Quoted in M Loughlin, *Public Law and Political Theory* (1992), p 147.

the most influential and has to an extent marked out the parameters of the debate
which has gone on ever since.

AV Dicey, *An Introduction to the Study of the Law of the Constitution*, 10th edn (1959), pp xxxiv–xxxv (introduction by ECS Wade)

The principle of parliamentary sovereignty was repeated by the author in each edition of this book
up to 1914, when he emphasised that the truth of the doctrines had never been denied. They
were:

(1) Parliament has the right to make or unmake any law whatever [referred to as 'the positive
aspect'].

(2) No person or body is recognised by the law of England as having a right to override or set
aside the legislation of Parliament [referred to as 'the negative aspect'].

(3) The right or power of Parliament extends to every part of the Queen's dominions.

Despite recent criticism, it is still true today as a proposition of the law of the UK to say that
Parliament has the right to make or unmake any law whatever. Nor can any court within the UK
set aside the provisions of an Act of Parliament. All that a court of law can do with such an Act is
to apply it, ie to interpret the meaning of the enactment. This is enough to satisfy the lawyer, but it
must be admitted that the conception is purely a legal one.

Notes

1   Whatever the controversies surrounding Dicey's views of sovereignty, one thing is
    certain: it is no longer true to say that '[No] court within the [UK] [can] set aside ...
    an Act of Parliament'. This has in fact happened in relation to certain provisions of
    two statutes, the Merchant Shipping Act 1988 and the Employment Protection
    (Consolidation) Act 1978.[13] The impact of EC law on parliamentary sovereignty is
    discussed in the next chapter, but this important caveat to the traditional view must
    be borne in mind during this chapter.

2   Dicey's view is in fact not as monolithic as first appears. Munro 'unpacks' the
    various strands of the Diceyan conception of sovereignty after citing the classical
    formulation quoted above.

Colin Munro, *Studies in Constitutional Law*, 2nd edn (1999), pp 130–33

The negative aspect, more fully expounded, is that 'there is no person or body of persons who can,
under the English constitution, make rules which override or derogate from an Act of Parliament,
or which (to express the same thing in other words) will be enforced by the courts in
contravention of an Act of Parliament' [Dicey, p 40]. We may notice that this is no more than a
recognition that Acts of Parliament are supreme within the hierarchy of laws and *a fortiori* prevail
over any principles or rules which are not laws. Dicey demonstrates the point by reference to the
absence of any legislative power able to compete with Parliament [Dicey, pp 50–61]: the Crown's
authority to legislate had, since the *Case of Proclamations* [(1611) 12 Co Rep 74] been restricted;
judge-made law was recognisably subordinate to statute; one of the Houses of Parliament acting
alone, even the House of Commons, could not make law, as *Stockdale v Hansard* [(1839) 9 Ad and
El 1] showed; the electorate, which chose the members of the Commons, had no other role in the
legislative process. All of these points were uncontroversial, for they were already well established.

---

13   The cases were, respectively: *R v Secretary of State for Transport ex p Factortame* [1990] 2 AC 85;
     ex p Factortame (No 2) [1991] 1 AC 603; and *R v Secretary of State for Employment ex p Equal
     Opportunities Commission* [1994] 2 WLR 409.

The positive aspect of sovereignty, however, is made to carry much more weight. 'It means not only that Parliament may legislate upon any topic, but also that any parliamentary enactment must be obeyed by the courts' [Dicey, pp 87–91 and Chapter 2]. In a further reworking, sovereignty is said to involve first, that there is no law which Parliament cannot change, so that even constitutional laws of great importance may be changed in the same manner as other laws; secondly, the absence of any legal distinction between constitutional and other laws; and thirdly, that there exists no person or body, executive, legislative or judicial, which can pronounce void any enactment of Parliament on the ground of its being opposed to the constitution or any other ground.

Dicey's treatment of all these points as attributes of a sovereign legislature, and his referring to the positive and negative 'sides' of sovereignty, imply that we have here a number of corollaries flowing from the same proposition. Such an inference, however, would be wrong. That statute law is superior to other forms of law in the hierarchy does not necessarily entail that Parliament may legislate upon any topic or repeal any law; for example, it would be possible to maintain (and some do) that some parts of the Acts of Union between England and Scotland are unalterable, without doubting that Acts of Parliament prevail over other kinds of law. Again, the absence of a judicial power to hold Acts of Parliament void does not of itself mean that the legislature is unlimited, for in some countries excess of legislative authority may be left as a matter between the legislature and the electors, or may be dealt with by a non-judicial process. Dicey did recognise this last point, but the general impression left by his account is that the different attributes he ascribes to Parliament are all of a piece. This is not so, and it is instructive to unpack Dicey's doctrine. When we do, we see that, while the 'negative side' of sovereignty was uncontroversial, the other propositions advanced by Dicey were more wide-reaching and not so obviously justified.

In purporting to show that Parliament's legislative authority was unlimited, Dicey offered evidence of a different sort [Dicey, pp 41–50, 61–80]. He cited the opinions of Coke, Blackstone and De Lolme. He exhibited historical instances of the width of Parliament's powers; it could alter the succession to the throne, as it did in the Act of Settlement; it could prolong its own life, as with the Septennial Act of 1715; it could make legal past illegalities by Acts of Indemnity. He argued that some supposed limitations on Parliament's capacity were not real – the existence of inalienable prerogative powers could no longer be maintained; that doctrines of morality or the rules of international law could prevail against Acts of Parliament found no support in case law. Finally, Dicey denied that earlier Acts had ever limited what a Parliament could do. The language of certain enactments, such as the Acts of Union, suggested an intention to restrict later Parliaments, but their subsequent history demonstrated the futility of the attempts. Therefore, Parliament's authority was not only unlimited, but illimitable, for attempts to bind succeeding Parliaments would be ineffective.

These matters, informative as they are, scarcely compel us to accept Dicey's case … Dicey does not really establish that Parliament is unlimited, still less that it is illimitable. But if his propositions are not verifiable, they are falsifiable by appropriate evidence. No evidence to that effect existed at Dicey's time. We may see whether it has been thrown up in the 100 years since.

Notes

1 The actual record of matters which have been affected by legislation is undoubtedly impressive:

Parliament has in fact passed retroactive penal legislation, prolonged its own existence, transformed itself into a new body by the Acts of Union with Scotland and Ireland, repealed and amended provisions of those Acts which were to have permanent effect, altered the procedure for making laws (under the Parliament Acts) and followed the new procedure, and changed the succession to the throne (by the Bill of Rights, the Act of Settlement 1700, and Declaration of Abdication Act 1936).[14]

---

14 SA de Smith, *Constitutional and Administrative Law*, 6th edn (1994), pp 77–78.

However, as Professor Henry Calvert has pointed out:

> One no more demonstrates [that the powers of the UK Parliament are unlimited] by pointing to a wide range of legislative objects than one demonstrates the contrary by pointing to matters on which Parliament has not, in fact, ever legislated.[15]

2   Clearly, a more systematic approach is required, in which all the main possible limitations on sovereignty are examined in turn. It is to this task that the rest of this chapter is devoted.

POSSIBLE LIMITATIONS ON SOVEREIGNTY

There are a number of ways in which, theoretically, Parliament's legislative omnipotence could be limited. These fall into three main categories: first, limitations as to the *form* of the measure passed by Parliament – such limitations would arise if the courts were empowered to make an authoritative determination as to what was to count as a valid Act of Parliament; secondly, limitations based on the *substance* of the Act, for example, its conflict with other legal systems, or with fundamental constitutional principles; thirdly, limitations imposed on sovereignty by Parliament itself. These matters will be examined in turn.

Limitations based on form

An Act of Parliament is an expression of the sovereign will of Parliament. If, however, Parliament is not constituted as Parliament or does not function as Parliament within the meaning of the law, it would seem to follow that it cannot express its sovereign will in the form of an Act of Parliament. However, the courts have declined opportunities to declare an Act a nullity where it has been asserted that something which appears to be an Act of Parliament and which bears the customary words of enactment is not authentic, or is tainted by bad faith or fraud.

Nevertheless, the fact that any Act must bear the customary words of enactment is significant. The courts will not apply the doctrine of sovereignty to motions of the constituent bodies of Parliament that do not constitute actual enactments. Bradley and Wade note that: '... the courts do not attribute legislative supremacy to ... resolution[s] of the House of Commons[16] ... [nor] instrument[s] of subordinate legislation which appear to be issued under the authority of an Act of Parliament,[17] even though approved by the resolution of each House of Parliament[18] ... and will if necessary decide whether or not they have legal effect.' Thus, for example: 'If it should appear that a measure has not been approved by one House, then (unless the Parliament Acts 1911–49 apply) the measure is not an Act.'[19]

Notes

1   Dicey considered that it was partly due to the fact that 'the commands of Parliament can be uttered only through the combined actions of its three

---

15   H Calvert, *Constitutional Law in Northern Ireland* (1968), p 14.
16   *Stockdale v Hansard* (1839) 9 A & E 1; *Bowles v Bank of England* [1913] 1 Ch 57.
17   For example, *Chester v Bateson* [1920] 1 KB 829; [1920] Ch 27.
18   *Hoffman-La Roche v Secretary for Trade and Industry* [1975] AC 295.
19   Bradley and Wade, *op cit*, pp 70, 82.

constituent parts'[20] which made the doctrine of parliamentary sovereignty compatible with the Rule of Law. Parliament would not in practice wield arbitrary power because, as GW Keeton puts it, 'it was a combination of diverse elements, linked together by an intricate system of "checks and balances" '.[21] It should be noted that since Dicey wrote, this balance has been tipped markedly in favour of the Commons as a result of the Parliament Acts 1911–49 (see Part III Chapter 2).

2   As already indicated, the courts combine this very limited but important role of distinguishing Acts of Parliament from other emanations of the legislature with a refusal to enquire into the manner and means by which an apparently authentic Act was passed by the constituent parts of Parliament. The rationale for this refusal is partly the fear that such an enquiry, which could for example involve determining whether the House of Commons' own Standing Orders had been complied with, could bring the courts into conflict with Parliament, which would undoubtedly have made its own enquiry on the matter, the finding of which could differ from that made by the courts.

The other reason is Article 9 of the Bill of Rights 1688, which provides that 'Freedom of speech and debates or proceedings in Parliament ought not to be impeached or questioned in any court or place out of Parliament', the most important effect of which is to confer complete civil and criminal immunity upon those speaking during proceedings in Parliament (for full discussion, see Part III Chapter 3). However, Article 9 has also been construed so as to forbid any 'questioning' in the courts of the procedures used in Parliament to pass legislation: hence the refusal to consider finding an Act of Parliament to be invalid on the grounds of defective procedure, deception of the House, etc.

3   In *Edinburgh and Dalkeith Railway Co v Wauchope* (1842) 8 Cl and F 710, the court was asked to find that the legislation in question, a private Act, had been improperly passed in that Standing Orders of the House of Commons had not been complied with, and that the Act was therefore invalid. Lord Campbell said, *obiter*, that if according to the Parliament roll an Act has passed both Houses of Parliament and has received the royal assent, a court cannot enquire into the manner in which it was introduced into Parliament nor into what passed in Parliament during its progress through the various parliamentary stages.

4   This rule, now known as 'the enrolled Bill rule', was relied upon in *Pickin v British Railways Board* [1974] AC 765. Mr Pickin had sought to challenge a private Act of 1836 on the basis that Parliament had been misled by fraud. The House of Lords held that he was not entitled to examine proceedings in Parliament to show that the Act had been passed due to fraud. The action therefore failed.

Pickin v British Railways Board [1974] AC 765, 786–88

Lord Reid: ... In my judgment the law is correctly stated by Lord Campbell in *Edinburgh and Dalkeith Railway Co v Wauchope* (1842) 8 Cl and F 710; 1 Bell 252 ... Mr Wauchope appears to have maintained in the Court of Session that the provisions of [the Act in question] should not be applied because it had been passed without his having had notice as required by Standing Orders. This contention was abandoned in this House. Lord Brougham and Lord Cottenham said that want of notice was no ground for holding that the Act did not apply. Lord Campbell based his opinion on more general grounds. He said, 1 Bell 252, 278–279:

---

20   AV Dicey, *An Introduction to the Study of the Law of the Constitution*, 10th edn (1959),. p 402.
21   GW Keeton, *The Passing of Parliament* (1952), p 6, quoted in Loughlin, *op cit*, p 152.

... all that a court of justice can look to is the parliamentary roll; they see that an Act has passed both Houses of Parliament, and that it has received the Royal Assent, and no court of justice can inquire into the manner in which it was introduced into Parliament, what was done previously to its being introduced, or what passed in Parliament during the various stages of its progress through both Houses of Parliament. I therefore trust that no such inquiry will hereafter be entered into in Scotland, and that due effect will be given to every Act of Parliament, both private as well as public, upon the just construction which appears to arise upon it.

No doubt this was *obiter* but, so far as I am aware, no one since 1842 has doubted that it is a correct statement of the constitutional position.

The function of the court is to construe and apply the enactments of Parliament. The court has no concern with the manner in which Parliament or its officers carrying out its Standing Orders perform these functions. Any attempt to prove that they were misled by fraud or otherwise would necessarily involve an inquiry into the manner in which they had performed their functions in dealing with the Bill which became the British Railways Act 1968.

In whatever form the respondent's case is pleaded he must prove not only that the appellants acted fraudulently but also that their fraud caused damage to him by causing the enactment of s 18. He could not prove that without an examination of the manner in which the officers of Parliament dealt with the matter. So the court would, or at least might, have to adjudicate upon that.

For a century or more both Parliament and the courts have been careful not to act so as to cause conflict between them. Any such investigations as the respondent seeks could easily lead to such a conflict, and I would only support it if compelled to do so by clear authority. But it appears to me that the whole trend of authority for over a century is clearly against permitting any such investigation.

Notes

1   Lord Reid might also have cited *Lee v Bude & Torrington Junction Railway Co* (1871) LR 6 CP 576, *per* Willes J in support of his finding: 'If an Act of Parliament has been obtained improperly, it is for legislature to correct it by repealing it; but so long as it exists in law, the courts are bound to obey it.'

2   Lord Reid appears to leave the possibility open that the courts might be prepared to question whether the purported statute before them was in fact an Act of Parliament, indeed this is arguably implicit in his reference to the fact that the courts will 'apply the *enactments* of Parliament' (emphasis added). However, he also states that the courts will not enquire into 'the way in which' Parliament or its officers carry out its Standing Orders. The problem here is that it is the Standing Orders of the two Houses which go much of the way towards defining what 'enactments' of Parliament are. Lord Reid leaves it unclear whether the courts will enquire into whether Standing Orders had been complied with *at all*.

Limitations based on substance

Possible limitations here could be based on two grounds: first, that the statute conflicted with laws derived from other legal systems; secondly, that it contravened fundamental liberties or other constitutional principles. It is important to note that such limitations could take the form of a refusal to apply the statute in question, the imposition of the requirement of express words on Parliament or the employment of a restrictive interpretation of the statute.

Conflict with other legal systems

If UK law conflicts with international law, or with a provision in a treaty to which the British government is a signatory, the position seems clear.

In the Scottish case of *Mortensen v Peters* (1906) 14 SLT 227, a direct conflict arose between domestic and international law. Mortensen, a Norwegian fisherman, was charged with illegal fishing in the Moray Firth, contrary to a bylaw passed under s 7 of the Herring Fishery (Scotland) Act 1889. The bylaw extended to the whole of the Moray Firth, even though much of the Firth comprised international waters. Mortensen had been fishing in international waters, but inside the banned area and was convicted under the bylaw. He appealed.

Mortensen v Peters 1906 14 SLT 227

The Lord Justice General: In this court we have nothing to do with the question of whether the legislature has or has not done what foreign powers may consider a usurpation in a question with them. Neither are we a tribunal sitting to decide whether an act of the legislature is *ultra vires* as in contravention of generally acknowledged principles of international law. For us an Act of Parliament, duly passed by Lords and Commons and assented to by the King, is supreme, and we are bound to give effect to its terms . . .

It is said by the appellant . . . that international law has firmly fixed that a locus such as this is beyond the limits of territorial sovereignty; and that consequently it is not to be thought that in such a place the legislature could seek to affect any but the King's subjects.

It is a trite observation that there is no such thing as a standard of international law, extraneous to the domestic law of a kingdom, to which appeal may be made. International law, so far as this Court is concerned, is the body of doctrine regarding the international rights and duties of states which has been adopted and made part of the law of Scotland.

Notes

1 Lord Kyllachy in his judgment in the case noted that 'the language of the enactment . . . is fairly express . . . to the effect of making an unlimited and unqualified prohibition, applying to the whole area specified, and affecting everybody, whether British subjects or foreigners' (*ibid*). It may be inferred that, if the words of the Act had been less unambiguous, the courts might have attempted an interpretation which either exempted foreign nationals or limited the ambit of the Act to territorial waters, or both. Indeed, it was confirmed in *Treacy v DPP* [1971] AC 537, 552 that: 'It is . . . a general rule of construction that, unless there is something which points to a contrary intention, a statute will be taken to apply only to the UK . . . clear and express terms [would be needed to go against this rule].'

2 The finding in *Mortensen* was confirmed by the Privy Council in *Croft v Dunphy PC* [1933] AC 156, in which it was said (*per* Lord MacMillan at p 164): 'Legislation of Parliament, even in contravention of generally acknowledged principles of international law, is binding upon, and must be enforced by, the courts of this country.' The point may be regarded as settled (the position is of course wholly different if the conflict is with European Community law – see Chapter 5 of this Part).

3 The courts apply the same principle even if contravention of the international provision in question would result in the UK breaching its treaty obligations. In *Cheney v Conn* [1968] All ER 779, a taxpayer appealed against an assessment of income tax made under the Finance Act 1964 on the basis that part of the money

would be used for the construction of nuclear weapons, contrary (so it was argued) to the Geneva Convention, to which the UK was a party. His appeal was dismissed and Ungoed-Thomas J said: 'What the statute itself enacts cannot be unlawful, because what the statute says and provides is itself the law, and the highest form of law that is known to this country.'

Question
Did this *dicta* go further than was necessary to decide the case?

Note
Numerous other decisions have confirmed that domestic law overrides conflicting treaty obligations; see, for example, *Re M and H (Minors)* [1988] 3 WLR 485, 498 and *R v Secretary of State for the Home Department ex p Brind and Others* [1991] 1 AC 696. However, the latter case, amongst others, also confirmed that it is a general principle of statutory interpretation that the courts will strive to construe a statute in such a way as to be consistent with the UK's treaty obligations where possible.

Limitations based on protection of constitutional principles?

At first sight, the notion that the courts could refuse to apply a statute on the basis that it violated fundamental constitutional or moral principles seems both to fly in the face of theory, and to be flatly contradicted by authority. For example, the question of finding a statute to be invalid was rapidly dismissed in *R v Jordan* [1967] Crim LR 483.

R v Jordan [1967] Crim LR 483
The defendant was sentenced to 18 months' imprisonment for offences under the Race Relations Act 1965. He applied for legal aid to apply for a writ of *habeas corpus* on the ground that the Act was invalid as being a curtailment of free speech.

Held, dismissing the application, that Parliament was supreme and there was no power in the courts to question the validity of an Act of Parliament. The ground of the application was completely unarguable.

Notes
1   Such decisions highlight the apparently stark contrast between the UK and other jurisdictions where judicial review of legislation is a well accepted aspect of the constitution. For example, in the famous US case of *Marbury v Madison* (1803) 1 Cranch 137, 177, Chief Justice Marshall said:

> The constitution is either a superior paramount law, unchallengeable by ordinary means, or it is on a level with ordinary legislative acts, and, like other acts, is alterable when the legislature shall be pleased to alter it. If the former part of the alternative is true, then a legislative act contrary to the constitution is not law; if the latter part be true, then written constitutions are absurd attempts, on the part of the people, to limit a power in its own nature illimitable.

As Bradley sums up the case: '[The finding was therefore that] it was for the court where necessary to hold that an Act of Congress was void should it conflict with the terms of the constitution.'[22] Bradley goes on to note that a similar approach is adopted in many other countries where there is a written constitution, including the Republic of Ireland, Canada, Australia, and Germany.

2   However, the contrast may not be as stark as would first appear. Whilst there is no precedent for a refusal to apply a statute on such grounds, and many *dicta* against the notion, the courts are in certain cases prepared to impose on Parliament very strong presumptions that it cannot have intended to violate certain principles through the interpretation the courts give to statutes. This may lead them to require that Parliament must in some way make its meaning clear beyond doubt if it wishes to violate such principles.

3   Thus, in *Phillips v Eyre* (1870) LR 6 QB 1, 23 it was said: '... the courts will not ascribe retrospective force to new laws affecting rights unless by express words or necessary implication it appears that such was the intention of the legislature.' A similar rule relating to statutes intended to have extra-territorial effect has already been noted (above). Furthermore, in the administrative law field, the courts have shown themselves willing effectively to disregard an apparently clear statutory attempt to oust their power of supervisory review.[23]

4   In a recent series of cases involving human rights, the courts have begun to develop what may be termed a jurisprudence of common law fundamental rights, independent of the European Convention on Human Rights and the Human Rights Act. The main areas in which this development has taken place are access to the courts and freedom of expression, as illustrated by the following two decisions.

R v Lord Chancellor ex p Witham [1998] QB 575

The Lord Chancellor, in purported exercise of his powers under s 130 of the Supreme Court Act 1981 ('The Lord Chancellor may by order under this section prescribe the fees to be taken in the Supreme Court ...') made the Supreme Court Fees (Amendment) Order 1996, which increased the fees for issuing a writ and other processes and, in Art 3, removed from litigants-in-person in receipt of income support their exemption from payment of such fees and the Lord Chancellor's power under Art 5(3) of the 1980 Order exceptionally to reduce or remit fees in cases of financial hardship. The applicant was an unemployed man in receipt of income support who wished to issue proceedings in person for defamation, for which legal aid was not available. Such proceedings have to be brought in the High Court and the fee would, under the new regime, be £500. He was not able to afford the fee and, by virtue of Art 3, was no longer eligible for waiver. He sought judicial review by way of a declaration that Art 3 was beyond the Lord Chancellor's powers under s 130 of the Act of 1981 and was thus unlawful. The basis of his argument was that the Lord Chancellor's actions had the effect of denying him access to the courts.

> **Laws LJ** [summarising the argument of the Lord Chancellor]: 'The power conferred by section 130 of the Act of 1981 is not subject to any implied limitation of the kind for which the applicant contends. Parliament has conferred on the Lord Chancellor a wide discretion to prescribe fees for the Supreme Court ... the level and structure of fees are matters of judgment for him. The judgment that he makes is open to scrutiny on *Wednesbury* grounds [that is, that they were so unreasonable as to be perverse].'
>
> The common law does not generally speak in the language of constitutional rights, for the good reason that in the absence of any sovereign text, a written constitution which is logically and legally prior to the power of legislature, executive and judiciary alike, there is on the face of it no

23   *Anisminic Ltd v Foreign Compensation Commission* [1969] 2 All ER 147, see pp 702 and 710–11.

hierarchy of rights such that any one of them is more entrenched by the law than any other and if the concept of a constitutional right is to have any meaning, it must surely sound in the protection which the law affords to it ... In the unwritten legal order of the British state, at a time when the common law continues to accord a legislative supremacy to Parliament, the notion of a constitutional right can in my judgment inhere only in this proposition, that the right in question cannot be abrogated by the state save by specific provision in an Act of Parliament, or by regulations whose *vires* in main legislation specifically confers the power to abrogate. General words will not suffice and any such rights will be creatures of the common law, since their existence would not be the consequence of the democratic political process but would be logically prior to it.

... the right to a fair trial, which of necessity imports the right of access to the court, is as near to an absolute right as any which I can envisage. It seems to me, from all the authorities to which I have referred, that the common law has clearly given special weight to the citizen's right of access to the courts. It has been described as a constitutional right, though the cases do not explain what that means. In this whole argument, nothing to my mind has been shown to displace the proposition that the executive cannot in law abrogate the right of access to justice, unless it is specifically so permitted by Parliament; and this is the meaning of the constitutional right. But I must explain, as I have indicated I would, what in my view the law requires by such a permission. A statute may give the permission expressly; in that case it would provide in terms that in defined circumstances the citizen may not enter the court door. In *Ex parte Leech* [1994] QB 198 the Court of Appeal accepted, as in its view the ratio of their Lordships' decision in *Raymond v Honey* [1983] I AC I vouchsafed, that it could also be done by necessary implication. However for my part I find great difficulty in conceiving a form of words capable of making it plain beyond doubt to the statute's reader that the provision in question prevents him from going to court (for that is what would be required), save in a case where that is expressly stated. The class of cases where it could be done by necessary implication is, I venture to think, a class with no members ...

In my judgment the effect of the Order of 1996 is to bar absolutely many persons from seeking justice from the courts. [Counsel for the Lord Chancellor] ... says that the statute's words are unambiguous, are amply wide enough to allow what has been done, and that there is no available *Wednesbury* complaint. That submission would be good in a context which does not touch fundamental constitutional rights. But I do not think that it can run here. Access to the courts is a constitutional right; it can only be denied by the government if it persuades Parliament to pass legislation which specifically – in effect by express provision – permits the executive to turn people away from the court door. That has not been done in this case ...

I would allow this application and grant the relief sought, which is a declaration that Article 3 of the Order of 1996 is unlawful.

R v Secretary of State for the Home Department ex p Simms [2000] 2 AC 115, 131–32

Lord Hoffman: Parliamentary sovereignty means that Parliament can, if it chooses, legislate contrary to fundamental principles of human rights ... The constraints upon its exercise by Parliament are ultimately political, not legal. But the principle of legality means that Parliament must squarely confront what it is doing and accept the political cost. Fundamental rights cannot be overridden by general or ambiguous words. This is because there is too great a risk that the full implications of their unqualified meaning may have passed unnoticed in the democratic process. In the absence of express language or necessary implication to the contrary, the courts therefore presume that even the most general words were intended to be subject to the basic rights of the individual. In this way the courts of the United Kingdom, though acknowledging the sovereignty of Parliament, apply principles of constitutionality little different from those which exist in countries where the power of the legislature is expressly limited by a constitutional document ...

Note

This presumption was taken further in a series of *obiter* comments made by Laws LJ in a case which raised the issue of the impact of EC law on parliamentary sovereignty. That aspect of the decision is considered in the next chapter, but his Lordship also took the opportunity to make some more general remarks about the ability of the common law to impose certain restrictions upon Parliament.

Thoburn v Sunderland City Council [2002] 1 CMLR 50 (extracts)

In the present state of its maturity the common law has come to recognise that there exist rights which should properly be classified as constitutional or fundamental. [His Lordship cited authority, including *Simms*, *Pierson* [1998] AC 539 and *Witham* (above).] And from this a further insight follows. We should recognise a hierarchy of Acts of Parliament: as it were 'ordinary' statutes and 'constitutional' statutes. The two categories must be distinguished on a principled basis. In my opinion a constitutional statute is one which (a) conditions the legal relationship between citizen and State in some general, overarching manner, or (b) enlarges or diminishes the scope of what we would now regard as fundamental constitutional rights. (a) and (b) are of necessity closely related: it is difficult to think of an instance of (a) that is not also an instance of (b). The special status of constitutional statutes follows the special status of constitutional rights. Examples are the Magna Carta, the Bill of Rights 1689, the Act of Union, the Reform Acts which distributed and enlarged the franchise, the HRA, the Scotland Act 1998 and the Government of Wales Act 1998.

Ordinary statutes may be impliedly repealed. Constitutional statutes may not. For the repeal of a constitutional Act or the abrogation of a fundamental right to be effected by statute, the court would apply this test: is it shown that the legislature's *actual* – not imputed, constructive or presumed – intention was to effect the repeal or abrogation? I think the test could only be met by express words in the later statute, or by words so specific that the inference of an actual determination to effect the result contended for was irresistible. The ordinary rule of implied repeal does not satisfy this test. Accordingly, it has no application to constitutional statutes.

This development of the common law regarding constitutional rights, and as I would say constitutional statutes, is highly beneficial. It gives us most of the benefits of a written constitution, in which fundamental rights are accorded special respect. But it preserves the sovereignty of the legislature and the flexibility of our uncodified constitution.

Notes

1 The propositions put forward in *Simms* find echoes in other cases concerning freedom of expression. In particular, in cases where journalistic material raises political issues, broadly defined,[24] the courts have strongly emphasised the high status freedom of speech holds in the common law, as 'a constitutional right' or 'higher legal order foundation'.[25]

2 If the courts are thus, as Laws LJ asserts, prepared to impose requirements on the *form* in which Parliament expresses itself, in order to protect fundamental constitutional principles, might they be prepared to go further, *in extremis*? Bradley and Wade consider that:

24 *Reynolds v Times Newspapers* [1999] 4 All ER 60; *Derbyshire County Council v Times Newspapers* [1993] AC 534; *ex p Simms* [2000] 2 AC 115. However, deference to widely drafted primary legislation (*R v Secretary of State for Home Affairs ex p Brind* [1991] 1 AC 696) or arguments of national security (*Attorney-General v Guardian Newspapers* [1987] 1 WLR 1248 and *Brind*) have resulted in the ready upholding of restrictions on directly political speech.

25 *Reynolds, ibid*, at 628–29, *per* Lord Steyn; *Simms, ibid*, at 411, *per* Lord Steyn and 412, *per* Lord Hoffman.

It is not possible, by legal logic alone to demonstrate the [the courts] have utterly lost the power to 'control' an Act of Parliament, or to show that a judge who is confronted with a statute fundamentally repugnant to moral principle (for example, a law condemning all of a certain race to be executed) must either apply the statute or resign his office.[26]

It is often not recognised that statements in cases such as *Simms* or others, to the effect that Parliament can enact any statute, however repugnant are, by their nature, strictly *obiter*.[27]

3   Some commentators believe that it is when one starts considering such questions that the supposedly water-tight distinction between 'legal' and 'political' views of sovereignty start to break down. Martin Loughlin, writing from a stance critical of the traditional position, concludes that, even in Dicey's thought, the political and legal aspects of sovereignty are in fact interdependent:

I do not consider that Dicey's beliefs on the nature of political authority can be, or should be, divorced from his conception of legal sovereignty. In Bernard Crick's words: 'the legal doctrine of sovereignty was almost consciously confused with the empirical, pseudo-historical doctrine: that political stability, indeed law and order themselves, depended on parliamentary sovereignty.'[28]

Loughlin notes that Blackstone, whose analysis predated Dicey's and influenced the latter, drew no strict distinction between the legal and political aspects of the doctrine.

4   By contrast, Munro insists that clarity demands the maintenance of a strict distinction.

. . . the concept of parliamentary sovereignty is only indicative of the legal relationship between the legislature and the courts, nothing less but nothing more.

. . . Dicey not only did his best to make clear the sense in which he was employing the term, but additionally sought to dispose of one of the most obvious sources of possible confusion:

The word 'sovereignty' is sometimes employed in a political rather than in a strictly legal sense. That body is 'politically' sovereign or supreme in a state the will of which is ultimately obeyed . . . In this sense of the word the electors of Great Britain may be said to be . . . the body in which sovereign power is vested . . . But this is a political, not a legal fact . . . The political sense of the word 'sovereignty' is, it is true, fully as important as the legal sense or more so. But the two significations . . . are essentially different . . . [Dicey, pp 73–74].

. . . It is perfectly obvious that utterly abhorrent legislation is unlikely to be enacted by the UK Parliament; that governments are influenced by political considerations in deciding what legislation to propose; that international law and international obligations and relations are factors which affect the making of legislation; and that certain conventions are customarily observed by Parliament, so that, to give one example, it does not normally seek to legislate for the Channel Islands in domestic affairs. But these are not legal limitations, and there should be no need to mention them in a discussion of this sort, provided again that it is understood that sovereignty is only a legal conception.[29]

5   This debate is returned to at the conclusion of this chapter. For present purposes, it may be noted that even if one accepted in full Munro's contention that the legal/political distinction ought to be borne in mind when considering sovereignty, it is also helpful to be aware that the views of contributors to the debate on the

26   Bradley and Wade, *op cit*, p 75.
27   See Goldsworthy, *op cit*, at pp 239–40.
28   Loughlin, *op cit*, p 148.
29   Munro, *Studies in Constitutional Law*, 2nd edn (1999), pp 134–36.

legal aspect of sovereignty are likely to be affected by political considerations, such as their theory of democracy and its practice at Westminster. As Bradley puts it:

The democratic basis for legislation, regarded as a constitutional fundamental, serves *inter alia* to validate the whole legal system and the role of the courts. Indeed, one's approach to the legal doctrine of legislative sovereignty is likely to be coloured by one's perception of the democratic element in the composition and functioning of the legislature.[30]

Questions

1 Is what Bradley calls the 'constitutional fundamental' of the democratic basis for legislation a notion that would be recognised as part of constitutional law by the courts?

2 Is Bradley's notion that such a 'constitutional fundamental' exists compatible with his statement that, 'In reality, the doctrine of legislative sovereignty does not in itself imply any particular degree of democracy in the structure of Parliament itself'?

Note

TRS Allan sees a direct link between the democratic foundation provided for the constitution by Parliament and the legal basis for the courts' obedience to statute; but he argues that the very nature of the link implies that that such obedience can never be absolute.

TRS Allan, 'The limits of parliamentary sovereignty' [1985] PL 614, 620–22, 623–24 and 627

The legal doctrine of legislative supremacy articulates the courts' commitment to the current British scheme of parliamentary democracy. It ensures the effective expression of the political will of the electorate through the medium of its parliamentary representatives. If some conception of the nature and dimensions of the relevant political community provides the framework for the operation of the doctrine, equally some conception of democracy must provide its substantive political content. In other words, the courts' continuing adherence to the legal doctrine of sovereignty must entail commitment to some irreducible, minimum concept of the democratic principle. That political commitment will naturally demand respect for the legislative measures adopted by Parliament as the representative assembly, a respect for which the legal doctrine is in almost all likely circumstances a suitable expression. That respect cannot, however, be a limitless one. A parliamentary enactment whose effect would be the destruction of any recognisable form of democracy (for example, a measure purporting to deprive a substantial section of the population of the vote on the grounds of their hostility to Government policies) could not consistently be applied by the courts as law. Judicial obedience to the statute in such (extreme and unlikely) circumstances could not coherently be justified in terms of the doctrine of parliamentary sovereignty since the statute would plainly undermine the fundamental political principle which the doctrine serves to protect. The practice of judicial obedience to statute cannot itself be based on the authority of statute: it can only reflect a judicial choice based on an understanding of what (in contemporary conditions) political morality demands. The limits of that practice of obedience must therefore be constituted by the boundaries of that political morality. An enactment which threatened the essential elements of any plausible conception of democratic government would lie beyond those boundaries. It would forfeit, by the same token, any claim to be recognised as law.

---

30 Bradley, *op cit*, p 81.

Although, therefore, Dicey's sharp distinction between the application and interpretation of statute suffices for most practical purposes, it ultimately breaks down in the face of changing views of the contours of the political community or of serious threats to the central tenets of liberal democracy. Presumptions of legislative intent, which draw their strength from judicial perceptions of widely held notions of justice and fairness, cannot in normal circumstances override the explicit terms of an Act of Parliament. This is because a commitment to representative government and loyalty to democratic institutions are themselves fundamental constituents of our collective political morality. Judicial notions of justice must generally give way to those expressed by Parliament where they are inconsistent. The legal authority of statute depends in the final analysis, however, on its compatibility with the central core of that shared political morality. If Parliament ceased to be a representative assembly, in any plausible sense of the idea, or if it proceeded to enact legislation undermining the democratic basis of our institutions, political morality might direct judicial resistance rather than obedience. Answers [to such questions] can only be supplied as a matter of political morality and in terms of the values which the judges accept as fundamental to our constitutional order ...

A residual judicial commitment to preserving the essentials of democracy does not provide the only constraint on parliamentary supremacy. The political morality which underlies the legal order is not exhausted by our attachment to democratic government. It consists also in attitudes about what justice and fairness require in the relations between government and governed, and some of these must be fundamental. If these attitudes authorise a restrictive approach to the interpretation of statutes which, more broadly construed, would threaten fundamental values, they might equally justify rejection of statutes whose infringement of such values was sufficiently grave. If an ambiguous penal provision should, as a matter of principle, be narrowly construed in the interests of liberty and fairness, a criminal statute which lacked all precision – authorising the punishment of whatever conduct officials deemed it expedient to punish – should, on the same principle, be denied any application at all. It would be sufficient for the court to deny its application to the particular circumstances of the case before it: there would in practice be no need to make a declaration of invalidity. The result, however, would be the same: the strength of the principle of interpretation, in effect denying the statute any application at all, would reflect the scale of the affront to the moral and political values we accept as fundamental.

The limits of the principle which requires recognition of foreign penal or confiscatory legislation provide a good illustration. Legislation by a foreign, sovereign state in respect of its own nationals or assets situated within its own territories will normally be accorded recognition in English courts even when it is considered immoral or unjust. Refusal to accord it validity as part of the relevant foreign law would be considered a serious breach of international comity [*Aksionairnoye Obschestro AM Luther v James Sagor and Co* [1921] 3 KB 532]. In *Oppenheimer v Cattermole (Inspector of Taxes)* [1976] AC 249, however, a majority of the House of Lords refused to recognise a Nazi decree of 1941, depriving expatriate German Jews of their citizenship and providing for the confiscation of their property. Respect for the claims of international comity gave way in the face of grave iniquity. The court was confronted with 'legislation which takes away without compensation from a section of the citizen body singled out on racial grounds all their property on which the state passing the legislation can lay its hands and, in addition, deprives them of their citizenship.' In the view of Lord Cross, 'a law of this sort constitutes so grave an infringement of human rights that the courts of this country ought to refuse to recognise it as a law at all' [*ibid*, at p 278B–C]. Both the rule according legal validity to Acts of Parliament and the rule requiring the recognition of foreign penal legislation are alike important components, or products, of the political morality which informs judicial decision. Neither rule has absolute force, but is necessarily subject to certain ultimate constraints imposed by that morality.

... In each and every such case, the indeterminacy of the fundamental rule necessitates a thoroughgoing examination of the moral and political imperatives of the situation. The jurist cannot escape his moral responsibilities by seeking shelter in a formal doctrine providing legal neutrality – he is forced by events to set the boundaries of his doctrine.

Question

Allan states that: 'The practice of judicial obedience to statute cannot itself be based on the authority of statute: it can only reflect a judicial choice based on an understanding of what ... political morality demands.' Might not such obedience be attributable rather to more mundane matters, such as historical fact, the weight of tradition and the inherent conservatism of the judiciary?[31]

Note

Allan's thesis could strike one as theoretically interesting, but unrealistic as a prediction of how the judiciary would react to abhorrent Acts of Parliament. But his view that sovereignty is itself subject to higher order considerations has recently received influential and important judicial support, albeit by judges speaking extrajudicially. Lord Woolf first of all considers how the courts would and should react if confronted with an Act of Parliament which purported to abolish the system of judicial review.

The Rt Hon Lord Woolf of Barnes, *'Droit public* – English style' [1995] PL 57, 67, 68, 69

But what happens if a party with a large majority in Parliament uses that majority to abolish the courts' entire power of judicial review in express terms? It is administratively expensive, absorbs far too large a proportion of the legal aid fund and results in the judiciary having misconceived notions of grandeur. Do the courts then accept that the legislation means what it says? I am sure this is in practice unthinkable. It will never happen. But if it did, for reasons I will now summarise, my own personal view is that they do not ...

Our parliamentary democracy is based on the Rule of Law. One of the twin principles upon which the Rule of Law depends is the supremacy of Parliament in its legislative capacity. The other principle is that the courts are the final arbiters as to the interpretation and application of the law. As both Parliament and the courts derive their authority from the Rule of Law so both are subject to it and cannot act in a manner which involves its repudiation ...

I see the courts and Parliament as being partners both engaged in a common enterprise involving the upholding of the Rule of Law. It is reflected in the way that frequently the House of Lords in its judicial capacity will stress the desirability of legislation when faced with the new problems that contemporary society can create rather than creating a solution itself.

There are, however, situations where already, in upholding the Rule of Law, the courts have had to take a stand. The example that springs to mind is the *Anisminic* case [1969] [2 AC 147]. In that case even the statement in an Act of Parliament that the Commission's decision 'shall not be called in question in any court of law' did not succeed in excluding the jurisdiction of the court. Since that case Parliament has not again mounted such a challenge to the reviewing power of the High Court. There has been, and I am confident there will continue to be, mutual respect for each other's roles.

However, if Parliament did the unthinkable, then I would say that the courts would also be required to act in a manner which would be without precedent. Some judges might chose to do so by saying that it was an unrebuttable presumption that Parliament could never intend such a result. I myself would consider there were advantages in making it clear that ultimately there are even limits on the supremacy of Parliament which it is the courts' inalienable responsibility to identify and uphold. They are limits of the most modest dimensions which I believe any democrat would accept. They are no more than are necessary to enable the Rule of Law to be preserved.

---

31   For the best known analysis of alleged judicial Conservative bias, see JAG Griffith, *The Politics of the Judiciary*, 4th edn (1991).

Note

Lord Woolf thus issues quite a clear warning that Parliament, being itself bound by the Rule of Law, may not transgress its basic requirements. Sir John Laws (a Court of Appeal judge) has approached the same question of possible limitations on parliamentary sovereignty. He considers the issue from a rather broader perspective than Lord Woolf, examining the consequences following from the imperative of protecting fundamental human rights and democracy itself, and the restraints placed upon Parliament by the fact that it is itself constituted by law.

Sir John Laws, 'Law and democracy' [1995] PL 72, 84, 85–86, 87–88, 92

Now it is only by means of compulsory law that effective rights can be accorded, so that the medium of rights is not persuasion, but the power of rule; the very power which, if misused, could be deployed to subvert rights. We therefore arrive at this position: the constitution must guarantee by positive law such rights as that of freedom of expression, since otherwise its credentials as a medium of honest rule are fatally undermined. But this requires for its achievement what I may call a higher-order law: a law which cannot be abrogated as other laws can, by the passage of a statute promoted by a Government with the necessary majority in Parliament. Otherwise the right is not in the keeping of the constitution at all; it is not a guaranteed right; it exists, in point of law at least, only because the Government chooses to let it exist, whereas in truth no such choice should be open to any Government . . .

It is also a condition of democracy's preservation that the power of a democratically elected Government – or Parliament – be not absolute. The institution of free and regular elections, like fundamental individual rights, has to be vindicated by a higher-order law; very obviously, no Government can tamper with it, if it is to avoid the mantle of tyranny; no Government, therefore, must be allowed to do so.

But this is not merely a plea to the merits of the matter, which can hardly be regarded as contentious; the need for higher-order law is dictated by the logic of the very notion of government under law. If we leave on one side a form of society in which a single ruler rules only by the strength of his arm, and where the only law is the ruler's dictat, we can see that any Government holds office by virtue of a framework of rules. The application of the rules determines what person or party is entitled (or, under some imaginable systems, obliged) to become the Government. This is a necessary, not a contingent, truth, since the institution of government is defined by the rules; were it otherwise, we are back to the case we have proposed to set aside. Richard Latham of All Souls said this over 40 years ago:

> When the purported sovereign is anyone but a single actual person, the designation of him must include the statement of rules for the ascertainment of his will, and these rules, since their observance is a condition of the validity of his legislation, are rules of law logically prior to him.

. . . The thrust of this reasoning is that the doctrine of Parliamentary sovereignty cannot be vouched by Parliamentary legislation; a higher-order law confers it, and must of necessity limit it . . .

So the rules which establish and vindicate a Government's power are in a different category from laws which assume the existence of the framework, and are made under it, because they prescribe the framework itself. In states with written constitutions the rules are of course to be found in the text of the constitution, which, typically, will also contain provisions as to how they may be changed. Generally the mechanisms under which the framework may be changed are different from those by which ordinary laws, not part of the framework, may be repealed or amended; and the mechanisms will be stricter than those in place for the alteration of ordinary law.

But in Britain the rules establishing the framework possess, on the face of it, no different character from any other statute law. The requirement of elections at least every five years may in theory be altered by amending legislation almost as readily   though the 'almost' is important – as a provision defining dangerous dogs. The conventions under which Cabinet Government is carried on could in theory be changed with no special rules at all, as could any of the norms by which the Government possesses the authority to govern. The rules by which the power of a Government is conferred are in effect the same as the rules by which the Government may legislate upon other matters after it has gained power.

Parliament ... possesses what we may indeed call a political sovereignty. It is a sovereignty which cannot be objected to, save at the price of assaulting democracy itself. But it is not a constitutional sovereignty; it does not have the status of what earlier I called a sovereign text, of the kind found in states with written constitutions. Ultimate sovereignty rests, in every civilised constitution, not with those who wield governmental power, but in the conditions under which they are permitted to do so. The constitution, not the Parliament, is in this sense sovereign.

Can Parliament limit its own powers?

According to orthodox theory, Parliament cannot limit its own powers. Parliament can expressly repeal any Act which it has previously passed, and, by the doctrine of implied repeal, if there is any inconsistency between the provisions of two different statues, the later statute is deemed impliedly to repeal any inconsistent provisions of the earlier statute. No Parliament can protect its enactments from future express or implied repeal. As Munro explains:

It is evident that, if every succeeding Parliament is to enjoy the same degree of legislative authority as its predecessors, then attempts to bind subsequent Parliaments do not succeed. Acts which purport to bind later Parliaments, assuming Dicey was correct in his view, are not invalid, but merely ineffective (like, in varying degrees many other provisions) and, like all other enactments, liable to repeal.[32]

Notes

1 There is a clear distinction between three ways in which, theoretically, future Parliaments could be bound: first, they could be bound as to the substance, the *content* of future enactments; secondly, a requirement could be imposed that any legislation on a certain subject must bear a particular *form* (for example, use express words); or thirdly that a piece of legislation will be valid only if passed in a certain *manner*, for example, by a two-thirds majority, or with the approval of some outside body. The decisions usually cited for the proposition that Parliament cannot bind its successors in either way are *Vauxhall Estates v Liverpool Corporation* [1932] 1 KB 733 and *Ellen Street Estates v Minister of Health* [1934] 1 KB 590, CA, which, as Munro states:

'... concerned a provision in the Acquisition of Land (Assessment of Compensation) Act 1919 which, in regulating the compensation to be paid when land was compulsorily acquired, said that if land was acquired under the terms of any other statute, then so far as inconsistent with this Act those provisions shall cease to have or shall nor have effect. These words could be read as an attempt to preclude repeal, and since the compensation allowed for under the later Housing Act 1925 was less generous, it was in the interests of the companies involved in the two cases to plead the invalidity of the 1925 Act on that ground.'[33]

The argument was rejected by the courts. In *Vauxhall Estates* it was said (*per* Avory J):

---

32 Munro (1987), *op cit*, pp 86–87.
33 *Ibid*, p 91.

It must be admitted that such a suggestion as that is inconsistent with the principle of the constitution of this country. Speaking for myself, I should certainly hold, until the contrary were decided, that no Act of Parliament can effectively provide that no future Act shall interfere with its provisions.

In the *Ellen Street Estate* case, it was said (*per* Maugham LJ):

The legislature cannot, according to our constitution, bind itself as to the form of subsequent legislation and it is impossible for Parliament to enact that in a subsequent statute dealing with the same subject-matter there can be no implied repeal. If in a subsequent Act Parliament chooses to make it plain that the earlier statute is being to some extent repealed, effect must be given to that intention just because it is the will of the legislature [(1934) 1 KB 590 at 597].

2   It should be noted that Avory J is hardly bullish about his view of sovereignty. He states only that he would hold it 'until the contrary were decided'.

3   Neither case dealt with an attempt by Parliament to impose the requirement that any future legislation on the same subject must bear a particular *form*. Hence Bradley and Wade's comment that 'Maugham LJ went far beyond the actual situation' in stating that such an attempt would fail. They also note that there were only 'very weak grounds for suggesting that in 1919 Parliament had been attempting to bind its successors'.[34] The decisions were hardly surprising therefore, in the circumstances. Munro agrees, remarking: 'It should, however, be said that the *dicta* in [these] cases hardly settle the question finally with regard to all possible circumstances. It is at best doubtful whether, in that instance, Parliament had intended to prevent repeal, and it was scarcely an issue which would tempt judges to break new ground.'[35]

It seems therefore that the traditionally cited authority for the proposition that Parliament cannot bind itself as to either form or substance is not conclusive. The two possibilities will therefore now be considered in more detail.

Attempts to bind as to the substance of future legislation

The Acts of Union with Scotland (1707) and Ireland (1800) expressed certain aspects of the constitutions of the newly created states to be fixed, variously, 'for ever', for 'all time coming' or as 'established and ascertained for ever'.[36] The theory behind the argument that certain aspects of the Act of Union are not susceptible to repeal by the UK Parliament is simple. The Act was passed not by the UK Parliament but by the English and Scottish Parliaments.[37] By passing the Act, they abolished themselves and created a successor which was constituted from the start as limited by the provisions of the Act which created it. The problem with this theory is that, as Munro notes, the UK Parliament appears to have felt free to enact, and the courts appear to have felt themselves compelled to give effect to, legislation derogating from virtually all the fundamental principles of the Act of Union with Ireland and many of those contained in the Scottish Union Act.[38] However, it appears that the Scottish judiciary, at least, may regard certain aspects of the Act of Union with Scotland as immune from ordinary repeal.

---

34   Bradley and Wade, *op cit*, p 77.
35   *Munro* (1999), *op cit*, p 160.
36   For a general discussion of these Acts, see Munro (1999), *op cit*, pp 137–42.
37   Respectively, the Union with England Act 1707 and the Union with Scotland Act 1706.
38   Munro (1999), *op cit*, Chapter 4.

MacCormick v Lord Advocate 1953 SC 396

The Lord President (Cooper): ... The principle of the unlimited sovereignty of Parliament is a distinctively English principle which has no counterpart in Scottish constitutional law ... Considering that the Union legislation extinguished the Parliaments of Scotland and England and replaced them by a new Parliament, I have difficulty in seeing why it should have been supposed that the new Parliament of Great Britain must inherit all the peculiar characteristics of the English Parliament but none of the Scottish Parliament, as if all that happened in 1707 was that Scottish representatives were admitted to the Parliament of England. That is not what was done. Further, the Treaty and the associated legislation, by which the Parliament of Great Britain was brought into being as the successor of the separate Parliaments of Scotland and England, contain some clauses which expressly reserve to the Parliament of Great Britain powers of subsequent modification, and other clauses which either contain no such power or emphatically exclude subsequent alteration by declarations that the provision shall be fundamental and unalterable in all time coming, or declarations of a like effect. I have never been able to understand how it is possible to reconcile with elementary canons of construction the adoption by the English constitutional theorists of the same attitude to these markedly different types of provisions.

The Lord Advocate conceded this point by admitting that the Parliament of Great Britain 'could not' repeal or alter such 'fundamental and essential' conditions ... I have not found in the Union legislation any provision that the Parliament of Great Britain should be 'absolutely sovereign' in the sense that that Parliament should be free to alter the Treaty at will ...

Notes

1   The Lord President went on to find the issue non-justiciable: 'The making of decisions upon what must essentially be a political matter is no part of the function of the court, and is highly undesirable that it should be.'

2   It is interesting to note that, in the devolution legislation granting differing measures of self-government to Scotland, Wales and Northern Ireland (considered in Chapter 1 of this Part), Parliament chose to make a deliberate statement affirming its continuing sovereignty over the areas devolved to the subordinate legislatures created. Whether, despite such statements, Parliament has, as a matter of political reality, and perhaps as a matter of constitutional convention, ceded sovereignty at least over the areas devolved to the Scottish Parliament is considered in Chapter 1.

3   By contrast with the devolved areas, it is clear that when it came to granting independence to former colonies, Parliament clearly purported to divest itself of authority to legislate at all in respect of them. Section 2 of the Canada Act provides that, 'No Act of the Parliament of the UK passed after the Constitution Act 1982 (Canada) comes into force shall extend to Canada as part of its law'. No one doubts that the Canadian courts would ignore any legislation subsequently passed by the UK Parliament which purported to extend to Canada, but how would the British courts react? In *Manuel v Attorney-General* [1983] Ch 77, a case concerning the issue of whether the Canada Act had itself been properly passed, the following opinion was given (*per* Megarry VC).

Manuel v Attorney-General [1983] Ch 77, 87, 88

I do not think that, as a matter of law, it makes any difference if the Act in question purports to apply outside the UK. It matters not if a convention had grown up that the UK Parliament would not legislate for that colony without the consent of the colony. Such a convention would not limit the powers of Parliament, and if Parliament legislated in breach of the convention, 'the courts could not hold the Act of Parliament invalid': (*Madzimbamuto v Lardner-Burke* [1969] I AC 645, 723). Similarly if the other country is a foreign state which has never been British, I do not think that any

English court would or could declare the Act *ultra vires* and void. No doubt the Act would normally be ignored by the foreign state and would not be enforced by it, but that would not invalidate the Act in this country. Those who infringed it could not claim that it was void if proceedings within the jurisdiction were taken against them. Legal validity is one thing, enforceability is another … Plainly, once statute has granted independence to a country, the repeal of the statute will not make the country dependent once more; what is done is done, and is not undone by revoking the authority to do it. Heligoland did not in 1953 again become British. But if Parliament then passes an Act applying to such a country, I cannot see why that Act should not be in the some position as an Act applying to what has always been a foreign country, namely, an Act which the English courts will recognise and apply but one which the other country will in all probability ignore.

Notes

1   Munro cites this *dicta* with approval, to support his view that if, using Sir Ivor Jennings' example, a law was passed in the UK Parliament making it an offence for Frenchmen to smoke in the streets of Paris, 'English courts, if a guilty Frenchman could be apprehended while visiting Folkestone, would enforce it'.[39] It should be noted however that Megarry VC's remarks were strictly *obiter* and that the Court of Appeal did not take the opportunity to endorse them.

2   Lord Denning, in *Blackburn v Attorney-General* [1971] 1 WLR 137, considers the case of the Acts 'which have granted independence to the dominions and territories overseas'. He asks: 'Can anyone imagine that Parliament could or would reverse those laws and take away their independence? Most clearly not. Freedom once given cannot be taken away. Legal theory must give way to practical politics [p 140].' Megarry VC in *Manuel*, however, opined that 'it is clear from the context that Lord Denning was using the word "could" in the sense of "could effectively"; I cannot read it as meaning "could as a matter of abstract law"' (p 89). *Is* this clear?

3   The case of *Madzimbamuto v Lardner Burke* [1969] 1 AC 526 concerned the attempt by Parliament to reassert its right to legislate for Southern Rhodesia, after that country, having 'in practice enjoyed self-government and legislative autonomy for many years'[40] unilaterally declared full independence. The Privy Council found that the UK Parliament was, as a matter of law, still competent to legislate for Rhodesia. It should be noted, however, that there had, in that case, been no formal renunciation by Parliament of legislative competence, along the lines of s 2 of the Canada Act. This case did not therefore really answer the question whether Parliament can deprive itself of legislative competence; it stated only that the unilateral act of a dependant territory could not do so, a scarcely surprising finding.

Attempts to bind as to the manner and/or form of future legislation

Evidence from decided cases

Here, we look at the courts' likely response to attempts by one Parliament to provide that any subsequent Acts dealing with a given subject must have a particular form, for example, bear certain words, or be passed in a certain manner, for example, with a two-thirds majority or with the consent of some outside body. For example, s 1 of the Northern Ireland Act 1998[41] provides that Northern Ireland will not cease to be

---

39   Munro (1999), *op cit*, p 153.
40   *Ibid*, p 151.
41   This is the Act which puts in place the legislative framework for the Good Friday Agreement (see further Part I Chapter 1); the provision it contains was previously set out in s 1 of the Northern Ireland Constitution Act 1973.

part of her Majesty's dominions without the consent of the majority of the people of Northern Ireland voting in a poll. How would the courts treat this provision? Some guidance may be gleaned from cases in which the Privy Council or courts in other common law jurisdictions have had to rule on the lawfulness of such provisions. One of the key cases is *Attorney-General for New South Wales v Trethowan* [1932] AC 526, PC, a decision of the Privy Council which concerned the New South Wales legislature. That legislature was subject to s 5 of the Colonial Laws Validity Act 1865, which provided:

> ... every representative legislature shall, in respect to the colony under its jurisdiction, have, and be deemed at all times to have had, full power to make laws respecting the constitution, power and procedure of such legislature; provided that such laws shall have been passed in such manner and form as may from time to time be required by any Act of Parliament, letters patent, order in council, or colonial law for the time being in force in the said colony.

The facts were as follows.

> In 1929 the Parliament of New South Wales passed an Act which provided that no Bill for abolishing the upper house of the legislature (the Legislative Council) should be presented for the royal assent unless it had been approved at a referendum by a majority of the electors. [It did this by amending the Constitution Act 1902, previously passed by that Parliament, adding a new s 7A.] It was further provided that this requirement of a referendum might not itself be repealed except by the same process. The aim of the right-wing Government which sponsored the legislation was to 'entrench' the position of the upper house, which the Labour Party had declared its intention to abolish. In 1930, however, a new Parliament was elected in which the Labour Party held the majority of seats in the lower house. Two Bills were passed through both Houses, the first purporting to repeal the referendum requirement, and the second purporting to abolish the Legislative Council. Neither Bill was submitted to the electors, and accordingly two members of the threatened Legislative Council sought an injunction to restrain the submission of these Bills for royal assent. The Supreme Court of New South Wales granted the injunction and the decision was appealed to the High Court of Australia.[42]

Attorney-General of New South Wales v Trethowan (1931) 44 CLR 401

Dixon J: ... This question must be answered upon a consideration of the true meaning and effect of the written instruments from which the Parliament of New South Wales derives its legislative power. It is not to be determined by the direct application of the doctrine of parliamentary sovereignty, which gives to the Imperial Parliament its supremacy over the law. It is the law derived ... from the Imperial Parliament which gives to the Legislature of New South Wales its powers, and it is that law which determines the extent of those powers and the conditions which govern their exercise. The incapacity of the British Legislature to limit its own power otherwise than by transferring a portion or abdicating the whole of its sovereignty has ... been explained as a necessary consequence of a true conception of sovereignty. But in any case it depends upon considerations which have no application to the Legislature of New South Wales, which is not a sovereign body and has a purely statutory origin. Because of the supremacy of the Imperial Parliament over the law, the Courts merely apply its legislative enactments and do not examine their validity, but because the law over which the Imperial Parliament is supreme determines the powers of a legislature in a Dominion, the Courts must decide upon the validity as well as the application of the statutes of that legislature.

---

42 Munro (1999), *op cit*, p 158.

It must not be supposed, however, that all difficulties would vanish if the full doctrine of parliamentary supremacy could be invoked. An Act of the British Parliament which contained a provision that no Bill repealing any part of the Act including the part so restraining its own repeal should be presented for the royal assent unless the Bill were first approved by the electors, would have the force of law until the Sovereign actually did assent to a Bill for its repeal. In strictness it would be an unlawful proceeding to present such a Bill for the royal assent before it had been approved by the electors. If, before the Bill received the assent of the Crown, it was found possible, as appears to have been done in this appeal, to raise for judicial decision the question whether it was lawful to present the Bill for that assent, the Courts would be bound to pronounce it unlawful to do so. Moreover, if it happened that, notwithstanding the statutory inhibition, the Bill did receive the royal assent although it was not submitted to the electors, the Courts might be called upon to consider whether the supreme legislative power in respect of the matter had in truth been exercised in the manner required for its authentic expression and by the elements in which it had come to reside.

The High Court dismissed the appeal and the case then went to the Privy Council.

Attorney-General of New South Wales v Trethowan [1932] AC 526, PC

Viscount Sankey LC: The question to be determined is in substance whether the legislature of the State of New South Wales has power to abolish the Legislative Council of the State or to alter its constitution or powers without first taking a referendum of the electors upon the matter ...

The appellants urge: (1) That the King, with the advice and consent of the Legislative Council and the Legislative Assembly, had full power to enact a Bill repealing s 7A (2). That sub-s 6 of s 7A of the Constitution Act is void, because: (a) The New South Wales legislature has no power to shackle or control its successors, the New South Wales constitution being in substance an uncontrolled constitution; (b) It is repugnant to s 4 of the Constitution Statute of 1855; (c) It is repugnant to s 5 of the Colonial Laws Validity Act, 1865.

For the respondents it was contended: (1) That s 7A was a valid amendment of the constitution of New South Wales, validly enacted in the manner prescribed, and was legally binding in New South Wales. (2) That the legislature of New South Wales was given by Imperial statutes [that is, those passed by the UK Parliament] plenary power to alter the constitution, powers and procedure of such legislature. (3) That when once the legislature had altered either the constitution or powers and procedure, then the constitution and powers and procedure as they previously existed ceased to exist, and were replaced by the new constitution and powers. (4) That the only possible limitations of this plenary power were: (a) it must be exercised according to the manner and form prescribed by any Imperial or colonial law, and (b) the legislature must continue a representative legislature according to the definition of the Colonial Laws Validity Act, 1865. (5) That the addition of s 7A to the Constitution had the effect of: (a) making the legislative body consist thereafter of the King, the Legislative Council, the Assembly and the people for the purpose of the constitutional enactments therein described, or (b) imposing a manner and form of legislation in reference to these constitutional enactments which thereafter became binding on the legislature by virtue of the Colonial Laws Validity Act, 1865, until repealed in the manner and mode prescribed. (6) That the power of altering the constitution conferred by s 4 of the Constitution Statute, 1855, must be read subject to the Colonial Laws Validity Act, 1865, and that in particular the limitation as to manner and form prescribed by the 1865 Act must be governed by subsequent amendments to the constitution, whether purporting to be made in the earlier Act or not ...

...The answer depends in their Lordships' view entirely upon a consideration of the meaning and effect of s 5 of the Act of 1865, read in conjunction with s 4 of the Constitution Statute, assuming that latter section still to possess some operative effect. Whatever operative effect it may still possess must, however, be governed by and be subject to such conditions as are to be found in s 5 of the Act of 1865 in regard to the particular kind of laws within the purview of that section. Section 5 is therefore the master section to consider for the purpose here in hand.

... Reading section [5] as a whole, it gives to the legislature of New South Wales certain powers, subject to this, that in respect of certain laws they can only become effectual provided they have been passed in such manner and form as may from time to time be required by any Act still on the statute book. Beyond that, the words 'manner and form' are amply wide enough to cover an enactment providing that a Bill is to be submitted to the electors and that unless and until a majority of the electors voting approve the Bill it shall not be presented to the Governor for His Majesty's assent.

In their Lordships' opinion the legislature of New South Wales had power under s 5 of the Act of 1865 to enact the Constitution (Legislative Council) Amendment Act, 1929, and thereby to introduce s 7A into the Constitution Act, 1902. In other words, the legislature had power to alter the constitution of New South Wales by enacting that Bills relating to specified kind or kinds of legislation (eg, abolishing the Legislative Council or altering its constitution or powers, or repealing or amending that enactment) should not be presented for the Royal assent until approved by the electors in a prescribed manner. There is here no question of repugnancy. The enactment of the Act of 1929 was simply an exercise by the legislature of New South Wales of its power (adopting the words of s 5 of the Act of 1865) to make laws respecting the constitution, powers and procedure of the authority competent to make the laws for New South Wales.

The whole of s 7A was competently enacted. It was *intra vires* s 5 of the Act of 1865, and was (again adopting the words of s 5) a colonial law for the time being in force when the Bill to repeal s 7A was introduced in the Legislative Council.

The question then arises, could that Bill, a repealing Bill, after its passage through both chambers, be lawfully presented for the Royal assent without having first received the approval of the electors in the prescribed manner?

In their Lordships' opinion, the Bill could not lawfully be so presented. The proviso in the second sentence of s 5 of the Act of 1865 states a condition which must be fulfilled before the legislature can validly exercise its power to make the kind of laws which are referred to in that sentence. In order that s 7A may be repealed (in other words, in order that that particular law 'respecting the constitution, powers and procedure' of the legislature may be validly made) the law for that purpose must have been passed in the manner required by s 7A, a colonial law for the time being in force in New South Wales.

... A Bill, within the scope of sub-s 6 of s 7A, which received the Royal assent without having been approved by the electors in accordance with that section, would not be a valid Act of the legislature. It would be *ultra vires* s 5 of the Act of 1865. Indeed, the presentation of the Bill to the Governor without such approval would be the commission of an unlawful act. In the result, their Lordships are of opinion that s 7A of the Constitution Act, 1902, was valid and was in force when the two Bills under consideration were passed through the Legislative Council and the Legislative Assembly. Therefore these Bills could not be presented to the Governor for His Majesty's assent unless and until a majority of the electors voting had approved them.

Note
Munro suggests that there are two possible views of this case:

The first is that there is a general rule that legislation may be enacted only in such manner and form as is laid down by law, and that the UK Parliament is just as subject to that rule as was the New South Wales legislature. This view gains support from the *dicta* in the second paragraph of Dixon J's judgment in the High Court. However, the opposing view is that the decision has no relevance at all. The Privy Council said that the case depended 'entirely upon a consideration of the meaning and effect of s 5 of the Act of 1865' [*ibid*, at 539], and it is hard to see how this can tell us anything about the UK Parliament, whose powers are not defined in or derived from any statute [(1999), *op cit*, p 158].

Questions

1   In relation to the Northern Ireland Act 1998, how would the courts react if:

    (a) the UK Parliament passed an Act ceding Northern Ireland to the Republic of
        Ireland, and the Act did not recite that a majority of Northern Ireland citizens
        had approved the change in a poll?

    (b) the UK Parliament passed an Act repealing the s 1 guarantee without taking a
        poll?

2   In relation to (b), would it make any difference if s 1 had stated that its own
    provisions could not be repealed without taking a poll?

Manner and form: the theory

A number of writers have taken the view that while Parliament may not bind itself in
such a way as to prevent itself outright from changing the law in a given area (a
content-based restriction), it may pass legislation (as did the New South Wales
Parliament) which establishes that future legislation on a given area must conform to a
'manner and form' requirements laid down in the original statute. As Geoffrey
Marshall puts it:

> Parliament ... might conceivably bind the future or circumscribe the freedom of future legislators,
> not by laying down blanket prohibitions or attempting to enact a fundamental Bill of Rights, but by
> using their authority to provide different forms and procedures for legislation. A referendum or a
> joint sitting, for example, might be prescribed before certain things could be done. Or a two-thirds
> majority. Or a 75% or 80% majority. If it is also provided that any repeal of such provisions should
> not be by simple majority, the courts may be able to protect the arrangements laid down by
> declaring in suitable proceedings that any purported repeal by simple majority of a protected
> provision is *ultra vires* as being not, in the sense required by law, an 'Act of Parliament'. In this
> finding they would not be in any way derogating from parliamentary sovereignty but protecting
> Parliament's authority from usurpation by those not entitled for the purpose in hand to exercise
> it.[43]

This view, had, by the 1970s received support from a number of distinguished
commentators.[44] RFV Heuston has produced a well known formulation of the theory.

RFV Heuston, *Essays in Constitutional Law*, 2nd edn (1964), pp 6–7

It is suggested that the new view can be summarised thus:

(1) Sovereignty is a legal concept: the rules which identify the sovereign and prescribe its
    composition and functions are logically prior to it.

(2) There is a distinction between rules which govern, on the one hand, (a) the composition, and
    (b) the procedure, and, on the other hand, (c) the area of power, of a sovereign legislature.

(3) The courts have jurisdiction to question the validity of an alleged Act of Parliament on grounds
    2(a) and 2(b), but not on ground 2(c).

(4) This jurisdiction is exercisable either before or after the Royal Assent has been signified – in
    the former case by way of injunction, in the latter by way of declaratory judgment.

---

43 *Constitutional Theory* (1971), p 42.
44 RFV Heuston, *Essays in Constitutional Law*, 1st edn (1961), 2nd edn (1964), Chapter 1; G
    Marshall, *Parliamentary Sovereignty and the Commonwealth* (1957); *ibid*, Chapter 3; JDB Mitchell,
    Constitutional Law, 2nd edn (1968), Chapter 4; and SA de Smith, *Constitutional and
    Administrative Law*, 2nd edn (1973), Chapter 4.

Notes

1   The major difficulty with this view is that it does not provide an answer as to *what kinds* of laws Parliament should be able to protect in this manner. As Marshall's comments show, this kind of restriction is usually considered in relation to the protection of a Bill of Rights or other aspects of the constitutional order. The difficulty is that the assertion that Parliament can bind itself as to manner and form is not by its nature inherently limited in this way but is put *in general terms*, as if any law passed by Parliament could be thus protected. The problem with such a view, of course, is that to grant such a power to Parliament would amount to a direct and comprehensive threat to democracy. For if Parliament could, whenever it wished, provide that a given law could only be repealed by a two-thirds majority, then what would stop one Parliament, controlled, say, by a Conservative government, from passing a Finance Act cutting income tax to 20% and including a provision that the Act could not be repealed or modified except by that majority? In such a case, a new government, elected on a policy of increasing spending and raising tax, would find a statute increasing the level of income tax, but passed in the ordinary manner, declared *ultra vires* in the courts.

Thus, the rule that Parliament cannot bind itself is not merely a technical matter of constitutional law: it protects the democratic rights of future majorities to reverse the decisions of previous ones. Any proponent of the 'manner and form' school must therefore incorporate within his or her argument some suggested definition as to the areas of law which Parliament should be able to protect and those which it must *not* be able to.

2   We have been discussing a possible 'rule' or 'law' that Parliament cannot bind itself. What is the source of this law? The answer, interestingly enough, is directly related to the question of whether Parliament can change or 'break' this law. As Bradley notes:

... In the absence of a written constitution for the UK, where is the source of the legal rule that there are no limits on the legislative capacity of Parliament and that the courts may not review the validity of legislation? For reasons of logic, we should not expect to find this rule created by an Act of Parliament. As was said by the jurist Salmond, 'No statute can confer this power upon Parliament, for this would be to assume and act on the very power to be conferred' [*Salmond on Jurisprudence* (PJ Fitzgerald (ed)), 12th edn, (1966), p 111] ... It is to the decisions of the courts that we must look to discover propositions about the legislative powers of Parliament.[45]

3   Sir Ivor Jennings has argued on this point as follows: the rules governing sovereignty are derived from the common law; Parliament can change the common law in any way; therefore Parliament can change the rules which relate to its own sovereignty.[46] Wade has replied to this argument as follows.

HWR Wade, 'The basis of legal sovereignty' [1955] CLJ 186–89

At the heart of the matter lies the question whether the rule of common law which says that the courts will enforce statutes can itself be altered by a statute. Adherents of the traditional theory, who hold that future Parliaments cannot be bound, are here compelled to answer 'no'. For if they answer 'yes', they must yield to Jennings' reasoning.

But to deny that Parliament can alter this particular Rule of Law is not so daring as it may seem at first sight; for the sacrosanctity of the rule is an inexorable corollary of Parliament's continuing sovereignty. If the one proposition is asserted, the other must be conceded. Nevertheless some

45   Bradley, *op cit*, p 87.
46   This formulation of Jennings' argument is given by Wade, *op cit*, p 103.

further justification is called for, since there must be something peculiar about a rule of common law which can stand against a statute.

The peculiarity lies in this, that the rule enjoining judicial obedience to statutes is one of the fundamental rules upon which the legal system depends ...

Once this truth is grasped, the dilemma is solved. For if no statute can establish the rule that the courts obey Acts of Parliament, similarly no statute can alter or abolish that rule. The rule is above and beyond the reach of statute, as Salmond so well explains, because it is itself the source of the authority of statute. This puts it into a class by itself among rules of common law, and the apparent paradox that it is unalterable by Parliament turns out to be a truism. The rule of judicial obedience is in one sense a rule of common law, but in another sense – which applies to no other rule of common law – it is the ultimate political fact upon which the whole system of legislation hangs. Legislation owes its authority to the rule: the rule does not owe its authority to legislation. To say that Parliament can change the rule, merely because it can change any other rule, is to put the cart before the horse.

What Salmond calls the 'ultimate legal principle' is therefore a rule which is unique in being unchangeable by Parliament – it is changed by revolution, not by legislation; it lies in the keeping of the courts, and no Act of Parliament can take it from them. This is only another way of saying that it is always for the courts, in the last resort, to say what is a valid Act of Parliament; and that the decision of this question is not determined by any rule of law which can be laid down or altered by any authority outside the courts. It is simply a political fact. If this is accepted, there is a fallacy in Jennings' argument that the law requires the courts to obey any rule enacted by the legislature, including a law which alters this law itself. For this law itself is ultimate and unalterable by any legal authority.

Notes

1   Bradley notes the core of Wade's argument, 'If no statute can establish the rule that the courts obey Acts of Parliament, similarly no statute can alter or abolish that rule', and goes on: '... Wade's argument at this crucial point depends for its logical strength upon the word "similarly" (consider the argument "No person can bring his own life into being; similarly, no person can bring his own life to an end"), and it does not take adequate account of the fact that Parliament's legislative power includes power to make constitutional changes.'[47]

2   A more thorough examination of the argument that sovereignty is a common law doctrine and may therefore be changed by the judiciary has been provided by Goldsworthy. His explanation depends upon an understanding of Hart's theory of a Rule of Recognition, advanced in his seminal work, *The Concept of Law* (1961).

JD Goldsworthy, *The Sovereignty of Parliament: History and Philosophy* (1999), pp 237–41, 243–46 (extracts)

Fundamental human laws can come into existence either by express agreement among the members of a community, or at least the most powerful of them, as in the case of the adoption of a written constitution, or by the gradual development of customs, as in the case of rules of succession governing traditional monarchical systems. In both cases, the continued existence of such laws depends on their being accepted as binding, at least by people who are able to force others to comply with them. To accept that such a law is binding is to have what Hart called the 'internal point of view' towards the law: it is to believe that there are good reasons for insisting that it be obeyed, and for criticising those who fail to obey it.

Hart argued that for a legal system to exist, its most fundamental laws must be accepted as binding by its most senior officials, and the system as a whole must be generally obeyed, for whatever

47   Bradley, *op cit,* p 88.

reason, by those subject to it. Indeed, the most fundamental laws of any legal system simply are whatever laws are accepted as binding, and routinely applied in administering the system, by its most senior officials. The most important of these laws is a 'rule of recognition', which specifies the criteria that determine what other laws should be recognised as members of the system or, in other words, as valid laws. While the existence, as valid laws, of all the other laws of the system depends on their satisfying those criteria, the existence of the rule of recognition itself depends on its being accepted as binding by the most senior officials of the system, and on their decisions being generally obeyed by everyone else. Those officials must adopt the internal point of view, but ordinary citizens need not.

According to Hart, the content of the rule of recognition, in any legal system, is entirely a matter of fact. It is whatever rule that system's most senior officials, including its judges, do in fact accept and apply in identifying valid laws of the system, irrespective of its merits from the perspective of political morality. That we might regard as morally repugnant the rule of recognition actually accepted and applied by the most senior officials of some legal system cannot alter the fact that it is a fundamental law of that system. If it confers sovereign law-making authority upon some person or institution, their unworthiness to exercise such authority cannot diminish the fact that they have it. Denying that fact would be as futile as denying that Hitler was Chancellor of Germany, because of the iniquity of his actions.

In Britain, the most senior legal officials, including judges, have for a very long time recognized as legally valid whatever statutes Parliament has enacted, and have often said that they are bound to do so. In applying Hart's theory to the British legal system, the ease for regarding the sovereignty of Parliament as a central component of its rule of recognition seems clear cut, as Hart himself apparently believed. Fear that Parliament might one day grossly abuse its authority might be a good reason to change the rule, but that is a different matter.

[Having set out this framework, Goldsworthy then goes on to consider what he regards as the fallacious argument that parliamentary sovereignty is judge-made law. While in doing so, he in part agrees with Wade in viewing the law of sovereignty as a unique kind of rule, he rejects Wade's view that it cannot be changed, save by revolution.]

Now it is true that Parliament did not, and could not, confer sovereign authority on itself by statute. But it is less often noted that for similar reasons the doctrine of parliamentary sovereignty cannot be a product of judicial law-making. The argument that it is judge-made consists of four steps: first, that there are only two kinds of law in Britain, statute law and common law: secondly, that the doctrine could not have been established by statute, because that would have been question-begging: thirdly, that it must therefore be a matter of common law: and fourthly, that the common law is judge-made law.

The argument fails because of the conjunction of the first and fourth steps. To say both that there are only two types of law in Britain, statute law and common law, and that the common law has been made by judges, is to say that all law in Britain has been deliberately made, either by Parliament, or by the judges. But if so, what could be the legal source of the judges' authority to make the common law? It could not be statute, because that would create a vicious circle (since the point of the argument is that Parliament's authority to enact statutes was conferred by the judges). The only alternative consistent with the argument is to think that the judges conferred authority on themselves. But that would be just as question-begging as the discredited idea that Parliament conferred authority on itself by statute.

The source of these logical difficulties is the Hobbesian assumption that every law, including those conferring authority on Parliament, and on the judges, must originally have been deliberately made by someone, and if it was not Parliament, then it must have been the judges. That assumption leads to the question-begging conclusion that either Parliament, or the judges, originally conferred legal authority on themselves. But the truth is that the judges are no more qualified than Parliament to be regarded as a Hobbesian sovereign, ultimately responsible for the creation of all law. The authority of either Parliament, or the judges, or both, must be based on laws that neither was solely responsible for creating. Those more fundamental laws are what Hart called the 'secondary rules' of the legal system, comprising rules of recognition, change, and adjudication. A necessary condition for the existence of such rules is a consensus among the most senior officials of the legal system, in all three branches of government, legislative, executive, and judicial. This avoids the question-begging that is implicit in any one branch of government purporting to confer law-making authority on itself. Parliament's sovereignty was not created by the judges alone, and its continued existence depends only partly, and not solely, on their willingness to accept it.

A common mistake in the interpretation of Hart's theory is to think that the rule of recognition is constituted by the practices and convictions of the judiciary alone. This is clearly not what Hart meant in the first edition of *The Concept of Law*. In describing the rule of recognition, he continually referred to its being constituted by the practices of legal officials in general: it 'rests simply on the fact that it is accepted and used as such a rule in *the judicial and other official* operations of a [legal] system whose rules are generally obeyed' [at p 117, emphasis added]. The reason why Hart insisted that no legal system can exist unless its officials adopt the internal point of view towards its most fundamental rules, and particularly its rule of recognition, is that 'the characteristic unity and continuity of a legal system' depends on the acceptance of 'common standards of legal validity' [at p 113].

He pointed out that if only some judges accepted the sovereignty of Parliament, and they made no criticisms of those who did not, ordinary citizens would sooner or later be faced with contradictory legal directives. The legal system would disintegrate into chaos. But this reasoning extends to all of the most senior officials of the system: the same disastrous consequences would flow from a rift between the judiciary as a whole, and the other branches of government.

. . . It follows that either the first or the fourth steps of the fallacious argument previously criticized must be rejected, either parliamentary sovereignty is a matter of neither statute law nor common law, or it is a common law doctrine that was not made by the judges. The second alternative is certainly arguable. The term 'common law' is now somewhat ambiguous. Until relatively recently, it meant customary law, which judges discovered and enunciated but did not make, whereas today, it usually means judge-made law. It is wrong to describe the doctrine of parliamentary sovereignty as a matter of common law in the modern sense of judge-made law. But it can be described as a matter of common law in the old sense of the term, meaning a custom that the courts have recognized, but did not create, and therefore cannot unilaterally change. It is indeed a creature of custom – or at least, of custom among senior legal officials – that gradually evolved from the sovereignty of the medieval King. Nevertheless, it might help prevent confusion if the doctrine were not described as one of common law, because its nature and status are so different from those of all other common law doctrines, as we understand them today.

. . . It does not follow that the doctrine of parliamentary sovereignty cannot be changed. There are many examples of fundamental legal rules changing as a result of official consensus changing. In the Australia Act 1986 (UK), the United Kingdom Parliament relinquished its authority to alter Australian law. If it attempted to resume that authority by repealing the Act, Australian courts would almost certainly refuse to accept the validity of the repeal, even if this meant repudiating the doctrine of parliamentary sovereignty that they themselves accepted many years ago. But this change in the allegiance of Australian courts is part of a change in the allegiance of all senior legal officials, and citizens, in Australia, and would therefore be universally accepted there as legitimate. Indeed, a refusal by Australian courts to subscribe to that general change in allegiance would provoke political conflict between them and the other branches of government.

. . . Of course, a change in a fundamental legal rule has to start somewhere: someone has to initiate the requisite change in the official consensus that constitutes it. Parliament can do so, by enacting legislation such as the Australia Act, or the European Communities Act, provided that the courts are willing to accept the change. Alternatively, the courts can initiate change, provided that the other branches of government are willing to accept it. An example of this is the way in which the courts today are increasingly subjecting the exercise of royal prerogatives to judicial review. In past centuries, this would have been vehemently opposed by the executive branch of government, and blocked by legislation. The courts have been permitted to expand their authority to control the exercise of power by the executive government only because its attitudes, as well as their own, have changed.

It is sometimes suggested that any change in the fundamental rules of a legal system, brought about by a change in official consensus, must be described as 'extra-legal' or even 'revolutionary' [Wade, above]. This is debatable. There are important differences between abrupt changes to fundamental legal rules, imposed on many senior officials through their coercion or removal from office, and gradual changes resulting from a voluntary change of mind on their part in response to broader social developments. In the latter case, it may be appropriate to say that the rules have evolved legally. Be that as it may, there is nothing necessarily wrong with one group of officials attempting to initiate change in the fundamental rules of their legal system. But great caution is needed. If significant numbers of other officials are unlikely to agree with them, the result may be conflict endangering the stability of the system ... A unilateral rejection by British courts of the doctrine of parliamentary sovereignty is unlikely to be meekly accepted by the other branches of government. Instead, they are likely to condemn it as an illegitimate attempt to alter the currently accepted balance of power, in favour of the courts. By unsettling what has for centuries been regarded as settled, the courts would risk conflict with the other branches of government that might dangerously destabilize the legal system.

Note
In summary, then, Goldsworthy's view is that alterations of the law of sovereignty lie beyond the unilateral action of either Parliament or the courts, since the law of sovereignty was produced by neither acting alone. However, Goldsworthy avoids Wade's implausible attitude that the law of parliamentary sovereignty is unalterable, save by revolution. Wade's view was placed in some difficulty by the decision in *Factortame*, which, as we have noted, amounted to a change to that law, whereas Goldsworthy is able to encompass it as an example of a change 'tacitly agreed' between Parliament and the courts.[48] The impact of that decision on traditional understandings of sovereignty is further explored below.

May Parliament now bind itself as to the form of future legislation? Recent evidence

As seen above, the literature in this area tends to discuss whether Parliament can bind itself as to 'manner and form', as if the two types of restrictions may readily be lumped together. In fact, they are very distinct, in two ways. First of all, there is now clear evidence that Parliament *can* bind itself, at least as to the *form* of future legislation; there is no such evidence in relation to restrictions as to *manner*. Cases from the Commonwealth, such as *Attorney-General for New South Wales v Trethowan* [1932] AC 526, PC (see above) are inconclusive when applied to the UK Parliament. Secondly, it should be recognised that a restriction based merely on form – that is, a requirement that a future statute must use express words in order to undo a previous statute – amounts to no real restriction upon the freedom of action of a future Parliament. It is a moment's work for a draftsman to insert such words into a statute. As Goldsworthy puts it, 'a Parliament that can only effectively legislate if it uses a particular form of words, to ensure that its intentions are unmistakeable, is still free to legislate whenever it wishes to do so'.[49] By contrast, a requirement, say, that a two-thirds majority must be

---

48 *Op cit*, at p 244.
49 Goldsworthy, *op cit*, p 245.

used to overturn a previous statute amounts to a very real fettering of future Parliaments, and thus a very real entrenchment of the provision in question, because such majorities, unlike the strokes of a draftsman's pen, are not at the disposal of a government.

What then is the evidence that Parliament may now restrict itself as to the *form* of future legislation? The clearest example relates to the European Communities Act 1972 and its interpretation in the case of *R v Secretary of State for Transport ex p Factortame (No 2)* [1992] 3 WLR 285. The case is considered in detail in the next chapter, but, in brief, s 2(4) European Communities Act 1972 (ECA) amounted to an attempt of some kind by the Parliament of 1972 to fetter its successors. Section 2(4) stated, 'any enactment passed *or to be passed* shall be construed and have effect subject to the foregoing provisions of this section' (emphasis added).

The 'foregoing provisions' were those that made European Community law enforceable in the UK. By saying that any enactment *to be passed*, that is any future enactment, must take effect 'subject to' the provisions of this Act, Parliament appeared to be suggesting that the courts must allow EC law to prevail over subsequent Acts of Parliament. This was clearly an attempt to suspend the normal doctrine of implied repeal – instead of any later statute which conflicted with EC law impliedly repealing it, such a later statute would have to either be 'construed', that is, interpreted so that it did not conflict with EC law, or if it could not be so interpreted, deprived of effect insofar as it conflicted with EC law (given effect 'subject to').

Parliament was quite evidently, therefore, trying to alter the rule of parliamentary sovereignty itself and the decision in *Factortame (No 2)* appears to indicate that the courts are quite willing to allow it to do so, quite contrary to Wade's view that 'this rule is ultimate and unalterable by any legal authority' (see above).

The case arose because the Merchant Shipping Act 1988 placed restrictions on the abilities of non-British fishermen to fish in British waters. As such it was in clear conflict with the non-discrimination principle of EC law. The House of Lords held that, notwithstanding the requirement that the Merchant Shipping Act postdated the European Communities Act 1972, the latter would prevail: the Merchant Shipping Act must be disapplied to the extent of its inconsistency with EC law.

The clear finding of law to be drawn from the decision is that if Parliament wishes to legislate contrary to EC law it must use express words, either instructing the court to disregard EC law when applying the particular statute, or, possibly, by repealing the ECA first. In any event, it is clear that the courts accepted that Parliament could change the law of sovereignty. As Lord Bridge remarked, the decision was not 'a novel and dangerous invasion by a community institution of the sovereignty of Parliament' because Parliament had 'voluntarily accepted' a diminution in its sovereignty by passing the ECA in 1972.

Recently however, Laws LJ, in his judgment in *Thoburn v Sunderland City Council* [2002] 1 CMLR 50 suggested, *obiter*, that in fact the restriction placed upon Parliament in relation to the ECA was not achieved by the Parliament of 1972, as Lord Bridge appeared to suggest, but by the common law:

Parliament cannot bind its successors by stipulating against repeal, wholly or partly, of the ECA. It cannot stipulate as to the manner and form of any subsequent legislation. It cannot stipulate against implied repeal any more than it can stipulate against express repeal. Thus there is nothing in the ECA which allows the Court of Justice, or any other institutions of the EU, to touch or qualify the conditions of Parliament's legislative supremacy in the United Kingdom. Not because the legislature chose not to allow it; because by our law it could not allow it. That being so, the legislative and judicial institutions of the EU cannot intrude upon those conditions. The British Parliament has not the authority to authorise any such thing. Being sovereign, it cannot abandon its sovereignty [para 59].

This, however, is not particularly persuasive. Laws LJ fails to draw the distinction between a mere restriction upon *form*, which, as argued above, leaves the legislature's freedom of action substantively unconstrained, and restrictions as to the *content* of acts or the manner of their passage. Moreover, if the UK Parliament is sovereign, he offers no justification as to why the courts, subordinate to Parliament precisely under that doctrine, may introduce a restriction upon form, while Parliament itself may not.

The other area in which Parliament may have limited itself as to form is in the area of those rights guaranteed under the European Convention on Human Rights, now incorporated into UK law under the Human Rights Act 1998 (HRA) (see further Part VI Chapter 1). The Act does not make any formal attempt to entrench itself. Indeed it provides that if any statutes contain provisions found to be inconsistent with any of the Convention rights, such statutes will remain valid and of full effect (ss 3(2)(b) and 4(6)). Section 4 states:

(1) Subsection (2) applies in any proceedings in which a court determines whether a provision of primary legislation is compatible with a Convention right.

(2) If the court is satisfied that the provision is incompatible with a Convention right, it may make a declaration of that incompatibility.

. . .

(6) A declaration under this section ('a declaration of incompatibility')—

(a) does not affect the validity, continuing operation or enforcement of the provision in respect of which it is given . . .

In part, the Act in effect simply confirms the orthodox constitutional position, that later statutes override previous inconsistent ones. In this respect, the HRA is of the same status as any other Act of Parliament although it introduces the innovation of the formal judicial declaration of incompatibility under ss 4 and 10. Such a declaration can trigger the parliamentary 'fast track' procedure for amending the offending legislation by means of secondary legislation but this leaves Parliament entirely free as to whether to remedy the incompatibility which the courts have found to exist.

However, in relation to statutes passed *prior* to the HRA, the Act provides for a departure from orthodoxy. Under the doctrine of implied repeal, one would expect, where it was found that a provision in a statute *pre-dating* the HRA was incompatible with one or more of the Convention rights, that the provision would be impliedly repealed. However, ss 3(2)(b) and 4(6) do not take this route: by stating that the provisions of *any* statute found to be incompatible with Convention rights remain valid and in force, they have the effect that the doctrine of implied repeal will not apply to the HRA. In other words, where a provision of an *earlier* statute is found to be incompatible with a Convention right, it will nevertheless remain in force. In this respect, then, the HRA makes a quite clear alteration to the normal rules of parliamentary sovereignty.

It may, however, make a further and more important alteration. Section 3(1) of the Act provides: 'So far as it is possible to do so, primary legislation and subordinate legislation must be read and given effect in a way which is compatible with the

Convention rights.' The meaning and effect of this provision were considered by the House of Lords in *R v A (No 2)* [2001] 2 Cr App R 21, now the leading decision on s 3. The case concerned the interpretation to be given to s 41 of the Youth Justice and Criminal Evidence Act 1999 which prohibited the giving of evidence in a rape trial of the woman's sexual history, including any previous sexual history with the alleged rapist, except in very limited circumstances.[50] This was thought to raise an issue of compatibility with Article 6 of the European Convention on Human Rights (ECHR) which provides:

1. In the determination of his civil rights and obligations or of any criminal charge against him, everyone is entitled to a fair and public hearing within a reasonable time by an independent and impartial tribunal established by law ...

3. Everyone charged with a criminal offence has the following, minimum rights:

...

   (d) to examine or have examined witnesses against him and to obtain the attendance and examination of witnesses on his behalf under the same conditions as witnesses against him ...

The argument essentially was that to refuse to allow the defence to admit evidence of previous sexual relations between the alleged victim and the defendant would violate the defendant's right to a fair trial. The House of Lords found first of all, 'that on ordinary principles of construction, s 41 of the Youth Justice and Criminal Evidence Act 1999 was *prima facie* capable of preventing an accused person from putting forward evidence critical to his defence and, thus construed, was incompatible with Article 6 of the ECHR' (headnote). The key part of s 41 was s 41(3)(c) which permitted evidence of the women's previous sexual history with the defendant where:

   (c) it is an issue of consent and the sexual behaviour of the complainant to which the evidence or question relates is alleged to have been, in any respect, so similar ... to any sexual behaviour of the complainant which ... took place as part of the event which is the subject matter of the charge against the accused ... that the similarity cannot reasonably be explained as a coincidence.

On its face, this allowed evidence to be given only in severely restricted circumstances. However, this was before the application of s 3(1) of the HRA.

R v A (No 2) [2001] 2 Cr App R 21 (extracts)

Lord Steyn: In my view ordinary methods of purposive construction of section 41(3)(c) cannot cure the problem of the excessive breadth of the section 41, read as a whole, so far as it relates to previous sexual experience between a complainant and the accused ...

On the other hand, the interpretative obligation under section 3 of the [HRA] is a strong one. It applies even if there is no ambiguity in the language in the sense of the language being capable of two different meanings. It is an emphatic adjuration by the legislature: *R v DPP ex p Kebilene* [2000] 2 AC 326, *per* Lord Cooke of Thorndon, at 373F; and my judgment, at 366B. The White Paper made clear that the obligation goes far beyond the rule which enabled the courts to take the Convention into account in resolving any ambiguity in a legislative provision: see 'Rights Brought Home: The Human Rights Bill' (1997) (Cm 3782), paragraph 2.7. The draftsman of the Act had

---

50 These included instances where that history was said to be relevant to the defendant's *belief* in consent. The discussion in the text concerned the circumstances in which such evidence could be admitted as to whether the women *did in fact* consent.

before him the slightly weaker model in section 6 of the New Zealand Bill of Rights Act 1990 but preferred stronger language. Parliament specifically rejected the legislative model of requiring a reasonable interpretation. Section 3 places a duty on the court to strive to find a possible interpretation compatible with Convention rights ...

Undoubtedly, a court must always look for a contextual and purposive interpretation: section 3 is more radical in its effect. It is a general principle of the interpretation of legal instruments that the text is the primary source of interpretation: other sources are subordinate to it: compare, for example, Articles 31 to 33 of the Vienna Convention on the Law of Treaties (1980) (Cmnd 7964). Section 3 qualifies this general principle because it requires a court to find an interpretation compatible with Convention rights if it is possible to do so. In the progress of the Bill through Parliament the Lord Chancellor observed that 'in 99 per cent of the cases that will arise, there will be no need for judicial declarations of incompatibility' and the Home Secretary said 'We expect that, in almost all cases, the courts will be able to interpret the legislation compatibility with the Convention': *Hansard* HL, February 5, 1998, col 840 (3rd Reading) and *Hansard* HC, February 16, 1998, col 778 (2nd Reading) ... In accordance with the will of Parliament as reflected in section 3 it will sometimes be necessary to adopt an interpretation which linguistically may appear strained. The techniques to be used will not only involve the reading down of express language in a statute but also the implication of provisions. A declaration of incompatibility is a measure of last resort. It must be avoided unless it is plainly impossible to do so. If a clear limitation on Convention rights is stated in terms, such an impossibility will arise: *R v Secretary of State for the Home Department* ex p *Simms* [2000] 2 AC 115 at 132A–B per Lord Hoffmann. There is, however, no limitation of such a nature in the present case.

In my view section 3 requires the court to subordinate the niceties of the language of section 41(3)(c), and in particular the touchstone of coincidence, to broader considerations of relevance judged by logical and common sense criteria of time and circumstances. After all, it is realistic to proceed on the basis that the legislature would not, if alerted to the problem, have wished to deny the right to an accused to put forward a full and complete defence by advancing truly probative material. It is therefore possible under section 3 to read section 41, and in particular section 41(3)(c), as subject to the implied provision that evidence or questioning which is required to ensure a fair trial under Article 6 of the Convention should not be treated as inadmissible. The result of such a reading would be that sometimes logically relevant sexual experiences between a complainant and an accused may be admitted under section 41(3)(c). On the other hand, there will be cases where previous sexual experience between a complainant and an accused will be irrelevant, eg, an isolated episode distant in time and circumstances. Where the line is to be drawn must be left to the judgment of trial judges. On this basis a declaration of incompatibility can be avoided. If this approach is adopted, section 41 will have achieved a major part of its objective but its excessive reach will have been attenuated in accordance with the will of Parliament as reflected in section 3 of the 1998 Act. That is the approach which I would adopt.

Lord Hutton: This subsection [s 3(1)] enacts a strong interpretative obligation ... It is clearly desirable that a court should seek to avoid having to make a declaration of incompatibility under section 4 of the 1998 Act unless the clear and express wording of the provision makes this impossible ...

[**Lord Hope** took a different approach, considering that in this case s 41(3)(c) did not in any event prevent the defendant from having a fair trial. But he went on: I should like to add however that I would find it very difficult to accept that it was permissible under section 3 of the Human Rights Act 1998 to read into section 41(3)(c) a provision to the effect that evidence or questioning which was required to ensure a fair trial under Article 6 of the Convention should not be treated as inadmissible. The rule of construction which section 3 lays down is quite unlike any previous rule of statutory interpretation. There is no need to identify an ambiguity or absurdity. Compatibility with Convention rights is the sole guiding principle. That is the paramount object which the rule seeks to achieve. But the rule is only a rule of interpretation. It does not entitle the judges to act as legislators. As Lord Woolf CJ said in *Poplar Housing and Regeneration Community Association Ltd v*

Donoghue [2001] EWCA Civ 595, section 3 does not entitle the court to legislate; its task is still one of interpretation. The compatibility is to be achieved only so far as this is possible. Plainly this will not be possible if the legislation contains provisions which expressly contradict the meaning which the enactment would have to be given to make it compatible. It seems to me that the same result must follow if they do so by necessary implication, as this too is a means of identifying the plain intention of Parliament: see Lord Hoffmann's observations in *R v Secretary of State for the Home Department, ex p Simms* [2000] 2 AC 115 at 131F–G.

In the present case it seems to me that the entire structure of section 41 contradicts the idea that it is possible to read into it a new provision which would entitle the court to give leave whenever it was of the opinion that this was required to ensure a fair trial. The whole point of the section, as was made clear during the debates in Parliament, was to address the mischief which was thought to have arisen due to the width of the discretion which had previously been given to the trial judge. A deliberate decision was taken not to follow the examples which were to be found elsewhere ... of provisions which give an overriding discretion to the trial judge to allow the evidence or questioning where it would be contrary to the interests of justice to exclude it. Section 41(2) *forbids* the exercise of such a discretion *unless* the court is satisfied as to the matters which that subsection identifies. It seems to me that it would not be possible, without contradicting the plain intention of Parliament, to read in a provision which would enable the court to exercise a wider discretion than that permitted by section 41(2). I would not have the same difficulty with a solution which read down the provisions of subsections (3) or (5), as the case may be, in order to render them compatible with the Convention right. But if that were to be done it would be necessary to identify precisely (a) the words used by the legislature which would otherwise be incompatible with the Convention right and (b) how these words were to be construed, according to the rule which section 3 lays down, to make them compatible. That, it seems to me, is what the rule of construction requires.

Notes

1   It may therefore be seen that Lords Steyn and Hutton were prepared to hold that the only way in which Parliament could legislate contrary to a Convention right would be by 'a clear limitation on Convention rights ... stated in terms'. This approach lead them simply to read into s 41(3)(c) words which were not there, namely that evidence was to be admitted where that was necessary to achieve a fair trial. It may be noted that Lord Hope, in contrast, considered that this approach went too far, crossing the line from interpretation to legislating. He considered, in what is certainly the more usual understanding of the word 'interpretation', that the judge's task was limited to identifying specific words which would otherwise lead to incompatibility and then re-interpreting those words, clearly not something which Lords Steyn and Hutton – and for that matter Lord Slynn – undertook.

2   Lord Hope's approach found more support in a more recent House of Lords' decision, *Re S and Re W (Care Orders)* [2002] 2 AC 291; [2002] 2 WLR 720 (also known as *Re S and W (Care Orders)*), endorsing a more restrained reading of s 3(1). Lord Nicholls observed that a reading of legislation under s 3(1) should not 'depart substantially from a fundamental feature of an Act of Parliament' (at para 40). To like effect are the *dicta* of Lord Woolf CJ in *Poplar Housing* [2002] QB 48, cited by Lord Hope in *R v A* (above) and of Lord Hope himself in *R v Lambert* [2002] AC 545; [2001] 3 WLR 206, 233–35. This indicates that the markedly activist approach adopted in *R v A* will not be consistently adopted. The basic point, however remains: where the judges chose to, they can use s 3(1) to require Parliament to use express words when it wishes to legislate incompatibly with the Convention rights.

3   Is there a further way in which, while as a matter of law the Act represents no threat to sovereignty, it may nevertheless amount to a kind of *de facto* 'higher law'? In this respect, the duty of ministers introducing legislation under s 19 of the HRA

is of relevance. Under s 19, a minister must make a statement when introducing legislation into Parliament that the legislation does not infringe Convention rights, or that he or she believes it does but wishes to proceed in any event. Statements of the latter kind would amount to a declaration that the UK intended deliberately to violate its treaty obligations and breach international law. The need to make such statements, which could cause immediate international condemnation, will inevitably act as a powerful deterrent against the introduction of clearly incompatible legislation. Overt infringements of the Convention will therefore become almost inconceivable. At the same time, the possibility of *inadvertent* legislative infringements should be removed, since parliamentary counsel will have to scrutinise the Bill prior to its introduction into Parliament to ensure its compatibility with the Convention, so that the minister responsible can make the statement of compatibility to Parliament under s 19. What is likely to slip through both these safeguards is ambiguously worded legislation, which *may* infringe Convention rights, depending upon how it is interpreted by the courts. Such legislation should, however, be dealt with by the courts under s 3(1) of the Act, which should ensure that ambiguous legislation is always interpreted compatibly with Convention rights. Thus, since openly incompatible legislation is most unlikely to be introduced by any government, inadvertent incompatibilities weeded out prior to parliamentary scrutiny, and ambiguities resolved in favour of the Convention by the courts, the effect may be that, in practice, Parliament no longer passes legislation which, once interpreted, infringes Convention rights.

4   However, all this could of course theoretically be removed simply by repeal of the HRA. Whether this happens or not depends upon whether some convention of respect develops in relation to the HRA. At present, it seems clear that such a convention is far from developing and indeed some Conservative politicians have recently been urging repeal of the HRA to facilitate action thought necessary to deal with terrorism in the aftermath of the attacks in the US on 11 September 2001.[51] Recent comments by the Home Secretary and the Prime Minister about the possibility of entering a reservation to Article 3 of the ECHR, in order to allow the UK to deport asylum seekers even where they would face a risk of inhuman treatment or torture upon arrival, and about the need to restrain judges from using the HRA to override the will of Parliament, seem to indicate that no real culture of respect has grown up amongst the government either.

FURTHER READING

J Jaconelli, 'Comment' [1985] PL 630

G Winterton, 'The British *Grundnorm*: parliamentary supremacy re-examined' (1976) LQR 591

Sir Robin Cooke, 'Fundamentals' (1988) NZLR 158

Lee [1985] PL 633

Goldsworthy, *The Sovereignty of Parliament* (1999)

---

51   See Prime Minister's Questions, 24 October 2001, cols 278–79. Iain Duncan Smith, Leader of the Opposition: 'Does the Prime Minister recognise that the European Convention on Human Rights as incorporated into United Kingdom law is proving an obstacle to protecting the lives of British citizens?'

CHAPTER 5

THE EUROPEAN UNION AND PARLIAMENTARY SOVEREIGNTY

INTRODUCTION

The most important practical application of the debate as to whether the UK Parliament may limit its own powers or have legal limitations imposed upon it by external sources of legal authority arises from the UK's membership of the European Union. The UK became a member of the European Community with effect from 1 January 1972 by virtue of the Treaty of Accession 1972. Treaties and Community law capable of having direct effect in the UK were given domestic legal effect by the European Communities Act 1972 (ECA) which, by s 2(1), incorporated all existing Community law into UK law.

The problem posed by Britain's prospective membership of the Community was obvious. The purposes of the Community meant that uniformity in the laws of the different Member States had to be guaranteed in those areas regulated by the Community. An Act of Parliament would obviously be required, providing that Community law was binding in Britain. That Act was the European Communities Act 1972. But, suppose that Parliament either deliberately, or inadvertently, later passed an Act that was inconsistent with Community law? The traditional doctrine of implied repeal states, as discussed above in Chapter 4, that if there is any inconsistency between the provisions of two different statutes, the later statute is deemed to repeal any provisions of the earlier statute that are inconsistent with it. Thus, no Parliament can protect its enactments from future express or implied repeal. So some device was needed in the European Communities Act to protect Community law from being gradually repealed in this way.

The device chosen was simple. No express declaration of the supremacy of Community law is included in the Act. The words intended to achieve this are contained in s 2(4), which reads as follows: 'any enactment passed *or to be passed* ... shall be construed and have effect subject to the foregoing provisions of this section ...' (emphasis added). 'The foregoing' are those provisions referred to in s 2(1) giving the force of law to 'the enforceable Community rights' there defined. Section 3(1) provides that questions as to the meaning or effect of Community law are to be determined 'in accordance with the principles laid down by any relevant decision of the European Court'.

Clearly, any Community law provision would prevail over UK legislation enacted before 1 January 1973. Authority for this can be found in rulings such as those in *Henn* [1981] 2 All ER 166 and *Goldstein* [1982] 1 WLR 804. This is uncontroversial and merely accords with the ordinary operation of the orthodox doctrine of parliamentary sovereignty. The problem arises in respect of statutes passed after 1 January 1972. By saying that any enactment 'to be passed', that is, any *future* enactment, must take effect 'subject to' the provisions of this Act, Parliament seemed to be suggesting that the courts must allow Community law to prevail over subsequent Acts of Parliament. This was evidently an attempt to suspend the normal doctrine of implied repeal – instead of any later statute which conflicted with EC law impliedly repealing it, such a later statute would have to be either 'construed', that is, interpreted so that it did not conflict with EC law, or if it could not be so interpreted, simply set aside ('have effect subject to'). In other words, Parliament was quite clearly seeking to bind its successors.

According to orthodox understandings of parliamentary sovereignty, as expressed in cases such as *Ellen Street Estates Ltd v Ministry of Housing* [1934] 1 KB 590 and *Vauxhall Estates v Liverpool Corporation Ltd* [1932] 1 KB 733, it had no legal power to do so (see pp 149–50, below).

THE POSITION OF THE EUROPEAN COURT OF JUSTICE

The European Court of Justice (ECJ) had early made clear its view that Community law should prevail over national law.

Costa v ENEL (Case 6/64) [1964] ECR 585, 586, ECJ

By creating a Community of unlimited duration, having its own institutions, its own personality, its own legal capacity and capacity of representation on the international plane, and, more particularly, real powers stemming from a limitation of sovereignty or a transfer of powers from the states to the Community, the Member States have limited their sovereign rights and have thus created a body of law which binds both their nationals and themselves.

The integration into the laws of each Member State of provisions which derive from the Community and, more generally the terms and the spirit of the Treaty, make it impossible for the states, as a corollary, to accord precedence to a unilateral and subsequent measure over a legal system accepted by them on a basis of reciprocity. Such a measure cannot therefore be inconsistent with that legal system. The law stemming from the Treaty, an independent source of law, could not because of its special and original nature, be overridden by domestic legal provisions, however framed, without being deprived of its character as Community law and without the legal basis of the Community itself being called into question.

The transfer by the states from their domestic legal system to the Community legal system of the rights and obligations arising under the Treaty carries with it a permanent limitation of their sovereign rights.

Amministrazione delle Finanze dello Stato v Simmenthal SpA (Case 106/77) [1978] ECR 629, 645–46, ECJ

[The Court ruled:] A national court which is called upon, within the limits of its jurisdiction, to apply provisions of Community law is under a duty to give full effect to those provisions, if necessary refusing of its own motion to apply any conflicting provision of national legislation, even if adopted subsequently, and it is not necessary for the court to request or await the prior setting aside of such provisions by legislative or other constitutional means.

Note
The far-reaching finding in *Amministrazione delle Finanze dello Stato v Simmenthal SpA* was to the effect that conflict between provisions of national law and directly applicable Community law must be resolved by rendering the national law inapplicable, and that any national provision or practice withholding from a national court the jurisdiction to apply Community law even temporarily was incompatible with the requirements of Community law.

THE POSITION OF THE UK COURTS

The purposive approach

How have the UK courts approached this conflict? In *Felixstowe Dock and Railway Co v British Transport Docks Board* [1976] 2 CMLR 655, Lord Denning MR disposed of a challenge to UK law on the basis that 'once a Bill is passed by Parliament and becomes a statute, that will dispose of all discussion about the Treaty. These courts will have to abide by the statute without regard to the Treaty at all'. This was the traditional approach. However it then gave way to what has been termed a 'rule of construction' approach to s 2(4) ECA. In *Garland v British Rail Engineering* [1983] 2 AC 751, Lord Diplock suggested (without resolving the issue) that, even where the words of the domestic law were on their face incompatible with the Community law in question, they should be construed so as to comply with it. He said that national courts must strive to make domestic law conform to Community law however 'wide a departure from the *prima facie* meaning may be needed to achieve consistency'. However, he added that they should do so only while it appeared that Parliament wished to comply with EC law.

This approach was applied in *Pickstone v Freemans* [1988] 3 WLR 265; [1988] 2 All ER 803[1] in the House of Lords, although not in the Court of Appeal. The Court of Appeal ruled that domestic legislation – the Equal Pay Amendment Regulations made under s 2(2) of the European Communities Act – was inconsistent with Article 119 of the EC Treaty. It then treated Art 119 as having more authority than the Amendment Regulations and made a ruling consistent with Art 119 (extracts from this case can be found in the next chapter). Thus, the House of Lords avoided the controversial approach of finding that EC law prevailed over national law but, by a less overtly contentious route, achieved the same result. It adopted a purposive interpretation of the domestic legislation which was not in conflict with Article 119. This was done on the basis that Parliament must have intended to fulfil its EC law obligations in passing the Amendment Regulations once it had been compelled to do so by the ECJ.

This decision provided authority for the proposition that plain words in a statute will be ignored if they involve departure from the provisions of European Community law, albeit under the guise of 'interpretation' rather than by a naked refusal to apply the words of an inconsistent UK statute. It might appear to follow that Parliament had succeeded in partially 'entrenching' s 2(1) of the European Communities Act, by means of s 2(4), by imposing a requirement of form (express words) on future legislation designed to override Community law. It should be noted that the House of Lords in *Pickstone* justified its disregard of statutory words by the finding that Parliament intended them to bear a meaning compatible with Community obligations.

The unequivocal primacy of Community law?

Lord Denning in *Macarthys v Smith* (Case 129/79) [1981] 1 All ER 111 suggested more clearly that partial 'entrenchment' of s 2(1) of the 1972 Act had occurred: '... we are entitled to look to the Treaty ... not only as an aid but as an overriding force. If ... our legislation ... is inconsistent with Community law ... then it is our bounden duty to give priority to Community law.' These *dicta* were to be tested in the decisive – and still leading – case on the issue, *R v Secretary of State for Transport ex p Factortame* (*Nos 1–3*) (1989) and (1992). *Factortame* required the courts to go a significant step further than previous cases because the UK courts for the first time had to confront directly an irreconcilable conflict between EC law and domestic law. The UK statute, the Merchant Shipping Act 1988, was plainly incompatible with clear and fundamental principles of

---

1   For comment see (1988) 51 MLR 221; [1988] PL 483.

Community law and thus, since there was no question of 'interpreting' the two into compatibility, the courts were faced with a stark choice – either uphold the statute, thus plunging the UK into direct conflict with the Community authorities, or take the unprecedented step of simply refusing to follow provisions of primary legislation. The background to the case is described by Erika Szyszczak.

> *Factortame* concerned the compatibility of national legislation with the Common Fisheries Policy and the availability of immediate protection and enforcement of Community rights. Briefly, in order to prevent 'quota hopping', whereby the UK's fishing quotas were drained by ships registered in the UK but owned and operated by non-British companies, the UK introduced the Merchant Shipping Act 1988. This stipulated that, in order to register as British fishing vessels, ships had to be British owned and, in the case of ships owned by companies, 75% of shareholders had to be British citizens, resident and domiciled in the UK. As a result of this Act, 95 fishing vessels registered in the UK, but controlled by Spanish companies, were effectively banned from fishing in British waters. Facing economic ruin, the Spanish companies applied to the High Court for judicial review of the measures contained in the Merchant Shipping Act 1988 and for a declaration that the measures relating to nationality and residence requirements should not be applied since they contravened Community law.[2]

R v Secretary of State for Transport ex p Factortame [1990] 2 AC 85, HL (extracts)

The Community law rights in issue included the prohibition of discrimination on grounds of nationality, the prohibition of restrictions on exports between Member States, the provision for the free movement of workers and the requirement that nationals of Member States are to be treated equally with respect to participation in the capital of companies established in one of those states. A ruling on the substantive questions of Community law was requested from the European Court of Justice and pending that ruling, which could not be expected for another two years, the Divisional Court made an order by way of interim relief, setting aside the relevant part of the 1988 Regulations and allowing the applicants to continue to operate their vessels as if they were British registered.

This order was set aside by the Court of Appeal. Bingham LJ said, however, that where the law of the Community is clear 'whether as a result of a ruling given on an Article 177 [now 234] reference or as a result of previous jurisprudence or on a straightforward interpretation of Community instruments, the duty of the national court is to give effect to it in all circumstances ... To that extent a UK statute is not as inviolable as it once was'. In the instant case it had not yet been established that the statute was inconsistent with Community law and in those circumstances it was held that the court had no power to declare a statute void.

The applicants appealed to the House of Lords which upheld the ruling of the Court of Appeal and referred to the European Court of Justice for a preliminary ruling the question whether Community law required a national court should grant the interim relief sought. Lord Bridge said that if it appeared after the European Court of Justice had ruled on the substantive issue that domestic law was incompatible with the Community provisions in question, Community law would prevail.

> **Lord Bridge:** ... By virtue of s 2(4) of the Act of 1972, Part II of the Act of 1988 is to be construed and take effect subject to directly enforceable Community rights and those rights are,

---

2   E Szyszczak, 'Sovereignty: crisis, compliance, confusion, complacency?' (1990) 15(6) EL Rev 480–81.

by s 2(1) of the Act of 1972, to be 'recognised and available in law, and ... enforced, allowed and followed accordingly;' ... This has precisely the same effect as if a section were incorporated in Part II of the Act of 1988 which in terms enacted that the provisions with respect to registration of British fishing vessels were to be without prejudice to the directly enforceable Community rights of nationals of any Member State of the EEC. Thus it is common ground that, in so far as the applicants succeed before the ECJ in obtaining a ruling in support of the Community rights which they claim, these rights will prevail over the restrictions imposed on registration of British fishing vessels by Part II of the Act 1988, and the Divisional Court will, in the final determination of the application for judicial review, be obliged to make appropriate declarations to give effect to these rights.

The European Commission then successfully sought a ruling in the European Court of Justice that the nationality requirement of s 14 of the Merchant Shipping Act should be suspended (*Re Nationality of Fishermen: EC Commission v UK* (Case C-248/89) [1989] 3 CMLR 601; [1991] 3 CMLR 706) pending the delivery of the judgment in the action for a declaration. This decision was given effect in the UK by means of the Merchant Shipping Act 1988 (Amendment) Order 1989. The European Court of Justice then ruled on the question of interim relief relying on *Amministrazione delle Finanze dello Stato v Simmenthal SpA* (Case 106/77) [1978] ECR 629. Predictably, it found that a national court must set aside national legislative provisions if that were necessary to give interim relief in a case concerning Community rights (*R v Secretary of State for Transport ex p Factortame Ltd* (1989)). As Szyszczak notes:

> Although invited to, the European Court did not issue any guidelines as to when interim relief should be available. Thus the circumstances and the form in which interim relief is granted are left to the discretion of the national courts, subject to the ruling in *Amministrazione delle Finanze dello Stato v SpA San Giorgio* [(Case 199/82) [1983] ECR 3595], that the conditions must not render the right to interim relief virtually impossible. It may be justifiable to subject the grant of interim relief against primary legislation to more stringent conditions than those applied to secondary legislation and administrative decisions. This may be a matter for the national court to assess alongside other issues such as whether damages may be an appropriate remedy.[3]

The House of Lords then considered the application for interim relief, and decided to grant it.

Factortame Ltd v Secretary of State (No 2) [1991] 1 AC 603 (extracts)

Lord Bridge of Harwich: My Lords, when this appeal first came before the House in 1989 (see *Factortame Ltd v Secretary of State for Transport* [1989] 2 All ER 692, [1990] 2 AC 85) your Lordships held that, as a matter of English law, the courts had no jurisdiction to grant interim relief in terms which would involve either overturning an English statute in advance of any decision by the Court of Justice of the European Communities that the statute infringed Community law or granting an injunction against the Crown. It then became necessary to seek a preliminary ruling from the Court of Justice as to whether Community law itself invested us with such jurisdiction.

In June 1990 we received the judgment of the Court of Justice replying to the questions we had posed and affirming that we had jurisdiction, in the circumstances postulated, to grant interim relief for the protection of directly enforceable rights under Community law, and that no limitation on our jurisdiction imposed by any rule of national law could stand as the sole obstacle to preclude the grant of such relief. In the light of this judgment we were able to conclude the hearing of the appeal in July and unanimously decided that relief should be granted in terms of the orders which the House then made, indicating that we would give our reasons for the decision later.

---

3   *Ibid*, p 482.

Some public comments on the decision of the Court of Justice, affirming the jurisdiction of the courts of Member States to override national legislation, if necessary, to enable interim relief to be granted in protection of rights under Community law, have suggested that this was a novel and dangerous invasion by a Community institution of the sovereignty of the UK Parliament. But such comments are based on a misconception. If the supremacy within the European Community of Community law over the national law of Member States was not always inherent in the EEC Treaty it was certainly well established in the jurisprudence of the Court of Justice long before the UK joined the Community. Thus, whatever limitation of its sovereignty Parliament accepted when it enacted the European Communities Act 1972 was entirely voluntary. Under the terms of the 1972 Act it has always been clear that it was the duty of a UK court, when delivering final judgment, to override any rule of national law found to be in conflict with any directly enforceable rule of Community law. Similarly, when decisions of the Court of Justice have exposed areas of UK statute law which failed to implement Council directives, Parliament has always loyally accepted the obligation to make appropriate and prompt amendments. Thus there is nothing in any way novel in according supremacy to rules of Community law in those areas to which they apply and to insist that, in the protection of rights under Community law, national courts must not be inhibited by rules of national law from granting interim relief in appropriate cases is no more than a logical recognition of that supremacy.

Notes

1 In *R v Secretary of State for Transport ex p Factortame Ltd (No 3)* [1992] QB 680, the ECJ had to consider the substantive issue in this case. It ruled that, while at present competence to determine the conditions governing the nationality of ships was vested in the Member States, such competence must be exercised consistently with Community law. It then determined that Part II of the Merchant Shipping Act 1988 was discriminatory on the grounds of nationality contrary to Article 52 and therefore did not so conform. Thus, the ECJ found that Article 52 had been breached due to the nationality and residence requirements laid down in the Act for registration of owners of fishing vessels. The ruling meant that Community law must be applied in preference to the Merchant Shipping Act 1988, which must be disapplied.

2 Once the issue as to the question of interim relief was resolved in the House of Lords it appeared that the UK courts had come to accept that, where Community law is certain, it should be applied in preference to domestic law. If Community law is unclear, and applicants who wish to rely on it have a seriously arguable case, domestic law should be disapplied if that is necessary to give interim relief pending a ruling on the issue from the European Court.

3 In relation to the grant of interim relief against a Minister of the Crown, Lord Bridge considered (i) that as a matter of domestic law injunctions could not be granted in judicial review proceedings against a minister of the Crown, although he accepted (ii) (after the ruling of the ECJ on the matter) that there was an overriding principle of Community law requiring the grant of interim relief to a party whose claim to be entitled to directly effective rights under Community law was seriously arguable. In the subsequent decision in *M v Home Office* [1994] 1 AC 377,[4] the Lords departed from this finding as regards point (i).

4 As Ian Loveland notes,[5] the *Factortame* decisions, radical though they were, left two practical issues open: first, could a statute be disapplied only after the ECJ on a reference had held that it was incompatible with EC law; secondly, was the novel

---

4 For the judgment see Part I Chapter 3, pp 83–84.
5 I Loveland, *Constitutional Law: A Critical Introduction,* 2nd edn (2000), p 388.

power to 'disapply' statutes confined to the House of Lords, or could it be exercised by any court, however lowly? These questions were decisively answered, and the basic principle laid down in *Factortame* affirmed, in the House of Lords' decision in *R v Secretary of State for Employment ex p EOC* [1995] 1 AC 377. Certain provisions of the Employment Protection (Consolidation) Act 1978 governed the right not to be unfairly dismissed, compensation for unfair dismissal and the right to statutory redundancy pay. These rights did not apply to workers who worked less than the specified number of hours a week. The Equal Opportunities Commission (EOC), considered that since the majority of those working for less than the specified number of hours were women, the provisions operated to the disadvantage of women, and were therefore discriminatory and in breach of EC law. The EOC accordingly wrote to the Secretary of State for Employment expressing this view. The Secretary of State replied by letter that the conditions excluding part-time workers from the rights in question were justifiable and therefore not indirectly discriminatory. The EOC applied for judicial review of the Secretary of State's refusal to accept that the UK was in breach of its obligations under EC law. The Secretary of State argued that no decision or justiciable issue susceptible of judicial review existed. However, the House of Lords found that, although the letter itself was not a decision, the provisions themselves could be challenged in judicial review proceedings. Judicial review was found to be available for the purpose of securing a declaration that certain UK primary legislation was incompatible with EC law, following *Factortame*. The requisite declarations were duly made.

5   After the *Factortame* litigation it may be said that the courts clearly have the power to refuse to obey an Act of Parliament if it conflicts with Community law, and Parliament is therefore effectively constrained in its freedom to legislate on any subject. If it wishes to avoid this restraint it will have to use express words demonstrating its intention to override any inconsistent EC law, though it is by no means clear that this would guarantee judicial obedience to such a statute. In contrast to *dicta* of Lord Denning in *Macarthys v Smith* [1979] 3 All ER 325 to the effect that a domestic court would give regard to express words in a statute requiring it to override Community law, Lord Bingham in *Factortame* did not enter a caveat that effect would have been given to express words used in the Merchant Shipping Act 1988 declaring that its provisions should prevail over those of Community law. He came close to suggesting that effect would not be given to such words in observing 'any rule of domestic law which prevented the court from giving effect to directly enforceable rights established in Community law would be bad'. In any event, since in practice it is highly improbable that such express words would be used, it appears to be impossible for Parliament to depart from the principle of the primacy of Community law unless it decides to withdraw from the Community.

6   The change in attitude of the UK judiciary over the last 20 years is very notable. Like the judiciary in the other Member States, the UK judiciary has gradually come to a full realisation of the need to achieve a uniform application of Community law throughout the Member States. However, this has taken some time, as can be seen by comparing a case such as *HP Bulmer Ltd v J Bollinger SA* [1974] Ch 401 with *Factortame*. The *Bulmer* case is in this sense similar to a German case: *Internationale Handelsgesellschaft mbH* [1974] 2 CMLR 540.

7   What then is the final result of the *Factortame* and *EOC* cases? Do they amount to an unequivocal acceptance of the primacy of Community law by the British courts and the consequent fettering of the legislative competence of the UK Parliament?

And on what basis did the House of Lords justify such an apparently radical departure from the orthodox, Diceyan understanding of sovereignty? These questions are considered in the following section.

Assessing *Factortame*; reconsidering sovereignty

The judicial reasoning and its critics

If Lord Bridge's explanation for what happened in the *Factortame* cases is examined, it is apparent that his reasoning represents a very typically British piece of judicial manoeuvring, allowing their Lordships to avoid facing up to the wider constitutional, even jurisprudential implications of the decision reached. It will be recalled that his Lordship justified what occurred on the basis that Parliament had accepted limitations on its sovereignty but that it had done so voluntarily. That explanation was clearly something of an exercise in pouring oil on politically troubled waters – as his comments made clear, there had been an angry response from the Euro-sceptic Right at the over-riding of a UK statute by Community law and the loss of national sovereignty this indicated. In response, his Lordship was pointing out, if you like, that the UK may indeed have lost some of its sovereignty but that the loss had not been imposed from outside, but voluntarily accepted, since everyone had been fully aware of the consequences of joining the European Community before the UK made the decision to join in 1972. It does therefore answer one question: their Lordships indicated clearly that in their view the limitation placed upon parliamentary sovereignty came from *Parliament itself*, not from some outside body. In other words, as far as the UK courts are concerned, the supremacy of EC law in the UK arises simply and solely from the provisions of a UK Act of Parliament, the European Communities Act 1972, not from the Treaties signed by the UK, nor from the judgments of the ECJ independently of the effect they are given in UK law via s 3(1) of the ECA. As Sir John Laws (now Laws LJ) put it, speaking extra-judicially, 'the law of Europe is not a higher-order law, because the limits which for the time being it sets to the power of Parliament are at the grace of Parliament itself'.[6] This therefore affirms one of the essential planks of the traditional view: Parliament's will cannot be overridden by any outside source of power.

However, what the judgment completely fails to do, as Loveland points out,[7] is explain how it was that Parliament managed in 1972 to achieve this voluntary, partial surrender of its sovereignty. The orthodox view, or course, was that if Parliament tried to bind its successors by providing that later legislation would not override an earlier measure – as they did in s 2(4) of the ECA – the courts would simply not enforce it. So how was it that Parliament managed in 1972 to achieve the constitutionally impossible? Lord Bridge does not even attempt to answer this question. In fact he speaks as if the judgment represented nothing of any great significance, denying that it was in anyway 'novel'. His Lordship was also slightly disingenuous in asserting that it had always been absolutely obvious that Parliament was accepting a limitation on its powers in 1972. In fact, in articles published shortly after the ECA was passed in 1972, Lord Diplock and Lord Denning both took the view that the rules of implied repeal would operate perfectly normally in relation to EC law.

---

6   J Laws, 'Law and democracy' [1985] PL 72, 89.
7   *Op cit*, pp 388–89.

It is also noteable that their Lordships carefully placed all the responsibility for this change to the accepted constitutional order upon Parliament,[8] which, they implied, had freely chosen to limit its own sovereignty. The real issue, which their Lordships quite simply ducked, was that in the past Parliament had enacted provisions which appeared to have the aim of binding its successors – as perhaps in the *Ellen Street Estates* and *Vauxhall Estates* cases,[9] and in the Acts of Union with Scotland and Ireland[10] – but that, faced with later provisions that were incompatible with them, the courts had simply refused to uphold the purported binding force of the earlier statute and applied the later provisions in the normal manner. The courts in the *Factortame* case clearly decided to change *their* approach; but by pretending that they were simply and loyally enforcing the will of Parliament, they avoided having to explain what lay behind this change. As we will see below, Laws LJ, in a more recent decision, has provided an alternative, and much more explicit account of the effect of the ECA upon parliamentary sovereignty.

Two views as to the nature of the change to constitutional doctrine represented by *Factortame* are put forward below. In the first, Wade, who had earlier argued that sovereignty was the 'ultimate political fact' of the UK constitutional order, unchangeable by legal means, draws the conclusion logically required by such a stance: *Factortame* was a technical revolution. Since the change made could not take place legally, it was by definition an extra-legal shift in the constitutional order. TRS Allan offers an alternative view, arguing that *Factortame* rather represents an evolutionary adaptation of a legal principle, itself based on deeper political values, in legitimate response to changing political circumstances. Wade's argument is couched partly in response to the views of Sir John Laws, speaking extra-judicially. Laws has made it plain that, in his view, all that has occurred is a suspension of the doctrine of implied repeal in relation to directly effective EC law,[11] and, as he notes, the courts in other areas of law may require express words, for example, for a statute to have retrospective effect or impose a tax. The decision in *Factortame* is therefore, he suggests, 'hardly revolutionary'.

HWR Wade, 'Sovereignty – revolution or evolution?' (1996) 112 LQR 568 (extracts)

When in the second *Factortame* case the House of Lords granted an injunction to forbid a minister from obeying an Act of Parliament, and the novel term 'disapplied' had to be invented to describe the fate of the Act, it was natural to suppose that something drastic had happened to the traditional doctrine of Parliamentary sovereignty ... The Parliament of 1972 had succeeded in binding the Parliament of 1988 and restricting its sovereignty, something that was supposed to be constitutionally impossible ...

[Wade then goes on to consider – and dismiss – what he terms the 'construction' view, suggested as a possible perspective in an article by Craig. Taking this view, what occurred in *Factortame* was merely the application of 'a rule of interpretation to the effect that Parliament is presumed not to intend statutes to override EEC law ...'; a view also favoured by Sir John Laws (see above). Wade cites a crucial part of Lord Bridge's speech in which he said that the effect of the 1972 Act was: '... as if a section were incorporated in Part II of the Act of 1988 which in terms enacted that the

---

8   As Craig points out: [1991] YBEL 221 at 252.
9   See Chapter 4 of this part, pp 149–50.
10   See Chapter 4 of this part, pp 150–51.
11   Laws, *op cit*, at, 89.

provisions with respect to registration of British fishing vessels were to be without prejudice to ... directly enforceable Community rights ...,' and comments:]

But this is much more that an exercise in construction. Lord Bridge's hypothetical section would take effect by authority of the Parliament of 1988, not the Parliament of 1972. To hold that its terms are putatively incorporated in the Act of 1988 is merely another way of saying that the Parliament of 1972 has imposed a restriction upon the Parliament of 1988. This is precisely what the classical doctrine of sovereignty will not permit. Sir John Laws [argues] that Parliament has only to provide expressly for the later Act to prevail over any conflicting Community law. But ... if there had been any such provision in the Act of 1988 we can be sure that the [ECJ] would hold that it was contrary to Community law and that holding would be part of the Community law to which by the Act of 1972 the Act of 1988 is held to be subject ... While Britain remains in the Community we are in a regime in which Parliament has bound its successors and which is nothing if not revolutionary.

[Wade goes on to note that Lord Bridge's speech in *Factortame (No 2)* (above) does not suggest a mere rule of construction but something much more radical.]

He takes it for granted that Parliament can 'accept' a limitation of its sovereignty which will be effective both for the present and for the future. It is a statement which could hardly be clearer: Parliament can bind its successors. If that is not revolutionary, constitutional lawyers are Dutchmen ... Neither does Lord Bridge's theory fit well with any theory based upon statutory construction, such as the theory that every post-1972 statute is to be construed as impliedly subject to Community law, subject only to express provision to the contrary. Nothing of that kind is suggested by Lord Bridge's doctrine of 'voluntary acceptance' by Parliament of Community law as a 'limitation of its sovereignty.' The truth is, apparently, that so far from containing 'nothing in any way novel' the new doctrine makes sovereignty a freely adjustable commodity whenever Parliament chooses to accept some limitation. The effect may be similar to implying limitations into future statutes, as Lord Bridge himself explains. But 'voluntary acceptance' goes much deeper into the foundations of the constitution, suggesting by its very novelty that the courts are reformulating the fundamental rules about the effectiveness of Acts of Parliament ...

But is 'revolutionary' the right word as a matter of law? Has the House of Lords adopted a new rule of recognition or ultimate legal principle as to the validity and effects of Acts of Parliament? As Craig puts it, 'The entry of the United Kingdom into the EEC might therefore be regarded as a catalyst for a partial change in the ... ultimate legal principle, as it operates in the UK'. As previously supposed, the rule was that an Act of Parliament in proper form had absolutely overriding effect, except that it could not fetter the corresponding power of future Parliaments. It is a rule of unique character, since only the judges can change it. It is for the judges, and not for Parliament, to say what is an effective Act of Parliament. If the judges recognise that there must be a change, as by allowing future Parliaments to be fettered, this is a technical revolution. This is what happens when the judges, faced with a novel situation, elect to depart from the familiar rules for the sake of political necessity ... in *Factortame* the House of Lords elected to allow the Parliament of 1972 to fetter the Parliament of 1988 in order that Community law might be given the primacy which practical politics obviously required. This in no way implies that the judges ... decided otherwise than for what appeared to be good legal reasons. The point is simply that the rule of recognition is itself a political fact which the judges themselves are able to change when they are confronted with a new situation which so demands ...

To predict just what that change may entail can only be guesswork. Is it now to be possible at any time, and to any extent, for Parliament to signify its 'voluntary acceptance' of limitations on its successors' sovereignty in the manner stated by Lord Bridge? Or, at the other extreme, was accession to the Community a unique legal event, demanding concessions of sovereignty for obvious political reasons, but otherwise setting no precedent of any kind? Or might there be intermediate positions ...? [Wade discusses possibilities of entrenchment of statutes only after approval via referendum, or entrenchments via a requirement of a two-thirds majority but not a larger one, or entrenchment being possible only for 'basic constitutional enactments'.] It is idle to speculate ... the prudential course may be to follow the example of the House of Lords and turn a blind eye to constitutional theory altogether. Unsatisfying as that may be to the academic mind, it at least provides a further example of the constitution bending before the winds of change, as in the last resort it will always succeed in doing.

Questions

1 Which of the possibilities outlined above by Wade do you find most plausible? Why?

2 Does the *Factortame* case really establish, as Wade argues, that 'the new doctrine makes sovereignty a fully adjustable commodity whenever Parliament chooses to accept some limitation'?

Note

Below, TRS Allan, whose alternative viewpoint on the issue of sovereignty was noted in Chapter 4 (above) takes issue with Wade's analysis and suggests what he considers to be a more subtle and satisfactory account of the significance of *Factortame* than the crude and dramatic tag of 'revolution'. Having summarised Wade's view, and pointed out some difficulties in the notion of the Rule of Recognition, on which Wade's view depends, he goes on to the heart of his critique.

TRS Allan, 'Parliamentary sovereignty: law, politics and revolution' (1997) 113 LQR 443 (extracts)

The difficulty with Professor Wade's thesis is immediately apparent from his reassurance that despite the change of fundamental rule [of parliamentary sovereignty] 'for reasons of political necessity'... we should not assume that in ... *Factortame* the judges 'decided otherwise than for what appeared to them to be good legal reasons'. Now it is scarcely possible to argue both that changes in the rule of recognition are made or acknowledged for 'good legal reasons' and that such a rule constitutes only 'a political fact' subject to alteration for reasons of 'political necessity'. Legal reasons are usually understood to ground a legitimate judicial decision by invoking settled doctrine or principle: they serve to justify it by explaining the sense in which it was required by the standards of the existing legal order. A revolution occurs, or is cemented, only when a new source of authority is acknowledged, or fundamental rule adopted, which is *not* justified by the existing order, from which the courts have for whatever reason withdrawn their allegiance.

If legal reasons exist, drawn from accepted legal principles or constitutional doctrine, they can be inspected and weighed. If sufficiently strong they will justify a judicial decision: if not, the judges will either have erred in law or abandoned law for politics. Which alternative does Professor Wade envisage as the appropriate explanation for *Factortame*? The preservation of a distinction between legal principle, on the one hand, and political expediency, on the other, is surely essential to any coherent understanding of the Rule of Law. Judges who make political decisions which violate accepted constitutional principles plainly act improperly: their conduct, when properly so described, should be condemned as illegitimate even if it is expedient or popular ...

The existence of good legal reasons for the *Factortame* decisions shows that, far from any dramatic, let alone unauthorised, change in the 'rule of recognition', the House of Lords merely determined what the existing constitutional order required in novel circumstances. The view that the acknowledgments of exceptions or qualifications to the rule that courts should give unconditional obedience to statutes amounts to 'revolution' is simply dogmatic and ultimately incoherent ...

However, it cannot really be supposed that the House of Lords was [as Wade argues] acknowledging an unrestricted freedom for Parliament to fetter the legislative authority of subsequent Parliaments. A Parliament which was strongly influenced by an authoritarian government might seek to entrench all kinds of provision whose vulnerability to repeal (by ordinary majority) it would be important for the courts to preserve on grounds of democratic principle ... The principle of voluntary acceptance by Parliament of limits on sovereignty must clearly be confined to the present context. Whether any such voluntary acceptance of limits would be permitted in another context would depend on the circumstances: the reasons for and against such limits would have to be weighed ... *Factortame* represents a rational attempt to explore the boundaries of legislative sovereignty within the contemporary constitution – even if each decision is presented in largely technical terms, with little serious attempt to articulate the constitutional considerations at stake.

Once we free ourselves of the idea that every qualification of the principle of judicial obedience to statutes constitutes a revolution inspired by political considerations which resist ordinary legal analysis, we can see that the reference to the 'rule of recognition' is really an excuse for shirking the explicit analysis of constitutional principle. The requirements of such a 'rule' are those which constitutional considerations dictate in the particular context under review. The absence of relevant discussion in the *Factortame* judgments can only be explained by the judge's understandable reluctance to risk political controversy, seeking to attribute all responsibility to Parliament, or else by the assumption that they were in some way bound by a 'rule of recognition' beyond the reach of rational, legal analysis. Neither explanation reflects much credit upon what is our highest, constitutional court ...

... When constitutional debate is opened up to ordinary legal reasoning, based on fundamental principles, we shall discover that the notion of unlimited parliamentary sovereignty no longer makes any legal or constitutional sense ... It is not so much, as [Craig] has suggested that the UK's entry into the EC might 'be regarded as a catalyst for a partial change in the ... ultimate legal principle' [(1991) 11 YBEL 21 at 251] but rather that membership of the Community reveals the nature of the ultimate principle in all its existing complexity – integral to a larger, if mainly implicit, constitutional theory.

[Allan then considers – and rejects – analogies between the position of the courts in changing their allegiance to statutes with those of courts in countries formerly subject to British rule as part of the British Empire deciding to reject the legal authority of British statutes – a state of affairs he refers to as 'autochthony'.]

It is intrinsic to a claim of autochthony, when made by the courts of a foreign state, that its independent sovereignty does not (whatever the history of the matter) derive from Westminster: it now has an indigenous root. A surrender of legislative power to the Community, by contrast, could only be justified, if at all, on the basis of the existing legal order: it is the legal consequence, primarily, of the 1972 Act. If the 1975 referendum [approving the UK's membership of the Community] is treated as an additional justification, its significance derives, necessarily, from the official status it acquired under the rules of the prevailing legal order. Even on the most radical interpretation no legal discontinuity arises. For British courts, if not for foreign ones, law and politics remain distinct ...

Foreign judges may choose, if they think it either morally desirable, or politically expedient, to transfer their allegiance from the former British legal order to a newly independent one; but British judges must continue to recognise the constitution which they were appointed to defend ... The extent to which Parliament may cede legislative power over domestic affairs to supra-national institutions is a question of British constitutional law, to be determined by fundamental analysis of the existing legal order ...

If therefore we are to treat the nature of parliamentary sovereignty as a matter for legitimate judicial exegesis, and not merely a matter of agreement between politicians, we cannot evade the task of developing a systematic theory of the constitution. Judicial decisions which settle doubts about the scope of parliamentary sovereignty must inevitably draw on such a theory, if they are rational and legitimate ... Talk of revolution falsely implies that the courts' role is merely to accept, on grounds of expediency, whatever the politicians decide. The implications for the future of the legal order of insisting on the courts' inescapable constitutional role are surely profound. Wade's suggestion that 'the prudential course may be to follow the example of the House of Lords and turn a blind eye to constitutional theory altogether' must, then, be firmly rejected. Such a pusillanimous course would disarm us just when recourse to theory becomes more essential than even, when political change induces even orthodox lawyers to abandon the simple faith that parliamentary omnipotence can be the governing principle for a modern constitutional democracy.[12]

Question

Allen, then, suggests that the reasons which led the courts to decide *Factortame* as they did were 'legal' not 'political', but what, if any, criteria does he suggest to distinguish the two?

Note

In the recent decision of *Thoburn v Sunderland City Council* [2002] 1 CMLR 50, Laws LJ put forward a quite different analysis of the position of the ECA. The facts are not particularly material: they concerned an alleged incompatibility between the Weights and Measures Act 1985 and the ECA 1972, which the judge found not to exist.[13] It should therefore be noted that his comments on whether a later incompatible act would nevertheless have prevailed are, strictly, *obiter*.

Thoburn v Sunderland City Council [2002] 1 CMLR 50 (extracts)

Parliament cannot bind its successors by stipulating against repeal, wholly or partly, of the ECA. It cannot stipulate as to the manner and form of any subsequent legislation. Thus there is nothing in the ECA which allows the Court of Justice, or any other institutions of the EU, to touch or qualify the conditions of Parliament's legislative supremacy in the United Kingdom ... The British Parliament has not the authority to authorise any such thing. Being sovereign, it cannot abandon its sovereignty ...

The present state of our domestic law is such that substantive Community rights prevail over the express terms of any domestic law, including primary legislation, made or passed after the coming into force of the ECA, even in the face of plain inconsistency between the two. This is the effect of *Factortame* ... In *Factortame* Lord Bridge said this at 140:

> By virtue of section 2(4) of the Act of 1972 Part II of the [Merchant Shipping] Act of 1988 is to be construed and take effect subject to directly enforceable Community rights ... This has precisely the same effect as if a section were incorporated in Part II of the Act of 1988 which in terms enacted that the provisions with respect to registration of British fishing vessels were to be without prejudice to the directly enforceable Community rights of nationals of any Member State of the EEC.

So there was no question of an implied *pro tanto* repeal of the ECA of 1972 by the later Act of 1988; on the contrary the Act of 1988 took effect subject to Community rights incorporated into our law by the ECA. In *Factortame* no argument was advanced by the Crown in their Lordships' House to suggest that such an implied repeal might have been effected. It is easy to see what the argument might have been: Parliament in 1972 could not bind Parliament in 1988, and section 2(4) was therefore ineffective to do so. It seems to me that there is no doubt but that in *Factortame* the House of Lords effectively accepted that section 2(4) could not be impliedly repealed, albeit the point was not argued.

[Laws LJ then went on to argue that the common law could denote certain statutes as 'constitutional' statutes, and thus not vulnerable to implied repeal (see the passage quoted in

---

12   Allan's ideas are more fully developed in his book, *Law, Liberty and Justice* (1993).
13   [2002] 1 CMLR 50, at para 50.

Chapter 4 of this part) and found]: The ECA clearly belongs in this family. It incorporated the whole corpus of substantive Community rights and obligations, and gave overriding domestic effect to the judicial and administrative machinery of Community law. It may be there has never been a statute having such profound effects on so many dimensions of our daily lives. The ECA is, by force of the common law, a constitutional statute.

...

In my judgment (as will by now be clear) the correct analysis of that relationship involves and requires these following four propositions. (1) All the specific rights and obligations which EU law creates are by the ECA incorporated into our domestic law and rank supreme: that is, anything in our substantive law inconsistent with any of these rights and obligations is abrogated or must be modified to avoid the inconsistency. This is true even where the inconsistent municipal provision is contained in primary legislation. (2) The ECA is a constitutional statute: that is, it cannot be impliedly repealed. (3) The truth of (2) is derived, not from EU law, but purely from the law of England: the common law recognises a category of constitutional statutes. (4) The fundamental legal basis of the United Kingdom's relationship with the EU rests with the domestic, not the European, legal powers. In the event, which no doubt would never happen in the real world, that a European measure was seen to be repugnant to a fundamental or constitutional right guaranteed by the law of England, a question would arise whether the general words of the ECA were sufficient to incorporate the measure and give it overriding effect in domestic law. But that is very far from this case.

Notes

1 It is important to be clear about what Laws LJ means when he asserts that the specific rights and obligations created by EC law 'rank supreme'. It would seem that a UK statute which specifically stated that it was intended to override any such right or obligation would have that effect. But any other statute inconsistent with such rights or obligations will have no effect, even if passed *after* the ECA 1972.

2 Laws LJ's analysis of the position is far clearer than that in *Factortame*. In that decision, the House of Lords appeared to suggest that Parliament had somehow imposed a requirement of form upon future Parliaments, such that the ECA could not be impliedly repealed, but Laws LJ robustly rejects this suggestion. Instead, he suggests that the courts have the ability to designate certain statutes as 'constitutional', and thus immune from implied repeal. What he does not explain, however, is why it is any more acceptable for a sovereign body to have such a restriction imposed upon it from an outside body than it would be for it to be able to impose such a restriction upon itself. Only time will tell whether Laws LJ's analysis finds more favour.

Sovereignty after Factortame: how much has changed?

Some commentators take the view that, even where express words were used in a statute demonstrating Parliament's intention to legislate in conflict with EC law, a UK court might not give them effect. This suggests that if a UK statute is to override Community law, s 2(4) of the European Communities Act must first be repealed.

The contrary view, that the doctrine of express repeal has been unaffected by the primacy of Community law, rests on the proposition that the judges, in disapplying statutory provisions, are simply carrying out Parliament's will as expressed in s 2(4) of the 1972 Act. This notion becomes harder to sustain in the face of provisions which appear to be intended to infringe Community law, such as the nationality requirements under the Merchant Shipping Act 1988. Nevertheless, in the face of such provisions, the judges appear to take the view that (i) Parliament in passing such provisions had in mind an interpretation of them which would render them compatible with Community law, and (ii) Parliament would not have wished the provisions to override Community law once the ECJ had ruled that they were incompatible.

If express words were used in a statute, such as 'these provisions are to take effect notwithstanding Article 52 of the Treaty', Parliament would appear to be expressing its intention that such provisions should be applied, regardless of a finding of the ECJ to the effect that they breach Article 52. In such an instance, judges would therefore be unable to hide behind the notion of fulfilling Parliament's will in disapplying the domestic provisions. If it is assumed that those provisions contained an implied term that the requirements they laid down were to be without prejudice to directly enforceable Community rights, such a term would directly contradict the express wording of the statute. Since a term may only be implied into a statute where there is room to do so under its express wording, it would seem that the judges would have to allow the express words to prevail and therefore the requirements in question would override Community rights.

Since Parliament retains the power to repeal the ECA expressly, it arguably still retains its ultimate sovereignty. It may be concluded that, where Community law conflicts with domestic law, the traditional doctrine of implied repeal will not be applied but, although the doctrine of parliamentary sovereignty has been greatly affected, it is arguable that it would revive in its original form if the UK withdrew from the EU.

It may be useful to conclude by examining how far the traditional Diceyan view of sovereignty can be said to have survived the ECA and its interpretation in *Factortame*. It will be recalled that the traditional doctrine had a positive and a negative aspect – Parliament has the right to make or unmake any law whatever ('the positive aspect') and no person or body outside Parliament is recognised by the law as having a right to override or set aside any legislation of Parliament at all ('the negative aspect'). The positive aspect was said to entail three propositions:

(a) there is no law which Parliament cannot change;

(b) there is therefore no distinction between constitutional and other laws;

(c) an enactment of Parliament cannot be pronounced void on the grounds that it conflicts with any principles of the constitution (see pp 134–35 above).

If these propositions are examined in turn, the results are instructive. First of all, then, is it still true to say that no person or body outside Parliament is recognised by the law as having a right to override or set aside any legislation of Parliament at all? It would appear not. The courts have 'disapplied' an Act of Parliament, surely the equivalent of setting it aside? Is it still the case that there is no law which Parliament cannot change? The answer is that we do not know for sure, but this is probably still the case, in the sense that Parliament can ultimately repeal the ECA and then proceed to legislate as it chooses, inconsistently with EC law. The position on the second part of the positive aspect – there is no distinction between constitutional and other laws – seems clearer. Such a distinction now clearly exists – the law of the EC may be seen as 'constitutional' in character because, at the least, the doctrine of implied repeal does not apply. This is indeed expressly asserted by Laws LJ in *Thoburn*, as seen above. It may be that express repeal does not apply either – or rather that Parliament would have to repeal the ECA before the courts would allow EC law to be overridden by statute. The third proposition – an enactment of Parliament cannot be pronounced void on the grounds that it conflicts with any principles of the constitution – remains technically correct. In the *Factortame* and *EOC* cases, the courts 'disapplied' the offending legislation; they did not pronounce it void. It has been pointed out that the Merchant Shipping Act was not 'struck down' by the courts – it remained of full effect in relation to non-EC nationals. However, the result in the *EOC* case was effectively that the courts pronounced the legislation in question a dead letter on the basis that it conflicted with basic principles of EC law.

FURTHER READING

See Part I Chapter 4.

PART II

EUROPEAN LAW & INFLUENCE

THE EC LEGAL SYSTEM IN NATIONAL COURTS: DIRECT AND INDIRECT EFFECTS OF EC LAW IN DOMESTIC LAW; THE *FRANCOVICH* PRINCIPLE

INTRODUCTION

The European Coal and Steel Community was established by the Treaty of Paris in 1951, which was signed by Belgium, France, Germany, Italy, Luxembourg and the Netherlands, with the objective of creating a single market in coal and steel. These six states decided to widen their economic co-operation by extending the notion of the single market beyond coal and steel. To this end they created two new Communities, the European Economic Community and the European Atomic Energy Community by two Treaties of Rome signed on 25 March 1957.

The UK became a member of the European Communities in 1973 by signing the Treaty of Rome. At present there are three Communities, of which the most significant is the European Community (formerly the European Economic Community). The others are the European Atomic Energy Community and the European Coal and Steel Community. The Communities became known as the European Union under the Treaty of European Union signed at Maastricht. The Treaty of Rome, together with the Single European Act 1986 and the Treaty of European Union, creates the constitutional framework of the Union.

The Treaty on European Union was signed at Maastricht on 7 February 1992. However, due to delays in the ratification of the Treaty by some of the Member States, including the UK, the European Union established by the Treaty only came into existence on 1 November 1993. The Treaty was adopted into the UK by the European Communities (Amendment) Act 1993. The Treaty on European Union established the European Union (EU) without displacing the three existing Communities, of which, as noted above, the most important is the European Community with its own founding Treaty, amended by the Single European Act 1986, a Treaty signed by all the Member States. The EU is founded on the three Communities and has been said to provide an 'umbrella' for them. The European Union has also been compared to a temple supported by three pillars. The main pillar is made up of the three Communities each of which has its own founding Treaty, as amended. The other pillars are Common Foreign and Security Policy (CFSP) and Co-operation in Justice and Home Affairs (CJHA).

The Amsterdam Treaty was signed on 2 October 1997. It renumbers the EC Treaty and the Treaty on European Union, and it introduces a new part into the EC Treaty on visas, asylum and immigration and other policies relating to the free movement of persons[1] within the third pillar. The Treaty of Nice was signed in February 2001 by all Member States but is not in force at the time of writing, its ratification having been initially rejected by the Irish people in a referendum. The changes it will make, if and when it comes into force, are beyond the scope of this work, being concerned primarily with the re-weighting of votes in the Council of Ministers, the extension of Qualified Majority Voting therein and matters concerning the Commission.

---

1   C Boch, *EC Law in the UK* (2000), p 2.

The treatment of EU matters in this book does not attempt to provide students with the information they will require to study the institutions and legal order of the EU as a 'core subject' and nor does it contain any discussion of substantive law (for example, free movement of goods, persons, etc) or the law governing actions brought against the institutions of the Community or Union, or enforcement action by the Community against Member States. It is limited to an examination of how the EU legal order interacts with that of its Member States, in particular the UK. We have already examined, in Part I Chapter 5, the supremacy doctrine, and how that has been accommodated within the UK constitution.

In this chapter, discussion will concentrate on the extent to which individuals can rely on Community law directly before national courts. It will ask which Community instruments can be relied on and against whom. A movement will be traced towards the surer enforcement of EC provisions in national law and towards further protection of individuals under EC provisions. The extracts from the various European treaties, included below, will therefore be limited to these areas of relevance, although the general aims of the Community and Union will be given, in order to give some idea as to the scope of Community and Union law. The provisions giving general legislative competency are also included for this reason, as are the provisions governing the jurisdiction of the European Court of Justice (ECJ), and the basic aspirations of the Union, including its commitment to the Rule of Law and respect for fundamental rights.

As mentioned above, the Amsterdam Treaty renumbered both the EC Treaty and the Treaty on European Union: because many of the most important decisions of the ECJ use the old numbering, because of when they were decided, the old numbering is given in square brackets throughout.

FUNDAMENTALS OF THE EC LEGAL ORDER

The short extracts from the treaties which follow are intended to indicate the fundamental aims of the Community and Union; the different types of legal instrument that the Community may produce; the various legal bases laid down for legislative action by the Community; the concept of citizenship of the Union; the role and powers of the ECJ; and the basic principles of the Treaty on European Union. Reading the Treaty is also illuminating, because one notices the key principles of the Community *not* mentioned in the Treaty, notably the supremacy of EC law, the doctrine of direct effect and the principle of state liability for breach of Community law (the *Francovich* principle, see below).

Treaty Establishing the European Community (as amended by the Amsterdam Treaty)

Preamble

HIS MAJESTY THE KING OF THE BELGIANS, THE PRESIDENT OF THE FEDERAL REPUBLIC OF GERMANY, THE PRESIDENT OF THE FRENCH REPUBLIC, THE PRESIDENT OF THE ITALIAN REPUBLIC, HER ROYAL HIGHNESS THE GRAND DUCHESS OF LUXEMBOURG, HER MAJESTY THE QUEEN OF THE NETHERLANDS (I),

DETERMINED to lay the foundations of an ever closer union among the peoples of Europe,

RESOLVED to ensure the economic and social progress of their countries by common action to eliminate the barriers which divide Europe,

AFFIRMING as the essential objective of their efforts the constant improvements of the living and working conditions of their peoples,

RECOGNISING that the removal of existing obstacles calls for concerted action in order to guarantee steady expansion, balanced trade and fair competition,

ANXIOUS to strengthen the unity of their economies and to ensure their harmonious development by reducing the differences existing between the various regions and the backwardness of the less-favoured regions,

DESIRING to contribute, by means of a common commercial policy, to the progressive abolition of restrictions on international trade,

INTENDING to confirm the solidarity which binds Europe and the overseas countries and desiring to ensure the development of their prosperity, in accordance with the principles of the Charter of the United Nations,

RESOLVED by thus pooling their resources to preserve and strengthen peace and liberty, and calling upon the other peoples of Europe who share their ideal to join in their efforts,

DETERMINED to promote the development of the highest possible level of knowledge for their peoples through a wide access to education and through its continuous updating,

HAVE DECIDED to create a EUROPEAN COMMUNITY and to this end have designated as their Plenipotentiaries:

(1) The Kingdom of Denmark, the Hellenic Republic, the Kingdom of Spain, Ireland, the Republic of Austria, the Portuguese Republic, the Republic of Finland, the Kingdom of Sweden and the United Kingdom of Great Britain and Northern Ireland have since become members of the European Community.

PART ONE – PRINCIPLES

Article 1

By this Treaty, the High Contracting Parties establish among themselves a European Community.

Article 2

The Community shall have as its task, by establishing a common market and an economic and monetary union and by implementing common policies or activities referred to in Articles 3 and 4, to promote throughout the Community a harmonious, balanced and sustainable development of economic activities, a high level of employment and of social protection, equality between men and women, sustainable and non-inflationary growth, a high degree of competitiveness and convergence of economic performance, a high level of protection and improvement of the quality of the environment, the raising of the standard of living and quality of life, and economic and social cohesion and solidarity among Member States.

Article 3

1. For the purposes set out in Article 2, the activities of the Community shall include, as provided in this Treaty and in accordance with the timetable set out therein:

(a) the prohibition, as between Member States, of customs duties and quantitative restrictions on the import and export of goods, and of all other measures having equivalent effect

(b) a common commercial policy

(c) an internal market characterised by the abolition, as between Member States, of obstacles to the free movement of goods, persons, services and capital

(d) measures concerning the entry and movement of persons as provided for in Title IV

(e) a common policy in the sphere of agriculture and fisheries

(f) a common policy in the sphere of transport

(g) a system ensuring that competition in the internal market is not distorted

(h) the approximation of the laws of Member States to the extent required for the functioning of the common market

(i) the promotion of coordination between employment policies of the Member States with a view to enhancing their effectiveness by developing a coordinated strategy for employment

(j) a policy in the social sphere comprising a European Social Fund

(k) the strengthening of economic and social cohesion

(l) a policy in the sphere of the environment

(m) the strengthening of the competitiveness of Community industry

(n) the promotion of research and technological development

(o) encouragement for the establishment and development of trans-European networks

(p) a contribution to the attainment of a high level of health protection

(q) a contribution to education and training of quality and to the flowering of the cultures of the Member States

(r) a policy in the sphere of development cooperation

(s) the association of the overseas countries and territories in order to increase trade and promote jointly economic and social development

(t) a contribution to the strengthening of consumer protection

(u) measures in the spheres of energy, civil protection and tourism.

2. In all the activities referred to in this Article, the Community shall aim to eliminate inequalities, and to promote equality, between men and women.

Article 4 [ex Article 3a]

1.   For the purposes set out in Article 2, the activities of the Member States and the Community shall include, as provided in this Treaty and in accordance with the timetable set out therein, the adoption of an economic policy which is based on the close coordination of Member States' economic policies, on the internal market and on the definition of common objectives, and conducted in accordance with the principle of an open market economy with free competition.

2.   Concurrently with the foregoing, and as provided in this Treaty and in accordance with the timetable and the procedures set out therein, these activities shall include the irrevocable fixing of exchange rates leading to the introduction of a single currency, the ecu, and the definition and conduct of a single monetary policy and exchange rate policy the primary objective of both of which shall be to maintain price stability and, without prejudice to this objective, to support the general economic policies in the Community, in accordance with the principle of an open market economy with free competition.

3.   These activities of the Member States and the Community shall entail compliance with the following guiding principles: stable prices, sound public finances and monetary conditions and a sustainable balance of payments.

Article 5 [ex Article 3b]

The Community shall act within the limits of the powers conferred upon it by this Treaty and of the objectives assigned to it therein.

In areas which do not fall within its exclusive competence, the Community shall take action, in accordance with the principle of subsidiarity, only if and in so far as the objectives of the proposed action cannot be sufficiently achieved by the Member States and can therefore, by reason of the scale or effects of the proposed action, be better achieved by the Community.

Any action by the Community shall not go beyond what is necessary to achieve the objectives of this Treaty.

Article 7 [ex Article 4]

1. The tasks entrusted to the Community shall be carried out by the following institutions:

– a EUROPEAN PARLIAMENT,

– a COUNCIL,

– a COMMISSION,

– a COURT OF JUSTICE,

– a COURT OF AUDITORS.

Each institution shall act within the limits of the powers conferred upon it by this Treaty.

2. The Council and the Commission shall be assisted by an Economic and Social Committee and a Committee of the Regions acting in an advisory capacity.

Article 10 [ex Article 5]

Member States shall take all appropriate measures, whether general or particular, to ensure fulfilment of the obligations arising out of this Treaty or resulting from action taken by the institutions of the Community. They shall facilitate the achievement of the Community's tasks.

They shall abstain from any measure which could jeopardise the attainment of the objectives of this Treaty.

Article 12 [ex Article 6]

Within the scope of application of this Treaty, and without prejudice to any special provisions contained therein, any discrimination on grounds of nationality shall be prohibited. The Council, acting in accordance with the procedure referred to in Article 251, may adopt rules designed to prohibit such discrimination.

PART TWO – CITIZENSHIP OF THE UNION

Article 17 [ex Article 8]

1. Citizenship of the Union is hereby established.

 Every person holding the nationality of a Member State shall be a citizen of the Union.

2. Citizens of the Union shall enjoy the rights conferred by this Treaty and shall be subject to the duties imposed thereby.

Article 18 [ex Article 8a]

1. Every citizen of the Union shall have the right to move and reside freely within the territory of the Member States, subject to the limitations and conditions laid down in this Treaty and by the measures adopted to give it effect.

2. The Council may adopt provisions with a view to facilitating the exercise of the rights referred to in paragraph 1; save as otherwise provided in this Treaty the Council shall act unanimously on a proposal from the Commission and after obtaining the assent of the European Parliament.

Article 19 [ex Article 8b]

1. Every citizen of the Union residing in a Member State of which he is not a national shall have the right to vote and to stand as a candidate at municipal elections in the Member State in

which he resides, under the same conditions as nationals of that State. This right shall be exercised subject to detailed arrangements to be adopted before 31 December 1994 by the Council, acting unanimously on a proposal from the Commission and after consulting the European Parliament; these arrangements may provide for derogations where warranted by problems specific to a Member State.

2. Without prejudice to Article 190(4) and to the provisions adopted for its implementation, every citizen of the Union residing in a Member State of which he is not a national shall have the right to vote and to stand as a candidate in elections to the European Parliament in the Member State in which he resides, under the same conditions as nationals of that State. This right shall be exercised subject to detailed arrangements acting unanimously on a proposal from the Commission and after consulting the European Parliament; these arrangements may provide for derogations where warranted by problems specific to a Member State.

Article 20 [ex Article 8c]

Every citizen of the Union shall, in the territory of a third country in which the Member State of which he is a national is not represented, be entitled to protection by the diplomatic or consular authorities of any Member State, on the same conditions as the nationals of that State. Before 31 December 1993, Member States shall establish the necessary rules among themselves and start the international negotiations required to secure this protection.

Article 21 [ex Article 8d]

Every citizen of the Union shall have the right to petition the European Parliament in accordance with Article 194.

Every citizen of the Union may apply to the Ombudsman established in accordance with Article 195.

PART THREE COMMUNITY POLICIES

...

CHAPTER 3 APPROXIMATION OF LAWS

Article 94 [ex Article 100]

The Council shall, acting unanimously on a proposal from the Commission and after consulting the European Parliament and the Economic and Social Committee, issue directives for the approximation of such laws, regulations or administrative provisions of the Member States as directly affect the establishment or functioning of the common market.

Article 95 [ex Article 100a]

1. By way of derogation from Article 100 and save where otherwise provided in this Treaty, the following provisions shall apply for the achievement of the objectives set out in Article 14. The Council shall. acting in accordance with the procedure referred to in Article 251 and after consulting the Economic and Social Committee, adopt the measures for the approximation of the provisions laid down by law, regulation or administrative action in Member States which have as their object the establishing and functioning of the internal market.

...

PART TWO: INSTITUTIONS OF THE COMMUNITY

CHAPTER 1 THE INSTITUTIONS

The Treaty describes the main institutions of the Community: the Parliament, directly elected by the peoples of Europe, which participates in the legislative process and scrutinises the work of the Commission; the Council, made up of Ministers from each of the Member States, which is the main policy-formulating and legislative body (it now shares legislative power with the Parliament under the most important of the Community's legislative procedures); the Commission, independent of the Member States, with the task of ensuring that Community law is implemented and observed and with the ability to bring actions against defaulting states, and with its own power to formulate policy proposals for consideration by the Council and Parliament. The Treaty then describes the Court of Justice, and the Court of First Instance, our concern here.

Article 220 [ex Article 164]

The Court of Justice shall ensure that in the interpretation and application of this Treaty the law is observed.

Article 221 [ex Article 165]

The Court of Justice shall consist of 15 Judges.

The Court of Justice shall sit in plenary session. It may, however, form chambers, each consisting of three, five or seven Judges, either to undertake certain preparatory inquiries or to adjudicate on particular categories of cases in accordance with rules laid down for these purposes.

The Court of Justice shall sit in plenary session when a Member State or a Community institution that is a party to the proceedings so requests ...

Article 222 [ex Article 166]

The Court of Justice shall be assisted by eight Advocates-General ...

It shall be the duty of the Advocate-General, acting with complete impartiality and independence, to make, in open court, reasoned submissions on cases brought before the Court of Justice, in order to assist the Court in the performance of the task assigned to it in Article 220.

Article 255 [ex Article 168a]

1. A Court of First Instance shall be attached to the Court of Justice with jurisdiction to hear and determine at first instance, subject to a right of appeal to the Court of Justice on points of law only and in accordance with the conditions laid down by the Statute, certain classes of action or proceeding defined in accordance with the conditions laid down in paragraph 2. The Court of First Instance shall not be competent to hear and determine questions referred for a preliminary ruling under Article 234.

...

The Treaty then sets out the Courts' jurisdiction: to hear actions alleging breach of Community law by a Member State brought by the Commission (Article 226) or another state (Article 227); to award fines for failure to comply with its judgements (Article 228); and, under Article 230 (formerly Article 173), to 'review the legality' of legislation produced by the Community and of individual acts of Council, Commission and Central Bank at the instance of another Member State, Community institution, or 'any natural or legal person complaining of a decision addressed to them or against a decision which, although in the form of a regulation or a decision addressed to another person, is of direct and individual concern to the former' and pronounce the said act void. The Courts also have jurisdiction to hear cases brought alleging failure to act by the Parliament, Council or Commission. The provision of greatest concern for our purposes follows.

Article 234 [ex Article 177]

The Court of Justice shall have jurisdiction to give preliminary rulings concerning:

(a) the interpretation of this Treaty;

(b) the validity and interpretation of acts of the institutions of the Community and of the ECB;

(c) the interpretation of the statutes of bodies established by an act of the Council, where those statutes so provide.

Where such a question is raised before any court or tribunal of a Member State, that court or tribunal may, if it considers that a decision on the question is necessary to enable it to give judgment, request the Court of Justice to give a ruling thereon.

Where any such question is raised in a case pending before a court or tribunal of a Member State, against whose decisions there is no judicial remedy under national law, that court or tribunal shall bring the matter before the Court of Justice.

CHAPTER 2 – PROVISION COMMON TO SEVERAL INSTITUTIONS

The Treaty then sets out its main legislative provision, which describes the different legislative measures the Community may adopt.

Article 249 [ex Article 189]

In order to carry out their task and in accordance with the provisions of this Treaty, [the European Parliament acting jointly with the Council,] the Council and the Commission shall make regulations and issue directives, take decisions, make recommendations or deliver opinions.

A regulation shall have general application. It shall be binding in its entirety and directly applicable in all Member States.

A directive shall be binding, as to the result to be achieved, upon each Member State to which it is addressed, but shall leave to the national authorities the choice of form and methods.

A decision shall be binding in its entirety upon those to whom it is addressed.

Recommendations and opinions shall have no binding force.

The Treaty on European Union grafts a Union onto the existing Community structures.

Treaty on European Union

His Majesty the King of the Belgians,

Her Majesty the Queen of Denmark,

The President of the Federal Republic of Germany,

The President of the Hellenic Republic,

His Majesty the King of Spain,

The President of the French Republic,

The President of Ireland,

The President of the Italian Republic,

His Royal Highness the Grand Duke of Luxembourg,

Her Majesty the Queen of the Netherlands,

The President of the Portuguese Republic,

Her Majesty the Queen of the United Kingdom of Great Britain and Northern Ireland,

RESOLVED to mark a new stage in the process of European integration undertaken with the establishment of the European Communities,

RECALLING the historic importance of ending of the division of the European Continent and the need to create firm bases for the construction of the future Europe,

CONFIRMING their attachment to the principles of liberty, democracy and respect for human rights and fundamental freedoms and of the Rule of Law,

DESIRING to deepen the solidarity between their peoples while respecting their history, their culture and their traditions,

DESIRING to enhance further the democratic and efficient functioning of the institutions so as to enable them better to carry out, within a single institutional framework, the tasks entrusted to them,

RESOLVED to achieve the strengthening and the convergence of their economies and to establish an economic and monetary union including, in accordance with the provisions of the Treaty, a single and stable currency,

DETERMINED to promote economic and social progress for their peoples, within the context of the accomplishment of the internal market and of reinforced cohesion and environmental protection, and to implement policies ensuring that advances in economic integration are accompanied by parallel progress in other fields,

RESOLVED to establish a citizenship common to nationals of the countries,

RESOLVED to implement a common foreign and security policy including the eventual framing of a common defence policy, which might in time lead to a common defence, thereby reinforcing the European identity and its independence in order to promote peace, security and progress in Europe and in the world,

REAFFIRMING their objectives to facilitate the free movement of persons, while ensuring the safety and security of their peoples, by including provision on justice and home affairs in this Treaty,

RESOLVED to continue the process of creating an ever closer union among the peoples of Europe, in which decisions are taken as closely as possible to the citizen in accordance with the principle of subsidiarity,

IN VIEW of further steps to be taken in order to advance European integration,

HAVE DECIDED to establish a European Union . . .

TITLE I – COMMON PROVISIONS

Article 1 [ex Article A]

By this Treaty, the High Contracting Parties establish among themselves a European Union, hereinafter called 'the Union'.

This Treaty marks a new stage in the process of creating an ever closer union among the people of Europe, in which decisions are taken as closely as possible to the citizen.

The Union shall be founded on the European Communities, supplemented by the policies and forms of cooperation established by the Treaty. Its task shall be to organise, in a manner demonstrating consistency and solidarity, relations between the Member States and between their peoples.

Article 2 [ex Article B]

The Union shall set itself the following objectives:

1   to promote economic and social progress and a high level of employment and to achieve which is balanced and sustainable development, in particular through the creation of an area without internal frontiers, through the strengthening of economic and social cohesion and through the establishment of economic and monetary union, ultimately including a single currency in accordance with the provisions of this Treaty;

2   to assert its identity on the international scene, in particular through the implementation of a common foreign and security policy including the eventual framing of a common defence

policy, which might in time lead to a common defence in accordance with the provisions of Article 17;

3   to strengthen the protection of the rights and interests of the nationals of its Member States through the introduction of a citizenship of the Union;

4   to maintain and develop the Union as an area of freedom, security and justice, in which the free movement of persons is assured in conjunction with appropriate measures with respect to external border controls, immigration, asylum and the prevention and combating of crime

5   to maintain in full the 'acquis communautaire' and build on it with a view to considering to what extent the policies and forms of cooperation introduced by this Treaty may need to be revised with the aim of ensuring the effectiveness of the mechanisms and the institutions of the Community.

The objectives of the Union shall be achieved as provided in this Treaty and in accordance with the conditions and the timetable set out therein while respecting the principle of subsidiarity as defined in Article 5 of the Treaty establishing the European Community.

Article 3 [ex Article C]

The Union shall be served by a single institutional framework which shall ensure the consistency and the continuity of the activities carried out in order to attain its objectives while respecting and building upon the 'acquis communautaire'.

The Union shall in particular ensure the consistency of its external activities as a whole in the context of its external relations, security, economic and development policies. The Council and the Commission shall be responsible for ensuring such consistency. They shall ensure the implementation of these policies, each in accordance with its respective powers.

Article 4 [ex Article D]

The European Council shall provide the Union with the necessary impetus for its development and shall define the general political guidelines thereof.

The European Council shall bring together the Heads of State or of Government of the Member States and the President of the Commission. They shall be assisted by the Ministers for Foreign Affairs of the Member States and by a Member of the Commission. The European Council shall meet at least twice a year, under the chairmanship of the Head of State or of Government of the Member State which holds the Presidency of the Council.

The European Council shall submit to the European Parliament a report after each of its meetings and a yearly written report on the progress achieved by the Union.

Article 5 [ex Article E]

The European Parliament, the Council, the Commission and the Court of Justice shall exercise their powers under the conditions and for the purposes provided for, on the one hand, by the provisions of the Treaties establishing the European Communities and of the subsequent Treaties and Acts modifying and supplementing them and, on the other hand, by the other provisions of this Treaty.

Article 6 [ex Article F]

1.   The Union is founded on the principles of liberty, democracy, respect for fundamental rights and fundamental freedoms, and the rule of law, principles which are common to the Member States.

2.   The Union shall respect fundamental rights, as guaranteed by the European Convention for the Protection of Human Rights and Fundamental Freedoms signed in Rome on 4 November 1950 and as they result from the constitutional traditions common to the Member States, as general principles of Community law.

3.   The Union shall respect the national identities of its Member Sates

4. The Union shall provide itself with the means necessary to attain its objectives and carry through its policies.

The relationship between national and European Courts and the nature of EC law

One of the key provisions of the EC legal order is Article 234 (formerly Article 177), above, under which national courts refer questions of EC law for authoritative determination by the ECJ.[2] Many of the famous cases in which the ECJ established the foundational principles of EC law came about as a result of references by national courts. Crucially, Article 234 also ensures the uniform interpretation of EC law throughout the different Member States. Questions of EC law can arise in a great variety of legal proceedings in Member States: the procedure basically allows national courts, once an issue of EC law has arisen, to stay proceedings and refer a specific issue or issues to the Court (the national courts certify specific questions to be answered by the ECJ). Once the answer is obtained, the national court will then apply the ruling to the case before it. It should be noted that the ECJ does *not*, as such, instruct national courts as to what decisions to reach in the particular case before it: it simply provides an answer to the certified questions of EC law, though in some cases the ruling it gives is so detailed and specific as to leave little or no discretion to the national court in its final determination of the EC aspects of the case.[3]

It should also be noted that the ECJ has no power to annul or disapply national legislation found to be incompatible with EC law. Where this issue arises, the Court will simply make a finding that the legislation in question is incompatible, but only the national court can disapply or strike down the legislation in question. Conversely, national courts have no power to find EC legislation *ultra vires* or void.[4]

It will be seen from Article 234 that it distinguishes between the highest court of a country (courts from whose decisions there is no appeal), which *must* refer questions of EC law, and lower courts, which have a discretion to do so. The only exception to the obligation of the highest court in a country to refer is the so called *acte claire* doctrine: essentially this means that the national court need not refer a question of EC law if, as a result of previous rulings of the ECJ, it is obvious what the answer to the question would be.[5] In the UK, higher national courts have laid down guidance for lower courts on when to refer: in *R v International Stock Exchange ex p Else* (1993), Lord Bingham MR suggested that 'the appropriate course is ordinarily to refer the issue to the [ECJ] ... unless the national court can with complete confidence resolve the issue itself', guidance which sets up something close to a presumption of reference.

Students of EC law need to grasp some basic distinctions between the types of legislation the EC produces, set out in Article 249 (formerly Article 189) above. *Regulations* are measures of general application which have legal force directly and automatically in the laws of the Member States. They do not need to be implemented

---

2   Note that the Treaty of Nice, which at the time of writing is not in force, and will not be so until ratified by referendum in Ireland, allows for certain references to be heard by the Court of First Instance (CFI).

3   Sionaidh Douglas-Scott cites the decision in *Stoke on Trent CC v B & Q plc* [1992] ECR-I 6635 as an example: *Constitutional Law of the European Union* (2002), p 229.

4   *Foto-Frost* [1987] ECR 4199.

5   *CILFIT* [1982] ECR 3415.

by national measures (though this is occasionally needed, for practical reasons).[6] They are thus said to be 'directly applicable'. This does not mean quite the same as 'directly effective'. As one commentator puts it, 'Directly applicable is best understood as meaning that a regulation automatically becomes part of the law of the land, without the need for further implementation, whereas direct effect [means] ... capable of giving rise to individual rights enforceable in the national courts, or justiciability'.[7] *Treaty provisions* can also have this effect, if sufficiently clear, precise and unconditional. *Directives* are different: they tend to be more general measures, setting out objectives to be achieved by the Member State, but leaving to each individual State the particular form and method used to implement them. As Prechal explains:

> The theory expounded by the ECJ was ... [that] the Community's legal system should be considered as an integral part of the legal systems of the Member States and, consequently, the whole body of Community law is as such incorporated in the national legal orders, ie 'the law of the land'. However, it appeared that, on the one hand, not all Community law that is part of the national legal system is directly effective, since for having direct effect, certain additional conditions had to be satisfied. On the other hand, non-directly effective provisions cannot be ignored and treated as being non-existent.[8]

It should also be noted, although discussion is outside the scope of this work, which does not deal with substantive EC law, that Community law also includes what are known as 'general principles of law'.[9] These are used by the ECJ (and by national courts when applying EC law) as interpretative tools when applying Community law, and, in particular, as grounds of review for assessing the legality of acts of the Community institutions. They may be summarised very briefly as: fundamental human rights,[10] including, but not limited to, those set out in the European Convention on Human Rights, which, as seen above, is cited in Article 6 of the Treaty on European Union as a foundation of the Union; the principle of proportionality; the principle of legal certainty, or legitimate expectations; the principle of equality; and the principle of fair procedure or 'the rights of defence' as it is commonly known.

The EU adopted a Charter of Fundamental Rights as part of the Treaty of Nice, though it is not to be directly justiciable and indeed its legal status remains unclear. At present it appears that it will figure as a source of 'soft law', that is as a source of principle to guide the interpretation and application of existing law; it is also intended to be declaratory of existing rights – a codification – rather than a source of new rights. The Charter may be made directly enforceable in future, if so agreed between the Member States.

---

6   It should be noted that the ECJ has held that, unless a Regulation either expressly states that it requires national implementation, or this is clearly apparently from its terms, it is improper for a state to use national implementing measures, rather than simply enforcing the Regulation directly: *Commission v Italy* [1973] ECR 101.

7   Douglas-Scott, *op cit*, p 288. It will be noted later that the concept of 'direct effect' can in fact be seen as extending beyond just the creation of 'individual rights' (see below, pp 211–12).

8   S Prechal, 'Does direct effect still matter?' (2000) 37 CMLR 1047.

9   See T Tridimas, *The General Principles of EC Law* (1999); Douglas-Scott, *op cit*, Chapters 10 and 13.

10 At the time of writing, the Convention on the Future of Europe, chaired by Giscard d'Estaing and charged with drawing up a 'constitution' for the EU, is beset by arguments between the Member States as to whether the EU Charter should be made binding in the new constitution. The UK is leading the argument that it should not. against strong opposition from most other States. For discussion of the Charter, see Douglas-Scott, *op cit*, pp 470–78.

There were perhaps three main stages in the movement towards surer enforcement of EC provisions in national courts. These three stages are discussed in the next three sections below. First, the ECJ identified those EC instruments which would have direct effects in national courts and determined when they would have such effects. Secondly, the ECJ found that if a particular instrument – usually a Directive – does not produce direct effects (since it is being invoked against an individual or non-state body or does not in any event satisfy the requirements for direct effect) it may produce 'indirect effects' (that is influence the interpretation and application of existing domestic law). Thirdly, the ECJ decided that, where an individual has suffered due to the failure of a state to implement a Directive properly, the individual may have a claim against the state in damages (the *Francovich* principle – see below).

THE POLICY OF THE EUROPEAN COURT OF JUSTICE: DIRECT EFFECT AND THE DIRECT EFFECT OF DIRECTIVES

Van Gend en Loos (Case 26/62) [1963] ECR 1 was the case in which the ECJ first held that EC law could have direct effect in Member States. The case arose out of a challenge by the Van Gend company that the imposition of an increased customs duty by the Dutch government was contrary to Article 25 (formerly Article 12) which prohibits the introduction by Member States of any new customs duties on imports or exports from other EC countries. Van Gend wished to rely on the Treaty article in its national courts in order to have the customs duties declared void. The question was whether it could. Article 25 states: 'Member States shall refrain from introducing between themselves any new customs duties on imports or exports or any charges having equivalent effect. . . .'

It should be noted first of all that, as Douglas-Scott puts it:

The suggestion that EEC law might give rise to individual rights which could be invoked in the national courts could not be derived from the specific provision in the treaty. Nothing in the EC treaty specifies that individually enforceable rights can be derived from international obligations imposed on the member states. The Netherlands government submitted [in *Vand Gend en Loos*] that interpreting [Article 25] in this way would be contrary of the intentions of its drafters. In this they were backed by Advocate General Roemer.[11]

The Court, however, took a different view.

NV Algemene Transport- en Expeditie Onderneming van Gend en Loos v Netherlands Inland Revenue Administration (Case 26/62) [1963] ECR I (extracts)

The first question . . . is whether Article 12 of the Treaty has direct application in national law in the sense that nationals of Member States may on the basis of this Article lay claim to rights which the national court must protect.

To ascertain whether the provisions of an international Treaty extend so far in their effects it is necessary to consider the spirit, the general scheme and the wording of those provisions.

The objective of the EEC Treaty, which is to establish a common market, the functioning of which is of direct concern to interested parties in the Community, implies that this Treaty is more than an agreement which merely creates mutual obligations between the contracting states. This view is

---

11 *Op cit*, p 282.

confirmed by the preamble to the Treaty which refers not only to governments but to peoples. It is also confirmed more specifically by the establishment of institutions endowed with sovereign rights, the exercise of which affects Member States and also their citizens. Furthermore, it must be noted that the nationals of the states brought together in the Community are called upon to cooperate in the functioning of this Community through the intermediary of the European Parliament and the Economic and Social Committee.

In addition the task assigned to the Court of Justice under Article 177, the object of which is to secure uniform interpretation of the Treaty by national courts and tribunals, confirms that the states have acknowledged that Community law has an authority which can be invoked by their nationals before those courts and tribunals. The conclusion to be drawn from this is that the Community constitutes a new legal order of international law for the benefit of which the states have limited their sovereign rights, albeit within limited fields, and the subjects of which comprise not only Member States but also their nationals. Independently of the legislation of Member States, Community law therefore not only imposes obligations on individuals but is also intended to confer upon them rights which become part of their legal heritage.

These rights arise not only where they are expressly granted by the Treaty, but also by reason of obligations which the Treaty imposes in a clearly defined way upon individuals as well as upon the Member States and upon the institutions of the Community.

The wording of Article 12 contains a clear and unconditional prohibition which is not a positive but a negative obligation. This obligation, moreover, is not qualified by any reservation on the part of states which would make its implementation conditional upon a positive legislative measure enacted under national law. The very nature of this prohibition makes it ideally adapted to produce direct effects in the legal relationship between Member States and their subjects.

The implementation of Article 12 does not require any legislative intervention on the part of the states. The fact that under this Article it is the Member States who are made the subject of the negative obligation does not imply that their nationals cannot benefit from this obligation.

In addition the argument based on Articles 169 and 170 of the Treaty put forward by the three governments which have submitted observations to the court in their statements of case is misconceived. The fact that these Articles of the Treaty enable the Commission and the Member States to bring before the court a state which has not fulfilled its obligations does not mean that individuals cannot plead these obligations, should the occasion arise, before a national court, any more than the fact that the Treaty places at the disposal of the Commission ways of ensuring that obligations imposed upon those subject to the Treaty are observed, precludes the possibility, in actions between individuals before a national court, of pleading infringements of these obligations.

A restriction of the guarantees against an infringement of Article 12 by Member States to the procedures under Article 169 and 170 would remove all direct legal protection of the individual rights of their nationals. There is the risk that recourse to the procedure under these Articles would be ineffective if it were to occur after the implementation of a national Decision taken contrary to the provisions of the Treaty.

The vigilance of individuals concerned to protect their rights amounts to an effective supervision in addition to the supervision entrusted by Articles 169 and 170 to the diligence of the Commission and of the Member States.

It follows from the foregoing considerations that, according to the spirit, the general scheme and the wording of the Treaty, Article 12 must be interpreted as producing direct effects and creating individual rights which national courts must protect.

Notes

1   TC Hartley comments that Article 12 'was addressed to Member States: it imposed an obligation on them [not to impose additional customs duties] but did not expressly grant any corresponding right to individuals to import goods free from any duty imposed after the establishment of the EC: nor did it state explicitly that

any such duty would be invalid'.[12] This did not stop the ECJ finding it to be directly effective. As Douglas-Scott remarks: '[The Court's] disposition to look to the spirit of the Treaty means that [it] could transform provisions which were intended to guide actions of member states and Community institutions into fundamental freedoms which can be invoked by parties before their national courts.'[13]

2   Hartley goes on to comment that the claim by the ECJ that 'the states have limited their sovereign rights' is a 'very bold and ambitious claim' but one which has by no means been accepted by all the Member States. The view of the UK courts, for example, is that EC law has effect in the UK solely and simply because of the provisions of the European Communities Act 1972 (see Part I Chapter 5).

3   The next significant stage in the development of the doctrine of direct effect was the decision in *Van Duyn v Home Office* (1975) in which the question of whether directives could have direct effects was raised. The UK government, the respondent in the case, argued that, 'if directives were directly effective, what would there be to distinguish them from regulations, and yet Article 249 defines them quite differently'.[14] Again, the Court took a different view.

Van Duyn v Home Office (Case 41/74) [1974] ECR 1337, ECJ (extracts)

[11] The UK observes that, since Art 189 of the Treaty distinguishes between the effect ascribed to regulations, directives and decisions, it must therefore be presumed that the Council, in issuing a directive rather than making a regulation, must have intended that the directive should have an effect other than that of a regulation and accordingly that the former should not be directly applicable.

[12] If, however, by virtue of the provisions of Art 189 regulations are directly applicable and, consequently, may by their very nature have direct effects, it does not follow from this that other categories of acts mentioned in that Article can never have similar effects. It would be incompatible with the binding effect attributed to a directive by Art 189 to exclude, in principle, the possibility that the obligation which it imposes may be invoked by those concerned. In particular, when the Community authorities have, by directive, imposed on Member States the obligation to pursue a particular course of conduct, the useful effect of such an act would be weakened if individuals were prevented from relying on it before their national courts and if the latter were prevented from taking it into consideration as an element of Community law. Art 177, which empowers national courts to refer to the Court questions concerning the validity of the interpretation of all acts of the Community institutions, without distinction, implies furthermore that these acts may be invoked by individuals in the national courts. It is necessary to examine, in every case, whether the nature, general scheme and wording of the provisions in question are capable of having direct effects on the relations between Member States and individuals.

[13] By providing that measures taken on grounds of public policy shall be based exclusively on the personal conduct of the individual concerned, Art 3(1) of Directive 64/221 is intended to limit the discretionary power which national laws generally confer on the authorities responsible for the entry and expulsion of foreign nationals. Firstly, the provision lays down an obligation which is not subject to any exception or condition and which, by its very nature, does not require the intervention of any act on the part either of the institutions of the community or of Member States. Secondly, because Member States are thereby obliged, in implementing a clause which derogates from one of the fundamental principles of the Treaty in favour of individuals, not to take account of factors extraneous to personal conduct, legal certainty for the persons concerned

---

12   TC Hartley, *The Foundations of European Community Law*, 4th edn (1998), p 191.
13   *Op cit*, p 283.
14   *Ibid*, p 289.

requires that they should be able to rely on this obligation even though it has been laid down in a legislative act which has no automatic direct effect in its entirety.

[14] If the meaning and exact scope of the provision raise questions of interpretation, these questions can be resolved by the courts, taking into account also the procedure under Art 177 of the Treaty.

[15] Accordingly, in reply to the second question, Art 3(1) of Council Directive 64/221 of 25 February 1964 confers on individuals rights which are enforceable by them in the courts of a Member State and which the national courts must protect.

Notes

1   As one scholar has commented, direct effect 'provided a mechanism which made Community law "the law of the land"; at least in practical terms. By placing Community law directly before the national courts, it has *de facto* and decisively contributed to the acceptance of Community law as law which must be applied by national courts.'[15] Nevertheless, it was almost certainly contrary to the intention of the drafters of the Treaty; both the distinction drawn between Regulations and directives (with the latter not being said to be directly applicable) and the fact that directives are expressed to be binding only as to the result to be achieved are strong indications that the direct effect of directives was not intended, a view which was 'generally accepted in the early days of the EC'.[16]

2   The arguments put forward by the Court in *Van Duyn* were certainly tendentious. As Douglas-Scott notes, the first contention, that 'It would be incompatible with the binding effect attributed to a directive by Art 189 to exclude, in principle' direct effect is 'not a very strong argument' (Hartley calls it 'unsound'),[17] simply because 'there are many EC laws which are binding at interstate level without being directly effective'.[18] The argument that it would weaken the effectiveness of a measure if it could not be invoked by individuals is a stronger one; though it is clearly a consequentialist argument (that is, producing a reading which the court thought would best further the effective development of EC law), rather than one based on the text of the Treaty itself. Hartley points out that it is based on the fact that Member States are often remiss at implementing directives; that the only way of enforcing them if they were held *not* to be directly effective would be through enforcement action by the Commission or another Member State and that the Commission 'is able to handle only a small number of such cases every year' and would find it 'quite impossible' to bring actions in respect of every unimplemented directive.[19]

3   As Douglas-Scott goes on to note, the strongest argument for direct effect was not adverted to in the *Van Duyn* case at all. It was not introduced until a later case – *Ratti* – and was, in essence, a species of estoppel argument: a Member State should not be able to rely on its own failure to implement a directive in order to benefit from its lack of enforceability.[20]

4   What characteristics, then, must a measure have for it to have direct effect? Hartley states:

15   Prechal, *op cit*.
16   Hartley, *op cit*, pp 199–200.
17   *Ibid*.
18   Douglas-Scott, *op cit*, p 289.
19   *Ibid*, p 200.
20   *Ibid*, pp 289–90.

The test may now be stated succinctly as follows:

1. The provision must be clear and unambiguous

2. it must be unconditional

3. its operation must not be dependent on further action being taken by Community or national authorities.[21]

5 Hartley goes on to explain that the first test refers not to ambiguity as such, since the ECJ can resolve ambiguities through interpretation, but rather to precision. 'If the provision merely lays down a general objective or policy to be pursued, without specifying the appropriate means to attain it, it can hardly be regarded as a legal rule suitable for application by a court of law.'[22] Hartley instances Article 10 (formerly Article 5) as a broad, non-justiciable provision of this type.

6 The second test – 'unconditionality' – means, as Hartley explains,[23] that there must be no intervening discretion between the Community norm and its enforcement. If such a norm applies only after a decision by the Commission (say) that it should apply in the particular case, then it cannot be directly effective.

7 The third test simply means that, if a provision specifically states that it will only come into force when further executive or legislative action is taken, it cannot come into force without that action being taken. However, as Hartley points out,[24] most Community provisions give a time limit for such action, and if that time limit passes and the required action has not been taken, the provision can then become directly effective: the classic example is directives, which can start to have direct effect only after the date for the implementation has been passed without this being done, or if they have been mis-implemented by the member state.

Against whom can one enforce a directive? Vertical and horizontal effect

The next question with which the ECJ was confronted was the issue of whether provisions in directives could be relied upon against other individuals (as could Regulations and applicable Treaty articles) – what is known as 'horizontal effect' – or whether they could only be relied upon as against emanations of the state – 'vertical effect'.[25] This issue arose when a question was referred to the ECJ asking whether the appellant in the following case could rely on the Equal Treatment Directive as against a Health Authority, which, the UK government contended, should be treated as being, in effect, a private employer, rather than a governmental body.

Marshall v Southampton and South West Hampshire Area Health Authority (Teaching) (Case 152/84) [1986] ECR 723, ECJ (extracts)

... it is necessary to consider whether Art 5(1) of Directive 76/207 may be relied upon by an individual before national courts and tribunals.

The appellant and the Commission consider that that question must be answered in the affirmative. They contend in particular, with regard to Arts 2(1) and 5(1) of Directive 76/207, that those provisions are sufficiently clear to enable national courts to apply them without legislative intervention by the Member States, at least so far as overt discrimination is concerned.

---

21 *Op cit*, p 191.
22 *Ibid*, p 192.
23 *Ibid*.
24 *Ibid*, p 195.
25 See further, J Steiner, 'Coming to terms with EEC Directives' (1990) 106 LQR 144.

In support of that view, the appellant points out that directives are capable of conferring rights on individuals which may be relied upon directly before the courts of the Member States; national courts are obliged by virtue of the binding nature of a directive, in conjunction with Art 5 of the EEC Treaty, to give effect to the provisions of directives where possible, in particular when construing or applying relevant provisions of national law (judgment of 10 April 1984 in Case 14/83 *von Colson and Kamann v Land Nordrhein-Westfalen* [1984] ECR 1891).

. . .

The respondent and the UK propose, conversely, that the second question should be answered in the negative. They admit that a directive may, in certain specific circumstances, have direct effect as against a Member State in so far as the latter may not rely on its failure to perform its obligations under the directive. However, they maintain that a directive can never impose obligations directly on individuals and that it can only have direct effect against a Member State *qua* public authority, and not against a Member State *qua* employer. As an employer a state is no different from a private employer. It would not therefore be proper to put persons employed by the state in a better position than those who are employed by a private employer.

With regard to the legal position of the respondent's employees, the UK states that they are in the same position as the employees of a private employer.

. . .

With regard to the argument that a directive may not be relied upon against an individual, it must be emphasised that, according to Art 189 of the EEC Treaty, the binding nature of a directive, which constitutes the basis for the possibility of relying on the directive before a national court, exists only in relation to 'each Member State to which it is addressed'. It follows that a directive may not of itself impose obligations on an individual and that a provision of a directive may not be relied upon as such against such a person. It must therefore be examined whether, in this case, the respondent must be regarded as having acted as an individual.

In that respect it must be pointed out that, where a person involved in legal proceedings is able to rely on a directive as against the state, he may do so regardless of the capacity in which the latter is acting, whether employer or public authority. In either case it is necessary to prevent the state from taking advantage of its own failure to comply with Community law.

It is for the national court to apply those considerations to the circumstances of each case; the Court of Appeal has, however, stated in the order for reference that the respondent, Southampton and South West Hampshire Area Health Authority (Teaching), is a public authority.

The argument submitted by the UK that the possibility of relying on provisions of the directive against the respondent *qua* organ of the state would give rise to an arbitrary and unfair distinction between the rights of state employees and those of private employees, does not justify any other conclusion. Such a distinction may easily be avoided if the Member State concerned has correctly implemented the directive in national law.

. . . the provision contained in Art 5(1) of Directive 76/207, which implements the principle of equality of treatment set out in Art 2(1) of the directive . . . is . . . sufficiently precise to be relied on by an individual and to be applied by the national courts . . .

and . . . is sufficiently precise and unconditional to be capable of being relied upon by an individual before a national court in order to avoid the application of any national provision which does not conform to Art 5(1).

Consequently, the answer to the second question must be that Art 5(1) of Council Directive 76/207 of 9 February 1976, which prohibits any discrimination on grounds of sex with regard to working conditions, including the conditions governing dismissal, may be relied upon as against a state authority acting in its capacity as employer, in order to avoid the application of any national provision which does not conform to Art 5(1).

Notes

1   In the above decision, the ECJ thus limited the principle of direct effect to 'vertical' application. In other words, individuals could rely on a directive against a state body but not against a private body.[26] Perhaps in order to mitigate to an extent the effect of this decision, the last paragraph of this judgment held that directives can be enforced against state bodies whether they are carrying out governmental functions or simply acting as an employer like any other.

2   Thus directives do *not* have direct effect in 'horizontal' situations, that is direct effect as against non-state bodies, private companies or individuals. This was confirmed in the following, well-known case which was concerned with the issue of whether the provisions of the Directive in question – concerning the right of cancellation – could be invoked in proceedings between a consumer and a trader.

Faccini Dori v Recreb (Case C-91/92) [1994] ECR I-3325, ECJ (extracts)

[21] The national court observes that, if the effects of unconditional and sufficiently precise but transposed directives were to be limited to relations between state entities and individuals, this would mean that a legislative measure would operate as such only as between certain legal subjects, whereas, under Italian law as under the laws of all modern states founded on the Rule of Law, the state is subject to the law like any other person. If the directive could be relied on only as against the state, that would be tantamount to a penalty for failure to adopt legislative measures of transposition as if the relationship were a purely private one.

[22] It need merely be noted here that, as is clear from the judgment in *Marshall*, cited above (paras 48–49), the case law on the possibility of relying on directives against state entities is based on the fact that under Art 189 a directive is binding only in relation to 'each Member State to which it is addressed'. That case law seeks to prevent 'the state from taking advantage of its own failure to comply with Community law'.

[23] It would be unacceptable if a state, when required by the Community legislature to adopt certain rules intended to govern the state's relations – or those of state entities – with individuals and to confer certain rights on individuals, were able to rely on its own failure to discharge its obligations so as to deprive individuals of the benefits of those rights. Thus the Court has recognised that certain provisions of directives on conclusions of public works contracts and of directives on harmonisation of turnover taxes may be relied on against the state (or state entities) (see the judgment in Case 103/88 *Fratelli Costanzo v Comune di Milano* [1989] ECR 1839 and the judgment in Case 8/81 *Becker v Finanzamt Münster-Innenstadt* [1982] ECR 53).

[24] The effect of extending that case law to the sphere of relations between individuals would be to recognise a power in the Community to enact obligations for individuals with immediate effect, whereas it has competence to do so only where it is empowered to adopt regulations.

[25] It follows that, in the absence of measures transposing the directive within the prescribed time-limit, consumers cannot derive from the directive itself a right of cancellation as against traders with whom they have concluded a contract or enforce such a right in a national court.

[28] The directive on contracts negotiated away from business premises is undeniably intended to confer rights on individuals and it is equally certain that the minimum content of those rights can be identified by reference to the provisions of the directive alone (see para 17 above).

[29] Where damage has been suffered and that damage is due to a breach by the state of its obligation, it is for the national court to uphold the right of the aggrieved consumers to obtain reparation in accordance with national law on liability.

---

26   See further J Stuyck and P Wytinck (1991) 1 CMLR 205.

[30] So, as regards the second issue raised by the national court, the answer must be that in the absence of measures transposing the directive within the prescribed time limit, consumers cannot derive from the directive itself a right of cancellation as against traders with whom they have concluded a contract or enforce such a right in a national court. However, when applying provisions of national law whether adopted before or after the directive, the national court must interpret them as far as possible in the light of the wording and purpose of the directive.

Note

Once it is decided that directives can have direct effect only against state bodies, it becomes necessary to ask what constitutes a state body; this issue is particularly pertinent in view of the radical programme of privatisation, contracting out and marketisation in the UK. This question was addressed in the following case, concerning British Gas, then still a nationalised industry. The issue was whether British Gas could be treated as a state body or not, and, as such, could be subject to the direct effect of Article 5(1) of Directive 76/207.

Foster v British Gas (Case C-188/89) [1990] ECR I-3313, ECJ (extracts)

By virtue of the Gas Act 1972 which governed the BGC [British Gas Corp] at the material time, the BGC was a statutory corporation responsible for developing and maintaining a system of gas supply in Great Britain, and had a monopoly of the supply of gas.

The members of the BGC were appointed by the competent Secretary of State. He also had the power to give the BGC directions of a general character in relation to matters affecting the national interest and instructions concerning its management.

The members of the BGC were obliged to submit to the Secretary of State periodic reports on the exercise of its functions, its management and its programmes. Those reports were then laid before both Houses of Parliament. Under the Gas Act 1972 the BGC also had the right, with the consent of the Secretary of State, to submit proposed legislation to Parliament.

The BGC was required to run a balanced budget over two successive financial years. The Secretary of State could order it to pay certain funds over to him or to allocate funds to specified purposes.

The BGC was privatised under the Gas Act 1986. Privatisation resulted in the establishment of British Gas plc, the respondent in the main proceedings, to which the rights and liabilities of the BGC were transferred with effect from 24 August 1986.

. . .

. . . the House of Lords stayed the proceedings and referred the following question to the Court for a preliminary ruling:

> Was the BGC (at the material time) a body of such a type that the appellants are entitled in English courts and tribunals to rely directly upon Council Directive 76/207 of 9 February 1976 on the implementation of the principle of equal treatment for men and women as regards access to employment, vocational training and promotion, and working conditions so as to be entitled to a claim for damages on the ground that the retirement policy of the BGC was contrary to the directive?

The jurisdiction of the court

Before considering the question referred by the House of Lords, it must first be observed as a preliminary point that the UK has submitted that it is not a matter for the Court of Justice but for the national courts to determine, in the context of the national legal system, whether the provisions of a directive may be relied upon against a body such as the BGC.

The question was what effects measures adopted by Community institutions have and, in particular, whether those measures may be relied on against certain categories of persons necessarily involves interpretation of the articles of the Treaty concerning measures adopted by the institutions and the Community measure in issue.

It follows that the Court of Justice has jurisdiction in proceedings for a preliminary ruling to determine the categories of persons against whom the provisions of a directive may be relied on. It is for the national courts, on the other hand, to decide whether a party to proceedings before them falls within one of the categories so defined.

Reliance on the provisions of the directive against a body such as the BGC

...

The Court has ... held in a series of cases that unconditional and sufficiently precise provisions of a directive could be relied on against organisations or bodies which were subject to the authority or control of the state or had special powers beyond those which result from the normal rules applicable to relations between individuals.

The Court has accordingly held that provisions of a directive could be relied on against tax authorities (the judgments in Case 8/81 *Becker*, cited above, and in Case C-221/88 *ECSC v Acciaierie e Ferriere Busseni (in liquidation)* [1990] ECR I-495), local or regional authorities (judgment in Case 103/88 *Fratelli Costanzo v Comune di Milano* [1989] ECR 1839), constitutionally independent authorities responsible for the maintenance of public order and safety (judgment in Case 222/84 *Johnston v Chief Constable of the Royal Ulster Constabulary* [1986] ECR 1651), and public authorities providing public health services (judgment in Case 152/84 *Marshall*, cited above).

It follows from the foregoing that a body, whatever its legal form, which has been made responsible, pursuant to a measure adopted by the state, for providing a public service under the control of the state, and has for that purpose special powers beyond those which result from the normal rules applicable in relations between individuals, is included in any event among the bodies against which the provisions of a directive capable of having direct effect may be relied upon ...

Notes

1 When the case came back to the House of Lords, it held that British Gas fell within the definition of a state body laid down by the ECJ in the case. As Douglas-Scott points out, the wide definition of state body adopted creates problems of unfairness: if the key rationale for the direct effect of directives is that the state should not be able to rely upon its own failure to implement directives, there is no justification for imposing, through direct effect, obligations upon bodies such as British Gas, which plainly bear no responsibility for such failures.[27]

2 It may be seen that the ECJ adopted a wide definition of 'state body', thereby extending the ambit of the doctrine of vertical direct effect. But, whatever the definition of 'state body', it was clear that private citizens and private companies providing non-public services, and without the 'special powers' referred to, fell outside it. This created an anomaly since a citizen could claim Community rights only if the body claimed against fell within the borders of the definition of a state body, which, as has been found above, was a complex one.[28] The definition appeared to create arbitrary distinctions between citizens in terms of their entitlements to such rights.

3 As de Burca notes:

This limitation on direct effect [ie that directives do not have horizontal direct effect] remains an awkward problem for the Community, since the effectiveness of its laws and their equal and uniform application in all of the Member States is a prerequisite to the attainment of the objectives

27 *Op cit*, p 297.
28 See D Curtin (1990) 15 EL Rev 195.

which the Community was founded to achieve. The combination of the states' frequent non-implementation of directives, with the fact that directives cannot in themselves be directly enforced against individuals, means that their effectiveness as a legislative form is seriously undermined. In practical terms, many of the Community's important legislative policies, such as that embodied in the Equal Treatment Directive [76/207, OJ No 39, p 40] have been hindered or frustrated.[29]

For further discussion of the arguments for and against maintaining the horizontal/vertical distinction in relation to direct effect, see D Colgan, 'Triangular situations: the coup de grace for the denial of horizontal direct effect of Community directives' (2002) 8(4) EPL 545, pp 562–68.

4   However, recent case law of the ECJ appears to have progressed the position: while the ECJ still affirms the basic principle that directives cannot be relied upon to give rights as against other individuals, recent case law has served to create a species of quasi-horizontal, or what some writers refer to as 'triangular' effect.[30] There have been a number of decisions in which legal relations between private parties have been affected by directives, although not through straightforward reliance on a directive as a source of rights against another party. Rather, directives have been relied upon in order to disapply provisions of national law which were unhelpful to one party to private litigation. *CIA Security* (1996) concerned the applicability of Directive 83/189 to a dispute between private parties. Directive 83/189 is designed to protect the free movement of goods by providing that national regulations which could impact on such free movement must be notified in draft to the Commission for comment. CIA Security[31] had taken action in libel against two rival companies which in their promotional literature had claimed that CIA's burglar alarms did not comply with domestic (Belgian) law. However, the provisions of domestic law with which the alarms were said not to comply should have been notified to the EC Commission under Article 8 of Directive 83/189. On a reference from the Belgian courts, the ECJ ruled that the breach of the Directive's notification requirement meant that the national court had to disregard the unnotified rules. Consequently, CIA's rivals found themselves with no defence to the company's action against them. The effect of the ruling was therefore to effect an important change in the legal position of one private party vis à vis another, though this occurred through the means of holding national regulations to be invalid, not by allowing one private party to rely positively on a provision of a directive against another, which would be the 'pure' and still forbidden form of horizontal direct effect of directives.[32] However, the case of *Unilever Italia*, which concerned the same Directive, appeared to progress the position closer towards this purportedly forbidden ground. Michael Dougan summarises the facts.

Unilever Italia concerned a dispute between two private undertakings over a contract for the supply of extra virgin olive oil. Central Food refused to accept delivery because the goods did not comply with labelling requirements as regards the origin of olive oil imposed by recent Italian legislation. Unilever claimed that the Italian rules were themselves governed by the provisions of

---

29   G de Burca, 'Giving effect to European Community directives' (1992) 55 MLR 215.
30   See eg, K Lackhoff and H Nyssens, 'Direct effect of directives in triangular situations' (1998) 23 EL Rev 397; M Lenz, DS Tynes and L Young, 'Horizontal what? Back to basics' (2000) 25 EL Rev 121; D Colgan, 'Triangular situations: the coup de grace for the denial of horizontal direct effect of Community directives' (2002) 8(4) EPL 545.
31   Not the American intelligence service, but an Italian company which made security systems.
32   In *Lemmens* (Case C-226/97) [1998] ECR I-3711, the ECJ, rather confusingly held that in a similar case of non-notification of national rules (in this case rules specifying the use of a breathalyser) a person convicted using evidence obtained by the breathalyser could not rely on the non-notification so as to have the evidence obtained through the use of the breathalyser disregarded.

Directive 83/189. Under Article 8 of the Directive, Member States must notify draft technical regulations to the Commission. Italy had notified its draft labelling rules to the Commission as required by Article 8, but nevertheless continued to enact those proposals into law contrary to the standstill obligations contained in Article 9 [ie the obligation not to bring the draft regulations into force until the Commission and/or other Member States have had time to comment within the relevant time limits]. Unilever [which had commenced proceedings against Central Foods for the contractual price of the olive oil] argued that the principle in *CIA Security* should extend also to a failure to comply with Article 9, rendering the national rules on labelling non-applicable and thus obliging Central Food to accept delivery in accordance with its contractual duties. The Italian court sought guidance from the ECJ under Article 234 EC.[33]

Unilever Italia v Central Food (Case C-443/98) [2000] ECR I-7535

After dealing with some preliminary issues, the Court had to consider whether the failure to observe the stand-still period in Article 9 rendered the national law which laid down the labelling requirements (which Central Foods complained had not been observed) void, even though such a ruling would have a direct impact on the rights and duties of private parties vis à vis each other. It noted the arguments against such a finding.

> The Italian Government ... observes that, whilst the Court has indeed attributed direct effect to certain provisions of directives in that individuals, in the absence of proper transposition, may rely on such provisions as against the defaulting Member State, it has also held that to extend such a precedent to relationships between individuals would be tantamount to granting the Community power to impose, with immediate effect, obligations on individuals, even though it has no such competence except where it is empowered to adopt regulations. Thus, it is clear from settled case-law of the Court that a directive cannot of itself impose obligations on individuals and cannot therefore be relied on as such against them. No derogation from that principle can be based on the judgment in *CIA Security*. The operative part of that judgment discloses no intention to reverse the principle according to which a directive cannot have direct effect in horizontal relations between individuals.
>
> . . .
>
> 45 It is ... necessary to consider ... whether the inapplicability of technical regulations adopted in breach of Article 9 of Directive 83/189 can be invoked in civil proceedings between private individuals concerning contractual rights and obligations.
>
> 46 First, in civil proceedings of that nature, application of technical regulations adopted in breach of Article 9 of Directive 83/189 may have the effect of hindering the use or marketing of a product which does not conform to those regulations.
>
> 47 That is the case in the main proceedings, since application of the Italian rules is liable to hinder Unilever in marketing the extra virgin olive oil which it offers for sale.
>
> 48 Next, it must be borne in mind that, in *CIA Security*, the finding of inapplicability as a legal consequence of breach of the obligation of notification was made in response to a request for a preliminary ruling arising from proceedings between competing undertakings based on national provisions prohibiting unfair trading.
>
> 49 Thus, it follows from the case-law of the Court that the inapplicability of a technical regulation which has not been notified in accordance with Article 8 of Directive 83/189 can be invoked in proceedings between individuals for the reasons set out in paragraphs 40 to 43 of this judgment. The same applies to non-compliance with the obligations laid down by Article 9 of the same directive, and there is no reason, in that connection, to treat disputes between individuals relating

---

to unfair competition, as in the *CIA Security* case, differently from disputes between individuals concerning contractual rights and obligations, as in the main proceedings.

50 Whilst it is true, as observed by the Italian and Danish Governments, that a directive cannot of itself impose obligations on an individual and cannot therefore be relied on as such against an individual (see *Faccini Dori* [1994] ECR 1-3325, paragraph 20), that case-law does not apply where non-compliance with Article 8 or Article 9 of Directive 83/189, which constitutes a substantial procedural defect, renders a technical regulation adopted in breach of either of those articles inapplicable.

51 In such circumstances, and unlike the case of non-transposition of directives with which the case-law cited by those two Governments is concerned, Directive 83/189 does not in any way define the substantive scope of the legal rule on the basis of which the national court must decide the case before it. It creates neither rights nor obligations for individuals.

52 In view of all the foregoing considerations, the answer to the question submitted must be that a national court is required, in civil proceedings between individuals concerning contractual rights and obligations, to refuse to apply a national technical regulation which was adopted during a period of postponement of adoption prescribed in Article 9 of Directive 83/189.

Notes

1   It may be noted that the Advocate General in the case argued *against* rendering the national rules inapplicable in this context. As Dougan summarises his argument:

The Advocate General observed at several points that the procedural code laid down by Directive 83/189 was designed to regulate relations between the Commission and the Member States; it was intended neither to confer rights on, nor to create obligations for, individuals. As such, the consequences of a Member State's failure to comply with Directive 83/189 were best determined not through the case law on the direct effect of un- or incorrectly implemented directives, but rather on the basis of the general principles of Community law. From this perspective, fundamental Community interests relating directly to the effectiveness of Commission supervision and indirectly to the free movement of goods justified a decision that the Member State cannot enforce against individuals technical regulations adopted in breach of Article 8 Directive 83/189. Moreover, the special procedural circumstances of *CIA Security* vindicated the Court's view that the same sanction of inapplicability should extend to civil proceedings between competitors based on national rules prohibiting unfair trading practices – which were comparable to the Member State's own enforcement activities acting in its capacity as public prosecutor or administrative authority. However, the Court in *CIA Security* could not have intended that the sanction of inapplicability should apply in all types of proceedings between individuals, including civil actions concerning contractual rights and obligations.

First, such a possibility would be detrimental to legal certainty in the day-to-day conduct of trade – especially given the practical difficulties in ascertaining whether the Member State has fully complied with its procedural obligations under Directive 83/189. Secondly, it would also threaten to generate injustice – as regards both the individual forced to bear the cost of, and the individual permitted to profit from, the Member State's default.[34]

2   Dougan goes on to comment on the decision:

M Dougan, 'Case comment' (2001) 38 CMLR 1503–17 (extracts)

... It may ... be true that the black letter of the Directive does not define the substantive legal rules for determining the dispute at hand and does not in that sense seek to create rights or obligations for individuals. Yet the very consequence of rendering offending national regulations inapplicable is *precisely* to transform the Directive into a measure which determines the

34   *Ibid.*

substantive legal rules applicable to the case and whose effect is *precisely* to create rights and obligations for the relevant protagonists – for example, to the extent that Unilever could enforce entitlements and Central Foods would be bound by duties not recognized as such under existing Italian law.

... as regards the interests of the private parties involved in the relevant dispute: the sanction of inapplicability under Directive 83/189 could well spell financial ruin for those individuals who relied on the apparent security of existing domestic rules; while straightforward horizontal direct effect for 'ordinary' directives need not aggravate to any such degree the legal responsibilities incumbent upon those private parties who currently benefit from the *Dori* rule.

As it stands, the outcome in both *CIA Security* and especially in *Unilever Italia* was that a private individual suffered the consequences of the Member State's failure to comply with the terms of a Community directive ...

Indeed, the Court's reasoning in *Unilever Italia* operates, in effect, to alter the underlying legislative nature of Directive 83/189: it becomes less like a directive ... and more akin to a regulation in its ability to produce binding legal effects between private parties independently of implementation by the Member State ... the odd result of the Court's approach in *Unilever Italia* is that a measure (such as Directive 83/189) which is intended to govern inter-institutional relations between Member State and Commission can legitimately produce binding effects for the legal position of third parties, whilst a measure (such as the Equal Treatment Directive or the Doorstep Selling Directive) which is specifically intended to govern relations between private individuals is prohibited from having any such consequences – surely the opposite of what a coherent legal system should seek to achieve.

Notes
1   Colgan agrees, arguing that, 'the most useful definition of triangular situations must place the emphasis on the *impact* of a decision, rather than taking a purely technical view ...'[35]

2   The above commentary brings out the extent to which this decision places in some jeopardy the stability of the rule against horizontal direct effect of directives, by opening the way towards the carving out of further 'bold exceptions' to it as and when the ECJ finds that course desirable. Colgan indeed considers that, 'The limitation of the direct effect of directives has thus – in the triangular situations – been shown to have been drawn at an utterly arbitrary point'[36] and therefore concludes that the only resolution to this artificial and unprincipled situation is to abolish the 'unsustainable distinction between vertical and horizontal direct effect'.[37]

What are the legal effects produced by direct effect?

As Sacha Prechal notes, 'the orthodox understanding of direct effect was that ... wherever national rules are incompatible with Community law (or where there are no national rules at all), the Community law provisions must be able to be applied instead'.[38] However, he goes on point out that reliance upon Community law in substitution of national law is not the only aspect of direct effect:

35 *Op cit*, p 546.
36 *Ibid*, p 562.
37 *Ibid*, p 561.
38 *Op cit*, p 1059.

... judicial activity is not limited to the 'positive' application of the Community law provisions to the facts of the case. Often, the courts may confine themselves to reviewing the national law in the light of Community law provisions and, where appropriate, disapplying the national provisions, without it being necessary to apply the Community law provision instead. The same holds true *mutatis mutandis* where the applicant merely seeks a declaration, such as that a Member State has acted contrary to Community law.[39]

A well known example is the *EOC*[40] case decided by the House of Lords, in which the Lords granted a declaration that provisions of the Employment Protection (Consolidation) Act 1987 were incompatible with EC law, on the basis that they amounted to indirect, unjustified sex discrimination, contrary to Article 141 (formerly Article 119) EC.

Prechal continues:

in other cases, in particular where the disapplication results in a gap, it may be necessary for the domestic court to be able to apply a Community law provision instead in order to resolve the case before it. In discrimination cases ... the Court has provided the national courts with an aid to fill the gap, if it occurs: the same rules must be applied to the disadvantaged group as those which are applicable to the persons who are 'better off'.[41]

He then goes on to point out that Community law can still be directly effective where there is a discretion to be exercised by a national body, whether a court or executive authority: in such a case, the Community norm provides a standard by which to assess the legality of the exercise of the discretion; the question will be whether it has stayed within the limits set by Community law.[42]

DIRECTIVES: INDIRECT EFFECTS

The doctrine of vertical effect seemed to create unfairness since it meant *inter alia* that an individual who happened to be employed by a state body might be able to claim a remedy for denial of rights which would not be available to an individual employed by a non-state body. In response to this perception of unfairness, the ECJ developed the doctrine which has been termed the doctrine of indirect effect, explained in the following case.

Marleasing SA v La Comercial Internacional de Alimentación SA (Case C-106/89) [1990] ECR I-4135, I-4157–60, ECJ

Those questions arose in a dispute between Marleasing SA, the plaintiff in the main proceedings, and a number of defendants including La Commercial Internacional de Alimentación SA (hereinafter referred to as 'La Commercial'). The latter was established in the form of a public limited company by three persons, including Barviesa SA, which contributed its own assets.

It is apparent from the grounds set out in the order for reference that Marleasing's primary claim, based on Arts 1261 and 1275 of the Spanish Civil Code, according to which contracts without cause or whose cause is unlawful have no legal effect, is for a declaration that the founders' contract establishing La Commercial is void on the ground that the establishment of the company lacked cause, was a sham transaction and was carried out in order to defraud the creditors of

---

39 *Ibid.*
40 *R v Secretary of State for Employment ex p Equal Opportunities Commission and Another* [1994] 2 WLR 409.
41 *Op cit*, p 1060.
42 *Ibid*, p 1061. Prechal goes on to provide numerous examples.

Barviesa SA, a co-founder of the defendant company. La Commercial contended that the action should be dismissed in its entirety on the ground, in particular, that Art 11 of Directive 68/151, which lists exhaustively the cases in which the nullity of a company may be ordered, does not include lack of cause amongst them.

The national court observed that in accordance with Art 395 of the Act concerning the Conditions of Accession of Spain and the Portuguese Republic to the European Communities (*Official Journal* (1985) L 302, p23) the Kingdom of Spain was under an obligation to bring the directive into effect as from the date of accession, but that that had still not been done at the date of the order for reference. Taking the view, therefore, that the dispute raised a problem concerning the interpretation of Community law, the national court referred the following question to the Court:

> Is Art 11 of Council Directive 68/151/EEC of 9 March 1968, which has not been implemented in national law, directly applicable so as to preclude a declaration of nullity of a public limited company on a ground other than those set out in the said article?

With regard to the question whether an individual may rely on the directive against a national law, it should be observed that, as the Court has consistently held, a directive may not of itself impose obligations on an individual and, consequently, a provision of a directive may not be relied upon as such against such a person (judgment in Case 152/84 *Marshall v Southampton and South-West Hampshire Area Health Authority* [1986] ECR 723).

However, it is apparent from the documents before the Court that the national court seeks in substance to ascertain whether a national court hearing a case which falls within the scope of Directive 68/151 is required to interpret its national law in the light of the wording and the purpose of that directive in order to preclude a declaration of nullity of a public limited company on a ground other than those listed in Art 11 of the directive.

In order to reply to that question, it should be observed that, as the Court pointed out in its judgment in Case 14/83 *Von Colson and Kamann v Land Nordrhein-Westfalen* [1984] ECR 1891, para 26, the Member States' obligation arising from a directive to achieve the result envisaged by the directive and their duty under Art 5 of the Treaty to take all appropriate measures, whether general or particular, to ensure the fulfilment of that obligation, is binding on all the authorities of Member States including, for matters within their jurisdiction, the courts. It follows that, in applying national law, whether the provisions in question were adopted before or after the directive, the national court called upon to interpret it is required to do so, as far as possible, in the light of the wording and the purpose of the directive in order to achieve the result pursued by the latter and thereby comply with the third paragraph of Art 189 of the Treaty.

It follows that the requirement that national law must be interpreted in conformity with Art 11 of Directive 68/151 precludes the interpretation of provisions of national law relating to public limited companies in such a manner that the nullity of a public limited company may be ordered on grounds other than those exhaustively listed in Art 11 of the directive in question.

With regard to the interpretation to be given to Art 11 of the directive, in particular Art 11(2)(b), it should be observed that that provision prohibits the laws of the Member States from providing for a judicial declaration of nullity on grounds other than those exhaustively listed in the directive, amongst which is the ground that the objects of the company are unlawful or contrary to public policy.

According to the Commission, the expression 'objects of the company' must be interpreted as referring exclusively to the objects of the company as described in the instrument of incorporation or the articles of association. It follows, in the Commission's view, that a declaration of nullity of a company cannot be made on the basis of the activity actually pursued by it, for instance defrauding the founders' creditors.

That argument must be upheld. As is clear from the preamble to Directive 68/151, its purpose was to limit the cases in which nullity can arise and the retroactive effect of a declaration of nullity in order to ensure 'certainty in the law as regards relations between the company and third parties, and also between members' (sixth recital). Furthermore, the protection of third parties 'must be ensured by provisions which restrict to the greatest possible extent the grounds on which obligations entered into in the name of the company are not valid'. It follows, therefore, that each ground of nullity provided for in Art 11 of the directive must be interpreted strictly. In those circumstances the words 'objects of the company' must be understood as referring to the objects of the company as described in the instrument of incorporation or the articles of association.

The answer to the question submitted must therefore be that a national court hearing a case which falls within the scope of Directive 68/151 is required to interpret its national law in the light of the wording and the purpose of that directive in order to preclude a declaration of nullity of a public limited company on a ground other than those listed in Art 11 of the directive.

Note

In this case, there was a very clear clash between the Spanish Civil Code, under which contracts would be void if they lacked a cause, and EC law which provided an exhaustive list of grounds under which the incorporation of a company could be void, none of which included anything equivalent to the provision in Spanish law. Nevertheless, the ECJ's judgment implied that national courts had to give effect to indirectly effective directives regardless of the terms of the national legislation, an interpretation which would, as Hartley points out, have created 'horizontal direct effect under another name'.[43] In the following case, however, the ECJ seemed to draw back from such an extreme version of indirect effect.

Faccini Dori v Recreb (Case C-91/92) [1994] ECR I-3325, ECJ

It must also be borne in mind that, as the Court has consistently held since its judgment in Case 14/83 *Von Colson and Kamann v Land Nordrhein-Westfalen* [1984] ECR 1891, para 26, the Member States' obligation arising from a directive to achieve the result envisaged by the directive and their duty under Art 5 of the Treaty to take all appropriate measures, whether general or particular, is binding on all the authorities of Member States, including, for matters within their jurisdiction, the courts. The judgments of the Court in Case C-106/89 *Marleasing v La Comercial Internacional de Alimentación* [1990] ECR I-4135, para 8, and Case C-334/92 *Wagner Miret v Fondo de Garantía Salarial* [1993] ECR I-6911, para 20, make it clear that, when applying national law, whether adopted before or after the directive, the national court that has to interpret that law must do so, as far as possible, in the light of the wording and the purpose of the directive so as to achieve the result it has in view and thereby comply with the third paragraph of Art 189 of the Treaty.

Notes

1 The key limiting qualification to the obligation to interpret domestic legislation compatibly with EC law appears in the words 'so far as possible'.

2 A further question relates to the question of how indirect effect can apply horizontally, that is, be relied upon in disputes between private parties. It is clear that it can, in principle (as in *Marleasing*), but an exception appears to apply where the impact of interpreting national law in line with relevant Community law would be to impose an obligation on an individual, especially criminal liability. This exception arises from the case of *Arcaro*[44] in which the Court said:

the obligation of the national court to refer to the content of the directive when interpreting the relevant rules of its own national law reaches a limit where such an interpretation leads to the imposition on an individual of an obligation laid down by a directive which has not been

---

43 *Op cit*, p 213.
44 *Criminal Proceedings against Luciano Arcaro* [1996] ECR I-4705.

transposed or, more especially, where it has the effect of determining or aggravating, on the basis of the directive and in the absence of a law enacted for its implementation, the liability in criminal law of persons who act in contravention of that directive's provisions (see *Kolpinghuis Nijmegen* Case 80/86 [1987] ECR 3969.)

3   Thus, the doctrine of indirect effect, whilst a potentially powerful tool in the service of the effective domestic enforcement of EC law, has clear limitations. As Josephine Steiner puts it:

Whilst national courts might be prepared to construe domestic law to comply with Community law when the former was ambiguous, and capable of an interpretation in conformity with the directive, or where domestic law had been introduced, either before or after the directive, in order to comply with the directive [eg *Litster v Forth Dry Dock and Engineering Co Ltd* [1990] 1 AC 546], there were circumstances in which they not unnaturally felt that they had no discretion to give a directive indirect effect. Such might be the case where:

(a)   ... national law was perhaps compatible with Community law, but there was evidence that domestic law was not intended to have the meaning contended for [eg *Duke v GEC Reliance Ltd* [1988] AC 618, HL];

(b)   national law was clearly incompatible with Community law, and there was no evidence that domestic law was intended to comply with the directive; or

(c)   there was no domestic law to 'interpret' in accordance with the directive.

Furthermore, in these types of case it could be argued, with some justice, that it would be unfair, in breach of individuals' legitimate expectations [see *Kolpinhuis Nijmegen* Case 80/86 [1987] ECR 3969], to 'interpret' domestic law to comply with Community law. To do so would be to introduce direct effects by the back door.[45]

FRANCOVICH AND STATE LIABILITY

Introduction

EC law, whether primary (deriving from Treaty articles) or secondary (in the form of Regulations or directives) often does not lay down the remedies that should be made available for an aggrieved party if the provisions are breached. As de Burca puts it:

in the case of directives which are directly enforceable, but which do not themselves specify any particular remedy for breach, the ECJ has stressed that there is an obligation upon national courts to provide adequate and effective remedies.[46]

But the details of these remedies and the legal procedures required to change them have always remained, in principle, a matter for national law. As the ECJ said in *Comet v Produktschap voor Siergewassen* (Case 45/76) [1976] ECR 2045 and *Rewe v Landwirtschaftskammer Saarland* (Case 33/76) [1976] ECR 1805:

It is for the national legal order of each Member State to designate the competent courts and to lay down the procedural rules for proceeding designed to ensure the protection of the rights which individuals acquire through the direct effect of Community law [*Comet*, p 2043].

There are, though, two basic principles of EC law relating to remedies: first, the principle of *equality*: Community law claims must not be treated less favourably than comparable national law claims; secondly, the principle of *effectiveness*: there must be

---

45   J Steiner, 'From direct effects to *Francovich*: shifting means of enforcement of Community law' (1993) 18(3) EL Rev 3, 5.
46   de Burca, *op cit*.

an effective remedy before national courts and this requires that the national rules must not be framed in such a way as to render virtually impossible or very difficult the exercise of the rights conferred by EC law.[47] This has been a problem for the enforcement of EC law. As de Burca puts it:

> ... even where a directive is sought to be enforced against the state and has been held to confer a right directly upon an individual, the Member State in question may not have provided a suitable domestic remedy for the enforcement of that right. National courts have frequently had to grapple with the problem of what to do when faced with a directly enforceable Community right for which no national remedy exists (a celebrated example in the UK being the case of *Factortame Ltd v Secretary of State for Transport* [1990] 2 AC 85 and [1991] 1 AC 603).[48]

In *Factortame* [1990] 2 AC 85, under English law there was no means of granting interim relief[49] by suspending the statute which infringed rights deriving from EC law. Lord Bridge said: 'I am clearly of the opinion that as a matter of English law, the court has no power to make an order which has these consequences.'[50] When the ECJ was asked by the House of Lords what to do in this situation it said: '... a court which in those circumstances would grant interim relief, if it were not for a rule of national law, is obliged to set aside that rule.'[51] In this case, that rule was that the courts may not grant an injunction against the Crown, as was needed in this case so as to prevent it from enforcing a statute which was probably incompatible with EC law (it would not be established that it was definitely incompatible until the ECJ had made its ruling).

But, as Steiner goes on to explain, the means of enforcement, in particular of directives, were not proving adequate; there was a crisis of compliance with EC law:

> With the move towards completion of the internal market by 31 December 1992, to be achieved largely through harmonisation by directive [under Article 100a EEC], the problem of enforcement became acute. States were failing increasingly to implement directives on time. Despite redoubled efforts by the Commission under Art 169, states continued to neglect their duties of implementation and even successful proceedings failed to secure compliance. In 1989, 26 Art 169 proceedings were brought for the second time. If the internal market programme were to succeed, something more had to be done.[52]

The *Francovich* principle was the means by which this problem could be ameliorated.

The establishment of the principle of state liability: the *Francovich* decision

Francovich v Italy (Joined Cases C-6/90 and C-9/90) [1991] ECR I-5357, ECJ

Mr Francovich, a party to the main proceedings in Case C-6/90, had worked for CDN Elettronica SnC in Vicenza but had received only sporadic payments on account of his wages. He therefore brought proceedings before the Pretura di Vicenza, which ordered the defendant to pay approximately LIT 6 million. In attempting to enforce that judgment the bailiff attached to the Tribunale di Vicenza was obliged to submit a negative return. Mr Francovich then claimed to be

---

47 See, eg, *Amministrazione delle Finanze dello Stato v San Giorgio* (Case 199/82) [1983] ECR 3595.
48 *Op cit.*
49 Whilst reference was made to the ECJ.
50 *Ibid.*
51 *Secretary of State for Transport v Factortame I* [1990] ECR I-2433 at paras 18–21.
52 Steiner (1993), *op cit.*

entitled to obtain from the Italian State the guarantees provided for in Directive 80/987 or, in the alternative, compensation.

In Case C-9/90 Danila Bonifaci and 33 other employees brought proceedings before the Pretura di Bassano del Grappa, stating that they had been employed by Gaia Confezioni Srl, which was declared insolvent on 5 April 1985. When the employment relationships were discontinued, the plaintiffs were owed more than LIT 253 million, which was proved as a debt in the company's insolvency. More than five years after the insolvency they had been paid nothing, and the receiver had told them that even a partial distribution in their favour was entirely improbable. Consequently, the plaintiffs brought proceedings against the Italian Republic in which they claimed that, in view of its obligation to implement Directive 80/987 with effect from 23 October 1983, it should be ordered to pay them their arrears of wages, at least for the last three months, or in the alternative to pay compensation.

. . .

. . . The national court seeks to determine whether a Member State is obliged to make good loss and damage suffered by individuals as a result of the failure to transpose Directive 80/987.

The national court thus raises the issue of the existence and scope of a state's liability for loss and damage resulting from breach of its obligations under Community law.

That issue must be considered in the light of the general system of the Treaty and its fundamental principles.

(a) The existence of state liability as a matter of principle

It should be borne in mind at the outset that the EEC Treaty has created its own legal system, which is integrated into the legal systems of the Member States and which their courts are bound to apply. The subjects of that legal system are not only the Member States but also their nationals. Just as it imposes burdens on individuals, Community law is also intended to give rise to rights which become part of their legal patrimony. Those rights arise, not only where they are expressly granted by the Treaty, but also by virtue of obligations which the Treaty imposes in a clearly defined manner both on individuals and on the Member States and the Community institutions (see the judgments in Case 26/62 *Van Gend en Loos* [1963] ECR 1 and Case 6/64 *Costa v ENEL* [1964] ECR 585).

Furthermore, it has been consistently held that the national courts whose task it is to apply the provisions of Community law in areas within their jurisdiction must ensure that those rules take full effect and must protect the rights which they confer on individuals (see in particular the judgments in Case 106/77 *Amministrazione delle Finanze dello Stato v Simmenthal* [1978] ECR 629, para 16, and Case C-213/89 *Factortame* [1990] ECR I-2433, para 19).

The full effectiveness of Community rules would be impaired and the protection of the rights which they grant would be weakened if individuals were unable to obtain redress when their rights are infringed by a breach of Community law for which a Member State can be held responsible.

The possibility of obtaining redress from the Member State is particularly indispensable where, as in this case, the full effectiveness of Community rules is subject to prior action on the part of the state and where, consequently, in the absence of such action, individuals cannot enforce before the national courts the rights conferred upon them by Community law.

It follows that the principle whereby a state must be liable for loss and damage caused to individuals as a result of breaches of Community law for which the state can be held responsible is inherent in the system of the Treaty.

A further basis for the obligation of Member States to make good such loss and damage is to be found in Art 5 of the Treaty, under which the Member States are required to take all appropriate measures, whether general or particular, to ensure fulfilment of their obligations under

Community law. Among these is the obligation to nullify the unlawful consequences of a breach of Community law (see, in relation to the analogous provision of Art 86 of the ECSC Treaty, the judgment in Case 6/60 *Humblet v Belgium* [1960] ECR 559).

It follows from all the foregoing that it is a principle of Community law that the Member States are obliged to make good loss and damage caused to individuals by breaches of Community law for which they can be held responsible.

(b) The conditions for state liability

Although state liability is thus required by Community law, the conditions under which that liability gives rise to a right to reparation depend on the nature of the breach of Community law giving rise to the loss and damage.

Where, as in this case, a Member State fails to fulfil its obligation under the third paragraph of Art 189 of the Treaty to take all the measures necessary to achieve the result prescribed by a directive, the full effectiveness of that rule of Community law requires that there should be a right to reparation provided that three conditions are fulfilled.

The first of those conditions is that the result prescribed by the directive should entail the grant of rights to individuals. The second condition is that it should be possible to identify the content of those rights on the basis of the provisions of the directive. Finally, the third condition is the existence of a causal link between the breach of the state's obligation and the loss and damage suffered by the injured parties.

Those conditions are sufficient to give rise to a right on the part of individuals to obtain reparation, a right founded directly on Community law.

Subject to that reservation, it is on the basis of the rules of national law on liability that the state must make reparation for the consequences of the loss and damage caused. In the absence of Community legislation, it is for the internal legal order of each Member State to designate the competent courts and lay down the detailed procedural rules for legal proceedings intended fully to safeguard the rights which individuals derive from Community law (see the judgments in Case 60/75 *Russo v AIMA* [1976] ECR 45, Case 33/76 *Rewe v Landwirtschaftskammer Saarland* [1976] ECR 1989 and Case 158/80 *Rewe v Hauptzollamt Kiel* [1981] ECR 1805).

Further, the substantive and procedural conditions for reparation of loss and damage laid down by the national law of the Member States must not be less favourable than those relating to similar domestic claims and must not be so framed as to make it virtually impossible or excessively difficult to obtain reparation (see, in relation to the analogous issue of the repayment of taxes levied in breach of Community law, *inter alia* the judgment in Case 199/82 *Amministrazione delle Finanze dello Stato v San Giorgio* [1983] ECR 3595).

In this case, the breach of Community law by a Member State by virtue of its failure to transpose Directive 80/987 within the prescribed period has been confirmed by a judgment of the Court. The result required by that directive entails the grant to employees of a right to a guarantee of payment of their unpaid wage claims. As is clear from the examination of the first part of the first question, the content of that right can be identified on the basis of the provisions of the directive.

Consequently, the national court must, in accordance with the national rules on liability, uphold the right of employees to obtain reparation of loss and damage caused to them as a result of failure to transpose the directive.

The answer to be given to the national court must therefore be that a Member State is required to make good loss and damage caused to individuals by failure to transpose Directive 80/987.

Note

The principles of direct and indirect effects had limitations, as suggested above, in terms of securing compliance with EC law. The decision in *Francovich* provided a new and surer means of enforcing EC law, as explained by Steiner.

Josephine Steiner, 'From direct effects to _Francovich_: shifting means of enforcement of Community law' (1993) 18(3) EL Rev 9–12, 19–22

Assessment of Francovich

The decision in _Francovich_ is undoubtedly consistent with, and a natural and logical extension of, the Court's case law. Having established that Community law can give rise to rights for individuals, and that national courts are obliged to ensure the full effectiveness of such provisions, it was but a small step to guarantee their full effect by holding states liable in damages for infringements of those rights for which they were responsible.

The breakthrough in _Francovich_ lay not so much in the fact that individuals were held entitled to claim damages against the state – in the context of actions based on directly effective Community law against 'public' bodies that had long been possible [for example, _Bourgoin v Minister for Agriculture and Fisheries_ [1985] 3 All ER 585, CA], but that their claim to compensation was independent of the principle of direct effects. Provided the criteria for _Francovich_ are met, the individual may now proceed against the state for breach not of substantive, directly effective Community provisions, but for the state's primary failure to comply with its obligation to implement Community law. ... In this way, the problems associated with directives arising from their lack of horizontal effect would be largely circumvented. If Community rights could not be enforced against private parties, compensation would at least be provided for individuals wrongfully deprived of their Community rights. At the same time the prospect of liability to all parties suffering damage as a result of their failures to implement Community law would provide states with a powerful incentive fully to comply with their Community obligations.

A principle of state liability as applied in _Francovich_ is arguably more legitimate as a means of enforcement of Community law than the principle of direct effects. Under the latter principle, Treaty provisions, the scope of which may not be clear (eg, Art 119), may be enforced against the legitimate expectations of 'private' parties. The majority of 'public' bodies, against which directives may be invoked, can hardly be seen as responsible for non-implementation. The element of public authority or control to which they are subject simply renders them liable by association. If that authority or control should have ensured compliance by the defendant organisation with the obligations imposed by directives and failed to do so, the fault lies less with the local authority or public enterprise than with the central authorities, the legislative or executive organs of the state.

The development of the _Francovich_ doctrine: beyond liability for failure to implement directives

In the following case, the ECJ was asked certain questions relating to the scope of the _Francovich_ principle in relation to the _Factortame_ litigation and the compensation claimable by the Spanish fishing companies who had sustained loss because of the Merchant Shipping Act 1988. The facts were as follows:

The intention [of the Act] was to protect British fishing communities by preventing foreign nationals from fishing against the United Kingdom's quota under the common fisheries policy adopted by the European Community. Before introducing the Act the British Government had conducted a process of consultation and obtained legal advice, including leading counsel's opinion, that there was a reasonably good chance that the proposed legislation would be upheld by the European Court of Justice. However, the European Commission had warned that provisions of the Act appeared to infringe Community law. Under the Act a vessel could be registered as a British fishing vessel only if its owners and 75 per cent of its shareholders were British citizens resident and domiciled in the United Kingdom, and all previously registered vessels required to be reregistered. The applicants, companies incorporated under UK law, and their directors and shareholders, most of whom were Spanish nationals, owned between them 95 deep-sea fishing vessels which had previously been registered as British. They were unable to re-register their vessels because they failed to satisfy one or more of the conditions imposed by the Act. The applicants commenced judicial review proceedings to challenge the legality of the provisions of the Act which were based on nationality and domicile, on the grounds that they were incompatible with the EEC Treaty. The European Commission also brought infringement proceedings against the UK. The European Court of Justice held that the registration conditions were contrary to Community law. The applicants claimed from the United Kingdom legislature damages in respect of expenses and losses allegedly incurred by them in consequence of the relevant provisions of the Act. The Divisional Court made a reference to the European Court of Justice as to whether, as a matter of Community law, the claimants had an entitlement to damages and if so, what considerations national courts should apply in determining claims.[53]

(In its decision, the ECJ also answered certain questions asked of it by a German court in the *Brasserie du Pêcheur* case.)

R v Secretary of State for Transport, ex p Factortame (No 4); Brasserie du Pêcheur SA v Germany (Joined Cases C-48/93 and C-46/93) [1996] ECR I-1029

51 Community law confers a right to reparation where three conditions are met: the rule of law infringed must be intended to confer rights on individuals; the breach must be sufficiently serious; and there must be a direct causal link between the breach of the obligation resting on the state and the damage sustained by the injured parties.

...

55 As to the second condition, as regards both Community liability under Art 215 and Member State liability for breaches of Community law, the decisive test for finding that a breach of Community law is sufficiently serious is whether the Member State or the Community institution concerned manifestly and gravely disregarded the limits on its discretion.

56 The factors which the competent court may take into consideration include: the clarity and precision of the rule breached; the measure of discretion left by that rule to the national or Community authorities; whether the infringement and the damage caused was intentional or involuntary; whether any error of law was excusable or inexcusable; the fact that the position taken by a Community institution may have contributed towards the omission, and the adoption or retention of national measures or practices contrary to Community law.

57 On any view, a breach of Community law will clearly be sufficiently serious if it has persisted despite a judgment finding the infringement in question to be established, or a preliminary ruling or settled case law of the court on the matter from which it is clear that the conduct in question constituted an infringement.

58 While, in the present cases, the court cannot substitute its assessment for that of the national courts, which have sole jurisdiction to find the facts in the main proceedings and decide how to characterise the breaches of Community law at issue, it will be helpful to indicate a number of circumstances which the national courts might take into account.

...

61 The decision of the UK legislature to introduce in the Merchant Shipping Act 1988 provisions relating to the conditions for the registration of fishing vessels has to be assessed differently in the case of the provisions making registration subject to a nationality condition, which constitute direct discrimination manifestly contrary to Community law, and in the case of the provisions laying down residence and domicile conditions for vessel owners and operators.

62 The latter conditions are *prima facie* incompatible with Art 52 of the Treaty in particular but the UK sought to justify them in terms of the objectives of the common fisheries policy. In the

---

53 This summary of the facts of the case is taken from *Factortame (No 5)* [2000] 1 AC 524, HL.

judgment in *Secretary of State for Transport, ex p Factortame Ltd (No 3)* (Case C-221/89) [1992] QB 680, the court rejected that justification.

63 In order to determine whether the breach of Art 52 thus committed by the UK was sufficiently serious, the national court might take into account *inter alia*, the legal disputes relating to particular features of the common fisheries policy, the attitude of the Commission, which made its position known to the UK in good time, and the assessments as to the state of certainty of Community law made by the national courts in the interim proceedings brought by individuals affected by the Merchant Shipping Act.

64 Lastly, consideration should be given to the assertion made by Rawlings (Trawling) Ltd, the 37th applicant in Case C-48/93, that the UK failed to adopt immediately the measures needed to comply with the order of the President of the Court of Justice of 10 October 1989 in *Commission of the European Communities v United Kingdom of Great Britain and Northern Ireland* (Case 246/89R) [1989] ECR 3125, and that that needlessly increased the loss it sustained. If that allegation – which was certainly contested by the UK at the hearing – should prove correct, it should be regarded by the national court as constituting in itself a manifest and, therefore, sufficiently serious breach of Community law.

65 As for the third condition, it is for the national courts to determine whether there is a direct causal link between the breach of the obligation borne by the state and the damage sustained by the injured parties.

66 The aforementioned three conditions are necessary and sufficient to found a right in individuals to obtain redress, although this does not mean that the state cannot incur liability under less strict conditions on the basis of national law.

67 As appears from *Francovich v Italian Republic* (Joined Cases C-6 and 9/90) [1995] ECR 722, 772-773, paras 41-43, subject to the right to reparation which flows directly from Community law where the conditions referred to in the preceding paragraph are satisfied, the state must make reparation for the consequences of the loss and damage caused in accordance with the domestic rules on liability, provided that the conditions for reparation of loss and damage laid down by national law must not be less favourable than those relating to similar domestic claims and must not be such as in practice to make it impossible or excessively difficult to obtain reparation (see also *Amministrazione delle Finanze dello Stato v SpA San Giorgio* (Case 199/82) [1983] ECR 3595).

68 In that regard, restrictions that exist in domestic legal systems as to the non-contractual liability of the state in the exercise of its legislative function may be such as to make it impossible in practice or excessively difficult for individuals to exercise their right to reparation, as guaranteed by Community law, of loss or damage resulting from the breach of Community law.

. . .

70 While the imposition of such restrictions may be consistent with the requirement that the conditions laid down should not be less favourable than those relating to similar domestic claims, it is still to be considered whether such restrictions are not such as in practice to make it impossible or excessively difficult to obtain reparation.

. . .

73 . . . any condition that may be imposed by English law on state liability requiring proof of misfeasance in public office, such an abuse of power being inconceivable in the case of the legislature, is also such as in practice to make it impossible or extremely difficult to obtain effective reparation for loss or damage resulting from a breach of Community law where the breach is attributable to the national legislature.

74 Accordingly, the reply to the questions from the national courts must be that, where a breach of Community law by a Member State is attributable to the national legislature acting in a field

in which it has a wide discretion to make legislative choices, individuals suffering loss or injury thereby are entitled to reparation where the rule of Community law breached is intended to confer rights on them, the breach is sufficiently serious and there is a direct causal link between the breach and the damage sustained by the individuals. Subject to that reservation, the state must make good the consequences of the loss or damage caused by the breach of Community law attributable to it, in accordance with its national law on liability. However, the conditions laid down by the applicable national laws must not be less favourable than those relating to similar domestic claims or framed in such a way as in practice to make it impossible or excessively difficult to obtain reparation.

The Court then went on to consider the question whether 'the national court is entitled to make reparation conditional on the existence of fault (whether intentional or negligent) on the part of the organ of the state to which the infringement is attributable' (para 75).

76 As is clear from the case file, the concept of fault does not have the same content in the various legal systems.

77 Next, it follows from the reply to the preceding question that, where a breach of Community law is attributable to a Member State acting in a field in which it has a wide discretion to make legislative choices, a finding of a right to reparation on the basis of Community law will be conditional, inter alia, on the breach having been sufficiently serious.

78 So, certain objective and subjective factors connected with the concept of fault under a national legal system may well be relevant for the purpose of determining whether or not a given breach of Community law is serious: see the factors mentioned in paragraphs 56 and 57 above.

79 The obligation to make reparation for loss or damage caused to individuals cannot, however, depend on a condition based on any concept of fault going beyond that of a sufficiently serious breach of Community law. Imposition of such a supplementary condition would be tantamount to calling in question the right to reparation founded on the Community legal order.

80 Accordingly, the reply to the question from the national court must be that, pursuant to the national legislation which it applies, reparation of loss or damage cannot be made conditional on fault (intentional or negligent) on the part of the organ of the state responsible for the breach, going beyond that of a sufficiently serious breach of Community law.

The actual extent of the reparation (question (4)(a) in Case C-46/93 and the second question in Case C-48/93)

81 By these questions, the national courts essentially ask the court to identify the criteria for determination of the extent of the reparation due by the Member State responsible for the breach.

82 Reparation for loss or damage caused to individuals as a result of breaches of Community law must be commensurate with the loss or damage sustained so as to ensure the effective protection for their rights.

83 In the absence of relevant Community provisions, it is for the domestic legal system of each Member State to set the criteria for determining the extent of reparation. However, those criteria must not be less favourable than those applying to similar claims based on domestic law and must not be such as in practice to make it impossible or excessively difficult to obtain reparation.

84 In particular, in order to determine the loss or damage for which reparation may be granted, the national court may inquire whether the injured person showed reasonable diligence in order to avoid the loss or damage or limit its extent and whether, in particular, he availed himself in time of all the legal remedies available to him.

85 Indeed, it is a general principle common to the legal systems of the Member States that the injured party must show reasonable diligence in limiting the extent of the loss or damage, or risk having to bear the damage himself: *Mulder v Council and Commission of the European Communities* (Joined Cases C-104/89 and C-37/90) [1992] ECR I-3061, 3136, 3137, para 33.

. . .

89 As regards in particular the award of exemplary damages, such damages are based under domestic law, as the Divisional Court explains, on the finding that the public authorities concerned acted oppressively, arbitrarily or unconstitutionally. In so far as such conduct may constitute or aggravate a breach of Community law, an award of exemplary damages pursuant to a claim or an action founded on Community law cannot be ruled out if such damages could be awarded pursuant to a similar claim or action founded on domestic law.

Notes

1 In the above case, the ECJ provided some clarification of the application of the *Francovich* principle. Most significantly, it found that the *Francovich* principle of state liability held good regardless of which organ of the state was responsible for the breach; liability was not dependent on fault on the part of the relevant organ of the state, and exemplary damages could be awarded against the State in claims founded on Community law if they could be awarded in similar claims founded on domestic law. Guidance was given in para 56 (above) as to when a breach would be 'sufficiently serious' (the second *Francovich* criterion). A breach of Community law would always be sufficiently serious if it persisted, despite a judgment by the ECJ finding the breach to be established. In *R v HM Treasury ex p British Telecommunications plc* (Case C-392/93) [1996)] QB 615 the ECJ found that the failure of the UK to implement correctly Directive 90/531 did not involve a sufficiently serious breach of Community law since the Directive was worded imprecisely and the Commission had not given guidance on the subject.

2 In *Factortame (No 5)* [2001] 1 AC 524, the House of Lords had to determine whether, as the lower courts had held, the conditions for liability set out by the ECJ in its case law were satisfied in relation to the enactment of the Merchant Shipping Act 1988 and the loss it had caused. The decision in this case appears in the next section.

3 For recent application of the *Francovich* principle and commentary thereon, see T Tridimas, 'Liability for breach of Community law: growing up and mellowing down?' (2001) 38 CMLR 301–32.

EC LAW IN UK COURTS: DIRECT EFFECT, INDIRECT EFFECT AND *FRANCOVICH* APPLIED

Introduction

As noted in Part I Chapter 5, in order for Community law to become part of UK domestic law, it had to be incorporated into domestic law through an Act of Parliament, the European Communities Act 1972.

European Communities Act 1972.

2–(1) All such rights, powers, liabilities, obligations and restrictions from time to time created or arising by or under the Treaties, and all such remedies and procedures from time to time provided for by or under the Treaties, as in accordance with the Treaties are without further enactment to be given legal effect or used in the United Kingdom shall be recognised and available in law, and be enforced, allowed and followed accordingly; and the expression 'enforceable Community right' and similar expressions shall be read as referring to one to which this subsection applies.

(2) Subject to Schedule 2 to this Act, at any time after its passing Her Majesty may by Order in Council, and any designated Minister or department may by regulations, make provision—

(a) for the purpose of implementing any Community obligation of the United Kingdom, or enabling any such obligation to be implemented, or of enabling any rights enjoyed or to be enjoyed by the United Kingdom under or by virtue of the Treaties to be exercised; or

(b) for the purpose of dealing with matters arising out of or related to any such obligation or rights or the coming into force, or the operation from time to time, of subsection (1) above; and in the exercise of any statutory power or duty, including any power to give directions or to legislate by means of orders, rules, regulations or other subordinate instrument, the person entrusted with the power or duty may have regard to the objects of the Communities and to any such obligation or rights as aforesaid.

In this subsection 'designated Minister or department' means such Minister of the Crown or government department as may from time to time be designated by Order in Council in relation to any matter or for any purpose, but subject to such restrictions or conditions (if any) as may be specified by the Order in Council.

. . .

(4) The provision that may be made under subsection (2) above includes, subject to Schedule 2 to this Act, any such provision (of any such extent) as might be made by Act of Parliament, and any enactment passed or to be passed, other than one contained in this part of this Act, shall be construed and have effect subject to the foregoing provisions of this section; but, except as may be provided by any Act passed after this Act, Schedule 2 shall have effect in connection with the powers conferred by this and the following sections of this Act to make Orders in Council and regulations.

. . .

3 (1) For the purposes of all legal proceedings any question as to the meaning or effect of any of the Treaties, or as to the validity, meaning or effect of any Community instrument, shall be treated as a question of law (and, if not referred to the European Court, be for determination as such in accordance with the principles laid down by and any relevant decision of the European Court or any court attached thereto).

(2) Judicial notice shall be taken of the Treaties, of the Official Journal of the Communities and of any decision of, or expression of opinion by, the European Court or any court attached thereto and any such question as aforesaid; and the Official Journal shall be admissible as evidence of any instrument or other act thereby communicated of any of the Communities or of any Community institution.

Note

Section 3(1), by rendering the decisions of the ECJ determinative in relation to all questions of EC law, was crucial in giving effect in the UK to the supremacy of EC law and in ensuring the obedience of UK courts to decisions of the European Court. It dovetails nicely with Article 234 (formerly Article 177) EC – the discretion/obligation to refer points of EC law to the ECJ for determination.

Direct effect – determining what is a state body in the UK

In the following case, the Court of Appeal had to grapple with the question of whether a voluntary aided school was an emanation of the state such that the provisions of a Directive could be enforced against it.

National Union of Teachers and Others v Governing Body of St Mary's Church of England (Aided) Junior School and Others [1997] 3 CMLR 630

Schiemann LJ: ... It is clear from [the decision of the ECJ] that the concept of an emanation of the state for the purposes of the doctrine of vertical effect is a very broad one and certainly in my judgment extends to local authorities.

[16] The European Court of Justice has not promulgated a formula which can be applied to all situations. It has preferred to adopt the approach of the Common Law and of the French Conseil d'Etat of moving from case to case to establish principles and refine them as it goes along. Most of the case law has been developed on references to the European Court of Justice under Article 177 EEC. The only ineluctable task of the European Court of Justice on such a reference is to provide a ruling in sufficiently wide terms to enable the national court to reach a decision in the case in which the reference was made ... It is ... important to remember that while the decision whether or not a particular body is properly regarded as an emanation of the state is a matter for the national court the proper development of the Community requires that all national courts should proceed upon the same principles when applying Community law. Van Gerven AG in *Foster* ... said [at para 21]:

> ... it is not entirely possible to give [these] expressions a precise Community meaning: whether someone forms part of the government, whether a particular duty is a public duty and whether someone derives his authority from the state (whether or not in the sense that he exercises authority delegated by the state) are difficult matters to define, and their meaning differs significantly not just from one Member State to another and within each Member State from one period to another but also in Community Law, in so far as they are used there, according to the matter in issue.

In the cases I have referred to, the court did not attempt to define those concepts in the abstract, and I think it was right not to do so. Nevertheless it appears from those cases that the concept of a public body must be understood very broadly and that all bodies which pursuant to the constitutional structure of a Member State can exercise any authority over individuals fall within the concept of 'the state'. In that respect it is immaterial how that authority (which I shall call public authority) is organised and how the various bodies which exercise that authority are related ...

... Lord Templeman delivering a judgment with which all the other members of the Judicial Committee concurred stated this in *Foster v British Gas Plc* [[1991] 2 AC 306.]:

> ... I can see no justification for a narrow or strained construction of the ruling of the European Court of Justice which applies to a body 'under the control of the state' ... I decline to apply the ruling of the European Court of Justice, couched in terms of broad principle and purposive language characteristic of Community law in a manner which is, for better or worse, sometimes applied to enactments in the United Kingdom parliament.

[22] The respondent relied heavily on the decision of this court in *Rolls Royce Plc v Doughty*. [[1992] ICR 538.]

That was a case in which the applicant sought to sue the company relying on the same Council Directive 76/207. At the relevant time all the shares in the company were held by nominees of the Crown. Mustill LJ, delivering a judgment with which other members of the court agreed, stated at page 550 that there were two questions confronting the court [the first was not relevant, the second was]:

> 2. ... to what extent does the answer furnished by the Court of Justice in paragraph [22] of its judgment in *Foster* constitute an exhaustive statement of the criteria for determining the status of the entity; and if it is not exhaustive, what test should be applied to the present case?

[23] He ... said this at page 552:

> On behalf of the employer Mr Pannick was disposed to accept, rightly in my view, that this test was not intended to provide the answer to every category of case. The words 'is included

among' in paragraph make this clear enough. Nevertheless, at least in a case of the same general type as *Foster* the court's formulation must always be the starting point and will usually be the finishing point. If all the factors identified by the court are present it is likely to require something very unusual to produce the result that an entity is not to be identified with the state. Conversely, although the absence of a factor will not necessarily be fatal, it will need the addition of something else not contemplated by the formula, before [the body in question will be considered an emanation of the state].

The Position of Voluntary Aided Schools in the State School System

[24] ... The problem before the court springs from the fact that we are not concerned with county schools established and maintained by a [Local Education Authority] but rather with voluntary aided schools – schools over which the Church has some measure of control ... It is common ground that a LEA is an emanation of the state for the purposes of this doctrine. But the respondents assert that the connection between the governors of the junior school and the State is too loose for the former to be regarded as an emanation of the latter ...

[26] ... So far as teaching is concerned the primary provisions are now contained in the Education Reform Act 1988 ('the ERA'). Section 1 provides: (1) It shall be the duty— (a) of the Secretary of State as respects every maintained school; (b) of every local education authority as respects every school maintained by them; and (c) of every governing body or head teacher of a maintained school as respects that school; to exercise their functions ... with a view to securing that the curriculum for the school satisfies the requirements of this section. (2) The curriculum for a maintained school satisfies the requirements of this section if it is a balanced and broadly based curriculum which— (a) promotes the spiritual, moral, cultural, mental and physical development of pupils at the school and of society; and (b) prepares such pupils for the opportunities, responsibilities and experiences of adult life.

[27] The body with primary responsibility for the provision of education in a given area is the local education authority ('LEA'). The Education Acts place various duties on LEAs relating to the provision of education in their area and LEAs have a wide range of powers to enable them to perform these duties. Under section 8 EA 1944, for example, there is a duty 'to secure that there shall be available for their area sufficient schools' for providing primary and secondary education in their area. In the fulfilment of that duty the LEA relies on schools provided by them and schools provided by others. Some of those others are wholly independent of LEA funds; others are dependent to a small degree; others to a very large degree.

[28] Section 9 EA 1944 empowers LEAs 'for the purpose of fulfilling their functions under this Act ... to maintain ... schools whether established by them or otherwise'.

[29] Schools which are maintained by the LEA for this purpose but which were not actually established by the LEA are known as voluntary schools (section 9(2) EA 1944).

[30] The concept of 'maintaining' a school is defined under the 1944 Act section 114(2). Essentially it means that the LEA defrays the expenses of maintaining the school, save for those expenses that, by virtue of the Act or any agreement thereunder, the governors are required to meet. In the context of the present case it is noteworthy that, by virtue of section 46 of the ERA 1988, the costs of meeting redundancy payments for teachers are carried by the LEA. The system of local government finance is such that those costs are largely if not entirely met by the grant from central government. Until the ERA 1988 one of the distinctions between schools provided by the LEA and voluntary schools which had opted into the state system was that the LEA had much tighter control over the management of County Schools than over voluntary schools. Thus the LEA was responsible for managing that part of the expenses of schools which it provided pursuant to section 9 EA 1944 whereas voluntary schools had a board of governors who were responsible for the management. Under the provisions of Chapter 3 ERA 1988 provision was made for very much more devolution of responsibility in the case of County Schools.

[31] Voluntary schools, choose of their own volition to come within the state system. However, once within the system, they are subject to a very considerable degree of control and influence by the Secretary of State for Education and the LEA. [His Lordship went on to give examples of such controls.]

...

The Case in the Tribunals Below

[37] The Employment Appeals Tribunal concluded that ... the Directive cannot be enforced by the applicants against the governing body of a voluntary aided school. Their reasons [were] as follows:

(1) The rationale for the doctrine that provisions of a Directive, which are unconditional and sufficiently precise may have vertical effect is that the state, to whom the Directive is addressed, cannot properly rely, as against an applicant, on its own failure to implement the Directive addressed to it.

(2) The (emphasis supplied) *test* of the European Court of Justice for determining whether the body, against whom it is sought to enforce the Directive is an emanation of the state consists of a tripartite, cumulative set of criteria namely:

(a) Has the body been made responsible pursuant to a measure adopted by the state for providing a public service?

(b) Is that service under the control of the state?

(c) Does the body for that purpose have special powers beyond those which apply between individuals?

(3) The provision of education in voluntary aided schools is a public service. But at a voluntary aided school, that service is provided by the governing body, not by the state or pursuant to its measures or under its control. The governing body is not under the control of the state. It exists by virtue of the constitution in the form of articles of government made under the authority of legislation. The governing body does not have a monopoly of education. It is not an agency of the state. The provision of state funds is not determinative of control. The state has no right to require the governors to adopt an employment position (for example, as stated in the Directive) which is not incorporated into the general law by legislation of the Member State. It is for the governing body to adopt an employment position in conformity with the general law applicable as between individuals and non state bodies. It has no special powers.

(4) The cases in which a body has been held to be an emanation of the state for the purposes of the doctrine of direct effect are far removed from the present case [the EAT cited *Marshall* (an area health authority) and *Foster* (British Gas) ...

(5) The state is the supreme civil power of a nation. Under its law and through its institutions, it is vested with ultimate effective political control of the organisation and machinery of the government of its affairs, both internal and external. The state and its agencies have special legal powers, exceptional in quality and degree and different from powers exercisable by individuals and non-state bodies. The powers exercised in the organisation and running of a voluntary aided school are a far cry from state powers of this kind. Its governors' powers are not exceptional in a relevant sense. They are only special in the sense that those who govern schools have powers which pupils, teachers and parents do not have. The governing body of a voluntary aided school exists within a state, providing a public service, but it is not an emanation or agency of the organisation of the state. It is under the control of the state only in the same sense that other citizens are. Like the Industrial Tribunal, we have been unable to find any 'special powers' in the sense used in the case of *Foster*. So far as the articles of government are concerned they provide that the conduct of the school, its internal organisation and management, should be under the direction of the governing body. The governing body, though financially maintained by the

local education authority, is not established or controlled by it. We have been unable to find any 'special powers' of the governing body in the relevant education legislation ranging from the 1944 Act to the 1993 Act.

Conclusions

[38] The appellants submit that:

1. Since the present case is not of 'the same general type' as *Foster*, the tripartite test promulgated therein and adopted in *Rolls Royce* is not directly applicable;

2. If the tripartite test is applicable then it is fulfilled in the present case.

. . .

[40] I do not regard the present case as of the same general type for present purposes as *Foster*. That case and *Rolls Royce* were both concerned with commercial undertakings in which the Government had a stake. The present case is not concerned with any commercial undertaking but rather with the provision of what would generally in the Community be regarded as the provision of a public service . . .

[41] . . . What emerges from the case law is a number of indicia which point to the appropriateness of treating the body in question as an emanation of the state, none of which indicia is conclusive. To quote the Advocate General in *Foster*,

> . . . The point of departure must be the reasoning behind *Marshall's* case and *Johnston's case* [[1986] 3 CMLR 240]. A Member State, but also any other public body charged with a particular duty by the Member State from which it derives its authority, should not be allowed to benefit from the failure of the Member State to implement the relevant provision of a directive in national law.

[42] In the present case, the Governors of the old junior school derived their authority from the Diocese of Rochester Voluntary Aided Schools (Instrument of Government) No 2 Order made by the Secretary of State for Education in the exercise of powers conferred by section 17(2) and 11 of the EA 1944. The governors of the new primary school derive their authority from an amendment to that Instrument of Government which was made by the LEA under powers given to the LEA by section 1(2) of the Education No. 2 Act 1986. True it is that in each case the governors volunteered for the task and true it is that the diocese might have chosen not to subject the school to the regime set out in that Order. But the diocese did not so choose but chose instead to enter the state system. True it is that, in certain circumstances and subject to certain conditions, the diocese was still free to withdraw the school from the state system, but it did not do so. Whilst the school was in the state system the governors were a public body charged by the state with running the school and with exercising their functions with a view to securing that the school provided the national curriculum.

[43] The legislation already referred to gives extensive powers which may be exercised by the LEA or the Secretary of State to control the actions of the governors. Duties are imposed on the Governors both by the general legislation and by the statutory instrument by virtue of which they exercise their powers. The financial position is that the failure to transpose the Directive will, if the present appeal is dismissed, have the effect of allowing the LEA and the State to benefit from the failure to transpose the Directive. The *Rolls Royce* case indicates that the mere fact that some incidental benefit may arise to the State from a failure to implement a Directive does not necessarily bring the doctrine of vertical direct effect into play. In the present case the benefit is direct to the LEA, as is conceded because of the provisions of section 46 of the ERA, and the LEA, as is further conceded, is an emanation of the State for the purposes of the doctrine of direct vertical effect.

[44] The Employment Appeal Tribunal rightly identified in its first finding the rationale behind the doctrine of direct effect. In my judgment it was wrong in adopting the tripartite test in *Foster* as if it were a statutory definition of an emanation of the State. It was understandable that it did so since the parties before it all proceeded on that basis. In my judgment it did not fully appreciate the

significance of the undoubted fact that the Community case law indicates that a body may be an emanation of the State although it is not under the control of central government. Its failure to appreciate the significance of this point is shown by the disquisition on the nature of the State at the beginning of paragraph 5 of its reasoning. In my judgment it is not appropriate to apply the tripartite test in *Foster* as though it were a statutory definition. However I ought briefly to record the parties' submissions on each of the three elements of that test and my reaction to them.

1. *Have the governors been made responsible pursuant to a measure adopted by the State for providing a public service?*

Mr Straker submits that they have not because the diocese was free to decide whether or no to apply to make the school a voluntary aided school. He submitted that in England no one person was responsible for the provision of education. That responsibility was shared between parents, schools, LEAs and the Secretary of State. Mr Hand, for the appellants, submits that once the diocese asks for and obtains voluntary aided status for one of its schools then the governors have been made responsible. As indicated above, I prefer the latter submission. The statutory instrument, made by the LEA under Statutory powers, can be regarded as a measure adopted by the State. Education can be regarded as a public service.

2. *Is that service under the control of the State?*

Mr Straker submits that education is not under our complicated statutory system under the control of the State. I am not inclined to accept that submission. As I have sought to show, the Secretary of State has duties and powers in respect of the provision of education and so do LEAs. Those powers amount to sufficient control by the State for present purposes to come within the concept of control.

3. *Do the governors have special powers beyond those which apply between individuals?*

Mr Hand submitted that the governors had the power to spend public money and that this was a special power for present purposes. I am not presently persuaded that this was the sort of power which the European Court of Justice had in mind in *Foster*.

[45] However, as I have already indicated, I think it inappropriate to apply the tripartite test as though it were a definition section. In my judgment for the purposes of the doctrine of direct vertical effect the governors of the schools must be regarded as emanations of the state and I therefore consider that this appeal must be allowed.

Note

For comment on this decision, see V Kvjatkovski, 'What is an "emanation of the state"? An educated guess' (1997) 3(3) EPL 329–38; P Spink, 'Direct effect: the boundaries of the state' (1997) 113 LQR 524–29; J Eady, 'Emanation of the state' (1997) 26(3) ILJ 248–52.

Indirect effect

The UK courts have at times seemed reluctant to engage fully with the doctrine of indirect effect, particularly when seeking to interpret provisions of the Equal Pay Act 1970 and the Sex Discrimination Act 1975 so as to render them compatible with the Community Directives on equal pay and equal treatment, which were introduced after those Acts, as the following commentary makes clear.

Erika Szyszczack, 'Sovereignty: crisis, compliance, confusion, complacency?' (1990) 15(6) EL Rev 483–87

... in *Duke v GEC Reliance Ltd* [1988] AC 618 the House of Lords rejected the use of a purposive construction of s 6(4) of the Sex Discrimination Act 1975 since it pre-dated the directive. Therefore there was no discretion vested in the national courts to construe the Act in conformity with the directive which in this instance did not give rise to direct effects. Counsel for Ms Duke had argued that s 2(4) of the European Communities Act 1972 provided the legal basis for the purposive construction of the Sex Discrimination Act 1975 but this argument was rejected by Lord Templeman (with whom the rest of the House of Lords concurred):

> [Section 2(4)] does no more than reinforce the binding nature of legally enforceable rights and obligations imposed by appropriate Community law. [It] does not enable or constrain a British court to distort the meaning of a British statute in order to enforce against an individual a Community directive which has no direct effect between individuals. Section 2(4) applies, and only applies, where Community provisions are directly applicable. [*ibid* at p 680]

Central to ... criticism [of this decision] was the failure of the House of Lords to apply the rulings of the European Court, whereby national courts are directed to interpret national implementing legislation in accordance with Community law. In *Von Colson* the European Court limited the purposive interpretation only to legislation enacted specifically to implement a directive. This may not have been a deliberate limitation since, in subsequent cases, the Advocates-General have argued that the obligation is wider, embracing more than implementing legislation [see Advocate General Mischo in Case 80/86, *Criminal Proceedings against Kolpinghuis Nijmegen BV* [1987] ECR 3639; Advocate General van Gerven in Case C-262/88, *Barber v Guardian Royal Exchange Assurance Group*]. This would seem to be a tenable position to take since Member States do not always need to introduce implementing legislation in order to comply with a directive. However, when informing the Commission, either under obligations to notify contained in a directive, or as part of the Commission's implementation review of a directive, a Member State is forced into a position of identifying the relevant national legislation it claims fulfils the Community obligations. It would be absurd to allow legislation predating a directive to be immune from the *Von Colson* principle of purposive interpretation, and a denial of Community obligations to prevent individuals from enforcing their Community rights, simply because there was no need for amendment of existing national legislation.

Note

The case of *Finnegan*, as Erika Szyszczack notes, 'gave the House of Lords opportunity of extricating itself from the morass it had led itself into in *Duke*'.

> The House of Lords chose not to grasp this opportunity. Ms Finnegan had been retired by her employers soon after her 60th birthday. The normal retirement age for men was 65. A Northern Ireland Industrial Tribunal upheld her complaint of sex discrimination by interpreting the parallel provisions to s 6(4) of the Sex Discrimination Act 1975, namely Art 8(4) of the Sex Discrimination (Northern Ireland) Order 1976, to comply with the Equal Treatment Directive as interpreted in *Marshall*. The decision was reversed by the Northern Ireland Court of Appeal, following the ruling in *Duke*. When the issue came before the House of Lords, their lordships could have seized upon two distinctions between the *Duke* and *Finnegan* litigation. First, the Northern Ireland Order 1976 had been enacted *after* the Equal Treatment Directive. Secondly, the European Court had already ruled in Case 222/84, *Johnston v Chief Constable of the Royal Ulster Constabulary* [1986] ECR 1651 that the Order should be interpreted in the light of the Equal Treatment Directive.[54]

Finnegan v Clowney Youth Training Programme Ltd [1990] 2 AC 407, 415–17, HL

Lord Bridge of Harwich: ... On the face of it ... the enactment applicable to the circumstances of the present employee's claim is indistinguishable from the enactment which fell to be applied in *Duke v GEC Reliance Systems Ltd* [1988] AC 618 and would appear, therefore, to dictate the inevitable result that the appeal must fail. This was the view of the Court of Appeal in Northern Ireland. Counsel for the employee submits, however, that a crucial distinction is to be derived from

---

54   E Szyszczack, 'Sovereignty: crisis, compliance, confusion, complacency?' (1990) 15(6) EL Rev 483–87.

the chronology, in that the English Act 1975 was passed before the Council of the European Communities adopted the Equal Treatment Directive, on 9 February, whereas the Order of 1976 was not made until July of that year. He referred us to a familiar line of authority for the proposition that the national legislation of a Member State of the European Community which is enacted for the purpose of implementing a European Council directive must be construed in the light of the directive and must, if at all possible, be applied in a sense which will effect the purpose of the directive ...

I entirely accept the validity of the proposition, but I do not accept that it has any application here. Before the decision in the *Marshall* case [1986] QB 401 it is apparent from the history I have recounted that neither the UK Parliament nor the UK Government perceived any conflict between the provisions of s 6(4) of the Sex Discrimination Act 1975 and s 6(1A) of the Equal Pay Act 1970 on the one hand, and the provisions of the European Equal Treatment Directive on the other hand, such as to call for amendment of the English statutes after the adoption of the directive. Accordingly, it would appear to me to be wholly artificial to treat the Order of 1976 enacting identical provision for Northern Ireland, because it was made after the directive, as having been made with the purpose of implementing Community law in the same sense as the regulation which fell to be construed in the *Pickstone* and *Litster* cases. The reality is that Art 8(4) of the Order of 1976 being in identical terms and in an identical context to s 6(4) of the English Act of 1975, must have been intended to have the identical effect. To hold otherwise would be, as in *Duke v GEC Reliance Systems Ltd* [1988] AC 618, most unfair to the employers in that it would be giving retrospective operation to the amending Order of 1988 and effectively eliminating the distinction between Community law which is of direct effect between citizens of Member States, and Community law which only affects citizens of Member States when it is implemented by national legislation.

...We were further invited to make a reference to the European Court of Justice under Art 177 of the EEC Treaty. In my opinion, however, the determination of the appeal does not depend on any question of Community law. The interpretation of the Order of 1976 is for the UK courts and it is not suggested that the Equal Treatment Directive is of direct effect between citizens.

I would dismiss the appeal.

Appeal dismissed

Notes
1   However, in other cases, the UK courts have shown themselves willing to engage in quite drastic changes of interpretation to UK legislation. In *Pickstone v Freemans* [1988] 3 WLR 265, Mrs Pickstone and other warehouse operatives were paid less than male warehouse checkers, but one man was employed as an operative. The defendant [employers] therefore argued that her claim to equal pay was barred due to the wording of s 1(2)(c) of the Equal Pay Act 1970, as amended: 'where a woman is employed on work which, not being work to which (a) or (b) applied is ... of equal value ...'. Paragraph (a) did apply because one man was employed doing the same work and therefore it could be argued that a like work claim arose but not an equal value one. The House of Lords considered that allowing this argument to succeed would mean that Parliament had failed once again to implement its obligations under Article 119 (the Equal Pay Directive); and it could not have intended such a failure. In such circumstances any interpretation should take into account the terms in which the 1983 amending regulations were presented to Parliament; in other words, a purposive approach should be adopted. As their Lordships noted:

The debate on the draft regulations in the House of Commons which led to their approval by resolution was initiated by the Under Secretary of State for Employment, who, in the reports of the House of Commons for 20 July 1983 (46 HC Official Report (6th series) col 479), said:

The Equal Pay Act allows a woman to claim equal pay with a man ... if she is doing the same or broadly similar work, or if her job and his have been rated equal through job evaluation in effort, skill and decision. However, if a woman is doing different work from a comparable man, or if the jobs are not covered by a job evaluation study, the woman has at present no right to make a claim for equal pay. This is the gap, identified by the European Court, which we are closing.

... In the course of the debate in the House of Commons, and in the corresponding debate in the House of Lords, no one suggested that a claim for equal pay for equal work might be defeated under the regulations by an employer who proved that a man who was not the subject of the complaint was employed on the same or on similar work with the complainant.

2   In the following case, an even more radical approach to re-interpreting national law that was *prima facie* incompatible with Community law was adopted.

Litster v Forth Dry Dock and Engineering Co Ltd [1990] I AC 546, HL

Lord Templeman: ... My Lords, by article 3 of the Council Directive (77/187/EEC) dated 14 February 1977 the Council of Ministers of the European Community directed that upon the transfer of a business from one employer to another, the benefit and burden of a contract of employment between the transferor ('the old owner') and a worker in the business should devolve on the transferee ('the new owner'). The Directive thus imposed on the new owner liability for the workers in the business although the member states were authorised by article 3 to continue the liability of the old owner to the workers in the business 'in addition to the transferee.' The object of the Directive was expressed to be:

'to provide for the protection of employees in the event of a change of employer, in particular, to ensure that their rights are safeguarded; ...'.

Article 4(1) of the Directive provided:

The transfer of an undertaking, business or part of a business shall not in itself constitute grounds for dismissal by the transferor or the transferee. This provision shall not stand in the way of dismissals that may take place for economic, technical or organisational reasons entailing changes in the workforce.

The result of article 4(1) is that the new owner intending to dismiss the workers cannot achieve his purpose by asking the old owner to dismiss the workers immediately prior to the transfer taking place. The new owner cannot dismiss the workers himself after the transfer has taken place. Any such dismissal, whether by the old owner or the new owner, would be inconsistent with the object of protecting the rights of the workers and is prohibited by article 4(1).

The Transfer of Undertakings (Protection of Employment) Regulations 1981 were approved by a resolution of each House of Parliament in pursuance of paragraph 2(2) of Schedule 2 to the European Communities Act 1972, for the express purpose of implementing Council Directive (77/187/EEC). Regulation 5(1) provides, in conformity with article 3 of the Directive, that:

A relevant transfer shall not operate so as to terminate the contract of employment of any person employed by the transferor in the undertaking or part transferred but any such contract which would otherwise have been terminated by the transfer shall have effect after the transfer as if originally made between the person so employed and the transferee.

... Regulation 8 provides, in conformity with article 4, that:

(1) Where either before or after the relevant transfer, any employee of the transferor or transferee is dismissed, that employee shall be treated ... as unfairly dismissed if the transfer or a reason connected with it is the reason or principal reason for his dismissal.

... The appellants were dismissed at 3.30 pm on 6 February by Forth Dry Dock and the business was transferred to Forth Estuary at 4.30 pm on the same day. It is argued, on behalf of Forth Estuary, that despite the Directive and the Regulations, they are not liable to the appellants in respect of their unfair dismissal because regulation 5(3) provides:

> Any reference in paragraph (I) . . . above to a person employed in an undertaking or part of one transferred by a relevant transfer is a reference to a person so employed immediately before the transfer, including, where the transfer is effected by a series of two or more transactions, a person so employed immediately before any of those transactions.

Thus, it is said, since the workforce of Forth Dry Dock were dismissed at 3.30 pm, they were not employed 'immediately before the transfer' at 4.30 pm and therefore regulation 5(1) did not transfer any liability for the workforce from Forth Dry Dock to Forth Estuary. The argument is inconsistent with the Directive. In P Bork International A/S v Foreningen af Arbejdslederei Danmark (Case 101/87) [1989] IRLR 41, 44 the European Court of Justice ruled that:

> the only workers who may invoke Directive [(77/187/EEC)] are those who have current employment relations or a contract of employment at the date of the transfer. The question whether or not a contract of employment or employment relationship exists at that date must be assessed under national law, subject, however, to the observance of the mandatory rules of the Directive concerning the protection of workers against dismissal by reason of the transfer. It follows that the workers employed by the undertaking whose contract of employment or employment relationship has been terminated with effect on a date before that of the transfer, in breach of article 4(1) of the Directive, must be considered as still employed by the undertaking on the date of the transfer with the consequence, in particular, that the obligations of an employer towards them are fully transferred from the transferor to the transferee in accordance with article 3(1)of the Directive.

His Lordship then went on to cite the principle that 'in applying the national law and in particular the provisions of a national law specifically introduced in order to implement Directive 76/207/EEC, national courts are required to interpret their national law in the light of the wording and the purpose of the Directive' (Von Colson [1984] ECR 1891, 1909).

> Thus the courts of the United Kingdom are under a duty to follow the practice of the European Court of Justice by giving a purposive construction to Directives and to Regulations issued for the purpose of complying with Directives. ... In the present case, in the light of Council Directive (77/187/EEC) and in the light of the ruling of the European Court of Justice in Bork's case [1989] IRLR 41, it seems to me, following the suggestion of my noble and learned friend, Lord Keith of Kinkel, that paragraph 5(3) of the Regulations of 1981 was not intended and ought not to be construed so as to limit the operation of regulation 5 to persons employed immediately before the transfer in point of time. Regulation 5(3) must be construed on the footing that it applies to a person employed immediately before the transfer or who would have been so employed if he had not been unfairly dismissed before the transfer for a reason connected with the transfer.

Note
As Szyszczack comments, the greater receptivity to Community principles and flexibility in interpretative technique displayed by the Lords in Litster and Pickstone as compared to Duke and Finnegan makes little sense in Community law terms.

> In their enthusiasm to adopt this 'greater flexibility' in statutory interpretation, it seems to have escaped their lordships' attention that in this situation, like the situation in Duke and Finnegan, the directive only gave rise to indirect effects and not direct effects. The only difference between the two situations was that in Litster the directive had necessitated implementing legislation.[55]

---

55   Szyszczack, *op cit*, at 483–87.

The *Francovich* principle in the UK courts

The leading UK decision on the *Francovich* principle is *Factortame (No 4)* (below)[56] which concerned a claim for damages made by 97 different Spanish fishing companies in respect of losses sustained by being unable to fish in UK waters as a result of the Merchant Shipping Act 1988. (The facts appear above, at pp 219–20.)

R v Secretary of State for Transport ex p Factortame Ltd and Others (No 5) [2000] I AC 524

Lord Slynn summarised the relevant principles of EC law laid down by the ECJ starting with the *Francovich* decision and going on to *Factortame (No 3)*, noting the Courts' consistent rulings to the effect that the conditions for state liability should be the same as those for liability of the Community itself under (former) Article 215.

Lord Slynn: . . . The question, therefore, is what constitutes being [a] 'sufficiently serious' [breach of EC law][57] . . . In *Factortame III* [1996] QB 404, the [ECJ] . . . said, at p 498, para 43:

> The system of rules which the court has worked out with regard to article 215 of the Treaty, particularly in relation to liability for legislative measures, takes into account, inter alia, the complexity of the situations to be regulated, difficulties in the application or interpretation of the texts and, more particularly, the margin of discretion available to the author of the act in question.

The strict approach towards the liability of the Community in the exercise of legislative functions was due in part to the need not to hinder legislative action, 'whenever the general interests of the Community requires legislative measures to be adopted which may adversely affect individual interests'.

. . . .

Accordingly, at p 499:

> 55. As to the second condition, as regards to both Community liability under article 215 and member state liability for breaches of Community law, the decisive test for finding that a breach of Community law is sufficiently serious is whether the member state or the Community institution concerned manifestly and gravely disregarded the limits on its discretion.

> 56. The factors which the competent court may take into consideration include the clarity and precision of the rule breached; the measure of discretion left by that rule to the national or Community authorities; whether the infringement and the damage caused was intentional or involuntary; whether any error of law was excusable or inexcusable; the fact that the position taken by a Community institution may have contributed towards the omission, and the adoption or retention of national measures or practices contrary to Community law.

More recent cases show the working out of these rules. Thus in *R v HM Treasury, Ex parte British Telecommunications Plc* (Case C-392/93) [1996] QB 615 the court held that, where the interpretation adopted by the United Kingdom was arguable on the basis of an imprecisely worded article of the relevant directive and where there was no case law to give guidance the state was not liable in damages. In *R v Ministry of Agriculture, Fisheries and Food, Ex parte Hedley Lomas (Ireland) Ltd* (Case C-5/94) [1997] QB 139 where there was no or very little room for discretion in granting a licence that could in itself be a sufficiently serious breach. In *Dillenkofer v Federal Republic of Germany* (Case C-178/94) [1997] QB 259 it was held that a failure to implement

---

56 [2000] 1 AC 524.
57 Note that it was conceded by the government that the rule of Community law concerned – Article 52 of the EC Treaty – was intended to confer rights upon individuals – while the issue of causation was deferred for later consideration.

a directive, where no or little question of legislative choice was involved, the mere infringement may constitute a sufficiently serious breach. In *Denkavit Internationaal BV v Bundesamt für Finanzen* (Case C-283/94) [1996] ECR I-5063 the court held that other member states, after discussion with the Council had adopted the same interpretation of the Directive as Germany and as there was no relevant case law of the court it was held that the breach was not sufficiently serious.

It was also clear from the cases that it is not necessary to establish fault or negligence on the part of the member state going beyond what is relevant to show a sufficiently serious breach.

Application of the principle in this case.

In the present case the United Kingdom was entitled to consider how it would exercise the margin of discretion left to it under Community law in the application of the common fisheries policy and in particular of the quota system and also, subject to those limits, how it would exercise its rights under international law to provide for registration as a British fishing vessel. Although the three conditions (nationality, domicile, residence) held in *Factortame II* [1992] QB 680 to be a breach of the Treaty taken in conjunction reflect what the British Government was seeking to do, for the purposes of liability to compensate, the conditions have been considered separately. The first question is, therefore, whether in imposing a nationality requirement the United Kingdom committed a sufficiently serious breach in that it had manifestly and gravely disregarded the limits of its discretion.

In the first place it is to be noted that the relevant rule of Community law is not to be found in an ambiguous directive but in a clear and fundamental provision of the Treaty. By article 7 it is provided that 'Within the scope of application of this Treaty, and without prejudice to any special provisions contained therein, any discrimination on the grounds of nationality shall be prohibited.' The importance of this principle in the present context is underlined in article 40(3) of the EEC Treaty since any common organisation of the market set up under article 39 'shall exclude any discrimination between producers and consumers within the community.'

It is obvious that what was done here by the Government was not done inadvertently. It was done after anxious consideration and after taking legal advice. I accept that it was done in good faith and with the intention of protecting British fishing communities rather than with the deliberate intention of harming Spanish fishermen and those non-British citizens with financial stakes in British registered fishing vessels. The inevitable result of the policy adopted, however, was to take away or seriously affect their rights to fish against the British quota.

The nationality condition was obviously discriminatory and in breach of article 52 as *Factortame II* [1992] QB 680 decided. Indeed as far as article 52 was concerned, this was already clear from *Commission of the European Communities v Italian Republic* (Case 63/86) [1988] ECR 29. Although the question whether this was a sufficiently serious breach justifying the award of damages is a matter for the national courts, and therefore for your Lordships, to decide it is to be noted that in *Factortame III* [1996] QB 404, 500, para 61 the European Court stated bluntly that the nationality condition constituted direct discrimination which was manifestly contrary to Community law.

Can it be said that, even if the Act of 1988 was deliberately adopted, it was an, unintentional and 'excusable' breach which should prevent what was done being 'a sufficiently serious breach' in that it was a manifest and grave disregard of the limits of the United Kingdom's discretion?

The appellant relies on the history of the discussions leading up to the enactment of the Act of 1988 and the making of regulations under it. He explains the problem and the understandable aim of seeking to protect British fishing communities and the British quota. Licensing rules having not been adequate, the only solution they felt was to change the rules on registration by primary legislation (letter Ministry of Agriculture, Fisheries and Food to Foreign Secretary on 14 November 1986). They were, however, aware from the beginning of the legal problems involved . . .

Professor Francis Jacobs QC and other counsel were asked to advise . . . on 24 February 1987 they said:

... In our view the proposed legislation should, if challenged, be held to be compatible with Community law on the basis that such legislation is a necessary consequence of the Common Fisheries Policy.

On 31 March 1987 the Law Officers advised: 'that there is a reasonably good prospect that the proposed legislation would be upheld by the European Court.'

On 18 November 1988 Mr Advocate General Mischo gave his opinion (a) in *R v Ministry of Agriculture, Fisheries and Food, Ex parte Jaderow Ltd* (Case C-216/87) [1990] 2 QB 193 208, para 7 that 'Community law does not therefore restrict the power which each member state has under public international law to determine the conditions on which it allows a vessel to fly its flag' and (b) in *R v Ministry of Agriculture, Fisheries and Food, Ex parte Agegate Ltd* (Case C-3/87) [1990] 2 QB 151 that the residence requirement in the crewing condition in the Act of 1983 was compatible with Community law because of the quota system and other features of the fisheries regulation.

On the other hand it is to be remembered that the power of member states in this area is subject to the extensive control exercised by the Community institutions under the common fisheries policy. On 28 March 1988, before the bill received the royal assent the Commission (DG XV) told the United Kingdom Government that the proposed conditions were prima facie contrary to the right of establishment under article 52. The Commission continued to state its opposition to the nationality condition and subsequently to the domicile and residence conditions. The article 169 proceedings against the United Kingdom in respect of the nationality condition, led to the President's order of 10 October 1998 as an interim measure suspending that condition. Moreover it is to be recalled that the Divisional Court had initially suspended all three conditions [1989] 2 CMLR 353 as the House of Lords was to do on 10 July 1989 following *Factortame I*: see [1991] 1 AC 603 The decisions of the European Court in the *Agegate case* [1990] 2 QB 151 and the *Jaderow case* [1990] 2 QB 193 gave the Government no comfort or encouragement.

It was, moreover, obvious as the Divisional Court [1989] 2 CMLR 353 and the Court of Appeal [1989] 2 CMLR 392 thought on the initial hearing in 1988, and as the House of Lords [1990] 2 AC 85 thought on the hearing following *Factortame I* [1990] ECR I-2433 that the damage which would be suffered by the respondents would be serious and immediate.

How far the views of the Commission ought to be taken into account has been much debated in argument. ... [His Lordship noted the views of the Divisional Court and Court of Appeal, which considered them very important].

It is in my view clear that the views of the Commission are not conclusive (a) as to whether there has been a breach of Community law and (b) as to whether the breach is a sufficiently serious breach to justify an award of damages ... The considered view of the Commission in a case of this kind, where the Community has a substantial role, is however of importance. Indeed in an area so closely subject to Community control as is the common fisheries policy, it is not only wise but often a necessary step to consult the Commission. The Government did here consult the Commission. A member state may choose to ignore the advice given but if it does so, it incurs the risk that, if it proves to be wrong and the Commission to be right, the member state will be found to have gone ahead deliberately, well aware of the Commission's views, and that a court will be more likely to find that the breach has been manifest and grave and thus sufficiently serious. In the present case, the Commission's view was firm, consistent and hostile to the Government.

It seems to me that the appellant can rely on the fact that it took legal advice although that is but one factor in having regard, as I think one must, to all the circumstances. However, the advice of Professor Jacobs QC and others in 1987 was to some extent qualified and was based on the instructions that there would be a dispensing power not just for the residence but also for the nationality and domicile conditions. Moreover as time went on, there was clearly doubt as to whether the Government could really succeed before the European Court and the Commission's letters, to which I have referred, were not it seems the subject matter of any further discussion with counsel ... The shortness of the transitional period, the fact that there was, it seemed, no way in domestic law of challenging the statute, and that the respondents were obliged, not merely to avoid being removed from the old register, but to apply to be put on the new register all emphasise the determination of the Government to press ahead with this scheme despite the strong opposition of the Commission and the doubts of some of its officials. When the judgments in the *Agegate* and *Jaderow* cases [1990] 2 QB 151 and 193 were delivered they gave the Government no encouragement to continue and the view of some government officials (eg Mr. Timothy Pratt on 14 December 1989 which in retrospect seemed prophetic) and the opinion of Andrew Macnab of counsel on 16 March 1990 made the difficulties more clear. There is indeed, in my view, considerable justification for the Divisional Court's finding that by January 1990 there was really little hope of saving the three conditions.

Accordingly, despite the arguments of the United Kingdom and the advice it received, it seems to me clear that the deliberate adoption of legislation which was clearly discriminatory on the ground of nationality and which inevitably violated article 52 of the Treaty (since it prevented establishment in the United Kingdom) was a manifest breach of fundamental Treaty obligations. It was a grave breach of the Treaty both intrinsically and as regards the consequences it was bound, or at the least was most likely, to have on the respondents. It has not been shown to have been excusable. The Commission opposed it and despite the view of Mr Advocate General Mischo, on the Act of 1983 there was no decision of the European Court to support the Government. What was done, therefore, in regard to nationality plainly constituted a sufficiently serious breach for the purposes of the second condition of liability. Moreover to maintain the legislation in operation after the court's decisions in the cases of *Agegate* and *Jaderow* and to allow such a short transitional period itself constituted a sufficiently serious breach.

It is agreed that 'domicile' falls to be treated in the same way as nationality. That condition, therefore, was also a sufficiently serious breach.

As to residence, the European Court said [1996] QB 404, 500:

> 62. The latter conditions are prima facie incompatible with article 52 of the Treaty in particular, but the United Kingdom sought to justify them in terms of the objectives of the common fisheries policy. In the judgment in *R v Secretary of State for Transport, Ex parte Factortame Ltd (No 3)* (Case C-221/89) [1992] QB 680 the court rejected that justification.

> 63. In order to determine whether the breach of article 52 thus committed by the United Kingdom was sufficiently serious, the national court might take into account, inter alia, the legal disputes relating to particular features of the common fisheries policy, the attitude of the Commission, which made its position known to the United Kingdom in good time, and the assessments as to the state of certainty of community law made by the national courts in the interim proceedings brought by individuals affected by the Merchant Shipping Act.

I have had some doubt about the condition as to residence. If the aim of protecting the livelihood of British fishing communities, including allied trades such as preparing and processing landed fish, is justified then it is arguable that to require active fishermen to live in these communities might be excusable. The condition here was not however, limited to such fishermen or to such areas. It covered shareholders and directors of companies owning fishing vessels. It allowed the fishermen to live anywhere. It seems to me that this condition cannot be justified where the discrimination is, as it is here, clear ...

It is, moreover, somewhat artificial to separate out the various conditions and in the end I agree with the Court of Appeal that the conditions should be treated as cumulative.

... I, therefore, conclude that the United Kingdom's breach of its Community obligations by imposing and applying the conditions of nationality, domicile and residence in and pursuant to the Merchant Shipping Act 1988 was a sufficiently serious breach so as to entitle the respondents to compensation for damage directly caused by that breach. I consider also that the United Kingdom was in breach of Community law by failing to give effect to the order of the President of the European Court of 10 October 1989 until 2 November 1989 and that this also constituted a serious breach of Community obligations which would, had they not succeeded on the first ground, have entitled Rawlings (Trawling) Ltd to compensation for damage directly caused by that breach.

Note

The UK government was therefore found to be liable in damages to the Spanish fishermen who had suffered loss from the imposition of the illegal requirements contained in the Merchant Shipping Act 1988.[58]

FURTHER READING

M Andenas and J Usher, *The Treaty of Nice* (2003)

A Arnull, A Dashwood, M Ross, and D Wyatt, *Wyatt & Dashwood's European Union Law,* 4th edn (2000)

T Birtwistle, *Principles of European Union Law,* 3rd edn (2002)

G de Burca and P Craig, *EU Law: Text, Cases and Materials,* 3rd edn (2002)

G de Burca and J Scott (eds), *Constitutional Change in the EU: From Uniformity to Flexibility?* (2000)

K Lenaerts and P Van Nuffel, *Constitutional Law of the European Union* (1999)

J Shaw, 'The Treaty of Nice: Legal and Constitutional Implications' (2001) 7(2) EPL 195

J Steiner, L Woods and C Twigg-Flesner, *Textbook on EC Law,* 8th edn (2003)

S Weatherill, *Cases and Materials on EU Law,* 6th edn (2003)

---

58 For commentary on this decision, see L Williams, 'Defining a sufficiently serious breach of Community law: the House of Lords casts its net into the waters' (2000) 25(4) EL Rev 2000, 452–459.

CHAPTER 2

THE EUROPEAN CONVENTION ON HUMAN RIGHTS

INTRODUCTION

The European Convention on Human Rights was conceived after the Second World War as a means of preventing the kind of violation of human rights seen in Germany during and before the war. It has not generally been invoked in relation to large scale violations of rights, but instead has addressed particular deficiencies in the legal systems of the Member States which on the whole create regimes of human rights which are in conformity with the Convention. Drafted in 1949, it was based on the United Nations Declaration of Human Rights,[1] and partly for that reason, and partly because it was only intended to provide basic protection for human rights, it appears today as quite a cautious document, less far reaching than the 1966 International Covenant on Civil and Political Rights. Nevertheless, it has had far more effect on UK law than any other human rights treaty due to its machinery for enforcement which includes a Court with the power to deliver a ruling adverse to the government of a Member State. Thus, the machinery for the enforcement of the Convention is impressive compared to that used in respect of other human rights treaties, particularly the 1966 International Covenant on Civil and Political Rights which, as far as the UK is concerned, has been enforceable only through a system of assessment of national reports.

The Court insists upon the dynamic nature of the Convention and adopts a teleological or purpose-based approach to interpretation, which has allowed the substantive rights to develop until they may cover situations unthought of in 1949. At the same time, the Court is greatly influenced by general practice in the Member States as a body and will interpret the Convention to reflect such practice, so that a state which is clearly out of conformity with the others may expect an adverse ruling. Where practice is still in the process of changing and may be said to be at an inchoate stage as far as the Member States generally are concerned, it may not be prepared to place itself at the forefront of such changes. There is general agreement that its jurisprudence has had an enormous impact, not only through the outcome of specific cases, but in a general symbolic, educative and preventive sense. Its function in raising awareness of human rights was of particular significance in the UK since, until the enactment of the Human Rights Act 1998, no equivalent domestic instrument had such a role. Since the Human Rights Act has afforded the Convention further effect in UK law, its interpretation, the values it encapsulates and the development of the control machinery have become of even greater significance. An understanding of the workings of the Convention is crucial since the jurisprudence is now being very frequently relied on in the domestic courts. The Strasbourg jurisprudence relating to a number of the Convention guarantees is considered further, in relation to domestic law, in Part VI.

---

1 The Declaration was adopted on 10 December 1948 by the General Assembly of the United Nations.

THE CONVENTION AND ITS PROTOCOLS

The substantive rights may be said to fall into two groups: Articles 2–7, covering the most fundamental human rights and containing no express exceptions, or narrow express exceptions; and Articles 8–12, which may be said to cover a more sophisticated or developed conception of human rights and which are subject to a broad range of express exceptions. Thus, under Articles 2–7, argument will tend to concentrate on the question of whether a particular situation falls within the compass of the right in question, whereas under Articles 8–11 it will largely concentrate on determining whether the interference with the guarantee can be justified (Article 12 only contains one exception, but of a very broad nature). There is an enormous amount of overlap between the Articles and it may be found that weaknesses or gaps in one can be remedied by another, although the Convention will be interpreted as a harmonious whole.[2] It will also be found that invocation of a substantive right in order to attack a decision in the national courts on its merits may sometimes fail, but that a challenge to the *procedure* may succeed under one of the Articles explicitly concerned with fairness in the adjudicative process – Articles 5, 6 and 7.[3] The rights and freedoms are largely concerned with civil and political rather than social and economic matters; the latter are governed by the 1961 European Social Charter and the 1966 International Covenant on Economic, Social and Cultural Rights.

The Convention has grown by way of additional protocols so that it now creates a more advanced human rights regime based on Articles 2–14 with the First Protocol[4] in conjunction with the Fourth,[5] Sixth[6] and Seventh[7] Protocols. The very significant Protocol Twelve was opened for ratification in November 2000 (see below, p 245). The UK has not yet ratified the rights contained in the Fourth and Seventh Protocols, and at present does not intend to ratify the Twelfth Protocol.

Convention for the Protection of Human Rights and Fundamental Freedoms

The Governments signatory hereto, being Members of the Council of Europe,

Considering the Universal Declaration of Human Rights proclaimed by the General Assembly of the United Nations on 10 December 1948;

Considering that this Declaration aims at securing the universal and effective recognition and observance of the Rights therein declared;

Considering that the aim of the Council of Europe is the achievement of greater unity between its Members and that one of the methods by which that aim is to be pursued is the maintenance and further realisation of Human Rights and Fundamental Freedoms;

---

2 P Van Dijk and GJH Van Hoof, *Theory and Practice of the European Convention on Human Rights*, 1998, Chapter II.

3 See C Gearty, 'The European Court of Human Rights and the protection of civil liberties: an overview' [1993] CLJ 89.

4 Cmnd 9221. All the parties to the Convention except Switzerland are parties to this Protocol, which came into force in 1954.

5 Cmnd 2309. It came into force in 1968; the UK is not yet a party.

6 (1983) 5 EHRR 167. It came into force in 1985. The UK is now a party to it and it is included in the Human Rights Act 1998, Sched 1. See below, pp 244–45 and Part VI Chapter 1, p 866.

7 (1984) 7 EHRR 1. It came into force in 1988. The UK is not a party but proposes to ratify it imminently: see the White Paper, *Rights Brought Home: The Human Rights Bill*, Cm 3782 (1997), paras 4.14–4.15, and the Home Office Review of Human Rights Instruments (amended), 26 August 1999. Note that the other Protocols are concerned with the procedural machinery of the Convention.

Reaffirming their profound belief in those Fundamental Freedoms which are the foundation of justice and peace in the world and are best maintained on the one hand by an effective political democracy and on the other by a common understanding and observance of the Human Rights upon which they depend;

Being resolved, as the Governments of European countries which are like-minded and have a common heritage of political traditions, ideals, freedom and the Rule of Law to take the first steps for the collective enforcement of certain of the Rights stated in the Universal Declaration,

Have agreed as follows:

Article 1

The High Contracting Parties shall secure to everyone within their jurisdiction the rights and freedoms defined in s 1 of this Convention.

Section 1 Rights and freedoms

Article 2 Right to life

1. Everyone's right to life shall be protected by law. No one shall be deprived of his life intentionally save in the execution of a sentence of a court following his conviction of a crime for which this penalty is provided by law.

2. Deprivation of life shall not be regarded as inflicted in contravention of this Article when it results from the use of force which is no more than absolutely necessary:

    (a) in defence of any person from unlawful violence;

    (b) in order to effect a lawful arrest or to prevent the escape of a person lawfully detained;

    (c) in action lawfully taken for the purpose of quelling a riot or insurrection.

Article 3 Prohibition of torture

No one shall be subjected to torture or to inhuman or degrading treatment or punishment.

Article 4 Prohibition of slavery and forced labour

1. No one shall be held in slavery or servitude.

2. No one shall be required to perform forced or compulsory labour.

3. For the purpose of this Article the term 'forced or compulsory labour' shall not include:

    (a) any work required to be done in the ordinary course of detention imposed according to the provisions of Article 5 of this Convention or during conditional release from such detention;

    (b) any service of a military character or, in the case of conscientious objectors of compulsory military service;

    (c) any service exacted in case of an emergency or calamity threatening the life or well-being of the community,

    (d) any work or service which forms part of normal civic obligations.

Article 5 Right to liberty and security

1. Everyone has the right to liberty and security of person. No one shall be deprived of his liberty save in the following cases and in accordance with a procedure prescribed by law:

    (a) the lawful detention of a person after conviction by a competent court;

    (b) the lawful arrest or detention of a person for non-compliance with the lawful order of a court or in order to secure the fulfilment of any obligation prescribed by law;

    (c) the lawful arrest or detention of a person effected for the purpose of bringing him before the competent legal authority on reasonable suspicion of having committed an offence or when it is reasonably considered necessary to prevent his committing an offence or fleeing after having done so;

(d) the detention of a minor by lawful order for the purpose of educational supervision or his lawful detention for the purpose of bringing him before the competent legal authority;

(e) the lawful detention of persons for the prevention of the spreading of infectious diseases, of persons of unsound mind, alcoholics or drug addicts or vagrants;

(f) the lawful arrest or detention of a person to prevent his effecting an unauthorised entry into this country or of a person against whom action is being taken with a view to deportation or extradition.

2. Everyone who is arrested shall be informed promptly, in a language which he understands, of the reasons for his arrest and of any charge against him.

3. Everyone arrested or detained in accordance with the provisions of paragraph 1(c) of this Article shall be brought promptly before a judge or other officer authorised by law to exercise judicial power and shall be entitled to trial within a reasonable time or to release pending trial. Release may be conditioned by guarantees to appear for trial.

4. Everyone who is deprived of his liberty by arrest or detention shall be entitled to take proceedings by which the lawfulness of his detention shall be decided speedily by a court and his release ordered if the detention is not lawful.

5. Everyone who has been the victim of arrest or detention in contravention of the provisions of this Article shall have an enforceable right to compensation.

Article 6 Right to a fair trial

1. In the determination of his civil rights and obligations or of any criminal charge against him, everyone is entitled to a fair and public hearing within a reasonable time by an independent and impartial tribunal established by law. Judgment shall be pronounced publicly but the press and public may be excluded from all or part of the trial in the interests of morals, public order or national security in a democratic society, where the interests of juveniles or the protection of the private life of the parties so require, or to the extent strictly necessary in the opinion of the court in special circumstances where publicity would prejudice the interests of justice.

2. Everyone charged with a criminal offence shall be presumed innocent until proved guilty according to law.

3. Everyone charged with a criminal offence has the following minimum rights:

(a) to be informed promptly, in a language which he understands and in detail, of the nature and cause of the accusation against him;

(b) to have adequate time and facilities for the preparation of his defence;

(c) to defend himself in person or through legal assistance of his own choosing or, if he has not sufficient means to pay for legal assistance, to be given it free when the interests of justice so require;

(d) to examine or have examined witnesses against him and to obtain the attendance and examination of witnesses on his behalf under the same conditions as witnesses against him;

(e) to have the free assistance of an interpreter if he cannot understand or speak the language used in court.

Article 7 No punishment without law

1. No one shall be held guilty of any criminal offence on account of any act or omission which did not constitute a criminal offence under national or international law at the time when it was committed. Nor shall a heavier penalty be imposed than the one that was applicable at the time the criminal offence was committed.

2. This Article shall not prejudice the trial and punishment of any person for any act or omission which, at the time when it was committed, was criminal according to the general principles of law recognised by civilised nations.

Article 8 Right to respect for family and private life

1. Everyone has the right to respect for his private and family life, his home and his correspondence.

2. There shall be no interference by a public authority with the exercise of this right except such as is in accordance with the law and is necessary in a democratic society in the interests of national security, public safety or the economic well-being of the country, for the prevention of disorder or crime for the protection of health or morals, or for the protection of the rights and freedoms of others.

Article 9 Freedom of thought, conscience and religion

1. Everyone has the right to freedom of thought, conscience and religion; this right includes freedom to change his religion or belief and freedom, either alone or in community with others and in public or private, to manifest his religion or belief, in worship, teaching, practice and observance.

2. Freedom to manifest one's religion or beliefs shall be subject only to such limitations as are prescribed by law and are necessary in a democratic society in the interests of public safety, for the protection of public order, health or morals, or for the protection of the rights and freedoms of others.

Article 10 Freedom of expression

1. Everyone has the right to freedom of expression. This right shall include freedom to hold opinions and to receive and impart information and ideas without interference by public authority and regardless of frontiers. This Article shall not prevent States from requiring the licensing of broadcasting, television or cinema enterprises.

2. The exercise of these freedoms, since it carries with it duties and responsibilities, may be subject to such formalities, conditions, restrictions or penalties as are prescribed by law and are necessary in a democratic society, in the interests of national security territorial integrity or public safety, for the prevention of disorder or crime, for the protection of health or morals, for the protection of the reputation or rights of others, for preventing the disclosure of information received in confidence, or for maintaining the authority and impartiality of the judiciary.

Article 11 Freedom of assembly and association

1. Everyone has the right to freedom of peaceful assembly and to freedom of association with others, including the right to form and to join trade unions for the protection of his interests.

2. No restrictions shall be placed on the exercise of these rights other than such as are prescribed by law and are necessary in a democratic society in the interests of national security or public safety, for the prevention of disorder or crime, for the protection of health or morals or for the protection of the rights and freedoms of others. This Article shall not prevent the imposition of lawful restrictions on the exercise of these rights by members of the armed forces, of the police or of the administration of the State.

Article 12 Right to marry

Men and women of marriageable age have the right to marry and to found a family, according to the national laws governing the exercise of this right.

Article 13 Right to an effective remedy

Everyone whose rights and freedoms as set forth in this Convention are violated shall have an effective remedy before a national authority notwithstanding that the violation has been committed by persons acting in an official capacity.

Article 14 Prohibition of discrimination

The enjoyment of the rights and freedoms set forth in this Convention shall be secured without discrimination on any ground such as sex, race, colour, language, religion, political or other opinion, national or social origin, association with a national minority, property, birth or other status.

Article 15 Derogation in time of emergency

1. In time of war or other public emergency threatening the life of the nation any High Contracting Party may take measures derogating from its obligations under this Convention to the extent strictly required by the exigencies of the situation, provided that such measures are not inconsistent with its other obligations under international law.

2. No derogation from Article 2, except in respect of deaths resulting from lawful acts of war, or from Articles 3, 4 (paragraph 1) and 7 shall be made under this provision.

3. Any High Contracting Party availing itself of this right of derogation shall keep the Secretary-General of the Council of Europe fully informed of the measures which it has taken and the reasons therefor. It shall also inform the Secretary-General of the Council of Europe when such measures have ceased to operate and the provisions of the Convention are again being fully executed.

Article 16 Restrictions on political activity of aliens

Nothing in Articles 10, 11 and 14 shall be regarded as preventing the High Contracting Parties from imposing restrictions on the political activity of aliens.

Article 17 Prohibition of abuse of rights

Nothing in this Convention may be interpreted as implying for any State, group or person any right to engage in any activity or perform any act aimed at the destruction of any of the rights and freedoms set forth herein or at their limitation to a greater extent than is provided for in the Convention.

Article 18 Limitation on use of restrictions on rights

The restrictions permitted under this Convention to the said rights and freedoms shall not be applied for any purpose other than those for which they have been prescribed.

First protocol (1952) Cmnd 9221

Article 1 Protection of property

Every natural or legal person is entitled to the peaceful enjoyment of his possessions. No one shall be deprived of his possessions except in the public interest and subject to the conditions provided for by law and by the general principles of international law.

The preceding provisions shall not, however, in any way impair the right of a State to enforce such laws as it deems necessary to control the use of property in accordance with the general interest or to secure the payment of taxes or other contributions or penalties.

Article 2 Right to education

No person shall be denied the right to education. In the exercise of any functions which it assumes in relation to education and to teaching, the State shall respect the right of parents to ensure such education and teaching in conformity with their own religious and philosophical convictions.

Article 3 Right to free elections

The High Contracting Parties undertake to hold free elections at reasonable intervals by secret ballot, under conditions which will ensure the free expression of the opinion of the people in the choice of the legislature.

Sixth protocol (1983) 5 EHRR 167, entry into force 1985

Article 1 Abolition of the death penalty

The death penalty shall be abolished. No one shall be condemned to such penalty or executed.

Article 2 Death penalty in time of war

A State may make provision in its law for the death penalty in respect of acts committed in time of war or of imminent threat of war; such penalty shall be applied only in the instances laid down in the law and in accordance with the relevant provisions. The State shall communicate to the Secretary of the Council of Europe the relevant provisions of that law.

Article 3 Prohibition of derogations

No derogation from the provisions of this Protocol shall be made under Article 15 of the Convention.

Article 4 Prohibition of reservations

No reservation may be made under Article 57 of the Convention in respect of the provisions of this Protocol.

Notes

1   Articles 8–11 have a second paragraph enumerating certain restrictions on the primary right. An exception may only be relied upon if it has a legitimate aim, is 'prescribed by law'[8] and 'necessary in a democratic society'. The latter phrase was interpreted in *Handyside v United Kingdom* (1976) 1 EHRR 737 and *Silver v UK* (1983) 5 EHRR 347 as meaning that, to be compatible with the Convention, the interference must, *inter alia*, correspond to a pressing social need and 'be proportionate to the legitimate aim pursued'. The interests covered by the restrictions are largely the same in all these Articles and, apart from the 'rights of others' exception, reflect general societal concerns.

2   The Convention rights must be secured without discrimination under Article 14. Article 14 does not provide a general right to freedom from discrimination, only that the rights and freedoms of the Convention must be secured without discrimination. Thus, if discrimination occurs in an area which is not covered by the Convention, Article 14 will be irrelevant. Thus, Article 14 remains of limited value since it is not free standing and does not cover social and economic matters lying outside the protected rights. But these weaknesses will eventually be addressed by the Twelfth Protocol, which will provide a free standing right to freedom from discrimination in relation to rights protected by law.[9] The protection from discrimination under the Twelfth Protocol will render Article 14 redundant. However, at present, the UK government has not ratified it and, strangely for a Labour government committed to anti-discrimination policies, it does not currently intend to do so.

Under Article 14 an applicant may allege violation of a substantive right taken alone and also that he or she has been discriminated against in respect of that right. However, even if no violation of the substantive right taken alone is found and even if that claim is manifestly ill-founded, there could still be a violation of that Article and Article 14 taken together so long as the matter at issue is covered by the other Article. This was found in *X v Federal Republic of Germany* Application 4045/69 (1970) Yearbook XIII, ECHR. It may be noted that the Convention may be of particular value as a source of general principles in sex discrimination cases before the European Court of Justice.[10]

3   Article 13 provides a right to an effective remedy for breach of another Convention right before a national authority. Even if no violation of the other Article is eventually found, it can still be argued that the national courts should have

---

8   This phrase includes unwritten law; see *The Sunday Times v United Kingdom* (1979) 2 EHRR 245.
9   For further discussion of the draft Discrimination Protocol, see G Moon (2000) 1 EHRLR 49.
10 See, eg, *Johnstone v Chief Constable of the RUC* [1986] ECR 1651.

provided an effective means of considering the possible violation. In *Leander v Sweden* (1987) 9 EHRR 433 it was found that 'the requirements of Article 13 will be satisfied if there exists domestic machinery whereby, subject to the inherent limitations of the context, the individual can secure compliance with the relevant laws'.[11] This machinery may include a number of possible remedies. It has been held that judicial review proceedings will not be sufficient. In *Smith and Grady v UK* (2000) 29 EHRR 493, the Court said of the concept of *Wednesbury* unreasonableness:

... the threshold at which the ... Court of Appeal could find the Ministry of Defence policy irrational was placed so high that it effectively excluded any consideration by the domestic courts of the question whether the interference with the applicants' rights answered a pressing social need or was proportionate to the national security and public order aims pursued, principles which lie at the heart of the Court's analysis of complaints under Article 8 of the Convention.[12]

4   The state is allowed a 'margin of appreciation' – a degree of discretion – as to the measures needed to protect an interest which falls within one of the exception clauses. The doctrine of the margin of appreciation has a particular application with respect to para 2 of Articles 8–11, but it can affect all the guarantees. In different cases, a wider or narrower margin of appreciation has been allowed. A narrow margin may be allowed, in which case a very full and detailed review of the interference with the guarantee in question will be conducted. This occurred in *Sunday Times v UK* (1979) 2 EHRR 245 (see further Part VI Chapter 2, pp 925–27). It was held that Strasbourg review was not limited to asking whether the state had exercised its discretion reasonably, carefully and in good faith; its conduct must also be examined in Strasbourg to see whether it was compatible with the Convention. If a broader margin is allowed, Strasbourg review will be highly circumscribed. For example, the minority in the *Sunday Times* case (nine judges) wanted to confine the role of Strasbourg to asking only whether the discretion in question was exercised in good faith and carefully, and whether the measure was reasonable in the circumstances.

It is quite hard to predict when each approach will be taken, but it seems to depend on a number of factors. Some restrictions are seen as more subjective than others, such as the protection of morals. It is therefore thought more difficult to lay down a common European standard, and the Court and Commission have, in such instances, shown a certain willingness to allow the exceptions a wide scope in curtailing the primary rights. For example, Article 10 contains an exception in respect of the protection of morals. This was invoked in the *Handyside* case (1976) 1 EHRR 737 (see further Part VI Chapter 2, pp 943–44) in respect of a booklet aimed at schoolchildren which was circulating freely in the rest of Europe. It was held that the UK government was best placed to determine what was needed in its own country in order to protect morals, and therefore no breach of Article 10 had occurred. Some restrictions, particularly national security, fall more within the state's domain than others, and therefore the Strasbourg authorities may think that the state authorities are best placed to evaluate the situation and determine what is needed. In *Civil Service Unions v UK* (1987) 10 EHRR 269, the European Commission of Human Rights, in declaring the unions' application inadmissible, found that national security interests should prevail over freedom of association, even though the national security interest was weak while the infringement of the primary right was very clear; an absolute ban on joining a trade union had been imposed.

---

11   Note that if such machinery exists, but is of doubtful efficacy, a challenge under Article 6(1) may be most likely to succeed (*de Geouffre de la Pradelle v France* (1993) HRLJ 276).
12   *Ibid*, para 138.

The margin of appreciation doctrine clearly has the power to undermine the Convention, and therefore its growth has been criticised.[13]

5 Further general restrictions on Convention rights are allowed under Articles 17, 15 and 64. Under Article 15(2), derogation is allowed in respect of most, but not all, of the rights. In order to derogate, the state in question must show that there is a state of war or public emergency, and in order to determine the validity of this claim two questions should be asked. First, is there an actual or imminent exceptional crisis threatening the organised life of the state? Secondly, is it really necessary to adopt measures requiring derogation from the Articles in question and do the measures go no further than the situation demands? A margin of discretion is allowed in answering these questions because it is thought that the state in question is best placed to determine the facts, but it is not unlimited; Strasbourg will review it if the State has acted unreasonably.

The UK entered a derogation in the case of *Brogan* (1989) 11 EHRR 117 after the European Court of Human Rights had found that a violation of Article 5, which protects liberty, had occurred. At the time of the violation there was no derogation in force in respect of Article 5 because the UK had withdrawn its derogation. However, after the decision in the European Court, the UK entered the derogation stating that there was an emergency at the time. This was challenged as an invalid derogation but the claim failed on the basis that the exigencies of the situation did amount to a public emergency,[14] and the derogation could not be called into question merely because the government had decided to keep open the possibility of finding a means in the future of ensuring greater conformity with Convention obligations. The fact that the emergency measures had been in place since 1974 did not mean that the emergency was not still in being. That derogation formed part of the Human Rights Act 1998 (Sched 3, Part I), but the Act was amended once the derogation was withdrawn.

The Anti-Terrorism, Crime and Security Act 2001, introduced as a response to the 11 September attacks in New York, contains provisions in Part 4 allowing for the indefinite detention without trial of non-British citizens subject to immigration controls suspected of international terrorism, with an initial appeal to the Special Immigration Appeals Tribunal (SIAC) set up under the Special Immigration Appeals Commission Act 1997. The government considered that the new provisions would be incompatible with Article 5(1) of the Convention, which protects the right to liberty and security of the person, afforded further effect in domestic law under the Human Rights Act, and therefore entered a derogation to Article 5(1), under s 14 of the Human Rights Act,[15] within the terms of Article 15 of the Convention. The government made an Order under s 14, the Human Rights Act (Designated Derogation) Order 2001.[16] The Schedule to the Order states that there is a domestic public emergency, which is especially present since there are foreign nationals in the UK who threaten its national security. On this basis, therefore, it argues, the measures in Part 4 are clearly and strictly required by the very grave nature of the situation.

---

13 See T Jones, 'The devaluation of human rights under the European Convention' [1995] PL 430; P Mahoney, 'Marvellous richness or invidious cultural relativism?' (1998) 19 HRLJ 1.

14 *Brannigan and McBride v UK* (1994) 17 EHRR 539.

15 Section 14(1)(b), (4) and (6) provide power for the Secretary of State to make a 'designation order', designating any derogation from an Article or Protocol to the Convention; it can be made in anticipation of the making of the proposed derogation.

16 SI 2001/3644. It was laid before Parliament on 12 November 2001, coming into effect on the following day. It designates the proposed derogation as one that is to have immediate effect.

In the *Greek* case, Report of 5 November 1969, Yearbook XII, the Commission was prepared to hold an Article 15 derogation invalid. Greece had alleged that the derogation was necessary due to the exigencies of the situation; it was necessary to constrain the activities of Communist agitators due to the disruption they were likely to cause. There had been past disruption which had verged on anarchy. Greece therefore claimed that it could not abide by the Articles in question: 10 and 11. Apart from violations of those Articles, violations of Article 3, which is non-derogable, were also alleged. The Commission found that the derogation was not needed; the situation at the decisive moment did not contain all the elements necessary under Article 15.

6   Extracts from certain significant decisions of the Court and Commission regarding breaches of the substantive rights are set out, with criticism of them, in Part VI.

THE INSTITUTIONS FOR THE SUPERVISION OF THE CONVENTION AND THE RIGHT OF COMPLAINT

The European Commission of Human Rights and the European Court of Human Rights

Under Article 19 the Convention set up the European Commission of Human Rights and the European Court of Human Rights. This machinery for the enforcement of the Convention is impressive compared to that used in respect of other human rights treaties, particularly the 1966 International Covenant on Civil and Political Rights, which, as far as the UK is concerned, has been enforceable only through a system of assessment of national reports.[17]

The main role of the Commission, which has now been abolished, was to filter out applications as inadmissible, thereby reducing the workload of the Court. However, it also had another role; it tried to reach a friendly settlement between the parties and could give its opinion on the merits of the case if it was not intended that a final judgment should be given. It also referred the case to the Court or (occasionally) the Committee of Ministers for the final judgment. Creation of the Commission represented a compromise: when the Convention was drafted in 1949 it was thought too controversial merely to allow citizens to take their governments before the Court. There was a feeling that a political body composed of government representatives might be more sympathetic to states' cases; the state might feel less on trial than in the Court. Therefore, the Commission was created as an administrative barrier between the individual and the Court and has been used as a means of filtering out a very high proportion of cases, thus considering far more cases than the Court.

The role of the Commission came under review for a number of reasons. It was barely able to deal with the number of applications it received, and as states which used to be part of the Soviet Union or Yugoslavia became signatories to the Convention, this problem was exacerbated. Moreover, although the notion of involvement of an administrative body in dealing with cases may have been acceptable in 1950, it arguably detracted from the authority of the Convention. The Parliamentary Assembly of the Council of Europe therefore recommended that the

---

17   The Optional Protocol to the Covenant governs the right of individual petition; but it has not been ratified by the UK. For comment on the general efficacy of the reporting system, see (1980) HRLJ 136–70.

Commission and the Court should be merged into one body which would sit full time
– a new Court of Human Rights.[18] The new arrangements governing the control
mechanism[19] are contained in the Eleventh Protocol, which has had a radical effect on
the Convention procedure. Its most significant reform was to set up the single Court,[20]
which now sits full time in place of the Court and Commission (under Article 19).
Now that the Court and Commission have merged, it may be argued that the authority
of the Convention will increase because its jurisprudence will no longer be influenced
by the decisions of an administrative body; the control system has become, in this
respect, more akin to that of a domestic legal system. Although the Commission has
been abolished, it has had a considerable influence on the Strasbourg jurisprudence.

The European Court of Human Rights has increased enormously in standing and
efficacy over the last 30 years, partly due to its activism and creativity in interpreting
the Convention[21] and its willingness to find that Member States have violated the
rights of individuals. It has already brought about a number of important reforms in
human rights matters in the UK.[22]

The right of complaint: individual applications

Article 34, widely viewed as the most important Article in the Convention since it
governs the right of individual complaint, enables citizens of Member States to seek a
remedy for a breach of Convention rights by petitioning the European Court. The right
of complaint was not intended to mimic the working of a domestic legal system. The
Court hears very few cases in comparison with the number of applications made.[23] The
route to Strasbourg is lengthy and discourages applicants from using it. It is still a slow
and cumbersome route owing to the number of applications, despite improvements in
the mechanisms for considering them.[24] The fact that an application may take, at
present, five years to be heard is perhaps one of the main deficiencies of the
Convention enforcement machinery.[25]

Section II of the Convention

European Court of Human Rights

Article 27

Committees, Chambers and Grand Chamber

1. To consider cases brought before it, the Court shall sit in committees of three judges, in
    Chambers of seven judges and in a Grand Chamber of 17 judges. The Court's Chambers shall
    set up committees for a fixed period of time.

    ...

---

18 See 'Reform of the control systems' (1993) 15 EHRR 321.
19 *Ibid*. For comment, see A Mowbray [1993] PL 419.
20 See 'Reform of the control systems', *op cit*.
21 For discussion of the role of the Court in interpreting the Convention, see Gearty, *op cit*, at 89.
22 See DJ Harris, M O'Boyle and C Warbrick, *Law of the European Convention on Human Rights*,
    1995, p 648.
23 Eg, in 1991, the Commission registered 1,648 applications; it referred 93 cases to the Court,
    which gave judgment in 72: European Court of Human Rights, Survey of Activities 1959–91.
24 Eg, new procedures were introduced under the Eighth Protocol including a summary
    procedure for rejecting straightforward cases.
25 The average time is a little over four years: see 'Reform of the control systems', *op cit*, at 360,
    para 7.

Article 28

Declarations of inadmissibility by committees

A committee may, by a unanimous vote, declare inadmissible or strike out of its list of cases an individual application submitted under Article 34 where such a decision can be taken without further examination. The decision shall be final.

Article 29

Decisions by Chambers on admissibility and merits

1. If no decision is taken under Article 28, a Chamber shall decide on the admissibility and merits of individual applications submitted under Article 34.

. . .

Article 30

Relinquishment of jurisdiction to the Grand Chamber

Where a case pending before a Chamber raises a serious question affecting the interpretation of the Convention or the protocols thereto or where the resolution of a question before it might have a result inconsistent with a judgment previously delivered by the Court, the Chamber may, at any time before it has rendered its judgment, relinquish jurisdiction in favour of the Grand Chamber, unless one of the parties to the case objects.

Article 31

Powers of the Grand Chamber

The Grand Chamber shall

(a) determine applications submitted either under Article 33 or Article 34 when a Chamber has relinquished jurisdiction under Article 30 or when the case has been referred to it under Article 43; and

(b) consider requests for advisory opinions submitted under Article 47.

Article 32

Jurisdiction of the Court

1. The jurisdiction of the Court shall extend to all matters concerning the interpretation and application of the Convention and the protocols thereto which are referred to it as provided in Articles 33, 34 and 47.

2. In the event of dispute as to whether the Court has jurisdiction, the Court shall decide.

. . .

Article 34

Individual applications

The Court may receive applications from any person, non-governmental organisation or group of individuals claiming to be the victim of a violation by one of the High Contracting Parties of the rights set forth in the Convention or the protocols thereto. The High Contracting Parties undertake not to hinder in any way the effective exercise of this right.

Article 35

Admissibility criteria

1. The Court may only deal with the matter after all domestic remedies have been exhausted, according to the generally recognised rules of international law, and within a period of six months from the date on which the final decision was taken.

2. The Court shall not deal with any individual application submitted under Article 34 that

    (a) is anonymous; or

(b) is substantially the same as a matter that has already been examined by the Court or has already been submitted to another procedure of international investigation or settlement and contains no relevant new information.

3. The Court shall declare inadmissible any individual application submitted under Article 34 which it considers incompatible with the provisions of the Convention or the protocols thereto, manifestly ill-founded, or an abuse of the right of application.

4. The Court shall reject any application which it considers inadmissible under this Article. It may do so at any stage of the proceedings.

Article 36

Third party intervention

1. In all cases before a Chamber or the Grand Chamber, a High Contracting Party one of whose nationals is an applicant shall have the right to submit written comments and to take part in hearings.

...

Article 38 [which replaced Article 28]

Examination of the case and friendly settlement proceedings

1. If the Court declares the application admissible, it shall

   (a) pursue the examination of the case, together with the representatives of the parties, and if need be, undertake an investigation, for the effective conduct of which the States concerned shall furnish all necessary facilities;

   (b) place itself at the disposal of the parties concerned with a view to securing a friendly settlement of the matter on the basis of respect for human rights as defined in the Convention and the protocols thereto.

2. Proceedings conducted under paragraph 1.b shall be confidential.

Article 40

Public hearings

... Hearings shall be public unless the Court in exceptional circumstances decides otherwise.

Article 41

Just satisfaction

If the Court finds that there has been a violation of the Convention or the protocols thereto, and if the internal law of the High Contracting Party concerned allows only partial reparation to be made, the Court shall, if necessary, afford just satisfaction to the injured party.

...

Article 43

Referral to the Grand Chamber

1. Within a period of three months from the date of the judgment of the Chamber, any party to the case may, in exceptional cases, request that the case be referred to the Grand Chamber.

2. A panel of five judges of the Grand Chamber shall accept the request if the case raises a serious question affecting the interpretation or application of the Convention or the protocols thereto, or a serious issue of general importance.

3. If the panel accepts the request, the Grand Chamber shall decide the case by means of a judgment.

Article 44

Final judgments

1. The judgment of the Grand Chamber shall be final.

2. The judgment of a Chamber shall become final

   (a) when the parties declare that they will not request that the case be referred to the Grand Chamber; or

   (b) three months after the date of the judgment, if reference of the case to the Grand Chamber has not been requested; or

   (c) when the panel of the Grand Chamber rejects the request to refer under Article 43.

3. The final judgment shall be published.

Article 45

Reasons for judgments and decisions

1. Reasons shall be given for judgments as well as for decisions declaring applications admissible or inadmissible.

2. If a judgment does not represent, in whole or in part the unanimous opinion of the judges, any judge shall be entitled to deliver a separate opinion.

Article 46

Binding force and execution of judgments

1. The High Contracting Parties undertake to abide by the final judgment of the Court in any case to which they are parties.

2. The final judgment of the Court shall be transmitted to the Committee of Ministers, which shall supervise its execution.

Notes

1 The requirement that domestic remedies must have been exhausted refers to the 'legal remedies available under the local law which are in principle capable of providing an effective and sufficient means of redressing the wrongs for which [the respondent state is said to be responsible]'.[26] If there is a doubt as to whether a remedy is available, Article 35 (previously Article 26) will not be satisfied unless the applicant has taken proceedings in which that doubt can be resolved.[27] This generally means that judicial procedures must be instituted up to the highest court which can affect the decision but also, if applicable, appeal must be made to administrative bodies.

2 An application will be found to be manifestly ill-founded if the facts obviously fail to disclose a violation. In the past, when the Commission decided on this matter, the ill-founded character of the application was not always as manifest as this would imply. Under the current arrangements, it is necessary to have unanimity if a committee declares the application inadmissible (r 53(3) of the Rules of the Court), but a majority if a Chamber of the Court does so. Although it is more satisfactory that the decision is being taken judicially, it is arguable that it should have been necessary to have unanimity or a two-thirds majority as to a finding of manifest ill-foundedness by a Chamber, even though a bare majority suffices in respect of the other conditions.

3 The proceedings before the Chamber of seven judges will consist of a written stage, followed by a hearing.[28] Chambers designate Judge Rapporteurs to examine applications. The arrangements are characterised by their flexibility: within the Rules, the Court is free to decide on a procedure which can be tailored to the nature of a particular application (see r 42(2)) and this may include visiting a particular

---

26 *Nielsen v Denmark* Application No 343/57, (1958–59) 2 YB 412.
27 *De Vargattirgah v France* Application No 9559/81.
28 Under Article 55, the Court shall draw up its own rules and determine its own procedure.

place, such as a prison. An on-the-spot inquiry can be conducted by a delegate of the Court. The Court can also order a report from an expert on any matter. After this initial stage, the Chamber will normally conduct an oral hearing if there has been no oral admissibility hearing.

4   The Court is not bound by its own judgments (r 51, para 1). Nevertheless, it usually follows and applies its own precedents unless departure from them is indicated in order to ensure that interpretation of the Convention reflects social change. Under Article 46, the judgment of the Court is binding on the State Party involved. The Court is not ultimately a coercive body and relies for acceptance of its judgments on the willingness of states to abide by the Convention. The Court can award compensation under Article 41. The purpose of the reparation is to place the applicant in the position he would have been in had the violation not taken place. It will include costs unless the applicant has received legal aid. It can also include loss of earnings, travel costs, fines and costs unjustly awarded against the applicant. It can also include intangible or non-pecuniary losses which may be awarded due to unjust imprisonment or stress.[29]

5   The Committee of Ministers consists of one representative from the government of each Member State of the Council of Europe, usually the Minister for Foreign Affairs. Under Article 46, the Committee is charged with supervising the execution of the Court's judgment. If the state fails to execute the judgment, the Committee decides what measures to take: it can bring political pressure to bear, including suspension or even, as a final sanction, expulsion from the Council of Europe. However, doubts have been raised over the fitness of the Committee to oversee one of the key stages in the whole Convention process, namely the implementation of national law to bring it into line with the findings of the Court.

Questions

1   Will the new control mechanism be likely to inspire confidence in applicants?

2   Is further reform of the control mechanisms of the Convention needed? Examples might include abolition of the supervision of the Court's judgment by the Committee of Ministers with a view to ensuring more effective judicial supervision, or allowing the Court to fine Member States who fail to implement the judgment of the Court fully.

3   What significance may be found in the steady improvement in the position of the individual applicant in proceedings before the Court?

4   Why are Member States willing to submit to judgments of the Court of Human Rights which may require a radical change in national law?

THE INFLUENCE OF THE CONVENTION ON EUROPEAN UNION LAW

The influence of the Convention on EU law became increasingly important due to acceptance of the principle enunciated in *Amministrazione delle Finanze dello Stato v Simmenthal* (Case 106/77) [1978] ECR 629 and *Nold v Commission* (Case 4/73) [1974] ECR 491, namely, that respect for fundamental rights should be ensured within the

---

29   Eg, in *Young, James and Webster v United Kingdom* (1981) 4 EHRR 38, pecuniary and non-pecuniary costs were awarded: the Court ordered £65,000 to be paid. See further Part VI Chapter 1, pp 874–75.

context of the EU. The Convention has come into a closer relationship with EU law as the process of European integration has continued.

J Nold, Kohlen- und Baustoffgroßhandlung v Commission of the European Communities (Case 4/73) [1974] ECR 491, ECJ
Judgment of the Court of 14 May 1974

Fundamental rights are an integral part of the general principles of law the observance of which the Court ensures. In safeguarding these rights the Court is bound to draw inspiration from the constitutional traditions common to the Member States and cannot uphold measures which are incompatible with the fundamental rights established and guaranteed by the constitutions of these states.

Similarly, international treaties for the protection of human rights, on which the Member States have collaborated or of which they are signatories, can supply guidelines which should be followed within the framework of Community law.

Johnston v Chief Constable of the RUC (Case 222/84) [1986] ECR 1651, paras 17 and 18, ECJ

Article 6 of the [equal treatment] directive requires Member States to introduce into their internal legal systems such measures as are needed to enable all persons who consider themselves wronged by discrimination 'to pursue their claims by judicial process'. It follows from that provision that the Member States must take measures which are sufficiently effective to achieve the aim of the directive and that they must ensure that the rights thus conferred may be effectively relied upon before the national courts by the persons concerned.

The requirement of judicial control stipulated by that article reflects a general principle of law which underlies the constitutional traditions common to the Member States. That principle is also laid down in Articles 6 and 13 of the European Convention for the Protection of Human Rights and Fundamental Freedoms of 4 November 1950. As the European Parliament, Council and Commission recognised in their joint declaration of 5 April 1977 (*Official Journal* Ch 103 p 1) and as the court has recognised in its decisions, the principles on which that Convention is based must be taken into consideration in Community law.

Notes

1   The Treaty on European Union, Article 6(2) states that the EU will respect fundamental rights as recognised by the Convention and as resulting from the constitutional traditions common to Member States.[30] But although Article 6 states that the EU will respect fundamental rights as recognised by the Convention, the ECJ, in Opinion 2/94 (28 March 1996),[31] held that the EU cannot accede to the Convention, on the ground that an amendment to the EU Treaty would be required in order to bring about this change. Under the Treaty of Amsterdam, voting rights of Member States who fail to observe the principle embodied by Article 6(2) can be suspended. Thus, in all the Member States, implementation of EU measures in national law is clearly subject to respect for the Convention rights, although an individual cannot make an application to Strasbourg against the Union alleging that the Union has violated the Convention. Even though formal accession of the Union to the Convention has not yet occurred, the Convention will control Union

---

30   For enforcement of the Convention by this means, see P Craig and G de Burca, *European Law: Text and Materials*, 2nd edn (1998).
31   (1996) *The Times*, 16 April.

conduct. Thus, the decision of the European Court of Human Rights in *Rees* (1986) 9 EHRR 56 was relied upon by the ECJ in deciding, in *P v S and Cornwall CC* (Case 13/94) (1996) *The Times*, 7 May, that transsexuals fall within the Equal Treatment Directive. This was found on the basis that the Directive was simply the expression of the principle of equality, which was one of the fundamental principles of European law.[32]

2 Pronouncements of the ECJ such as that in *Nold* suggest that protection for fundamental rights in the European Community is likely to increase due to the respect for such rights apparently evinced by the ECJ. Below, Jason Coppel and Aidan O'Neill question this assumption.

3 The EU Charter of Fundamental Rights was agreed at Nice.[33] The Charter, published in May 2000, contains those rights recognised under the European Convention on Human Rights together with a number of new social rights, including the right to strike, guarantees of maximum working hours, worker consultation and trade union membership. The rights could, potentially, bind the EU institutions. Certain Member States and the European Commission proposed that the Charter should be included in the Treaty of Nice in December 2000. Britain considers that the Charter should not become part of the Treaty, and therefore have binding effect, but should have a merely declaratory status. At present, this is the position; although not of binding force, the Charter will aid in the interpretation of EU law. The future status of the Charter is considered below, at p 258, by Arnull.

J Coppel and A O'Neill, 'The European Court of Justice: taking rights seriously?' (1992) 12(2) LS 227–30, 231–36, 244–45

I Introduction

... References to fundamental rights are now being made by the court in order to extend its jurisdiction into areas previously reserved to Member States' courts and to expand the influence of the Community over the activities of the Member States. This shall be termed the 'offensive' use of fundamental rights, to be contrasted with the earlier 'defensive' use.

It will be argued that the court is using fundamental rights 'offensively' in two ways. On the one hand, it is extending the use of the concepts of fundamental rights in specific areas of Community law previously untouched by those concepts. On the other hand, it is undertaking a more general expansion of its jurisdiction, in the guise of fundamental rights protection, into areas previously the preserve of Member States, by means of subtle changes in its formulation of a crucial jurisdictional rule.

With respect to both the offensive and defensive uses of fundamental rights, it must be questioned whether the court has ever been motivated by a concern for any supposed lack of adequate protection of fundamental rights within the European Communities. It is the argument of this paper that the court has employed fundamental rights instrumentally, so as to accelerate the process of legal integration in the Community. It has not protected these fundamental rights for their own sake. It has not taken these rights seriously.

2 The defensive use of human rights

Starting in the late 1960s, increasing concern was expressed in the courts in Germany and Italy on the question of whether or not the fundamental rights entrenched in their respective national constitutions were recognised and protected within European Community law [for a summary of

---

32 These developments had particular significance in the UK since the Convention was not part of UK law. See further Part VI Chapter 1.

33 See for discussion, E Wicks [2001] PL 527.

the relevant German case law see especially Brinkhorst and Schermers, *Judicial Remedies in the European Community*, 4th edn (1987), pp 144–54]. Their fear was that these fundamental rights would gradually be eroded as the competences of the Community increased.

In response to the threat that national courts would resolve their dilemma by opting for the supremacy of their own national constitutional provisions on fundamental rights protection, the European Court discovered that the protection of fundamental rights was indeed a general principle of European Community law. This development contradicted its own previous case law rejecting the idea of fundamental rights protection within the Community legal order [see *Friedrich Stork and Co v High Authority of the ECSC* (Case 1/58) [1959] ECR 17; *Geitling v High Authority of the ECSC* (Cases 36–38, 40/59) [1960] ECR 523; *Sgarlata v Commission of the EC* (Case 40/64) [1965] ECR 215], and was effected notwithstanding the absence of any mention or list of fundamental rights within the texts of the Community treaties.

The European Court's policy on fundamental rights appears, thus far, to have averted any significant damage by the courts of the Member States to the integrity, unity and supremacy of the Community legal order.

3 The offensive use of human rights

One feature of the defensive use of fundamental rights was that these rights were applied only to Community acts. Initially, at least, human rights were not applied directly to the activities of Member States [see eg *Defrenne v Sabena* (Case 149/77) [1978] ECR 1365, and *Demirel* (Case 12/86) [1987] ECR 3719]. It is arguable that the Court no longer feels itself constrained to observe any distinction between Community acts and Member State acts, at least in relation to fundamental rights protection. The Court has increasingly been applying fundamental rights considerations to the acts of Member States.

It is not until 1989 that the court was seen openly to take the step of assessing the validity of an act of a Member State on the basis of fundamental rights considerations [*Wachauf v Federal Republic of Germany* (Case 118/75) [1976] ECR 1185, 1207 is discussed coming to the following conclusion].

The decision in *Wachauf* is of significance because, for the first time, the European Court applied fundamental rights principles to national acts formulated in implementation of Community legislation. The court held that, where a Community provision incorporates the protection of a fundamental right, national measures which implement that provision must give effect to the provision in such a way that the fundamental right is respected.

This may indeed be a conservative interpretation of the implications of *Wachauf*. The European Court itself, in the subsequent case of *Elleniki Radiophonia Tileorasi (ERT) v Dimotiki Etairia Pliroforissis* [(Case 260/89) [1991] ECR 2925], interpreted *Wachauf* in broader terms [*ibid*, para 41]. '[M]easures which are incompatible with respect for human rights, which are recognised and guaranteed [in Community law], could not be admitted in the Community.' It is not clear from the terms of the judgment in *ERT* whether the court in this passage is referring to Community measures or Member State measures, but given that *ERT* concerned measures instituted by Greece, a Member State, in derogation from Community law, the latter conclusion is not unjustifiable.

Further, in *ERT* the court adopted a more forthright fundamental rights approach to the question of the admissibility of public policy derogations by Member States from Community law than is evidenced by *Rutili*. The court held [para 43] that: 'When a Member State invokes Articles 56 and 66 of the Treaty in order to justify rules which hinder the free movement of services, this justification, which is provided for in Community law, must be interpreted in the light of general principles of law, notably fundamental rights. The national rules in question may only benefit from the Article 56 and 66 exceptions insofar as they are compatible with fundamental rights, the observance of which the court ensures.' And, the court went on [para 45 – authors' translation]: 'The limitations imposed on the power of Member States to apply the provisions of Articles 66 and 56 of the treaty for reasons of public order, public security and public health must be understood in the light of the general principle of freedom of expression, enshrined in Article 10 of the European Convention.'

In *ERT*, the European Court is once more seen to be extending its jurisdiction in the matter of fundamental rights. The court is, in effect, applying the text of the European Convention not only to the acts of Community institutions but also to any attempts by Member States to derogate from the market freedoms assured by Community law. It is a development of *Rutili* precisely in that it uses the European Convention on Human Rights as an additional standard on the basis of which to judge Member State action, rather than, as in *Rutili*, merely a declaration which happens to echo general principles of existing Community law.

4 Changing formulations of the general jurisdictional rule

The line of cases from *Wachauf* through to *Grogan* also evinces an incremental expansion of the area of law and of Member State action which is subject to fundamental rights validation by the European Court of Justice.

In *Cinéthèque v Fédération nationale des cinémas français*, Case 60/84 [1985] ECR 2605, para 26 the court stated:

> Although it is true that it is the duty of this court to ensure observance of fundamental rights in the field of Community law, it has no power to examine the compatibility with the European Convention of national legislation which concerns, as in this case, an area which falls within the jurisdiction of the national legislator.

... the *Cinéthèque* formula was reworded in *Demirel v Stadt Schwaebisch Gmund* [(Case 12/86) [1987] ECR 3719, 3754, para 28]: '[The Court] has no power to examine the compatibility with the European Convention on Human Rights of national legislation lying outside the scope of Community law'. This change of emphasis from that which is within the jurisdiction of the national legislator to that which is within the jurisdiction of Community law is a subtle one, but one which may nevertheless have revolutionised the impact of fundamental rights considerations on national administrative and legislative action. For one thing it paved the way for the decision in *Wachauf*, which applied fundamental rights standards to a Member State act in implementation of a Community rule. Such an act is one which clearly falls within the jurisdiction of the national legislator and also falls within the scope of Community law. The application of fundamental rights criteria in this case would not have been consistent with the reasoning of *Cinéthèque* but fell within the *Demirel* formulation.

In *ERT*, the court appeared to go further, stating the following [see note [24], para 42]: 'According to its jurisprudence [see the decisions in *Cinéthèque* and *Demirel*] ... the court cannot assess, from the point of view of the European Convention on Human Rights, national legislation which is not situated within the body of Community law. By contrast, as soon as any such legislation enters the field of application of Community law, the court, as the sole arbiter in this matter, must provide the national court with all the elements of interpretation which are necessary in order to enable it to assess the compatibility of that legislation with the fundamental rights – as laid down in particular in the European Convention on Human Rights – the observance of which the court ensures'.

The implication of the court is that it would examine all matters which did fall within the area of Community law. The only Member State actions which the court might decline to vet on human rights grounds are, therefore, those which occur in an area of exclusive Member State jurisdiction. This concept of exclusive Member State jurisdiction may itself be open to future redefinition by the court.

This implication was spelt out by Advocate General Van Gerven in *Grogan* when he stated [see note [29], para 31 of the opinion of the Advocate General of 11 June 1991]: 'In [*Cinéthèque*] ... it was stated that the court's power of review did not extend to "an area which falls within the jurisdiction of the national legislator", a statement which, generally speaking, is true. Yet once a national rule is involved which has effects in an area covered by Community law (in this case

Article 59 of the EEC Treaty) and which, in order to be permissible, must be able to be justified under Community law with the help of concepts or principles of Community law, then the appraisal of that national rule no longer falls within the *exclusive jurisdiction* of the national legislature'.

The court in *Grogan* did not expressly adopt the advocate general's formulation, asserting [*ibid*, para 30 of the judgment of the court] that it was competent to pronounce on fundamental rights issues 'where national legislation falls within the field of application of Community law', but that 'the court has no such jurisdiction with regard to national legislation lying outside the scope of Community law.' Nevertheless, the implication as to the requirement of exclusive national jurisdiction remains. This represents, in practice, a major expansion of the *Cinéthèque* reasoning, and a doctrine of much wider application than the strict terms of the decision in *Wachauf*.

5 Conclusion

Given the jurisdictional expansion seen in the reformulation of the *Cinéthèque* dictum in *ERT* and *Grogan*, the court now sees itself as being able to review national legislation wherever this operates in an area touched by Community law. *ERT* reveals that such assessment of the validity of national law will be made from a point of view of its respect for human rights. Similarly, national courts would now seem to be obliged to give effect to the European Convention on Human Rights, as this would be interpreted by the European Court of Justice, if not the European Court of Human Rights in Strasbourg, in all questions before them which fall within the field of Community law [see Hall (1991) EL Rev 466]. Article F(2) of the common Provisions of the Maastricht Treaty may encourage this trend.

At times the court has seemed willing to apply human rights as if they were superior to (and hence grounds for invalidating) the acts of Member States. However, at the same time, it clearly subordinates human rights to the end of closer economic integration in the Community. In doing so the court has treated human rights, and in particular their place in any normative hierarchy, in a confused and ambiguous way.

Evidently it is economic integration, to be achieved through the acts of Community institutions, which the court sees as its fundamental priority. In adopting and adapting the slogan of protection of human rights the court has seized the moral high ground. However, the high rhetoric of human rights protection can be seen as no more than a vehicle for the court to extend the scope and impact of European law.

By using the term 'fundamental right' in such an instrumental way the court refuses to take the discourse of fundamental rights seriously. It thereby both devalues the notion of fundamental rights and brings its own standing into disrepute.

A Arnull, 'From Opinion 2/94 to the future of Europe' (2002) 27(1) EL Rev 1–2

When the Court of Justice ruled in Opinion 2/94 ([1996] ECR I-1759) that the European Community lacked the power to accede to the European Convention on Human Rights, few could have predicted quite how profound the consequences would be. Opponents of Community accession doubtless congratulated themselves on the outcome. They may even have been tempted to think that their success at the 1996 IGC in resisting pressure for the Court's Opinion to be reversed meant that the question was now closed. But advocates of reinforcing protection for fundamental rights in the Union were not to be so easily thwarted. Barely was the ink dry on the Treaty of Amsterdam when the European Council agreed at Cologne in June 1999 to establish a charter of fundamental rights, 'in order to make their overriding importance and relevance more visible to the Union's citizens.' A draft of the charter was to be drawn up by a body – subsequently entitled a Convention – comprising not just representatives of the members of the European Council but also European and national parliamentarians. (The European Council dealt with the composition and working methods of the Convention in more detail at Tampere in October 1999.) Rejectionist Member States might have remained relatively sanguine. The Cologne conclusions left open the question of the legal status of the charter and made it possible to argue that it should be nothing more than a restatement of existing rights. However, the genie was out of the bottle. Although at Nice the Charter which had been agreed by the Convention was not made formally binding, its status was identified in a declaration on the future of the Union as a question to be addressed at the next IGC in 2004. The Nice declaration stated that, at its meeting in Laeken in December 2001, the European Council would decide how to take forward the debate on the future of the Union. What the European Council did (see the Laeken Declaration on the future of the European Union) was to convene a new Convention, modelled on the one which drew up the Charter, to consider not just the Charter's status but also a series of far-reaching questions affecting the accountability and legitimacy of the Union ... The final document will provide a starting point for discussions at the 2004 IGC. Although the Laeken Declaration makes it clear that it is at the IGC that the final decisions will be taken, the Convention's deliberations are likely to have a significant impact on the tenor of the negotiations. Its composition, like that of the Convention which drew up the Charter, will endow it with considerable moral authority. It will be chaired by a former French President assisted by two Vice-Chairmen. In addition, the Convention will comprise one representative of each Head of State or Government, two members of each national parliament, 16 MEPs and two Commission representatives. Candidate countries will be represented in the same way as current Member States, although they will not be entitled to block any consensus which may emerge among the latter. The Heads of State and Government recognised in their declaration at Nice 'the need to improve and to monitor the democratic legitimacy and transparency of the Union and its institutions, in order to bring them closer to the citizens of the Member States.' They will therefore have little choice but to treat the Convention's conclusions with the utmost seriousness ... The Union's legitimacy deficit, now widely acknowledged, and the potential difficulty of making changes to the Treaties after enlargement may produce a 'constitutional moment' in 2004. The result could be a treaty even more significant than Maastricht.

Questions

1   Coppel and O'Neill argue that in protecting rights the ECJ is motivated primarily by the desire to accelerate the process of legal integration in the Community. What limitations might this motivation impose on the level of rights protection provided by the ECJ?

2   Given the founding principles of the EU, would it be a legitimate development for it now to base its rights protection on any ground other than legal integration?

3   What are the implications of the EU Charter of Fundamental Rights for the UK?

FURTHER READING

R Clayton and H Tomlinson, *The Law of Human Rights* (2000)

H Fenwick, *Civil Liberties and Human Rights*, 3rd edn (2002), Chapter 2

D Harris, K O'Boyle and C Warbrick, *Law of the European Convention on Human Rights* (1995), 2nd edn (expected 2004)

M Janis, R Kay and A Bradley, *European Human Rights Law*, 2nd edn (2000)

P Van Dijk and F Van Hoof, *Theory and Practice of the European Convention on Human Rights*, 3rd edn (1998)

PART III

PARLIAMENT AND ITS REFORM

THE COMMONS: ELECTIONS, PARTIES, LEGISLATION AND SCRUTINY[1]

INTRODUCTION: THE ELECTORAL SYSTEM

This chapter considers the role of the House of Commons in the UK constitution in relation to the legislative process and, importantly, scrutiny of the executive. Its emphasis will be on the constitutional relationship between the Commons and government; on the functions Parliament can realistically be attempted to perform, the extent of its domination by government and an evaluation of its work. Recent reforms and proposals for further reform will also be considered. Since the Commons is also the principal democratic forum of the UK, from which governments are formed, and which ultimately holds the key to their continued existence, this chapter also considers the effect of the electoral system which plays such an important part in determining the make-up and behaviour of both Commons and government and the vital role of political parties, not least in subverting the traditional, constitutional relationship between MPs and government. Because of the vast range and scale of changes elsewhere in the UK constitution which this book must cover, and the fact that there is currently little prospect of any reform to the UK Parliament's electoral system, this chapter does not consider alternatives to the 'first past the post' electoral system used in the UK for elections to the Westminster Parliament in detail. What then is that system, how does it work in practice, and what are some of the alternatives to it?

G Ganz, *Understanding Public Law*, 3rd edn (2001), pp 4–8

Historically the electoral system is based on the representation of communities. This is still reflected in the qualification for voting and the method of voting. Everyone who is 18, a Commonwealth citizen (who is legally in the UK) or a citizen of [Ireland], not a peer who is entitled to sit in the House of Lords (see below Chapter 2) and not serving a sentence of imprisonment or held in a mental institution as a consequence of criminal activity is entitled to be placed on the electoral register in a constituency where he is resident. Residence does not now involve a qualifying period or residence on a particular date (formerly October 10). It may not even now require a degree of permanence, which was sufficiently manifested by the women protesting at Greenham Common *(Hipperson v Newbury Electoral Registration Officer,* 1985). A person can be resident where he is staying at a place otherwise than on a permanent basis if he has no home elsewhere (Representation of the People Act 2000, s 3). This could apply, for example, to travellers. Similarly, a homeless person, who is not resident at any address, can be registered if he gives an address of a place where he spends a substantial part of his time. Patients in mental

---

1 General reading for this part (additional to that cited elsewhere in it) relevant chapters in the following: C Turpin, *British Government and the Constitution,* 4th edn (1999); R Holme and M Elliott, *Time for a New Constitution* (1988); IPPR, *The Constitution of the United Kingdom* (1991); A Bradley and K Ewing, *Constitutional and Administrative Law,* 13th edn (2002); O Hood Phillips, *Constitutional and Administrative Law,* 8th edn (2001); J McEldowney, *Public Law,* 2nd edn (1999); R Pyper and L Robins (eds), *Governing the UK in the 1990s* (1995) Part II; J Griffith, *Parliamentary Scrutiny of Government Bills* (1974); I Burton and G Drewry, *Legislation and Public Policy* (1981); SA Walkland and M Ryle, *The Commons Today* (1981); M Franklin and P Norton, *Parliamentary Questions* (1993); M Rush, *Parliamentary Government in Britain* (1981); P Norton, *The Commons in Perspective* (1981); P Norton, *Legislatures* (1990); A Tomkin, "'Conclusion", in *Government Unwrapped: the Constitution after Scott* (1998); D Oliver, "The Reform of the United Kingdom Parliament", in J Jowell and D Oliver, *The Changing Constitution,* 4th edn (2000); Hansard Commission, *The Challenge for Parliament: Making Government Accountable* (2001).

hospitals, other than those detained there for criminal activity can now be treated as resident at the mental hospital and those remanded in custody, who have not been convicted of an offence, can be treated as resident at the place of detention. Those who cannot satisfy the residence qualification may be entitled to be registered in a constituency where they were resident, e.g. if they are absent because they are members of the armed forces or British citizens living abroad who have been registered there within the preceding 20 years (Representation of the People Act 1989). In such cases entitlement to vote is based on citizenship rather than residence to which lip-service is paid through registration in the constituency where the citizen was previously resident. Such a notional residence is essential as all voters must be on an electoral roll in a constituency

The constituency is the linchpin of our electoral system. Its origin lies in the representation of communities which is still an important part of an MP's work. There is, however, a constant tension between this concept of representation and the modern party system which affects so many facets of our representative democracy It manifests itself at the outset when the constituency boundaries are drawn. These are now reviewed every eight to twelve years (Boundary Commissions Act 1992) by four politically impartial Boundary Commissions, one for each part of the United Kingdom (Parliamentary Constituencies Act 1986). Their functions will be taken over in due course by the Electoral Commission set up under the Political Parties, Elections and Referendums Act 2000. Their terms of reference enjoin them to create constituencies as near as possible to the electoral quota which is obtained by dividing the electorate of that part of the United Kingdom by the number of constituencies in it without crossing county or London borough boundaries (unless there are exceptional circumstances) and taking into account local ties. The number of seats has increased with each review and is now 659 but the changes in population are not evenly spread throughout the country. This has profound implications for the political parties but political considerations cannot be taken into account by the Commissions and, therefore, political arguments are put to them cloaked in arguments about local ties (Home Affairs Committee Report, HC 97 (1986–87), p 80). Not surprisingly nearly every review since 1945 has given rise to political controversy. In 1969 the Labour government refused to implement the Boundary Commissions' recommendations and in 1983 unsuccessfully challenged them in Court (*R. v Boundary Commission for England ex parte Foot*, 1983).

The crucial importance of constituency boundaries to the outcome of elections is the result of our electoral system, called first past the post, under which an MP is elected for a constituency if he receives one vote more than his nearest rival however small his percentage of the total vote. This not only enables MPs to be elected on a minority vote (312 MPs in 1997) but on two occasions since the war (1951 and February 1974) the party gaining most seats polled fewer votes than the main opposition party. Most disadvantaged by our electoral system are the Liberal Democrats, whose support is fairly evenly spread throughout the country and who come second in a large number of seats but only win a handful of seats where their support is concentrated. In 1997 they gained 46 seats for 17 per cent of the vote, whilst Labour gained 418 seats for 43 per cent and the Conservatives 165 seats with 31 per cent of the vote. It is this glaring discrepancy between seats and votes since the revival of the Liberal party in 1974 which has fuelled the pressure for electoral reform. The result of the 2001 election has left this situation virtually unchanged.

As these figures illustrate the system can also be unfair to the major parties. Labour obtained over 60 per cent of the seats with 43 per cent of the vote whilst the Conservatives gained 25 per cent of the seats with 31 per cent of the vote. Even more startling is that Labour polled fewer votes in 1997 (13.5 million) than the Conservatives in 1992 (14 million) and achieved an overall majority of 179 seats, whereas the Conservatives only managed a majority of 21 in 1992. There were several reasons for this. The turnout of voters was much lower in 1997 (only 71.5 per cent against 77.7 per cent in 1992) and some of the lowest polls were in Labour seats. Liberal Democrat voters switched to Labour in greater numbers than to Conservatives. Most importantly the election was won in approximately 100 seats where the lowest swing of votes was needed to win the seat. By targeting these seats Labour achieved better than average results where they counted most. Election campaigns have, therefore, become highly professional operations focused on a narrow band of voters, who are canvassed and cajoled, often at the expense of the party's traditional supporters. The 2001 election with a record low turnout of 59 per cent confirmed these trends.

The concentration on these marginal seats highlights the importance of constituency boundaries and their review by the Boundary Commissions. These reviews have to reflect the movement of population from the North to the South and out of the cities to the rural hinterland. This has traditionally been unfavourable to the Labour party but at the latest review Labour was able to avoid the worst effects by skilful presentations to the Commissions. Such deleterious effects as remained were more than neutralised by the 10 per cent swing against the Conservatives and the factors discussed above which were weighted against the Conservatives.

In fulfilment of a pre-election agreement with the Liberal Democrats, which was embodied in its manifesto, Labour set up a Commission under the chairmanship of Lord Jenkins, a leading Liberal Democrat peer and former Labour Minister, to recommend the best alternative system to the existing system of voting. They thus became the first government elected triumphantly under the present system to set in train the process of reform. Whether the choice between the existing system and an alternative system is put to the electorate in a referendum after the 2001 election remains to be seen.

The fairness of an electoral system must be judged not only by the proportionality of votes to seats but by the proportionality of power. If seats had been allocated in proportion to votes in Britain, the third party (now the Liberal Democrats) would have held the balance of power since 1974, as its counterpart did in Germany for 30 years. This gives disproportionate power to a minority party. The Jenkins Commission was asked to take into account both proportionality of votes and stable government (which is not the hall-mark of coalitions) as well as the link between an MP and a geographical constituency.

The Commission in its report (Cm 4090, 1998) rejected the Alternative Vote which retains single member constituencies but where voters list candidates in order of preference and which ensures that an MP is elected by more than 50 per cent of the votes including second-preference votes. One of its main reasons was that it would have disadvantaged the Conservatives in 1997 disproportionately because of the strength of the anti-Conservative vote. It also rejected the Single Transferable Vote, where votes are cast for candidates in order of preference in multi-member constituencies and seats are allocated according to a complicated formula, partly because of its complexity. It came down in favour of a version of the Additional Member System used in Germany, where a proportion of MPs are elected in single member constituencies and these are then topped-up by MPs elected from a party list so as to achieve proportionality – each voter having two votes, one for a constituency MP and one for the party. The constituency MP would be elected by the Alternative Vote system. For the top-up MPs Britain would be divided into 80 areas returning one or two MPs so as to provide between 15 per cent and 20 per cent of MPs. The Commission calculated that this degree of proportionality would have produced single party majority governments in three out of the last four elections and a hung Parliament, where no party has a majority only in 1992. The Liberal Democrat party would be the main beneficiary of the change by receiving a more proportional share of seats. The boundary changes necessitated by these recommendations made it impossible for it to come into effect at the next election regardless of when the referendum was held.

Notes

1   At the time of writing, reform to the electoral system of Westminster seems to be firmly off the agenda. It is likely to reappear if the Labour Party loses its overall majority and needs to form a coalition with the Liberal Democrats, or possibly if it is returned with a very small majority, such that it needs Liberal Democrat support in order to secure the passage of at least some of its legislation. The Conservatives remain implacably opposed to any form of electoral reform for Westminster at present.

2 The workings and effect of the electoral system, as described above, are crucial to the work of the Commons: the basic fact of the Commons is that the government will normally have a majority of its own party in the House; the struggle of Parliament against the executive tends to play very much second fiddle to the struggle between the parties.

3 The role of the Opposition receives some recognition in the constitution. The Leader of Her Majesty's Opposition (invariably the Leader of either the Conservative or Labour Parties) is paid a salary and public funding, known as 'Short money', assists the Opposition in its task.[2] As Ganz notes,[3] in debate, the Speaker must call for contributions alternately from the Opposition parties and the government, while the membership of parliamentary committees is proportionate to party strengths.

4 Philip Norton has summarised the four main changes to Parliament generally since the early 1970s as: increased independence (of backbench MPs); greater professionalism (that is, more MPs are now career politicians); increased specialisation (the introduction of permanent Select Committees has given MPs the opportunity to build up expertise in particular areas); and greater accessibility (both greater visibility, through broadcasting of the Commons' proceedings, and a more active relationship between MPs and the public and pressure groups).[4]

5 One recent change to the Commons worthy of note is the setting up of Westminster Hall, which functions as a parallel but subordinate chamber to the Commons. The report below recommending its establishment also notes some of the pressures and problems the current Commons labours under. The establishment of Westminster Hall was recommended in the *Second Report of the Select Committee on Modernisation of the House of Commons*, HC 194 (1998–99) and was approved by the House on 24 May 1999. Sittings in Westminster Hall began on Tuesday 30 November 1999. After the experiment had been running for some time, the Committee reviewed the effectiveness and use of the new opportunities for debate.

Fourth Report of the Select Committee on Modernisation of the House of Commons, HC 906 (1999–2000) (extracts)

24 ... Westminster Hall has provided valuable additional opportunities for both private Members and select committees ...

25 ... It has not enabled the Government to expand its legislative programme: the business taken in Westminster Hall has been additional business which would otherwise not have taken place at all. Overwhelmingly it is accepted that Westminster Hall has not detracted from the primacy of the Chamber: the House has had no difficulty in keeping the business in the main Chamber going on Thursday afternoons when the parallel Chamber has also been in operation.

...

27 ... there can be little doubt that the creation of Westminster Hall is a radical innovation, the importance of which is recognised in many other Parliaments ...

...

40 Accordingly, ... we recommend that the experiment with sittings in Westminster Hall should be continued ...

---

2 See HC Deb col 1869 (20 March 1975), and col 427 (26 May 1999).
3 G Ganz, *Understanding Public Law*, 3rd edn (2001), at p 30.
4 P Norton, 'Parliament's changing role', in Pyper and Robins *op cit*, esp pp 85–95.

Note

The Committee also made a number of recommendations including increasing the proportion of time available for debate of Select Committee reports, seen as one of the most important and well-attended types of debate carried out by Westminster Hall. The issue of debating Select Committee reports is returned to below. The Westminster Hall experiment is now firmly established.

THE COMMONS: APPROVAL OF LEGISLATION AND GOVERNMENT POLICY

Primary legislation

The role of the Commons in relation to executive policy

The doctrine of the separation of powers (first postulated by John Locke in 1690 and expanded by Montesquieu in the 18th century), which demanded that a body separate from the executive be vested with legislative power, has been extremely influential in general terms but seldom has a constitution been fashioned which accords with its precepts. At least in theory, Parliament is pre-eminently a legislative body, and as the dominant partner in Britain's tri-partite legislature,[5] the contribution of the Commons should be of great importance. It is, however, elementary that a government with an overall majority will be able to ensure that the vast majority of its Bills will reach the statute books, often with little modification. There have been five full sessions of Parliament since the present government came to power in 1997; during that time there have been 1,640 Divisions in the House of Commons.[6] The government has suffered no defeats at all on single whipped votes, let alone defeats on the Second Reading of a Bill (that is, wholesale rejection of the entire Bill). If Parliament is not then in fact a separate legislature, what is its proper role? In order to be able to analyse properly the functions that the Commons performs in relation to legislation, it is necessary to place it into a comparative perspective, by examining how legislatures can be classified.

Philip Norton, 'Parliament and policy in Britain: the House of Commons as a policy influencer' (1984) 13(2) Teaching Politics 198 (extracts)

... I would distinguish between legislatures which have a capacity, occasionally or regularly exercised, for policy-making, for policy-influencing, and for having little or no policy impact.

1 *Policy-making* legislatures are those which can not only modify or reject Government measures but can themselves formulate and substitute a policy for that proposed by Government.

2 *Policy-influencing* legislatures can modify or reject measures put forward by Government but cannot substitute a policy of their own.

3 Legislatures with *little or no policy impact* can neither modify or reject measures, nor generate and substitute policies of their own.

'Policy' has been subject to different definitions. I would define it as a related set of proposals which compromise a recognisable whole, based ideally but not necessarily (in practice probably rarely) on conscious and tested assumptions as to costs, needs, end products and implications.

---

5   Commons, Lords, Monarch.
6   See the speech of Lord Phillips, HL Deb col 627 (21 January 2003).

'Policy-making' is the generation of that recognisable whole. Once 'made', policy can then be presented for discussion, modification, acceptance or rejection, application and evaluation. 'Policy influence' can be exerted at these later stages. It may take the form of formal modification or even rejection. It may work through a process of anticipated reaction: that is, the policy-makers may be influenced by expectations of whether or not a particular policy will gain approval. In such instances, the 'making' of policy is influenced by, but is not in the hands of, the legislature. In cases of little or no policy impact, a legislature has no appreciable influence upon policy-making nor upon the later stages of the policy cycle.

If we liken policy to a small (or not so small) jigsaw the picture becomes clearer. Policy-makers put the jigsaw together. They may do so in a clumsy and haphazard manner. They may produce a well-structured piece. Whichever, the responsibility for putting it together is theirs. A policy-making legislature can modify or reject that jigsaw, substituting one it has compiled itself. A policy-influencing legislature can reject the jigsaw or, more likely, reject or move about some of the pieces, but has not the capacity to reconstruct it or create a new jigsaw. A legislature with little or no policy impact looks upon and approves the jigsaw, with or without comment.

This classification of legislatures has two advantages. Firstly, it provides a useful framework for distinguishing between the US and UK legislatures. Congress is a policy-making legislature. That is, not only can it amend or reject executive policy, it can – and occasionally does – substitute a policy of its own. It has the leadership capable of formulating a policy as a substitute to that of the executive. In the House of Commons, the equivalent leadership is the executive. Though it has the capacity, recently exercised, to modify and even reject executive proposals, the House does not have the capacity to generate alternative policies. It is a policy influencer, not a policy-maker. [One problem with this assertion arises in the context of private members' legislation. However, procedural and political constraints ensure that such legislation is not used as a major policy-making medium.] ... Secondly, the distinction is useful in helping understand recent developments ...To make sense of their impact upon the House of Commons it is helpful to draw the distinction between the making and the influencing of public policy. Without it, the changes of recent years may appear confused and shapeless....

Question
Elsewhere, Norton notes that his second category – policy-influencing legislatures – is 'the most crowded of the three'; into it fall 'most legislatures of Western Europe ... of the Commonwealth [and] of the new legislatures of east and central Europe' whilst the first category – policy-making legislatures – 'is almost empty', its only members being the US Congress and the US state legislatures.[7] Why has Montesqueiu's model been so overwhelmingly rejected?

Notes
1 Norton states that the House of Commons does not have a leadership 'capable of formulating a policy as a substitute to that of the executive', but on one level this is inaccurate. The Opposition can and does formulate alternative policies. What it does not have is the administrative back-up (civil servants, parliamentary draftsmen) to allow it to produce a large volume of alternative legislation, though it could presumably produce some. The essential difference is that the Opposition will only rarely have a majority in the Commons whereas the US Congress is quite often controlled by a party which does not also make up the executive.

2 Even if it is accepted that the legislative role of the Commons lies in *responding* to government measures, if it is thought that this role demands that the House provide independent assessment of the merit of government Bills and make

---

7 P Norton, *Does Parliament Matter?* (1993), pp 50–51.

numerous amendments to them, then clearly it is not fulfilling this role. As Henry Calvert puts it, 'the substantial task of legislating will have been largely discharged before the Bill is read in the House', or again, 'Before the formally dramatic part of the legislative process even begins almost all the terms of almost all [government] Bills are settled'.[8] However, on one view, the argument which states that the Commons is redundant because it is largely powerless to amend or reverse the government's programme is wrongheaded; it is contended that the Commons would be undermining democratic accountability if it substantially changed government Bills, since the legislative programme of the party which attracted the greatest proportion of votes should be enacted, in accordance with the electorate's presumed wishes. This argument was undoubtedly what Professor Bernard Crick had in mind when he wrote, '... the phrase "parliamentary control" should not mislead anyone into asking for a situation in which Governments can have their legislation changed or defeated' (*The Reform of Parliament* (1964), p 80).

3   Crick's point of view is clearly open to a number of objections: it can be plausibly argued that many people vote, not after a careful assessment of which legislative programme they would like to see enacted, but on the basis of traditional loyalty, misinformation, misunderstanding or their reaction to politicians' perceived personalities. Further, it is undoubtedly true that people may vote for a party even though they may object to some of its specific legislative proposals.[9] Finally, Crick's argument applies in its purest form only to manifesto government Bills; as Michael Zander notes (below), these in fact form only a small percentage of enacted legislation; the argument is certainly wholly inapplicable to legislation which actually appears to reverse the policies which the electorate thought the party introducing it stood for: an example can be seen in the increases in taxation introduced by the Major administration subsequent to the 1992 General Election in which a key Conservative campaigning theme was its opposition to the higher taxes it alleged Labour would introduce.

4   During the last years of the Major government (ending in 1997), when its overall majority dwindled in the end to only one, the force of Crick's argument was perhaps more apparent than usual. As a government's majority decreases, it must perforce have more regard to the views of its backbenchers. However, when a majority reaches a low enough level, small groups of dissident MPs become able to force the government to depart from its pre-planned policy which was the platform on which it was elected. Of course, most of its legislative policies are not directly mandated (see below) but, to take the example of the Major government's policy on the European Union, the government stood on a platform of a general attitude towards Europe which could perhaps be described as cautious engagement. This was the publicly declared, official policy of the Conservative Party. If a number of anti-EU MPs are able to force the government into a far more thorough-going scepticism,[10] this could be viewed as a welcome example of greater parliamentary

---

8   *British Constitutional Law* (1985), p 84.

9   For general discussion of voting patterns, see Dennis Kavanagh and Bill Jones, 'Voting behaviour', in B Jones (ed), *Politics UK* (1994).

10   For example, the Major government at various points came under intense pressure from right-wing backbenchers to take action against the EU over its ban on British beef and associated products (see, for example, the treatment of Douglas Hogg, the Agriculture Minister, on 1 May 1996, in which his call for further persuasion and negotiation was greeted with 'near derision' by backbenchers (see 'Back bench beef fury boils over', *The Independent*, 30 April 1996). The government did indeed adopt a policy of non-cooperation with the EU in retaliation for the ban, which did not, however, last very long.

control over the executive. But it may also be seen, in Crick's terms, as an undermining of the democratic mandate.

5   In another sense, it is of course wholly unrealistic to expect the House of Commons to subject government Bills to independent scrutiny. The government *is* the government precisely because it is the party with an overall majority in the Commons. Therefore, by definition, the majority of MPs in the House will be pre-disposed to support legislation introduced by the government, so that it is built into the nature of the Commons that most of its members will precisely *not* be impartially minded. The House can be seen to be poised between two possible roles, fulfilling neither of them. Because, formally, the Commons is the law-making body, it must be composed of democratically elected members, that is, those tied to political parties, thus ensuring that in practice the Cabinet legislates. But again, because MPs are tied to political parties, they are unable to carry out properly the actual task of the House, scrutiny of legislation, in a fair-minded and impartial manner.

6   It should be borne in mind that the Commons still provides a constitutional safeguard, albeit one of mainly theoretical importance, in that governments could presumably not rely on it to pass legislation which removed the basic liberties of the citizen. However, confidence in this safeguard was for many people gravely weakened when, in November 2001, the Commons passed the present government's Anti-Terrorism, Crime and Security Bill 2001, which *inter alia* allowed for the detention without trial for an indefinite period of suspected international terrorists.[11] The Bill was purportedly an emergency measure, introduced into Parliament in response to the perceived greater threat from international terrorism following the attacks on America on 11 September 2001. However, a very large number of its provisions did not in fact deal with specifically anti-terrorism measures. It included a new offence of incitement to religious hatred, which, in itself would clearly provide no assistance in the fight against terrorism, new powers of the police compulsorily to photograph criminal suspects – not just suspected terrorists (Part 10), a new procedure whereby Third Pillar EU criminal measures would become part of UK law via secondary legislation (Part 13) and measures to put in place a new Code of Practice on retention of communications data – websites visited, mobile phone calls made and so on (Part 11).[12] The Bill was a very lengthy one – 126 clauses and eight lengthy schedules – and indeed took the government two months to prepare. Nevertheless, it was rushed through the Commons with almost indecent haste: MPs first of all accepted a timetable of only 16 hours in which to scrutinise a Bill of 124 pages and then imposed not a single defeat on the government, though the government did accept amendments tabled by chairs of Select Committees which had scrutinised the Bill in draft. The Common's spineless performance in relation to this Bill caused one respected commentator to remark: 'In a long record of shaming fealty to whips, never have so many MPs showed such utter negligence towards so impressive a list of fundamental principles.'[13]

---

11   Very broadly defined, using the definition in the Terrorism Act 2000, for which see H Fenwick, *Civil Rights, New Labour and the Human Rights Act* (2000), Chapter 3.

12   For analysis of the Act's provisions, see A Tomkins, 'Legislating against terror: the Anti-Terrorism, Crime and Security Act 2001' [2002] PL 205 and H Fenwick, 'The Anti-Terrorism, Crime and Security Act 2001: a proportionate response to 11 September?' (2002) 65(5) MLR 724.

13   Hugo Young, 'Once lost, these freedoms will be impossible to restore', *The Guardian*, 11 December 2001.

7   There are in fact many precedents for draconian and illiberal legislation being passed by the Commons in such indecent haste. The most dramatic example was the Official Secrets Act 1911, which made it a criminal offence to reveal virtually any official government information without proper authorisation. Its passage is described by the minister responsible for piloting it through the Commons.

EB Seely, *Adventure* (1930), p 145[14]

I got up and proposed that the bill be read a second time, explaining, in two sentences only, that it was considered desirable in the public interest that the measure should be passed. Hardly a word was said and the bill was read a second time; the Speaker left the Chair. I then moved the bill in committee. This was the first critical moment; two men got up to speak, but both were forcibly pulled down by their neighbours after they had uttered a few sentences, and the committee stage was passed. The Speaker walked back to his chair and said: 'The question is, that I report this bill without amendment to the House.' Again two or three people stood up; again they were pulled down by their neighbours, and the report stage was through. The Speaker turned to me and said: 'The third reading, what day?' 'Now, sir,' I replied. My heart beat fast as the Speaker said: 'The question is that this bill be read a third time.' It was open to anyone of all the members in the House of Commons to get up and say that no bill had ever yet passed through all its stages in one day without a word of explanation from the minister in charge. . . . But to the eternal honour of those members, to whom I now offer, on behalf of that and all succeeding Governments, my most grateful thanks, not one man seriously opposed, and in a little more time than it has taken to write these words that formidable piece of legislation was passed.

Notes

1   John F McEldowney suggests that the main role of the Commons is to legitimise legislation (echoing Norton's view that most legislatures exist not to make laws but to assent to them) and also to provide the 'life blood of party politics' through its 'debates, votes and censure[s]'.[15] This latter suggestion may be seen as a variant on the publicising role of Parliament suggested by some commentators (see below).

2   If it is accepted that due to its make-up and the party system, the Commons cannot be expected either to take on the role of policy-maker or provide genuinely independent assessment of government Bills, by what criteria may it be assessed? Putting it another way, what can we reasonably expect it to do? It is suggested that four main functions may be identified. The first is the education of both the government and electorate through the publicising effects of debate in Parliament: the electorate will become aware of the issues surrounding a particular policy, whilst the reaction of newspapers, commentators and the public to debates on the proposed legislation will help keep the government informed of the drift of public opinion. The second is the influence on the pre-legislative process which both backbenchers and Opposition MPs may have. The third is the limited amount of improvement and amendment which, despite the partisan nature of the Commons, still does take place. The fourth is the clarification as to the meaning and operation of a given piece of legislation which may take place during debate. This may, since *Pepper v Hart* [1993] 1 All ER 42, go to the interpretation a Bill receives in the courts; it may also provide ammunition for future political attack if things do not go as planned. It is clear that in relation to the first, third and fourth of these functions, the amount of time and resources which Members have available to them to devote

---

14   This passage was cited by DGT Williams, in 'Statute law and administrative law' (1984) Statute Law Review 166 and in M Zander, *The Law-Making Process* (1994).

15   *Public Law* (1994), p 45.

to scrutiny of legislation will be crucial; the importance of the second and third will be closely tied to the size of the government's majority.

3   The ability of backbench MPs to influence government policy is obviously dependent upon the degree to which (within the context of the basic loyalty which the party system demands) they are prepared to view their own party's policy with a critical eye, and vote against legislation it has brought forward. Philip Norton notes an interesting trend here.

Philip Norton, *Does Parliament Matter?* (1993), p 21

The behaviour of MPs has changed in recent decades. Most significantly of all ... has been the change in behaviour in the division (voting) lobbies. Members have proved relatively more independent in their voting behaviour. As we have seen, cohesion was a marked feature of parliamentary life by the turn of the century. That cohesion has been maintained throughout the 20th century, reaching its peak in the 1950s. In the 1960s, one distinguished American commentator was able to declare that cohesion had increased so much 'until in recent decades it was so close to 100% that there was no longer any point in measuring it' (Beer, 1969: 350–51). Shortly afterwards, it did become relevant to measure it.

The early years of the 1970s saw a significant increase in cross-voting by Conservative MPs. They voted against their own leaders more often than before, in greater numbers and with more effect. On six occasions, cross-voting resulted in the Government being defeated. Cross-voting also became a feature of Labour MPs after the party was returned to office in 1974, contributing to most of the 42 defeats suffered by the Government in the 1974–79 Parliament. The number of defeats on the floor of the House, combined with defeats in standing committee, ran into three figures. Some degree of independent voting has been maintained in succeeding Parliaments. In 1986, the Government lost the second reading of the Shops Bill, the first time in the 20th century a Government with a clear overall majority had lost a second reading vote.

Note

There was a widespread perception, at least during the Parliament of 1997–2001, that Labour backbenchers were amongst the most party-minded in recent history, a perception challenged below by Philip Cowley. As he notes, Labour MPs were criticised as '"Daleks", "clones" and "spineless" ... for leaking [critical] Select Committee reports [to assist the government in rebutting them and] ... asking patsy questions for Ministers.'[16] He notes that, in some ways, the accusation may be seen to be true, but it leaves out of account the effect which the damaging lack of cohesion had on a Labour Party out of power for 18 years on attitudes of MPs and also the huge size of Mr Blair's majority (179) which tended to mask the quite large rebellions that did in fact occur.

Philip Cowley, 'The Commons: Mr Blair's lapdog?' (2001) 54 Parl Aff 815 (extracts)

... the Parliamentary Labour Party [PLP] elected in May 1997 proved the most cohesive for a generation. There were fewer revolts by government MPs between 1997 and 2001 than in any full-length Parliament since the 1950s. And Blair's was the first government since that of 1966 not to be defeated at least once by its own backbenchers.

[But] most of the criticism was misplaced. For one thing, high levels of cohesion did not mean absolute cohesion ... A third of the PLP – that is, around half of all backbenchers – voted against the government at least once. Moreover, the average (mean) size of rebellions was the third highest of any Parliament since 1945. Labour MPs may not have rebelled very often, but when they

16   P Cowley, 'The Commons: Mr Blair's lapdog?' (2001) 54 Parl Aff 815, at 818–19.

did, they rebelled in numbers and across a wide range of issues [he notes some of the largest rebellions, eg, 74 against the Welfare Reform Bill 1999, 47 against the Social Security Bill 1997 and 41 against the Freedom of Information Bill 2000].

[Cowley goes on to note first of all the effect of being out of power for 18 years and broad sympathy with much of what the government was doing as reasons for a high level of self-discipline and loyalty, respectively, and goes on:]

The [other] reason ... is that, despite its reputation as autocratic, the government was usually willing to negotiate with its backbench critics ... Where genuine consultation did not take place, or where the government adopted a macho stance – as with lone-parent benefit or disability benefit – rebellions were noticeable, but where it adopted a more consultative approach, rebellions were muted or non-existent. A good example came in the second session of the Parliament, with the government's plans for dealing with asylum seekers. Some 61 Labour MPs signed an Early Day Motion opposing the proposals, and *The Times* (19 June 1999) claimed that the government faced potential defeat. Yet after concessions granted by ... the Home Secretary, just seven MPs voted against the bill.

Seen in this light, the lack of rebellions is rather more positive. Rather than being a Bad Thing – caused by MPs who are too scared to defy their leaders – it is a Good Thing, the result of agreement and consultation as much as coercion.

Note
There are also signs that the backbenchers of the 2001 Parliament are somewhat more assertive than even their colleagues of 1997. As Philip Cowley and Mark Stuart note: '... the government faces a potentially tougher ride from its backbenchers this Parliament ... The first 44 votes saw 10 backbench Labour rebellions against the whips; the comparable figure for the last Parliament was zero.'[17] Nevertheless, it remains the case that the Blair government has not, to date, suffered a single legislative defeat, in marked contrast to the position in the much more independent House of Lords, which has imposed important legislative reversals on the government; however, at the time of writing, the government is facing a possible serious defeat on its controversial policy of Foundation Hospitals.[18]

Parliament and the war on Iraq in 2003: a reassertion of parliamentary power?

Such predictions of greater backbench independent-mindedness were spectacularly borne out by the parliamentary reaction to the Blair government's policy on military action against Iraq in early 2003. The UN Security Council on 25 November 2002 passed resolution 1441, which found Iraq to be in material breach of its disarmament obligations under numerous previous resolutions and threatened 'serious consequences' if Iraq failed fully to co-operate with UN Inspectors seeking to investigate whether Iraq had, as it claimed, fully dismantled its prohibited nuclear, chemical and biological weapons programmes. Blair's policy, in the light of less than full cooperation from the Iraqi government was to seek to obtain a further Security Council resolution, expressly endorsing military action against Iraq to disarm it of such weapons. However, he also repeatedly refused to rule out taking such action, in partnership with the US, even if there was no such further resolution because, for example, of what he termed an 'unreasonable veto' by one of the five permanent

---

17 P Cowley and M Stuart, 'Parliament: mostly continuity, but more change than you'd think' (2002) 55 Parl Aff 271, at 284.
18 A very large Labour rebellion is expected.

members of the Security Council. In a debate held shortly before conflict began, but by which time it was looking as if Blair might fail to secure a second UN resolution, a rival motion was put forward by Chris Smith, a former Labour Cabinet minister, stating that the case for military action was 'as yet unproven'. Extracts from the debate follow:

HC Deb cols 265 et seq (26 February 2003) (extracts)

The Secretary of State for Foreign and Commonwealth Affairs (Mr Jack Straw): I beg to move,

> 'That this House takes note of Command Paper Cm 5769 on Iraq; reaffirms its endorsement of United Nations Security Council Resolution 1441, as expressed in its Resolution of 25th November 2002; supports the Government's continuing efforts in the United Nations to disarm Iraq of its weapons of mass destruction; and calls upon Iraq to recognise this as its final opportunity to comply with its disarmament obligations.'

The situation that we face is plainly grave. It is a matter that, across a range of beliefs, arouses great concern and anxiety. So in this debate I want to answer what I think are the central and continuing questions in people's minds. Why Iraq? Why now? Why not more time, more inspectors? Why a second resolution? Why not persist with the policy of containment, rather than contemplate military action? And finally, is not the west guilty of double standards, especially in relation to Israel/Palestine?

Let me deal with those questions in turn. First, why Iraq? The best answer to that question is to be found in the 42 pages of text of the 13 Security Council resolutions that form the first section of the Command Paper [called 'Iraq' – put before the House]. There we see, paragraph by paragraph, the exceptional danger posed by Iraq, and its continued defiance of the United Nations. On 2 August 1990, resolution 660 tells Iraq to withdraw from Kuwait. On 29 November 1990, resolution 678 offers Iraq a 'final opportunity' – interesting words – to comply, which it fails to take. On 3 April 1991, resolution 687 gives Iraq until 18 April 1991 to make a full declaration of the 'locations, amount and types' of all chemical and biological weapons and of all medium and long-range ballistic missiles. That resolution bars Iraq from ever developing biological, chemical or nuclear weapons.

On and on the resolutions go. Resolution 688 is 'gravely concerned' about the repression of the civilian population in many parts of Iraq. In 1994, resolution 949 'condemns military deployments by Iraq in the direction of the border with Kuwait', three years after the original invasion. In 1999, nine years after the invasion of Kuwait, resolution 1284 establishes a further inspection regime, 'as a result of Iraq's failure to implement the Security Council Resolutions fully.' Iraq flatly and completely refuses to comply. Last November, resolution 1441 recognised

> 'the threat which Iraq's non-compliance with Council Resolutions and proliferation of Weapons of Mass Destruction and long range missiles poses to international peace and security' –

and gave Iraq its 'final opportunity to comply'.

So, for the United Nations, the answer to the 'Why Iraq?' question is very clear. Iraq is the only country in such serious and multiple breach of mandatory UN obligations. It is the only country in the world to have fired missiles at five of its neighbours, the only country in history to have used chemical weapons against its own people, and the only country in the region that has invaded two of its neighbours in recent years ...

The next question that I raised was, 'Why now?' All the resolutions of the Security Council, 12 years of them, also help us answer that question.

Saddam's aim is that 'now' shall never arrive. His tactics all along have been to prevaricate in the hope that by exploiting people's natural anxieties about military action he can string out the process for ever and keep his arsenal for good.

Let us look at the recent evidence. On 10 September last year, Iraq declared – I was there in the General Assembly when this was said – that it would never, ever readmit weapons inspectors under any circumstances. Then President Bush made his important and most welcome speech to the General Assembly. Four days later, Iraq said that it would after all readmit weapons inspectors, but made its offer subject to 19 spurious conditions of the kind that it has often come forward with. Fortunately, those were rejected.

There were then two months of intense negotiations inside the Security Council. In response, the international community united, resolution 1441 was passed unanimously and the Security Council agreed to back its diplomacy with the credible threat of force. The inspectors finally entered Iraq on 27 November, looking, as the resolution required, for full, active and immediate co-operation from Iraq.

But since the inspectors' return the story has been all too familiar. We saw first a 12,000-page Iraqi declaration, which Dr Blix called

'rich in volume but poor in new information ... and practically devoid of new evidence.'

... as Dr Blix himself indicates, in 15 weeks, the inspectors have not been able to close a single outstanding issue. There have been no answers to what has happened to the 8,500 litres of anthrax; no answers to what has happened to the 360 tonnes of bulk chemical warfare agent; no answers to what has happened to the 3,000 tonnes of precursor chemicals; no answers to what has happened to the 1.5 tonnes of the completely deadly VX nerve agent or to the 6,500 chemical bombs identified by Dr Blix on 27 January. The intimidation of scientists and their families so that they do not give full evidence has continued ...

The next question that I raised was about more time and more inspections. I understand why there are calls for more time and more inspections, but Saddam has not shown that he is ready to break with the past. That is exactly what Dr Blix said today. At present, it is not even clear whether the Iraqis really want to co-operate. In these circumstances, in the absence of active and immediate Iraqi co-operation, more time will not achieve anything of substance. Nor, without that active co-operation, can it be a question of more inspectors.

It took just nine inspectors to verify the disarmament of South Africa's nuclear weapons programme at the end of apartheid. It did not take 12 years. It did not take hundreds of inspectors. It did not take endless Security Council resolutions. It took three years, nine inspectors and no resolutions. Why? Because South Africa was complying with the inspectors.

... The next question is why do we need a second resolution now? Resolution 1441 required Iraq's full, active and immediate compliance, as indeed did resolution 687, which was passed 12 years ago. Fifteen weeks after 1441, Saddam's response has been neither full, nor active, nor immediate. He has not complied, and not a single member of the Security Council says otherwise. In place of active voluntary co-operation, we have had a string of cynically timed concessions that are calculated to divide and to delay.

Unless we bring this game to a halt, it will go on for as long as Saddam wants. ... We have waited 110 days already, which is stretching the meaning of 'immediately' to breaking point.

I ask our friends in France and Germany – who share our goal of Iraqi disarmament, and who fully support resolution 1441 – why Saddam is more likely to co-operate actively, fully and immediately in the further 120 days that they now propose than he was in the past 110 ... No. Saddam would use a further 120 days to bring the authority of the United Nations lower week by week, to tie the weapons inspectors in knots, and to create further divisions within the international community. We know that this is what he will do, because it is what he has always done.

... Time is pressing, so let me turn to the next question, which in many ways is at the heart of the amendment [put down by Chris Smith, saying that the case for war is not yet made]. Why not persist with the policy of containment, rather than contemplate military action? After all, some argue that Iraq has not invaded any of its neighbours or used chemical and biological weapons in the past 12 years, and that these weapons have either been destroyed, or do not present a sufficient threat to Iraq's neighbours or to the wider world to justify the use of force to remove them if Saddam refuses to do so peacefully.

I understand the containment argument, even if I do not agree with it. However, let no one be under any illusions: the policy of containment is not the policy of disarmament as set out in resolution 1441 or any of the preceding resolutions. There can be no stable, steady state for Iraq unless it is properly disarmed, and nor can there be stability for the region and the international community. What may appear to be containment to us is rearmament for Saddam.

We do not need to speculate on this, as we have witnessed it. A de facto policy of containment existed between 1998 and 2002 following the effective expulsion of inspectors by Iraq, and Iraq's refusal to comply with resolution 1284.

Far from keeping a lid on Saddam's ambitions, that period allowed him to rebuild his horrific arsenal, his chemical and biological weapons, and the means of delivering them against his enemies at home and abroad. UNMOVIC inspectors chart in their recent reports, which are before the House, how Iraq has refurbished prohibited equipment that had previously been destroyed by UNSCOM, the earlier inspectors …

… I turn now to the next question. I am often asked, 'Isn't the west guilty of double standards, especially in relation to Israel and Palestine?' [Hon Members: 'Yes.'] Some of my hon Friends say yes. I accept, as does my right hon Friend the Prime Minister, that there has been a considerable amount to this charge, and to the perception of double standards, which extends well beyond the Arab and Islamic world. However, we deal with this charge not by ignoring outstanding UN obligations, but by working even harder to see all of them implemented. The key ones on Israel/Palestine – 242, 338, 1397 – impose obligations on three sets of parties – on the Palestinians to end terrorism, on the Arab countries to end support for terrorism and to recognise the state of Israel, and on Israel fully to co-operate in the establishment of a viable state of Palestine with borders broadly based on those of 1967.

… It must also never be forgotten, however, that the obligations on Saddam are singular, unilateral, and not for negotiation by him. We increase, not undermine, respect for the authority of the UN as a whole – and the prospects of a peace settlement in the middle east – if we implement fully the resolutions on Iraq, and do not shy away from their consequences.

… International terrorism and the proliferation of weapons of mass destruction are the crucial strategic questions of our time. Our answer to these threats will determine the stability of the world for decades to come. This is an awesome responsibility. It calls for courageous leadership. And it requires the vision and foresight to act decisively and, if necessary, with military force.

[This] is … a moment of choice for the UN. As I told the Security Council on 5 February, the UN's pre-war predecessor, the League of Nations, had the same fine ideals as the UN. Yet the League failed because it could not create actions from its words: it could not back diplomacy with a credible threat and, where necessary, the use of force. Small evils therefore went unchecked, tyrants became emboldened, then greater evils were unleashed. At each stage good men and women said, 'Not now, wait, the evil is not big enough to challenge.' Then before their eyes, the evil became too big to challenge. We had slipped slowly down a slope, never noticing how far we had gone until it was too late. We owe it to our history as well as to our future not to make the same mistake again.

Mr Chris Smith: I beg to move, To leave out from 'destruction' to end and add

'but finds the case for military action against Iraq as yet unproven.'

The amendment stands in my name and the names of 115 hon Members …

Three main arguments appear to be mounted in support of early military intervention in Iraq. The first is: 'They have had the time to comply; they don't need more time.' Actually, Iraq has had 11 weeks since the weapons inspectors went in this time round. Let us not forget that, from 1991 to

1996–97, the weapons inspection process produced substantial results. Substantial amounts of chemical and biological warfare capacity were destroyed by the process. I would argue that a strongly supported weapons inspection process – one that is given the time to complete the job – is what the international community should be arguing for.

The second argument is that there has not been full and complete co-operation with the weapons inspection process. That is true. However, there has been a substantial amount of co-operation. Are we seriously saying that, because Saddam Hussein has complied by 70 per cent rather than 100 per cent, that is a cause for going to war?

Mr Straw: There is no basis whatsoever – from any sentence of the Blix reports or any other evidence – for saying that Saddam has complied by 70 per cent or by any fraction approaching that.

Mr Smith: I have to disagree with my right hon Friend. Everyone agrees that Saddam Hussein has not given full co-operation and is not complying completely. However, in such a situation, we must ask ourselves whether the degree of co-operation that he has given and which has undoubtedly been extorted out of him by the pressure from the international community falls so far short of what is required that it is a cause for going in and wreaking substantial havoc and destruction on Iraq. That case, as yet, is not made.

... The third major argument that is used is that we will give comfort to Saddam Hussein by sending the wrong message. That is true only if we fail to maintain the pressure on him. There may well be a time for military action ...

The other argument that has been made is that those of us who urge caution are failing to be strong and that, by doing so, we are somehow appeasing a tyrant. That is the shallowest argument of all. Strength does not lie simply in military might. Strength lies in having an unanswerable case. It lies in making the right moral choices. It lies in maintaining the pressure, and it lies in securing the fullest possible international agreement. That is where our efforts should now be directed, but I fear that we may be cutting short those efforts by the timetable that is now upon us.

Let us not forget what we are talking about. We are talking about going to war. We are talking about thousands – possibly hundreds of thousands – of innocent lives being lost. We are talking about casualties almost inevitably among our own forces. We are talking about instability across the whole middle east. We are talking about making the achievement of a solution to the Israel/Palestine question infinitely more difficult. We are talking about the alienation of moderate Muslim opinion across the world. One does not undertake such things lightly. One must have the clearest possible reasons for doing them, and I do not believe that those reasons are there.

Mr Kenneth Clarke (Rushcliffe): Let me make clear the origin of my doubts about the very persuasive case that the Prime Minister and the Foreign Secretary sometimes put. I cannot rid myself of doubts that the course to war upon which we are now embarked was decided on many months ago, primarily in Washington, and there has been a fairly remorseless unfolding of events since that time. I am not alone in having heard and met American politicians of great distinction who gave the impression that a change of regime in Iraq was determined upon long ago and that the use of military force in a pre-emptive strike was justified in order to achieve that ...

Although other concerns cannot be brushed aside, the revolting nature of the Iraqi regime and its cruelty, much though we deplore it, is not a legal basis for war. We must concentrate on whether there are weapons of mass destruction, whether disarmament can be induced and, if not, whether force will be used to effect it.

The question that we must ask is whether a material breach has occurred. To me, that means considering whether demonstrable evidence exists to show that biological and chemical weapons are held in conditions and circumstances in which they pose a current threat to neighbours or to us. There is no evidence of links with al-Qaeda and I do not believe that Iraq poses a threat to New York or London. To claim that is to insult our intelligence. However, I wish to know whether demonstrable evidence exists of sufficient quantities of weapons to pose a threat. I doubt that.

However, we should consider alternatives because of the consequences of war. How many terrorists will we recruit in the greater, long-standing battle against international terrorism? It will be far harder to win. What will we do to the stability of Saudi Arabia, Pakistan or Egypt? What sort of leadership will replace that which might be deposed? The Government never address those questions satisfactorily, as my right hon Friend the shadow Foreign Secretary said. However, they will have to live with the answers.

The next time a large bomb explodes in a western city, or an Arab or Muslim regime topples and is replaced by extremists, the Government must consider the extent to which the policy contributed to it. That is why hon Members should pause and why, unless evidence is produced for a breach and a material threat, my judgment today is that we should not go to war.

Ann Clwyd (Cynon Valley): In 1991, I stood at the Opposition Dispatch Box and described what I had seen on the mountains of Iran and Iraq when the Kurds fled from the bombardment of Saddam Hussein. I am afraid that people have very short memories. The scenes were appalling and typical of the attacks made by the Iraqi regime on its own people. The victims include Arabs as well as Kurds. They also include Assyrians, Turkomans and the Shi'as in the south of the country who were forced to flee from the marshes into Iran.

I have spent the past two days travelling and I have come back for this debate so that I can tell the House what I have seen and heard. As the House knows, I have continually argued the case over the years for indicting the regime for war crimes, crimes against humanity and genocide. I am grateful to 201 of my colleagues on both sides of the House who supported my proposal. I believe that the regime should be removed and that it could have been removed by using international law and indictment. It is a great regret to me that this country, which could have led the way, did not do so. After two years of our making the case and providing evidence from the victims of the regime, the Attorney-General felt that there was not sufficient evidence. I do not know how much evidence one needs, because it abounds. Human Rights Watch and Amnesty International have the evidence, and the Kurds captured documents from the torture centre that they eventually liberated. Thousands of their citizens died there.

On my latest visit, I opened the first genocide museum in Iraq. It was snowing and quite dark on that day and people had come from all over the area. Their relatives had died in that torture chamber. Inside the museum were photographs that the Kurds had taken. The images were of skulls and shreds of clothing, and of the type of thing that one sees in genocide museums elsewhere in the world. I have been to similar museums in Rwanda and Cambodia, and I have seen the holocaust exhibition in London, but I am afraid that, on this occasion, I just cried. I do not think that I have ever cried in public before, but I did so because the regime's victims were all around me. One old woman came up to me with a piece of plastic and pushed it into my hand. I unwrapped it and saw three photographs. They were of her husband and two sons who had died in that torture centre.

... The victims were all around me, and I have been involved for 25 years – including before I became a politician – with the Iraqi opposition. For those 25 years, I have heard the tales of Saddam Hussein's regime and its repression of the Kurds and other minorities. People seem to think that that all came to an end in 1991, but that is a big mistake. Repression, torture and ethnic cleansing have continued throughout the time since then.

On my latest visit, I met some of the victims of torture who had, in the past few months, come out of the Abu Ghraib prison in Baghdad under the so-called amnesty. One man told me stories that I hardly like to repeat, but we at Indict have taken victims' statements over the past seven years. This victim was a youngish man who said that he had been in prison for eight years. He said that almost every day, people were executed at that prison – not one person, but hundreds. When there was an attack on Uday Hussein's life some time ago, 2,000 prisoners in the prison were executed on the same day. That is the reality of Saddam's Iraq. When I hear people calling for more time, I say 'Who will speak up for those victims?'

. . . Ethnic cleansing goes on all the time. I visited a UN camp where there were hundreds of recent victims of ethnic cleansing who had been kicked out of Kirkuk. The men, women and little children in the camp had been told that they had 24 hours to get out of Kirkuk because they would not agree that they were not Kurds, but Arabs, as part of arabisation. In other countries, we have taken action against people responsible for ethnic cleansing, so I say to my colleagues, please, who is to help the victims of Saddam Hussein's regime unless we do?

I believe in regime change. I say that without hesitation, and I will support the Government tonight because I think that they are doing a brave thing.

Notes

1 In the event, the rebellion of Labour MPs came to 122, apparently the largest single rebellion against a government since the modern party system was put in place. There was a further debate on 18 March 2003[19] on the eve of military action; by this time, the attempt to obtain a Security Council resolution explicitly authorising the use of force had been abandoned in the face of implacable opposition from France, Germany and Russia and lack of support from other members of the Security Council, representing a major failure of Anglo-American diplomacy and a serious reverse for the government. It was now faced with its worst case scenario – taking the country to war with no explicit UN backing, without even a majority of the UN Security Council in favour, and with massive protests sweeping the country and the rest of Europe. An anti-war march in March 2003 attracted over a million protestors, making it the largest ever demonstration in Britain; the polls showed a majority of the public against war in the absence of explicit UN authorisation. Robin Cook, former Foreign Secretary, and now Leader of the House of Commons – a Cabinet post – resigned, and made a powerful speech attacking government policy on war with Iraq (see further Part IV Chapter 2, pp 520–21).[20]

2 It was in these circumstances that the government asked Parliament to back it in going to war against Iraq. The Prime Minister opened the debate with an impassioned plea for support, having intimated that he would resign should the party fail to back him. One of the principal government defences of its actions in taking action without explicit UN backing was that the French President, by expressly stating that his government would veto *any* resolution authorising force, whatever the circumstances, had made it effectively impossible for the Security Council to enforce the 'final' demand to the Iraqi regime to disarm contained in resolution 1441, since there was now no credible threat of UN-mandated force to back it up. Thus, it could be argued that the French government had stymied the UN process, rendering it pointless to pursue it further, given the plausible assumption that it was only the threat of such force which had forced Saddam Hussein to allow the UN inspectors back into Iraq (they had left in 1998 in the face of the regime's persistent failure to co-operate with them). In the event, the rebellion – those voting for a backbench amendment opposing war – was even larger than last time (139 Labour MPs voted for the anti-war amendment), but not as bad as had been feared, given the fact that a number of Labour MPs who voted with the government in the previous debate did so because at that point it was hoped that the government would still obtain explicit Security Council authorisation for the use of force. On the separate vote on the substantive government motion, the government won by 412 votes to 149, a majority of 263.

19 HC Deb cols 760 *et seq* (18 March 2003).
20 For Robin Cook's resignation statement, see HC Deb cols 726 *et seq* (17 March 2003).

This outcome meant that Blair could lead the country into war with the legitimacy of a clear parliamentary mandate for military action.

3   The episode, to many commentators, represented a major reassertion of parliamentary power against the executive: whilst in theory it would have been possible for the government to take the country to war without parliamentary approval, given that the power to do so resides in the Royal Prerogative (see further Part IV Chapter 1), given the enormity of the issues at stake, and the huge unease in the Labour Party and the country at large, such an action would have been politically unthinkable. To many, the fact that the Blair government had refused to give Parliament a chance to vote on a substantive motion[21] on the military action in Kosovo in 1999[22] was evidence of the administration's contempt for Parliament, and the weakness of Labour MPs in allowing Parliament thus to be sidelined. In retrospect, however, it is perhaps apparent that the government only felt able to take such action in the knowledge that its policy on Kosovo had broad support in the Parliamentary Labour Party and, indeed, across the parties. Where such support was lacking, the government was forced to bow to Parliament's will, in giving MPs the chance to vote against war *before* military action was taken: in fact, by so doing, Blair's premiership was actually placed at risk and he was faced with the prospect of resigning should his policy have been opposed by a majority of the Parliamentary Labour Party.[23] The episode thus reveals the simple truth that, as Adam Tomkin has argued,[24] there *is* in fact no *government* majority in Parliament even at the current time. The government vote in Parliament in fact consists only of the payroll of government *ministers*, who are bound by the convention of collective responsibility to vote for government policy or resign. Backbench MPs do not, strictly, form part of this majority: whilst they are arguably under an obligation to vote for measures contained in the government's manifesto, they are free to use their judgement on other matters, although, of course, the normal expectation will be that they will vote with their party. But the episode illustrates that all that is needed for Parliament to re-assert its will over the executive is for MPs to have the necessary resolve to do so, a resolve that can be generated where, as in this case, Members feel sufficiently strongly about the issue in question and there is widespread and deeply-felt public opposition to government policy. The episode presented the relationship between Parliament and the executive in a markedly different light from that normally seen: rather than Parliament as the obedient lapdog of the government, the public saw the Prime Minister forced to seek Parliament's assent, having to persuade by force of argument, not just by invoking party loyalty, and with a credible threat to his premiership should he lose that argument. As Mr Blair put it:

At the outset, I say that it is right that the House debate this issue and pass judgment. That is the democracy that is our right, but that others struggle for in vain ... Here we are, the Government, with their most serious test, their majority at risk, the first Cabinet resignation over an issue of policy, the main parties internally divided ... The country and the Parliament reflect each other ...

---

21   That is a motion explicitly approving government policy, as opposed to a motion simply to adjourn the House, which allows dissent to be expressed, but not a chance to vote directly against the government.

22   Debates were held after the conflict began, on 24 March and 19 April, 1999.

23   Mr Blair revealed in an interview with *The Sun* newspaper on 18 April 2003 that he had drawn up contingency plans for his resignation and the withdrawal of British forces from the Gulf, should the vote in the Parliamentary Labour Party have gone against him.

24   A Tomkin, 'Conclusion', in *Government Unwrapped: The Constitution after Scott* (1998).

It will determine the way in which Britain and the world confront the central security threat of the 21st century, the development of the United Nations, the relationship between Europe and the United States, the relations within the European Union and the way in which the United States engages with the rest of the world. So it could hardly be more important. It will determine the pattern of international politics for the next generation.[25]

The legislative work of the Commons

In view of the fact that the Commons makes so little impact upon legislation in terms of scrutiny and amendment during the legislative passage of Bills, this volume omits the lengthy consideration of the work of the Commons in this area that was contained in the first edition of this work. Space precludes such analysis, particularly as the more important work of the Commons in constitutional terms is its role in holding the government to account through scrutiny in the form of questions, debates and select committee work has undergone a certain amount of change in recent years. Accordingly, what follows is limited to a brief overview of the legislative role of the Commons, with prominence given to two important recent innovations: a much greater use of pre-legislative scrutiny; and the introduction of timetabling of Bills (whereby they are allotted a fixed amount of time to complete all their stages) as standard procedure.

The pre-legislative stage

As Zander points out:

The belief that most bills derive from a Government's manifesto commitments is mistaken. It has been estimated that only 8% of the Conservative Government's bills in the period from 1970 to 1974 came from election commitments and that in the 1974–79 Labour Government the proportion was only a little higher at 13% (Richard Rose, Do Parties Make a Difference?, 2nd edn (1984), pp 72–73). The great majority of bills originated within Government departments, with the remainder being mainly responses to particular and unexpected events such as the Prevention of Terrorism (Temporary Provisions) Act 1974 in response to the Birmingham IRA bombings, or the Drought Act 1976.[26]

However, Zander also goes on to point out that pre-legislative consultation is patchy and unsystematic. In terms of parliamentary influence, governments must take account of the likely response of its own backbenchers to legislation, as ascertained by the Whips, at the pre-legislative stage. If backbenchers are aware of widespread public discontent at proposed legislation, this will be relayed to the government which will wish to avoid the embarrassment of hearing its own supporters expressing public dissent – dissent which, as Norton remarks, 'provides good copy for the press'.[27] The effect of this anticipated response may be to force the government into modifying its proposals, the most dramatic example being the Labour government's abandonment of its proposed industrial relations legislation in 1969 when it became clear to it that its own MPs did not support the measure. Similarly, in October 1992, John Major's administration was forced to abandon its plans for immediate closure of 31 coal pits in order to avoid near certain defeat by Conservative backbenchers, whilst Michael

---

25 HC Deb col 761 (18 March 2003).
26 Zander, op cit, p 2.
27 The Commons in Perspective (1981), p 119.

Heseltine's plans to sell off the Post Office suffered a similar fate in 1994. A more recent example relates to legislation on asylum proposed by the Blair government in 1999 (see the comments above by Cowley (at p 273)).

The most important recent example of such pre-legislative influence occurred in relation to the government's White Paper on comprehensive reform of the House of Lords,[28] considered in the next chapter. In brief, when the White Paper was debated in the Commons, virtually no support for its proposals, which were seen as a significant weakening of the guarantees of independence contained in the Royal Commission's Report on reform of the Lords,[29] could be found, even amongst normally loyal Labour MPs. As a result, the government abandoned its proposals entirely, setting up a Joint Committee with broad terms of reference to bring forward a fresh set of proposals, although these too failed to secure agreement. See further, Chapter 2 of this part.

However, as a Select Committee recently noted:

... there has hitherto been little, if any, consultation with Members or with the House as a whole before Bills are formally introduced. In recent years some draft Bills have been produced for prior consultation, and the present Government has specifically undertaken in the Queen's Speech to extend this process. The House itself has however made no attempt to undertake any systematic consideration of such draft Bills. There has as a result been no formal channel to allow time and opportunity for Members to receive representations from interested parties. Consultations between Government and those outside Parliament with a legitimate concern in the legislation has also been criticised as patchy and spasmodic.[30]

One aspect of the Labour government's modernisation reform programme for the House of Commons has been a very significant increase in the number of Bills published in draft for pre-legislative scrutiny by committees of the House. Important examples have included Bills on the Food Standards Agency, freedom of information, tobacco advertising, financial services, anti-terrorism and media and communications. This experiment has generally been seen as a partial success.

First Report of the Liaison Committee, *The Work of Select Committees*, HC 590 (2001–02) (extracts)

14 Select committees contain a pool of knowledge and experience in their membership which should be used effectively to consider legislative proposals ... scrutiny of draft bills by departmental select committees needs early notice, adequate documentation and the avoidance by the Government of unrealistic deadlines for committees to complete their work.

15 In recent months, committees have taken the initiative and have usually received substantial co-operation from Whitehall. Thanks to a quick reallocation of resources, three committees were able to comment on the Anti-terrorism, Crime and Security Bill introduced after the events of September 11. The Home Affairs Committee took evidence on the policy proposals in advance of the Bill's publication, and then further evidence after the Bill was published. Its Report was issued in time for Second Reading on 19 November. Such initiatives make for better-informed debate on the Floor of the House.

---

28   *The House of Lords: Completing the Reform*, Cm 5291 (2001).
29   Known as the 'Wakeham Report' after its chairman, Lord Wakeham: *A House for the Future*, Cm 4534 (2000).
30   Modernisation Committee, HC 190 (1997–98), paras 5 and 6.

16 Indeed, the Committee's approach went further: its Chairman tabled amendments to implement some of its conclusions, two of which were accepted by the Government. This effective involvement was complemented by a Report from the Defence Committee which reviewed the Bill's provisions covering the Ministry of Defence Police.

17 Less satisfactory was the case of the Animal Health Bill. The Environment, Food and Rural Affairs Committee wished to report to the House on its provisions, but the Bill was not published in draft, so the Committee only had time to take evidence shortly after the Bill's presentation to the House. It then published the evidence before the Second Reading debate, in order to inform the House's deliberations. Such a rushed procedure could have been avoided by publication of the Bill in draft, permitting detailed scrutiny and informed comment.

Note

In its Annual Report for 2002,[31] the Liaison Committee noted that: 'there are already encouraging signs that one of the preconditions for pre-legislative scrutiny – a steady flow of draft Bills – is beginning to be met (para 30).' It picked out in particular the pre-legislative scrutiny of the important, and controversial, Communications Bill 2002:

By common consent, this was a highly successful exercise, at least defined in terms of the thoroughness and openness of the process and the extent to which the Committee was able to secure the Government's agreement to significant and wide-ranging changes in the draft bill [para 31].

The important role of the Joint Committee on Human Rights is to engage in pre-legislative scrutiny of Bills in order to determine their compatibility or otherwise with the European Convention on Human Rights and, if necessary, suggest amendments needed to ensure such compatibility. The work of the Committee is considered further in the next chapter on the House of Lords.

Legislation: through the House of Commons

Michael Zander, *The Law-Making Process* (1994), pp 53–57, 58–64

The sequence of events in the legislative process from the introduction of a bill to Royal Assent has been described by a senior member of the office of Clerk to the House of Commons, most kindly written for the second edition of this book:

A bill must be given 'three readings' in each House before it can be submitted for the Royal Assent. The first reading is purely formal when the Clerk of the House reads the title from a dummy bill and a day is named for second reading.

The debate on second reading is the main consideration of the general principles of a bill, at the end of which a vote [though it need not] be taken on the bill as a whole. Although a bill can be lost at many stages in its career, the second reading is undoubtedly the most important, and the vast majority of bills which get a second reading and proceed into committee also get on to the statute book . . .

Unless a Member moves that the bill be sent to a committee of the whole House (or to a Select Committee if a detailed examination with witnesses is required or to a Special Standing Committee which combines both Select Committee and Standing Committee procedure) all bills after second reading (with the exception of certain financial measures) are automatically sent upstairs to a Standing Committee. These committees consist of from 16 to 50 Members and, in a session, over 500 Member are called upon to serve on them. Appointments to

Standing Committee are made by a Select Committee, called the Committee of Selection, which is charged with having regard to the 'qualifications of those Members nominated and to the composition of the House'. The Government thus keeps its majority, but the opposition and minority parties so far as possible are fully represented. The chair is taken by a Member selected by the Speaker from a panel of chairmen, who maintains the same standard of impartiality in committee as the Speaker does in the House. The task of the committee is to go through the bill and amend it where desirable, bearing in mind that the general principle of the bill has been approved by the House.

A bill in committee is considered clause by clause and the question that the clause 'stand part of the bill' is put on each one. Before the question is put on a clause, however, amendments may be moved – provided that they are relevant, not 'wrecking', and conform to various technical requirements, such as the limitation imposed by any accompanying financial resolution passed by the House. Members of most Standing Committees are showered with suggestions for amendments from interested bodies to add to any ideas of their own for amendment of the bill. The Government's amendments are drafted by the Parliamentary Counsel who prepare their bills; the private member usually seeks the advice of the Public Bill Office....

A bill which has been considered by a committee of the whole House and emerges un-amended goes straight on to third reading. Any other bill must have a consideration or 'report' stage, when further amendments may be moved, and attempts made either to restore parts lost in committee or to remove parts added. The Government frequently use the report stage to introduce, in a form acceptable to them, amendments the principle of which they have accepted in committee ... The report stage is a useful safeguard ... against a small committee amending a bill against the wishes of the House, and a necessary opportunity for second thoughts....

There remains the third reading; and here, unlike the second reading, when a bill may be reviewed in the context of the subject to which it relates, debate must be confined to the contents of the bill....

Safely read the third time ... the Clerk of the House proceeds to the 'other place' and hands in the bill at the bar of the House....

After a Commons bill has been through the Lords, it is returned with the Lords amendments to it, which then must be considered in the House. On any bill, the two Houses must finally reach agreement on the amendments made by each other if the bill is not to fall during that session. Under the Parliament Acts 1911 and 1949, disagreement between the two Houses can delay a bill only for a year if the Commons persist with it; and in the case of a money bill, a bill passed by the Commons can go for Royal Assent after only one month's delay. Where one House cannot agree to the other's amendments, it sends a message to that effect giving reasons. A bill can go back and forth several times but it is only rarely that a bill has had to be reintroduced in a second session in order to become law, because of the failure of the two Houses to agree ...

The final stage in the enacting process is Royal Assent.

... From this account of the customary procedures for the passage of a bill, it will be seen that, if proper consideration is given at each stage to a substantial measure, whether or not it is opposed in principle, its passage takes a considerable time. In fact, major bills will take six months or more to pass. On the other hand a small bill can, if urgency requires it, pass through both Houses in a day ... The key to the productivity of Parliament lies in control of the timetable of the House of Commons by the Government and the willingness of the House to entrust the Chair with discretion to select amendments for debate, and to accept or reject motions for the closure of debate.

Notes

1   Clarification as to the meaning and implementation of a Bill was put forward at the beginning of this chapter as a useful product of parliamentary debate; the passage

of the Prevention of Terrorism (Additional Powers) Act 1996 is instructive in this respect. Despite the fact that the Bill was guillotined (see below), a few important points emerged from the Home Secretary's speeches during the debate. The most controversial provision in the Bill allowed for the police to stop and search persons for items related to terrorist offences without any reasonable suspicion. In response to numerous questions during the debate about the safeguards balancing the new power, two key points were made: first, guidance as to the operation of the powers would be issued by the Home Secretary to the police;[32] secondly, and more specifically, the Home Secretary would instruct the police to apply the PACE Code for stop and search to all searches under the new power.[33] The second point is particularly important, and given the silence of the new Act itself as to the applicability of the Code, may enable the courts to decide, through perusal of *Hansard*,[34] that Parliament's intention was that the Code should be applied. Thus, significant legal consequences could flow from this assurance.

2   The committee stage is often perceived as a time in which party loyalties are less strong and more constructive debate may take place. However, as appears from Zander's account, MPs lack the resources that would give them the expertise required to challenge increasingly complex government legislation from a position of sufficient knowledge. As Griffith and Ryle comment, 'the Opposition has no back up comparable to that of the minister's departmental staff'.[35] Norton, whilst noting that MPs' resources have increased dramatically since 1960, remarks that: 'By international standards [their] office, secretarial and research facilities remain poor.'[36]

3   Adversarial debate may be used in committee as on the floor of the House and the style is particularly unsuited to examining the factual and technical background to the Bill. Vernon Bogdanor has recently described Standing Committees as 'mere *ad hoc* debating committees within which second reading speeches are repeated at tedious length interspersed with the reading of well-rehearsed briefs helpfully supplied by interested organisations'.[37] The Study of Parliament Group recognised both this problem and that of the lack of sufficient information for MPs, and, on a very few occasions, the Standing Committees have been allowed to follow the recommendations of the group and call expert witnesses, ministers and records before going on to the usual clause-by-clause examination of the Bill and amendments. This procedure was followed during the passing of the Criminal Attempts Act 1981, and substantial changes were made during the committee stage.

4   In general, however, the committee stage results in the acceptance of government amendments only because, as Griffith's examination of Standing Committees found, 'party discipline is largely maintained'.[38] Further, many Opposition amendments are designed not to increase the effectiveness of the Bill but to

32   HC Deb col 265 (2 April 1996).
33   *Ibid*. The Code gives a number of important procedural safeguards; for details see Part VI Chapter 4.
34   *Pepper v Hart* [1993] 1 All ER 42 provides that the court may look to *Hansard* to assist it in construing ambiguous statutes.
35   *Op cit*, p 316.
36   P Norton, *Does Parliament Matter?* (1993), p 20.
37   'The Westminster malaise', *The Independent*, 15 May 1996.
38   'Standing Committees in the House of Commons', in Walkland and Ryle, *op cit*, p 130.

embarrass the government; the political role of Opposition MPs can prevent them undertaking *constructive* criticism. The Standing Committee stage for the poll tax legislation – a hugely controversial change to local government finance, which eventually had to be scrapped, at a total cost of £1.5 billion, and which was so unpopular that it lead to rioting in London and contributed heavily to the downfall of Margaret Thatcher – has been described as 'a futile marathon ... mostly a matter of posturing ... scrutiny by slogan and sound bite'.[39] However, where Opposition MPs are able to offer constructive criticism, it may have an indirect effect; whilst nearly all Opposition amendments are rejected, 'Ministers in committee do agree to reconsider proposals from the Opposition (often in order to make progress), and this sometimes results in government amendment at a late stage which more or less accept the Opposition's argument'.[40]

5   The debate on ratification of the Maastricht Treaty[41] showed the efficacy of the Commons as a means of publicising issues surrounding legislation. Because of the newsworthiness of the drama generated during the debates, the pros and cons of both Maastricht generally and the UK opt-out from the Social Protocol in particular were given a thorough airing.

6   The greatest threat to the ability of the Commons to generate such publicity through debate (or to propose amendments) comes from the devices available to the government to reduce the time available for debate. The use of the 'closure' allows debate to be simply cut off at the instance of government Whips (if supported on a vote which must be passed with at least 100 members in favour), while the 'guillotine' allows the government to allocate a set amount of time for each stage of debate.

7   As Ganz comments,

the use of the guillotine or timetabling of Bills goes to the heart of our democratic process, ie, the relationship between government and Parliament ... Guillotines used to be regarded as weapons of last resort to be imposed only after the opposition had filibustered to delay the Bill becoming law. They have been used increasingly to structure debate in committee so that discussion is not prolonged on the initial clauses and curtailed on the later ones after the guillotine has fallen.[42]

8   It is by no means unknown for the guillotine to be used in relation to legislation with serious implications for civil liberties. In 1996 the Commons passed in a single day the Prevention of Terrorism (Additional Powers) Bill, introduced in the wake of the IRA's bomb attack on Canary Wharf, and allowing for stop and search without reasonable suspicion for terrorist offences.[43] The episode vividly illustrates that if both main parties are behind a populist measure, scrutiny can be reduced to negligible proportions, leaving individual backbenchers largely impotent. Since, in fact, measures which are seen as 'tough' on crime or terrorism are likely in the future to have all party support, given their populist appeal, it can be seen how the party system not only facilitates executive dominance of the Commons at the expense of the Opposition, but perhaps as importantly can result in the almost total withdrawal of sustained backbench scrutiny if such an action is perceived to be politically advantageous by the Opposition leadership. Similarly rushed Bills were

---

39   Butler, *Failure in British Government*, quoted in HC Deb col 1098 (13 November 1997).
40   JAG Griffith and M Ryle, *Parliament: Functions, Practice and Procedures* (1989), p 317.
41   For extended analysis of this debate, see R Rawlings [1994] PL 258.
42   *Op cit*, pp 32–33.
43   See HC Deb cols 159–66, 181 (2 April 1996).

passed in the wake of the Omagh bombing in 1998[44] and the 11 September attacks on America in 2001, in spite of the fact that, only a year before, the UK Parliament had passed the Terrorism Act 2000 which had placed on a permanent basis, and massively extended the scope of, the UK's previous 'temporary, emergency' anti-terrorism legislation.[45] For details of the debate of the 2001 legislation in the Lords, which did impose a series of defeats on the government, see Chapter 2 of this part, under the heading 'Case Study'.

9   An alternative to the imposition of the guillotine or closure are 'programming' Bills, whereby a timetable for the Bill's passage is agreed between the party Whips. This technique is discussed in a series of reports from the Modernisation Select Committee which, as appears below, proposed greater use of programming, which, however, was to prove controversial.

Second Report of the Modernisation Committee: *Programming of Legislation and Timing of Votes,* HC 589 (1999–2000)

5 . . . The basic requirements of a reformed system as identified in our First Report were:

- The Government of the day must be assured of getting its legislation through in reasonable time (provided that it obtains the approval of the House).

- The Opposition in particular and Members in general must have a full opportunity to discuss and seek to change provisions to which they attach importance.

- All parts of a bill must be properly considered.

But now there should be added:

- Bills need to be properly prepared so as not to require a mass of new Government amendments.

These objectives remain central to the proposals which we are making to the House.

. . .

12 Our own analysis confirms that even with programme motions the third of our aims – scrutiny of all parts of a bill – is hardest to deliver. Although it is clear that programmed bills have been rather more comprehensively discussed than have old-style guillotined bills, there remain some gaps and omissions.

The case for agreed programming

13 While we acknowledge that there remain deficiencies in the agreed programming procedures used since 1997, it remains our firm judgment that, whilst voluntary informal agreements will continue to have a role to play, agreed programming of legislation can have a role to play in ensuring a more effective and efficient use of parliamentary time and improvement in the scrutiny of legislation. Its benefits extend across the range of interests in Parliament and beyond:

– It allows the Government to know when it can obtain approval of each piece of its programme.

– It offers the Opposition the opportunity to determine the structure and focus of the debate.

– Backbenchers from all parties may be given more certainty of voting times.

– In the longer term legislation will be better drafted because of the pressure on the Government to reduce the number of amendments which are tabled at the last minute.

---

44 See C Walker, 'The bombs in Omagh and their aftermath: the Criminal Justice (Terrorism and Conspiracy) Act 1998' (1999) 62(6) MLR 879.

45 For details, see Fenwick (2000), *op cit*, Chapter 3.

14 It is said that the Opposition's main weapon is time. Whilst it is the case that the Government can be inconvenienced if controversial provisions are debated at some length, it has often been assumed that the strength of this weapon was in the wasting of time by obstructing discussion of important issues on which there is disagreement. While a long-cherished weapon, it has long been clear that it is massively ineffective in its declared aim of preventing Government legislation from reaching the statute book, although it does at times provide a negotiating position for Opposition parties.

15 In recent years, it has increasingly been recognised that in practice the most effective use of time is when it is used to focus on the issues of greatest importance to the Opposition, which are most commonly the issues of greatest difficulty for the Government. Agreed programmes are the key to such a structured use of time. This would also allow Members on all sides to have greater certainty in planning the working day.

16 Fundamental to our approach is the view that change is not a 'zero sum' game in which gains by one participant are inevitably matched by losses by others. Properly constructed it should bring benefits for all participants in the legislative process, including those outside the House with legitimate interests, the Government, Opposition, and backbenchers in all parties.

Notes

1   The Committee's recommendation in this Report that programming be used for all Bills was only made at the cost of splitting the Committee. The non-Labour minority on the Committee issued a scathing minority Report. Nevertheless, the use of programming as an experiment for one session was approved by the House on 7 November 2000.[46] The Committee was later forced to report, however,[47] that the attempt to find overall support for programming had failed:

Despite all party agreement on the value of programming early in the Parliament and strong attempts to reach agreement in preparing our Second Report of last Session, it was not possible to reach agreement across the House or with all backbenchers on the current Sessional Orders. In practice, every programme motion in this Session has faced opposition, irrespective of content.

2   In fact, considerable hostility had been raised towards programming, which was widely perceived across the parties as amounting in practice to merely another means whereby government limited and controlled opposition in Parliament. A particularly notorious incident occurred in relation to the Criminal Justice and Police Bill in 2001, described here by two Conservative members of the Modernisation Committee:

Appendix to a Report of the Modernisation Committee on Programming of Legislation, HC 382 (2000–01): Memorandum submitted by Mrs Angela Browning MP and Mr Richard Shepherd MP

As many feared, the Sessional Order [setting out the arrangements for programming of Bills] has increased the power of the Executive over the timetable of bills in Standing Committee and denied the House the ability to cover shortfalls on consideration.

Every bill this session has been guillotined. Few enquiries if any are made of the Official Opposition or opposition parties as to what time may be necessary to properly discharge the duty of scrutiny. This may perhaps best be illustrated by reference to the Criminal Justice and Police Bill. The out time from Standing Committee, which had been set immediately after Second Reading and without

46   HC Deb cols 209 *et seq*.
47   HC 382 (2000–01), para 3.

any reference to the weight of issues raised at Second Reading, simply proved inadequate. When the guillotine fell at 7 pm in Standing Committee, the Committee had only reached Clause 90 out of 132. There were amendments yet to be considered, including Government amendments. Those experienced members who chaired the Committee were clear that there had been no filibustering. The whole of Part III, from Clause 49 to Clause 69, had also not been considered. The Guillotine arrangements for Report Stage were also so tight that clauses and amendments which had not been considered in Standing Committee were not considered at Report.

As Mr Simon Hughes said on the floor of the House:

Debate on the early parts of the Bill was often guillotined and we did not fully consider the rest, so it is true to say that we had not properly considered many measures, including significant clauses. (*Hansard*, col 750.)

As the House knows, the Government tabled a Motion stating that:

... the Bill shall be deemed to have been reported to the House, as amended by the Committee and as if those Clauses and Schedules the consideration of which has not been completed by the Committee has been ordered to stand part of the Bill with the outstanding Amendments which stood on the Order Paper in the name of Mr Charles Clarke.

The Speaker advised the House that there is *no* precedent for such a Motion (*Hansard*, col 728).

The Shadow Leader of the House said at col 738:

If we are to accept tonight that a Committee and all its outstanding business, which I shall mention in a moment, are deemed to have been considered and concluded, why do we not deem Second Reading debates to have been completed? Why do we not deem Report stages to have been completed? Why do we not deem ourselves to be elsewhere, and allow some robots to sit on these Benches and legislate on behalf of the people of this country?

We do not believe that it is in the interest of the House and of its standing among those whom we are elected by to pass a motion that is an untruth. Nor is it proper to consign to the Lords an unconsidered bill.

The Select Committee in writing its Report would permit no analysis of what has actually happened to consideration of bills under the Sessional Order of 7 November 2000. We believe this would have been a helpful exercise to the Select Committee and the House in assessing whether the Sessional Order has achieved the aim of properly scrutinising bills.

Of the 'beliefs' expressed in the Select Committee Majority Report, in paragraph 7:

We believe that if these procedural approaches are supported by all we will have improved the legislative 'terms of trade' to the benefit of everyone: *et seq*.

We reject the view that it improves the 'terms of trade' for everyone. It is clearly to the disadvantage of the Official Opposition, to the expressed disadvantage of backbenchers and minorities and to the balance between the majority and the minority within the House. It has strengthened the Government's control over procedures with no discernible concession to the Opposition. It is true that the Government will get greater certainty for this legislative timetable. The proposition that Opposition parties and backbenchers will get greater opportunities to debate and vote on the issues of most concern to them simply has not been borne out by experience in this Session of the experiment of systematic guillotining of all bills. Similarly the evidence of this Session is that the House has not scrutinised legislation better and we would refer back to the Government Motion of 12 March, to which we have previously made reference, as indicative of this failure.

The efficient working of the House is dependent on a degree of tolerance and forbearance by the majority towards Opposition and minority opinion. The present Sessional Order, brought in contrary to the expressed principled opposition of the Opposition and minorities, has denied the House its central role of properly examining Government legislation.

Note

One reform which should help relieve the pressure on parliamentary time is the notion of carry-over, here explained in a memo by Robin Cook, Leader of the House:

> 20 The major pressure to rush legislation through Parliament is the rule that any Bill which has not completed every procedural stage falls in the autumn with the end of the Session. As a result few Bills are introduced after May as there is little prospect of them completing all stages by November. The consequence is a spate of Bills earlier in the Session and congestion in the legislative process.
>
> 21 The Commons would have much more opportunity to carry out scrutiny of legislation if Bills were carried over from one Session to the next. Plainly there must be a time limit on the period within which any Bill must complete all stages, and the *quid pro quo* for greater flexibility on the carry-over between Sessions should be a requirement that all Bills must complete all stages within a fixed period of months.
>
> 22 This reform would enable a more even flow in the introduction of new bills and would remove the need to rush them through scrutiny.[48]

For further discussion of the mechanics and implications of carry-over, see the Third Report of the Modernisation Committee: HC 543 (1997–98). Carry-over of Bills, subject to certain safeguards, was agreed by the Commons in 2002.

Delegated legislation

As Zander notes:

> Each year over 2,000 sets of rules and regulations are made by ministers or the Crown in Council or other central rule-making authorities – by comparison with less than 100 public Acts of Parliament. This form of legislation is under the authority of powers delegated by Parliament. The reason is usually to avoid having too much detail in the main Act [referred to below as the 'Parent Act'] and thereby to waste the time of parliamentarians in minutiae. The delegated power to make regulations also enables the responsible minister to respond to new circumstances by amplifying the original rules without troubling Parliament with matters of detail that are within principles dealt with in the original legislation. Sometimes, however, Parliament leaves to ministers power to issue regulations on matters of principle.
>
> The most sweeping grant of delegated legislative power to the executive is undoubtedly that in s 2(2) of the European Communities Act 1972, which permits Orders in Council and regulations by designated ministers and Government departments to be made to give effect to Community instruments and provisions of the treaties which do not have direct effect. The Act provides that such delegated powers are to have the effect of Acts of Parliament and can include any provision that could have been included in an Act of Parliament except that they may not impose or increase taxation; have retroactive effect; sub-delegate legislative powers; or create new criminal offences punishable with more than two years' imprisonment or fines of over £400.[49]

In some cases the parent Act may also grant to the Minister a discretion to delay bringing in the proposed new scheme until he or she thinks it appropriate to do so. What will be the position if the Secretary of State disregards the will of Parliament and decides not to bring in such a scheme at all, and, without seeking to procure the repealing of the Act in question, attempts to implement an alternative policy, relying on his prerogative powers? In *Secretary of State for the Home Department ex p Fire*

---

48 *Modernisation of the House of Commons: a Reform Programme for Consultation*, HC 440 (2001–02).
49 Zander, *op cit*, pp 92–93.

Brigades Union and Others [1995] 2 WLR 464,[50] the House of Lords upheld the finding of the Court of Appeal that the Home Secretary, Michael Howard, was wrong to decide not to bring into force the statutory scheme for criminal injuries compensation which had been laid down in the Criminal Justice Act 1988 and to bring in a 'radically different' tariff scheme since that decision involved him in setting aside the duty laid upon him in the Act to consider when to bring the legislation into force.

The House of Lords was thus, as it were, enforcing the constitutional rights of Parliament against the executive, thus preventing the abuse of the latter's powers. In actual fact, of course, it was the Conservative government which had procured the passage the original legislation, and the same Conservative government which later decided that it wished to disregard that legislation. The gap between constitutional theory and political reality can be seen in the fact that the majority of MPs, as Conservatives, probably regarded the decision of the House of Lords as a source of acute political embarrassment, rather than a vindication of their constitutional rights.

But there is a broader issue of constitutional principle at stake in the increasing use of Acts which lay down merely a skeletal framework for legislation whereby extremely important matters are decided by secondary legislation (the most important contemporary example is undoubtedly the Regulatory Reform Act 2001).[51] The enactment of broad enabling powers by Parliament which give ministers *de facto* powers to legislate may also be seen as a significant erosion of parliamentary sovereignty. So called 'Henry VIII' clauses, in giving ministers the power to amend primary legislation by regulations which may never be seen or debated by Parliament,[52] offend against one of the fundamental principles of parliamentary sovereignty, that 'no person or body is recognised by the law of England as having a right to override or set aside the legislation of Parliament'.[53]

Scrutiny of delegated legislation: efficacy

The following report from the Procedure Committee outlines the standard methods of scrutiny for delegated legislation, and the special methods used for the scrutiny of European Union legislation (all of which is delegated legislation under the European Communities Act 1972) and for Orders made under the Deregulation and Contracting Out Act 1994 (and now also the Regulatory Reform Act 2001) which are of special significance because they amend primary legislation.

First Report of the Procedure Committee, *Delegated Legislation*, HC 48 (1999–2000) (extracts)

5 ...The present system, which has grown up over many years, is founded on the distinction between two categories of statutory instrument: 'affirmative instruments', which require a positive Resolution of each House to come into effect, and 'negative instruments', which can be annulled by a Resolution of either House if passed within 40 days of their laying.

---

50 For the case itself, see Part IV Chapter 1, pp 490–93.
51 See Phillips (2001), *op cit*, pp 679–80; on deregulation orders made under the previous legislation, see D Miers, 'The deregulation procedure: an expanding role' [1999] PL 477.
52 On the power to make such Orders contained in s 10 of the Human Rights Act 1998, in order to repeal or amend legislative provisions found to be incompatible with the European Convention on Human Rights, see Part I Chapter 3, at pp 107–9.
53 AV Dicey, *An Introduction to the Study of the Law of the Constitution*, 10th edn (1959), pp xxxiv.

6 An affirmative instrument stands automatically referred for debate in a Standing Committee on Delegated Legislation ('DL Committee') unless the Government agrees that it be debated on the Floor of the House. Debate in Committee arises on a formal and un-amendable motion, 'That the Committee has considered the draft XYZ Order 2000', and after a maximum of one and a half hour's debate, the Chairman reports the instrument to the House irrespective of whether or not the motion has been agreed to. A motion to approve the instrument is then put to the House, without further debate. Instruments taken on the Floor are debated for up to an hour and a half, also on an un-amendable motion.

7 Negative instruments are not debated unless a motion is tabled seeking ('praying') that the instrument be annulled, and the Government agrees either that the instrument be debated in a DL Committee or, much more rarely, on the Floor of the House. For many years the Government has accepted no obligation so to agree. Proceedings in committee are the same as for an affirmative instrument; however, in the case of negatives referred to committee there are no subsequent proceedings on the Floor (a point of some significance given that negatives can only effectively be annulled by a vote on the Floor).

8 All statutory instruments laid before Parliament are scrutinised by the Joint Committee on Statutory Instruments (JCSI). The committee's task is to consider technical but important issues such as whether the instrument is made within the powers conferred by the parent legislation, and whether its drafting is defective. The committee is precluded from considering the actual merits of instruments or the policy underlying them. It has the assistance of Speaker's Counsel and regularly reports to both Houses.

9 In the last complete Session, 1998–99, 178 affirmative instruments were laid before the House, of which 150 were considered in committee, 21 were considered on the Floor, and seven were withdrawn. In the same Session, 1,266 negative instruments were laid before the House, of which 28 were considered in committee and one on the Floor.

48 **The European Scrutiny Committee** (until 1998 the European Legislation Committee) is charged with the task of considering a range of EU documents, as defined in Standing Order No 143. These include EU Regulations, Directives, Decisions of the Council, budgetary documents, Commission proposals, reports and recommendations, documents submitted to the European Central Bank, various inter-governmental proposals, and reports of the Court of Auditors. About 1,000 EU documents a year are deposited in Parliament for scrutiny. The Committee's functions are to assess the political and/or legal importance of these documents and decide which merit further scrutiny, either in European Standing Committee or on the Floor; to report in detail on each document the Committee considers important (some 475 a year), taking written and oral evidence if necessary; to monitor business in the Council of Ministers and the negotiating position of UK Ministers; to review EU legal, procedural and institutional developments which may have implications for the UK and the House; and to police the scrutiny system.

49 When a document is referred by the Committee to one of the three *European Standing Committees*, that committee will meet to hear a Government Minister make a statement and answer questions put by Members for up to 1 hour (extendable by a further 30 minutes at the Chairman's discretion); this is followed by a debate on an amendable motion for up to a further 1 hour 30 minutes. The Chairman reports to the House any resolution to which the committee has come, or that it has come to no resolution. A Government motion couched in similar terms is usually moved in the House a few days later; the Question on this is put forthwith.

Notes

1   There has been a long history of parliamentary committees complaining that the system for parliamentary scrutiny and control of delegated legislation is grossly inadequate. In 1978, the Select Committee on Procedure 1977–78 warned, '... the system provides only vestigial control of statutory instruments and is in need of complete reform'. The fundamental problem identified with the system was that

instruments subject to negative affirmation were increasingly becoming law without ever having been debated by the Commons. Since that Report, this phenomenon increased sharply: in 1978–79, 71.7 per cent of prayers for annulment were debated; in the 1985–86 Session, this percentage had dropped to 30.6 per cent.

2 As mentioned above, an important mechanism for the scrutiny of delegated legislation is the Joint Committee on Statutory Instruments, established by the following Standing Order.

House of Commons Standing Order No 151

151(1) A select committee shall be appointed to join with a committee appointed by the Lords to consider ... every instrument which is laid before each House of Parliament and upon which proceedings may be or might have been taken in either House of Parliament, in pursuance of an Act of Parliament, being –

(a) a statutory instrument, or a draft statutory instrument;

(b) a scheme, or an amendment of a scheme, or a draft thereof, requiring approval by statutory instrument;

(c) any other instrument (whether or not in draft), where the proceedings in pursuance of an Act of Parliament are proceedings by way of an affirmative resolution; or

(d) an order subject to special parliamentary procedure,

but excluding any Order in Council or draft Order in Council made or proposed to be made under paragraph 1 of Schedule 1 to the Northern Ireland Act 1974 [ie, legislation for Northern Ireland] and any draft Order proposed to be made under section 1 of the Deregulation and Contracting Out Act 1994 or under section 1 of the Regulatory Reform Act 2001 [considered by the Deregulation and Regulatory Reform Committee – see Standing Order No 141], or any subordinate provisions order made or proposed to be made under that Act ... with a view to determining whether the special attention of the House should be drawn to it on any of the following grounds:

(i) that it imposes a charge on the public revenues or contains provisions requiring payments to be made to the Exchequer or any government department or to any local or public authority in consideration of any licence or consent or of any services to be rendered, or prescribes the amount of any such charge or payment;

(ii) that it is made in pursuance of any enactment containing specific provisions excluding it from challenge in the courts, either at all times or after the expiration of a specific period;

(iii) that it purports to have retrospective effect where the parent statute confers no express authority so to provide;

(iv) that there appears to have been unjustifiable delay in the publication or in the laying of it before Parliament;

(v) that there appears to have been unjustifiable delay in sending a notification under the proviso to section 4(1) of the Statutory Instruments Act 1946, where an instrument has come into operation before it has been laid before Parliament;

(vi) that there appears to be a doubt whether it is *intra vires* or that it appears to make some unusual or unexpected use of the powers conferred by the statute under which it is made;

(vii) that for any special reason its form or purport calls for elucidation;

(viii) that its drafting appears to be defective;

or on any other ground which does not impinge on its merits or on the policy behind it; and to report its decision with the reasons thereof in any particular case.

(6)　　　The committee and any subcommittee appointed by it shall have power to require any
government department concerned to submit a memorandum explaining any instrument
which may be under its consideration or to depute a representative to appear before it as
a witness for the purpose of explaining any such instrument ...

Notes

1　JD Hayhurst and P Wallington argue that the use of delegated legislation has
changed significantly, especially in the previous decade or so. 'It is no longer the
technical implementation of detail in a legislative mosaic, although undoubtedly
the majority of statutory instruments are in this category. More of the policy of a
legislative proposal is likely to be delegated, the legislation being enabling not just
at a specific but at the broadest level.'[54]

2　For a sustained analysis of the inadequacies of the current system, and proposals
for reform, see the First Report of the Procedure Committee, *Delegated Legislation*,
HC 48 (1999–2000). The key elements of these proposals still await enactment.[55] The
Procedure Committee has recently recommended[56] the establishment of a Joint
Committee of both Houses to act as a 'sifting committee', to identify instruments
'which it considers to be of sufficient political importance ... to merit debate' in the
House or in a Standing Committee. The Lords has already established such a
Committee[57] and the Procedure Committee, in line with the view of the Lords,
thought that it would be preferable for the Houses to have a Joint Committee for
this task (paras 8–11).

THE COMMONS AS SCRUTINISER OF THE EXECUTIVE

It is an axiom of any theory of responsible government that thorough scrutiny of the
executive arm of the state is vital to a democratic system; an important part of this
scrutiny is undertaken by Parliament, to which, at least theoretically, all ministers are
responsible.[58] As Norton has pointed out, in the House of Commons, 'Unlike [in] many
legislatures, the government of the day is obliged to explain its actions continually and
open itself to constant criticism. The US President does not face a critical Congress and
can even hide away from the press if he so chooses. The British Prime Minister,
however, has to face the Leader of the Opposition twice a week over the despatch
box.'[59]

However, there is a central problem for the Commons in an acting as a scrutiniser
of the executive: that MPs from the governing party – nearly always that majority in

---

54　'The parliamentary scrutiny of delegated legislation' [1988] PL 547–76, at p 573.
55　For further comments on this issue and suggestions for reform, see P Tudor (clerk to the House
　　of Lords Delegated Powers and Deregulation Committee), 'Secondary legislation: second class
　　or crucial?' (2000) 21(3) SLR 149.
56　First Report, *Delegated Legislation: Proposals for Sifting Committee*, HC 501 (2002–03).
57　House of Lords Procedure Committee, 5th Report, 2001–02, HL Paper 148, para 10. The report
　　was agreed by the House of Lords on 24 July 2002.
58　It should be noted that changes in the organisation of the Civil Service, the 'Next Steps'
　　initiative, and the rise in the number of government services carried out by semi-autonomous
　　agencies, has raised serious questions as to the extent to which ministers in charge of the
　　relevant departments can still be held accountable to Parliament. This issue is discussed in the
　　chapter on the executive (Part IV Chapter 2).
59　Norton, 'Parliament I: the House of Commons', in Jones, *op cit*, p 319. Prime Minister's
　　Questions now only takes place once a week, but for the same total time period.

the House – tend to place their loyalty to their political party above their rather abstract duty, as members of the legislature, to hold the executive to account. In addition, the dual imperative driving opposition members – to exact such accountability, but also to score as many political points as they can – tends to make the government overly defensive in relation to the Commons. It can also have the effect of causing MPs from the governing party to 'rally round' the government in its defence, thus siding with the very body they are supposed to be scrutinising and holding to account. In the extract below from a recent important report of the Hansard Society Commission, this tension is explored.

Hansard Society Commission on Parliamentary Scrutiny, *The Challenge for Parliament: Making Government Accountable* (2001), Chapter 2 (extracts)

2.5   The Commission recognises that the institutional structure of Parliament and the dominance of parties means that MPs have very different and often contradictory views about their own role, and that of Parliament. Many of these problems relate to the absence of separation of powers and the Commission recognises that for as long as the political parties are the forum for organising parliamentary business, the executive will dominate Parliament. The Commission's recommendations seek to redress some of the imbalance between the executive and Parliament in the Commons. The Commission also sought recommendations which would promote cultural change by offering MPs greater opportunities and incentives to reconcile their roles in a manner that does not lose sight of the public interest.

The institutional structure of the Commons and parliamentary roles

2.6   What MPs do at Westminster is, of course, decided by the individual MP. There are few obligations on the Member of Parliament, there is no job description and MPs enjoy a great deal of leeway in defining who they represent, and how they represent them. In a landmark survey of Members of Parliament Donald Searing found eight distinct roles which individual MPs could play whilst in the Commons, four of these were backbench roles – policy advocate, ministerial aspirant, constituency member, Parliamentarian – and four were leadership roles – parliamentary private secretaries, whips, junior ministers, senior ministers.

2.7   He found that in so far as MPs consciously chose a particular role, their decisions were based on both institutional and political factors. The opportunities provided by the institution were obviously a significant factor but these were tempered by MPs' own political ambitions, which rely on the support and patronage of the political party. In short, the structure of the institution, and its formal and informal rules, will 'define the essential tasks that need to be performed.' At Westminster the two most important factors which determine activity are the dominance of the governing party over the activity of the Commons, and the influence of the parties over their MPs.

2.8   Westminster is characterised by the dominance of the executive. Although this is common in many democracies, especially where the executive is drawn from the legislature, evidence to the Commission from Professor Thomas Saalfeld shows the extent of executive dominance at Westminster is far greater than for many other parliaments. The extent of this control is conveyed in Standing Order 14 of the House of Commons which states that 'save as provided in this order, government business shall have precedence at every sitting'.

2.9   The organisation of business in the chamber of the Commons is determined by the governing party. It allocates the timing for all debates and legislation, and although in practice this relies on negotiation with the Opposition parties through the 'usual channels', the Government will time debates to its own advantage. The notion that the Government shall get its business dominates procedures in the chamber and standing committees. This has a number of implications for Parliament as an institution. It means that Parliament is informed of its business by a Cabinet minister, the Leader of the House, on a weekly basis who announces the content for each day the following week and provisional business for the week after. Although the Labour Government has introduced reforms which seek to bring a greater predictability to parliamentary business, the current system means that it is impossible for MPs to plan their work too far ahead.

2.10   The effect on the ethos of the Commons is to emphasise the distinction between executive and legislature. MPs conceive their role according to their position, and the position of their party, in relation to the Government. There is little sense that Parliament owns its business or determines its own workload, nor much sense of Parliament acting collectively as an institution In some respects this atomises and individualises the work of MPs, with each MP acting as 'his own public relations officer.' Although Parliament has certain collective functions, its ability to deliver them is limited by the fact that it has no collective ethos, 'The idea of "Parliament" as a political force, or as a whole, is simply a myth. Parliament in this sense simply does not exist.'

2.11   The only collective activity inside the Commons is orchestrated by the political parties and the only realistic career path for the ambitious MP is through the structures of the political party. The vast majority of activity in the Commons chamber is organised along party lines and the whips on both sides play a significant role in marshalling the contributions of their MPs. The knowledge that whips and party leaders will determine their political career has a significant bearing on MPs' behaviour, and it is those traits which emphasise the party political divide that are most likely to get a backbencher noticed. Promotion is more likely to be the result of partisan activity – toeing the party line, asking the right questions, scoring points off the Opposition – than pursuing the accountability functions of Parliament.

Note

The Commission made a number of proposals for enhancing Parliament's role. Some of these have in fact now been implemented, as will be seen below.

Scrutiny on the floor of the Commons

As Michael Ryle points out, the opportunities for scrutiny in the Commons have increased markedly over the last 50 years.

Michael Ryle, 'The changing Commons' (1994) Parl Aff 647, pp 658–59

In addition to their Opposition days, the official Opposition choose the subject for debate on all but the first of the five or six days debate on the Queen's speech at the beginning of each session. They have debates – in practice, less than one a session – on motions of censure. They can have debates on 'prayers' to annul statutory instruments on the floor of the House or in standing committees. They can apply for emergency debates (in recent years the Speaker has only allowed one or two such debates each session). Scottish and Welsh matters of the Opposition's choosing have, since 1957, been debated in the Scottish and Welsh Grand Committees. Opposition front bench spokesmen are asking an increasing number of private notice questions on urgent matters. And Prime Minister's Question Time is used increasingly by Leaders of the Opposition to give a public airing, at prime time for media attention, to matters of their choosing. In a wide range of ways, the opportunities for the Opposition to set the agenda have increased to some extent over the past 50 years.

Opportunities for backbenchers have expanded considerably more. Time for private members' bills and motions has been increased. Backbench Members choose which European documents to debate. They can raise any matter for which ministers are responsible on numerous adjournment motions. They choose the subjects for estimate days. Backbenchers also bring in many more bills under the '10 minute rule', which permits a short speech at prime media time, than they did in the 1940s and 50s. Backbenchers also have many opportunities to raise matters without debate. Aided by their research assistants, Members have made fuller use of questions for written answer to obtain information and to press ministers for action, and the back pages of *Hansard* are a mine of information on an amazingly wide range of matters; that was not the case 40 or 50 years ago.

The conduct of Question Time itself has changed markedly. Far fewer questions are reached for oral answer: some 45–50 a day in the 1940s and 1950s; about 15 a day today. Oral questions have become broader and more political and Speakers have been willing to allow more supplementaries; today they are really opportunities for Members on both sides to make political points rather than to seek for information as originally conceived. There has also been the development of the syndication of questions, whereby Members – inspired, it may be thought, by their Whips – put down very similar questions on arranged topics in the attempt to get as many questions favourable to ministers, or hostile (as the case may be), high on the list and likely to be called.

Another development has been the adoption, since about 1977, of 'open' questions to the Prime Minister which enable Members to raise whatever matters they wish. Again, the tabling is often syndicated. Prime Minister's Question Time is covered live on television and Members – particularly the Leader of the Opposition – regularly seek to highlight current political issues of their choosing and hope to get coverage on the evening television news programmes. This is a far cry from the intimate, sometimes searching, sometimes lightly teasing, exchanges between Attlee and Churchill in the years after the war; quite often in those days there would be no questions to the Prime Minister (they only came up after 44 questions to other ministers) or there would be no supplementaries.

Other expanding opportunities for backbenchers include almost daily applications for emergency debates when a matter which a Member considers urgent may be given publicity, occasional private notice questions, and the right to table early day motions; little used until the mid-1960s, today up to 2,000 such motions are tabled each session. The Speaker tries to call as many Members as possible – certainly more than in the years up to 1983 – to speak in debates and to ask supplementary questions on ministerial statements. There has been one restriction of backbenchers' rights, however; because more and more Members want to speak in some important debates, it became necessary in 1984 to give the Speaker power to impose 10 minute limits on speeches for part of some debates.

Notes

1 To the above developments should be added the advent of Westminster Hall, considered above, which has markedly increased the opportunities for scrutiny.

2 Whilst the floor of the House now has increased potential as a forum for scrutiny of the executive, it is here that scrutiny can still sometimes be at its most ineffective. At the end of each day, half an hour is set aside for adjournment debates. This provides opportunities for backbenchers to make extended criticisms of government policy. Unfortunately, the House tends to be almost empty at this time, and very little publicity is afforded to these debates which consequently lose much of their sting. Standing Order No 20 in respect of emergency debates allows a further opportunity to raise urgent issues on the floor of the House, but requests for such debates are rarely granted. Similarly, Early Day Motions allow for cross-party expressions of concern or criticism of government policy; opportunities for debate of these Motions have markedly increased with the advent of Westminster Hall as an alternative forum for debate, but the situation is still far from satisfactory.

3 Far more publicity is given to the questioning of ministers on the floor of the House; 45–50 minutes are set aside every day, except Friday, for oral answers to be given to Members' questions. A recent report by the Procedure Committee revealed

the enormous growth in the use of questions for both oral and written answers[60] from just 3,525 in 1946–47 to 28,739 in 1999–2000.

Limitations on the obligation to reply to questions

The basic principles governing ministerial replies to any form of questioning in Parliament are set out in the Ministerial Code (Cabinet Office, 1997) which replicates the wording of a resolution passed by Parliament in 1997:[61]

(1) Ministers have a duty to Parliament to account and be held to account, for the policies, decisions and actions of the Departments and next Steps Agencies.

(2) It is of paramount importance that Ministers give accurate and truthful information to Parliament, correcting any inadvertent error at the earliest opportunity. Ministers who knowingly mislead Parliament will be expected to offer their resignation to the Prime Minister.

(3) Ministers must be as open as possible with Parliament and the public, refusing to provide information only when disclosure would not be in the public interest, which should be decided in accordance with relevant statute, and the Government's *Code of Practice on Access to Information*.

The content of the duty of ministerial responsibility and accountability are explored in Part IV Chapter 2, pp 522–73, while the Code of Practice itself, together with commentary, appears in Part IV Chapter 3, pp 620–40 and readers are referred to those chapters at this point. However, a few brief comments will be made here though, since it is the Code that represents the main limitation upon governmental willingness to answer questions in the House.

The Code sets out a general obligation to provide information (not documents) relating to government activity including background information to policy decisions and information about public services. However, it specifies a large number of areas where information should not be given, including where it would harm defence, national security, international relations, or where it would involve disclosing commercial confidences, or would harm the frankness and candour of internal policy discussion, including advice given by officials to ministers, or would prejudice legal investigations or infringe an individual's privacy, or where the information was supplied in confidence. Answers will also be refused where the Minister considers that the information requested would prejudice the proper and efficient conduct of the operations of any government department or other public authority. Examples of questions being refused under the Code are set out in Part IV Chapter 3, pp 633–37.

4   The Freedom of Information Act 2000 will for the first time introduce a general right of access to government information, policed by an independent Information Commissioner and which is ultimately enforceable through the contempt jurisdiction of the High Court (s 52). MPs will of course be able to make as much use of the Act as anyone. It will therefore deal with the basic problem that ministers cannot at present ultimately be compelled to release information. However, the Act is riddled with extremely wide ranging exemptions – broader even than those in the Code, in the view of some commentators. In particular, there is a class exemption in s 35 in relation to all information relating to 'the formulation or development of government policy'. The only limitation to this astonishingly broad

---

60   Annex C to the Third Report of the Procedure Committee, Parliamentary Questions, HC 622 (2001–02).
61   HC Deb cols 1046–47 (19 March 1997).

exemption – which is not subject to any burden on ministers to prove that any harm would be caused by releasing the information in question – is that statistical information relating to a decision is no longer exempted once the decision is made. But, for example, evidence of other policy options considered, and the reasons for rejecting them, would be covered by the exemption. The Information Commissioner can order release of the information concerned if satisfied that the public interest in withholding information does not outweigh the interest in its reception (s 2); however, because the information relates to a central government department, its release can ultimately be vetoed by a Cabinet minister (s 53). Moreover, the Act does not come fully into force until 2005. See further on the Act, Chapter 3 of this part, pp 639–61

5   In relation specifically to parliamentary questions, in addition to the specific grounds for refusing questions set out in the Code of Practice, there is also the ground of excessive cost: successive governments have refused to answer questions deemed disproportionately expensive to research. The figure above which a question will be deemed too expensive to answer is currently £600.[62] There are also more general limitations on the use of questioning, explained by the Public Administration Committee which also goes on to note problems with the use of these restrictions by Ministers as well as complaints as to the promptness and quality of answers.[63]

Report of the Public Administration Committee, *Ministerial Accountability and Parliamentary Questions*, HC 61 (2000–01)

4 The House's principal rules on what may be asked in a written Parliamentary Question are derived from decisions by successive Speakers on individual Questions, endorsed from time to time by Select Committees on Procedure. They can be crystallised in three essential points:

● Questions should seek information or press for action, ie, they should not become a form of debate, giving Members the opportunity to make statements, or political points, directly;

● Questions should be on matters for which the Government has responsibility, and should be directed to the Minister within the Government who is responsible; and

● Questions should not repeat recently answered Questions.

The last of these points is one of the reasons for the operation of the system of what has been generally known as 'blocking'. A Question may not be asked if that same Question has already been asked and answered in the current Session (unless there is a reason to believe that the situation has changed). If a Minister declines to provide information in answer to a Parliamentary Question (or refuses to take a particular action, if that is what has been asked), the same Question cannot be asked again for the next three months (again, unless there is reason to believe that circumstances have changed).

...

9 The proportion of questions 'blocked' by each Department in Session 1998–99 was as follows:

[The table shows that departments blocked between 0.37 and 2.52 per cent of questions asked. Many departments blocked less than 1 per cent: only two, Defence, and Attorney-General's, blocked 2 per cent or more.]

Evidence from Departments

...

11 We have said in our two latest reports that in many cases, when a Department withholds information in response to a question on the grounds that the information is confidential, it fails to

---

62   Third Report of the Procedure Committee, HC 622 (2001–02), para 20.
63   HC 61 (2000–01), para 4.

mention the relevant exemption of the Code of Practice on Access to Government Information. This happens despite the fact that the Government accepted a recommendation of the Public Service Committee in July 1996 that the relevant exemption should be specified when departments gave such answers. Practice still does not appear to have improved much in this respect, although there are one or two departments which are quite punctilious in giving the specific exemption.

12 **We continue to be disappointed by the failure of many departments to adopt a practice recommended by this Committee and accepted by the Government, and recommend again that the Government ensure that where Departments withhold information under an exemption in the Code of Practice (or later under the Freedom of Information Act 2000) they invariably cite the relevant exemption.**

13 This year we decided to try to find out from Members what displeased them about Ministerial replies to Questions ...

...

15 The complaints we received fell into six main categories: dissatisfaction with the rules or conventions of the House regarding Parliamentary Questions and answers to them; complaints that these were not being followed; complaints about partial or misleading answers; complaints that questions were not being addressed at all; complaints of discrepancies between Departments or within the same Department over time; and complaints about delays in answering letters to Ministers.

...

17 Only a small proportion of questions in reality elicit 'disproportionate cost' answers. When they are given they undoubtedly cause disproportionate annoyance. In 1997–1998, out of 51,982 written questions, 1,441 received such answers; in 1998–1999 it was 732 out of 32,286 and in 1999–2000, 871 of 36,850.

18 Perhaps inevitably, Members and others suggested to us that 'disproportionate cost' is sometimes used as an excuse for not answering. Dr Lowry, a researcher, drew our attention to an exchange in the Chamber in which Mr Campbell-Savours said as much. Mr Garnier thought that it might hide bureaucratic laziness and Mr Field gave an example of a question which originally received this answer only to be answered after evidence before a Select Committee made it clear that the information could, in fact, be made available ...

...

19 **We recommend that when Departments are considering refusing to answer a question on the grounds of 'disproportionate cost', there should be a presumption that any of the requested information which *is* readily available should be given.**

...

21 One of the conventions that some Members feel is being broken is that concerning the day by which written questions should be answered. Briefly, if a question is tabled for ordinary written answer, one clear day's notice must be given and the question should be answered within a working week. If a more urgent reply is required it may be tabled for a 'named day', in which case two clear days notice must be given; an answer, even if only a 'holding answer', should be given on the day named and a substantive reply within a month ...

...

24 [But] sometimes the answer to a Parliamentary Question is long delayed, and we have reason to believe that some are never answered at all. It is, of course, open to Members to pursue the matter by a question on the lines of 'when I may expect an answer' but we believe this puts the onus unfairly on the Member. We recommend that Departments should overhaul their systems for ensuring that all questions receive a timely answer.

25 It occasionally happens that a Member tables a question to which the answer is delayed until another Member tables a similar one, in which case the second Member receives a substantive answer and the first an answer by reference. **We deplore this practice and recommend that in these cases the Member who tabled the earlier question should receive the substantive answer.**

26 We received, in response to our request to Members, a number of responses complaining that part of a question had been ignored. Miss Widdecombe, for instance, asked the Home Secretary 'what estimate he has made of the average cost to public funds of a drug abstinence order made under Part III of the Criminal Justice and Court Services Bill; what estimate he has made of the number of orders that will be made annually; what estimate he had made of the number of other community orders that will include drug abstinence orders; if magistrates' courts will be able to make such an order; and if he will make a statement'. She received the answer 'the average cost of a Drug Abstinence Order/Requirement under community supervision is estimated at £1,500. The new drug-testing regime will be piloted in the first instance. It is estimated that initial piloting in three areas would result in 3,500 offenders being made subject to the drug abstinence requirements'. No mention was made of the magistrates' courts . . .

27 In some cases, failure to answer part of a complex question results from the fact that an element of it falls outside ministerial responsibility, or could only be answered at disproportionate cost. Even so, we would expect that where this is so, it will be clearly stated in the answer. Failure even to address part of a question is at best sloppy; at worst it may be symptomatic of what Lord Phillips in his inquiry into BSE described as a 'culture of secrecy'. **We deplore the practice of answering part only of a question and ignoring the rest, whether it arises out of policy or slackness; we recommend that Departments should introduce stringent checks to ensure that all parts of a question are addressed.**

. . .

29 Some questions receive partial answers; others receive answers which are almost insulting. Mr Loughton asked 'how much of the change in the figures for carbon emission savings from fuel duties, set out in the Pre-Budget Report, relies on (i) reduced mileage travelled by vehicles and (ii) reduced emissions resulting from technological improvements in car engines'. He received the reply 'the Pre-Budget report set out that the fuel duty escalator from 1996 to 1999 is estimated to produce carbon savings of 1 to 2.5 million tonnes of carbon by 2010'. This is an answer not to the question asked but to one which the Table Office might well have refused to accept on the grounds that the information was readily available.

Notes

1 The government response to this report[64] accepted the recommendations it made and promised improvements, saying:

In the light of the concerns raised by the Committee, the Government has reissued the *Guidance to Officials on Drafting Answers to Parliamentary Questions* and reminded Ministers and civil servants of their responsibilities in this area.

2 The relevant parts of this guidance (it is returned to in the chapter on ministerial accountability (Part IV Chapter 2) state:

4. Where information is being refused on the grounds of disproportionate cost, there should be a presumption that any of the requested information which is readily available should be provided

. . .

5. Do not omit information sought merely because disclosure could lead to political embarrassment or administrative inconvenience.

---

64 HC 464 (2001–02).

6. Where there is a particularly fine balance between openness and non-disclosure, and when the draft answer takes the latter course, this should be explicitly drawn to the Minister's attention. Similarly, if it is proposed to reveal information of a sort which is not normally disclosed, this should be explicitly drawn to Ministers' attention.

7. If you conclude that material information must be withheld and the PQ cannot be fully answered as a result, draft an answer which makes this clear and which explains the reasons in equivalent terms to those in the Code of Practice, or because of disproportionate cost or the information not being available.

3   For the latest report of the Public Administration Committee on parliamentary accountability, see the Ninth Report of the Committee for 2001–02 (HC 1086). In that report, the Committee noted that some departments were *still* failing to cite the relevant Code exemption when refusing answers (para 8). In response,[65] the government pledged again to tackle this problem. The Committee said:

The Government's response says that it will in future insist that the relevant exemption is mentioned in Ministers' answers when requested information is not given. **We regard this as an important step towards openness and the protection of the public interest, and we warmly welcome it** [para 4].

The Committee was also particularly concerned about the use of the 'commercial confidentiality' exemption in the Code, observing:

The issue of commercial confidentiality is of particular relevance at this time due to the Government's plans for reform of public services, an issue upon which the Prime Minister said he will be judged at the next election. The Government want to use private sector finance and knowledge to improve public service delivery. The main vehicles for this process are Public Private Partnerships (PPP) and the Private Finance Initiative (PFI). These projects use private sector finance as capital and then the private sector earns profit from managerial efficiency or ownership of the capital project after a period of time. The contracts for these projects are long-term, up to 30 years. The length of the contracts means that once they are signed there is little chance for public influence. The Capita Group, one of the major private companies involved with PPPs, has estimated the market to be worth £50 billion. This indicates to us that the public interest is best served by as much information as possible being made public before the contracts are signed [para 14].

3   The Committee also noted that there is ultimately no means of compelling ministers to answer parliamentary questions or to give fuller replies where MPs are dissatisfied with the replies received. The Ombudsman has no role in the matter under the statute governing his powers (see Part V Chapter 3), the Speaker has indicated unwillingness to become involved in seeking to force ministers to reply (HC 1086 (2001–02), para 21) and it would be 'inappropriate' to involve the politically impartial Cabinet Secretary in a matter which should be resolved by Parliament (*ibid*, paras 21–22). The Committee therefore recommended that:

this Committee, through its Chairman, should be asked by the Speaker to refer unsatisfactory answers to questions to the Department concerned if requested to do so by a Member, and if such answers are deemed appropriate for such a referral [para 26].

4   Oral questioning of ministers is now often afforded live television coverage, and Prime Minister's questions are always covered on terrestrial television stations. Oral questions and their supplementaries tend to be used as an opportunity to probe ministers' grasp of their portfolios or to attack government policy. They thus have some effect in ensuring that ministers are kept up to the mark; they provide an

---

65   First Report, *Ministerial Accountability and Parliamentary Questions: The Government Response to the Committee's Ninth Report of Session 2001–02*, HC 136 (2002–03).

opportunity for weak elements in government policy to be publicly exposed, and are one of the few times in which ordinary backbenchers can raise matters directly with Cabinet ministers. The following extract provides examples of oral questions to the Home Office on a variety of controversial subjects and subsequent debate.

HC Deb cols 593 et seq (8 July 2002)

Mr Michael Clapham (Barnsley, West and Penistone): What plans he has to propose reforms to the law on rape; and if he will make a statement. [64747]

The Secretary of State for the Home Department (Mr David Blunkett): We all accept that rape is a particularly heinous crime. The legislative framework must enable us to take firm action wherever and whenever we can. We intend to publish our proposals for strengthening legislation on sex offences and sex offenders in the autumn, and to legislate as soon after that as parliamentary time allows.

A working group has been formed with representatives from the police, the Crown Prosecution Service and the court service, in response to the joint report published on 8 April on the investigation and prosecution of rape. We recognise that there is a great deal more to do and I am very pleased that the Attorney-General and the Solicitor-General are giving us their full support in dealing with the present very low prosecution and conviction rates.

Mr Clapham: I thank my right hon Friend for that answer and am pleased to hear that a working party has been set up. However, as he is aware, between only 2 and 5 per cent of rape cases result in a conviction. Research shows that as many as 80 per cent of people who suffer this crime do not report it to the police. That is not good enough. Just last week I spoke to staff at the Rape Crisis offices In Barnsley and in Yorkshire, and was told that three factors really worry them – cross-examination procedures; the use of past histories to denigrate the character of the victim and make it appear that she encouraged the rape; and the increase in the date rape drug. Will my right hon Friend consider referring these matters to the Sentencing Advisory Panel with a view to making progress and ensuring protection for rape victims?

Mr Blunkett: The figure for reported rapes resulting in conviction to which my hon Friend referred is 7 per cent. The number of those taken to court is staggering: in 1977, 68 per cent of defendants were found guilty; by 2000, the figure had dropped to 29 per cent. There are clearly serious issues: first, encouraging people to report; secondly, the way that they are handled; and, importantly, finding the right balance for both the male and female involved.

My hon Friend's question was partly dealt with by the Sentencing Advisory Panel when, earlier this year, it came down firmly on avoiding differentials between one type of rape and another, and we accept the panel's judgment. The proposed sentencing guidelines council will assist us in taking a broader look at both crime and sentences so that, we hope, we can get things right.

Mr Andrew MacKay (Bracknell): Does the Home Secretary accept that recent high profile cases have made it clear that both the alleged victim and the person accused should remain anonymous throughout a trial, otherwise there is dreadful adverse publicity for people who are often found innocent? That cannot be right.

Mr Blunkett: It would be a great mistake if we made a judgment on the back of one case. In the case of Mr Hann, we should be prepared to think a little during the summer and, when we make our proposals on the revision of sex offences, we should do so in the light of all the evidence. I do not think that there is disagreement about the fact that victims should remain anonymous; the real issue for all of us is whether, in the transparent society where the media expect us to be honest and open about what is taking place in relation to criminality, it would be acceptable for a particular type of perpetrator to remain anonymous when that was not the case for others. In the light of the campaign for a free society, I shall be interested to hear from Opposition spokesmen whether they feel that is the case.

Vera Baird (Redcar): The cross-departmental inquiry reporting on the thematic investigation into rape was announced in April and it has been said that it would report at the end of June or the beginning of July. Can my right hon Friend give any indication of when there will be a report as to how the three relevant departments intend to take forward the recommendations made by the inspectors? Can he tell us what input the Lord Chancellor's Department had in that cross-departmental inquiry, granted that the report was highly critical of the judiciary, especially its excessive readiness to include previous sexual history?

Mr Blunkett: My hon and learned Friend is right: the report announcing the inquiry was published on 8 April. The action plan has been completed and we shall shortly be able to publish it. I am convinced of the commitment of the Lord Chancellor and his Ministers to join the Attorney General, the Solicitor General and me in ensuring that we get this right. Given that the Lord Chancellor, the Attorney General and I are males, we should keep the lack of understanding of many men strongly in mind when addressing this critical issue.

Mr Julian Brazier (Canterbury): Does the Home Secretary agree that the most tragic and awful rapes are those affecting children, and that we need to reconsider the operation of the court process since it delivers an even lower conviction rate for those accused of those even more terrible offences? May I suggest to the right hon Gentleman that there should be more training for judges and, in particular, that they should be discouraged from allowing defence barristers to bully and confuse already extremely frightened children and from using points of order to get the case deferred from day to day and hour to hour in order to break down a frightened and demoralised child?

Mr Blunkett: The hon Gentleman and I are in entire agreement: we should and will address the need to avoid the adversarial judicial system being applied to juveniles, and I look forward to all-party support.

Notes

1   The ability of members to put down really probing questions is reduced by the lack of information and support staff available to backbenchers. Ministers, by contrast, have the aid of a skilled team of civil servants who provide them with answers to the tabled questions and undertake research into the questioner's known interests and concerns in an attempt to anticipate and prepare the minister for possible supplementaries. (The cost of this preparation in officials' time amounts to an average of £299 per oral answer.) This inequality has led some observers to call for the establishment of a Department of the Opposition to improve the efficiency of Opposition MPs by giving them a staff of civil servants which would go some way to redressing the imbalance between ministers and MPs. Needless to say, no such department has yet been created. However, various disadvantages might result from such a reform. Douglas Wass, in a lecture proposing a Department of the Opposition, conceded that there were fears that the department might inhibit the emergence of new parties, and that the department's civil servants might 'capture the minds' of the Opposition front bench, encouraging a drift to the middle ground commonly presumed to be favoured by the Civil Service.[66]

2   This is perhaps one area in which television coverage has, whilst being helpful in terms of publicity, perhaps given a misleading impression. The kind of 'Commons clash' at Prime Minister's Question Time (PMQT) between the Leader of the Opposition and the Prime Minister which routinely gains television coverage may give the impression that ritual baiting, party point scoring and, above all, a complete lack of information transmission are the outstanding characteristics of

---

66   Quoted in C Turpin, *British Government and the Constitution*, 3rd edn (1993), p 451.

PMQT. What needs to be borne in mind is that PMQT is by far the most politicised of all oral questioning of ministers. A more comprehensive examination of Prime Minister's Questions reveals that, whilst oral questions are often put and dealt with on a purely party political basis, they can yield useful results in terms of scrutiny as well. Information can be gained; useful concessions or statements of intent to which the government can later be held are extracted; inadequacies in government thinking is exposed.

3   The Hansard Society Commission's recent report[67] was highly critical of Question Time, particularly Prime Minister's Questions. The Commission commented:

[Question Time] is dominated by point scoring and the vast majority of questions on both sides of the House are planted by the whips. The high level of political management of questions is illustrated by the fact that in the first 21 PMQs in 1997 the Prime Minister's 'standard reply to [planted questions] – "My honourable friend is absolutely right" – was used 35 times' [S Weir and D Beetham, *Political Power and Democratic Control in Britain: The Democratic Audit of the United Kingdom* (1999), p 432].

4   As a way of simply obtaining information, questions for written answers are generally to be much more effective.

HC Written Answers to Questions, Wednesday 3 July 2002
DEFENCE

Mr Beard: To ask the Secretary of State for Defence what the latest estimate is of the cost of the Trident Acquisition Programme; and if he will make a statement. [67206]

Mr Hoon: The current estimate of the total acquisition cost of the Trident programme, with payments already made expressed at the prices and exchange rates actually incurred and future spend at the current financial year rate (the hybrid) estimate, is now £9,800 million. Since the 2001 estimate and leaving aside the effects of price inflation and exchange rate variation (+£11 million), there has been a real cost increase of £25 million. This increase derives principally from additional costs associated with dockyard projects and with missiles and related equipment, offset by a reduced acquisition cost for the four submarines. Expenditure on the Trident acquisition programme to 30 September 2001 represented over 98 per cent of the total estimate. If all expenditure, past and projected, is brought up to this current year's economic conditions (the non-hybrid estimate) the estimate is £14,376 million.

The programme continues to show an overall reduction in real terms on its original 1982 estimate. This reduction, including the savings resulting from the decision to process missiles at the United States facility at Kings Bay, Georgia, now stands at over £3.7 billion at current prices.

The proportion of the estimate for work undertaken in the United Kingdom continues to be around 70 per cent.

Three in-service Vanguard class submarines are successfully maintained continuous at-sea deterrence, with the fourth, HMS Vanguard, now undergoing planned major overhaul ...

Dr Tonge: To ask the Secretary of State for Defence what new agreements have been reached regarding the Ballistic Missile Early Warning Station at RAF Fylingdales following the end of the 1972 ABM Treaty. [66684]

Mr Ingram: None.

Notes
1   It may be seen from the above that the style of answering written questions is far more straightforward and factual, and a great deal of information of use both in

---

67   *Op cit*, paras 4.19–4.23.

informing debate about public policy in particular areas and in assisting backbenchers and the Opposition in pressing for action from government, as well as exposing flaws in government policy, may be obtained.

2   Whilst, in general, questions of ministers, speeches and debates on policy may have little impact, they may on occasions be decisive. The careers of ministers, even Prime Ministers, can be severely damaged or destroyed during such occasions, whilst the reputation of an administration as a whole may be dented. One example is the famous speech of Norman Lamont, made after his forced resignation, in which he described the Major administration as giving the impression of being 'in office, but not in power'; a similarly wounding attack was made by Sir Geoffrey Howe on Mrs Thatcher in his unexpectedly ferocious resignation speech in November 1990. Conversely, if a minister manages to acquit him or herself with aplomb during a testing debate, his or her stature may be increased. Michael Howard's performance in the debate in October 1995 on his dismissal of the Director of the Prison Service, Derick Lewis (following the publication of the highly critical Learmont report on prisons), was widely regarded as a crucial moment in his career, given that he had been accused of misleading the House. The fact that he was generally regarded to have decisively rebutted the attack on him by Jack Straw, the Shadow Home Secretary, in the debate – one verdict was that 'in ... one of the fiercest prize fights of recent years ... Howard wiped the floor with Jack Straw',[68] – apparently greatly increased his standing amongst Conservative MPs and party activists.[69]

3   The government is of course generally as sure of winning votes taken after debates on policy as it is of carrying its own legislation. But just as with legislation, who wins the actual votes is not the end of the story. An important policy debate was occasioned by the publication of the Scott Report in February 1996. The main formal debate on Scott was in the form of an adjournment debate,[70] but was effectively one of confidence in the government's record on the arms-to-Iraq affair and specifically in Sir Nicholas Lyell and William Waldegrave. Two Conservative MPs and all eight Ulster Unionists voted against the government but it won the division by one vote. It seems therefore that in the final analysis, despite appeals to them by Robin Cook to see the vote as deciding not whether the government was defeated but one which decided 'the quality of democracy in which we live', Conservative MPs perceived the occasion as ultimately a struggle between parties rather than between executive and backbencher. As the Conservative Sir Michael Marsh saw it, 'this debate has been a straight party political battle'.[71]

4   However, quite apart from the narrowness of the result,[72] the outcome cannot be seen simply as a government victory. The threat of rebellion, of possible defeat, had its impact: the government made a 'massive last minute effort to secure the support of waverers and dissident MPs',[73] part of which involved a shift in the government's public stance on Scott. Greater preparedness to admit that mistakes had been made became evident, together with increased willingness to promise

---

68   'Bitter revenge of the uncivil servant', *The Sunday Times*, 22 October 1995.
69   See *The Sunday Times*, 15 October 1995.
70   HC Deb 26 cols 589 *et seq* (February 1996).
71   *Ibid*, col 678.
72   This was generally emphasised in the broadsheet newspapers (which were broadly hostile to the government on the issue). See for example 'Major scrapes in by a single vote', *The Independent*, 27 February 1996.
73   *Ibid*.

(albeit in fairly non-committal terms) to review areas of policy and practice criticised by Scott.

5 One extremely important aspect of government policy-making, namely its decision to bind the UK to international treaties, has historically received very little attention from Parliament, since the power to enter into treaties derives from the royal prerogative and does not require parliamentary assent *per se*. This matter is considered below.

THE SELECT COMMITTEES

Introduction

It was precisely to give backbenchers more in-depth knowledge of government departments that 14 Select Committees were set up in 1979, covering between them each of the major government departments with the exception of the Law Officers' Department and the Lord Chancellor's Department which were brought within the system later.

The current list of Select Committees is as follows: Agriculture; Culture, Media and Sport; Defence; Education and Skills; Transport; Foreign Affairs; Health; Home Affairs; International Development; Northern Ireland Affairs; Scottish Affairs; Work and Pensions; Trade and Industry; Treasury; Lord Chancellor's Department (added in 2003); Welsh Affairs; Environment, Food and Rural Affairs. The following committees cut across departments: Deregulation; Environmental Audit; European Scrutiny; Public Accounts; Public Administration; Science and Technology; Statutory Instruments; Joint Committee on Human Rights.

The Committees were set up due to widespread dissatisfaction with procedures on the floor of the House of Commons as a means of scrutinising the workings of government and a consequent perception that the balance of power between the executive and Parliament was not being maintained under the then current arrangements, as Ryle explains below.

Memorandum by Mr Michael Ryle (SC 35)

. . .

2 At the heart of the functions of the House of Commons today lies the task of scrutinising the policies and acts of the Government. Ministers must explain and defend – or be prepared to explain and defend – everything they do or propose to do. Their principal critics, the Opposition parties, must equally explain and defend their alternative policies. Parliament is essentially a critical forum through which the powers of Government are exercised and in which they are publicly examined.

3 The influence of Parliament depends on the extent to which its critical process both reflects and conditions public opinion. To be effective the House of Commons must both listen to and speak to the people it represents.

4 This public criticism, to be effective, requires the use of procedures which enable ministers, civil servants and others to be examined in detail on their responsibilities and, above all, which provide access to the information necessary to assets their conduct. The great growth in this century in the range, volume and complexity of modern government has meant that this criticism in depth can no longer be achieved by the simple process of debate followed by vote, and that there is not enough time for the actions of ministers to be fully considered on the floor of the House. Hence the development of a range of committee systems.

The new Committees were better equipped and organised than their predecessors, set up in the 1966–70 Parliament. Their function was expressed to be 'to examine the expenditure, administration and policy of the principal government departments'. The Committees allow officials and ministers to be questioned in a systematic and searching manner, which is not always possible on the floor of the House of Commons. Furthermore, the members of the Committees are comparatively well informed and can call on the assistance of expert advisors. The published reports of Committees constitute a significant and valuable source of information about the workings of government. The Committees show an impartiality remarkable in the contentious atmosphere of the Commons; they 'seek to proceed by a more non-partisan approach',[74] conducting their business in an inquisitorial as opposed to adversarial manner on party lines. As the Hansard Society Commission found:

> The strength of the select committees is that they are largely free from the interference of the political parties ... once they are established, the committees tend to derive their influence from effective cross-party collaboration. As a result, the committees provide a forum which allows MPs from all parties to reconcile their conflicting roles in the pursuit of the public interest.[75]

The following is a general description of the work of the Committees.

The Committee System of the House of Commons (from the House of Commons website: www.parliament.uk)

24 Select committees are appointed by the House to perform a variety of tasks on the House's behalf, including scrutinising the work of Government Departments and advising on the procedures and domestic administration of the House. The findings and recommendations of select committees are submitted to the House as printed reports. Members of committees are nominated by the House; for departmental select committees and domestic committees, the necessary motion is made by a member of the Committee of Selection, and for other committees it is usually made by the Government after consultation with the Opposition ...

...

26 A select committee chooses its own chairman, although there is usually an informal understanding about the party from which each chairman will be chosen. Members speak seated around a horse-shoe shaped table, and refer to each other by name. Most select committees call witnesses, and usually meet in public whilst hearing evidence, but always sit in private when deliberating.

27 Most select committees are appointed by standing order, either without a time limit or for the lifetime of a Parliament, and the members, once chosen, usually serve for the remainder of the Parliament, unless changes become necessary. In total, the party membership of all the select committees approximately reflects party proportions in the House.

The work of the departmental committees varies greatly but their general operation can be described. The committee selects a topic or series of topics for inquiry. It may begin by having private briefings and taking specialist advice. It then embarks on a process of information gathering, taking oral and written evidence. Normally, government ministers and officials will give evidence at some stage. The oral and written evidence is published (sometimes omitting material on the grounds of confidentiality). In addition, most inquiries lead to the committee making a report to the House and most committees agree several reports each session. These will make recommendations, most of which will be addressed to the Government. The Government is expected to publish a reply to the report within two months. Many reports, if not formally the subject of motions for debate in the House, are referred to by a 'tag' on the Order Paper as being

---

74   P Craig, *Administrative Law*, 2nd edn (1989), p 69.
75   *Op cit*, para 2.25.

relevant to debates. Between 1979–80 and 1987–88 almost a quarter of all select committee reports were the subject of debates on the floor of the House; since 1987, more than a third of reports from departmental select committees have been debated. Since 1995, provision has also been made for committee reports to be debated on three Wednesday mornings each session.

...

37 Committees are supported by staff of the Department of the Clerk of the House. All the departmental select committees are staffed by the Committee Office and the Clerk of Committees also acts as Clerk of the Liaison Committee ...

38 The staff of each select committee is led by the committee clerk. The number of other staff varies. The average departmental select committee has three or four other staff: typically, another clerk in a training grade and/or a specialist assistant on a short term contract of up to four years, a committee assistant and a secretary ...

Determining membership of the Select Committees: their independence

This relative lack of partisanship, widely seen as one of the most valuable aspects of the Select Committees, can be partly explained by the fact that the Committees' members are chosen from the backbenches: by Convention, no front bench spokespersons are appointed to them, although former ministers may be. However, members of the Committee of Selection, which nominates the MPs to the Committees, are themselves chosen by the whips, so that the government can still exercise partial control in an attempt to keep known outspoken and independently minded MPs off the Committees. The role of the Committee of Selection in seeking to manipulate the membership of Select Committees to the (perceived) advantage of governments has come under sustained scrutiny over the last few years, particularly from the Liaison Committee, made up of the chairs of each departmental Select Committee to oversee and evaluate their work and remit. The following report, which received much publicity and support for its proposals outside Parliament,[76] analyses the problem and proposes a solution.

First Report of the Liaison Committee, *Shifting the Balance: Select Committees and the Executive*, HC 300 (1999–2000)

10 When the 1979 system was introduced, the Committee of Selection was given the responsibility of picking Members to serve on the departmental select committees. If the committees were to be independent monitors of Government, the argument ran, then their membership should not be in the hands of government or party organisation – in practice the Whips. They should be selected to do a job on behalf of the House as a whole. On the same reasoning, this procedure was also applied to the domestic committees appointed in the wake of the Ibbs Report of 1990.

11 In practice, however, the Committee of Selection – itself heavily influenced by the Whips – has nominated Members to serve on select committees in the same way as Members to serve on standing committees or private bill committees – primarily on the basis of lists supplied by the Whips.

12 This has had three unwelcome results:

---

76 See, eg, M Brown, 'Withdraw the whip and give backbenchers power', *The Independent*, 6 March 2000.

- on some occasions there have been long delays – whatever their cause – in setting up select committees at the beginning of a Parliament, at the very time when committees need to put in maximum effort to establish their approach, plan their programme and begin work. These delays are of course convenient for the government of the day.

- when a Member decides to leave a committee there have been long delays – for no good reason – in making the change of membership. Some committees have been as many as three Members short for a matter of months, when there has been no shortage of volunteers.

- Members have undoubtedly been kept off committees, or removed from them, on account of their views. Oppositions as well as governments have been guilty of this, but of course if committees are to be effective scrutineers of government it is the influence of the governing party that causes us the greater concern.

13 It is wrong in principle that party managers should exercise effective control of select committee membership. We propose a new system.

14 The Liaison Committee should be renamed and reconstituted as the Select Committee Panel, mirroring for select committees the role of the Chairmen's Panel for standing committees. It should have a crucial additional task: proposing to the House the names of Members to serve on select committees.

15 In the early weeks of a Parliament there has been no Liaison Committee because there have been no committees and so no Chairmen. Just as the House appoints the Chairman and Deputy Chairmen of Ways and Means at the very beginning of a Parliament, so it should, at the same time and after similar consultation, appoint a Chairman of Committees and two Deputy Chairmen of Committees. The Chairman of Committees should not serve as a Chairman of any other select committee, but the Deputies should not be so restricted. All three would be senior and respected Members of the House, prepared to work in a wholly non-partisan way.

16 Immediately upon appointment, the Chairman and Deputies would invite names for membership of committees, with a deadline for submissions. They would propose to the House the membership of each committee not more than a fortnight after that deadline.

17 Members would be free to propose themselves, or others, with information about qualifications and suitability; and the Whips could make their own suggestions; but the final decisions on nomination would be made by the Chairmen and Deputies. The party managers would also be free to give their views on the division of Chairmanships; but, once again, it would be for the first three members of the Select Committee Panel to decide how to reflect those views in their proposals. It is, after all, up to each committee independently to elect its Chairman.

18 The proposals would be put to the House in amendable, debatable motions, as is already the case. . .

. . .

20 We are sure that this system would be transparent and fair, and that it would protect the independence of select committees.

Notes

1 This report of the Liaison Committee was debated in the House on 9 November 2000 and again on 12 February 2001. In the latter debate, the House endorsed the government's view that 'concentrating patronage in the hands of three senior Members of the House' would not 'increase the transparency or effectiveness of the Committee system'.

2 However, further impetus for change to the present system was given by events in July 2001, following the June 2001 General Election. The government sought to remove two chairs of Select Committees whom it saw as being particularly critical of government policy: Gwyneth Dunwoody, previously chair of the Transport

Committee; and Donald Anderson, former chair of the Foreign Affairs Committee. Extracts from the debate follow.

HC Deb cols 50 *et seq* (16 July 2001)

Mr Andrew Stunell (Hazel Grove): Select Committees are a fundamental method of holding the Executive to account, and if they do not work effectively they cannot exercise scrutiny ... we deprecate the purge – the cull – of senior critics of the Government through the Committee of Selection's work.

In [relation to both Committees] a stern and effective critic of the Government has been dealt a blow by respective Governments. Not only were they stern and effective critics in their own right but they spoke for the Committee. The Select Committee is a representative body of this Parliament. We require it to hold the Government to account; the Chairman is its representative and spokesman. An attack on the Chairman, in this way, is an attack on the House.

Mr Alan Williams (Swansea, West): ... Under our system, democracy does not exist if accountability does not exist. Accountability cannot exist with the current scale of business, the scale of Departments and the volume of money unless we have a working, informed and effective Committee system. That is what this debate is all about – scrutiny.

Committees inevitably develop expertise that can match that of the Departments, so one can understand why Ministers regard them as a threat ... The most important role of Select Committees is to be a bulwark against ministerial diktat ... the departmental Select Committees [are] ... the best innovation in my years in this place. They have enabled Back Benchers in a way that the generalist Committees, such as those on the nationalised industries, did not.

Members on both sides of the House must ensure that Select Committees are independent from the patronage of the Whips. It is glaringly inconsistent that the Government can appoint on any Committee the majority of their scrutineers, which can produce all sorts of nonsense ...

The method of appointment is not just inconsistent: it will be an insult to those who dedicate much of their time and effort to the Committee structure and to Committee work if Committee chairmanships are seen as compensation for ex-Ministers ... It is nonsense and outrageous that Committee chairmanships should be regarded as palliatives for injured pride.

Sir George Young (North-West Hampshire): ... There is a convention among Whips [on the Committee of Selection] that they do not challenge the nominations of other parties. If the other side wants to put someone on a Committee or to keep someone off whose interests may be relevant but unhelpful, that is not challenged ...

Unlike other Committees, the substance of the discussion is not circulated beforehand. We know what Committees we are going to appoint, but we do not know the nominations. They are produced like rabbits out of a hat at the meeting and agreed, usually without discussion or division. The meetings last a matter of minutes.

There needs to be a more rigorous and transparent process, leading to an output that commands greater confidence. The Committees should be better balanced, without being over-dominated by the Whips ...

My second point is that the nominations matter; they are vital. All the recent reports on reform of the House focus on the role of independent Select Committees. They should not be selected by the Government whom they are holding to account. Let us consider the Select Committee on Transport, Local Government and the Regions, which we are appointing tonight. One of the key political issues in coming months will be the tube – the private finance initiative, Bob Kiley, the Greater London assembly and so on. That requires no legislation. It will be covered briefly at Question Time and we can have an Opposition day on it, but that does not provide the opportunity to scrutinise the Executive. The Select Committee will be the only way in which the House can get behind the PFI for the tube.

Mrs Gwyneth Dunwoody (Crewe and Nantwich): ... I do not intend to detain the House long tonight, but I have to say that I am astonished by what has happened ... The fact is that outside the House, the current Parliament is perceived as not doing its job properly, and the Select Committees are regarded as a means of carefully examining not only what Whitehall and the Government are doing but what all the arms of government and their myriad agencies are doing. There is no other comparable form of machinery in the House of Commons. There is no other way of doing the job.

... What the Select Committees do matters. It matters because the House of Commons must never become a great morass of people doing what they are told not by the electorate but by the Executive. That is why it is important that we vote tonight on who serves on which Committee. That is why it is important to say to the electorate as a whole that we do a vital job....

Notes

1 The government was defeated on the motions relating to the composition of the Foreign Affairs Committee (that is, on the chairmanship of Anderson) by 301 votes to 232 and the Transport Committee (chairmanship of Dunwoody) by 308 to 221. Well over 100 Labour MPs rebelled. While this was widely seen in the media as evidence of a new vigour and independent spirit amongst the previously 'robotic' Parliamentary Labour Party, it should be noted that the vote was a free one, and not on a matter of policy.[77]

2 Whatever the wider significance of this rebellion, it helped keep the issue of selection of Select Committee members firmly on the parliamentary agenda. The matter was returned to by the Liaison Committee in 2002,[78] considering a report by the Modernisation Committee on the matter. It suggested an alternative, a Committee of Nomination, made up of senior backbench MPs, with no whips. The proposal to change to the new system was debated by the House on 14 May 2002.[79] Robin Cook urged members to:

welcome the fact that the [Nomination] Committee will reinforce the standing of Select Committees and make it clear that nomination is independent of the control of party or Executive machine. As a result, the Select Committees of the House will carry greater legitimacy, command greater confidence and bring greater authority to their task of scrutiny.

(3) In the event, the proposal to replace the Committee of Selection with one of Nomination was narrowly defeated, by 209 votes to 195. As an example of attempts by the government to control and limit the independence of Select Committees (ironically enough, since that was the very mischief which the change was designed to limit) it should be noted that, although the proposal was brought forward by Robin Cook, a member of the government, not one Cabinet Minister voted in favour of the change and, as one Member pointed out after the vote, although it was a free vote, members of the whips office were present, directing members of the Labour Party to vote against this proposal (see Mr Prentice's point of order at col 720).

77 See further, Cowley and Stuart, *op cit*, at 282–84.
78 Second Report of the Liaison Committee, *Select Committees: Modernisation Proposals*, HC 692 (2001–02).
79 HC Deb cols 666 *et seq*.

The remit and work of the Select Committees

Jurisdiction of the Committees

Second Report from the Select Committee on Procedure, HC 19-II (1989–90), para 5

The general terms of reference of these committees are as set out in Standing Order No 130. . . . The committees are responsible for the interpretation of their own terms of reference. The committees are entitled to examine the expenditure, administration and policy of the principal Government departments, and also of their 'associated public bodies'. The terms of the standing orders do not define 'associated public bodies', but the then Chancellor of the Duchy of Lancaster said in his speech on 25 June 1979 that:

> The Government also accept the Procedure Committee's view that the committees must be able to look at the activities of some public bodies that exercise authority of their own and over which ministers do not have the same direct authority as they have over their own departments. The test in every case will be whether there is a significant degree of ministerial responsibility for the body concerned.

Associated public bodies therefore include all nationalised industries, fringe bodies and other Governmental organisations within the responsibilities of the department or departments concerned for which ministers are ultimately answerable. They do not, however, include bodies for which ministers are not answerable to Parliament, even though these bodies may be in receipt of Government funds. There will no doubt be borderline cases, but in general the existing principles of parliamentary accountability can be applied.

Notes

1   As the Liaison Committee noted:[80]

> All committees examine the work of non-departmental public bodies within their remit. For some, such as the Culture, Media and Sport Committee, this is a considerable task: the Department of Culture, Media and Sport is a small department but sponsors more such bodies than any other; and 95% of its programme expenditure is spent by quangos. The Agriculture Committee and the Defence Committee have begun rolling programmes to examine the agencies for which they are responsible, and other committees are following a similar pattern.

2   Parliament agreed on 14 May 2002 upon a set of 'core tasks' for Select Committees, following suggestions of the Liaison[81] and Modernisation[82] Committees. This was also something strongly recommended by the Hansard Society Commission,[83] which argued that this would make 'scrutiny more systematic'. The following extract sets out those tasks, together with guidance on them from the Liaison Committee.

---

80   First Report of the Liaison Committee, *Shifting the Balance: Unfinished Business* HC 321-II (2000–01), para 79.
81   HC 692 (2001–02), para 16.
82   HC 224 (2001–02), para 34.
83   *Op cit*, paras 3.23–3.46.

Departmental Select Committee Objectives and Tasks: An Illustrative Template,
Appendix 3 to the First Report of the Liaison Committee for 2002-03,
Annual Report, **HC 558 (2002–03)**

OBJECTIVE A: TO EXAMINE AND COMMENT ON THE POLICY OF THE DEPARTMENT

Task 1: To examine policy proposals from the UK Government and the European Commission in Green Papers, White Papers, draft Guidance etc, and to inquire further where the Committee considers it appropriate

This calls for more systematic scrutiny of proposals made. It is not intended to involve formal written or oral evidence as a matter of course, but to ensure that a Committee is at least apprised of proposals and has the opportunity to consider whether detailed scrutiny of them should form part of their programme of work.

Departments must ensure that Committees are informed directly of policy proposals and provided with the necessary documentation, rather than waiting to be asked.

Task 2: To identify and examine areas of emerging policy, or where existing policy is deficient, and make proposals

This calls for Committees to identify areas where, based on judgement of Members, views of others etc, a Committee inquiry would be worthwhile.

Ministers must be prepared to give proper consideration to policy proposals from committees. This may involve revision of the practice on instant reaction/rebuttal.

Task 3: To conduct scrutiny of any published draft bill within the Committee's responsibilities

This calls for Committees to commit time for necessary oral evidence and reporting, subject to its timetable for other inquiries.

Ministers must ensure that committees are warned early on the likely appearance of draft bills: must consult with committee chairmen on how they are to be handled: and must allow a decent time for committee consideration.

Task 4: To examine specific output from the department expressed in documents or other decisions

This calls for a formal framework for being informed of secondary legislation, circulars and guidance, treaties and previously identified casework decisions, so that they can if needed be drawn to a Committee's attention.

Departments will have to engage in co-operative discussions with committee staff on the best means of ensuring that committees are kept abreast of such outputs.

OBJECTIVE B: TO EXAMINE THE EXPENDITURE OF THE DEPARTMENT

Task 5: To examine the expenditure plans and out-turn of the department, its agencies and principal NDPBs

This calls for a systematic framework for committee scrutiny of the Department's Main and Supplementary Estimates: its expenditure plans; and its annual accounts.

Departments will as a matter of course have to produce more explanatory material on financial matters, eg on Supplementary Estimates, underspends etc.

OBJECTIVE C: TO EXAMINE THE ADMINISTRATION OF THE DEPARTMENT

Task 6: To examine the department's Public Service Agreements, the associated targets and the statistical measurements employed, and report if appropriate

This calls for an established cycle of written scrutiny and annual reporting of results.

Ministers must be prepared to be genuinely responsive to committee concerns on PSAs etc.

Task 7: To monitor the work of the department's Executive Agencies, NDPBs, regulators and other associated public bodies

This calls for a systematic cycle of scrutiny of annual reports. It does not require either written or oral evidence except where a Committee judges it to be necessary.

The bodies concerned must ensure that their accountability to Parliament is recognised by full and regular provision of information, including annual reports and other publications.

Task 8: To scrutinise major appointments made by the department

This would call for scrutiny of all major appointments made.

Departments would have to systematically notify committees in advance of all major appointments pending and/or made.

Task 9: To examine the implementation of legislation and major policy initiatives

This would call for a framework of detailed annual progress reports from departments on Acts and major policy initiatives so that committees could decide whether to undertake inquiry.

Ministers must be more willing to provide for annual reports on particular pieces of legislation, and departments to provide detailed annual reports on identified policy areas or initiatives.

OBJECTIVE D: TO ASSIST THE HOUSE IN DEBATE AND DECISION

Task 10: To produce Reports which are suitable for debate in the House, including Westminster Hall, or debating committees.

This could call for committees to come to an explicit view when deciding on an inquiry as to whether a debate was in due course envisaged.

Examination of treaties

One area of Select Committee work that has been of increasing importance over the last few years has been the examination of treaties which the government proposes to enter into.

Second Report of the Procedure Committee, *Parliamentary Scrutiny of Treaties*, HC 210 (1999–2000)

Introduction

1 The power to make treaties is a prerogative power vested in the Crown and exercised on the advice of the Secretary of State for Foreign and Commonwealth Affairs in consultation with other Ministers; there is no constitutional requirement for treaties to be laid before or approved by Parliament. While many treaty obligations necessitate the introduction of primary or secondary legislation which must be passed by Parliament, treaties which require no such legislation (or which require only secondary legislation subject to negative resolution) may come into force without any parliamentary debate having taken place. Over time a number of conventions have evolved regarding Parliamentary input into treaty-making – in particular the so-called 'Ponsonby Rule', first formulated in 1924 – but it has been observed that 'the lack of formal parliamentary involvement in treaty-making distinguishes the British Parliament from most other national legislatures'. [Richard Ware, '*Parliament and Treaties*', in C Carstairs and R Ware (eds), *Parliament and International Relations*, 1991.]

...

The Ponsonby Rule

4 The Ponsonby Rule is a convention whereby almost all treaties which do not come into force on signature are laid before Parliament for 21 days before they are ratified ... In a debate in the House in 1924 Mr Ponsonby affirmed that ...:

In the case of important treaties, the Government will, of course, take an opportunity of submitting them to the House for discussion within this period ... if there is a formal demand for discussion forwarded through the usual channels from the Opposition or any other party, time will be found for the discussion of the treaty in question. [*Hansard*, 1.4.1924, c 1999.]

5 ... Over time the requirement for a treaty to lie on the table for 21 days has hardened into a requirement for all treaties to be laid for at least 21 *sitting* days before ratification. The FCO interprets the Ponsonby Rule as applying to acceptance, approval and accession as well as to ratification, and since 1998 the FCO has also applied the Rule to treaties subject only to the mutual notification of the completion of necessary internal procedures by each contracting party. Whilst almost every British government has respected this convention since its inception in 1924, it has no statutory or otherwise enforceable basis. However, the present Government has strongly reaffirmed its commitment to the Rule ...

9 The Minister of State was unable to give us a categorical assurance that a formal request from a select committee – whether expressed through a Report to the House, and EDM signed by the Members, or a request endorsed by the Liaison Committee – would of itself trigger a debate. His view was that this was necessarily a matter for the business managers. However, he also stated that if a select committee sought a debate on a treaty involving major issues, 'I do not see that there would be the kind of resistance that we might imagine'. He also told us that the Government was willing to show flexibility in regard of timing, for instance if a select committee wished to conduct an inquiry that was likely to take more than the 21 days specified under the Ponsonby Rule.

[The Committee then considered the limited exceptions to the Ponsonby Rule finding that they were not of great importance and alternative means of scrutiny were generally found.]

Other countries' experiences

13 The Defence Committee pointed out in its report on NATO enlargement that in most other Allied countries the consent of the legislature is required before treaties can be ratified, and that in many cases parliamentary committees make recommendations to the legislature before ratification is debated. This is also the case in most OECD countries. Of the current 16 NATO member states, only Canada shares with the UK a ratification process which requires no formal involvement from the legislature. In other member countries treaties are ratified by the head of state upon authorisation of the legislature, usually by a simple majority (although in the case of the United States a two-thirds majority in the Senate is required for final approval of the resolution of ratification). Although in most of these countries the assent of the legislature is required for the ratification of all international agreements, in Norway, for example, the consent of Parliament is needed only for issues of 'special importance'.

Note

The Committee then went on to make recommendations. The government's response to this Report[84] accepted its main recommendations, stating that:

The FCO will ensure that a copy of each Command Paper and accompanying Explanatory Memorandum (EM) for treaties laid before Parliament under the Ponsonby Rule is sent to what the FCO judges to be the relevant departmental select committee.

It added:

In accordance with the 'Ponsonby Rule' time for consideration of a treaty by a select committee should normally be within 21 sitting days, but in cases where a committee wished to conduct an inquiry that was likely to take more than 21 days, it is open to a committee to ask for an extension. The Government would aim to respond positively to such requests provided circumstances permit and cases are justified.

---

84 Published by the Procedure Committee, HC 990 (2000–01).

It also gave a positive response to the request for an undertaking 'that if a select committee requests that a debate should be held on the floor of the House before ratification of a treaty involving major political, military or diplomatic issues ... and if that request is supported by the Liaison Committee, then that request would normally be acceded to'.

Scrutiny of departmental expenditure

Clearly, scrutiny over the national finances is a vital link in the chain of Commons control of the executive; it is, however, patchy.[85] As Colin Turpin comments, government borrowing 'largely escapes scrutiny' while detailed parliamentary examination of departmental supply expenditure 'was abandoned long ago'.[86] However, in the area of verifying the authorisation of expenditure and ascertaining that value for money has been obtained, the Public Accounts Committee has been notably effective. It is, as Stanley de Smith notes, 'scrupulously non-partisan',[87] while the value of its investigations is greatly enhanced by the fact that the Comptroller and Auditor-General, an officer of the House and therefore independent from the government and assisted by a staff of several hundreds, sits with it. One of its most influential recent reports, which received a great deal of attention, was concerned with the controversial issue of the effectiveness of the Private Finance Initiative (PFI).[88]

The departmental Select Committees are also making greater efforts in terms of financial scrutiny, although the Liaison Committee recently reported that the situation remained unsatisfactory.

Second Report of the Liaison Committee, *Select Committees: Modernisation Proposals* HC 692 (2001–02)

10 ... At present some limited examination of expenditure plans is undertaken by most departmental select committees. Greater provision of specialist assistance from the scrutiny unit should enable committees to ensure that Departments are made accountable and transparent in more policy areas.

11 The pressure for select committees to engage in more thorough scrutiny of expenditure – which should range more widely than just a review of the Estimates – is not new. But these hopes have not been realised. This is the fault of select committees. As early as 1978 the Procedure Committee Report which led to the establishment of departmentally related select committees recommended that [those Committees] 'should be encouraged to examine the ... Estimates referred to them in the conduct of their scrutiny of departmental policy and administration ...'. In 1981 the Select Committee on Procedure (Supply), which recommended the establishment of Estimates Days, stated in its Report that the departmentally related committees 'should allot some time each session to the examination of their departmental Estimates, but ... the amount of time and depth of such scrutiny should be a matter for each committee to determine'. This view was reinforced by the Procedure Committee in 1990 in its Report on The Working of the Select Committee System. These recommendations were taken a stage further by our predecessors in 1997 when they proposed that select committees 'should intensify examination of their departmental reports'.

---

85 See further J McEldowney, 'The control of public expenditure', in J Jowell and D Oliver, *The Changing Constitution*, 4th edn (2000).
86 *British Government and the Constitution* (1990), p 482.
87 SA de Smith, *Constitutional and Administrative Law*, 6th edn (1994), p 287.
88 Forty-Second Report of the Public Accounts Committee, *Managing the Relationship to Secure a Successful Partnership in PFI Projects*, HC 460 (2001–02).

12 The 1999 Procedure Committee Report on Procedure for Debate on the Government's Expenditure Plans adopted a more prescriptive approach, recommending that, by Standing Order, the main Estimates and the departmental plans and annual reports should be referred to the relevant select committee, who would be obliged to report on them to the House. From outside the House, the most recent impetus in favour of extending the financial scrutiny role of select committees came from the *Hansard* Society whose principal new recommendation was that each committee should 'pilot and evaluate a ... Finance and Audit Sub-Committee [which would] consider ... Estimates and departmental allocations, audit and value for money inquires, Public Service Agreements, performance indicators and outcomes'.

13 **The Modernisation Committee is right to re-emphasise the importance of financial scrutiny within the overall remit of the departmental select committees. The fact that their record so far has been relatively patchy should strike a cautionary note. Committees have to remember that they belong to the House. The House has the right to spell out what it expects of them.**

We recommend that the National Audit Office be invited to help assess the need for specialist and other support staff for select committees and to advise on how this could best be provided, and that the House of Commons Commission should look favourably on funding for staffing increases which may be proposed [para 29].

14 We are glad that the Modernisation Committee accepted this proposal which our Chairman put forward when he gave evidence. **Staffing levels** for the new scrutiny unit will need to be agreed by the House of Commons Commission in time for its introduction in the financial year 2002/03. Staffing is to include secondments as well as permanent and short term staff. We understand that the National Audit Office, which already supplies secondees to the Committee Office, is prepared to consider providing further expert staff, particularly to assist with financial scrutiny. We understand also that it would be willing to help assess how extra specialist and support staff might best be provided to meet any needs identified by the House.

Notes

1   A major problem for Select Committees, noted by the Liaison Committee in its Annual Report for 2002, was that draft copies of estimates of departmental expenditure were not being made available to Select Committees in time for them to be scrutinised before Parliament was called upon to approve them:

for the 2002 Winter Supplementary Estimates, committees received no effective advance warning at all.

... a similarly unsatisfactory position has arisen over the Spring Supplementary Estimates for 2002–03. These were presented on 28 February 2003 and taken in the House on 11 March 2003. This situation is unacceptable. Effective scrutiny is a two-way process, requiring the active co-operation of the Government in ensuring that committees have adequate time to complete their work.[89]

2   A new role for Select Committees has also been found in holding confirmation hearings for key public appointments made by government, though the Committees have no veto over the decision.[90] As seen above, this is now one of the core tasks of Select Committees. The Liaison Committee in 2003 noted by way of example that 'The Treasury Committee has already established an effective role by scrutinising each appointment made by the Chancellor to the Bank of

89   HC 558 (2002–03), paras 27 and 28.
90   See the First Report of the Liaison Committee, *Shifting the Balance: Unfinished Business*, HC 321-II (2000–01), paras 90–93.

England's Monetary Policy Committee. During 2002 there were three such appointments'.[91]

Powers of the Select Committees

The Procedure Committee sets out the basic position:[92]

7   Select Committees (and their sub-committees) normally have the power to 'send for persons, papers and records'. This power is understood as a power to 'order' the attendance of persons and the submission of papers ...

8   Any official who appears before a Select Committee or who submits papers to it does so on behalf of his ministers. As the Procedure Committee emphasised in its report:

The over-riding principle concerning access to Government information should be that the House has power to enforce the responsibility of ministers for the provision of information or the refusal of information. It would not, however, be appropriate for the House to seek directly or through its committees to enforce its rights to secure information from the executive at a level below that of the ministerial head of the department concerned (normally a Cabinet minister), since such a practice would tend to undermine rather than strengthen the accountability of ministers to the House.

In practice, committees normally proceed on the basis of 'requests' for departmental witnesses and evidence rather than through the exercise of formal powers ...

17   ... The departmental committees have ... been given power to appoint specialist advisors either to supply information which is not readily available or to elucidate matters of complexity within the committee's orders of reference....

As the description of the Committees on the House of Commons website clarifies:

36(a) ... with the exception of the Committee on Standards and Privileges with regard to Members of the Commons, a committee cannot order the attendance of Members of either House of Parliament; but Members may attend voluntarily. While a committee cannot, therefore, insist on Ministers attending one of its hearings, Ministers will normally accept an invitation to give evidence. Similarly the committees can only request that government departments send papers and records. The Government has frequently reaffirmed that ministers and civil servants will attend committees when requested and provide committees with the information necessary to their inquiries. The power to send for persons, papers and records is not given to the Joint Committee on Statutory Instruments, nor to the Standing Orders Committee.

The ability to obtain Government documents

The record of the Committees in obtaining the government records they require gives rise to most concern: in the words of the 1997 Liaison Committee Report, 'It is in [this area] that most difficulties have arisen'.[93] Select Committees have the formal power to send for papers; however, Parliament can compel the production of documents from a department headed by a Secretary of State (that is, most departments) only through an address to the Crown.[94] Furthermore, as Tomkin notes,[95] the current draft of the

---

91   HC 558 (2002–03), para 20.
92   HC 19-II (1989–90).
93   *Op cit*, para 14.
94   Erskine May, *Treatise on the Law, Privileges, Proceedings and Usage of Parliament*, 21st edn (1989), p 630.
95   *Op cit*, pp 79–80.

Cabinet Office memorandum *Departmental Evidence and Response to Select Committees* states (at para 50):

> The Government's commitment to provide as much information as possible to Select Committees is met largely through the provision of memoranda, written replies to Committees' questions and oral evidence from Ministers and officials. It does not amount to a commitment to provide access to internal files, private correspondence, including advice given on a confidential basis or working papers. Should a Committee press to see such documents, rather than accepting written or oral evidence on the subject, departments should consult their Ministers and the Cabinet Office Central Secretariat.

The Liaison Committee found that governmental promises to make time for a Commons debate on a refusal to provide requested documentation have not been honoured: 'There have been a significant number of cases where committees have been refused specific documents but the government has not provided time for the subject to be debated.' The reference to a debate is to the House's formal power to make a finding that a refusal to supply requested documents – or indeed a refusal to attend a Committee at all – represented a contempt of Parliament. Such a finding could only be made after a debate and the Committee recommended that 'The onus should be shifted onto the government to defend in the House its refusal to disclose information to a select committee' (para 16) and that the power of the Privileges Committee 'to require that specific documents or records in the possession of a Member relating to its inquiries be laid before the Committee' be extended to all Committees.

A recent example deriving from the 'Arms to Sierra Leone' affair[96] illustrates the growing assertiveness of Select Committees in relation to this issue. Problems arose between the Foreign Affairs Committee and the Foreign Secretary, Robin Cook, during the Committee's investigation into the affair in which it appeared that Foreign Office officials had been aware that arms shipments from the UK were in breach of a UN embargo on the export of arms to Sierra Leone. The Minister refused to provide the Committee with a number of key telegrams from the UK's High Commissioner in Sierra Leone to the Foreign Office; the objection was the usual one of the need to preserve confidences. A compromise formula, that a summary of the telegrams would be made available to the Committee and members of it would be able to visit the Foreign Office to examine the actual documents to verify the accuracy of the summaries, was eventually reached.[97]

Below, the Liaison Committee reviews the success of Committees in obtaining government documents.

First Report of the Liaison Committee, *Shifting the Balance: Unfinished Business,* HC 321-II (2000–01)

121 The Treasury Sub-committee faced a number of problems in securing documents. During its inquiry into HM Customs and Excise it was refused an internal report on the possibility of merging the revenue departments and a report on measures to combat tobacco smuggling. The Treasury Committee commented:

... we remain mystified as to why the Government felt forced to employ a range of spurious and conflicting excuses to explain its reluctance to hand over to parliamentary scrutiny an old report

---

96 For a lively account, see A Rawnsley, *Servants of the People: the Inside Story of New Labour* (2001), below, p 345.
97 See the Committee's Reports, HC 760 and 1057(I) (1997–98).

on a routine matter concerning departmental administration. With regard to the Taylor report, we deplore the manner in which the Government has published those snippets of Mr Taylor's advice which support the new strategy for dealing with tobacco smuggling when it has refused to publish, in any form, his advice in full.

122 By contrast, in the Home Affairs Committee's investigation of events at Blantyre House it was able to draw upon confidential internal documents, which contributed to the authority and quality of the report which resulted.

123 The Treasury Sub-committee also identified a point which potentially affects all committees. In an inquiry into the Government's debt and cash management it was refused sight of the non-confidential responses to consultation documents, because those consulted had not been warned that there was a possibility that their responses might be made public. The Sub-committee secured an undertaking from the Treasury that future consultations would make clear the possibility of publication unless confidentiality were requested.

124 The Treasury Committee and its Sub-committee invite us to consider the circumstances in which select committees should have access to consultation responses. We understand that, if those consulted had not been warned of the possibility of publication, a department would be reluctant to break a *de facto* relationship of confidentiality, even if responses contained nothing sensitive. However, the results of a consultation can be very useful to a select committee inquiry; and such access can also benefit a department, for example in demonstrating the grounds for subsequent action. We note that the Deregulation Committee routinely receives the responses to consultation on proposals for deregulation orders.

125 We think that the approach adopted by the Treasury Sub-committee is the right one. All Government consultation documents should make clear the possibility that the responses may be passed to the relevant select committee, and may be published, unless confidentiality is requested. We are glad to see this provision in Criterion 2 of the Cabinet Office code on written consultation, and trust that this will now be standard practice in all Government consultations

...

103 Committees report generally good relations with departments, although some difficulties have been identified. The Culture, Media and Sport, Agriculture, and Welsh Affairs Committees reported poor or delayed responses to requests for evidence or information. Although the Agriculture Committee found improvements over the last year in the general level of information it received from the Ministry of Agriculture, Fisheries and Food, it had experienced particular difficulties with submission of written evidence by the Ministry. Over the last year only two submissions had arrived on time, and one arrived the day after the evidence session for which it was intended. The memorandum updating progress on recommendations, of which several months' notice had been given, arrived nearly three weeks late, and the one update for which DETR was responsible arrived nearly six weeks late.

...

105 A failure by departments to inform committees of relevant developments is a theme running through the annual reports. This should be simple enough to resolve with clear instructions from Ministers to parliamentary branches, liaison officers and private offices.

The ability to call witnesses

As the Procedure Committee noted in 1990:[98]

Officials appearing before Select Committees do so on behalf of their ministers. It is customary, therefore, for ministers to decide which officials (including members of the armed services) should

---

98 HC 19-II (1989–90).

appear to give evidence. Select Committees have in the past generally accepted this position. Should a committee invite a named official to appear, the minister concerned, if he did not wish that official to represent him, might suggest that another official could more appropriately do so, or that he himself should give evidence to the committee. If a committee insisted on a particular official appearing before them – whether serving in the UK or overseas – they could issue a formal order for his attendance. In such an event the official would have to appear before the committee. In all circumstances, the official would remain subject to ministerial instructions as to how to answer questions.

It should be noted that, in addition to examining the expenditure, administration and policy of Government departments and associated public bodies, Select Committees are free to seek evidence from whomsoever they please, and are entitled to require the production of papers by private bodies or individuals so long as these are relevant to the committees' work.

Note

Up until very recently, a convention prevented the Select Committees from questioning the most important member of the executive – the Prime Minister. The Liaison Committee proposed a once a year session.

First Report of the Liaison Committee, *Shifting the Balance: Unfinished Business,* HC 321-II (2000–01)

143 A central theme of *Shifting the Balance* is a more integrated approach to the work of select committees in scrutinising Government. When reviewing progress on our recommendations, we therefore also considered how the scrutiny of Government as a whole might be improved. Now that the Government produces an Annual Report on its policies and performance, we thought that the logical response in terms of scrutiny was for the Liaison Committee to take evidence following the publication of each Annual Report. There is, after all, no other select committee which is able to consider the whole range of select committee responsibilities. By the same token, the only Minister who would be able to give evidence on the overall direction and performance of the Government would be the Prime Minister himself.

...

145 Our invitation to the Prime Minister took this factor into account: we proposed that he should give evidence once a year, and it was clear that this occasion would be *sui generis* and would not provide a general precedent. We also thought that Parliamentary questioning of the nation's Chief Executive, not in the noisy and adversarial atmosphere of the Chamber but in the calmer surroundings of a committee room, with the ability to pursue lines of questioning, would be very welcome to the voters who put us here.

This invitation was refused by the Prime Minister at the time, on 29 January 2001, mainly on the basis of convention. However, as the Committee commented:[99]

No Prime Minister can be expected to carry a detailed knowledge of the whole range of Government responsibilities, and detailed questioning is not our intention. Our proposal was to explore exactly those broad strategic themes which are raised in the Government's Annual Report and with which the Prime Minister is closely concerned; and we suggested that a single session each year, with advance indication of the themes, should rule out a request from any other committee to the Prime Minister to give evidence ...

150 ... if we were for the purposes of argument to accept that responsibilities lie with Secretaries of State and other Departmental Ministers, and not with the Prime Minister, this would surely lead one to ask: for what is the Prime Minister responsible, if he is not responsible for the Government's performance and programme? Where does this particular buck stop?

---

99   HC 321-II (2000–01), para 149.

Note

However, in a recent innovation, perhaps intended to deflect criticism that Mr Blair's administration had little respect for Parliament, it was announced that the Prime Minister would make himself available for questioning, once a year, by the Liaison Committee, a Select Committee composed of the chairs of the departmental Select Committees.

Liaison Committee Press Notice No 4 of Session 2001–02, 26 April 2002

The Rt Hon Alan Williams, MP (Labour, Swansea West), Chairman of the Liaison Committee, said . . .:

While the Liaison Committee as a whole has not yet had time to consider the Prime Minister's proposal, I know they will be delighted with this very significant extension of accountability to Parliament.

The Chairs of all the House's investigative Committees are on this large Committee. By definition, they are all very knowledgeable in their own Committee's specialism. So several hours of wide-ranging questioning over domestic and international issues will be a demanding session.

To the best of my knowledge, this is the first time in the whole of the post-war period that a Prime Minister has appeared before a Committee of the House for intensive questioning.

Notes

1   The first of these sessions took place on 16 July 2002; the second on 4 February 2003.[100] They were generally seen as providing for far more revealing, probing questioning of the Prime Minister than that allowed for by parliamentary questions. The Liaison Committee itself has commented[101] that the sessions 'met our aim of achieving a "more productive and informative" event than is possible under the current operation of Prime Minister's Questions in the Chamber' (para 9).

2   The power to question members of the executive is clearly crucial to the efficacy of the Committees and, not surprisingly, has caused controversy. As Tomkin notes,[102] whilst MPs and ministers can be required to attend by committees if an initial request is refused, and, in the last resort, ordered to attend by the House, no MP has been ordered to attend 'this century' and no minister has ever been ordered to attend. In 1979, the Leader of the House pledged that '. . . every minister . . . will do all in his or her power to co-operate with the new system of committees'. Despite this promise, the Committees have sometimes found themselves frustrated when investigating areas of acute sensitivity by the refusal of certain key witnesses to attend. For example, in 1984, the government would not allow the Director of Government Communications Headquarters (GCHQ) to give evidence to the Select Committee on Employment which was enquiring into the trade union ban at GCHQ. Similarly, in 1986, the Defence Committee, in the course of its enquiry into the Westland affair, wished to interview certain officials; again the minister in question would not allow them to attend.

3   Successive administrations have set out their views on the attendance of civil servants before Select Committees in the following document, first issued by the Cabinet Office in 1994 and subsequently updated.

---

100 See www.parliament.the-stationery-office.co.uk/pa/cm200203/cmselect/cmliaisn/334-i/
3012101.htm and www.publications.parliament.uk/pa/cm200102/cmselect/cmliaisn/1065/
106501.htm for transcripts.

101 In its Annual Report for 2002, HC 558 (2002–03).

102 *Op cit*, p 75.

Cabinet Office, *Departmental Evidence and Response to Select Committees* (1999) (extracts)[103]

1 This memorandum gives guidance to officials from Departments and their Agencies who may be called upon to give evidence before, or prepare memoranda for submission to, Parliamentary Select Committees. It replaces the December 1994 edition.

2 In providing guidance, the memorandum attempts to summarise a number of long-standing conventions that have developed in the relationship between Parliament, in the form of its Select Committees, and successive Governments. As a matter of practice, Parliament has generally recognised these conventions. It is important to note, however, that this memorandum is a Government document. Although Select Committees will be familiar with its contents, it has no formal Parliamentary standing or approval, nor does it claim to have.

. . .

Section 3: Role of Officials giving evidence to Select Committees

Summoning of Named Officials

40 ... it is customary for Ministers to decide which official or officials should represent them. Select Committees have generally accepted this position.

41 Where a Select Committee indicates that it wishes to take evidence from a particular named official, Ministers will usually agree to meet such a request, but this is subject to two important qualifications:

(a) Ministers retain the right to suggest an alternative official to that named by the Committee if they feel that the former is better placed to represent them. While the Committee is under no obligation to accept the Minister's proposal, it is open to the Minister to appear personally before the Committee in the unlikely event of there being no agreement about which official should most appropriately give evidence.

(b) It has been agreed that it is not the role of Select Committees to act as disciplinary tribunals (see paragraphs 70–74). A Minister will therefore wish to consider carefully a Committee's request to take evidence from a named official where this is likely to expose the individual concerned to questioning about their personal responsibility or the allocation of blame as between them and others. This will be particularly so where the official concerned has been subject to, or may be subject to, an internal departmental inquiry or disciplinary proceedings. Ministers may, in such circumstances, wish to suggest either that he give evidence personally to the Committee or that a designated senior official do so on their behalf.

42 If a Committee nonetheless insists on a particular official appearing before them, contrary to the Minister's wishes, the formal position remains that it could issue an order for attendance, and request the House to enforce it. In such an event (so far unprecedented) the official, as any other citizen, would have to appear before the Committee but, in all circumstances, would remain subject to Ministerial instruction under the terms of this Guidance and of the Code.

Agency Chief Executives

43 Where a Select Committee wishes to take evidence on matters assigned to an Agency in its Framework Document, Ministers will normally wish to nominate the Chief Executive as being the official best placed to represent them. While Agency Chief Executives have managerial authority to the extent set out in their Framework Documents, like other officials they give evidence on behalf of the Minister to whom they are accountable and are subject to that Minister's instruction.

---

103 The full text of the Code is available from the Cabinet Office website: www.cabinet-office. gov.uk/central/1999/selcom/intro.htm.

Position of Retired Officials

44 Given the above, it is extremely rare, but not unprecedented, for Committees to request evidence from officials who have retired. A Committee could, again, issue an order for attendance if it chose. However, retired officials cannot be said to represent the Minister and hence cannot contribute directly to his accountability to the House. It is primarily for these reasons, as well as for obvious practical points of having access to up to date information and thinking, that Ministers would expect evidence on Government matters to be given by themselves or by serving officials who report to them.

Notes

1   This ability of ministers to control which of their officials appear before Select Committees is justified in terms of ministerial responsibility; since ministers, not civil servants, are responsible to Parliament and civil servants give advice only on behalf of ministers, it is for ministers to choose which civil servants they think are appropriate to 'represent' them. However, this interpretation of ministerial responsibility has recently run into renewed controversy. During the Scott Inquiry, two retired officials in the Ministry of Defence (MoD), Mr Primrose and Mr Harding, had important first-hand information about aspects of the Supergun affair, and the Trade and Industry Select Committee (TISC), which was investigating the affair, wished to interview them. The MoD refused to allow them to attend.[104] Sir Richard Scott has commented[105] on the wider significance of this episode, turning on its head the notion that ministerial responsibility justifies this kind of control by ministers:

Given that ministers have not got personal knowledge of a vast number of things that happen within their department ... their obligation I think is to facilitate the giving of information by those who do have personal knowledge of the matter. [Scott then goes on to note the Osmotherly rules – allowing ministers to prevent civil servants from giving evidence to Select Committees.] I think that ministerial accountability does require ministers to facilitate Select Committees obtaining first-hand evidence from those with first-hand knowledge of the matter in question.[106]

2   More recent examples of refusals by ministers and others to appear before Committees are not hard to find. In a Special Report of the Transport, Local Government and the Regions Committee, *The Attendance of a Minister from HM Treasury before the Committee*,[107] the Committee was enquiring into London Underground and was informed that:

important decisions about the future funding of improvements were being taken by HM Treasury. This is a concern which had been raised in earlier inquiries on the subject. In particular, it has been alleged that the Treasury made:

(i)   the principal decision to fund improvements to London Underground by a Public Private Partnership (PPP); and

(ii) key decisions about the scope and nature of the deal: it was responsible for deciding the timing and level of funding, and for delaying vital improvements to the network.

Its report went on:

---

104 See Inquiry into Exports of Defence Equipment and Dual-Use Goods to Iraq and Related Prosecutions, HC 115 I (1995–96), paras F4 61–F4 66.
105 See the minutes of evidence taken before the Public Services Committee on 8 May 1996, HC 313 (1995–96).
106 *Ibid*, QQ 394–97.
107 HC 771 (2001–02).

If the claims made to the Transport Sub-Committee are right, there could be no better example of the excessive influence of the Treasury than the decision to plump for a PPP scheme for London Underground to the exclusion of other options, and then to interfere with the bidding process. It is argued that one man has been principally responsible for this choice, the Chancellor of the Exchequer. The Secretary of State for Transport, Local Government and the Regions has been little more than a messenger. The Chancellor has imposed the PPP scheme despite the opposition from a wide range of experts. It is a scheme which will not provide the capacity enhancements which Londoners and the national economy require. It has not been proved to offer better value for money than other options, which could be rapidly developed. It fails to adequately transfer risk and it is needlessly complex [para 7].

Despite this, its request for a Treasury Minister to appear before its Committee was refused. The Committee concluded that, as a result, 'Treasury Ministers have treated this Committee with disdain'.

3   A further important example of refusal to appear before a Committee, in this case in relation to one of the Prime Minister's more controversial 'special advisers' is detailed below.

Fourth Report of the Transport, Local Government and the Regions Committee, *The Attendance of Lord Birt at The Committee*, HC 655 (2001–02)

1 In December 2001 the Committee announced its inquiry into the Review of the Government's Ten Year Plan for Transport. As part of this inquiry we wrote to Lord Birt, inviting him to give oral evidence in his capacity as the Prime Minister's adviser to the Forward Strategy Unit at No 10 Downing Street where he is engaged in 'blue skies thinking', looking at transport over the next 15 to 20 years.

2 ... We were informed that the Department for Transport, Local Government and the Regions was responsible for the matters covered by our inquiry and that the appropriate civil servant, Mr Willy Rickett, would represent Ministers in answering any questions about longer term issues relating to transport ...

...

4 We would have summoned Lord Birt. We are prevented from doing so because of a long-standing convention that Members of the other House are not compelled to appear before Committees of the House of Commons ...

...

6 While Lord Birt pursues the long term future of transport in secret, the Committee is examining the Government's Ten Year Plan for Transport through a series of public evidence sessions. We have been seeking to discover if the Government has the right objectives, and if its assumptions about how those objectives will be achieved are well founded. Any sensible plans for the next ten years must take account of forecasts or analysis of what happens thereafter. We have only a sketchy view of what Lord Birt is doing: even those experts he has spoken to have little idea. But his work seems likely to be highly relevant to our inquiry. It is therefore appropriate that he appear before us, all the more so because of the high regard the Prime Minister appears to hold him in. The questions which need to be pursued are:

- what bearing his work has on the Review of the Ten Year Plan for Transport;
- what is the scope of his project;
- as a man with no previous experience of transport policy, what grasp he has of the subject;
- what he will be able to add to the work of the Department for Transport, Local Government and the Regions (DTLR), which is by no means evident, since the Department must be considering the future of transport after 2010 in its review of the Ten Year Plan;

- what assumptions he is making about patterns of demand and costs, technologies and expenditure levels.

An evidence session would also play a valuable role in making his work public.

...

Who should decide who appears before Departmental Select Committees

17 One of the most surprising aspects of this episode is that the Prime Minister and his Department should take it upon themselves to decide who should give oral evidence to Select Committees. **In a democratic Parliament the Prime Minister and his advisers should not obstruct a Select Committee from taking evidence from a relevant witness. If the Prime Minister does not want them to give oral evidence, he should appear himself. Select Committees themselves should determine who should and should not give evidence to them. We consider that No 10 Downing Street's refusal to allow Lord Birt to attend this Committee to discuss the future of transport amounts to a deliberate attempt to undermine the Departmental Select Committee system.**

...

V CONCLUSIONS

19 There are a growing number of units and staff attached to No 10 Downing Street. In effect a Prime Minister's Department has been created. It, and the advisers within it, like Lord Birt, are increasingly influential, although we readily admit that he is far from the most significant. There is a serious danger that in their endless meddling in the work of departments, they reduce rather than increase the effectiveness of Government.

...

21 The Prime Minister's advisers should be accountable to departmental Select Committees. If the Department for Transport, Local Government and the Regions, can account to this Committee for its review of the transport plan up to 2010, so Lord Birt should for his review of transport after 2010. It should be for House of Commons' Committees themselves to decide who should or should not give evidence to them, not the Prime Minister, his Department, or advisers. Of course, Committees in most circumstances can do this by summoning witnesses to appear.

22 Unfortunately, this is not possible because Lord Birt, like so many of the Prime Minister's advisers, is a Member of the Other House. He is therefore able to take advantage of the ancient convention, established in quite different circumstances, that he will not be summoned to appear before a Commons' Committee. **We recommend that this convention be modified to ensure that the Prime Minister's or other Minister's advisers do not abuse it to evade scrutiny.** We endorse the recommendation of the Modernisation Committee that the Procedure Committees of both Houses examine this matter.

23 It should not, however, be necessary for the Prime Minister and the Central Unit to hide behind an ancient convention. Even at this late stage we urge Lord Birt to give oral evidence to the Committee.

Note

It is noteworthy that the Standards and Privileges Committee has recently been given power to order the attendance of any Member. The Liaison Committee recommended in its 1997 Report that this power should be given to the departmental Select Committees (HC 323-I (1996–97), para 12).

The ability to question witnesses present before the Committee

The main restrictions upon what witnesses will disclose are those set out in the government's *Code of Practice on Access to Information* (above). Additional restrictions, purportedly designed to protect civil service neutrality and the principles of ministerial responsibility, apply to civil servants, as explained below.

Cabinet Office, *Departmental Evidence and Response to Select Committees* (1999) (extracts)

4A Provision of Evidence by Officials: Central Principles

46 The central principle to be followed is that it is the duty of officials to be as helpful as possible to Select Committees. The Government's wider policies on openness to Parliament and the public are set out in the Code of Practice on Access to Government Information (Annex A). Officials should be as forthcoming as they can in providing information under the terms of the Code, whether in writing or in oral evidence, relevant to a Select Committee's field of inquiry. Any withholding of information should be limited to reservations that are necessary in the public interest; this should be decided in accordance with the law and the exemptions as set out in the Code.

Accuracy of Evidence

47 Officials appearing before Select Committees are responsible for ensuring that the evidence they give is accurate. They will therefore need to be fully briefed on the main facts of the matters on which they expect to be examined. This can be a major exercise as a Committee's questions can range widely and can be expected to be testing. Should it nevertheless be discovered subsequently that the evidence unwittingly contained factual errors, these should be made known to the Committee, usually via the Clerk, at the earliest opportunity. Where appropriate, a correcting footnote will appear in the published transcript of the evidence.

Discussion of Government Policy

48 Officials should as far as possible confine their evidence to questions of fact and explanation relating to government policies and actions. They should be ready to explain what those policies are; the justification and objectives of those policies as the Government sees them; the extent to which those objectives have been met; and also to explain how administrative factors may have affected both the choice of policy measures and the manner of their implementation. Any comment by officials on government policies and actions should always be consistent with the principle of civil service political impartiality. Officials should as far as possible avoid being drawn into discussion of the merits of alternative policies where this is politically contentious. If official witnesses are pressed by the Committee to go beyond these limits, they should suggest that the questioning should be referred to Ministers.

49 A Select Committee may invite specialist (as opposed to administrative) officials to comment on the professional or technical issues underlying government policies or decisions. This can require careful handling where Committees wish to take evidence from, for example, government economists or statisticians on issues which bear on controversial policy questions and which are also matters of controversy within the respective profession. Such specialists may find themselves in some difficulty if their own judgement on the professional issues has, or appears to have, implications that are critical of Government policies. It is not generally open to such witnesses to describe or comment upon the advice which they have given to Departments, or would give if asked. They should not therefore go beyond explaining the reasoning which, in the Government's judgement, supports its policy. The status of such evidence should, if necessary, be made clear to the Committee. If pressed for a professional judgement on the question the witness should, if necessary, refer to the political nature of the issue and, as above, suggest that the line of questioning be referred to Ministers.

Consulting Ministers on Evidence

53 Because officials appear on behalf of their Ministers, written evidence and briefing material should be cleared with them as necessary. It may only be necessary for Ministers to be consulted if

there is any doubt among officials on the detail of the policy to be explained to the Committee, or on what information should be disclosed. However, as Ministers are ultimately accountable for deciding what information is to be given and for defending those decisions as necessary, their views should be sought if a question arises of withholding information which a Committee has asked for.

Excessive Cost

65 Although the provisions under the Code for charging applicants do not apply in the case of Select Committees, it may occasionally prove necessary to decline requests for information which would involve the Department in excessive cost or diversion of effort. Ministers should always be consulted on their priorities in such cases.

66 Requests for named officials who are serving overseas to attend to give evidence should not be refused on cost grounds alone if the official is the one best placed to represent the Minister. Committees will generally be willing to arrange for such witnesses to give evidence on a mutually acceptable date.

Matters which may be *sub judice*

67 Committees are subject to the same rules by which the House regulates its conduct in relation to matters awaiting the adjudication of the courts (although the bar on debating such matters may be lifted if a Committee is meeting in closed session). If a matter already before the courts is likely to come up for discussion before a Committee at a public session, the Clerk will usually be aware of this and will draw the attention of the Chairman to the relevant rules of the House. Nonetheless, if a Department has reason to believe that such matters may arise, the Liaison Officer may wish to check with the Clerk that the Committee is also aware. It should be noted, however, that the Committee Chairman has an overriding discretion to determine what is appropriate in the hearing of evidence.

68 Officials should take care in discussing or giving written evidence on matters which may become the subject of litigation but which, at the time, do not strictly come under the rules precluding public discussion of *sub judice* questions. Such caution should be exercised whether or not the Crown is likely to be a party to such litigation. If such matters seem likely to be raised, officials should first consult their departmental legal advisers or the Treasury Solicitor on how to handle questions which might arise. In any case of doubt about the extent to which details may be disclosed of criminal cases, not currently *sub judice*, the Law Officers are available for consultation.

69 Similar considerations apply in cases where a Minister has or may have a quasi-judicial or appellate function, for example in relation to planning applications and appeals.

Conduct of Individual Officials

70 Occasionally questions from a departmentally-related Select Committee may appear to be directed to the conduct of individual officials, not just in the sense of establishing the facts about what occurred in making decisions or implementing Government policies, but with the implication of allocating individual criticism or blame.

71 In such circumstances, and in accordance with the principles of Ministerial accountability, it is for the Minister to look into the matter and if necessary to institute a formal inquiry. Such an inquiry into the conduct and behaviour of individual officials and consideration of disciplinary action is properly carried out within the Department according to established procedures designed and agreed for the purpose, and with appropriate safeguards for the individual. It is then the Minister's responsibility to inform the Committee of what has happened, and of what has been done to put the matter right and to prevent a recurrence. Evidence to a Select Committee on this should be given not by the official or officials concerned, but by the Minister or by a senior official designated by the Minister to give such evidence on the Minister's behalf.

72 In this context, Departments should adhere to the principle that disciplinary and employment matters are a matter of confidence and trust (extending in law beyond the end of employment). In

such circumstances, public disclosure may damage an individual's reputation without that individual having the same 'natural justice' right of response which is recognised by other forms of tribunal or inquiry. Any public information should therefore be cast as far as possible in ways which do not reveal individual or identifiable details. Where Committees need such details to discharge their responsibilities, they should be offered in closed session and on an understanding of confidentiality. Evidence on such matters should normally be given on the basis that:

(a) information will not be given about Departmental disciplinary proceedings until the hearings are complete;

(b) when hearings have been completed, the Department will inform the Committee of their outcome in a form which protects the identity of the individual or individuals concerned except insofar as this is already public knowledge;

(c) where more detail is needed to enable the Committee to discharge its responsibilities, such detail will be given but on the basis of a clear understanding of its confidentiality;

(d) the Committee will thereafter be given an account of the measures taken to put right what went wrong and to prevent a repeat of any failures which have arisen from weaknesses in the Departmental arrangements.

73 Select Committees have agreed that it is not their task to act as disciplinary tribunals. Accordingly, if in the course of an inquiry a Select Committee were to discover evidence that called into question the conduct (in this sense) of individual named officials, the Committee should be asked not to pursue their own investigation into the conduct of the person concerned, but to take up the matter with the Minister.

74 If it is foreseen that a Select Committee's line of enquiry may involve questions about the conduct of named officials, it should be suggested to the Committee that it would be appropriate for a Minister or a senior official designated by the Minister to give evidence, rather than the named officials in question. If an official giving evidence to a Committee is unexpectedly asked questions which are directed at his or her individual conduct, or at the conduct of another named official, the official should indicate that he wishes to seek instructions from Ministers, and the Committee should be asked to allow time for this.

Papers of a Previous Administration

75 There are well established conventions which govern the withholding of policy papers of a previous Administration from an Administration of a different political complexion. These were set out in a Parliamentary answer from the Prime Minister on 24 January 1980 (Official Report, Columns 305–307). Since officials appear before Select Committees as representatives of their Ministers, and since Select Committees are themselves composed on a bipartisan basis, it follows that officials should not provide a Committee with evidence from papers of a previous Administration which they are not in a position to show to their present Ministers. If such evidence is sought, Ministers should be consulted. Where Ministers propose to make an exception, it would be necessary to consult a representative of the previous Administration before either showing the papers to present Ministers or, with Ministers' authority, releasing information from them to a Committee.

[There is also further guidance on the handling of evidence given in confidence to Committees.]

Note
Failure to attend has generally been less of a problem than failure to answer questions properly. As Norton puts it, 'Whilst the committees normally get the witnesses they want, they do not always get the answers they want . . .'.[108] As the above extract made clear, the areas on which officials will refuse to answer questions are wide, and

---

108 P Norton, *Does Parliament Matter?* (1993), p 108.

constitute a severe restriction on freedom of information.[109] How far they are justified by the doctrines of civil service neutrality and ministerial responsibility to Parliament is a question considered elsewhere in this book (see Part IV Chapter 2, at pp 571–73). Nevertheless, the overall verdict of the Liaison Committee in 2003 was that, 'Overall the relationships between committees and departments are reported as good, with a high level of co-operation and openness'.[110]

The problem of self-incrimination

Where the Committees seek to question individuals about suspected serious wrongdoing, a conflict may arise between the public interest in seeking the information in question, and the individual privilege against self-incrimination. This problem arose out of the investigation by the Social Security Select Committee of the Maxwell pension fund. When the Committee called Kevin and Ian Maxwell, both refused to answer certain key questions.

First Special Report from the Social Security Committee, HC 353 (1991–92) (extracts)

8   During the meeting both QCs [representing the Maxwells] argued that the committee should not proceed with its questions. Mr Carman, in defending his client's right to silence, introduced the concept of a person being 'on the threshold of charges' [Q389]. He also said that Mr Kevin Maxwell had been 'advised by me and by others that imminently he faces the risk of a criminal prosecution' [Q384], and Mr Jarvis, with reference to Mr Ian Maxwell, argued that the committee should not proceed with its questioning. There was, they said, a very real possibility of charges being made in the near future and that a public, televised committee session could jeopardise the prospects of a fair trial. It was further argued that Mr Ian Maxwell and Mr Kevin Maxwell had a right in common law not to incriminate themselves, a possibility that might exist if they answered the committee's questions, and also that under the terms of the House's own *sub judice* rule the committee should agree to postpone the meeting. Mr Jarvis did say that Mr Ian Maxwell would be prepared to answer written questions provided that no public use was made of the answers (he later added that another condition was that the answers should not be released to the Serious Fraud Office) [QQ 336, 405]. Mr Carman said that this was something that Mr Kevin Maxwell was also prepared to consider [QQ 393–94]. The committee then went into private session to consider the points made.

9   The committee decided that it was reasonable for the meeting to continue and for questions to be put in public. We were quite clear that the House's *sub judice* rule was not brought into play by any current legal proceedings. It is also the case that there is no right to silence in front of a Select Committee, whatever the position in common law. We also believed that, despite the legal difficulties Mr Ian Maxwell and Mr Kevin Maxwell faced, there were questions that they could answer without there being any danger of them incriminating themselves.

. . .

12   . . . To opt not to undertake an inquiry into the operation of pension funds in the wake of Robert Maxwell's plundering of the pension funds he controlled would not merely be a betrayal of those citizens who have lost or may still lose their pensions. We believe it would have struck the public as an example of politicians unwilling to grapple with difficult issues which are of major importance to them . . .

. . .

---

109 R Brazier, *Constitutional Practice* (1994), p 227.
110 HC 558 (2002–03), para 42.

17 The committee is mindful that the primary task of the Serious Fraud Office is to collect evidence on whether the law has been broken and, if so, to press charges, rather than to trace the missing funds and to secure their return. From the outset, the committee therefore was anxious, not only to play the historic role given to the House of Commons of voicing the grievance of constituents (in this instance, the grievance naturally felt by those contributors to the pension schemes run by Mr Robert Maxwell who have been defrauded) but also to open up these events to public scrutiny.

18 It is in carrying out this side of its inquiry that the refusal of the Maxwell brothers to give evidence has been most harmful to the committee's activities.

20 There is no doubt that to refuse to answer questions in front of a Select Committee is a serious matter. The House of Commons expressed its view in a resolution agreed *nem con* on the 12 August 1947 'that the refusal of a witness before a Select Committee to answer any question which may be put to him is a contempt of the House and an infraction of the undoubted right of this House to conduct any inquiry which may be necessary in the public interest' [Commons Journal (1946–47), p 378].

Note

Any punishment imposed by the House for contempt, in refusing to answer questions which the witness believed would incriminate him or her, would be likely to infringe Article 6 of the European Convention on Human Rights, which guarantees the presumption of innocence.[111] However, an action could not be brought directly against Parliament under the Human Rights Act 1998, since Parliament is expressly included from the definition of 'public authorities' which are bound by the Convention rights.[112]

Evaluation of the Select Committees and Reform

We start this section with comment by Giddings on the Select Committees during the previous Conservative era.

P Giddings, 'Select Committees and parliamentary scrutiny: *plus ça change?*' (1994) 47(4) Parl Aff 668, pp 682–85

... taken as a whole the work of the committees has been unsystematic and its coverage of the work of Government patchy, not to say idiosyncratic. In spite of the existence of the Liaison Committee with a co-ordinating brief, each committee is a law unto itself in the choice of topics for investigation. And the same political dynamic is often evident in the pattern of questioning, which does not always follow a coherent strategy. Members are first and foremost political animals and generalists. They will pursue those topics and lines of inquiry which fit with their perception of the political needs of the moment, which may not immediately relate to the requirements of rational or systematic analysis of policy issues, expenditure priorities or administrative systems, nor to the brief which has been put before them by the clerk.

'The evolution of Select Committees has proceeded in a manner which maintains the continuity of institutional forms in the House of Commons. It has been a work of cautious adaptation, sensitive to the susceptibilities of those in Government but bringing renewed vitality to the traditional critical functions of Parliament.' That assessment in 1988 remains true today. Caution, continuity and adaptation have been hallmarks of the development of the Select Committee system in the last 50 years. ... Indeed, the principal features of that system remain untouched: the Chamber of the House of Commons remains the primary forum for debate and decision; the mode of

---

111 See Part VI Chapter 1, at pp 886–89 (*Brown v Stott*).
112 See s 6(1) and (3) and Part VI Chapter 1, at pp 859 and 871–72.

behaviour and discourse in the House is still that of cohesive, adversarial parties; single party majority Government remains the norm; the executive is still dominant.

Whilst Select Committees have grown and become more prominent, they do not provide an alternative career structure to ministerial office, even if they do provide a useful staging-post in the career of some ambitious younger MPs as well as for some of those whose ministerial days are over. On the other hand, they do provide an outlet for the increased professionalisation which has been so marked in British parliamentary politics in the last 30 years.

Although the fundamentals remain the same, change there has certainly been. Select Committees have grown in number and significance, particularly if one takes the quantity of activity and published output as an indicator. Scrutiny has been extended, accountability deepened and policy debate widened. A substantial and continuous process of explanatory dialogue between ministers and their officials on the one side and backbench MPs on the other is taking place across the whole range of Government, absorbing a significant and growing amount of the energies and time of all concerned.

How might the Select Committee system develop? If, as seems most likely whilst the present party and electoral systems remain intact, they continue as scrutiny rather than decision-making committees, the obvious developments are those which would build upon the existing system. A further extension of the range of scrutiny, including, for example, the security services, is desirable. Deeper scrutiny of administration and expenditure would be possible with more staff resources and, in particular, if the services of the National Audit Office could be made more widely available and perhaps extended in coverage . . .

A more radical development would be for the committees to engage with the passage of parliamentary business, such as legislation or expenditure. One of the reasons for Governments' relatively benign attitude to Select Committees has been that, if necessary, they can afford to ignore them, at least as far as the dispatch of Government business is concerned. Whilst it is helpful for Governments to have the support of Select Committees (on which, of course, their nominal supporters are normally in a majority), it is not necessary. Adverse or critical reports from scrutiny committees are an irritant or an embarrassment, but no more. However, should the committees become engaged with the legislative or expenditure process, the Government – and hence the whips – would be bound to take a much closer interest in their work, and especially in their votes. This would undoubtedly lead to a very significant shift away from the consensual mode of Select Committee work towards the adversarial.

Notes

1   Professor Peter Hennessy has argued[113] that, leaving aside formal changes to their powers and jurisdiction, the Select Committees could still achieve far more simply by being more bold in their aspirations:

Now the problem with the Select Committees . . . is really what Ernie Bevin once said of his beloved working class, that it is the 'poverty of their aspirations' that is so breathtaking and disappointing because they will not push things beyond a certain point. They will not keep at it. It is not entirely their fault . . . in that you cannot talk to these people about this or talk about that because it is national security and so on and you cannot talk to the officials that actually did it . . . Yet I have always thought that, in the end, if Select Committees really pushed this, perhaps having to go to votes in the House or orders from the floor and so on for people to attend, the whole climate would change. Apart from the Public Accounts Committee, you see, those who are steeped in executive convenience do not really walk in fear of these bodies. . . and they should do because, apart from anything else, [they] . . . are all we have got.[114]

---

113 See the minutes of evidence taken before the Public Services Committee on 20 March 1996, HC 313 (1995–96).
114 *Ibid*, Q 90.

2   It can be difficult to assess the impact of the Committees on departmental policy-
    making because Committee reports may merely contribute to debate which is
    already taking place, but it is clear that, particularly where reports are unanimous,
    as is generally the case, they may have some impact on the policy debate. One of
    the few examples of a Select Committee report apparently resulting in a clear
    change in government policy can be seen in the decision to repeal the 'sus' law by
    means of the Criminal Attempts Act 1981 after a critical report from the Home
    Affairs Select Committee. It has to be conceded that such examples are very much
    the exception. Griffith and Ryle's blunt conclusion is that 'Select Committees have
    not made a general impact on Government policies'.[115] As Norton notes, they are
    essentially 'advisory bodies' only[116] and, as Gavin Drewry comments, 'in the
    business of scrutiny and exposure, not Government'.[117] Where their activities do
    impact on policy, this is more likely to happen in relatively 'non political' areas. To
    expect Select Committees to be able to change contentious party-driven policies is
    clearly unrealistic.

3   More recently, the Labour government responded very positively to the report of
    the Home Affairs Select Committee on police complaints and the disciplinary
    procedure for officers guilty of misconduct (HC 258-I (1997–98); the government's
    response appears as HC 683. The government accepted a large number of the
    Committee's findings and recommendations, including the broad thrust of the
    Committee's report that the present procedures of the Police Complaints Authority
    were inadequate and that significant reform was required to strengthen the
    complaints system.

4   A further example of Select Committee influence is provided below.

First Report of the Liaison Committee, *Shifting the Balance: Unfinished Business*, HC 321-II (2000–01)

131 Committees' annual reports give an encouraging, and indeed impressive, demonstration of
the influence and effect they have had. We said in *Shifting the Balance* that audits of committee
effectiveness can be misleading. Analysis and criticism can often have as much effect as formal
recommendations; and the influence of committees can be as much through the public debate
that they initiate and inform as it is in their relationship with Government. In this respect, we
commend the study of effectiveness and influence in the report of the Environment Audit
Committee, which looks at a wide range of indicators and also draws upon independent
studies ...

...

133 In *Shifting the Balance* we said that it was important to distinguish between the 'soft'
recommendation already halfway to implementation and the 'hard' recommendation which may
change thinking and which may be adopted months or years later. One striking example of this was
reported by the Home Affairs Committee. In 1990 the Committee's recommendation to set up a
Criminal Records Bureau was not accepted by the then Government. Subsequently, an Efficiency
Scrutiny advanced the case, a White Paper made it Government policy in 1996, and the necessary
legislation was passed in 1997. The Home Affairs Committee is now about to report on the
administrative and financial arrangements of a body which it recommended three Parliaments and
eleven years ago.

---

115 *Op cit*, p 430.
116 *Does Parliament Matter?* (1993), p 108.
117 *The New Select Committees* (1989).

Notes

1   There is no doubt that a number of very recent Select Committee reports that were critical of government policy have had a very marked impact, receiving extensive publicity in the media, always forcing the government further to explain and defend its policies from the criticisms made and, on occasion, causing it to reconsider its policies. Particularly influential were a number of trenchant reports by the Transport Committee. Its most important[118] was a forensic dissection of the government's 10 Year Transport Plan – its master-plan for tackling the hugely difficult issue of reducing car usage and improving public transport as an alternative. The Report[119] was widely viewed in the media as sounding the death knell for the plan as originally conceived by John Prescott, while some viewed it as partly responsible for the resignation, in June 2002, of the then Transport Secretary, Stephen Byers.[120]

2   The Hansard Society Commission was strongly of the view that, in order to enhance their impact, the Committees should pursue recommendations made in their reports with much greater perseverance:

    The impact of committee reports will be determined by the assiduity with which their recommendations are monitored and followed up. Committees should publish a periodic review (two to three years after the original report) assessing how far their recommendations have been implemented.[121]

3   Ganz argues that whilst Select Committee reports can be influential, especially when unanimous, the key problem is that 'they exist as an oasis in an adversarial system'. This gives rise to 'the most fundamental weakness ... the difficulty in transferring the consensus of the committee to the House itself'. Thus, when Select Committee reports on proposed legislation are cited on the floor of the House, and an acute conflict arises between loyalty to the Committee on the one hand and to the party on the other, the party almost invariably[122] triumphs. Ganz instances the 'open disagreement' between members of the Trade and Industry Committee on the interpretation of their unanimous report on proposed pit closures and the ease with which the government was able to buy off the rebels with the minimum of concessions,[123] a pattern repeated when a hostile report by the same Committee[124] over rail privatisation was considered during the report stage of the legislation.[125]

4   A package of proposals to strengthen Select Committees was recently agreed[126] between the Liaison and Modernisation Committees. The report of the former sets out the main proposals of the Modernisation Committee (in italics) and comments on them.

---

118 Another hard-hitting report concerned the adoption of a Public Private Partnership for the London Underground: HC 680 (2001–02).

119 Eighth Report of the Select Committee on Transport, Local Government and the Regions, *Ten Year Plan for Transport*, HC 558-I (2001–02).

120 See further Part IV Chapter 2, p 554.

121 *Op cit*, para 3.40.

122 A notable exception, as Ganz points out (*op cit*, p 32) was during the debate on the 'sus' report (HC Deb col 1763 (5 June 1980)).

123 HC Deb col 25 (29 March 1993).

124 HC 375 and 245 (1992–93).

125 HC Deb cols 758 *et seq* (25 May 1993).

126 There were some areas of disagreement, notably over a recommendation to increase the size of Select Committees and to rename them 'Scrutiny Committees'.

Second Report of the Liaison Committee, *Select Committees: Modernisation Proposals*, HC 692 (2002) (extracts)
More Resources

5 We recommend that the House of Commons Commission should make available the necessary funds for a central unit of specialist support staff to be in place in the next financial year. [Paragraph 28]

6 The Modernisation Committee compares the resources available to select committees with those available to Government, and rightly seeks a better balance. It notes the 'very limited specialist advice' which is provided, and considers that effectiveness could be enhanced by 'direct access to further specialist advice independent of Government'.

7 We are glad that the Report specifically endorses the Liaison Committee's recommendation for a central unit within the Committee Office to support specialist scrutiny functions. . . .

PRE-LEGISLATIVE SCRUTINY

9 Pre-legislative work imposes extra burdens on Members, and will create a problem of priorities for the committee and for committee staff. So it is welcome to have the endorsement of the Modernisation Committee for the provision of extra specialist support that could help enhance committees' examination of legislation. The staff of the unit could provide briefing to individual committee staffs, or augment a committee secretariat for a particular pre-legislative study.

. . .

We recommend that the National Audit Office be invited to help assess the need for specialist and other support staff for select committees and to advise on how this could best be provided, and that the House of Commons Commission should look favourably on funding for staffing increases which may be proposed. [Paragraph 29]

14 We are glad that the Modernisation Committee accepted this proposal which our Chairman put forward when he gave evidence. Staffing levels for the new scrutiny unit will need to be agreed by the House of Commons Commission in time for its introduction in the financial year 2002/03. Staffing is to include secondments as well as permanent and short term staff. We understand that the National Audit Office, which already supplies secondees to the Committee Office, is prepared to consider providing further expert staff, particularly to assist with financial scrutiny. We understand also that it would be willing to help assess how extra specialist and support staff might best be provided to meet any needs identified by the House.

SUPPORT FOR CHAIRMEN

We recommend that within the Committee Office there should be sufficient staff to assist with the function of supporting the administrative workload of the select committee chairmen. [Paragraph 30]

15 The Modernisation Committee's Report considers support to committee chairmen, in the light of representations from some of them that 'running an active select committee generates considerable demands for secretarial services'. We are only too conscious of these demands, although there are different views within our own membership as to how best these burdens might be supported. We are glad that the Report has recognised that it is not reasonable to expect this burden to be met from the resources available within the general range of Members' allowances. The Modernisation Committee's solution, which is helpful, is to recommend that the Committee Office should have sufficient staff 'to assist with the function of supporting the administrative workload of the select committee chairmen'. Such support would probably best be available within individual committee secretariats, as the staff would be familiar with the issues and with the chairman's manner of working. The duties to support chairmen, many of which are carried

out already, would be likely to be shared across the staff of each committee, but a fuller service will require extra staffing levels.

...

CORE TASKS FOR SELECT COMMITTEES

We recommend that select committees should experiment with appointing one of their number as a rapporteur on a specific task, such as for example financial scrutiny. [Paragraph 34]

We recommend that as part of the process of producing an annual report each departmental select committee should submit to the Liaison Committee a statement of how it has met each core task in the scrutiny of its department. [Paragraph 35]

We recommend that there should be an agreed statement of the core tasks of the departmental select committees. [Paragraph 33]

We recommend the following model as an illustration of what we would regard as the principal objectives of departmental select committees [the Report then sets out the core tasks of Select Committees reproduced above (pp 314–15)].

17 ... One other task which we and our predecessors and the *Hansard* Society Commission considered crucial is the need for committees to follow up previous reports in a systematic way. Although not mentioned in the Modernisation Committee's list of 'principal objectives', we continue to believe that reviewing their earlier work is something which the House has a right to expect its committees to do on a regular basis, with assistance from the proposed central scrutiny unit where appropriate.

...

Witnesses

We recommend that, in the light of the recommendations of the Joint Committee on Parliamentary Privilege, this limitation on the power to require witnesses to give evidence should be reviewed by the appropriate committees of both Houses. [Paragraph 36]

22 This review might also usefully consider the position of named civil servants, where no difficulties have arisen recently but where agreement between the Government and this Committee has been lacking in the past. It could also consider special advisers and civil servants who work directly for the Prime Minister, whose staff is not currently covered by one of the departmental select committees. We note that the Public Administration Committee's current inquiry into the Government Information and Communications Service includes consideration of the role of special advisers. We would expect its eventual recommendations to be taken into account in the proposed review.

...

An Alternative Career Structure

We recommend that the value of a parliamentary career devoted to scrutiny should be recognised by an additional salary to the chairmen of the principal investigative committees. [Paragraph 41]

27 We fully support the aim of creating an alternative career structure to counterbalance the pull of the prospect of ministerial office. The Report rightly seeks to increase the status of chairmen in order to make committee work more attractive to Members as a long term commitment.

28 The proposal is that the salary should, if agreed, be payable to the chairmen of the 'principal investigative committees'. Which committees are to be included needs clarification before the House takes a final decision in the light of any recommendation from the SSRB.

29 A large majority of chairmen are in favour of the principle of an additional salary. But they also emphasise that those who receive this would have to relinquish outside interests, as now occurs with the Deputy Speakers and other non-ministerial postholders who are paid an additional salary.

Notes

1   Robin Cook described the above proposals as: 'The most comprehensive package to strengthen the Select Committee system in the 20 years since it was set up.'[127] They were debated by the House of Commons on 14 July 2002. As noted above, the proposal to replace the Committee of Selection with a Committee of Nomination, intended to be more independent of party influence, was defeated, unfortunately so in the eyes of many parliamentary observers.

2   The House also rejected the proposal that minority parties (the SNP, Plaid Cymru) and the Northern Ireland parties should be guaranteed some places on Select Committees (col 712). It then accepted the main proposal regarding core tasks for Select Committees, greater resources and more specialist support staff (cols 715–16) and was also in favour of payment for Chairs of Select Committees in an attempt to encourage members to see this as an alternative career path, something also strong recommended by the Hansard Commission.[128] The proposals should represent a significant enhancement of the effectiveness of Select Committees. The most recent report from the Liaison Committee[129] stated: 'Much of our earlier agenda for improvement has been accepted. Our main focus is no longer campaigning on the principles, but monitoring progress in their implementation' (para 2).

3   It may be noted that, with the recent innovations to Select Committees both already agreed and implemented by the Commons in May 2002, many of Giddings' suggestions for improving the system have been met: there is an attempt at greater co-ordination of the Committee's activities; a much greater involvement in pre-legislative scrutiny and an extension of resources and availability of the services of the National Audit Office to the Committees. The Liaison Committee found that the new Scrutiny Unit, as proposed above:

> has already established itself as a useful source of support to select committees in their pre-legislative and financial scrutiny roles. It comprises ten staff at present and will expand during 2003 to the 18 approved by the House of Commons Commission. The current staff include one Estimates specialist, two auditors, a statistician, a lawyer and a social policy expert.[130]

4   Ganz's view is that such reforms will have little impact, because they:

> could not cure the lack of a separation of powers between the government and Parliament in the UK which is root cause of the weakness of these committees in contrast to US Congressional Committees. The tyranny of party has ensured that the Committees have not altered the balance of power between the government and Parliament ... The balance of power cannot be changed by improving procedures by select committees but by MPs using their votes.[131]

5   Ganz is correct to say that the Committees cannot alter the *balance of power* between government and Parliament, in the sense of shifting power over policy implementation, but it is doubtful whether they were ever intended to achieve this. The Committees certainly *have* greatly enhanced critical scrutiny over government, in terms of information gathering, critical policy analysis, and identifying weaknesses in government administration and policy. At times, and particularly where their voice is amplified by that of the press, they are able to have at least an influence on policy: the Report of the Home Affairs Select Committee on reforming

---

127   HC Deb col 655 (14 July 2002).
128   *Op cit*, paras 2.34–2.36.
129   First Report, *Annual Report for 2002*, HC 558 (2002–03).
130   HC 558 (2002–03).
131   *Op cit*, p 41.

the law relating to illegal drugs[132] is a clear example, in that it appeared to be a significant 'push' towards the downgrading of cannabis from a Class B to a Class C drug which the Home Secretary announced in July 2002. The next edition of this book will be able to judge how far the changes considered above have enhanced the quality and influence of the Select Committees' work.

FURTHER READING

P Bennet and S Pullinger, *Making the Commons Work* (1991)

R Blackburn and A Kennon, *Griffith & Ryle on Parliament: Functions, Practice and Procedures*, 2nd edn (2002)

A Bradley and K Ewing, *Constitutional and Administrative Law*, 13th edn (2002)

I Burton and G Drewry, *Legislation and Public Policy* (1981)

B Crick, *The Reform of Parliament* (1964)

M Franklin and P Norton, *Parliamentary Questions* (1993)

J Griffith, *Parliamentary Scrutiny of Government Bills* (1974)

O Hood Phillips, *Constitutional and Administrative Law*, 8th edn (2001)

Hansard Commission, *The Challenge for Parliament: Making Government Accountable* (2001)

R Holme and M Elliott, *Time for a New Constitution* (1988)

IPPR, *The Constitution of the United Kingdom* (1991)

D Judge (ed), *The Politics of Parliamentary Reform* (1984)

J McEldowney, *Public Law*, 2nd edn (1999)

P Norton, *The Commons in Perspective* (1981)

P Norton, *Legislatures* (1990)

Norton Commission, *Strengthening Parliament* (2000)

D Oliver, 'The reform of the United Kingdom Parliament', in J Jowell and D Oliver (eds), *The Changing Constitution*, 4th edn (2000)

R Pyper and L Robins (eds), *Governing the UK in the 1990s* (1995), Part II

Rush, *Parliamentary Government in Britain* (1981)

M Ryle and P Richards (eds), *The Commons under Scrutiny* (1988)

J Seaton and BK Winetrobe, 'Modernising the Commons' (1999) 70 Political Quarterly 152

A Tomkin, 'Conclusion', in *Government Unwrapped: the Constitution after Scott* (1998)

C Turpin, *British Government and the Constitution*, 4th edn (1999)

SA Walkland and M Ryle, *The Commons Today* (1981)

S Walkland (ed), *The House of Commons in The Twentieth Century* (1979)

---

132 HC 318 (2001–02).

THE HOUSE OF LORDS AND REFORM

INTRODUCTION

Reform of the House of Lords, at the time of writing, remains firmly on the political agenda, though many see it as having lost its way. Labour's first term of office saw it achieve an historic Labour Party goal with the passage of the House of Lords Act 1999, which removed all but 92 of the hereditary peers, who, for centuries, had comprised the large majority of the membership of the Lords. The process of reform, following reports from the Royal Commission on Reform of the House of Lords, under the chairmanship of Lord Wakeham[1] (hereafter 'Wakeham') the government's White Paper in response,[2] an influential report from the Public Administration Select Committee,[3] and two from the new Joint Committee on Lords Reform[4] is still seemingly ongoing, though the failure of the two Houses of Parliament in February 2003 to agree upon a basic blueprint for the composition of a new second chamber seems to many to have left the reform process in limbo.

This chapter will consider the constitutional role of the House of Lords. It will examine its membership, the pattern and extent of party control over it, its effectiveness in scrutinising legislation and policy, and the constraints, both legal and conventional, which restrict its powers. In the context of that inquiry it will then consider the various proposals for reform discussed above and lessons from overseas that may help resolve the debate as to the best way forward for this still unfinished part of Labour's constitutional reform programme.

The House of Lords is very different from the Commons, and very distinctive, as JAG Griffith and M Ryle bring out:

> The differences between the Houses derive from the source of political authority of the Lords – based on prescription and immemorial antiquity rather than popular election; the retention of its old procedures, which have not as yet been forced into radical change (as were those of the Commons in the late nineteenth century by the Irish Nationalists); the lack of a Speakership with effective powers ... an absence of priority for government business; the maintenance of freedoms for the individual member, resulting from the comparative lack of pressures on the time of the House; the lack of power on financial matters; the presence of bishops, law lords and life peers and the consequent specialist experience of many members; and the distinctive and idiosyncratic contribution of the hereditary peerage. These factors contribute to the peculiar, indeed unique, quality of the House of Lords.[5]

---

1   Wakeham Report, *A House for the Future*, Cm 4534 (2000), available at www.official-documents.co.uk/document/cm45/4534/4534.htm.
2   This appeared in the White Paper, *The House of Lords: Completing the Reform*, Cmd 5291 (2001) available at www.lcd.gov.uk/constitution/holref/holreform.htm and in a further document published by the Lord Chancellor's Department, *House of Lords Reform: Supporting Documents* (6 December 2001), available at www.lcd.gov.uk/whatsnfr.htm.
3   Fifth Report, HC 494-i (2001–02), esp at paras 6 and 36 (hereafter PASC).
4   For the resolutions appointing it see: HC Deb cols 338–80 (19 June 2002); HL Deb cols 354–62 (4 July 2002). Its terms of reference may be found at: www.parliament.uk/parliamentary_committees/joint_committee_on_house_of_lords_reform.cfm. Its reports are discussed below.
5   JAG Griffith and M Ryle, *Parliament: Functions, Practice and Procedures* (1989), p 455.

COMPOSITION OF THE HOUSE OF LORDS AND PARTY BALANCE

As indicated above, the make-up of the Lords has recently undergone a significant change; this extends both to its membership and to the method of appointing independent ('cross-bench') peers. We start with consideration of the unreformed House.

The unreformed House of Lords

To most commentators in this area, the outstanding feature of the unreformed House of Lords was its wholly undemocratic character and particularly the presence of some 750 hereditary peers.

> **Donald Shell, 'The House of Lords: time for a change?' (1994) 47(4) Parl Aff 721, 721–23**
>
> Imagine the task of conducting around Westminster a delegation of officials from eastern Europe here in the UK to learn the ways of democracy. Explaining the House of Lords must present something of a challenge. That most of those entitled to sit, to speak, and to vote in the second chamber do so simply because they inherited this right seems extraordinary. That Britain, a country thought to have pioneered the development of democracy, should retain as part of its Parliament a second chamber still dominated by the aristocracy, seems paradoxical. That towards the close of the twentieth century, far from feeling embarrassed about this state of affairs, many seem to take pride in the continued existence of the House of Lords as a sort of tribute to English genius, or the triumph of English pragmatism, must surely bemuse overseas observers.
>
> Having perhaps parried some difficult questions from those seeking know-how about democracy on the place of hereditary legislators, it would then have to be explained that the remaining members of the House are not elected, either directly or even indirectly, that they are not appointed by the House of Commons, or by local Councils, or even by a committee of any kind. Rather, every single one of them has become a member of the second chamber because the Prime Minister of the day had decided to recommend them for a peerage . . .
>
> Inquirers about the party breakdown in the House might be told that whatever the complexion of the government of the day, the Conservative Party always enjoys control in the House of Lords . . . Conservative spokesmen may emphasise that their party does not have an overall majority, but with over 48% of the House taking the Conservative whip, and around 30% sitting on the cross-benches, Conservative preponderance is assured. When Prime Minister Mrs Thatcher took care to recommend almost twice as many Conservatives as Labour party supporters for elevation to the House, far from evening up the party balance in the House, she seemed determined to ensure an increased Conservative majority. That she was allowed to do this is surely curious; that no outcry greeted such behaviour is remarkable.
>
> To say that such a House is deeply offensive to democratic values is surely a truism. But what is remarkable as the continued existence of the House is the fact that so much satisfaction is expressed with it and that so little public debate surrounds the survival of this feudal relic.

Notes

1   The membership of the House of Lords was thus drawn from a number of sources: the hereditary peers, 26 Bishops of the Church of England (other Christian denominations and non-Christian faiths are not represented); the Law Lords, and the life peers. On the creation of life peerages in 1958, Griffith and Ryle comment:

> Life peers have transformed the House. Instead of a House consisting predominantly of landowners and retired politicians (with a sprinkling of lawyers and bishops) the range of

occupations and interests has been vastly increased. The number of life peers created has been large, and the variety of persons selected for life peerages has been extensive. Those appointed are not representative in the sense that they are appointed to speak for their colleagues, but they do provide a wide spectrum of expertise.[6]

2   The following description was given by a peer during a recent debate on reform of the Lords:

> You form a unique pool of expertise and experience. Casual research reveals that 20 per cent of you came from the [Commons], including two former Prime Ministers, five former Chancellors of the Exchequer and more than 60 other former Ministers; another 20 per cent come from business, international commerce and financial services; and some 14 per cent are lawyers and judges. Other well represented sectors are local government, the Civil and Foreign Services, trades unions, teachers, professors, doctors, nurses, the voluntary services, the armed forces and police, agriculture, the religious faiths and the media.[7]

3   The make-up of the House of Lords prior to the removal of the hereditary peers is set out in the following White Paper, which preceded the House of Lords Act 1999.

Modernising Parliament – Reforming the House of Lords, Cm 4183 (1999), Chapter 3 (extracts)

3 . . . At 4 January 1999, the structure of the House of Lords was:

Life peers	510

(of whom 7 are on leave of absence)

Hereditary peers	
– of first creation	9
– by succession	750

(of whom 67 are without a Writ of Summons and 56 are on leave of absence)

Archbishops and Bishops	26
TOTAL	1,295

Hereditary peers, including those without a Writ of Summons and those on leave of absence, command a clear absolute majority in the present House of Lords:

Hereditary peers by succession	750
Others	545

Only 103 peers are women, 16 of whom are hereditary peers. Nearly 40 per cent of the House (excluding those without Writs of Summons or on leave of absence) were born before 1930 – about one-third of hereditary peers and nearly half of life peers.

4. But the nominal membership of the House of Lords is misleading. It is perhaps not widely understood that membership of the House of Lords is not a salaried job. Peers may claim only reimbursement of expenses incurred in undertaking parliamentary duties. Many members of the House attend only rarely. For example, in the 1997–98 session, only 40 per cent of life peers attended more than two-thirds of the House's sessions and 34 per cent attended less than one-third. The equivalent figures for the hereditary peers are 20 per cent and 67 per cent respectively. Nearly 200 hereditary peers never attended at all, not counting those on leave of absence. The average daily attendance in 1997 was around 400, and a division involving more than 300 peers is

---

6   *Ibid*, pp 462–64 (extracts).
7   HL Deb col 651 (9 January 2002).

rare. The majority of the business of the House is carried out by peers who regularly attend the House, the majority of whom are life peers ...

18. Political parties operate within the overall structure of the House of Lords. But unlike the House of Commons, there is a significant independent element – the cross-bench peers. At 4 January 1999, the political make-up of the House, broken down by component group and excluding those on leave of absence or without a Writ of Summons, was:

Party	Life Peers	Hereditary Peers	Bishops	Total
Conservative	172	304	–	476
Labour	157	18	–	175
Liberal Democrat	45	24	–	69
Cross-bench[1]	119	198	–	317
Other[2]	10	92[3]	26	128
TOTAL	**503**	**636**	**26**	**1,165**

1 Includes 28 Law Lords

2 Peers who have not taken a party whip

19. As can be seen, the Conservatives have a clear majority over the other parties overall, and an overwhelming majority among the hereditary peers. They constitute nearly 50 per cent of the total of hereditary peers, including the politically non-affiliated. They also form the largest single party among the life peers. The Conservatives' share of the House of Lords far exceeds the Party's vote in recent general elections:

	House of Lords (% of House)[1]	General Election 1997 (% of vote)[2]	General Election 1992 (% of vote)
Conservative	66	34	44.5
Labour	24	48	36.5
Liberal-Democrat	10	18	19

1 Of those taking a party whip

2 Excluding nationalist and regional parties

Note
As the above analysis highlights, when one looks instead of total membership, at those who attended more than 50% of the sessions, a slightly different picture emerges. First, only about a third of peers attended 50% or more – the figures were 399 for 1996–97. Second, the peers were distributed as follows: Conservatives have 195, or 49%; Independents (cross-benchers) 21%; Labour 83 or 21%; Liberal Democrats 37 or 9%. So to defeat the Conservatives, nearly all the Independents had to vote with Labour and the Liberal Democrats – given that these three put together only have a bare 51% of the votes. So unless the Independents voted overwhelmingly with the non-Conservative parties (which they very seldom do – see below), the Conservatives always had a majority.

The composition of the Lords after the removal of the hereditary peers

The first part of the reform of the House of Lords came with the removal of most hereditary peers from the House of Lords. This was achieved through the short House of Lords Act 1999, which provided, in s 1, that 'No-one shall be a member of the House of Lords by virtue of a hereditary peerage'.

As Stephen Tierney notes:

> Labour's attempt to remove the right of hereditary peers to sit and vote in the House of Lords was only a partial success ... the Act, which in the end preserved the right of ninety-two hereditary peers to remain in the House of Lords, emerged as the result of an agreement between the Government and Lord Cranborne, leader of the Conservative Party in the Lords ... The Government was prepared to reach a settlement with the dominant Conservative Party in the Lords in order to avoid disruption not only to this proposal but to other important elements of the Government's legislative programme.[8]

2   The deal over how many hereditaries to retain was apparently the subject of some remarkable haggling between Irvine and Cranborne and indicates the utter *'ad hoc-ery'* that constitutional reform in the UK can descend into. The latter could threaten 'the complete buggerisation of your legislative programme'[9] if Labour didn't come to a compromise; the former, the dismissal of the entire grouping of hereditaries if the price for buying Conservative cooperation in their demise became too high. Irvine's initial offer was for 10 hereditaries to be retained; Cranborne demanded 150. After conferring, negotiations resumed.

A Rawnsley, *Servants of the People: The Inside Story of New Labour* (revised edn, 2001), p 202

Irvine was sanctioned to up his offer to the survival of 75 of the hereditary peers pending the second stage of Lords' reform. 'We really do want a deal.' Cranborne had come down to 100. To bridge the gap between them, the Viscount wondered if the government would throw in the 15 hereditaries who held offices. 'I'll talk to young Blair,' replied Irvine. The next day, Cranborne heard from Irvine: 'Done.' Cranborne asked: 'Will you give me the Earl Marshall and the Lord Great Chamberlain?' Irvine: 'Done.' The Viscount and the Cardinal, these peers of the realm, bargained about the future composition of one half of parliament with the sophistication of a couple of used-car dealers. Thus was British constitutional history made.

To seal the bargain, on Thursday 26 November, Cranborne was smuggled into Downing Street and up to the Prime Minister's flat ... Blair frowned at him: 'But will Hague [then Conservative Leader] back this?' Cranborne was operating behind enemy lines: ... Hague and his fellow Tories in the Shadow Cabinet had told him they didn't want a deal with the government. Cranborne ... expressed himself relaxed. He ... expected Hague to come round.

... When the deal was announced, Hague renounced it and sacked Cranborne. Then, confronted with a rebellion by Conservative peers, Hague was abjectly forced to swallow the fix done with the government ... A year later, 650 of the hereditaries were gone from the Lords ...

Notes

1   As Tierney notes:

> [This] was widely perceived as a tactical deal compromising the principle of no hereditary representation which Labour had categorically and repeatedly asserted in the manifesto, the Queen's Speech and the White Paper [see D Shell (2000) Parl Aff 290–310, at 298–99]. The hasty way in which this compromise was reached has resulted in a very ad hoc process of selection for the ninety-two hereditary peers and an even more inchoate arrangement for their replacement, provoking one prominent observer to label the entire process as 'nonsense' ... [*ibid*, at 305]. It has been ordained that vacancies arising when a peer retires or dies are to be filled through an election by the other members of his party group. Donald Shell points out the absurdity of the

---

8   S Tierney, 'The Labour government and reform of the House of Lords' (2000) 6(4) EPL 506, at 508–09.

9   A Rawnsley, *Servants of the People: The Inside Story of New Labour* (2000), p 202.

only remaining Labour member being in a position to choose his new colleague, and of the possibility that the two surviving Liberal Democrats might disagree on a replacement to complete their triumvirate. In general he is scathing of these arrangements: 'If these were decisions about granting membership of a private club, it could well be argued that they do not really matter, but these are decisions about membership of Parliament, the legislature for the United Kingdom.' [*Ibid.*][10]

2   One of the few plausible arguments made for the retention of the hereditary peers was that the work of some talented and distinguished peers (such as the Russell family) would be lost to the nation as a result of the reform. The retention of the 92, assuming that peers voted for those with a proven record as able and committed scrutinisers, answered this concern, as well as easing the passage of the Bill through the Lords.

3   A second point is of more importance. Given that all life peers are appointed by the Prime Minister of the day, this reform actually *increased* executive influence over Parliament. However, an examination of the party balance immediately after the 1999 Act revealed that fears that removal of the hereditary peers would lead to the House overnight becoming packed with 'Tony's cronies', thus becoming 'the Government's poodle', to be largely groundless. Immediately after the departure of the hereditaries, the party balance was as follows: Conservatives 35%, Labour 27.5%, cross-benchers 24.5%, Liberal Democrats, 8%, Bishops and others, 5%. The Conservatives thus remained the biggest group by a comfortable margin; Labour were only slightly ahead of the cross-benchers – indeed the independent members outnumbered Labour if the Bishops were counted in. Thus, in theory, in order to move its legislation through the House, the government still needed to persuade no less than 151 non-Labour peers to support it. The figures also reveal that the strong cross-bench element in the Lords, far from being reduced, was strengthened, in terms of proportion of membership. Around 14% of the total eligible membership of the unreformed Lords were cross-benchers (1998 figures); as a result of the House of Lords Act, that figure rose to 24.5%, or virtually a quarter of the total.

4   Clearly, however, the use of prime ministerial patronage, in relation to the transitional House was, and continues to be crucial. It would have been quite possible for this power, unrestrained save by some rather vague conventions relating to the appointment of peers from other parties, to have been used over time to pack the Lords with Labour placemen, giving Labour an eventual overall majority. To counter this fear, the government set out a series of principles in the White Paper to govern Mr Blair's appointments to the transitional House.[11]

In our manifesto we said:
'*Our objective will be to ensure that over time party appointees as life peers more accurately reflect the proportion of votes cast at the previous general election. We are committed to maintaining an independent cross-bench presence of life peers. No one political party should seek a majority in the House of Lords.*'
Our present intention is to move towards broad parity between Labour and the Conservatives. The principle of broad parity and proportionate creations from the Liberal Democrat and other parties would be maintained throughout the transitional period.

5   In pursuit of this goal of broad parity with the Conservatives the government has so far appointed an average of 66 life peers a year – three times higher than the previous average. As Tierney notes: 'By June 2000 [Blair] had appointed 214 peers

---

10   Tierney, *op cit*.
11   *Modernising Parliament: Reforming the House of Lords*, Cm 4183 (1999), Chapter 6.

compared to a total of 203 appointed by Margaret Thatcher in her eleven years in office.'[12] By November 2001, this had risen to 248 peers, meaning, as *The Times* commented, that 'In a House ... containing just over 700 peers, more than a third owe their places in Parliament to one Prime Minister'.[13] However, fewer than half of these peers, 113, are Labour peers.

6　The more important concern with the present House is that it is, and always has been, objectionable on constitutional grounds that the Prime Minister, the effective head of the executive, should appoint members of one chamber of the legislature, and this objection gains far more force now that the large majority of that chamber – rather than as, previously, a minority – are appointed. In response to this concern, the government proposed a new, non-statutory, independent appointments commission, which would appoint the cross-bench peers.

Modernising Parliament – Reforming the House of Lords, Cm 4183 (1999), Chapter 6 (extracts)

9. ... The Government proposes to set up an Appointments Commission to take over from the Prime Minister the function of nominating cross-bench peers ... The Commission will be an advisory non-departmental public body. It will consist of representatives of the three main political parties, and independent figures who will comprise a majority, one of whom will become the Chairman. It will operate an open and transparent nominations system for cross-bench peers, both actively inviting public nominations and encouraging suitable bodies to make nominations. The general qualities being sought and the type of information required to support a nomination will be made public. It will seek to cast its net wider than the present system to achieve successful nominations. ...

10. The Appointments Commission will also take on and reinforce the present function of the Political Honours Scrutiny Committee in vetting the suitability of all nominations to life peerages. It will continue to include scrutiny on the grounds of propriety in relation to political donations, as endorsed by Lord Neill in his report on the funding of official parties ... The Prime Minister will have no right to refuse a nomination the Commission had passed.

11. The Appointments Commission itself will be appointed in accordance with the rules of the Commissioner for Public Appointments. It will also seek his advice about best practice in the area of attracting and assessing potential nominees.

12. Awards of peerages will continue to be made by The Queen. In accordance with the normal conventions for the exercise of the prerogative, the names of those recommended will have to be submitted by the Prime Minister. The Prime Minister will decide the overall number of nominations to be made to The Queen and the Commission will be asked to forward to the Prime Minister the same number of recommendations. The Prime Minister will pass these on to Her Majesty in the same way as he will pass on the recommendations of other party leaders to fill the vacancies on their benches. Therefore, except in the most exceptional of circumstances, such as those endangering the security of the realm, the only nominations which the Prime Minister will be able to influence are those from his own party...

Notes

1　Thus, the current position is that the Prime Minister still appoints all those peers who take a party whip (the large majority) while the non-statutory Appointments Commission appoints the others; this nevertheless represents an appreciable diminution of his power of patronage and also a form of guarantee that the cross-benchers appointed genuinely will be independent of party.

12　Tierney, *op cit*, at 509.
13　*The Times*, 8 November 2001.

2   The political composition of the House of Lords at the time of writing is as follows:

ANALYSIS OF COMPOSITION – 1 May 2003
By party strength

Party	Life peers	Hereditary: elected by party	Hereditary: elected office holders	Hereditary: * royal office holders	Bishops	Total
Conservative	163	41	9			213
Labour	182	2	2			186
Liberal Democrat	60	3	2			65
Cross-bench	146	29	2	2		179
Archbishops and Bishops					25	25
Other	7					7
TOTAL	**558**	**75**	**15**	**2**	**25**	**675**

NB Excludes 14 peers on leave of absence.

Notes

1   It may be seen that the Conservatives are still quite comfortably the biggest party, although Labour has succeeded in closing the gap substantially since 1999, having now only 27, rather than 50 less members, but still making up only 27.5% of the total membership. The independent element, at 179 members, is only slightly smaller than the Labour contingent, indeed it is larger, if the Bishops are counted in (giving a total 204 independent peers). It is hard not to conclude that in removing (most of) those with no claim at all to be there, the hereditary peers, reducing the permanent dominance of the Conservative party, whilst denying dominance to any other party, and retaining a strong independent element, the new House is a significant improvement over the old. The hereditary peers were the most objectionable feature of the Lords since they had nothing at all to recommend them as a class, though of course individual hereditary peers might happen to be useful members of the House. The transitional House is not more democratic, but it is more meritocratic.

2   The actual appointments made by the new Appointments Commission were subject to some criticism for elitism,[14] one Labour MP describing the appointments as 'a complete farce'[15] – though mainly, it seems, because the phrase 'people's peers', apparently used by one Labour spin doctor to describe the expected creations of the Commission, had created expectations that ordinary people, including working class people with no particular achievements, would be appointed. In fact, the Commission appointees represented, roughly speaking, 'the great and the good' who might have been expected to have been rewarded peerages anyway.[16] It is suggested, however, that the criticism of the Commission's choices is misplaced: the work of the Lords is often technical and requires expertise; no one questions the calibre of those appointed, nor their ability to make useful

---

14   See, eg, 'No Joe Soaps among the people's peers', *The Telegraph*, 27 April 2001; 'Lords: business as usual', *The Guardian*, 27 April 2001.

15   Gordon Prentice, on BBC R4 'The World at One', quoted in *The Telegraph*, 27 April 2001.

16   The 15 appointed included seven knights and three professors.

contributions to the work of the Lords. The Chairman of the Commission said that 'the process unearthed a wider variety of candidates than the old system'.[17] A more important concern is that it is over two years since the Commission recommended a batch of cross-bench peers in April 2001. As the Joint Committee on Lords Reform recently remarked, 'There is, therefore, a growing need to top up the stock of expertise and of younger members'.[18]

3   While the removal of most of the hereditary peers and the setting up of the Appointments Commission clearly represented an improvement on the unreformed House, it is worth noting the enormous problems, in terms of legitimacy, that still dog the Lords. It remains entirely unelected, dominated by the legally unrestrained patronage of the Prime Minister, and given that the Conservatives are still the largest party within it, despite having been twice decisively rejected at general elections, very unrepresentative. It is also male-dominated, very under-representative of ethnic minorities, of the working class, of most of the regions of England and, with a membership whose average age is 68, of the young and indeed the middle-aged.

The political behaviour of the House of Lords, before and after reform

How did the Lords' historical in-built Conservative weighting affect its work in practice? The Lords were clearly aware of the fact that if they were to create serious difficulties for Labour governments, demand among Labour MPs for reform of the Lords would become more pressing. Commentators suggest that although the House has traditionally been generally sympathetic to Conservative governments, it has tended to adopt a more even-handed approach to legislation emanating from a Labour administration than would have been expected. It was particularly noticeable that the House's general sympathy towards Conservative administrations did not result in servile obedience to the Conservative administrations of 1979–97. Writing in 1985, Donald Shell found that the Lords were proving unexpectedly difficult for the Thatcher government:

Donald Shell, 'The House of Lords and the Thatcher government' (1985) Parl Aff 16, 28–29

There seems something paradoxical in a Conservative Government experiencing real difficulties with the House of Lords. After all, hereditary peers out-number created peers by almost two to one, and the Conservative Party remains far and away the largest single party in the House. Yet by Summer 1984 it was apparent that Mrs Thatcher's legislation was more at risk in the Lords than in the Commons.

In the 1983–84 session there were indications of a more determined and self-confident mood amongst peers. With a Commons majority of 146 and a leader more ascendant within the Conservative Party than for many years (perhaps since Disraeli), it was peers rather than MPs (either Government back-benchers or opposition MPs) who could exert parliamentary checks upon Government. Following the election, the Labour leader in the Lords emphasised that the House had a 'much heavier responsibility' because of the huge Government majority in the Commons and even though this view was firmly repudiated by the Lord Chancellor, peers were undoubtedly conscious that they could more readily oblige governments to reconsider legislative

---

17   *The Telegraph,* 27 April 2001.
18   HL 97, HC 668 (2002–03), para 30.

proposals than MPs could. As this situation became more widely recognised, peers were put on their mettle. 'It is an interesting constitutional situation that gives an unelected chamber a greater influence than the elected chamber to change the minds of the executive on legislation', bemoaned a senior Tory MP.

[Shell goes on to find that the Lords' lack of obedience to the wishes of Conservative Governments is not simply due to the fact that there is no overall Conservative majority in the House.]

... Conservative back-benchers in the House have on some issues proved unreliable. Such unreliability may be expressed by voting with the opposition (and on average in 22 major defeats from 1979–84, 154 Conservative peers did enter the opposition lobby), or by abstention or absence.

... there is nothing like the machinery for whipping which exists in the Commons: there are no 'area Whips' though subjects may be allocated as the special responsibility of certain individual whips. This is also true of the other parties, though they do use three line whips more frequently.

Whipping in the Lords remains essentially low-key. It may be possible to persuade peers, but they cannot be coerced, commanded or bullied. Apart from a handful of office-holders, they receive no salaries; the vast majority are part-timers in the House, and very few can have ambitions for office. In such circumstances heavy whipping is unlikely to be effective.

... once the Government has gone down to a clear defeat, a significant compromise will usually have to be made, as it was on the Local Government Paving Bill in 1984. If that compromise is again rejected, then the Government will probably have to give way, as it did on accommodation for the elderly in the 1984 Housing and Building Control Bill.

Notes

1   The Lords did not display any more obedience to the Major administration, as examples given below of major government defeats on televising of sport, splitting of pensions and other matters indicate.

2   However, any claim that the Lords have been even-handed as between Conservative and Labour administrations would be going much too far, as the figures reveal. In the six years 1964–70, the Lords inflicted 116 defeats on the Labour government; between 1970–74, by contrast, they inflicted a mere 26 defeats on the Conservative administration. The contrast with the next two administrations is still more dramatic: the Lords imposed 355 defeats on the 1974–79 Labour government compared with less than a third of that figure (100) over the seven years 1979–86 of the Thatcher government. As Mr Straw (then Home Secretary) noted in the Queen's Speech debate in 1998, 'In an average Session when the Conservatives have been in power, there have been 13 defeats of government business in the [Lords]. In an average Session when Labour has been in power the figure has been five times that – on average 60 defeats.'[19] Thus, the Lords cannot be described as 'independent' of party influence, indeed it is very far from such a state; what can be sustained is the much more modest claim that peers display far more independence from party than do MPs.

3   Ultimately, however, major points of government legislation will usually be carried, even if the Lords oppose them. This is due to a mixture of legal and conventional restraints on the powers of the House, which will be examined in the next section.

---

19   HC Deb cols 573–74 (30 November 1998).

LIMITATIONS ON THE POWERS OF THE HOUSE OF LORDS

Legal limitations

The *legal* constraints on the power of the Lords arise under the Parliament Act 1911, as amended by the Parliament Act 1949. As AW Bradley and ECS Wade note, the Act of 1911 was brought in after the 'rather uncertain convention' that the Lords should give way to the Commons when the people's will was behind that body broke down when the Lords rejected Lloyd George's budget in 1909.[20]

Parliament Act 1911 (as amended by the Parliament Act 1949)[21]
Powers of House of Lords as to Money Bills

1. (1) If a Money Bill, having been passed by the House of Commons, and sent up to the House of Lords at least one month before the end of the session, is not passed by the House of Lords without amendment within one month after it is so sent up to that House, the Bill shall, unless the House of Commons direct to the contrary, be presented to His Majesty and become an Act of Parliament on the Royal Assent being signified notwithstanding that the House of Lords have not consented to the Bill.

(2) A Money Bill means a Public Bill which in the opinion of the Speaker of the House of Commons contains only provisions dealing with all or any of the following subjects, namely, the imposition, repeal, remission, alteration, or regulation of taxation; the imposition for the payment of debt or other financial purposes of charges on the Consolidated Fund, or on money provided by Parliament, or the variation or repeal of any such charges; supply; the appropriation, receipt, custody, issue or audit of accounts of public money; the raising or guarantee of any loan or the repayment thereof; or subordinate matters incidental to those subjects or any of them. In this subsection the expressions 'taxation,' 'public money,' and 'loan' respectively do not include any taxation, money, or loan raised by local authorities or bodies for local purposes . . .

Restriction of the powers of the House of Lords as to Bills other than Money Bills

2. (1) If any Public Bill (other than a Money Bill or a Bill containing any provision to extend the maximum duration of Parliament beyond five years) is passed by the House of Commons [in two successive sessions] (whether of the same Parliament or not), and having been sent up to the House of Lords at least one month before the end of the session, is rejected by the House of Lords in each of those sessions, that Bill shall, on its rejection [for the second time] by the House of Lords, unless the House of Commons direct to the contrary, be presented to His Majesty and become an Act of Parliament on the Royal Assent being signified thereto, notwithstanding that the House of Lords have not consented to the Bill: Provided that this provision shall not take effect unless [one year has elapsed] between the date of the second reading in the first of those sessions of the Bill in the House of Commons and the date on which it passes the House of Commons [in the second of those sessions].

(2) When a Bill is presented to His Majesty for assent in pursuance of the provisions of this section, there shall be endorsed on the Bill the certificate of the Speaker of the House of Commons signed by him that the provisions of this section have been duly complied with.

---

20 See AW Bradley and ECS Wade, *Constitutional and Administrative Law,* 11th edn (1993), p 204.
21 Amendments made by the 1949 Act appear in square brackets.

(3) A Bill shall be deemed to be rejected by the House of Lords if it is not passed by the House of Lords either without amendment or with such amendments only as may be agreed to by both Houses.

(4) A Bill shall be deemed to be the same Bill as a former Bill sent up to the House of Lords in the preceding session if, when it is sent up to the House of Lords, it is identical with the former Bill or contains only such alterations as are certified by the Speaker of the House of Commons to be necessary owing to the time which has elapsed since the date of the former Bill, or to represent any amendments which have been made by the House of Lords in the former Bill in the preceding session, and any amendments which are certified by the Speaker to have been made by the House of Lords [in the second session] and agreed to by the House of Commons shall be inserted in the Bill as presented for Royal Assent in pursuance of this section:

Provided that the House of Commons may, if they think fit, on the passage of such a Bill through the House [in the second session], suggest any further amendments without inserting the amendments in the Bill, and any such suggested amendments shall be considered by the House of Lords, and, if agreed to by that House, shall be treated as amendments made by the House of Lords and agreed to by the House of Commons but the exercise of this power by The House of Commons shall not affect the operation of this section in the event of the Bill being rejected by the House of Lords.

Certificate of Speaker

3. Any certificate of the Speaker of the House of Commons given under this Act shall be conclusive for all purposes, and shall not be questioned in any court of law.

Notes

1   The Parliament Acts thus allow the House of Commons to assert political supremacy over the Lords in two very important instances. First, s 2 of the Parliament Act 1911 makes various provisions to present a Bill for the Royal Assent despite the opposition of the Lords. When a Bill has been passed by the Commons in two successive sessions and it is rejected for a second time by the Lords it can be presented on its second rejection for the Royal Assent. One year must elapse between the second reading of the Bill in the Commons at the first session and its passing in the Commons in the second. Note that a Bill is deemed rejected by the Lords if it is either not passed unamended by it, or only with such amendments as are agreed to by both Houses (s 2(3)).

2   Secondly, if a Bill is a money Bill as defined in s 1(2) of the Parliament Act 1911, and is passed by the Commons but is not passed by the Lords without amendment within one month after their receiving it, it shall be presented to the Queen for the Royal Assent and become an Act of Parliament. This provision, adopted with a view to stopping the Lords blocking the passing of essential financial legislation and contained in s 1(1) of the 1911 Act, was brought forward after the Lords had rejected the Finance Bill 1909.

3   However, the limits on the Lords' power under the Parliament Acts are not as significant as may at first appear. First, not all Bills are subject to the Parliament Acts. Exemption extends to private Bills, Statutory Instruments, Bills prolonging the life of Parliament beyond five years and Bills originating in the House of Lords (around a third of government Bills). Secondly, in practice, the government will not want to wait for over a year before securing the passage of its legislation and so will be prepared to accept compromise amendments.

4   As previously mentioned, the Lords are generally circumspect in the use of their formal powers. They will, however, on occasion use their powers of suspension fully as in relation to the Trade Union and Labour Relations (Amendment) Bill 1974–75. In the debate in the Lords in relation to their amendments to this Bill, Lord Carrington said:

> In our system we have hitherto taken the view that the will of the elected house must in the end prevail, but that there should be a second House which has the opportunity ... to enforce a delay in which there can be reassessment by Government ... If we now decide to use that very limited power we are not thwarting the will of the people for, in so far as it is represented by the House of Commons, it will and must prevail in a comparatively short time. [HL Deb vol 365 col 1742 (11 November 1975).]

The Lords eventually allowed the Bill to go for Royal Assent only because the government threatened to pass it under the Parliament Acts procedure. By delaying the Bill the Lords had ensured that it would receive greater scrutiny. The suspensory powers were again used to the full in relation to the War Crimes Bill 1991, which had to be passed under the Parliament Acts procedure, as did the European Elections Act 1999 and the Sexual Offences (Amendment) Act 2000 (see further below).[22]

5   As Meg Russell points out, while it is commonly thought that the Parliament Acts allow the Lords to impose a delay of one year to a Bill, in practice, the period of delay may be much shorter:

> One of the difficulties with the current system is that the delay which can be imposed by the House of Lords is indeterminate. The Parliament Act stipulates only that a bill may be reintroduced in the next parliamentary session, if more than a year has passed since its second reading in the House of Commons. However, in practice the period of delay imposed by the upper house may be relatively short, particularly if a bill is sent to the House of Lords late in the parliamentary session.

> For example, the European Parliamentary Elections Bill – to introduce a proportional voting system for European elections – was only the second bill since 1949 to be forced through the house under the Parliament Act procedures. However, objections in the House of Lords, which repeatedly tried to amend the bill to provide for 'open' rather than 'closed' lists of candidates delayed the bill by only about a month. Although the bill was introduced in the House of Commons in October 1997, it did not pass to the Lords until the spring of 1998. Its third reading in the house was then not until October that year. This is when the disagreement between the chambers became clear. During the months of October and November 1998 the bill was repeatedly amended in the Lords, and shuttled back and forth to the House of Commons, where the amendments were rejected each time. The Houses failed to agree by the end of the parliamentary session in November. However the bill was able to be reintroduced only eight days later, at the start of the new session. The bill's opponents in the House of Lords were, ironically, being co-operative when they ensured the bill was rejected outright in December, as it was then able to be sent for royal assent. The inconvenience caused to government by this episode in the end was relatively minor, and the elections held in June 1999 used the 'closed' list system.[23]

6   Examination of the powers of the House of Lords should be put in comparative context. The following table indicates the powers of second chambers overseas over ordinary legislation. It should be noted that virtually all second chambers overseas have additional powers over legislation altering the constitution, a matter discussed further below.

---

22 At the time of writing, it appears that the Parliament Acts may be used in relation to legislation banning fox-hunting.
23 M Russell, *Reforming the House of Lords: Lessons from Overseas* (2000), p 266.

M Russell and R Cornes, 'The Royal Commission on Reform of the House of Lords: a House for the future?' (2001) 64 MLR 82, 84

Table 1: Power of the upper house over ordinary and financial Bills in 10 democracies

Country	Power over ordinary Bills	Power over financial Bills
Australia	Total veto	As for ordinary Bills
Canada	Total veto	As for ordinary Bills
France	6–12 months' delay	As little as 15 days' delay
Germany	Total veto over Bills affecting states, delay over others	As for ordinary Bills
Ireland	Three months' delay	Three weeks' delay
Italy	Total veto	As for ordinary Bills
Japan	Two months' delay	One month's delay
Spain	Two months' delay	As for ordinary Bills
Switzerland	Total veto	As for ordinary Bills
UK	Approximately one year's delay	One month's delay for 'Money Bills'
USA	Total veto	As for ordinary Bills

The Bryce Commission, established in 1917 by David Lloyd George to study options for House of Lords reform, wisely stated that one of the four main functions of an upper house was 'The interposition of so much delay (and no more) in the passing of a Bill into law as may be needed to enable the opinion of the nation to be adequately expressed upon it.' The chamber's current powers could be said to meet this requirement.

Conventional restraints upon the Lords

The conventions and their observation

The Lords accept a number of self-imposed informal constraints that have developed into conventions designed to avoid accusations that they are thwarting the will of the people. One of the most important conventions has been termed 'the doctrine of the mandate'. This doctrine was explained by Lord Salisbury in 1964: 'as a guiding principle, where legislation had been promised in the party manifesto, the Lords would not block it on the ground that it should be regarded as having been approved by the British people.'[24] This doctrine was developed during the post-war Labour administration but now normally applies to 'mandated' Bills of either party. However, this doctrine does not mean that the Lords will refrain from insisting on an amendment to a Bill even though the effect will almost certainly be to kill it. This occurred in relation to the House of Commons (Redistribution of Seats) Bill in 1968–69.

When the Lords oppose a Bill sent up by the Commons they nearly always propose amendments at the committee stage rather than vote against the second reading, but there is a (weak) convention that amendments at the committee stage should not re-open matters of principle already accepted by the Commons. The Lords will rarely insist on their amendments to a government Bill if a compromise can be reached, although of course they may do so when the government lacks an effective majority to

---

24   HL Deb vol 261 col 66 (4 November 1964).

ensure their rejection in the Commons. O Hood Phillips has also argued[25] that there is almost a convention that the Lords will not return a government Bill to the Commons for reconsideration more than once, though the behaviour of the Lords in relation to legislation sponsored by the Blair administration (below) casts this assertion somewhat into doubt.

Donald Shell considers that the combined effect of these legal and conventional restraints on the Lords means that it is unable to provide an appreciable check on the government-dominated Commons. The experience of the Thatcher government is again used as an example:

> To the Thatcher Governments of the 1980s the House was frequently an irritant but never a serious obstacle. In particular, legislation relating to local government and its various responsibilities, notably education and housing, was frequently amended against the will of the government. Ministers regularly gave ground to the Lords, with the House even being described as the real opposition during the 1983 Parliament when the Labour opposition in the Commons was at its lowest ebb. But in the late 1980s there appeared to a hardening of ministerial attitudes to the Lords, with the Government endeavouring wherever possible to overturn any defeat it suffered there. This culminated in the used of the Parliament Act procedures to pass the War Crimes Act of 1991, a Bill which the Government chose to persist with notwithstanding strong opposition in the Lords, not least from the judicial peers, as well as much opposition from within Conservative Party ranks. It was certainly not a manifesto Bill, and not at all the kind of legislation envisaged as appropriate for Parliament Act procedures when these had first been formulated. [26]

Notes

1   Shell's view here (expressed in 1994) that the Lords were 'an irritant but never a serious obstacle' to the Thatcher government seems at odds with his opinion in 1985 that the government was then experiencing 'real difficulties' with the Lords (above, pp 349–50). The inference is presumably that the 'more determined and self-confident mood amongst peers' in 1983 which he noted in his earlier article was a product of the peers' knowledge that the Commons opposition was at that time relatively ineffectual, given the huge Conservative majority after the 1983 General Election; and further that as the Conservatives' majority was progressively reduced in subsequent elections, the peers retreated towards a more facilitative and anodyne approach. If this explanation is correct, it may be concluded that the Lords are capable of taking a flexible approach towards their self-imposed restraints, adopting a more bullish approach when the political situation seems to demand it. This is one argument in favour of leaving such restraints on a self-imposed basis only.

2   However, any notion that as a government's majority decreases[27] the House of Lords is content to leave real opposition to government proposals to the Commons seems hard to square with the important series of defeats inflicted by the Lords on the Major government's legislation – defeats on matters of controversial policy relating to television rights to sport (described as 'the biggest Government upset in the Lords since 1988'),[28] pensions and rights of asylum seekers. While it is tempting to try to formulate general rules about the behaviour of the Lords which relate it to

25   *Constitutional and Administrative Law*, 7th edn (1987), p 148.
26   Donald Shell, 'The House of Lords: time for a change?' (1994) Parl Aff 721, 733.
27   John Major's administration was reduced to a majority of just one in 1996.
28   'Peers inflict huge defeat on TV sport', *The Independent*, 7 February 1996. The defeat in 1988 referred to was the 133 vote defeat over the 'poll tax' in May of that year.

the situation in the Commons, it is quite possible that, the Salisbury Convention excepted,[29] the most important factor in determining the assertiveness of the Lords is simply the nature of the legislation put before them.

3   The House of Lords has shown a fair degree of assertion in relation to the present Labour government, even before the removal of the hereditary peers. One peer recently compared the performance of the Lords with the Commons since 1997.

HL Deb cols 627–628 (21 January 2003)

Lord Phillips of Sudbury: What is the best demonstration of effective holding to account of a Government? Most people would say that it is the ability of the Opposition in the House of Commons to vote down measures by the Government which they think are bad or misconceived. Perhaps we may look at the statistics. In the five Sessions of Parliament since the present Government came to power in 1997, there have been 1,640 Divisions in the House of Commons. On how many occasions were the Government defeated in a whipped vote? The answer is not one.

I put it to the House that for all the grand talk about legitimacy, the reason that there is a decline in democratic allegiance in this country is that the House of Commons is no longer able to hold the executive to account at all.

In the same period, in this place, we had 639 whipped votes. The Government won 475; they were defeated in 164 Divisions. Therefore, in one in four Divisions throughout the five-year period, the Government in this place have been defeated, whereas in another place, on not one single occasion have they been defeated in a whipped Division. In the past year, the number of defeats has risen from one in four to one in three. The Divisions are not the end of the matter because on the back of defeats governments tend to be much more pliant towards opposition amendments. If one were to add up the number of forced amendments, it would be seen to be a huge number; more than [in the Commons]. In looking to legitimacy, it is reasonable to look at those statistics.

Notes

1   A striking example of the Lords' assertiveness was the European Elections Bill 1998 discussed by Russell above. Defending themselves against the charge that their insistence on the amendment to introduce 'open' rather than 'closed lists' for the elections breached the Convention, Lord Mackay cited the relevant pledge in Labour's 1997 manifesto: 'We have long supported a proportional voting system for election to the European Parliament.' He commented: 'There is no mention of the system to be used. There is no mention of a closed list [or of] ... an open list. Therefore this Bill, if we amend it with the open list, honours in every possible way the commitment given by the Labour Party in its manifesto ... your Lordships are not breaching [the Salisbury] Convention.'[30] Eventually, the Bill was passed using the Parliament Acts procedure.

2   The Lords took a similarly assertive stance over the Teaching and Higher Education Bill 1998; widespread opposition in the Lords to a provision in the Bill which waived the payment of fees for the fourth year of a degree taken at a Scottish university for Scottish students, but not those from the rest of the UK, led the Lords to restore on three occasions an amendment rejected by the Commons which equalised the position for students from all parts of the UK. The government was

---

29   See p 354, above.
30   HL Deb cols 1343–34 (18 November 1998).

eventually forced to promise an independent review of the system within six months of its establishment, an important concession.

3   Much more controversially, the House of Lords in 1998 and again in 2000 decisively rejected the Commons' attempt to legalise the age of consent between homosexuals and heterosexuals.[31] Their Lordships were warned in clear terms by both Lord Lester and Lord Williams for the government that a failure to equalise the age of consent would almost certainly result in the UK being found in breach of the ECHR, but undeterred, the House voted by 290 to 122 against the clause to equalise. When the government again brought the change in under the Sexual Offences Amendment Bill 2000, the Lords again voted it down.[32] Eventually the government used the Parliament Acts procedure to make the reform without the Lords' consent, only the fifth time that the procedure has been used.

The effect of removal of the hereditary peers

What was unknown at the time that the House of Lords Act 1999 was passed was whether the reformed House would react to its small increase in legitimacy by becoming more assertive in its relations with the Commons. As seen above, it is the *conventional* restraints on the exercise of its own powers that, in practice, keep it firmly subordinate to the Commons, and thus the government. One aspect of this restraint, which figures as at the least an entrenched *custom*, if not exactly a constitutional *convention*, was the notion that the Lords would not use their powers – left untouched by the Parliament Acts – to vote down subordinate legislation. It appears that the Lords had only in fact rejected secondary legislation once in the 20th century,[33] in 1968 in relation to a sanctions order against Rhodesia. That in fact was an order requiring positive approval from the Lords: Erskine May reveals that they have *never* voted down orders requiring only the negative approval procedure. Up until recently, the Lords had not voted on any item of subordinate legislation submitted to them for consideration. However, when this was pointed out to them and it was suggested that a convention had come into being that the Lords would not vote down items of subordinate legislation, their Lordships response was bullish: a motion by Lord Simon of Glaisdale to the effect that the House had unfettered freedom to vote on any subordinate legislation before them was overwhelmingly approved.[34]

Nevertheless, the Lords still held back from exercising this freedom until after the partial reform of their House. The dispute which eventually caused them to exercise it related to the refusal of the government, in its legislation governing the London Mayor and Assembly, to give candidates a free 'mail shot' to the electorate. The Lords chose to express their discontent on the matter in a novel way: they voted upon a piece of delegated legislation (the Greater London Authority (Election Expenses) Order 2000), which dealt with the nuts and bolts of the London mayoral and assembly elections, in particular the amount of electoral expenditure which candidates would be allowed to incur; the Order required only negative approval, that is, it would go through automatically unless voted against. To the consternation of the government, the Lords

---

31   For the 1998 debate, see HL Deb vol 592 cols 936 *et seq* (22 July 1998).
32   HL Deb vol 619 cols 19 *et seq* (13 November 2000).
33   See R Brazier, *Constitutional Practice*, 2nd edn (1994), p 254, fn 119.
34   HL Deb vol 559 col 356 (20 October 1994).

threw the Order out and in doing so quite clearly relied upon their newly reformed status. During the debate, there was some disagreement about whether the practice of the Lords not to reject secondary legislation had achieved the status of a constitutional convention. Some peers certainly took this view. Lord Hughes, for example, said: '... in relation to orders [it was my understanding] that secondary legislation may be challenged only on the grounds that it is not in accord with primary legislation.'[35] Others firmly rejected such a notion, pointing to the House's resolution of October 1994 cited above. Others still, such as Lord Cranbourne, for the Conservatives,[36] appeared to believe that while there may have been convention that the House would not reject such legislation, it would not apply now, the House being a reformed chamber which was not necessarily bound by the conventions of the unreformed House.

In general, there was strong support for a more assertive attitude on the part of the new House. Lord Mackay noted that a government spokesperson (the Lord Privy Seal) had stated in the *House Magazine* on 27 September 1999 that the 'new' House of Lords 'will be more legitimate, because its members have earned their places, and therefore more effective'.[37] The Earl of Onslow said emphatically:

> ... this House now has legitimacy, which it has not had since 1911 ... I can do what I would not have done [in the old House]. Then ... the House lacked legitimacy, and also ... there was an imbalance in the House. The imbalance has been rightly destroyed and we have been given new legitimacy.[38]

Such attitudes could also be seen in the response of the Lords to a controversial piece of *primary* legislation, which would have restricted the right of a defendant to choose trial by jury. The heart of the government's Criminal Justice (Mode of Trial) Bill was clause 1, which removed the right of defendants to choose jury trial in 'either way' offences, such as theft and burglary. The crucial part of the debate took part in Committee stage in January 2000[39] and only got as far as clause 1. The very first amendment put down restored the right of the defendant to be tried by a jury in such cases at his election, and thus ripped the heart out of the Bill. It was therefore what is commonly referred to as a 'wrecking amendment' since it altered the fundamental principle of the legislation. This amendment was carried by the Lords by a large majority: 222 votes to 126. The government spokesperson, Baroness Jay, immediately announced that since the Bill 'no longer represented Government policy' it would be withdrawn.[40] It is important to note that the Bill started life in the Lords, not the Commons. Therefore, by effectively throwing out the Bill, the Lords had prevented the Commons being able even to see it. A report in *The Times* remarked that this was the 'first time in memory' that 'a mainstream Bill' had been 'killed ... before it had reached the elected House'. As Lord Windlesham put it: 'This [was] a significant moment in the short life of the reformed House.'[41]

---

35   HL Deb col 164 (22 February 2000).
36   *Ibid*, cols 151–52.
37   *Ibid*, col 143.
38   *Ibid*, cols 163–64.
39   HL Deb col 1246 *et seq* (20 January 2000).
40   *Ibid*, col 1297.
41   *Ibid*, col 1273.

A further example of assertiveness by the Lords, which provoked rather less enthusiasm by many constitutional observers, was its rejection of the notorious 'section 28' of the Local Government Act. This provision is actually contained in s 2A of the LGA 1986 and it prohibits local authorities from 'promoting homosexuality' generally and in particular from 'promoting the teaching in any maintained school of the acceptability of homosexuality as a pretended family relationship' (sub-s (2)). This provision had long been controversial, with many seeing it as enshrining discrimination against, or at least official disapproval for homosexuality in the law. Labour sought to remove this through a clause in what became the Local Government Act 2000. This was opposed by many – particularly Conservative – peers in the Lords. Baroness Young, proposing an amendment to keep clause 2A, said:

> Lady Jay [of the Government] ... has said on more than one occasion that the new House is more legitimate. We are perfectly entitled to take a view on this matter.[42]

The attempt to abolish the clause was defeated by 270 to 228 votes in a debate that illustrated that whilst the Lords can act as a bulwark against the erosion of civil liberties they also have a tendency to be much more conservative – even reactionary – in matters of morality, perhaps not surprisingly, given that the average age of those who sit in the Lords is 68. For the full debate see HL Debs vol 616 cols 97–130 (24 July 2000).

THE WORK OF THE HOUSE OF LORDS

The work of the House and its effectiveness will be examined in this section. Broadly, the House has two roles, undertaking detailed scrutiny of both legislation and government policy and administration. These roles include the House's important functions of initiating legislation and scrutinising and reporting on the policy and legislative output of the institutions of the European Union. As Brigid Hadfield notes:

> The White Paper of 1968 on reform of the Lords listed the following main functions–
>
> (a) the provision of a forum for full and free debate on matters of public interest;
>
> (b) the revision of public bills brought from the House of Commons;
>
> (c) the initiation of public legislation, including in particular those Government bills which are less controversial in party political terms, and private members' bills;
>
> (d) the consideration of subordinate legislation;
>
> (e) the scrutiny of the activities of the executive; and
>
> (f) the scrutiny of private legislation.
>
> To this must now be added – most importantly – the scrutiny of (proposed) legislation emanating from the European Economic Community ... which last function takes place mainly in Committee and sub-committee rather than on the floor of the House. (B Hadfield, 'Whither or whether the House of Lords' (1994) 35(4) NILQ 320).
>
> It is important to note that while the Lord Chancellor is the Speaker of the House of Lords, 'his role is quite unlike that of other Speakers. He has no effective and controlling powers, and the

---

42   HL Deb vol 616 col 103 (24 July 2000).

standing orders of the House deny him power to maintain order. His role is 'ornamental and symbolic';[43] the responsibility for maintaining order rests with the House as a whole.'[44]

Scrutiny of legislation

The work of the House in considering public Bills constitutes its single most time-consuming task, reflecting the fact that such scrutiny is generally regarded as the Lords' most important role. Philip Norton has suggested three main features of the House of Lords which render it 'particularly suitable' for the task of detailed consideration of legislation.

Philip Norton, 'Parliament II: the House of Lords', in B Jones (ed), *Politics UK* (1994), p 354

First, as an unelected House, it cannot claim the legitimacy to reject the principle of measures agreed by the elected House. Thus, basically by default, it focuses on the detail rather than the principle. Secondly, its membership includes people who have distinguished themselves in particular fields – such as the sciences, the law, education, industry industrial relations – who can look at relevant legislation from the perspective of practitioners in the field rather than from the perspective of party politicians. And, third, the House has the time to debate non-money bills in more details than is usually possible in the Commons – unlike in the Commons there is no provision for a guillotine and all amendments are discussed. The House thus serves as an important revising chamber, trying to ensure that a bill is well drafted and internally coherent. In order to improve the bill, it will suggest amendments, most of which will be accepted by the Commons. In terms of legislative scrutiny, the House has thus developed a role which is viewed as complementary to, rather than one competing with (or identical to) that of the Commons.

Notes

1   Two of the positive attributes which Norton identifies arise from the fact that the House is not elected; the first directly, the second from the fact that it cannot consider money Bills, which is a reflection of its lower, because undemocratic, status. (Such a wide disability does not apply, for example, to the elected US Senate.) The paradoxical notion that much of the value which commentators perceive in the Lords is attributable to the one characteristic which most lays it open to attack – its unelected status – is a recurring theme in the literature on the subject.

2   To the above positive attributes can be added the following: the greater age of members in the Lords, which arguably gives them a more mature and experienced outlook; their long terms of office, which mean they can take a more independent line, not being subject to re-selection; their comparative lack of political ambition, flowing from the fact that most peers are at the end of their political careers.[45]

3   What is the *nature* of the legislative work of the Lords?:

The legislative work of the Lords relates mainly to public Bills, on the consideration of which it expends half its time. The formal delaying power of the House is probably less important in real terms than the fact that its presence means a prolongation of the parliamentary consideration of

---

43   HL 9 (1987–88), para 13.
44   Griffith and Ryle, *op cit*, p 464.
45   See, eg, Russell, *op cit*, pp 248–49.

Bills, providing opportunity for more detailed scrutiny and for second thoughts on the part of the Government, in the light of comments made both inside and outside Parliament. Also, its existence enables Bills to be initiated elsewhere than in the Commons, which tends to suffer from a glut of Bills at the beginning of a session (especially after a general election) and from the Finance Bill in the second part of a session.

... it would seem from a consideration of the 12 parliamentary sessions since 1972 that the Lords do have a valuable revising role, albeit a more limited role than is usually appreciated.

It should be noted, first, that many of the Commons' Bills go through the Lords 'on the nod'. This is probably best explained by the subject-matter of those Bills, although a partial explanation may be found in the fact that these Bills arrive in the Lords later rather than earlier in the parliamentary session. The conclusion is, however, that the Lords concentrate their revising efforts on only a limited number of Commons' Bills. Secondly, the majority of amendments proposed and accepted are of the technical or drafting kind; these cause no difficulties to any Government of any complexion and this is the main explanation for their high level of acceptability to the Commons. Some amendments are, however, of substantive importance.[46]

4   The picture that emerges from examining the Lords' legislative work is one of a House that is concerned not so much with the broad policy behind Bills, but rather with ensuring that measures will be workable in practice. In this sense, the Lords may be seen as complementary to the House of Commons, which is regarded as unsuitable for the detailed scrutiny of legislation, due to its combative style of debate, and the fact that the opposition will oppose much government legislation as a matter of course.[47] However, such a division of labour by the two Houses arguably leaves a lacuna in the scrutiny provided by Parliament as a whole: if the Commons opposition attacks policy wholesale, whilst the Lords largely ignore it, measured and discriminating criticisms of policy may never receive consideration.

5   Clarke and Shell compare the ability of the House of Lords to revise and amend legislation with that of the Commons.

DN Clarke and D Shell, 'Revision and amendment by the House of Lords: a case study' [1994] PL 409, 410–14

The House of Lords and government legislation

Increasingly in recent years attention has focused on the role of the House in making a seemingly ever growing number of amendments to an ever expanding quantity of legislation. In the early 1950s the number of pages of primary legislation enacted each year rose to around 1,000; by the 1970s it had reached almost 2,000, and in the 1980s up to 1987 the average was over 2,500, after which the page size for legislation altered, though it would seem volume continued to increase. Far from reducing the quantity of legislation, and improving its quality, as the Conservatives in opposition in the 1970s had argued was necessary, the Conservatives in office since 1979 steadily increased the quantity. Nor would many accept that there had been any improvement in quality in the sense of clarity and precision and the avoidance of unnecessary complexity and obscurity. It has been widely argued that this has been the main reason underlying the vast growth in the number of amendments made to Bills in the revising chamber. [In the three sessions 1970–73 the House of Lords made (on average) some 950 amendments per session to government Bills; by 1979–82 the average had risen to almost 1,300 per session, but by 1987–90 it had gone up to an average of over 2,600.] Overwhelmingly these were amendments introduced by ministers

---

46   B Hadfield, 'Whither or whether the House of Lords' (1994) 35(4) NILQ 320, pp 325, 326.
47   See Part III Chapter 1.

themselves, though many were of course responses to representations made to Government by the many interests typically affected by legislation, such representations being made both within and outside of parliament. Twenty years ago a major study of parliamentary scrutiny of legislation concluded that many Bills emerge from the House of Commons 'in a state unfit to be let loose on the public' [JAG Griffith, *Parliamentary Scrutiny of Government Bills* (1974), p 231]. Since then the situation has deteriorated considerably. As a result the House of Lords sits longer hours and spends an increasing proportion of its time tidying up legislation brought to it from the Commons in a highly unsatisfactory form. In the 1992–93 session the House of Lords spent almost half its sitting time dealing with Government legislation, and made 2,056 amendments to Government Bills, of which only 18 were subsequently rejected by the Commons.

The ability to revise and amend

... it is the way the legislative procedure operates in the Upper House which facilitates the submission and consideration of amendments. The student of Parliament is taught at an early stage that a Bill goes through the same stages in each House; a second reading to debate the principles of the Bill, a committee stage to consider the detail, a report stage to report on and consider final amendments before the third reading completes the process. The keen student may even take note that the Lords always sits as a committee of the whole House, the Commons rarely so. The reality is that the procedure is similar only in form. In the case of the passage of the [Leasehold Reform, Housing and Urban Development Act 1993] through the Commons, for example, only 32 MPs were assigned to the Standing Committee. Though the report stage occupied about 10 hours, the third reading debate, following on immediately [the usual practice], lasted barely 40 minutes. Some of the themes and concerns that were to surface in the Upper House had an earlier rehearsal in the Commons – but by no means all. Amendments to the Bill in the Commons were few; at the committee stage, some threats were headed off by promises to reconsider and then by making no change at the report stage. Where divisions were called at report the House divided largely on party lines. This procedure is, in reality, highly ritualised. The Government has its majority, even in committee; the divisions called by the Opposition at report stage on the 1993 Act were set pieces on a few issues of principle. Where amendments were put down by Conservative back-bench opponents at the report stage, the arguments were largely markers for later debate in the Lords.

It is the different way the same format of committee stage, report, and third reading is used that permits the Lords to make the best use of the time to consider amendments. Since the committee stage involves the whole House and amendments are also allowed at the third reading stage in the Lords [four and a half hours on the 1993 Act], any peer who has a concern can put down an amendment at the committee stage knowing that there are two further occasions to return to the issue. Indeed, many such amendments are acknowledged to be 'probing'; seeking to elucidate the meaning of a particular section; or to judge the Government's attitude to some change; or, by listening to other contributions to the debate, to gauge the degree of support from elsewhere in the House. Many amendments are withdrawn, with consent, without a vote thus enabling private discussions, redrafting and resubmission at report or third reading. These three genuine opportunities permit a process which allows proposals to be aired, reconsidered and reformulated in a way that is not possible in the Commons.

The Upper House is also jealous of the opportunity to debate those changes proposed by the Government itself. Thus Lord Williams of Elvel, for the Opposition, insisted upon an explanation of a Government change to the 1993 Act stating:

> It is part of the job of this House, as a revising chamber, to correct the Government when it tries to slide through amendments without any proper debate.

This can be compared, on this legislation, to a whole series of amendments at report stage in the Commons, not all of them technical, which received no explanation whatsoever. [*Hansard* vol 218 cols 927–32. Given the decision in *Pepper v Hart* [1993] AC 593, allowing reference to statements in Parliament by the courts where legislation is ambiguous or obscure, it may be that there will be more chance of a relevant explanation by a Minister in the Lords being of relevance than in the Commons, where nothing may have been said.]

Notes

1 The House of Lords has recently agreed an important package of proposals designed to render its scrutiny more effective.[48] As well as changes to the timing of sittings and the parliamentary year, the changes include:

scrutinising virtually all major government Bills in draft; carry-over of Bills that have received pre-legislative scrutiny (so that they do not fall automatically at the end of a parliamentary session if not passed), subject to certain safeguards; scrutiny of the Finance Bill (the Bill implementing the Budget) by a sub-committee of the Economic Affairs Committee; creation of a new Select Committee to scrutinise the merits of all statutory instruments subject to parliamentary scrutiny, the latter proposal being designed to ensure that statutory instruments of political importance were properly considered by [the] House.[49]

2 The Lords are often seen as having a particularly important role to play in the protection of civil liberties, an issue to which the Commons may often show little sensitivity when both main parties feel obliged to show their 'toughness' on law and order issues. The Lords inserted an important amendment to the Police and Criminal Evidence Bill 1984 allowing evidence unfairly obtained to be excluded; this eventually prompted the government to put forward its own amendment which became s 78 of the Act. The War Crimes Bill 1990 was rejected outright by the Lords, on the grounds that the convictions of former Nazi war criminals, which it aimed to facilitate, would be inherently unsafe. The government was forced to use the Parliament Act procedure to enable the Bill to become law. Similarly, in January 1997, the Lords defeated the government to procure an important amendment of principle to the Police Act 1997. As originally conceived, the Bill gave police officers power to enter premises to plant listening devices to assist in the detection of crime. Authorisation was to be given by the Chief Constable; by contrast when the police want to tap phones they must obtain a warrant from the Home Secretary. There was also no exception in relation to bugging premises where conversations involving legal professional privilege might take place – listening devices could therefore have been planted at lawyer's offices. The Lords inserted amendments to force the police to seek prior *judicial* approval before installing listening devices, forcing the government to bring forward its own, similar proposals.

3 One of the most important recent parliamentary innovations in relation to the protection of civil liberties and human rights is the Joint Committee on Human Rights, whose basic remit is to scrutinise Bills for compatibility with the ECHR, and report on changes that may be needed to achieve some compatibility. The Committee was particularly influential in relation to the Anti-Terrorism Bill 2001 and detailed examples of its work on that Bill are discussed below. For further detail of the Committee's work, see D Feldman,

---

48 First proposed by a Leader's Group to consider the working practices of the House; its report was considered by the House on 21 May 2002: HL Deb cols 641 *et seq*. Their recommendations were remitted to the Procedure Committee, which arrived at detailed proposals to put them into practice in their Fifth Report: HL 148 (2001–02). They were approved by the House on 24 July 2002: HL Deb cols 373 *et seq*.

49 HL Deb col 656 (21 May 2002), Lord Roper.

'Parliamentary scrutiny of legislation and human rights' [2002] PL 323 and Lord Lester, 'Parliamentary scrutiny of legislation under the Human Rights Act 1998.' (2002) 4 EHRLR 432.

4   The legislative role of the House of Lords is not confined to scrutiny of measures originating in the Commons. Bills which are not seen as contentious in party political terms are regularly introduced into the Lords, thus relieving pressure on the Commons. This work is by no means small in scale: Griffith and Ryle have compiled figures showing that in 1978, 58 Public General Acts were introduced in the Lords, 60 in 1979, 67 in 1980 and 57 in 1982.[50] From consideration of Acts from some sessions between 1978 and 1982, Hadfield has identified four (not exclusive) broad categories into which Public Bills introduced in the Lords can be placed:

(a) law reform measures, including consolidating Acts and Acts dealing with the administration of justice;

(b) international Acts, including the implementation of treaties;

(c) Acts relating solely to Northern Ireland or Scotland; and

(d) matters of non-controversial substance (in the party-political sense).[51]

5   Members of the Lords, unlike members of the Commons, are free to introduce Private Members' Bills into the House and there is usually enough time for them to be debated fully, although of course if they are passed this does not ensure that time will be found for them in the Commons. As the Lords have no constituents to whom they are accountable they may feel free to bring forward Private Members' Bills on emotive and contentious subjects such as homosexuality and abortion. The initiative for relaxing the law relating to homosexual conduct, which eventually resulted in the passing of the Sexual Offences Act 1967, came from the Lords, not the Commons. Similarly, the Anti-Discrimination (No 2) Bill 1972–73 raised interest when being discussed by the Lords' Select Committee. This led to espousal of the Bill first by backbenchers and then by the government. The eventual result was the Sex Discrimination Act 1975.

6   In 1992, the House of Lords created for itself an important new scrutinising mechanism for overseeing the use of delegated legislation, the scrutiny of which, as noted above, is generally thought to be inadequate in the Commons.[52] This is a new Select Committee on the Scrutiny of Delegated Powers (DPSC), since renamed the Delegated Powers and Regulatory Reform Committee. The remit of the Committee is 'to report whether the provisions of any Bill inappropriately delegate legislative powers; or whether they subject the exercise of legislative power to an inappropriate degree of parliamentary scrutiny';[53] the Committee itself has indicated that it will pay particular attention to Bills containing 'Henry VIII' clauses (giving ministers powers to repeal or amend primary legislation through order) and skeleton legislation which in effect gives ministers power to 'legislate' their own chosen policy through secondary legislation. The Committee has expressed

---

50   Griffith and Ryle, op cit, p 353.
51   Hadfield, op cit, p 325. For an example of a legislative debate in the Lords see below, pp 365–72.
52   We give here only a very brief summary of the Committee's work, drawing on C Himsworth's interesting analysis, 'The Delegated Powers Scrutiny Committee' [1995] PL 34. All quotes in the text are from this article, unless otherwise indicated.
53   First Report of the Select Committee on the Procedure of the House, HL Deb col 11 (1992–93) quoted ibid, p 36.

satisfaction with its own work; government has co-operated with it by producing a memorandum for most pieces of delegated legislation, which explains the purpose of a given provision and why delegated legislation has been used for it. The Committee has a particularly significant role examining orders made under the Henry VIII clause in the Regulatory Reform Act 2001. As a briefing note on the Committee explains:

regulatory reform orders may be made by any minister to amend or repeal any enactment of primary legislation with a view to removing or reducing any administrative or bureaucratic burden. Both Houses of Parliament must be satisfied that the technical requirements of the 2001 Act have been met. The 2001 Act provides for a two-stage process of parliamentary scrutiny:

1. The proposal, together with explanatory material is laid before Parliament in the form of a draft order. The Committee and its Commons equivalent have 60 days in which to report.

2. The government lays a draft order before Parliament, either in its original form or amended to take account of the two Committees' views, for approval by resolution of each House. This can only be done in the Lords after the Committee has made a second report on it.[54]

The Committee may be regarded as having made an important contribution to the scrutiny provided by the Lords, and to have provided a welcome focusing of attention on the increasing use of delegated legislation for matters of principle and substance.

The work of the House of Lords in practice: a case study

The following extracts from debate in the House of Lords illustrate the work of the second chamber in scrutinising and revising government legislation. The Bill in question was the Home Secretary's Anti-Terrorism, Crime and Security Bill 2001, introduced into Parliament in response to the perceived greater threat from international terrorism following the attacks on the United States on 11 September 2001. The Bill was a long one: 126 clauses and eight lengthy Schedules. Much of it did not in fact deal with specifically anti-terrorism measures. It included a new offence of incitement to religious hatred which, in itself, would clearly provide no assistance in the fight against terrorism, new powers of the police compulsorily to photograph criminal suspects – not just suspected terrorists (Part 10), a new procedure whereby Third Pillar EU criminal measures would become part of UK law via secondary legislation (Part 13) and measures to put in place a new Code of Practice on retention of communications data – websites visited, mobile phone calls made and so on (Part 11). Its most controversial part, which was aimed at terrorism, was Part 2. This gave power to the Home Secretary to detain non-British nationals suspected of involvement with international terrorism, who, it is thought, could not be convicted of any offence, but who also could not be deported to their country of origin because there were grounds to think that they would there be subject to torture or inhuman and degrading treatment, because to do so would violate Article 3 of the European Convention on Human Rights (ECHR), which is not derogable. In order to allow for such detention, the government decided to derogate from Article 5 ECHR which provides for the right to personal liberty. The Bill provided that the Home Secretary's determinations that a person was involved with international

---

54   Available at www.parliament.the-stationery-office.co.uk/pa/ld199798/ldbrief/lddeleg.pdf.

terrorism and his decisions to detain them could not be questioned in any court, but only in the Special Immigration Appeals Commission (SIAC), which is, however, a fully-fledged judicial tribunal.[55]

The approach of the Lords may be contrasted with the Commons, which first of all accepted a timetable of only 16 hours in which to scrutinise a Bill 124 pages long and containing an important derogation from the UK's international obligations under the ECHR, and then imposed not a single amendment on the government. One peer himself remarked upon the far heavier burden the Lords had taken up in scrutinising the legislation:[56]

> What concerns me most is that, had this House not had the time and the ability to scrutinise it, the legislation would have gone through. It is a matter of concern that a Bill containing 126 clauses should be sent to this House without most of them having been properly considered. It is no good the Home Secretary or any other Cabinet Minister complaining about this House, when it has done its job – a job which should have been done by the House of Commons in the first place, it having been elected to do so. It is entirely reprehensible that an elected House of Commons should have less concern than this House for the freedoms and the rights of the people of this country ... unless the House of Commons does its job, this House has to spend a great deal more time on the Bill – more than three times as much – and has to do the job for it.

In contrast, their Lordships imposed a series of major defeats on the government,[57] including a record five in one session[58] and, as is apparent from any reading of the debates, this was done in no narrow partisan spirit – imposing defeats on a governing party just because they are the other side – but out of genuine concern for basic liberties. The extract below focuses on an issue which was controversial in terms of its impact on human rights. It concerned clause 17 of the Bill which applied to some 66 existing statutes which allowed disclosure of information by one public authority to another (clause 19 gave similar powers to Customs and Excise). It amounted to an enormous broadening of that power, allowing any public authority to require from another information for any of the following purposes:

(2) (a) the purposes of any criminal investigation whatever which is being or may be carried out, whether in the United Kingdom or elsewhere;

(b) the purposes of any criminal investigation whatever which have been or may be initiated, whether in the United Kingdom or elsewhere;

(c) the purposes of the initiation or bringing to an end of any such investigation or proceedings;

(d) the purposes of facilitating a determination of whether any such investigation or proceedings should be initiated or brought to an end.

The extracts from debate that follow concern amendments that would have limited clause 17 to offences relating to terrorism or threats to national security.

---

55 Joint Committee on Human Rights, Second Report, HL 37, HC 372 (2001–02), para 46.
56 HL Deb col 1155 (10 December 2001), Lord Stoddart.
57 These included: restricting the scope of information sharing by government agencies to that relevant to possible terrorist offences; rejecting the proposed offence of incitement to religious hatred; insisting on shorter 'sunset clauses' for controversial parts of the Bill (provisions whereby they automatically lapsed after a space of time); rejecting the proposed exclusion of judicial review (see text); on transposing EU criminal legislation into domestic law via secondary legislation; on retention of communications data.
58 See 'Labour accuses Lords of wrecking anti-terror Bill', The Guardian, 7 December 2001.

HL Deb cols 949–72 (6 December 2001) (extracts)

Lord Phillips of Sudbury ...The issue is whether the extensive powers reserved by the state should be confined to threats to national security. It is all about reconciling our duty to safeguard our traditional civil liberties with our duty to forestall as best we can any emergency threats to our national security.

... It is counter-intuitive to believe that civil liberties are best preserved by suspending them. That tends to be a poor way of winning the battle for hearts and minds, here or abroad, without which no long-term national security is possible, particularly post-September 11th.

What does Clause 17 allow? As its title says, it extends existing disclosure powers in the 66 statutes listed in Schedule 4. Each of those statutes was carefully considered and contains differing and often highly detailed regimes of required confidentiality and permitted disclosure. The core of our disagreement with Clause 17, and the other clauses to which this group relates – Clause 19 and in particular Clauses 103 and 104 – is that this widespread extension of existing disclosure is not confined to the protection of national security or to the fight against terrorism.

It is instructive briefly to look at the precise effect of Clause 17 in relation to the 66 scheduled statutes, as that has not been done so far ... I refer briefly to the Health Act which is also specified. On considering that Act, one realises what an intricate and carefully balanced web of protections is provided which will, frankly, be blown apart if Clause 17 as drafted is approved. It provides a comparable framework to the Companies Act, so that there can be no disclosure for the purposes of criminal proceedings outside the United Kingdom, and disclosure for criminal offences within it is confined to serious arrestable offences. I need hardly say that nothing like that is included in Clause 17.

As I am sure the House is aware, Clause 17 will override those restrictions. It is extraordinarily wide. First, any public authority here or abroad can request information from the commissions and bodies connected with the 66 statutes I mentioned. However, what some noble Lords may not appreciate is that 'public authorities' in this context are extremely widely defined and include private bodies and companies in so far as they have public functions such as running schools, prisons or railways here or abroad. Secondly, contrary to what [we] first understood in debate, a request for disclosure from any of those public authorities at home or abroad can be refused only on good grounds or what are known to lawyers as *Wednesbury* principles; that is, such bodies are judicially reviewable if they refuse a request for disclosure. Thirdly, the scope is not confined to serious offences but extends to any offence whatever. Those can include private prosecutions. Moreover, the list of 66 statutes is not exhaustive and can be added to by statutory instrument.

Where requests are made by public authorities or individuals abroad there is no safeguard that the legal system, procedures or integrity of the relevant foreign jurisdiction are comparable to our own and provide comparable protection. Furthermore, the citizen does not have the safeguard that exists in the Regulation of Investigatory Powers Act which requires prior authorisation before any request for disclosure can be made.

The Government say, and have said repeatedly, that none of those matters should be too worrisome due to the provisions of the Human Rights Act. However, in normal cases a citizen whose rights of confidentiality have been breached will never be aware of that. Even where he or she is aware of it, resort to Human Rights Act remedies is extremely uncertain and expensive. One can exercise those rights only in the course of proceedings and, what is more, the rights themselves are extremely generally framed. I put it to the House that few indeed will treat that as a real and effective protection against disclosure of confidential information.

Above all – I have hinted at this – Clause 17 is not confined to disclosure in connection with prosecutions, public or private, or investigation of prosecutions, but extends to decisions as to whether to initiate an investigation and even to inquiries before that stage. These amendments endeavour to rectify some of those defects, particularly as regards the issue of scope.

I believe that the unanimous view of this House is that the Government are fully entitled to endeavour to deal with unexpected and emergency threats of terrorism. We have endeavoured to define the scope of disclosure in a practical way that will give the police and other authorities the scope they need in order to do their work. Therefore, we have stipulated that whether disclosure is voluntary or is supplied on request it can be provided where the public authority 'believes or suspects' that the relevant information, 'may relate directly or indirectly to any risk to national security or to a terrorist'.

The lowest hurdle, therefore, under the amendment to this and the other clauses in the group, is that there must be a suspicion that disclosure may indirectly relate to such a risk . . .

The Earl of Northesk: The Minister has been studious in advising us that thus far communications data have been central to the investigation into the events of September 11th and that the assistance afforded by CSPs has been 'excellent'. All of us are delighted to hear that. However, if investigations have proceeded and are proceeding so successfully and without compromise under the existing law, what need do the Government have of such a broad scope of data retention powers on the face of the Bill?

Earl Ferrers: My Lords, perhaps I may be permitted to make an intervention. I have not done so yet in relation to this Bill; perhaps I may be permitted to do so now. As I understand the position, under the Bill the Government are permitting the police, investigating authorities and even courts to investigate people's financial affairs – that is, their bank balances, VAT records and all such other information. That may well be fine for the purposes of terrorism.

I believe that we are all agreed that, where prospective terrorists are at large, such information should be made available to those who are investigating them. But . . . it is quite a different thing to permit that type of investigation to be carried out for civil offences, such as, as she suggested, motoring offences. I cannot believe that any government would want that to happen . . .

Supposing information is gathered and persons are found to be innocent of the offence they were thought to have committed, what will happen to that information? Will it remain on file to be used on other occasions?

Lord Elton: . . . We have here machinery that can result in confidential information being released to a foreign public authority. That could be the police or another body, certainly anywhere in Europe and arguably anywhere in the world. The proposal goes much further than the matter with which we are concerned. A public authority is also defined as any public authority, not merely the police. The ramifications of that are enormous and quite unnecessary. They would be curtailed by this group of amendments and I hope that noble Lords will support them.

Viscount Goschen: My Lords, during the Bill's passage through this House, there has been widespread – almost total – support for the Government's intention of combating terrorism. There has been an acceptance that they need additional powers and that those powers are valid. However, they are valid solely for the specific purpose of preserving national security and combating terrorism.

As we have heard, the Bill is drawn much more widely than that. The argument that the Government deployed in Committee was that their intention was to focus the use of the Bill's powers on combating threats to national security and on countering terrorism, but that they needed wider, broader powers because terrorists are involved in many other crimes – which is, of course, true. As we have heard, terrorists can be involved in drug running, people trafficking, money laundering and a broad spread of other crimes. That is why the amendments, which were drafted by my noble friends and the noble Lord, Lord Phillips, sought to preserve the Government's ability to tackle terrorists who are involved in other crimes by ensuring that whatever crime the Bill's powers are focused on, such powers must be related to combating terrorism.

. . .

Lord Rooker: . . . The amendment would severely limit disclosure. Clause 19 allows Customs and the Inland Revenue to disclose information to law enforcement and intelligence agencies for the investigation of crime. Reducing that gateway simply to cases of terrorism or threats to national security would be counter-productive and reduce the effectiveness of fighting terrorism.

Perhaps I may give an example. There is a proven link between terrorists groups and criminal activities for which Customs are responsible. We know that some terrorist groups have been engaged for some time in large-scale drug smuggling and in the massive evasion of excise duties on cigarettes and alcohol. At the time Customs become aware of that, they may not have appreciated the significance of what is involved in terms of terrorist investigation and may not immediately recognise the connection with a terrorist group. They may simply believe that the Inland Revenue has been ripped off, the Chancellor is charging too much in tax and the criminals are trying to make a buck on the side with bucket shops around the country.

Under the gateway, as drafted, if the safeguards are satisfied, the information could be passed to the police. Under the amendment the information would remain with Customs and a potentially vital piece of the jigsaw of intelligence would be denied and never reach the police. The same applies to Customs as regards the money laundering regulations . . .

It is important that, in bringing forward this legislation, we are able to do so in such a way that it helps in the fight against terrorism internationally in co-operation with our partners or on our own and is recognised as the precautionary response that we need to make on behalf of the public who would never forgive us if something happened and we had decided that the appropriate legislation was not worth it because we did not want to bother Parliament and we could not guarantee that a particular clause was directly related to the act that had taken place. We do not want to take a narrow view of the purposes of the legislation because it would hamper our effectiveness in combating crime.

I said in Committee that we cannot meaningfully distinguish between terrorism and other forms of crime for a couple of reasons. Terrorists are criminals anyway and other criminal acts foster and resource terrorism. One example that I have given, which I do not need to repeat, is the importation of cigarettes. Some 40 million cigarettes were seized from a ship and it was known that a large proportion of that consignment was destined to criminals linked to paramilitary organisations. The idea that criminals are not connected to terrorism is wrong. We need to be able to consider all the pieces of the jigsaw . . .

Lord Phillips of Sudbury: My Lords, we are grateful to the Minister for endeavouring to defend the Government's position in relation to the amendments. When he started he made a lively analogy with a jigsaw. A jigsaw has a big picture. It can be pieced together by reference to a clear picture. Clause 17, and the other clauses to which the group of amendments relate, has no picture. It has no limits. It does not even mention national security or terrorism.

So while the Minister made a strong case for Clause 17 with such a limitation, he made no case whatever for Clause 17 un-amended. I put to your Lordships that it was perfectly legitimate, but wholly unrealistic, for the Minister to spend the past hour talking purely about terrorism and about the things with which we are all concerned. The clause goes to any criminal offence, however petty, wherever, whenever and by whomsoever. It is not confined to the police and security authorities. Any public authority, here or abroad, whether hybrid or not, can make any request for disclosure under this hugely wide Clause 17. And the good Minister cannot stop them.

Once this is through the net he cannot stop them. It will be no good him then saying, 'Oh my goodness, I did not intend it to relate to some appalling regime abroad trying to use these powers to force disclosure from some public authority here under this Act'. It will be no use at all.

I wish to test the opinion of the House.

On Question, Whether the said amendment (No 1) shall be agreed to?

Their Lordships divided: Contents, 227; Not-Contents, 145.

[The amendment was thus carried, and the government defeated.]

[A similar amendment was then carried in relation to clause 19 which gave a new, broad power relating to disclosure of information held by revenue departments for the same wide purposes as those in cl 17 (this amendment was also agreed to and the government again defeated).]

Notes

1   It may be observed that the debate genuinely illustrates those qualities of independent-mindedness, non-partisanship and expertise which the House of Lords is so valued for. The speeches also indicate a concern with the longer-term view, and a willingness to look behind the short term political concerns with which the Commons was more concerned (the Commons passed the Bill with no amendments carried against the government).

2   On some points, the government was forced to accept complete defeat: the proposed creation of an offence of incitement to religious hatred was repeatedly rejected by the Lords[59] and eventually dropped from the Bill altogether. The Lords also procured the insertion of 'sunset' clauses against government resistance, whereby the more draconian aspects of the legislation would automatically lapse after a specified period,[60] as well as statutory provision for a review of the detention powers specifically by a person appointed by the Home Secretary[61] and a full review of the operation of the whole legislation by Privy Counsellors.[62] On retention of communications data, the Lords scored a significant victory by insisting on their amendment[63] that the Code of Practice which the Secretary of State would draw up could only contain provisions necessary '. . . for the purposes of prevention or detection of crime or the prosecution of offenders *which may relate directly or indirectly to national security'*,[64] not any criminal offences as the government had wanted.

3   The Lords eventually accepted compromises from the government on other issues. On provisions to allow EU criminal legislation to become law in the UK without primary legislation, the government dropped its original proposal whereby the provisions would cover all such legislation, accepting instead that they would cover only a limited and specified set of measures agreed by EU leaders[65] and would lapse in July 2002.[66] The Lords also eventually accepted the exclusion of judicial review of SIAC decisions in return for a government concession – to make the SIAC a superior court of full record[67] – which essentially gives it the same powers as the High Court, as well as placing its reasons on the public record.[68] On s 17 – the extraordinarily broad powers given to public authorities to share

---

59   See, eg, HL Deb vol 629 cols 1163–95 (10 December 2001) and HL Deb vol 629 cols 1449 *et seq* (13 December 2001).

60   Sections 21–23, giving the power of detention without trial, will lapse 15 months from the date on which the Act was passed; see also text to fn 66 below.

61   Section 28. The review must be made within 14 months of the date of the passage of the Act, and the report produced laid before Parliament (ss 4).

62   Their report may specify particular provisions which will then lapse within six months, unless the report is debated in each House within that period: s 122.

63   See HL Deb vol 629 cols 1474 *et seq* (13 December 2001).

64   Section 102(3)(b).

65   Listed in s 111(2).

66   Section 111(1).

67   Section 35(1).

68   See HL Deb vol 629 cols 1435 *et seq* (13 December 2001).

information (above) – a weak compromise was reached which was designed to ensure that large amounts of information could not be gathered purely on the basis of a fishing expedition by police or other prosecuting authorities: the Bill as amended by the Lords provides that public authorities may not disclose information unless satisfied 'that the making of the disclosure is proportionate to what is sought to be achieved by it'.[69] This in particular represented a major climbdown by the Lords. The crucial point on which they had repeatedly insisted was that the clause as drafted did not restrict the scope of the information-sharing provision to terrorist-related offences; this amendment left that problem substantially untouched.[70] The requirement on the public authority to consider proportionality adds nothing as a matter of law – Lord Lester described it as 'window dressing'[71] because s 6(1) HRA[72] would impose the same obligation via Article 8 ECHR.[73] The amendment thus '... merely restate[d] the existing duty under the Human Rights Act ...'[74] so that on the major issue – the breadth of the power – the Lords essentially collapsed.[75]

4 Nevertheless, the contrast between the approach of the elected – and thoroughly whipped – Commons and the unelected, and relatively independent-minded Lords was marked. As one respected commentator remarked: 'In a long record of shaming fealty to whips, never have so many MPs showed such utter negligence towards so impressive a list of fundamental principles.' In contrast, as he noted, the Lords engaged in a thorough and painstaking examination of the Bill: 'Their debate is serious, their resilience formidable and their morality alive. They don't oppose the anti-terrorism campaign, but they want to keep it within sane limits. They scrutinise, question and amend.'[76] It is suggested that this contrast between the approach of the two Houses must be borne in mind when considering the debate as to the democratic element within any reformed second chamber (below).

Scrutiny of EU policy and legislation

Given the ever-growing impact of EU legislation, this task is clearly of great importance, particularly as it has been suggested that the British MEPs in the European Parliament are not particularly effective in this role.[77] The main

---

69 This is now sub-s (5) of s 17; an identical provision was also included as sub-s (3) of s 19, which deals with disclosure of information held by revenue departments.

70 The Lords inserted an amendment at report stage as follows: 'Information may only be disclosed ... if the public authority concerned believes or suspects that the disclosure may be of information which directly or indirectly relates to a risk to national security or to a terrorist.' See HL Deb vol 629 cols 949–75 (6 December 2001). For the debate in which the Lords accepted instead the government amendment, see HL Deb vol 629 cols 1142 et seq (13 December 2001).

71 Ibid, col 1425.

72 Section 6(1) states: 'It is unlawful for a public authority to act in a way that is incompatible with a Convention right.'

73 That is, assuming that the disclosure in question related to private life and so engaged Article 8. If it did so, under para 2 of that Article, the disclosure could only lawfully be made if it pursued a legitimate aim and was 'necessary in a democratic society', ie proportionate to the pressing social need that the legislation sought to address.

74 HL Deb vol 629 col 1423 (13 December 2001), Lord Thomas of Gresford.

75 As one peer remarked: 'It is rather sad that we ... have been seen to cave in to what I would describe as waffle.' Ibid, col 1424, the Earl of Onslow.

76 H Young, 'Once lost, these freedoms will be impossible to restore', The Guardian, 11 December 2001.

77 See V Bogdanor, 'Britain and the European Community', in J Jowell and D Oliver (eds), The Changing Constitution, 3rd edn (1994), pp 18–19.

responsibility for this area of the Lords' work lies with the House of Lords Select Committee on the European Communities, considered by Bogdanor below.

V Bogdanor, 'Britain and the European Community', in J Jowell and D Oliver (eds), *The Changing Constitution*, 3rd edn (1994), pp 10–13

The House of Lords Select Committee is a more influential body than its Commons counterpart. It is chaired by a salaried office-holder of the House, who as Principal Deputy-Chairman of Committees, ranks third in the Lords after the Lord Chancellor and the Chairman of Committees. Whereas in the Commons, the Committee before 1991 sifted legislation for the House as a whole to consider, in the Lords it is the Chairman of the Select Committee, assisted by a legal adviser and the Clerk, who sifts legislation for the Select Committee and its sub-committees to consider. This sift is later endorsed by the Select Committee itself. On average, around one-third of the Community documents received are selected for further consideration, and around one-tenth are the subject of reports to the House.

The House of Lords Select Committee calls upon a wide range of sources, including MEPs, for both written and oral evidence. MEPs giving evidence to the House of Lords Committee are not confined to those representing Britain, but will include members of other nationalities, so enabling the House of Lords Committee to establish links with the Rapporteur of the relevant Committee of the European Parliament. Moreover, the House of Lords Committee also takes evidence from Commission officials, and representatives of interest groups, academics, etc. in all the countries of the Community.

Around one-half of the reports from the House of Lords Committee are debated in the House. Since the Government does not enjoy control over the order paper in the House of Lords as it does in the Commons, the Select Committee could always, in the last resort, *insist* upon a debate. These debates are in no way dominated, as those in the Commons have been, by the division between pro- and anti-Community opinions, and a leading part is played in debates on the floor of the House by members of the Select Committee and the sub-committees ....In the Lords, it is the reports which are important, not least because they attract a wide readership throughout the Community and its institutions, and not the debates.

There is widespread agreement that the scrutiny procedures adopted by the Lords are amongst the most effective in the Community. In 1977, a Committee established by the Hansard Society for Parliamentary Government was 'struck by the relevance and businesslike nature of the results of the Lords' work in this field, and think it significant that the Commons, who are meant to represent the people of this country, have taken in contrast to the Lords, a largely inward-looking and conservative attitude where the opposite was required.' And in 1982 a Report of the Study Group of the Commonwealth Parliamentary Association on 'The Role of Second Chambers' concluded that the Lords offered 'the only really deep analysis of the issues that is available to the parliamentary representatives of the [then] ten countries in the Community ... The Lords' reports are far more informative and comprehensive than those produced by the Commons committee on European legislation.' The Study Group attributed this to the greater specialist knowledge of peers and comparative absence of partisanship.

[The Committee] has the advantage, because of the system of nominating to life peerages men and women of eminence, of containing experts in almost every field covered by Community activity. Whether the subject-matter be agriculture, law, or economics, some of the leading authorities in the country will be found in the Lords; and since much Community legislation is technical, this means that the Lords is peculiarly suited to considering it. Thus the scrutiny procedures of the House of Lords owe their effectiveness to factors which it would be difficult to replicate in any legislature dominated primarily by party politicians. They depend upon the peculiarities of a chamber whose members are there either by hereditary right or by nomination.

Notes

1   Once again the conclusion is reached that the Lords' effectiveness in this area is strongly linked to its undemocratic nature. It is *not* of course dependent on the particular method for selecting life peers, that is, prime ministerial patronage.

2   Philip Norton broadly concurs with Bogdanor's favourable assessment of the work of the Lords in this area:

> The EC Committee has built up an impressive reputation as a thorough and informed body, issuing reports which are more objective and extensive than its counterpart in the Commons, and which are considered authoritative both within Whitehall and the institutions of the EC. The House, like the chambers of other national legislatures, has no formal role in the EC legislative process, and so has no power, other than that of persuasion, to affect outcomes. The significance of the reports, therefore, has tended to lie in informing debate rather than in changing particular decisions.[78]

3   Similarly, the Hansard Society Commission has praised the scrutiny of EU issues by the above Committees as 'an example of very highly effective scrutiny work undertaken by the Lords'.[79] However, a more sceptical note was struck by a member of the EU Committee in a recent debate. While not disputing the excellent work done by the Committee, he was concerned that its antiquated methods of procedure and lack of an efficient publicity machine substantially detract from its effectiveness and impact:

> As for the Select Committees, never has so much talent been assembled for so little return. As a proud member of European Union Sub-Committee C ... I am appalled that the wonderful array of talent, experience and expertise found among my fellow committee members leads us to write reports on foreign common and security policy which frequently fail to reach the Floor of the House for engaged debate; whose tired and unserviceable presentation makes them an unappetising read. These reports are seldom read outside the House or sent to those who might benefit from them, such as British Members of the European Parliament, because little attention is given to who might be their core audience.

> ... My anxieties ... were brought to a head last autumn when the media became hot under the collar about the so-called European army – the European rapid reaction force. Sub-Committee C had published an excellent and informative report on this subject a couple of months previously, but because of the lack of resources and the absence of an established press officer for the Lords, our report was rendered impotent for the purposes of enlightening and enlivening the public debate. No one had heard of it and certainly we had done little to promote it. Our Olympian aloofness means that our report stayed with the gods.[80]

Scrutiny of domestic administration and policy

The House also scrutinises government policy. Peers can debate policy in a less partisan atmosphere than the Commons and are not subject to the constituency and party influences that dominate in the elected House. They are therefore in a position to debate issues of public policy that may not be at the heart of the partisan battles and which, consequently, receive little attention in the Commons. Given their backgrounds,

---

78   Philip Norton, 'Parliament II: the House of Lords', in B Jones (ed), *Politics UK* (1994), p 359.
79   *The Challenge for Parliament: Making Government Accountable* (2001), para 6.21
80   HL Deb cols 576–77, Lord Harrison.

peers are also often – though not always – able to debate public policy from the perspective of those engaged in the subject. 'The House, for example, is able to debate science policy with an authority denied the lower House – it contains several distinguished scientists. When discussing education, the House will normally hear from peers who are professors, university chancellors, vice-chancellors, and former Secretaries of State for Education.'[81]

The Lords have other methods by which they scrutinise policy: questions of Ministers and the Select Committees. These are intended to complement, not duplicate the work of the Commons Select Committees and so are not departmental, but rather cross-cutting in their remit. Of these, as Rodney Brazier observes, those on the European Union, considered above, and on Science and Technology 'are generally acknowledged to be outstanding successes'.[82] Recent additions to the Lords committees include the Constitution Committee, whose remit, as well as reporting on the process of ongoing constitutional reform, requires them to report on Bills that raise an important question of principle about a principal part of the constitution, and the Economic Affairs Committee. However, since the methods of scrutiny used are broadly similar to those in the House of Commons, considered in detail in Chapter 1 of this part, no further material is offered here, due to constraints of space. Methods of making Lords scrutiny more effective are considered under reform proposals, below.

FURTHER REFORM OF THE HOUSE OF LORDS

Labour's programme of reform for the Lords was never meant to finish with removal of the hereditary peers. Certainly, a considerable amount of government attention has been paid to the issue of further reform since the House of Lords Act 1999. The Royal Commission on Reform of the House of Lords, under the chairmanship of Lord Wakeham produced a comprehensive, if unpopular blueprint for reform;[83] the government's long-awaited response[84] broadly accepted Wakeham's rather conservative proposals but watered down considerably the independence that the Royal Commission had sought to give the reformed House. A powerfully argued Public Administration Select Committee[85] (PASC) report criticised the White Paper strongly and called for a majority elected House instead. So unpopular did the White Paper prove (it had a very hostile reception from all sides, including a very substantial part of the parliamentary Labour Party, as well as the opposition parties, and virtually all the press) – that the government eventually abandoned it and a Joint Committee of both Houses,[86] set up to find an alternative way forward, produced a report giving various options on composition of a reformed second chamber at the end of December 2002.[87] Free votes in both Houses on these options

81 Norton, *op cit*, p 354.
82 R Brazier, *Constitutional Reform*, 2nd edn (1998), p 90.
83 Wakeham Report, *op cit*.
84 Cmd 5291 (2001); see sources at fn 2.
85 Fifth Report, HC 494-I (2001–02), esp at paras 6 and 36.
86 For the resolutions appointing it see the references given in fn 4.
87 First Report, HL 17, HC 171 (2002–03).

were held in January 2003[88] but no agreement was found either in the Commons or between the two Houses. The Joint Committee is now seeking to find ways of advancing the reform agenda in the absence of agreement on the most important issue of all – the composition of a new House.[89] It is required by its terms of reference to have regard to the reports of Wakeham, the PASC and the government's White Paper.

This section will consider the possibilities for further reform of the House of Lords. It will first set out a series of general principles to guide reform that may be gleaned from second chambers overseas; it will then consider the proposals set out in the Wakeham report; together with a brief mention of how far the government's (now discarded) White Paper deviated significantly from Wakeham. Criticism of Wakeham and the counter-proposals set out in the Fifth Report of the PASC will also be considered. The final main section will explore particular aspects of the reform proposals now on the table. Throughout, suggestions and findings of the Joint Committee on Lords Reform will be given, where relevant, but it should be noted that the Committee has not, to date, offered a comprehensive alternative blueprint for Lords reform as an alternative to those offered by Wakeham and the PASC.

Reform: general principles and lessons from overseas

The following extract from Russell's authoritative study of overseas second chambers is illuminating both in pointing out how some of the valuable features which one might assume were unique to the Lords are in fact shared by other second chambers, and in helping to pin-point factors common to such second chambers which make them distinctive and valuable.

M Russell, *Reforming the Lords: Lessons from Overseas* (2000) (extracts – references omitted)

Many ... factors mean that, despite the diverse nature of these chambers [those in France, Canada, Australia, Spain, Italy, Ireland and Germany] in measurable terms, there is a certain atmosphere that tends to be common to them all. This is critical to their work and the impact that they have.

First, they are all smaller than their respective first chambers, some considerably so. This results in a more intimate atmosphere, in the chamber itself and in both party groups and committees. Coupled with longer parliamentary terms, which apply in Canada, France and Australia, this means that the members of the chamber are likely to know each other better than the members of the lower house. Once the higher average age of Senators is taken into account a picture already begins to emerge of more mature and deliberative parliamentary chambers with a less adversarial atmosphere. [Moreover] ... in several cases the power of the upper house over legislation, and particularly over making and breaking governments, tends to be less than that of the first chamber ... This means that the outcome of votes in the second chamber may be less critical, and that political leaders will tend to be concentrated in the first chamber. Even in Italy and Australia, where

---

88 For the debate in the Lords see HL Deb vol 643 cols 575–688 (21 January 2003) and 721–838 (22 January 2003). For debate in the Commons see HC Deb vol 398 cols 187–274 (21 January 2003) and for the debates and votes on composition specifically, HC Deb vol 399 cols 152–243 and HL Deb vol 644 cols 115–40.

89 For its latest, Second Report, see HL 97, HC 668 (2002–03)

the power of the chambers over legislation is more or less equal, party leaders and senior cabinet members will tend to be drawn more from the lower house. These factors tend to add to a calmer, less adversarial chamber which is not under such intense media scrutiny as the lower house. This could certainly be said to apply to all the chambers considered here.

Party discipline in upper chambers may also be less strict. This particularly applies where the upper house can be overridden by the lower chamber, as has been demonstrated on occasion by the British House of Lords. But this can also be a result of the stature of upper house members. The House of Lords is an example of a chamber where members are less bound by the party whip because they are at the end of their political careers, are not subject to re-selection, and have confidence in their own mature judgment. A similar situation applies, for example, in the French Senat, where members are mature and well-established political figures. The slower, more stately, pace of the Senat is also influenced by the nine-year terms served by its members ...

In Canada a similar situation applies. Here, as in Britain, France, Germany, and Australia (other than in exceptional circumstances) the chamber cannot be dissolved. This helps to give it an independent authority. The long-serving members of the Canadian Senate are socialised over time into a less partisan culture. There is thus a higher incidence of 'cross voting' in the Senate, as compared to the lower house where party discipline is extraordinarily strict. This is one factor which makes Canadians a little more tolerant of their otherwise unpopular, unelected Senate.

The Irish Seanad, which generally has a weak position within the parliamentary system, also exhibits similar traits. The lack of pressure and adversarialism in the Seanad, its very small size and its independent members, all help provide 'a less hurried forum for discussion of the issues facing Irish society and the implications of legislative proposals.' The Seanad, which is less subject to media attention, is often used to debate new and controversial issues on which the parties do not have established positions. The university Senators regularly play a leading role in such debates.

The Australian Senate offers a counter-example on party discipline, given that the outcome of votes in the upper house is crucial to the success of the government's legislation. The political numbers in the Senate generally mean that its members must attend every vote and stick rigidly to the party line – something which need not apply in the lower house. However, the fact that political negotiations must take place in the Senate, whilst the lower house is strictly adversarial, means that relations between its members are none the less better. The rowdy debates and question periods in the House of Representatives lead Senators to dub it 'the monkey house', whilst its members refer to the Senate as 'the mortuary'. The following quote further emphasises the distinct personality of the Australian Senate, and could refer to any one of these seven second chambers:

> Candidates with Prime Ministerial aspirations, with talent for scoring points from the opposing party and divining the moods of the electorate, will recognise the House of Representatives as the place where they can shine. Candidates whose aspirations lie in the direction of independent thought and research, who really want to come to grips with the issues confronting the nation, and to do something about them will see the Senate as the place where they can be most effective (Lucy, *The Australian Form of Government* (1993), p 195).

... In all seven parliaments, even where the upper house has less time available for legislative consideration than the lower house, it generally has a reputation for more detailed scrutiny. This is a product both of the chamber's composition and its powers. The concentration of party leaders and ministers in the lower house, and consequently the focus of media attention on that chamber, means that lower houses tend to focus on big political issues, and high-profile point-scoring and debate. Thus although most bills may start their legislative passage in the lower house, many details often remain ill-considered when they reach the upper house. Meanwhile, by the time the bill arrives, groups both inside and outside of parliament will have had time to consider its detail and bring forward proposed amendments. These will often be debated in the less frenetic atmosphere of the upper house.

The fact that the upper house has lesser powers than the lower house also places it, at times, in a stronger position to negotiate legislative changes. Whilst members of the lower house must toe the party line, and government defeats may be seen as a confidence issue, the same pressure does not apply in the upper house. Thus even members of the government side in the second chamber may be more prone to question the content of bills, and threaten to vote against the government. In upper houses where government does not have a majority, the threat of defeat is very real. Although the chamber may have only a limited delaying power, the inconvenience and embarrassment which is caused by government defeats may result in compromise. Governments will, in any case, often make concessions more easily in the upper house than they can in the lower house, where every amendment may be viewed by the media as a defeat or a U-turn. For all of these reasons the upper house is often the site of genuine negotiation between the parties, and a higher degree of consensus than is generally found in the lower house ...

[Russell later summarises the effectiveness of the lower chambers in dealing with legislative detail as being dependent on four key factors: longer terms of office and rolling membership; non-renewable terms of office; no ministers (or less important) ministers in the chamber; more mature members. She then goes on to consider public perceptions of her seven chambers.]

The most embattled of the chambers is probably the Senate of Canada. Although it is responsible for much detailed legislative and investigative work, the 'accepted image of the Senate [is] as a dusty, obscure Arcadia filled with aged and retired political war horses ... whose main concern, apart from enjoying a good, comfortable, life, is to preserve private wealth and the interests of big business.' This is an image that is perpetuated by the media, who periodically question the working hours and lifestyles of Senators. The upper house is also widely criticised by the provinces, which have no involvement in choosing its members, despite its formal role as the territorial house. These criticisms are damaging to the Senate, whose views are less likely to be listened to as a result. The results of many Senate committee investigations, for example, have been left to gather dust. As Franks has observed, 'it is clear that appointment by the Prime Minister from among party supporters has by now reduced the legitimacy of the Senate to the point where it harms not only the Senate but also parliament as a whole and even the government'.

In Ireland 'mainstream opinion is tolerant of the Seanad rather than supportive of it.' There is little to indicate that many of the public understand the chamber as 'the absence of any feeling of urgency or of momentous political cut and thrust, and the comparatively poor publicity it gets, all emphasise its lack of importance and contribute to its low prestige'. However, there are times when the media focuses on the Seanad, and helps to generate negative feelings towards it. For example during the 1997 election campaign the Irish Times ran a piece entitled 'There is no point in the Seanad' and opening 'Hundreds of candidates are engaged in another frenetic election campaign, this time for a redundant institution.' It remarked that 'if there is to be no fundamental change in the Seanad's role and composition there is no reason to retain it' (Irish Times, 2 July 1997).

Viewed as equally pointless is the powerful Italian Senate. Generally controlled by the same political parties as the lower house, and carrying out identical functions, the upper house is seen to add little to the system apart from delay. In a system where parliament is generally considered inefficient and problematic, 'the sternest criticisms of bicameralism have stemmed from its having come to be identified as one of the major causes of the malfunctioning of the whole institutional system'. Although this may not be entirely justified, 'for the most part – and here there is substantial agreement – it is the structure of a perfectly equal bicameralism that is held responsible for the crisis of representation – in Italian politics'.

Of the seven chambers, the German Bundesrat is the only one that receives general public support. Germany appears to be almost unique in having no campaign that seeks to reform the upper house. In fact there are even moves to extend the structure of the Bundesrat to create second chambers in the states, attended by representatives of local government. This is because the Bundesrat is acknowledged as a genuine forum where state and federal interests are represented, and agreements are reached. Although disputes between the chambers can be fuelled by party politics, this is not seen as an overriding concern.

This is in stark contrast to the situation in Spain, where 'the Senate, initially intended as a chamber for territorial representation in central government, is widely seen as a useless body'. Even senior officials of the upper house are prepared to admit that 'practically since the moment the constitution was approved, there has been talk of a less-than-ideal Senate, proposing the need for its reform, because it is felt that the chamber does not meet the requirements of full territoriality'. It had been hoped that the addition of autonomous community Senators, as devolution progressed, would strengthen the territorial basis of the house. However, these Senators make up only one in five of the total, and after almost 20 years there is a lively debate in Spain on upper house reform.

In some countries the view of the upper house is more equivocal. France is an example. Despite some attempts by the Senat authorities to modernise its image, most commentators recognise that the upper house is essentially a conservative institution. For example, on the day after the Senat blocked the *Parite* legislation to give women equal rights to elected office the leader column of *Le Monde* was headed 'A Senat from another age'. The piece said that:

> ... the Senat boasts that it is a temple of 'wisdom' against the extremes of the [lower house] and the swings of universal suffrage. Carefully protecting a mode of scrutiny from another age, the Senators themselves are not unhappy to present themselves as the guardians of a sepia, rural, unchanging France ... at the [Senat], 'wisdom' becomes conservatism.' [*Le Monde*, 27 January 1999.]

These sentiments echoed the earlier comments of Lionel Jospin, who has described the Senat as 'an anomaly amongst modern democracies'. [*Le Monde*, 21 April 1998.]

However, the French public seem less convinced about the need to reform the upper house. The only two constitutional referendums that have ever been rejected by the French people – in 1946 and 1969 – included weakening or removal of the Senat. The second of these resulted in the fall of President de Gaulle. Opinion polls demonstrate that the Senat is relatively popular. In 1990, 46 per cent of voters believed the upper house performed its role well, compared to 38 per cent who believed the same about the lower house. This may, however, simply indicate a lack of understanding of the work of the Senat – because of its claimed role in protecting liberties it may be confused by some people with the Constitutional Council.

Opinions over the Australian Senate are equally split. Governments never welcome the powerful interventions of the elected Senate, which they do not politically control. However, oppositions always embrace the opportunity to use the Senate – in partnership with minor parties – to modify government proposals. Thus the major parties tend to have a schizophrenic attitude to the upper house – in government they resent its interference, but in opposition they appreciate its benefits. Prime Minister Paul Keating famously referred to members of the Senate as 'unrepresentative swill' and to the house itself as a 'spoiling chamber'. Nevertheless his party, upon entering opposition in 1996, began to use exactly the same tactics as the previous opposition in the Senate to rein back government. This fluctuating attitude to the upper house is shared by the press, which at times lambasts and at other times celebrates its role. Much of the debate in Australia centres around the concept of *mandate* with the government claiming that its majority in the lower house gives it a mandate to govern, and the opposition and minor parties claiming that their combined forces in the proportionally elected Senate have a mandate to question and modify government proposals. The press keenly joins in the debate, with headlines such as 'Will of the people: yes, but which people?' and 'End the mandate muddle' [*The Sunday Telegraph*, 4 October 1998].

All the evidence suggests that voters in Australia are fairly happy with the way things are. Votes for small parties are always higher for the Senate than for the lower house, and analysis of voting patterns shows that some Australians operate 'split ticket' voting – supporting one party in the lower house elections and another in the Senate. It has been suggested that voters do this in order to ensure that, even if their own party is elected, the Senate operates as a brake on government.

When polled, 45 per cent of voters say they believe it is better when government does not control both houses of parliament, compared to 41 per cent who would prefer government to do so.

[Russell later summarises what her research has indicated are the key factors in ensuring a successful upper house.]

The UK is clearly far from being alone in seeking to reform its upper house. Reform movements around the world have led to numerous parliamentary committees, Royal Commissions, study groups, conferences, and reports, which have all grappled with the question of how to design an effective upper house. The proliferation of reform proposals which has resulted leads to an interesting question: is an agreed second chamber model emerging? Are there common themes from these debates from which the UK can learn? ... there do appear to be some features which are generally supported. These are either accepted features of existing second chambers which are seen to work successfully, or proposals which are made by reformers in other countries, or both. In many cases a feature which works in one country is proposed for introduction in another. There is a growing tendency for reformers to learn from international examples, and the UK can potentially do the same.

Some of the features which attract a large degree of support are as follows:

That the upper house should represent the territorial nature of the state.

Probably the most striking aspect of reform debates overseas is the extent to which there is a movement towards 'territorial' upper houses. In these systems the second chamber represents the provinces, regions, or states in the national parliament. The proposal to move towards a more territorial model has emerged in reform debates in both federal and unitary states. This remains an aspiration in Italy, for example, where the original intention that the Senate should be a house of the regions has never been realised. Even in countries where the upper house is nominally territorial – such as Canada and Spain – there is strong pressure for reform to create a more genuine connection to sub-national institutions.

The two chambers should have distinct functions.

It is relatively common in parliaments overseas – as at Westminster – for the lower chamber to focus on the broad direction of policy, while the upper house takes more responsibility for detailed legislative scrutiny. However, where the upper house is territorial this offers an added opportunity for specialisation, which helps make it distinctive from the lower house. Proposals in Italy and Spain, for example, would give the upper house particular responsibility for territorial matters. This builds on the German model. In Ireland it has been proposed that the upper chamber specialises by concentrating on European and delegated legislation, and detailed inquiries, whilst government ministers are restricted to membership of the lower house.

No powers to remove government from office.

A specialisation that receives universal support is the system whereby government must retain the confidence of the lower house only. Like the UK, most countries follow this model. The exception is Italy, where the upper house can vote government out of office. However, reform proposals include the removal of this power from the Senate.

Lesser powers over financial legislation, more over constitutional change.

As in Britain, most parliaments give reduced powers to the upper house over financial legislation. Australia is an exception, but since a constitutional crisis was caused by the Senate in 1975 it has been proposed that its powers be reduced in this area. On the other hand, it is common for the upper house to have powers to block constitutional change. These powers have only been weakened (for example in Canada) where other constitutional safeguards apply.

Government should not control the chamber.

An important way in which the two chambers may be distinct in composition is through their political balance. Government generally has a majority in the lower house, but this need not apply in the upper house. In countries where government does have a majority in the upper house – notably Ireland and Spain – the limited impact of the chamber is criticised. In contrast, the distinct political complexion of the Australian upper house adds to its impact. In Australia government is frustrated by its lack of control over the Senate, but the Australian people seem largely to support the existing party balance, which results in legislative negotiation and compromise. Polls in other countries suggest that this is a common public response.

Direct election is supported, although indirect election may provide better territorial links.

In countries where the upper chamber is directly elected, this feature generally has public support. For example, the reform debate in Italy emphasises the importance of a distinct upper house, but few would suggest that the Senate cease to be directly elected. Neither have any serious reform proposals of this type been made in Australia. Meanwhile most recent proposals in Canada have focused on the need for an elected chamber, and directly elected Senators were also included in the recent proposals in Ireland. However, in Spain, where the majority of upper house members are directly elected, it is proposed by some that territorial links would be strengthened through an expansion in the number of indirectly elected members in the chamber.

• *The second chamber should be smaller than the first.*

In all countries except the UK, the second chamber of parliament is smaller than the first. This is a completely non-controversial feature, and is generally cited as one of the upper house's assets. A smaller chamber is generally more manageable and efficient, more friendly and courteous, and has smaller and more effective committees.

Long parliamentary terms, and a chamber renewed in parts.

Many second chambers have a membership which is renewed in parts – for example the French Senat, where one-third of members are elected every three years, and the Australian Senate, where half are elected every three years. This means that the chamber has a rolling membership, and cannot be dissolved by government. Where this system applies it appears to be supported, and in some countries where it does not apply there are suggestions that it be introduced.

Note

Many of the specific points made by Russell above are returned to below. With the broad outline of what she sees as the generally agreed features of an effective second chamber in mind, we may turn to consideration of the Royal Commission's proposed outline of a new second chamber.

The Wakeham Report – basic recommendations[90]

A House for the Future, Cm 4534 (2000), Executive Summary

5. We began our work by looking at the *roles* which the reformed second chamber could play. We then considered the *powers* it should have and the specific *functions* it should perform. Our

---

90   The Commission's terms of references were: '*Having regard to the need to maintain the position of the House of Commons as the pre-eminent chamber of Parliament* and taking particular account of the present nature of the constitutional settlement, including the newly devolved institutions, the impact of the Human Rights Act 1998 and developing relations with the European Union: To consider and make recommendations on the role and functions of the second chamber; To make recommendations on the method or combination of methods of composition required to constitute a second chamber fit for that role and those functions [emphasis added].'

conclusions on these matters gave us the basis for determining the *characteristics* which the reformed second chamber should possess and it was this assessment that shaped our recommendations on how the second chamber should be *constituted.*

6. We needed to find a way of building on the strengths of the existing House of Lords while creating a new second chamber better adapted to modern circumstances. Change must be in a direction, and at a pace, which goes with the grain of the traditional British evolutionary approach to constitutional reform, while taking this once-in-a-lifetime opportunity to produce a coherent blueprint for the second chamber of Parliament.

7. We were also determined to define the role and functions of the new second chamber in terms which demonstrated that it has a real and important part to play in the political life of the country. At the same time we needed to allay fears that it could undermine the pre-eminence of the House of Commons as the United Kingdom's primary democratic forum.

8. In particular, we wanted to produce recommendations which would illustrate the crucial trilateral relationship between the Government, the House of Commons and the new second chamber. We took into account the fact that the stability of the trilateral relationship could be affected by the powers of the new second chamber and also by the way its members are selected.

9. We saw the need for a new second chamber with the authority and confidence to function effectively and to use its powers wisely. At the same time we recognised the danger of setting up an institution which could threaten the status of the House of Commons and cause constitutional conflict or whose members could rival those of the House of Commons (for example, in the discharge of their constituency representative role).

10. Above all, we were keen to make proposals that would produce a new second chamber distinctively different from the House of Commons, whose members were more representative of the whole of British society and who could bring a wider range of expertise and experience to bear on the consideration of public policy questions.

11. We acknowledged from the outset that it would be wrong – as well as futile – to try to make the second chamber a politician-free zone. Parliament is a place where political issues are debated and fought over, and the second chamber cannot and should not be disengaged from that process. It will need a cadre of men and women with appropriate political experience to help it play a constructive role. But the new second chamber should not simply be a creature of the political parties, and the influence of the parties on individual members should be minimised. We wanted to create a new second chamber which was politically astute but not a home for yet another group of professional politicians; which provided an appropriate role for the political parties but discouraged sterile partisan confrontation; and which included members of the political parties but was designed to limit the parties' influence and foster the exercise of independent judgment.

Roles

12. The new second chamber should have four main roles:

- It should bring a range of different perspectives to bear on the development of public policy.

- It should be broadly representative of British society. People should be able to feel that there is a voice in Parliament for the different aspects of their personalities, whether regional, vocational, ethnic, professional, cultural or religious, expressed by a person or persons with whom they can identify.

- It should play a vital role as one of the main 'checks and balances' within the unwritten British constitution. Its role should be complementary to that of the House of Commons in identifying points of concern and requiring the Government to reconsider or justify its policy intentions. If necessary, it should cause the House of Commons to think again ...

- It should provide a voice for the nations and regions of the United Kingdom at the centre of public affairs.

Powers

13. No radical change is needed in the balance of power between the two Houses of Parliament. The new second chamber should retain the 'suspensory veto' set out in the Parliament Acts. This will give it the power to delay the enactment of proposed legislation but not to prevent the passage of a Commons Bill which has been approved by the House of Commons in two successive sessions of Parliament.

14. The corollary of recommending that the new second chamber should have the same powers as the present House of Lords is that it should continue to consider all Government business within a reasonable time and that the principles underlying the 'Salisbury Convention' should be maintained. The second chamber should respect a governing party's general election manifesto and be cautious about challenging the clearly expressed views of the House of Commons on major issues of public policy.

15. The absolute (but unused) power of the House of Lords to veto Statutory Instruments should be adapted so that any vote against a Statutory Instrument in the new second chamber could be overridden by an affirmative vote in the House of Commons. While this would represent a diminution in the formal power of the second chamber, it would give it a mechanism which it could use in order to delay, and demonstrate its concern about, specific Statutory Instruments. The House of Commons should have the last word but would have to take full account of the second chamber's concerns, Ministers' responses and public opinion.

Making law

16. There should be no significant changes in the second chamber's law-making functions. Parliament should continue to derive the benefits of being bicameral, with a second chamber capable of bringing a distinctive range of perspectives to bear. There should be more pre-legislative scrutiny of draft Bills. The new second chamber should consider how to promote the consideration of law reform Bills drawn up by the Law Commission. The valuable work of the Delegated Powers and Deregulation Committee should continue.

Protecting the constitution

17. The second chamber's role in protecting the constitution should be maintained and enhanced. It should no longer be possible to amend the Parliament Acts using Parliament Act procedures, as was done in 1949. Such a change would maintain the current balance of power between the two Houses of Parliament and reinforce the second chamber's power of veto over any Bill to extend the life of a Parliament.

18. There should be no extension of the second chamber's formal powers in respect of any other matter, whether 'constitutional' or concerning human rights. But an authoritative Constitutional Committee should be set up by the second chamber to scrutinise the constitutional implications of all legislation and to keep the operation of the constitution under review.

19. A Human Rights Committee should be set up by the second chamber to scrutinize all Bills and Statutory Instruments for human rights implications ...

Giving a voice to the nations and regions

20. The new second chamber should be able to play a valuable role in giving a voice to the nations and regions, whatever pattern of devolution and decentralisation may emerge in future. The chamber must serve the interests of the whole of the United Kingdom and contain people from all over the United Kingdom. It should contain a proportion of 'regional members' to provide a direct voice for the nations and regions of the United Kingdom at the centre of national affairs. These 'regional members' should not be drawn from the devolved administrations, or from the Scottish

Parliament and the other devolved Assemblies, but should be able to speak for each national or regional unit of the United Kingdom. Because the 'regional members' would share a regional perspective with MEPs, members of the devolved institutions, the English Regional Chambers and the existing local government groupings, they could encourage and facilitate greater contact across different levels of Government and a stronger 'regional' voice, in Europe as well as at Westminster.

Scrutinising secondary legislation

21. Secondary legislation is increasingly pervasive and voluminous but currently subject to inadequate Parliamentary scrutiny. The House of Lords has shown a conscientious interest in the grant and exercise of delegated powers. The new second chamber should maintain and extend this function, using the new procedure referred to in paragraph 15 [above].

Scrutinising EU business

22. The existing arrangements for scrutinising Ministers' handling of European Union business should be maintained and improved in the new second chamber, with additional resources being made available to its European Union Committee. United Kingdom MEPs should not be represented in the new second chamber, but the chamber should promote greater contact and co-operation between Parliament and the United Kingdom's MEPs.

Holding the Government to account

23. Some Ministers should continue to be drawn from and be directly accountable to the new second chamber. Senior Ministers based in the House of Commons should make occasional statements to and take questions from an appropriate second chamber Committee.

24. The new second chamber should continue to be a relatively non-polemical forum for national debate, informed by the range of different perspectives which its members should have. Its specialist investigations (eg, in respect of scientific and technological issues) should continue, drawing on its members' broad spread of expertise. There is no distinct role for the second chamber to play in scrutinising public appointments.

25. A Committee should be established to scrutinise Treaties laid before Parliament and draw attention to any implications which merit Parliamentary consideration before ratification takes place.

The Law Lords and the judicial role of the second chamber

26. ... as long as certain basic conventions (which we recommend should be set out in writing) continue to be observed, there is insufficient reason to change the present arrangements. Indeed, we see some advantage in having senior judges in the legislature where they can be made aware of the social developments and political balances which underlie most legislation ...

Characteristics

28. Taking account of the roles and functions we think the new second chamber should perform, we believe it should, above all, be:

- authoritative;
- confident; and
- broadly representative of the whole of British society.

It should also contain members with:

- a breadth of experience outside the world of politics and a broad range of expertise;
- particular skills and knowledge relevant to the careful assessment of constitutional matters and human rights;
- the ability to bring a philosophical, moral or spiritual perspective to bear;
- personal distinction;

- freedom from party domination. A significant proportion of the members should belong to no political party and sit on the Cross-Benches, so that no one party is able to dominate the second chamber;

- a non-polemical and courteous style; and

- the ability to take a long-term view.

29. A new second chamber with these characteristics should remedy the deficiencies of the old House of Lords, which lacked the political legitimacy and confidence to do its job properly, while preserving some of its best features.

Composition

30. ... we do not recommend:

- a wholly or largely directly elected second chamber;

- indirect election from the devolved institutions (or local government electoral colleges) or from among United Kingdom MEPs;

- random selection; or

- co-option.

31. While the principle of vocational or interest group representation is attractive, the objective would be more effectively achieved through an independent appointments system. On the other hand, total reliance on an independent appointments system to nominate members of the new second chamber would leave no voice for the electorate in its composition. It would be unsatisfactory as a basis for identifying people to provide a voice for the nations and regions of the United Kingdom.

32. We also believe the proposed arrangements for making appointments to the interim House of Lords through the mechanism of an independent Appointments Commission would not be satisfactory as a long-term solution. They leave too much power in the hands of the Prime Minister of the day and they confine the role of the Appointments Commission to the nomination of Cross-Benchers.

33. We therefore recommend that a new second chamber of around 550 members should be made up as follows:

- A significant minority of the members of the new second chamber should be 'regional members' chosen on a basis which reflects the balance of political opinion within each of the nations and regions of the United Kingdom. The regional electorates should have a voice in the selection of members of the new second chamber. Those members in turn will provide a voice for the nations and regions.

- Other members should be appointed on the nomination of a genuinely independent Appointments Commission with a remit to create a second chamber which was broadly representative of British society and possessed all the other characteristics mentioned above.

- The Appointments Commission should be responsible for maintaining the proportion of independents ('Cross-Benchers') in the new second chamber at around 20 per cent of the total membership.

- Among the politically-affiliated members, the Appointments Commission would be required to secure an overall political balance matching the political opinion of the country as a whole, as expressed in votes cast at the most recent general election.

34. To facilitate a smooth transition to the new arrangements, the existing life peers should become members of the new second chamber.

35. Untrammelled party patronage and Prime Ministerial control of the size and balance of the second chamber should cease. The Appointments Commission should ensure that the new second chamber is broadly representative of British society. It should make early progress towards achieving gender balance and proportionate representation for members of minority ethnic groups. In order to identify appropriate candidates for the second chamber it should maintain contacts with vocational, professional, cultural, sporting and other bodies. It should publish criteria for appointment to the chamber and invite nominations from the widest possible range of sources.

36. We present three possible models for the selection of the regional members. Each model has the support of different members of the Commission. Model B has the support of a substantial majority of the Commission.

- Model A – a total of 65 regional members, chosen at the time of each general election by a system of 'complementary' election. Votes cast for party candidates in each constituency at general elections would be accumulated at regional level. The parties would secure the number of regional members for each region proportional to their shares of the vote in that region, drawing the names from a previously published party list. Regional members would be selected for one-third of the regions at each general election.

- Model B – a total of 87 regional members, elected at the time of each European Parliament election. One-third of the regions would choose their regional members at each election. The system of election used for electing members of the second chamber should be the same as that used for electing the United Kingdom's members of the European Parliament, although a majority of those supporting this model would prefer a 'partially open' list system of proportional representation (PR).

- Model C – a total of 195 regional members elected by thirds, using a 'partially open' list system of PR, at the time of each European Parliament election.

37. To promote continuity and a longer-term perspective, all members (under all three models) should serve for three electoral cycles or 15-year terms, with the possibility of being reappointed for a further period of up to 15 years at the discretion of the Appointments Commission.

Religious faiths

38. A substantial majority of the Commission recommends a broadening and deepening of religious representation in the second chamber. Representation should be extended beyond the Church of England to embrace other Christian denominations in all parts of the United Kingdom and representatives of other faiths.

Remuneration

39. To make participation in the work of the new second chamber possible for people who do not have other sources of income and who come from outside the South East of England, there should be a review of the current system of paying expenses. A modest payment related to attendance in the new second chamber should be introduced.

Notes

1   Specific aspects of the Wakeham proposals will be examined in more detail below. First, however, we turn to the government's response to the report. It is fair to say that the government broadly accepted the main thrust of the Wakeham proposals, in some cases fleshing them out. However, in certain areas of some significance it departed from Wakeham, and in yet other areas it left questions open for consultation.

2   The key controversial changes which the White Paper proposed to Wakeham in relation to composition then were:

- leaving the parties to nominate the political non-elected members; Wakeham had proposed that the Appointments Commission should do this;

- allowing both nominated and elected members to stand again;

- reducing the long terms proposed by Wakeham.

These changes were controversial, because, taken together, their effect would have been radically to increase party control over both the selection of members and their likely behaviour – since the threat of not being re-selected for membership could be used to enforce obedience to the Whips. Shorter terms would make the threat of de-selection a more pressing one. It was these changes which the parliamentary members of the Royal Commission refused to support.[91]

3   The proposals of the PASC,[92] which appear to represent the views of most MPs, are also for a mixed House, made up of elected and appointed members, independents and party political members. It backs Wakeham over the remit of the independent Appointments Commission, the 20% independent element, who should be picked for their expertise and authority in their fields, especially human rights and constitutional matters, and the targets for making the House more representative in terms of gender, race etc, aiming by these methods to preserve the House's current qualities of relative independence from party and expertise in a variety of fields. It sided with Wakeham against the government in recommending two parliament terms for all classes of members to bolster their independence, and on barring second terms.

Where the PASC's report makes a major departure from Wakeham is in its suggestion that 60% of its membership should be elected, a figure which they thought represented the 'centre of gravity' amongst the views of MPs.[93] These members would be elected using an open list PR system based on the European constituencies. The existing life peers would be compulsorily retired to make room for the new elected members, while, in line with the recommendation of both Wakeham and the government, the rump of the hereditary peers would be removed from the House. A further 20% of the House would be nominated party-political members, appointed by the Appointments Commission in proportion to the parties' share of the vote at the most recent second chamber election, in order to allow for the inclusion in the House of former senior Ministers and backbenchers and of distinguished experts who also take a party whip.[94]

4   Finally, the Reports of the Joint Committee may be mentioned, though they are short on specific recommendations at present. Clear recommendations included the following: that no one party should dominate the House;[95] that a strong independent element should be retained in any new House;[96] that there should be no greater control by the parties over peers taking a whip than at present, if possible;[97] that the remaining hereditary peers should be removed as part of a further reform package; that the Committee was 'not attracted to' compulsory

---

91 Lord Hurd, Lord Wakeham, Baroness Dean and Gerald Kaufman MP all said they could not support the White Paper as it stood.
92 HC 494-I (2001–02).
93 *Ibid*, paras 96 and 97.
94 The PASC instanced Lord Winston, Professor of Gynaecology (Labour), Lord Wallace, Professor of International Relations (Liberal Democrat), and Lord Norton, Professor of Government (Conservative).
95 First Report, HL 17, HC 171 (2002–03), para 34.
96 *Ibid*, para 40
97 *Ibid* and para 35.

retirement for existing life peers (para 55), so that the House would number around 600 (para 46); and that there should be a statutory Appointments Commission, as recommended by the Royal Commission (para 52).

5   In terms of moving towards a more general, preliminary evaluation of the Wakeham proposals, it is worth recalling Russell's analysis above as to the crucial factors which make for an effective second chamber. As summarised by the PASC,[98] the reformed Lords should have:

Distinct composition: There are various ways in which the membership of the new upper house can be made distinct from that of the House of Commons. The method of composition may be different, but the party balance in the chamber will also be particularly important.

Adequate powers: If the new upper house is to be able to make an impact, and have bargaining power with the government and the lower house, it will need to have moderate to strong powers.

Perceived legitimacy: In order to use its powers the new chamber – unlike the existing House of Lords – will need to be seen to have legitimacy, and be able to carry public support.[99]

The Joint Committee arrived at five key qualities that a reformed House should have: legitimacy; representativeness; no domination by one party, independence and expertise.[100] In substance, it is suggested, these coincide with the first two of Russell's criteria: representativeness goes to legitimacy, while independence, freedom from party domination and expertise are qualities that render the Lords distinct from the Commons.

6   The Wakeham proposals clearly fulfil the criterion of distinct composition: the proposed membership would be markedly different from that of the Commons in a number of ways. First, the 20% independent members would provide a bedrock of expertise, experience and alternative perspectives from those held by professional politicians. Secondly, the exclusive jurisdiction of the Appointments Commission over the party political appointments should also have the effect of providing at least some party members of a different character from those found in the Commons: strong party loyalty would not be a key criterion for the Appointments Commission, as it is for the political parties themselves, so that those it selected might well tend to be those more experienced and independently-minded party members who might not recommend themselves to the parties but who yet could make a valuable contribution to the work of the second chamber. Long, non-renewable terms would further bolster their independence from party. Thirdly, and just as significantly, party balance in the Lords would, under the Wakeham proposals, form a strong contrast to the position in the Commons, since neither the government, nor any other party in the Lords would have an overall majority, the position which, as discussed below, research suggests is the best option.[101] The Wakeham proposals thus also fulfil each of the three 'distinctiveness' criteria of the Joint Committee – no domination by one party, independence and expertise.

7   The current *powers* of the Lords are recognisably in the moderate end of the international spectrum, as Russell finds, though the removal of the absolute veto over delegated legislation would amount to a significant weakening of the House,

98   Fifth Report, HC 494 (2001–02), para 8.
99   *Ibid.*
100 *Op cit*, para 30.
101 See below, pp 388–89.

and the lack of any proposal to the give the Lords special powers over constitutional matters would keep it significantly less powerful in that area than most overseas chambers. Both issues are discussed further below.

8 It is Russell's third factor and the Joint Committee's first – legitimacy – that is problematic in relation to the Wakeham/White Paper proposals. Certainly the general response to Wakeham and *a fortiori* the White Paper in the press and elsewhere suggests that a House with only a small elected element would simply not be seen as sufficiently legitimate; however, the current political climate suggests that if the elected element were increased to half, this would probably suffice. But any reformed House that had some elected element and a significant element appointed by an independent body would have overwhelmingly greater legitimacy than the unreformed, or even the current, House.

9 In the next section, specific issues that would need to be resolved in any reform programme are examined in the light of academic and parliamentary viewpoints.

Party balance

M Russell, *Reforming the Lords: Lessons from Overseas* (2000) (extracts)

In modern systems the most important difference between the chambers is liable to be in terms of political balance. This will have a critical impact on the relationship between the two chambers, and the relationship between the upper house and government. We have seen that there are three patterns of party balance demonstrated by the seven chambers surveyed. The first is for government to control the upper house, as well as the lower house – this is generally the case in Ireland, Italy, and Spain. This holds the danger that the upper house will simply act as a 'rubber stamp' for government decisions. In France and Canada, as in the UK, the upper house is sometimes dominated by the governing party and at other times by the opposition. This leads to the prospect of periods of great tension, interspersed with periods where the upper house does not play a particularly effective scrutiny role. The most interesting pattern is that in Australia and Germany, where neither government nor opposition generally win control of the upper house. This provides an opportunity for genuine bargaining between the upper house and the government . . .

. . . Critically, political balance has at least as great an effect on an upper house's impact as [its formal powers and legitimacy]. Upper chambers which are controlled by government will tend to be of limited impact, whilst those which are sometimes controlled by the opposition win occasional bloody victories. But an upper house will tend to be at its most genuinely influential when controlled by neither government nor opposition. When the balance of power is held by other forces, government will be more inclined, and more able, to negotiate in order to secure its bills. This is seen in particular in the Australian and German upper houses. Whilst governments may find this process frustrating, a powerful upper house which is controlled by forces independent of government can help create a form of consensus politics which results in better political outcomes in the longer term.

Notes

1 There are, then, three logical alternatives for party balance in a parliamentary chamber:

Government control: Spain, Italy and Ireland are examples, and as Russell notes above, are some of the most widely derided chambers with the lowest levels of public confidence and satisfaction in them. 'It is difficult for a chamber with a permanent government majority to play an effective review role.'[102]

---

102 Russell, *op cit*, p 298.

Opposition control: as Russell notes, 'while providing a strong check upon government, this amounts to a potentially unstable situation as an opposition-controlled chamber may seek to disrupt all government legislation. The unreformed Lords, which often faced Labour governments with a House effectively under the control of the Conservative Opposition, has not on the whole sought to do this, because of the conventions noted above, which proceed partly from a widely shared recognition of its own lack of legitimacy. The Canadian Senate is similar'.

Neither opposition nor government controlled. According to Russell, this 'appears to be the most effective option according to overseas experience'. It is frustrating to governments, as in Australia, but popular with the public and approved by commentators. 'Even in Ireland, where the upper house has weak powers, the chamber worked effectively during one isolated period when independent members had control'.[103]

2   The arguments of Wakeham on this point were as follows:

A House for the Future, Cm 4534 (2000) (extracts)

10.24 As we observed in Chapter 3, it would be unrealistic to think that the second chamber could somehow be insulated from party politics or that it could function effectively without the involvement of political parties. As long as the second chamber retains a role in the determination of public policy and legislation, the political parties will demand access to it and find ways of securing a role for themselves.

10.25 It is nevertheless crucial that no one political party should be able to dominate the second chamber. If it were to be controlled by the party of Government it might become nothing more than a rubber stamp. If the main Opposition party were to gain control, it could be used to produce legislative deadlock and so trigger a series of constitutional conflicts. There should be a fair balance between the main political parties in the second chamber and no one party should ever be able to secure a majority. We accept, however, that the party of Government should have significant representation in the chamber so that it has a substantial pool of supporters to call on. The Government needs people who can serve as Ministers, explain and defend Government policies and provide some assurance that Government business will get through without undue delay or disruption.

10.26 We see advantages in preserving a strong independent element such as that represented in the present House of Lords by the Cross-Benchers – members who are not affiliated to any political party. The existence of such an independent element would of course be consistent with our desire to see a second chamber which was more broadly representative of British society. People in all walks of life have political views, but the net should be cast sufficiently wide to ensure that a proportion of those selected to be members of the second chamber are not formally affiliated to any particular party and will sit on the Cross-Benches. If the proportion of Cross-Benchers were large enough, it would provide an absolute guarantee that no one political party could ever come to control the second chamber. The fact that the Cross-Benchers might hold the 'balance of power' would encourage the parties' spokespersons to seek to win any arguments on their merits rather than by appealing to party loyalty or partisan interests. The authority of the second chamber would be reinforced if decisions were taken at least to some extent on the basis of an independent judgment of the merits of each case.

10.27 It would be wrong, however, to place the onus for ensuring independent-mindedness solely on Cross-Benchers. During the consultation exercise our attention was repeatedly drawn – with

---

approval – to examples of members of the House of Lords who were affiliated to a party but had not voted invariably in accordance with their party whip. We share the view that even those members of the second chamber who are affiliated to a party should be prepared to deal with issues on their merits and should exercise a certain independence of judgment.

10.28 More generally, members of the second chamber should not be beholden to or capable of being mandated by any other person or organisation. They should be 'representatives' in the Burkean tradition, not delegates. They should think and speak for themselves.

. . .

11.14 ... During the course of our work we commissioned two papers from the Public Policy Group at the London School of Economics that discussed what principles might be applicable to elections to the second chamber and what options might be explored. They used general and European election data going back to 1974 to model the outcomes that might be expected from the use of different electoral systems to select members of the second chamber. One of the points to emerge most clearly was that if the overall political balance of the second chamber had been determined by reference to the parties' shares of the vote at national or regional level in any general or European election since the mid-1970s, it would always have produced a chamber in which every party had a proportional share of the seats, the Government party was normally the largest but no single party ever had a majority. This observation holds true for every general election since 1901, except for the two in the 1930s in which governing coalitions won more than 50 per cent of the popular vote. As we want to achieve a second chamber with exactly those characteristics, this finding seemed highly relevant to our work.

Note

While neither the government nor Wakeham received much praise or even positive recognition for this aspect of their plans for reform of the Lords, their proposal that that the government of the day would never control the Lords, so that the balance of power will lie either with independents, or with smaller parties, deserves to be welcomed by those wishing to see an effective and assertive second chamber. This recommendation has been approved by both the PASC in its Fifth Report,[104] which, in arguing for a 20% appointed independent element, and a proportional electoral system, wished to minimise the possibility of one party gaining overall control of the chamber. Under this system, the largest party, with a typical 43% or 44% of the national vote, would have around a third of the seats in the second chamber, compared to a possible very large majority in the first, as at present. The Joint Committee recommended that: 'any arrangements for the reformed House must take account of the importance of maintaining the principle that no one political party should be able to be dominant in it,'[105] and this principle now seems to command universal acceptance: as the Joint Committee noted in its Second Report:

> Many Members [in debate] emphasised the need for lack of domination by one party and worry was expressed about the degree of political patronage in the existing system of appointments. In his remarks on the second day of the debate in the House of Lords, the Lord Chancellor said that reform of the Lords should produce a House which was not 'a rival nor a pale imitation' of the Commons and one that is not 'dominated by the political parties either collectively or singly; that brings to its deliberations distinctive expertise and experience'.[106]

104 HC 494 (2001–02), para 80.
105 First Report, HL 17, HC 171 (2002–03), para 36.
106 HL 97, HC 668 (2002–03), para 24.

Elected, appointed or a mixed House?

Ultimately, it was in failing to decide this crucial question in the votes held in February 2003 that the two Houses of Parliament probably stymied the current drive towards comprehensive reform of the Lords. The options on which they voted were as follows: *Option 1* – fully appointed; *Option 2* – fully elected; *Option 3* – 80% appointed, 20% elected (the Wakeham option); *Option 4* – 80% elected, 20% appointed; *Option 5* – 60% appointed, 40% elected; *Option 6* – 60% elected, 40% appointed (the PASC option); *Option 7* – 50% appointed, 50% elected. An amendment in the Commons called for the Lords to be abolished.

	Amendment	Option 1	Option 2	Option 3	Option 4	Option 5	Option 6	Option 7
Lords								
For		335	106	39	93	60	91	84
Against		110	329	375	338	358	317	322
Commons								
For	172	245	272	[no vote]	281	[no vote]	253	[no vote]
Against	390	323	289		284		316	

Essentially, then, the Lords backed a wholly appointed House, while the Commons rejected that option, but also failed to agree upon either a wholly elected House, or any of the 'hybrid' options. In this section, the arguments on this essential matter of composition, which were essentially echoed in the debates in both Houses, are examined.

An objection to any mixed House?

Since the two solutions of an entirely appointed or entirely elected House both seem to have obvious drawbacks one might expect that the obvious solution would have been some form of mixed House. The Royal Commission, the government White Paper and the PASC all recommended such a proposal; one might therefore expect that such an option would be seen as commending a clear consensus. Remarkably, however, this option seems suddenly to have fallen out of favour. A large number of MPs and even more Peers expressed opposition to a mixed House during the debate on the Joint Committee report on this ground.

Perhaps what caused this basic idea to lose support, apart from the Prime Minister's making known that he was against a mixed House himself,[107] was the view that a hybrid House would be unworkable in practice. This view was first expressed by Bogdanor.

V Bogdanor, 'Reform of the House of Lords: a sceptical view' (1999) 70(4) Political Quarterly 375 (extracts)

There are especial difficulties, it may be suggested, in a mixed second chamber, combining directly or indirectly elected members with a nominated element. For a mixed chamber would, by definition, contain members enjoying different degrees of democratic legitimacy. The danger then is that any vote carried by a group with a lesser degree of democratic legitimacy will be seen as less

---

107 See Prime Minister's Questions col 877 (29 January 2003).

valid than a vote carried by a group with greater democratic legitimacy. In the past, the Labour party has regarded votes carried by the hereditary peers as having less weight than votes carried by the life peers, since it regards the former as less legitimate than the latter. In a new second chamber composed of an elected element and a nominated element, votes carried by the latter would be regarded as carrying less weight than those carried by the former. Who elected you? would be the cry directed at the hapless nominated members whenever they carried a vote against their elected colleagues.

Notes

1   Russell cautiously agrees that this could be a problem:

> The greatest potential difficulty in a new upper house that combines elected and appointed members is that it could become controversial whenever the appointed members decide the outcome of a vote . . . A similar situation applied towards the end of the life of the previous House of Lords, when commentators were quick to point out the occasions that the hereditary members were in this decisive position. Hereditary members were seen as less legitimate than life members, and it is possible that appointed members would bear the same stigma in a new chamber where most members had been elected.[108]

She points out that the only parallel here would be the Italian Senate, which has a small number of *ex officio* appointed members; because their numbers are small, their votes are rarely determinate. However, 'On the one recent occasion when this happened, in 1994, it caused considerable controversy'.

2   This point was echoed in Parliament by some of the more thoughtful objectors to a mixed House in the parliamentary debates on the Joint Committee report in January 2003 and indeed seemed to be used as the chief argument against having a mixed House. 'The compromises of part-election are the worst option, with the invidious outcome of two classes of members – elected and appointed'[109] 'A partly elected second Chamber would . . . create two classes of Member. We can imagine the cries of "Foul!" when elected Members are outvoted by unelected Members'.[110] 'It will be the nominated upper Members of Parliament who will be responsible for stopping the popular will of the elected Members of the House of Lords.[111] However, the extent to which this would be a problem for a mixed House should not be too readily assumed. The reaction of the elected members to such an eventuality is a matter of speculation.[112] If a mixed House had been approved by both Houses of Parliament on a free vote, and so had received all-party endorsement, it would be difficult for elected members to carp at the presence and influence of the non-elected members which Parliament itself had agreed should be there.

3   More importantly, those arguing against hybridity on these grounds miss a simple, but important point: if the elected members constituted a *majority* of the House, as the PASC suggests should be the case, then they would rarely or never be defeated by the unelected; thus the danger Bogdanor foresees would simply never

108 Russell, *op cit*.
109 HC Deb col 204 (21 January 2003).
110 *Ibid*, col 250, Mr Clelland.
111 HL Deb col 631 (21 January 2003), Lord Hughes.
112 As Russell has pointed out, only two chambers out of 58 bi-cameral legislatures worldwide have a substantial amount of appointed members in the second chamber, so there is little evidence from which to predict with any confidence the dynamics of such chambers ('Second chambers overseas' (1999) 70(4) Political Quarterly 411, 417).

materialise. Yet this simple point seemed to go largely unrecognised in the debates: as one peer said,

The crucial point about a hybrid system is that, *whatever* the percentage—20/80, 60/40, 50/50—it would not be stable. The first time the unelected Members defeated the elected Members there would be increasing pressure to have more elected Members.[113]

How his Lordship envisaged, say, a 20% unelected contingent defeating an 80% elected one is not clear. Moreover, it is unlikely that any given issue would split the two groups of members squarely down the middle as Bogdanor suggests. In nearly all cases, there would be bound to be some elected members siding with their unelected colleagues (particularly perhaps Liberal Democrat and non-partisan party members generally). This would preclude the isolation and exposure of the unelected members.

4   In any event, there are ways of minimising the problem. Both Wakeham[114] and the PASC recommended that everything should be done to ensure that all members enjoy parity of esteem, whether elected or appointed. Thus Wakeham recommended:

Once members have arrived in the chamber, by whatever route, they should so far as possible serve the same terms, benefit from the same allowances and facilities and be treated in all respects identically.[115]

Similarly the PASC[116] said:

... however individual members enter the House, they should enjoy equal status and parity of esteem, whether they are elected, nominated by the parties or appointed to sit on the Cross-Benches.

99. In furtherance of this principle, we recommend that all members of the second chamber should serve for similar periods and for long terms; should enjoy equal facilities; and should receive the same pay and conditions of service.

What proportion (if any) of the new House should be elected?

In this section we consider the arguments advanced for and against the four main options of a fully elected, fully appointed, mainly elected and mainly appointed House. We start with Wakeham, which advocated a mainly appointed House.

A House for the Future, Cm 4534 (2000) (extracts)

11.3 In a democracy there is a natural presumption in favour of election as the appropriate way of constituting the second chamber. There was considerable support for direct election among respondents to our consultation exercise. Election implies direct accountability to the electorate. It was also argued that, if the second chamber were to retain the power to veto, or at least delay, legislation passed by the House of Commons and to act as a check on the executive, it should have some electoral authority to justify the exercise of such power and to give it the confidence to use that power. A second chamber with at least a significant proportion of directly elected members would have the necessary political weight to carry out the responsibilities we propose it should have and its decisions would be more widely seen as politically legitimate. There is a danger

---

113 *Ibid*, col 726 (22 January 2003), Lord Higgins (emphasis added).
114 Wakeham Report, *op cit*, paras 12.4–12.6.
115 *Ibid*, para 12.5.
116 *Op cit*, paras 98–99.

that, without a directly elected element, the reformed second chamber might decline into an assemblage of respected but politically ineffective dignitaries ...

11.4 These points led us to the view that the second chamber should contain at least some members who would be chosen on a basis which directly reflects the balance of political opinion within each nation and region of the United Kingdom; but, in reaching that view, we were conscious of the arguments against direct election. A review of those arguments ... reveals the strength of the case against having a wholly – or even a largely – directly elected second chamber.

11.5 A second chamber which was wholly or largely directly elected would certainly be authoritative and confident, but the source of its authority could bring it into direct conflict with the House of Commons. There would be a risk that the second chamber would have a different political complexion from the House of Commons. Such a divergence would, whatever the formal distinctions between the chambers in terms of their powers and pre-eminence, be bound to give rise to constitutional conflicts. A different risk would arise if the second chamber had the same political complexion as the House of Commons because that could cause it to act as a compliant rubber stamp for whatever any future Government might want to do.

11.6 ... There would, in particular, be no justification for a continuation of the Salisbury Convention (see Chapter 4). If a directly elected second chamber were to be opposed to a Bill, it would not be easy to argue that it should, save in exceptional circumstances, defer to the views of the other directly elected chamber.

...

11.8 A wholly directly elected second chamber could not be broadly representative of the complex strands of British society. The fact is that elections can only be fought effectively by organised political parties which can attract large blocks of voters and who have the resources to organise television broadcasts, publicity, canvassing, public meetings and the like. While most major political parties are broad churches whose members and supporters are generally representative of British society, it is inevitable that in choosing electoral candidates they will select people who will epitomise the party's distinct ethos and who have demonstrated both their long-term loyalty to the party and their effectiveness in advancing its interests. Successful candidates for any direct elections to the second chamber would almost certainly come from a narrow class of people who are politically aware and highly partisan and who have to a very considerable degree already committed their lives to political activity. Putting it bluntly but accurately, a wholly elected second chamber would in practice mean that British public life was dominated even more than it is already by professional politicians.

11.9 By the same token, total reliance on direct election would in practice be incompatible with securing membership for people with relevant experience of and expertise in other walks of life. Such people would generally be reluctant to commit themselves to a party platform or engage in electioneering and would therefore be unlikely to put themselves forward as candidates for election. They would also be unlikely to be successful if they did so. While they might be well known in their field, such people rarely achieve widespread popular recognition or support. They lack the skills necessary to fight an electoral battle. Direct election would therefore be unlikely to produce members with the ability to speak directly for the voluntary sector, the professions, cultural and sporting interests and a whole range of other important aspects of British society.

11.10 In addition, most systems of direct election deliver results which may be geographically representative but which are seldom gender-balanced or provide appropriate representation for ethnic, religious or other minorities.

11.11 Direct elections are also not well suited to securing membership of the second chamber for those with specific expertise and authority in constitutional matters and the protection of human rights. Indeed, it could be counter-productive to base the selection of people with such characteristics on a popular election. There would be some risk that successful candidates would find it difficult to maintain the necessary detached and quasi-judicial approach to their responsibilities. Nor is it easy to see how direct election could reliably produce members of the second chamber who could make a specialist contribution to the discussion of philosophical, moral or spiritual issues.

11.12 Another fundamental criticism of any proposal that the membership should be wholly or largely elected is that it would significantly reduce the prospects for securing a second chamber which was relatively independent of the influence of political parties. Very few independents, if any, would secure election, even using a highly proportional system such as Single Transferable Vote (STV). Successful candidates for election would nearly all be closely associated with political parties and essentially dependent on those parties. Under the current system for appointing life peers to the House of Lords, the parties have been good at nominating at least some people who are not professional politicians, who are personally distinguished in their own right and who sometimes take a relatively independent line. But if the parties were nominating candidates for election, their criteria would be likely to change. The emphasis would be on selecting people with the political commitment and campaigning skills likely to bring out the vote and win the election. Moreover, such elections would be fought on manifestos or programmes which would bind those who were elected and reinforce the extent to which they would be creatures of party rather than relatively dispassionate individuals, albeit with party allegiances.

11.13 Another real obstacle to the use of direct election is the risk that the introduction of yet another round of elections, possibly involving yet another electoral system, would contribute to what has become known as 'voter fatigue'. A very low turnout for any election to the second chamber could serve to undermine its authority. Voters are currently expected to vote in local government elections, Westminster elections, European Parliament elections and, where relevant, for the Scottish Parliament and the Welsh or Northern Ireland Assemblies. Shortly, some of them will be voting for the London Assembly and the Mayor for London. The only two pairs of elections in that list which use the same electoral system are local government (in Great Britain) and Westminster elections and those for the Scottish Parliament and the National Assembly for Wales. There is also a growing practice of inviting the electorate to express its views in referendums. Any increase in the number or variety of elections would be a recipe for voter alienation as well as confusion. In the light of US experience, which has seen the extension of opportunities to vote accompanied by a steady decline in turnout, we would be reluctant to propose an additional electoral contest, especially one using yet another electoral system.

Notes

1   A critical weakness in the arguments expressed above are that they are often expressed as being arguments directed against 'a wholly or mainly' elected body, as if the same considerations apply to each, while in other instances it is not made clear which scenario is being envisaged; however the two clearly have profoundly different implications. Exactly the same, possibly deliberate confusion can be seen in a recent comment of the Lord Chancellor:

> ... a wholly or substantially elected House ... would be a House of equal legitimacy to the House of Commons, since it would be elected. The rationale for the conventions by which this House came to accept that it is subordinate to the House of Commons, as the sole elected Chamber, would be gone for ever.[117]

---

117 *Ibid*, col 832 (22 January 2003) (emphasis added).

The points made in paras 11.5 and 11.6 – the challenge to the pre-eminence to the Commons – in reality applies only to a wholly elected second chamber or one in which all but a very small minority were elected. If, for example, 60% of the second chamber were elected, the House of Commons, as wholly elected body, could still claim a significantly stronger democratic mandate for its decisions. The arguments in paras 11.8 and 11.9 about representativeness and expertise are only expressed to apply to a *wholly* elected chamber, and this is clearly the case. The same is true of para 11.11, since a minority of appointed members could provide the necessary constitutional expertise; they could also supply the independent members whose admitted desirability is canvassed in para 11.12. The concern as to gender and ethnic representation (para 11.10) could be answered by having a substantial minority of appointed members, where a duty lay upon the appointing body to secure such equality of representation (as Wakeham in fact proposes). The 'voter fatigue' concern, aired in para 11.13, since it goes to the process of having to engage in a further round of electioneering and voting, rather than the proportion of elected to non-elected members in the chamber for which the elections were held, would presumably apply to *any* elections for a second chamber, regardless of that proportion. Ironically, voter apathy would probably in fact be most marked if the elected element of the second chamber was so small as to give rise to a perception that the elected element was tokenistic and the elected members impotent, because constantly out-voted by appointees, a point made recently by the Joint Committee:

We cannot see an election for a small proportion of the new House raising any enthusiasm or contributing to a sense of the importance of the reformed House in the eyes of the electorate.[118]

This point, rather ironically in view of Wakeham's actual proposals, therefore argues for at the least a substantially elected element.

2   In the result, Wakeham's arguments against an elected House do not appear to apply with any force against a chamber composed of the 60% elected element that the PASC recommended. The White Paper included similarly unpersuasive arguments of this kind (see para 36).

3   The PASC report was representative of the Commons' attitudes in its robust dismissal of such fears:

The Government, and some members of the Lords, have laid particular stress on the threat which would allegedly be posed to the pre-eminence of the Commons by a more legitimate reformed second chamber. We are satisfied that the Parliament Acts provide sufficient safeguards against that. The differences in powers between the Houses are already very clear. These have only to be identified for any argument on this point to be removed. The Commons can pass legislation without the consent of the Lords, after delay of about one year. But the Lords cannot pass legislation without gaining the consent of the Commons. The Commons only has to wait one month before passing a money bill without the consent of the Lords. Governments are formed, tested and held to account in the Commons. They have to retain the confidence of the Commons if they are to retain office. Only the Commons can make or break governments. We therefore do not believe that a reformed, more representative second chamber will pose a threat to that status. Moreover, our proposals are intended further to strengthen the distinctiveness of the second chamber, and so increase the effectiveness of Parliament as a whole.[119]

---

118 First Report, HL 17, HC 171 (2002–03), para 70.
119 *Op cit*, para 51.

4   A more sophisticated argument against an elected House is put forward by Dawn
     Oliver, one of the members of the Royal Commission.

D Oliver, 'The reform of the UK Parliament', in J Jowell and D Oliver (eds), *The Changing Constitution*, 4th edn (2000), pp 288–89

The Royal Commission claimed that its proposals would produce a House that was authoritative, confident, and broadly representative of the whole of British society. It would be more democratic and more representative than the present House of Lords. More democratic because it would reflect the overall balance of political opinion within the country, and regional members would directly reflect the balance of political opinion in the regions. And more representative because it would contain members from all parts of the country and all walks of life, broadly equal numbers of men and women, and representatives of all the country's main ethnic and religious communities.

These proposals imply a novel concept of 'democracy', since the elected or electorally related element in the chamber would range, depending on precisely which method of selecting regional members was elected, between only about 16 per cent and 33 per cent. Behind the claim to the quality of democracy for the reformed chamber lies a view that democracy requires more than election of representatives and of a government, which is what elections to the House of Commons provide. It also requires that the functioning of the legislature be supportive of democracy and democratic values, for instance in providing constitutional and human rights protection. A legislature should also be representative of the country at large. The House of Commons, dominated by party and in particular by the party of government, is not equipped to perform these watchdog functions. And systems of election, even highly proportional ones such as the Single Transferable Vote or list systems, do not secure render balance or fair representation of ethnic minorities. Nor can elections produce many people who can represent particular aspects of British life and make valuable contributions to the legislative process and the process of holding the government to account and debating matters of national concern, since many such people are not politically affiliated or, if affiliated, are not politically ambitious or would not want to stand for election.

Against this the point could of course be made that it is essential that our legislators are accountable to the electorate: the unelected members of the reformed second chamber would not be so accountable and this can hardly be democratic. Even the elected members would not be re-electable under the Royal Commission's proposals, and would thus not be accountable in the sense of being liable to be dismissed by the electorate. This raises the question of exactly what it is about a second chamber in a system such as that of the UK that requires it to be elected, and what 'democracy' entails. The reformed second chamber – like the present one – will not be responsible for the choice of government, nor for maintaining the government in power, nor for financial matters. Those are matters for the House of Commons and, it is suggested, it is largely for that reason that the lower house needs to be elected. These arguments do not apply with the same force to the second chamber.

The reformed second chamber will be a hybrid body in many respects: in protecting the constitution and human rights it will be performing functions that non-political, non-elected, unaccountable bodies such as constitutional courts or councils perform elsewhere: it is accepted that such bodies should not be democratically accountable. In much of what it does it will be performing a technical scrutiny function and holding government to account, activities that are also performed by other non-elected bodies such as the press and pressure groups, advisory committees, and the like, and in which political affiliation or accountability is not essential. And its powers are limited – in primary legislation to a one-year suspensory veto. This is quite different from the position in the Commons, whose consent is always required for legislation. The true legislator in the system, or at least the body which has the last word on legislation, is – and under the proposals will remain – the House of Commons. This is the body that needs to be accountable to the electorate. In other words, the arguments surrounding the reform of the House of Lords also raise issues about what makes an institution a 'legislative chamber' and when the notion of 'legislative chamber' ends and runs into that of council of state, constitutional court or constitutional council.'

Notes

1   The weakness in the Commission's argument on this point, more articulately put forward here by Oliver than in the report itself, is clear. As Russell and Cornes put it: 'Whilst there are arguments for the inclusion of both groups within the House, the Commission does little to justify the *dominance* of the chamber by appointed members, the majority of whom would continue to take a party whip.'[120]

2   Oliver's argument above justifies the predominance of non-elected members on the basis that they will primarily be undertaking a technical, scrutinising function, which does not require an impeccable democratic mandate. A similar point was made by Robin Cook, for the government:

> The limited functions of a second Chamber do not require it to mirror the democratic mandate of the House of Commons. On the contrary, the second Chamber will be better able to fulfil its role of deliberation and a more valuable forum in which difficult issues can be discussed openly if its debates are informed by the expertise and authority of people with a lifetime of distinction.[121]

However, if this is the justification for a mainly non-elected House, with the implication that the skills required are those of expertise and objectivity, rather than those of the politician, then it would surely point to the non-elected element being made up of independent rather than party political members, whereas Wakeham suggests a mainly appointed House but with only a 20% independent element: in other words one would have party members deciding constitutional and human rights issues – but without the legitimacy given by election. This seems a crucial weakness in the Wakeham proposals.

3   The key point which those who argue for a relatively small – or no – elected element dismiss too readily, particularly where a large proportion of the other members were appointed by the government and other political parties rather than any independent body, as the White Paper proposed, is that such a body would be neither *perceived* to be, nor see it itself as, sufficiently legitimate to assert its powers fully against a government-controlled Commons. As one MP put it:

> Why should a small group choose the representatives of 60 million people? We have just heard that we got rid of Old Sarum, where seven people elected two MPs, and Dunwich under the sea, where 14 did ... do they really want to go back not just centuries but to a different millennium?[122]

Or as Lord Goodhart put it, an all appointed House would mean: '... one House of Parliament being elected by an electorate of eight, nine or 10 people. That I regard as a totally incredible idea.'[123]

4   Even if the House was not fully appointed, if the elected element were a small minority, as Wakeham and the government suggested, the House as a whole would

---

120   M Russell and R Cornes, 'The Royal Commission on Reform of the House of Lords: A House for the Future?' (2001) 64 MLR 82, p 86.

121   HC Deb (10 March 2002).

122   HC Deb col 239 (21 January 2003), Malcom Savidge.

123   HL Deb col 825 (22 January 2003).

arguably still lack such perceived legitimacy. The example discussed above by Russell[124] of the appointed Canadian Senate, a potentially very powerful House, but one which in practice is so crippled by the perception of its lack of legitimacy as to make little effective contribution to the legislative process, is apposite. The Wakeham report observed on this point:

The reformed second chamber should also be sufficiently confident to use its powers in what it judges to be the most effective and appropriate manner. Throughout the 20th century the House of Lords was inhibited both by its lack of authority and its lack of confidence. The reformed second chamber must be free of such debilitating inhibitions.[125]

Of the unreformed House, Donald Shell wrote in 1994 that its lack of legitimacy meant that: 'It would now be foolish to rely on the House to provide satisfactory protection for the fundamentals of the constitution.' This view was arguably borne out by the response of the Lords in April 1996 to the Prevention of Terrorism (Additional Powers) Act, passed in the wake of the IRA's bomb attack on Canary Wharf, breaking its ceasefire; *inter alia*, the Act gives the police new powers to stop and search pedestrians for terrorist-related items without having to have reasonable suspicion (s 1). The fundamental principle at stake (it has of course been violated before) was that measures threatening the liberty of the subject should be given a decent period for scrutiny and that debate should not be subject to severe time constraints. The Act passed all its stages in the Commons in a single day and the Lords were requested by the government to follow suit. As the debate made clear, many peers expressed considerable disquiet at what they were being asked to do, but ultimately appeared to think it their duty to acquiesce.[126] Thus the House felt itself unable either to reject the Bill or to extend time for consideration, although peers clearly expressed a sense of constitutional impropriety in the way in which the matter had been handled.

5   However, as suggested above, the response of the Lords to the 2001 Anti-Terrorism Bill was much more bullish; the greater preparedness to resist the government on crucial issues probably flowed from the Lords' own perception of their greater legitimacy, following the removal of the hereditary peers. Ministers were no longer able to lambast the House simply as an anachronistic impediment to the democratic process, dominated by Conservative hereditary peers; as commentators pointed out, the government was now dealing with an institution which it had reformed, albeit limitedly, precisely to make it more legitimate and representative.[127] Nevertheless, as seen above, the Lords did give way on a number of crucial issues; doubtless this was, at least in part, due to the Lords' own perception of their lack of legitimacy. A fully-reformed Lords, with a substantially elected element, would no doubt have felt far more able to stick to its guns. The clear lesson to be learned is that the crucial factor in the readiness of the Lords to provide a substantial check upon the government is not so much its formal powers – which are, in any event, likely to remain substantially unchanged in any process of further reform – but its own perception of its legitimacy. Increasing its legitimacy will markedly increase its impact as a constitutional check in practice even without any formal increase in its powers.

---

124 See the extract from her book, at p 377, above.
125 *Op cit*, para 10.8.
126 See HL Deb vol 571 no 73 cols 298, 301–04, 337–38 (3 April 1996).
127 See 'Blunkett "bully on terror bill"', *The Guardian*, 10 December 2001.

6   *Perceived* legitimacy is therefore crucial. The Royal Commission, as seen above,
     recognised this. However, in the view certainly of the PASC, the Commission
     simply misjudged the public mood in considering that a mainly appointed House
     with a small elected element would garner to itself sufficient apparent legitimacy to
     be truly effective. While their arguments as to other means of obtaining legitimacy
     and authority (expertise, representativeness, personal distinction, independent-
     mindedness and so on)[128] are not without some merit, they arguably fail to
     recognise that the direct political power that the House of Lords exercises requires
     it to have a direct electoral mandate from the people, as the press and
     parliamentary reaction to Wakeham and the White Paper indicated. As the PASC
     put it, in proposing a predominately appointed chamber, Wakeham and the
     government 'are bravely swimming against the tide of political and public
     opinion'. In the following extract, the PASC explains this point and puts forward an
     alternative suggestion.

Select Committee on Public Administration, Fifth Report, HC 494 (2001–02) (extracts)

85. The debate in the House of Commons on 9 January, the support for the Early Day Motion, our own survey of MPs, and public opinion surveys show that having a minority elected element is no longer a credible option ... there has been a revulsion against party patronage. The main criticism of the White Paper voiced again and again in the parliamentary debates and in the media was that it is no longer acceptable for most of the second chamber to be party placemen, who owe their place to their party leader. Even if these appointments were not made directly by party leaders but mediated by the Appointments Commission, a largely appointed second chamber would still be 'the biggest quango in the land'. The public is no longer willing to accept patronage on that scale.'[129] ...

94. The Royal Commission and the White Paper both proposed a predominantly appointed second chamber. Although we also support a mixed chamber, we believe that the balance between election and appointment needs to be tipped in the opposite direction. This is not just because we believe that this is where the centre of gravity of opinion now lies, but because we think that the legitimacy of the institution requires it. Without sufficient legitimacy, the second chamber will not be as effective as it needs to be. This consideration has also led us to conclude that the superficially attractive option of parity between election and appointment, reflecting the merits and purposes of each, is not sufficient to guarantee legitimacy and effectiveness.

95. That is why we have concluded that the new second chamber must be predominantly elected. But we also believe that there should still be a significant appointed element. The cross-benchers will only get there by appointment. Scientists, industrialists, public servants, academics and other experts who would not normally stand for election will only get there by that means. We are proposing the continuation of an appointed element not simply to accommodate those opposed to election, but because there are those who genuinely believe that the appointed members add value through their distinct expertise and experience from outside politics, which should not be lost ...

96. To fulfil the condition that the second chamber should be predominantly elected, we therefore recommend that 60 per cent of its members should come by election. Of the remainder, half (20 per cent of the total) should be nominated by the political parties; and half (20 per cent of the

128 See Wakeham Report, *op cit*, para 10.6.
129 Wakeham Report, *op cit*, paras 85 and 86.

total) should be independent, non-aligned members; both categories should be appointed by the Appointments Commission ...

97. [This] would deliver a chamber with the confidence and the authority (to repeat again the final and most important principle of composition from the White Paper) to fulfil its constitutional role.

Notes

1 One practical obstacle in the way of increasing the number of elected members beyond the 20% or so recommended by the government is the existing life peers, a problem spelt out very clearly by Lord Irvine:

Today we have 587 life peers, 92 hereditaries and 26 bishops. So the start position is 705. If we take away 92 hereditaries we are left with 613; we add 120 elected and reach a total of 733. The maximum transitional House that we contemplate is 750, reducing to 600 over 10 years. Many would say that anything in excess of 700, even on a transitional basis, is excessive.

What these figures show is that there is no scope at present for more than 120 elected. Those who say that there should be more than 120 elected should explain where the scope for them exists. All that is on the assumption that the rights of the 587 life peers are to be respected; we believe they must.[130]

Unless the life peers, then, are removed, they will leave only through death, or possibly early retirement, leaving very little scope for the addition of many more elected members, and also leaving the House in its current, grossly over-sized guise. In this respect, the Joint Committee has said that it was 'not attracted to' compulsory retirement for existing life peers,[131] so that the House would number around 600; that there should be a statutory Appointments Commission, as recommended by the Royal Commission which, however, could take nominations from the parties and others; that members should serve a term of 12 years, and be barred from standing for the Commons for three years.

2 There remains considerable argument as to the mechanics of elections to the second chamber, whatever the proportion of the elected element, which cannot be addressed in detail here. One of these is the day on which the election should be held, whether teamed with the European elections (which produce a very low turn-out) or with the general election as favoured by the government and the PASC[132] (which could produce a House with too strong a resemblance in political balance to the Commons – unless voters operated a 'split ticket' in casting their votes for Commons and Lords). Another is the electoral system used. As one MP remarked:

If the ... elected element is elected using the closed-list system that operates for the European Parliament, the power of patronage would apply not just to the political appointments but to the elected element as well. The party bosses would determine who was top of the list. The second Chamber would be almost entirely created by patronage and appointment.[133]

3 The PASC also came out strongly against the use of a closed list system, which they described as 'not acceptable and a turn-off for voters'.[134] They added a number of useful principles which should guide the selection of an electoral system. It should, they said:

---

130 HL Deb col 564 (9 March 2002).
131 First Report, HL 17, HC 171 (2002–03), para 55.
132 PASC, Fifth Report, HC 494 (2001–02), paras 114–116.
133 HC Deb col 770 (10 March 2002), Norman Lamb.
134 HC 494 (2001–02), para 110.

- be complementary to the voting system for the House of Commons;

- minimise the risk of one party gaining an overall majority;

- maximise voter choice, by enabling voters to vote for individual candidates, within and across parties;

- encourage a more diverse chamber; and

- encourage the election of independent-minded people.

They concluded that:

These principles will best be realised by using multi-member constituencies, and a proportional voting system. This could be either STV [single transferable vote] or regional lists, so long as the lists are fully open lists, which maximise voter choice. We would not support limited open lists, which present an appearance of choice for the voter, but almost never affect the outcome.[135]

These recommendations were taken up by the Joint Committee, which recommended that any elections should use open regional list or STV, *not* first past the post.[136]

4   The PASC also recommended that elections to the new chamber should be staggered, as in most overseas chambers, partly to ease the Appointment Commission's task of achieving diversity in the Chamber and also to avoid instability and promote a long term view.[137]

5   The elected element in the new chamber was designed partly to ensure proper regional representation, one of the classical functions of a second chamber (see Russell, above, at p 379). Some chambers in federal systems use a system of indirect election to achieve this, whereby regional assemblies elect members to serve in the second chamber: such members thus act at least partly as representatives of their region, rather than their party only. The problem with seeking to implement such a proposal in the UK at present, as all the reports considered above recognised, was that in the absence of English regional assemblies, there would be no bodies that could elect members to represent the regions of England. There would be little point in having members nominated by the Scottish Parliament if there were no equivalents from Northumberland or Yorkshire.

Size of the chamber, the appointment of members and the terms of service

The Appointments Commission

A House for the Future, Cm 4534 (2000) (extracts)

13.8 The Appointments Commission should not only be independent of the political parties in practice, but should also be seen to be so. A number of safeguards should therefore be set in place to ensure the independence of the Appointments Commission. These relate to its legal status, the means by which its members are appointed and their security of tenure, the procedures by which members of the second chamber are appointed and the reporting arrangements set in place.

---

135 *Ibid*, paras 111–12.
136 *Op cit*, para 53.
137 *Ibid*, para 118.

...

13.13 We recommend therefore that the Appointments Commission should be established by primary legislation. Amendment of the legislation would require open debate in Parliament and the approval of the second chamber itself. Such amending legislation would also come under close scrutiny from the proposed Constitutional Committee of the second chamber. We doubt that any Government would risk the embarrassment of attempting to use the Parliament Acts to force through such legislation against the will of a second chamber. Establishing the Appointments Commission through primary legislation would therefore offer considerable entrenchment ...

Number of Appointments Commissioners

13.14 The interim Appointments Commission will include representatives of the three main political parties and a number of independents. The latter will form a majority among the Commissioners and will provide the chairman, implying a total of at least seven Commissioners. Experience from other public bodies working in politically controversial areas, such as the Committee on Standards in Public Life, suggests that there would be significant merit in including nominees from each of the main political parties. While they would be expected not to behave in a partisan manner, their understanding of how Parliament and the political parties work and think would be of considerable benefit to the Appointments Commission. We therefore recommend that three of the Appointments Commissioners should be nominees from the main political parties. A Commissioner nominated by the convenor of the Cross-Benchers would be a logical corollary. These four members should be balanced by four independent members, of whom one should be the chairman. The resulting total of eight should allow scope for representation from Scotland, Wales or Northern Ireland, thereby ensuring that the Appointments Commission was not a solely English body.

Selection of Appointments Commissioners

13.15 Since the first report of the Nolan Committee in 1995, both Conservative and Labour Governments have committed themselves to filling the majority of public appointments according to what have become known as the 'Nolan principles', notably that appointments should be made strictly on merit and should be free of the taint of favouritism or bias ... The Government has committed itself to applying the Nolan principles in selecting the independent members of the Appointments Commission which will operate during the interim stage of House of Lords reform. The Home Office has taken the same view with regard to the membership of the new Electoral Commission. We recommend that this approach should also be adopted

in connection with the independent members of the Appointments Commission. Such an approach does not, of course, preclude 'head hunting' and the taking of private soundings.

Appointment of Commissioners

13.17 For most public appointments, the decision will be taken by the responsible Minister. Such direct Ministerial control would be unacceptable in the case of the Appointments Commission for the second chamber. The most common approach for appointments of a constitutional nature is for them to be made by the Queen, on the advice of the Prime Minister. The process is subject to certain controls, designed to ensure that the Prime Minister's advice has cross-party support.

13.18 ... Since the Appointments Commission will operate in respect of the second chamber, it would be most appropriate for it to be that chamber whose approval is required, on a motion moved by the Leader of the House, following the normal consultation with the leaders of the other party groupings and the Convenor of the Cross-Benchers.

Length and Security of Tenure

13.19 All Appointments Commissioners, including party nominees, should have a long period in office with security of tenure in order to protect them against undue influence and encourage them to bring a long-term perspective to bear on their work. The Commissioner for Public Appointments has recommended that no one should hold a public office for more than ten years. The Government proposes to write such a limit into the legislation for the Electoral Commission. We recommend that the same limit should apply to Appointments Commissioners.

13.20 While members should have security of tenure during their period in office, there should be a procedure for removing an individual whose behaviour has become inappropriate. Corrupt activity on the part of individual members would already be covered by the criminal law. The Government proposes that Electoral Commissioners should be removable only on a resolution of the House of Commons. Since the

Appointments Commission will to some extent stand in the same position with regard to the second chamber, removal of an Appointments Commissioner should require a resolution of the second chamber.

Scrutiny of reports

13.21 An important aspect of the Appointments Commission's work will be the information given in its annual report. This report will act as the vehicle by which the Appointments Commission will set out the characteristics required of members of the second chamber and its strategy for ensuring that there is an appropriate balance of members from all parts of society and among the political parties. This strategy might include setting out the types of nomination that would be particularly welcome over the coming year. The report should also provide a detailed breakdown of the composition of the chamber, in terms of party, gender, ethnicity, age and region and the extent to which the chamber's membership as a whole reflects the characteristics set out in the Appointments Commission's published specification. An important element of this information would be to report on changes in the political and other balances which the Appointments Commission will be required to strike, arising from the departure of members at the end of their term of office, the characteristics of the regional members and the results of each general election.

13.22 The report would provide the main means by which the Appointments Commission could be held to account. Such scrutiny should consider three aspects of the Commission's operation:

- whether the specification of the characteristics required of members of the second chamber was appropriate and whether the estimate of the number of members required was correct;

- whether the selection process was effective in identifying individuals with the required characteristics and whether the resulting composition of the second chamber, including the regional members, achieved the appropriate balances; and

- whether the Appointments Commission was using public funds efficiently and the expenditure involved had been made properly.

13.23 Since the Appointments Commission would be a statutory body, its reports should be presented to Parliament. It should not be possible to enquire into individual cases, but it would be right for the Appointments Commission to be held to account on its fulfilment of its statutory duties.

Note

As noted above, it was in proposing, contrary to Wakeham's recommendations, that the political members should be appointed by the parties rather than the Appointments Commission, that the terms served by both appointed and elected members should not be the 15 years proposed by Wakeham but some shorter period, and that elected appointed members should be eligible for re-election that the government attracted most criticism. These matters are now explored further below.

Should the Appointments Commission appoint all non-elected members and what should be the terms of appointment for all members?

The suggestion by the government that the nominated party members should be selected by the parties themselves, rather than the Appointments Commission, as Wakeham had suggested, was widely seen as being nothing more than a typical example of New Labour's desire to retain as much control as possible over possible political rivals. The only principled argument put forward by the government on the point was voiced by the Lord Chancellor, in evidence to the PASC:

> Now we took the view, and I think all parties actually would agree with this, that an Appointments Commission should no more decide who should represent a party in the Houses of Parliament, should no more decide that than an appointments committee should decide who wins in the short list for a constituency selection for membership of the House of Commons. We thought that was not one of the most politically switched on suggestions of the Wakeham Commission ... Just as political parties select who stands for parliament and – unless there is a fantastic shift – certainly in safe seats it is known that when a political party selects it is selecting the next MP. I do not see any difference in that between the political party selecting who it wants to put forward to be a member of the Lords.[138]

Notes

1 One clear difference between the two scenarios which Lord Irvine cannot apparently see is, of course, the impact on legitimacy. Selecting members to stand for a party in an election is *not*, in this sense, the same as selecting them directly to sit in a chamber of Parliament, for a very obvious reason: in the former case, the members derive legitimacy from the imprimatur of the electorate, however much of a formality that may be, in practical terms, if they are standing in a 'safe seat.' Selected members derive no such legitimacy; rather they are tainted with the imprimatur of patronage. The other matter that Lord Irvine does not appear to recognise is that members appointed by the party leaders will inevitably be seen as placemen – anxious merely to do their leaders' bidding and moreover that such a method of selection will be guaranteed to keep talented, thoughtful but maverick figures – those taking a party whip but often thinking outside its confines – away from the second chamber.

2 Adverse comments on the government's proposals in this respect appear below.

HL Deb 9 March 2002 and HC Deb 10 March 2002 (extracts)[139]

Mr Worthington MP: The proposed powers of the Prime Minister and other political leaders are worth examination. The number of nominated political Members in the second Chamber will probably be 332, and page 21 of the White Paper makes it clear that the Government want them to serve for terms of only four to five years ... If it had been established in time

---

138 Evidence (24 January 2002).
139 Footnotes in the extract give the appropriate reference.

to reflect the pattern of voting at the last election, my right hon. Friend the Prime Minister would have been required to find about 140 Members of the proposed new House of Lords. The Tory leader would have had to choose about 100 names, and the Liberal Democrats would have had to find more people than they have MPs ... As at present, Members of the new House of Lords would receive no salary, only expenses. There would be no pension or resettlement allowance, so Members would be totally dependent on the patron. The motto would be, 'Vote with me, or you're out. I shall not renew your licence.' ... In my view, that is far worse than the rotten borough system – at least Old Sarum had seven voters. For 140 Members of the future House of Lords, there would be one voter. He or she would decide whether a Member remained in the other Chamber.[140]

...

Lord Strathclyde: [The Government] has sought out all the devices put in by ... Lord Wakeham to buttress the independence of Peers and brutally struck them out ... There are two which go to the very heart of the matter. First ... the Royal Commission wanted the Appointments Commission to appoint all nominated Members, including political ones ... the Government rejected [this] ... Second[ly] the Royal Commission [proposed] ... that Peers, whether elected or appointed, should have long terms to ensure their independence of party Whips. The power to select and deselect is the power by which patronage dominates another place and, if the Government have their way, is set to dominate this House too. It was an ingenious proposal, like the Commission's suggestion that Members of this House should not be re-elected or be allowed to move immediately to another place. But the Government rejected each one of those crucial proposals.[141]

...

Lord Wakeham: The Government want[s] the political parties to determine who should represent them. That creates two problems. That would preclude the appointments of politicians who might make an excellent contribution to the work of this House but who happen to be out of favour with their party leadership – and we can all think of examples. It would also inhibit the Appointments Commission in proactively seeking out good quality candidates from different walks of life if it were prevented from appointing people who happen to have political affiliations. There are many good and suitable people who would not get on to a political list, but who have expertise and experience in other areas, but are members of one party or another and cannot be considered Cross-Benchers.

I also have major concerns about the Government's provisional views on the arrangements for electing 'regional' members. If 'regional' members have only a short tenure and remain dependent on their party for re-nomination, they are less likely to apply independent judgment in their contribution to the House. If they perceive membership of the second Chamber as a stepping-stone to a wider political career in another place, they would be inclined to behave in a partisan fashion that would alter very substantially the nature of the second Chamber[142] ...

Notes

1   Dawn Oliver wrote of the notion that the parties, rather than the Commission, should appoint the party members:

---

140 HC Deb col 762 (10 March 2002).
141 HL Deb cols 567–68 (9 March 2002).
142 *Ibid*, col 583.

The party leaders could not be required to secure that 'their' members in the reformed second chamber produced the required gender balance and representation of ethnic minorities. Nor could a system of nomination by party leaders secure the presence of the broad range of people for all sections of society and with the skill and expertise the House would need and which the Commission's model for a the reformed House required.[143]

2   The PASC agreed; though they also thought, contrary to the proposal of the Conservative Party leadership,[144] that, in addition to the 20% appointed *independent* element, there should be a further 20% appointed party-political element. Whether this proposal in reality represents a shrewd political calculation that the government would not be prepared to accept an 80% elected chamber is impossible to assess.

Select Committee on Public Administration, Fifth Report HC 494-I (2001–02) (extracts)

128 ... For the new second chamber to be credible and have authority, its appointed members must be independent minded people, not just perceived as the recipients of party patronage. They must bring expertise from the professions, science, the arts and other walks of life which are under-represented in politics. And they must help to redress the imbalances amongst the elected members and to promote diversity.

Balance between independent members and party nominees

129. With 60 per cent of the members elected, the balance remaining to be appointed is 40 per cent. Of the appointed members, we propose that half (20 per cent of the total) should be party nominees, and half (20 per cent of the total) should be independent members sitting on the Cross-Benches.

Justification for retaining party nominees

130. In their separate proposals published during our inquiry, both the Conservatives and the Liberal Democrats have proposed that all the party representatives in the new House should be elected members, leaving appointment only for the Cross-Benchers. We believe there continues to be a justification for some party nominees, but not in the proportion (55 per cent) proposed in the White Paper. That is why in our proposals we have reduced the proportion of party nominees to 20 per cent.

131. We expect the parties to continue to nominate members of two kinds. First, former Prime Ministers, Cabinet Ministers, party leaders and other senior MPs who want to continue to serve in Parliament, but to retire from the House of Commons. In future such figures would have no routine expectation of a seat in the second chamber, but would have to take their chance within their party's quota. However, those who have served with distinction in Parliament and Government can and should be able to make a contribution in the second chamber. We do not subscribe to the denigration of party politicians and believe that they may have a valuable role to play in the reformed second chamber. Second, the parties will continue to nominate experts similar to those who sit on the Cross-Benches, but who have a party affiliation. Not all experts are non-political: to take examples from three recent appointments, Lord Winston professor of gynaecology (Labour), Lord Wallace of Saltaire, professor of international relations (Liberal Democrat), and Lord Norton of Louth, professor of government (Conservative) are all

143 D Oliver, 'The reform of the UK Parliament', in J Jowell and D Oliver (eds), *The Changing Constitution*, 4th edn (2000), p 287.
144 Iain Duncan Smith came out in favour of an 80% elected House with the remaining 20% appointed by an Independent Appointments Commission. See 'Tories to turn Lords into elected Senate', *The Telegraph*, 13 January 2001; and Duncan Smith, 'Trust the people – that's the Tory message', *ibid*. There was, however, very strong opposition to these proposals amongst the Conservative peers: see 'Tory peers attack Duncan Smith's "80pc elected" Lords plan'.

distinguished experts in their respective fields who take the party whip. We hope the parties will continue to nominate such people, and not take an unduly narrow view of who is 'sound' politically, and not simply use their lists to recycle MPs. Examples of MPs 'selling' their seats to the party managers, often just before General Elections, in exchange for places in the Lords, is the sort of practice that brings discredit on all concerned, and on the institution itself.

132. We believe that there should be a robust filter to ensure that those nominated by parties are acceptable, and that the Appointments Commission (see below) should have the final say. This would help to underpin the credibility of these appointments, by subjecting them to a check that would ensure that they were people of merit and not merely the recipients of party patronage. This recommendation was fundamental to the Royal Commission's report, and we very much regret that it was not accepted by the Government in the White Paper . . .

133. We recommend that the parties should submit lists of party nominees to the Appointments Commission, ranked if they wish in order of preference, but that the Commission should make the final selection. If the Prime Minister can choose the Archbishop of Canterbury from names submitted to him by the Church of England, there should be no difficulty about an independent appointments commission choosing from names submitted by the parties. The Appointments Commission would take the final decision on those who are to represent their parties. If the Government is unable to agree to this recommendation, which we regard as fundamental, then we recommend that there should be no separate element of party nominees in the second chamber and that its composition should consist of 70 per cent directly elected members and 30 per cent independent appointees.

134. We note that the Government is completely silent about the process by which nominations from the parties will be found. We find this a disturbing omission. There is no mention of the 'Nolan' principles on public appointments or of the need for the selection process to be open to public scrutiny. We believe that the parties should be required to publish the details of their procedures for selecting their nominees for the second chamber and that these procedures should be monitored by the Appointments Commission.

Notes
1   The problem with the Committee's proposal here is that they seek to ensure that party-affiliated but independent-minded members will still find their way, through nomination, into the chamber, something which they fear would not happen if the parties had the final word. However, if the Appointments Commission merely selects members from lists supplied by the parties, with no ability to appoint party members save from those lists, then parties determined to ensure that only members likely to prove compliant to the party line can achieve this aim simply by keeping known mavericks off the lists supplied to the Commission. Wakeham, it should be noted, recommended a stronger system: the Commission would be able to appoint party-affiliated members without the approval or support of their political party.[145]

2   The Joint Committee's view on the Appointments Commission was closer to Wakeham's than the White Paper: it envisaged the Commission making party-political appointments as well as independents, but did allow that the Prime Minister should have the right to have some appointments confirmed by Commission,[146] effectively allowing the Prime Minister to *make* some appointments. It appears to envisage that these would only amount to a few appointments a year,

---

145 Wakeham Report, *op cit*, Recommendation 98, paras 13.42–13.43.
146 First Report, HL 17, HC 171 (2002–03), paras 51–52.

to allow the Prime Minister to appoint Ministers from the Lords, but no clear limits to the Prime Minister's power of patronage are expressed, making the Joint Committee's report somewhat unsatisfactory in this respect.

3   On the length of term to be served by both classes of members, Wakeham proposed 15 years for both, with no right of re-election for the elected members. The aim was clearly to bolster members' independence. As noted above, the government was of the view that 15 years was excessively long, and there should be no bar on re-election, purportedly on the grounds that this would encourage greater accountability. The PASC favoured Wakeham, though it suggested a compromise:

121. We believe that a renewable term as short as five years would both seriously jeopardise the independence of second chamber members and increase the risk of conflict with the members of the Commons. There would be greater likelihood of claims that the second chamber members were as legitimate as the MPs. Such a move would be a fundamental departure from the Royal Commission recommendations . . .

126. We recommend that elected second chamber members should serve a single term extending to two Parliaments. No member of the second chamber should be permitted to stand for election to the Commons for ten years after leaving the second chamber. These restrictions would apply from the next general election. Political parties should not be allowed to nominate for appointment anyone who has served as an elected member of the second chamber.[147]

Its suggested compromise of two parliamentary terms would mean an average term of eight years, while the Joint Committee recommended in its First Report a term of 12 years with members then being banned from standing for the Commons for three years.[148]

Size of the Second Chamber

The government's proposals were that:

There should be a statutory cap on the total size of the House of 600 members, to come into force after 10 years (para 91).

The maximum target size during the transition should be 750, declining to 600.

In any rebalancing, the first duty of the Appointments Commission should be to achieve a lead for the governing party over its main opposition (para 93)[68].

The Public Administration Committee suggested a much smaller House, in common with the Conservatives and Liberal Democrats:

161. By international standards the UK legislature and in particular the second chamber is very large. The 600-member reformed house proposed in the White Paper would still be by a big

147 *Op cit.*
148 First Report, HL 17, HC 171 (2002–03), para 48.

margin the biggest second chamber in the world. Only five others have more than 200 members . . .

163. There are a number of very sound arguments in favour of a small second chamber. For instance, it is said that co-operation between members is better in smaller chambers than in large ones. A small, expert, well-resourced house might also be preferable as a revising chamber to a larger body in which each member has little support . . .

164. Against this runs the feeling, which is strongly held in the House of Lords, that to maintain its expertise on a wide range of subjects the House needs to continue to allow at least some of its members to work part-time.

165. It is also hard to imagine that national and regional representatives, and some of the more diverse membership we propose, will find it easy to attend Westminster full-time. The second chamber should be flexible enough to accommodate these members.

166. The statistics reveal that only a minority of peers are currently active in the House of Lords. In the current Session, 25 per cent of peers had asked 87 per cent of the Questions and made 76 per cent of the speeches and interventions.[70] This suggests that a smaller House need not suffer a diminution of expertise.

167. We have considered this issue, as we have others, with accountability in mind. We see a continuing role for expertise in the chamber. Thus we believe that part-time membership should continue to be possible. That implies a somewhat larger chamber than would otherwise be the case. However, we believe that the size proposed by the Government is far too large, and unnecessarily so.

168. We recommend that the size of the second chamber when all elected members have joined should be clearly established and that it be set at up to 350. This figure would be very much the upper limit of the acceptable range.

The position of the Law Lords

It was noted in the Rule of Law chapter[149] that the decision of the European Court of Human Rights in *McGonnell v United Kingdom*[150] indicated that it may no longer be possible for the Lord Chancellor to sit as a Law Lord, given Art 6(1) of the European Convention on Human Rights, which provides:

> In the determination of his civil rights and obligations, or of any criminal charge against him, everyone is entitled to a fair and public hearing within a reasonable time by an independent and impartial tribunal established by law.

But this decision also has implications for the participation of the Law Lords in legislative debates concerning instruments on which they may then be called upon to give judicial rulings. It is clearly capable of casting doubt upon their independence and impartiality under Article 6 ECHR. This issue is covered as an aspect of the separation of powers in the UK constitution (see Part I Chapter 3, pp 115–18).

---

149 Part I Chapter 3.
150 (2000) 30 EHRR 289.

Changing the *powers* of the Lords?

As Hadfield[151] has pointed out, the powers of a second chamber cannot be considered in isolation from its composition and legitimacy. Broadly speaking, the more legitimate a second chamber is, the greater its powers may permissibly be. Now since, the aim of any reform to the Lords, in particular the introduction of some elected element, would be greatly to increase its legitimacy, one might have expected that increases in the powers of the Lords would be on the agenda. But in this area, as in others, Wakeham was cautious. The report said:

> 17. The second chamber's role in protecting the constitution should be maintained and enhanced. It should no longer be possible to amend the Parliament Acts using Parliament Act procedures, as was done in 1949. Such a change would maintain the current balance of power between the two Houses of Parliament and reinforce the second chamber's power of veto over any Bill to extend the life of a Parliament.

> 18. There should be no extension of the second chamber's formal powers in respect of any other matter, whether 'constitutional' or concerning human rights (from the *Executive Summary*)

There now seems little prospect of any substantial change to the powers of the Lords, in particular giving it special powers over legislation that alters the constitution or abrogates fundamental rights, as is the norm in other Western democracies. Indeed, the PASC stated in their report that one of the areas of consensus was that 'there should be no major change in the powers of either House'.[152] The Joint Committee, having considered the possibility of giving the reformed House special powers over 'constitutional legislation' simply recommended that 'no new powers [be] given to the House of Lords at this stage.'[153]

What seems to be going unrecognised in Parliament is that such a no-change policy, even if reform in other areas occurs, would leave the Lords in a glaringly anomalous position compared to nearly all second chambers overseas. As Russell remarks:

> The most basic constitutional role which a new upper house could play would be to exert a greater power over bills to amend the constitution than over ordinary bills. This is standard practice overseas ... [Out of] 20 Western democracies ... aside from the UK, the only countries where the upper house does not have special powers over constitutional amendments are those where other safeguards – such as automatic referendums on constitutional change – are built into the system.

The following table indicates the position overseas; comment on this matter by the author follows.

---

151 *Op cit*, p 349.
152 *Ibid.*
153 HL 17, HC 171 (2002–03), para. 29. The Committee left open the possibility of returning to the Royal Commission's proposal to amend the Parliament Acts to prevent their change without the Lords' approval: *ibid*, note 36.

M Russell and R Cornes, 'The Royal Commission on Reform of the House of Lords: a house for the future?' (2001) 64 MLR 82, p 86

Table 2: Procedures for constitutional change in 10 democracies

Australia	Must be passed by referendum.
Canada:	Must be passed by provincial assemblies.
France:	Must pass both chambers, then either joint sitting by 3/5 majority, or a referendum.
Germany:	Must pass both chambers by 2/3 majority.
Ireland:	Must be passed by referendum.
Italy:	Must pass both chambers by absolute majority, and if not by 2/3 majority referendum may be called by 1/5 of members of either house, 500,000 electors or five regional assemblies.
Japan:	Must pass both chambers by 2/3 majority.
Spain	Must pass both chambers by 3/5 majority, or lower house by 2/3 majority and upper house by absolute majority. Referendum may be requested by 1/10 of members of either house.
Switzerland	Must pass both chambers, else referendum.
UK	Treated as ordinary legislation.
USA	Must pass both chambers by 2/3 majority, plus States' approval by referendum.

G Phillipson, 'The powers of a reformed second chamber' [2003] PL 32 (extracts)

The Royal Commission's sole ground of principle for rejecting any proposal to bring the Lords into line with this almost unanimous Western consensus is as follows:

> Our fundamental concern about any such proposal is that it would alter the current balance of power between the two chambers and could be exploited to bring the two chambers into conflict. It would be inconsistent with the requirement in our terms of reference 'to maintain the position of the House of Commons as the pre-eminent chamber of Parliament' and with our view of the overall role that the second chamber should play [para 5.7]

The Commission put forward this remarkable position even though they clearly recognised the risk of the Parliament Acts being used to push through ill-considered constitutional change. The weaknesses of this argument are, it is suggested, three-fold. First, giving the House extra powers over constitutional legislation would *not* as the Commission asserts (without argument) be 'inconsistent' with maintaining the Commons as the 'pre-eminent' House. In the vast majority of legislative instances – all those unconnected with significant constitutional or human rights matters – the Commons would remain the superior House, able to bypass Lords opposition after the delay of only a year, or, in the case of money bills, a month only. This would clearly maintain its pre-eminence, whatever the position was in relation to 'constitutional' legislation.

Second, the Lords *already have* special powers under the Parliament Acts in relation to one type of constitutional legislation – a Bill to extend the life of a Parliament – and the Royal Commission supported retention of this power and indeed, strengthening it, so that the Parliament Acts themselves could not be amended to remove or weaken this safeguard using the procedure they themselves provide for bypassing the Lords [paras 5.13–5.16]. The Royal Commission supported the retention of this power, presumably because it represents an important democratic safeguard.

But once it is accepted that the Lords should have special powers to safeguard democracy in this basic manner, then logic suggests extending the scope of such powers to cover other matters equally important to the maintenance of a liberal democracy, such as rights to freedom of expression and assembly, habeas corpus, the franchise and the like. The Royal Commission proposals would leave the Lords with an absolute veto over a proposal, say, to extend a Parliament by a year during wartime, but with nothing but their normal delaying power over a peacetime Bill abolishing habeas corpus or criminalizing all public protest. Such a position is hard to defend on principled grounds.

Third, and perhaps most importantly, the Royal Commission fails to situate its reasoning on this matter within the wider constitutional context: that the UK, unusually amongst Western democracies, has no provision for primary legislation that abrogates fundamental human rights to be annulled on such grounds in the courts or even to be subject to pre-legislative audit in some form of Constitutional Council, as in France. There are numerous recent examples of Parliament being asked to rush through legislation threatening civil liberties in hasty response to short term crises, legislation which, once on the statute book, cannot be challenged in the courts. [The author cites the Prevention of Terrorism (Additional Powers) Bill 1996, Criminal Justice (Terrorism and Conspiracy) Bill 1998, and the 2001 Anti-Terrorism, Crime and Security Bill – all discussed above at pp 365–72 – and goes on]:

Such casual attitudes towards internationally recognised human rights norms arguably spring from the historic absence of a codified constitution and a Bill of Rights. The UK's entrustment of the protection of such rights to the unfettered discretion of a governing party representing the majority of the day – or rather, typically around 43–45% of it – has traditionally meant that there has been no set of clearly constitutionalised standards around which the different political parties and political commentators can unite. Neither the ECHR nor the Human Rights Act yet represents such a unifying point: the Conservatives and much of the right-wing press remain sceptical about the HRA, and it and the Convention is often presented in the tabloid newspapers as a 'foreign', European imposition, frequently confused with the EU and thus a target for the Euro-scepticism of much of the popular press. Even the Labour Government that introduced the HRA appears profoundly ambivalent about the limitations on governmental power that it seeks to impose. Commentators on other state-power legislation introduced by this Government, including the Terrorism Act 2000 and the Regulation of Investigatory Powers Act 2000, have concluded that the Government has, at best, a highly qualified attitude of respect for fundamental human rights, especially where they clash with crime control values [see, eg, H Fenwick, *Civil Rights: New Labour and the Human Rights Act* (2000)].

In short, within the context of a political order that both culturally and constitutionally represents the principle of unbridled majoritarianism, it is of particular importance that the second chamber should be able to enforce at the least a thoughtful and considered decision in relation to the abridgement of basic human rights and the necessity of garnering a broad consensus that such action is truly necessary. [The PASC was open to this proposal: *op cit*, paras 74 and 75..]

The practical problem that the Royal Commission highlighted – the lack of a mechanism for identifying the provisions that should trigger the Lords' special powers in a country without a codified constitution – does not seem an insuperable problem. Perhaps the best practical solution would be to give the power to certify a Bill as 'constitutional' to the Constitution Committee of the second chamber ... There would be numerous instances in which the classification of the Bill would be obvious, for example, changes to any of the devolution Acts, the franchise, the Freedom of Information Act, the European Communities Act 1972, the Human Rights Act, any legislation introduced with a negative statement under section 19 HRA [meaning that the Government thinks some of its provisions may be incompatible with the ECHR], any further derogation Orders in relation to the ECHR, and the legislation establishing the new second chamber itself. In order to avoid the special powers being triggered where no real issue was at stake, legislation could state that the changes made to such legislation or generally to the constitution must be 'significant' or 'of principle' to activate those powers, so that they would not be brought into play by, say, minor consequential amendments to the devolution legislation, or Bills which raised only doubtful claims of incompatibility with the ECHR. The *power* triggered by a positive finding of the Constitution Committee could be any one of the following: an extended power of delay – say two years; the removal of the application of the Parliament Acts (ie, an absolute veto); the need for special majorities in both Houses; or for a referendum.

[The author also considers the only substantive proposal made by Wakeham on powers: to reduce the Lords' powers of delegated legislation.]

The proposal before the Joint Committee is that the House's current absolute veto should be reduced to the ability to impose what is presented as a three-month delay. The Royal Commission put the argument thus:

> **7.11** ... there has (so far) been no serious challenge since 1968 to the convention that the House of Lords does not reject Statutory Instruments ...

> **7.31** ... Its *influence* over secondary legislation is therefore paradoxically less than its influence over primary legislation ...

> **7.33** [Its] powers [over delegated legislation] ... are too drastic. That is the reason why they are not in practice used now and we would not suggest that a reformed second chamber should be more willing than the present House of Lords to persist in blocking an instrument altogether.

> **7.35** ... the second chamber should be given a tool which it can use to *force* the Government and the House of Commons to take its concerns seriously. There is ... not much point in the second chamber having a theoretically greater power which it does not in reality exercise ... It should have powers which it can actually exercise, and which would require the Government and the House of Commons to take some positive action either to meet its concerns or override its reservations.

> **7.36** We therefore recommend that changes be made by legislation, so that:
>
> - where the second chamber votes against a draft instrument, the draft should nevertheless be deemed to be approved if the House of Commons subsequently gives (or, as the case may be, reaffirms) its approval within three months; and
>
> - where the second chamber votes to annul an instrument, the annulment would not take effect for three months and could be overridden by a resolution of the House of Commons.

Three rejoinders to the above may be suggested. First, as argued above, it seems perverse to *reduce* the House's powers at the very time that its legitimacy is being substantially *increased.* Second, the Royal Commission offers no argument at all for the proposal that the Lord's power of delay over delegated legislation should be only three months, rather than a year, as with primary legislation. It is in fact misleading even to refer to it as a three month power of delay, since, as the PASC report pointed out [at para 78], under the above proposals, the Commons could revive delegated legislation annulled by the Lords in a vote that could be held within days – or even hours – of its rejection by the Lords. Why should delegated legislation attract such an extraordinarily emasculated power of delay? Third, the argument above appears to assume that the historic behaviour of the unreformed House in this area would be continued by the new second chamber. Or rather, at one point the Report says that it *should* be continued [para 7.33 above], thereby seeming to conflate the *likelihood* of future behaviour with the Commission's view on the *desirability* of that behaviour. In fact, there is every reason to suppose that the reason for the Lords' historic reluctance to reject delegated legislation outright was at least partly attributable to precisely the same cause as the restraint the House shows towards primary legislation, namely the general perception of its lack of legitimacy. Were this legitimacy deficit to be cured, by the reforms the Royal Commission suggested, presumably this historic reticence would decrease substantially and the theoretical power used far more frequently. Such a view has already received support from the greater assertion displayed by the Lords since the removal of the hereditary peers gave them a sense of enhanced legitimacy: the Lords abandoned the very convention which the Royal Commission refers to when they rejected the Greater London Authority (Election Expenses) Order 2000 [see HL Deb vol 610 col 143 et seq, 22 February 2000].

It may be that a total veto over delegated legislation is too drastic a power for a second chamber not intended to be co-equal to retain. But no argument has been made against the more evidently rational reform: simply giving the Lords the same powers over delegated as primary legislation.

Notes

1 In relation to the highly important conventional restraints upon the Lords, discussed above,[154] both the government and Wakeham suggested that the Salisbury Convention should continue to be observed: this is arguably a sensible compromise between the need for an effective check upon government and the necessity for a government of the day to be able to implement, at least in substance, the main points of its manifesto programme, thus ensuring that the basic link between elections and subsequent policy changes remains in place, provided it did not apply to 'constitutional' legislation, as discussed above. The Lords do not often have a key role in relation to manifesto commitments, which at least have been thought through to some extent and formulated after consultation within the party concerned and sometimes more widely, rather their checking function is at its most valuable when government, reacting to political pressures, seek to rush through Parliament ill-considered and short-termist legislation. The Anti-Terrorism Act 2001 is a prime example. The Joint Committee's view on this was that:

The continuing operation of the existing conventions in any new constitutional arrangement will be vital in avoiding deadlock between the Houses – which could all too easily become an obstacle to continuing good governance. **We therefore strongly support the continuation of the existing conventions.**[155]

2 In terms of new mechanisms for scrutiny, here again, save for some modest proposals for extensions of the House's Committee system to include new Committees on constitutional matters,[156] devolution, human rights[157] and the scrutiny of treaties, Wakeham had nothing very new to suggest. Its most interesting idea was that 'a mechanism should be developed which would require Commons Ministers to make statements to, and deal with, questions from members of the second chamber',[158] although cautiously again the Commission

154 See pp 354–59.
155 First Report, HL 17, HC 171 (2002–03), para 12.
156 See Wakeham Report, *op cit*, Chapter 5.
157 Wakeham suggested that the devolution and human rights committees could be sub-committees of an overarching Constitutional Committee.
158 Wakeham Report, *op cit*, Recommendation 45 (para 8.7).

proposed that this would have to meet off the floor of the House, in order to respect the long-standing convention that members of one House do not speak in another.[159] This would significantly enhance ministerial accountability: at present, because of the convention that Cabinet Ministers[160] must be drawn from the Commons, the House of Lords is often able to scrutinise only relatively junior Ministers, who have to answer questions on a very wide area, due to the relatively small number of Ministers who are members of the Lords. As Russell notes, 'the convention barring House of Commons ministers from the House of Lords is highly unusual. In most countries ministers may speak in either chamber, irrespective of whether they are a member of that chamber'.[161] The Hansard Society Commission approved this proposal, remarking that it would allow much greater use to be made of the Lords' expertise, enhancing parliamentary scrutiny of the executive overall.[162]

Prospects for reform[163]

At present, following rejection by the Commons of all the options for composition put forward by the Joint Committee in its First Report, and the absence of any clear lead from the government, Lords reform seems unlikely to make any significant progress. In its latest report, the Joint Committee said that:

> This Committee remains unanimous in its view that simply to maintain the status quo is undesirable. The differences between us as to the long-term future structure of the second Chamber inevitably reflect those in Parliament and Government alike.
>
> Whatever may or may not be decided later – perhaps some considerable time ahead, perhaps not – about the long-term composition of the second Chamber, there are possible changes affecting the effectiveness, representative quality and credibility of the House that can and should be considered and decided now. Things should not simply be left as they are.[164]

Note
However, whilst the Joint Committee clearly wished to keep the reform process alive, its report was very short on specific proposals or even specific arguments of principle. Time after time, issues are raised, only to be disposed of by saying merely that they will need 'careful attention' or 'will need to be worked out' at some point in the future. It called upon the government to respond to it, but there is actually very little to respond to. The only concrete recommendation the report makes is for:

> a new and manifestly independent Appointments Commission, ... endorsed – as an interim alternative to primary legislation – by an Order in Council, approved by both Houses [para 30].

More ominously, the Committee's minutes of proceedings indicated that it divided on a large number of issues: far more than most Select Committees. This does not bode

---

159 *Ibid*, paras 8.7–8.8.
160 Save for the Lord Chancellor.
161 Russell, *op cit*, p 274.
162 *The Challenge for Parliament: Making Government Accountable* (2001), para 6.15.
163 A number of other issues are raised by the debate over Lords reform, including religious representation and the resources and payment to be devoted to members of the Lords. On grounds of space, these have not been discussed here.
164 HL 97, HC 668 (2002–03), paras 3 and 4.

well for its being able to achieve unanimous recommendations on the most contentious issues, and with deep divisions between the two Houses on the question of introducing elected members into a reformed House and no lead from the government, at present reform of the Lords appears to have hit an impasse.

FURTHER READING

R Blackburn and A Kennon, *Griffith & Ryle on Parliament: Functions, Practice and Procedures*, 2nd edn (2002)

B Dickson and P Carmichael (eds) *The House of Lords: Its Parliamentary and Judicial Roles* (1999)

D Oliver, *Constitutional Reform in the UK* (2003)D Oliver, *United Kingdom Government and Constitution* (1990)

I Richards and D Welfare, *Unfinished Business: Reforming the House of Lords* (1999)

D Shell, 'Reforming the House of Lords' [1990] PL 193

D Shell, *The House of Lords* (1992)

CHAPTER 3

PARLIAMENTARY PRIVILEGE

INTRODUCTION

This chapter will consider the privileges of Parliament. The examples used will mainly relate to the House of Commons, but the privileges of the two Houses are substantially identical.[1] It will touch on all the main privileges, concentrating on freedom of speech as by far the most important and contentious privilege claimed. Conflict between Parliament and the courts will also be discussed and criticisms of the current state of affairs in this field will be considered.

> 'The sole justification for the present privileges of the House of Commons is that they are essential for the conduct of its business and maintenance of its authority', according to one clerk of the House of Commons. If the constant general purpose has been the maintenance of Parliament's independence, the threats to that independence have come from various quarters: at times from the ordinary courts seeking to enforce the general law of the land, at times from the Crown, at times from other persons or bodies, including the mass media. Sometimes the enemy is within, and then privilege enables the House to deal with members who abuse their office or seek to obstruct its business.[2]

The Joint Committee on Parliamentary Privilege summarised parliamentary privilege thus:

> Parliamentary privilege consists of the rights and immunities which the two Houses of Parliament and their members and officers possess to enable them to carry out their parliamentary functions effectively. Without this protection members would be handicapped in performing their parliamentary duties, and the authority of Parliament itself in confronting the executive and as a forum for expressing the anxieties of citizens would be correspondingly diminished.

The clerk of the House of Commons has aptly captured the unique nature of privilege:

> Privilege is ... a great many things at once, not all of them always easy to reconcile with the others. For example, privilege:
>
> – is a legal concept which is simultaneously part of the general law and an exception to it;
>
> – is partly set out in statute, but is also to be deduced from the traditional claims of the House, and the freedoms granted by the Sovereign at the beginning of every Parliament;
>
> – is interpreted both by the courts and by the House. The courts perform a quasi-legislative role when they define 'proceedings in Parliament' and in other areas of privilege the House acts in what can be seen as a judicial way. These two great authorities of the state have often not been entirely at one in the application of privilege law;
>
> – is a central constitutional fact, whose origins (and some of its elements) are nearly immemorial (the earliest privilege citation in Erskine May is of 1290) part of the very fabric of the state, not capable of being added to by the Parliament it seeks to protect, short of legislation, but also a matter of political sensitivity, so that its nature and boundaries have radically shifted over the years;

---

1   Erskine May, *Treatise on the Law, Privileges, Proceedings and Usage of Parliament*, 1st edn (1844), p 44, referring to William Hakewill, *Modus Tenendi Parliamentum*, 'All the privileges which do belong to those of the Commons House of Parliament *a fortiori* do appertain to all the Lords of the Upper House.'

2   C Munro, *Studies in Constitutional Law*, 2nd edn (1999), p 216.

– is a defence for Members of the House, often against rights which the law would otherwise allow to citizens, but also exists to protect the citizen; and

– is in essence a simple functional protection for the institution of Parliament and does not confer a special status on individual Members, though many of its incidents attach to and claims are made by individual Members and others who are not Members.[3]

As Colin Munro emphasises, parliamentary privilege has a unique status in law; while some parts of it may be found in statute,[4] and some in common law,[5] others are part of the law of Parliament itself:

Its origin is customary; it is recognised as having the status of law; but it will be found, for the most part, not in statutes or cases, but in parliamentary proceedings ... Since it is enforced primarily by the Houses themselves, it is defined principally in resolutions of the Houses and rulings by the Speakers. Of course, like any other part of the law, parliamentary privilege is subject to the supremacy of Acts of Parliament. Acts have curtailed the scope of privilege [and] ... may regulate the exercise of privilege ... But it is also possible for statute to maintain or extend the scope of privileges. The privileges of freedom of speech and exclusive cognisance of internal proceedings were given a statutory foundation when included as Article 9 of the Bill of Rights: 'That the freedom of speech, and debates or proceedings in Parliament, ought not to be impeached or questioned in any court or place out of Parliament.'[6]

Notes

1 The justification for privilege offered by the clerk of the Commons cited by Munro offers a stringent test: only those matters which are 'essential' for the proper conduct of the business of the House should be claimed as privileges. The Committee on Standards and Privileges has given its own view of the *raison d'être* of parliamentary privileges (in its report on the 'cash for questions affair'). It regards their purpose as 'not to protect individual Members of Parliament but to provide the necessary framework in which the House in its corporate capacity and its Members as individuals can fulfil their responsibilities to the citizens they represent',[7] a definition which also stresses that 'privileges' are not in fact to do with the personal aggrandisement of MPs but simply necessary adjuncts to their role as public servants. Given that one of the fundamental principles of the British Constitution is supposed to be equality before the law, it seems right that those who argue in favour of placing some in a uniquely privileged position should have to adduce compelling evidence that such protection is indeed necessary. It is worth bearing these tests in mind when examining the arguments put forward in cases in which the proper scope of privilege has been contested.

2 Munro's definition is somewhat more wide-ranging and imports the rather nebulous concept of 'dignity'; it will become apparent that the House of Commons sometimes appears to take a rather expansive view of what the protection of its dignity demands; a view which might be thought to sit rather uneasily with the sometimes childishly combative mode of debate which, as noted in Chapter 1 of this Part, is not unknown in that House.

---

3 HLP 43-1 (1998–99).
4 Eg, the Defamation Act 1996, s 13; Article 9 Bill of Rights 1689, Parliamentary Papers Act 1844.
5 Cases such as *Bradlaugh v Gossett* (1884) 12 QBD 271, as well as numerous cases on the interpretation of Article 9, Bill of Rights.
6 Munro, *op cit*, p 217.
7 Quoted in D Oliver, 'The Committee on Standards in Public Life: regulating the conduct of Members of Parliament' (1995) PA 590, 596.

THE 'INTERNAL' PRIVILEGES OF PARLIAMENT

The privileges in general

Many questions of privilege have been relatively uncontentious; those which affect only members of Parliament in their capacity as MPs have been agreed by Parliament and the courts to be under the sole jurisdiction of Parliament. As Coleridge J said in *Stockdale v Hansard* (1839) 9 Ad & El 233:

> ... that the House should have exclusive jurisdiction to regulate the course of its own proceedings and animadvert upon any conduct there in violation of its rules or derogation from its dignity, stands upon the clearest ground of necessity.

The case of *Bradlaugh v Gossett* (1884) 12 QBD 271 is also instructive; it was summarised in *Rost v Edwards* [1990] 2 WLR 1280.

Rost v Edwards [1990] 2 WLR 1280, 1287

In *Bradlaugh v Gossett* (1884) 12 QBD 271 the Parliamentary Oaths Act of 1866 required Charles Bradlaugh, who had been elected to Northampton as a Member of the House of Commons, to take the oath. The question had arisen whether Mr Bradlaugh was qualified himself to sit by making an affirmation instead of taking the oath. Subsequently, following re-election, he was prevented from taking the oath by order of the House. The sergeant was ordered to exclude him from the House until he undertook not to disturb the proceedings further. Mr Bradlaugh sought a declaration from the courts that the order of the House was *ultra vires* and also an injunction restraining the Sergeant at Arms from preventing him from entering the House and taking his oath. The court decided against Mr Bradlaugh, taking the view that what was in issue was the internal management of the House procedure and therefore the court had no jurisdiction. Lord Coleridge CJ said at p 275:

> What is said or done within the walls of Parliament cannot be inquired into in a court of law. On this point all the judges in the two great cases which exhaust the learning on the subject – *Burdett v Abbott* (1811) 14 East 1, 148 and *Stockdale v Hansard*, 9 Ad & El 1 – are agreed, and are emphatic. The jurisdiction of the Houses over their own members, their right to impose discipline within their walls, is absolute and exclusive. To use the words of Lord Ellenborough, 'They would sink into utter contempt and inefficiency without it'.

> The House of Commons is not subject to the control of ... [the] courts in its administration of that part of the statute law which has relation to its own internal proceedings ... Even if that interpretation should be erroneous, [the] court has no power to interfere with it, directly or indirectly (at 278, 286).

Note

As Munro notes, whilst disputed elections (an area previously falling within the House's right to regulate its own proceedings) are now determined by High Court judges, the 'form' of privilege is preserved, as their findings are merely certified to the Speaker for him to act as he thinks fit; in fact the findings of the court are invariably complied with.[8] Despite this erosion of privilege in the area of elections, the question of whether a candidate may take his seat having been clearly elected still falls to be determined solely by the House,[9] as recent examples make clear.

8   Munro, *op cit*, p 227.
9   *Ibid*.

Colin Munro, *Studies in Constitutional Law*, 2nd edn (1999), pp 227 *et seq*

... when Mr Tony Benn became Viscount Stansgate in succession to his father in 1960, his seat was declared vacant by the House of Commons and he was barred from the chamber (the law was subsequently changed to permit hereditary peerages to be disclaimed). Similarly, it is for the House of Lords to determine whether a peerage entitles the holder to sit in that House. A life peerage had been created for the judge Sir James Parke in 1855, presumably so as to strengthen judicial expertise in the House of Lords without at the same time diluting its ranks for the future with the descendants of lawyers. But the House decided that a peerage of that sort did not entitle the holder to sit in Parliament.

The House of Commons may also expel a member for grounds other than disqualification, if it considers him unfit to continue in that capacity A sufficient cause would be conviction of a criminal offence involving turpitude ... In 1947 when Garry Allighan was expelled, it was his gross contempt of the House which caused it. He had made unsubstantiated allegations that details of confidential party meetings, held within the precincts of Parliament, were being revealed by members to journalists for money or while under the influence of drink. He was himself receiving payments for doing just that, and had lied to the Committee of Privileges.

It is interesting to consider that, if the Government were to use its majority in the House to vote to expel all members who opposed it, no objection could be heard by the courts in this country. It is usually said in response to this that there is nothing to prevent expelled members, if not disqualified from standing, from being re-elected, as John Wilkes was by the electors of Middlesex in the eighteenth century. That is true, but the real protection against abuse lies in conventional self-restraint. The calling of an election is itself at the wish of a Commons majority, for another aspect of privilege is the House's right to determine when casual vacancies will be filled. When a vacancy arises through a member's death, expulsion or disqualification, it is for the House to resolve that a writ be issued for the holding of a by-election.

Exclusive cognisance of internal affairs

Each House collectively claims the right to control its own proceedings and to regulate its internal affairs and whatever takes place within its walls. The claim was partly protected by the provision in the Bill of Rights to the effect that 'the freedom of speech and debates or proceedings in Parliament ought not to be impeached or questioned in any court or place out of Parliament', and so this aspect of privilege is linked to the freedom of speech. It is also linked to the privilege concerning composition, for the Houses regard their membership as their own affair.

The claim has been accepted by the courts, at least provided they can agree that 'internal concerns' are involved. 'Whatever is done within the walls of either assembly must pass without question in any other place', said Lord Denman in *Stockdale v Hansard* [at 114]. In *Bradlaugh v Gossett*, Stephen J observed that 'the House of Commons is not a court of justice, but the effect of its privilege to regulate its own internal concerns practically invests it with a judicial character', and held that 'we must presume that it discharges this function properly and with due regard to the laws, in the making of which it has so great a share' [at 285]. Indeed, the doctrines upon which claims to privilege are based, and upon which the jurisdiction of courts is denied or restricted have much in common with those which are expressed as the sovereignty of Parliament. When, for example, the validity of an Act of Parliament is challenged on the ground of alleged defects of parliamentary procedure, and the courts refuse to investigate, their refusal might be justified on grounds of sovereignty or privilege. In *British Railways Board v Pickin* [1974] 1 All ER 609 ... the sovereignty aspect was emphasised, but privilege was also adduced as a justification in the speeches of Lord Simon of Glaisdale and Lord Morris of Borth-y-Gest ...

However, if matters happen 'within the walls', but are unconnected with the business of Parliament, the ordinary courts may be entitled to assume jurisdiction without being in breach of privilege, or at least are allowed to. 'I know of no authority for the proposition that an ordinary crime committed in the House of Commons would be withdrawn from the ordinary course of criminal justice', said Stephen J in *Bradlaugh v Gossett* [at 283]. In practice it has been left to the ordinary authorities and courts to deal with incidents such as the killing of the Prime Minister by a madman in the lobby of the House of Commons (in 1812) and the projection of CS gas into the chamber by a protester in the public gallery (in 1970). Sometimes there would be concurrent jurisdiction, as where one member assaults another in the course of proceedings . . .

Notes

1   It is hard to see why the House requires its ability to allow or disallow Members at its pleasure. Apart from the hypothetical (but still disturbing) possibility that the House *could* resolve, quite legally, to expel all Opposition MPs, a more realistic concern relates to its power to determine when vacancies (caused by death or bankruptcy) should be filled. Complaints have been directed at government dilatoriness in moving writs for by-elections at which they expect to be defeated, and it is not fanciful to suggest that a government with a majority of only one could procure a delay in a by-election which could wipe out its majority so that the election only took place after a crucial Commons vote which was expected to be very close. There seems to be no reason why the law should not provide that all by-elections must take place within a fixed time of a seat becoming vacant.

2   A case which, as Munro puts it,[10] took a 'generous' view of the scope of the House's internal affairs was *R v Graham-Campbell ex p Herbert* [1935] 1 KB 594, in which the High Court considered whether a magistrate had been right in finding that he lacked jurisdiction to prosecute Members for selling alcohol without a licence in the Members' Bar.

R v Graham-Campbell ex p Herbert [1935] I KB 594, 602

Lord Hewart CJ: Here, as it seems to me, the magistrate was entitled to say, on the materials before him, that in the matters complained of the House of Commons was acting collectively in a matter which fell within the area of the internal affairs of the House, and, that being so, any tribunal might well feel, on the authorities, an invincible reluctance to interfere. To take the opposite course might conceivably be, in proceedings of a somewhat different character from these, after the various stages of those proceedings had been passed, to make the House of Lords the arbiter of the privileges of the House of Commons.

Notes

1   This decision cannot be justified by arguing that the privilege found here to exist, of flouting the licensing laws,[11] was necessary to allow the House to carry on its business properly. (Such a notion could, for example, justifiably be used to protect Members from criminal liability incurred by speeches or questions in the House.) Even if some notion of protecting the dignity of Parliament is invoked, it is hard to see how that is protected by shielding Members from the ordinary criminal law in a matter as unrelated to their constitutional activities as illegal drinking.

2   It seems almost certain that if more serious offences were committed, the House would hand over the matter to the courts, for as Stanley de Smith comments, its penal powers 'are inadequate to deal with ordinary crime';[12] in any event Parliament would be anxious to avoid the unfavourable publicity that would undoubtedly ensue from an attempt to protect such an offender through an assertion of immunity by virtue of privilege. In the unlikely event of such an assertion being made by the Commons, the outcome must be in doubt.

---

10   *Op cit*, p 230.
11   Note that Avory J also found that the Licensing Acts were not intended to apply to Parliament (at p 603).
12   SA de Smith, *Constitutional and Administrative Law*, 6th edn (1994), p 325.

3   The Joint Committee on Parliamentary Privilege has made a series of
    recommendations on the possible immunity of Members from the ordinary
    criminal law. It recommended that MPs should be included within the scope of
    future legislation on bribery,[13] a proposal energetically backed by the Wicks Report[14]
    and supported by the government,[15] though this proposal has not as yet been
    enacted in law. The Joint Committee also made more general recommendations.

    19. Each House of Parliament should continue to exercise control over its own affairs. Statute
    should provide that the privilege of each House to manage its internal affairs within its precincts
    applies only to activities directly and closely relating to proceedings in Parliament.

    20. It should also be made clear in statute that every law applies to Parliament unless Parliament
    has been expressly excluded. The precincts of Parliament should not be a statute-free zone.[16]

Note
The reasoning and recommendations of the Joint Committee show a clear attempt to
pare away from the ambit of privilege those areas of parliamentary activity which do
not require protection. It should be remembered that a basic principle of the Diceyan
version of the Rule of Law is equality before the law; as the Joint Committee notes,
exempting law-makers from the laws they make which bind others appears a
particularly unfortunate derogation from this principle and not one which can be
justified by arguments as to the sovereignty and efficacy of the legislature.

Members' financial interests: the Nolan Report and its aftermath

The problem of Members' outside interests

One further, important aspect of the Commons' internal regulatory rules lies in the
regulations governing Members' financial interests. As Alan Doig notes, this issue has
implications which go well beyond mere internal self-regulation.

**Alan Doig, 'Full circle or dead end? what next for the Select Committee
on Members' Interests?' (1994) 47(3) Parl Aff 355, 356**

It is generally accepted, and certainly among MPs, that MPs may have other occupations and
sources of income in addition to their parliamentary salary. It is also not in dispute that in
representing interests and opinions, MPs can help bridge the gap between government and
organisations affected by its activities. Government policy-making and decision-taking need a
continuing bilateral relationship of information, co-operation and mutual understanding, for
example in the oil industry, it's not a case that we have a choice, the politics of energy and oil draw
us into very close relationships with government. Such organisations, ranging from multinationals
like ICI or British Airways to representative organisations like the National Farmers' Union or the
Royal College of Nursing will have offices and staff to monitor, liaise with and report back on the
decision-making processes of Whitehall and Westminster. Those without a permanent
governmental relations office can hire professional lobbyists. Whatever the means, however, the
purpose is to get that interest's message to the policymakers and the legislators.

---

13   For the government's proposals, see Cm 4759 (2000).
14   Wicks Committee, Sixth Report, Cm 4557-I (2000), paras 3.8–3.11.
15   In evidence to the Wicks Committee, see *ibid*, para 3.10.
16   HLP 43–41 (1998–99), paras 19 and 20.

Concern about the activities of interests and of professional lobbyists and the involvement of MPs with those activities has been growing. What MPs do in Parliament, or say to ministers or government departments, should be in accordance with their perceptions of the public or national interest, of the promises of party manifestos and of the expectations of their constituencies. At the same time, in representing the views of interests, what they say and do may be felt to be compromised because they are being paid to sell the interest's views to colleagues, ministers and civil servants, whether or not they themselves are convinced of the intrinsic value of that interest's case. The underlying expectations of political decision-making processes, and the public's acceptance of the outcomes, are not best served by suspicions or allegations of hidden influence, the exploitation of insider contacts and information, the role of money to secure privileged access to the decision-making procedures and, above all, the conflict of interest for MPs who may serve two masters.

Notes

1   A public perception that the existing rules on this matter were either inadequate or were being flouted with impunity arose after various incidents, in which MPs were perceived as having used their office for improper gain, attracted intense media interest. The most notorious event was the 'cash for questions' affair in which *The Sunday Times* reported[17] that two MPs had been willing to table questions in Parliament in return for payments of money. Another episode of concern was the tabling by one MP in another MP's name of an amendment which would have benefited an association for which he acted as a parliamentary adviser.[18]

2   As a result of this concern, a Standing Committee was set up to enquire generally into the issue of standards in public life (not into specific instances) under the chairmanship of Lord Nolan.[19] The first report of the Nolan Committee was published in May 1995[20] and dealt with MPs, ministers and civil servants, executive quangos and NHS bodies. We are concerned here only with the first of these matters. The Second Report from the Select Committee on Standards in Public Life,[21] which was set up to consider Nolan's proposals, summarises the recommendations made by Nolan which were accepted in principle by the House of Commons, when the Report was debated on 19 July as follows:

> ... the Appointment of a Parliamentary Commissioner for Standards; the establishment [from the 1995–96 session] of a new Select Committee on Standards and Privileges [replacing the old Committee on Members' Interests and the Committee of Privileges]; the introduction of a Code of Conduct, coupled with a review of the wording of the 1947 Resolution [see below].[22]

5   The Code of Conduct recommended by Nolan was drafted by the new Committee on Standards and Privileges, which reported in July 1996.[23] Its proposed draft of the Code was accepted by the House after a short debate without a division.[24] The

---

17   10 July 1994. On the Hamilton affair, see A Doig, 'The offence that dare not speak its name: cash, corruption and the Hamilton affair' (1998) Parl Aff, January.

18   See HC Deb col 612 (22 May 1995), for the MPs' apology.

19   Its members were appointed for three years in the first instance. On the Nolan Committee and the issue of standards in public life generally, see articles in 48(4) Parl Aff which is devoted to this issue; see also D Oliver, 'Standards of Conduct in Public Life – what standards?' [1995] PL 497.

20   First Report of the Committee on Standards in Public Life, Cm 2850 (1995) (Nolan Report).

21   HC 816 (1994–95), para 3.

22   *Ibid.*

23   Third Report, HC 604 (1995–96).

24   HC Deb cols 392–407 (24 July 1996).

Code itself, in line with Nolan's recommendation that it amount to a statement of broad principle accompanied by detailed guidance, is brief – amounting to only two pages – and accompanied by a much more lengthy Guide to the Rules relating to the Conduct of Members, which also includes the text of all relevant House resolutions. It should be noted that some significant changes to the Guide were made in 2002, following a series of reports both by the Committee on Standards in Public Life[25] and the Committee on Standards and Privileges.[26] Specific sections of the Guide which deal with the advocacy rule, the Register of Members' interests and the procedure to be used for investigating alleged infringements of the Rules are quoted below in the relevant sections of this chapter. The Code itself is as follows:

The Code of Conduct for Members of Parliament
Prepared pursuant to the Resolution of the House of 19 July 1995
Purpose of the Code

The purpose of the Code of Conduct is to assist Members in the discharge of their obligations to the House, their constituents and the public at large.

The Code applies to Members in all aspects of their public life. It does not seek to regulate what Members do in their purely private and personal lives.

Public duty

By virtue of the oath, or affirmation, of allegiance taken by all Members when they are elected to the House, Members have a duty to be faithful and bear true allegiance to Her Majesty the Queen, her heirs and successors, according to law.

Members have a duty to uphold the law and to act on all occasions in accordance with the public trust placed in them.

Members have a general duty to act in the interests of the nation as a whole; and a special duty to their constituents.

Personal conduct

Members shall observe the general principles of conduct identified by the Committee on Standards in Public Life as applying to holders of public office:—

Selflessness

Holders of public office should take decisions solely in terms of the public interest. They should not do so in order to gain financial or other material benefits for themselves, their family, or their friends.

Integrity

Holders of public office should not place themselves under any financial or other obligation to outside individuals or organisations that might influence them in the performance of their official duties.

Objectivity

In carrying out public business, including making public appointments, awarding contracts, or recommending individuals for rewards and benefits, holders of public office should make choices on merit.

---

25 In two main reports, the first known as the Neill Report after its then Chair: Sixth Report, Vol 1, Cm 4557-I (2000); the second known as the Wicks Report under Lord Wicks: Eighth Report, Cm 5663 (2002).
26 See below.

Accountability

Holders of public office are accountable for their decisions and actions to the public and must submit themselves to whatever scrutiny is appropriate to their office.

Openness

Holders of public office should be as open as possible about all the decisions and actions that they take. They should give reasons for their decisions and restrict information only when the wider public interest clearly demands.

Honesty

Holders of public office have a duty to declare any private interests relating to their public duties and to take steps to resolve any conflicts arising in a way that protects the public interest.

Leadership

Holders of public office should promote and support these principles by leadership and example.

Members shall base their conduct on a consideration of the public interest, avoid conflict between personal interest and the public interest and resolve any conflict between the two, at once, and in favour of the public interest.

Members shall at all times conduct themselves in a manner which will tend to maintain and strengthen the public's trust and confidence in the integrity of Parliament and never undertake any action which would bring the House of Commons, or its Members generally, into disrepute.

The acceptance by a Member of a bribe to influence his or her conduct as a Member, including any fee, compensation or reward in connection with the promotion of, or opposition to, any Bill, Motion, or other matter submitted, or intended to be submitted to the House, or to any Committee of the House, is contrary to the law of Parliament.

Members shall fulfil conscientiously the requirements of the House in respect of the registration of interests in the Register of Members' Interests and shall always draw attention to any relevant interest in any proceeding of the House or its Committees, or in any communications with Ministers, Government Departments or Executive Agencies.

In any activities with, or on behalf of, an organisation with which a Member has a financial relationship, including activities which may not be a matter of public record such as informal meetings and functions, he or she must always bear in mind the need to be open and frank with Ministers, Members and officials.

No Member shall act as a paid advocate in any proceeding of the House.

No improper use shall be made of any payment or allowance made to Members for public purposes and the administrative rules which apply to such payments and allowances must be strictly observed.

Members must bear in mind that information which they receive in confidence in the course of their parliamentary duties should be used only in connection with those duties, and that such information must never be used for the purpose of financial gain.

We now turn to the two main areas of controversy: first, employment of Members by outside bodies and its influence on their conduct; secondly, the issue of disclosure of outside interests. These issues will be dealt with in turn.

Parliamentary consultancies: permissibility, payment for advocacy

Nolan first of all recommended that 'Members should remain free to have paid employment unrelated to their role as MPs'[27] – a freedom which remains *existant* today

---

27 *Op cit*, para 21.

– and then went on to consider the thorny issue of Members entering into agreements with and receiving payment not from ordinary employment, such as law or journalism, but as part of consultancy agreements made with lobbying firms (what Nolan referred to as 'multi-client consultancies') and campaigning groups, which were clearly related to their activities in Parliament.

First Report of the Committee on Standards in Public Life, Cm 2850 (1995)

...

26. In 1947 the House declared that:

> ... it is inconsistent with the dignity of the House, with the duty of a Member to his constituency and with the maintenance of the privilege of freedom of speech, for any Member of the House to enter into any contractual agreement with an outside body controlling or limiting the Member's complete independence and freedom of action in Parliament or stipulating that he shall act in any way as the representative of such outside body in regard to any matters to be transacted in Parliament; the duty of a Member being to his constituency and to the country as a whole, rather than to any particular section thereof ...

...

48. If a Member is engaged to advise a client on Parliamentary matters affecting the client, and is at the same time free to speak, lobby and vote on those same matters in the House, it is not merely possible but highly likely that the Member will use Parliamentary opportunities in a way consistent with that advice.

49. It is more likely than not that Members who enter into consultancy agreements will do so with clients to whose viewpoints they are sympathetic, although Members who have such agreements have been at pains to tell us that they would not hesitate both to make clear to their clients where their views differed, and to express views in the House which their clients did not share. Nevertheless the impression can easily be gained, however unfair this may be in individual cases, that not only advice but also advocacy have been bought by the client. The evidence which we have received leaves us in little doubt that this is the impression which many people have. It is one of the most potent sources of public suspicion about the true motivation of Members of Parliament. In recent years Members have acquired paid consultancies on a large scale. Over the same period public scepticism about MPs' financial motives has increased sharply. It must be more likely than not that these two developments are related, but in any case their combination can only tend to undermine the dignity of Parliament as a whole.

50. We would consider it thoroughly unsatisfactory, possibly to the extent of being a contempt of Parliament, if a Member of Parliament, even if not strictly bound by an agreement with a client to pursue a particular interest in Parliament, was to pursue that interest solely or principally because payment, in cash or kind, was being made. A Member who believes in a cause should be prepared to promote it without payment; equally a Member ought not to pursue a cause more forcefully than might otherwise have been the case as a result of a financial interest. We believe that such action would breach the spirit if not the letter of the 1947 resolution, and we cannot be confident that all Members are as scrupulous in this respect as some have claimed to be.[28]

Second Report from the Select Committee on Standards in Public Life, HC 816 (1994–95)

11. The main source of public anxiety, as identified by Nolan, is the notion that influence, whether real or imagined, can be bought and sold through Members. This suggests that any remedial action,

---

28 In the event, Nolan recommended against a general advocacy ban (paras 51–55, above) but only on multi-client consultancies.

rather than seeking to draw a line of legitimacy between different types of outside body with which Members should or should not be allowed to have paid relationships, ought to concentrate on defining as closely as possible those *actions* by Members which, because they give rise to suspicions about the exercise – or attempted exercise – of improper influence, need to be prohibited ...

13. We propose that the rules of the House should now distinguish between paid advocacy in Parliament (unacceptable for the reasons outlined above) and paid advice (acceptable provided it is properly registered and declared).

Note

The recommendations of the Committee in this area, specifically the addendum to the 1947 Resolution, were accepted by the House on 6 November 1995[29] and now appear in the Rules of the House.

Guide to the Rules Relating to the Conduct of Members (extract)
3. Lobbying for reward or consideration

53. On 6th November 1995 the House agreed to the following Resolution relating to paid advocacy:

> It is inconsistent with the dignity of the House, with the duty of a Member to his constituents, and with the maintenance of the privilege of freedom of speech, for any Member of this House to enter into any contractual agreement with an outside body, controlling or limiting the Member's complete independence and freedom of action in Parliament or stipulating that he shall act in any way as the representative of such outside body in regard to any matters to be transacted in Parliament; the duty of a Member being to his constituents and to the country as a whole, rather than to any particular section thereof: and that in particular no Members of the House shall, in consideration of any remuneration, fee, payment, or reward or benefit in kind, direct or indirect, which the Member or any member of his or her family has received is receiving or expects to receive—
>
> > (i) advocate or initiate any cause or matter on behalf of any outside body or individual, or
> >
> > (ii) urge any other Member of either House of Parliament, including Ministers, to do so,
>
> by means of any speech, Question, Motion, introduction of a Bill or Amendment to a Motion or a Bill or any approach, whether oral or in writing, to Ministers or servants of the Crown.
>
> (Resolution of the House of 15th July 1947, amended on 6th November 1995 and on 14th May 2002)

54. This Resolution prohibits paid advocacy. It is wholly incompatible with the advocacy rule that any Member should take payment for speaking in the House. Nor may a Member, for payment, vote, ask a Parliamentary Question, table a Motion, introduce a Bill or table or move an Amendment to a Motion or Bill or urge colleagues or Ministers to do so.

55. The Resolution does not prevent a Member from holding a remunerated outside interest as a director, consultant, or adviser, or in any other capacity, whether or not such interests are related to membership of the House. Nor does it prevent a Member from being sponsored by a trade union or any other organisation, or holding any other registrable interest, or from receiving hospitality in the course of his or her parliamentary duties whether in the United Kingdom or abroad.

...

---

29   HC Deb cols 659–61.

57. In addition to the requirements of the advocacy rule, Members should also bear in mind the long established convention that interests which are wholly personal and particular to the Member, and which may arise from a profession or occupation outside the House, ought not to be pursued by the Member in proceedings in Parliament.

Guidelines on the application of the ban on lobbying for reward or consideration

If a financial interest is required to be registered in the Register of Members' Interests, or declared in debate, it falls within the scope of the ban on lobbying for reward or consideration. The Committee on Standards and Privileges has provided the following Guidelines to assist Members in applying the rule:

- **Parliamentary proceedings:** When a Member is taking part in any parliamentary proceeding or making any approach to a Minister or servant of the Crown, advocacy is prohibited which seeks to confer benefit exclusively upon a body (or individual) outside Parliament, from which the Member has received, is receiving, or expects to receive a pecuniary benefit, or upon any registrable client of such a body (or individual). Otherwise a Member may speak freely on matters which relate to the affairs and interests of a body (or individual) from which he or she receives a pecuniary benefit, provided the benefit is properly registered and declared.

- **Constituency interests:** Irrespective of any relevant interest which the Member is required to register or declare, he or she may pursue any constituency interest in any proceeding of the House or any approach to a Minister or servant of the Crown, except that:

  - where the Member has a financial relationship with a company in the Member's constituency the guidelines above relating to parliamentary proceedings shall apply;

  - where the Member is an adviser to a trade association, or to a professional (or other representative) body, the Member should avoid using a constituency interest as the means by which to raise any matter which the Member would otherwise be unable to pursue. [The above Guidelines supersede the Guidelines in force until 14 May 2002 which reflected the distinction drawn by the Select Committee on Standards in Public Life between the initiation of, and participation in, parliamentary proceedings].

The current Guidelines give effect to a recommendation from the Committee on Standards in Public Life in the following terms:

> In recommending in the First Report a ban on agreements between MPs and multi-client consultancies, we were concerned to avoid a situation in which MPs could be presented as participating in 'a hiring fair'. We retain that concern. On the other hand, we are anxious that the rules should not unnecessarily inhibit the ability of MPs to become well informed and to use their expertise and experience effectively. Bearing in mind the evidence that we have heard about the present guidelines on 'initiation' and the ban on paid advocacy, we believe that they are operating unnecessarily harshly and that they should be amended. We recommend that the ban on paid advocacy should remain in place, but that the restriction on initiation should be removed and the guidelines relating to participation extended to include both participation and initiation. The effect of this would be that an MP who had a personal interest would be permitted to initiate proceedings in the same way that he or she is able to participate in proceedings under the current guidelines, but that the MP (a) would not be able to engage in 'paid advocacy' or seek to confer benefits exclusively on a particular individual or body and (b) would be required to register and declare the benefit in accordance with the guidelines. We recommend a further safeguard (c) that, reinforcing present practice regarding the declaration of interests when tabling a written notice, in addition to registration and oral declaration, the MP would also be required to identify his or her interest on the Order Paper (or Notice Paper) by way of an agreed symbol. [Sixth Report of the Committee on Standards in Public Life, Reinforcing Standards, Cm 4557-I, January 2000, para 3.96.]

The Committee on Standards and Privileges has made it clear that it would regard it as a very serious breach of the rules if a Member failed to register or declare an interest which was relevant to a proceeding he had initiated [Fourth Report, HC 478 (2001–02)].

[Note:'Initiating a parliamentary proceeding' includes: presenting a Bill; presenting a Petition; tabling and asking a Parliamentary Question; asking a supplementary question to one's own Question; initiating, or seeking to initiate an adjournment (or other) debate; tabling or moving any Motion (eg an 'Early Day Motion', a Motion for leave to introduce a Bill under the 'Ten Minutes Rule' or a Motion 'blocking' a Private Bill; tabling or moving an Amendment to a Bill; proposing a draft Report, or moving an Amendment to a draft Report, in a Select Committee; giving any written notice, or adding a name to such notice, or making an application for and introducing a daily adjournment debate, or an emergency debate. A similar consideration applies in the case of approaches to ministers or civil servants.]

Parameters to the operation of the ban on lobbying for reward or consideration

62. The Committee on Standards and Privileges has also agreed to the following parameters to the operation of the advocacy rule:—

Registrable interests: The ban on lobbying for reward or consideration is to apply with equal effect to any registrable or declarable pecuniary benefit irrespective of the source of that benefit (ie no distinction is drawn between financial benefits received from a company, a representative organisation, a charity, a foreign government or any other source). Similarly, no distinction should be drawn in the application of the advocacy rule to different categories of registrable or declarable benefit (except for the provision below relating to ballot bills, to overseas visits, and to membership of other elected bodies). Non-pecuniary interests registered by Members do not fall within the scope of the Resolution agreed by the House on 6th November 1995 and the rule does not apply to them.

Past, present, and future benefits: Unlike the Register, which lists current benefits, or benefits received in the immediate past, the Resolution on lobbying of 6th November 1995 also refers, as does the rule on declaration, to past and expected future benefits ...

Continuing benefits: Continuing benefits, ie directorships, other employment, and sponsorship, can be divested to release a Member with immediate effect from the restrictions imposed by the rule, providing that the benefit is disposed of and there is no expectation of renewal.

'One-off' benefits: The rule applies to 'one-off' registrable benefits, both visits and gifts, from the day upon which the interest was acquired until one year after it is registered.

. . .

Ministers: The restrictions imposed by the rule do not apply to Ministers when acting in the House as Ministers.

The financial interests of Members are extremely varied, as the Register demonstrates. Each Member will need to apply the rule and the Guidelines to his or her particular circumstances. When in doubt, Members will be able to seek the advice of the Commissioner, or the Committee on Standards and Privileges. However, some illustrative examples of the application of the Guidelines may be of value:—

A Member who is director of a company may not seek particular preference for that company (eg tax relief, subsidies, restriction of competition) in any proceeding of the House or any approach to Ministers or officials.

In the case of trade associations, staff associations, professional bodies, charities (or any similar representative organisation):

Membership alone of any representative organisation does not entail any restrictions under the rule.

A Member who is, for example, a remunerated adviser:

- may not advocate measures for the exclusive benefit of that organisation; nor speak or act in support of a campaign exclusively for the benefit of the representative organisation or its membership (eg a campaign for special tax relief, or for enhanced pay and numbers);

- may speak or act in support of a campaign which is of particular interest to the representative organisation (eg in the case of an animal welfare organisation, a campaign to prohibit the importation of animal fur, or prohibit blood sports; in the case of a charity for cancer research, a campaign for the prohibition of smoking).

When a Member has a problem involving a company within his or her constituency the Member may take any parliamentary action to resolve that problem, even though he or she may hold a remunerated position with a body representing the relevant sector of the industry regionally or nationally, or with another company outside the constituency in the same industrial sector.

Similarly a Member who has a remunerated position with a representative association is not restricted in any way in taking up the case of a constituent who is a member of that association, or is employed by a member of that association. The only circumstances when the Member's actions are restricted are when the Member has a registrable interest with the company concerned when the guidelines provide that the Member forfeits the special position he or she has as a constituency Member.

Members are reminded that when accepting foreign visits they should be mindful of the reputation of the House. However, the knowledge obtained by Members on such visits can often be of value to the House as a whole. While it is desirable that Members should be able to use that knowledge in debate in the House there is a point at which promoting the interests, of eg a foreign Government from which hospitality has been received, crosses the line between informed comment and lobbying. Members may not, for example, advocate in debate increased United Kingdom financial assistance to a Government from which they have recently received hospitality. Nor may the Member advocate any other measure for the exclusive benefit of the host Government. . . .

A Member whose visit was funded by a non-governmental organisation (NGO) or other agency would not be inhibited in speaking about its work or the problems it was dealing with. Only a matter which was for the exclusive benefit of the NGO or agency, e.g. a request for a grant-in-aid to the particular organisation, could not be pursued.

. . .

Responsibility of the Member

In common with the rules of the House relating to registration and declaration of interest the main responsibility for observation of the ban on lobbying for reward or consideration lies with the individual Member. The Select Committee on Standards in Public Life stated in its Second Report that 'it is important to make clear that it will not be the function of the Chair to enforce the ban ... during speeches, either by interrupting a Member thought to be contravening it, or by declining to call him. Complaints will be a matter for the Commissioner to investigate in the first instance'. The Speaker has declined to receive points of order relating to registration or lobbying.

Delegations

'. . . a Member with a paid interest should not initiate or participate in, including attendance, a delegation where the problem affects only the body from which he has a paid interest.' (Part of a Resolution of the House of 6th November 1995).

Note

This reform was probably the most important change to the rules of the House resulting from the Nolan Report. As noted above, it was changed in May 2002[30] by a

---

30 For the history of the proposals on changes to the Advocacy Rule, see: Committee on Standards in Public Life, Sixth Report, Vol 1, Cm 4557-I (2000), summarised in A Doig, 'Sleaze: picking up the threads or "Back to Basics" scandals?' (2001) 54 Parl Aff 360, 370. See also the changes proposed by the Committee on Standards and Privileges, Fifth Report, HC 267 (2000–01). For the debate approving the motion see HC Deb cols 730 *et seq* (14 May 2002).

resolution of the House approving the Ninth Report of the Committee on Standards and Privileges, which included a draft new Code of Conduct and Guide.[31] Essentially, the previous position was as follows: a distinction was drawn between (a) *initiating* a parliamentary proceeding, for example, presenting a Bill, moving an amendment, or putting one's name to it; and (b) simply *participating* in a debate started by others. A Member could not *initiate* any proceeding if it 'relate[s] specifically and directly to the affairs and interests of [the body from whom he receives the benefit]' (old version of the Guide, para 58.1). However, Members could participate in a debate already under way, provided that their speech did not 'seek directly to confer a benefit *exclusively* upon a body' from which the Member received the payment (the Guide, para 58.2). Under the new position:

> advocacy is prohibited which seeks to confer benefit exclusively upon a body (or individual) outside Parliament, from which the Member has received, is receiving, or expects to receive a pecuniary benefit, or upon any registrable client of such a body (or individual). Otherwise a Member may speak freely on matters which relate to the affairs and interests of a body (or individual) from which he or she receives a pecuniary benefit, provided the benefit is properly registered and declared (Guide to the Rules, above).

Disclosure of interests

Before the Nolan saga began, there was already in existence a Register of Members' Interests. The detail of the requirements on MPs to disclose interests is laid down in the Code of Conduct together with the Guide to the Rules Relating to the Conduct of Members. This covers the types of interests that must be registered; the means by which disclosure must be made in the Register; the obligation to disclose interests orally and by notice during parliamentary proceedings; the special rules relating to parliamentary consultancy agreements; guidance on all the above. It should be noted that the resolution of the House in May 2002 referred to above also relaxed slightly the registration requirements by setting a threshold below which interests need not be registered.

Guide to the Rules Relating to the Conduct of Members, as approved by Parliament on 14 May 2002 (extract)[32]

1. Registration of Members' Interests

Rules of the House

> 'Every Member of the House of Commons shall furnish to a Registrar of Members' Interests such particulars of his registrable interests as shall be required, and shall notify to the Registrar any alterations which may occur therein, and the Registrar shall cause these particulars to be entered in a Register of Members' Interests which shall be available for inspection by the public.'
>
> (Resolution of the House of 22nd May 1974)
>
> 'For the purposes of the Resolution of the House of 22nd May 1974 in relation of disclosure of interests in any proceeding of the House or its Committees, any interest declared in a copy of the Register of Members' Interests shall be regarded as sufficient disclosure for the purpose of taking part in any division of the House or in any of its Committees.'
>
> (Part of the Resolution of the House of 12th June 1975)

---

31 HC 763 (2001–02).
32 For commentary on the interpretation of the then proposed new rules see: Committee on Standards and Privileges, Fifth Report, HC 267 (2000–01).

Definition of the Register's purpose

The main purpose of the Register of Members' Interests is 'to provide information of any pecuniary interest or other material benefit which a Member receives which might reasonably be thought by others to influence his or her actions, speeches or votes in Parliament, or actions taken in his or her capacity as a Member of Parliament.' [Select Committee on Members' Interests, First Report, HC 326 (1991–92), para 27.] The registration form specifies ten Categories of registrable interests which are described below. Apart from the specific rules, there is a more general obligation upon Members to keep the overall definition of the Register's purpose in mind when registering their interests. The purpose of registration is openness. Registration of an interest does not imply any wrongdoing.

Members of Parliament are required to complete a registration form and submit it to the Commissioner for Standards within three months of taking their seats after a general election. For a Member returned at a by-election, the time limit is also three months. After the initial publication of the Register (or, in the case of Members returned at by-elections, after their initial registration) it is the responsibility of Members to notify changes in their registrable interests within four weeks of each change occurring.

Any Member having a registrable interest which has not at the time been registered, shall not undertake any action, speech or proceeding of the House (save voting) to which the registration would be relevant until notification has been given to the Commissioner for Standards of that interest.

Members are responsible for making a full disclosure of their interests, and if they have relevant interests which do not fall clearly into one or other of the specified categories, they are nonetheless expected to register them.

A reference in any Category to a spouse includes a Member's partner.

Interests the value of which does not exceed 1 per cent of the current parliamentary salary do not have to be registered. All single benefits of whatever kind which exceed that threshold should be registered in the appropriate Category (unless a higher threshold is specified in the relevant Category). All benefits received from the same source in the course of a calendar year, which cumulatively amount to more than 1 per cent of the current parliamentary salary, should also be registered. In addition, if a Member considers that any benefit he or she has received falls within the definition of the main purpose of the Register set out in paragraph 9, even though it does not exceed the 1 per cent threshold, the Member should register it in the appropriate Category or under Category 10 (Miscellaneous).

13. The Register is published soon after the beginning of a new Parliament, under the authority of the Committee on Standards and Privileges, and annually thereafter. Between publications the Register is regularly updated in a loose leaf form and, in that form, is available for public inspection in the Committee Office of the House of Commons. It is also available on the internet.

The Categories of Registrable Interest

[The Code then sets out 10 categories of interests, including (1) directorships; (2) remunerated employment; (3) consultancies providing service as an MP; (4) sponsorships or any other form of financial or material support; (5) gifts, benefits and hospitality; (6) overseas visits related to MP's status; (7) overseas benefits and gifts; (8) land/property other than a home; (9) shareholdings greater than a specified value (over 15% of the issued share capital of the company or greater in value than the current MPs salary); (10) other interests not falling within one of the other categories, but which fall within the main purpose of register (see above); this will generally mean that non-remunerative interests do not have to be registered unless 'a Member considers that an unremunerated interest which the Member holds might be thought by others to influence his or her actions in a similar manner to a remunerated interest'. Each of the specific categories above is subject to detailed specification and exceptions.]

2. Declaration of Members' Interests

Rules of the House

'In any debate or proceeding of the House or its Committees or transactions or communications which a Member may have with other Members or with Ministers or servants of the Crown, he shall disclose any relevant pecuniary interest or benefit of whatever nature, whether direct or indirect, that he may have had, may have or may be expecting to have.' (Resolution of the House of 22nd May 1974.)

'For the purposes of the Resolution of the House of 22nd May 1974 in relation to disclosure of interests in any proceeding of the House or its Committees,

(i) Any interest declared in a copy of the Register of Members' Interests shall be regarded as sufficient disclosure for the purpose of taking part in any division of the House or in any of its Committees.

(ii) The term "proceeding" shall be deemed not to include the asking of a supplementary question.' (Resolution of the House of 12th June 1975, amended on 19th July 1995.)

[section omitted]

37. In 1974 the House replaced a long standing convention with a rule that any relevant pecuniary interest or benefit of whatever nature, whether direct or indirect, should be declared in debate, or other proceeding. The same rule places a duty on Members to disclose to Ministers, or servants of the Crown, all relevant interests. The term 'servants of the Crown' should be interpreted as applying to the staff of executive agencies as well as to all staff employed in government departments.

Past and potential interests

38. The rule relating to declaration of interest is broader in scope than the rules relating to the registration of interests in two important respects. As well as current interests, Members are required to declare both relevant past interests and relevant interests which they may be expecting to have. In practice only interests held in the recent past, ie, those contained in the current printed edition of the Register, need normally be considered for declaration. Expected future interests, on the other hand, may be more significant. Where, for example, a Member is debating legislation or making representations to a Minister on a matter from which he has a reasonable expectation of personal financial advantage, candour is essential. In deciding when a possible future benefit is sufficiently tangible to necessitate declaration, the key word in the rule which the Member must bear in mind is 'expecting'. Where a Member's plans or degree of involvement in a project have passed beyond vague hopes and aspirations and reached the stage where there is a reasonable expectation that a financial benefit will accrue, then a declaration explaining the situation should be made.

Agreements for the provision of services

Such agreements, whereby Members enter into a contract to provide parliamentary assistance to a particular firm were seen as requiring particular transparency, since it is such agreements that are thought to be most likely to influence Members in their actions as MPs. Again, the new rules approved by the resolution of 14 May 2002 had the effect of relaxing the old rules significantly so that agreements do not need to be registered if the remuneration gained from them is seen as *de minimis* – specifically, no more than 1 per cent of the current parliamentary salary.

Guide to the Rules Relating to the Conduct of Members, as approved by Parliament on 14 May 2002 (extract)

Any Member proposing to enter into an agreement which involves the provision of services in his capacity as a Member of Parliament shall conclude such an agreement only if it conforms to the Resolution of the House of 6th November 1995 relating to Conduct of Members; and a full copy of any such agreement including the fees or benefits payable in bands of: up to £5,000, £5,001–£10,000, and thereafter in bands of £5,000, shall be deposited with the Parliamentary Commissioner for Standards at the same time as it is registered in the Register of Members' Interests and made available for inspection and reproduction by the public.

[Existing agreements also to be placed in such form by 31 March 1996.]

Provided that the requirement to deposit a copy of an agreement with the Commissioner shall not apply

(a) if the fees or benefits payable do not exceed 1 per cent of the current parliamentary salary; nor

(b) in the case of media work (but in that case the Member shall deposit a statement of the fees or benefits payable in the bands specified above).

(Part of a Resolution of the House of 6th November 1995, amended on 14th May 2002)

35. Under a Resolution of the House of 6th November 1995 the House agreed that Members should deposit certain employment agreements with the Parliamentary Commissioner for Standards. The two Resolutions set out above have continuing effect. Any Member who has an existing agreement or proposes to enter into an agreement which involves the provision of services in his or her capacity as a Member of Parliament should:

• ensure that the agreement does not breach the advocacy rule (see paragraphs 53–65);

• put any such agreement in written form;

• deposit a full copy of the agreement with the Parliamentary Commissioner for Standards. The agreement should indicate the nature of the services to be provided and specify the fees or benefits the Member is to receive in bands of (1) up to £5,000; (2) £5,001 to £10,000 (and thereafter in bands of £5,000).

• make the appropriate entry in the Register of Members' Interests; and

• declare the interest when it is appropriate to do so (see below) . . .

36. The Select Committee on Standards in Public Life [Second Report, Session 1994–95, HC 816, p xi] gave the following guidance in respect of their application of the rule:

. . .

The new requirement for employment agreements to be put in writing will apply principally to any arrangement whereby a Member may offer advice about parliamentary matters. We think it right, however, that it should also include frequent, as opposed to merely occasional, commitments outside Parliament which arise directly from membership of the House. For example, a regular, paid newspaper column or television programme would have to be the subject of a written agreement, but ad hoc current affairs or news interviews or intermittent panel appearances would not.

It may not always be immediately obvious whether a particular employment agreement arises directly from, or relates directly to, membership of the House. At one end of the spectrum are those Members whose outside employment pre-dates their original election, whilst at the other extreme are those who have taken up paid adviserships since entering the House. In between there will be many cases which are difficult to classify. Some Members, for example, may provide advice on Parliamentary matters incidentally as part of a much wider employment agreement covering matters wholly unrelated to the House. In these circumstances, it would be for an individual Member to decide how far it would be proper to isolate the Parliamentary services within a separate, depositable agreement; in reaching that decision he may wish to consult the Commissioner.

On the basis of this guidance the Committee on Standards and Privileges has agreed that: disclosing the remuneration for parliamentary services separately from remuneration for other services would be justified only in exceptional circumstances; e.g. where the parliamentary services are separately identifiable and form only a small proportion of the services as a whole. In any such case the entry in the Register should make it clear that the remuneration is for parliamentary services as part of a wider agreement.

The scope of the Resolutions is not limited to employment registered under Category 2 (Remunerated employment, office, profession, etc.) but includes other forms of employment, such as directorships (including non-executive directorships), when these involve the provision of services by the Member in his or her capacity as a Member of Parliament.

The following provisions apply to media work (journalism, broadcasting, speaking engagements, media appearances, training, &c):

- The deposit of an agreement for the provision of services is not required.

- Instead Members who register any form of media work under Category 2 (Remunerated employment, office, profession, etc) should declare the remuneration, or value of the reward, they receive for each commitment, or group of commitments for the same organisation or audience in the same calendar year, in bands of (1) up to £5,000; (2) £5,001–£10,000 (and thereafter in bands of £5,000).

But such declarations are not required—

- for media work which is wholly unrelated to parliamentary affairs, such as a sports column in a newspaper, or

- in any case where in the course of a calendar year total remuneration received from an employer or client, or through an agency, does not exceed 1 per cent of the current parliamentary salary.

Note

The reasons for the special rules relating to the disclosure of agreements for the provision of parliamentary services are well set out in the following extract from the original Nolan Committee Report.

First Report of the Committee on Standards in Public Life, Cm 2850 (1995)

66. Full declaration is especially important in respect of paid activities related to Parliament. We consider that in those cases, because the risk of impropriety is greater, it is essential that the full terms of all consultancy and sponsorship agreements, if not already in writing, should be reduced to writing and deposited along with the Register, so as to make them open for public inspection in full.

67. The need to deposit the contract in full is illustrated by the recent 'cash for questions' case. At several places in the evidence there is discussion of the form of entry which would have been put in the Register, and it is clear that whether or not payment was being made for a single question, or for a consultancy, the entries would have been wholly uninformative ...

69. Depositing the agreement will inevitably involve disclosure of the remuneration. We believe that the public, and in particular Members' constituents, have a right to know what financial benefits Members receive as a consequence of being elected to serve their constituencies. We consider it right, therefore, that remuneration should be disclosed in these cases. We also believe that information about the remuneration or other financial consideration received by a Member for Parliamentary services, or by way of sponsorship, should be entered in the register itself, possibly in banded form. It has been argued that actual remuneration is irrelevant, and that the mere existence of a financial relationship is what matters. That argument is not at all convincing. A Member who gets £1,000 a year as a parliamentary adviser is less likely to be influenced by the prospect of losing that money than one who receives £20,000 a year. The scale of the remuneration is in practice relevant to a full understanding of the nature of the service expected.

We have noted that several MPs with whom we raised this issue did not object to disclosure of remuneration so long as this related strictly to parliamentary services.

Notes

1 The House of Commons accepted in the debate of 6 July 1995 'the extension of the requirement for ... relevant interests to be declared by means of symbols on the Order Paper, previously applied only to the proposers of Early Day Motions, to all written parliamentary Proceedings except Division lists', also recommended by Nolan.[33] In political terms, this was seen as uncontroversial, as merely extending the range of a given type of disclosure to encompass other activities. In fact, this was quite an important change, allowing possible motivations behind the initiation of written parliamentary proceedings to be immediately ascertained.

2 The proposal that agreements with outside bodies relating to parliamentary activities should be put in writing – in particular that the amounts earned should be revealed – was thought to require further consideration by the Committee on Standards in Public Life. That Committee reawakened the party political aspect of the debate by splitting sharply on party lines on the issue: the motion now set out in the Rules of the House (the resolutions set out at pp 435–36, above, requiring the publication of parliamentary consultant agreements including the amount of remuneration), supported by the opposition members, was defeated by the Conservative majority on the Committee.[34] This aspect of its deliberations was emphasised in the extensive media coverage of its findings[35] and the party political aspect of the debate was further accentuated when the Prime Minister publicly gave his support to the view of the Conservative majority on the Committee.[36]

3 In the Commons debate, Labour motions were put forward on the same lines as that quoted above and were carried, by 322 votes to 271 (on disclosing amounts) and by 325 votes to 202 (on making the agreements open to inspection by the public). Thirty-three Conservative MPs voted with the Opposition and a further 31 abstained or did not vote. The rest (around 220) followed the lead of the then Prime Minister, John Major, and voted against the proposal. The Opposition was united behind support for the proposal. For the debate, see HC Deb cols 608–82 (6 November 1995).

Enforcement of the rules – the mechanisms and compliance by MPs

The enforcement procedures

It is important to appreciate that the ability of the House to enforce the standards rules is merely part of both Houses' general jurisdiction to punish both Members and non-Members for breaches of privilege – contempts of Parliament. As Munro puts it:

> The Houses are able to deal with offenders and enforce their privileges because they are the High Court of Parliament, and so have an inherent jurisdiction. When any of the rights and immunities known as privileges are disregarded or attacked by anybody, the offence is called a breach of privilege, and is punishable under the law of Parliament. By virtue of the same

---

33 As summarised in the Second Report from the Select Committee on Standards in Public Life, HC 816 (1994–95), para 3.

34 The motion therefore passed.

35 See, eg, 'Tories block Nolan plan for disclosure of earnings', *The Guardian*, 1 November 1995.

36 In Question Time on 2 November, HC Deb cols 387–89.

jurisdiction, each House may punish offences against its authority or dignity, even if they do not involve breaches of specific privileges. Such offences are contempts of Parliament: the concept is analogous to contempt of court ...[37]

The mechanisms to police adherence to the new rules are a new Committee on Standards and Privileges (hereinafter 'the Committee') and a Parliamentary Commissioner for Standards ('the Commissioner'). The Committee also has the general role of investigating contempts of the House not related to breaches of the Code of Conduct. It should be noted, however, that the Committee decided[38] to draw a distinction, in terms of the procedure it would adopt, between cases involving alleged breaches of privilege – which generally involve non-Members – and those involving breach of the Code of Conduct (by Members). The former cases, as Rush notes,[39] would 'continue to be dealt with in the traditional way, in that the committee takes oral and written evidence from those involved and the Commissioner is not involved'. The latter would entail an initial investigation by the Commissioner, whose report would then form the basis of the Committee's own investigation. The Standing Orders governing these bodies are as follows.

HC Deb cols 610–12 (6 November 1995)

Standing Order (Committee on Standards and Privileges)

(1) There shall be a select committee, called the Committee on Standards and Privileges:

   (a) to consider specific matters relating to privileges referred to it by the House;

   (b) to oversee the work of the Parliamentary Commissioner for Standards; to examine the arrangements proposed by the Commissioner for the compilation, maintenance and accessibility of the Register of Members' Interests and any other registers of interest established by the House; to review from time to time the form and content of those registers; and to consider any specific complaints made in relation to the registering or declaring of interests referred to it by the Commissioner; and

   (c) to consider any matter relating to the conduct of Members including specific complaints in relation to alleged breaches in any code of conduct to which the House has agreed and which have been drawn to the committee's attention by the Commissioner; and to recommend any modifications to such code of conduct as may from time to time appear to be necessary.

(2) The committee shall consist of 11 Members, of whom five shall be a quorum.

(3) Unless the House otherwise orders, each Member nominated to the committee shall continue to be a member of it for the remainder of the Parliament.

(4) The committee shall have power to appoint sub-committees consisting of no more than seven Members, of whom three shall be a quorum, and to refer to such sub-committees any of the matters referred to the committee; and shall appoint one such sub-committee to receive reports from the Commissioner relating to investigations into specific complaints.

(5) The committee and any sub-committee shall have power to send for persons, papers and records, to sit notwithstanding any adjournment of the House, to adjourn from place to place, to report from time to time and to appoint specialist advisers either to supply information

---

37 Munro, *op cit*, p 216.
38 First Special Report, HC 34 (1996–97), para 6.
39 M Rush, 'The law relating to Member's conduct', in D Oliver and G Drewry, *The Law and Parliament* (1998), p 116.

which is not readily available or to elucidate matters of complexity within the committee's order of reference.

(6) The committee shall have power to order the attendance of any Member before the committee or any sub-committee and to require that specific documents or records in the possession of a Member relating to its inquiries, or to the inquiries of a sub-committee or of the Commissioner, be laid before the committee or any sub-committee.

(7) The committee shall have power to refuse to allow proceedings to which strangers are admitted to be broadcast.

(8) Mr Attorney General, the Lord Advocate, Mr Solicitor General and Mr Solicitor General for Scotland, being Members of the House, may attend the committee or any sub-committee, may take part in deliberations, may receive committee or sub-committee papers and may give such other assistance to the committee or sub-committee as may be appropriate, but shall not vote or make any motion or move any amendment.

Standing Order (Parliamentary Commissioner for Standards)

(1) There shall be an officer of this House, called the Parliamentary Commissioner for Standards, who shall be appointed by the House.

(2) The principal duties of the Commissioner shall be:

(a) to maintain the Register of Members' Interests and any other registers of interest established by the House, and to make such arrangements for the compilation, maintenance and accessibility of those registers as are approved by the Committee on Standards and Privileges or an appropriate sub-committee thereof;

(b) to provide advice confidentially to Members and other persons or bodies subject to registration on matters relating to the registration of individual interests;

(c) to advise the Committee on Standards and Privileges, its sub-committees and individual Members on the interpretation of any code of conduct to which the House has agreed and on questions of propriety;

(d) to monitor the operation of such code and registers, and to make recommendations thereon to the Committee on Standards and Privileges or an appropriate sub-committee thereof; and

(e) to receive and, if he thinks fit, investigate specific complaints from Members and from members of the public in respect of:

(i) the registration or declaration of interests, or

(ii) other aspects of the propriety of a Member's conduct,

and to report to the Committee on Standards and Privileges or to an appropriate sub-committee thereof.

(3) The Commissioner may be dismissed by resolution of the House.

Guide to Rules relating to the Conduct of Members (extract)

4 Procedure for Complaints

66. Complaints, whether from Members or from members of the public, alleging that the conduct of a Member is incompatible with the Code of Conduct or with this Guide, should be addressed in writing to the Parliamentary Commissioner for Standards.

67. Both the Commissioner and the Committee on Standards and Privileges will be guided by the view of the former Select Committee on Members' Interests that 'it is not sufficient to make an unsubstantiated allegation and expect the Committee to assemble the supporting evidence', and that it 'would not normally regard a complaint founded upon no more than a newspaper story or

television report as a substantiated allegation'.[22] The Commissioner will not entertain anonymous complaints.

68. Communications between a member of the public and the Commissioner are not covered by Parliamentary privilege nor privileged at law unless and until the Commissioner decides the case has some substance to merit further inquiry. If he decides to the contrary, he may at his discretion reject the complaint without further reference to the Committee. The receipt of a complaint by the Commissioner is not to be interpreted as an indication that a *prima facie* case has been established.

69. If the Commissioner is satisfied that sufficient evidence has been tendered in support of the complaint to justify his taking the matter further, he will ask the Member to respond to the complaint and will then conduct a preliminary investigation. If he decides, after some inquiry, that there is no *prima facie* case, he will report that conclusion briefly to the Select Committee. If he finds that there is a *prima facie* case or that the complaint raises issues of wider importance, he will report the facts and his conclusions to the Committee.

70. The Committee on Standards and Privileges will consider any matter relating to the conduct of Members, including specific complaints in relation to alleged breaches of the Code of Conduct or Guide to which the House has agreed and which have been drawn to the Committee's attention by the Commissioner.

71. The Committee has power under its Standing Order to send for persons, papers and records; to order the attendance of any Member before it; and to require that specific documents in the possession of a Member relating to its inquiries or to the inquiries of the Commissioner be laid before it.

72. While it is the practice of the Committee to deliberate in private, the Committee determines for itself whether sessions at which evidence is to be taken shall be held publicly or in private, and is empowered to refuse leave for the broadcasting of any public sessions.

73. On specific complaints for which the Commissioner has decided there is a *prima facie* case, the Committee will make recommendations to the House on whether further action is required. It may also report to the House on other complaints if it thinks fit.

Notes

1   It is important to note the unique powers enjoyed by the Committee, those over and above those enjoyed by Parliament's other Select Committees. The Committee may order the attendance of Members and require papers to be laid before it. In contrast, other Select Committees may force the attendance of a Member before it only though obtaining a Resolution of the House as a whole.

2   For a detailed explanation of the procedure followed by the Commissioner, see the Ninth Report of the Select Committee on Standards and Privileges, HC 403 (1999–2000), Appendix.

The efficacy of the new procedures[40]

It was presumed when the new procedures were set up that the Committee would be reluctant to overturn findings made by the Commissioner, particularly where doing so would lay it open to charges of party political bias. While the Committee does not often overturn such findings, it has done so in a number of cases[41] and in some cases, where

---

40   For a recent survey of the Commissioner's work, see Doig (2001), *op cit*, at 360–75.

41   Some recent examples were the rejection by the Committee of the Commissioner's findings on Roy Beggs (Third Report, HC 320 (2000–01)) and on John Maxton (Second Report, HC 319 (2000–01)).

the Commissioner reported that she had been unable to obtain satisfactory co-operation from the Member in question, has reacted simply by admonishing the Member, but dropping the complaint. An example occurred when, after the 1997 election, the Labour-dominated Committee was investigating complaints against Labour Members, including Labour ministers in some cases.[42] One of the most important cases was the report on Dr John Reid, a senior Labour Minister, and Mr John Maxton.[43]

It may be noted that the Commissioner has no powers to send for persons or papers. She also has, of course, no power to compel Members to answer questions, and indeed such powers, where the answers could incriminate the Member, might be breach of Article 6 of the European Convention on Human Rights (ECHR).[44] This situation raised the question as to whether the Commissioner has sufficient powers to investigate cases involving recalcitrant 'suspects' satisfactorily. The most notorious case in which this issue was raised was the investigation into a total of 18 complaints against Keith Vaz,[45] then Minister for Europe in the Labour government. The case was a complex one and the outcome problematic. As the Committee commented:

> In this case, uniquely, the Commissioner has been unable to complete her investigations because some witnesses have refused to provide her with the information she needed. We have therefore had to take evidence, not to assist us in considering the Commissioner's conclusions, but to enable us to reach conclusions at all on a number of outstanding complaints.[46]

The outcome was somewhat unsatisfactory: in three of the eight cases, the Commissioner was unable to complete her inquiries because of lack of co-operation from the parties, in some cases, including Mr Vaz or his supporters in the Labour Party. The Committee found:

> Mr Colin Hall, Chairman of the Leicester East CLP [Constituency Labour Party], threatened a witness with possible disciplinary and legal action because of allegations the witness had made to the Commissioner. The Committee found itself unable to uphold the complaint. We took the view that in putting improper pressure on a witness Mr Hall had committed a serious contempt, and asked him to appear before us to explain his actions. Mr Hall apologised unreservedly for any contempt that had been committed and undertook not to commit any further such actions in the future. Intimidation that comes to our attention will be dealt with severely.[47] Both Councillor John Thomas and Councillor Piara Singh Clair, officers of the CLP, refused to provide the Commissioner with information that she needed. We experienced delay in getting information from Councillor Singh Clair, and he declined our invitation to appear before us. **We conclude that the consistently unhelpful attitude displayed by officers of the CLP was intended to frustrate the Commissioner's investigation.**[48]

The Committee concluded that such intimidation was a serious contempt and promised to deal with future examples 'severely'. However, it may be thought that merely requiring an apology from the culprit (Mr Hall in this case) is hardly 'severe' punishment.

One of the complaints in relation to which there was arguably an unsatisfactory resolution related to an allegation that Mr Vaz was provided by a businessman with

---

42   See, eg, the report of the Committee on Keith Vaz, Third Report HC 314-I (2000–01).
43   Second Report, HC 89 (2000–01).
44   See further Part VI Chapter 4, pp 1044–47 and 886–89.
45   Third Report, HC 314 (2000–01).
46   *Ibid*, para 4.
47   *Ibid*, paras 68 and 69.
48   *Ibid*, para 70.

cheques prior to 1997.[49] The Commissioner said that she was unable to complete her enquiries satisfactorily in relation to the complaint (para 40), due to what appears to have been a pattern of deliberate obstruction by Mr Vaz and of his local constituency Labour Party. This was then repeated in a further investigation into Mr Vaz,[50] in which the Commissioner found that his refusal to answer questions satisfactorily relating to his financial interests with Mapesbury Communications Limited meant that she could not complete her enquiry. The Committee was forced to find the complaint not upheld (para 20). The same outcome resulted from a complaint that Mr Vaz had employed an illegal immigrant and had held her passport (paras 28–30).

The Committee was concerned at the attitude of Mr Vaz to the Commissioner, in particular his eventual refusal to answer further questions from her:

> In her memorandum the Commissioner drew attention to 'the failure on the part of Mr Vaz to provide full and accurate answers to certain of [her] questions (in some cases, throughout the inquiry, in others until evidence was produced from other sources)', and she said she had found it necessary, even where she had not upheld a complaint, to express some criticism of Mr Vaz's approach to her inquiry.

> Mr Vaz was wrong to say to the Commissioner last December that he was not prepared to answer further questions from her. All Members have a duty to co-operate with the Commissioner and to assist her with her inquiries. We consider that in this respect Mr Vaz's behaviour was not in accordance with his duty of accountability under the Code of Conduct.[51]

It may be noted that, in response to this apparently deliberate attempt by Mr Vaz to obstruct the work of the Commissioner, the Committee did no more than issue a rebuke. In the wake of this report, there were sustained calls for Mr Vaz's resignation as a minister, both from the Conservative Opposition and the press. No resignation was forthcoming. To many, the outcome of the case shook the belief in the independence of the Committee from party interest, and its determination to impose sanctions likely to deter future obstruction of the Commissioner. There were then a fresh series of complaints against Mr Vaz:

Fifth Report, HC 605-I (2001–02)

40. The Commissioner concluded that—

(i) by providing inaccurate information which he had not sought to correct,

(ii) by avoiding answering questions fully, and

(iii) by giving the Commissioner inaccurate information about complainants and witnesses,

Mr Vaz had seriously misled and sought to obstruct the Committee and her.

. . .

47. We should record that, while the current investigation was under way Mr Vaz suffered two periods of illness, fought a general election, resigned from his Ministerial position, and was subjected to stress as a result of media speculation. He clearly feels both that the investigation process is unfair and that his relationship with the Commissioner has broken down.

48. Whether or not Mr Vaz thought the process was fair, he had a responsibility to co-operate. Mr Vaz has failed to answer questions fully, directly, clearly and promptly.

---

49 For full details see the Third Report, HC 314 (2000–01), paras 40–47.
50 Fifth Report, HC 605-I (2001–02).
51 Third Report, HC 314 (2000–01), paras 65–66.

49. Mr Vaz's failure to co-operate is made more serious by the failings on his part which were identified by the last Committee following the investigation of numerous complaints against him less than a year ago.

50. In his response to the investigation of the complaints against him since February 2000 Mr Vaz failed in his duty of accountability under the Code of Conduct by refusing to submit himself to the scrutiny appropriate to his office as a Member.

[The Committee then considered a complaint that Mr Vaz had attempted to discredit one of those who had made a complaint against him, Miss Eggington, by wrongfully accusing her of harassing his mother.]

69. We conclude that Mr Vaz recklessly made a damaging allegation against Miss Eggington to the Commissioner, which was not true, and which could have intimidated Miss Eggington or undermined her credibility. Miss Eggington and Mrs Gresty were interviewed by the police as a direct result of his intervention. Having set the Commissioner on a false line of inquiry Mr Vaz then accused her of interfering in a criminal investigation and threatened to report her to the Speaker.

71. Mr Vaz failed in his public duty under the Code of Conduct 'to act on all occasions in accordance with the public trust placed in [him]'. By wrongfully interfering with the House's investigative process he also committed a contempt of the House.

Conclusion

72. Of the original eleven allegations made against Mr Vaz we have upheld three, two of which we do not regard as serious. If that had been all, we would have recommended an apology to the House. Regrettably two further matters have arisen from the way Mr Vaz responded to the allegations against him investigated by the Commissioner. We have found that Mr Vaz committed serious breaches of the Code of Conduct and a contempt of the House.

73. **We recommend that Mr Vaz be suspended from the service of the House for one month.**

Notes

1   By the time this punishment was imposed, Mr Vaz was no longer a minister. The perception thereby created that the Committee was prepared to impose a more severe punishment once the member concerned was no longer a minister hardly helped the reputation of the Committee for impartiality. Such a perception might be unfair, however: the matters of which Mr Vaz was found guilty on this occasion, particularly the allegation of intimidation, were arguably more serious.

2   As noted above, there have been a number of cases in which adverse findings by the Commissioner have not been upheld by the Committee. Oliver noted, that in the May 1995 debate on Nolan, 'some hostility [was shown by Members] directed mainly to concern that the House's 'sovereignty' might be undermined if independent outsiders were involved in policing conduct';[52] which suggested that at least some Members may be minded to view the work and findings of the Commissioner with a sceptical eye.

3   This fear was to a certain extent borne out by the whispering campaign directed against the reappointment of Elizabeth Filkin, the Commissioner in June–July 2001, by certain Labour MPs. This culminated in a decision by the House of Commons to force the Commissioner, Ms Filkin, to reapply for her job when the initial term of three years expired. As one commentator noted, whilst Ms Filkin's job description

stated that the post was for three years 'initially', forcing her to reapply after that term was 'hardly usual. Ms Filkin's predecessor, Gordon Downey, was positively urged to stay on for a second term, but declined to do so. Within the Nolan rubric, most public jobs of this kind carry an implicit bias in favour of a second term, unless there's a powerful reason, or inadequacy of age (Filkin is 61. Downey was 70) against it.'[53] Whilst various pretexts for the hostility shown towards her were given,[54] as Young notes: 'Not a single complaint has been made about the talents she brought to [her job]. No one has charged her with political partiality. Her diligence is beyond reproach. Her forensic intellect is tireless. Several MPs, like Tony Baldry, have commended her fairness even as she was finding fault.'[55] The real reason therefore appeared to be a perception in some quarters that the Commissioner had been overzealous in investigating complaints against MPs: that she had been *too* independent an enforcer. Perhaps for the same reason, when the post was readvertised in November 2001, it appeared that its importance was being downgraded. The post was advertised only as a part-time one, at three days a week (even though Ms Filkin had found it necessary to work full-time to discharge her duties properly) and at a reduced salary. Once again, suspicion was aroused that elements within the Commons quite simply wished to have a less rigorous investigator looking over their shoulder.[56]

4   As has been seen, the rationale adopted by Nolan for recommending disclosure of amounts earned demanded that the requirement to disclose be limited only to remuneration which the MP acquires as a result of being an MP. As is readily apparent, however, whether a particular source of remuneration is from an occupation unrelated to a member's activities is an issue which is open to debate – the Committee noted that 'there will be many cases which are difficult to classify'[57] – and following the vote on 6 November 1995 there were immediate signs that a number of MPs (mainly from the Conservative benches) were planning to exploit the ambiguity in the rules in order to avoid full disclosure; others hinted at open defiance.[58] Fears of recalcitrance were borne out when the new Register was first published on 7 May 1996 and between 30 and 40 MPs declared only some of their earnings. Principal amongst the refusenik MPs were Sir Edward Heath, who claimed that most of his earnings were related only to his previous post as Prime Minister, and David Mellor, who claimed that his earnings were also unrelated to his work as an MP. Since then, however, there has been a gradual acceptance of the need for full registration, with both main political parties finding allegations of 'sleaze' – often related to non-registration of interests – a useful weapon of political attack.

The fairness of investigations by the Committee on Standards and Privileges: compatibility with Article 6, ECHR

Concern has recently been mounting as to the compliance of the Committee with basic standards of procedural fairness. The 1967 Select Committee on Parliamentary Privilege recommended a number of procedural changes, which were not enacted.

---

53   H Young, 'A brilliant public servant is being hounded from office', *The Guardian* 3 July 2001.
54   See Leader, *The Guardian*, 3 July 2001.
55   Young, *op cit*.
56   See 'MPs downgrade sleaze watchdog', *The Guardian*, 12 November 2001.
57   *Op cit*, para 42.
58   See 'Commons vote to disclose earnings', *The Guardian*, 7 November 1995.

More recently, the Committee itself recommended an appeals procedure, to be available where a member wished to appeal against a finding of the Commissioner.[59] The Joint Committee on Parliamentary Privilege also recognised serious problems with the Committee and called for change (see the extract below). It drew attention to the fact that such criticisms have now taken on a legal dimension, with the incorporation into UK law of Article 6 of the ECHR,[60] noted above. In particular, the following case, which concerned the Maltese House of Representatives, has raised concerns as to the compatibility of the system for disciplining MPs with Article 6. In *Demicoli v Malta* (1992) 14 EHRR 47, the editor of a political satirical magazine criticised the parliamentary behaviour of two members of the House. He was found guilty of contempt by the House. The two members whose conduct was criticised, and who had raised the breach of privilege claim in the House, participated throughout in the contempt proceedings of the House. Mr Demicoli was convicted under s 11 of the Ordinance concerning the privileges of the House of Representatives which provided as follows:

> The House shall have the power to punish with a reprimand or with imprisonment for a period not exceeding sixty days or with a fine ... any person, whether a Member of the House or not, guilty of any of the following acts:
>
> ...(k)   the publication of any defamatory libel on the Speaker or any Member touching anything done or said by him as Speaker or as a Member in the House or in a Committee thereof.

Demicoli v Malta (1992) 14 EHRR 47 (extracts)

30. The Government submitted that in Maltese law the breach of privilege proceedings taken against the applicant for defamatory libel were not 'criminal' but disciplinary in character. This view, contested by the applicant, was not supported by the Commission. It considered that the proceedings in question involved the determination of a 'criminal charge' and that Article 6 para 1 (Art 6-1) was therefore applicable.

31 ... In order to determine whether the breach of privilege of which Mr Demicoli was found guilty is to be regarded as 'criminal' within the meaning of Article 6 (Art 6), the Court will apply the three criteria which were first laid down in the *Engel and Others* judgment of 8 June 1976 (Series A no 22, pp 34–35, para 82) and have been consistently applied in the Court's subsequent case-law ...

32. It must first be ascertained whether the provisions defining the offence in issue belong, according to the legal system of the respondent State, to criminal law, disciplinary law or both concurrently. [This was found to be unclear and the Court went on ...]

33. However, as already noted above, the indication afforded by national law is not decisive for the purpose of Article 6. A factor of greater importance is 'the very nature of the offence' in question. Mr Demicoli was not a Member of the House. In the Court's view, the proceedings taken against him in the present case for an act of this sort done outside the House are to be distinguished from other types of breach of privilege proceedings, which may be said to be disciplinary in nature in that they relate to the internal regulation and orderly functioning of the House. Section 11(1)(k)

---

59   Twenty-first Report of the Committee on Standards and Privileges, Appeal Procedures, HC 1191 (1997–98).
60   Article 6(1), so far as relevant, provides: 'In the determination of his civil rights and obligations, or of any criminal charge against him, everyone is entitled to a fair and public hearing ... by an independent and impartial tribunal established by law ...'

potentially affects the whole population since it applies whether the alleged offender is a Member of the House or not and irrespective of where in Malta the publication of the defamatory libel takes place. For the offence thereby defined the Ordinance provides for the imposition of a penal sanction and not a civil claim for damages. From this point of view, therefore, the particular breach of privilege in question is akin to a criminal offence under the Press Act 1974

34. The third criterion is the degree of severity of the penalty that the person concerned risks incurring. The Court notes that in the present case, whilst the House imposed a fine of 250 Maltese liri on the applicant which has not yet been paid or enforced, the maximum penalty he risked was imprisonment for a period not exceeding sixty days or a fine not exceeding 500 Maltese liri or both. What was at stake was thus sufficiently important to warrant classifying the offence with which the applicant was charged as a criminal one under the Convention

35. In conclusion, Article 6 applied in the present case.

36. The applicant submitted that in the proceedings before the House of Representatives he did not receive a fair hearing by an independent and impartial tribunal. The political context in which the proceedings against him were conducted 'made a mockery of the whole concept of the independence and the impartiality of the judiciary'. This, he claimed, was evident from statements made by Members of the House in relation to his case in the official record of the parliamentary sittings ... He maintained that in breach of privilege proceedings Members of Parliament sit as victims, accusers, witnesses and judges. In his case it was the privilege of the individual Members concerned that was in issue and not, as the Government suggested, that of the whole House. Even if the Government's view on this point were accepted, that would mean, in his view, that 'each and every Member of the House of Representatives is a *judex in causa sua*'.

37. The Government argued that the House of Representatives was 'an independent and impartial tribunal established by law' for the purpose of hearing the disciplinary charge against Mr Demicoli. The Maltese House of Representatives was an independent authority 'par excellence'. The House was independent of the executive and of the parties, its Members were elected for a term of five years and its proceedings afforded the necessary guarantees. Accordingly it fulfilled all the requirements of a tribunal set out in the *Ringeisen* judgment of 16 July 1971 (Series A no 13, p 39, para 95). The independence of the House was sufficient to exclude any legitimate doubt as to its impartiality. Moreover, the Members directly satirised by the article intervened to defend the dignity of the House and not just their own reputations ...

39. The Court ... notes that the power of the Maltese Parliament to impose disciplinary measures and to govern its own internal affairs is not in issue. Moreover, the Court's task is not to review the relevant law and practice *in abstracto*, but to determine whether the manner in which the proceedings against Mr Demicoli were conducted gave rise to a violation of Article 6 para 1 (Art 6-1).

According to its case-law, 'a 'tribunal' is characterised in the substantive sense of the term by its judicial function, that is to say determining matters within its competence on the basis of rules of law and after proceedings conducted in a prescribed manner ... It must also satisfy a series of further requirements – independence, in particular of the executive; impartiality; duration of its members' terms of office; guarantees afforded by its procedure – several of which appear in the text of Article 6 para 1 (Art 6-1) itself.

40. In the circumstances of the present case the House of Representatives undoubtedly exercised a judicial function in determining the applicant's guilt. The central issue raised in this case is whether the requirement of impartiality was duly respected. For the purposes of Article 6 para 1 (Art 6-1) this must be determined according to a subjective test, that is on the basis of the personal conviction or interest of a particular judge in a given case, and according to an objective test, namely ascertaining whether the judge offered guarantees sufficient to exclude any legitimate doubt in this respect. In this context even appearances may be of a certain importance, particularly as far as criminal proceedings are concerned.

41. The two Members of the House whose behaviour in Parliament was criticised in the impugned article and who raised the breach of privilege in the House (see paragraph 11 above) participated throughout in the proceedings against the accused, including the finding of guilt and (except for one of them who had meanwhile died) the sentencing. Already for this reason, the impartiality of the adjudicating body in these proceedings would appear to be open to doubt and the applicant's fears in this connection were justified.

42. Accordingly, there has been a breach of Article 6 para 1.

Notes

1 It should be noted that the Court deliberately distinguished the proceedings taken against Mr Demicoli in the case which related to 'an act ... done outside the House' from 'other types of breach of privilege proceedings, which may be said to be disciplinary in nature in that they relate to the internal regulation and orderly functioning of the House'. This implies that the latter may be regarded as not falling within Article 6 of the Convention. It is clear also that the finding of a breach of Article 6 rested primarily upon the simple and obvious problem that the two MPs criticised participated in the proceedings against the editor. The ruling was not based upon the fact that they were politicians *per se*. The direct applicability of this ruling is therefore clearly quite limited. However, the Joint Committee on Parliamentary Privilege considered that the judgment, amongst other considerations, impelled some reform to the way in which the Committee operated.

2 There are two main concerns with the Committee: one is the lack of procedural safeguards; the other is the potential problem of bias or perceived bias.

Joint Committee on Parliamentary Privilege, HLP 43–41 (1998–99) (extracts)

280. Contempt is a serious matter. A finding of contempt of either House against a member may have adverse consequences of a high order, particularly when it relates to the member's personal conduct ... in a particularly serious case a member of the House of Commons faces the prospect of suspension and significant financial loss and, which may be more worrying for him, the destruction of his political career. Even when a member is not suspended, the electorate may react adversely to his conduct as revealed during investigation of a complaint made against him. It is important, therefore, that the procedures followed in the investigation and adjudication of complaints should match contemporary standards of fairness.

281. While fairness is fundamental to any disciplinary procedure, the more serious the consequences, the more extensive must be the safeguards if the procedure is to be fair. Some allegations of contempt are more serious than others. In dealing with specially serious cases, we consider it is essential that committees of both Houses should follow procedures providing safeguards at least as rigorous as those applied in the courts and professional disciplinary bodies. At this level the minimum requirements of fairness are for the member who is accused to be given:

  – a prompt and clear statement of the precise allegations against the member;

  – adequate opportunity to take legal advice and have legal assistance throughout;

  – the opportunity to be heard in person;

  – the opportunity to call relevant witnesses at the appropriate time;

  – the opportunity to examine other witnesses;

  – the opportunity to attend meetings at which evidence is given, and to receive transcripts of evidence.

In determining a member's guilt or innocence, the criterion applied at all stages should be at least that the allegation is proved on the balance of probabilities. In the case of more serious charges, a higher standard of proof may be appropriate . . .

283. Further, any person who has a personal interest in the matter under investigation, including a person who made the complaint, should be disqualified from participating in relevant proceedings of the committee or the House, other than as a witness. Again, this is elementary fairness, because those accused are entitled to a hearing by an impartial tribunal: no one should be judge in his own cause. This is also in accordance with the European Convention of Human Rights [the Committee cited the *Demicoli v Malta* case (above)] . . . In that case the person charged with contempt was a non-member, but it would be unwise to assume the requirements of fairness would be significantly less for members.

284. Although proceedings in Parliament are excluded from the Human Rights Act 1998 and from the jurisdiction of United Kingdom courts,[61] they may nevertheless be within the jurisdiction of the European Court of Human Rights. The existence of this jurisdiction is a salutary reminder that, if the procedures adopted by Parliament when exercising its disciplinary powers are not fair, the proceedings may be challenged by those prejudiced . . .

Notes

1   As suggested above, the Committee might be considered to determine what are essentially criminal charges matters by its decisions (see the *Demicoli* case, above). As the Joint Committee on Parliamentary Privilege pointed, out, it does not, at present, follow what would generally be regarded as the basics of fair procedure. The more significant point, perhaps, and one not addressed by the *Demicoli* case, is that since it is a body made up of party politicians, and its decisions have in the past clearly been influenced by party political considerations, it may not be regarded as 'an independent and impartial tribunal' as Article 6 requires. While it could be argued that the Committee does not itself 'determine' any criminal charge, since it merely makes recommendations and it is the Commons which makes the final decision on any action to be taken against a Member, this merely moves the problem up the line, as all the objections which could be levelled at the Committee as a decision-making body apply equally, if not *a fortiori*, to the Commons.

2   The Wicks Report returned to this problem in 2002, in which it made a series of recommendations designed, broadly, to strengthen the current, self-regulatory system. It found that the Committee's procedures conformed to four out of six of the recommendations of the Joint Committee on Parliamentary Privilege on the minimum requirements of fairness, noted above – the two not complied with were the ability to call witnesses and cross-examine witnesses. In order to deal with this problem, the Wicks Report suggested as follows:

6.25 **We recommend**, therefore, that the House should have available the option of an Investigatory Panel for serious, contested cases. In such cases, which could be rare, the Panel would be a forum in which witnesses can be called and examined by both the accused Member as well as by the Panel itself. This would provide the Committee with a body better suited than itself to conduct hearings on the most serious and contested cases whilst ensuring fairness to the individual Member.[62]

---

61   This is because the Human Rights Act 1998 binds only 'public authorities' with the duty to act compatibly with the Convention rights and the definition of 'public authority' in s 6 specifically excludes 'either House of Parliament or a person exercising functions in connection with proceedings in Parliament' (s 6(3)).

62   The Committee went on to note that in its Sixth Report it had 'recommended that there should be a disciplinary tribunal to deal with serious, contested cases [but] the House did not accept this recommendation'.

6.27 We ... propose [however] that the Committee should retain the final power to decide whether the facts as found by the Panel amount to a breach of the Code, even if the Panel itself has reached the conclusion that a breach has occurred. We have reached the view that the centrality of the Committee's role in the self-regulatory process makes it vital that the Committee be the final arbiter before the matter is put before the full House of Commons.

6.28 The main elements of the Investigatory Panel as recommend it are set out below.

The Panel would be involved only in cases where the facts are disputed by the MP, and which carry the potential, if proved, of a serious penalty. The Committee would have the final decision on whether a case should be referred to the Panel. The criteria would be that proof of the complaint would be likely to lead to the imposition of a serious penalty on the Member and that there appeared to be significant contested issues of fact which could not properly be decided [by the Committee]

The Panel should be chaired by a lawyer of substantial seniority who is not a Member of the House ...

The remaining membership of the Panel should be two MPs ... [of] substantial seniority, [and] be drawn from different parties.

The Panel should call and examine witnesses, including the accused MP. As a measure of fairness, the accused MP would have the right to call and question witnesses before the Panel and the right to receive financial assistance to enable him or her to fund legal representation at the hearings of the Panel.

The Panel would produce a report to the Committee on Standards and Privileges on the same basis as the Commissioner. That is, a report of the facts that it has identified, and its own conclusion on whether the Code has been breached (Cm 5663 (2002)).

Note
This recommendation, designed to introduce an independent element into the regulatory process, and to ensure that cross-examination and calling of witnesses would be available where required, thus made the most modest of inroads into the principle of self-regulation, since it left the parliamentary Committee free not to accept the panel's findings. Nevertheless, it was too much for the Committee to accept.

Eighth Report of the Committee on Standards and Privileges, HC 403 (2002–03)

29. We have given very careful consideration to this recommendation. We recognise the force of the arguments that have led the Wicks Committee to make it, but consider that it poses a fundamental difficulty. It would mean that the Commissioner, who in all other cases has the prime responsibility for establishing the facts, and expressing an opinion on whether these point to a breach of the Code, would have no responsibility for the final investigative stages of the most serious cases and no opportunity to express an opinion on whether these point to a breach of the Code.

30. We do not believe that the recommendation will advance the Wicks Committee's aim of providing 'a clear framework within which the Commissioner can discharge [his] functions with authority, working with the Committee on Standards and Privileges within the overall process of upholding and maintaining high ethical standards'.

[The Committee then went on to propose its own preferred mechanism.]

37. We have therefore considered a further option, under which the responsibility for establishing the facts in such cases would remain with the Commissioner, assisted by a legally-qualified assessor of seniority and standing, who might be a retired judge, and a senior Member of the House.

38. In such cases, the Commissioner would prepare his report on the facts as at present unless, having first sought all available avenues for resolving factual disagreements with the Member, areas

remained in dispute. In that eventuality, the Commissioner would invoke the procedure set out below if he was satisfied that the case met both the prescribed tests, and would report to the Committee that he was doing so. The present practice of the Commissioner of sharing his factual analysis with the Member before coming to a view as to whether the complaint was substantiated would continue and it would be open to the Member, at this stage, to inform the Commissioner that he disputed some of the facts, to identify these and to request that the same procedure was invoked. If the Commissioner did not agree that the case merited referral, the matter could be referred to the Committee for decision. It would also be open to the Committee to invoke the procedure if it considered that the prescribed tests were met, whether or not the Commissioner or the Member under investigation had sought this course of action.

39. For the purpose of resolving the factual disputes, we propose a panel of the Commissioner with two assessors, who would advise the Commissioner but have no responsibility for the findings. One would be a legal assessor, who would advise the Commissioner on legal matters, and the other would be a senior Member of the House, who would advise on parliamentary matters. The legal assessor would report to the Committee that he was satisfied that the Commissioner had followed proper procedures. The assessor Member would also have the right to report to the Committee.

40. The Member under investigation could be heard in person; would have the opportunity to call relevant witnesses; and to examine other witnesses. That Member would be entitled to legal advice and help as at present, and to be present throughout the taking of evidence, of which a verbatim record would be taken.

41. At the conclusion of the proceedings, the Commissioner would prepare a report (or further report) setting out the facts of the case as now established and expressing an opinion on whether the Code had been breached. The Member would have the option to be heard by the Committee, but only in the most exceptional circumstances would new evidence be permitted. The Committee would then come to a decision, based on the facts as revealed in the Commissioner's report or reports, on whether the Code had been breached, and recommend any penalty to the House. The Commissioner's reports, together with all the evidence taken, would be appended to the Committee's report to the House, together with the report of the legal assessor and any report of the assessor Member.

42. We prefer this option because the determination of the facts remains with the Commissioner, as in all other cases. It would strengthen the role of the Commissioner, in the current arrangement, as the independent investigator of the facts. We believe that this procedure would meet the Joint Committee on Parliamentary Privilege's six minimum requirements for fairness in handling serious cases. It would also mean that all members of the Committee could be involved in the crucial judgement of whether the facts as revealed in the Commissioner's report pointed to a breach of the Code of Conduct by the Member concerned.

The response of Lords Wicks to this alternative proposal was as follows:

You prefer a different approach—a panel comprising the Commissioner, assisted by a legally qualified assessor and a senior Member of the House. Such an approach would provide a further instrument to help the Commissioner, and indirectly therefore your Committee, to ascertain the facts of a case. It would also, we believe, meet the two tests of fairness and we welcome that.[63]

Notes

1   Despite this proposed introduction of at least some independent element, giving the possibility of greater procedural protection for Members, another problem remained: the fact that the political nature of the Committee prevents it from being considered an 'independent and impartial tribunal' under Article 6, and also leaves it open to charges of political partiality especially when investigating government

63   First Special Report, HC 516 (2002–03).

ministers. The Committee, like other Select Committees, is nominated in proportion to party strengths, thus normally giving it an in-built majority of Members belonging to the governing party. The Wicks Report found in evidence that:

7.4 [A] former member of the Committee on Standards and Privileges, Martin Bell had said, 'I think most of the members managed to leave their party allegiances behind, but some did not' ... Robert Kaye from the London School of Economics, who carried out a detailed study of the Committee on Standards and Privileges, thought it clear that 'The Committee has shown itself a lot more willing to overturn decisions of the Commissioner when they have been dealing with a Minister.'

...

7.7 Rightly or wrongly, such perceptions are damaging, and have contributed to an undermining of the Committee's credibility when it has disagreed with the conclusions of the Commissioner. Tony Wright MP illustrated this point when he said, 'the Standards and Privileges Committee I think has been revealed as having shortcomings too and certainly should have no role in relation to changing reports and recommendations from the Commissioner.'

2   However, Wicks found that the involvement of outside Members would not be accepted by Parliament. They therefore resolved to tackle directly the problem of the government majority on the Committee, noting the comments of Dawn Oliver:

'In the case of the House of Commons it will be essential that the Government does not have oversight of the self-regulatory process since this would enable it to capture the regulatory process, which it may wish to do when it is directed against people who are also ministers or government backbenchers' (para 7.13).

  ... Even if this is a matter of perception rather than practice, the fact that the Government has an overall majority on the Committee leaves the Committee particularly vulnerable to such a charge.

  7.16 ... We return to the fundamental point that the Committee on Standards and Privileges should be seen as one of the most important committees of the House, fulfilling a unique and highly valuable role in sustaining the reputation of the House. We believe that, to do so successfully, its position would be greatly strengthened by making clear the politically impartial nature of the Committee. We therefore **recommend** that no one party should hold an overall majority membership on the Committee.

  [It also recommended that a majority of the members on it should be of senior standing and the exclusion from the Committee of Parliamentary Private Secretaries (PPPs) – unpaid assistants to government ministers – the lowest level of government post.]

The Committee agreed with this finding, though it strongly rejected any notion that its current composition in fact led to any party feeling entering its deliberations or findings. However, it agreed that the perception of such possible bias required a change:

Although we would reject the assertion that our composition colours our decisions, we believe that our unique role as a quasi-judicial body, and the responsibility that we discharge equally on behalf of every Member of the House, would justify our composition being different if that improved Members' or public confidence in the regulatory process. We note that there are precedents in other legislatures that would support taking such a step: for example, the Standards Committees in both Houses of the US Congress are composed of equal numbers of Republican and Democrat members.[64]

---

64   HC Deb 516 (2002–03), para 57.

3   The Committee also agreed, reluctantly, to the exclusion of Parliamentary Private Secretaries (the lowest type of ministerial office), again on grounds of perception of possible bias. Wicks also proposed (para 7.29), and the Committee agreed[65] that the Committee should have the services of an independent legal adviser. The Committee also agreed to the proposal that no MP should seek to lobby the Committee on behalf of a friend or colleague that the Committee was advising and that the Committee should keep its deliberations confidential until it issued its report on a complaint, to avoid the possibility of pressure being brought to bear upon it.[66]

4   Finally, the Committee agreed to a series of measures designed to bolster the independence of the Commissioner. These included making it explicit in Standing Orders that the Commissioner was an office holder, not merely an employee of the Commons, and giving her security of tenure by a longer term (at least five years) with a non-renewable contract.[67] The Commissioner would also be given the same formal powers as the Committee, that is, to compel the attendance of members and the production of records (paras 79–82).

5   A point that none of the above reports seemed willing to seriously consider was the manifest drawbacks of the Commons as a final arbiter on questions of misconduct and breaches of privilege. On this, the Joint Committee on Parliamentary Privilege was defensive:

Joint Committee on Parliamentary Privilege, HLP 43–41 (1998–99) (extracts)

293. At present, a finding of contempt by a committee and any recommendation for punishment comes before the House for decision. This procedure has the attraction, from the parliamentary point of view, that a decision involving a penalty is always that of the whole House and not merely a committee. The House remains in control throughout. But this practice raises difficulties of procedural fairness.

294. The Joint Committee believes it would be wrong if the ultimate decision were no longer made by the whole House. We consider the least unsatisfactory way of achieving this is for each House to have power to endorse the report of the committee, or to depart from it by ordering a reduced penalty or no penalty at all. The House should have no power to increase the penalty above that recommended by the committee. This solution is imperfect and untidy, but no better course has been suggested or has occurred to us whereby a body, as large as the whole House and subject to partisan pressures, may continue to be involved in making decisions on the exercise of disciplinary powers in a particular case.

295. A decision by the whole House also provides the member with an opportunity to have the report of the standards and privileges committee reviewed by another body. The existence of this opportunity is in line with the general expectation today that persons found guilty of disciplinary offences should have some avenue of appeal: there should be some means, internal or external, enabling them to have the finding against them reviewed. Thus, professional organisations normally provide an internal appeal procedure. In some professions, such as the medical, dental and veterinary professions, disciplinary decisions can be appealed to the judicial committee of the Privy Council. While neither House, as a constituent body of a sovereign Parliament, can be equated with a professional organisation, members of the House who are being disciplined ought equally to be able to have recourse to an appeal procedure.

296. It was suggested to the Joint Committee that in cases where a person who was subject to parliamentary jurisdiction disputed a decision that his actions were a contempt, or claimed the

---

65   *Ibid*, para 71.
66   *Ibid*, paras 73 and 74.
67   *Ibid*, paras 76 and 77.

penalty was disproportionate, an appeal should be considered by the judicial committee of the Privy Council. The procedure would be similar in character to the review of disciplinary decisions by a professional body. The Joint Committee has considered whether some such right of appeal to the judicial committee or some other outside body is called for.

297. So far as disputed issues of fact are concerned, a right of appeal, as recommended by the standards and privileges committee of the House of Commons, would render unnecessary a further appeal on questions of fact in 'conduct' cases in that House. The position would be the same in 'privilege' cases (and cases in the House of Lords) if comparable procedures were introduced to deal with disputes of fact.

298. On all other matters calling for review, such as the procedures adopted and penalty imposed, we consider that the review by the House of the committee's report furnishes reasonable and adequate protection for a member. The member has an opportunity to address the House and raise any matter he wishes. Although the committee's decision is only a recommendation, and not itself a final decision, we believe that in substance a right to challenge this recommendation is equivalent to a right of appeal. Accordingly, none of the members of the committee should vote in the House, although the chairman and other members of the committee should be eligible to participate in the debate. Traditionally, such debates are well attended, and members do not divide on party lines. We see no reason to doubt that this tradition will be carefully respected.

299. In reaching our conclusion we have been influenced by the constitutional implications of a member having a right of appeal, even of a limited nature, from a decision of the House of Commons to a court of law or other tribunal. Such a right of appeal would detract from the sovereignty of Parliament over proceedings in Parliament, and accordingly it is intrinsically undesirable. Had we considered that fairness to a member called for such an innovation, we would have so recommended. Since fairness does not so require, we do not recommend that Parliament should embark upon such a course, inherent in which is a real prospect of conflict between the courts of law and Parliament.

Note

The problem, however, is that the Commons does not always follow the Committee's recommendations, nor is it bound by its previous decisions, drawbacks illustrated by the case of *GR Strauss*,[68] considered below at p 457. Whilst the Commons as a whole is not ideally suited to make the final decisions on matters of privilege, the Committee itself has been subject to criticisms as a forum for trying issues which, at least theoretically, could result in the imprisonment of those it finds to have been in breach of privilege or to have committed contempts. First, it is nominated in proportion to party strengths. It is, as de Smith notes,[69] unusual for it to divide along party lines, but it did so in the *WJ Brown* case,[70] in delivering a verdict which favoured the government MP concerned, and more recently, as described above, split dramatically over the Nolan Report. One could envisage such considerations intruding in the case of, for example, a senior government figure sued for libel; in determining whether the minister's publishing of the libel was covered by privilege, government MPs might well be more concerned with possible embarrassment to the government than with following expert recommendation. A similar issue could arise where the Committee determined a complaint of a breach of the rules governing Members' interests by a government minister: the complaint would be determined by a Committee with a majority (in some cases a large majority) of MPs of the same party as the minister. As noted above, this happened in relation to the cases against Keith Vaz, Dr John Reid,

---

68 See Report of the Committee of Privileges, HC 308 (1956–57).
69 *Op cit*, p 320.
70 HC 188 (1946–47).

and also Geoffrey Robinson, the former Paymaster General.[71] If the Committee reports are unanimous, this may be sufficient to rebut the suspicion of bias in observers' minds – though this may not satisfy the requirements of Article 6 of the ECHR. This problem – inherent in the system of self-regulation – would only be solved if the contempt jurisdiction were transferred altogether to another body, perhaps the ordinary courts, or the Judicial Committee of the Privy Council. However, as the attitude of the Joint Committee on Parliamentary Privilege towards giving the Privy Council any role in hearing appeals from decisions of the Commons on privilege indicates, this is an unlikely course of action.

2. It might be thought that changes to this unsatisfactory position could be forced on Parliament by an aggrieved MP taking action under the HRA for a declaration that proceedings of the CSP amounted to a breach of Art 6 of the ECHR, and possibly claiming damages; however, it is submitted that this is a remote prospect. Although it is true that in extreme cases, the sanctions recommended by the Committee could, through expulsion of a Member, lead to loss of his livelihood (making the consequences of an adverse judgment more grave than those of many a criminal conviction), nevertheless, Art 6 refers to 'the determination of [a citizen's] civil rights and obligations or ... any criminal charge against him', a wording which would not appear to be apt to cover the Committee's remit (as indicated above, the decision in the *Malta* case found that the determinations of Parliament in that case were covered chiefly because they affected the whole population, not just MPs). Furthermore, even if it *could* be argued that the Committee's activities were *prima facie* covered by Art 6, it appears that no action could be brought under the HRA, quite apart from the fact that one would expect a court to be minded to refuse jurisdiction in a matter affecting Parliament's regulation of its own affairs. This is because the Act: makes it 'unlawful for a *public authority* to act in a way which is incompatible with a Convention right' (s 6); provides that proceedings may be brought in respect of such an act (s 7); and provides that damages or other remedies may be awarded to the aggrieved claimant (s 8). However, s 6(3) specifically states that neither House of Parliament nor 'a person exercising functions in connection with proceedings in Parliament' count as 'public authorities' for the purposes of the Act. No action could therefore be brought against either the Committee or the House itself by an aggrieved Member. If the action were struck out, or simply lost, the claimant could of course still take his case to the European Court of Human Rights under the right of individual petition enshrined in Art 34 of the Convention, provided that all domestic avenues had been exhausted.

FREEDOM OF SPEECH

The general parameters of the privilege

In terms of creating conflict outside the political realm it is, not surprisingly, those privileges that, in their exercise, can affect the legal rights of those *outside* Parliament which have caused difficulties. Principal amongst these is freedom of speech. As Munro explains:

Colin Munro, *Studies in Constitutional Law*, 2nd edn (1999)

The privilege ... was effectively secured at the Revolution. Its inclusion in the Bill of Rights gave it a statutory foundation. Article 9 of the Bill of Rights proclaimed: 'That the freedom of speech, and debates or proceedings in Parliament ought not to be impeached or questioned in any court or place out of Parliament'. ...

Article 9 applies equally to both Houses, and its effect is that no action or prosecution can be brought against a Member for anything said or done in the course of proceedings in Parliament.

---

71   See First Report of the Committee, HC 297 (2001–02).

The most important application of this is that it invests members with an immunity from the law of defamation, when they are speaking in Parliament and on some other occasions. So, when an action for defamation was brought against a Member of the Commons for words spoken in the House, the court recognised that it had no jurisdiction in the matter, and ordered that the writ should be removed from the records [*Dillon v Balfour* (1887) 20 LR Ir 600]. In the same way, the courts would be unable to entertain prosecutions or actions of other kinds. In 1938, when Mr Duncan Sandys raised a matter of national security in a parliamentary question, and refused to reveal the sources of his information, a prosecution on an Official Secrets charge was threatened. The House asserted its privilege in order to avert the threat [HC 146 (1937–38), HC 173 (1937–38)]. In 1977, at a trial on Official Secrets Act charges, a judge had allowed a witness, an officer in the Security Services, to be identified only as 'Colonel B'. When some organs of the press referred to the officer by his real name, in disregard of the judge's wishes, proceedings for contempt of court were brought against them. However, four Members of the Commons, who named the officer during questions in the House, were, under the shelter of privilege, immune from such proceedings themselves. Article 9 also means that matters arising in the course of parliamentary proceedings cannot be relied on for the purpose of supporting an action or prosecution based on events occurring elsewhere. For example, the Church of Scientology, bringing a libel suit against an MP for remarks made in a television interview, was unable to refer to his speeches in the House of Commons in seeking to prove his malice [*Church of Scientology of California v Johnson-Smith* [1972] 1 QB 522; [1972] 1 All ER 378.]

Parliament's official reports and papers enjoy a corresponding privilege. Following *Stockdale v Hansard* [(1839) 9 Ad & El 1], the Parliamentary Papers Act 1840 was passed, which bars proceedings, criminal or civil, against persons for the publication of papers or reports printed by order of either House of Parliament, or copies of them ...

Notes

1   Whilst extracts from *Hansard* will be covered by s 3 of the Parliamentary Papers Act 1840, protection does not extend to headlines under which the extract appears (*Mangena v Lloyd* (1908) 99 LT 824).

2   A parliamentary sketch will be covered by qualified privilege if it is fair and accurate and published without malice (*Cook v Alexander* [1974] 1 QB 279).

Areas of uncertainty and controversy

Wason v Walter (1868) QB 73 confirmed that Article 9 of the Bill of Rights provides complete civil and criminal immunity for Members in respect of words spoken by them during proceedings in Parliament.[72] This is a remarkably wide privilege, considering the numerous constraints on freedom of expression of the rest of the population (see Part VI Chapter 2). Regrettably, however, as was evident from the above, the scope of the privilege is by no means clear. This is partly due to the fact that, as Munro noted, the phrase 'proceedings in Parliament' is of uncertain meaning. It is fairly clear, as the Joint Committee on Parliamentary Privilege remarked, that it covers:

... Debates (expressly mentioned in Article 9), motions, proceedings on bills, votes, parliamentary questions, proceedings within committees formally appointed by either House, proceedings within sub-committees of such committees, and public petitions, once presented, statements made and

---

72   Note, however, the interesting comment of Laws J on Article 9 (speaking extra-judicially): 'I am not myself convinced that if [an MP] were motivated by reasons of actual personal malice to use his position to defame, in the course of debate, an individual outside Parliament, he should not as a result be subject to the ordinary laws of defamation, and Article 9 could readily be construed comfortably with such a state of affairs' (J Laws, 'Law and democracy' [1995] PL 72, 76, note 14).

documents produced in the course of these proceedings, and notices of these proceedings ... internal House or committee papers of an official nature directly related to the proceedings, and communications arising directly out of such proceedings, as where a member seeks further information in the course of proceedings and another member agrees to provide it [as well as] ... the steps taken in carrying out an order of either House.[73]

The difficulty really arises over what may be counted as 'proceedings in Parliament'. Something is not a 'proceeding in Parliament' merely because it happens there. A defendant's defamatory statements about his former wife, put in letters to MPs, were not protected by reason of having been posted within the Palace of Westminster (*Rivlin v Bilankin* [1953] 1 All ER 534). Even a conversation between Members, if on private affairs, would probably not be privileged (HC 101 (1938–39)). Rather the phrase seems intended to cover what is the business of Parliament or its Members. The matter has been considered by the Commons, but decisions by the House on matters of privilege set no binding precedent. The London Electricity Board case in 1958 is one well-known example:

Mr George Strauss MP, in a letter written to a minister, described the Board's practices in selling scrap metal as 'a scandal which should be instantly rectified'. The letter was passed on to the Board, which threatened to sue Mr Strauss for libel. The House determined that the letter was not a 'proceeding in Parliament', although the Committee of Privileges had taken the opposite view [HC 305 (1956–57), HC 227 (1957–58), 591, HC *Official Report* (5th series), col 208]. However, it is difficult to infer much from this, for the vote was narrow and the decision is not binding on the House. It may too have been significant that the subject of the letter (being a matter of day-to-day administration of a nationalised industry) was not within ministerial answerability, and therefore could not have formed the basis of a parliamentary question. The Speaker ruled that if a Member tabled a question, and a minister invited him to discuss it with him, the correspondence or discussions were covered by privilege [591 HC *Official Report* (5th series), col 808].[74]

Subsequent events have suggested that the matter would now be differently decided. In 1967 the Select Committee on Parliamentary Privilege strongly recommended that legislation be enacted to reverse the Commons decision in *Strauss* (1970); the Joint Committee on Publication of Proceedings in Parliament proposed a definition of 'proceedings in Parliament', which *included* letters sent between MPs for the purpose of allowing them to carry out their duties. Their proposed definition was subsequently approved by the Faulks Committee on Defamation 1975, and the Committee of Privileges 1976–77. Further, in the *Strauss* case, the vote on whether the Electricity Board had committed a breach of privilege, which went against Strauss, an Opposition MP, divided substantially along party lines. This phenomenon was seen even more clearly in the Report of the Committee of Privileges on implementation of the Nolan Committee's recommendations: both the Committee and the House as a whole split on clearly defined party lines.[75] If the Commons is going to be influenced by party

---

73 *Op cit*, para 102.
74 Munro, *op cit*, p 222
75 As noted above, the issue which split the parties was the proposed disclosure of the *amount* of outside earnings. All of the Conservative Members on the Committee voted against the proposal, whilst all Opposition Members voted in favour. In the Commons vote on the issue, 33 Conservative MPs voted with the Opposition and a further 31 abstained or did not vote. The rest (around 220) followed the Prime Minister's lead and voted against the proposal. The Opposition was united behind support for the proposal. For the debate, see HC Deb cols 608–82 (6 November 1995); for the crucial divisions showing how the Committee and the House voted, see the Second Report from the Select Committee on Standards in Public Life, HC 816 (1994–95), pp xx–xxi and HC Deb cols 661–62, *op cit*, respectively.

political principles when making such determinations, this will clearly hinder any attempt to deduce a set of consistent principles from its decisions.

The problem of whether a particular speech or letter is covered by absolute privilege assumes a more pressing aspect when a litigant sues in defamation in respect of words which Parliament has deemed to be absolutely privileged, that is, immune from civil or criminal proceedings. When this happens, Parliament can regard the action as a contempt and attempt to prevent the litigant from exercising his legal right to sue and enforce the judgment of the court. As Munro points out:

> In the London Electricity Board case, it was taken for granted in parliamentary discussion that the commencement of proceedings in a court in respect of a 'proceeding in Parliament' was in itself a breach of privilege. That assumption may be criticised, and the assumption that a mere threat to institute proceedings amounts to a breach of privilege is even more doubtful. It may be noted too that the Select Committee on Parliamentary Privilege recommended in 1967 that, save in exceptional circumstances, such matters should be left to the ordinary processes of the courts [HC 34 (1967–68)]. But it is by no means certain that the House might not take a similar view again.[76]

The difficulty was illustrated in 1839 in the case of *Stockdale v Hansard* (1839) 9 Ad & El 1. Stockdale brought an action in respect of allegedly defamatory words in a report of prison inspectors published by Hansard, by order of the Commons. When the action was tried, the court decided that Hansard's reports were *not* covered by absolute privilege, so that Stockdale could proceed. Parliament, however, refused to accept this judgment and so an impasse developed (see below), which was finally resolved only when the Parliamentary Papers Act 1884 was passed. Alternatively, as in the *Church of Scientology* case mentioned above, the issue can arise where a defendant to a libel action wishes to defend the proceedings brought against him by referring to matters which have taken place in Parliament: in such a case it will be necessary to ascertain what amounts to 'proceedings in Parliament'. This issue arose in *Rost v Edwards* [1990] 2 WLR 1280, in which Popplewell J had 'no hesitation' in saying (*obiter*) that correspondence between Members was covered, but cited no authority, and indeed no argument of principle to support his view.

2 The issue of Member's correspondence was addressed in some detail by the Joint Committee.

Joint Committee on Parliamentary Privilege, HLP 43–41 (1998–99)

110. There is another consideration. Article 9 provides an altogether exceptional degree of protection ... In principle this exceptional protection should remain confined to the core activities of Parliament, unless a pressing need is shown for an extension. There is insufficient evidence of difficulty, at least at present, to justify so substantial an increase in the amount of parliamentary material protected by absolute privilege. Members are not in the position that, lacking the absolute immunity given by Article 9, they are bereft of all legal protection. In the ordinary course a member enjoys qualified privilege at law in respect of his constituency correspondence. In evidence the Lord Chief Justice of England, Lord Bingham of Cornhill, and the Lord President of the Court of Session, Lord Rodger of Earlsferry, both stressed the development of qualified privilege at law and the degree of protection it provides nowadays to those acting in an official capacity and without malice. So long as the member handles a complaint in an appropriate way, he is not at risk of being held liable for any defamatory statements in the correspondence ...

---

76   C Munro, *Studies in Constitutional Law*, 1987, p 140.

112. Constituency correspondence has burgeoned over the last 30 years, but since *Strauss* there have been remarkably few, if any, instances of defamation actions against members who were acting on behalf of their constituents. We recommend that the absolute privilege accorded by Article 9 to proceedings in Parliament should not be extended to include communications between members and ministers.

Notes

1 It is interesting that, at this point, the Joint Committee applied a very rigorous test for what would, admittedly have been, a probable extension of the scope of parliamentary privilege: was there a 'pressing need' for such extension? – a test almost on all fours with the 'pressing social need' test used in the European Convention on Human Rights to justify restrictions on certain Convention rights (see further Part II Chapter 2). In other places, particularly with regard to the Joint Committee's findings on the need to continue the embargo on any form of questioning of the propriety of proceedings in Parliament, it is arguable that the Joint Committee was far more readily satisfied of the need to maintain what many have seen as an unjustifiable aspect of privilege.

2 As Munro remarks:

When Members of Parliament are not clothed by parliamentary privilege, they may benefit from some other privilege or defence. For example, under the Parliamentary Commissioner Act 1967, communications between MPs and the Parliamentary Commissioner for Administration are protected by absolute privilege (which is a defence to actions for defamation). Actions by Members in pursuit of their parliamentary duties would seem generally to be protected by qualified privilege, which is a defence in the law of defamation unless lost by proof of malice. In *Beach v Freeson* [[1971] 2 All ER 854], an MP's letters to the Lord Chancellor and to the Law Society, reporting complaints about a solicitors' firm in his constituency, were held to be so protected ... By statute, a similar defence applies to the publication of extracts from, or abstracts of, parliamentary papers, and by common law to the fair and accurate reporting of parliamentary proceedings [Parliamentary Papers Act 1840, s 3; Defamation Act 1952, s 9; *Wason v Walter* (1868) LR 4 QB 73].[77]

3 A part of the judgment in *Rost* which was later to become controversial was Popplewell J's finding that the Register of Members' Interests was *not* part of 'proceedings in Parliament' for the purposes of Article 9. This issue arose again in *Hamilton v Al Fayed*, now the leading case in this area.

Hamilton v Al Fayed [1999] 1 WLR 1569; [1999] 3 All ER 317, CA; [2001] 1 AC 395, HL

Neil Hamilton made a number of parliamentary interventions, including questions in the defendant [Al Fayed's] interests, and on October 20, 1994 *The Guardian* published a front page story which alleged that Al Fayed had paid tens of thousands of pounds to the plaintiff ... through the agency of IGA [Ian Greer Associates], in return for asking questions in Parliament on his behalf. The article also alleged that the plaintiff and his wife had enjoyed a week's stay at the Ritz Hotel in Paris free of charge, and had had free shopping trips to Harrods at the defendant's invitation.

The plaintiff issued proceedings for libel against *The Guardian*, as did IGA and Mr Ian Greer, on the same day as the publication, October 20, 1994. *The Guardian* pleaded justification, alleging *inter alia* that over the two-year period 1987 to 1989 the plaintiff sought and received from the defendant in the form of either cash or Harrods gift vouchers a total of £28,000, for the most part in cash, and that such sums represented payments by the defendant for the plaintiff's services in tabling parliamentary questions and motions and other parliamentary services. In his reply the plaintiff asserted that he had never received any payment in cash or kind for any action taken by him in support of the defendant's cause.

On July 21, 1995 May J (as he then was) stayed both the plaintiff's and Greer-IGA's actions, holding that 'the claims and defences raised issues whose investigation would infringe parliamentary privilege to such an extent that they could not fairly be tried'. A significant part of his ratio was that *The Guardian* would be inhibited in presenting its plea of justification since it would be precluded on grounds of parliamentary privilege from linking the alleged payments made to the plaintiff with the admitted tabling of the parliamentary questions. That seemed to be the end of the matter. But on July 4, 1996 the Defamation Act 1996 received Royal Assent ... Section 13 [of the Act] was undoubtedly prompted by the stay of Mr Hamilton's action in the preceding July ... [It allows Members to waive privilege so as to allow them to take proceedings which would otherwise be stayed as contrary to Article 9.] On July 31, 1996 May J lifted the stay imposed by him on July 21, 1995 ... Section 13 of the Defamation Act 1996 provides as follows:

Defamation Act 1996, s 13

(1) Where the conduct of a person in or in relation to proceedings in Parliament is in issue in defamation proceedings, he may waive for the purposes of those proceedings, so far as concerns him, the protection of any enactment or rule of law which prevents proceedings in Parliament being impeached or questioned in any court or place out of Parliament.

(2) Where a person waives that protection:

    (a) any such enactment or rule of law shall not apply to prevent evidence being given, questions being asked or statements, submissions, comments or findings being made about his conduct, and

    (b) none of those things shall be regarded as infringing the privilege of either House of Parliament.

(3) The waiver by one person of that protection does not affect its operation in relation to another person who has not waived it ...

(4) Nothing in this section affects any enactment or rule of law so far as it protects a person (including a person who has waived the protection referred to above) from legal liability for words spoken or things done in the course of, or for the purposes of or incidental to, any proceedings in Parliament.

(5) Without prejudice to the generality of subsection (4), that subsection applies to:

    (a) the giving of evidence before either House or a committee;

    (b) the presentation or submission of a document to either House or a committee;

    (c) the preparation of a document for the purposes of or incidental to the transacting of any such business;

    (d) the formulation, making or publication of a document, including a report, by or pursuant to an order of either House or a committee; and

    (e) any communication with the Parliamentary Commissioner for Standards or any person having functions in connection with the registration of members' interests.

In this subsection 'a committee' means a committee of either House or a joint committee of both Houses of Parliament.

The Hamilton saga then continued:

On October 1996, after the end of *The Guardian* case, the CSP asked the Commissioner to investigate allegations concerning the plaintiff and a number of other MPs. The Commissioner conducted a detailed inquiry involving some 60 witnesses including the plaintiff and the defendant,

13 oral hearings and some 14,000 pages of documents. Evidence was not given on oath and witnesses were not permitted to cross-examine each other, but the evidence was tested by counsel to the inquiry and the Commissioner. The Commissioner described his approach as inquisitorial not adversarial. In his report of July 1997 the Commissioner concluded that the plaintiff had received cash payments from the defendant and hospitality at the Ritz as a reward for lobbying. .... In its report of November 1997 the Standards Committee held that the plaintiff's conduct had fallen seriously and persistently below the standards which the House was entitled to expect . . . Later in November 1997 the House resolved to approve the Standards Committee's report.

Meanwhile in January 1997 Channel 4 broadcast a programme in its *Dispatches* strand which contained an interview with the defendant in which he repeated his allegations concerning the cash payments, the holiday in the Ritz and the shopping trips to Harrods. In January 1988 the plaintiff commenced fresh proceedings for libel against the defendant. The defendant applied to strike out the action on the grounds that (1) to allow the action to proceed would necessarily involve questioning proceedings in Parliament in contravention of Article 9 of the Bill of Rights 1689 or a wider rule of which Article 9 was merely one manifestation and/or (2) the action constituted a collateral attack upon Parliament's decision upon allegations of misconduct against the plaintiff in resolving to adopt the Standards Committee's report.

Notes

1   One point which the litigation raised was whether the investigation and report of the Commissioner and Committee which had both made findings against Hamilton in the 'cash for questions affair' were 'proceedings in Parliament' and so protected under Article 9 from being 'impeached or questioned' in court. Some doubt was cast on the contention that they were such 'proceedings' by the findings of Popplewell J at first instance. Indeed his conclusion was that the findings (or as he saw it, non-findings) of the Committee on the key issue and the investigation of the Commissioner were not 'proceedings in Parliament' such as to oust the jurisdiction of the court to consider them critically. These matters were then considered in the Court of Appeal (*Hamilton v Al Fayed* [1999] 1 WLR 1569, CA, which found that: 'The [Commissioner's] inquiry and report, the hearings before the CSP [the Committee] and its report, as well as the resolution of the House, amounted individually and collectively to "proceedings in Parliament" whether for the purposes of Article 9 of the Bill of Rights or of any wider rule which enjoins the protection of such proceedings.' This part of the Court of Appeal judgment was explicitly endorsed by the House of Lords [2001] 1 AC 395.

2   The Joint Committee on Parliamentary Privilege made a number of recommendations on what should amount to 'proceedings in Parliament' for the purposes of Article 9 and recommended that the term should be defined in statute.

129. The Joint Committee recommends the enactment of a definition on the following lines:

(1) For the purposes of Article 9 of the Bill of Rights 1689 'proceedings in Parliament' means all words spoken and acts done in the course of, or for the purposes of, or necessarily incidental to, transacting the business of either House of Parliament or of a committee.

(2) Without limiting (1), this includes:

(a) the giving of evidence before a House or a committee or an officer appointed by a House to receive such evidence;

(b) the presentation or submission of a document to a House or a committee or an officer appointed by a House to receive it, once the document is accepted;

(c) the preparation of a document for the purposes of transacting the business of a House or a committee, provided any drafts, notes, advice or the like are not circulated more widely than is reasonable for the purposes of preparation;

(d) the formulation, making or publication of a document by a House or a committee;

(e) the maintenance of any register of the interests of the members of a House and any other register of interests prescribed by resolution of a House.[78]

Two points in particular may be noted about this definition: first, it explicitly *includes* the Register of Members' Interests in what would be a direct statutory reversal of the decision in *Rost* on the point; secondly, it is intended, as noted above, to *exclude* letters sent by MPs whether to constituents or ministers.

'Impeached or questioned'

It is not merely the phrase 'proceedings in Parliament' which has caused disagreement. Article 9 of the Bill of Rights states that freedom of speech, debates and proceedings in Parliament ought not to be 'impeached or questioned in any court or place outside Parliament'. It is accepted that this means that no legal liability may arise in respect of words spoken in Parliament, but what further meanings do the words have? Do they mean that words spoken, or matters taking place in Parliament cannot even be adduced in evidence in legal proceedings? Or that they may be so adduced, but cannot be subject to *critical* scrutiny? While *Rost v Edwards* [1990] 2 WLR 1280, 1289–90 suggested the former interpretation, it now appears tolerably well settled that the second is correct. The Privy Council in *Prebble v Television New Zealand Ltd* [1994] 3 All ER 407 said that '[i]t is questionable whether *Rost* was rightly decided' on this point, commenting that such decisions 'betray some confusion between the right to prove the occurrence of parliamentary events and the embargo on questioning their propriety' (at 418). From this *dicta*, and the House of Lords' finding in *Pepper v Hart* [1993] 1 All ER 42 that the courts may, contrary to a long-standing prohibition, consult Hansard as an aid to statutory interpretation, one may conclude that non-critical examination of affairs in Parliament does not, after all, fall within the prohibition on 'questioning' in Article 9 and is therefore not a breach of privilege.

However, it appears that any form of examination of proceedings in Parliament which entails any form of criticism of the parliamentary actors is still flatly prohibited. The leading cases are *Prebble v Television New Zealand Ltd*; and, now, *Hamilton v Al Fayed*.

Prebble v Television New Zealand Ltd [1994] 3 All ER 407 (extracts)

The defendant, Television New Zealand, made certain allegations of impropriety in a broadcast against the fourth Labour Government of New Zealand which were alleged by the plaintiff, a minister within that Government, to carry a meaning defamatory of him. In libel proceedings in New Zealand the defendant alleged, *inter alia*, that the defamatory meanings were mostly true. Certain of the particulars of the justifications relied on statements and actions which took place in Parliament. The plaintiff applied to strike out those particulars which concerned matters taking place in the House and which were therefore, under Article 9 of the Bill of Rights 1689, subject to Parliamentary privilege. The judge agreed that the particulars should be struck out and the Court of Appeal upheld that decision but considered it unjust that the plaintiff should be able to continue the action given that the defendant's ability to substantiate his justification plea was thereby substantially impaired, and so ordered a stay of proceedings until the Committee of Privileges could determine whether the privileges protected by Article 9 could be waived.

The plaintiff appealed against the stay of proceedings and the defendant against the decision to strike out the particulars. The questions for decision by the Privy Council were:

(a) would the allegations, if pursued, infringe Article 9;

(b) if so, should a stay have been ordered?

Lord Browne-Wilkinson: ... The defendants submit, first, that [parliamentary privilege] only operates to protect the questioning of statements made in the House in proceedings which seek to assert legal consequences against the maker of the statement for making that statement.

[His Lordship found against this submission] The important public interest protected by such privilege is to ensure that the Member or witness at the time he speaks is not inhibited from stating fully and freely what he has to say. If there were any exceptions which permitted his statements to be questioned subsequently, at the time when he speaks in Parliament he would not know whether or not there would subsequently be a challenge to what he is saying. Therefore he would not have the confidence the privilege is designed to protect.

Moreover to allow it to be suggested in cross-examination or submission that a Member or witness was lying to the House could lead to exactly that conflict between the courts and Parliament which the wider principle of non-intervention is designed to avoid. Misleading the House is a contempt of the House punishable by the House: if a court were also to be permitted to decide whether or not a Member or witness had misled the House there would be a serious risk of conflicting decisions on the issue.

The defendants' second submission [is] that the rules excluding parliamentary material do not apply when the action is brought by a Member of Parliament. Their Lordships cannot accept that the fact that the maker of the statement is the initiator of the court proceedings can affect the question whether Art 9 is infringed. The privilege protected by Art 9 is the privilege of Parliament itself ...

Their Lordships are acutely conscious (as were the courts below) that to preclude reliance on things said and done in the House in defence of libel proceedings brought by a Member of the House could have a serious impact on a most important aspect of freedom of speech, viz the right of the public to comment on and criticise the actions of those elected to power in a democratic society: see Derbyshire CC v Times Newspapers Ltd [1993] I All ER 1011; [1993] AC 534. If the media and others are unable to establish the truth of fair criticisms of the conduct of their elected Members in the very performance of their legislative duties in the House, the results could indeed be chilling to the proper monitoring of Members' behaviour. But the present case ... illustrates how public policy, or human rights, issues can conflict. There are three such issues in play in these cases: first, the need to ensure that the legislature can exercise its powers freely on behalf of its electors, with access to all relevant information; second, the need to protect freedom of speech generally; third, the interests of justice in ensuring that all relevant evidence is available to the courts. Their Lordships are of the view that the law has been long settled that, of these three public interests, the first must prevail. But the other two public interests cannot be ignored and their Lordships will revert to them in considering the question of a stay of proceedings.

For these reasons (which are in substance those of the courts below) their Lordships are of the view that parties to litigation, by whomsoever commenced, cannot bring into question anything said or done in the House by suggesting (whether by direct evidence, cross-examination, inference or submission) that the actions or words were inspired by improper motives or were untrue or misleading. Such matters lie entirely within the jurisdiction of the House ...

However, their Lordships wish to make it clear that this principle does not exclude all references in court proceedings to what has taken place in the House. ... Since there can no longer be any objection to the production of Hansard, the Attorney General accepted (in their Lordships' view rightly) that there could be no objection to the use of Hansard to prove what was done and said in

Parliament as a matter of history ...Thus, in the present action, there cannot be any objection to it being proved what the plaintiff or the Prime Minister said in the House (particulars 8.2.10 and 8.2.14) or that the State-Owned Enterprises Act 1986 was passed (particulars 8.4.1). It will be for the trial judge to ensure that the proof of these historical facts is not used to suggest that the words were improperly spoken or the statute passed to achieve an improper purpose.

Stay of proceedings

...Their Lordships are of the opinion that there may be cases in which the exclusion of material on the grounds of parliamentary privilege makes it quite impossible fairly to determine the issue between the parties. In such a case the interests of justice may demand a stay of proceedings. But such a stay should only be granted in the most extreme circumstances ...

Note

Commentary on the reasoning in this case appears below. First, however, it is necessary to examine the implicit challenge to aspects of the reasoning made by the Court of Appeal in *Hamilton*, and the explicit reassertion of the *Prebble* view by the House of Lords in the same case: a matter of some importance, given that *Prebble*, being a Privy Council decision, was of only persuasive value. The facts of the case appear above (at pp 459–61). It will be recalled that Hamilton had issued proceedings against Fayed, and others, for defamation, when Fayed repeated the allegation that he had given Hamilton sums of money in return for asking questions in the House, an allegation which, by this time, had been found to be true by the Commissioner, a finding endorsed by the Committee. The point at issue in the following extract was Fayed's argument that to allow the defamation action to continue would involve the court in reassessing these findings of the Commissioner and the Committee and that this would constitute a breach of the Article 9 embargo on impeaching or questioning proceedings in Parliament. On this the Court of Appeal's finding was as follows.

Hamilton v Al Fayed [1999] 1 WLR 1569, CA (extracts)

Lord Woolf MR: The vice to which Article 9 is directed (so far as the courts are concerned) is the inhibition of freedom of speech and debate in Parliament that might flow from any condemnation by the Queen's courts, being themselves an arm of government, of anything there said. The position is quite different when it comes to criticisms by other persons (especially the media) of what is said in Parliament. Lord Browne-Wilkinson himself drew this distinction in the passage we have cited from *Pepper v Hart*. The courts could only have legitimate occasion to criticise anything said or done in parliamentary proceedings if they were called on to pass judgment on any such proceedings; but that they clearly cannot and must not do. Nor therefore should they issue such criticisms on any occasion, for to do so would be gratuitous.

... [Thus] as long as the requirement to avoid any such criticism is observed, Article 9, properly understood, does not mean the plaintiff's proceedings cannot be allowed to continue ... Manifestly the court would never make any order striking down what has been done by Parliament, or attaching legal sanctions or consequences to it. The defamation proceedings create no risk of this. The most that can be said is that the court might arrive at a different result on some aspects of the factual merits of the 'cash for questions' issue from that arrived at by the Commissioner and (at least) not departed from or objected to by the CSP or the House of Commons.

... The court should only decline to hear the plaintiff's libel claim if it were persuaded that the possibility of a result being arrived at which was inconsistent with the Commissioner's conclusions would be to undermine the authority of Parliament so that the action should on that ground be condemned as abusive. It cannot credibly be maintained that such a power ought to be exercised in every single case where litigation covers or overlaps the same ground as has been trodden by an investigation by Parliament into some aspect of its own affairs.

Notes

1   It is clear that the crucial – and controversial – passage in this judgment is the assertion:

> The court should only decline to hear the plaintiff's libel claim if it were persuaded that the possibility of a result being arrived at which was inconsistent with the Commissioner's conclusions would be to undermine the authority of Parliament so that the action should on that ground be condemned as abusive.

The passage arguably represented a narrowing in the scope of Article 9; the prior orthodoxy, which the Court of Appeal had earlier appeared to endorse, was that Article 9 prevented 'direct criticism by the courts of anything said or done in the course of parliamentary proceedings'. It is a narrower interpretation of Article 9 because it is perfectly possible that there could be criticism by the courts of something said or done in Parliament by an *individual member* that yet, arguably, would not 'undermine the authority of Parliament' collectively. Such an interpretation could lead to a distinction being drawn in future between a finding in court that an individual Member had made an untruthful statement to Parliament, for example, or had had an improper motive for anything he or she said – which could be thought merely to damage the credibility of that Member but not realistically that of Parliament as a whole – and a finding in court that an *official organ or officer of Parliament* – a Select Committee or the Commissioner for example – had reached a mistaken or even dishonest or biased conclusion. The latter, but not the former, would raise an Article 9 issue. There would be an even stronger argument for a more limited reinterpretation of Article 9: namely that it was not infringed where the 'questioning' in court was directed *not* at the conduct or evidence given in Parliament by any *MP*, but by a stranger to the House, in this case, by Al Fayed himself, in the evidence he gave to the Commissioner. For it is very hard to see that a finding in court that a stranger to the House had misled it in evidence given to it somehow undermined the authority of the House itself.

2   The Court of Appeal judgment had thus left the door open to a narrowing in the interpretation placed on the scope of Article 9; it was on this point that the House of Lords took issue with the Court of Appeal. Their Lordships also considered the point that the Court of Appeal had erred in not considering whether a stay on the proceedings should be granted, if it was felt that a prohibition on questioning the findings of the Commissioner and Committee (on the grounds that such questioning would breach Article 9) would render it impossible for the action to be fairly tried.

Hamilton v Al Fayed [2001] I AC 395, HL

Lord Browne-Wilkinson: ... I am far from satisfied that the views of the Court of Appeal on this point are correct ... The normal impact of parliamentary privilege is to prevent the court from entertaining any evidence, cross-examination or submissions which challenge the veracity or propriety of anything done in the course of parliamentary proceedings. Thus, it is not permissible to challenge by cross-examination in a later action the veracity of evidence given to a parliamentary committee. If that approach had been adopted in the present case, there can be no doubt that, apart from section 13, the trial of the action would from the outset have proved completely impossible. All evidence by Mr Hamilton that he had not received money for questions would have conflicted directly with the evidence of Mr Al Fayed which was accepted by the parliamentary committees. Any attempt to cross-examine Mr Al Fayed to the effect that he was lying to the parliamentary committees when he said that he had paid money for questions would have been stopped forthwith as an infringement of parliamentary privilege.

Presumably because of the way the case was presented to them, the Court of Appeal never considered the relevant question (viz whether there should be a fair trial stay) ... The only way in which Mr Al Fayed could justify his defamatory statements was by detailed challenge to Mr Hamilton's conduct in Parliament, which challenge would be precluded by parliamentary privilege. That being so it would in my judgment have been impossible for Mr Al Fayed to have had a fair trial in this action if he had been precluded from challenging the evidence produced to the parliamentary committees on behalf of Mr Hamilton. Had it not been for section 13, the court should, in my judgment, have stayed the libel action brought by Mr Hamilton ...

Notes

1 Thus, the decision was that the courts were unable to hear any evidence or permit any cross-examination which implied any criticism of MPs *or others giving evidence to Parliament* about what had gone on in Parliament, without Parliament's permission, unless the MP concerned decided to waive privilege under the Defamation Act 1996, s 13. Whether the evidence should be admitted would therefore be decided by a resolution of the House of Commons, which could be subject to party political considerations. It seems far from satisfactory that matters of admissibility of evidence should be decided by such a partisan body.

2 For a similar case in which the defendant newspaper wished to rely upon pleading impropriety connected with the handling of certain Early Day Motions in Parliament in defending an action brought by an MP, see *Allison v Haines* (1995) *The Times*, 25 July. The defence was found to be contrary to Article 9, but it was held that since the defence pleaded was the only one available to the defendant, it would be manifestly unfair to allow the action to proceed; it was therefore struck out.

3 The Joint Committee on Parliamentary Privilege took a firmly conservative view on this point: they recommended a statutory definition of the meaning of 'impeached or questioned' based on s 16 of the Parliamentary Privileges Act 1987 (Commonwealth legislation), namely:

a statutory enactment to the effect that no court or tribunal may receive evidence, or permit questions to be asked or submissions made, concerning proceedings in Parliament by way of, or for the purpose of, questioning or relying on the truth, motive, intention or good faith of anything forming part of proceedings in Parliament or drawing any inference from anything forming part of those proceedings.

4 It is evident from *Prebble* and *Fayed* taken together that the Privy Council and the House of Lords (Lord Browne-Wilkinson delivered the relevant speeches in both cases) saw two reasons as to why critical scrutiny of proceedings in Parliament cannot take place. One was that, if the courts found that the Member had lied to the House (a contempt of Parliament) but Parliament found he or she had not, there would be a conflict between Parliament and the courts. But all the serious conflicts which have arisen between the courts and Parliament (see below) have arisen because the courts have tried to attach *legal liability* to things done or said in Parliament and Parliament has sought to protect its Members from such liability. No such liability was in question in this case. The second reason given was that, if Members anticipated that their statements made in the House would later be subject to 'challenge' or questioning, they would not have the confidence to speak out freely. Two things may be said about this. First, it seems, with respect, simply incorrect. If a Member is telling the truth, or giving his honest opinion, why should the realisation that his statements may later be scrutinised inhibit him from speaking? Maybe such a realisation would inhibit him from telling lies, but is this a bad thing? Presumably, no one wishes to encourage members to be dishonest. But

secondly, what members say in the House is *already the subject of critical and probing scrutiny*, as carried on by journalists and political commentators. What possible justification is there for saying that a member who may be savaged in the press for misleading the House – as William Waldegrave was repeatedly[79] in respect of misleading answers given by him to the House in relation to government policy on arms sales to Iraq – must be exempt from such criticism if it would be voiced by a barrister in a courtroom? In neither case is he or she in danger of incurring legal liability for what he or she says.

5 The arguments of the Joint Committee on this point seem manifestly unpersuasive: reacting to a proposal by Dr Marshall that statute should make clear that Article 9 only had the effect of forbidding the imposition of actual legal liability in respect of words spoken in Parliament, it said:

[Such] a provision ... would mean that members, although not facing legal liability, could find themselves called to account in court for what they said in Parliament and why they said it. We believe that, in general, this would not be desirable. Legal immunity may be the principal function of Article 9 today, but it is not the only purpose. Although the phrase 'impeached or questioned' perhaps supports the view that the Article 9 prohibition is co-terminous with legal liability, a wider principle is involved here, namely, that members ought not to be called to account in court for their participation in parliamentary proceedings. This is, and should remain, the general rule.[80]

It may be noted that no argument is given for allowing MPs to be fully exposed to the vitriolic and often inaccurate or politically biased criticism of MPs' conduct which may appear in the press, but prohibiting the far more measured and scrupulous criticism which might take place in court.

6 Thus, it is suggested that the arguments for maintaining such a draconian bar on, for example, any suggestion being made in court that a parliamentary committee may have received untruthful or inaccurate evidence from a person who may not even be an MP come nowhere near supporting it. This is all the more evident when comparison is made with the arguments and evidence that may be put in judicial review proceedings. It is a well established law that if a minister made a decision for an improper purpose, or took into account irrelevant considerations in making it, then that decision would be unlawful. But it is obvious that, since ministers generally announce both decisions and the reasons for them to the House of Commons, the suggestion that there was an ulterior and improper motive for the decision will involve precisely the suggestion being made in court that a Member of Parliament made a false or misleading statement during parliamentary proceedings, exactly what *Prebble* and now *Hamilton* say cannot be done in the different context of defamation proceedings. The Joint Committee recognised this anomaly and tried to justify it, but with respect, had little success.[81] The point is that ministerial statements made to the House are regularly 'questioned' in judicial review proceedings; this does not in itself appear to have had any adverse consequences for the authority of Parliament.

7 The injustice which appears to arise from privilege, where the person claiming privilege is the one who has made the defamatory statements concerned, was adverted to in the following Australian decision.

---

79 See, eg, 'Five steps to save us from the contempt of our rulers', *The Independent*, 16 February 1995.
80 *Op cit*, para 77.
81 *Ibid*, paras 46–55.

Wright and Advertiser Newspapers Ltd v Lewis (1990) 53 SASR 416, 421–22

King CJ: A Member of Parliament could sue for defamation in respect of criticisms of his statements or conduct in the Parliament. The defendant would be precluded however from alleging and proving that what was said by way of criticism was true. This would amount to a gross distortion of the law of defamation ... [which] in law is by definition an *untrue* imputation against the reputation of another ... If the defendant were precluded from proving the truth of what is alleged, the Member of Parliament would be enabled to recover damages ... for an imputation which was perfectly true [King CJ went on to consider how the defences of fair comment and qualified privilege might well also not be available in such a situation]. If this is the true legal position, it is difficult to envisage how a court could apply the law of defamation in a rational way to an action by a Member of Parliament in respect of an imputation relating to his statements or conduct in the House, or could try such an action fairly. [Original emphasis.]

Note

Section 13 of the Defamation Act 1996, which in essence allows an MP to waive privilege in relation to defamation proceedings, was designed to remedy the apparent injustice which occurs when MPs are forced out of office as a result of allegations relating to their parliamentary conduct, but have no way of clearing their name through defamation proceedings (any action would be struck out as contrary to Article 9). Al Fayed, in *Hamilton v Al Fayed*, sought to argue that s 13 did not apply in the circumstances of that case: the point was considered by the House of Lords:

Hamilton v Al Fayed [2001] 1 AC 395, HL

Lord Browne-Wilkinson: The effect of [s 13] [is] entirely clear. It deals specifically with the circumstances raised by Mr Hamilton's case against 'The Guardian'. He could waive his own protection from parliamentary privilege and in consequence any privilege of Parliament as a whole would fall to be regarded as not infringed ... The privileges of the House are just that. They all belong to the House and not to the individual. They exist to enable the House to perform its functions. Thus section 13(1) accurately refers, not to the privileges of the individual MP, but to 'the protection of any enactment or rule of law' which prevents the questioning of procedures in Parliament. The individual MP enjoys the protection of parliamentary privilege. If he waives such protection, then under section 13(2) any questioning of parliamentary proceedings (even by challenging 'findings ... made about his conduct') is not to be treated as a breach of the privilege of Parliament. I can see no way, following the waiver by Mr Hamilton of his parliamentary protection in relation to the parliamentary inquiry into his conduct, that it can be said that such waiver does not also operate under subsection (2)(b) so as to override any privilege belonging to Parliament as a whole.

Notes

1   Whilst many MPs and peers welcomed the advent of s 13, two clear objections to it are apparent. The first is the apparent unfairness of the new position: if an MP is defamed about his parliamentary activities, he or she can lift the cloak of privilege to sue. By contrast, a newspaper or journalist defending an action brought by an MP, who needs to adduce evidence as to proceedings in Parliament as part of his defence (as in *Prebble*) will find that privilege will prevent him from doing so. In addition, of course, citizens defamed by MPs will continue to be unable to clear their names as only MPs will be able to waive privilege.

2   Arguments in favour of the asymmetry of position under s 13 attempt to justify it by reference to the public interest in freedom of speech in Parliament which requires immunity for MPs but not for those who defame them. For example, the response of the Joint Committee on Parliamentary Privilege to the asymmetry objection was as follows:

The ... Committee considers the answer lies in appreciating that the ... power of waiver [does] not create an imbalance. The basic 'imbalance' between members and everyone else, the lack of symmetry, is created by Article 9 itself. Members are shielded from legal liability for defamatory statements made in the course of parliamentary proceedings. This is an essential concomitant of parliamentary freedom of speech.[82]

It is apparent that, while this may partly answer criticisms of the situation whereby citizens are not able to sue MPs, it does not tell us why journalists who *prima facie* defame MPs should not be able to defend themselves by adducing evidence of proceedings in Parliament in order to prove the truthfulness of what they said. This aspect of privilege still stands to be justified by the reasons put forward in *Prebble*, which as argued above seem manifestly unpersuasive.

3   The second main objection to the change was argued by Lords Lester and Richards in the debate on s 13; as the former put it, '[t]he immunities written into Article 9 were not included simply for the personal ... benefit of Members ... but to protect the integrity of the legislative process by ensuring the independence of individual legislators'.[83] Since the rationale for privilege is supposed to be its necessity to each House as a whole, it follows that waiver of its protection should be a matter for the House only, not a power in the hands of individual Members to be used for their personal benefit.

4   The Joint Committee found this criticism of s 13 persuasive and recommended legislative change to it:

Joint Committee on Parliamentary Privilege, HLP 43–41 (1998–99)

68. Unfortunately the cure that section 13 seeks to achieve has severe problems of its own and has attracted widespread criticism, not least from our witnesses. A fundamental flaw is that it undermines the basis of privilege: freedom of speech is the privilege of the House as a whole and not of the individual member in his own right, although an individual member can assert and rely on it. Application of the new provision could also be impracticable in complicated cases; for example, where two members, or a member and a non-member, are closely involved in the same action and one waives privilege and the other does not. Section 13 is also anomalous: it is available only in defamation proceedings. No similar waiver is available for any criminal action, or any other form of civil action.

69. The Joint Committee considers these criticisms are unanswerable. The enactment of section 13, seeking to remedy a perceived injustice, has created indefensible anomalies of its own which should not be allowed to continue. The Joint Committee recommends that section 13 should be repealed.

70. Yet there is a problem here. In practice, neither House now treats the libel of one of its members as a contempt, nor is either House equipped to hear libel cases even if such a course were publicly acceptable. In the *Hamilton* type of case it is, on the one hand, unthinkable that if the media criticise those who have been elected to power, the media should not be free to establish the truth of their criticisms. As was pointed out by Lord Browne-Wilkinson in the *Prebble* decision, were this not so the results could be 'chilling' to the proper monitoring of members' behaviour. On the other hand, if the law is left as enunciated in *Prebble*, members criticised outside Parliament and accused of misconduct in the performance of their parliamentary duties can find themselves wholly unable to clear their names. This undesirable state of affairs could even, in turn, encourage irresponsible media comment. Commentators would rest secure in the knowledge they could not be called to account in court for allegations of parliamentary misconduct. The difficulty lies in resolving this conflict.

---

82   HLP 43–41 (1998–99), para 76.
83   Quoted *ibid.*

...

72. We have considered whether there is [an] alternative, which will enable justice to be done to both parties: to permit the courts to investigate the alleged misconduct. One way of achieving this in a principled fashion would be that, instead of a member having power to waive Article 9, as is the position under section 13 of the Defamation Act 1996, the House itself should be empowered to waive the Article 9 privilege in any case where no question arises of the member making the statement being at risk of incurring legal liability. The existence of such a power would enable Parliament to meet the perceived injustice in the *Hamilton* type of case and in its criminal counterpart. If a member, placed as was Mr Hamilton, started a defamation action, the defendant newspaper would be entitled to seek to prove the truth of its allegations. The member, in turn, would have an opportunity to vindicate himself. In this way justice would be done to both parties, but at the same time the vital constitutional principle of freedom of speech in Parliament would be preserved. When they speak in Parliament members would have, as now, complete confidence that no legal liability could attach to them in consequence.

...

89. Section 13 should be replaced by a short statutory provision empowering each House to waive Article 9 for the purpose of any court proceedings, whether relating to defamation or to any other matter, where the words spoken or the acts done in proceedings in Parliament would not expose the speaker of the words or the doer of the acts to any legal liability.

Notes

1   A final problem with the embargo on any form of questioning of proceedings in parliament is that it may represent a violation of Article 6 of the ECHR. Article 6(1) states: 'In the determination of his civil rights and obligations ... everyone is entitled to a fair and public hearing within a reasonable time by an independent and impartial tribunal established by law.' As we have seen above, it is possible that the judicial interpretation of Article 9 of the Bill of Rights (as precluding any evidence to be given, or cross-examination engaged in which expressly or impliedly constitutes any kind of criticism of anyone engaged in parliamentary proceedings) may effectively prevent a litigant from being able to have his or her cause of action determined. The action may be struck out, *not* on the basis that the litigant has no cause of action, but that the hearing of it would involve an infringement of parliamentary privilege. Since the litigant would be wholly denied judicial determination of his or her rights, it is hard to see how this could not constitute a violation of Article 6 of the ECHR. Whether it would definitively do so is a matter of European Convention law, which cannot be determined here. But it is at the least a strong possibility, and one which the UK courts have not begun to grapple with.

2   Now the Human Rights Act is in force, the courts are bound under s 6(1) to act compatibly with the Convention,[84] and this will require them to interpret and apply the common law compatibly with the Convention. Whether this duty will apply when both parties before the court are private parties – as would be likely in a defamation action – is a matter of some controversy (see Part VI Chapter 1, pp 872–73) but it seems likely that, at the least, a positive action of the court, such as granting a stay to defamation proceedings would be caught by s 6(1). The Court of Appeal in *Fayed v Hamilton* did not need to consider the point, since it allowed the action to proceed, but it did at least mention the issue, unlike the House of Lords. They said simply, '... had we been of the view that this libel action ought to be stayed as an assault on the privileges of Parliament, we do not believe that the

---

84   The exception under s 6(2) would not apply in this case. See Part VI Chapter 1, p 871.

Strasbourg jurisprudence would have required the court to disapply a rule or principle of such general constitutional importance', an assertion which must be seriously open to doubt.

3   In contrast, should a person seek to sue in defamation, alleging that the defamatory statement was published during parliamentary proceedings, the action would be struck out, but there would (probably) be no breach of Article 6 of the ECHR because in this case, parliamentary privilege does not prevent the case being heard, it *determines its outcome* as a matter of substantive law by acting as an absolute defence.[85]

4   In conclusion, it is suggested that Article 9 of the Bill of Rights, as currently interpreted, is both riddled with anomalies in its interpretation and, more importantly, contains a serious and arguably unjustifiable restriction on access to justice. In what appears to be an obsessive quest to prevent courts from having to entertain any criticism of any actor in parliamentary proceedings, the courts have contrived to undermine one of the basic tenets of the rule of law: the right of a citizen to have his or her rights determined in an ordinary court, or as Article 6 of the ECHR puts it, to have his or her civil rights 'determined by an independent and impartial tribunal'.

Competing jurisdictions over the scope of privilege: Parliament versus the courts

One peculiar characteristic of parliamentary privilege is the fact that both the courts and Parliament have at times claimed the right to determine what is the law in this area. As Leopold puts it, in the context of the scope of the privilege of free speech, 'the problem is that [a ruling on the matter] could be made by both Parliament and the courts with not necessarily the same result'.[86] Should conflict flow from such a different result, the outcome remains uncertain, as illustrated by a case already mentioned, *Stockdale v Hansard* (1834) 9 Ad & El 1. This convoluted and colourful litigation is described by Erskine May.

Erskine May, *Treatise on the Law, Privileges, Proceedings and Usage of Parliament*, 20th edn (1983), pp 151–54

Messrs Hansard, the printers of the House of Commons, had printed by order of that House a report made by an inspector of prisons against which a Mr Stockdale brought an action for libel. The court did not consider Messrs Hansard's proof of the House's order to print a sufficient defence. Lord Denman CJ observed that the House's direction to publish all parliamentary reports was no justification for Hansard or anyone else.

[The House passed resolutions] declaring that the publication of parliamentary reports, votes and proceedings was an essential incident to the constitutional functions of Parliament; that the House had sole and exclusive jurisdiction to determine upon the existence and extent of its privileges; that to dispute those privileges by legal proceedings was a breach of privilege; and that for any court to assume to decide upon matters of privilege inconsistent with the determination of either House of Parliament was contrary to the law of Parliament.

... Messrs Hansard in this case relied entirely upon the privileges of the House and its order to print. The defence was unsuccessful. The Attorney General argued the case for regarding the High

---

85   The case of *Osman v UK* (1998) 29 EHRR 245, in which a principle of substantive tort law – that the police had a public policy immunity from actions in negligence – was found to constitute a violation of Article 6 suggests that in some cases, rules of substantive law may be regarded as breaches of Article 6. For discussion see C Gearty, 'Unraveling *Osman*' (2001) 64(2) MLR 159.

86   [1990] PL 30.

Court of Parliament as a superior court of exclusive jurisdiction binding on other courts, and its law a separate law. Each House separately, it was contended, possessed the whole power of the mediaeval High Court of Parliament, and so subordinate were the courts of law to each that a writ of error ran from them to Parliament. Furthermore, were the privileges of the Commons subject to review by the courts, the Lords would be the arbiter not only of their own privileges but also of those of the Commons. Once again, an appeal was made to the principle that the constitution supposed that the *lex parliamenti*, like the law administered in equity, ecclesiastical and admiralty courts, was a system different from the common law, the judges of which had no means of arriving judicially at knowledge of it. In such circumstances the courts must respect the general rule that they should follow the law of the court of original jurisdiction. Finally, the Attorney General cited instances of the Commons exercising its inquisitorial powers as a court by examining and committing judges.

The court rebutted nearly all these contentions. It was accepted that over their own internal proceedings the jurisdiction of the Houses was exclusive: but it was (in Lord Denman's view) for the courts to determine whether or not a particular claim of privilege fell within that category. Though the Commons had claimed that the publication of certain types of papers was essential to its constitutional functions, and the Attorney General argued that the court was bound to accept such a declaration as evidence of the law, Lord Denman held that the court had a duty to inquire further. There was, in his opinion, no difference between a right to sanction all things under the name of privilege and the same right to sanction them by merely ordering them to be done. This would amount to an 'arbitrary and irresponsible' superseding of the law'.

Lord Denman denied further that the *lex parliamenti* was a separate law, unknown to the judges of the common law courts. Either House considered individually was only a part of the High Court of Parliament, and neither could bring an issue within its exclusive jurisdiction simply by declaring it to be a matter of privilege. Any other proposition was 'abhorrent to the first principles of the constitution'. The declaration of the House ... was not the action of a court, legislative, judicial or inquisitorial, so that the superiority of the House of Commons over other courts had nothing to do with the question. In any case, there was, it seemed to the judges, no basis for regarding the courts of law as in principle incapable of reviewing any decision of the House of Commons. Conversely, there was no parliamentary revision of court judgments for error. The Commons was not a court of law in the sense recognised in the courts, and was unable to decide a matter judicially in litigation between parties, either originally or by appeal.

Having received an unfavourable verdict, the House of Commons, again despite their strong view expressed in the resolutions referred to above, ordered to be paid the damages and costs for which Messrs Hansard were declared liable. It was however agreed that, in case of future actions, the firm should not plead and that the parties should suffer for their contempt of the resolutions and defiance of the House's authority.

When therefore a third action was commenced for another publication of the original report, judgment was given against Messrs Hansard by default. Damages were assessed and the sheriffs of Middlesex levied for the amount, though they delayed paying the money to Stockdale for as long as possible. In 1840, the Commons committed first Stockdale and then the sheriffs, who had declined to repay the money to Messrs Hansard. Proceedings for the sheriff's release on a writ of habeas corpus proved unsuccessful. Howard, Stockdale's solicitor, was also proceeded against, but escaped with a reprimand.

While in prison, the persistent Stockdale commenced a fourth action, for which both he and Howard were committed. Messrs Hansard were again ordered not to plead, and judgment was entered against them. At this point, the situation was in part resolved by the introduction of what became the Parliamentary Papers Act 1840, affording statutory protection to papers published by order of either House ...

The case of *Howard v Gosset* (1845) may be viewed however as a continuation of the conflict in some of its aspects. Howard, Stockdale's solicitor, brought an action against the Serjeant at Arms and others for having taken him into custody and committed him to prison in obedience of the House's order and the Speaker's warrant. Leave to appeal was given to the defendants and the Attorney General was directed to defend them. The court favoured the plaintiff, on the grounds of the technical informality of the warrant. The judges proceeded on the principle that the warrant might be examined with the same strictures as if it had issued from an inferior court ... while at the same time concluding that they might adjudge it to be bad in form 'without impugning the authority of the House or in any way disputing its privileges'.

A select committee roundly condemned this doctrine, but advised the House 'that every legitimate mode of asserting and defending its privileges should be exhausted before it prevented by its own authority, the further progress of the action'. [Select Committee on Printed Papers, Second Report, HC 397 (1845), p vi.] The House accepted the advice and an appeal was lodged. In order, however, to avoid submission to any adverse judgment on appeal, the Serjeant was not authorised to give bail and execution was levied on his goods. In the event, the decision of the lower court was overturned, and the court found that the privileges involved were not in the least doubtful. The warrant of the Speaker was valid as a protection to the officer of the House, and the warrant should be construed as if it were a writ from a superior court.

Notes

1 In giving a return which did not state the facts upon which the allegation of contempt was based, Parliament had clearly learned from *Paty's case* (1704) 2 Ld Raym 1105 in which the Speaker gave the grounds for the finding of contempt: one of the judges (Holt CJ) hearing the application for habeas corpus dissented from the finding that the writ could not be granted, stating that where the reasons given could not amount in law to a breach of privilege or contempt, habeas corpus ought to be granted.

2 It is not certain that the matter could again be resolved as it was in *Stockdale v Hansard*. Henry Calvert considers it uncertain 'that a court of law would meekly accept a general return to a writ' in similar circumstances.[87] David Keir and Frederick Lawson, in contrast, take the view that the courts 'yielded the key to the fortress'[88] by refusing to question the legality of imprisonment for contempt where no reason is given, implying that a precedent has been set. Further, if the House of Lords (Judicial Committee) was asked to grant a writ of habeas corpus, it could not avoid questioning the Commons' actions on the grounds that the Commons was a superior court. An appeal was in fact made to the Lords in *Paty's case*, but the counsel preparing it was promptly imprisoned by the Commons.

3 In *Bradlaugh v Gossett* (1884) 12 QBD 271, 279 Stephen J said that 'the principal result of [*Stockdale*] is to assert in the strongest way the right of the Court of Queen's Bench to ascertain in case of need to the extent of the privileges of the House and to deny emphatically that the court is bound by resolution of the House declaring any particular matter to fall within their privilege ...'. More recently in *Rost v Edwards* [1990] 2 WLR 1280, 1293, the question of the courts' role as determiner of the boundary of privilege was addressed:

The approach I have to this aspect of the case is this. There are clearly cases where Parliament is to be the sole judge of its affairs. Equally there are clear cases where the courts are to have exclusive jurisdiction. In a case which may be described as a grey area a court, while giving full attention to the necessity for comity between the courts and Parliament, should not be astute to find a reason for ousting the jurisdiction of the court and for limiting or even defeating a proper

87 *British Constitutional Law* (1985), p 115.
88 *Cases in Constitutional Law*, 6th edn (1979), p 225.

claim by a party to litigation before it. If Parliament wishes to cover a particular area with privilege it has the ability to do so by passing an Act of Parliament giving itself the right to exclusive jurisdiction. Ousting the jurisdiction of the court has always been regarded as requiring the clearest possible words.

4   How should this conflict be resolved? De Smith has suggested that jurisdiction over breaches of privilege and contempts should be handed over to the courts.[89] It seems clear that the present state of affairs is unsatisfactory, as discussed above. It has been noted that the present competition for jurisdiction makes for uncertainty in this area, whilst the view that the party political nature of the Commons renders it unsuitable for deciding what are in effect legal issues has also been touched on. But, as discussed above, there are also serious grounds for dissatisfaction with the Commons as a decision-making body itself; its procedures not only fall foul elementary principles of natural justice; they may also constitute a breach of Article 6 of the ECHR, as discussed above.

FURTHER READING

C Boulton (ed), *Erskine May's Treatise on the Law, Privileges, Proceedings and Usage of Parliament*, 21st edn (1989)

A Doig, 'Cash for Questions: Parliament's response to the offence that dare not speak its name' (1998) 51(1) Parl Aff 36

A Doig, 'Sleaze: picking up the threads or "Back to Basics" scandals?' (2001) 54 Parl Aff 360

A Doig, 'Sleaze fatigue in "the House of ill-repute"' (2002) Parl Aff 389.

D Oliver, 'The Committee on Standards in Public Life: regulating the conduct of Members of Parliament' (1995) Parl Aff 591

A Sharland and I Loveland, 'The Defamation Act 1996 and Political Libels' [1997] PL 113

D Woodhouse, 'The Parliamentary Commissioner for Standards: lessons from the Cash for Questions Inquiry' (1998) 51(1) Parl Aff

---

89   *Constitutional and Administrative Law*, 6th edn (1994), p 332.

PART IV

THE CENTRAL EXECUTIVE:
POWERS AND ACCOUNTABILITY

CHAPTER I

PREROGATIVE POWERS

INTRODUCTION

In his *Commentaries on the Laws of England*, Blackstone wrote that the prerogative is 'that special pre-eminence which the King has, over and above all other persons, and out of the ordinary course of the common law, in right of his royal dignity'. The term 'prerogative', then, refers to powers which are unique to the sovereign and which he or she has by common law as opposed to statute. Prerogative powers are sometimes referred to as the 'royal prerogative'; this is technically correct, as in law these powers belong to the monarch. However, by convention, they are in practice exercised by the Prime Minister; in some cases by the Cabinet. However, certain prerogatives remain which are generally exercised by the monarch personally. These are sometimes known as the 'personal prerogatives' and will be examined below.

It should be stressed at the outset that it is one of the unique and disturbing features of the UK constitution that, by means of this historical relic, it allows powers of such great breadth, magnitude and importance to be wielded by the executive alone: as a Labour Party paper of 1993 commented: 'It is where power is exercised by government under the cover of royal prerogative that our concerns are greatest ... Massive power is exercised by executive degree without accountability to Parliament.'[1] Ironically enough, this area, which most concerned Labour in 1993 has remained entirely untouched by the great wave of constitutional reform enacted by the Blair administration from 1997 on, save for the impact of the Human Rights Act 1998 on judicial control of the prerogative.

This chapter first considers the nature of prerogative powers, and then goes on to examine the more important prerogatives: the power to dissolve Parliament, to assent to Bills, to declare war, to dismiss and appoint ministers; personal prerogatives of the monarch; and various immunities such as the Queen's personal immunity from suit or prosecution, and property rights.[2] Secondly, it considers the extent to which the prerogative, unchecked by Parliament, has been subject to control through judicial review.

THE NATURE AND EXTENT OF THE PREROGATIVE

Colin Munro, *Studies in Constitutional Law*, 2nd edn (1999), pp 256–59 (extracts)

The royal prerogative may be defined as comprising those attributes peculiar to the Crown which are derived from common law, not statute, and which still survive.

---

1   Labour Party, *A New Agenda for Democracy* (1993), p 33.
2   This chapter does not consider the arcane and rarely invoked prerogative power known as 'act of state', defined by O Hood Phillips as 'an act done by the Crown as a matter of policy in relation to another state, or in relation to an individual who is not within the allegiance to the Crown' (O Hood Phillips and P Jackson, *Constitutional and Administrative Law*, P Jackson and P Leopold (eds), 8th edn (2001), p 321. For discussion, see *ibid*, pp 320–26.

Some of these points need to be amplified, so that we may see what sort of creature we are dealing with. First, notice that the prerogative consists of legal attributes, not matters merely of convention or practice. The courts will recognise, in appropriate cases, that these attributes exist, and, when necessary, enforce them. So, when a university archaeological team excavated a treasure hoard from St Ninian's Isle in the Shetlands, an action was brought to establish that the treasure belonged to the Crown [*Lord Advocate v University of Aberdeen* 1963 SC 533]. The courts will rule, in other cases, that a prerogative which has been claimed does not exist or that Government action falls outside the scope of the prerogative ...

Strictly speaking, the prerogatives are recognised, rather than created, by the common law, for their source is in custom. By origin, royal prerogatives were attributes which of necessity inhered in kings as the governors of the realm. It is natural to think of the prerogative as composed of powers, for it is in the exercise of the Crown's discretionary powers, and the control of that exercise, that our chief interest lies. But rules affected the Crown in a variety of ways. Some gave rights to the Crown, such as the right to treasure trove. Some gave immunities, such as the Crown's immunity from being sued. Some even imposed duties, such as the Crown's duty to protect subjects within the realm.

Strictly speaking, it may be maintained that the term 'prerogative' should be reserved for rules peculiar to the Crown, as Blackstone expounded:

> It signifies ... something that is required or demanded before, or in preference to, all others. And hence it follows, that it must be in its nature singular and eccentrical; that it can only be applied to those rights and capacities which the king enjoys alone, in contradistinction to others, and not to those which he enjoys in common with any of his subjects; for if once any one prerogative of the Crown could be held in common with the subject, it would cease to be prerogative any longer [*Commentaries*, I, p 239].

On this view, the prerogative properly describes matters, such as the power to declare war or the granting of royal assent to Bills, which are peculiar to the Crown ... These special legal attributes are a residue, a remnant of what was possessed by medieval kings and queens. What remains is left to the executive by the grace of Parliament, for Parliament can abrogate or diminish the prerogative, like any other part of the common law.

The prerogatives that remain are relics. But they are not unimportant relics.

Notes

1   Munro admits that there is more than one view on the scope of the prerogative but arguably understates the definitional vacuum surrounding the term. Moreover, it is not as if there has not been more than adequate time for clarification. As John F McEldowney and Patrick McAuslan put it, 'Notwithstanding that the royal prerogative as a source of power of the government antedates Acts of Parliament, has been at the root of a civil war and a revolution in England and has been litigated about on countless major occasions in respect of its use both at home and overseas, its scope is still unsure'.[3]

2   Professor HWR Wade believes that this lack of clarity (for which he partly blames AV Dicey – see below) has resulted in many exercises of power being wrongly labelled as examples of the prerogative. He notes a number of examples of government actions that have been misdescribed by the courts as acts of 'prerogative' power.

---

3   'Legitimacy and the constitution: the dissonance between theory and practice', in P McAuslan and JF McEldowney, *Law, Legitimacy and the Constitution* (1985), p 12.

HWR Wade, *Constitutional Fundamentals* (1989), pp 58–66

But what does 'prerogative' mean? I have felt disposed to criticise the use of this term in some recent judgments and other contexts where, as it seemed to me, no genuine prerogative power was in question at all. If prerogative power is to be brought under judicial control, and if ministers are to be condemned for abusing it unlawfully, it is worth finding out what it really is. In the first place, the prerogative consists of legal power – that is to say, the ability to alter people's rights, duties or status under the laws of this country which the courts of this country enforce. Thus when Parliament is dissolved under the prerogative it can no longer validly do business. When a man is made a peer, he may no longer lawfully vote in a parliamentary election. When a university is incorporated by royal charter, a new legal person enters the world. All these legal transformations are effected in terms of rights, duties, disabilities, etc, which the courts will acknowledge and enforce. The power to bring them about is vested in the Crown by the common law, so it clearly falls within the definition of the royal prerogative as 'the common law powers of the Crown'. But when the Government cancels the designation of Laker Airways by making a communication to the Government of the United States under the terms of an international agreement, that has no effect under the law of this country whatsoever and has nothing to do with any power conferred by common law or recognised by British courts. It may be, as the Court of Appeal held, an act prohibited by a British statute. But it is not an act of power in any British constitutional sense, since it involves no special power that a British court will recognise. Whatever powers the Government may have had under the Bermuda Agreement were powers in the sphere of international law, and their capacity to make the Agreement came not from common law but from their status in international law as an international person. In the Laker Airways case the Attorney General claimed that the Crown was entitled to cancel the designation under the royal prerogative, and there was much talk about prerogative in the judgments. But if there was no power, in the correct legal and constitutional sense, there was no prerogative either. There was merely a piece of administrative action on the international plane.

Another example shows another species of inaccuracy. The Criminal Injuries Compensation Board is an instance of the practice, dear to the administrative heart, of doing things informally and extra-legally if means can be devised. This Board pays out several million pounds of public money annually to the victims of violent crime. But until recently it had no statutory authority. [The Board was made statutory by the Criminal Justice Act 1988.] Parliament simply voted the money each year, and the Board dispensed it under the rules of the scheme, which were laid before Parliament by the Home Secretary but had no statutory force. Nevertheless, by a feat no less imaginative than in the Laker Airways case, the courts assumed jurisdiction to quash decisions of the Board which did not accord with the rules of the scheme. In doing so, they described the Board as 'set up under the prerogative' [*R v Criminal Injuries Compensation Board ex p Lain* [1967] 2 QB 864, at 881, 883]. But one essential of 'prerogative', if I may be forgiven for saying so, is that it should be prerogative. Its etymology means that it should be some special power possessed by the Crown over and above the powers of an ordinary person, and by virtue of the Crown's special constitutional position.

... Now if we apply this test to the constitution of the Criminal Injuries Compensation Board, it is surely plain that the Government, in establishing it, was merely doing what ... any of us could do if we had the money ready to hand. We could set up a board, or a committee, or trustees with authority to make grants according to whatever rules we might please to lay down. Thousands of foundations or trusts have been set up in the exercise of exactly the same liberty that the Government exercised in the case of the criminal injuries scheme. So far as the Crown came into the picture at all, it was exercising its ordinary powers as a natural person, which of course include power to transfer property, make contracts and so on. [In *R v Panel on Take-overs and Mergers ex p Datafin plc* [1987] QB 815, at 848, Lloyd LJ expressed his agreement with this argument.] Blackstone was quite right, in my opinion, in saying that such powers are not prerogative at all.

Much the same might be said of other powers of the Crown which writers on constitutional law are fond of cataloguing as prerogative, without regard to Blackstone's doctrine. The power to appoint and dismiss ministers, for instance, appears to me to be nothing else than the power which all legal persons have at common law to employ servants or agents, so that it lacks any 'singular and eccentrical' element. Ministers as such have no inherent powers at common law and must therefore be counted as ordinary servants. It is otherwise with judges, who have very great legal powers, and their appointment and dismissal were undoubtedly within the true prerogative before Parliament gave them a statutory basis. I will not go through the whole catalogue of the powers commonly classed as prerogative in textbooks and elsewhere, though I suspect that a number of them would not pass the Blackstone test. A collector's piece comes from a hopeless case of 1971. Mr Clive Jenkins, the trade union leader, sued the Attorney General in an attempt to stop the Government from distributing a free pamphlet on the Common Market at a cost to the taxpayer of £20,000. The judge is reported to have held that the issue of free information is 'a prerogative power of the Crown' which the court cannot question [*Jenkins v Attorney General* (1970) 115 SJ 674]. Since all the Crown's subjects are at liberty to issue as much free information as they like (and many of them issue much too much of it), I offer you this as a choice example of a non-prerogative.

The truth seems to be that judges have fallen into the habit of describing as 'prerogative' any and every sort of Government action which is not statutory. It may be, also, that the responsibility for this solecism can be loaded onto that popular scapegoat, Dicey. For his well known definition of prerogative is 'the residue of discretionary power left at any moment in the hands of the Crown'. He makes no distinction between the Crown's natural and regal capacities, indeed at one point he says [*The Law of the Constitution*, 10th edn, p 425]:

> Every act which the executive Government can lawfully do without the authority of an Act of Parliament is done in virtue of this prerogative.

So the judges and authors whose wide statements I have ventured to criticise could quote Dicey against me. But if we match Dicey against Blackstone, I think that Blackstone wins. Nor do I think that the criticism is mere pedantry. The true limits of the prerogatives of the Crown are important both in constitutional and in administrative law. This is all the more so now that the courts are showing signs, as in the Laker Airways case, of bringing the exercise of the prerogative under judicial control. It may well be easier to extend control to the few genuine prerogative powers which may possibly admit it, for example an improper use of *nolle prosequi*, if the court is not by the same token committed to extend it to all sorts of pretended prerogatives, such as the control of the civil service and the making of contracts or treaties

Notes

1   Wade's contention that 'Ministers as such have no inherent powers at common law' is perhaps open to question. Whilst theoretically all prerogative powers are vested in the sovereign, the courts recognise clearly enough that the powers are in fact exercised by ministers: in *R v Secretary of State for the Home Department ex p Northumbria Police Authority* [1988] 2 WLR 590 (discussed below), the court referred to 'the prerogative powers available to the Secretary of State [for the Home Department] to do all that is reasonably necessary to preserve the peace of the nation' (at p 609). Nor is this a case where the courts were mistakenly labelling 'prerogative' a power in fact belonging to any ordinary citizen.

2   The prerogative covers a quite startlingly wide range of areas. Harry Calvert gives a useful list.

Harry Calvert, *An Introduction to British Constitutional Law* (1985), pp 163–65

The potential range of prerogative powers is ... enormous and no attempt will be made to set out a comprehensive list of them. Some are, however, more important or, at all events, better known than others.

For purposes of description, it is helpful to list individual prerogative powers in this way and convenient, also, to classify them as, eg, legislative, executive and judicial. This process of rationalisation is aided by the work of commentators and judges in examining the scope and nature of the prerogative. The reality, however, is that the prerogative is residual and unsystematic.

Amongst the best-known examples are the following:

(a) The power to summon, prorogue and dissolve Parliament ('proroguing' being the act of adjourning a Parliament at the end of a session).

(b) The power to declare war and peace, not legally a prerequisite to the institution or termination of hostilities, but having legal consequences (such as rendering certain persons 'enemy aliens' and thus subjecting them to certain legal disabilities, eg in relation to trade).

(c) The prerogative of pardon – the dispensing power to release a particular individual from the obligation to obey a particular law, was the subject of great controversy in the seventeenth century and the Bill of Rights 1689 contains a dubious partial prohibition of it. The power, however, to erase a conviction after the event survived and may be exercised absolutely, as is most common today, or conditionally, as was formerly common where a person convicted of murder and sentenced to death was reprieved and the sentence commuted to one of life imprisonment. This power remains peculiar in that it is exercised, in England, on the advice not of the Prime Minister but of the Home Secretary.

(d) The power to confer peerages and other honours – the vast majority of peerages (and few hereditary ones are created) are today almost invariably created on the advice of the Prime Minister, the most common occasions by far being those of the Birthday Honours and New Year's Honours lists. Exceptionally, the monarch may confer a peerage without advice and certain honours are in the gift of the monarch personally.

(e) The power to conclude treaties. This is merely a particular, though important, facet of the power of the Crown in relation to foreign affairs. Its exercise is commonplace; each year the United Kingdom becomes a party to a host of international arrangements simply by the exercise of the prerogative power and without any need for endorsement by Parliament. Amongst the most striking exercises of this power in recent years have been the acceptance by the United Kingdom of the compulsory jurisdiction of the Commission and Court established under the European Convention of Human Rights and Fundamental Freedoms ... and accession to the Treaty of Rome leading to United Kingdom membership of the European Community.

Whilst the exercise of the prerogative power in this way effectively renders the United Kingdom a party to such a treaty in the eyes of international law, one extremely important limitation on effectiveness should be noted. Notwithstanding that it is the clear purport of the treaty in question to confer rights or to impose obligations on the individual subject within the realm, mere accession to it by the Crown in the exercise of its prerogative power will not, by itself, have this effect, a point vividly illustrated in a number of cases such as *Civilian War Claimants Association Ltd v The King* [1932] AC 14, where the treaty in question had as its clear purport the provision of compensation for individuals suffering loss or injury as a result of the actions of the Axis powers during the First World War and where the funds for this purpose were actually handed over to the Crown. This, however, by itself conferred no right to compensation upon particular persons allegedly so injured.

A corollary of this doctrine is that individual subjects within the United Kingdom have no means of enforcing, as of right, an award in their favour by the organs of the European human rights regime established under the Convention above, under United Kingdom law. They may confidently expect compliance by Her Majesty's Government for the Government will not wish to court the consequences of non-compliance, the ultimate sanction of which is expulsion from the Council of Europe. Until Parliament legislates so as to provide otherwise, however, the individual has a mere spes, rather than a right, that he will benefit.

It follows that if it is intended to implement a treaty regime into the domestic law of the United Kingdom so as to affect the rights and duties of the subject, Parliament must intervene. Thus, although the United Kingdom acceded to the Treaty of Rome by prerogative act, and thus became a member of the European Community in the eyes of European and international law, parliamentary action was necessary if that membership was to be more than a sham. It is a central feature of the European Community that its laws apply to individuals in respect of their legal relationships within the Community. If subjects in the United Kingdom were to be able to assert their rights under or be fixed with obligations arising out of Community law, that law had to be incorporated into the domestic law of the United Kingdom by Act of Parliament and this end was achieved by the European Communities Act 1972.

The surviving prerogative powers of the Crown extend over an area vastly more wide than is indicated in this short list of examples. The power to declare war and peace, for example, may be viewed as merely a particular aspect of a wider prerogative concerning, amongst other things, the conduct of war, control over the armed forces generally (in so far as this is not now regulated by statute) and, incidentally thereto, the requisitioning and even destruction of property for these purposes. The treaty-making power relating to the conduct of foreign and colonial affairs involving matters such as the recognition of foreign states and governments, the organisation of diplomatic services and the reception and accreditation of the representatives of foreign states.

Notes

1 To Calvert's list, one could add (as RFV Heuston[4] points out), the fact that the assent of the monarch is a necessary element in legislation.

2 Calvert's concentration on the treaty-making aspect of the prerogative's ambit in foreign affairs deflects attention from the rather more drastic actions which may be taken in under it. Heuston quotes Walter Bagehot on the subject:

> I said in this book it would very much surprise people if they were really told how many things the Queen could do without consulting Parliament. Not to mention other things, she could disband the army ... dismiss all the officers from the General commanding-in-chief downwards ... [and] all the sailors too; she could sell off all our ships of war and all our navy stores; she could make a peace by the sacrifice of Cornwall and begin a war for the conquest of Brittany ... She could make every parish in the United Kingdom a university ... In a word, the Queen could by prerogative upset all the action of civil government.[5]

Of course, these powers are, by convention, exercised on the advice of ministers, but since conventions are not enforced by the courts,[6] it is still correct to say that the Queen *could*, as a matter of strict legal theory, do all the above.

PARLIAMENTARY CONTROL OVER THE PREROGATIVE

One of the most remarkable features of the prerogative, to foreign observers, must be the way in which it allows 'almost the whole terrain of foreign policy in the UK [to be] carried on by the government ... [without] the need to secure any formal [parliamentary] approval to its diplomatic agreements and executive decisions'.[7] Perhaps the most remarkable aspect of this situation is the complete absence of any formal parliamentary control over two of the most important types of decision which

4   RFV Heuston, *Essays in Constitutional Law* (1964), p 66.
5   Walter Bagehot, *The English Constitution*, pp 282–84, quoted *ibid*, p 72.
6   See Part I Chapter 2.
7   R Blackburn, 'The House of Lords', in R Blackburn and R Plant (eds), *Constitutional Reform: The Labour Government's Constitutional Reform Agenda* (1999), p 33.

government may make: the signing of treaties, and the deployment of the armed forces abroad. As to the former, Blackburn notes:

> The UK now has the only Parliament in the European Union that lacks any formal mechanism for securing scrutiny and approval to treaties. The 1924 Ponsonby 'Rule' – now a Foreign Office circular – is clearly inadequate as a basis for effective scrutiny. It involves the voluntary practice of governments laying treaties signed by the UK before Parliament as Command Papers after their entry into force, and in the case of treaties requiring legal ratification a copy being placed on the Table of the house 21 days beforehand.[8]

He notes the complaint of the Labour Party, when in opposition: 'Treaty after treaty is concluded without the formal consent of Parliament. Indeed foreign policy as a whole is an area virtually free from democratic control and accountability.'[9]

The lack of any necessity to seek approval from, or even consult with Parliament before committing the country's armed forces to battle abroad, whether in a formal state of war or not, is perhaps the other most remarkable feature of the use of the prerogative, as Brazier notes.

R Brazier, *Constitutional Reform*, 2nd edn (1999), p 123

On three occasions since 1945 the Cabinet has committed large military forces to actual or possible armed conflict, although not, in legal parlance, to war. In none of these cases was Parliament formally consulted before the decision to send forces was made. Suez, the Falklands, and the Gulf all received British armed forces on ministerial direction under the royal prerogative power to dispose those forces as the Crown thinks fit. How odd – perhaps bizarre – it is that the approval of both Houses of Parliament is required for pieces of technical, and often trivial, subordinate legislation, whereas it is not needed at all before men and women can be committed to the possibility of disfigurement or death! Speed of military response may, of course, be vital . . . To insist on prior approval of all military deployments would be absurd, especially when Parliament is in recess, as it was at start of the Gulf emergency. But the commitment of military forces is an act which may have such terrible consequences that the approval of Parliament ought to be required within a specified period. Even under the present arrangements, no British government is going to take the country to the brink of, or to actual, fighting unless it is reasonably confident that it can carry Parliament with it . . . The UK needs a War Powers Act, under which Parliament would have to be informed and its consent obtained with in a specified number of days in order that the armed services could be deployed lawfully overseas . . .

Notes

1   To Brazier's examples could be added the deployment and use of the RAF in Bosnia in the 1990s by the Major government, and the prolonged campaign of air-strikes against the targets in Kuwait and Serbia authorised by the Blair government, neither of which were the subject of formal parliamentary approval.

2   To make matters worse, in the absence of legal requirements to obtain parliamentary approval of actions taken under the prerogative, there are not even any clear *conventions* on the matter. As Munro notes: 'John Major, as Prime Minister, was merely stating how things were when he replied to a question by saying that "it is for individual Ministers to decide on a particular occasion whether and how to report to Parliament on the exercise of prerogative powers".'[10] See further, Part III, Chapter 1, pp 315–17.

---

8   *Ibid.*
9   Labour Party, *A New Agenda for Democracy* (1993), p 33.
10   C Munro, *Studies in Constitutional Law*, 2nd edn (1999), p 276.

3   The most recent example, at the time of writing, relates to the possibility of armed action against Iraq in Spring 2003. The Prime Minister, Tony Blair, found himself in the position of having a foreign policy – favouring military action against Iraq, possibly even in the absence of specific Security Council authorisation – that was sharply opposed to the views of many within the parliamentary Labour Party. In January, he was questioned on the issue of whether Parliament would be given a chance to debate and vote on military action before any was taken, and the wider issue of whether the historical power to use the royal prerogative to commit the country to war without Parliament's approval now required reform.

Oral Evidence Given by the Prime Minister to the Liaison Committee, 21 January 2003[11]

122. Will you give an undertaking that there will be a vote in the Commons in the event of military action being decided upon?

(Mr Blair) I have got absolutely no doubt at all that in the event of us having military action there will be a vote in the House of Commons. What I am not promising is that you can necessarily do that in all sets of circumstances before the action is taken, for the reasons again that we have gone through a thousand times. But ... in the conflicts we have been involved in in Kosovo and Afghanistan, Parliament has been consulted at every opportunity, and we will continue to do that. It is unthinkable that – I mean, no government could engage in a conflict if Parliament was against it ...

123. So even if, as you say, there may not be a vote before military action, then, very much like the Major Government at the time of the Gulf War in 1991, there would be a vote within days of military action taking place?

(Mr Blair) Do not tie me down to an absolute, specific time, but I have got no doubt that as soon as possible it is right that Parliament expresses its view. As I say, I have never had any difficulty at all with Parliament either being consulted and informed or expressing its view. The only reason I put in a caveat on this in relation to when exactly is that if you had a situation where you had to take action fairly quickly for any reason, the security of the troops obviously comes first, but I think that is accepted by people.

124. There is much talk – and we have had some today – of this country following America, but of course in one crucial respect constitutionally we do not follow the United States. President Bush has to go to Congress before he can wage war. We have this mysterious thing called the Royal Prerogative which enables Prime Ministers and Governments to wage war without Parliament. Is it not time that we had a War Powers Act as well?

(Mr Blair) I think we are about to get to one of these areas where we may have a disagreement with the United States. I think we have different systems, and I do not really see any reason to change the present system.

125. Well you say that, but you do not think it is constitutionally bizarre that the House of Commons can have endless votes on whether it wants to kill foxes, but has no right at all to have a vote on whether we kill people?

(Mr Blair) Well, as I said to you a moment or two ago, I cannot think of a set of circumstances in which a Government can go to war without the support of Parliament, so I do not think it is real. I think you can get into a great constitutional argument about this, but the reality is that Governments are in the end accountable to Parliament, and they are, and they are accountable for any war that they engage in, as they are for anything else.

---

11 Available at the parliamentary website: www.publications.parliament.uk/pa/cm200203/cmselect/cmliaisn/uc334-i/uc33402.htm.

126. Let me just try this one more time from a different angle, which is that Winston Churchill in 1950, in the context of Korea, argued that much better than having just a vote, where sometimes you can get a misrepresentative slice of opinion expressed in the House of Commons, if you have a vote then it can give authority to Governments in acting. Is it not both right for Parliament that it should vote and good for Government that there should be a right to vote too?

(Mr Blair) Yes, and there is a right to vote. The question is, do you take that one step further and get rid of the Royal Prerogative? I do not see any reason to change it, but I do really think that in the end it is more theoretical than real, this issue, because the truth is, if Parliament were to say to any Government — Supposing in relation to any conflict Parliament voted down the Government over the conflict, as I say, it is just not thinkable that the Government would then continue the conflict. That has been the case all the way through. So I think that even though it may be strictly true to say that the Royal Prerogative means you do it and in strict theory Parliament is not the authority, in the end Parliament is the authority for any Government ...

127. ... but the fact is that if you go through post-war conflicts you will find endless instances of demands for votes in Parliament which may or may not have been granted. It is a question of Government. It is surely much better to turn it round and make sure that Parliament simply has the right to vote on any military action taken by its Government?

(Mr Blair) There always are constant votes ... I do not really have very much to add to what I have said.

Notes
1   In the event, several debates took place, most recently on 26 February 2003, when there was a full scale vote on a substantive motion, in which no less than 122 Labour MPs rebelled against a three-line whip by voting for an anti-war amendment to the government motion. For extracts from the debate, see Part III Chapter 1, pp 273–79.
2   As Munro notes, there are a number of prerogatives upon which it is not even possible to raise a question in Parliament:

> When Members have tried to ascertain ... what advice the Prime Minister has given to the Queen as to the dissolution of Parliament, the question is ruled out on the ground that the Prime Minister is not responsible to Parliament for that advice ... Questions cannot be asked which bring the name of the Sovereign or the influence of the Crown before Parliament. The advice given to the Sovereign about some wider matters has similarly been ruled out of bounds: not only the dissolution of Parliament, but also the grant of honours, the ecclesiastical patronage of the Crown, and the appointment and dismissal of Privy Councillors.[12]

PERSONAL PREROGATIVES

Some of the more important prerogatives which the monarch may exercise personally relate to her powers over Parliament and the appointment of a Prime Minister. Sir Ivor Jennings notes:

> There are, however, certain prerogative powers which the Queen exercises on her own responsibility, and which may fitly be called 'the personal prerogatives'. Exactly what they are is by no means clear; for there are differences of opinion in respect of several of them. There is no controversy that she need not accept advice as to the appointment of a Prime Minister or as to the creation of peers so as to override the opposition of the House of Lords. There is controversy as to whether she can dismiss a Government or dissolve Parliament without advice, or whether she can refuse to dissolve Parliament when advised to do so.[13]

12   *Ibid*, p 277.
13   *Cabinet Government*, 3rd edn (1959), p 394, quoted in R Brazier, *Constitutional Texts* (1990), p 437.

The power to dissolve Parliament, independently of a request to do so by the Prime Minister, is by no means obsolete.

R Brazier, *Constitutional Texts* (1990), pp 438–39

In the wholly unlikely events of a Government losing a vote of confidence in the House of Commons but refusing either to recommend a dissolution or to resign, or of a Government which tried improperly to extend the life of Parliament beyond the statutory maximum of five years, the Queen would be justified in insisting on an immediate dissolution. There has been royal insistence on a dissolution twice this century in the context of the Prime Minister's request to create peers so as to coerce the House of Lords: in both cases the Prime Minister unreservedly acquiesced.

(1) EDWARD VII

'He began by saying', Nash recorded, 'that the King had come to the conclusion that he would not be justified in creating new peers (say 300) until after a second general election and that he, Lord Knollys, thought you should know of this now, though, for the present he would suggest that what he was telling me should be for your ear only. The King regards the policy of the Government as tantamount to the destruction of the House of Lords and he thinks that before a large creation of peers is embarked upon or threatened the country should be acquainted with the particular project for accomplishing such destruction as well as with the general line of action as to which the country will be consulted at the forthcoming election.'

[Note made on 15 December 1909 of a conversation between Asquith's secretary, Vaughan Nash, and the King's Private Secretary, Lord Knollys, quoted in Roy Jenkins, *Asquith* (Fontana edn, 1967), p 225.]

(2) GEORGE V

Mr Asquith did not ask for an immediate reply. It seems, however that King George and his private secretary misunderstood the purport of the discussion. Mr Asquith intended to prepare the King for the advice which he would subsequently receive from the Cabinet, while the King thought that no guarantee for the creation of peers would be sought before the election. Three days later Lord Knollys discovered that the King was mistaken, and Sir Arthur Bigge was instructed to telegraph that it would be impossible for the King to give contingent guarantees. The King 'much resented the implication' that in the event of a Liberal Government being returned he might fail to act constitutionally; and he considered that Mr Asquith was seeking to use his name to secure a Liberal victory. On 15 November the Cabinet gave the following advice in a formal minute:

> An immediate dissolution of Parliament – as soon as the necessary parts of the Budget, the provision of old age pensions, and one or two other matters have been disposed of. The House of Lords to have the opportunity, if they demand it, at the same time, but not so as to postpone the date of the dissolution, to discuss the Government Resolution. HM ministers cannot, however, take the responsibility of advising a dissolution unless they may understand that in the event of the policy of the Government being approved by an adequate majority in the new House of Commons, HM will be ready to exercise his constitutional powers (which may involve the prerogative of creating peers) if needed to secure that effect shall he given to the decision of the country.

> HM ministers are fully alive to the importance of keeping the name of the King out of the sphere of party and electoral controversy. They take upon themselves, as is their duty, the entire and exclusive responsibility for the policy which they will place before the electorate. HM will doubtless agree that it would be inadvisable in the interest of the State that any communication of the intentions of the Crown should be made public unless and until the actual occasion should arise.

Mr Asquith and Lord Crewe (as leader of the House of Lords) saw the King on the following day. The King, after much discussion, 'agreed most reluctantly to give the Cabinet a secret understanding that, in the event of the Government being returned with a majority at the general election, I should use my prerogative to make peers if asked for. I disliked having to do this very much, but agreed that this was the only alternative to the Cabinet resigning, which at this moment would be disastrous'.

[I Jennings, *Cabinet Government*, 3rd edn (1959), pp 440–41.]

Note
For the powers of the monarch in relation to Parliament and the Prime Minister, see further Part I Chapter 2 on Constitutional Conventions.

CONTROL OF THE PREROGATIVE BY THE COURTS

Determining the existence of a prerogative power

Two key questions clearly arise here. First, will the courts be prepared to make a finding as to whether the prerogative claimed actually exists in law; secondly, will they be prepared to adjudge whether an admittedly existent power was properly exercised? The courts have clearly answered the first question in the affirmative. As far back as the early 17th century, in the famous *Case of Proclamations* (1611) 12 Co Rep 74, it was said that: '... the King hath no prerogative, but that which the law of the land allows him'. Furthermore, the courts will not allow new prerogatives to be created by executive fiat, although they may allow a recognised prerogative to broaden in adapting itself to new situations. In *BBC v Johns* [1964] 1 All ER 923, the BBC claimed that a new prerogative had come into existence; in response Diplock LJ said, 'It is 350 years and a civil war too late for the Queen's courts to broaden the prerogative. The limits within which the executive government may impose obligations or restraints on the citizens of the United Kingdom without any statutory authority are now well settled and incapable of extension' (at 941). However, Lord Diplock's statement must be treated with some caution: in *Malone v Metropolitan Police Commissioner* [1979] Ch 344, the assertion that a prerogative power existed to authorise telephone tapping was based on the argument that no new power was being created although an old one was being extended to a new situation. It could be argued that the boundary between creating a new power and adapting an old one is not always clear, and that *Malone's* case is an example of an instance in which it is arguable that a new power was being claimed since it was very doubtful whether a prerogative power to intercept communications between citizens had ever existed.

It appears that in other areas the courts may approach the question of whether a prerogative to do a certain act exists not by considering whether it is authorised by some clearly defined and specific aspect of the prerogative but rather by first accepting the presence of a rather expansive and broadly defined general prerogative power and then finding that the specific act in question falls within that broad power. In the following case,[14] one issue which arose was whether there was, as the Home Secretary claimed, a general prerogative to do all that is reasonably necessary to keep the Queen's peace:

---

14   The facts appear below, at p 489.

R v Secretary of State for the Home Department ex p Northumbria Police Authority [1988] 2 WLR 590, 609–10

Mr Keene referred us to *Chitty's Prerogatives of the Crown* (1820) for the purposes of demonstrating that there was then no recognisable 'prerogative to provide or equip a police force.' With respect to Mr Keene, in my judgment this argument begs the question. One is not seeking a prerogative right to do this. The prerogative power is to do all that is reasonably necessary to keep the Queen's peace. This involves the commissioning of justices of the peace, constables and the like. The author clearly identifies the prerogative powers inherent in the Crown in relation to the duty placed on the Sovereign to protect his dominions and subjects . . .

After considering the principle and transcendent prerogatives with respect to foreign states and affairs, as supreme head of the church as the fountain of justice the author turns to the question of the protection of the realm in these terms, at p 71:

> The duties arising from the relation of sovereign and subject are reciprocal. Protection, that is, the security and governance of his dominions according to law, is the duty of the sovereign; and allegiance and subjection, with reference to the same criterion, the constitution and laws of the country, form, in return, the duty of the governed, as will be more fully noticed hereafter. We have already partially mentioned this duty of the sovereign, and have observed that the prerogatives are vested in him for the benefit of his subjects, and that His Majesty is under, and not above, the laws.

The up-to-date position is summarised in *Halsbury's Laws of England* (4th edn, 1981), vol 36, p 200, para 320:

> General functions of constables. The primary function of the constable remains, as in the 17th century, the preservation of the Queen's peace. From this general function stems a number of particular duties additional to those conferred by statute and including those mentioned hereafter. The first duty of a constable is always to prevent the commission of a crime. If a constable reasonably apprehends that the action of any person may result in a breach of the peace it is his duty to prevent that action. It is his general duty to protect life and property. The general function of controlling traffic on the roads is derived from this duty.

. . . In my judgment, the prerogative powers to take all reasonable steps to preserve the Queen's peace . . . include the supply of equipment to police forces which is reasonably required for the more efficient discharge of their duties.

Note

At times, the question of whether a claimed prerogative power is recognised by the law will be complicated by the enactment of a statute covering the same area. What happens when an area formerly regulated by the prerogative becomes covered by a statute?

Attorney-General v De Keyser's Royal Hotel Ltd [1920] AC 508, 526, 539, 575

Lord Dunedin: Inasmuch as the Crown is a party to every Act of Parliament it is logical enough to consider that when the Act deals with something which before the Act could be effected by the prerogative, and specially empowers the Crown to do the same thing, but subject to conditions, the Crown assents to that, and by that Act, to the prerogative being curtailed.

Lord Atkinson: It is quite obvious that it would be useless and meaningless for the Legislature to impose restrictions and limitations upon, and to attach conditions to, the exercise by the Crown of the powers conferred by a statute, if the Crown were free at its pleasure to disregard these provisions, and by virtue of its prerogative do the very thing the statutes empowered it to do. One cannot in the construction of a statute attribute to the Legislature (in the absence of compelling words) an intention so absurd. It was suggested that when a statute is passed empowering the Crown to do a certain thing which it might theretofore have done by virtue of its prerogative, the prerogative is merged in the statute. I confess I do not think the word 'merged' is happily chosen. I should prefer to say that when such a statute; expressing the will and intention of the King and of the three estates of the realm, is passed, it abridges the Royal Prerogative while it is in force to this extent: that the Crown can only do the particular thing under and in accordance with the statutory provisions ... and subject to all the limitations, restrictions and conditions by [them] imposed.

Lord Parmoor: The constitutional principle is that when the power of the executive to interfere with the property or liberty of subjects has been placed under Parliamentary control, and directly regulated by statute, the executive no longer derives its authority from the Royal Prerogative of the Crown but from Parliament, and that in exercising such authority the executive is bound to observe the restrictions which Parliament has imposed in favour of the subject.

Notes

1   In the *Northumbria Police Authority* case (above), the court had to consider whether s 4 of the Police Act 1964, which authorised Police Authorities to maintain vehicles, apparatus and equipment required for police purposes, effectively granted them a monopoly of this power, so that the Home Secretary had had his pre-existing prerogative power to keep the peace (which included the power to maintain and supply equipment to the police) abridged by the statute. Section 4(4) of the Police Act 1964 provided that the police authority for a police area 'may ... provide and maintain such vehicles, apparatus, clothing and other equipment as may be required for police purposes of the area'. It was argued that since the Home Secretary had an undoubted power under the statute to supply equipment, subject to certain requirements, he could not claim a parallel prerogative power to supply such equipment without any safeguards. The court rejected this argument on the basis that the statute did not expressly state that equipment was not to be supplied under any other power. Purchas LJ held:

Where [an exercise of the prerogative is directed towards the benefit or protection of the individual ... express and unequivocal terms must be found in the statute which deprives the individual from receiving the benefit or protection intended by the exercise of prerogative power ...

This appears to come close to stating that statute will only oust the prerogative if it uses express words in doing so; this would make it actually harder to abolish parts of the prerogative than to repeal previous Acts of Parliament, since previous Acts can be impliedly repealed, and thus seem to elevate the status of the prerogative over Acts of Parliament in direct opposition to the basic principle that statute is the highest form of law known in this country.

2   Croom-Johnson LJ's judgment was less controversial. He thought that s 4 'does not expressly grant a monopoly' and that in the circumstances 'there [was] every reason not to imply' such a monopoly, which does at least appear to admit of the possibility that the monopoly necessary to oust the prerogative could have been impliedly granted. Clarity appears to be lacking in this case, but the impression gained is that the courts were reluctant to allow erosion of the prerogative in the absence of a clear intent (express *or* implied?) to do so. In other words, any ambiguity – and there clearly was ambiguity in this case – seems to be resolved in favour of preservation of the prerogative.

3   Will the disabling of the prerogative by statute still take effect even where the statute in question only gives 'enabling' powers, allowing a scheme under the statutory provisions to be set up in the future? If it does not, could the government set up an alternative scheme, inconsistent with the statutory one, acting under the prerogative? These were the issues which the House of Lords had to consider in *R v*

Secretary of State for the Home Department ex p Fire Brigades Union and others [1995] 2 WLR 464. The Criminal Justice Act 1988, ss 108–17 and Scheds 6 and 7 provided for a statutory scheme to replace the old non-statutory scheme for compensating victims of violent crime. The statutory scheme would have compensated victims under the tort measure of damages. Section 171 of the Act permitted the Secretary of State for the Home Department to choose when the scheme was to come into force. He decided not to bring it in and instead set up a tariff system (acting under the prerogative) which was radically different from the scheme envisaged by the Act.

4   Ian Leigh describes the background to the case ([1995] 3 Web JCLI – below):

The applicants in the *Fire Brigades Union* case argued that introduction of a new non-statutory scheme was unlawful in the sense either that the minister was in breach of the provisions for the introduction of the 1988 scheme, or that the existence of the unimplemented, but unrepealed, statutory scheme prevented the introduction of a wholly different scheme. ... Either the case could be understood as an attack on the (non-)use of the Home Secretary's power to make a commencement order under the Criminal Justice Act 1988, s 171. Or it could be understood as being concerned with limiting the prerogative power to introduce a new scheme, because of the existence of unimplemented amending legislation. Broadly, the second was the view taken by the majority in the Court of Appeal *(R v Secretary of State for the Home Department, ex parte Fire Brigades Union and Others* [1995] 1 All ER 888), while the majority in the House of Lords preferred the first approach. A majority of the Court of Appeal held that the commencement section created no enforceable duty in the Home Secretary to bring the legislation into force at any particular time. However, a different majority held (Hobhouse LJ dissenting) that the Home Secretary had acted unlawfully in using the prerogative to introduce the new scheme since the 1988 Act suspended the prerogative in this area. Both points were cross-appealed to the House of Lords.

R v Secretary of State for the Home Department ex p Fire Brigades Union [1995] 2 All ER 244, 252–56

Lord Browne-Wilkinson found that the Home Secretary did not have an absolute duty to bring the scheme in, but continued as follows:

Lord Browne-Wilkinson: It does not follow that, because the Secretary of State is not under any duty to bring the section into effect, he has an absolute and unfettered discretion whether or not to do so. So to hold would lead to the conclusion that both Houses of Parliament had passed the Bill through all its stages and the Act received the royal assent merely to confer an enabling power on the executive to decide at will whether or not to make the parliamentary provisions a part of the law. Such a conclusion, drawn from a section to which the sidenote is 'Commencement', is not only constitutionally dangerous but flies in the face of common sense. The provisions for bringing sections into force under s 171(1) apply not only to the statutory scheme but to many other provisions. For example, the provisions of Pts I, II and III relating to extradition, documentary evidence in criminal proceedings and other evidence in criminal proceedings are made subject to the same provisions. Surely, it cannot have been the intention of Parliament to leave it in the entire discretion of the Secretary of State whether or not to effect such important changes to the criminal law. In the absence of express provisions to the contrary in the Act, the plain intention of Parliament in conferring on the Secretary of State the power to bring certain sections into force is that such power is to be exercised so as to bring those sections into force when it is appropriate and unless there is a subsequent change of circumstances which would render it inappropriate to do so.

If, as I think, that is the clear purpose for which the power in s 171(1) was conferred on the Secretary of State, two things follow. First, the Secretary of State comes under a clear duty to keep under consideration from time to time the question whether or not to bring the section (and therefore the statutory scheme) into force. In my judgment he cannot lawfully surrender or release the power contained in s 171(1) so as to purport to exclude its future exercise either by himself or by his successors. In the course of argument, the Lord Advocate accepted that this was the correct view of the legal position. It follows that the decision of the Secretary of State to give effect to the statement in para 38 of the 1993 White Paper (Cm 2434) that 'the provisions in the 1988 Act will not now be implemented' was unlawful. The Lord Advocate contended, correctly, that the attempt by the Secretary of State to abandon or release the power conferred on him by s 171(1), being unlawful, did not bind either the present Secretary of State or any successor in that office. It was a nullity. But, in my judgment, that does not alter the fact that the Secretary of State made the attempt to bind himself not to exercise the power conferred by s 171(1) and such attempt was an unlawful act.

There is a second consequence of the power in s 171(1) being conferred for the purpose of bringing the sections into force. As I have said, in my view, the Secretary of State is entitled to decide not to bring the sections into force if events subsequently occur which render it undesirable to do so. But if the power is conferred on the Secretary of State with a view to bringing the sections into force, in my judgment, the Secretary of State cannot himself procure events to take place and rely on the occurrence of those events as the ground for not bringing the statutory scheme into force. In claiming that the introduction of the new tariff scheme renders it undesirable now to bring the statutory scheme into force, the Secretary of State is, in effect, claiming that the purpose of the statutory power has been frustrated by his own act in choosing to introduce a scheme inconsistent with the statutory scheme approved by Parliament.

THE LAWFULNESS OF THE DECISION TO INTRODUCE THE TARIFF SCHEME

The tariff scheme, if validly introduced under the Royal Prerogative, is both inconsistent with the statutory scheme contained in ss 108 to 117 of the 1988 Act and intended to be permanent. In practice, the tariff scheme renders it now either impossible or at least more expensive to reintroduce the old scheme or the statutory enactment of it contained in the 1988 Act. The tariff scheme involves the winding up of the old Criminal Injuries Compensation Board together with its team of those skilled in assessing compensation on the common law basis and the creation of a new body, the Criminal Injuries Compensation Authority, set up to assess compensation on the tariff basis at figures which, in some cases, will be very substantially less than under the old scheme. All this at a time when Parliament has expressed its will that there should be a scheme based on the tortious measure of damages, such will being expressed in a statute which Parliament has neither repealed nor (for reasons which have not been disclosed) been invited to repeal.

My Lords, it would be most surprising if, at the present day, prerogative powers could be validly exercised by the executive so as to frustrate the will of Parliament expressed in a statute and, to an extent, to pre-empt the decision of Parliament whether or not to continue with the statutory scheme even though the old scheme has been abandoned. It is not for the executive, as the Lord Advocate accepted, to state as it did in the White Paper (para 38) that the provisions in the 1988 Act 'will accordingly be repealed when a suitable legislative opportunity occurs'. It is for Parliament, not the executive, to repeal legislation. The constitutional history of this country is the history of the prerogative powers of the Crown being made subject to the overriding powers of the democratically elected legislature as the sovereign body. The prerogative powers of the Crown remain in existence to the extent that Parliament has not expressly or by implication extinguished them. But under the principle in *A-G v De Keyser's Royal Hotel Ltd* [1920] AC 508; [1920] All ER Rep 80 if Parliament has conferred on the executive statutory powers to do a particular act, that act can only thereafter be done under the statutory powers so conferred: any pre-existing prerogative power to do the same act is *pro tanto* excluded ...

In his powerful dissenting judgment in the Court of Appeal, Hobhouse LJ decided that, since the statutory provisions had not been brought into force, they had no legal significance of any kind. He held, in my judgment correctly, that the *De Keyser* principle did not apply to the present case: since the statutory provisions were not in force they could not have excluded the pre-existing prerogative powers. Therefore the prerogative powers remained. He then turned to consider whether it could be said that the Secretary of State had abused those prerogative powers and again approached the matter on the basis that since the sections were not in force they had no significance in deciding whether or not the Secretary of State had acted lawfully. I cannot agree with this last step. In public law the fact that a scheme approved by Parliament was on the statute book and would come into force as law if and when the Secretary of State so determined is in my judgment directly relevant to the question whether the Secretary of State could in the lawful exercise of prerogative powers both decide to bring in the tariff scheme and refuse properly to exercise his discretion under s 171(1) to bring the statutory provisions into force.

I turn then to consider whether the Secretary of State's decisions were unlawful as being an abuse of power. In this case there are two powers under consideration: first, the statutory power conferred by s 171(1); second, the prerogative power. In order first to test the validity of the exercise of the prerogative power, I will assume that the 1988 Act, instead of conferring a discretion on the Secretary of State to bring the statutory scheme into effect, had specified that it was to come into force one year after the date of the royal assent. As Hobhouse LJ held, during that year the *De Keyser* principle would not apply and the prerogative powers would remain exercisable. But in my judgment it would plainly have been an improper use of the prerogative powers if, during that year, the Secretary of State had discontinued the old scheme and introduced the tariff scheme. It would have been improper because in exercising the prerogative power the Secretary of State would have had to have regard to the fact that the statutory scheme was about to come into force: to dismantle the machinery of the old scheme in the meantime would have given rise to further disruption and expense when, on the first anniversary, the statutory scheme had to be put into operation. This hypothetical case shows that, although during the suspension of the coming into force of the statutory provisions the old prerogative powers continue to exist, the existence of such legislation basically affects the mode in which such prerogative powers can be lawfully exercised.

Does it make any difference that the statutory provisions are to come into effect, not automatically at the end of the year as in the hypothetical case I have put, but on such day as the Secretary of State specifies under a power conferred on him by Parliament for the purpose of bringing the statutory provisions into force? In my judgment it does not. The Secretary of State could only validly exercise the prerogative power to abandon the old scheme and introduce the tariff scheme if, at the same time, he could validly resolve never to bring the statutory provisions and the inconsistent statutory scheme into effect. For the reasons I have already given, he could not validly so resolve to give up his statutory duty to consider from time to time whether to bring the statutory scheme into force. His attempt to do so, being a necessary part of the composite decision which he took, was itself unlawful. By introducing the tariff scheme he debars himself from exercising the statutory power for the purposes and on the basis which Parliament intended. For these reasons, in my judgment the decision to introduce the tariff scheme at a time when the statutory provisions and his power under s 171(1) were on the statute book was unlawful and an abuse of the prerogative power.

Notes

1   The House of Lords held by a majority of three to two (Lord Keith and Lord Mustill dissenting) that it was an abuse of power for the Home Secretary to purport to use the prerogative to set up a scheme inconsistent with the statutory one. The decision to do so was therefore unlawful.

2   As Leigh notes:

The Lords' decision in effect treats the prerogative as a source of law equivalent to legislation: it can only be repealed by later legislation which is itself in force. This is appealing on grounds of symmetry and logic, but can be criticised as an overly mechanical approach, which attributes more clarity and certainty to prerogative power than is justified. Although it may be too late to create new prerogatives, the exact scope of many prerogative powers remains wholly unclear until litigated. In effect, therefore, as a source of law, the prerogative is given a latent potential which greatly exceeds that of unimplemented (but precise and detailed) statutory provisions.[15]

3   It will be noted that notwithstanding the view of Professor Wade (above) that the whole Criminal Injuries Compensation Scheme had nothing to do with the prerogative, it was common ground that the prerogative was in fact being used.

4   One important argument of the dissenting minority was that, since any scheme the minister put in place could be changed (albeit with difficulty) by Parliament in the future, the minister could not be said to be frustrating Parliament's intent as he had not put an end to the statutory scheme, something only Parliament itself could do (*per* Lord Mustill at p 267). With respect, this view seems to be clearly mistaken. By bringing in a scheme which differed radically from that envisaged by Parliament, the minister was clearly contravening their will: the fact that such contravention could later be reversed is beside the point. Lord Mustill seems to think that Parliament's will is not frustrated as long as it is not permanently frustrated.[16]

5   Below, Leigh draws out the wider constitutional implications of the judgment.

I Leigh, 'The prerogative, legislative power, and the democratic deficit: the *Fire Brigades Union* case' [1995] 3 Web JCLI

In the words of Sir Thomas Bingham MR, legislation is 'the most solemn form for which constitution provides' ([1995] I All ER at 896). The broad principle that the government should not be free to obtain legislation from Parliament on the understanding that it will be used and then to decide unilaterally that it will not, is surely unimpeachable, even within the impoverished British versions of the rule of law and the separation of powers (cf Lord Mustill [1995] 2 WLR at 487–88). Although of fundamental importance, the implications are in a sense procedural: a requirement that a government which changes its mind should at least seek amending legislation before introducing changes. Normally, of course, it will be required to do so by the absence of legal authority for its new position. It is fairly common, for instance, after a change in government for unimplemented legislation at variance with the new government's policies to be first moth-balled, and then repealed. Where the power in question is a prerogative one this formality may be avoided. Although it may be a formality, it is an important one, on grounds of the enhanced scrutiny, public debate and legitimacy which legislation enjoys within a democracy when compared to use of the prerogative. These are strong arguments for codifying prerogative powers wherever possible. They are stronger still when codifying legislation has in fact been passed. In these circumstances to resort to the prerogative rather than amending legislation is strongly indicative of executive ennui with the democratic niceties.

This analysis suggests that judges who see their role as buttressing Parliamentary government ought, whenever possible, to give a restricted reading to the prerogative, and so force the executive to use the better (if more circuitous) route for implementing its policies. In the great constitutional battles of the seventeenth century the use of the prerogative by the Stuart monarchs to avoid inconvenient legislation was one of the abuses which culminated in the declaration in the Bill of Rights against the suspension of statutes. The inter-action between prerogative and statute is less a matter of constitutional crisis in current circumstances, not least because the prerogative is exercised by a government minister responsible to a Parliament elected through universal franchise. Nevertheless, the issues for the rule of law are fundamentally the same. The principle of legality demands that statutes cannot be set aside on a discretionary basis by the Crown.

---

15   I Leigh, 'The prerogative, legislative power, and the democratic deficit: the *Fire Brigades Union* case' [1995] 3 Web JCLI.
16   For further comment on the decision, see TRS Allan [1995] CLJ 491.

Reviewing the *exercise* of prerogative powers

Note

Our second question was how far the courts would be prepared to question the *exercise* of prerogative powers as opposed to their legal existence. The traditional view was, as Munro puts it, 'that courts lacked jurisdiction to review the manner of exercise of prerogative powers, or the adequacy of the grounds upon which they had been exercised'.[17] In relation to prerogative powers which are not classifiable as 'acts of state', before the decision in the *GCHQ* case (*CCSU v Minister for Civil Service* [1985] AC 374, below), the most important revision of the non-reviewability principle was made by Lord Denning in the following case.

Laker Airways Ltd v Department of Trade [1977] QB 643, 705

Lord Denning: ... The prerogative is a discretionary power exercisable by the executive Government for the public good, in certain spheres of governmental activity for which the law has made no provision, such as the war prerogative (of requisitioning property for the defence of the realm), or the treaty prerogative (of making treaties with foreign powers). The law does not interfere with the proper exercise of the discretion by the executive in those situations: but it can set limits by defining the bounds of the activity: and it can intervene if the discretion is exercised improperly or mistakenly. That is a fundamental principle of our constitution. It derives from two of the most respected of our authorities. In 1611 when the King, as the executive Government, sought to govern by making proclamations, Sir Edward Coke declared that: 'the King hath no prerogative, but that which the law of the land allows him': see the *Proclamations Case* (1611) 12 Co Rep 74, 76. In 1765 Sir William Blackstone added his authority, *Commentaries*, vol I, p 252: 'For prerogative consisting (as Mr Locke has well defined it) in the discretionary power of acting for the public good, where the positive laws are silent, if that discretionary power be abused to the public detriment, such prerogative is exerted in an unconstitutional manner.'

Question

This *dictum* was cited with approval by Purchas LJ in *R v Secretary of State for the Home Department ex p Northumbria Police Authority* (see above) at p 603. His comment was, 'The question whether once the power exists the courts will interfere with its exercise is still open'. If this is correct, should not Purchas LJ have expressly overruled at least part of what Lord Denning said?

Note

Did *GCHQ* leave this question open? In this case, the House of Lords had to consider a challenge to an Order in Council made by the Prime Minister which prevented staff at GCHQ belonging to national trade unions. Six members of staff and the union involved applied for judicial review of the Prime Minister's instruction on the ground that she had been under a duty to act fairly by consulting those concerned before issuing it. It had first to be determined whether the decision was open to judicial review. In general, a person affected by a decision concerning public law matters made under statutory powers may challenge it by way of judicial review.

CCSU v Minister for Civil Service [1985] AC 374, 417–18, HL

Lord Roskill: ... In short the orthodox view was ... that the remedy for abuse of the prerogative lay in the political and not in the judicial field. But fascinating as it is to explore this mainstream of our legal history, to do so in connection with the present appeal has an air of unreality. To speak

---

17   *Op cit*, p 279.

today of the acts of the sovereign as 'irresistible and absolute' when modern constitutional convention requires that all such acts are done by the sovereign on the advice of and will be carried out by the sovereign's ministers currently in power is surely to hamper the continual development of our administrative law by harking back to what Lord Atkin once called, albeit in a different context, the clanking of mediaeval chains of the ghosts of the past: see *United Australia Ltd v Barclays Bank Ltd* [1941] AC 1, 29. It is, I hope, not out of place in this connection to quote a letter written in 1896 by the great legal historian FW Maitland to Dicey himself: 'The only direct utility of legal history (I say nothing of its thrilling interest) lies in the lesson that each generation has an enormous power of shaping its own law': see Richard A Cosgrove, *The Rule of Law: Albert Venn Dicey, Victorian Jurist* (1980), p 177. Maitland was in so stating a greater prophet than even he could have foreseen for it is our legal history which has enabled the present generation to shape the development of our administrative law by building upon but unhampered by our legal history.

My Lords, the right of the executive to do a lawful act affecting the rights of the citizen, whether adversely or beneficially, is founded upon the giving to the executive of a power enabling it to do that act. The giving of such a power usually carries with it legal sanctions to enable that power if necessary to be enforced by the courts. In most cases that power is derived from statute though in some cases, as indeed in the present case, it may still be derived from the prerogative ... If the executive in pursuance of the statutory power does an act affecting the rights of the citizen, it is beyond question that in principle the manner of the exercise of that power may today be challenged on one or more of the three grounds which I have mentioned earlier in this speech. If the executive instead of acting under a statutory power acts under a prerogative power and in particular a prerogative power delegated to the respondent under Article 4 of the Order in Council of 1982, so as to affect the rights of the citizen, I am unable to see, subject to what I shall say later, that there is any logical reason why the fact that the source of the power is the prerogative and not statute should today deprive the citizen of that right of challenge to the manner of its exercise which he would possess were the source of the power statutory.

In either case the act in question is the act of the executive. To talk of that act as the act of the sovereign savours of the archaism of past centuries.

But I do not think that that right of challenge can be unqualified. It must, I think, depend upon the subject matter of the prerogative power which is exercised. Many examples were given during the argument of prerogative powers which as at present advised I do not think could properly be made the subject of judicial review. Prerogative powers such as those relating to the making of treaties, the defence of the realm, the prerogative of mercy, the grant of honours, the dissolution of Parliament and the appointment of ministers as well as others are not, I think, susceptible to judicial review because their nature and subject matter are such as not to be amenable to the judicial process. The courts are not the place wherein to determine whether a treaty should be concluded or the armed forces disposed in a particular manner or Parliament dissolved on one date rather than another.

In my view the exercise of the prerogative which enabled the oral instructions of 22 December 1983 to be given does not by reason of its subject matter fall within what for want of a better phrase I would call the 'excluded categories' some of which I have just mentioned. It follows that in principle I can see no reason why those instructions should not be the subject of judicial review
...

I find considerable support for the conclusion I have reached in the decision of the Divisional Court (Lord Parker CJ, Diplock LJ (as my noble and learned friend then was) and Ashworth J in *Criminal Injuries Compensation Board ex p Lain* (1967) 2 QB 864), the judgments in which may without exaggeration be described as a landmark in the development of this branch of the law.

Notes

1   The House of Lords went on to find that the applicants had had a legitimate expectation that they would be consulted, and that the Prime Minister had, *prima*

facie, 'acted unfairly'[18] in failing so to consult, but that reasons of national security justified the failure. Diplock LJ, in a well known *dicta*, remarked:

National security is the responsibility of the executive government; what action is needed to protect its interest is ... a matter on which those on whom the responsibility rests, and not the courts of justice must have the last word. It is par excellence a non-justiciable process. The judicial process is totally inept to deal with the sort of problems which it involves.

McEldowney and McAuslan note that the national security ground was not advanced by the Prime Minister 'until she had lost at first instance'.[19]

2 *GCHQ* then set out an (*obiter*) list of prerogatives which were to remain not subject to review. These included 'the making of treaties, the defence of the realm, the prerogative of mercy, the grant of honours, the dissolution of Parliament and the appointment of ministers as well as others ...'. *R v Secretary of State for the Foreign Office ex p Rees Mogg* [1994] QB 552 confirmed that the courts would not entertain challenges to the prerogative power to conclude treaties (in this case the Treaty of Maastricht). However, in other cases, the courts have begun to whittle away at that list.

3 *R v Secretary of State for Foreign and Commonwealth Affairs ex p Everett* [1989] 2 QB 540 concerned a challenge to the refusal to issue a passport. Passports are issued by the Passport Office (now a government agency, then a government department) under the royal prerogative. The government can therefore exercise a discretion to withhold a passport where a person wishes to travel abroad to engage in activities which are politically deplored, although legal. Because these powers arise under the royal prerogative, it was thought that they would not be open to review until the ruling noted above in the *GCHQ* case. The applicant, who was living in Spain, applied for a new passport when his old one expired. The Secretary of State refused to grant him one, on the basis that there was an outstanding warrant for his arrest in the UK and it was government policy not to give passports to such people. The applicant applied for judicial review on the basis that no details of the warrant had been given to him. It was held that the Secretary of State was obliged to provide the applicant with details of the warrant and that if there were exceptional reasons why the normal policy should not be applied, they would be taken into account. The government had argued that the grant of a passport came under the umbrella of foreign policy and so was in the area of 'high policy' in which courts could not interfere. Taylor J said that he agreed that matters of high policy would not now be reviewable. But, he argued, the grant of passport was an administrative decision, affecting the rights of individuals and their freedom of travel.

4 A further incursion into previously excluded territory occurred in *R v Secretary of State for the Home Department ex p Bentley* [1994] QB 349, which concerned the prerogative of mercy, one of the prerogatives on Lord Roskill's list. The issue was whether the Home Secretary's refusal to recommend a posthumous pardon for Derek Bentley, executed in 1953 for the murder of a policeman, was subject to judicial review. The Home Secretary had said that his personal view was that Bentley should not have been hanged, but that he could not exercise the prerogative of mercy since he had not been given any evidence indicating that Bentley was innocent. The court found, plainly against Lord Roskill's *dicta* in *GCHQ*, that the prerogative of mercy *was* reviewable, though on rather limited

---

18 *Per* Lord Scarman, at p 949.
19 *Op cit*, p 31.

grounds. While they said it would be difficult or impossible to assess the complex balancing act of political, moral and legal motives which the Home Secretary might engage in, in deciding whether to grant a pardon, in this case the issue was narrower and more technical, thus more suited to judicial oversight: that is, had the Home Secretary misdirected himself in failing to consider all the different types of action he could take under the prerogative. The court found that he had wrongly considered that the only option open to him was a full pardon; instead he should have considered whether some lesser action – a formal, public declaration that an injustice had been done to Bentley – could properly be carried out. It was thus held that the decision was at least partially open to review; the court dealt with Roskill's suggestion in *GCHQ* by simply dismissing it as *obiter*. However, the court was cautious when it came to remedies: instead of making any order, it simply issued a formal 'invitation' to the Home Secretary to reconsider his decision, an invitation which the Home Secretary did not decline.

5 Perhaps the most important of the post-*GCHQ* cases on the prerogative is the decision in *R v Ministry of Defence ex p Smith* [1995] 4 All ER 427. The case concerned a challenge to the ban on homosexuals serving in the armed forces, a policy which it was found was maintained by the prerogative. It was argued for the Ministry of Defence that (*inter alia*) the case was 'concerned with the exercise of a prerogative power in an area – the defence of the realm – recognised by the courts to be unsuitable for judicial review' (at p 441). This contention was directly addressed by the court of first instance, as follows.

R v Ministry of Defence ex p Smith and Others [1995] 4 All ER 427, 445, 446

Simon Brown LJ: In so far as Mr Richards [for the MOD] relies upon this being an irrationality challenge to the exercise of the prerogative – which I am satisfied it is, the broad statutory framework being to my mind immaterial in identifying the true source of this power – Mr Pannick [for the applicants] points to a series of cases since *CCSU* in which, despite Lord Diplock's doubts, the courts have accepted the reviewability on *Wednesbury* grounds of decisions taken in the exercise of prerogative power: see in particular *Secretary of State for Foreign and Commonwealth Affairs ex p Everett* [1989] 1 All ER 655, [1989] QB 811 (a Court of Appeal decision concerning passports), *Secretary of State for the Home Dept ex p Bentley* [1993] 4 All ER 442, [1994] QB 349 (a decision of the Divisional Court with regard to the prerogative of mercy), and *Criminal Injuries Compensation Board ex p P* [1995] 1 All ER 870, [1995] 1 WLR 845 (where the Court of Appeal by a majority found the CICB scheme reviewable even though it involved the distribution of 'bounty' on behalf of the Crown). True, only in *Bentley* did the applicant succeed, and even then only on a narrow issue concerning the scope of the prerogative. But it can no longer be suggested that the exercise of prerogative power is on that ground alone outside the court's supervisory jurisdiction.

As to Mr Richards' reliance on Parliament's examination and implicit approval of the existing policy, Mr Pannick reminds us that the executive decision under challenge in *Brind* had itself been debated in both Houses of Parliament, a consideration that did not deflect the House of Lords from considering the competing arguments on irrationality.

Brind is also the decision upon which Mr Pannick most heavily relies in response to Mr Richards' submissions on the particular nature of the policy here sought to be impugned – a military judgment upon the requirements of the armed services and thus a decision affecting the defence of the realm. *Brind* too, Mr Pannick stresses, involved policy considerations as to the way in which the United Kingdom should respond to the terrorist threat in Northern Ireland – a highly sensitive political issue affecting the security of the state. *Brind*, moreover, as many of the speeches emphasised, involved only the most limited interference with freedom of speech (a restriction ultimately found insufficient even to get past the admissibility threshold at Strasbourg); contrast the substantial interference with the right of privacy in the present case.

Mr Pannick refers us also to the Divisional Court's judgment in *Army Board of the Defence Council ex p Anderson* [1991] 3 All ER 375, [1992] QB 169 in which a decision of the Secretary of State for Defence was held reviewable in relation to a complaint of racial discrimination in the army, albeit on the ground of unfair procedure and not irrationality.

It is time to state my conclusions on these issues.

(1) I have no hesitation in holding this challenge justiciable. To my mind only the rarest cases will today be ruled strictly beyond the court's purview – only cases involving national security properly so-called and where in addition the courts really do lack the expertise or material to form a judgment on the point at issue. This case does not fall into that category. True, it touches on the defence of the realm but it does not involve determining 'whether ... the armed forces [should be] disposed of in a particular manner' (which Lord Roskill in *CCSU* thought plainly unreviewable – as indeed had been held in *China Navigation Co Ltd v A-G* [1932] 2 KB 197, [1932] All ER Rep 626). No operational considerations are involved in this policy. Now, indeed, that the 'security implications' have disappeared, there appears little about it which the courts are not perfectly well qualified to judge for themselves.

Notes

1   Having found the issue justiciable, the court went on to find that the policy of excluding homosexuals could not be held to be *Wednesbury* unreasonable. Clearly, the last part of the judge's remarks were *obiter*; when the Court of Appeal heard the appeal of the servicemen and women it made no such general remarks about the availability of review against the prerogative, but nor did it disapprove of Simon Brown LJ's comments, and indeed it appeared to take it for granted that the issue was justiciable. Clearly, therefore, *ex p Smith* indicates that the unreviewable areas of the prerogative were perhaps smaller than had been previously thought, whilst Simon Brown LJ's *dicta* that only 'the rarest cases' will be non-justiciable is an emphatic statement of judicial intention to enforce the fundamentals of the Rule of Law through the courts save in those cases where it would be clearly inappropriate.

2   Support for this view can be found in the following important recent decision of the Court of Appeal. The case arose from the detention by the US military authorities of a British national, Abbasi, whom they suspected of being a member of Al Qa'eda, in Guantanamo Bay. The US government's position was (and is) that those being held were 'unlawful combatants' and so can be held by the US throughout the duration of the 'war on terrorism', which in practice could well mean indefinite detention. Detainees have no access to a court to challenge their detention, US courts having refused jurisdiction, and nor has their status been determined by a competent tribunal, as the Geneva Convention arguably requires. Abbasi argued that, since he was being subject, in effect, to arbitrary detention, in violation of habeas corpus, the Foreign Office had a duty either to make representations on his behalf to the US government or, at the least, to explain why they had in fact taken no action in relation to his case. The court first of all found that it was obliged to approach the application for judicial review on the basis that: 'in apparent contravention of fundamental principles recognised by both jurisdictions and by international law, Mr Abbasi is at present arbitrarily detained in a "legal black-hole"' (para 64). However, one of the apparent stumbling blocks in the way of the applicant was the government's argument that the exercise of prerogative powers in the field of foreign affairs was non-justiciable (in reliance on the *dicta* from *GCHQ*, considered above). Extracts from the decision follow: the court first considers other *dicta* apparently excluding judicial review in this field.

R on the Application of Abbasi and another v Secretary of State for Foreign and Commonwealth Affairs and Secretary of State for the Home Department (2002) WL 31452052

37   [Mr Greenwood, for the Government] submitted that the courts have repeatedly held that the decisions taken by the executive in its dealings with foreign states regarding the protection of British nationals abroad are non-justiciable. He cited the following passages from recent decisions in support of this proposition:

> (1) *R v Secretary of State for Foreign and Commonwealth Affairs ex p Pirbhai* (1985) 107 ILR 462: '... in the context of a situation with serious implications for the conduct of international relations, the courts should act with a high degree of circumspection in the interests of all concerned. It can rarely, if ever, be for judges to intervene where diplomats fear to tread.' (p 479, *per* Sir John Donaldson MR).
>
> (2) *R v Secretary of State for Foreign and Commonwealth Affairs ex p Ferhut Butt* (1999) 116 ILR 607: 'The general rule is well established that the courts should not interfere in the conduct of foreign relations by the Executive, most particularly where such interference is likely to have foreign policy repercussions (see *ex parte Everett* [1989] 1 QB 811 at 820). This extends to decisions whether or not to seek to persuade a foreign government of any international obligation (eg to respect human rights) which it has assumed ... In such matters the courts have no supervisory role.' (p 615, *per* Lightman J).
>
> 'Whether and when to seek to interfere or to put pressure on in relation to the legal process, if ever it is a sensible and a right thing to do, must be a matter for the Executive and no one else, with their access to information and to local knowledge. It is clearly not a matter for the courts. It is clearly a high policy decision of a government in relation to its foreign relations and is not justiclable by way of judicial review.' (p 622, *per* Henry LJ).
>
> (3) *R (Suresh and Manickavasagam) v Secretary of State for the Home Department* [2001] EWHC Admin 1028 (unreported, 16 November 2001): '... there is, in my judgment, no duty upon the Secretary of State to ensure that other nations comply with their human rights obligations. There may be cases where the United Kingdom Government has, for example by diplomatic means, chosen to seek to persuade another State to take a certain course in its treatment of British nationals; but there is no *duty* to do so.' (para 19, *per* Sir Richard Tucker).

38   To the above he added a citation from the judgment of Laws LJ in the matter of *Foday Saybana Sankoh* (2000) 119 ILR 389 at 396 where he described as a hopeless proposition that 'the court should dictate to the executive government steps that it should take in the course of executing government foreign policy'.

[The court went on to find that Abbasi could rely neither on the HRA (since the Convention did not apply, Abbasi being outside the UK government's jurisdiction) nor on general principles of international law; however, it did find that the applicant had a legitimate expectation, based upon Government statements, that the Foreign Office would at least *consider* intervening on his behalf, as a British national subject to arguably illegal detention abroad, and that the Foreign Office was thus obliged so to consider his case. (Legitimate expectations are an accepted head of judicial review: see Part V Chapter 2.) It then went on to consider the justiciability point: citing *GCHQ*, the court found:] ...

Those extracts indicate that the issue of justiciability depends, not on general principle, but on subject matter and suitability in the particular case ...

99   What then is the nature of the expectation that a British subject in the position of Mr Abbasi can legitimately hold in relation to the response of the government to a request for assistance? The policy statements that we have cited underline the very limited nature of the expectation. They indicate that where certain criteria are satisfied, the government will 'consider' making representations. Whether to make any representations in a particular case,

and if so in what form, is left entirely to the discretion of the Secretary of State. That gives free play to the 'balance' to which Lord Diplock referred in *GCHQ*. The Secretary of State must be free to give full weight to foreign policy considerations, which are not justiciable. However, that does not mean the whole process is immune from judicial scrutiny. The citizen's legitimate expectation is that his request will be 'considered', and that in that consideration all relevant factors will be thrown into the balance.

100 One vital factor, as the policy recognises, is the nature and extent of the injustice, which he claims to have suffered. Even where there has been a gross miscarriage of justice, there may perhaps be overriding reasons of foreign policy which may lead the Secretary of State to decline to intervene. However, unless and until he has formed some judgment as to the gravity of the miscarriage, it is impossible for that balance to be properly conducted ...

104 The extreme case where judicial review would lie in relation to diplomatic protection would be if the Foreign and Commonwealth Office were, contrary to its stated practice, to refuse even to consider whether to make diplomatic representations on behalf of a subject whose fundamental rights were being violated. In such, unlikely, circumstances we consider that it would be appropriate for the court to make a mandatory order to the Foreign Secretary to give due consideration to the applicant's case.

105 Beyond this we do not believe it is possible to make general propositions. In some cases it might be reasonable to expect the Secretary of State to state the result of considering a request for assistance, in others it might not. In some cases he might be expected to give reasons for his decision, in others he might not. In some cases such reasons might be open to attack, in others they would not.

106 We would summarise our views as to what the authorities establish as follows:

(i) It is not an answer to a claim for judicial review to say that the source of the power of the Foreign Office is the prerogative. It is the subject matter that is determinative.

(ii) Despite extensive citation of authority there is nothing which supports the imposition of an enforceable duty to protect the citizen. The European Convention on Human Rights does not impose any such duty. Its incorporation into the municipal law cannot therefore found a sound basis on which to reconsider the authorities binding on this court.

(iii) However the Foreign Office has discretion whether to exercise the right, which it undoubtedly has, to protect British citizens. It has indicated in the ways explained what a British citizen may expect of it. The expectations are limited and the discretion is a very wide one but there is no reason why its decision or inaction should not be reviewable if it can be shown that the same were irrational or contrary to legitimate expectation; but the court cannot enter the forbidden areas, including decisions affecting foreign policy.

(iv) It is highly likely that any decision of the Foreign and Commonwealth Office, as to whether to make representations on a diplomatic level, will be intimately connected with decisions relating to this country's foreign policy, but an obligation to consider the position of a particular British citizen and consider the extent to which some action might be taken on his behalf, would seem unlikely itself to impinge on any forbidden area.

(v) The extent to which it may be possible to require more than that the Foreign Secretary give due consideration to a request for assistance will depend on the facts of the particular case.

Are the applicants entitled to relief in the present case?

107 We have made clear our deep concern that, in apparent contravention of fundamental principles of law, Mr Abbasi may be subject to indefinite detention in territory over which the United States has exclusive control with no opportunity to challenge the legitimacy of his detention before any court or tribunal. However, there are a number of reasons why we consider that the applicants' claim to relief must be rejected:

(i)   It is quite clear from Mr Fry's evidence that the Foreign and Commonwealth Office have considered Mr Abbasi's request for assistance. He has also disclosed that the British detainees are the subject of discussions between this country and the United States both at Secretary of State and lower official levels. We do not consider that Mr Abbasi could reasonably expect more than this. In particular, if the Foreign and Commonwealth Office were to make any statement as to its view of the legality of the detention of the British prisoners, or any statement as to the nature of discussions held with United States officials, this might well undermine those discussions.

(ii) On no view would it be appropriate to order the Secretary of State to make any specific representations to the United States, even in the face of what appears to be a clear breach of a fundamental human right, as it is obvious that this would have an impact on the conduct of foreign policy, and an impact on such policy at a particularly delicate time.

(iii) The position of detainees at Guantanamo Bay is to be considered further by the appellate courts in the United States. It may be that the anxiety that we have expressed will be drawn to their attention ... As is clear from our judgment, we believe that the United States courts have the same respect for human rights as our own ...

Notes

1   This judgment is evidently a mixture of boldness and caution: the court accepted that there were still 'forbidden areas' of prerogative immune from review; but it was bold in carving out an exception to an area traditionally thought forbidden in this case, and left open the possibility that it might be possible to require 'more than that the Foreign Secretary give due consideration to a request for assistance': a radical proposition, given that this could potentially amount to a direct intervention by the courts in the conduct of foreign affairs.

2   In spite of these welcome recognitions by the courts that the mere fact that a power can be labelled 'prerogative' does not immediately oust their jurisdiction to consider the legality of its exercise, the degree of judicial control in this area should not be exaggerated. The *Malone* and *Northumbria Police Authority* cases demonstrate a willingness on the part of the courts to recognise the existence of prerogative powers of doubtful origin, whilst as Professor Patrick Birkinshaw notes, '... it is ironic to realise that the exercise of some of the most important prerogatives is devoid of any control save political rebellion or insurrection – declaration of war for instance or the appointment of a Prime Minister'.[20]

Impact of the Human Rights Act 1998

The Human Rights Act 1998 (HRA) is considered fully in Part VI Chapter 1, but it would be wrong to leave any discussion of judicial control of the prerogative without at least a reference to the changes the Act will bring about. The relevant provision is s 6(1), which simply provides: 'It is unlawful for a public authority to act in a way which is incompatible with a Convention right' (that is, a right contained in the European Convention on Human Rights, as defined in the HRA itself). The partial definition of 'public authority' includes courts (s 6(3)) and will clearly also include the Crown exercising the prerogative. What effect then will this have? The most important and basic effect will be to put an end to the notion of there being areas of prerogative powers which are non-justiciable *per se*. The HRA states that it is unlawful for public

20   'Decision-making and its control', in McEldowney and McAuslan, *op cit*, p 152.

authorities to contravene Convention rights and gives a right to bring proceedings for such a breach (s 7) and to seek remedies (s 8). An exercise of the prerogative which breaches a Convention right will therefore be as justiciable as any other executive action, simply because there has been no attempt to exclude the prerogative from the general duty under s 6(1): such an attempt would plainly have been incompatible with the Convention itself.

On the face of it, this sounds like a radical change, and it is, in principle. However, a number of factors are likely to reduce the impact of the HRA. The most stark and obvious of these is the fact that the HRA specifically protects acts of the prerogative from being annulled by the courts where they are expressed as Orders in Council. This is because such Orders are included within the definition of 'primary legislation' (s 21(1)) which, by virtue of ss 3(2)(b) and 4(6), may not be struck down by the courts if found to be incompatible with Convention rights. Whether Orders in Council made under the prerogative may at present be struck down by the courts appears to be a matter of doubt; what is clear is that the HRA will allow acts of prerogative power made in this way to be insulated from successful assault on Convention grounds. While the courts may make a purely declaratory finding that the Order in question is in breach of the Convention, the sections cited provide that such a declaration will not affect the Order's continuing effect and validity.[21]

The second factor is a simple one: the exercise of many, perhaps most, of the areas of the prerogative currently regarded as non-justiciable will not engage the Convention at all. It is hard to see, for example, how the powers to conclude treaties, appoint ministers, grant honours, and for that matter, dissolve Parliament could raise serious Convention points.

The third factor is a little more complex. While the HRA will require the courts to decide whether ministerial action breached a Convention right, *as a matter of law*, it is already clear that in certain areas they will take a deferential approach to this assessment, particularly in relation to Articles 8–11 of the ECHR which set out broad exceptions allowing lawful interference with the primary rights granted, provided that the interference is prescribed by law, in pursuit of an aim specified in the Article in question and is 'necessary in a democratic society', by which it is meant that there was a 'pressing social need' to take the complained of action and the interference was proportionate to the legitimate aim pursued.[22] In determining whether a given interference *was* 'necessary', it is apparent that courts may consider themselves bound to recognise and respect an 'area of discretionary judgment'[23] when reviewing the decisions of ministers in some areas. A deferential approach may be taken to their decisions, either on democratic grounds, or on the well-established and familiar basis

---

21 For criticism of this provision see P Billings and B Pontin [2001] PL 21.
22 *Olsson v Sweden* (1988) 11 EHRR 259.
23 In *R v DPP ex p Kebilene* [1999] 3 WLR 972, Lord Hope rejected any domestic application of the margin of appreciation doctrine but went on: 'In some circumstances it will be appropriate for the courts to recognise that there is an area of judgment within which the judiciary will defer, on democratic grounds, to the considered opinion of [the democratic body or person] whose act or decision is said to be incompatible with the Convention.' This approach has now been confirmed in a number of cases decided after the HRA came into force: see, eg, *R (on the application of Alconbury Developments Ltd) v Secretary of State of the Environment, Transport and the Regions and Other Cases* [2001] 2 WLR 1389, HL; *Brown v Stott* [2001] 2 WLR 817, PC, at 835.

that the courts do not have the ability to assess the complex policy considerations in play (see further Part VI Chapter 1, pp 886–94). It may be noted that in the pre-HRA era, while the areas excluded from review were shrinking, the approach of the courts in a number of the key cases (*GCHQ, Smith, Bentley*) was very cautious, the applicant failing in two of them and achieving only a partial victory in the third. If this approach prevails, the extension of review in these areas may turn out to be a symbolic, rather than a real increase in legal accountability. Much may depend on how the courts apply the HRA in practice.

REFORM OF THE PREROGATIVE

In any event, is the existence of the prerogative itself satisfactory? If not, what is to be done? A number of commentators have suggested that the answer lies in simply abolishing certain prerogatives, and the codification of others in statute. The Labour Party in 1993 committed itself to:

> ... [ensuring] that all actions of government are subject to political and parliamentary control, including those actions now governed by the arbitrary use of the Royal Prerogative to legitimize actions which would otherwise be contrary to law. [The party reaffirms its] intention to review the Royal Prerogative and to identify particular areas of government activity which should be regulated by statute or excluded from its protection. (*A New Agenda for Democracy* (1993)).

Munro gives the example of the power to dissolve Parliament:

> The prerogative, nominally exercised by the Crown, is in reality exercised on the Prime Minister's advice, at least in the ordinary course of events. This effectively enables the Prime Minister to choose the date of the next general election, and it is notorious that the choice is influenced not by considerations of the public interest but by calculations of party advantage. That is surely an abuse of power, but it is a power the exercise of which seems to be impossible to challenge, whether in Parliament or in the courts.[24]

In this respect, it may be noted that the government, in legislating for a Scottish Parliament, did not give the Queen (and thereby the Scottish First Minister), the power to dissolve it. Instead, the Parliament may be dissolved only upon its own vote, and then requires a two-thirds majority, or if the First Minister dies or resigns and no replacement can be found within 28 days (s 3 of the Scotland Act 1998). The deliberate choice not to replicate the unfettered power of the UK Prime Minister in designing the new institutions surely reflects an implicit acceptance that the UK position cannot be defended in terms of principle.

Other powers, such as those concerning the regulation of the Civil Service, the control of the armed forces, and the conduct of foreign policy must evidently be retained, but, as suggested above, could be placed on a statutory basis.

Question
Are there any arguments *against* replacing prerogative powers with statutory provisions?

---

24 *Op cit*, pp 290–91.

FURTHER READING

R Brazier, *Constitutional Practice* (1994)
R Brazier, *Ministers of the Crown* (1997)
RHS Crossman, *Diaries of a Cabinet Minister* (1975)
T Daintith and A Page, *The Executive in the Constitution: Structure, Autonomy, and Internal Control* (1999)
P Greer, 'The Next Steps initiative' (1992) Political Quarterly 63
C Harlow (ed), *Public Law and Politics* (1984)
IPPR, *The Constitution of the United Kingdom* (1991)
S Jenkins, *Accountable to None: The Tory Nationalisation of Britain* (1995)
I Jennings, *The Law and the Constitution*, 5th edn (1959) and *Cabinet Government* (1959)
N Lawson, *The View from No 11* (1992)
JF McEldowney and P McAuslan, *Law, Legitimacy and the Constitution* (1985)
JP Mackintosh, *The British Cabinet* (1977)
G Marshall, *Constitutional Theory* (1971)
G Marshall and GC Moodie, *Some Problems of the Constitution* (1971)
R Pyper and L Robins (eds), *Governing the UK in the 1990s* (1995), Part I
S Sunkin and S Payne, *The Nature of the Crown* (1999)
Baroness Thatcher, *The Downing Street Years* (1993)

CHAPTER 2

THE CENTRAL EXECUTIVE: STRUCTURES AND ACCOUNTABILITY

INTRODUCTION

This chapter does not attempt a description of the everyday workings of the institutions that make up the central executive, for that would amount to a description of a system of government, rather than an analysis of the constitution. Insofar as a distinction can be maintained,[1] a work on the constitution should be looking for a normative framework within which government is supposed to be carried on; simply describing the practice of government *per se* is not therefore the aim. What we are looking for, then, are informing and pervasive ideas and conventions which purport to regulate government activity according to an idea of constitutionalism.[2] Since the core of the notion of constitutionalism are the ideas of limited government, checks on government power, and the accountability of government, these themes determine the topics considered here. Attention will focus therefore on two main themes: first, the increased concentration of power into a few hands within government, and, secondly, a cluster of concepts about responsibility and accountability – the responsibility of ministers for their departments, their responsibility to be open with Parliament and not to mislead it, and the responsibilities of civil servants to ministers and possibly to Parliament. The impact on traditional notions of accountability of the 'Next Steps' reforms will be considered in depth. The whole topic of accountability will be informed by the evidence thrown up by the Scott Inquiry and its conclusions and by developments in ministerial responsibility under the Blair government.

THE PRIME MINISTER AND THE CABINET

Three main issues will be discussed here. First, the debate as to the actual importance of the Cabinet in the system of government; secondly and clearly connected to the first matter, the ways in which the Prime Minister can (a) control and manipulate, and (b) effectively bypass Cabinet; and thirdly, the relevance of collective responsibility to these first two issues. We start with a brief outline of the position of the Cabinet and the manner of the appointment of a Prime Minister.

Harry Calvert, *An Introduction to British Constitutional Law* (1986), pp 146, 150–51, 155

... the Cabinet, as an institution, does not rest on parliamentary authority but rather on practice developed over the centuries. It is true that the existence of the Cabinet is now acknowledged in parliamentary legislation – the Parliamentary Commissioner Act 1967, for example, creates a privilege for Cabinet papers in connection with proceedings before the 'ombudsman' – but this no more puts the Cabinet on a statutory, legal, basis than does the Dogs Act create dogs.

---

1   There is some debate as to what matters properly belong in a work on constitutional law. For a critical analysis of recent trends in this respect, see FF Ridley, 'There is no British constitution: a dangerous case of the emperor's clothes' (1988) 41 Parl Aff 40, esp pp 342 *et seq*.
2   See Part I Chapter 1.

Important consequences attend the fact that the composition, powers and procedures of the Cabinet are not fixed by law.... It may meet more or less regularly; it may discharge business in plenary session or sit in committees. We are told that decisions are usually arrived at by consensus, but there is nothing to stop a vote being taken, or simply for the Prime Minister to divine the 'sense of the meeting' and proceed accordingly....

[Calvert then goes on to consider the increased power of modern Prime Ministers, starting with the manner of their appointment.]

Appointment of a Prime Minister

Legally, the position is simple. The monarch may, if he wishes, appoint any number of persons he likes to be 'Minister of the Crown' and may, if he wishes, appoint one of them to be his 'Prime' Minister. Acts of Parliament assume but do not require that there will be a 'Prime Minister'.

The efficient functioning of the constitution, however, does require that there should be a Prime Minister and, since any Government is heavily dependent upon Parliament, and particularly the House of Commons, especially for the authority to raise taxes, it follows that if a Prime Minister is to do the job properly, he must be a person who enjoys the confidence or support of a stable majority of the House of Commons. Under the modern party system, a party leader is that party's candidate for the office of Prime Minister and when, in a general election, the electorate returns to the House of Commons a majority of members of a particular party it in substance elects a Prime Minister. The words 'in substance' have been used because formally the choice remains that of the monarch but the constitutional role of the monarch in this regard is now accepted as being nothing more than formally appointing the person who commands a majority in the House of Commons, and in the usual situation above envisaged there will be no room for doubt on the matter. The electorate will have made it abundantly clear who should be appointed.

In exceptional situations, however, it may be less clear. Suppose:

● ... a Prime Minister resigns or dies in office and the majority party is divided as to who his successor shall be; or

● although a particular party secures a majority in a general election, its leader is defeated.

Who is to be appointed?

For the monarch, the basic criterion remains the same. He must seek to ensure that he appoints a person who will enjoy the confidence of a majority of Members of the House of Commons. Usually, the monarch will be spared a controversial decision. All major political parties now have procedures for electing a leader and would, if circumstances compelled it, find ways of removing an old one and appointing a new. Once the leaders of the various factions are identified, then either one commands a majority, in which case, the problem disappears; or, if there is no majority, a wise monarch will await reliable information as to what has emerged as a result of the horsetrading and dealing which would inevitably attend the business of trying to form a coalition or, at least, a minority Government with the tacit support of a majority.

There is no 'proper' course for a monarch in such unusual circumstances, there is merely a prudent course. If the monarch made the 'wrong' choice, ie appointed a person who, in the event, could not command the support of a majority in the House of Commons, that appointment would nevertheless remain valid although effective government would be impossible and crisis would result. The monarch would then have to consider a dissolution if advised or, if not, consider whether to dismiss the Prime Minister wrongly chosen and appoint another in his place, or to muddle on. Controversy would attend any chosen course of action and the stature of the monarch would be demeaned. In an extreme case, the existence of the monarchy itself would be threatened.

These considerations effectively mean that in exceptional cases, the monarch's role might well go beyond simply doing what he is told. There can be room for substantial individual judgment by a monarch and if caution does not attend its exercise, crisis with unpredictable consequences may result.

Notes

1   See further on the monarch's powers in relation to the choice of a Prime Minister Part I Chapter 3.

2   It is illuminating to contrast the position in relation to the importance of the Prime Minister, the leader of the UK government, governed as it is entirely by convention, with the statutory provisions of the Scotland Act, which govern the choice of the First Minister of the Scottish Executive, in some sense Scotland's Prime Minister. In the UK, as we have seen, the position in law is very simple: the Prime Minister is simply the Queen's chief minister. He becomes Prime Minister not by virtue of the results of general elections, which simply determine the make up of the House of Commons, but solely and simply by being chosen by the Queen. It is only through the conventions discussed by Calvert above that the Queen's unfettered legal powers are exercised so as to match up the appointment of the Prime Minister with the democratic will of the people. Under the Scotland Act, in contrast, the First Minister is nominated by the Scottish Parliament within 28 days of an election or vacancy and appointed by the Queen (s 46). While the Queen is not legally *obliged* to appoint the nomination of the Parliament, there is at least a clear legal role for the Parliament to play in nominating the First Minister and the Queen may in law appoint only a member of the Scottish Parliament as First Minister (s 45(1)), something that is only a matter of convention in relation to the House of Commons and the Prime Minister. It is perhaps rather incongruous that, in shaping a Parliament for the 21st century, the Queen was still given the legal power to appoint. By contrast, the Welsh and Northern Ireland assemblies *elect* rather than nominate ministers – there is no role for the Queen to play at all.

3   Walter Bagehot, writing in 1867, called the Cabinet 'the most powerful body in the nation' (*The English Constitution* (1963 edn)) and considered that collective responsibility meant that every member of the Cabinet had the right to take part in Cabinet discussion but was bound by the decision eventually reached. In contrast, John Mackintosh in *The British Cabinet* (1977) wrote: 'the principal policies of a government may not be and often are not originated in Cabinet.'

4   A number of writers, including Richard Crossman, have considered that Cabinet government has shown signs of developing into prime ministerial government and that therefore collective decision-making has suffered (see, for example, his *Diaries of a Cabinet Minister* (1975)). Crossman argued that the power of the Prime Minister to sack ministers, and to determine the Cabinet agenda and the existence and membership of Cabinet committees meant that his or her control over the Cabinet was the most important force within it. Mrs Thatcher, Prime Minister between 1979 and 1990, is generally considered to have (at least temporarily) increased the power of the Prime Minister by using the available power to the full. The Blair premiership is also generally seen to be marked by the sidelining of Cabinet.

5   However, other commentators point out that in diluting and fragmenting the power of the Cabinet in this fashion it might be argued that Thatcher and Blair were merely taking further a process which had already begun. The use of gatherings other than Cabinet to make decisions – inner Cabinets, Cabinet committees, ministerial meetings – had been growing for the last 30 years and had arguably undermined the Cabinet as a decision-making body, though many considered this inevitable. In what follows, by discussing the three issues outlined at the start of this section,[3] we will attempt to reach some balanced conclusions on these matters and to root out their significance in constitutional terms.

---

3   The importance of Cabinet; prime ministerial control over it; collective responsibility.

The changing role of the Cabinet

As Rodney Brazier notes, 'Meeting only once a week for a couple of hours ... and being composed entirely of Ministers with heavy departmental responsibilities, the Cabinet could not possibly now be the forum either for the close control of activities of government or for the co-ordination of the departments of state'.[4] Neither, clearly does it have time either to formulate, approve or even discuss much policy. 'Since the Second World War all but a tiny proportion of decisions have been taken by individual ministers, by correspondence and by committees.'[5] These last have assumed an increasingly important role: much of the major policy-making work of government which requires either the co-operation of more than one department or is so important that it requires wider discussion has long been carried out through the Cabinet committee system which in its formal guise 'has been in existence since the First World War, [comprising] some 30 to 40 standing committees ... and well over 100 *ad hoc* committees' which both settle points of detail and isolate fundamental questions for decision by Cabinet.[6]

The Ministerial Code, the official statement of rules and principles governing ministerial conduct, issued by the Cabinet Office, and redrafted by the Prime Minister of the day,[7] has this to say about the role of the Cabinet:

3. The business of the Cabinet and Ministerial Committees consists in the main of:

a. questions which significantly engage the collective responsibility of the Government because they raise major issues of policy or because they are of critical importance to the public;

b. questions on which there is an unresolved argument between Departments.

Matters wholly within the responsibility of a single Minister and which do not significantly engage collective responsibility as defined above need not be brought to the Cabinet or to a Ministerial Committee unless the Minister wishes to inform his colleagues or to have their advice. A precise definition of such matters cannot be given: in borderline cases a Minister is advised to seek collective consideration. Questions involving more than one Department should be examined interdepartmentally, before submission to a Ministerial Committee, so that the decisions required may be clearly defined.

James discusses the changing role of the Cabinet since the 1940s.

S James, 'The Cabinet system since 1948: fragmentation and integration' (1994) 47(4) Parl Aff 613, 619–20

From 1945 until the arrival of Mrs Thatcher, Cabinet meetings followed a standard format: first came a standing item on parliamentary business, under which the Leaders of both Houses would detail business for the following week; then a report on overseas developments, in which the Foreign Secretary sketched out the dominant issues of the moment. The rest of the agenda consisted of items referred up by committees. Occasionally these came because, although the Committee supported the proposal unanimously, the issue was so important that it was felt Cabinet should look at the subject. But in most cases ministers had disagreed at committee and the chairman had allowed an appeal. Most of these appeals were straightforward arbitration exercises: the ministers who had argued the issue in committee would rehearse their cases, and in

---

4   R Brazier, *Constitutional Practice*, 2nd edn (1994), p 104.
5   S James, 'The Cabinet system since 1948: fragmentation and integration' (1994) 47(4) Parl Aff 613, 619.
6   R Brazier, 'Reducing the power of the Prime Minister' (1991) 44(4) Parl Aff 453, 456.
7   For comment on the status of the Code, see below pp 524–25.

effect appeal to the judgement of their colleagues who had not been there and who were asked to screen the proposal, not from an expert point of view but for its good sense and public acceptability in a sort of political litmus test.

Although the Cabinet's court of appeal role gave it a say on some key decisions, the system had serious faults. The Cabinet became almost entirely reactive to the proposals of ministers and committees. There was little discussion of general political developments. There was no item of 'any other business' to allow discussion of other issues that might be worrying ministers. The Cabinet's role was essentially negative: it could block, amend or qualify proposals, but of itself did not initiate policy. It was a brake, not a dynamo. Furthermore, by the time an issue reached it, it had often gained irreversible momentum. Hailsham observed, after serving under Macmillan and Heath: 'The ground has usually carefully been prepared by discussion between civil servants, correspondence between ministers, in formal meetings, Cabinet committee meetings ... By the time the Cabinet is brought in as a whole, it may be that only one decision is possible even when, had it been consulted at the outset, the policy would have been unacceptable.'

Question

Some correction will need to be made to this view below, but for now it is sufficient to note the Cabinet's relative lack of importance, except perhaps *in extremis*. What are the consequences of this for the exercise of power within government?

Prime ministerial control over Cabinet and government

Two main issues are in play here: first, the Prime Minister's power of patronage; and secondly, his or her control over the agenda and meeting of Cabinet and its committees – crudely speaking, over who discusses what and when.

Prime ministerial patronage

Whilst the Queen formally appoints all ministers of the Crown, this power is of course exercised in practice by the Prime Minister who has the absolute power of appointment and dismissal of ministers.[8] The Prime Minister's freedom to choose who he or she wants will be limited by the need to maintain some sort of balance in the Cabinet between different wings of the parties and to appease powerful personalities within it, but still the Prime Minister, and the Prime Minister alone, makes these decisions. Similarly, the Prime Minister may – subject to political constraints – get rid of any ministers he or she does not want at any time in response to major mistakes made by that minister or simply because he or she finds the views of the particular minister uncongenial. This is of course normally achieved through 'reshuffling' rather than outright dismissal, which is comparatively rare. The skill and judgment – and ruthlessness – of a Prime Minister in exercising this power is of key importance: Clement Atlee famously observed that a vital characteristic of any Prime Minister was the ability to be a good butcher.

The political constraints on this power are most marked in one area. As James remarks, 'This discretion [to dismiss or reshuffle] may be less when dealing with the most senior two or three members of the Cabinet who can more or less insist on one of the top jobs. For something like two-thirds of the post-war era, the Exchequer and the Foreign Officer have been held by party magnates who were effectively irremovable.

---

8   Note, though, that Prime Ministers will generally leave junior appointments to the minister at the head of the department concerned, through lack of knowledge if nothing else.

Once someone has reached that level in the Cabinet, there are few other places to which they can be transferred'.[9] Such would certainly appear to be the case in relation to the current Chancellor, Gordon Brown. So important is Brown to the government that it is virtually unthinkable that he could be moved against his will from the Treasury.

Nevertheless, in spite of this exception (which is not absolute – both Mrs Thatcher and Mr Major managed to lose Chancellors from government) the Prime Minister, if determined enough, can make quite extensive use of this power in order to achieve a Cabinet which reflects the Prime Minister's particular political outlook. Mrs Thatcher, as is well known, made particular use of this power, having come to power in 1979 with a Cabinet initially balanced between moderates and Thatcherites. However, by 1981 Mrs Thatcher had shuffled five of the seven moderates out of her Cabinet, leaving her with a Cabinet that reflected her own political convictions pretty closely.[10] But this cannot be put down merely to the excesses of an extreme ideology. As Brazier notes,[11] there were clear precedents for this type of behaviour. When Neville Chamberlain came to power in 1937, he ruthlessly excluded from his Cabinet anyone who was opposed to his policy of appeasing the European dictators. This power that the Prime Minister has over the careers of ministers obviously gives him or her enormous influence over ministers, aware as they are that their continuing in office is, broadly speaking, dependent upon their retaining the Prime Minister's favour. Blair has perhaps not used his powers of appointment and dismissal as ruthlessly as Thatcher, partly because he has always felt the need not to alienate his exceptionally powerful Chancellor, Gordon Brown, by openly removing ministers loyal to the Chancellor from key positions.

Prime ministerial allocation and control of government business

The Prime Minister can determine what the Cabinet does and does not discuss, both specifically, in that its written agenda for its weekly meetings is set by him or her, and more generally, through the manipulation of Cabinet committees. As well as using the official Cabinet committees, which have formal procedures and are serviced by the Civil Service in respect of minutes, agendas etc, the Prime Minister can make use of *ad hoc* informal groups of ministers, convened to discuss a particular issue. Meetings of these groups will not be attended by civil servants and they will often not have formal agendas or minutes. The use of the formal committees is, as noted above, well established, and, given that it allows proper discussion of the issue by a fair number of ministers, is generally seen as a necessary and reasonable way of doing business. Thus, as a former minister recalls, when an issue already discussed by a committee (relating to British military presence in Suez and defence procurement) was put before the Cabinet in 1966:

It soon became clear that all the details were now cut and dried ... so the whole thing was fixed. All Cabinet could do was express opinions and influence to some extent the general tone of the white paper by drafting amendments. Of course there were some ministers like Barbara Castle who took up postures of protest. But the rest of us felt that there was nothing we could do and

---

9   James, *op cit*, p 625.
10   See Brazier (1994), *op cit*, p 79.
11   *Ibid*, pp 72–73.

that the procedure under which we had been excluded was not unreasonable. Fourteen of our twenty-three members of Cabinet are members of the Cabinet committee. To the preparation of this white paper this fourteen had devoted nineteen meetings and two Chequers weekends. After all this, it was natural enough that they should expect Cabinet to give formal authorisation to the recommendations that they had worked out.[12]

By contrast, the heavy use made by Mrs Thatcher of *ad hoc* groups of ministers to discuss key issues raised more concern.

M Doherty, 'Prime ministerial power and ministerial responsibility' (1988) 41(1) Parl Aff 49, 54

The role of the Cabinet under Mrs Thatcher is to endorse rather than to make decisions. This was evident in a statement by Geoffrey Howe, Secretary of State for Foreign and Commonwealth Affairs since 1983, during an interview with the *Daily Mail* on the 6th February 1984. When asked whether or not the full Cabinet had discussed the decision to ban trade unions at the Government Communication Headquarters at Cheltenham, he replied, 'No. It was discussed, as almost every Government decision is discussed, by the group of ministers most directly involved. There are very few discussions of Government decisions by full Cabinet'. Mrs Thatcher favours decision-making by means of informal *ad hoc* sessions at Number 10. The behaviour of a Cabinet committee, led by Lord Whitelaw, at the time Lord President of the Council and from 1979–1983 Home Secretary, which was set up in 1985 to consider the teachers' pay dispute, is informative. Instead of making a report to the Cabinet, it reported back to the Prime Minister at a meeting she chaired at Number 10. James Prior, who was Secretary of State for Employment (1979–81) and Secretary of State for Northern Ireland (1981–84), tells us that the use of such groups developed gradually; that she used the formal machinery of Cabinet government at first, but then, 'after a few years, the formal Cabinet committees were very much downgraded and she began to operate much more in small groups dominated by her "cronies".'

Notes

1 The use of such informal groups was not an innovation of Thatcher, as James notes:[13] 'In the 1960s and 70s ... [Prime Ministers] managed [issues] by secret committees. Barbara Castle's diaries recorded that for years Wilson prevented his Cabinet from discussing Rhodesia and devaluation; similarly, the head of Callaghan's policy unit recalls his Prime Minister running economic policy through a secret committee called "the seminar"'.

2 Mrs Thatcher appears to have taken this technique further, by making much greater use of such groups as a deliberate way of disabling the views of those opposed to her policies. In one sense, this more ruthless procedural style was the natural corollary of her more radical policies. The greater than usual internal dissent and opposition caused by such policies necessitated either the more domineering style she adopted or the abandonment or dilution of the more radical aspects of her New Right programme, which Mrs Thatcher was not prepared to countenance. She thus made use of informal groups quite specifically in order to ensure that particular issues were handled by groups sympathetic to her. Because Prime Ministers can hand-pick these groups, they can (within limits) ensure that a given sensitive issue is discussed only by those ministers with whom they wish to discuss it. Thus, for example, in the early 1980s Michael Heseltine put forward proposals for a radical programme of investment in the inner cities, to tackle the poverty, unemployment and crime which was causing serious social unrest. Mrs

---

12 R Crossman, *Diaries of a Cabinet Minister: Minister of Housing 1964–66* (1975), pp 455–56.
13 *Op cit*, p 621.

Thatcher, who was opposed to the plan, convened a special group of ministers to discuss it, selecting ministers she knew would be hostile to Heseltine's proposals. The group duly came up with recommendations that involved nothing like the investment Heseltine had proposed.[14]

3   But whatever the procedural imperatives of her radical policies, the point is that Mrs Thatcher's way of doing business starkly illustrated the enormous powers which the flexible nature of the Cabinet and committee system gives to *any* Prime Minister. As Brazier notes, the power to decide 'whether to set up a committee and when to dissolve it . . . its terms of reference . . . members and chairman [and to] lay down rules which restrict appeal to the full Cabinet' means that 'Significant parts of the British machinery of Government are . . . within the personal control of the Prime Minister . . .'.[15] The treatment of the budget provides a vivid illustration of this point:

> . . . the Chancellor's budget proposals are of major economic and political importance, but they are arrived at in great secrecy in the Treasury, in consultation with the Prime Minister. Individual ministers can and do make representations to the Chancellor . . . which may or may not be heeded. But the first which the Cabinet hears of the detail of the budget are on the morning . . . the Chancellor presents it to the House [by which time] it is obviously too late . . . for ministers to be able to insist on more than minor changes. This astonishing procedure is justified by the need for secrecy [to prevent] damaging leaks.[16]

4   As noted above, the general view is that the Blair premiership has been perhaps even more presidential than Thatcher's, that the Cabinet has been marginalised as never before, and that the Prime Minister has sought and gained control over the rest of government to a greater extent than any previous premier. Key decisions are taken by Cabinet committees or just small groups of ministers. For example, the crucial decision in May 1997 to give the Bank of England independence and the power to set interest rates – one of the most important decisions in economic policy for decades – was apparently taken by the Prime Minister and the Chancellor of the Exchequer alone, in consultation with their special advisers. Other members of the Cabinet were not even consulted.

Brady notes how in a recent lecture:

> Peter Hennessy quoted a number of sophisticated and experienced Whitehall insiders who had declared the death of traditional Cabinet government. One stated that 'This is not a collective government: we have to accept that the old model of Cabinet government is dead as a doornail'; a second that the 'Prime Minister has killed off Cabinet government very effectively'; a third, comparing Blair with that other murder of Cabinet government Margaret Thatcher, that 'Blair makes Margaret Thatcher look like a natural consulter; to be a minister outside the inner loop is hell'.[17]

Hennessy's own comments on the Blair style of premiership are as follows:

P Hennessy, 'The Blair style and the requirements of twenty-first century premiership' (2000) Political Quarterly 386, 387–89 (extracts)

. . .

> Both personal temperament *and* ambition are central to the Blair style. For his is a command premiership, perhaps the most commanding of all since the Second World War – and self-

---

14   See P Hennessy, *Cabinet* (1986), p 102.
15   Brazier (1991), *op cit*, pp 456–57.
16   *Ibid*, p 456.
17   C Brady, 'Collective responsibility of the Cabinet: an ethical, constitutional or managerial tool?' (1999) 52(2) Parl Aff 214.

consciously so, if his use of political language is any guide. 'I will decide the issue of monetary union,' he declared to Sir David Frost on BBC television in January 2000; 'I'm the Prime Minister who's got responsibility for it, according to the British national interest' (to which my immediate reaction, as an old believer in collective Cabinet government, was, 'Not according to the British constitution you haven't').

. . .

Talking to students from Queen Mary and Westfield College at the House of Commons just before Easter 2000, the Home Secretary, recalling the last Wilson administrations, said:

> A lot of decisions went to Cabinet. The fundamental distinction is between Cabinet now and then. Cabinet still has an important role, but fewer decisions are formally endorsed there. The key fundamental difference is that the Labour party in the 1970s had a pretty schismatic division inside it. And the leadership, therefore, in a fundamental way, was unstable.

. . .

From his seat in the Cabinet Room, what did he make of the Blair style as the third anniversary of the government's formation approached? 'Our Prime Minister', he explained to the students, 'has adopted the mode' developed by Mrs Thatcher in the 1980s whereby fewer decisions were made at full Cabinet level, with more devolved to Cabinet committees. 'What Mrs Thatcher did was develop the idea of bilaterals with ministers,' an approach extended by her successor-but-one in Number Ten.

Summing up the Blair style, Jack Straw said, 'The Prime Minister is operating as chief executive of . . . various subsidiary companies and you are called in to account for yourself.' It was, he added, loyally, 'a good process'. . . .

. . .

On the central terrain of Cabinet and premiership, I have come to the conclusion that the traditional collective model, developed albeit in a haphazard way since the late seventeenth century, refashioned under the pressure of two world wars in the twentieth, and consciously adapted for the peace on the back of that wartime experience, has finally disappeared as the governing norm in Whitehall. The model developed by the Anderson Committee during the Second World War and presented to Churchill as the war in Europe ended – in essence, an upper tier of co-ordinating Cabinet committees just beneath the full Cabinet itself – and operated to varying degrees and with variable geometries by all Prime Ministers (Mrs Thatcher included) up to April 1997, has gone under Mr Blair. There are exceptions, such as the Cabinet committees dealing with future legislation and the swathe of constitutional reform committees chaired by Lord Irvine, the Lord Chancellor. But overall we have moved to a new command model in which the distinction between Number Ten and the Cabinet Office, the supposed instrument of the Cabinet as a collective, is more and more blurred.

A shrewd and careful inside observer spoke privately about this in early 1999:

> Do we need a Prime Minister's Department? It's largely an academic debate now because we already have one. It's a properly functioning department with a departmental head [Mr Blair's chief of staff, Jonathan Powell; a political appointee, not a career civil servant], with a sense of being *the* central machinery of government. We do now, in effect, have a PMD, *but* (and it's a crucial 'but') it is not formalised. This is an advantage because it makes it extremely flexible.
>
> It makes it possible to bring in a large number of advisers at very short notice. Almost all the people in this structure hold office at the pleasure of the PM. It is *sui generis* – a case apart from the rest of the Whitehall machine. The centre is not just a person, the Prime Minister, and a small staff – it is a machinery around him.

The best-known parts of the enhanced Prime Minister's office are its presentation and communications aspects. The Prime Minister's press secretary, Alastair Campbell, is much written about and outstrips, in my view, any of his predecessors (Joe Haines under Wilson and Bernard

Ingham under Thatcher being the chief contenders) as the most influential figure in *policy* as well as presentational terms to have held the post.

My thoughtful observer of the Prime Minister's Department-that-will-not-speak-its-name alluded to this, too, when he said:

> The key part of the job is to keep the PM informed – to be the PM's early warning mechanism on policy developments. And when the government changed, Number Ten became much more central to the presentation of policy. The area where there has been a big increase in staffing is the Press Office and the Strategic Communications Unit. That represents a determination that Number Ten shall not just be *primus inter pares* but *the* dominant department in putting forward the message of the government.
>
> . . .
>
> Not only does the Prime Minister agree an annual work programme with each of his Cabinet ministers (with regular progress-chasing sessions as described by Jack Straw), he has instituted an equivalent system for the permanent secretaries at the head of the more important departments. . . . 'We', declared Blair and the then Minister for the Cabinet Office, Jack Cunningham, in the White Paper, 'will ensure that permanent secretaries and heads of department have personal objectives, on which their performance will be assessed, for taking forward the government's modernisation agenda and ensuring delivery of the government's key targets.' Place such procedural accretions alongside the policy reach of a 'big picture', keeper-of-the-government's-strategy premier like Mr Blair and you see a raising of the personal prime ministerial impulse in turn-of-the-century central government and the effective downgrading of what is supposed to be a collective executive.
>
> . . .

Notes

1   See further on the Prime Minister's office, M Burch and I Holliday, 'The Prime Minister's and Cabinet offices: an executive office in all but name'.[18]

2   Perhaps the most bitter attack upon Blair's style of governing came from Clare Short, upon her resignation from the Cabinet as International Development Secretary. Her resignation concerned the UN resolution to reconstruct Iraq (see below), but she also took the opportunity to attack the government's general style.

> The problem is the centralisation of power into the hands of the Prime Minister and an increasingly small number of advisers who make decisions in private without proper discussion. It is increasingly clear, I am afraid, that the Cabinet has become, in Bagehot's phrase, a dignified part of the constitution – joining the Privy Council. There is no real collective responsibility because there is no collective; just diktats in favour of increasingly badly thought through policy initiatives that come from on high.
>
> The consequences of that are serious. Expertise in our system lies in Departments. Those who dictate from the centre do not have full access to that expertise and do not consult. That leads to bad policy. In addition, under our constitutional arrangements, legal, political and financial responsibility flows through Secretaries of State to Parliament. Increasingly, those who are wielding power are not accountable and not scrutinised. Thus we have the powers of a presidential-type system with the automatic majority of a parliamentary system. My conclusion is that those arrangements are leading to increasingly poor policy initiatives being rammed through Parliament, which is straining and abusing party loyalty and undermining the people's respect for our political system.[19]

---

18   (1999) 52 Parl Aff 32.
19   HC Deb col 38 (12 May 2003).

Charges very like these were put to the Prime Minister when he submitted himself for questioning before the Liaison Committee (a committee consisting of the chairs of all the Select Committees).

Liaison Committee, Evidence presented by the Rt Hon Tony Blair MP, Prime Minister, on 16 July 2002, HC 1095 (2001–02)

4. (Sir George Young) Traditionally a government department would work up a policy because that is where the expertise was, that is where the ministers were, and if it involved sensitive issues or other government departments it would be brokered through sub-committees, possibly ending with Cabinet. This process seems to be short-circuited under your administration. Can I just quote what one of your former Cabinet Ministers [Mo Mowlam] said: 'More and more decisions were being taken by Number 10 without consultation with the relevant Minister or Secretary of State. He makes decisions with a small coterie of people, advisers, just like the President of the United States. He doesn't go back to Cabinet, he isn't inclusive'. Is there any substance in what one of your former colleagues said about this style of Government?

(Mr Blair) I truly believe not, no. I think that is unfair and wrong. I think we have roughly doubled the number of Cabinet sub-committees that we inherited in 1997. I think there are now over 40 Cabinet sub-committees. I have regular bilateral stock-takes with Ministers. The Departments, of course, are charged with policy, but the reality is for any modern Prime Minister you also want to know what is happening in your own Government, to be trying to drive forward the agenda of change on which you were elected. It is true that at Cabinet, yes, I would be surprised if the first time I knew of a problem is that it suddenly surfaced around the Cabinet table. But I regard that as good management. That is not to say when critical issues come up that the Cabinet does not sit and discuss them; but if there were particularly very contentious issues and the first I ever heard of it was at Cabinet then I would think some process of communication between Departments and the centre had broken down. I do not actually accept that we have changed fundamentally principles at all; but I do probably place a lot more emphasis on bilateral stock-takes—although there are, as I say, the Cabinet sub-committees and of course I chair groups of ministers myself.

5. (Sir George Young) If Mo Mowlam has got it wrong, what about Sir Richard Packer, a former Permanent Secretary? 'They have shaken up Departments and there's a lot more power at the centre. There are groups at the centre with the Prime Minister's ear ... if something goes wrong, departmental responsibility is clear; but if something goes right, they read in the newspaper it is all the Prime Minister's idea'?

(Mr Blair) I do not accept that either! ... One thing I do say though very strongly is that I make no apology for having a strong centre. [But] before I came to the Committee, I was looking through some of the facts and figures in relation to this and we worked out that my Number 10 office has roughly the same or perhaps even fewer people working for it than the Irish Taoiseach's. To put this in context, there are far fewer people than either the French Prime Minister, never mind the [French President] and the Prime Minister combined, or the German Chancellor.

6. (Tony Wright) ... If you look at what has happened, just the sheer growth of Number 10, more than doubling of the number of special advisers inside government, about a third of those are inside Number 10, we cannot pretend this is the same kind of government that is going on now, can we?

(Mr Blair) ... in relation to foreign policy ... it is correct that we have changed and brought in, for example, Sir Stephen Wall, and Sir David Manning who are now my advisers there. That has expanded from where we were before. When I first came to office John Holmes, who was the adviser to John Major and to me ... was literally handling all foreign policy matters, all European matters, all defence and security matters and Northern Ireland. It just is not possible to do the job effectively with that much pressure being placed on one person. In relation to policy, yes, again it is true that we have expanded the number of policy advisers, but that is because I think it is the right thing to do. I think it is important that in these big public service reform areas we are in constant dialogue, keeping up an exchange of views and partnership with the departments to drive forward the process of change. The short answer to your question is, I am not disputing the fact that we have strengthened the centre considerably; but I say that is the right thing to do; it is necessary if we are wanting to deliver the public service reform that is essential for us and given the totally changed foreign policy and security situation.

...

8. (Tony Wright) What I want you to say is, that we now have a different way of doing government here. Peter Hennessy talks about 'Washington has now come to Whitehall'. All the people who know about these things say something similar. Why can we not just say, there may be good reasons for having it, we have a Prime Minister's Department. The fact you have come here today means we are moving towards a Prime Minister's Department. Why be so coy about it?

(Mr Blair) I think to say that is not either constitutionally or practically correct. You mentioned the United States of America, let us set this in context: in the United States of America there are 3,500 or even 4,000 political appointments; we have 80 special advisers for the whole of Government. There are 3,500 senior civil servants; there are 80 special advisers; there are 400,000 civil servants as a whole. I think we need to get this in context ... There is another thing ... I cannot believe there is a single Prime Minister ... who has not wanted the Prime Minister's writ to run. I cannot believe there is a Prime Minister sitting in Downing Street saying, 'Let them just get on with it, I don't mind much'. It is not the real world. The real world is that with the Prime Minister the buck stops with you; that is the top job and that is how it should be.

Note

1   At least two correctives to the picture of Blair as a command premier are pointed out by Hennessy:[20]

    ...

    Tony Blair has presided over an administration which, to a degree contemplated by no other, has dispersed power through a range of constitutional measures. Two of these – devolution in Scotland and Wales, and the Human Rights Act 1999 – mark but the start of a long process of change and adjustment in both the structures and the culture of British government. However reluctant a devolver he may be, if the Prime Minister resigned tomorrow he could lay claim to be the greatest ever constitutional reformer to have occupied Number Ten.

    ... Second ... the Prime Minister's ... neighbour, Gordon Brown, is a contender for the title of most commanding Chancellor of the Exchequer since 1945. (One probably has to go back to Chamberlain in the 1930s, if not to Lloyd George before the First World War, to find a comparator wielding such a range and degree of power over policy.) To a remarkable degree, Blair's is a twin-stellar government. The Chancellor's constellation revolves around the comprehensive spending reviews and their detailed public service agreements which give the Treasury a degree of control over *departmental* policy outcomes of a kind previous Chancellors could only dream of.

2   It should also further be noted that Blair was careful to gain the full backing of the Cabinet for the highly controversial policy of taking military action against Iraq in Spring 2003 – see further below. Moreover, in May/June 2003, Blair and Brown were careful to consult fully with Cabinet ministers before formally announcing the government's decision not to join the euro at this stage, a decision which was formally endorsed by the full Cabinet.

3   Two more general correctives to the picture of prime ministerial power being painted should also be noted: first of all, the power of Prime Ministers depends greatly on (a) the size of their majority in Parliament, and (b) their perceived popularity and the popularity of their policies. Secondly, the powers outlined above do not mean that the Prime Minister has the capacity to control the detailed

---

20   Hennessy, *op cit*, p 389.

policy-making and day-to-day administration of all government departments. Simple lack of knowledge and insufficient time preclude this.

4   Nevertheless, despite this caveat, this ability to bypass Cabinet has a wider significance: its adverse affect on two important aspects of government. First, there is internal consultation and scrutiny: if an issue is discussed in a small, informal and carefully selected group, the number of people – and particularly unpersuaded, possibly sceptical people – to whom proposed government policy has to be explained is decreased, as is the variety of critical perspectives which have the chance of influencing that policy. This might be seen as a negative effect in constitutional terms since the effect is that power is concentrated in fewer hands and policy (arguably) becomes less honed and tested. However, the corollary of this process is a reduction in the risk of leaks, and a decrease in the chances of controversial policies suffering modification or even abandonment – that is, a gain in political terms. Clearly, as we have seen, these political considerations tend to trump the constitutional ones. This is not surprising given that the person who manipulates and determines the particular system of government used, the Prime Minister, is before all else a politician. The second aspect of government adversely affected is the notion of collective responsibility, to which we now turn.

Prime Minister, Cabinet and collective responsibility

Collective responsibility as an aspect of government accountability will be considered briefly below. Here, its significance in relation to the issues discussed above is considered. According to Brazier:

> The doctrine of collective ministerial responsibility requires that all ministers, and usually parliamentary private secretaries, must accept Cabinet decisions, or dissent from them privately while remaining loyal to them publicly, or dissent publicly and resign, unless collective responsibility is waived by the Cabinet on any given occasion. If a minister does not resign over an issue of policy or procedure he will be collectively responsible for it, in the sense that he will have to support it publicly through his votes in Parliament and through his speeches.[21]

As the Ministerial Code puts it:

> 16. The internal process through which a decision has been made, or the level of Committee by which it was taken, should not be disclosed. Decisions reached by the Cabinet or Ministerial Committees are binding on all members of the Government . . .
>
> 17. Collective responsibility requires that Ministers should be able to express their views frankly in the expectation that they can argue freely in private while maintaining a united front when decisions have been reached. This in turn requires that the privacy of opinions expressed in Cabinet and Ministerial Committees should be maintained. Moreover Cabinet and Committee documents will often contain information which needs to be protected in the public interest. It is therefore essential that, subject to the guidelines on the disclosure of information set out in the Code of Practice on Access to Government Information, Ministers take the necessary steps to ensure that they and their staff preserve the privacy of Cabinet business and protect the security of Government documents.

Colin Turpin, 'Ministerial responsibility', in J Jowell and D Oliver (eds), The Changing Constitution, 3rd edn (1994), pp 147–50

The rigour of collective responsibility is, as is well known, mitigated by the practice of 'unattributable leaking' by ministers to the press, in this way rallying support outside for their

---

21   Brazier (1994), *op cit*, pp 129–30.

position in arguments within Government, or letting it be known that they have opposed a decision unwelcome to sections of their party or to interest groups. Gordon Walker defended this practice as necessary to the preservation of collective responsibility [*The Cabinet* (1972), p 32]. It has not diminished in frequency since his time and must be counted an established, if not entirely 'correct', feature of the constitutional system. Prime Ministers try to curb the practice, but have been known to resort to it themselves.

A more radical remedy for the strains which may be caused in party and government by the demands of collective solidarity is the *suspension* of the obligation, so as to allow open dissent, within specified limits, on a strongly contested question. The 1932 'agreement to differ' was seen as something unique until collective responsibility was again suspended in 1975 for the referendum campaign on membership of the European Communities, and in 1977 for the second reading of the European Assembly Elections Bill. There are those who deprecate this sort of expedient as undermining the basis of parliamentary government, but it is questionable whether the public interest is always well served by the concealment of differences on policy within government. In particular, when the Opposition leadership is in agreement with the official Government view on an important issue facing the country, public debate is devalued if the dissenting opinions of senior politicians on both sides are stifled by insistence on collective responsibility.

In any event it may be impossible to maintain a public show of ministerial solidarity when there are sharp ideological differences, or an especially keen contest on some particular question of policy, between Cabinet ministers. This became evident in the periods of Labour government in the 1960s and 1970s. In the earlier years of Mrs Thatcher's premiership there were ministers who openly expressed their disagreement with Government policies and who were not, with one or two exceptions, visited with immediate loss of office as a result. Leading dissentients were, however, progressively removed in Cabinet reshuffles and dissension became less persistent – but when it occurred, was more portentous … When Mr Nigel Lawson resigned as Chancellor of the Exchequer in 1989, he did so on the ground that the exchange-rate policy he was seeking to further was not being supported by the Prime Minister, who was instead giving rein to the contrary opinions of her personal economic adviser, Sir Alan Walters. Mr Lawson too, in his resignation speech, insisted on the need for the collective resolution of policy differences in government. Disagreement between ministers on policy towards the European Community precipitated the resignation in 1990 of Sir Geoffrey Howe, Leader of the House of Commons and Deputy Prime Minister, who protested in his letter of resignation that 'Cabinet government is all about trying to persuade one another from within' [*The Times*, 2 November 1990].

Despite the recurring note struck by these three ministers in their public statements, they did not resign for the purpose of defending a constitutional principle of collective decision-making, but for a variety of convoluted and partly unavowed reasons. Nevertheless that principle is essential to the effective working of Cabinet government. Although, as we have seen, the responsibility of ministers does not depend on their having taken part in the making of the decision or policy in question, the convention of collective solidarity finds its most secure anchorage, and its most convincing justification, in executive arrangements which allow for full discussion and the representation of contrary viewpoints. A style of administration – like that of Mrs Thatcher's premiership – which is not favourable to collective decision-making may be seen as undermining the basis of the convention.

Notes
1   A recent example of the flexibility of the doctrine of collective responsibility lay in the attitude of Clare Short, Secretary of State for International Development, to government policy on the use of force against Iraq,[22] specifically the government's eventual, and hugely controversial, decision to take military action against Iraq in

---

22   See Part III Chapter 1 for more on Parliament and the Iraq conflict, at pp 273–81.

March 2003 without an explicit mandate from the UN Security Council.[23] The Security Council on 25 November 2002 had passed resolution 1441, which found Iraq to be in material breach of its disarmament obligations under numerous previous resolutions and threatened 'serious consequences' if Iraq failed fully to cooperate with UN inspectors seeking to investigate whether Iraq had, as it claimed, fully dismantled its prohibited nuclear, chemical and biological weapons programmes. government policy, in the light of less than full cooperation from the Iraqi government, was to seek to obtain a further Security Council resolution, expressly endorsing military action against Iraq to disarm it of such weapons. However, by mid-March, the attempt to obtain a Security Council resolution explicitly authorising the use of force had been all but abandoned in the face of implacable opposition from France, Germany and Russia and lack of support from other members of the Security Council, representing a major failure of Anglo-American diplomacy and a serious reverse for the government. The government was now faced with the prospect of taking the country to war with no explicit UN backing, without even a majority of the UN Security Council in favour, and with massive protests sweeping the country and the rest of Europe. At this point, Clare Short launched an extraordinary public attack on the government's policy – a policy for which she had collective responsibility – warning that she would resign from the government if no such resolution was secured. In a radio interview she said:

The whole atmosphere of the current situation is deeply reckless; reckless for the world, reckless for the undermining of the UN in this disorderly world, which is wider than Iraq, reckless with our government, reckless with his own future, position and place in history. It's extraordinarily reckless. I'm very surprised by it.[24]

2   However, once the government finally decided that it would take military action even without such a UN resolution, Short did *not* resign, losing a great deal of political credibility thereby, but then resigning over a related issue only a few months later (see below). The episode demonstrates, it is suggested, that there is no *automatic* sanction of enforced resignation, or dismissal, for breaches of collective responsibility: all will depend upon the Prime Minister's calculation of the best course of action for the government (and/or his or her own position) at the time. Blair obviously took the view that it would be better to keep Short in the Cabinet, at least for the present, despite her extraordinary attack upon government policy.

3   As Turpin notes, collective responsibility implies not only a duty of public acquiescence to official government policy but, as a corollary to this, a reasonable chance for government ministers to at least discuss key policies which the convention will demand they later defend. As the Ministerial Code now puts it, 'Collective responsibility requires that Ministers should be able to express their views frankly in the expectation that they can argue freely in private while maintaining a united front when decisions have been reached' (para 17). As James notes, the lesson of the Heseltine affair is that 'the enforcement against ministers of the rule of collective responsibility implies an obligation on the Prime Minister ... to ensure that colleagues are consulted, at least on major issues'.[25] Brady comments that Thatcher did not recognise these two aspects of the convention, rather

---

23   Clare Short and Robin Cook were the two Cabinet ministers to resign; there were a number of lower level resignations also over the issue.
24   See 'Short spearheads rebellion with threat to quit over war', *The Guardian*, 10 March 2003.
25   James, *op cit*, p 627.

regarding 'collective responsibility as something owed to a Prime Minster and not something which had to be earned and nurtured'.[26] The problem is that these two basic aspects of the convention (the duty to present a united front and the duty on the PM to consult) derive unequal levels of support from the political imperatives of government. Whilst, with exceptions, the basic survival of government depends upon the first aspect, giving maximum incentive for its enforcement by the Prime Minister, by contrast, as discussed above, the Prime Minister may often have strong reasons *not* to allow fulfilment of the second, since denial of full ministerial participation in policy formation will clearly assist a Prime Minister bent on forcing through controversial policies. Further, the first part of the convention arguably provides a disincentive for honouring the second: the Prime Minister's motivation for allowing full participation is hardly increased by his knowledge that (provided things are not pushed too far) ministers will have to support a given policy regardless of whether they supported, opposed or even discussed it. Once again, in an important aspect of British governmental practice, politics may be seen to trump constitutionalism.

4 Of course, in a sense, some version of collective responsibility is a prerequisite for any kind of recognisable government. Any collection of individual people is inevitably going to disagree over at least some important issues, and if all those disagreements were on public show, if ministers could constantly disclaim responsibility for decisions they did not like, then we would hardly have recognisable 'government' policy at all – only different policies, held by different individuals. But it is important nevertheless to recognise clearly all the implications and consequences of the convention, necessary as it may be to an extent.

5 Tony Blair's government has been unusual in seeing two high profile resignations – by Robin Cook and Clare Short – made on a point of principle: a policy of the government which members of the Cabinet felt that they could not support. When the government finally decided to support US military action against Iraq without a second UN resolution, Robin Cook, Leader of the House of Commons, resigned from the government. His statement follows:

Personal Statement of Robin Cook, HC Deb cols 736 et seq (17 March 2003)

Mr Robin Cook (Livingston): This is the first time for 20 years that I have addressed the House from the Back Benches. . . . I have chosen to address the House first on why I cannot support a war without international agreement or domestic support.

I applaud the heroic efforts that the Prime Minister has made in trying to secure a second resolution. I do not think that anybody could have done better than the Foreign Secretary in working to get support for a second resolution within the Security Council. But the very intensity of those attempts underlines how important it was to succeed. Now that those attempts have failed, we cannot pretend that getting a second resolution was of no importance.

. . . It is not France alone that wants more time for inspections. Germany wants more time for inspections; Russia wants more time for inspections; indeed, at no time have we signed up even the minimum necessary to carry a second resolution. We delude ourselves if we think that the degree of international hostility is all the result of President Chirac. The reality is that Britain is being asked to embark on a war without agreement in any of the international bodies of which we are a leading partner—not NATO, not the European Union and, now, not the Security Council.

---

26 Brady, *op cit*, at 221.

To end up in such diplomatic weakness is a serious reverse. Only a year ago, we and the United States were part of a coalition against terrorism that was wider and more diverse than I would ever have imagined possible. History will be astonished at the diplomatic miscalculations that led so quickly to the disintegration of that powerful coalition. The US can afford to go it alone, but Britain is not a superpower. Our interests are best protected not by unilateral action but by multilateral agreement and a world order governed by rules. Yet tonight the international partnerships most important to us are weakened: the European Union is divided; the Security Council is in stalemate. Those are heavy casualties of a war in which a shot has yet to be fired.

... [It is unfair] to accuse those of us who want longer for inspections of not having an alternative strategy. For four years as Foreign Secretary I was partly responsible for the western strategy of containment. Over the past decade that strategy destroyed more weapons than in the Gulf war, dismantled Iraq's nuclear weapons programme and halted Saddam's medium and long-range missiles programmes. Iraq's military strength is now less than half its size than at the time of the last Gulf war.

Iraq probably has no weapons of mass destruction in the commonly understood sense of the term – namely a credible device capable of being delivered against a strategic city target. It probably still has biological toxins and battlefield chemical munitions, but it has had them since the 1980s when US companies sold Saddam anthrax agents and the then British Government approved chemical and munitions factories. Why is it now so urgent that we should take military action to disarm a military capacity that has been there for 20 years, and which we helped to create? Why is it necessary to resort to war this week, while Saddam's ambition to complete his weapons programme is blocked by the presence of UN inspectors?

Only a couple of weeks ago, Hans Blix told the Security Council that the key remaining disarmament tasks could be completed within months. I have heard it said that Iraq has had not months but 12 years in which to complete disarmament, and that our patience is exhausted. Yet it is more than 30 years since resolution 242 called on Israel to withdraw from the occupied territories. We do not express the same impatience with the persistent refusal of Israel to comply. I welcome the strong personal commitment that the Prime Minister has given to middle east peace, but Britain's positive role in the middle east does not redress the strong sense of injustice throughout the Muslim world at what it sees as one rule for the allies of the US and another rule for the rest.

... From the start of the present crisis, I have insisted, as Leader of the House, on the right of this place to vote on whether Britain should go to war. It has been a favourite theme of commentators that this House no longer occupies a central role in British politics. Nothing could better demonstrate that they are wrong than for this House to stop the commitment of troops in a war that has neither international agreement nor domestic support. I intend to join those tomorrow night who will vote against military action now. It is for that reason, and for that reason alone, and with a heavy heart, that I resign from the Government. [Applause.]

Note

Clare Short, having failed to resign over the failure to secure UN backing for the conflict, resigned only a few months later over the terms of a proposed UN resolution on the reconstruction and interim government of Iraq, after Saddam Hussein's government had been overthrown in the conflict. Her resignation statement made plain her reasons for so doing.

Personal Statement of Clare Short, HC Deb cols 736 et seq (12 May 2003)

... I have decided to resign from the Government. ... The House will be aware that I had many criticisms of the way in which events leading up to the conflict in Iraq were handled. I offered my resignation to the Prime Minister on a number of occasions but was pressed by him and others to stay. I have been attacked from many different angles for that decision but I still think that, hard as it was, it was the right thing to do.

The reason why I agreed to remain in the Government was that it was too late to put right the mistakes that had been made. I had throughout taken the view that it was necessary to be willing to contemplate the use of force to back up the authority of the UN. The regime was brutal, the people were suffering, our Attorney-General belatedly but very firmly said there was legal authority for the use of force, and because the official Opposition were voting with the Government, the conflict was unavoidable. [Interruption.] There is no question about that. It had to carry.

I decided that I should not weaken the Government at that time and should agree to the Prime Minister's request to stay and lead the UK humanitarian and reconstruction effort. However, the problem now is that the mistakes that were made in the period leading up to the conflict are being repeated in the post-conflict situation. In particular, the UN mandate, which is necessary to bring into being a legitimate Iraqi Government, is not being supported by the UK Government. This, I believe, is damaging to Iraq's prospects, will continue to undermine the authority of the UN and directly affects my work and responsibilities.

... I believe that it is the duty of all responsible political leaders right across the world – whatever view they took on the launch of the war – to focus on reuniting the international community in order to support the people of Iraq in rebuilding their country, to re-establish the authority of the UN and to heal the bitter divisions that preceded the war. I am sorry to say that the UK Government are not doing this. They are supporting the US in trying to bully the Security Council into a resolution that gives the coalition the power to establish an Iraqi Government and control the use of oil for reconstruction, with only a minor role for the UN.

... Both in the run-up to the war and now, I think the UK is making grave errors in providing cover for US mistakes rather than helping an old friend, which is understandably hurt and angry after the events of 11 September, to honour international law and the authority of the UN. American power alone cannot make America safe. Of course, we must all unite to dismantle the terrorist networks, and, through the UN, the world is doing this. But undermining international law and the authority of the UN creates a risk of instability, bitterness and growing terrorism that will threaten the future for all of us.

I am ashamed that the UK Government have agreed the resolution that has been tabled in New York and shocked by the secrecy and lack of consultation with Departments with direct responsibility for the issues referred to in the resolution. I am afraid that this resolution undermines all the commitments I have made in the House and elsewhere about how the reconstruction of Iraq will be organised. Clearly this makes my position impossible and I have no alternative [other] than to resign from the Government.

GOVERNMENT ACCOUNTABILITY AND RESPONSIBILITY

What then are the mechanisms by which the exercise of the vast powers of central government may be scrutinised and made accountable? The traditional panacea for all ills is the convention of the accountability of ministers to Parliament. The detailed *mechanisms* by which the actions of ministers and their departments are scrutinised (Parliamentary Questions, Select Committees, etc) are examined in Part III Chapter 1. The normative content of the convention itself, and sanctions for its breach are examined here. We start with an account of the historical development of the convention of ministerial responsibility.

Privy Council Office, Canada, *Responsibility in the Constitution* (1977), Chapter 2 (extracts)

The origins of ministerial responsibility

By the close of the 17th century, more particularly through the *Bill of Rights*, the *Mutiny Act*, and the *Act of Settlement*, the Crown's dependency on the Commons for the imposition of taxes was embedded in the constitution. The king's advisers continued to be appointed by the Crown, but they found it necessary to work in harmony with the Commons because it exercised control over the financial and military power of the Crown. If the king's ministers, those in charge of the principal offices of state, were to function successfully, if money was to be granted, they had to get along with a majority of members of the Commons. Gradually ministers saw the importance of – and a considerable number, particularly those with financial responsibilities, profited from – being members of the House of Commons.

Control over ways and means (taxation) and supply (expenditure) enabled the House of Commons to hold ministers responsible for their actions, which is to say that ministers, appointed by the Crown, were held responsible for the actions they took in the name of the Crown. This individual responsibility was manifested not only in the accounting that ministers might be required to give to Parliament, but also in the impeachment procedures that were used to force the Crown to dismiss a minister who ceased to enjoy the confidence of Parliament.

There was little respect for the concept of 'the Government', and ministers entered and left office individually as the king (occasionally at the behest of Parliament) saw fit.

The ability of the king to pick and choose ministers was circumscribed by political forces at work in Parliament and among ministers. The growth of political parties favouring particular groups of ministers further reduced the exercise of the Crown's prerogative. George I, the beneficiary of the Hanoverian Settlement, owed his throne to the new Whig party, and was constrained to select his ministers from this group. George I had the additional handicap of speaking little English. The powers of royal patronage were now increasingly exercised on the advice of the principal Treasury Lord, who became the first of the king's ministers. In short, the Hanoverian Settlement began the process of substituting prime ministerial control for the king's control' over the selection of ministers.

By the time of the Seven Years War the First Lord of the Treasury had begun to be known as first or prime ministers. By the end of the century the prime minister had taken effective control over the appointment although not necessarily the dismissal of ministers and some other senior office holders. This development made possible and was accompanied by the emergence of the cabinet as a device for co-ordinating the views of ministers in order to enable them to support one another in the House of Commons. In this way the critical convention of collective responsibility was added to the individual responsibility of ministers, which in the 18th century was a legal matter rendering them liable to impeachment. Individual responsibility remains the primary legal basis of the system today. The possibility of impeachment has been replaced by the threat of loss of office, which usually takes place through voluntary resignation in order not to invoke the collective responsibility of colleagues that would result in removal from office of the ministry as a whole.

Note

The contemporary concept of ministerial responsibility is complex. Essentially the idea of ministerial responsibility involves two concepts: first, the duty of ministers to give an account and explanation of their actions and of the decisions taken by their department to Parliament; and, secondly, the obligation to accept responsibility for mistakes made personally by them or by their department. A corollary to both these aspects of the doctrine is the duty of ministers not to mislead Parliament. The above summary indicates the order in which the various elements of this topic will be considered.

The duty of accountability

We start then with the duty to give an account. The traditional doctrine will be considered first, possible modification of it in the light of the increasing complexity of government business and the 'Next Steps' reforms will then be noted and, finally, areas of uncertainty and difference of opinion relating to the 'new' position will be considered. In this section, therefore, we are considering what the duty of accountability means, by contrasting it with the notion of personal responsibility for policy or other failings and the implications of that distinction for the accountability split between ministers and officials. In the last major section of this chapter, the *content* of the duty to give an account is explored, by which is meant an examination of *what* ministers must tell Parliament and their duty not to mislead it.

It should be noted that the difficulties in this area commence at once, with terminology. In the above introduction, we have distinguished between what we have called 'the duty to give an account' and the 'obligation to accept responsibility'. This broadly follows a distinction in terminology put forward by Sir Robin Butler, when he was Head of the Home Civil Service, and accepted by both the Major and Blair governments (see below) in which 'accountability' denotes the duty to explain, whilst 'responsibility' means the obligation to accept personal blame for error. Unfortunately, Turpin, in an important essay on this topic,[27] written before Sir Robin's suggested distinction, treats the two terms as 'synonymous' whilst noting that others treat the imposition of sanctions on a minister for his personal fault as a strong form of responsibility sometimes described as 'accountability'. The matter is further confused by the fact that 'ministerial responsibility' or 'individual responsibility of ministers' is generally used as a shorthand to denote both aspects of the doctrine. In what follows, the terminology put forward by Sir Robin Butler (though not necessarily the propositions lying behind it) is followed.

The accountability/responsibility distinction

We need to ask what exactly is a minister accountable for? Theoretically, the answer is everything that goes on in his or her department. That this obligation is indeed formally present can be seen in the official government definition of ministerial responsibility, which we will return to again later in this chapter. That definition, appearing in the Ministerial Code, a Cabinet Office document containing guidance for Ministers, formerly known as Questions of Procedure for Ministers (QPM) is as follows:

> 1. (ii)   Ministers have a duty to Parliament to account for, and be held to account, for the policies, decisions and actions of their departments and Next Steps Agencies.

It should be noted that, whilst as the Nolan report remarked, 'QPM has no particular constitutional status',[28] Professor Hennessy, giving evidence to the Public Service Committee in April 1996[29] described QPM as the 'strand of DNA which determines the proper conduct of central government ... as both the Nolan and Scott Inquiries discovered as they went along ...'. Moreover, the above paragraph (together with others relating to the extent of the duty to account to Parliament considered below) was approved by a resolution of both Houses in 1997,[30] giving it far greater significance than mere guidance from the executive to its own. Tomkins comments:

---

27   'Ministerial responsibility', in J Jowell and D Oliver (eds), *The Changing Constitution*, 3rd edn (1994), p 112.
28   First Report of the Committee on Standards in Public Life, Cm 2850-I (1995), Chapter 3, para 9 (p 92).
29   HC 313-1 (1995–96), Minutes of Evidence, 20 March 1996, Q 66.
30   HC Deb vol 292 cols 1046–47 (19 March 1997); HL Deb vol 579 col 1055 (20 March 1997).

No longer is ministerial responsibility merely an unwritten constitutional Convention ... It is now a clear parliamentary rule, set down in resolutions by both Houses of Parliament ... The government acting on its own cannot now change the terms on ministers' responsibility to Parliament in the way that the Conservative government did throughout its period in office.[31]

The Public Administration Select Committee recently spoke of the Code thus:

The Ministerial Code is a vital part of the constitution. It sets out what citizens should expect of those who govern them, and provides an important means by which they should be held to account. It is an important safeguard against abuse and incompetence.[32]

In a previous report, it said:

We believe that the development of such codes of conduct across public life reinforces the need for the constitutional status of the Ministerial Code to be properly recognised. It is not a legal document but a set of guidelines. It does not necessarily cover all aspects of what should be considered acceptable Ministerial practice or behaviour and should not substitute for the Prime Minister's judgement, for which he must account to Parliament. It is unsatisfactory for its status still to be in doubt. It is the rule book for ministerial conduct, including the responsibilities of Ministers to Parliament, and its status should reflect its importance. It may have developed in a private and ad hoc way, but it is now an integral part of the new constitutional architecture. It is time for it to be recognised as such.[33]

The Ministerial Code, as it now is, is also a useful starting point, partly because it gives the governmental view of its own responsibility and partly because it is interesting to note what it leaves unsaid. As a matter of fact and common sense, clearly a minister will not be able to give an account of everything going on within a large and complex government department in which hundreds of decisions may be taken every day by civil servants, often at quite a low level. But the Code does not say how this affects the minister's accountability. Presumably, a minister is accountable for the actions of civil servants in that he or she can be required to investigate a matter and report to the House on it, but can there be a parallel accountability of the civil servants themselves? In the chapter on the House of Commons (Part III Chapter 1, pp 327–31), the restrictions on what kinds of questions civil servants would respond to when being questioned by Select Committees – restrictions which suggested that they did not need to account for their own personal decisions – were noted and will not be rehearsed here. As the government sees the position from the point of view of the convention of ministerial responsibility, the civil servant is accountable not to Parliament but to the minister. This view is summed up – and critiqued – in the following important Select Committee report which starts by considering the basic problem that it is unrealistic to expect ministers to take responsibility for every action taken in their departments.

Second Report from the Public Service Committee, HC 313 (1995–96) (extracts)

...

12. The standard solution to this problem is contained in the speech by Sir David Maxwell-Fyfe, the then Home Secretary, on the Crichel Down Affair in 1954. Maxwell-Fyfe's speech was intended to scotch the notion (which might be regarded as being fostered by the Bridges memorandum, quoted above) that 'the principle operates so as to oblige Ministers to extend total protection to

---

31 A Tomkin, *The Constitution after Scott: Government Unwrapped* (1998), p 62.
32 Second Report, HC 439 (2001–02), para 1.
33 Third Report, HC 235 (2000–01), para 15.

their officials and to endorse their acts, and to cause the position that civil servants cannot be called to account and are effectively responsible to no-one.' 'That is a position', he went on to say, 'which I believe is quite wrong, and I think it is the cardinal error, that has crept into the appreciation of this situation'. Maxwell-Fyfe identified four different situations to indicate the boundaries of Ministers' responsibility for the actions of civil servants. These are:

— 'in the case where there is an explicit order by a Minister, the Minister must protect the civil servant who has carried out his order';

— 'when the civil servant acts properly in accordance with the policy laid down by the Minister, the Minister must protect and defend him';

— where an official makes a mistake or causes some delay, but not on an important issue of policy and not where a claim to individual rights is seriously involved, the Minister acknowledges the mistake and he accepts the responsibility, although he is not personally involved. He states that he will take corrective action in the Department ... he would not, in those circumstances, expose the official to public criticism';

— 'where action has been taken by a civil servant of which the Minister disapproves and has no prior knowledge, and the conduct of the official is reprehensible, then there is no obligation on the part of the Minister to endorse what he believes to be wrong, or to defend what are clearly shown to be errors of his officers. The Minister is not bound to defend action of which he did not know, or of which he disapproves. But, of course, he remains constitutionally responsible to Parliament for the fact that something has gone wrong, and he alone can tell Parliament what has occurred and render an account of his stewardship'.

13. This has become regarded as an authoritative statement of how the convention is to be interpreted. It is nonetheless confusing and ambiguous, particularly so on the extent to which a Minister's responsibility for the conduct of his officials extends to the general oversight of the work of the department. Maxwell-Fyfe appears to argue that a Minister has no responsibility for the conduct of his officials where they are not explicitly or implicitly following his policy; on the other hand, he said that a Minister remains 'constitutionally responsible to Parliament for the fact that something has gone wrong, and he alone can tell Parliament what has occurred and render an account of his stewardship'. In another part of his speech, he said that 'it is part of a Minister's responsibility to Parliament to take necessary action to ensure efficiency and the proper discharge of the duties of his department ... He can lay down standing instructions to see that his policy is carried out. He can lay down rules by which it is ensured that matters of importance, of difficulty, or of political danger are brought to his attention'.

14. Some of the difficulty on the discussion of the roles and responsibilities of Ministers derives from the vagueness and ambiguity of what is meant by the word 'responsible'. Since 1954, the issue of the extent to which Ministers can be regarded as 'responsible' for the activities of their departments has been raised regularly, often in the context of the giving of evidence by civil servants to Select Committees. Successive governments have tried to bring greater clarity by introducing a distinction between *responsibility* and *accountability* – although, as the Treasury and Civil Service Committee were told in 1994, the distinction has not been used consistently, and the words 'can and often have been used interchangeably' ...

15. The last few years have seen further attempts to clarify the point, some in the context of the controversy concerning the extent of Ministerial responsibility for the work of Next Steps agencies – something which will be examined later – and some in the context of the Scott Inquiry. These have largely been directed towards applying the word 'accountability' to a Minister's duty as the representative in Parliament of part of the executive, while limiting 'responsibility' to actions taken personally by the Minister. The Cabinet Office in a memorandum submitted to the Treasury and Civil Service Committee in April 1994 distinguished between 'the constitutional fact of Ministerial accountability for all that a department does, and the limits to the direct personal responsibility (in the sense of personal involvement) of Ministers for all the actions of their departments and agencies, given the realities of delegation and dispersed responsibility for much

business'. In his memorandum to this Committee, the Chancellor of the Duchy of Lancaster has sought to cast this distinction back into the statements by Maxwell-Fyfe and Bridges by defining the occasions on which they used the words 'responsible', 'answerable' or 'account' as meaning either 'constitutionally accountable' or 'personally responsible'.

16. The most recent, and most elaborate, interpretation of the doctrine and the distinction has come in the Government's reply to the Treasury and Civil Service Committee's 1994 Report on the Role of the Civil Service. The Government says that:

> 'In the Government's view, a Minister is 'accountable' to Parliament for everything which goes on within his department, in the sense that Parliament can call the Minister to account for it. The Minister is responsible for the policies of the department, for the framework through which those policies are delivered, for the resources allocated, for such implementation decisions as the Framework Document may require to be referred or agreed with him, and for his response to major failures or expressions of Parliamentary or public concern. But a Minister cannot sensibly be held responsible for everything which goes on in his department in the sense of having personal knowledge and control of every action taken and being personally blameworthy when delegated tasks are carried out incompetently, or when mistakes or errors of judgement are made at operational level. It is not possible for Ministers to handle everything personally, and if Ministers were to be held personally responsible for every action of the department, delegation and efficiency would be much inhibited. It was for this reason that evidence suggested the use of the word 'accountable' for the first of these two meanings of the word responsible, to distinguish it from the second'.

17. This is undoubtedly clearer than the interpretation of the convention given in the Armstrong Memorandum. Yet the distinction remains somewhat confusing because it makes use of common words in different ways. Sir Robin Butler admitted in evidence to this Committee that the distinction 'has actually caused more confusion than clarity'. Part of the problem is that in normal usage, the words 'responsibility', 'accountability', 'answerability' and 'liability' can often be taken to mean roughly the same thing'. An alternative might be to stick to a single term (either accountability or responsibility) and to distinguish different forms of it as Geoffrey Marshall, Provost of The Queen's College, Oxford, suggests. However, this does not seem much to improve on the Government's approach of erecting accountability and responsibility into distinguishable terms of art, with assigned meanings. Sir Michael Quinlan, Director of the Ditchley Foundation and former Permanent Under-Secretary of State in the Ministry of Defence, told us:

> A good deal of public discussion seems to me needlessly hampered by the attempt to identify in the normal usage of the words 'accountability' and 'responsibility' (and also sometimes 'answerability') tidy and precise meanings, distinct as between one word and another. But words derive their meaning from usage, and the usage of these words in common parlance is not tidy and precise – they are used in overlapping and indeed sometimes interchangeable ways. It may be that there would be value in establishing, for the context of public-service analysis, term-of-art conventions whereby such words would be assigned, by customary agreement among those engaged in such discourse, exact meanings. I interpret the recent use of the words 'responsibility' and 'accountability' by Sir Robin Butler, Cabinet Secretary and Head of the Home Civil Service, as seeking to encourage a term-of-art precision not hitherto present in ordinary parlance.

The Government's distinction now receives some support. Professor Rodney Brazier has recommended its acceptance:

> 'there should be an unqualified principle that a Minister is accountable for everything which happens (or does not happen) in his or her department, in the sense that he or she *owes a duty to account to Parliament and the public* for departmental policies, for what has taken place in the department or its agencies, and for the conduct of officials, and to demonstrate what has been done to correct mistakes and to ensure that they will not recur. . . . The principle that a Minister is *responsible* to Parliament and public, and that he or she should bear personal blame

for acts and omissions (and in appropriate cases resign), should be narrowed down to cases in which the Minister has some personal responsibility for, or some personal involvement in, a blameworthy act or omission. It is absurd nowadays to try to continue the fiction that a Minister is personally responsible, and should bear personal obloquy, for every occurrence in the department, even if he was unaware of it and had no reason to be aware of it.'

Lord Howe said the distinction was 'helpful'; 'I think accountability is an obligation, as I understand it, to explain, to say what happened, to be accountable for it; responsibility implies some more potentially disciplinary response for it, and to that extent I think that is a useful distinction.'

18. We are less certain that the distinction between 'accountability' and 'responsibility' is always a useful one. For the substance of it is a distinction between those matters on which Ministers have merely to provide an explanation to the House, and those matters on which failures may be regarded as their own fault and which may justifiably lead to the Minister's resignation. In many, probably most, cases that distinction is easily made. A Minister is obviously responsible for deciding on what policy to follow, or the resources allocated to particular budgets, for example. But in other cases, the distinction is hard to draw. The most difficult area is the one with which Maxwell-Fyfe grappled: to what extent can Ministers be said to be responsible (in the sense that it may be regarded proper that they lose their job if something goes wrong) for essentially *administrative* failures within a department?

19. The issue has been a battleground over which successive Governments and Oppositions (and private members) have fought. Mr Enoch Powell put the case for a broader interpretation of Ministerial responsibility in the debate in 1984 over an escape from the Maze prison in Belfast. Rejecting the Minister's refusal to accept blame for the escape, he said:

'[The Secretary of State] drew a distinction, which I believe to be invalid, between responsibility for policy and responsibility for administration. I believe that this is a wholly fallacious view of the nature of Ministerial responsibility ... even if all considerations of policy could be eliminated, the responsibility for the administration of a department remains irrevocably with the Minister in charge.'

Mr Powell makes an extreme case for the extent to which Ministers should take personal blame for failures in their department, which will not be generally accepted. Yet Ministers must accept in some degree that they are personally responsible for the overall way in which their Department is administered. They cannot, indeed, be blamed for individual failures at operational level; but they might be blamed for a broader pattern of incompetence. Indeed, the Chancellor of the Duchy of Lancaster has referred to a Minister's responsibility for the organisation and resource framework of a Department. Ministers cannot be blamed for each failure connected with the work of the department; but if such a failure were great enough, many may feel it proper that the Minister resign.

20. What Ministers must never do is to put the blame onto civil servants for the effects of unworkable policies and their setting of unrealistic targets. If, when things go wrong, it is held that Ministers are not to blame because they did not (knowingly) mislead Parliament, and civil servants are not to blame because they acted as servants of Ministers, then the unsatisfactory outcome is that nobody is to blame. There is clearly something unsatisfactory about a doctrine of Ministerial Responsibility that can issue in such a conclusion.

21. If the point of drawing a distinction between 'accountability' and 'responsibility' is to limit the extent to which blame might be attached to Ministers for failings in their departments, then it is unsuccessful. To the extent that it protects Ministers from being seen as personally to blame for minor failings (an incorrect social security payment, for example) it is no more than a statement of the obvious: few would seriously advance the proposition that a Minister should resign in such circumstances. To the extent that it implies that it is possible to draw in practice a clear line between minor failings at operational level and a more systemic failure, experience suggests that it is, at best, hopeful. **It is not possible absolutely to distinguish an area in which a Minister**

is personally responsible, and liable to take blame, from one in which he is constitutionally accountable. Ministerial responsibility is not composed of two elements with a clear break between the two. Ministers have an obligation to Parliament which consists in ensuring that government explains its actions. Ministers also have an obligation to respond to criticism made in Parliament in a way that seems likely to satisfy it – which may include, if necessary, resignation.

. . .

32. The theory of Ministerial responsibility should keep pace with the contemporary reality, if it is to retain its credibility. It would give greater clarity if the Government were less coy in its definition of what Ministerial responsibility means. As we have said, we believe that Ministers have a general responsibility to Parliament for the work of their departments which cannot be neatly divided into spheres of 'personal responsibility' and 'constitutional accountability'. There are, it is time to say, two sides to the obligation of Ministers for those matters which come within their responsibility – even if they cannot be simply distinguished. They may be referred to as the obligation to *give an account*; and the liability *to be held to account*. **We believe that the following represents a working definition of 'Ministerial responsibility'.**

> **Ministers owe a fundamental duty to account to Parliament. This has, essentially, two meanings. First, that the executive is obliged to give an account – to provide full information about and explain its actions in Parliament so that they are subject to proper democratic scrutiny. This obligation is central to the proper functioning of Parliament, and therefore any Minister who has been found to have knowingly misled Parliament should resign. While it is through Ministers that the Government is properly accountable to Parliament, the obligation to provide full information and to explain the actions of government to Parliament means that Ministers should allow civil servants to give an account to Parliament through Select Committees when appropriate – particularly where Ministers have formally delegated functions to them, for example in the case of Chief Executives of Executive Agencies.**

> **Second, a Minister's duty to account to Parliament means that the executive is liable to be held to account: it must respond to concerns and criticism raised in Parliament about its actions because Members of Parliament are democratically-elected representatives of the people. A Minister's effective performance of his functions depends on his having the confidence of the House of Commons (or the House of Lords, for those Ministers who sit in the upper House). A Minister has to conduct himself, and direct the work of his department in a manner likely to ensure that he retains the confidence both of his own party and of the House. It is for the Prime Minister to decide whom he chooses as Ministers; but the Prime Minister is unlikely to keep in office a Minister who does not retain the confidence of his Parliamentary colleagues.**

. . .

Notes

1 In its response to this report,[34] the government rejected the suggestion in the final sentence of the first paragraph of this definition of ministerial responsibility, saying that it was not prepared to breach:

the longstanding basic principle that civil servants, including the Chief Executives of Next Step Agencies [see below] give an account to Parliament on behalf of the Ministers whom they serve.

---

34   First Special Report of the Committee, HC 67 (1996–97).

Were civil servants to go beyond this, they would inevitably be drawn into matters on which, as the Committee itself acknowledges (para 114) they must refer Select Committees to the Minister.

2 It is apparent, however, that the duty on *ministers* to explain extends to answering criticisms, to defending the record of the department in question, even to promising investigation and remedial action if necessary. The duty to explain therefore goes beyond the mere neutral transmission of information: 'accountability' means not only 'giving an account' but also 'being held to account' with the proviso that this kind of being held to account does not include the acceptance of personal fault by the minister. (Acceptance of such fault means acceptance of 'responsibility' and resignation may then become an issue – a matter we will examine below.) Therefore, 'accountability' in the government sense also covers what Turpin described as 'strong responsibility' – the ability for redress (short of personal redress) to be exacted by Parliament. Lord Armstrong explained it thus to the Public Service Committee. In cases in which the minister cannot fairly be held to be personally responsible:

> ... the responsibility of the minister is to take the action which is required to ensure that it does not happen again. I do not think the minister is exempted from a measure of responsibility. I do not think that responsibility is necessarily a resigning matter for the minister concerned, but I think he is responsible for taking action which will both deal with the situation that has occurred and make sure that, as far as possible, it is not repeated in the future.[35]

Woodhouse, writing in 2002, sees recognition by Cook (in relation to the Sandline affair in 1998) and Straw (in relation to the passports crisis of 1999) of this principle of what she calls 'explanatory and amendatory responsibility', in that both ministers provided a full account of what had gone wrong (though Cook is criticised for some initial obstruction of the investigation by the Foreign Affairs Select Committee) and put in place remedial action which, in turn, they invited Parliament to scrutinise, thus 'completing the accountability cycle' ([2002] PL 73, 83–85).

3 Is the present position satisfactory? Dawn Oliver thinks not:

> Ministerial responsibility, it is suggested, has become a governmental defence against accountability instead of a weapon against government and a mechanism for accountability. Civil servants remain for the most part anonymous, without personal responsibility to members of the public with whom their departments deal or, most importantly, to Parliament and its select committees. They can never express their own views about Government action, for which ministers alone are 'responsible'. Nor do ministers have to answer questions about these matters, because they are Members of Parliament and MPs cannot be compelled by select committees to answer questions. Hence Parliament encounters barriers against the effective investigation of areas of Government activity because of the doctrine of ministerial responsibility and its flipside – parliamentary government.[36]

4 It is worth noting that the Canadian position appears to be substantially identical to the above, as the following extract makes clear. (Note that 'deputy ministers' in the Canadian government are not elected ministers, but the most senior civil servants of a department, equating roughly to Permanent Secretaries in the British Civil Service.)

---

35 Minutes of Evidence Taken Before the Public Service Committee, HC 313 (1995–96), 3 April 1996, Q 115. Lord Armstrong is a former Secretary to the Cabinet, and Head of the Home Civil Service. He held these positions during the launch of the 'Next Steps' initiative.

36 D Oliver, 'Parliament, ministers and the law' (1994) 47(4) Parl Aff 630 at 643.

Privy Council Office, Canada, *Responsibility in the Constitution* (1977), Chapter 7 (extracts)

Officials are not of course constitutionally responsible, but they play and have played a role *vis-à-vis* Parliament that in some important respects complements the role of ministers. Although officials do not have constitutional responsibility nor share the responsibility of their ministers, they do share to a degree in the answerability of their ministers to Parliament. A traditional preserve has been established that protects officials from answering to Parliament on matters of policy or matters involving political controversy. Apart from the obvious reasons of political sensitivity, matters of policy and political controversy have been reserved more or less exclusively for ministers principally because political answerability on the part of officials would inevitably draw them into controversy, destroy their permanent utility to the system, and, indeed, undermine the authority and responsibility of their ministers. Ministers are, furthermore, most closely associated with policy, and conflicting views expressed by officials could give rise to chaos and embarrassment. Deputies may, however, in the presence of their ministers explain and answer questions having to do with complex policy matters, but they do not defend policy against political attack. In other matters, principally those having to do with the administration of the department and its programs, officials answer directly on behalf of their ministers.

The answerability of deputies and other officials is rendered in the committees of both houses, and is best seen in the Public Accounts Committee, where it is now customary for officials rather than ministers to appear. In other committees officials are supposed to appear in support of the minister or his or her parliamentary secretary. The practice is that officials answer questions of administration directly, with the minister or parliamentary secretary (although regrettably sometimes neither is present) intervening if the proceedings threaten to turn into political debate, raising the possibility of the minister's responsibility being involved overtly.

Officials are, therefore, in a sense accountable *before* Parliament for matters of administration. This is a matter of observation. It does not detract from the responsibility of ministers, which will be invoked in cases where administration infringes on matters of policy or political controversy. Even in the days before officials answered before committees, it was normal for ministers to be accompanied by officials to brief them in answering administrative questions. This practice extended to the committee of the whole on supply, where for the first 70-odd years of this century the deputy regularly sat in conference with his or her minister when the department's estimates were under consideration. Nowadays committee of the whole is seldom used except for tax bills. Instead, officials appear before select committees, where they answer directly in the manner described.

Conclusion

Officials are *accountable to their ministers*, who must answer to the House for their use of the authority conferred upon them in law and by virtue of their responsibility to the House of Commons. It is, however, possible to distinguish between a deputy's accountability *to* the minister for all that occurs under the minister's responsibility, and the deputy's accountability *before* parliamentary committees for administrative matters so long as they do not call directly into question the exercise of the minister's responsibility. The accountability of officials before parliamentary committees for administrative matters cannot be said to alter the *formal* and *direct* responsibility of ministers personally to Parliament for any matter within their discipline for which the House chooses to hold them answerable.

Note

An area of particular contemporary concern is the seeming complete lack of parliamentary accountability of ministerial special advisers. The parliamentary view of the fact that ministers have refused to allow special advisers to appear for questioning before Select Committees, despite their undoubted great influence on policy formation, was given in Part III Chapter 1, at pp 326–27.

However, it is of interest to note the Prime Minister's view on this matter when he was questioned by the Liaison Committee.

Liaison Committee, Evidence presented by the Rt Hon Tony Blair MP, Prime Minister, 16 July 2002, HC 1095 (2001–02)

16. Prime Minister, some people have argued that the Select Committee system is one way to re-energise the parliamentary initiative and if we are to do that, we have got to be able to scrutinise, and indeed our method of scrutiny can actually help in your own ambition for putting public service investment in, but demanding reform. We are at the very heart of being able to help in that scrutiny process in terms of evaluating whether the extra money that was announced yesterday is actually effective, but the problem we have very often when we are trying to scrutinise the Executive is that many of the decisions are still seen to be made not in departments and our writ does not run. We cannot get anyone from the Performance and Innovation Unit to come before a Select Committee, we cannot get anyone from your Policy Unit before a Select Committee, and you say the media takes interest, but the media would take much greater interest if I could get Andrew Adonis in front of my Committee or other senior advisers when we suspected they were making very important policy decisions in Number 10 or in the PIU.

(Mr Blair) I suspect you would get quite a lot of interest, though whether for the right reasons I do not know. I do not recognise this as what is happening. For example, in the Department of Education, on education policy you are better talking to Estelle Morris than you are to anybody else, whether in my Policy Unit or elsewhere, and I simply do not recognise this notion that policy is not made in departments.

17. Why are you so reluctant to allow it? This is going to be every six months, it is going to be very useful and I welcome it, so why are you so reluctant to allow senior policy influences, if I can call them that, to come before a Committee? It is not going to be life-threatening, is it, to have a frank discussion with a Select Committee?

(Mr Blair) No, but I think that there is a reason why no government has ever done it, and the reason is that in the end Ministers are accountable and it is Ministers that should be held to account. No government has ever done this and I think it would change quite significantly for reasons I know Richard Wilson gave in some evidence I was reading the other day. I think it would change the relationship quite significantly. If I may say to you really bluntly, they are not the people who will tell you what the policy is; Ministers are ... and ultimately it is those Ministers that take the decisions.

Note

The above explanation is clearly unconvincing: civil servants appear before Committees even though they do not make policy either. The real objection is presumably that allowing such scrutiny of policy advisers would inevitably reveal, if it did anything at all, the advice they were giving to ministers, something which the government has always been extremely wary about disclosing. See further Chapter 3 of this part on the Code of Practice on Access to Government Information, at 620–39, and Part III Chapter 1, pp 298–306.

The impact of the Next Steps agencies

The term 'Next Steps' refers to the changes in the organisation of certain government departments which came out of proposals put forward by the Prime Minister's Efficiency Unit in the late 1980s. The nature of the reforms themselves will first of all be considered and we will then turn to their impact on ministerial accountability.

Next Steps: the nature of the reforms

A Gray and B Jenkins, 'The management of central government services', in B Jones (ed), *Politics UK* (1994), pp 433–34

One of the most frequent complaints of managers in the UK civil service has been of the hierarchical financial regimes in which they have had to operate. Purchasing, appointing temporary staff and even painting the office often seemed impossible without reference to principal finance officers. More fundamentally, the annual limits on the budget and controls over capital investment decisions hampered efficiency and effectiveness. The Financial Management Initiative, with its philosophy of accountable management, was intended to move departments from this position, and the Next Steps to take these changes in delegation and financial freedom even further.

There is no doubt that these developments are crucial in shaping the management regimes negotiated in framework documents. Twelve agencies, for example, are now treated as trading funds, ie as commercial businesses with concomitant accounting practices and financial freedoms over capital investment. Such bodies are those with identifiable products and markets (eg Her Majesty's Stationery Office, the Royal Mint and the Vehicle Inspectorate). However, financial freedoms are not the only management systems of importance. Encouraged by the Treasury's policy of local rather than national pay bargaining, agencies are developing their own personnel management regimes. Thus, from April 1994, all agencies with over 2,000 staff have responsibility for their own pay bargaining. The Treasury has also urged that all new systems link pay with performance. Meanwhile, in the wider field of human resource and personnel management, the Civil Service (Management Functions) Act, passed in December 1992, has given scope for the Treasury to delegate to agencies powers to alter the terms and conditions of staff without further reference to the centre.

Notes

1   After an initially hesitant start, the reforms gathered pace. As Gray and Jenkins note:

> By the autumn of 1993, a total of 89 agencies, as well as similar units in Customs and Excise and the Inland Revenue, employing over 350,000 civil servants (nearly two-thirds of the total), had been established. Numbers of employees ranged from 64,215 in the Social Security Benefits Agency to 25 in the Wilton Park Conference Centre. The plan is to launch the remaining agencies by April 1995 by which time 75 per cent of civil service personnel will be employed in agencies.[37]

2   A key quote from the report which inspired the reforms makes their aim clear:

> The aim should be to establish a quite different way of conducting the business of government. The central civil service should consist of a relatively small core engaged in the function of servicing ministers and managing departments, who will be the 'sponsors' of particular government policies and services. Responding to these departments will be a range of agencies employing their own staff, who may or may not have the status of Crown servants, and concentrating on the delivery of their particular service, with clearly defined responsibilities between the Secretary of State and the Permanent Secretary on the one hand and the Chairmen or Chief Executives of the agencies on the other. Both departments and their agencies should have a more open and simplified structure.[38]

3   The key question surrounding the introduction of the reform from the constitutional point of view was what effect they would have on the traditional accountability of ministers to Parliament for the work of their departments. If

---

37   A Gray and B Jenkins, 'The management of central government services', in B Jones (ed), *Politics UK* (1994), p 432.
38   Prime Minister's Efficiency Unit, *Improving Management in Government: The Next Steps* (1988), para 44.

ministers were no longer running the departments, who would answer to Parliament for their work? The original Next Steps report recognised that the issue was of concern.

Next Steps: the impact on accountability

Prime Minister's Efficiency Unit, *Improving Management in Government: The Next Steps* (1988), Annex A: Accountability to Ministers and Parliament on operational matters

Evidence we gathered in the scrutiny suggested that when individuals had to answer personally to Parliament, as well as to ministers, their sense of personal responsibility was strengthened. The accountability of permanent secretaries to the Public Accounts Committee, as accounting officers, is long established. It includes direct personal accountability for financial propriety. Another instance of officials having specific functions which may require them to answer directly to Parliament (though on behalf of their minister) is the case of principal officers, and of bodies with independent or delegated authority, answering to the Select Committee on the Parliamentary Commissioner for Administration.

2 In paragraph 23 we point out that if the concept of agencies developed in the report is to succeed, some extension of this pattern of accountability is likely to be necessary. The principal reasons are, first, that the management of an agency is unlikely in practice to be given a realistically specified framework within which there is freedom to manage if a minister remains immediately answerable for every operational detail that may be questioned; and second, that acceptance of individual responsibility for performance cannot be expected if repeated ministerial intervention is there as a ready-made excuse.

3 The precise form of accountability for each agency would need to be established as part of drawing up the framework for agencies. Any change from present practice in accountability would, of course, have to be acceptable to ministers and to Parliament. It is axiomatic that ministers should remain fully and clearly accountable for policy. For agencies which are Government departments or parts of departments ultimately accountability for operations must also rest with ministers. What is needed is the establishment of a convention that heads of executive agencies would have delegated authority from their ministers for operations of the agencies within the framework of policy directives and resource allocations prescribed by ministers. Heads of agencies would be accountable to ministers for the operations of their agencies, but could be called – as indeed they can now – to give evidence to Select Committees as to the manner in which their delegated authority had been used and their functions discharged within that authority. In the case of agencies established outside departments, appropriate forms of accountability to ministers and to Parliament would need to be established according to the particular circumstances.

4 There is nothing new in the suggestion that ministers should not be held answerable for many day-to-day decisions involving the public and public services. Apart from services delivered by local authorities, there are large numbers of central Government functions carried out at arm's length from ministers. The main categories are:

- decisions on individual cases, where these need to be protected from the risk of political influence, eg tax cases, social security cases;
- some management and executive functions, eg in Customs and Excise, Regional and District Health Authorities, Manpower Services Commission (MSC);
- quasi-judicial or regulatory functions, eg Office of Fair Trading, Immigration Appeals;
- nationalised industries.

5 A variety of different structures exist to cover these functions, for example:

- Customs and Excise and the Inland Revenue are non-ministerial departments with boards which have defined statutory responsibilities;

- the MSC and the other main bodies in the Employment Group (Health and Safety Executive, and ACAS) are non-departmental public bodies. The Chairman of the MSC is Accounting Officer for the MSC's expenditure;

- HMSO and some other internal services bodies (eg Crown Suppliers) are established as trading funds and work on a commercial basis;

- the PSA, the Procurement Executive and the NHS Management Board are agencies within departments;

- a range of quasi-judicial functions is carried out by a statutory tribunals (eg Rent Tribunals, Industrial Tribunals).

6 Agencies outside departments generally operate within a statutory framework which lays down the constitution of the particular agency and the powers of ministers in relation to it. In answer to Parliamentary Questions about matters within the control of the agency, ministers often preface their reply by saying 'I am advised by the Chairman of the Board that ... '. Most operations currently carried out within departments operate under statute. Where it is necessary to change the arrangements for formal accountability for operations currently carried out within departments, legislation (normally primary legislation) would generally be required, and in instances where this is needed it should be considered. Provided that the objective of better management is clearly explained and understood, and that an appropriate form of accountability to ministers and to Parliament is retained, the Government should be able to present such proposals in a positive light.

7 As regards the Public Accounts Committee, as explained in paragraph 22 of the report, the modification of accountability we propose should not immediately affect accountability to the PAC. This would remain, as now, with the Accounting Officer, who may still be, but need not be, the Permanent Secretary. (Of the 76 Accounting Officers appointed by the Treasury, only 18 are First Permanent Secretaries.) However, the practice might develop of the Accounting Officer being accompanied at a PAC hearing by the manager of the agency. The Accounting Officer would answer questions about the framework within which the agency operated; the manager would answer questions about operations within the framework. This would give the PAC the ability to question in detail the person who had firsthand knowledge of the particular operation. It would also in the process put a clear pressure on the agency head to be responsible for his or her agency and to strive for good value from his or her spending.

8 In the case of other select committees it is existing practice for officials with operational responsibility to give evidence before them. It would be normal in the future for the agency head to give evidence before a select committee about operational matters within his or her responsibility.

9 The powers of the Parliamentary Commissioner for Administration could continue to apply to agencies.

10 Quite apart from the issue of improving Civil Service management, there is a good case for trying to reduce the degree of ministerial overload that can arise from questions about operations, as distinct from policy. For example, Social Security Ministers receive about 15,000 letters a year from MPs, many of which are about individual cases. In the future, MPs could be asked to write about operational matters directly to the Chairman of the Board or the local office manager. Arrangements of this sort could be promulgated by a letter from the relevant minister or the Leader of the House to all MPs. (In the past the Chancellor of the Exchequer has written to all MPs asking them to refer questions about constituents' tax to local tax offices, and the Secretary of State for Social Services has written similarly about referring social security cases to DHSS local office managers.) If an MP writes to an operational manager about matters which are essentially political, it is already normally practice for the manager to refer the letter to the minister.

11 It would be part of the framework drawn up between the department and the agency to have specific targets for promptness in dealing with correspondence with MPs. It should be possible for MPs to get a quicker answer when dealing direct with the responsible person, because the

intermediate stage of a headquarters branch calling for a report from a local manager before drafting a reply for the minister will have been cut out.

Notes

1 How have these suggested new arrangements for scrutiny of the agencies been realised in practice and what impact have these changes had? A parliamentary question which is perceived as raising matters within the remit of the Chief Executive of an agency will be answered by the Executive (subject to an exception, below), and his or her answers have (from October 1992) been published in *Hansard*. Chief Executives give evidence to the Public Accounts Committee in relation to their Agency's accounting policies. But what exactly *is* the allocation of responsibility between minister and Chief Executive, and does the fact that the Chief Executive has taken on greater levels of responsibility than civil servants were ever admitted to have relieve the minister of accountability for those areas? The government position is reiterated in the 1995 Next Steps Review:[39]

The introduction of Next Steps agencies has not changed the normal framework of ministerial accountability to Parliament. Ministers account to Parliament. The Next Steps programme has, however, built on the conventional relationships between ministers and those carrying out the executive functions of Government. The aim is that operational responsibilities should be clearly delegated, with the Chief Executive being personally responsible to the minister for the management and performance of the agency. The form and extent of this delegation is determined case by case in published framework documents. However, for ministers to provide an adequate account to Parliament and others, they need to keep in touch and do, of course, retain the right to look into, question and even intervene in the operations of an agency if public or Parliamentary concerns require it.

2 The government considers that the reforms have 'emphasised delegation and clarity of responsibility' and thus 'strengthened accountability'.[40] The Treasury and Civil Service Select Committee has given extensive consideration to this issue. Extracts from its Minutes of Evidence and its report appear below, starting with the issue of whether the Next Steps agencies have in fact improved accountability. The Public Service Committee's key report on this point follows.

Minutes of Evidence taken before the Treasury and Civil Service Select Committee on 23 November 1993, HC 27 (1993–94), QQ 1365 and 1366, and on 26 April 1994, QQ 2103 and 2104; Fifth Report, paras 163, 166–67, 170–71

Sir Robin Butler: I believe that [the Next Steps reforms] do increase accountability to Parliament for this reason: that, in the past, whereas the minister was accountable, and still is accountable, for the operation of every executive agency, below that it was a little difficult to see who was responsible for the quality of the services. Now there are Chief Executives who are appointed with terms of reference that are published; they publish their corporate plans; they publish their results; they can be called before select committees of Parliament; and in my view that greatly increases the total accountability of the system . . .

I think in no case are [the agencies] independent of ministers. A minister can always intervene with the agencies. Similarly, any Member of Parliament who is dissatisfied with the way in which an agency is performing, and the answer that they get from a Chief Executive, can take it up with the minister. In a sense there are two opportunities for Members of Parliament or the public to test these agencies . . .

---

39 Cm 3164, p iv.
40 Memorandum submitted by the Office of Public Science and Service, para 12.

I think there is a misunderstanding, particularly about Next Steps Agencies. People often refer to them as quasi-autonomous. They are not. They are part of the Civil Service. The Chief Executive of a Next Steps Agency is a civil servant like anybody else, responsible to the minister, and the minister is accountable for him. That is not often widely understood and that is part of the reason, part of the misunderstanding, why people have talked about an accountability gap. I say there is no accountability gap because a minister is accountable, in the sense that he can be called to account for everything that goes on in his Department; every exercise of the powers that Parliament has given to him.

Chairman

2104. It might be a responsibility gap.

Sir Robin Butler: There might be a responsibility gap, but that is what we have sought to close in the Next Steps arrangement by defining the responsibility of Chief Executives and civil servants down the line. So my whole argument about Next Steps is that it is an improvement in accountability because we have both retained the fact that Parliament can always ask a minister about anything under his control, but can recognise that some powers have, in a complex society, to be delegated.

[Fifth Report]

Mr Vernon Bogdanor argued that . . . 'the *actual* responsibility of the Chief Executive for the work of his or her agency should be accompanied by a direct *constitutional* responsibility for his work'. To give effect to this, ministers should state that the Osmotherly Rules did not apply to agency Chief Executives. The idea of giving agency Chief Executives greater authority personally to account for their actions gained wide support, including that of Sir Peter Kemp. The original Next Steps Report envisaged that legislation might be necessary to enable agencies to operate with sufficient independence and accountability. Several observers felt that the time had now arrived to give statutory backing to executive agencies, endowing their agreements with ministers with legal force. It was suggested that this would strengthen the division of responsibility between ministers and Chief Executives, facilitate improved public and Parliamentary scrutiny and make it more difficult to 'shift the goal posts' . . .

167. The Government argued that the establishment of executive agencies left the traditional doctrine of ministerial accountability unimpaired while increasing 'the accountability of whole areas of Civil Service work, through greater openness and clearer lines of responsibility'. According to the Government, Agencies did not 'undermine the key constitutional principle that it is ministers who are accountable to Parliament for all that their Departments do'. The Government emphasised the marked growth of information about the internal operations of Government available to Parliament and the public as a result of Next Steps and argued that the creation of agencies made accountability 'more effective' through enhanced transparency in Government. Mr Waldegrave described the previous arrangements for ministerial replies on operational matters as 'a fiction', a view which has also been expressed by another minister. The Government saw the new arrangements as an improvement on previous practice, because a Member of Parliament had an opportunity both to receive a reply from the responsible civil servant and to seek a reply from a minister if he remained dissatisfied. Mr Waldegrave added that it was important that a minister or his office scanned replies to ensure that issues were not emerging which related to policy . . .

171. We do not believe that ministerial power to intervene in the actions and decisions of agencies justifies the retention of ministerial accountability for the actions and decisions of agencies for which Chief Executives are responsible. The theoretical separation of accountability and responsibility is nowhere more untenable than in the operation of agencies; continued adherence to the theory behind such a separation might jeopardise the durability of the delegation at the heart of Next Steps. The delegation of responsibility should be accompanied by a commensurate delegation of accountability. **We recommend that agency Chief Executives should be directly and personally accountable to select committees in relation to their annual performance**

agreements. Ministers should remain accountable for the framework documents and for their part in negotiating the annual performance agreement, as well as for all instructions given to agency Chief Executives by them subsequent to the annual performance agreement. To this end, we recommend that all such instructions should be published in agency annual reports, subject only to a requirement to preserve the personal confidentiality or anonymity of individual clients.

Note

It will be seen that the Select Committee made quite a radical proposal – to end the ministerial obligation to answer for all operational matters. This would be replaced by a parallel obligation of the Chief Executive which would be enforced by Select Committees, in effect ending the 'parallel' system of accountability which currently exists. The proposal was rejected by the government on the grounds that it would undermine ministerial accountability. In evidence before the Public Service Committee, Peter Hennessy said:

> I actually think the ... Committee was right to say that agency Chief Executives would come and give evidence ... in their own right. ... If you have got named responsibilities in framework documents ... publicly-assigned responsibilities, you have got to be publicly accountable for them, no caveats ... If you really are going to follow through the logic of the Next Steps, you have to go that far. ... [41]

Derek Lewis (former Director General of the Prison Service) made more radical proposals in 1996[42] to alter fundamentally the status and organisation of certain politically contentious government agencies, in particular the prison service; his proposals reflect elements of Oliver's analysis. Key features of the new arrangements would be:

- an independent board, established by statute, which would have responsibility for oversight of the prison service and for its management through a Chief Executive and management board that it would appoint (and if necessary remove);

- policy would be set by ministers through secondary legislation; ... this would ensure there was absolute clarity about what was policy and Parliament would be given a proper opportunity to scrutinise and take action on policy changes; ...

- the sponsoring department would have the responsibility for monitoring efficiency through systematic and rigorous performance audits conduced by an independent inspectorate ... with powers for the sponsoring department to intervene in the case of serious deficiencies.

The Committee's views on these suggestions and others appear in their report. The Committee begins by considering the option of making Chief Executives directly and fully accountable to Parliament, and the objection to it.

Second Report from the Public Service Committee, HC 313 (1995–96) (extracts)

109 Mr Heseltine put the case against this:

...

> 'that is incompatible with their status as civil servants because, as I think the words are, the civil servant is the Minister in this sense. If I have an agency, I am responsible for the policy and

---

41 Minutes of Evidence Taken Before the Public Service Committee, HC 313 (1995–96), 20 March 1996, Q 92.
42 *Ibid*, 22 May 1996.

so I have to lay down the policy, I have to set the targets and I have to account to this Committee or to Parliament for what goes on. What I cannot have in such circumstances is a Chief Executive coming here and giving a whole range of views about what he wants to do and all that in a way which conflicts with what I want him to do because then he becomes effectively another political force.'

Former and present civil servants were anxious not to disturb what Lord Armstrong called 'the line of accountability', through Ministers, to Parliament. Lord Howe suggested that the accountability of Chief Executives to Parliament through Select Committees was something which would happen anyway: 'de facto, accountability will grow along that line'.

. . .

112. This does not mean that Ministers should relinquish their overall responsibility to Parliament for the agencies. But we accepted earlier that there were two different sides to the obligation of Ministers to Parliament for those matters which come within their responsibility: the obligation to give an account – to provide full information about the actions of the Government: and the liability to he held to account – to respond to criticism and to concerns raised in Parliament. The second of these aspects of responsibility cannot be delegated. If an activity remains within a department, Ministers must always retain the ability and duty to make investigations in response to concerns raised with them, to put matters right where things have gone wrong, to ensure that if mistakes have been made, those responsible for making them are duly disciplined, even, if something has gone wrong which they might have been able to prevent, to take some of the blame themselves. But the other side of the obligation to Parliament – the obligation to give an account – can be (and in practice largely is) delegated, at least in part, to the agency Chief Executive. It is, admittedly, only a partial delegation of the accountability function, because the retention of the formal responsibility of Ministers means that, if a Member of Parliament is unsatisfied with the response he has received from the agency Chief Executive, he can always have recourse to the Minister. But in the first instance, at least, it is Chief Executives who give the account to Parliament of their stewardship.

. . .

114. The Osmotherly Rules say that Chief Executives give evidence on behalf of the Minister to whom they are accountable and are subject to that Minister's instruction (when doing so). We believe that this no longer accurately reflects the reality. As we have seen, Ministers rarely become involved in the answers given by Chief Executives to Parliamentary Questions; it is unclear, therefore, why Chief Executives should continue to be subject to Ministers' instruction when giving evidence to Select Committees. In practice, giving an account to Parliament – in the first instance – on the matters within the responsibility of a Chief Executive has become a function delegated to the Chief Executive. **We recommend that the Osmotherly Rules be amended to indicate that agency Chief Executives should give evidence to Select Committees on matters which are delegated to them in the Framework Document.** This does not, of course, mean that Chief Executives will speak without Ministerial approval on policy matters, as policy matters are not delegated to the Chief Executive. If asked questions about policy, or the impact of policy, the Chief Executive would, as now, refer the Committee to the Minister. Chief Executives would not therefore become, as Mr Heseltine suggests, an alternative political force.

The responsibilities of Ministers and Chief Executives

. . .

116. The Office of Public Service say that 'the clarity of the division of responsibilities between the Minister and Chief Executive is something that should be considered carefully in initially setting up an agency and subsequently in reviewing its Framework Document'; but they comment that 'no Framework Document could spell out in precise terms the division of responsibility in every theoretical set of circumstances'. Sir Peter Kemp seems to take a more hopeful view. He believes

that it would be possible to have a more direct form of accountability to Parliament if the respective roles of Minister and Chief Executive were clearer, perhaps in some form of explicit contract so that specific responsibilities are delegated to officials and put into statutory form, and Ministers would remain responsible only for the terms of the delegation. Then officials might speak more freely on their performance of their side of the contract. He argues that 'What is required . . . is a more specific and as may be detailed description, on a case by case basis, of what is down to who . . . It ought to be possible, given care and time and trouble, in the case of each and every agency to delineate and write down who does what'. Clearly, it is not always possible to decide in advance what issues will prove to be politically sensitive, and it is always open to a Minister to involve himself in any issue, however detailed, provided that his involvement is clearly recorded if it departs from the terms of the Framework Document and he takes full responsibility and accountability for his actions.

117. Not all agencies, as we have said (para 102) raise issues of this nature in any serious way. Most agencies appear to have little or no difficulty in working within the responsibilities as they are at present mapped out in the Framework Document. It was suggested by some of our witnesses, in fact, that agencies that were as politically controversial as the Prison Service were unsuitable for agency status at all, and should be pulled back into their parent departments. Areas of activity in which Ministers need to involve themselves so much should be retained within departments in order to ensure that their political accountability remained the priority. Making the Prison Service into an agency was, Lord Armstrong told us, 'a stage too far'. The function suitable for agency status was, he said 'a basic management task without a controversial political contact, whereas the Prison Service is anything but that'. He made a similar point about the Child Support Agency: 'So much of the devil lies in the detail of the way in which the individual cases are handled that it is very difficult to maintain this dichotomy between objectives and budgets, on the one hand, and day-to-day management on the other. In a sense the objectives of the agency are so closely related to, and are reflected in the day-to-day actions, that it may not have been a very good case for becoming an agency'. Lord Armstrong, former Cabinet Secretary and Head of the Home Civil Service, has said that the agency arrangement works satisfactorily 'where there is little political context'; and in evidence to us he said that this meant in cases where the Minister is unlikely to become involved on a day-to-day basis. Sir Robin Butler was less pessimistic: He accepted that the more politically controversial agencies were ones in which Ministers need to be involved much more closely than in the case of others, but it should still be possible to define separate roles. 'These are difficult lines to draw and they need to be reviewed, but I think it is well worth doing. Even in the Prison Service, he said, 'notwithstanding the difficulties, very considerable improvements in management have been made'.

118. Some have argued, on the other hand, that the difficulties of defining the separate roles and responsibilities of Ministers and managers would be eased if agencies were more formally divided from their departments, perhaps through placing them on a statutory basis. Statutory independence might be seen as a means of reducing the ability of a Minister to interfere in the work of the agency. Derek Lewis described a possible arrangement for the Prison Service in which agencies were non-departmental public bodies within a statutory framework, similar to that for the police [above]. . . .

119. In Sweden, we looked at the way a more formal relationship such as this might work in practice. Historically, a good deal of government services have been provided by agencies. There are over 300 agencies ranging from 30,000 employees to a mere handful. Although the Government appoints agency heads, the agencies are independent of the Government. Government control is exercised in the long term through decisions on agency functions and directions and by overall budgetary control. These are set out in a letter of regulation which the Government issues each year to every agency. In discussions with the Swedish Agency for Administrative Development and other bodies with experience of the agency sector in Sweden it was emphasised to us that, in the absence of formal contact with the Government agencies do

operate under legal rules and remain sensitive to changes in government and in government policy. Government frequently consults informally with them.

120. The difficulty with making agencies into bodies with statutory independence is, as Sir Robin Butler argued, that it could tend to reduce, rather than enhance, their accountability.

'If you gave an agency statutory independence what you would do is turn it into something else, which is perfectly familiar, which is a quango, and this is a body that has got independence, in areas defined by the statute, from the Minister, and there are plenty of bodies of that sort. But, of course, what one has got to recognise, by doing that, is that you do to that extent reduce Ministerial accountability, the Minister is no longer responsible for that matter of which the Chief Executive has been made statutorily responsible, so you would divorce something from Parliamentary Ministerial responsibility.'

As he added, 'While it is still an agency and accountable to Parliament, you certainly may get, and this, indeed, is part of the philosophy of agencies, a better account directly from the Chief Executive than from the Minister, in the first instance; but if Parliament is then dissatisfied with that, or an MP is dissatisfied with that, that MP always has the right to go to the Minister and ask the Minister to intervene'. This is perhaps an overly conservative view of the scope for improved accountability within such statutory bodies: a statutory relationship would probably require the Government to set down what it requires of the body in writing, perhaps even through statutory instrument, which might be approved in Parliament. Therefore the scope for Parliamentary control of the policy process could be enhanced, rather than reduced. Equally, Ministers would still, presumably, have powers to appoint and dismiss the body's head. But it is true that it would mean that Members of Parliament would be less easily able to influence the activities of the body; and the experience of the nationalised industries is often cited to suggest that statutory bodies or public corporations, while theoretically independent, could be subject to a considerable amount of pressure from Ministers. However, nationalised industries were not in fact normally subject to detailed legislative prescription: indeed pride was taken in the fact that they were left to operate in their markets as freely as possible .

121. An alternative way of making the division of responsibilities between agencies and departments more explicit would be to make it more contractual. This, to some extent, is happening already. As Dr Andrew Massey, Reader in Public Policy, University of Portsmouth, noted, 'the Market Testing initiative, in-service agreements, competitive tendering and privatisation all mark the transformation of the accountability function away from being rule-based and hierarchical. It tends to strengthen Ministerial control, in that the loss of a contract is a sobering discipline for Chief Executives operating under tight financial constraints'. Graham Mather, MEP, President of the European Policy Forum, advocates a more explicit contractual arrangement, akin to that introduced in New Zealand. The New Zealand model of public service reform was discussed by the Treasury and Civil Service Committee in its 1994 Report on the Role of the Civil Service. In New Zealand, the State Sector Act 1988 formally separated the functions of the Minister and officials. The relationship between them became subject to an annual performance agreement, under which Chief Executives undertook to perform certain outputs set by the Minister in return for control over inputs decisions – pay, appointments, organisational structures, and so on. The outputs could include both service delivery and policy advice. The Public Finance Act 1989 took the division further, by making Ministers into purchasers of outputs, and the departments and agencies into suppliers. Ministers purchase outputs in order to achieve the Government's desired outcomes. The system resembles 'the arrangements and incentives of the commercial marketplace'.

122. Sir Robin Butler argued that such a contractual approach would be too formal for many of the functions which agencies perform. His opposition reflects the resistance to introducing law into the machinery of Government to which Professor Lewis referred. Introducing legal rules as the way in which the relationship between Ministers and Chief Executives were determined would, undoubtedly, be one way of increasing accountability, particularly if such rules were

statutory instruments, subject to parliamentary procedure. But such formalism is not essential; what is essential is openness in the relationship. Mr Mottram told us that 'the great benefit' of agencies was 'that someone is in charge, they have a clear set of responsibilities, they must define who they are doing something for, and when we under-pin all that with resource budgeting and accounting, as we will be doing by the end of the decade, we will have these advantages even more'. This greater definition and greater clarity is the central benefit of the Next Steps initiative, and we believe that it needs to be enhanced, and enhanced openly. Therefore, **we recommend that Framework Documents should specify more precisely the respective roles of Ministers and Chief Executives.**

123. Agencies need to be able to engage in a constructive dialogue with Parliament through Select Committees. As Kate Jenkins, an independent consultant and former Head of the Prime Minister's Efficiency Unit, said, one thing that would make accountability really effective would be 'if Committees of the House of Commons are able to add value, so that a Chief Executive who has come and had a discussion with the Committee really does feel that they now have a Committee who understands what the problems are or has a Committee who has some ideas which it can contribute and it is not simply a process of asking why something has gone wrong and why it cannot go better'. Dr Philip Giddings made a similar comment: 'notwithstanding some important early work by the National Audit Office and the Public Accounts Committee and growing interest by some departmental Committees, it remains the case that the work of Committees as a whole has not yet taken on the character of a sustained and systematic performance audit of agencies which some would like to see'. This implies responsibilities both for the Committees (which we have dealt with above), for the agency, and for the department. This should begin with the establishment of the agency, and the drafting of its Framework Document. Professor Norman Lewis, Professor of Public Law at the University of Sheffield, argues that 'It would be a clear advance in terms of accountability if the departmental Select Committees were given a timely opportunity to comment on these documents and their renewals where appropriate. In doing so they might be able to influence the relationship between responsibility for outputs and outcomes in a way that Parliament has never attempted before'. Kate Jenkins made a similar suggestion, that Select Committees should become involved – in a quite informal way – in the way in which Framework Documents and agency Corporate Plans are put together. Sir Peter Kemp agreed. **We recommend that Government invites Select Committees to comment on Framework Documents and agency Corporate Plans before they are published and when they are reviewed.**

...

Notes

1   The issue of the blurring of responsibility between Chief Executive and minister will be returned to below when we consider the issue of ministerial resignation.

2   The situation as it relates to accountability therefore seems to be this – Chief Executives will answer parliamentary questions on operational matters and give evidence to Select Committees, but the minister can be asked all the same questions as the Chief Executive if Parliament is dissatisfied with the latter's replies. Also, the minister can intervene in any aspect of the running of agencies, though the expectation is that he or she will not do so and as we shall see, when errors and blunders in operational matters come to light, ministers will often distance themselves from mistakes which they claim are due to mistakes in running the agencies, not in the original policies themselves. Only the minister can be asked about matters of high policy. Although the Chief Executive gives an account to Parliament about operational matters, any disciplinary action against the Chief Executive is a matter for the minister only, not Parliament.

3   Is this a logically satisfactory position? Arguably not. The whole point of these agencies is that they are supposed to operate with a large degree of independence

from ministers; thus, they can determine their own spending priorities, and negotiate pay levels with the civil servants they employ. This is supposed to lead to greater efficiency and better delivery of public services, since the agencies should be run on much more business-like lines and be free from constant political interference by ministers. As Lord Armstrong said in evidence before a Select Committee:

It seemed to me absolutely clear at [the time the first agencies were set up] that ... Chief Executives were going to be given responsibility for day to day management ... and they would be left to get on with it and the letters of complaints and that kind of thing would be dealt with by the Chief Executive and the minister would not expect to be involved.[43]

Given that this is the whole point of the changes, it seems somewhat futile still to maintain that the minister should be accountable for everything going on in the agencies. Nevertheless, the present government, reformist in other areas of the constitution, has firmly maintained the traditional view on this matter, 'refusing to accept arguments that Chief Executives should be personally and directly accountable to Parliament for the matters assigned to them'.[44]

4 Oliver has gone further and alleges that there are reasons of principle, as well as internal consistency, for discarding, or at least radically revising, the doctrine of ministerial accountability.

Dawn Oliver, 'Parliament, ministers and the law' (1994) 47(4) Parl Aff 630, 644–45

We need to face up to the fact that alternatives are needed, are possible, are being devised and could be developed, as far better checks on government than ministerial responsibility can ever be ... Nor is it to exonerate ministers from responsibility for their own acts and policies or those of their departments. It is an argument for accepting explicitly the need to supplement existing arrangements with legally based, non-parliamentary mechanisms of control and accountability, and acknowledging that there are situations where ministerial responsibility can be involved inappropriately to protect Government against accountability rather than to expose Government to it.

... There are civilised countries in the world with comparable levels of development and sophisticated political cultures (and the British political culture is sophisticated, even if part of the sophistication lies in the scepticism of Britons about Government, anti-intellectualism and deep indifference to matters of governance) which manage, indeed are relatively effectively governed, without our level of reliance on this convention, our rejection of legal regulation in central government (local government is quite another matter in the UK) and our tendency to reject fully-fledged or full-blooded alternatives.

In New Zealand for example – the closest relative of the United Kingdom system – much of the public sector has been corporatised in state owned enterprises independent of ministers, thus breaking the unity of the Crown. Almost the whole of the remaining civil service is organised into executive agencies and ministers are responsible for formulating the policy within which these operate. Ministers, not Chief Executives, are responsible to Parliament. Appointments of Chief Executives and staff are on the recommendation of the State Services Commission, which is independent of the Government department, by the Governor General in Council – effectively the

---

43 Minutes of Evidence Taken Before the Public Service Committee, HC 313 (1995–96), 3 April 1996, Q 109. Lord Armstrong was Cabinet Secretary and Head of the Home Civil Service during the launch of the Next Steps initiative.

44 See C Turpin, *British Government and the Constitution*, 5th edn (2002), p 466. We are indebted to Turpin for the following references to government statements on this matter: *Taking Forward Continuity and Change*, Cm 2478, p 31; Government Response to the House of Lords Select Committee on the Public Service, Cm 4000, paras 14, 44–46.

Cabinet; the Chief Executive is the employer of agency staff. There is an Official Information Act 1982 and a Bill of Rights Act 1990. In Sweden executive agencies are independent of Government, they have representative boards, they report directly to Parliament and they are subject to audit by a range of independent auditing agencies. Ministers are not responsible to Parliament for them, although Sweden has a parliamentary executive. Sweden has a freedom of information regime. The United States, without a parliamentary executive, adopts a quite different model for controlling Government, with regulatory agencies concerned with rule-making and adjudication, and functions conceived quite differently from our framework of policy making, administration and management. There, too, is a government in the sunshine act.

The obligation to accept responsibility for errors and failures

The constitutional position

Here, we examine how developments in the duty to explain have affected responsibility for error and consider whether, as many commentators argue, a contraction of responsibility has occurred. As seen above, ministers are now considered by the government not to have to accept personal blame – and therefore possibly resign – unless matters of policy are involved. Certainly, resignations in the absence of such fault have always been few and far between.

The resignation of Sir Thomas Dugdale in respect of the Crichel Down Affair in 1954 is usually cited as an example of a resignation due to responsibility accepted by the minister for departmental errors. Land in Devon was acquired by compulsory purchase in 1938 for use as a bombing range. It was then transferred to the Ministry of Agriculture and by it to the Commissioners for Crown Lands who let it to a tenant of their choice. The former owner of the land was denied the right to buy it back and neighbouring landowners who had been led to believe that they would be able to bid for it were denied the opportunity to do so. When these events led to an enquiry it was concluded that civil servants in the Department of Agriculture had acted in a deceitful and high-handed manner. The Minister for Agriculture then resigned and said in the House: 'I as Minister must accept full responsibility to Parliament for any mistakes or inefficiency of officials in my Department.' In fact, this example of the operation of the doctrine may not be as clear cut as this example suggests: it became apparent that the minister had played a personal part in the decisions made.

One rare example of a ministerial resignation in the absence of personal fault was Lord Carrington's, in the aftermath of the Argentinian invasion of the Falkland Islands in 1982, though it was apparent that Carrington's decision was taken at least partly for political reasons – to assist the government in the difficult times ahead. In any event, if there ever was a time when ministers accepted that they should resign to atone for mistakes which were not their own, that time has certainly passed. The government's present position has been summarised thus:[45]

The Government contended that 'It has never been the case that ministers were required or expected to resign in respect of any and every mistake made by their departments, though they are clearly responsible to Parliament for ensuring that action is taken to put matters right and prevent a recurrence'. The resignation of Sir Thomas Dugdale over the Crichel Down Affair in 1954 was held to be the exception that proved the rule. The notion of ministers resigning for the mistakes of others was seen by Mr Waldegrave as 'a bad doctrine'. Mr Waldegrave suggested that

---

45   Fifth Report from the Treasury and Civil Service Select Committee, HC 27 (1993–94), para 121.

in cases which might possibly entail resignation, Select Committees might inquire into whether ministerial accountability was matched by actual ministerial responsibility for mistakes. The Government's position was broadly consistent with that outlined by Sir David Maxwell-Fyfe in the Crichel Down debate in July 1954. He listed categories of actions or events for which, in the view of the Government, it would and would not be appropriate to hold a minister responsible. He contended that 'a minister is not bound to defend action of which he did not know, or of which he disapproves', but he concluded that a minister 'remains constitutionally responsible to Parliament for the fact that something has gone wrong, and he alone can tell Parliament what has occurred and render an account of his stewardship'. Lord Jenkins and Lord Callaghan endorsed the Government's view that ministers should not be expected to resign for administrative failures in which they are not directly involved, the latter remarking that 'if we were to apply Thomas Dugdale's approach today we would not have the same Cabinet for three weeks running'.

2   The 'new' doctrine of responsibility for policy only appears to have gained ground: not only have the last Conservative and Labour governments both asserted it, but Parliament now seems to accept it. As Woodhouse notes,[46] when the 'new' doctrine was put forward by the then Home Secretary, James Prior, in 1983, after a break-out from the Maze Prison by IRA prisoners, in response to calls for his resignations, many MPs were not impressed. For example, Enoch Powell protested that the minister could not say to the House and to the public that the policy was excellent and was his, but that the execution was disastrous or defective and had nothing to do with him. However, when Kenneth Baker put forward the same argument in a similar situation in 1984, 'the House seemed to accept his division between policy and administration and the corresponding limitation of his responsibility'.[47] Lord Justice Scott also indicated in his report that he accepted the 'new' doctrine saying he found it 'difficult to disagree' with Sir Robin Butler's view that:

the conduct of government has become so complex and the need for ministerial delegation of responsibilities to and reliance on the advice of officials has become so inevitable as to render unreal the attaching of blame to a minister simply because something has gone wrong in the department of which he is in charge.[48]

3   The following questions are raised by the 'new' position on responsibility: (a) is the operational/policy division sustainable, an issue considered above; (b) is it liable to be abused by ministers anxious to avoid responsibility; and (c) how should persons other than ministers be held responsible? Points (b) and (c) are considered in turn.

Ministerial abuse of the operational/policy divide?

It is clear that there is room for doubt in trying to locate the operational/policy divide. Without being unduly cynical, it might be suggested that ministers are happy to leave the matter vague, in order to give themselves maximum scope for argument when faced with criticisms about failures in their department. When William Waldegrave was pressed by the Treasury and Civil Service Select Committee as to exactly when a minister should take responsibility, his replies did not suggest anxiety to clarify the position.

46   D Woodhouse, 'When do ministers resign?' (1993) 46(3) Parl Aff 277, 286–87.
47   Ibid, 287.
48   Inquiry into Exports of Defence Equipment and Dual-Use Goods to Iraq and Related Prosecutions, HC 115-I (1995–96), para K8.15.

Minutes of Evidence Taken Before the Treasury and Civil Service Select Committee on 26 April 1994, HC 27 (1993–94), QQ 1894–97

1894. When Sir Robin appeared in front of the Scott Inquiry he drew a distinction between ministerial accountability and ministerial responsibility. Do you draw the same distinction and, if so, could you define each?

Mr Waldegrave: I find all these words quite difficult because they are bound to overlap in ordinary language I think. There is a real sense in which ministers are accountable to Parliament and the electorate for policy, but are not responsible for every action taken in a common sense way by the thousands of people ultimately working within that policy. They are accountable for the structures, for the appointments, for the policy and accountable if they do not put things right properly when serious things go wrong and they are accountable if a lot of little things continuously go wrong and they do not see that something is done about that. However, I think there is a proper sense in which somebody carrying out a day to day policy can be said to be responsible for actually carrying out those things he has agreed to carry out.

Chairman

1895. So who is responsible then? If the minister is not responsible, then who is responsible?

Mr Waldegrave: The minister is ultimately accountable for everything.

1896. But you said he or she is not necessarily responsible? Who is responsible?

Mr Waldegrave: Again, you are going to have to take resort in common sense. It depends on the extent and importance and if something has gone wrong, and it is a serious thing, then committees like this inquire into whether it would be plausible to say the minister should have seen in advance that it was going to go wrong and should have done something in advance about it. If it is something that goes wrong, as things will go wrong in life with the best of intentions, then has he done something to put it right, if it is important? Or is it actually a matter of how that office is organised or how that delegated thing is carried out, in which case, in the first instance at least, it might be right to say this is within the normal conscientious carrying out of the duty by this agency head or civil servant of one kind or another, and part of his normal conscientious work would have been for him to get that right and it is unfair to blame the minister? It is terribly difficult to make general rules. Ultimately, of course, the minister is accountable to Parliament for everything.

Sir Thomas Arnold

1897. For you personally does accountability as a concept lack a blame element? This seems to be the principal point of distinction which was in Sir Robin's mind if I understood his evidence to Scott correctly.

Mr Waldegrave: I think you have again to look at individual cases. I find them rather difficult to categorise.

Notes

1 The advantages of this confusion to beleaguered ministers anxious to stay in government seems to be two-fold. First, it will very often be arguable as to whether failures in a given area are due to policy or its implementation. As Professor Hennessy had recently pointed out. 'There is not actually a proper division between [the two] ... These are seamless garments. If operationally you hit real trouble, it is usually because the policy is flawed'.[49] In other words, the day to day problems which occur in a department may in actuality be attributable to overall – but hidden – policy problems, such as insufficient funding. So, policy mistakes may

49 HC 27 (1993–94).

be *inferred* from widespread operational difficulties. Government has, however, tended to take the opposite line, relying on a 'bright line' distinction between the two, which serves in practice to exonerate ministers from blame after departmental failings have come to light. In particular, commentators saw a tendency during the last Conservative administration to narrow down the areas of 'policy' for which ministers conceded they were personally responsible to 'high government policy and overall political strategy'.[50] The suspicion that the area of departmental activity for which ministers will accept responsibility is an ever-shrinking one is, to an extent, borne out by events during the 18 years of the previous Conservative administration. Although there were a number of major failings in government policy, including the arms to Iraq affair, the BSE crisis, the poll tax and the Pergau Dam affair, only one minister, Lord Carrington, actually accepted responsibility for error in his department (the Foreign Office) and resigned; this took place in the wholly exceptional circumstance of the actual loss of British territory – the Falkland Islands – by an armed invasion. Other than this, the only examples of the areas for which ministers will take responsibility are negative ones, where the particular problems that had occurred in the department were found by the minister *not* to be ones which would engage his or her responsibility.

2   The reaction of ministers to the appalling performance in its first year of the Child Support Agency is also instructive, as Woodhouse points out.[51] Ministers refused to take any blame for the Agency's failure to meet its performance targets and its already long record of maladministration, despite the fact that, as Woodhouse argues, 'the ministers' failure to ensure that the Agency was properly established, staffed and resourced directly affected the ability of the Agency to operate effectively'. Similarly, Cook, in relation to the Sandline affair in 1998, and Straw, in relation to the passports crisis of 1999, both stated that essentially operational decisions were to blame for the problems that arose in their departments, assertions which to be fair to them were largely accepted by independent commentators.[52] Cook did recognise systemic and cultural problems with the Foreign Office but, given that he had been Foreign Secretary for less than a year, could not reasonably be expected to take personal responsibility for these. Woodhouse, writing in 2002, observed that 'in the second half of the 20th century, only the resignations of Dugdale (1954), Carrington (1982) and Brittan (1986) can, with any degree of certainty, be attributed to departmental fault'.[53] This pattern appears set to continue in the 21st century.

3   The further problem is that in the common case in which both policy and its application are at fault, ministers, because they control the flow of information to Parliament, can often ensure that only evidence of *administrative* failings reach Parliament. Civil servants may know first hand that policy was to blame as well, but will be unable to bring this to Parliament's attention against the wishes of their minister. As the FDA has pointed out:

Operational failures ... could all be laid at the door of Government agencies failing to deliver Government policies ... At the same time, policy failures and the reasons for them, for example lack of resources, remaining impenetrable because of the confidentiality which binds a civil servant

---

50   D Woodhouse, 'Ministerial responsibility: something old, something new' [1997] PL 262, 268.
51   *Ibid*, pp 169–70.
52   See, eg, D Woodhouse, 'The reconstruction of constitutional accountability' [2002] PL 73, 84–86.
53   *Ibid*, 74.

to ensure that any difference in the advice which she or he gives the Minster and the Government's ultimate decision is never revealed.[54]

4   Derek Lewis, in a memorandum submitted to the Public Services Committee in 1996,[55] voiced similar concerns. Noting that, at present, 'in speaking publicly about agencies, Chief Executives are either required to avoid comment on ... policy or to expound the policy of the Government of the day', he goes on to argue that the Chief Executive should be permitted to comment publicly and to Parliament on policy:

> If this is not permitted, the principle of ministerial responsibility is seriously distorted. Ministers would be free to impose half-baked impractical policies or to set wholly unrealistic performance targets, and then simply load the blame onto those running the agency for any failure to implement or achieve as a mere operational matter.

He notes by way of example that both chief constables of police and the Chair of the Bank of England are able, within limits, to express their views on government policies which they are actively involved in implementing, and expresses the view that, far from merely provoking 'destructive and intolerable conflict' between Chief Executives and ministers, allowing such 'reasoned public debate' would improve the quality of our democracy.[56]

5   Lord Justice Scott made an important point which addressed precisely this concern. Noting Sir Robin Butler's distinction between 'accountability' and 'responsibility', he argues that it has:

> ... an important bearing on the obligation of ministers to provide information to Parliament. If ministers are to be excused blame and personal criticism on the basis of the absence of personal knowledge or involvement, the corollary ought to be an acceptance of the obligation to be forthcoming with information about the incident in question. Otherwise Parliament (and the public) will not be in a position to judge whether the absence of personal knowledge and involvement is fairly claimed or to judge on whom responsibility for what has occurred ought to be placed. Any re-examination of the practices and conventions relied on by Government in declining to answer, or to answer fully, certain Parliamentary Questions should, in my opinion, take account of the implications of the distinction drawn by Sir Robin between ministerial 'accountability' and ministerial 'responsibility' and of the consequent enhancement of the need for ministers to provide, or to co-operate in the provision of, full and accurate information to Parliament.[57]

4   While the Freedom of Information Act 2000 will in theory give both MPs and the public a means of ascertaining the facts about such matters, there is a class exemption in s 35 in relation to all information relating to 'the formulation or development of government policy'. The only limitation to this astonishingly broad exemption – which is not subject to a burden on ministers to prove that harm would be caused by releasing the information in question – is that statistical information relating to a decision may be released once the decision is made. But, for example, evidence of other policy options considered and the reasons for rejecting them would not be. While the Information Commissioner can order release of the information concerned if satisfied (per s 2) that the public interest in withholding

---

54   Minutes of Evidence Taken Before the Public Service Committee (Memorandum), HC 313-I, (1995–96), 20 March 1996, para 24.

55   Minutes of Evidence Taken Before the Public Services Committee (Memorandum), HC 313 (1995–96), 22 May 1996.

56   *Ibid*, paras 10–12.

57   *Inquiry into Exports of Defence Equipment and Dual-Use Goods to Iraq and Related Prosecutions*, HC 115-I (1995–96), para K8.16.

information does not outweigh the interest in its reception because the information relates to a central government department, its release can ultimately be vetoed by a Cabinet minister (s 53). Moreover, the Act does not come fully into force until 2005. See further on the Freedom of Information Act, Chapter 3 of this part.

5   The other main advantage to ministers of the ambiguity surrounding the operational policy divide is this: because ministers have repeatedly asserted (particularly in relation to the Next Steps agencies) that operational matters are not their primary responsibility, it appears that they can have the best of both worlds. They can interfere with the day-to-day running of the agency in order to satisfy short-term political imperatives, but then if things go wrong step back and rely on the principle that policy only is their concern to deflect criticism on to the Chief Executive concerned. To many, this is what the Derek Lewis saga illustrates. When the highly critical Learmont Report on the state of Britain's prisons came out in October 1995, Michael Howard, the Home Secretary, found that all the problems identified therein were due not to his policies but to the way they had been put into practice by the head of the Prison Service, Derek Lewis, whom he promptly sacked. Lewis complained in vain that in fact much of his day-to-day work had been directed and controlled by Michael Howard and launched an action for wrongful dismissal against the Home Office which it eventually settled, paying the claimed damages in full.

6   There was evidence that Howard had in fact intervened in matters of day-to-day running. The Learmont Report contained a section devoted to the difficulties encountered by the Prison Service because of the political demands made on Lewis. The report found that 'ways and means must be found to overcome the problem' and that a new relationship was needed to 'give the Prison Service the greater operational independence that agency status was meant to confer'.[58] A newspaper reported a prison governor as saying, 'The idea that Howard has not been meddling is just nonsense ... We all know he's been messing everywhere'.[59] In an interview,[60] Lewis claimed that documents which he would demand from the Home Office to support his action would prove extensive ministerial interference: 'Lewis is calling for minutes of meetings which he says will show how he was summoned virtually every day to the Home Office by one minister or another, interfering in operational matters.' Examples he gave include the personal intervention of Mr Howard to try to procure the movement of Private Lee Clegg (the soldier convicted of murder following a shooting at a security checkpoint in Northern Ireland) to an open prison after a campaign on his behalf by the right-wing press. Further allegations were that 'ministers challenged the punishments meted out to particular prisoners – a matter that is the sole legal prerogative of prison governors' and also decisions on home leave for prisoners and the disciplining of staff.[61] When the Learmont Report came out, and the Opposition called for Mr Howard's head, Howard was protected politically by the support of his party and the Prime Minster, whilst constitutionally he was assisted in making his claim that the mistakes did not concern him by the presumption that operational matters were always the sole concern of Chief Executives. The problem is that the type of interference described above will often be covert: Parliament will not usually have access to the evidence which would reveal it.

---

58   Quoted in 'Bitter revenge of the uncivil servant', *Sunday Times*, 22 October 1995.
59   *Ibid*.
60   'My life with Michael Howard', *Independent*, 3 June 1996.
61   *Ibid*.

7 Most interestingly, Lord Armstrong, giving his views on these matters before the Public Service Committee[62] in April 1996 said:

I think that if you had asked me that day before I retired whether I thought the Prison Service should be made into an agency, I would have doubted it, because I should have felt that not only the objectives and the budget are matters of great political moment but there are many aspects of day to day management which inevitably become politically controversial ...

He contrasts the Prison Service with the Driver and Vehicle Licence Centre (DVLC) which was ideal because its work was only 'management activity'. The highly political nature of all aspects of penal policy and practice make it inevitable that ministers will be unable to resist the pressure to intervene in day-to-day management decisions, thus both undermining the basis of the Next Steps principle and creating confusion about responsibility and accountability. Interestingly, when the present Labour government came to power in 1997, Jack Straw announced that the Home Secretary and other Home Office ministers would take back responsibility for answering parliamentary questions on the Prison Service, perhaps in recognition of the particular problems thrown up by prisons policy.[63]

8 A recent episode concerning the Scottish Qualifications Agency, in which tens of thousands of examination marks for Scottish Highers were found to be suspect, shows that the issue of the extent of ministerial responsibility for 'arms-length' agencies is not going away. The head of the agency, Ron Tuck, accepted responsibility and resigned; ministers denied responsibility. The author of the following article draws some useful general lessons from the SQA episode, referring to ministerial responsibility as IMR; 'NDPBs' refers to Non-Departmental Public Bodies.

E Clarence, 'Ministerial responsibility and the Scottish Qualifications Agency' (2002) 80(4) Public Administration 791 (extracts)

Contested concepts of accountability and responsibility have evolved in parallel with the changing nature and structure of government activities. The concept of IMR is rooted in ideas of parliamentary sovereignty and top-down hierarchical control. Both of these have been compromised: parliamentary sovereignty by the ascendance of the party system and hierarchical control in favour of a focus on market-oriented service provision. Next Steps agencies were intended to revolutionize the delivery of services and became a feature of this shift towards market-oriented service provision. The introduction of agencies on a wide scale during the 1980s and 1990s has led to a lack of clarity as to whom is responsible, in practice, if not in theory. (Indeed, this article argues that the lack of clarity was recycled rather than invented: the issues were already clear in earlier problems over accountability and the nationalized industries, something which will be discussed below.) Nor had the (long) existence of NDPBs ... prior to the introduction of agencies established clear formal and operational lines of responsibility.

Agencies and NDPBs are not the same; important formal distinctions exist, including: NDPBs are usually founded by primary legislation; employees of agencies are civil servants while NDPB staff are not; the assets of an agency are within the ownership of the Secretary of State, those of the NDPB are vested in the relevant Board; and, auditing arrangements may be different. Informal factors have also contributed to the development of NDPBs – including the redefinition of some 'quangos' as NDPBs in order to avoid the use of the word 'quango' ... Broadly, as Heald and Geaughan have noted, it may be argued that NDPBs 'operate at 'greater arm's length' from the core department than do Executive Agencies'. ... These distinctions are important but

---

62 Minutes of Evidence Taken Before the Public Service Committee, HC 313 (1995–96), 3 April 1996, QQ 109–11, 116–20.
63 HC Deb col 397 (19 May 1997).

they do not detract from the issues of balancing ministerial control and administrative autonomy that are similar to both. Crucially, ministers are 'responsible' to Parliament for both agencies and NDPBs.

Rather than clouding issues of responsibility, the then Chancellor of the Duchy of Lancaster, William Waldegrave, argued that agencies would enhance responsibility and make 'transparent the *links* in the accountability chain which were pretty obscure before'. ... Such an argument was based on the belief that the establishment of agencies and the role and use of performance management indicators for agency senior management enabled a distinction to be drawn between operational and policy matters. ... This distinction required ministers to take responsibility for the policy/political failures but not any operational failings; operational responsibility would fall on chief executives who would be held responsible through the setting of performance targets.

The neat line drawn masks the reality of a complex and messy relationship between policy and the operationalization of policy. Furthermore, it ignores the role of agencies in the development of policy. ... The SQA's Management Statement and Financial Memorandum (MSFM) clearly states that '[t]he Secretary of State will look to the SQA for advice on the management and development of assessment structures, units [etc.]' (Enterprise and Lifelong Learning Committee – ELLC 2000a, Annex B, Annex C). Thus, while the policy/operation distinction was not central to the events surrounding the SQA, the MSFM indicates the paucity of such claims.

The role of agency chief executives in this distinction is further complicated by the insistence that they are subject to the convention of IMR and, when held to account for their actions by a Select Committee, bound by the Osmotherly Rules (whereby civil servants speak on behalf of the minister and indicate where questions should be referred to the minister). The Cabinet Office guidance on *Departmental Evidence and Response to Select Committees* explicitly sets out the duties of an agency chief executive in relation to Select Committees. The guidance states:

> While Agency Chief Executives have managerial authority to the extent set out in their Framework Documents, like other officials they give evidence on behalf of the Minister to whom they are accountable and are subject to that Minister's instruction. (Cabinet Office 1999)

Agency chief executives find themselves in a position whereby they are required to defend the actions of their agency but cannot comment (or defend themselves) on the failings of the agency if they believe that such failings are a result of ministerial 'interference' or under-resourcing. ...

Indeed, the distinction so coveted by proponents of agencies and NDPBs, was rejected by Mountfield, a former Permanent Secretary in the Cabinet Office, who argued that '[t]he distinction is a useful guide; but not a clear cut basis for deciding blame'. ... The responsibility remains with the minister. Crucially, Mountfield argues that ministerial intervention was always a potential feature of agencies. 'There could be no question of a self-denying ordinance. The responsible Minister must be able to shine his light anywhere into an Agency within his department, and direct the Chief Executive if necessary'. ...

It is clear that ministers always had the potential to 'interfere' or involve themselves in the day-to-day running of an agency while not being held accountable for the activities of the agency. ...

Contemporary responsibility and accountability

It is not simply the creation of agencies that have clouded the waters. The *ad hoc* development of these various systems ensures that more complex and opaque accountability structures are difficult to conceive. It is not only the shift to agency-driven government that has led to the accountability gap, but the wider move which the shift to agencies indicates: the shift from administration to management. With governments increasingly involving the private sector in service delivery and the new structures for management that have been created, the lines of accountability have become not only unclear, but at times hidden by issues of commercial confidentiality. ...

The shift to agencies and NDPBs has also altered what accountability means. It is no longer accountability to the people through Parliament, but rather to people as customers and consumers of services. Ministerial accountability can be and has been constructed as an unresponsive feature of government, unable to respond quickly or adequately to the needs of consumers. The needs of citizens for an accountable government can thus be side-stepped in favour of efficient and responsive government. ... the relationship between a minister and an NDPB in a period before and during a very public crisis. It confirms the lack of clarity that exists not only in terms of the policy/operation split, but also in the wider relationship of responsibility between ministers and NDPBs.

...

Implications

The SQA incident clearly illustrates that the responsibility and accountability structures between ministers and NDPBs as they currently exist are unsatisfactory. There is an inherent tension between the use of agencies, NDPBs and IMR. Davis and Willman have argued, convincingly, that the agency model cannot function 'within the present system of public accountability through Ministers'. ... As Wilding makes clear, the accountability of fringe bodies is ultimately a dilemma: increased accountability will involve increased ministerial activity, as ministers will seek to ensure that they are satisfactorily discharging their responsibilities. ... This runs counter to the purpose of NDPBs and agencies. ... 'You can have public accountability or you can have independence; you can usually achieve ... a balance of the two; but you cannot push one beyond a certain point without sacrificing the other. ...'

Note
The above leads directly to the issue of how officials and staff at departments, agencies and NDPBs can be held responsible.

How should officials other than ministers be held responsible?

This penchant of ministers to attribute failure not to their policy but to operational matters, and thus to officials, raises a question as to whether Parliament should have any part to play in protecting officials in danger of being scapegoated by ministers or even in disciplining them itself. Civil servants are employed under the royal prerogative which, as the FDA (First Division Association, representing Senior Civil Servants) recently noted,[64] 'legally ... gives the right to dismiss a civil servant at will and without compensation ... The Government in practice exercises [that] right'. The FDA went on to voice its concern over the manner in which Derek Lewis was dismissed:

> The Home Secretary dismissed Mr Lewis summarily, for no stated disciplinary reasons and outside the terms of the Civil Service Management Code and departmental procedures. Mr Lewis was given no notice of his dismissal [*ibid*].

We have already noted how the Treasury and Civil Service Select Committee suggested that Chief Executives should be directly accountable to them for their performance and Scott's suggestion that ministers must provide full information about any incident in respect of which they propose to 'delegate blame' to civil servants, which would undoubtedly assist the latter. The present government has repeatedly promised a Civil Service Act though no legislation, even in draft form, has appeared. When it does, the issues above will have to be revisited.

---

64   *Ibid*, para 10. For the prerogative generally, see Chapter 1 of this part.

Ministerial resignation in practice

It is important to note that it would be naive to talk of the above factors as if they were determinative of a minister's decision whether or not to resign. Whether or not a resignation actually occurs will of course depend upon a wide variety of other factors, and the actual record of resignations will not be seen to marry well with any constitutional theory that supposedly dictates when resignation should occur. One well known empirical study of resignations was Finer's:[65]

> SE Finer's classic analysis on this subject shows that three variables have to come into alignment: the minister must be compliant, the Prime Minister firm, and the party clamorous. Finer suggests that this conjunction is rare – and is quite fortuitous. Furthermore, from a normative (or constitutionalist) viewpoint, it is also indiscriminate in the sense that which ministers escape and which are caught has very little to do with the gravity of the offence.[66]

Notes

1 A more recent study,[67] citing a number of cases (Edwina Currie, David Mellor, Cecil Parkinson) in which the Prime Minister of the day tried unsuccessfully to hang on to the minister in question suggests that Finer's second requirement is not always necessary.[68]

2 As is well known, there were no resignations over the Scott Report, despite the findings that Sir Nicholas Lyell was 'personally at fault' and William Waldegrave had signed a string of untrue letters and deliberately chosen not to inform Parliament of the change in policy on arms-related exports to Iraq (see below). Clearly, John Major (and the Conservative Party generally) regarded the matter from the outset as a party political battle. The stream of criticisms from former senior government ministers directed at Scott's procedures,[69] the pointed failure of the Prime Minster to declare his confidence in the fairness of Scott's procedures,[70] and the presentation of the report to the press, using carefully prepared – and misleading – press briefings[71] whilst the Opposition had had only a few hours to read the report, had pre-figured this. The behaviour of Conservative MPs in the initial debate on Scott, described in one report as 'rall[ying] noisily round John Major and his ministers'[72] after having only 10 minutes to read the report suggests that for them simple party loyalty rather then what Scott actually said dictated their response to his findings. The substantive debate on the report was won by the Conservatives, admittedly only by one vote but with only two Conservative rebels.

3 So, even though there were no resignations, the point about the constitutional factors discussed above is that the government still has to justify a refusal to accept responsibility to the public and to Parliament in normative, constitutional terms. It does not say, 'We really don't care whether the minister should, constitutionally

---

65 SE Finer, 'The individual responsibility of ministers' (1956) 34 *Public Administration* 377.
66 M Loughlin, *Public Law and Political Theory* (1992), pp 52–3.
67 Woodhouse (1993), *op cit*, 277.
68 See further K Dowding and W-T Kang, 'Ministerial resignations 1945-97' (1998) 76(3) *Public Administration* 411.
69 See 'Furious Scott takes on Tory "smear campaign" ', *The Independent*, 8 February 1996.
70 HC Deb cols 466–67 (8 February 1996).
71 See for example 'Blind to blame', *Sunday Times*, 18 February 1996. Andrew Neil described the 'rigging' of the presentation of the report 'an awesome disgrace to democracy'. See 'Weasel words let guilty wriggle off Scott's hook', *Sunday Times*, 18 February 1996.
72 'Secretive, incompetent, chaotic', *Independent*, 18 February 1996.

speaking, resign. We've decided it would be better for political reasons for the minister to brazen it out'. Instead, as with Scott, it argues why the minister does not need to resign: there was no intention to mislead Parliament; the Attorney General's advice on PIIs is a matter of legal opinion and so on. The constitutional convention thus sets the parameters for the debate. Further, whilst a minister may cling on to power, if the government is seen to have a weak case in constitutional terms this will be apparent to the public, which will draw conclusions accordingly.[73]

4   A difficult case to classify, perhaps, is the resignation in May 2002 of the Secretary of State for Trade and Industry, Stephen Byers. Byers was forced out after months of hostile press coverage, particularly surrounding the circumstances of the dismissal of Byers' former press officer, Martin Sixsmith, and his refusal to sack another press adviser, Jo Moore, over her notorious 'good day to bury bad news' memo of 11 September 2001. It is not clear that serious problems in his department's *policy* can be laid at his door, though there was extreme discontent in various quarters over his decision to place Railtrack in administration and his plans for its replacement, as well as the state of the railways generally. Moreover he had, through inept presentation (in particular, by apparently misleading Parliament and the public over exactly when Sixsmith had been dismissed), lost the trust of the general public – principally by relentless media attacks upon him – and so had become a liability to the government. In that sense, Byers' resignation simply reflects the 'realist' interpretation of ministerial 'responsibility': that ministers will be forced to resign only when, on a hard-headed political calculation, their staying on will cause more damage to the governing party than their resignation.

5   Aside from resignation out of responsibility for errors and failures of policy, or for misleading Parliament, ministers may also be forced to resign because of personal errors of judgment, if sufficiently serious or, indeed, simply for personal reasons.[74] A recent example was the resignation of Ron Davies in October 1998, after an indiscretion of some sort took place on Clapham Common. However, the minister might of course be reinstated when it was thought that his misconduct had expiated itself. The prime example is the reinstatement of Peter Mandelson to the Cabinet less than two years after he had resigned in December 1998 following the revelation that he had been lent a very large sum of money from a fellow government minister, Geoffrey Robinson, and concealed the loan from the Prime Minister.

Enforcing ministerial responsibility: a new mechanism?

Under the current position, save for the highly unusual and uncertain sanction of enforced resignation, discussed above, the only person who can enforce the constitutional duties of ministers is the Prime Minister. The Ministerial Code stresses this, stating that ministers can only remain in office 'for as long as they retain the Prime Minister's confidence'. In response to a recommendation from the Neil Committee on Standards in Public Life,[75] the 2001 version of the Ministerial Code makes it clear that the ultimate responsibility for judging compliance with the Code lies with the Prime Minister:

---

73   Opinion polls taken shortly after the Scott Report showed that majorities of over 60 per cent thought Waldegrave and Lyell should resign.

74   Alan Milburn, the Health Secretary, resigned in June 2003 simply because he found that the job allowed him hardly any time with his family.

75   Sixth Report of the Committee on Standards in Public Life, *Reinforcing Standards* (2000) Cm 4557-I, paras 4.72–4.78, and Recommendation 13.

Ministers only remain in office for so long as they retain the confidence of the Prime Minister. He is the ultimate judge of the standards of behaviour expected of a Minister and the appropriate consequences of a breach of those standards, although he will not expect to comment on every allegation that is brought to his attention (Chapter 1, para 4).

As a Public Administration Select Committee report comments:

When asked about the present system for investigation, John Major described it as 'not perfect but I think it is the least imperfect system I have come across.' He added that 'there is an infinity of circumstances' and explained that the nature of the particular allegation would suggest the appropriate investigatory steps to be taken. He explained that the Prime Minister can call upon a wide variety of sources for advice and assistance and choose whichever is appropriate. These sources included the Cabinet Secretary, the Chief Whip, parliamentary colleagues, legal advisers and the police. Lord Butler [former Cabinet Secretary] told us that 'I do not think it is the case that there is a complete absence of means of inquiry, there is a vast range of them, but no one of them is suitable for every purpose'.[76]

Note

Nevertheless, many commentators believe that leaving assessment of compliance to the Prime Minister is no longer a satisfactory state of affairs. When ministers are accused of some form of impropriety, particularly where it is impropriety committed by a number of ministers, such as misleading Parliament on a number of occasions, the Prime Minister as leader of the government has an enormous vested interest in refuting the accusation. He is therefore very far from being an unbiased forum for adjudicating upon charges of breaches of the Code. The Neill Committee considered but rejected the idea of an independent ethics commissioner, who could investigate claims of ministerial misconduct, in the way that the Parliamentary Commissioner for Standards in the Commons investigates claims of misconduct by MPs.[77] The Committee said:

It has been suggested that the post of an ethics commissioner would have the following features:

• the commissioner would be a Crown servant, appointed by the Queen

• would report to the Queen and the Prime Minister

• would deal only with cases referred by the Prime Minister

• would publish his/her advice to the Prime Minister

• would not have an executive role

• would produce an annual report

• could be summoned to the House of Commons to give evidence to a Select Committee (para 4.35).

If such a commissioner were to be an independent investigator who could then advise the Prime Minister, the Committee saw the following advantages in such a system, indicating the witnesses to their enquiry who had put forward such advantages:

• proper investigative resources would improve the quality of the factual basis upon which the Prime Minister can make a judgement (Sir George Young Bt MP);

• it removes the complaint that Ministers provide their own defence, upon which they are then unchallenged – the 'circularity' point (Sir George Young Bt MP and Mr Preston);

---

76 Third Report, *The Ministerial Code: Improving the Rule Book*, HC 235 (2000–01), para 25.
77 Sixth Report, *op cit*, paras 4.59–4.71 and Recommendation 12. On the Standards Commissioner, see Part III Chapter 3.

- it would be fairer to Ministers (Mr Riddell, Mr Preston);

- it would provide an open system and one that was comprehensible to the public (Mr Riddell, Professor Hennessy and Mr Preston);

- although the process of investigation might take longer is some cases, this was not a crucial problem and was an inconvenience worth tolerating (Mr Davis MP, Sir George Young Bt MP and Professor Hennessy).[78]

Note

However, the Committee eventually decided against recommending any external investigatory body, party because it feared that it would become a political football because of the intense political significance of some complaints about ministers, but primarily on the ground that at present the Prime Minister has a wide discretion as to how to investigate any complaint, as described above, and that having a standard body to investigate complaints would fetter that discretion. As the Committee remarked:

> At the heart of the matter is the power of the Prime Minister to determine the dismissal of a Minister. In Professor Hennessy's words, the Prime Minister is 'can-carrier-in-chief.' It follows from that that he or she has the right to decide, in every case, how the allegation should be handled and to make his or her own judgement as to what would be the right course. We think it undesirable to make a recommendation that would fetter the Prime Minister's freedom in those respects and in our view, a new office of ethics commissioner or independent investigative officer would have that effect (para 4.71).

The above concern is arguably unpersuasive. The Prime Minister's ultimate responsibility for the position of ministers is answered by his or her having the final decision over the sanction for any breach of the Ministerial Code. Having a body to avoid the kind of ad hoc, hasty investigation carried out in the case of Peter Mandelson and the Hinduja brothers' passport applications would seem to be such a substantial advantage that, if there is anything to the concern about unfettering the Prime Minister's discretion, it is easily outweighed. That episode led to Mandelson's enforced second resignation over the issue of whether he had misled the public and the Prime Minister by denying having used his ministerial position to intervene with the Home Office in order to expedite the granting of passports to the Hinduja brothers as an informal quid pro quo for their large donation to the Millennium Dome. Here, the Cabinet Secretary was asked to investigate, at great speed, this extremely politically sensitive matter,[79] but Mandelson's resignation was forced on him primarily on a political judgment that it was necessary as a way of killing the story, which was obsessing the media at the time. It is notable that the Public Administration Committee, when it investigated the issue of enforcement of ministerial standards, came to a different view:

Public Administration Select Committee, Third Report, *The Ministerial Code: Improving the Rule Book*, HC 235 (2000–01)

25. If the Code is to be credible, there have to be effective mechanisms for the investigation of alleged breaches of its provisions, certainly in cases where the allegations are serious, rather than the spurious and frivolous allegations that form part of the daily political game. . . .

---

78 *Ibid*, para 4.69.
79 For an excellent account, see A Rawnsley, *Servants of the People: the Inside Story of New Labour* (2001), Chapter 22.

26. An issue which was examined by the Neill Committee was whether there was a case for an independent ethics commissioner. Peter Riddell, a long-standing advocate of such a post, raised the issue in evidence both to Lord Neill and to this Committee. He told us that 'there is no one-fits-all solution,' but an independent official could not only provide advice to the Prime Minister on allegations of breaches but would also provide a continuous source of reference for Ministers. In his view 'it is actually in the Civil Service's interest, the Prime Minister's interest and certainly in the Ministers' interest to have someone like that to provide an adviser. I know from my own conversations that some senior civil servants and some Ministers believe that an ethics adviser would have avoided some quite severe difficulties.' This view is supported by Professor Hennessy, who told us that 'one of the purposes for having this … is if you curb the anxious who give us all such headaches and produce such difficult cases for the Cabinet Secretaries and Prime Ministers and there were systems that increased the chances of it not getting out of hand and of deceit having to be undone.'

27. However, we also heard evidence that there was no real advantage in creating a new post of this kind. The Neill Committee came to the firm conclusion that 'no new office for the investigation of ministerial conduct should be established.' Lord Neill told us that the Prime Minister 'has available to him a whole armoury of investigative procedures and we saw no particular advantage in having one official called the ethics adviser or ethics commissioner, because the cry would always go up: Why have you not referred this issue to the ethics adviser? … it would become a sort of political football game and we did not see any great advantage.' John Major told us that 'I do not think that an external ethics commissioner would be the right way forward.' The Government welcomed the Neill Committee's recommendation that no new office for the investigation of ministerial conduct should be established.

28. The role of the Cabinet Secretary and Permanent Secretaries in investigating allegations of ministerial misconduct has received particular attention. Peter Riddell described the role of the Cabinet Secretary in this respect as 'invidious', while 'Permanent Secretaries are in a difficult position in relation to their political masters.' He cited an example, from his own journalistic contacts, of a permanent secretary feeling 'very uneasy about being an adviser.' When asked about the role of the Cabinet Secretary in investigations, Lord Neill agreed that 'this is not really a role for a Cabinet Secretary … it is an impossible situation'. John Major told us that 'It is the job of the permanent secretary to provide information that is readily available from within the Government. It is not the job of the permanent secretary to investigate.' Although the Cabinet Secretary clearly has a pivotal role, if such a role were to be extended to include responsibility for conducting independent investigation of alleged breaches of the Code, this would require fundamental changes to his existing position, including his relationship to Parliament.

29. Clarifying where the buck stops and establishing a requirement that the Prime Minister must answer for the Code to a Select Committee of Parliament would go some way to ensure that it is adequately policed and to reassure the public that breaches have been properly investigated. However, there is a case for going further, while avoiding a legalistic approach, and for bringing an independent element into the process. The Neill Committee asked the Parliamentary Commissioner on Standards if her office had a role to play in providing independent advice and investigation. The current Commissioner, Elizabeth Filkin, replied that 'the offer would be there, but I am agnostic about it'. We also considered whether there might be a role for the Parliamentary Ombudsman in investigating complaints of alleged ministerial misconduct. When we put this to the Ombudsman, Mr Buckley explained that under the current legislative framework he 'could not investigate unless some member of the public claimed to have sustained some injustice as a result … of malpractice by a minister'. However, when pressed further on a possible extension of his role, he added 'I can think of some similarities with the Local Government Ombudsman, who indeed investigates complaints involving suggestions that councillors have breached a local authority code of practice. It is not unthinkable but, obviously, I work within the statute as it is now and that is pretty much off limits … ministerial conduct as such is not a matter for me.' Mr

Buckley also acknowledged that in other countries the work of ombudsmen 'is devoted to investigating complaints of corruption of all sorts of levels in the public service.'

30. We do believe that having an independent parliamentary mechanism for advice and investigation would prove beneficial in strengthening accountability. Parliament lacks an investigatory officer to act on its behalf when there are allegations of ministerial failure or misconduct. It routinely demands inquiries, but has no effective means to put one in hand. This has been a concern of Select Committees for a number of years ... Parliament should not have to rely upon the executive to initiate inquiries into the executive's own alleged failings. We believe that the role of the select committees in scrutiny and accountability needs to be strengthened by an investigatory officer capable of finding out the facts of a case on Parliament's behalf. Equally, fairness to Ministers accused of breaching the Ministerial Code, and therefore subject to great political pressure, requires that they have the assurance of an independent investigation before there is a premature rush to judgement. A possible approach would be to create a new post of Ministerial Code Commissioner. Two precedents for such Commissioners already exist in the First Civil Service Commissioner and the Commissioner for Public Appointments. The first polices the Civil Service rules, the second the Nolan rules. The Commissioner might operate both by providing ex ante advice to Ministers thereby relieving Permanent Secretaries of this responsibility, and also have responsibility for ex post investigations. We do not, however, believe that a new office needs to be created. Parliament already possesses officers with the capacity to do what is required, both in terms of continuing advice and independent investigation. **We recommend that the remit of the Parliamentary Commissioner for Standards be expanded to include the provision of independent advice to Ministers on their responsibilities under the Code. We further recommend that, on referral from the Prime Minister, or by a resolution of the House proposed by the chair of the Liaison Committee, the Parliamentary Ombudsman should be empowered to conduct independent investigations on alleged breaches of the Ministerial Code and to report to the Prime Minister and to the House. Such reports should be published.**

Notes

1   Not surprisingly, having been let off the hook on this matter by the prestigious and influential Neill Committee, the government declined to accept this recommendation.

2   The essential weakness with the current system, it is suggested, was not addressed by any of the above reports. At present, ministerial survival depends primarily upon a political judgment made by the Prime Minister as to whether retaining a particular minister would cause more damage to the government than losing him or her; this in turn will be based upon the Prime Minister's reading of public opinion on the matter, and that public opinion is likely to be itself strongly influenced by newspapers, which tend to take a very strong line on such matters, as was clearly the case in relation to both Mandelson resignations and that of Stephen Byers. Since newspapers are clearly both openly political partisan and also often clearly prejudiced in relation to individual ministers on what may be flimsy or even bigoted grounds (Mandelson was a hate figure for much of the media for many years and some suspected that this was at least in part due to his homosexuality), in effect, important and highly influential investigations and recommendations are made by bodies that are blatantly partial and subject to very strong biases. Certain ministers in a Labour government, as at present, may be pursued by right-wing papers whose primary motive is simply to damage a centre-left government and thus assist the Conservative party. As *The Guardian* remarked in relation to the eventual resignation of Stephen Byers:

'Liar Byers' has been plastered everywhere, his face distorted by a Pinocchio nose in the Mirror, his constant tag 'embattled' or 'beleaguered'. In the end he could say nothing, he could do nothing about transport policy. He was the story. It was, apparently, no single issue that forced his resignation, just the constant grinding away by the media.[80]

Prime Ministers find it hard to resist such pressure from newspapers because it is obvious that they are biased too, for the reason given above. Indeed, the Prime Minister may actually be a personal friend of the minister concerned (as with Blair and Mandelson). An independent investigator would take some of the immediate political heat out of the situation by announcing what would quite evidently be an impartial investigation, and newspapers would find it much harder to attack its actual findings because, unlike the Prime Minister, it would evidently have no vested interest in either the departure or survival of the minister concerned.

3   As for the fear that its investigations would become politicised, the obvious reply is that this would be much less the case than is so at present. Moreover, the same thing happens, quite often, in relation to investigations of the Standards Commissioner in the Commons, and no one has suggested getting rid of the Standards Commissioner for that reason.

The content of the duty to give an account and not mislead Parliament

Until November 1995 – and therefore during the time in which the events which gave rise to the Scott inquiry took place – Questions of Procedure for Ministers (QPM) had this to say about the duty not to mislead Parliament:

> [Ministers' responsibility for their department] includes the duty to give Parliament ... and the public as full information as possible about the policies, decisions and actions of the Government, and not to deceive or mislead Parliament and the public [para 27].

The importance of the obligation to give full and truthful information to Parliament is clear, as noted in the Scott Report:[81]

> D4.58 The importance, if ministerial accountability is to be effective, of the provision of full and adequate information is, in my opinion, self-evident. If, and to the extent that, the account given by a minister to Parliament, whether in answering PQs, or in a debate, or to a Select Committee, withholds information on the matter under review, it is not a full account, and the obligation to account for what has happened, or for what is being done, has, *prima facie*, not been discharged. Without the provision of full information it is not possible for Parliament, or for that matter the public, to hold the executive fully to account. It follows, in my opinion, that the withholding of information by an accountable minister should never be based on reasons of convenience or for avoidance of political embarrassment and should always require special and strong justification.

The findings of the Scott Report

By far the most comprehensive and authoritative inquiry into the compliance by government with its duty to give an account in the context of a controversial defence exports policy, an enquiry which had unique access to highly confidential government papers and to government officials, was that undertaken by Lord Justice Scott into the export of defence-related equipment to Iraq. The report's[82] conclusion was that:

---

80   'Pressure that proved too much for the rubber man', *The Guardian*, 29 May 2002.
81   Inquiry into Exports of Defence Related Equipment and Dual-Use Goods to Iraq and Related Prosecutions, HC 115-I (1995–96).
82   *Ibid.* For articles generally on the Scott Report, see the Autumn 1996 edition of *Public Law*, and I Leigh and L Lustgarten, 'Five volumes in search of accountability: the Scott Report' (1996) 59(5) MLR 695.

Government statements made in 1989 and 1990 about policy on defence exports to Iraq consistently failed ... to comply with the standard set by paragraph 27 of [QPM] and, more important, failed to discharge the obligations imposed by the constitutional principle of ministerial accountability.[83]

In this section, the findings of the Scott Report which support this conclusion will be given; the significance of the justifications by the government for the – at the least – incomplete disclosure to Parliament of this policy will be explored; questions will be asked about the position of civil servants in this respect; and parliamentary and governmental reaction to the report's findings will be analysed.

The factual background to the Scott Inquiry

In order to understand Scott's condemnation of the government, the circumstances leading to the setting up of the Scott Inquiry and the government's changing policy on arms to Iraq needs to be understood. Essentially, the affair resolved around the guidelines governing the granting of export licences for sale of defence-related equipment to both Iran and Iraq. The parts of the Scott Report which are of relevance here concern the manner in which these guidelines were changed, or re-interpreted and the information that was given by ministers to Parliament about the changing face of government policy under the guidelines. The guidelines as originally drafted are described here by Richard Norton-Taylor.

Richard Norton-Taylor, *Truth is a Difficult Concept: Inside the Scott Inquiry* (1995), pp 40–41

The export guidelines which were to cause the Government so much anguish were drawn up in 1984, ironically in an attempt to make it easier for ministers to defend their policy in public. 'The Iran-Iraq war', William Waldegrave, former minister of state at the Foreign Office, was to tell the inquiry, 'was turning out to be a really major war. It was not just an incursion. Persians and Arabs had been squabbling with each other for 8,000 years, but this was turning out to be a really major war with hundreds of thousands of people killed'.

They were prompted by Sir Richard Luce, one of Waldegrave's predecessors at the FO, and one of the few members of the Government who expressed real anxiety about selling arms-related goods to Iraq and Iran ...

What became known as the Howe guidelines were designed to unravel the knots tying up the Government over attempts to draw distinctions between 'lethal' and 'non-lethal' exports. They stated:

(i) We should maintain our consistent refusal to supply any lethal equipment to either side.

(ii) Subject to that overriding consideration, we should attempt to fulfil existing contracts and obligations.

(iii) We should not, in future, approve orders for any defence equipment which, in our view, would significantly enhance the capability of either side to prolong or exacerbate the conflict.

(iv) In line with this policy, we should continue to scrutinise rigorously all applications for export licences for the supply of defence equipment to Iran and Iraq.

Note

When Iran and Iraq declared a ceasefire in 1988, the British government was eager to seize the 'big prize' of renewed exports sales to Iraq in particular. At this point,

---

83   *Op cit*, para D4.63.

therefore, a relaxed version of guideline (iii) was put forward (on 21 December). In future, defence equipment which *'would be of direct and significant assistance to either country in the conduct of offensive operations in breach of the ceasefire'* was not to be exported; the significance of this change is considered below. However, what happened next was the Iranian *fatwa* (sentence of death) against Salman Rushdie, which dealt such a blow to British-Iranian relations that it became politically impossible to export any defence-related equipment to Iran. A further modification of the policy was therefore agreed upon; at the same time it was also agreed that neither modification would be announced to Parliament. Scott traces the unfolding of government policy starting with the decision to adopt the new guideline (iii).[84]

Inquiry into Exports of Defence Equipment and Dual-Use Goods to Iraq and Related Prosecutions, HC 115-I (1995–96)

D3.65 The state of affairs, therefore, that had been reached by the end of February 1989 was (i) that the Ministers of State at the FCO, the MOD and the DTI had agreed that a more liberal policy towards defence equipment sales to Iraq and Iran should be implemented; (ii) that at MODWG and IDC level the liberal policy was being implemented by the application of the revised form of guideline (iii) 'on a trial basis for the time being'; and (iii) that it had been agreed that no public announcement of these changes would be made. These changes were regarded as temporary or provisional, pending final agreement being reached on the form the new, more liberal, policy should take. . . .

D3.42 Accordingly, Mr Waldegrave replied to Mr Clark by a letter dated 7 February 1989 from his Private Secretary to Mr Clark's Private Secretary. The letter said that '. . . DTI, MOD and FCO officials have agreed that the form of words tabled on 21 December [revised guideline (iii)] appears after all to meet our joint requirements, and should continue to be used on a trial basis for the time being' and that 'Mr Waldegrave is content for us to implement a more liberal policy on defence sales, without any public announcement on the subject'.

Following the 'tilt' to Iraq, Mr Waldegrave set out in a letter of 27 April 1989 the new policy:

> We agreed [ie at a meeting of junior ministers on 24 April] that we should continue to interpret the guidelines more flexibly in respect of Iraq, as we have done in practice since the end of last year; but that we should revert to a stricter interpretation for Iran, along the lines which operated before the ceasefire. This would, in effect mean, that we would not contemplate a major sale of defence equipment to the Iranian Armed Forces. This need not in principle preclude all sales to the Iranian Navy or to the IRGC, although in present circumstances I find it extremely difficult to envisage any major exports to those organisations.

Mr Waldegrave's letter then repeated the agreed form of answer to be used 'if we are now pressed in Parliament over the guidelines', namely:

> The Guidelines on the export of defence equipment to Iran and Iraq are kept under constant review, and are applied in the light of prevailing circumstances, including the ceasefire and developments in the peace negotiations.

D3.84 The essence of the agreement reached between the ministers at their 24 April 1989 meeting, as described in Mr Waldegrave's letter, was, so far as Iraq was concerned, that they would 'continue to interpret the guidelines more flexibly . . . as we have done in practice since the end of [1988]'. The 'flexible interpretation' since the end of 1988 had consisted, in practice, of the

---

84 The Scott Report uses a number of abbreviations. The most important are as follows: FCO – Foreign and Commonwealth Office; MOD – Ministry of Defence; DTI – Department of Trade and Industry; MODWG – Ministry of Defence Working Group; ELA – Export Licence Applications.

application of the revised guideline (iii) to Iraqi ELAs and AWP applications. This practice was, therefore, to continue ...

D3.89 The MODWG met on 10 May 1989. Lieut-Colonel Glazebrook's manuscript notes, made on the agenda for the meeting, record what the MODWG members were told about the ministerial agreement:

1. IRAQ. new relaxed Guidelines

2. IRAN. apply stringent Guidelines.

D3.90 On 15 June 1989 Mr Barrett followed up the remarks made at the 10 May MODWG meeting by sending a note to all MODWG members in order 'to confirm in writing the interpretation of the guidelines which ministers had agreed we should now use when considering ELAs and AWP applications for Iran and Iraq.' The written confirmation was as follows:

2. For both countries the normal security considerations should continue to apply. In addition the existing guidelines in respect of lethal equipment will still apply. For non-lethal equipment the following will apply:

a. Iran. – The existing guidelines strictly interpreted in the way that they were being used at the height of the conflict. There should not, however, be a blanket embargo against the Iranian Navy or IRGC; we should stop anything which we believe would pose a direct threat to the Armilla Patrol.

b. Iraq. – We should refuse applications only if they would be of direct and significant assistance in the conduct of offensive operations in breach of the ceasefire.

Note

This then was the new policy agreed upon by ministers. It is worth noting the view of 'one of the [Ministry of Defence's] most experienced assessor of weapons systems responsible for vetting arms exports'[85] (Lieutenant-Colonel Glazebrook) on what kind of equipment was actually cleared for export to Iraq under this new, undeclared policy:

... in his view, and that of his military colleagues, Matrix Churchill machine tools were 'lethal' and should never have been cleared for exports. Glazebrook was so concerned about the 'whittling away' of export controls that, in June 1989, he drew up a report to warn ministers of how 'UK Ltd is helping Iraq, often unwittingly, but sometimes not, to set up a major indigenous arms industry'. Britain's contribution to Iraq, he said, included setting up a major research and development facility to make weapons, machinery to make gun barrels and shells, and a national electronics manufacturing complex. Taken together, the exports represented 'a very significant enhancement to the ability of Iraq to manufacture its own arms and thus to resume the war with Iran'. Export guidelines should be tightened, he said, 'from the point of view of both military and security concerns' (*ibid*).

Scott's findings: the failure to disclose shifts in policy; the government's explanations

As Scott found, 'A conscious decision was taken by the junior ministers that there should be no public announcement [of the new policy]'. He goes on to note that 'As a consequence of this decision, answers given by ministers to Parliamentary Questions ['PQs'] and [their] letters ... to MPs ... were decidedly uninformative'.[86] In another part of the report he states, ' ... The answers to PQs ... failed to inform Parliament of

---

85 R Norton-Taylor, *Truth is a Difficult Concept: Inside the Scott Inquiry* (1995), p 52.
86 *Op cit*, para D3.107.

the current state of government policy on non-lethal arms sales to Iraq. This failure was deliberate . . .'[87]

The following extracts from the report show, first, Scott's analysis of this failure as displayed in certain ministerial letters to MPs[88] and, secondly, his discussion of the different rationale offered by various government spokespersons for the way in which the government handled replies to MPs on this issue.

Inquiry into Exports of Defence Equipment and Dual-Use Goods to Iraq and Related Prosecutions, HC 115-I (1995–96)

D4.1 Over the period February 1989 to July 1989, a number of letters, signed mainly by Mr Waldegrave but a few by Lord Howe, were sent to MPs whose constituents had asked questions about Government policy on defence sales to Iraq. . . .

D4.2 A form of response to be incorporated in the letters sent to the MPs in question was settled in the FCO. The response included the following two sentences (or the gist of them):

> British arms supplies to both Iran and Iraq continue to be governed by the strict application of guidelines which prevent the supply of lethal equipment or equipment which would significantly enhance the capability of either side to resume hostilities. These guidelines are applied on a case by case basis.

D4.3 Letters to MPs incorporating these sentences and signed by Mr Waldegrave numbered some seven in March 1989, five in April, twenty-three in May, one in June and two in July. Lord Howe signed two similar letters in May and two in July. In one of the April letters and in each of the May, June and July letters the formula was preceded by the statement that: 'The Government have not changed their policy on defence sales to Iraq or Iran.'

In one letter there was a reference to 'our firm and even-handed position over arms sales to Iran and Iraq'.

D4.4 The reference in each of these letters to the criterion that governed the supply of non-lethal defence equipment to Iraq was not accurate. Since the end of February 1989 the criterion for Iraq had been the new formulation, namely, that there would be no supply of equipment which would be of direct and significant assistance to Iraq in the conduct of *offensive* operations in breach of the ceasefire. The inaccuracy should have been noticed by Mr Waldegrave, who had been one of the midwives at the birth of this new formulation. Lord Howe, on the other hand, had not been informed of the junior ministers' agreement on the new formulation.

D4.5 The statement in the letters that 'The Government have not changed their policy on defence sales to Iraq or Iran' was untrue. . . .

D4.6 Mr Waldegrave knew first hand, the facts that, in my opinion, rendered the 'no change in policy' statement untrue. I accept that, when he signed these letters, he did not regard the agreement he had reached with his fellow ministers as having constituted a change in policy towards Iraq. In his evidence to the inquiry, he strenuously and consistently asserted his belief, in the face of a volume of, to my mind, overwhelming evidence to the contrary, that policy on defence sales to Iraq had, indeed, remained unchanged. I did not receive the impression of any insincerity on his part in giving me the evidence he did. But it is clear, in my opinion, that policy on defence sales to Iraq did not remain unchanged.

D4.7 The proposition that the Government's position over 'arms sales to Iran and Iraq' was 'even-handed' had been untrue ever since the decision, taken as a consequence of the Rushdie affair, to 'return to a more strict approach to Iran.'

87 *Op cit*, para D4.42.
88 Replies to PQs are analysed in Part III Chapter 1, pp 298–306.

This differential policy was already being implemented by 17 April. I could well understand that the reference in the letter to Mr Curry to the 'even-handed position' may have been an overlooked refugee from a common form sentence that would, two months earlier, have been unexceptionable. But the proposition that on 17 April, the date of the letter, it was a true statement is not, in my opinion, remotely arguable ...

D3.4 It has been strenuously argued by a number of ministers and officials who have given evidence to the inquiry that the many statements to the effect that Government policy remained unchanged after the ceasefire and that the Guidelines announced in 1985 remained in force were not invalidated by the fact of the changes that were agreed upon by the junior ministers in the period preceding July 1990. The essence of the argument proceeded on these lines:

(i)   Government policy, of which the Howe Guidelines announced in October 1985 were an important part, had been established by senior ministers with the concurrence of the Prime Minister.

(ii) It was not open to junior ministers on their own authority to alter the policy thus established.

(iii) to the manner in which in changing circumstances the established policy would be applied.

(iv) Changes in the manner in which established policy would be applied were, inevitably, necessitated by the ceasefire and by other events. But these changes did not, and could not, constitute any change in the established policy itself. They exemplified no more than a flexible application, geared to the new circumstances, of the established policy.

I accept ... that in deciding that the agreed approaches to defence exports to Iraq and Iran respectively could be described as being interpretations of the 1985 Guidelines, the junior ministers believed that they were avoiding a formal change of the 1985 Guidelines. But, however the agreement reached by the junior ministers be described, if the substance of the agreement was to change the criterion that would be applied to applications for licences to export defence equipment to Iraq, they were, in any ordinary use of language, agreeing on a change of policy. I regard the explanation that this could not be so because the approval of the senior ministers and the Prime Minister had not been obtained as sophistry ...

D4.52 A frank and sustained defence of the divergence between the Government's actual policy and the various ministerial statements of policy, whether in letters or in answers to PQs, was offered by Lord Howe in his oral evidence to the inquiry. He said:

> ... there is nothing necessarily open to criticism in incompatibility between policy and presentation of policy ... It [ie the Government] is not necessarily to be criticised for a difference between policy and public presentation of policy.

He explained:

> The fact is that, as soon as you are embarked upon the necessary policy, in competition with other nations, of enhancing a commercial position, a commercial position which is more inhibited than other nations, for reasons we have investigated, any attempt to enlarge that base is capable of being criticised by others ...
>
> Q. Can this not be explained to the public in a manner the public would understand?
>
> A. Not easily, not if you visualise, as the *Independent* pointed out, the extremely emotional way in which such debates are conducted in public ... if you look at the various reasons given by colleagues for caution in relation to the shifting nuances of policy, in the Spring of 1989, they all add up to a very good reason for not volunteering this, because the scope for misunderstanding is enormous.
>
> ... Q. [So the Government's approach was] 'We know what is good for you. You may not like it and, if you were made aware of it, you might protest, but we know what is best'?
>
> A. It is partly that, but it is partly 'If we were to lay specifically our thought processes before you, they are not just going before you; they are laid before a worldwide range of

uncomprehending or malicious commentators'. This is the point. You cannot choose a well balanced presentation to an elite Parliamentary audience.

In relation to the circumstance that, as a result of the re-formulation of guideline (iii) and the decision to apply the re-formulated guideline to Iraq but not to Iran, policy was no longer even-handed or impartial as between the two countries Lord Howe said: 'It cannot be seen like that. That is the point.' And

> Frankly the inaccuracy is intrinsic in the policy position that we are presenting. If you are saying that the Guidelines are still in place and being applied directly to Iran without any qualification, and being applied with modification to Iraq, then that is the thing you cannot disclose and you have to head back to 'The Guidelines are in place'. That is the point. The Guidelines are in place because the basic policy has not changed.

...

D3.121 I have referred earlier in this section of the report to arguments that have been put forward in support of the proposition that the Guidelines, as announced in 1985, remained in force and unchanged notwithstanding the agreement reached by the junior ministers over the period December 1988 to May 1989. For a number of reasons I do not accept that proposition or the arguments.

D3.122 First, it is argued that the relaxation of the Guidelines agreed upon by the junior ministers did not constitute a change in the Guidelines but was no more than a liberal, relaxed interpretation, or implementation, of them. ....

This 'interpretation' is said to be consistent with the flexibility inherent in the Guidelines from their inception. It was this 'interpretation' that had been applied to Iraq since February 1989 and was confirmed for Iraq at the end of April 1989. In Mr Waldegrave's written comments, the use of revised guideline (iii) is described as follows:

> The revised form of guideline (iii) was used by the MODWG and IDC in January and February 1989 as a temporary working premise on a trial basis. After the *fatwa*, ministers decided that the suggested change in the guidelines should not go ahead and that instead the original guidelines were to be applied with flexibility. Thereafter, the MODWG and IDC applied the original guidelines restrictively for Iran and liberally for Iraq. In the case of Iraq, this meant in practice that those groups used the suggested revised form of guideline (iii) as an interpretative gloss on the original guidelines.

D3.123 The viewpoint expressed in the passage from Mr Waldegrave's letter that I have cited, and exemplified in the passage cited from his written comments, is one that does not seem to me to correspond with reality. The revised formulation of guideline (iii) was intended to do two things; first. it was intended, in view of the termination of the conflict, to restate guideline (iii) in a manner that could make sense; second, it was intended to release from the guidelines non-lethal equipment whose military value was primarily defensive. If that second purpose had not been present, the reference to 'offensive operations in breach of the ceasefire' would not have been included and the limiting adjective 'direct' would not have been necessary. To describe this revised formulation as no more than an interpretation of the old, is, in my opinion, notwithstanding the many advocates who espoused the thesis, so plainly inapposite as to be incapable of being sustained by serious argument. In my opinion, the agreement to which Mr Waldegrave referred in his 28 March 1989 letter was, on any ordinary use of language, an agreement to adopt a new and more liberal policy towards sales of non-lethal defence equipment than had been in place during the conflict and to do so by applying a revised formulation of guideline (iii) in place of the original. The intended effect of applying the revised guideline was to release a certain class of non-lethal defence equipment from the Guidelines.

D3.124 I accept that Mr Waldegrave and the other adherents of the 'interpretation' thesis did not, in putting forward the thesis, have any duplicitous intention and, at the time, regarded the relaxed interpretation, or implementation, of guideline (iii) as being a justifiable use of the flexibility believed to be inherent in the Guidelines. But that that was so underlines, to my mind, the duplicitous nature of the flexibility claimed for the guidelines. Flexibility that reflects the differences of opinion that may arise whenever an attempt is made to apply a criterion that depends upon a value judgment is inevitable and desirable. For example, whether an enhancement of military capability is 'significant' is a matter on which opinions may differ. If opinions do differ, a decision falling within the spectrum created by those differences can legitimately be described as an application of the criterion. Guideline (iii) had, thus, an inherent and entirely acceptable flexibility. But the removal from the scope of guideline (iii) of non-lethal defence equipment of a primarily defensive nature is not a 'flexible interpretation' of the Guidelines. It is a decision that the Guidelines will not be applied so as to restrict the sale of a certain class of defence equipment. The description of that decision as being merely a flexible interpretation, or flexible implementation, of the Guidelines is bound to be misleading to anyone who does not know the substance of the decision.

D4.42 ... Having heard various explanations as to why it was necessary or desirable to withhold knowledge from Parliament and the public of the true nature of the Government's approach to the licensing of non-lethal defence sales to Iran and Iraq respectively, I have come to the conclusion that the overriding and determinative reason was a fear of strong public opposition to the loosening of the restrictions on the supply of defence equipment to Iraq and a consequential fear that the pressure of the opposition might be detrimental to British trading interests.

Note

It is worth commenting briefly on the differing justifications[89] put forward. The first one, that no change took place because no change was approved at a high level was described by Alan Clark as a 'slightly *Alice in Wonderland* suggestion' where '... because something was not announced, it could not have happened'.[90] In effect, one of the most disturbing aspects of the whole affair, that this important change in policy was never approved at a senior level, was being used to *defend* a failure to be open with Parliament. Nevertheless, the capacity of government ministers to indulge in such mental acrobatics is important, given the new subjective formulation of the duty not to mislead Parliament, considered below. The second justification, put forward by Lord Howe, is frankly paternalistic; it is significant in revealing a clear rejection by a former senior government figure of the basic principle of democratic accountability based upon the provision of full information to the public, not because that information would (say) threaten national security but simply because the public is not deemed to be capable of considering it in a sensible, rational way. The third is perhaps the most important; it rests on the notion that because only a minor change (a new interpretation of declared policy) had taken place and the main policy had already been declared, it was not necessary to declare any change, since Parliament already had most of the information.

After the Scott Report: the duty not to mislead Parliament

The remainder of this chapter will discuss what, post-Scott, appears to be the extent of the obligation not to mislead Parliament; this will not involve any attempt to find a consensus between the various differing viewpoints as to the extent of this obligation,

---

89 Another justification put forward was that if Iran heard of the 'tilt to Iraq', this could cause a further deterioration in Britain's relations with that country and thus put British hostages under the control of Iran at risk (*ibid*, paras 3.107–3.108). Scott finds that the contemporary documentation reveals no evidence that this was a 'significant factor' in the decision to conceal the change in policy from Parliament (*ibid*).

90 Norton-Taylor, *op cit*, pp 68–69.

for none presently exists. Rather, it will sketch the various positions taken in the new parameters of the debate. The findings of Scott take us to five key questions at the heart of the current debate over the duty not to mislead Parliament. The first is whether the current list of topics on which the government will refuse to supply information should be reviewed; this issue is dealt with in Chapter 3 of this part, which examines the Code of Practice on access to information and the provisions of the new Freedom of Information Act. The second issue is the question whether and if so when the giving of incomplete information is to be regarded as misleading; the third is the issue of when, if ever, it may be justifiable to lie to Parliament; the fourth is the significance of the minister's own belief as to whether he or she is saying something misleading; and the fifth is the constitutional position of civil servants who are asked to co-operate with the misleading of Parliament or become aware that it is occurring.

Since the time of the Scott Report, the obligation as set out in QPM, now the Ministerial Code, has changed quite significantly. The accountability obligation, now set out as a number of key constitutional principles in Chapter 1 of the Code, reads as follows:

iii) It is of paramount importance that Ministers give accurate and truthful information to Parliament, correcting any inadvertent error at the earliest opportunity. Ministers who knowingly mislead Parliament will be expected to offer their resignation to the Prime Minister;

iv) Ministers should be as open as possible with Parliament and the public, refusing to provide information only when disclosure would not be in the public interest which should be decided in accordance with the relevant statutes and the Government's Code of Practice on Access to Government Information;

v) Ministers should similarly require civil servants who give evidence before Parliamentary Committees on their behalf and under their direction to be as helpful as possible in providing accurate, truthful and full information in accordance with the duties and responsibilities of civil servants as set out in the Civil Service Code.[91]

'Ministers must not knowingly mislead Parliament'

Fifth Report from the Treasury and Civil Service Select Committee, HC 27 (1993–94), paras 124–26; Minutes of Proceedings of the same, 8 March 1994, QQ 1840, 1843, 1906, 1907 and 24 April 1994, Q 2148 (Sir Robin Butler)

124. . . . There has been considerable concern recently about the adequacy of, and adherence to [the guidance in Questions of Procedure for Ministers regarding openness with Parliament].

125. Sir Robin Butler informed the Scott Inquiry that there was a category of Parliamentary answers 'where it is necessary to give an incomplete answer, but one should, in these circumstances, seek not to mislead'. Mr Waldegrave, in evidence to the sub-committee, vividly asserted the need, in certain circumstances, not to disclose all relevant information: 'There are plenty of cases over the years, with both Governments, where the minister . . . will not mislead the House and will take care not to mislead the House, but may not display everything he knows about that subject . . . Much of Government activity is much more like negotiation, much more like playing poker than it is like playing chess. You do not put all the cards up all the time in the

91 Professor Hennessy in his opinion (given below) refers to this as 'the new front-end of QPM'.

interests of the country'. The necessity for non-disclosure has been asserted in the past, even in the case of civil servants appearing before select committees. In 1985 the then Head of the Home Civil Service said that, taking 'an extreme case', when a decision had been made to devalue the pound, a minister could instruct a civil servant appearing before a select committee not to reveal that devaluation in advance. Sir Robin Butler reaffirmed this in 1990, while emphasising that that 'would not extend to the minister instructing the civil servant to mislead the committee; that would be improper'. There is self-evidently a problem in determining the line between non-disclosure which is not misleading and a misleading answer or statement. This problem is more acute for ministers than for civil servants, since a civil servant appearing before a select committee can refer a committee to a minister. Both Mr Waldegrave and Sir Robin Butler gave examples of answers which they held to be incomplete but not misleading. In such cases there was a general duty 'to make clear that you have information which you cannot disclose', although there were circumstances when even this would not be appropriate. Even in the latter circumstances, ministers and civil servants had to 'frame their answer in a way which avoids misleading, if they possibly can'.

126. Sir Robin stressed that it was wrong for a minister or a civil servant to lie, to mislead intentionally or to give an answer which was known to be false. The Prime Minister has made it clear in a letter to the Chairman of the Sub-Committee that, in such circumstances, a minister would usually be expected to relinquish his office. However, Sir Robin Butler and Mr Waldegrave also contended that there were 'very rare occasions' when the wrong of lying to the House would be outweighed by the greater wrong consequent upon not lying. Three instances were adduced in support of this contention. First, Sir Stafford Cripps did not mislead Parliament over devaluation but said after the devaluation in 1949 that, if he had been asked just before devaluation whether he was going to devalue he would have told a lie to Parliament. Second, Mr Peter Thomas gave an untrue answer about whether Mr Greville Wynne, who had just been arrested by Soviet authorities, was working for British Intelligence; this was untrue but was considered necessary to save Mr Wynne's life. Finally, both Sir Robin Butler and Mr Waldegrave alleged that, on 16 November 1967, the then Mr James (now Lord) Callaghan gave an answer which was 'false'. Mr Waldegrave did not dissent from the proposition that Lord Callaghan had lied to the House. Sir Robin Butler, who had worked in the Treasury as Secretary to the Budget Committee at the time, argued that when Lord Callaghan said in answer to a question from Mr Stanley Orme about devaluation 'I have nothing to add to or subtract from anything I have said on previous occasions on the subject of devaluation' he was misleading the House since his previous answers had been that assertions that the Government was not going to devalue the pound and he therefore did have something to subtract from previous statements. He accepted that Lord Callaghan did not have an intention to mislead and was thus not 'deliberately lying to the House of Commons', but argued that he had made a 'slip', which Sir Robin Butler implied Lord Callaghan had acknowledged. In reply, Lord Callaghan vigorously contested Mr Waldegrave's implication that he had lied to the House, stating that 'none of my answers supports Mr Waldegrave's assertion that I lied to the House of Commons'. He did not admit to a false answer to Mr Orme, referring to 'one *possible* slip (which was not intended to deceive) in the reply I gave to Mr Orme'. He repudiated 'the attempt to put a construction on my replies by Sir Robin Butler and Mr Waldegrave, twenty five years after the event, that no one who was present ever did either at the time or later'....

134. Effective accountability depends in considerable measure upon adherence by ministers and civil servants to the duty set out in *Questions of Procedure for Ministers* to give Parliament, including its Select Committees, and the public as full information as possible about the policies, decisions and actions of the Government, and not to deceive or mislead Parliament and the public'. We are aware of considerable public cynicism about the honesty of politicians generally and in this context concern about the honesty and integrity of ministerial statements to and answers in Parliament might seem misplaced. However, the knowledge that ministers and civil servants may evade questions and put the best gloss on the facts but will not lie or knowingly mislead the House of Commons is one of the most powerful tools Members of Parliament have in holding the executive

to account. Not only is the requirement laid down clearly in Government guidance to ministers, it is a requirement which the House of Commons itself expects from all its Members, departure from which standard can be treated as a contempt. We accept that the line between non-disclosure and a misleading answer is often a fine one, not least because the avoidance of misleading answers requires not only strict accuracy but also an awareness of the interpretations which could reasonably be placed upon an answer by others, but ministers should be strengthened in their determination to remain the right side of that line by certainty about the consequences of a failure to do so. **Any minister who has been found to have knowingly misled Parliament should resign.**

[Evidence of Mr Waldegrave and Sir Robin Butler]

Mr Waldegrave: There are plenty of cases over the years, with both Governments, where the minister – and it very often has happened in relation particularly to diplomatic matters, but not only to diplomatic matters – will not mislead the House and will take care not to mislead the House, but may not display everything he knows about that subject, but he will answer the question accurately.

Chairman

1843. Let me get this right. You are saying, if a minister is criticised or found to be misleading the House, he or she should not necessarily resign?

Mr Waldegrave: There is a full range, is there not, from very serious things to totally trivial things. Far the best judge of this is surely the House at the time....

1906. Referring to Sir Robin Butler's answer, he went on to refer to a 'wider category of cases where it is necessary to give an incomplete answer'. The devaluation case is cut and dried, but I am interested in this wider category of cases where it is necessary to give an incomplete answer. Can you imagine circumstances where a minister could give an incomplete answer where he should actually have to resign?

Mr Waldegrave: It would depend again on whether the effect had been to seriously mislead the House about an important matter.

1907. So you can foresee that an incomplete answer would be a resignation issue?

Mr Waldegrave: You have to look at what the outcome would ultimately be for the House and for the judgment of the House. We had an example of what was alleged to be – I was not in the House at the time – an incomplete answer which the House accepted in relation to Northern Ireland [to whether the Government was making covert contacts with IRA/Sinn Fein] and the House very easily accepted that; both sides of the House accepted that....

Sir Robin Butler: The position is that the duty of ministers is always to give full and truthful information to Parliament and not to lie or to mislead. The duty of civil servants is the same. Only in the most exceptional circumstances – so exceptional, you may say, as to be virtually theoretical and of which I have quoted examples – can an even greater damage be done by telling the truth...

Notes

1   A senior member of the FDA in evidence to the Public Service Committee commented that: '... there is a commonly accepted culture that the function of [an answer to a PQ] is to give no more information than the minister thinks will be helpful to him or her, the minister, in the process of political debate in the House.'[92]

2   The giving of selective information is thus routine. During the Scott Inquiry, Sir Gore-Booth [a very senior civil servant] opined, in a similar manner to Sir Robin

---

92   Minutes of Evidence Taken Before the Public Service Committee, HC 313 (1995–96), 20 March 1996, Q 21.

Butler and William Waldegrave, that giving such incomplete information was not necessarily misleading – 'half a picture can be true'. Scott's comment on this view is as follows:

D4.55 The problem with the 'half a picture' approach is that those to whom the incomplete statement is addressed do not know, unless it is apparent from the terms of the statement itself, that an undisclosed half is being withheld from them. They are almost bound, therefore, to be misled by the statement, notwithstanding that the 'half a picture' may, so far as it goes, be accurate. The proposition is not that a statement to Parliament must include each and every fact relating to the subject in order to avoid being misleading. Such a requirement would clearly be impracticable. A fair summary of the 'full picture' would often, depending on the question that had been asked and the apparent purpose of the statement, be a complete and sufficient response. The proposition is that if part of the picture is being suppressed and the audience does not know it is being suppressed. The audience will be misled into believing the half picture to be the full picture.[93]

3   However, Scott was unworried about the reformulation of QPM noted above:

K8.5 The qualification of 'mislead' by the addition of the adverb 'knowingly' does not, to my mind, make any material difference to the substance of the obligation resting on ministers not to mislead Parliament or the public. It must, I believe, always have been the case that misleading statements made in ignorance of the true facts were not regarded as a breach of a minister's obligation to be honest with Parliament and the public. Questions might, of course, arise as to why the minister was ignorant of the true facts and thus unable to have rendered to Parliament an accurate account of his stewardship.[94]

4   Arguably, Scott is a little too sanguine here. A genuinely inadvertent mistake of fact should arguably not be viewed as serious misconduct (though as Scott notes, it may raise issues of competence) but the addition of the word 'knowingly' could have far wider consequences than this. In is worth remembering the case of Waldegrave himself: Scott found that he persisted in his view that the Guidelines had not changed 'in the face of overwhelming evidence to the contrary'. The position potentially is, therefore, that a minister who holds an honest but manifestly unreasonable – even bizarre – view that government policy has not changed is entitled simply to tell Parliament that there has been no change. Clearly the risk is that a minister will be able to refute charges of knowingly misleading the House as long as he or she is able to make up some argument, however flimsy, that he or she did not *realise* that that was what he or she was doing. The duty ought surely to be based on the requirement for a more objective assessment by the minister. To take the example of the change in the export guidelines: if the minister realised or ought to have realised that, despite his or her honest belief that government policy had not changed, others might well take a different view, and the information which gives rise to the possible inference that there has been a change ought to be disclosed to Parliament. Parliament can then make its own judgment on the matter. In short, ministers' duty should be neither to knowingly *or recklessly* mislead Parliament. As Leigh and Lustgarten put it, the real issue is whether 'a minister, who, though not intending to deceive, has failed in his duty to inform Parliament for reasons that are found to be indefensible and illogical should remain in post?'[95] Tomkin agrees:

... should William Waldegrave have been allowed to have continued in office simply because he wrongly failed to realise that his answers and letters were misleading? ... What happened to the

---

93   Scott Report, para D4.55.
94   *Ibid*, para K8.5.
95   *Op cit*, 706.

days when ministers were constitutionally responsible to Parliament for their incompetence as well as for their dishonesty? ... Limiting ministers' culpability to situations where they have knowingly and deliberately lied to Parliament is confining their responsibilities too narrowly and the Scott report erred in not saying so ... If ministers are only constitutionally responsible when they know that Parliament is being misled, who is constitutionally responsible when ministers do not know?[96]

5   The FDA certainly saw difficulties with the new subjectivist formulation:

38. The new Civil Service Code makes it clear that Parliament must not *knowingly* be misled. Equally, in his evidence to the Scott Inquiry, and indeed to the Select Committee, Sir Robin Butler indicated that both ministers and civil servants may be justified in giving only half the picture. He did not confine such withholding of information to questions of national security, matters affecting the national economy, nor foreign affairs. The implication is that ministers may withhold information, provided that the answer that they give is not misleading.

39. But Sir Richard takes the argument further. He says ministers deliberately withheld information and that in his judgment the reason for this was a fear of public opposition to what was really happening. However, he does not say Parliament was deliberately misled.

40. The question is how this position can sit alongside the duty clearly laid out in *Questions of Procedure* to give Parliament, including its Select Committees and the public, as full information as possible about the policies, decision and actions of the Government, and not deceive or mislead Parliament and the public.[97]

Note
Recently, Stephen Byers sought to rely on the defence that he had not 'knowingly' misled Parliament after he had wrongly announced in February 2002 that his former press officer, Martin Sixsmith, had agreed terms for his resignation, when in fact this had not been agreed. Byers' story, seemingly accepted by Labour colleagues during a Commons debate in May 2002, was that this had been his genuine, though mistaken, understanding at the time from discussions with his permanent secretary. Byers refused to resign, or even apologise, stating that at all times he had acted in good faith, representing to Parliament – and to the public – the position as he believed it to be. He escaped censure by Parliament, but was forced to resign later in the month. The causes of his resignation were complex but, in part, came from a widespread perception that he had in fact been duplicitous. The lesson drawn by commentators was, however, that it was the press and not Parliament that had forced the resignation, by making Byers a liability for the government through constant, negative reportage which served to prevent transport policy from being anything other than a 'bad news' story whilst he was in charge of it.[98]

Misleading Parliament: the position of civil servants

Two questions arise here. First, what does a civil servant do if he or she is asked to draft answers to Parliamentary Questions which he or she considers misleading, or is instructed to withhold certain information from Select Committees? Secondly, if civil servants willingly collude with ministers to mislead Parliament, can they be brought to account? One of the extremely rare cases in which a civil servant actually went public

---

96   Tomkin, *op cit*, pp 43–44.
97   HC 313 (1995–96), 20 March 1996; FDA memorandum, paras 38–41.
98   See, eg, 'Pressure that proved too much for the rubber man', *The Guardian*, 29 May 2002.

with allegations of ministerial deception of Parliament was the celebrated case of Clive Ponting.

Geoffrey Marshall, 'Ministers, civil servants, and open government', in C Harlow (ed), *Public Law and Politics* (1986), pp 86–89

Mr Ponting, a civil servant in the Ministry of Defence, was charged with disclosing to a Member of Parliament official information without authority, the information in question being two documents about the conduct of naval operations in the South Atlantic and the sinking of the Argentinian cruiser *General Belgrano* in May 1982. It was conceded by the prosecution that national security had not been prejudiced by the communication of the documents. An argument about national security was however involved in the issue between Ponting and his ministerial superiors since it was a potential danger to national security that the Secretary of State eventually relied upon as his reason for declining to answer questions put by Mr Tam Dalyell MP, and it was Ponting's disagreement with his minister on the question of danger to national security that persuaded him that ministers were unnecessarily and improperly concealing the truth from the House of Commons.

The factual members that were the subject of the alleged deception of the House were, on the face of it and in isolation, not of great moment. They related to the details of the *Belgrano's* course at various times in relation to the British task force, the precise date at which the submarine *Conqueror* sighted the *Belgrano* and the making of certain changes in the naval rules of engagement, not revealed at the time they were made. In order to answer Mr Dalyell's questions, Mr Ponting was asked to draft replies for the minister. His draft replies were not used. In his book Mr Ponting notes that as a civil servant he was accustomed to having drafts rejected or modified. That was 'a fact of life in a bureaucracy'. But in this case ministers, he thought, had decided to mislead Parliament. Errors had been made in the statements given on the points raised in Mr Dalyell's question and the minister, instead of conceding them, was intending to choke off further inquiries and the junior minister, Mr John Stanley, was claiming erroneously that none of the questions could be answered on grounds of national security. It was, Mr Ponting relates, against all his training to disclose Government information. Yet as a civil servant he could not be a party to the deliberate deception of Parliament. He therefore sent Mr Dalyell an unsigned note saying that the information he sought was unclassified and that he should press his questions and later he sent the two documents. Mr Dalyell passed the documents to the Chairman of the Foreign Affairs Committee, who returned them to the Ministry of Defence, and the Attorney-General, with no prompting from Mr Heseltine or Mrs Thatcher, instituted proceedings.

... What then should Mr Ponting have done other than what he did? In describing his moment of truth he said that he wondered about appealing to someone outside the department since he saw that ministers were not likely to change their minds and accept his advice and since no other senior civil servant in the department had protested about the ministers' conduct, and 'I had received no support from those high up in the Department'. There is no suggestion in his book however that he had explicitly asked for support on the issue as it finally presented itself to him. As to the external appeal (to the Head of the Home Civil Service perhaps) he remarks that all the methods of effective protest were cut off by people already involved in the cover up. The manner in which this 'cutting off' took place however is not detailed. Mr Ponting added that he remembered a note by the Treasury to the Public Accounts Committee saying that an officer who without authority corrected misleading evidence by publishing the true facts to the Committee or to the House would not be in breach of the Official Secrets Act since the publication would amount to a proceeding in Parliament and be absolutely privileged. That makes it somewhat harder to understand why Mr Ponting, if no one in the civil service would listen to him, did not approach the Foreign Affairs Committee or its chairman directly asking them to investigate the allegations, if necessary saying publicly that he had done so. Given that in Mr Ponting's belief at the time there was no major departmental plot or sinister cover up, he was dealing with a ministerial misjudgment about the need to classify information. So leaking to Mr Dalyell or to some other opponent of the Government if it had been Mr Ponting's last desperate throw need not have been his first.

Notes

1   Until very recently, civil servants owed no general duty not to mislead Parliament or the public. For the first time, in the New Civil Service Code, it is stated (para 5) that civil servants 'must not knowingly mislead Parliament or the public'.[99] Moreover, as noted above, the new formulation of the Ministerial Code instructs Ministers that they should:

> similarly require civil servants who give evidence before Parliamentary Committees on their behalf and under their direction to be as helpful as possible in providing accurate, truthful and full information in accordance with the duties and responsibilities of civil servants as set out in the Civil Service Code.

Nevertheless, it is clear that, as Ms Symons (Director of the FDA) noted that,[100] if they asked to do so, or are aware of deception by ministers, they are in 'no circumstances' to go public with this information: 'the civil servant should not leak information to the British public'. Instead, civil servants have the right under the Code to appeal ultimately to the Civil Service Commissioners (paras 11 and 12) but only after departmental procedures have failed to resolve the issue. As Mr Dunabin explained,[101] civil servants do see this as a 'very substantial benefit ... because one cannot suppose that the ... Commissioners will turn down such an appeal simply because they think that the information which is not being released is embarrassing to ministers and their party policy ... [but only] if they [thought] ... it was not in the public interest, properly so defined for that information to be released'.

2   Of course, if civil servants do not complain, this may not always be for fear of the consequences to them. They may simply not be concerned about whether Parliament is being misled or not, as long as they are carrying out instructions. Civil servants interviewed by Scott were quite blunt about where their loyalties lay. Mark Higson, for example, said, 'It was simply a matter of us not telling the truth, of knowingly not telling the truth to the public and Parliament. The policy was bent and we concealed that policy'. In such cases, civil servants' lack of accountability to Parliament means that they can effectively escape being brought to account in any way for colluding with ministers to deceive. Under the present constitutional understanding, only ministers, not Parliament, can 'punish' civil servants. But whilst ministers may be prepared to discipline civil servants for errors of administration, they are hardly likely to punish civil servants for carrying out their instructions to draft incomplete or misleading answers to questions. Another lacuna in Parliamentary accountability is thus apparent.

---

99   This came into force on 1 January 1996; its full text appears at HL Deb, 9 January 1996, WA 21.
100 Before the Public Service Committee, HC 313 (1995–96), 20 March 1996, QQ 33–35.
101 *Ibid*, Q 35.

FURTHER READING

R Brazier, *Constitutional Practice* (1994)

R Brazier, *Ministers of the Crown* (1997)

R Crossman, *Diaries of a Cabinet Minister* (1975)

T Daintith and A Page, *The Executive in the Constitution: Structure, Autonomy, and Internal Control* (1999)

P Greer, 'The Next Steps initiative' (1992) Political Quarterly 63

C Harlow (ed), *Public Law and Politics* (1984)

S Hogg and K Jenkins, 'Effective government and effective accountability' (1999) Political Quarterly 139

N Lawson, *The View from No 11* (1992)

JF McEldowney and P McAuslan, *Law, Legitimacy and the Constitution* (1985)

JP Mackintosh, *The British Cabinet* (1977)

C Polidano, 'The bureaucrats who almost fell under a bus: a reassertion of ministerial responsibility?' (2000) Political Quarterly 177

R Pyper and L Robins (eds), *Governing the UK in the 1990s* (1995), Part I

M Sunkin and S Payne, *The Nature of the Crown* (1999)

Baroness Thatcher, *The Downing Street Years* (1993)

CHAPTER 3

OFFICIAL SECRECY AND ACCESS TO INFORMATION

INTRODUCTION

It has often been said that the UK is more obsessed with keeping government information secret than any other Western democracy.[1] It is clearly advantageous for the party in power to be able to control the flow of information in order to prevent public scrutiny of certain official decisions and in order to be able to release information selectively at convenient moments.

The British government has available a number of methods of keeping official information secret, including use of the doctrine of Public Interest Immunity (PII), the deterrent effect of criminal sanctions under the Official Secrets Act 1989, the Civil Service Conduct Code,[2] around 80 statutory provisions engendering secrecy in various areas and the civil action for breach of confidence. (The use of the doctrine of confidence in this context is discussed in Part VI Chapter 2.) The situation of the civil servant in the UK who believes that disclosure as to a certain state of affairs is necessary in order to serve the public interest may therefore be contrasted with the situation of his or her counterpart in the US, where he or she would receive protection from detrimental action flowing from whistle-blowing[3] under the Civil Service Reform Act 1978. A weak form of a public interest defence might have been adopted under proposals in the government White Paper on freedom of information, published in July 1993.[4] It was proposed that the disclosure of information would not be penalised if the information was not 'genuinely confidential'. But when the Labour government introduced the Public Interest Disclosure Act 1998, crown servants involved in security and intelligence activities, or those whose 'whistle-blowing' breaches the 1989 Act, were expressly excluded from its ambit, leaving them unprotected from employment detriment.

The justification traditionally put forward for maintaining a climate of secrecy, which goes beyond protecting specific public interests such as national security, is that freedom of information would adversely affect 'ministerial accountability'. In other words, ministers are responsible for the actions of civil servants in their departments and therefore must be able to control the flow of information emanating from the department in question. However, it is usually seen as essential to democracy that government should allow a reasonably free flow of information so that citizens can be informed as to the government process and can therefore assess government decisions in the light of all the available facts, thereby participating fully in the workings of the democracy. A number of groups, including the Campaign for Freedom of Information,

---

1 See, eg, G Robertson, *Freedom, the Individual and the Law* (1989) pp 129–31.
2 See G Drewry and T Butcher, *The Civil Service Today* (1991). It should be pointed out that the Civil Service Code, which came into force on 1 January 1996, contains a partial 'whistle-blowing' provision in paras 11–12.
3 For discussion of the situation of UK and US civil servants and developments in the area, see Y Cripps, 'Disclosure in the public interest: the predicament of the public sector employee' [1983] PL 600; G Zellick, 'Whistle-blowing in US law' [1987] PL 311–13; JG Starke (1989) 63 ALJ 592–94.
4 *Open Government* (1993). See below, pp 625–26, for discussion.

have therefore advocated freedom of information and more 'open' government in Britain, as in most other democracies. They accept that certain categories of information should be exempt from disclosure, but argue that those categories should be as restricted as possible compatible with the needs of the interest protected, and that the categorisation of any particular piece of information should be open to challenge.

The citizen's 'right to know' is recognised in most democracies including the US, Canada, Australia, New Zealand, Denmark, Sweden, Holland, Norway, Greece and France. In such countries, the general principle of freedom of information is subject to exceptions where information falls into specific categories. Perhaps responding to the general acceptance of freedom of information, there was a shift in the attitude of the Conservative government of 1992–97 to freedom of information in the UK: that is, the principle was accepted, but the traditional stance as to the role of the law hardly changed. The UK has traditionally resisted freedom of information legislation and, until 1989, criminalised the unauthorised disclosure of any official information at all, however trivial, under s 2 of the Official Secrets Act 1911, thereby creating a climate of secrecy in the Civil Service which greatly hampered the efforts of those who wished to obtain and publish information about the workings of government. The 1989 Official Secrets Act decriminalised the disclosure of a range of government information, but did not provide rights of access to that information. Such rights were finally provided under the Freedom of Information Act 2000 (FoI Act) which therefore signalled a dramatic break with the traditional culture of secrecy: 'the principle that communication was the privilege of the State rather than of the citizen was at last ... reversed.'[5] The Act, introduced by the current Labour government, extends well beyond government departments. The part it may play once it is fully in force (by 2005) in introducing a climate of openness in the Civil Service, and in public authorities more generally, is one of the central concerns of this chapter.

OFFICIAL SECRECY

Introduction

During the 19th century, as government departments grew larger and handled more official information, the problem of confidentiality grew more acute. Internal circulars such as the Treasury minute entitled 'The premature disclosure of official information' 1873 urged secrecy on all members of government departments. The perceived need to enforce secrecy led to the passing of the Official Secrets Act 1889 which made it an offence for a person wrongfully to communicate information obtained owing to his employment as a civil servant. However, the government of the time grew dissatisfied with this measure; under its terms the state had the burden of proving both *mens rea* and that the disclosure was not in the interests of the state. It was thought that a stronger measure was needed and eventually the government passed the Official Secrets Act 1911, s 2(1) of which provided:

> ... If any person having in his possession or control [any information ...] which has been entrusted in confidence to him by any person holding office under His Majesty or which he has obtained [or to which he has had access] owing to his position as a person who is or has held of office under

---

5   D Vincent, *The Culture of Secrecy, Britain 1832–1998* (1998), p 321.

His Majesty, or as a person who holds or has held a contract made on behalf of His Majesty, or as a person who is or has been employed under a person who holds or has held such an office or contract ... (a) communicates the [code word, pass word,] sketch, plan, model, article, note, document, or information to any person, other than a person to whom he is authorised to communicate it, or a person to whom it is in the interest of the state his duty to communicate it, ... that person shall be guilty of a misdemeanour.

The criticism frequently levelled at s 2 was that it lacked any provision regarding the substance of the information disclosed, so that technically it criminalised, for example, disclosure of the colour of the carpet in a minister's office. There were surprisingly few prosecutions under s 2; it seems likely that it created an acceptance of secrecy in the Civil Service which tended to preclude disclosure. In one of the few cases which did come to court, *R v Fell* [1963] Crim LR 207,[6] the Court of Appeal confirmed that liability was not dependent on the contents of the document in question or on whether the disclosure would have an effect prejudicial to the interests of the state.

The decision in *R v Ponting* [1985] Crim LR 318[7] is usually credited with finally bringing about the demise of s 2.[8] Clive Ponting, a senior civil servant in the Ministry of Defence, was responsible for policy on the operational activities of the Royal Navy at a time when Opposition MPs, particularly Tam Dalyell, were pressing the government for information relating to the sinking of the *General Belgrano* in the Falklands conflict. Michael Heseltine, then Secretary of State for Defence, decided to withhold such information from Parliament and therefore did not use a reply to Parliamentary Questions drafted by Ponting. He used instead a much briefer version of it and circulated a confidential minute indicating that answers on the rules of engagement in the Falklands conflict should not be given to questions put by the Parliamentary Select Committee on Foreign Affairs. Feeling that Opposition MPs were being prevented from doing their job of scrutinising the workings of government, Ponting sent the unused reply and the minute anonymously to the Labour MP, Tam Dalyell, who disclosed the documents to the press.

Ponting was charged with the offence of communicating information under s 2. His defence rested on the provision in s 2(1)(a) of the 1911 Act that the information had been communicated 'to a person to whom it is in the interests of the state his duty to communicate it, or to a person to whom it is in the interests of the state his duty to communicate it'. The judge directed the jury that 'duty' meant official duty, meaning the duty imposed upon Mr Ponting by his position. In relation to the words, 'in the interests of the state', the judge said:

---

6   See David Hooper, *Official Secrets* (1987) for history of the use of s 2.

7   See also [1985] PL 203, at 212 and [1986] Crim LR 491.

8   It may be noted that, although a conviction was obtained in *R v Tisdall* (1984) *The Times*, 26 March, the decision created some adverse publicity for the government due to what was perceived as a draconian use of s 2. Sarah Tisdall worked in the Foreign Secretary's private office and in the course of her duties came across documents relating to the delivery of cruise missiles to the RAF base at Greenham Common. She discovered proposals to delay the announcement of their delivery until after it had occurred and to make the announcement in Parliament at the end of Question Time in order to avoid answering questions. Considering that this political subterfuge was morally wrong, she leaked the documents to *The Guardian* but they were eventually traced back to her. She pleaded guilty to an offence under s 2 and received a prison sentence of six months – an outcome which was generally seen as harsh: see Cripps, *op cit*.

I direct you that these words mean the policies of the state as they were in July 1984 ... and not the policies of the state as Mr Ponting, Mr Dalyell, you or I might think they ought to have been ... The policies of the state mean the policies laid down by those recognised organs of Government and authority ... While it has [the support of a majority in the House of Commons], the Government and its policies are for the time being the policies of the state.

The judge in *Ponting* effectively directed the jury to convict. Despite this direction they acquitted, presumably feeling that Ponting should have a defence if he was acting in the public interest in trying to prevent government suppression of matters of public interest. The prosecution and its outcome provoked a large amount of adverse publicity, the public perceiving it as an attempt at a cover-up which had failed, not because the judge showed integrity but because the jury did.[9]

The outcome of the *Ponting* case may have influenced the decision not to prosecute Cathy Massiter, a former officer in the security service, in respect of her claims in a Channel 4 programme screened in March 1985 (*MI5's Official Secrets*) that MI5 had tapped the telephones of trade union members and placed leading CND members under surveillance.[10] Section 2's perceived lack of credibility may also have been a factor in the decision to bring civil as opposed to criminal proceedings against *The Guardian* and *The Observer* in respect of their disclosure of Peter Wright's allegations in *Spycatcher*: civil proceedings for breach of confidence were in many ways more convenient and less risky than a s 2 prosecution (see Part VI Chapter 2, pp 908–18).

There is a long history of proposals for the reform of s 2. The Franks Committee, which was set up in response to Caulfield J's comments in *R v Aitken* (1971), recommended that s 2 should be replaced by narrower provisions which took into account the nature of the information disclosed.[11] The Franks proposals formed the basis of the government's White Paper on which the Official Secrets Act 1989 was based.

The Official Secrets Act 1989[12]

Once the decision to reform the area of official secrecy had been taken, an opportunity was created for radical change which could have included freedom of information legislation along the lines of the instruments in America and Canada. However, it was made clear from the outset that the legislation was unconcerned with freedom of information.[13] It de-criminalises disclosure of some official information, although an official who makes such disclosure may of course face an action for breach of confidence as well as disciplinary proceedings, but it will not allow the release of any

---

9 For comment on the case, see C Ponting, *The Right to Know* (1985); G Drewry, 'The *Ponting* case' [1985] PL 203.

10 The IBA banned the programme pending the decision as to whether Massiter and the producers would be prosecuted. The decision not to prosecute was announced by Sir Michael Havers on 5 March 1985. An enquiry into telephone tapping by Lord Bridge reported on 6 March that all authorised taps had been properly authorised. This of course did not address the allegation that some tapping had been carried out, although unauthorised.

11 Report of the Committee on s 2 of the Official Secrets Act 1911, Cmnd 5104; see W Birtles, 'Big Brother knows best: the Franks Report on s 2 of the Official Secrets Act' (1973) PL 100.

12 For comment on the 1989 Act see: S Palmer,, 'Tightening secrecy law' [1990] PL 243; J Griffith, 'The Official Secrets Act 1989' (1989) 16 JLS 273; D Feldman, *Civil Liberties and Human Rights*, 2nd edn (2002), Chapter 15.3; Bailey, Harris and Ormerod (2001), Chapter 8.2.

13 See White Paper on s 2, Cmnd 7285; Green Paper on Freedom of Information, Cmnd 7520; White Paper, Reform of the Official Secrets Act 1911, Cmnd 408.

official documents into the public domain. Thus, claims made, for example, by Douglas Hurd (the then Home Secretary) that it is 'a great liberalising measure' clearly rest on other aspects of the Act. Aspects which are usually viewed as liberalising features include the categorisation of information covered, the introduction of tests for harm, the *mens rea* requirement of ss 5 and 6, the defences available, and decriminalisation of the receiver of information. In all these respects the Act differs from its predecessor, but it is arguable that the changes have not brought about any real liberalisation. Other features of the Act have also attracted criticism: the categories of information covered are very wide and do not admit of challenge to the categorisation; the Act contains no defences of public interest or of prior disclosure, and no general requirement to prove *mens rea*.

Official Secrets Act 1989

Security and intelligence

1.–(1) A person who is or has been—

    (a) a member of the security and intelligence services; or

    (b) a person notified that he is subject to the provisions of this subsection,

is guilty of an offence if without lawful authority he discloses any information, document or other article relating to security or intelligence which is or has been in his possession by virtue of his position as a member of any of those services or in the course of his work while the notification is or was in force.

. . .

    (3) A person who is or has been a Crown servant or government contractor is guilty of an offence if without lawful authority he makes a damaging disclosure of any information, document or other article relating to security or intelligence which is or has been in his possession by virtue of his position as such but otherwise than as mentioned in subsection (1) above.

    (4) For the purposes of subsection (3) above a disclosure is damaging if—

    (a) it causes damage to the work of, or of any part of, the security and intelligence services; or

    (b) it is of information or a document or other article which is such that its unauthorised disclosure would be likely to cause such damage or which falls within a class or description of information, documents or articles the unauthorised disclosure of which would be likely to have that effect.

    (5) It is a defence for a person charged with an offence under this section to prove that at the time of the alleged offence he did not know, and had no reasonable cause to believe, that the information, document or article in question related to security or intelligence or, in the case of an offence under subsection (3), that the disclosure would be damaging within the meaning of that subsection.

. . .

    (9) In this section 'security or intelligence' means the work of, or in support of, the security and intelligence services or any part of them, and references to information relating to security or intelligence include references to information held or transmitted by those services or by persons in support of, or of any part of, them.

Defence

2.–(1) A person who is or has been a Crown servant or government contractor is guilty of an offence if without lawful authority he makes a damaging disclosure of any information, document or other article relating to defence which is or has been in his possession by virtue of his position as such.

(2) For the purposes of subsection (1) above a disclosure is damaging if—

(a) it damages the capability of, or of any part of, the armed forces of the Crown to carry out their tasks or leads to loss of life or injury to members of those forces or serious damage to the equipment or installations of those forces; or

(b) otherwise than as mentioned in paragraph (a) above, it endangers the interests of the United Kingdom abroad, seriously obstructs the promotion or protection by the United Kingdom of those interests or endangers the safety of British citizens abroad; or

(c) it is of information or of a document or article which is such that its unauthorised disclosure would be likely to have any of those effects.

(3) It is a defence for a person charged with an offence under this section to prove that at the time of the alleged offence he did not know and had no reasonable cause to believe, that the information, document or article in question related to defence or that its disclosure would be damaging within the meaning of subsection (1) above.

...

International relations

3.–(1) A person who is or has been a Crown servant or government contractor is guilty of an offence if without lawful authority he makes a damaging disclosure of—

(a) any information, document or other article relating to international relations; or

(b) any confidential information, document or other article which was obtained from a state other than the United Kingdom or an international organisation,

being information or a document or article which is or has been in his possession by virtue of his position as a Crown servant or government contractor.

(2) For the purposes of subsection (1) above a disclosure is damaging if—

(a) it endangers the interests of the United Kingdom abroad, seriously obstructs the promotion or protection by the United Kingdom of those interests or endangers the safety of British citizens abroad; or

(b) it is of information or of a document or article which is such that its unauthorised disclosure would be likely to have any of those effects.

(3) In the case of information or a document or article within subsection (1)(b) above—

(a) the fact that it is confidential; or

(b) its nature or contents, may be sufficient to establish for the purposes of subsection (2)(b) above that the information, document or article is such that its unauthorised disclosure would be likely to have any of the effects there mentioned.

(4) It is a defence for a person charged with an offence under this section to prove that at the time of the alleged offence he did not know, and had no reasonable cause to believe, that the information, document or article in question was such as is mentioned in subsection (1) above or that its disclosure would be damaging within the meaning of that subsection.

(5) In this section 'international relations' means the relations between states, between international organisations or between one or more states and one or more such organisations and includes any matter relating to a state other than the United Kingdom or to an international organisation which is capable of affecting the relations of the United Kingdom with another state or with an international organisation.

Crime and special investigation powers

4.–(1) A person who is or has been a Crown servant or government contractor is guilty of an offence if without lawful authority he discloses any information, document or other article to which this section applies and which is or has been in his possession by virtue of his position as such.

(2) This section applies to any information, document or other article—

    (a) the disclosure of which—

        (i) results in the commission of an offence; or

        (ii) facilitates an escape from legal custody or the doing of any other act prejudicial to the safekeeping of persons in legal custody; or

        (iii) impedes the prevention or detection of offences or the apprehension or prosecution of suspected offenders; or

    (b) which is such that its unauthorised disclosure would be likely to have any of those effects.

(3) This section also applies to—

    (a) any information obtained by reason of the interception of any communication in obedience to a warrant issued under section 2 of the Interception of Communications Act 1985 [or under the authority of an interception warrant under section 5 of the Regulation of Investigatory Powers Act 2000],[14] any information relating to the obtaining of information by reason of any such interception and any document or other article which is or has been used or held for use in, or has been obtained by reason of, any such interception; and

    (b) any information obtained by reason of action authorised by a warrant issued under section 3 of the Security Service Act 1989 [or under section 5 of the Intelligence Services Act 1994 or by an authorization under section 7 of that Act],[15] any information relating to the obtaining of information by reason of any such action and any document or other article

which is or has been used or held for use in, or has been obtained by reason of, any such action.

(4) It is a defence for a person charged with an offence under this section in respect of a disclosure falling within subsection (2)(a) above to prove that at the time of the alleged offence he did not know, and had no reasonable cause to believe, that the disclosure would have any of the effects there mentioned.

(5) It is a defence for a person charged with an offence under this section in respect of any other disclosure to prove that at the time of the alleged offence he did not know, and had no reasonable cause to believe, that the information, document or article in question was information or a document or article to which this section applies.

Information resulting from unauthorised disclosures or entrusted in confidence

5.–(1) Subsection (2) below applies where—

    (a) any information, document or other article protected against disclosure by the foregoing provisions of this Act has come into a person's possession as a result of having been—

---

14 Inserted by Sched 4, para 5 to the 2000 Act.
15 Inserted by Sched 4, para 4 to the 1994 Act.

      (i) disclosed (whether to him or another) by a Crown servant or government contractor without lawful authority; or

      (ii) entrusted to him by a Crown servant or government contractor on terms requiring it to be held in confidence or in circumstances in which the Crown servant or government contractor could reasonably expect that it would be so held;

      (iii) disclosed (whether to him or another) without lawful authority by a person to whom it was entrusted as mentioned in sub-paragraph (ii) above; and

    (b) the disclosure without lawful authority of the information, document or article by the person into whose possession it has come is not an offence under any of those provisions.

(2) Subject to subsections (3) and (4) below, the person into whose possession the information, document or article has come is guilty of an offence if he discloses it without lawful authority knowing, or having reasonable cause to believe, that it is protected against disclosure by the foregoing provisions of this Act and that it has come into his possession as mentioned in subsection (1) above.

(3) In the case of information or a document or article protected against disclosure by sections 1 to 3 above, a person does not commit an offence under subsection (2) above unless—

    (a) the disclosure by him is damaging; and

    (b) he makes it knowing, or having reasonable cause to believe, that

it would be damaging; and the question whether a disclosure is damaging shall be determined for the purposes of this subsection as it would be in relation to a disclosure of that information, document or article by a Crown servant in contravention of sections 1(3), 2(1) or 3(1) above.

    ...

(5) For the purposes of this section information or a document or article is protected against disclosure by the foregoing provisions of this Act—

    (a) it relates to security or intelligence, defence or international relations within the meaning of section 1, 2 or 3 above or is such as is mentioned in section 3(1)(b) above; or

    (b) it is information or a document or article to which section 4 above applies and information or a document or article is protected against disclosure by sections 1 to 3 above if it falls within paragraph (a) above.

(6) A person is guilty of an offence if without lawful authority he discloses any information, document or other article which he knows, or has reasonable cause to believe, to have come into his possession as a result of a contravention of section 1 of the Official Secrets Act 1911.

Information entrusted in confidence to other states or international organisations

6.–(1) This section applies where—

    (a) any information, document or other article which—

      (i) relates to security or intelligence, defence or international relations; and

      (ii) has been communicated in confidence by or on behalf of the United Kingdom to another state or to an international organisation,

    has come into a person's possession as a result of having been disclosed (whether to him or another) without the authority of that state or organisation or, in the case of an organisation, of a member of it; and

(b) the disclosure without lawful authority of the information, document or article by the person into whose possession it has come is not an offence under any of the foregoing provisions of this Act.

(2) Subject to subsection (3) below, the person into whose possession the information, document or article has come is guilty of an offence if he makes a damaging disclosure of it knowing, or having reasonable cause to believe, that it is such as is mentioned in subsection (1) above, that it has come into his possession as there mentioned and that its disclosure would be damaging.

(3) A person does not commit an offence under subsection (2) above if the information, document or article is disclosed by him with lawful authority or has previously been made available to the public with the authority of the state or organisation concerned or, in the case of an organisation, of a member of it.

...

(5) For the purposes of this section information or a document or article is communicated in confidence if it is communicated on terms requiring it to be held in confidence or in circumstances in which the person communicating it could reasonably expect that it would be so held.

Authorised disclosures

7.–(1) For the purposes of this Act a disclosure by—

(a) a Crown servant; or

(b) a person, not being a Crown servant or government contractor in whose case a notification for the purposes of section 1(1) above is in force,

is made with lawful authority if, and only if, it is made in accordance with his official duty.

(2) For the purposes of this Act a disclosure by a government contractor is made with lawful authority if, and only if, it is made—

(a) in accordance with an official authorisation; or

(b) for the purposes of the functions by virtue of which he is a government contractor and without contravening an official restriction.

(3) For the purposes of this Act a disclosure made by any other person is made with lawful authority if, and only if, it is made—

(a) to a Crown servant for the purposes of his functions as such; or

(b) in accordance with an official authorisation.

(4) It is a defence for a person charged with an offence under any of the foregoing provisions of this Act to prove that at the time of the alleged offence he believed that he had lawful authority to make the disclosure in question and had no reasonable cause to believe otherwise.

(5) In this section 'official authorisation' and 'official restriction' mean, subject to subsection (6) below, an authorisation or restriction duly given or imposed by a Crown servant or government contractor or by or on behalf of a prescribed body or a body of a prescribed class.

(6) In relation to section 6 above 'official authorisation' includes an authorisation duly given by or on behalf of the state or organisation concerned or, in the case of an organisation, a member of it.

...

Penalties

10.–(1) A person guilty of an offence under any provision of this Act other than section 8(1), (4) or (5) shall be liable—

    (a) on conviction on indictment, to imprisonment for a term not exceeding two years or a fine or both;

    (b) on summary conviction, to imprisonment for a term not exceeding six months or a fine not exceeding the statutory maximum or both.

  (2) A person guilty of an offence under section 8(1), (4) or (5) above shall be liable on summary conviction to imprisonment for a term not exceeding three months or a fine not exceeding level 5 on the standard scale or both.

    . . .

'Crown servant' and 'government contractor'

12.–(1) In this Act 'Crown servant' means—

    (a) a Minister of the Crown;

    (a)(a) a member of the Scottish Executive or a junior Scottish Minister;[16]

    (b) . . .[17]

    (c) any person employed in the civil service of the Crown, including Her Majesty's Diplomatic Service, Her Majesty's Overseas Civil Service, the civil service of Northern Ireland and the Northern Ireland Court Service;

    (d) any member of the naval, military or air forces of the Crown including any person employed by an association established for the purposes of the Reserve Forces Act 1996;

    (e) any constable and any other person employed or appointed in or for the purposes of any police force (including a police force within the meaning of the Police Act (Northern Ireland) 1970) [or of the National Criminal Intelligence Service or the National Crime Squad];[18]

    (f) any person who is a member or employee of a prescribed body or a body of a prescribed class and either is prescribed for the purposes of this paragraph or belongs to a prescribed class of members or employees of any such body;

    (g) any person who is the holder of a prescribed office or who is an employee of such a holder and either is prescribed for the purposes of this paragraph or belongs to a prescribed class of such employees.

  (2) In this Act 'government contractor' means, subject to subsection (3) below, any person who is not a Crown servant but who provides, or is employed in the provision of, goods or services—

    (a) for the purposes of any Minister or person mentioned in paragraph (a) or (b) of subsection (1) above, [of any office-holder in the Scottish Administration,][19] of any of the services, forces or bodies mentioned in that subsection or of the holder of any office prescribed under that subsection; or

    [(a)(a) for the purpose of the National Assembly for Wales];[20]

---

16 Inserted by the Scotland Act 1998, Sched 8, para 26(2),(3).
17 Repealed by the Northern Ireland Act 1998, Sched 13, para 9(2).
18 Inserted by the Police Act 1997, Sched 9, para 62.
19 Inserted by the Scotland Act 1998, Sched 8, para 26(2),(3).
20 Inserted by the Government of Wales Act 1998, Sched 12, para 30.

(b) under an agreement or arrangement certified by the Secretary of State as being one to which the government of a state other than the United Kingdom or an international organisation is a party or which is subordinate to, or made for the purposes of implementing, any such agreement or arrangement.

Lord Advocate v Scotsman Publications Ltd [1989] 2 All ER 852, 859, 860, 861, HL

This decision is not on the 1989 Act but concerns the civil action for breach of confidence. However, it indicates the approach that may be taken under s 5 of the 1989 Act.

Lord Templeman: My Lords, in this appeal the Lord Advocate, acting on behalf of the Crown, claims to restrain the respondent newspapers and television companies from disclosing certain information contained in a book written by one Cavendish, that information having been obtained by him in the course of his employment with the British security and intelligence services.

Any such restraint is an interference with the right of expression safeguarded by the Convention for the Protection of Human Rights and Fundamental Freedoms, Article 10 ...

The question ... is whether the restraint sought to be imposed on the respondents is 'necessary in a democratic society in the interests of national security' [para 2 of Article 10]. Similar questions were considered in *A-G v Guardian Newspapers Ltd (No 2)* [1988] 3 All ER 345, [1988] 3 WLR 776 (the *Spycatcher* case) but at that time Parliament had not provided any answer to the questions posed by the conflict between the freedom of expression and the requirement of national security.

In my opinion it is for Parliament to determine the restraints on freedom of expression which are necessary in a democratic society. The courts of this country should follow any guidance contained in a statute. If that guidance is inconsistent with the requirements of the convention then that will be a matter for the convention authorities and for the UK Government. It will not be a matter for the courts.

The guidance of Parliament has now been provided in the Official Secrets Act 1989. In my opinion the civil jurisdiction of the courts of this country to grant an injunction restraining a breach of confidence at the suit of the Crown should not, in principle, be exercised in a manner different from or more severe than any appropriate restriction which Parliament has imposed in the 1989 Act ...

In my opinion the respondents fall into the category described by s 5.

The information derived from Cavendish which the respondents may wish to publish and disclose is information embedded in a book of memoirs by Cavendish. Part of that book relates to the period between 1948 and 1953 when Cavendish was a security employee and is protected against disclosure by s 1 of the 1989 Act. The Crown concedes, however, that publication of that information by the respondents will not cause or be likely to cause damage to the work of the security or intelligence services, presumably because the information is inaccurate or unenlightening or insignificant. ... Nevertheless, the Crown contends that it is entitled to restrain the respondents from publishing this harmless information because the information is contained in the memoirs of a security employee. It is said that the publication of harmless information derived from a former security employee and protected by s 1 against disclosure by him, though not damaging in itself, would cause harm by encouraging other security employees to make disclosures in breach of s 1 of the 1989 Act and by raising doubts as to the reliability of the security service.

... If the 1989 Act had been in force when Cavendish circulated his book to a chosen band of readers, he would have committed an offence under s 1 of the Act notwithstanding that the information disclosed in his book is harmless. But it does not follow that third parties commit an offence if they disclose harmless information. Were it otherwise, the distinction between an offence by a security employee and an offence by a third party which appears from the 1989 Act would be eradicated. A security employee can commit an offence if he discloses any information. A third party is only guilty of an offence if the information is damaging in the sense defined by the Act.

I would affirm the decision of the Court of Session and dismiss the appeal of the Crown.

R v Shayler [2003] I AC 247; [2002] 2 WLR 754; [2002] 2 All ER 477, HL

This is a very significant decision since it indicates that ss 1(1) and 4(1) of the 1989 Act are not incompatible with Article 10 scheduled in the Human Rights Act 1998.[21] It is the only decision of the House of Lords on the 1989 Act. The facts and legal background appear in the speech of Lord Bingham.

LORD BINGHAM OF CORNHILL

My Lords,

1. Mr David Shayler, the appellant, is a former member of the Security Service. He has been indicted on three counts charging him with unlawful disclosure of documents and information contrary to sections 1 and 4 of the Official Secrets Act 1989. Moses J, exercising a power conferred by section 29(1) of the Criminal Procedure and Investigations Act 1996, ordered that a preparatory hearing be held before him. At that hearing the judge ruled under section 31(3)(b) of that Act that no public interest defence was open to the appellant under those sections, which he held to be compatible with article 10 of the European Convention for the Protection of Human Rights and Fundamental Freedoms. The appellant appealed to the Court of Appeal (Criminal Division) which upheld those rulings. The appellant now challenges these rulings of the judge and the Court of Appeal before the House.

. . .

The facts

5. On 24 August 1997, The Mail on Sunday published an article written by the appellant himself (according to the by-line) and a number of other articles by journalists purporting to be based on information disclosed by the appellant. The prosecution allege that the appellant was paid a substantial sum of money by the newspaper for these activities. The prosecution also allege that the information contained in and referred to in the articles relates to matters of security and intelligence to which the appellant could only have had access by reason of his employment with the service.

6. In reply to the charge he said: 'I have been living in Paris for three years and I have decided voluntarily to return to Britain to face charges under the Official Secrets Act. . . . Any disclosures made by me were in the public and national interests. In my defence I will rely on my right of freedom of expression as guaranteed by the common law, the Human Rights Act and Article 10 of the European Convention on Human Rights.'

. . .

8. At the preparatory hearing before the judge the first issue was whether, in law, the appellant would be entitled to be acquitted of the charges against him if (as he asserted on his arrest) his disclosures had (or, one should add, might have) been made in the public and national interest.

. . .

20. It is in my opinion plain, giving sections 1(1)(a) and 4(1) and (3)(a) their natural and ordinary meaning and reading them in the context of the OSA 1989 as a whole, that a defendant prosecuted under these sections is not entitled to be acquitted if he shows that it was or that he believed that it was in the public or national interest to make the disclosure in question or if the jury conclude that it may have been or that the defendant may have believed it to be in the public or national interest to make the disclosure in question. The sections impose no obligation on the prosecution to prove that the disclosure was not in the public interest and give the defendant no

21   For full discussion of the Human Rights Act 1998, see Part VI Chapter 1, pp 855–903.

opportunity to show that the disclosure was in the public interest or that he thought it was. The sections leave no room for doubt, and if they did the 1988 white paper quoted above, which is a legitimate aid to construction, makes the intention of Parliament clear beyond argument.

The right to free expression

21. The fundamental right of free expression has been recognised at common law for very many years: see, among many other statements to similar effect, *Attorney General v Guardian Newspapers Ltd* [1987] 1 WLR 1248, 1269B, 1320G; *Attorney General v Guardian Newspapers Ltd (No 2)* [1990] 1 AC 109, 178E, 218D, 220C, 226A, 283E; *R v Secretary of State for the Home Department, Ex p Simms* [2000] 2 AC 115, 126E; *McCartan Turkington Breen v Times Newspapers Ltd* [2001] 2 AC 277, 290G-291B. Modern democratic government means government of the people by the people for the people. But there can be no government by the people if they are ignorant of the issues to be resolved, the arguments for and against different solutions and the facts underlying those arguments. The business of government is not an activity about which only those professionally engaged are entitled to receive information and express opinions. It is, or should be, a participatory process. But there can be no assurance that government is carried out for the people unless the facts are made known, the issues publicly ventilated. Sometimes, inevitably, those involved in the conduct of government, as in any other walk of life, are guilty of error, incompetence, misbehaviour, dereliction of duty, even dishonesty and malpractice. Those concerned may very strongly wish that the facts relating to such matters are not made public. Publicity may reflect discredit on them or their predecessors. It may embarrass the authorities. It may impede the process of administration. Experience however shows, in this country and elsewhere, that publicity is a powerful disinfectant. Where abuses are exposed, they can be remedied. The role of the press in exposing abuses and miscarriages of justice has been a potent and honourable one. But the press cannot expose that of which it is denied knowledge.

22. Despite the high value placed by the common law on freedom of expression, it was not until incorporation of the European Convention into our domestic law by the Human Rights Act 1998 that this fundamental right was underpinned by statute. Section 12 of the 1998 Act reflects the central importance which attaches to the right to freedom of expression. The European Court of Human Rights for its part has not wavered in asserting the fundamental nature of this right. In paragraph 52 of its judgment in *Vogt v Germany (1995) 21 EHRR 205* the court said:

> (1) Freedom of expression constitutes one of the essential foundations of a democratic society and one of the basic conditions for its progress and each individual's self-fulfilment. Subject to article 10(2), it is applicable not only to 'information' or ' ideas' that are favourably received or regarded as inoffensive or as a matter of indifference, but also to those that offend, shock or disturb; such are the demands of that pluralism, tolerance and broadmindedness without which there is no 'democratic society'.

It is unnecessary to multiply citations to the same effect. Thus for purposes of the present proceedings the starting point must be that the appellant is entitled if he wishes to disclose information and documents in his possession unless the law imposes a valid restraint upon his doing so.

23. Despite the high importance attached to it, the right to free expression was never regarded in domestic law as absolute. The European Convention similarly recognises that the right is not absolute: article 10(2) qualifies the broad language of article 10(1) by providing, so far as relevant to this case:

> The exercise of these freedoms, since it carries with it duties and responsibilities, may be subject to such formalities, conditions, restrictions or penalties as are prescribed by law and are necessary in a democratic society, in the interests of national security, territorial integrity or public safety, for the prevention of disorder or crime, ..., for the protection of the ... rights of others, for preventing the disclosure of information received in confidence ...

It is plain from the language of article 10(2), and the European Court has repeatedly held, that any national restriction on freedom of expression can be consistent with article 10(2) only if it is prescribed by law, is directed to one or more of the objectives specified in the article and is shown by the state concerned to be necessary in a democratic society. 'Necessary' has been strongly interpreted: it is not synonymous with 'indispensable', neither has it the flexibility of such expressions as 'admissible','ordinary','useful','reasonable' or 'desirable': *Handyside v United Kingdom* (1976) I EHRR 737, 754, para 48. One must consider whether the interference complained of corresponded to a pressing social need, whether it was proportionate to the legitimate aim pursued and whether the reasons given by the national authority to justify it are relevant and sufficient under article 10(2): *The Sunday Times v United Kingdom* (1979) 2 EHRR 245, 277–278, para 62.

24 ... It was common ground below, in my view, rightly, that the relevant restriction was prescribed by law. It is on the question of necessity, pressing social need and proportionality that the real issue between the parties arises.

25. There is much domestic authority pointing to the need for a security or intelligence service to be secure. ... members of the service will feel unable to rely on each other; those upon whom the service relies as sources of information will feel unable to rely on their identity remaining secret; and foreign countries will decline to entrust their own secrets to an insecure recipient: see, for example, *Attorney General v Guardian Newspapers Ltd (No 2)* [1990] I AC 109, 118C, 213H–214B, 259A, 265F; *Attorney General v Blake* [2001] I AC 268, 287D–F. In the *Guardian Newspapers Ltd (No 2)* case, at p 269E–G, Lord Griffiths expressed the accepted rule very pithily:

> The Security and Intelligence Services are necessary for our national security. They are, and must remain, secret services if they are to operate efficiently. The only practical way to achieve this objective is a brightline rule that forbids any member or ex-member of the service to publish any material relating to his service experience unless he has had the material cleared by his employers. ... What may appear to the writer to be trivial may in fact be the one missing piece in the jigsaw sought by some hostile intelligence agency.

26. The need to preserve the secrecy of information relating to intelligence and military operations in order to counter terrorism, criminal activity, hostile activity and subversion has been recognised by the European Commission and the Court in relation to complaints made under article 10 and other articles under the convention: see *Engel v The Netherlands (No I)* (1976) I EHRR 647, paras 100–103; *Klass v Federal Republic of Germany* (1978) 2 EHRR 214, para 48; *Leander v Sweden* (1987) 9 EHRR 433, para 59; *Hadjianastassiou v Greece* (1992) 16 EHRR 219, paras 45–47; *Esbester v United Kingdom* (1993) 18 EHRR CD 72, CD 74; *Brind v United Kingdom* (1994) 18 EHRR CD 76, CD 83–84; *Murray v United Kingdom* (1994) 19 EHRR 193, para 58; *Vereniging Weekblad Bluf! v The Netherlands* (1995) 20 EHRR 189, paras 35, 40. The thrust of these decisions and judgments has not been to discount or disparage the need for strict and enforceable rules but to insist on adequate safeguards to ensure that the restriction does not exceed what is necessary to achieve the end in question. The acid test is whether, in all the circumstances, the interference with the individual's convention right prescribed by national law is greater than is required to meet the legitimate object which the state seeks to achieve. The OSA 1989, as it applies to the appellant, must be considered in that context.

27. The OSA 1989 imposes a ban on disclosure of information or documents relating to security or intelligence by a former member of the service. But it is not an absolute ban. It is a ban on disclosure without lawful authority. It is in effect a ban subject to two conditions. ... (1.) The former member may make disclosure to the staff counsellor, whose appointment was announced in the House of Commons in November 1987 (Hansard (HC Debates) 2 November 1987, written answers col 512), before enactment of the OSA 1989 and in obvious response to the grievances ventilated by Mr Peter Wright in Spycatcher. The staff counsellor, a high ranking former civil servant, is available to be consulted: 'by any member of the security and intelligence services who has anxieties relating to the work of his or her service which it has not been possible to allay through the ordinary processes of management – staff relations.' (2.) If the former member has concerns about the lawfulness of what the service has done or is doing, he may disclose his

concerns to (among others) the Attorney General, the Director of Public Prosecutions or the Commissioner of Metropolitan Police. (3.) If a former member has concerns about misbehaviour, irregularity, maladministration, waste of resources or incompetence in the service he may disclose these to the Home Secretary, the Foreign Secretary, the Secretary of State for Northern Ireland or Scotland, the Prime Minister, the Secretary to the Cabinet or the Joint Intelligence Committee. He may also make disclosure to the secretariat, provided (as the House was told) by the Home Office, of the parliamentary Intelligence and Security Committee. He may further make disclosure, by virtue of article 3 of and Schedule 2 to the Official Secrets Act 1989 (Prescription) Order 1990 (SI 200/1990) to the staff of the Controller and Auditor General, the National Audit Office and the Parliamentary Commissioner for Administration.

28. Since one count of the indictment against the appellant is laid under section 4(1) and (3) of the OSA 1989, considerable attention was directed by the judge and the Court of Appeal to the role of the commissioners appointed under section 8(1) of the Interception of Communications Act 1985, section 4(1) of the Security Service Act 1989 and section 8(1) of the Intelligence Services Act 1994. The appellant submits, correctly, that none of these commissioners is a minister or a civil servant, that their functions defined by the three statutes do not include general oversight of the three security services, and that the secretariat serving the commissioners is, or was, of modest size. But under each of the three Acts, the commissioner was given power to require documents and information to be supplied to him by any crown servant or member of the relevant services for the purposes of his functions (section 8(3) of the 1985 Act, section 4(4) of the 1989 Act, section 8(4) of the 1994 Act), and if it were intimated to the commissioner, in terms so general as to involve no disclosure, that serious abuse of the power to intercept communications or enter premises to obtain information was taking or had taken place, it seems unlikely that the commissioner would not exercise his power to obtain information or at least refer the warning to the Home Secretary or (as the case might be) the Foreign Secretary.

29. One would hope that, if disclosure were made to one or other of the persons listed above, effective action would be taken to ensure that abuses were remedied and offenders punished. But the possibility must exist that such action would not be taken when it should be taken or that, despite the taking of effective action to remedy past abuses and punish past delinquencies, there would remain facts which should in the public interest be revealed to a wider audience. This is where, under the OSA 1989 the second condition comes into play: the former member may seek official authorisation to make disclosure to a wider audience.

30. As already indicated, it is open to a former member of the service to seek authorisation from his former superior or the head of the service, who may no doubt seek authority from the secretary to the cabinet or a minister. . . . If the document or information revealed matters which, however, scandalous or embarrassing, would not damage any security or intelligence interest or impede the effective discharge by the service of its very important public functions, [authorisation] might be appropriate. Consideration of a request for authorisation should never be a routine or mechanical process: it should be undertaken bearing in mind the importance attached to the right of free expression and the need for any restriction to be necessary, responsive to a pressing social need and proportionate.

31. One would, again, hope that requests for authorisation to disclose would be granted where no adequate justification existed for denying it and that authorisation would be refused only where such justification existed. But the possibility would of course exist that authority might be refused where no adequate justification existed for refusal, or at any rate where the former member firmly believed that no adequate justification existed. In this situation the former member is entitled to seek judicial review of the decision to refuse, a course which the OSA 1989 does not seek to inhibit. In considering an application for judicial review of a decision to refuse authorisation to disclose, the court must apply the same tests as are described in the last paragraph. It also will bear in mind the importance attached to the convention right of free expression. It also will bear in mind the need for any restriction to be necessary to achieve one or more of the ends specified in article 10(2), to be responsive to a pressing social need and to be no more restrictive than is necessary to achieve that end.

32. For the appellant it was argued that judicial review offered a person in his position no effective protection, since courts were reluctant to intervene in matters concerning national security and the threshold of showing a decision to be irrational was so high as to give the applicant little chance of crossing it. Reliance was placed on the cases of *Chahal v United Kingdom* (1996) 23 EHRR 413 and *Tinnelly & Sons Ltd v United Kingdom* (1998) 27 EHRR 249, in each of which the European Court was critical of the effectiveness of the judicial review carried out.

33. There are in my opinion two answers to this submission. First the court's willingness to intervene will very much depend on the nature of the material which it is sought to disclose. If the issue concerns the disclosure of documents bearing a high security classification and there is apparently credible unchallenged evidence that disclosure is liable to lead to the identification of agents or the compromise of informers, the court may very well be unwilling to intervene. If, at the other end of the spectrum, it appears that while disclosure of the material may cause embarrassment or arouse criticism, it will not damage any security or intelligence interest, the court's reaction is likely to be very different. Usually, a proposed disclosure will fall between these two extremes and the court must exercise its judgment, informed by article 10 considerations. The second answer is that in any application for judicial review alleging an alleged violation of a convention right the court will now conduct a much more rigorous and intrusive review than was once thought to be permissible. The change was described by Lord Steyn in *R (Daly) v Secretary of State for the Home Department* [2001] 2 AC 532, 546 where after referring to the standards of review reflected in *Associated Provincial Picture Houses Ltd v Wednesbury Corporation* [1948] 1 KB 223 and *R v Ministry of Defence, Ex p Smith* [1996] QB 517, he said:

> 26. . . . There is a material difference between the Wednesbury and Smith grounds of review and the approach of proportionality applicable in respect of review where Convention rights are at stake.

> 27. The contours of the principle of proportionality are familiar. In *de Freitas v Permanent Secretary of Ministry of Agriculture, Fisheries, Lands and Housing* [1999] 1 AC 69 the Privy Council adopted a three-stage test. Lord Clyde observed, at p 80, that in determining whether a limitation (by an act, rule or decision) is arbitrary or excessive the court should ask itself: 'whether: (i) the legislative objective is sufficiently important to justify limiting a fundamental right; (ii) the measures designed to meet the legislative objective are rationally connected to it; and (iii) the means used to impair the right or freedom are no more than is necessary to accomplish the objective.'

> Clearly, these criteria are more precise and more sophisticated than the traditional grounds of review. What is the difference for the disposal of concrete cases? Academic public lawyers have in remarkably similar terms elucidated the difference between the traditional grounds of review and the proportionality approach: see Professor Jeffrey Jowell QC, 'Beyond the Rule of Law: Towards Constitutional Judicial Review' [2000] PL 671; Professor Paul Craig, *Administrative Law*, 4th ed (1999), pp 561–563; Professor David Feldman, 'Proportionality and the Human Rights Act 1998', essay in *The Principle of Proportionality in the Laws of Europe* edited by Evelyn Ellis (1999), pp 117, 127 et seq. The starting point is that there is an overlap between the traditional grounds of review and the approach of proportionality. Most cases would be decided in the same way whichever approach is adopted. But the intensity of review is somewhat greater under the proportionality approach. Making due allowance for important structural differences between various convention rights, which I do not propose to discuss, a few generalisations are perhaps permissible. I would mention three concrete differences without suggesting that my statement is exhaustive. First, the doctrine of proportionality may require the reviewing court to assess the balance which the decision maker has struck, not merely whether it is within the range of rational or reasonable decisions. Secondly, the proportionality test may go further than the traditional grounds of review inasmuch as it may

require attention to be directed to the relative weight accorded to interests and considerations. Thirdly, even the heightened scrutiny test developed in *R v Ministry of Defence, Ex p Smith* [1996] QB 517, 554 is not necessarily appropriate to the protection of human rights. It will be recalled that in *Smith* the Court of Appeal reluctantly felt compelled to reject a limitation on homosexuals in the army. The challenge based on article 8 of the Convention for the Protection of Human Rights and Fundamental Freedoms (the right to respect for private and family life) foundered on the threshold required even by the anxious scrutiny test. The European Court of Human Rights came to the opposite conclusion: *Smith and Grady v United Kingdom* (1999) 29 EHRR 493. The court concluded, at p 543, para 138:

> 'the threshold at which the High Court and the Court of Appeal could find the Ministry of Defence policy irrational was placed so high that it effectively excluded any consideration by the domestic courts of the question of whether the interference with the applicants' rights answered a pressing social need or was proportionate to the national security and public order aims pursued, principles which lie at the heart of the court's analysis of complaints under article 8 of the Convention.'

In other words, the intensity of the review, in similar cases, is guaranteed by the twin requirements that the limitation of the right was necessary in a democratic society, in the sense of meeting a pressing social need, and the question whether the interference was really proportionate to the legitimate aim being pursued.

28. The differences in approach between the traditional grounds of review and the proportionality approach may therefore sometimes yield different results. It is therefore important that cases involving Convention rights must be analysed in the correct way.

This approach contrasts sharply with that adopted in the authorities on which the appellant based his submission. In *Chahal*, on applications for both habeas corpus and judicial review, there was no effective judicial enquiry into the legality of the applicant's detention, and this was of even greater importance where the applicant faced the risk of torture or inhuman or degrading treatment: (1996) 23 EHRR 413, paras 132, 150–151. In *Tinnelly* the issue of conclusive certificates had effectively prevented any judicial determination of the merits of the applicants' complaints: (1998) 27 EHRR 249, para 77.

34. The appellant contended that even if, theoretically, judicial review offered a means of challenging an allegedly wrongful refusal of authorisation to disclose, it was in practice an unavailable means since private lawyers were not among those to whom disclosure could lawfully be made under section 7(3)(a), and a former member of the service could not be expected to initiate proceedings for judicial review without the benefit of legal advice and assistance. I would for my part accept that the fair hearing guaranteed by article 6(1) of the convention to everyone in the determination of their civil rights and obligations must ordinarily carry with it the right to seek legal advice and assistance from a lawyer outside the government service. But this is a matter to be resolved by seeking official authorisation under section 7(3)(b). The service would at that stage, depending on the nature of the material sought to be disclosed, be fully entitled to limit its authorisation to material in a redacted or anonymised or schematic form, to be specified by the service; but I cannot envisage circumstances in which it would be proper for the service to refuse its authorisation for any disclosure at all to a qualified lawyer from whom the former member wished to seek advice. If, at the hearing of an application for judicial review, it were necessary for the court to examine material said to be too sensitive to be disclosed to the former member's legal advisers, special arrangements could be made for the appointment of counsel to represent the applicant's interests as envisaged by the Court of Appeal in *Secretary of State for the Home Department v Rehman* [2000] 3 WLR 1240, 1250–1251, paras 31–32.

. . .

36. The special position of those employed in the security and intelligence services, and the special nature of the work they carry out, impose duties and responsibilities on them within the meaning of article 10(2): *Engel v The Netherlands (No 1)* (1976) 1 EHRR 647, para 100; *Hadjianastassiou v*

Greece (1992) 16 EHRR 219, para 46. These justify what Lord Griffiths called a bright line rule against disclosure of information of documents relating to security or intelligence obtained in the course of their duties by members or former members of those services. (While Lord Griffiths was willing to accept the theoretical possibility of a public interest defence, he made no allowance for judicial review: *Attorney General v Guardian Newspapers Ltd (No 2)* [1990] 1 AC 109, 269G.) If, within this limited category of case, a defendant is prosecuted for making an unauthorised disclosure it is necessary to relieve the prosecutor of the need to prove damage (beyond the damage inherent in disclosure by a former member of these services) and to deny the defendant a defence based on the public interest; otherwise the detailed facts concerning the disclosure and the arguments for and against making it would be canvassed before the court and the cure would be even worse than the disease. But it is plain that a sweeping, blanket ban, permitting of no exceptions, would be inconsistent with the general right guaranteed by article 10(1) and would not survive the rigorous and particular scrutiny required to give effect to article 10(2). The crux of this case is whether the safeguards built into the OSA 1989 are sufficient to ensure that unlawfulness and irregularity can be reported to those with the power and duty to take effective action, that the power to withhold authorisation to publish is not abused and that proper disclosures are not stifled. In my opinion the procedures discussed above, properly applied, provide sufficient and effective safeguards. It is, however, necessary that a member or former member of a relevant service should avail himself of the procedures available to him under the Act. A former member of a relevant service, prosecuted for making an unauthorised disclosure, cannot defend himself by contending that if he had made disclosure under section 7(3)(a) no notice or action would have been taken or that if he had sought authorisation under section 7(3)(b) it would have been refused. If a person who has given a binding undertaking of confidentiality seeks to be relieved, even in part, from that undertaking he must seek authorisation and, if so advised, challenge any refusal of authorisation. If that refusal is upheld by the courts, it must, however reluctantly, be accepted. I am satisfied that sections 1(1) and 4(1) and (3) of the OSA 1989 are compatible with article 10 of the convention; no question of reading those sections conformably with the convention or making a declaration of incompatibility therefore arises. On these crucial issues I am in agreement with both the judge and the Court of Appeal. They are issues on which the House can form its own opinion. But they are also issues on which Parliament has expressed a clear democratic judgment.

. . .

38. I would dismiss the appeal.

Lord Hope, Lord Hutton, Lord Hobhouse of Wood-Borough and Lord Scott of Foscote agreed that the appeal should be dismissed.

Notes

1 *Section 1(1): Information relating to the security services disclosed by members or former members.* Section 1(1) is intended to prevent members or former members of the security services (and any person notified that he is subject to the provisions of the subsection) disclosing anything at all relating or appearing to relate to[22] the operation of those services. It is a wide category and is not confined only to work done by members of the security and intelligence services. All persons covered thus come under a lifelong duty to keep silent even though their information might reveal a serious abuse of power by the security services or some operational weakness. There is no need to show that any harm will or may flow from the disclosure, and so all information, however trivial, is covered.

In *R v Shayler*, above, it was argued that since s 1(1) and s 4(1) are of an absolute nature, they are incompatible with Article 10 of the Convention, under the Human

---

22 Under s 1(2), misinformation falls within the information covered by s 1(1) as it includes 'making any statement which purports to be a disclosure of such information or which is intended to be taken as being such a disclosure'.

Rights Act 1998 (HRA), owing to the requirement that interference with expression should be proportionate to the legitimate aim pursued. In other words, it was argued that using s 3 of the HRA in a creative fashion to seek to resolve the incompatibility would be unfruitful, since compatibility could not be achieved. This argument was rejected by the House of Lords, on the basis that avenues of complaint were available to Shayler and that in particular judicial review could have been sought of a failure to authorise the release of the information in question. As Lords Bingham and Hope point out, the review would have been of a more intensive nature than in the pre-HRA era since the court would have to consider the requirements of proportionality. Therefore, although Shayler's freedom of expression was restricted by the operation of s 1(1), the interference was justified under Article 10(2). Thus, following this ruling, it is clear that Article 10 will have no impact on s 1(1). The decision in *Shayler* is discussed further below in relation to s 4(1) and the general question of implying a 'public interest defence' into the 1989 Act.

2. *Section 1(3): Information relating to the security services disclosed by Crown servants.* In contrast to s 1(1), s 1(3) is only satisfied if harm results from the disclosure, but taken at its lowest level under s 1(4)(b) it is clear that this test may be very readily satisfied: it is not necessary to show that disclosure of the *actual* document in question would be likely to cause harm, merely that it belongs to a class of documents disclosure of which would be likely to have that effect. Disclosure of a document containing insignificant information and incapable itself of causing the harm described under s 1(4)(a) can therefore be criminalised, suggesting that the importation of a harm test for Crown servants as opposed to members of the security services may not in practice create a very significant distinction between them. However, harm must be likely to flow from disclosure of a specific document where, due to its unique nature, it cannot be said to be one of a class of documents. The fact that there is a test for harm at all under s 1(3), however weak, affirms a distinction of perhaps symbolic importance between two groups of Crown servants because the first step in determining whether a disclosure may be criminalised is taken by reference to the *status* of the person making the disclosure rather than by the nature of the information, suggesting that s 1(1) is aimed at underpinning a culture of secrecy in the security services rather than at ensuring that no damaging disclosure is likely to be made.

The ruling of the House of Lords in *Lord Advocate v Scotsman Publications Ltd* [1990] 1 AC 812; [1989] 2 All ER 852, HL,[23] above, suggests that the test for harm under this subsection may be quite restrictively interpreted: it will be necessary to show quite a strong likelihood that harm will arise and the nature of the harm must be specified. As indicated, the ruling was given in the context of civil proceedings for breach of confidence, but the House of Lords decided the case on the basis of the principles under the 1989 Act even though it was not then in force. The ruling concerned publication by a journalist of material relating to the work of the intelligence services. Thus, the test for harm had to be interpreted, according to s 5, in accordance with the test under s 1(3) as though the disclosure had been by a Crown servant. The Crown conceded that the information in question was innocuous, but argued that harm would be done because the publication would undermine confidence in the security services. The House of Lords, noting that there had already been a degree of prior publication, rejected this argument as

---

23   For criticism of the ruling, see Walker [1990] PL 354.

unable alone to satisfy the test for harm. The case therefore gives some indication as to the interpretation the harm tests may receive. This ruling affords some protection for journalistic expression concerning the intelligence services which, under the HRA, would be in accordance with the high value Strasbourg has placed on expression critical of the workings of the state and state agents.[24]

3   *Information relating to defence.* The harm test under s 2 is also potentially extremely wide due to its open-textured wording. The first part of this test under s 2(2)(a), which is fairly specific and deals with quite serious harm, may be contrasted with that under (b), which is much wider. Bearing s 2(2)(c) in mind the test, at its lowest level, would be satisfied by showing that a disclosure of information in the category would be likely to endanger the interests of Britain abroad or seriously obstruct them. Again, in many cases it would be difficult for a Crown servant to determine beforehand whether or not a particular disclosure would be criminal.

4   *Section 3(1)(b): Information obtained from a foreign state or international organisation.* The harm test relating to information falling within s 3(1)(b), contained in s 3(3), is somewhat curious; once the information is identified as falling within this category, a fiction is created that harm *may* automatically flow from its disclosure. This implies that there are circumstances in which the only ingredient which the prosecution *must* prove is that the information falls within the category. Given that s 3(3) uses the word 'may', thereby introducing uncertainty into the section, there is greater leeway for imposing a Convention-friendly interpretation on it under s 3 of the HRA. If the word 'may' is interpreted strictly, the circumstances in which it would be unnecessary to show harm would be greatly curtailed. It could then be argued that since harm or its likelihood must be shown, the harm test itself must be interpreted compatibly with Article 10. It would have to be shown that the interference in question answered to a pressing social need (*Sunday Times v UK* (1979) 2 EHRR 245). Depending on the circumstances, it could be argued that if, ultimately, the 'interests of the UK abroad' would be benefited by the disclosure, or on balance little affected, no pressing social need to interfere with the expression in question could be shown.

5. *Information obtained by use of intercept and security service warrants.* Section 4(3) covers information obtained by use of intercept and security service warrants. There is no harm test under this category. It therefore creates a wide exception to the general need to show harm under s 1(3) when a Crown servant who is not a member of the security services makes a disclosure about the work of those services. But although s 4(1) appears to impose an absolute ban on disclosures falling within s 4(3), it is not incompatible with Article 10 under the HRA, according to the House of Lords in *Shayler*, since, as noted above, there are avenues which can be used to allow for disclosures of information falling within the category, in the public interest. This point is pursued below, at p 596.

6   *Section 5: Information resulting from unauthorised disclosures.* Section 5 does not refer to a new category of information. The section is primarily aimed at journalists who receive information leaked to them by Crown servants, although it could of course cover anybody in that position. Since s 5 is aimed at journalists and potentially represents an interference with their role of informing the public, it requires a very strict interpretation under s 3 of the HRA, in accordance with Article 10, bearing in mind the emphasis placed by Strasbourg on the importance of that role.[25] In

---

24   See *Thorgeirson v Iceland* (1992) 14 EHRR 843; *The Observer and the Guardian v UK* (1991) 14 EHRR 153.
25   See, eg, *Goodwin v UK* (1996) 22 EHRR 123.

contrast to disclosure of information by a Crown servant under one of the six categories, s 5 imports a requirement of *mens rea* under s 5(2). This provision affords some recognition to media freedom; nevertheless the burden of proof on the prosecution would be very easy to discharge if the information fell within ss 1(3), 3(1)(b) or 4(3) due to the nature of the tests for damage included in those sections; it would only be necessary to show that the journalist knew that the information fell within the category in question. Another apparent improvement in terms of media freedom is the decriminalisation of the receiver of information. However, this improvement might be said to be more theoretical than real in that it was perhaps unlikely that the mere receiver would be prosecuted under the 1911 Act even though that possibility did exist.

The fact that journalists were included at all in the net of criminal liability under s 5 has been criticised on the basis that some recognition should be given to the important role of the press in informing the public about government actions.[26] In arguing for a restrictive interpretation of s 5 under s 3 of the HRA, a comparison could be drawn with the constitutional role of the press recognised in America by the *Pentagon Papers* case:[27] the Supreme Court determined that no restraining order on the press could be made so that the press would remain free to censure the government. A court could afford recognition to the significance of the journalistic role, as required by Article 10, by placing a strong emphasis on the *mens rea* requirement. Where a journalist appeared to be acting in the public interest in making the disclosure, it would be possible for a court to interpret the *mens rea* requirement as disproved on the basis that it would be impossible to show that the defendant knew or should have known that the disclosure was damaging to the interest in question if on one view (even if mistaken) it could be seen as beneficial to it, and that was the view that the journalist took.

7   *Unauthorised publication abroad of information.* Section 6 covers the unauthorised publication abroad of information which falls into one of the other substantive categories apart from crime and special investigation powers. It covers the disclosure to a UK citizen of information which has been received in confidence from the UK by another state or international organisation. Typically, the section might cover a leak of such information to a foreign journalist who then passed it on to a UK journalist. However, liability will not be incurred if the state or organisation (or a member of the organisation) authorises the disclosure of the information to the public (s 6(3)). Again, since this section is aimed at journalists, a requirement of *mens rea* is imported: it must be shown under s 6(2) that the defendant made 'a damaging disclosure of [the information] knowing or having reasonable cause to believe that it is such as is mentioned in subsection (1) above and that its disclosure would be damaging'. However, it is important to note that under s 6(4), the test for harm under this section is to be determined 'as it would be in relation to a disclosure of the information, document or article in question by a Crown servant in contravention of s 1(3), 2(1) and 3(1) above'. Thus, although it appears that two tests must be satisfied in order to fulfil the *mens rea* requirement, the tests may in fact be conflated as far as s 3(1)(b) is concerned because proof that the defendant knew that the information fell within the relevant category may satisfy the requirement that he or she knew that the disclosure would be damaging. The requirement that *mens rea* be established is not, therefore, as favourable to the defendant as it appears to be

---

26   See, eg, KD Ewing and CA Gearty, *Freedom Under Thatcher* (1990), pp 196–201.
27   *New York Times Co v US* (1971) 403 US 713.

because – as noted in respect of s 5 – it may be satisfied even where the defendant believes that no damage will result. Once again, aside from this particular instance, this applies in all the categories due to the objective element in the *mens rea* arising from the words 'reasonable cause to believe'.

8 *A public interest defence?* The Act contains no explicit public interest defence and it follows from the nature of the harm tests that one cannot be implied into it; on the face of it, any good flowing from disclosure of the information in question cannot be considered, merely any harm that might be caused. The information may concern corruption at such a high level that internal methods of addressing the problem would be ineffective. However, s 3 of the HRA could be used creatively to seek to introduce such a defence – in effect – through the back door, by relying on Article 10. Whether or not this is possible in respect of categories of information covered by a harm test, it appears that it is not possible in respect of s 1(1) and s 4(1). In *Shayler* (2001), Judge Moses at first instance found that there was no need to rely on s 3 of the HRA since no incompatibility between Article 10 and s 1(1) arose (para 78 of the transcript). He reached the conclusion that s 3 could be ignored in reliance on the finding of the Lord Chief Justice in *Poplar Housing and Regeneration Community Association Ltd and Secretary of State for the Environment v Donoghue* [2002] WLR 183) (see Part VI Chapter 1); he said that 'unless legislation would otherwise be in breach of the Convention s 3 can be ignored; so courts should always first ascertain whether, absent s 3, there would be any breach of the Convention' (para 75).

The conclusion of the House of Lords that ss 1(1) and 4(1) are not in breach of Article 10 was reached on the basis that Mr Shayler did have an avenue by which he could seek to make the disclosures in question. There were various persons to whom the disclosure could have been made, including those identified in s 12. Also, the House of Lords found, a refusal of authorisation would be subject, the Crown accepted in the instant case, to judicial review. The refusal to grant authority would have to comply with Article 10 due to s 6 of the HRA; if it did not, the court in the judicial review proceedings would be expected to say so. The Lords found that the interference with freedom of expression was in proportion to the legitimate aim pursued under Article 10(2) – that of protecting national security. The Lords found that, for the reasons given, the absence of a 'public interest' defence in ss 1(1) and 4(1) of the 1989 Act does not breach Article 10 of the Convention. The decision means that s 3 need not be used in relation to s 1(1) and s 4(1). It is probable that the same arguments would apply if, in respect of disclosure of information falling within other categories, the defence sought to introduce a public interest defence, relying on Article 10.

The problem with the House of Lords' analysis is that the avenues available to members or former members of the security services to make disclosures are unlikely to be used. It seems, to say the least, highly improbable that such a member would risk the employment detriment that might be likely to arise, especially if he or she then proceeded to seek judicial review of the decision. One of the most important principles recognised at Strasbourg is that rights must be real, not tokenistic or illusory. It is argued that the right to freedom of expression – one of the central rights of the Convention – is rendered illusory by ss 1(1) and 4(1) of the 1989 Act in relation to allegedly unlawful activities of the security services – a matter of great significance in a democracy.

9 The situation of the civil servant in the UK who believes that disclosure as to a certain state of affairs is necessary in order to serve the public interest may be contrasted with the situation of his of her counterpart in the US where he or she

would receive protection from detrimental action flowing from whistle-blowing[28] under the Civil Service Reform Act 1978. However, the Civil Service Code, which came into force on 1 January 1996 and was revised in 1999, contains a partial 'whistle-blowing' provision in paras 11 and 12 (see Hansard, HL Deb (9 January 1996)). The duty of civil servants remains not to disclose any information to which they have acquired access as civil servants, without authorisation (para 10 of the Code). However, paras 11 and 12 provide that if a civil servant believes that he or she is being asked to act in a way which *inter alia* is improper, unethical or which raises fundamental issues of conscience, he or she should report the matter in accordance with departmental guidance (para 11). If the matter has been reported in this manner and the civil servant does not believe that a response is a reasonable response, he or she should report the matter to the Civil Service Commissioners (para 12). Where the matter cannot be resolved by resort to these procedures the civil servant should either resign or carry out his or her instructions (para 13 of the Code).[29] This is therefore a very limited provision since it only allows ultimate disclosure of information to the Civil Service Commissioners. No protection is offered in the Code if the disclosure is to an Opposition MP, as in *Ponting*.

10 *A defence of prior publication?* No express defence of prior publication is provided by the 1989 Act; the only means of putting forward such a defence would arise in one of the categories in which it was necessary to prove the likelihood that harm would flow from the disclosure; the prosecution might find it hard to establish such a likelihood where there had been a great deal of prior publication because no further harm could be caused. Prior publication would be irrelevant under s 1(1). Thus, where a member of the security services disclosed information falling within s 1 which had been published all over the world and in the UK, a conviction could still be obtained. If such publication had occurred but the information fell within s 1(3), the test for harm might be satisfied on the basis that, although no further harm could be caused by disclosure of the *particular document*, it nevertheless belonged to a class of documents disclosure of which was likely to cause harm. Where harm flowing from publication of a specific document is relied on, *Lord Advocate v Scotsman Publications Ltd* (above) suggests that a degree of prior publication may tend to defeat the argument that further publication can still cause harm. However, this suggestion must be treated with care as the ruling was not given under the 1989 Act and the link between the Act and the civil law of confidence may not form part of its ratio.[30]

Questions

1 Has the 1989 Act afforded any recognition to the important constitutional role of the journalist?

2 As things stand, a journalist who repeated allegations made by a member of the security services as to corruption or treachery in MI5 could be convicted if it could be shown, first, that he or she knew that the information related to the security services and, secondly, that disclosure of that type of information would be likely to cause damage to the work of the security services, regardless of whether the particular allegations would cause such damage. What would be the position under the Act, taking into account the impact of the HRA, of a journalist who

---

28 For discussion of the situation of UK and US civil servants and developments in the area, see Cripps, *op cit*; Zellick, *op cit*; Starke, *op cit*.
29 See further *Hansard*, HL Deb (29 November 1995).
30 Only Lord Templeman clearly adverted to such a link.

repeated allegations made by a future Cathy Massiter after they had been published in other countries?

Public interest immunity

Discovery may be needed by one party to an action of documents held by the other in order to assist in the action or allow it to proceed. Where a member of the government or other state body is the party holding the documents in question it may claim that it is immune from the duty to make such disclosure, asserting public interest immunity, a privilege based on the royal prerogative.[31] The immunity is expressly preserved in the Crown Proceedings Act 1947, but this means that the courts have had to determine its scope. Section 28(1) of the 1947 Act, which provides that the court can make an order for discovery of documents against the Crown and require the Crown to answer interrogatories, is qualified by s 28(2) which preserves Crown privilege to withhold documents on the grounds of public interest in a variety of cases.

Certain decisions demonstrate the development there has been in determining the scope of this privilege. The House of Lords in *Duncan v Camell Laird and Co* [1942] AC 624 held that documents otherwise relevant to judicial proceedings are not to be disclosed if the public interest requires that they be withheld. This test may be found to be satisfied either (a) by having regard to the contents of the particular document, or (b) by the fact that the document belongs to a category which, on grounds of public interest, must as a class remain undisclosed.[32] Crown privilege as formulated here was an exclusionary rule of evidence based on public interest and the minister was deemed the sole judge of what that constituted. In *Ellis v Home Office* [1953] 2 QB 135, a prisoner on remand who was severely injured by a mentally disturbed prisoner in the prison hospital sued the Crown for negligence. Privilege was claimed to prevent the disclosure of medical reports on his assailant and so the action had to fail. The danger clearly arose that, since the executive was the sole judge of what was in the public interest, matters embarrassing to government might be concealed. In *Conway v Rimmer* [1968] AC 910, the speeches in the House of Lords revealed the degree of concern which had arisen in the judiciary as to the danger of injustice created by the use of this privilege by ministers. In that case a police constable was prosecuted for theft. The charge was dismissed but he was dismissed from the police force. He brought an action for malicious prosecution against his former superintendent but the Home Office objected to the disclosure of reports relevant to the case. The House of Lords, in a landmark decision, overruled the minister's claim of Crown privilege and ordered disclosure.

This decision substituted judicial discretion for executive discretion regarding disclosure of documents. However, the judges have tended to exercise this discretion cautiously. Disclosure is unlikely to be ordered unless the party seeking it can show: first, that the material is clearly relevant to a specific issue in the case; secondly, that it will be of significant value in the fair disposal of the case; and thirdly, following *Air*

---

31 See R Cross and C Tapper, *Cross on Evidence*, 7th edn (1990), Chapter XII. For a discussion of the legal and historical background see: J Jacob, 'From privileged Crown to interested public' [1993] PL 121; A Bradley, 'Justice, good government and public interest immunity' [1992] PL 514; G Ganz, 'Matrix Churchill and public interest immunity' (1993) 56 MLR 564; TRS Allan, 'Public interest immunity and ministers' responsibility' (1993) CLR 661.

32 [1942] AC 624, at 636.

Canada v Secretary of State for Trade (No 2) [1983] 1 All ER 910, below, that it will assist the case of that party. The main issue for determination in *Air Canada* concerned the conditions which have to be satisfied before a court will inspect documents for which public interest immunity is claimed. If the court does not inspect it cannot order disclosure. The court considered that the documents were relevant in the case and necessary for its fair disposal. However, this did not lead the majority to find that inspection was necessary in order to determine whether non-disclosure would prevent the court from judging the issues. Instead, the majority found that the party seeking disclosure must show that 'the documents are very likely to contain material which would give substantial support to his contention on an issue which arises in the case'.[33] As Zuckermann points out below, this created a very serious obstacle to disclosure. Lord Scarman dissented from this view, although he agreed that inspection was unnecessary; extracts from his dissenting judgment are set out below.

Air Canada v Secretary of State for Trade (No 2) **[1983] I All ER 910, 923–25, HL(E)**

Lord Scarman: My Lords, the appeal raises an issue, not previously explored by the House, arising on the discovery of documents which belong to a class in respect of which the Crown has made a powerful claim in proper form for immunity from production in the public interest. The appeal illustrates, if illustration be needed, that the House's decision in *Conway v Rimmer* [1968] AC 910 was the beginning, but not the end, of a chapter in the law's development in this branch of the law.

The issue is specific and within a small compass. The Crown having made its objection to production in proper form, in what circumstances should the court inspect privately the documents before determining whether they, or any of them, should be produced?

The court, of course, has a discretion: but the discretion must be exercised in accordance with principle. The principle governing the production of disclosed documents is embodied in RSC, Ord 24, r 13. No order for the production of any documents for inspection or to the court shall be made unless the court is of the opinion that the order is necessary either for disposing fairly of the cause or matter or for saving costs: r 13(1). And the court may inspect the document for the purpose of deciding whether the objection to production is valid: r 13(2). The rule provides a measure of protection for a party's documents irrespective of their class or contents and independently of any privilege or immunity. While the existence of all documents in a party's possession or control relating to matters in question in the action must be 'discovered', that is to say disclosed, to the other party (or parties), he is not obliged to produce them unless the court is of the opinion that production is necessary.

Faced with a properly formulated certificate claiming public interest immunity, the court must first examine the grounds put forward. If it is a 'class' objection and the documents (as in *Conway v Rimmer* [1968] AC 910) are routine in character, the court may inspect so as to ascertain the strength of the public interest in immunity and the needs of justice before deciding whether to order production. If it is a 'contents' claim, eg a specific national security matter, the court will ordinarily accept the judgment of the minister. But if it is a class claim in which the objection on the face of the certificate is a strong one – as in this case where the documents are minutes and memoranda passing at a high level between ministers and their advisers and concerned with the formulation of policy – the court will pay great regard to the minister's view (or that of the senior official who has signed the certificate). It will not inspect unless there is a likelihood that the documents will be necessary for disposing fairly of the case or saving costs. Certainly, if, like

---

33   *Per* Lord Fraser [1983] 1 All ER 910, at 917.

Bingham J in this case, the court should think that the documents might be 'determinative' of the issues in the action to which they relate, the court should inspect: for in such a case there may be grave doubt as to which way the balance of public interest falls: *Burmah Oil Co Ltd v Governor and Company of the Bank of England* [1980] AC 1090, 1134–1135, 1145. But, unless the court is satisfied on the material presented to it that the documents are likely to be necessary for fairly disposing of the case, it will not inspect for the simple reason that unless the likelihood exists there is nothing to set against the public interest in immunity from production.

The learned judge, Bingham J, correctly appreciated the principle of the matter. He decided to inspect because he believed that the documents in question were very likely to be 'necessary for the just determination of the second and third issues in the plaintiffs' ... case'. Here I consider he fell into error. For the reasons given in the speech of my noble and learned friend, Lord Templeman, I do not think that the appellants have been able to show that the documents whose production they are seeking are likely to be necessary for fairly disposing of the issues in their 'constitutional' case. Indeed, my noble and learned friend has demonstrated that they are unnecessary. Accordingly, for this reason, but for no other, I would hold that the judge was wrong to decide to inspect the documents.

On all other questions I find myself in agreement with the judge. In particular, I am persuaded by his reasoning that the public interest in the administration of justice, which the court has to put into the balance against the public interest immunity, is as he put it:

> In my judgment, documents are necessary for fairly disposing of a cause or for the due administration of justice if they give substantial assistance to the court in determining the facts upon which the decision in the cause will depend.

... The Crown, when it puts forward a public interest immunity objection, is not claiming a privilege but discharging a duty. The duty arises whether the document assists or damages the Crown's case or if, as in a case to which the Crown is not a party, it neither helps nor injures the Crown. It is not for the Crown but for the court to determine whether the document should be produced. Usually, but not always, the critical factor will be whether the party seeking production has shown the document will help him. But it may be necessary for a fair determination or for saving costs, even if it does not. Therefore, although it is likely to make little difference in practice, I would think it better in principle to retain the formulation of the interests to be balanced which Lord Reid gave us in *Conway v Rimmer* [1968] AC 910, 940:

> It is universally recognised that here there are two kinds of public interest which may clash. There is the public interest that harm shall not be done to the nation or the public service by disclosure of certain documents, and there is the public interest that the administration of justice shall not be frustrated by the withholding of documents which must be produced if justice is to be done.

And I do so for the reasons given by Lord Pearce in the same case. Describing the two conflicting interests, he said of the administration of justice, at p 987, that the judge:

> can consider whether the documents in question are of much or little weight in the litigation, whether their absence will result in a complete or partial denial of justice to one or other of the parties or perhaps to both, and what is the importance of the particular litigation to the parties and the public.

Basically, the reason for selecting the criterion of justice, irrespective of whether it assists the party seeking production, is that the Crown may not have regard to party advantage in deciding whether or not to object to production on the ground of public interest immunity. It is its duty to bring the objection, if it believes it to be sound, to the attention of the court. It is for the court, not the Crown, to balance the two public interests, that of the functioning and security of the public service, which is the sphere within which the executive has the duty to make an assessment, and that of justice, upon which the executive is not competent to pass judgment.

For these reasons I would dismiss the appeal.

Chief Constable of West Midlands Police, ex p Wiley; Chief Constable of Nottinghamshire Police ex p Sunderland [1995] I AC 274, 281, 291–306

Mr Wiley was charged with robbery but at his trial the prosecution offered no evidence. He made a formal complaint against certain members of the West Midlands police force and he later commenced a civil action against the Chief Constable of the West Midlands force. Mr Sunderland was charged with assault but at his trial also the prosecution offered no evidence. He made a formal complaint that he had been assaulted by police officers and he indicated his intention to commence a civil action against the Chief Constable of Nottinghamshire Police. It was thought by lawyers acting for Mr Wiley and Mr Sunderland (following *Neilson v Laugharne* [1981] QB 736) that the documents compiled for the complaint which would come into the hands of the chief constables would attract public interest immunity. Therefore, in contesting the civil actions the chief constables could make use of the information contained in them but Mr Wiley and Mr Sunderland would not be able to do so. The lawyers, therefore, required the chief constables to give undertakings that the information would not be so used. The chief constables refused to do so and declarations were granted that they had acted unlawfully in so refusing; the chief constables appealed against grant of these declarations to the House of Lords.

All the parties concerned argued that public interest immunity did not attach to documents coming into existence during a police complaints investigation. The House of Lords had to consider whether *Neilson v Laugharne* and the decisions following it were wrongly decided. In *Neilson*, Lord Oliver had determined that a class immunity should attach to police complaints documents on the basis that the police complaints procedure would be placed in jeopardy if that was not the case.

Lord Templeman: ... I consider that when a document is known to be relevant and material, the holder of the document should voluntarily disclose it unless he is satisfied that disclosure will cause substantial harm. If the holder is in any doubt he may refer the matter to the court. If the holder decides that a document should not be disclosed then that decision can be upheld or set aside by the judge. A rubber stamp approach to public interest immunity by the holder of a document is neither necessary nor appropriate. ...

Lord Woolf: ... I turn to the decision of the Court of Appeal in *Neilson v Laugharne* [1981] QB 736. The case involved proceedings which have been commenced by the plaintiff in the county court claiming damages from a chief constable after the plaintiff had made a complaint which had resulted in the chief constable instituting the complaints procedure under section 49 of the Police Act 1964, which was the predecessor to the procedure which is now contained in Part IX of the Act of 1984. In the course of discovery the chief constable objected to the production of the documents on the ground that their production would be injurious to the public interest and on the ground that they were covered by legal professional privilege. The judge upheld the claim that the documents were covered by legal professional privilege. The Court of Appeal did not accept this was the case but dismissed the plaintiff's appeal on the grounds that the documents were entitled to public interest immunity on a class basis.

As to the reasoning in the Court, the first thing which has to be said is that the only evidence in support of the claim was apparently an affidavit of a deputy chief constable to the effect that an inquiry would be prejudiced if persons approached to make statements thought that such statements might be used in civil litigation and *revealed* to the parties. It was insubstantial material on which to establish a new class claim to public interest immunity. It was certainly not self-evident that the adverse consequences referred to would follow without establishing a new class claim. ... It is now necessary to refer to the cases in which *Neilson v Laugharne* [1981] QB 736 had not only been followed but also had been given an extended application ...

[In *Makanjuola*] Bingham LJ, after he had expressed his conclusion, went on to make the following comments [1992] 3 All ER 617, 623, which have since attracted considerable attention and probably explain why the case was belatedly reported:

> I would, however, add this. Where a litigant asserts that documents are immune from production or disclosure on public interest grounds he is not (if the claim is well founded) claiming a right but observing a duty. Public interest immunity is not a trump card vouchsafed to certain privileged players to play when and as they wish. It is an exclusionary rule, imposed on parties in certain circumstances, even where it is to their disadvantage in the litigation. This does not mean that in any case where a party holds a document in a class *prima facie* immune he is bound to persist in an assertion of immunity even where it is held that, on any weighing of the public interest, in withholding the document against the public interest in disclosure for the purpose of furthering the administration of justice, there is a clear balance in favour of the latter. But it does, I think, mean: (1) that public interest immunity cannot in any ordinary sense be waived, since, although one can waive rights, one cannot waive duties; (2) that, where a *litigant* holds documents in a class *prima facie* immune, he should (save perhaps in a very exceptional case) assert that the documents are immune and decline to disclose them, since the ultimate judge of where the balance of public interest lies is not him but the court; and (3) that, where a document is, or is held to be, in an immune class, it may not be used for any purpose whatever in the proceedings to which the immunity applies, and certainly cannot (for instance) be used for the purposes of cross-examination. (Emphasis added.)

This is a very clear statement as to the nature of public interest immunity, most of which I would unhesitatingly endorse ... I would be surprised if Bingham LJ was intending by these remarks to extend principles of public interest immunity or to make their application any more rigid than was required as a result of the previous authorities. ... If a Secretary of State on behalf of his department as opposed to any ordinary litigant concludes that any public interest in documents being withheld from production is outweighed by the public interest in the documents being available for purposes of litigation, it is difficult to conceive that unless the documents do not relate to an area for which the Secretary of State was responsible, the court would feel it appropriate to come to any different conclusion from that of the Secretary of State. The position would be the same if the Attorney-General was of the opinion that the documents should be disclosed. It should be remembered that the principle which was established in *Conway v Rimmer* [1968] AC 910 is that it is the courts which should have the final responsibility for deciding when both a contents and a class claim to immunity should be upheld. The principle was not that it was for the courts to impose immunity where, after due consideration, no immunity was claimed by the appropriate authority. What was inherent in the reasoning of the House in that case was that because of the conflict which could exist between the two aspects of the public interest involved, the courts, which have final responsibility for upholding the Rule of Law, must equally have final responsibility for deciding what evidence should be available to the courts of law in order to enable them to do justice. As far as contents of documents are concerned, I cannot conceive that their Lordships in *Conway v Rimmer* would have anticipated that their decision could be used, except in the most exceptional circumstances, so that a department of state was prevented by the courts from disclosing documents which it considered it was appropriate to disclose. As to class claims, it is interesting to note that Lord Reid in his speech in *Conway v Rimmer* referred to the announcement of the then Lord Chancellor in the House of Lords in June 1956 that in future reports of witnesses to accidents, medical reports and other documents which were previously the subject of a claim to privilege on a class basis would in future be disclosed. ... Where, however, parties other than government departments are in possession of documents in respect of which public interest immunity could be claimed on a class basis, there are practical difficulties in allowing an individual to decide that the documents should be disclosed. The indiscriminate and, indeed, any disclosure, of documents which are the subject of a class claim to immunity can undermine that class. If the reason for the existence of the class is that those who make the statement should be assured that the statement will not be disclosed, the fact that in some cases they are disclosed undermines the assurance. The assurance can never be absolute because of the residual power of the court to order disclosure in the interest of the administration of justice. However, if the assurance is to have any value the cases where disclosure occurs have to be restricted to situations where this is necessary. Here the court may have to intervene to protect the public interest ...

The next case to which it is necessary to refer is the decision of the Court of Appeal in *Halford v Sharples* [1992] 1 WLR 736 ... it was conceded in this case by all parties and accepted by the court, as a result of the *Hehir* [1982] 1 WLR 715 and *Makanjuola* [1992] 3 All ER 617 decisions (a transcript of the *Makanjuola* decision was available to the court), that if documents were protected from disclosure in the public interest, the chief constable was not entitled to make any *use* of information contained in the documents. It made no difference that both parties were well aware of the contents of the documents. They were not even entitled to rely on secondary evidence of the documents ... The case was one in which counsel for the Secretary of State appeared to assist the court. It is of interest to note the debatable approach which counsel for the Secretary of State considered it was appropriate to adopt having regard to the authorities. In the words contained in the judgment of Sir Stephen Brown J, at p 745:

> He accepted that there is a general duty to disclose everything that is relevant except that which the law prohibits. He explained that the Secretary of State's position was, and always has been, that it is not in the public interest that complaints and discipline files should be disclosed. He said that the Secretary of State was not making policy in taking the view but was *merely obeying the law*. The test was not 'Will it do any harm in this case?' The emphasis should be placed upon integrity of the files. Contributors to section 49 procedures were entitled to know and to be assured that what they had contributed will not be seen by anybody including the Inspectorate or the Secretary of State. He said that in this case the Secretary of State had not seen the files in question. (Emphasis added.)

If counsel was seeking to indicate that the Secretary of State no longer had responsibility for considering and assisting the court if necessary by providing evidence as to where the public interest lay, then I would disagree ...

The judgments in this case

In the Court of Appeal it was common ground that in civil proceedings public interest immunity applies on a class basis to the file of documents that came into existence as a result of the investigation into the complaints which had been made. The Court of Appeal therefore focused on the question whether the chief constables were entitled to use the information contained in the documents to assist their cases in the civil proceedings ... Nolan LJ, at p127, relied on the submissions which were made by counsel on behalf of the authority, that the use by chief constables of complaints investigation material in preparing their defence had 'a very detrimental effect on the important public interest of speedy and effective investigations into alleged police misconduct' ... Nourse LJ, at p128, was of the same opinion as Staughton and Nolan LJJ and shared the view of Popplewell J that the half-way house contended for by the chief constables 'has no logic'. The appeal was therefore unanimously dismissed.

Between the hearing in the Court of Appeal and the hearing before this House, as already indicated, the authority has accepted that in general the class immunity created by the *Neilson* decision can no longer be justified. The recognition of a new class-based public interest immunity requires clear and compelling evidence that it is necessary. Yet as the present case had demonstrated, the existence of this class tends to defeat the very object it was designed to achieve. The applicants only launched their proceedings for judicial review to avoid the existence of a situation where their position would be prejudiced as a result of their not being given access to material to which the police had access. Their non co-operation was brought about because of the existence of the immunity. Mr Reynold, on behalf of the applicants, made it clear that if there were to be disclosure of documents which came into existence as a result of the investigation, it would be inappropriate to grant injunctive relief. The restrictive nature of any assurance which could be given to a potential witness in relation to civil proceedings meant that it was unlikely to have significant effect on their decision as to whether to co-operate or not. The class was artificial in conception and this contributed to it having to be rigidly applied. The comments of Lord Taylor of Gosforth CJ in *Ex p Coventry Newspapers Ltd* [1993] QB 278, 292–3, which have already been cited, are likely to be equally appropriate in the great majority of cases. While I agree with Lord Hailsham of St Marylebone's statement in *National Society for the Prevention of Cruelty to Children* [1978] AC 171, 230, that: 'The categories of public interest are not closed, and must alter from time to time whether by restriction or extension as social conditions and social legislation develop' in my opinion no sufficient case has ever been made out to justify the class of public interest immunity recognised in *Neilson*.

The *Neilson* case [1981] QB 736 and the cases in which it was subsequently applied should therefore be regarded as being wrongly decided. This does not however, mean that public interest immunity can never apply to documents that come into existence in consequence of a police investigation into a complaint. There may be other reasons why because of the contents of a particular document it would be appropriate to extend immunity to that document. In addition, Mr Pannick submitted that the report which comes into existence as a result of a police investigation into a complaint is a candidate for public interest immunity on a narrower class basis. Mr Pannick did not, however have available the evidence which would be needed to succeed on this submission. Although I have considerable reservations as to whether it would be possible to justify a class claim to immunity as opposed to a contents claim in respect of some reports, it would not be right to close the door to a future attempt to establish that the reports are subject to class immunity.

The fact that documents coming into existence as a result of a police investigation are not entitled to public interest immunity from disclosure means that the decision of Popplewell J and that of the Court of Appeal [1994] 1 WLR 114 were wrong in these cases and the declarations and the injunction should not have been granted.

AAS Zuckerman, 'Public interest immunity – a matter of prime judicial responsibility' (1994) 57 MLR 703, 704, 705, 707–09, 714, 715, 717–20, 722–25

A Introduction – protecting private and public interest in litigation

The *Matrix Churchill* case, in which ministerial claims for public interest immunity were rejected and the accused acquitted, has given rise to an intense controversy concerning ministers' responsibilities in connection with public interest immunity. In addressing the issues raised by this case, we should not allow ourselves to be distracted from one fundamental and uncontroversial principle: that all relevant evidence is not only admissible but is also compellable.

The disclosure of the whole truth is as important to the administration of justice as it is to individual litigants. A judgment which is known to have been given, not on the basis of all the available evidence but on only part thereof, cannot inspire confidence in its correctness. . . .

There is, however, one exception to this observation: public interest immunity. An examination of judicial decisions in this area provides ample reason for doubting the courts' adherence to the idea that it is in the interests of justice that all relevant evidence should be made available in civil or criminal proceedings.

The doctrine that the courts are the sole arbiters of whether and when suppression of evidence is in the interests of justice has, paradoxically, encouraged ministers and public bodies to pay little or no regard to the interests of justice. Government ministers and other officials could legitimately reason that it is not for them but for the courts to decide whether justice required disclosure. Their task is limited to expressing the view that disclosure would be deleterious to the public interest. On their part, the courts have declined to place such claims under searching scrutiny, preferring to accept them at face value. Furthermore, the courts have shown a remarkable reluctance to investigate the effects that the withholding of evidence might have on the prospects of a litigant to prove his case and on their own ability to render correct judgments. These judicial attitudes have created fertile conditions for practices of the kind which the Scott Inquiry has been investigating.

B The judicial assumption of responsibility for the public interest

[In *Conway v Rimmer*] the House of Lords established three principles of great constitutional importance.

First, it held that the responsibility for deciding whether or not evidence should be withheld from a court of law rested with the courts and not the Crown. It was for the courts to determine whether the public interest necessitated suppression of evidence and, therefore, the matter was not one of Crown privilege. . . .

Second, the House of Lords laid down the process of reasoning which should be followed in the exercise of the judicial discretion to sanction the withholding of evidence. In arriving at its decision, the court has to weigh the public interest in the suppression of evidence against the public interest that the administration of justice shall not be frustrated. This balancing exercise requires the court to place on one side of the scales the potential harm to the public from the disclosure of the evidence in question. On the other side of the scales, the court has to place the consequences to the court's ability to administer justice, if the evidence were to be suppressed. This last aspect requires the court to take account of two separate, if closely related, factors. It requires the court to consider the likely effect that the absence of the evidence might have on the court's facility to ascertain the true facts. It also requires the court to take into account the effect that the withholding of the evidence will have on the appearance of justice and on confidence in the judicial system. It has been insufficiently appreciated that the need to conduct a balancing act in respect of every claim for immunity has greatly reduced the significance of the distinction between contents claims and class claims. Whether it is claimed that the contents of a particular document is sensitive and its disclosure would, *per se*, be harmful, or whether it is claimed that, notwithstanding the innocuousness of the information, it is desirable to maintain the confidentiality of the class to which it belongs, the court must consider whether the actual information in question is of importance to the determination of truth before it can allow the information to be withheld.

The third principle has to do with inspection. As we have just observed, the balancing exercise necessitates an assessment of the effect that the absence of a piece of information might have on the determination of truth. This raises the question: how is the court to determine the likely effect that the evidence would or would not have if it has been withheld? Mindful of this difficulty, the House of Lords held that a court was entitled to inspect in private materials for which immunity has been claimed for the purpose of deciding whether or not their suppression would have an adverse effect on the ascertainment of truth.

The *Conway v Rimmer* decision represents a bold and progressive step in the direction of establishing government accountability for the suppression of evidence ... The assumption of responsibility for deciding whether evidence should be withheld has had crucial implications for ministerial responsibility. When a minister's certificate was conclusive, the minister had to consider, at least in theory, what effect his certificate would have on the administration of justice. Under the new dispensation, ministers are relieved of this responsibility. For them it is only to decide whether they believe that the disclosure of the evidence would be harmful to the public interest. If it would be, they may claim immunity. It is then for the court to decide whether to accept the claim or overrule it, depending on the outcome of the balance of interests carried out by the judge. Ministers who appeared in the Scott inquiry were therefore correct in asserting that the responsibility for the suppression of evidence rested with the courts. Their task has been confined to determining whether there are grounds for believing that disclosure would be injurious to the public interest and to asserting that this is the case by issuing a certificate to this effect.

C Receding judicial scrutiny of claims for immunity

Blanket immunity

As we have seen, it was an important aspect of the decision in *Conway v Rimmer* that immunity from production in evidence should not be extended on an *a priori* basis to certain classes of documents. According to that decision, claims for immunity have to be balanced, in each individual case, against the interests of the administration of justice. This exercise necessitated consideration of the effect that the withholding of evidence would have on the court's ability to determine the factual issues in question. Notwithstanding the fact-dependent nature of the balancing test, the courts were soon tempted to extend blanket immunity to whole classes of documents and forgo altogether a case-by-case balancing exercise in respect of these classes. . . .

In relation to national security, blanket immunity subsisted both before and after *Conway v Rimmer*. In *Conway v Rimmer* itself there were *dicta* that could be interpreted as saying that decisions to withhold evidence on grounds of national security must be left to ministerial discretion [[1968] 1 All ER 874, 880, 888, 890]. Later, this view was clearly spelt out by the House of Lords in *Council of Civil Service Unions v Minister for the Civil Service* [1984] 3 All ER 935 where Lord Fraser stated:

> The decision on whether the requirements of national security outweigh the duty of fairness in any particular case is for the Government and not for the courts; the Government alone has access to the relevant information, and in any event the judicial process is unsuitable for reaching decisions on national security [[1984] 3 All ER 944; see also *per* Lord Diplock at 952].

Recently, this policy has been reiterated by Russell LJ, who held that 'once there is an actual or potential risk to national security demonstrated by an appropriate certificate, the court should not exercise its right to inspect' [*Balfour v Foreign and Commonwealth Office* [1994] 2 All ER 588 at 596]. Thus, the words 'national security' need only be uttered by a minister for the information in question to become inaccessible even in the interests of justice. In the United States, by contrast, the courts have kept the jurisdiction to judge claims of privilege on grounds of national security firmly in their hands [*United States v Reynolds*, 345 US 1 (1953)].

Acceptance of the argument from candour

The principle in *Conway v Rimmer* has been eroded, not only by the granting of blanket immunity, but also, and perhaps more significantly, by a ready acceptance of the argument from candour. It stands to reason that, for instance, it is in the public interest that military secrets should be kept inviolable. But what justification is there for according public interest immunity to, say, statements in the course of a police inquiry under s 49 of the Police Act 1964? Or, to take another example, what justification is there for according immunity to correspondence between social workers? The argument from candour provides the justification.

The argument from candour has two facets: internal and external. The internal facet proceeds as follows. For public institutions, such as government departments and local authority welfare agencies, to function properly, their officers must not be inhibited from expressing their candid professional views. In the absence of immunity, civil servants and other public employees would be inhibited in the expression of opinion. *Ergo,* immunity is in the public interest. The external facet proceeds on two assumptions: first, that to fulfil their functions, public bodies, such as the police, social workers or child welfare organisations, require information from the public. Second, if members of the public thought that such information might be made public, they would be reluctant to come forward. *Ergo,* immunity is necessary in order to encourage the divulgence of information. . . .

Obstacles to inspection

The conditions that have to be fulfilled before a court would inspect documents were more fully considered in *Air Canada v Secretary of State for Trade* [1983] 1 All ER 910.

The House of Lords proceeded from the assumption that it was in the public interest to protect from disclosure Government papers concerned with the workings of the Cabinet and with the formulation of Government policy. The court then turned to consider the other side of the scales. The documents were clearly relevant. Further, it was accepted that they were necessary for disposing fairly of the cause [[1983] 1 All ER 915]. But the court still had to determine whether non-disclosure would have a deleterious effect on the ability of the court to judge the issues fully and adequately. Bingham J felt, as we have seen, that he could not come to a decision on this point unless he looked at the documents, but the House of Lords thought otherwise.

It was not enough for the party seeking disclosure to show that the documents would help establish the truth one way or the other. The party seeking discovery it was held, must show that the documents are likely to assist his own case [per Lords Wilberforce, Edmund-David and Fraser; Lords Scarman and Templeman disagreeing].

This requirement presents a major obstacle to overcoming a claim for public interest immunity for, clearly, the party seeking disclosure has no access to the documents, does not know their contents and, ordinarily, cannot prove that the documents are likely to affect the outcome of the case, let alone that they would assist his own case. Carol Harlow and Richard Rawlings describe this as a '"Catch 22" dilemma: without the evidence the case cannot be won; without the case the evidence cannot be secured' [Pressure Through Law (1992), p 175].

This decision, perhaps more than any other decision, has seriously eroded the principle of judicial scrutiny of claims for public interest immunity propounded by Conway v Rimmer. It also amounts to a reversal of the principle that the party seeking to withhold documents from discovery bears the burden of showing that the public interest so requires [D v NSPCC [1977] 1 All ER 589 at 619]. Judicial scrutiny has been thus emasculated, not by an open change of policy, but by means of a technical ploy. Conway v Rimmer decided that no order should be made for the disclosure of documents in respect of which a prima facie valid claim for immunity has been made, except where the court is satisfied that disclosure is necessary in the interests of justice. To be so satisfied the court needs to inspect the documents to find out what they contain. Yet, on the Air Canada ruling, no inspection may take place unless the party seeking disclosure has shown that the documents will assist his case. Since, in the majority of cases, the party seeking disclosure is ignorant of the contents of the documents, this requirement is a bar to inspection, without which no order for disclosure can be made. It follows, in effect, that once a claim for immunity has been made, which is valid on the face of it, this is the end of the matter. Further, the rule in Air Canada has not remained confined to Cabinet papers and high level policy-making communications. It has even been applied where a citizen sued the police for wrongful arrest and false imprisonment [Evans v Chief Constable of Surrey Constabulary (Attorney General intervening) [1989] 2 All ER 594].

Not only did Air Canada undermine the Conway v Rimmer policy of judicial scrutiny of ministerial claims, it also tends to undermine the public interest in the administration of justice, which Conway v Rimmer set out to promote. Lord Wilberforce, this time a member of the majority in Air Canada. had this to say of the idea that it was in the interests of justice that judgments should be given on the basis of all existing and available evidence:

> In a contest purely between one litigant and another, such as the present, the task of the court is to do and to be seen to be doing, justice between the parties, a duty reflected in the word 'fairly' in the rule [RSC, Ord 24, r 13]. There is no higher additional duty to ascertain some independent truth. It often happens, from the imperfection of evidence, or the withholding of it sometimes by the party in whose favour it would tell if presented, that an adjudication has to be made which is not, and is known not to be, the whole truth of the matter: yet, if the decision has been in accordance with the available evidence and with the law, justice will have been fairly done [[1983] 1 All ER 919].

This reasoning is suspect. For while it is true that in an adversary system the court has no obligation, indeed no power, to seek to ascertain the facts independently of the evidence that the parties choose to present to it, it does not follow that the court has no duty to assist a party to obtain evidence relevant to the issue before the court. As has already been suggested, a court that is not prepared to assist a party to obtain relevant evidence fails in its obligation to afford that party an opportunity to prosecute his cause, because the facility of obtaining and presenting evidence is essential to the establishment of one's legal rights. The decisions in Burmah Oil Co and Air Canada place a clog on the administration of justice and should be reconsidered, especially now that the Court of Appeal has held that a claim for public interest immunity in criminal trials cannot be properly determined without inspection of the material in question [see R v Keane [1994] 2 All ER 479].

D Public interest immunity in criminal proceedings

In *Matrix Churchill*, itself a criminal prosecution, the court was concerned with the operation of public interest immunity in criminal proceedings. The position in criminal cases is, fundamentally, no different from that in civil proceedings [*Governor of Brixton Prison ex p Osman (No 1)* [1992] 1 All ER 108]. The interests at stake are, however, very different because, in criminal prosecutions, the accused runs the risk of punishment which may involve loss of liberty, of property and of reputation. Nevertheless, the balancing test of *Conway v Rimmer* is perfectly capable of according adequate weight to the interest of protecting the innocent from conviction [see eg *Keane* [1994] 2 All ER 478, 485]. ...

E Conclusion – prime judicial responsibility

The *Matrix Churchill* case has given rise to a lively debate concerning ministers' position with regard to the issue of public interest immunity certificates. The Attorney-General has stated that ministers have a duty to claim public interest immunity [House of Commons, 10 November 1992]. Some commentators have questioned this assertion. Others have advanced the view that, as the law stands at present, the Attorney-General was right in asserting that ministers have a duty to claim immunity [Smith, 'Public interest immunity in criminal cases' (1993) 52 CLJ 1; Tomkins, 'Public interest immunity after *Matrix Churchill*' (1993) PL 530; Allan, 'Public interest immunity and ministers' responsibility' (1993) CLR 661]. The commentators seem, however, to be united in the view that it is undesirable that ministers should claim immunity from disclosing evidence in criminal proceedings and their criticism has been tinged with a note of condemnation of the ministerial practices in the *Matrix Churchill* case.

In condemning ministers, critics have overlooked the role played by the courts in this regard. The courts have made it the law of the land that the responsibility for deciding whether evidence should be given in legal proceedings lies with judges and not with ministers. The role of ministers, it has been held, is confined to informing the courts by means of public interest immunity certificates, of the adverse consequences which may result from the disclosure of documents or information for which ministers are responsible. It is not for ministers to decide whether evidence should be disclosed in legal proceedings, nor do they possess the information necessary for such a decision.

In the field of public interest immunity, ministerial practices and judicial policies feed upon each other. Both, however, have to use statute as their starting point and take on board entrenched conventions of public administration. The law concerning public interest immunity has evolved against the background of the notorious catch-all provision of s 2 of the Official Secrets Act 1911. Although this provision has now been abolished and replaced by the more guarded and liberal provisions of the Official Secrets Act 1989, the administrative philosophy continues to embrace the tenet that secrecy is in the interest of good government. This philosophy has received judicial approval on countless occasions as many of the cases mentioned in this article demonstrate. In *Conway v Rimmer* itself, Lord Reid said:

> The business of government is difficult enough as it is, and no Government could contemplate with equanimity the inner workings of the Government machine being exposed to the gaze of those ready to criticise without adequate knowledge of the background and perhaps with some axe to grind. That must in my view also apply to all documents concerned with policy making within departments ... Further, it may be that deliberations about a particular case require protection as much as deliberations about policy [[1968] 1 All ER 888].

'In this country,' Carol Harlow and Richard Rawlings write [*Pressure Through Law* (1992)], 'a wall of silence blocks public access to information. Britain is almost alone in the Western world in possessing neither freedom of information legislation nor a general right to access to data held in official files.' On their part, the judiciary have shown remarkable willingness to bolster this wall of silence by placing their trust in the ability of ministers to judge what is in the public interest, as Stephen Sedley has recently pointed out ['The sound of silence: constitutional law without a constitution' (1994) 110 LQR 270]. Indeed, the courts have shifted the burden of proof with regard to public interest immunity. Once a claim for immunity has been made, which is within the accepted range of claims, the onus is on the party seeking disclosure to persuade the court that the interest in non-disclosure may be overcome. To make things worse, the ruling in the *Air Canada* case ensures that, in civil litigation, this onus is practically impossible to discharge.

Surely, when ministers read judicial decisions that exalt the importance of maintaining the secrecy of Cabinet papers, of promoting the confidentiality of advice given by civil servants to ministers, of screening high level policy-making processes from the public gaze, they are entitled to feel persuaded that they are rendering an important public service when they issue public interest immunity certificates. In some situations, the courts did not even require the advice of ministers in order to conclude that secrecy is important to the proper functioning of government and of other social organisations. Many decisions have involved no ministerial claim and no public interest immunity certificates.

One final point needs to be made in order to avoid misunderstanding. It is not suggested that the practices that have been developed since *Conway v Rimmer* are desirable or defensible. On the contrary, they are harmful to a healthy administration of justice and are inimical to good government in a democratic society. More specifically, they have undermined the sensible and enlightened principles of *Conway v Rimmer*. What is suggested, instead, is that ministers do not bear a major responsibility for this state of affairs. They have followed well-established practices which have had the courts' seal of approval. Clearly, then, if we are seriously interested in the reform of the law on public interest immunity, we must start by acknowledging that the judiciary are primarily responsible for the present state of affairs and not shrink from putting the courts themselves on trial and not just ministers.

Inquiry into Exports of Defence Equipment and Dual-Use Goods to Iraq and Related Prosecutions, HC 115-I (1995–96)

Below are extracts from the report of an enquiry chaired by Sir Richard Scott into government policy in relation to export of arms to Iraq. Directors of the company Matrix Churchill were accused of exporting arms to Iraq in breach of export regulations. They faced criminal proceedings although they alleged that government ministers had known of the exports. In the criminal trial ministers put forward public interest immunity certificates claiming that matters relevant to the defendants' defence should not be revealed. Mr Clarke's certificate made an exception for one witness who was to be called for the prosecution. The judge in the case ruled that a number of the matters covered by the PII certificates should be revealed and this led to the collapse of the case. The case caused a public and parliamentary outcry since it created the impression that the government had been prepared to allow three innocent men to be imprisoned rather than reveal its policy in relation to selling arms to Iraq. Sir Richard Scott was therefore appointed to head an enquiry into the matters at issue. The extracts set out below relate only to the claims of public interest immunity made by the ministers in question.

The first extract relates to the attitude of ministers and of the Attorney-General to signing the certificates.

G13.61 Mr Heseltine was of the clear view that the DTI documents ought not to be withheld from the defence. [Transcript, Day 69, pp 70–71: 'My view was that the documents should be released. If there was injury for the reasons that would flow from their class category, that, in my view, should be overwhelmed by the justice argument.'] He accepted that, in forming this view, he was exercising an element of judgment ... he was not prepared to assert the claim in a manner that might damage the conduct of the defence in the Matrix Churchill case.

G13.69 Mr Heseltine signed the Certificate in its redrafted form. Before doing so he read with some care the *All England Report* of the *Makanjuola* judgment and marked the passage at p 623 between g and h. The sentence '. . . the ultimate judge of where the balance of public interest lies is not him [*ie* the minister] but the Court' was, said Mr Heseltine, 'the clinching part as far as I was concerned'. [Transcript, Day 69, p 112.]

G13.71 There is, in my opinion, no doubt whatever but that Mr Heseltine signed the re-drafted Certificate on the footing that he had a duty in law to claim PII class protection for the DTI documents. He had been so advised by the Attorney-General. He had not been informed that if he took the view that the case for disclosure to the defence was a clear one, it was open to him to agree to the disclosure of the documents. He had signed the Certificate in the belief that the judge would be aware that in his (Mr Heseltine's) view some of the documents ought to be disclosed to the defence.

G13.100 The Attorney-General expressed the firm opinion that a minister's function in claiming PII was to decide whether documents placed before him fell into a PII class of documents that the Courts had in previous cases recognised as attracting PII. In the case of a class claim, the Attorney-General said, the damage to the public interest 'caused by disclosure of an individual document . . . flows from the fact that the document forms an integral part of a class which requires protection, rather than from the specific contents of that document or the specific damage that would be caused by disclosure of that document individually.' [Paragraph A.11.1(v) of Sir Nicholas Lyell's written statement (*ibid*).] It followed that it was not, in the Attorney-General's view, necessary for the minister to ask himself whether disclosure of the documents to the defence would be damaging to the public interest. If the Courts had, in previous cases, allowed PII claims in respect of documents falling within the class in question, then the minister had a duty to claim PII for such of his documents as he thought fell within the class. It was not, in the Attorney-General's view, for the minister to decide to disclose the documents to the defendant on the ground that the requirements of justice outweighed the damage to the public interest that might be caused by that disclosure. So to decide would be to perform the 'balancing' exercise that was, in the Attorney-General's view, the prerogative of the Courts.

G13.102 In the application to the Matrix Churchill case of the views described in the previous paragraphs, it was the Attorney-General's view:

(i) that each of the ministers (including Mr Heseltine) who signed a PII Certificate had been under a duty to claim PII for his department's documents falling within Categories B and C regardless of whether the minister thought that disclosure of the documents to the defendants would in fact be damaging to the public interest; and

(ii) that since Mr Alan Moses QC had not advised (and if asked would not have advised) in respect of any of the documents that Judge Smedley would be bound to order disclosure to the defence, it was not open to Mr Heseltine to treat the case as a clear one in which the interests of justice required the disclosure of the documents to the defence.

The Public Interest Immunity Claims

G18.43 The Public Interest Immunity claims that were made in the Matrix Churchill case raise the following issues:

(i) The claims made for PII included class claims of two separate varieties, namely, the Categories B and C described in Mr Garel-Jones' Certificate, as well as contents claims to cover the redacted parts of the Category C documents. The character of the documents for which Category B and Category C class claims were made raise the question whether class claims are appropriate in criminal cases, and, if so, whether the making of class claims with as wide a catchment net as the Treasury Solicitor's Department, and Mr Leithead in particular, appear to have regarded as necessary and proper can be justified.

(ii) What is the proper function of the minister (or senior official) who, by signing a PII Certificate, makes the claim for PII? Is it his function to exercise his judgment as to whether the public interest would suffer any significant damage if the documents in question were disclosed to the defence? If so, then, presumably, a minister must refrain from signing a Certificate unless he is so satisfied. Or is the minister's function to do no more than satisfy himself that the documents fall into the described class? If so, why is it necessary for a minister, as opposed to a departmental lawyer or official, to sign the certificate?

(iii) To what extent is it open to a minister, or to counsel, to authorise to be disclosed to the defence documents which are of the same general class or description as documents that in a previous case have been the subject of a successful PII claim?

Some of these questions are answered by the speeches in the House of Lords in *Chief Constable of the West Midlands Police, ex p Wiley* [1994] 3 All ER 420. Since, however, this case post-dated by some two years the PII decisions that were taken in the *Matrix Churchill* case, the justification for those decisions must be tested by reference to the case law as it stood at the time.

G18.44 The class claims made in the *Matrix Churchill* case were claims that, according to the Attorney-General and to Mr Leithead in the Treasury Solicitor's Department, it was the legal duty of the respective ministers to make. The ministers were not entitled, it was said, to exercise any judgment as to whether or not the class claims should be made or as to whether the damage that might be caused to the public interest by disclosure of the contents of the documents to the defence was of sufficient gravity to justify withholding from the defence documents that would otherwise have been disclosable.

G18.54 The proposition that a minister is ever under a legal duty to claim PII in order to protect documents from disclosure to the defence notwithstanding that in the minister's view the public interest requires their disclosure to the defence is, in my opinion, based on a fundamental misconception of the principles of PII law. To the extent that the proposition is sought to be supported by reference to Lord Justice Bingham's judgment in *Makanjuola*, it is based in my opinion, on a misreading of that judgment.

G18.67 ... Ministers had been accustomed, in civil cases at least, to claim PII without necessarily having had regard to the consequences on the administration of justice of their doing so. It does not, however, follow that a minister, with perhaps more of an instinct for justice than some of his fellows, might not from time to time have taken account of the requirements of justice before making a PII claim. Lord Reid's point was not that ministers were not entitled, or were not able, to take some account of the requirements of justice, but that they did not have a duty to do so. The contention that ministers are not entitled to take into account, or are not capable of taking into account, the requirements of justice seems to me, besides being an improbable one, to be contradicted by the submissions made in *Conway v Rimmer* by counsel for the Home Secretary. It was the Home Secretary who was objecting to the production of the documents on the ground that they fell within a class of documents the production of which would be injurious to the public interest. Counsel said this:

> In a conflict between the public interest in good government and the public interest in the administration of justice as between private litigants, the last word in the resolution of the conflict must lie with the executive and not with the judiciary which is not equipped to assess the effect of the production [of the documents]. [*Ibid*, p 926.]

Counsel putting forward this submission was the Attorney-General, Sir Elwyn Jones (later Lord Chancellor). In contending for the right of ministers to the last word in resolving the conflict between the two public interests, the Attorney-General (and the Home Secretary on whose behalf he was speaking) must have regarded ministers as capable of attributing some weight to the public interest in the administration of justice. If that was so in 1967, it is difficult to see why ministers' ability and willingness to do so should have in the meantime disappeared. It is, of course, the case that ministers and officials without any detailed knowledge of the issues in a case cannot weigh with any accuracy the extent to which the documents in question will, or may, assist the party claiming discovery. But they will at least know that the documents are within the criteria of relevance that would normally require their disclosure for the purposes of the litigation.

The second extract relates to the use of PII certificates in criminal cases.

K6.12 As to the documents whose potential to assist the defence is apparent, could a situation ever arise in which disclosure could properly be refused on PII grounds? This is not a question which needs to be asked in civil cases. In civil cases, where private interests are in competition, the interests in the litigation of one party may from time to time be required to be subordinated to the greater public interest. I have already cited passages in *Duncan v Cammell Laird* and *Conway v Rimmer* to that effect. Can there be any such subordination of the interests of a defendant in a criminal trial? In my opinion, there cannot. In civil cases, the weight of the public interest factors against disclosure may justify a refusal to order disclosure notwithstanding that without disclosure an otherwise sound civil action might fail. But, for the purposes of criminal trials, the balance must always come down in favour of disclosure if there is any real possibility that the withholding of the document may cause or contribute to a miscarriage of justice. The public interest factors underlying the PII claim cannot ever have a weight sufficient to outweigh that possibility. In a civil case, the heavier the weight of the public interest factors underlying the PII claim, the less likely it will be that the balance will come down in favour of disclosure. But if the fundamental principle underlying the rules of disclosure of documents in criminal cases is that documents should be disclosed 'in order to prevent the possibility that a man may ... be deprived of the opportunity of casting doubt on the case against him' (*per* Lord Lane in *Hallett*), it must follow that a document which might assist a defendant in a criminal trial cannot be withheld on the ground of some greater public interest. In criminal trials, once it has been decided that a document might be of assistance to the defence, that should be the end of the PII claim. If that is so, then there is no real balance to be struck. The only issue for decision is whether the document might be of assistance to the defence.

K6.18 For the reasons given above, the approach to PII claims in criminal trials should be as follows:

(i)   If documents are not within the criteria of relevance established by *Keane* and *Brown (Winston)*, they need not be disclosed.

(ii)   PII claims on a class basis should not in future be made. PII contents claims should not be made in respect of documents which it is apparent are documents which might be of assistance to the defence.

(iii) Before making a PII claim on a contents basis, consideration should be given to the use of redactions. The PII claim can then be confined to the redacted parts of the documents.

(iv)   PII claims on a contents basis should not be made unless in the opinion of the Minister, or person putting forward the claim, ' ... disclosure will cause substantial harm' (*per* Lord Templeman in *ex p Wiley*).

(v)   A PII claim should not be made if the responsible minister forms the opinion that notwithstanding the sensitivity of the documents the public interest requires that the documents should be disclosed.

(vi)   Save where the circumstances render it impracticable, a minister who is asked to sign a PII certificate should always be given adequate time to reflect upon the weight of the public interest factors alleged to require that the documents in question be not disclosed and on the relevance, so far as it is known, of the documents to the defence. It is undesirable that any minister should be placed in the position, in which, for example, Mr Garel-Jones was placed, of having to reach a decision overnight as to whether PII should be claimed.

(vii) If a disclosure issue in respect of documents the subject of a PII claim is referred to the judge, the judge should, unless the parties are in agreement on the point, be invited to rule, first, whether the documents are within the criteria of materiality so as to be disclosable.

(viii) If the documents are within the criteria of relevance established by *Keane* and *Brown (Winston)*, the judge should be asked to decide whether the documents might be of assistance to the defence. If a document satisfies this test, the document ought not to be withheld from a defendant on PII grounds. There is no true balance to be struck. The weight of public interest factors underlying the PII claim is immaterial. However, existing authority, with its apparent endorsement of the 'balancing exercise' while at the same time requiring the disclosure of any document which 'may prove the defendant's innocence or avoid a miscarriage of justice', suffers, in my opinion, from some degree of ambiguity. It would be important, in my opinion, if disclosure of a material document is to be withheld, that the defendant should know whether the decision was based on the judge's conclusion that the document would not be of any assistance to the defence or on the judge's conclusion that, despite meeting that test, the weight of public interest factors precludes disclosure. The latter conclusion would, in my opinion, be wrong in principle and contrary to authority.

(ix) For the purposes of any argument on the assistance that a document might give the defence, the defendant should specify the line or lines of defence which, in the defendant's contention, give the document its requisite materiality.

(x) If the documents, although relevant and *prima facie* disclosable, do not appear to be documents that might assist the defence, the judge may conclude that in view of the public interest factors underlying the PII claim, the documents need not be disclosed.

Notes

1 After *Air Canada*, in effect, three tests had to be satisfied before disclosure could be ordered. The documents in question must be relevant to the case; they must be of assistance in disposing of it and the party seeking disclosure must show that they will assist his or her own case. As Zuckermann points out, this means that if the party seeking disclosure does not know in detail what the documents contain he or she will not be able to satisfy the third test and the court will therefore refuse to inspect the documents to see if the second test is satisfied. The second test mentioned above has received an interpretation restrictive of disclosure; the need to show that the material in question will be of *substantial* assistance to the court was emphasised in *Bookbinder v Tebbit (No 2)* [1992] 1 WLR 217. Even where these three tests may be satisfied discovery may be refused due to the nature or 'class' of the material in question even where it clearly falls outside the protected categories covered by the Official Secrets Act 1989. In *Halford v Sharples* [1992] 1 WLR 736, the applicant claimed sex discrimination in that she had not been recommended for promotion, and sought discovery of documents from, *inter alia*, the police authority which had failed to interview her and the chief constable of her own force. The Court of Appeal found that all documents of any type relating to internal police enquiries were protected by public interest immunity and therefore production of the files would not be ordered. It also found that immunity from disclosure was also an immunity from use. Thus, no use at all could be made of the information contained in the documents in question regardless of the fact that both parties were aware of their contents.

The House of Lords in *Wiley* considered that there was insufficient evidence to support Lord Oliver's conclusion in *Neilson* as to the need for a new class claim to public interest immunity. Thus, it was found that *Neilson* must be regarded as wrongly decided but that did not mean that public interest immunity would never attach to police complaints documents: whether it did or not would depend on the particular contents of the document (see *Taylor v Anderton* [1995] 2 All ER 420). This decision emphasises that a clear case must be made out for use of a broad class claim to public interest immunity and as far as documents in the hands of public authorities are concerned it is preferable that each case be considered on its own facts and not on the basis of a class claim. Moreover, it is to be welcomed in the interests of justice as going some way towards ensuring that civil actions against the police are not undermined by claims that relevant information cannot be disclosed.

2   One of the most controversial assertions of public interest immunity occurred in
     the *Matrix Churchill* case,[34] as AAS Zuckermann indicates. Zuckermann observes
     that, after *Conway v Rimmer*, ministers were relieved of the responsibility of
     considering suppressing evidence by way of public interest immunity certificates
     on the administration of justice. On this basis, the responsibility for the
     suppression of evidence lies with the courts, not ministers, and therefore
     Zuckermann does not condemn the ministerial practices revealed in the Scott
     report (see further Part IV Chapter 2). He ends by arguing that the courts, 'not
     just ministers', should be put on trial for their part in the *Matrix Churchill* affair.
     On this view, judicial responsibility for the suppression of evidence, claimed in
     Conway, is in a sense a double-edged sword; on the one hand, it allows the judges
     to provide a check on the actions of the executive, but on the other, it frees the
     executive from keeping a check on itself as regards the potential effect of a PII
     certificate on the administration of justice. Zuckermann assumes that the only
     public interest which ministers can be expected to understand and evaluate – in
     the light of judicial approval of 'closed' government – is the interest in secrecy.
     Once that interest is established they can and perhaps should close their eyes to
     the likely consequences attendant on issuance of the certificate, such as the
     possibility that an innocent person might be convicted, even where such a
     possibility is self-evident due to the nature of the material sought to be
     suppressed (as it seems to have been in the *Matrix Churchill* case), and despite
     their knowledge of judicial timidity and reluctance to resist PII claims, especially
     in national security cases. Possibly, Zuckermann's understandable eagerness to
     condemn judicial bolstering of the 'wall of silence blocking access to public
     documents' has led him to accept too readily ministerial claims of inability to
     understand or take any responsibility for the requirements of the interests of
     justice so long as a public interest in non-disclosure can be made out. Possibly,
     he also displays a readiness to accept that ministers are seeking to act in the
     public rather than the government interest when a claim for suppression of
     evidence is made. In the light of Lord Templeman's comments in *Wiley*, above,
     it is suggested that both ministerial and judicial responsibility for creating 'the
     wall of silence' should be clearly condemned.

3   Zuckermann's conclusions as regards the use of PII certificates generally, and as
     regards their use in the *Matrix Churchill* case in particular, do not harmonise with
     those of Sir Richard Scott in the Scott report. Scott found that the government
     attitude 'to disclosure of documents to the defence was consistently grudging. The
     approach ought to have been to consider what documents the defence might
     reasonably need and then to consider whether there was any good reason why the
     defence should not have them ... the actual approach ... seems to have been to
     seek some means by which refusal to disclose could be justified'.[35] The danger in
     the argument, reiterated by Lord Scarman in *Air Canada* (above), that judges take
     the responsibility for considering the effect of suppression of evidence on the
     administration of justice, is that both judiciary and ministers succeed in shuffling
     off the responsibility for such suppression. The judges accept, as ministers strongly
     demand they should, that matters of public safety can be judged only by the
     executive, while ministers hide behind the fiction that the judiciary will weigh up

---

34   See I Leigh, *Betrayed: The Real Story of the Matrix Churchill Trial* (1993); A Tomkins, 'Public
     interest immunity after Matrix Churchill' [1993] PL 530.
35   Section G of the Scott Report. See also the debate in Parliament on the Scott Report, *Hansard*,
     HC Deb (26 February 1996); HC Deb vol 272 no 51, in particular col 612.

the interest in such matters against the interest in justice. Thus, ministers are able to adopt the convenient constitutional position of demanding, on the one hand, that the judiciary should not look behind PII claims based on national security interests, and on the other, that if judges accede to such demands they must take the responsibility for doing so. Clearly, there is a strong argument that judges should be less timid when faced with such claims, but there also appears to be merit in Scott J's argument (see para G18.67 of the Scott report) that ministers must take some responsibility for putting them forward, bearing in mind ministerial responsibility for upholding the proper administration of justice. It is suggested that the creation of a dichotomy between ministerial and judicial responsibility in this matter, in order to ensure that the latter prevails, is unnecessary and leads to situations such as the one which arose in *Matrix Churchill*. Thus, in the light of *Matrix Churchill* there is arguably a need for greater regulation of the issue of PII certificates which would be based on the acceptance of initial ministerial responsibility for their potential effects on justice, although the judiciary should remain the final arbiters in the matter.[36]

4   The argument, criticised by Scott J, that before signing a PII certificate ministers need do no more than satisfy themselves that documents fall into a prescribed class may be based partly on 'entrenched conventions of public administration' including the rule that 'secrecy is in the interests of good government'. In future this argument may become less sustainable in the face of the new culture of openness depending from the 1994 Code of Practice on Access to Government Information (see below). Although the Code excludes many matters from its ambit, including categories of information which would be likely to be the subject of PII claims, it is based on the principle that responsibility for ensuring access to official information lies with departments, not with the judiciary, thus suggesting not only that good government requires a degree of openness, but that it accepts sole responsibility for ensuring that openness is maintained. It may also be noted, in support of this point, that the duties and responsibilities of ministers set out in *Questions of Procedure for Ministers* include: 'the duty to give Parliament and the public as full information as possible about the policies, decisions and actions of the Government and not to ... knowingly mislead Parliament and the public ... [and] the duty to ... uphold the administration of justice.'

5   The then Conservative government responded to the Scott Report by announcing that changes would be made to the practice in respect of PII certificates issued by the government.[37] An immunity claim would be made only where a real danger to the public interest could be shown. The certificate itself would explain the harm which might be caused, unless to do so would in itself bring about the harm in question. Although these changes were expressed to apply only to government claims for immunity, it was accepted that they might apply in other instances.

6   Under the Human Rights Act 1998 (HRA), the use of PII certificates may have to be re-evaluated due to the demands of Article 6 of the European Convention on Human Rights. If the prosecutor considers that the material is sensitive, an application to a court for a ruling to protect it on grounds of PII must be made (see ss 3(6) and 7(5) of the Criminal Procedure and Investigations Act 1996). It can be made *ex parte* with notice to the defence or, in an exceptional case, without notice.

---

36   See further I Leigh, 'Reforming public interest immunity' (1995) (2) Web JCLI 49–71.
37   HC Deb vol 576 col 1507; HC Deb vol 287 col 949 (18 December 1996).

In any such application a judge, bound by s 6 of the HRA, would have to consider Article 6 requirements in respect of such disclosure.

7   Guidelines as to the use of public interest certificates were provided in *Davis, Rowe and Johnson* (1993). However, the use of PII in that case was found to breach Article 6 by the European Court of Human Rights[38] and, therefore, they will have to be re-examined. The domestic courts will have the opportunity of doing so now that the HRA is fully in force. The findings in the same context in *Fitt and Jasper v UK* (1999) 30 EHRR 223 will be relevant. The Court said that in those instances, the judge had been able to consider the sensitive material in question and therefore was able to conduct a balancing act between fairness to the defence and to the prosecution. On that basis, no breach of Article 6 was found. Disclosure of evidence raises a number of issues under Article 6. The fair hearing requirement of Article 6(1) has been found to connote equality between prosecution and defence[39] ('equality of arms') and, where relevant material is withheld from the defence, equality is unlikely to be assured. Moreover, failure to disclose evidence may prevent the defence challenging the credibility of a witness and therefore may not be reconcilable with the Article 6 guarantees.[40] However, the Strasbourg case law has left a discretion to the national court[41] as to the interpretation of the right to cross-examine witnesses under Article 6(3)(d) and so has deprived this right of some of its effect. The position appears to be that the rights of witnesses to life, liberty and security, which fall within the Convention, should be balanced against the rights of the defendant. Measures should be available to test the evidence, while recognising the need – where relevant – to protect the witness.[42] Where the aim of the failure to disclose evidence is, however, to protect governmental interests, as in *Matrix Churchill*, it is likely that the fair trial requirement would prevail.

Questions

1   'While the courts bear, and should bear, the ultimate responsibility for considering the effect of suppression of evidence on the administration of justice, ministers can nevertheless be expected, within current constitutional conventions, to take responsibility for considering the public interest in such administration in conjunction with the public interest in secrecy, when considering the issuance of a PII certificate.' Have the courts accepted this argument, or have they clearly taken the position that judicial responsibility for determining when evidence should be given precludes acceptance of initial ministerial responsibility?

2   To a layperson it might seem strange to assert that ministers should not balance the interests of justice against the need for secrecy in a particular sphere of government operation. This is tantamount to asserting that ministers are not responsible for the miscarriages of justice which may result from this policy. What is the basis for making this claim?

3   What constitutional and civil libertarian objections are there to the view that ministers have a duty and not a discretion to claim PII?

---

38   *Rowe and Davis v UK* (2000) 30 EHRR 1.
39   *Neumeister v Austria* (1968) 1 EHRR 91, para 43.
40   *Kostovski v Netherlands* (1989) 12 EHRR 434; *Windisch v Austria* (1990) 13 EHRR 281. See further Part II Chapter 2, p 242 and Part VI Chapter 4, pp 1038–47 on Article 6.
41   See, eg, *Asch v Austria* (1991) 15 EHRR 597; *Liefveld v Netherlands* (1995) 18 EHRR CD 103.
42   See *Doorson v Netherlands* (1996) 22 EHRR 330.

FREEDOM OF INFORMATION[43]

Almost all democracies have introduced freedom of information legislation[44] within the last 30 years. For example, Canada introduced its Access to Information Act in 1982 while America has had such legislation since 1967. The UK now has the FoI Act 2000, although it is not yet fully in force. Certain developments suggest that even prior to the introduction of the FoI Act 2000 a gradual movement towards more open government was taking place in the UK. The Data Protection Act 1984 allowed access to personal information held on computerised files. The Campaign for Freedom of Information had, from 1985 onwards, brought about acceptance of the principle of access rights in some areas including local government. Disclosure of a range of information was decriminalised under the Official Secrets Act 1989. A White Paper on Open Government (Cm 2290) was published in July 1993. In this section we will look briefly at the US freedom of information legislation and will go on to consider the current arrangements for the release of government documents to the public in the UK. The current arrangements largely depend on a Code of Practice, the Code of Practice on Access to Government Information, which is policed by the Ombudsman (the Parliamentary Commissioner for Administration – PCA).[45] This will be followed by consideration of the arrangements which will be in place once the Freedom of Information Act 2000 comes fully into force.

Freedom of information in the US

Freedom of Information Act 1967 (US)

5 US Code §552

§ 552.(a) Each agency shall make available to the public information as follows:

(1) Each agency shall separately state and currently publish in the Federal Register for the guidance of the public –

    (A) descriptions of its central and field organisation and the established places at which, the employees (and in the case of a uniformed service, the members) from whom, and the methods whereby, the public may obtain information, make submittals or requests, or obtain decisions;

    (B) statements of the general course and method by which its functions are channelled and determined, including the nature and requirements of all formal and informal procedures available;

    (C) rules of procedure, descriptions of forms available or the places at which forms may be obtained, and instructions as to the scope and contents of all papers, reports, or examinations;

    (D) substantive rules of general applicability adopted as authorised by law, and statements of general policy or interpretations of general applicability formulated and adopted by the agency; and

    (E) each amendment, revision, or repeal of the foregoing.

---

43 See generally: P Birkinshaw, *Freedom of Information: The Law, the Practice and the Ideal*, 3rd edn (2001); J Beatson, and Y Cripps, *Freedom of Expression and Freedom of Information* (2000); SH Bailey, DJ Harris and DC Ormerod, *Civil Liberties: Cases and Materials*, 5th edn (2001), Chapter 8.

44 See LJ Curtis, 'Freedom of information in Australia' (1983) 14 Fed LR 5; HN Janisch, 'The Canadian Access to Information Act' [1982] PL 534; For the US, see M Supperstone, *Brownlie's Law of Public Order and National Security* (1982), pp 270–87; P Birkinshaw, *Freedom of Information: The Law, the Practice and the Ideal*, 2nd edn (1996), Chapter 2.

45 See, for discussion of the Ombudsman, generally, Part V Chapter 3.

(3) Except with respect to the records made available under paragraphs (1) and (2) of this subsection, each agency, on request for identifiable records made in accordance with published rules stating the time, place, fees to the extent authorised by statute, and procedure to be followed, shall make the records promptly available to any person. On complaint, the district court of the United States in the district in which the complainant resides, or has his principal place of business, or in which the agency records are situated, has jurisdiction to enjoin the agency from withholding agency records and to order the production of any agency records improperly withheld from the complainant. In such a case the court shall determine the matter *de novo* and the burden is on the agency to sustain its action. In the event of non-compliance with the order of the court, the district court may punish for contempt the responsible employee, and in the case of a uniformed service, the responsible member.

(4) (b) This section does not apply to matters that are –

(1) specifically required by executive order to be kept secret in the interest of the national defence or foreign policy;

(2) related solely to the internal personnel rules and practices of an agency;

(3) specifically exempted from disclosure by statute;

(4) trade secrets and commercial or financial information obtained from a person and privileged or confidential;

(5) inter-agency or intra-agency memorandums or letters which would not be available by law to a party other than an agency in litigation with the agency;

(6) personnel and medical files and similar files the disclosure of which would constitute a clearly unwarranted invasion of personal privacy;

(7) investigatory files compiled for law enforcement purposes except to the extent available by law to a party other than an agency;

(8) contained in or related to examination, operating, or condition reports prepared by, on behalf of, or for the use of an agency responsible for the regulation or supervision of financial institutions; or

(9) geological and geophysical information and data, including maps, concerning wells.

Note

The US Freedom of Information Act applies to all parts of the federal government unless an exemption applies. Exempted categories include information concerning defence, law enforcement and foreign policy. The exemptions can be challenged in court and the onus of proof will be on the agency withholding the information to prove that disclosure could bring about the harm the exemption was intended to prevent. A number of reforms have been suggested since 1980 and in 1986 a major Freedom of Information Act reform was passed which extended the exemption available to law enforcement practices.

P Birkinshaw, *Freedom of Information: The Law, the Practice and the Ideal*, 1st edn (1988), pp 36–8

Freedom of information — overseas experience

The USA has possessed a Freedom of Information Act (FOIA) since 1966. All agencies in the executive branch of the federal government, including administrative regulatory agencies, are subject to FOIA. Excluded from the operation of the Act are the judicial and legislative branches of government. State government and local and city government are not included in this legislation. The aim of the Act, as amended in 1974, is to provide public access to an agency's records if it is covered by the Act. An applicant does not have to demonstrate a specific interest in a matter to view relevant documents – an idle curiosity suffices. Although the basic thrust of the Act is positive and supportive of openness, there are nine exemptions from the FOIA. Mandatory secrecy requirements rather than permissive ones have become more common, the 'balancing test' requiring the weighing of public access against the government need for secrecy has been eliminated, and systematic declassification has been cancelled. The order allows for its own mandatory 'review requests' of classified information as an alternative to FOIA actions. Internal rules and practices of an agency will be exempt but not the manuals and instructions on the interpretation of regulations. Other important exemptions include: trade secrets; commercial and financial information obtained by the Government that is privileged or confidential; inter- or intra-agency memoranda or letters which are not available by law; information protected by other statutes; personnel or medical files disclosure of which would constitute an invasion of privacy; and investigatory records compiled for law enforcement purposes if disclosure would result in certain types of harm. Reliance by an agency on an exemption is discretionary and not mandatory. Where there is a refusal to supply information, appeal procedures are specifically provided in each agency's FOIA regulations. A denial letter will inform the applicant of a right of appeal – usually within 30 days. The official refusing the appeal must be identified, and the exemption and reasons for refusal must be given.

Freedom of information in the UK

The Public Records Acts

Public Records Act 1958, as amended by the Public Records Act 1967

(3) The Lord Chancellor shall in every year lay before both Houses of Parliament a report on the work of the Public Record Office, which shall include any report made to him by the Advisory Council on Public Records.

. . .

Access to public records

5.–(1) Public records in the Public Record Office, other than those to which members of the public had access before their transfer to the Public Record Office, shall not be available for public inspection until they have been in existence for 30 years ... or such other period, either longer or shorter, as the Lord Chancellor may, with the approval, or at the request, of the Minister or other person, if any, who appears to him to be primarily concerned, for the time being prescribe as respects any particular class of public records.

(2) Without prejudice to the generality of the foregoing subsection, if it appears to the person responsible for any public records which have been selected by him under section three of this Act for permanent preservation that they contain information which was obtained from members of the public under such conditions that the opening of those records to the public after the period determined under the foregoing subsection would or might constitute a breach of good faith on the part of the Government or on the part of the persons who obtained the information, he shall inform the Lord Chancellor accordingly and those records shall not be available in the Public Record Office for public inspection even after the expiration of the said period. . . .

(3) ... it shall be the duty of the Keeper of Public Records to arrange that reasonable facilities are available to the public for inspecting and obtaining copies of public records in the Public Record Office.

. . .

Notes

1 Geoffrey Robertson has suggested that information is withheld to prevent embarrassment to bodies such as the police or civil servants rather than to descendants of persons mentioned in it; and in support of this he cites examples such as police reports on NCCL (1935–41), flogging of vagrants (1919), decisions

against prosecuting James Joyce's *Ulysses* (1924) as instances of material which in January 1989 was listed as closed for a century.[46]

2 In 1992–93, a review was conducted of methods of ensuring further openness in government and its results were published in a White Paper on Open Government (Cm 2290). The White Paper stated that a Code of Practice on Access to Information would be adopted (the Code is discussed below) and there would be a reduction in the number of public records withheld from release beyond 30 years. A review group established by Lord Mackay in 1992 suggested that records should only be closed for more than 30 years where their disclosure would cause harm to defence, national security, international relations and economic interests of the UK; information supplied in confidence; personal information which would cause substantial distress if disclosed. Under s 3(4) of the 1958 Act records may still be retained within departments for 'administrative' reasons or for any other special reason.[47]

3 The Freedom of Information Act (FoI Act) 2000 (see below), Part VI and Sched 8 amends the 1958 Act. Part VI amends the exemptions of Part II of the 1958 Act in respect of historical records, with a view to enhancing the ease of access to them. Section 63(1) of the FoI Act reduces the number of exemptions that apply to such records. This is done in three tranches. First, exemptions are removed after 30 years in respect of a number of categories of information, including information prejudicial to the economic interests of the UK, information obtained with a view to prosecution, court records, information prejudicial to public affairs and commercial interests. Secondly, one exemption is removed after 60 years – in respect of information concerning the conferring of honours. Thirdly, a large number of exemptions under s 31 relating to various investigations and the maintenance of law and order are removed after 100 years. These modest provisions are to be welcomed, as easing the task of historians, but their limited nature should be questioned; it must be asked why any absolute exemptions, in particular those relating to intelligence information, remain.[48]

The Code of Practice on Access to Government Information

A new Code of Practice on Access to Government Information was introduced from April 1994 as promised in the White Paper on Open Government. It was revised in 1997. The Code provides that certain government departments will provide information on request and will volunteer some information. The White Paper (Cm 2290) described the role of the PCA as follows:

> The Parliamentary Commissioner for Administration (PCA), the Parliamentary Ombudsman, has agreed that complaints that departments and other bodies within his jurisdiction have failed to comply with this code can be investigated if referred to him by a Member of Parliament. When he decides to investigate he will have access to the department's internal papers and will be able in future to report to Parliament when he finds that information has been improperly withheld. The Select Committee on the PCA will then be able to call departments and ministers to account for failure to supply information in accordance with the code, as they can now call them to account for maladministration or injustice. The ombudsman has the confidence of Parliament and is

---

46 See *Media Law* (1990), p 338.
47 The White Paper proposals in relation to public records are considered by Birkinshaw, '"I only ask for information" – the White Paper on Open Government' [1993] PL 557.
48 Cf the provision in respect of intelligence information held in the Public Record Office of Northern Ireland, which will no longer be subject to an absolute exemption, under the FoI Act, s 64(2).

independent of the Government. Parliamentary accountability will thus be preserved and enhanced. Ministers and departments will have a real spur to greater openness, and citizens will have an independent investigator working on their behalf.

However, no legal remedies are provided for citizens if the Code is breached and a number of matters were excluded from it, as can be seen in Part II of the Code which is set out below along with extracts from Part I. The extracts from the Code are followed by extracts from the White Paper (Cm 2290) describing the role of the PCA in relation to the Code. It is important to note that the PCA has no coercive powers: he cannot force government bodies to release information. Also, he can only investigate complaints about breaches of the Code if the body concerned is within his remit as determined by the Parliamentary Commissioner Act 1967. If a complaint is made about a body not within his remit there is nothing he can do.[49]

Criticisms of these arrangements follow the extracts from the Code and White Paper, from Patrick Birkinshaw and from the Select Committee on the PCA. This is followed by the government defence of the Code and of the role of the PCA in the *Minutes of Evidence Taken Before the Treasury and Civil Service Committee.*

Code of Practice on Access to Government Information
PART I
Purpose

1. This Code of Practice supports the Government's policy under the **Citizen's Charter** of extending access to official information, and responding to reasonable requests for information. The approach to release of information should in all cases be based on the assumption that information should be released except where disclosure would not be in the public interest, as specified in **Part II** of this Code.

2. The aims of the Code are:

   to improve policy-making and the democratic process by extending access to the facts and analyses which provide the basis for the consideration of proposed policy;

   to protect the interests of individuals and companies by ensuring that reasons are given for administrative decisions, except where there is statutory authority or established convention to the contrary; and

   to support and extend the principles of public service established under the **Citizen's Charter.**

   These aims are balanced by the need:

   to maintain high standards of care in ensuring the privacy of personal and commercially confidential information; and

   to preserve confidentiality where disclosure would not be in the public interest or would breach personal privacy or the confidences of a third party, in accordance with statutory requirements and **Part II** of the Code.

Information the Government will release

3. Subject to the exemptions in **Part II**, the Code commits departments and public bodies under the jurisdiction of the **Parliamentary Commissioner for Administration** (the Ombudsman):

---

49   See further Part V Chapter 3, pp 792–804 on the PCA's remit.

   i.   to publish the facts and analysis of the facts which the Government considers relevant and important in framing major policy proposals and decisions; such information will normally be made available when policies and decisions are announced;

   ii. to publish or otherwise make available, as soon as practicable after the Code becomes operational, explanatory material on departments' dealings with the public (including such rules, procedures, internal guidance to officials, and similar administrative manuals as will assist better understanding of departmental action in dealing with the public) except where publication could prejudice any matter which should properly be kept confidential under **Part II** of the Code;

   iii. to give reasons for administrative decisions to those affected;

   iv. to publish in accordance with the **Citizen's Charter:**

full information about how public services are run, how much they cost, who is in charge, and what complaints and redress procedures are available;

to release, in response to specific requests, information relating to their policies, actions and decisions and other matters related to their areas of responsibility.

4. There is no commitment that pre-existing documents, as distinct from information, will be made available in response to requests.

5. Information will be provided as soon as practicable. The target for response to simple requests for information is 20 working days from the date of receipt. This target may need to be extended when significant search or collation of material is required.

6. The Code applies to those Government departments and other bodies within the **jurisdiction of the Ombudsman** (as listed in Schedule 2 to the Parliamentary Commissioner Act 1967). The Code applies to agencies within departments and to functions carried out on behalf of a department or public body by contractors. The Security and Intelligence Services are not within the scope of the Code, nor is information obtained from or relating to them.

7. Departments, agencies and public bodies will make their own arrangements for charging.

Relationship to statutory access rights

8. This Code is non-statutory and cannot override provisions contained in statutory rights of access to information or records (nor can it override statutory prohibitions on disclosure) Where the information could be sought under an existing statutory right, the terms of the right of access take precedence over the Code. There are already certain access rights to health, medical and educational records, to personal files held by local authority housing and social services departments, and to personal data held on computer. There is also a right of access to environmental information.

Public records

9. The Code is not intended to override statutory provisions on access to public records, whether over or under thirty years old. Under s12(3) of the Parliamentary Commissioner Act 1967, the Ombudsman is not required to question the merits of a decision if it is taken without maladministration by a Government department or other body in the exercise of a discretion vested in it. Decisions on public records made in England and Wales by the Lord Chancellor, or in Scotland and Northern Ireland by the Secretary of State, are such discretionary decisions.

Investigation of complaints

11. Complaints that information which should have been provided under the Code has not been provided, or that unreasonable charges have been demanded, should be made first to the department or body concerned. If the applicant remains dissatisfied, complaints may be made

through a Member of Parliament to the **Ombudsman**. Complaints will be investigated at the Ombudsman's discretion in accordance with the procedures provided in the 1967 Act.[4]

[4] Separate arrangements will apply in Northern Ireland.

PART II

Reasons for confidentiality

The following categories of information are exempt from the commitments to provide information in this Code. In those categories which refer to harm or prejudice, the presumption remains that information should be disclosed unless the harm likely to arise from disclosure would outweigh the public interest in making the information available. References to harm or prejudice include both actual harm or prejudice and risk or reasonable expectation of harm or prejudice. In such cases it should be considered whether any harm or prejudice arising from disclosure is outweighed by the public interest in making information available.

1. Defence, security and international relations: Information whose disclosure would harm national security or defence. Information whose disclosure would harm the conduct of international relations or affairs. Information received in confidence from foreign governments, foreign courts or international organisations.

2. Internal discussion and advice: Information whose disclosure would harm the frankness and candour of internal discussion, including:

   • proceedings of Cabinet and Cabinet committees;

   • internal opinion, advice, recommendation, consultation and deliberation;

   • projections and assumptions relating to internal policy analysis; analysis of alternative policy options and information relating to rejected policy options;

   • confidential communications between departments, public bodies and regulatory bodies.

3. Communications with the Royal Household

4. Law enforcement and legal proceedings: Information whose disclosure could prejudice the administration of justice (including fair trial), legal proceedings or the proceedings of any tribunal, public inquiry or other formal investigations (whether actual or likely) or whose disclosure is, has been, or is likely to be addressed in the context of such proceedings. Information whose disclosure could prejudice the enforcement or proper administration of the law, including the prevention, investigation or detection of crime, or the apprehension or prosecution of offenders. Information relating to legal proceedings or the proceedings of any tribunal, public inquiry or other formal investigation which have been completed or terminated, or relating to investigations which have or might have resulted in proceedings.

   Information covered by legal professional privilege. . . .

5. Immigration and nationality: Information relating to immigration, nationality, consular and entry clearance cases. However, information will be provided, though not through access to personal records, where there is no risk that disclosure would prejudice the effective administration of immigration controls or other statutory provisions.

6. Effective management of the economy and collection of tax. Information whose disclosure would harm the ability of the Government to manage the economy, prejudice the conduct of official market operations, or could lead to improper gain or advantage. Information whose disclosure would prejudice the assessment or collection of tax, duties or National Insurance contributions, or assist tax avoidance or evasion.

7. Effective management and operations of the public service: Information whose disclosure could lead to improper gain or advantage or would prejudice:

   • the competitive position of a department or other public body or authority;

   • negotiations or the effective conduct of personnel management, or commercial or contractual activities;

   • the awarding of discretionary grants.

Information whose disclosure would harm the proper and efficient conduct of the operations of a department or other public body or authority, including NHS organisations, or of any regulatory body.

8. Public employment, public appointments and honours

9. Voluminous or vexatious requests

10. Publication and prematurity in relation to publication: Information which is or will soon be published, or whose disclosure, where the material relates to a planned or potential announcement or publication, could cause harm (for example, of a physical or financial nature).

11. Research, statistics and analysis: Information relating to incomplete analysis, research or statistics, where disclosure could be misleading or deprive the holder of priority of publication or commercial value. Information held only for preparing statistics or carrying out research, or for surveillance for health and safety purposes (including food safety), and which relates to individuals, companies or products which will not be identified in reports of that research or surveillance, or in published statistics.

12. Privacy of an individual: Unwarranted disclosure to a third party of personal information about any person (including a deceased person) or any other disclosure which would constitute or could facilitate an unwarranted invasion of privacy.

13. Third party's commercial confidences: Information including commercial confidences, trade secrets or intellectual property whose unwarranted disclosure would harm the competitive position of a third party.

14. Information given in confidence: Information held in consequence of having been supplied in confidence by a person who:

- gave the information under a statutory guarantee that its confidentiality would be protected; or

- was not under any legal obligation, whether actual or implied, to supply it, and has not consented to its disclosure.

Information whose disclosure without the consent of the supplier would prejudice the future supply of such information. . . .

15. Statutory and other restrictions: Information whose disclosure is prohibited by or under any enactment, regulation, European Community law or international agreement.

Information whose release would constitute a breach of Parliamentary Privilege.

Complaints about the operation of the Code and the role of the PCA

The White Paper on Open Government 1993 (Cm 2290) (extracts)

3   In investigating complaints that departments or public bodies within his jurisdiction have failed to observe the provisions of the Code of Practice on Government Information, the Parliamentary Commissioner will follow the same procedures as for other complaints investigated under the Act: . . .

     (viii) the commissioner has full discretion to set out the facts of the investigation, to explain his reasons for finding maladministration (if he upholds the complaint), to analyse and comment upon any disputed points about the interpretation of the code, to recommend what information should be published, to criticise the department (if appropriate), and otherwise to provide a full report on his investigation in accordance with his powers under the Parliamentary Commissioner Act;

     (ix) at present, where maladministration has led to unremedied injustice, the role of the commissioner is to recommend redress, but the giving of redress is normally a matter for the department; where a department accepts that maladministration has occurred — and even in those cases where it does not accept that charge — it is often possible for redress to be provided before the full process of investigation and report has been completed. By analogy, in cases relating to the Code of Practice, departments may similarly be able to provide information to the satisfaction of the person making a complaint once the commissioner has indicated that he is going to investigate or during the course of an investigation. In cases where the information in dispute has not been so provided by the department, the commissioner (in the light of sub paragraph (x) below) will not normally look to provide the redress himself by seeking to disclose the disputed information in his reports; if exceptionally he were minded to do so, he would first of all inform the principal officer of his intention;

(x)   Section 11(3) of the Act confers on ministers a power to give notice in writing to the commissioner with respect to any document or information or class of documents specified in the notice, that disclosure 'would be prejudicial to the safety of the state or otherwise contrary to the public interest' and where such a notice is given nothing in the Act shall be construed as authorising or requiring the commissioner or his staff to communicate to any person or for any purpose any document or information specified in the notice, or a document or information of a class so specified. Indiscriminate use of section 11(3) could inhibit the ability of the commissioner to carry out effective review of complaints relating to the Code of Practice on Government Information. Without fettering the discretion of ministers to use this power if the circumstances so demand, or of the commissioner to carry out his functions under the Act, neither the commissioner nor departments will act in such a way as to make the use of section 11(3) the usual means of resolving differences of opinion between the commissioner and departments. Normally the commissioner will make reasoned recommendations in his report without the specific information which is in dispute thereby being disclosed. Ministers will remain accountable to Parliament for the actions taken or refused in the light of the Parliamentary Commissioner's recommendations;

(xi)   the report mentioned above includes as appropriate:

 – the report of the results of the investigation the commissioner is required to send to the Member of the House of Commons (or If he is no longer a Member of the House to such other Member as he thinks appropriate) by whose request the investigation was made (s 10(1));

 – the special report to Parliament that may be made as the commissioner thinks fit under s 10(3) of the Act if, after conducting an investigation, it appears to the commissioner that injustice has been caused to the person aggrieved in consequence of maladministration (in these cases usually by a failure to provide information) and that the injustice has not been, or will not be, remedied; and the annual and other reports made under s 10(4) of the Act.

(For the purpose of the law of defamation, publications mentioned in s 10(5) of the Act are absolutely privileged.)

(xii)   once a report under s 10(3) or 10(4) has been laid before Parliament, it is then a matter for the House, or more usually in the first instance the Select Committee for the Parliamentary Commissioner for Administration, to consider that report and the action to be taken in the light of it. The commissioner would expect to take account of the views expressed by the Select Committee though he is not statutorily bound by them.

Criticism of the White Paper

P Birkinshaw, '"I only ask for information" – the White Paper on Open Government' [1993] PL 557, 559, 560

Analysis

In a government tradition that has been steeped in secrecy the White Paper on Open Government (WP) [Cm 2290] is a remarkable document. Remarkable both for announcing a significant *point de depart* from the culture of secrecy that has characterised the conduct of British Government – though it is well to remember that all Governments are secretive by nature, the British only more transparently so than most – and remarkable also for marking that departure, not in the form of legislation on freedom of information or open government, but largely through non-enforceable 'grace and favour' provisions. Access to government information, it should be emphasised, not papers, will be dependent upon the discretion of officials who will be guided by a Code in the exercise of their discretion. ....

Maintaining confidentiality

The WP specifies in Chapter 3, and the Code in Part II, the reasons and grounds for holding back public access for reasons of confidentiality. Some of the exemptions require a harm test to justify exemption; some do not, eg confidential communications between ministers and the Royal household, or information which could not be sought in a Parliamentary Question [prompting Maurice Frankel to write: 'Civil servants who have spent a lifetime perfecting techniques of evading MPs' questions, will now be free to practise on the general public' *(Secrets,* August 1993)], and information relating to immigration and nationality.

The exemption concerning the confidentiality of internal discussion, opinion and advice has caused much debate. This exemption seeks to protect the position of civil servants in their role as neutral advisers to Government. Were the advice revealed, civil servants would be reluctant to advise in complete candour fearing that their advice and their name could be used by the Opposition in attacking Government policies, or an incoming Government of a different party would single out civil servants with whom they could not work because of the tenor of their advice. The confidentiality of the relationship between ministers and civil servants would be eroded (para 3.15). As such it has long been supported by the First Division Association of Civil Servants and even included in Bills drafted or supported by the Freedom of Information Campaign. However, that campaign has drawn a distinction between policy advice and factual advice – as in the USA – and between policy advice and expert advice, ie advice offered on the basis of expertise and qualifications on a specific subject, very commonly of a scientific or economic nature [see *R v Secretary of State for Health, ex p US Tobacco Inc* [1992] 1 All ER 212 (QBD)]. What is common elsewhere is that factual evidence and expert evidence are available, as indeed are many forms of information once the policy-making process is over. The Freedom of Information Bill sponsored by Mark Fisher MP in the 1992/93 session, which was 'talked out' at report stage by the Government, would have allowed access to scientific and expert advice. Such advice would help to assess the strength of the options to the policies adopted by a Government.... One suspects an overkill in civil service sensitivity here. The WP dismissed the anonymising of papers when publishing them as 'not credible' without offering explanation (para 3.16). Where it is obvious who the adviser is, a lack of published documents will lead to ill-informed speculation about the nature of the advice which could be far more damaging to an individual. The reasoning is redolent of government sensitivity rather than civil service sensitivity.

Criticism of the introduction of the Code

Appendices to the Minutes of Evidence taken before the Select Committee on the PCA, HC 33 (1993–94), Vol II, p 258

Memorandum submitted by the Campaign for Freedom of Information (M31)

We regard the central proposal of the White Paper, the proposed Code of Practice on disclosure, as extremely disappointing. We do welcome some of the White Paper's proposals, particularly the proposed statutory rights to personal files and health and safety information. However, we believe that the factors that led the Government to propose broad statutory rights in these areas apply equally across the public sector and should have led the Government to accept the case for freedom of information legislation.

One aspect of the Code of Practice – the proposal that an independent arbitrator, the Parliamentary Ombudsman, should be able to investigate complaints – is a valuable step forward.

But the Code nevertheless suffers from weaknesses of such a fundamental nature that they cast doubt on whether it is capable of achieving its objectives. These features inevitably have implications for the work of the Ombudsman.

In particular we are concerned about:

- the limited scope of the disclosure Code, which is restricted to those areas subject to the Ombudsman's jurisdiction. These exclude many important parts of government;

- the lack of enforcement provisions. We recognise the value of the Ombudsman's approach. However, overseas experience with disclosure of information suggests that persuasion and reason are not enough – a legal remedy is also necessary;

- the fact that the Code only promises to answer applicants' questions – not allow them to see copies of documents. This is a fundamental flaw, which undermines the credibility of the proposals. It will generate considerable public suspicion and unnecessary work for the Ombudsman;

- the potentially large volume of complaints, and the possibility that the Ombudsman's office will not receive the resources to handle them efficiently. Long delays in dealing with complaints may frustrate applicants as effectively as outright refusals to disclose.

Scope

In our view the scope of the disclosure scheme is distorted by limiting it, as far as central government is concerned, to bodies subject to the Parliamentary Ombudsman's jurisdiction. ... The restrictions mean that parts of government which should be subject to any new access arrangements – and which are covered by freedom of information laws overseas – are excluded for essentially arbitrary reasons.

Enforcement

In our view an effective disclosure scheme requires an effective enforcement mechanism.

This is not to underestimate the value of a relatively informal remedy such as that offered by the Ombudsman. A complaint to the Ombudsman costs the applicant nothing and may, through a combination of persuasion and the threat of adverse publicity, often secure disclosure. However, it is unsatisfactory to rely exclusively on such an approach.

Many overseas freedom of information laws combine strict enforcement in a court or tribunal with the alternative of complaint to an ombudsman.

Interpreting exemptions

All the Code's exemptions raise definitional problems. Will a disclosure, in the words of the Code, 'harm defence', 'harm national security', 'harm the conduct of international affairs', 'prejudice the proper administration of the law', 'prejudice public inquiries', 'prejudice other formal proceedings', 'harm public safety', 'prejudice the conduct of official market operations', 'lead to improper gain or advantage', 'prejudice negotiations', 'prejudice the effective conduct of personnel management', 'harm the proper and efficient conduct of the operations of a department', constitute 'an unwarranted disclosure [which] would harm the competitive position of a third party'.

These terms are not clearly defined; their extent and limitations are not obvious; they are all potentially contentious. ... We doubt whether departments will find it difficult, or even embarrassing, to put forward and defend a different interpretation from the Ombudsman's. The broad exemptions provide ample, indeed almost unlimited, scope for differences of interpretation. The department need only explain that this is a matter of which there are legitimate differences of opinion; and that while it understands and respects the contrary view, it has the responsibility of deciding and feels obliged to follow its own judgment.

In the absence of a body capable of delivering and enforcing authoritative judgements we believe that it will be relatively easy for government departments to take this view and continue, in Mr Waldegrave's words 'to use secrecy for convenience if they can get away with it' [*Hansard*, HC Deb Col 598, 19 February 1993].

The exclusion of documents

What is apparently envisaged is that people will be supplied with a letter setting out the information they have requested, but will not be given access to existing reports or documents.

Minutes of Evidence Taken Before the Treasury and Civil Service Committee, 8 March 1994, HC 27 (1993–94), Vol II, p 176
Mr Davies:

1911. Mr Waldegrave ... Would you describe this White Paper and the draft Code as a reasonable compromise between the present position and the full Freedom of Information Act regime which applies in some other western countries?

Mr Waldegrave: Yes, I would, for the following reason. Presuming I get legislative time in a reasonable sense soon for the statutory things that need to be done in relation to personal records and health and safety records, if you look at the things which are then covered by statute and then you take that template and you say: 'Let's look at America. What are things about which people actually ask questions under the Freedom of Information Act?' about 80% of what in America or Canada is requested under the Freedom of Information Act will actually be statutorily based here. You are then left with the 20% or so which deals with central Government work and so on. It is possible, of course, as the Chairman very well knows, to have an Act covering that area too. I happen to think that the ombudsman route, policing a Code, is potentially a very swift and powerful and cheap way, both of improving the behaviour within the bureaucracies themselves and of giving a readier access, in terms of complaint to the citizen, without having to go through the courts. In this one area, the ombudsman holds the redress in his own hands; he sees the information. I think it will make much more of a change than people have yet realised.

1912. So you would see this really as a final solution, not just as a step along the road to full open Government?

Mr Waldegrave: ... I believe a real chance of doing what people want and if it does work it has the great merit of being cheaper, quicker and more accessible for the people who want to make a complaint.

1913. Do you accept, as a fundamental principle in a democracy where power by definition derives from the people, that all information should be open unless there are specific reasons to restrict the access to particular pieces of information?

Mr Waldegrave: I certainly do and some words very like those open the White Paper.

1914. Right. I wonder if I could come on to the issue of the role of the ombudsman? You describe the role of the ombudsman in very positive terms in contrast to Freedom of Information regimes around the world, but can we have your assurance that if the ombudsman rules that a piece of information should be revealed then the government department concerned will accept that ruling in all cases?

Mr Waldegrave: The Government has never, except in one very early case which it gave in on, tried to withstand the ombudsman. That is the first thing to say. The second thing to say is, as I said earlier, if a government was so silly then the ombudsman has the power – because he has the information – to take further steps. He has said himself that he would at that point try to negotiate, which would be sensible. He would try and say to the department: 'Come on'; that would be his first reaction, to say: 'Don't be so foolish'. In this case it is unlike other kinds of redress where you might have to order a bureaucracy to pay money or something. He actually holds the redress in his own hands. He has the bits of paper in his own hands.

The preliminary experience of the Code

The following two extracts concern the operation of the Code, and its enforcement by the Ombudsman in its early years. It is clear from the *Parliamentary Commissioner for*

Administration's Annual Report for 1995 that the Ombudsman did experience difficulties in persuading some government departments to abide by the Code, but that in general departments did show respect for the Code and the Ombudsman. However, as the Second Report from the Select Committee on the Parliamentary Commissioner for Administration, HC 84 (1995–96) indicates, concerns remained about the width of the exemptions, the limited scope of the Code and the narrowness of the Ombudsman's remit.

Parliamentary Commissioner for Administration's Annual Report for 1995, Cm 296

7. Three other investigations raised interesting and challenging issues. In the first [PCA: Ninth Report, HC 758 (1994–95), p 11] the Treasury ... refused to make available a 1994 report on frauds in Whitehall (one of an annual series) which they had prepared from departmental returns. When I took up the complaint they reconsidered the request. They then decided that, subject only to very minor excisions to avoid prejudice to investigations or legal proceedings, the report could be released ... I did not find all other departments as open-minded. In another case [PCA: First Report, HC 86 (1995–96), p 1] MAFF at first refused to release any information to a man who had bought at auction an imported heifer which had later had to be slaughtered after it had tested sero-positive for foot and mouth disease. They maintained that, irrespective of the Code, they owed the importer a common law duty of confidentiality – on the facts of the case I did not find that argument persuasive. After the referring Member's and my interventions, bit by bit all the information sought was released, except the name of the importer. I accepted that the name could be withheld under Exemption 13 of the Code ... The third case [PCA: Ninth Report, HC 758 (1994–95), p 1] involved DNH who were faced with a request that they should release information about the repeal of the broadcasting restrictions governing the interviewing of members of certain organisations in Northern Ireland. ... DNH refused the request relying on Exemption 2 of the Code (covering information whose disclosure would harm the frankness and candour of internal discussion). Having studied what was contained in the relevant Departmental papers I had no hesitation in upholding the department's view.

...

9. The one investigation which I discontinued [PCA: Ninth Report, HC 758 (1994–95), p 13] concerned a request made to HO to disclose information in their possession about records held by the Security Service. I decided to discontinue the investigation after the Permanent Secretary had confirmed to me that the decision not to release the information sought had been taken for the purposes of protecting the security of the State. That took the matter outside my jurisdiction (although I had come to the view that the existing wording in the Code did not match what was said to have been the Government's intentions) ...

12. What I have found disappointing are signs that, even within departments, knowledge of the Code's obligations can fall off quite rapidly as one moves away from those officials who have specific responsibilities in connection with information release; also there is a tendency in some departments to use every argument that can be mounted, whether legally-based, Code-based or at times simply obstructive, to help justify a past decision that a particular document or piece of information should not be released instead of reappraising the matter in the light of the Code with an open mind. I have found it time-consuming to have to consider a whole series of different defences, even when many of them prove to have no real foundation. That is one reason why it has taken longer than I would wish to complete my investigations during 1995. The other reason has been the complexity of some of the cases themselves. Some of them have been seen by the complainants and by the departments as test cases. Test cases make slow progress. In that sense they have not been typical information requests.

13. As my monitoring of the Code has developed, I have been encouraged to see signs of a change in the attitude to the release of information which the Code has produced. I have noticed this with

reference to the Treasury, the Inland Revenue and DSS. No doubt other departments have also made progress but I have detected in some departments an unawareness of the implications of the existence of the Code and an impermeability to its influence

14. Finally, I record certain other relevant developments. In the spring of 1995 the Cabinet Office produced a report [*Open Government: Code of Practice on Access to Government Information*, 1994 Report – Cabinet Office, March 1995] on the experience of departments, agencies and other public bodies in implementing the Code during the first nine months of its existence. Although there were some uncertainties over the statistics, what came out from that report was the low number of requests for information under the Code which had been made to departments. In other words, the low level of complaints to me cannot be taken to show that there is a high level of satisfaction with regard to requests for the release of information; it is simply a consequence of the fact that relatively few requests to departments are being made ...

Second Report from the Select Committee on the Parliamentary Commissioner for Administration, HC 84 (1995–96), *Open Government*

The Effect of the Ombudsman

34. The Ombudsman has concluded that the Code 'offers members of the public genuine benefits in terms of obtaining information'. [Second Report of the PCA, *Access to Official Information: The First Eight Months*, HC 91 (1994–95), p 7.] The Campaign for Freedom of Information also described its preliminary experience of the Code positively, 'it is capable of eliciting information which would previously not have been disclosed. The prospect of an investigation by the Ombudsman does appear to make departments whose objections to disclosure are not well-founded think again. The release of internal guidelines is likely to be valuable to individuals in their dealings with government and to organisations which advise them'. [Evidence p 37.] **We conclude that the Code has been an important and valuable contribution to more open government.**

The Immigration and Nationality Exemption

40. ... there is a sense of an exemption included as a result of special pleading from one department and with the suspicion that there is something to hide. The best way to dispel such assumptions would be to remove the Exemption. **We recommend that Exemption 5 'Immigration and Nationality' be removed from Part II of the Code.**

Publicity and the Office of Public Service

50. ... The Open Government 1994 Report gave statistics on the number of Code requests so made to Departments. The total to the end of 1994 (a nine month period) was 2600 requests. There are significant doubts as to the reliability of this statistic, to which we shall return. Any revision would only make it lower. The fact therefore remains that the number of requests in comparison with other countries is very low ...

59. We criticise the meagre publicity for government openness. ... **we recommend that there be a considerable increase in the funds devoted both at central and departmental level to the publicising of the Code.**

79. There has been criticism of the Code's refusal to grant a right of access to documents. The Campaign described this as 'a potentially overwhelming defect: the opportunities for selective editing are obvious ...' ... the refusal of a document can engender unnecessary suspicion. The terms of the letter sent to the complainants ... left the impression that information might be being held back. See [Eighth Report of the PCA, *Selected Cases 1995 – Volume 3: Access to Official Information*, HC 606 (1994–95), paras 8–9.]

82. We also accept the claim that there will always be a possibility, whether by design or oversight, that significant aspects of a document are removed or obscured in any paraphrase sent to a requester ...

83. **We recommend that the wording of the Code and the accompanying Guidance be amended to assert of right of access to documents, subject to the exemptions of the Code.**

External Review and the Ombudsman

96. Most FOI systems make provision for the external and independent review of a request for information. Such impartial scrutiny is perhaps particularly important in the case of FOI where the release of information can possibly be most inconvenient or embarrassing for a Government.

1. The Tribunal

97. Tribunal hearings are somewhat less adversarial than a court's and the tribunal is not bound by the normal rules of evidence. The Administrative Appeals Tribunal (AAT) is the main external review body for FOI matters at Commonwealth level in Australia . . .

2. The Court

98. In FOI regimes established by statute the court will always have a residual role through the possibility of judicial review of administrative decisions or appeal on a point of law (it is worth pointing out that even the United Kingdom's Ombudsman is susceptible to judicial review). In some instances, such as the Ontario legislation, it is made explicit that the courts cannot undertake *de novo* consideration of the case but only judicial review. Courts might also be involved as a means of enforcing the decision of the external review body. This is the case in Canada and Quebec.

99. There are also FOI regimes in which the court is the principle mechanism of external review. This is the case in the United States but is not common in Westminster-style systems. In Canada the court handles all cases claiming exemption on the grounds of commercial confidentiality.

3. The Ombudsman/Information Commissioner

100. The third model for external review is that of the Ombudsman/Information Commissioner. In New Zealand the Ombudsman was given sole responsibility for the external review of FOI decisions. In Australia the Ombudsman has external review powers but a complainant can also go to the AAT. Ombudsmen usually have power only to make recommendations . . .

Comparison of Options for External Review

104. The Government's arguments in favour of an Ombudsman, as opposed to a court or tribunal, can be summed up as follows:

- there are no costs to the complainant
- the investigation is quicker than a legal process
- the Ombudsman investigation avoids a confrontational and adversarial approach
- there is greater flexibility of approach than in a legal system
- the Ombudsman is already part of this country's political fabric, enjoying the respect of government departments and agencies
- the Ombudsman is able to make general recommendations for procedural improvements.

109. **We recommend that the Ombudsman/Information Commissioner model remain the external review mechanism for the consideration of FOI complaints.**

The Jurisdiction of the Ombudsman

112. Although there are strong arguments in favour of the Ombudsman/information Commissioner model for external review, there are problems with the Government's strategy of adding on FOI to the Ombudsman's other responsibilities without any change to his powers.

113. In addition to the restrictions placed on the Ombudsman's jurisdiction by the framing of Schedule 2 to the 1967 Act, there are also restrictions on the subject-matter he can investigate

found in Schedule 3. There are similar restrictions within the body of the Act. The Campaign gave an example of a request which had been foiled by such a restriction. The Campaign had applied to the Lord Chancellor's Department for the report of an interdepartmental working group which had considered the implications of a legal ruling (*Pepper v Hart*) of some constitutional significance. The request was refused by the Department, citing Exemption 2. The Campaign appealed to the Ombudsman who accepted their complaint for investigation. However, 'the investigation was abruptly discontinued after the Lord Chancellor's Department refused to supply the requested report to the Ombudsman'. Although the Ombudsman has wide powers of access to departmental information, section 8(4) of the Parliamentary Commissioner Act 1967 expressly denies him the right to obtain information or documents 'relating to proceedings of the Cabinet or of any committee of the Cabinet'. [Evidence, p 48.] The case raised a serious anomaly – as was pointed out earlier, Cabinet papers are not automatically exempted under the Code from release. A harm test applies. Yet the Ombudsman, the Government's preferred route of external appeal, cannot adjudicate in such cases because he has no access to the relevant documents. This is clearly unacceptable. **We note the recommendation previously made by this Committee in 1978 that 'no harm would be done by allowing the Commissioner access to Cabinet or Cabinet committee papers in the very rare cases where he considered it necessary, except where the Attorney-General certified that such access would itself be "prejudicial to the safety of the State or otherwise contrary to the public interest"'.** [Fourth Report from the Select Committee on the PCA, HC 615 (1977–78), para 34; see Evidence, p 107.] **This is also our view and we recommend to this effect.**

114. There is pressing need for the reform of the 1967 Act. Previous recommendations of this Committee, on the appointment and financing of the Ombudsman and on the redrafting of Schedule 2, still await enactment and are all the more urgent in the light of the Ombudsman's new FOI responsibilities. To these reforms we would add the removal of the absolute ban on access to Cabinet papers and a review of the provisions of Schedule 3 to the Act. Mr Freeman accepted that reform of the Ombudsman's jurisdiction was a 'third candidate' for legislation, along with two new proposed statutory rights, and he hoped to make progress [Q458]. The Government should conduct a thorough review of the current legislation along the lines we have indicated. **We recommend the thorough revision of the 1967 Act to remove the omissions in the Ombudsman's current jurisdiction, to implement the past recommendations of the Committee on the extension of his jurisdiction, and to ensure that the Ombudsman has comprehensive and effective powers in his consideration of FOI disputes.**

118. In its emphasis on the importance of the enforceability of Ombudsman decisions the Government clearly accepts that the decisions of an independent external adjudicator need at least to be *de facto* binding. This seems at present to be the case. We have stated above our preference for the Ombudsman to remain the external adjudicator in FOI cases. To give him powers to enforce his decisions on all matters investigated, both FOI and other cases of maladministration, would be a departure from the traditional concept of the Ombudsman and grant a general power that no one has asked for. It would upset a constitutional arrangement which over the last 29 years has been remarkable for its effectiveness and success.

A Freedom of Information Act

It is precisely because we accept the arguments advanced by the Government for an Ombudsman supervision that we conclude that there should be a single Freedom of Information Act encompassing all access rights. This would preserve the Ombudsman's important role, maintain the consistency of open government judgements and ensure that the various considerations that inform any decision on access all carry similar statutory weight. It would also give Parliament the opportunity to approve in detail the contents of the Code. We are convinced that on balance the advantage lies in favour of legislation. **We recommend, that the Government introduce a Freedom of Information Act.**

The current experience of the Code

At the present time, and until 2005, as explained above, the Code, with the PCA as the enforcement mechanism, represents the main method of providing access to government information. The following reports of the Select Committee on Public Administration provide patterns of answers to requests for information and detail a large number of refusals of requests for information; they indicate that public authorities have established practices of refusing such requests and can normally find a basis for such refusal within the Code. Most importantly, the extracts from the Special Report of the PCA for 2001–02 reveal that for the first time a government department has refused to accept that it should disclose information when recommended to do so by the PCA. This is significant since it reveals the impotence of the PCA system and therefore the need for an enforceable right of access to information. The report of the PCA for 2001–02 reveals that even where requests are not refused, there are often delays in the response to requests for information.

Second Report of the Select Committee on Public Administration, Prepared 17 January 2001

PATTERN OF ANSWERS LIST FOR SESSION 1998-99

HOME

Subject

Comment

Question no

Security Service (Shapurji Saklavala); Policy not to confirm or deny whether the Security Service holds records on a particular person. 61649

Operational matters (Police): Personal Security Arrangements (General Pinochet); Personal security arrangements are an operational matter for Chief Officers of Police. 62119

Official Advice

(Stephen Lawrence) Not practice to discuss advice to ministers from officials: and see 19.3 [76973]; 4.3 [73625] 74483

Immigration Records

(Pascal Lissouba) Not practice to disclose details of individuals' immigration records. 76140

Interception of Communications

Not policy and inconsistent with Interception of Communications Act 1985 to confirm or deny that warrant for or interception of communications has taken place; this includes revealing figures for interceptions in particular parts of the country. 78524

No details of reasons for issuing interception warrants given further than published in the Annual Report of the Commissioner appointed under the Interception of Communications Act 1985. 88718

Internal police inquiries: Lancet Inquiry. Operation Lancet inquiry supervised by the Police Complaints Authority—for them to monitor progress; length of the investigation for them and the investigating officer; no comment on criminal or disciplinary investigations, esp. because Home Secretary is appellate authority. 79094

PRIME MINISTER

MI5-MI6; Reports on purchase and fitting out of Vauxhall Cross and Thames House withheld under section I(a) of the Code of Practice on Access to Government Information. 63853

Cabinet Meetings, Information about Cabinet proceedings is not made public: and see 5.7 [89303] (JCCC); *but for partial unblocks see—30.4 [82878]; 27.4 [81665] (denying existence of War Cabinet).* 65517

Yugoslavia (NATO Bombing). Data on percentage of bombs and missiles which miss their target withheld under paragraph Ia of the Code on Access to Government Information. 80616

Departmental leak investigations, Not normal practice to disclose information on the outcome of leak investigations. 96344

DEFENCE

Iraq (accuracy of bombing and safety of diplomats in Baghdad). Refusal to discuss detailed operational issues under exemption I of the Code of Practice on Access to Government Information: and 16.12 [62657] 62656

Weight of ordnance fired; Approximate weight of ordnance fired at Iraq between certain dates withheld under Exemption I of Code of Practice on Access to Government Information: and see 10.5 [82592](weight of ordnance dropped on Yugoslavia). 78716

HMS Ark Royal. Estimate of the cost of refit of HMS Ark Royal commercially sensitive, as negotiations continue; information withheld under exemption 7 of the Code of Practice on Access to Government Information. 66700

CR Gas. Details of circumstances in which CR Gas used in the past withheld under Exemption I of the Code of Practice on Access to Government Information. 67629

NATO Summit. Details of UK's contribution to discussion of issues to be examined withheld under Exemption I of the Code of Practice on Access to Government Information. 81573

GM organisms research. Names of Universities and Institutes contracted to carry out GM research by DERA withheld. 84211

Flights of special nuclear material. Number of flights of special nuclear material between UK and US withheld under Exemption I of the Code of Practice on Access to Government Information. 88142

MOD hospital units. Contracts relating to NHS and MoD hospitals withheld in order to safeguard the effective management and operations of the public service. 88424

Officials attending meetings (Gulf War Veterans). Names of US officials attending meetings withheld under Exemptions I and I2 of the Code of Practice on Access to Government Information. 93940

Special Report of the PCA for 2001–02 (extracts)

This report of the PCA concerns the first occasion on which a government department has refused to accept that it should disclose information when recommended to do so by the PCA.

Access to Official Information Case No A28/01

Refusal to release the number of times Ministers had made declarations of interest and sought advice in accordance with guidelines set out in the Ministerial Code of Conduct

The attached report sets out the results of my investigation into a complaint that the then Home Secretary had refused to disclose the number of times Ministers in his Department had made a declaration of interest to colleagues under the Ministerial Code. I have concluded that there is no valid reason under the Code of Practice on Access to Government Information why this information should not be released, and that there is a public interest in making it available. I therefore much regret that Ministers have not agreed to the release of the information. As far as I can establish, this is the first occasion on which a Government department has refused to accept the conclusions of the Ombudsman on a question of disclosure of information under the Code of Practice. I therefore consider it appropriate to draw the case to the attention of Parliament by means of this report under section 10(4) of the Parliamentary Commissioner Act 1967.

MICHAEL BUCKLEY

Parliamentary Commissioner For Administration (the Ombudsman) November 2001

As part of a series of Parliamentary Questions to Secretaries of State, Mr Andrew Robathan MP asked the Home Secretary on how many occasions since May 1997 Ministers in his Department had made a declaration of interest to their colleagues under circumstances envisaged in paragraph 110 of the Ministerial Code of Conduct (the Ministerial Code). He also asked the Home Secretary how many times Ministers in his Department had sought the advice of the Permanent Secretary under the circumstances envisaged in Paragraphs 118, 121 and 123 of the Ministerial Code. The Home Secretary refused to provide the information and cited Exemption 2 and Exemption 12 of the Code of Practice on Access to Government Information. The Ombudsman found that neither of the two exemptions applied to the particular information sought by Mr Robathan. The Ombudsman upheld the complaint and recommended that the information be released to Mr Robathan. The Home Office would not agree to its release.

Departmental comments on the complaint

... the Permanent Secretary of the Home Office said that, having consulted other Departments and the Cabinet Secretary, he remained of the view that the information should not be disclosed. He said that the underlying reasons remained as set out in the then acting Permanent Secretary's comments on the complaint, namely that the purpose of the Ministerial Code would be frustrated by disclosure of this information and that it was important to maintain the separation between the public and private lives of Ministers. We remain convinced that the relationship between Ministers and Permanent Secretaries needs to be founded on full confidence. This is as provided for in the Ministerial Code of Conduct and to expose this, even in part, will eventually erode the ease with which consultations are carried out and inhibit the future operation of the Code. That is where the harm lies and it cannot be in the public interest.

[PCA's comments] 13. The purpose of Exemption 2 is to allow Government departments the opportunity to discuss matters, particularly those which are likely to be sensitive or contentious, on the understanding that their thinking will not be exposed in such a way as to impede their deliberations by inhibiting the frankness and candour of future discussion. However, Mr Robathan did not request the details of any declarations made or of advice sought, but simply the number of occasions on which they were made. He asked the Home Secretary on how many occasions since May 1997 Ministers within the Home Office had made a declaration of interest to their Ministerial colleagues or sought the advice of the Permanent Secretary under the circumstances envisaged in paragraphs 110, 118, 121 and 123 of the Ministerial Code. It is clear to me that Mr Robathan was not seeking anything other than a numerical response to his request. The question in this case, therefore, is whether or not the release of that information alone would affect the confidentiality of future discussion. I do not believe it would. I do not consider, therefore, that Exemption 2 can be held to apply to the information sought by Mr Robathan.

15. I now need to decide whether Exemption 12, also cited by the Home Office, can be held to apply to the information sought. They argued that disclosure of information relating to a possible conflict of interest between a Minister's public and private life would be an unwarranted invasion of privacy and would frustrate the purpose of the Ministerial Code. I must repeat that Mr Robathan's request was for nothing more than the number of occasions on which declarations were made or advice sought relating to a potential or actual conflict of interest. He did not request details of a Minister's private interest or even the name of any Minister who had made a

declaration or sought advice. As I see it, the purpose of the Ministerial Code is to clarify how Ministers should account to, and be held to account by, Parliament and the public. I do not agree that the release of this information would frustrate that purpose. In conclusion, I do not consider that the disclosure of the specific information requested by Mr Robathan would cause harm to the privacy of the individual concerned. Exemption 12 cannot therefore be held to apply.

Conclusion

17. I found that the two exemptions of the Code cited by the Home Office could not be held to apply to the specific information sought by Mr Robathan. I therefore upheld his complaint and recommended that the information should be disclosed to him. I am disappointed that the Home Office have not agreed to my recommendation.

Parliamentary Commissioner for Administration: ANNUAL REPORT 2001–2002

8th Report – Session 2001–2002, Presented to Parliament pursuant to Section 10(4) of the Parliamentary Commissioner Act 1967; Ordered by The House of Commons to be printed 2 July 2002; HC 897 (Session 2001–2002)

Chapter 5 – Access to Official Information

5.1 During the year the Ombudsman received 34 complaints that information had been wrongly withheld under the Code of Practice on Access to Government Information (the Code). This shows a slight reduction from 2000-01. In addition, as well as dealing with many enquiries (both written and over the telephone) about information issues, the Ombudsman commented on the information element of 79 maladministration cases submitted to him for consideration. The Ombudsman issued 20 statutory investigation reports and, for the first time, published a special report on the results of a single investigation under the Code.

Freedom of Information

5.2 As noted in the opening chapter of this report, the Government announced in November 2001 their intention to delay until January 2005 the bringing into force of those sections of the Freedom of Information Act 2000 which give a statutory right of individual access to information held by public bodies. Other things being equal, this means that until then the Code will remain in place and the Ombudsman will continue to investigate complaints that information has been incorrectly refused under it. The Ombudsman has also maintained contact with the Information Commissioner on matters of mutual interest and, more generally, has tried to ensure that the expertise gained by his Office in dealing with information complaints is made more widely available.

5.3 This has been a frustrating year for the Ombudsman in policing the Code.

5.4 A ... concern has been delay by departments involved in Code investigations. ... In case A33/01 (which involved a request for information relating to the Hinduja brothers and their applications for passports, aspects of which formed the subject of separate investigations by Sir Anthony Hammond QC), he issued his statement of complaint to the Home Office on 21 March 2001. Although he was able to examine some of the papers in this case relatively quickly, others were not provided to him because of a failure on the part of the Cabinet Office to respond, through the Home Office, to his request for a contact point for provision of their papers. Despite frequent letters and telephone calls, it was not until the Ombudsman wrote to the Home Office on 7 November, threatening to discontinue his investigation as a result of a lack of co-operation from both departments that, in December 2001, **nine months** later, papers were finally made available. In case A28/01 (see previous paragraph), the Ombudsman issued his draft report, again to the Home Office, on 20 March 2001. A response was not received until 19 October, a period of **seven months**, again despite regular prompting. The Home Office said that the delay in this case was caused by the need to consult other departments and the Prime Minister.

5.5. Such delays are completely unacceptable. The Ombudsman recognises that many of the cases he investigates under the Code involve sensitive material and difficult decisions; and that, inevitably, departments may not always welcome his conclusions. But he has become increasingly concerned at the difficulties being placed in his way in conducting some of his investigations, with consequences not only for the office's target times for the completion of investigations but, more importantly, for the complainant, who has to wait much longer for an answer than should be necessary even in the most finely-balanced of cases. In particular, it has become apparent that in some cases departments are resisting the release of information not because they have a strong case under the Code for doing so but because to release the information could cause them embarrassment or political inconvenience.

Notes

1   At the present time (2003), since the Code continues to be employed (as the Freedom of Information Act 2000 (see below) will not be fully in force until 2005), criticisms of both the Code and Ombudsman system are still pertinent. One of the key criticisms of the Code relates to the extensiveness of the list of exemptions and their breadth. Not only are the exemptions very broad, they are likely to give rise to grave difficulties of interpretation. If a department considers, on its interpretation of one of the exempting provisions, that the exemption applies, although the information seeker and Ombudsman disagree, the department cannot be compelled to release the information. No avenue of challenge to the exclusions from the Code is available. The patterns of answers to requests for information for 1998–99, given above, indicate that departments can readily find exemptions that apply to a very wide range of matters. (See also pp 298–306, above.)

2   Where an exemption clearly does not apply, a department nevertheless cannot be forced to disclose the information. If the Ombudsman recommends that a department should reveal information and the department does not accept the recommendation, it may be called upon to justify itself before the Select Committee on the Parliamentary Commissioner for Administration (PCA). However, this will not have the same impact as if the enforcement mechanism for the Code had been made legally binding since the Committee cannot compel a department to release information. In this context, the Annual Report of the PCA for 2001–02 and the Special Report for 2001 are of interest.

3   The Code is apparently based on the presumption that all useful government information will be released unless there are pressing reasons why it is in the public interest that it should remain secret. This is the general principle on which freedom of information is based. However, in relation to major policy decisions (Part I, s 3(i)), the Code only relates to information considered 'relevant' by the government. In countries which have FOI, the usefulness or relevance of documents containing information is determined by the person who seeks it rather than by government ministers or civil servants. Further, the Code promises only to afford release of information as opposed to documents. As pointed out in the memorandum submitted by the Campaign for Freedom of Information, and endorsed in the Second Report from the Select Committee on the PCA, the information seeker will be unable to ensure that all significant parts of the document in question have been disclosed.

4   As the Select Committee on the PCA points out, the government has made little effort to publicise the Code and this may be one reason for the lack of interest shown in it by individual citizens (see further the Second Report of the Parliamentary Commissioner for Administration, HC 91 (1994–95), para 5). Individual citizens who are aware of its existence may be deterred from using the

Code due to the charges which have been imposed for providing information, which have in some instances been excessive.[50] The delays in obtaining information noted by the PCA in his 2001–02 Annual Report are likely to discourage journalists and media bodies from using the Code.

5 Under the Parliamentary Commissioner Act 1967, s 5(1), the Ombudsman can take up a complaint only if the citizen has suffered injustice as a result of maladministration; both maladministration and injustice must be shown and there must be a causal link between them. These requirements are relaxed in relation to complaints relating to the Code of Practice. In relation to the Ombudsman's wider role in combatting maladministrative secrecy – where the Code makes no commitment to release particular information – these requirements must of course be met.

6 Certain matters set out in Sched 3 to the Parliamentary Commissioner Act 1967 are excluded from the investigation by the PCA. These include extradition and fugitive offenders, the investigation of crime by or on behalf of the Home Office, security of the state, action in matters relating to contractual or commercial activities, court proceedings and personnel matters of the armed forces, teachers, the civil service or police. The government has always resisted the extension of the Ombudsman system into these areas. The Code at present takes these exclusions into account and goes even further than they do in exempting a number of matters from the access which are within the jurisdiction of the PCA.

7 Criticism can also be made of the use of the MP filter in relation to Code-based complaints (for discussion and criticism of this aspect of the PCA's role in relation to his main function, see Part V Chapter 3). Citizens who need to obtain access to the Ombudsman system may not be able to do so because having contacted an MP with a complaint, the MP may decide not to refer the complaint on to the PCA. Furthermore, MPs may appear to be hampered by their political allegiance in contrast to the Ombudsman who is independent. Although MPs may not know the political allegiance of a constituent who makes a complaint regarding a refusal of access to politically sensitive information, and might in any event be uninfluenced by it, the constituent might assume that the complaint would be more forcibly pursued by an Opposition MP. In some instances MPs may have an interest in seeing that the information is withheld and therefore may face a conflict of interests.

8 It is of particular importance to note that findings and recommendations made by the PCA are not enforceable in law, so that the adverse publicity which would be generated by a refusal to comply with a recommendation is the only sanction for non-compliance. However, research indicates that the influence of the PCA is greater in practice than his limited formal powers might suggest. Rodney Austin noted in 1994 that 'Whitehall's record of compliance with the non-binding recommendations of the ombudsman is actually outstanding; on only two occasions have Government departments refused to accept the PCA's findings, and in both cases the PCA's recommendations were [nevertheless] complied with'. However, Austin goes on to note that 'compliance with the PCA's recommendations usually involves the payment of an *ex gratia* compensation, or an apology, or the reconsideration of a prior decision by the correct process. Rarely does it involve reversal on merits of an important policy decision. Governments will fight tenaciously to preserve secrets which matter to them ... there is little

---

50 See further the Citizen's Charter report on the operation of the Code, *Open Government* (1994).

ground for optimism that in a crucial case the Government would not choose to defy the PCA ...'.[51] The report of the PCA on the unprecedented refusal of the Home Office to supply information in November 2001 demonstrates that this contention is correct.

Questions

1   What avenues are available to a department which is subject to the Code to use in order to avoid complying with it in relation to embarrassing information?

2   Once the Code was in place, could it be argued that the UK citizen was in roughly the same position as regards gaining access to official information as the US citizen?

3   Consider the findings of the Scott Report (see Part IV Chapter 2, pp 559–70) and relate them to the case for placing freedom of information on a statutory basis, along US lines.

THE FREEDOM OF INFORMATION ACT 2000

Introduction

The criminalisation of the disclosure of official information under the Official Secrets Acts discussed above may be contrasted with the position in other democracies which have introduced freedom of information legislation within the last 30 years. Canada introduced its Access to Information Act in 1982, while, as indicated above, the US has had such legislation since 1967.

With the example set by other democracies in mind, commentators have been arguing for a number of years that the voluntary Code should be replaced by a broad statutory right of access to information, enforceable by another independent body or through the courts.[52] In particular, many commentators considered that one of the messages of the Scott report, published in February 1996, was that the UK needed an FoI Act, although it is impossible to know whether freedom of information could have prevented the Matrix Churchill affair.[53] The report tellingly revealed the lack of 'openness' in government: the system appeared to accept unquestioningly the need to tell Parliament and the public as little as possible about subjects which were seen as politically sensitive. It was apparent that the voluntary Code could not provide a sufficient response to the concerns which the report aroused. The Matrix Churchill affair, which led to the Scott Inquiry, would not, it seems, have come to the attention of the public but for the refusal of the judge in the *Matrix Churchill* trial to accept that the information covered by the PII certificates, relating to the change in the policy of selling arms to Iraq, could not be revealed. As the Select Committee on the PCA pointed out in its second report, an FoI Act would tend to change the culture of secrecy in government departments.

For the reasons given above, the general consensus was that merely placing the Code on a statutory basis was not a satisfactory course of action. The Conservative

51 'Freedom of information: the constitutional impact', in J Jowell and D Oliver (eds), *The Changing Constitution*, 3rd edn (1994), p 443 (currently in 4th edn (2000)).

52 See Birkinshaw (2001), *op cit*; A Tomkins, *The Constitution Unwrapped: Government after Scott* (1997), Chapter 3, pp 124–26.

53 See P Birkinshaw, 'Freedom of information' (1997) 50 Parl Aff 166; Tomkins, *ibid*, Chapter 3, pp 123–26.

governments of 1979–97 had no plans to enact freedom of information legislation. The Select Committee on the PCA recommended the introduction of an FoI Act (para 126), but this proposal was rejected by the then Conservative government.[54] The Labour government which came into office in 1997 had made a manifesto commitment to introduce an FoI Act. The White Paper, *Your Right to Know* (Cm 3818) was published on 11 December 1997. The White Paper stated: 'Unnecessary secrecy in government leads to arrogance in governance and defective decision-making ... the climate of public opinion has changed: people expect much greater openness and accountability from government than they used to.' A comprehensive statutory right of access to information was introduced with the inception of the Freedom of Information Act 2000. When it eventually comes fully into force citizens will have, for the first time, a statutory 'right' to information held by public authorities.

Freedom of Information Act 2000

An Act to make provision for the disclosure of information held by public authorities or by persons providing services for them and to amend the Data Protection Act 1998 and the Public Records Act 1958; and for connected purposes.

PART I

ACCESS TO INFORMATION HELD BY PUBLIC AUTHORITIES

Right to information

General right of access to information held by public authorities.

1.–(1) Any person making a request for information to a public authority is entitled—

(a) to be informed in writing by the public authority whether it holds information of the description specified in the request, and

(b) if that is the case, to have that information communicated to him.

(2) Subsection (1) has effect subject to the following provisions of this section and to the provisions of sections 2, 9, 12 and 14.

...

(6) In this Act, the duty of a public authority to comply with subsection (1)(a) is referred to as 'the duty to confirm or deny'.

Effect of the exemptions in Part II.

2.–(1) Where any provision of Part II states that the duty to confirm or deny does not arise in relation to any information, the effect of the provision is that where either—

(a) the provision confers absolute exemption, or

(b) in all the circumstances of the case, the public interest in maintaining the exclusion of the duty to confirm or deny outweighs the public interest in disclosing whether the public authority holds the information, section 1(1)(a) does not apply.

(2) In respect of any information which is exempt information by virtue of any provision of Part II, section 1(1)(b) does not apply if or to the extent that—

(a) the information is exempt information by virtue of a provision conferring absolute exemption, or

(b) in all the circumstances of the case, the public interest in maintaining the exemption outweighs the public interest in disclosing the information.

---

54   HC 75, HC 67 (1996–97).

(3) For the purposes of this section, the following provisions of Part II (and no others) are to be regarded as conferring absolute exemption—

    (a) section 21,

    (b) section 23,

    (c) section 32,

    (d) section 34,

    (e) section 36 so far as relating to information held by the House of Commons or the House of Lords,

    (f) in section 40—

        (i) subsection (1), and

        (ii) subsection (2) so far as relating to cases where the first condition referred to in that subsection is satisfied by virtue of subsection (3)(a)(i) or (b) of that section,

    (g) section 41, and

    (h) section 44.

Public authorities.

3.–(1) In this Act 'public authority' means—

    (a) subject to section 4(4), any body which, any other person who, or the holder of any office which—

        (i) is listed in Schedule 1, or

        (ii) is designated by order under section 5, or

    (b) a publicly-owned company as defined by section 6.

. . .

Fees.

9.–(1) A public authority to whom a request for information is made may, within the period for complying with section 1(1), give the applicant a notice in writing (in this Act referred to as a 'fees notice') stating that a fee of an amount specified in the notice is to be charged by the authority for complying with section 1(1).

. . .

(3) Subject to subsection (5), any fee under this section must be determined by the public authority in accordance with regulations made by the Secretary of State.

Time for compliance with request.

10.–(1) . . . a public authority must comply with s 1(1) . . . not later than the 20th working day following the date of receipt

. . .

Exemption where cost of compliance exceeds appropriate limit.

12.–(1) Section 1(1) does not oblige a public authority to comply with a request for information if the authority estimates that the cost of complying with the request would exceed the appropriate limit.

(2) Subsection (1) does not exempt the public authority from its obligation to comply with paragraph (a) of section 1(1) unless the estimated cost of complying with that paragraph alone would exceed the appropriate limit.

. . .

Vexatious or repeated requests.

14.–(1) Section 1(1) does not oblige a public authority to comply with a request for information if the request is vexatious.

(2) Where a public authority has previously complied with a request for information which was made by any person, it is not obliged to comply with a subsequent identical or substantially similar

request from that person unless a reasonable interval has elapsed between compliance with the previous request and the making of the current request.

...

The Information Commissioner and the Information Tribunal

The Information Commissioner and the Information Tribunal.

18.–(1) The Data Protection Commissioner shall be known instead as the Information Commissioner.

(2) The Data Protection Tribunal shall be known instead as the Information Tribunal.

Publication schemes

Publication schemes.

19.–(1) It shall be the duty of every public authority—

    (a) to adopt and maintain a scheme which relates to the publication of information by the authority and is approved by the Commissioner ...

PART II
EXEMPT INFORMATION

Information accessible to applicant by other means.

21.–(1) Information which is reasonably accessible to the applicant otherwise than under section I is exempt information.

(2) For the purposes of subsection (1)—

    (a) information may be reasonably accessible to the applicant even though it is accessible only on payment. . . .

Information intended for future publication.

22.–(1) Information is exempt information if—

    (a) the information is held by the public authority with a view to its publication, by the authority or any other person, at some future date, and ...

    (c) it is reasonable in all the circumstances that the information should be withheld from disclosure until the date referred to in paragraph (a).

(2) The duty to confirm or deny does not arise if, or to the extent that, compliance with section 1(1)(a) would involve the disclosure of any information ... which falls within subsection (1).

Information supplied by, or relating to, bodies dealing with security matters.

23.–(1) Information held by a public authority is exempt information if it was directly or indirectly supplied to the public authority by, or relates to, any of the bodies specified in subsection (3).

(2) A certificate signed by a Minister of the Crown certifying that the information to which it applies was directly or indirectly supplied by, or relates to, any of the bodies specified in subsection (3) shall, subject to section 60, be conclusive evidence of that fact.

(3) The bodies referred to in subsections (1) and (2) are—

    (a) the Security Service,

    (b) the Secret Intelligence Service,

    (c) the Government Communications Headquarters,

    (d) the special forces,

    (e) the Tribunal established under section 65 of the Regulation of Investigatory Powers Act 2000,

    (f) the Tribunal established under section 7 of the Interception of Communications Act 1985,

(g) the Tribunal established under section 5 of the Security Service Act 1989,

(h) the Tribunal established under section 9 of the Intelligence Services Act 1994,

(i) the Security Vetting Appeals Panel,

(j) the Security Commission,

(k) the National Criminal Intelligence Service, and

...

(5) The duty to confirm or deny does not arise if, or to the extent that, compliance with section 1(1)(a) would involve the disclosure of any information (whether or not already recorded) which was directly or indirectly supplied to the public authority by, or relates to, any of the bodies specified in subsection (3).

National security.

24.–(1) Information which does not fall within section 23(1) is exempt information if exemption from section 1(1)(b) is required for the purpose of safeguarding national security.

(2) The duty to confirm or deny does not arise if, or to the extent that, exemption from section 1(1)(a) is required for the purpose of safeguarding national security.

(3) A certificate signed by a Minister of the Crown certifying that exemption from section 1(1)(b), or from section 1(1)(a) and (b), is, or at any time was, required for the purpose of safeguarding national security shall, subject to section 60, be conclusive evidence of that fact.

...

Defence.

26.–(1) Information is exempt information if its disclosure under this Act would, or would be likely to, prejudice—

(a) the defence of the British Islands or of any colony, or

(b) the capability, effectiveness or security of any relevant forces.

(2) In subsection (1)(b) 'relevant forces' means—

(a) the armed forces of the Crown, and

(b) any forces co-operating with those forces,

or any part of any of those forces.

(3) The duty to confirm or deny does not arise if, or to the extent that, compliance with section 1(1)(a) would, or would be likely to, prejudice any of the matters mentioned in subsection (1).

International relations.

27.–(1) Information is exempt information if its disclosure under this Act would, or would be likely to, prejudice—

(a) relations between the United Kingdom and any other State,

(b) relations between the United Kingdom and any international organisation or international court,

(c) the interests of the United Kingdom abroad, or

(d) the promotion or protection by the United Kingdom of its interests abroad.

(2) Information is also exempt information if it is confidential information obtained from a State other than the United Kingdom or from an international organisation or international court.

(3) For the purposes of this section, any information obtained from a State, organisation or court is confidential at any time while the terms on which it was obtained require it to be held in confidence or while the circumstances in which it was obtained make it reasonable for the State, organisation or court to expect that it will be so held.

(4) The duty to confirm or deny does not arise if, or to the extent that, compliance with section 1(1)(a)—

(a) would, or would be likely to, prejudice any of the matters mentioned in subsection (1), or

(b) would involve the disclosure of any information (whether or not already recorded) which is confidential information obtained from a State other than the United Kingdom or from an international organisation or international court.

Relations within the United Kingdom.

28.–(1) Information is exempt information if its disclosure under this Act would, or would be likely to, prejudice relations between any administration in the United Kingdom and any other such administration.

(2) In subsection (1) 'administration in the United Kingdom' means—

(a) the government of the United Kingdom,

(b) the Scottish Administration,

(c) the Executive Committee of the Northern Ireland Assembly, or

(d) the National Assembly for Wales.

(3) The duty to confirm or deny does not arise if, or to the extent that, compliance with section 1(1)(a) would, or would be likely to, prejudice any of the matters mentioned in subsection (1).

The economy.

29.–(1) Information is exempt information if its disclosure under this Act would, or would be likely to, prejudice—

(a) the economic interests of the United Kingdom or of any part of the United Kingdom, or

(b) the financial interests of any administration in the United Kingdom, as defined by section 28(2).

(2) The duty to confirm or deny does not arise if, or to the extent that, compliance with section 1(1)(a) would, or would be likely to, prejudice any of the matters mentioned in subsection (1).

Investigations and proceedings conducted by public authorities.

30.–(1) Information held by a public authority is exempt information if it has at any time been held by the authority for the purposes of—

(a) any investigation which the public authority has a duty to conduct with a view to it being ascertained—

(i) whether a person should be charged with an offence, or

(ii) whether a person charged with an offence is guilty of it,

(b) any investigation which is conducted by the authority and in the circumstances may lead to a decision by the authority to institute criminal proceedings which the authority has power to conduct, or

(c) any criminal proceedings which the authority has power to conduct.

(3) The duty to confirm or deny does not arise in relation to information which is (or if it were held by the public authority would be) exempt information by virtue of subsection (1) or (2).

Law enforcement.

31.–(1) Information which is not exempt information by virtue of section 30 is exempt information if its disclosure under this Act would, or would be likely to, prejudice—

(a) the prevention or detection of crime,

(b) the apprehension or prosecution of offenders,

(c) the administration of justice,

(d) the assessment or collection of any tax or duty or of any imposition of a similar nature,

(e) the operation of the immigration controls,

(f) the maintenance of security and good order in prisons or in other institutions where persons are lawfully detained,

(g) the exercise by any public authority of its functions for any of the purposes specified in subsection (2),

(h) any civil proceedings which are brought by or on behalf of a public authority and arise out of an investigation conducted, for any of the purposes specified in subsection (2), by or on behalf of the authority by virtue of Her Majesty's prerogative or by virtue of powers conferred by or under an enactment....

(2) The purposes referred to in subsection (1)(g) to (i) are—

(a) the purpose of ascertaining whether any person has failed to comply with the law,

(b) the purpose of ascertaining whether any person is responsible for any conduct which is improper,

(c) the purpose of ascertaining whether circumstances which would justify regulatory action in pursuance of any enactment exist or may arise,

(d) the purpose of ascertaining a person's fitness or competence in relation to the management of bodies corporate or in relation to any profession or other activity which he is, or seeks to become, authorised to carry on,

(e) the purpose of ascertaining the cause of an accident....

(3) The duty to confirm or deny does not arise if, or to the extent that, compliance with section 1(1)(a) would, or would be likely to, prejudice any of the matters mentioned in subsection (1).

Court records, etc.

32.–(1) Information held by a public authority is exempt information if it is held only by virtue of being contained in—

(a) any document filed with, or otherwise placed in the custody of, a court for the purposes of proceedings in a particular cause or matter,

(b) any document served upon, or by, a public authority for the purposes of proceedings in a particular cause or matter, or

(c) any document created by—

(i) a court, or

(ii) a member of the administrative staff of a court,

for the purposes of proceedings in a particular cause or matter.

(2) Information held by a public authority is exempt information if it is held only by virtue of being contained in—

(a) any document placed in the custody of a person conducting an inquiry or arbitration, for the purposes of the inquiry or arbitration, or

(b) any document created by a person conducting an inquiry or arbitration, for the purposes of the inquiry or arbitration.

(3) The duty to confirm or deny does not arise in relation to information which is (or if it were held by the public authority would be) exempt information by virtue of this section.

Audit functions.

33.–(1) This section applies to any public authority which has functions in relation to—

(a) the audit of the accounts of other public authorities, or

(b) the examination of the economy, efficiency and effectiveness with which other public authorities use their resources in discharging their functions ...

Parliamentary privilege.

34.–(1) Information is exempt information if exemption from section 1(1)(b) is required for the purpose of avoiding an infringement of the privileges of either House of Parliament. . . .

Formulation of government policy, etc.

35.–(1) Information held by a government department or by the National Assembly for Wales is exempt information if it relates to—

(a) the formulation or development of government policy,

(b) Ministerial communications,

(c) the provision of advice by any of the Law Officers or any request for the provision of such advice, or

(d) the operation of any Ministerial private office.

(2) Once a decision as to government policy has been taken, any statistical information used to provide an informed background to the taking of the decision is not to be regarded—

(a) for the purposes of subsection (1)(a), as relating to the formulation or development of government policy, or

(b) for the purposes of subsection (1)(b), as relating to Ministerial communications.

(3) The duty to confirm or deny does not arise in relation to information which is (or if it were held by the public authority would be) exempt information by virtue of subsection (1).

(4) In making any determination required by section 2(1)(b) or (2)(b) in relation to information which is exempt information by virtue of subsection (1)(a), regard shall be had to the particular public interest in the disclosure of factual information which has been used, or is intended to be used, to provide an informed background to decision-taking.

Prejudice to effective conduct of public affairs.

36.–(1) This section applies to—

(a) information which is held by a government department or by the National Assembly for Wales and is not exempt information by virtue of section 35, and

(b) information which is held by any other public authority.

(2) Information to which this section applies is exempt information if, in the reasonable opinion of a qualified person, disclosure of the information under this Act—

(a) would, or would be likely to, prejudice—

(i) the maintenance of the convention of the collective responsibility of Ministers of the Crown, or

(ii) the work of the Executive Committee of the Northern Ireland Assembly, or

(iii) the work of the executive committee of the National Assembly for Wales,

(b) would, or would be likely to, inhibit—

(i) the free and frank provision of advice, or

(ii) the free and frank exchange of views for the purposes of deliberation, or

(c) would otherwise prejudice, or would be likely otherwise to prejudice, the effective conduct of public affairs.

(3) The duty to confirm or deny does not arise in relation to information to which this section applies (or would apply if held by the public authority) if, or to the extent that, in the reasonable opinion of a qualified person, compliance with section 1(1)(a) would, or would be likely to, have any of the effects mentioned in subsection (2).

(4) In relation to statistical information, subsections (2) and (3) shall have effect with the omission of the words 'in the reasonable opinion of a qualified person'.

(5) In subsections (2) and (3) 'qualified person'—

(a) in relation to information held by a government department in the charge of a Minister of the Crown, means any Minister of the Crown,

(b) in relation to information held by a Northern Ireland department, means the Northern Ireland Minister in charge of the department,

(c) in relation to information held by any other government department, means the commissioners or other person in charge of that department,

(d) in relation to information held by the House of Commons, means the Speaker of that House,

(e) in relation to information held by the House of Lords, means the Clerk of the Parliaments.
. . .

Personal information.
40.–(1) Any information to which a request for information relates is exempt information if it constitutes personal data of which the applicant is the data subject.

Information provided in confidence.
41.–(1) Information is exempt information if—

(a) it was obtained by the public authority from any other person (including another public authority), and

(b) the disclosure of the information to the public (otherwise than under this Act) by the public authority holding it would constitute a breach of confidence actionable by that or any other person.

(2) The duty to confirm or deny does not arise if, or to the extent that, the confirmation or denial that would have to be given to comply with section 1(1)(a) would (apart from this Act) constitute an actionable breach of confidence.

Report of the Lord Chancellor pursuant to section 87(5) of the Freedom of Information Act 2000, November 2001

The Freedom of Information Act received Royal Assent on 30 November 2000. The Act must be fully implemented by 30 November 2005. Some of the provisions of the Act are already in force. These provisions are, by and large, those which are needed in advance of implementation of the Act's main provisions. The provisions in force include those which:

Allow secondary legislation and codes of practice to be made under the Act;

- Establish the office of the Information Commissioner and relate to the appointment and period of office of the Information Commissioner;

- Allow the Information Commissioner to approve publication schemes and to prepare and approve model publication schemes;

- Allow the Commissioner to give advice and to arrange for the dissemination of information about the operation of the Act, about good practice, and any other matters within the scope of her functions under the Act;

- Require the Information Commissioner to lay an annual report before Parliament on the exercise of her functions under the Act.

Under section 87(1) certain provisions of the Act came into force on Royal Assent, ie 30 November 2000.

One of the advantages of the Data Protection Commissioner taking on expanded responsibility to oversee the Freedom of Information Act is that the extra costs of setting up a new body specifically to do this were avoided. This does not mean that no preparation is needed. On the contrary, the Office will be more than doubling in size over the next few years.

The Commissioner must be in a position to approve the Publication Schemes of all the authorities covered by the Act. With around 70,000 bodies having to meet this requirement, this is no minor task. Detailed guidance and model schemes will need to be prepared. Guidance on other areas of the Act will also need to be produced and wide consultation undertaken.

The Freedom of Information Act is a tool for culture change. It is challenged with the task of reversing the working premise that everything is secret unless otherwise stated to a position where everything is public unless it falls in to specified excepted cases. Such culture change requires more than just legislation; it takes time and effort.

Commitment at a senior level within organisations will be very important in achieving change.

Publication Schemes

A genuine open and active information policy will not just sit back and wait for requests for information to come in, but will look actively at how people can be offered information. Section 19 places a duty on every public authority to adopt and maintain a Publication Scheme. Publication Schemes give details of the classes of information that an authority publishes proactively and how. The plans indicate a commitment to proactively publish as much information as possible and will look at how best to transmit the information to those who need to know more. Many implementation teams are looking at the enormous potential for IT in this area.

Notes

1 The FoI Act 2000, which received royal assent on 30 November 2000, is one of the Labour government's major measures of constitutional reform.[55] As will be indicated below, the White Paper proposed a freedom of information regime that would have had a radical impact.[56] Had it been implemented, not only would it have brought the UK into line with other democracies as regards its freedom of information provision, but also in a number of respects the legislation would have been more bold and radical than that in place in other countries. When the Bill appeared, it was a grave disappointment,[57] but a number of improvements were made to it during the parliamentary process. The Act that has emerged cannot be termed radical, but it shows an adherence to the principle of openness which was absent in the Bill.

2 It may be noted that the Act does not extend to Scotland, with the exception of a few cross-border bodies. The Scottish Parliament passed in 2002 its own freedom of information legislation which was viewed as more liberal than the FoI Act.

3 At the time of writing, the main provisions of the Act are not yet in force, and need not come fully into force for five years (s 87(3)). It is expected that the provisions will come into force over this period so as to increase its coverage of public authorities gradually, starting with central government. The provisions already in force are indicated below and the current implementation timetable is also set out below. Importantly, it indicates, *inter alia*, that while central government bodies will have duties in relation to publication schemes by the end of 2002, they will not be subject to the right of access until 2005.

---

55 The best source of detailed critical analysis of the Bill may be found on the website of the Campaign for Freedom of Information (www.cfoi.org.uk), which contains numerous briefing notes and press releases. None of these is on the final text of the Act, but those prepared for the House of Lords' Committee, Report and Third Reading stages are extremely useful, provided they are read alongside the Act itself, and the following analysis has relied on those notes.

56 See P Birkinshaw, 'An "All singin' and all dancin'" affair: New Labour's proposals for freedom of information' [1998] PL 176.

57 See P Birkinshaw and N Parry, 'Every trick in the book: the Freedom of Information Bill 1999' (1999) 4 EHRLR 373.

Annual report on proposals for bringing fully into force those provisions of the Freedom of Information Act 2000 which are not yet fully in force. Presented to Parliament by the Lord Chancellor pursuant to section 87(5) of the Freedom of Information Act 2000, November 2001

HC 367

Implementation timetable

I announced to the House of Lords on 13 November 2001 that the Freedom of Information Act would be implemented in stages, according to the timetable set out below. The Freedom of Information Act 2000 will be implemented in full by January 2005; eleven months before the deadline set out in section 87(3) of the Act.

The Publication Scheme provisions of the Act will be implemented first, on a rolling programme, according to the timetable shown below.

November 2002: Central Government (except the Crown Prosecution Service and the Serious Fraud Office), Parliament, National Assembly for Wales, Non Departmental Public Bodies currently subject to the Code of Practice on Access to Government Information (Part I sections (1), (2), (3), and (5) and some of Part VI of Schedule 1)

February 2003: Local Government (except police authorities) (Part II)

June 2003: Police, police authorities, Crown Prosecution Service, Serious Fraud Office, Armed Forces (Part V not relating to Northern Ireland and Part I (6))

October 2003: Health Service (Part III relating to England and Wales)

February 2004: Schools, Universities, remaining NDPBs (Part IV relating to England and Wales and some of Part VI)

June 2004: Remaining public authorities

The Individual right of access to information will be brought into force for all public authorities in January 2005.

Public authorities in Northern Ireland will either be required to apply Publication Schemes at the same time as their counterparts in England and Wales, or alternative arrangements will be made. This is a matter for further discussion with the Northern Ireland Assembly.

4   The FoI Act 2000 gives UK citizens, for the first time, a statutory right to official information, which will extend to all such information except that which the Act defines as exempt. In terms of enforcement, there is a mixed picture: the right to information given by the Act is enforceable by an independent Information Commissioner, who, in the final resort, can enforce her orders through invoking the courts' power to punish for contempt of court. However, the Commissioner's power to force government to disclose information will not apply to some of the information that may be released under the Act: her disclosure orders can in some cases be quashed by ministerial veto (see below). This is perhaps the first major concern about the Act. The second is the great number and width of the exemptions it contains and the fact that many of these amount to 'class exemptions' where, in order to refuse release of the information, it is not necessary to satisfy a 'harm test', that is, show that release of the particular information requested would prejudice a particular interest, but merely that the information falls into a specified class and is, for that reason alone, exempt.

5   *The scope of the Act.* The Act covers 'public authorities'. Section 3 sets out the various ways in which a body can be a public authority. Instead of using the method adopted in the HRA, which, similarly, covers only 'public authorities' and which defines them by means of a very broad and general, non-exhaustive

definition, the FoI Act takes the different route of listing a number of public authorities in Sched 1. The list is divided into two halves. First, Parts I–V list those bodies that are clearly public authorities; under s 6 of the HRA they would be standard public authorities. Secondly, Parts VI–VII list those bodies that are only public authorities so long as they continue to meet the conditions set out in s 4(2) and (3) – that they have been set up by government and their members appointed by central government. Such bodies would probably also be viewed as standard public authorities under the HRA. But the list is not exhaustive, since s 4(1) gives the Secretary of State the power to add bodies to the list in Parts VI–VII if they meet the conditions set out in s 4(2) and (3), by Order. Under s 3(1)(b), a publicly owned company as defined in s 6 is automatically a public body; no formal designation is needed. Section 6 defines such bodies as those wholly owned by the Crown or any public authority listed in Sched 1, other than government departments. Some public authorities are covered only in respect of certain information they hold, in which case the Act only applies to that class of information (s 7(1)). Rather disturbingly, under s 7(3), the Secretary of State can amend Sched 1 so that a particular public authority becomes one which is subject only to such limited coverage by the Act – in effect potentially drastically limiting the range of information which can be sought from that authority.

6   *Public authorities covered.* The Act covers, in Sched 1, all government departments, the House of Commons, the House of Lords, quangos, the NHS, administrative functions of courts and tribunals, police authorities and chief officers of police, the armed forces, local authorities, local public bodies, schools and other public educational institutions, public service broadcasters. Under s 5, private organisations may be designated as public authorities in so far as they carry out statutory functions, as may the privatised utilities and private bodies working on contracted-out functions. The coverage of the Act is therefore far greater than that under the Code, above, and it is notable that some private sector bodies may be covered, although the government made it clear in debate on the Bill that a distinction between private and public bodies in terms of their obligations under the FoI Act should be strictly maintained and that s 5 should be used only to designate bodies discharging public functions.[58] The FoI Act is clearly *not* to be extended into the realm of business. The Act has been praised for the very wide range of bodies which it covers; in comparison with freedom of information regimes abroad, the coverage is very generous. But it should be noted that, in fact, its coverage of private bodies discharging public functions is subject to the exercise of a discretion by the Secretary of State.

7   *The rights granted by the Act.* The Act grants two basic rights under s 1(1): the right to be informed in writing by the public authority whether it holds information of the description specified in the request and, if that is the case, to have that information communicated to him or her. It may be noted that the right conferred under s 1(1)(b) can cover original documents as well as 'information',[59] and in this respect the Act is clearly an improvement on the Code. Both these fundamental rights are subject to the numerous exemptions the Act contains. Thus, where an authority is exempt from providing information under the Act, it is also entitled to refuse even to state whether it holds the information or not, although in some

---

58   HC Standing Committee B col 67 (11 January 2000).
59   Section 84 defines information broadly to cover information 'recorded in any form', and in relation to matters covered by s 51(8) this includes unrecorded information.

cases, it may only do this where stating whether it holds the information would have the effect of causing the prejudice that the exemption in question is designed to prevent. Such cases will be indicated below.

8 *Proposed exemptions under the White Paper.* Seven specified interests were indicated in the White Paper, which took the place of the exemptions under the Code. The test for disclosure was based on an assessment of the harm that disclosure might cause and the need to safeguard the public interest. The test was: will this disclosure cause substantial harm to one of these interests? The first of these interests covered national security, defence and international relations. Obviously, this interest covered a very wide range of information. A further five interests were: law enforcement, personal privacy, commercial confidentiality, the safety of the individual, the public and the environment, and information supplied in confidence. Finally, there was an interest termed 'the integrity of decision-making and policy advice processes in government'. In this category, a different test was used: it was not necessary to show that disclosure of the information would cause substantial harm; a test of simple harm only was used.

9 *Exemptions under the Act.* The exemptions proposed under the White Paper were relatively narrow and were subject to quite a strict harm test. They may be sharply contrasted with those that emerged under the Act which include a number of 'class'-based exemptions. The exemptions under the Act rely on the key distinction between 'class' and 'harm-based' exemptions mentioned above. The harm-based exemptions under the Act are similar to those indicated in the White Paper: they require the public authority to show that the release of the information requested would, or would be likely to, cause prejudice to the interest specified in the exemption. But a number are class-based, meaning that in order to refuse the request, the authority only has to show that the information falls into the class of information covered by the exemption, not that its release would cause or be likely to cause harm or prejudice. It may be noted that the class exemptions can be further divided into two groups: those that are content-based, in the sense that no access to the information under the FoI Act or any other instrument is available; and others, which relate not to the content of the information, but to the process of acquiring it. These distinctions are made clear below, in the first group of exemptions considered.

10 *The public interest test.* The Act complicates matters further by providing that, in relation to some, but not all, of the class exemptions, and almost all the 'harm exemptions', the authority, having decided that the information is *prima facie* exempt (either because the information falls into the requisite class exemption, or because the relevant harm test is satisfied, as the case may be), must still then go on to consider whether it should be released under the public interest test set out in s 2. This requires the authority to release the information unless 'in all the circumstances of the case, the public interest in maintaining the exemption outweighs the public interest in disclosing the information'. It should be noted that this provision was amended in the Lords so as to require release unless the interest in maintaining secrecy *'outweighs'* the interest in disclosure. This was thought to provide greater protection for freedom of information, since it must be demonstrated that the need for secrecy is the more compelling interest in the particular case. The Campaign for Freedom of Information (CFoI) noted that where information falls into a class exemption, and an authority objects to disclosure even under the public interest test, it will be able not only to argue that the specific disclosure would have harmful effects, *but also that the public interest would be harmed by any disclosure from within the relevant class of documents, regardless of the*

consequences of releasing the actual information in question.[60] By contrast, under a prejudice test, the authority must be able first to identify that harm would be caused by releasing the *specific information* requested, and then go on to show that that specific harm outweighs the public interest in disclosure.

11 *Categories of exemptions.* Four suggested categories are set out below. These categories are important not only in terms of the substantive legal tests which must be satisfied before information may be withheld: they also have crucial practical consequences in terms of time limits and enforcement. As explained below, the 20-day deadline for releasing information does not apply to information released only on public interest grounds. More importantly, the Commissioner's decision to order release on such grounds can, in relation to information held by certain governmental bodies, be vetoed by ministers (see further below).

(a) *Class exemptions not subject to the public interest test.* These exemptions can be referred to as 'total' or absolute exemptions: that is, class exemptions to which the public interest test in s 2 *does not apply.* The public authority concerned only has to show that information sought falls into the exempt class, not that its disclosure would cause any harm or prejudice; and there is no duty to consider whether the public interest in maintaining the exemption outweighs the public interest in disclosing the information. Most of these exemptions, such as those under ss 12, 14, 32, 34, 40 and 41 are self-explanatory. Section 21 covers information that is reasonably accessible to the applicant from other sources. Section 23(1) covers information supplied by or which relates to the intelligence and security services, GCHQ, the special forces and the various tribunals to which complaints may be made about their activities and about phone tapping. It should be noted that, as indicated above, the bodies mentioned in this exemption are not themselves covered by the Act at all. This exemption therefore applies to information which is held by *another public authority*, but which has been supplied by one of these bodies. Because it is a class exemption, it could apply to information which had no conceivable security implications, such as evidence of a massive overspend on MI5 or MI6's headquarters. The duty to confirm or deny does not apply to information in this category where complying with it would itself involve disclosure of information covered by this exemption. Bearing in mind the complete exclusion of the security and intelligence services from the Act, the use of this exemption unaccompanied by a harm test and not subject to the public interest test is likely to mean that sensitive matters of great political significance remain undisclosed, even if their disclosure would ultimately benefit those services or national security.

Information the disclosure of which would contravene any other Act of Parliament (for example, the Official Secrets Act 1989) or would be incompatible with any EU obligation or constitute a contempt of court (s 44) is exempt and the duty to confirm or deny does not apply to the extent that compliance with it would amount to a contravention, as described above. This exemption ensures that the FoI Act cannot be seen impliedly to repeal the numerous provisions that criminalise the release of information, but rather preserves them all.

(b) *Class exemptions subject to the public interest test.* The second category covers class exemptions subject to the public interest test. In relation to these exemptions, in practice, while the Commissioner will always have the last word on whether

---

60   Freedom of Information Bill, House of Lords, Third Reading, 21 November 2000, briefing notes, p 10.

the information falls into the class in question, she will not always be able to enforce a finding that it should nevertheless be released on public interest grounds if the information is held by certain governmental bodies, since the ministerial veto may be used.

The first of these exemptions arises under s 30(1); it is a sweeping exemption, covering all information, whenever obtained, which relates to investigations that may lead to criminal proceedings. It represents a specific rejection of the recommendation of the MacPherson Report[61] that there should be no class exemption for information relating to police investigations. It overlaps with the law enforcement exemption of s 31, which does include a harm test. The exclusion of police operational matters and decisions echoes the approach under s 4 of the Official Secrets Act, but unlike s 4, no harm test is included. There are certain aspects of information relating to investigations which would appear to require disclosure in order to be in accord with the principle of openness enshrined in the Act. For example, a citizen might suspect that his or her telephone had been tapped without authorisation or that he or she had been unlawfully placed under surveillance by other means. Under the Act, no satisfactory method of discovering information relating to such a possibility will exist. It is therefore unfortunate that telephone tapping and electronic surveillance were not subjected to a substantial harm or even a simple harm test.

This exemption extends beyond protecting the police and the CPS and will cover all information obtained by safety agencies investigating accidents. Thus, it will cover bodies such as the Health and Safety Executive, the Railway Inspectorate, the Nuclear Installations Inspectorate, the Civil Aviation Authority, the Marine and Coastguard Agency, environmental health officers, trading standards officers and the Drinking Water Inspectorate. It will cover routine inspections as well as specific investigations, since both can lead to criminal prosecution. Thus, anything from an inspection of a section of railway track by the Railway Inspectorate to a check upon hygiene in a restaurant by the Health and Safety Executive could be covered. The duty to confirm or deny does not apply (s 30(3)). As the CFoI commented:

Reports into accidents involving dangerous cars, train crashes, unsafe domestic appliances, air disasters, chemical fires or nuclear incidents will go into a permanently secret filing cabinet. The same goes for reports into risks faced by workers or the public from industrial hazards. The results of safety inspections of the railways, nuclear plants and dangerous factories would be permanently exempt. This is the information that most people assume FoI legislation exists to provide.[62]

The need for such a sweeping class exemption is hard to justify since s 31 specifically exempts information which could prejudice the prevention or detection of crime, or legal proceedings brought by a public authority arising from various forms of investigation. That exemption will ensure that no information is released which could damage law enforcement and crime detection, and it has been noted above that information which could amount to a contempt of court is also exempted. The CFoI noted that the recently retired Director General of the Health and Safety Executive has said publicly that the work of the HSE does not require such sweeping protection.[63] It should be noted

---

61 The MacPherson Report on the Stephen Lawrence Inquiry, Cm 4262 (1999), proposed that all such matters should be covered by the FoI Act, subject only to a substantial harm test.
62 Freedom of Information Bill, House of Lords, Committee Stage, 19 October 2000, briefing notes.

that, where it has been decided that the information falls into the protected class, the authority must then go on to consider whether it should be released under the public interest test. Since most of the information above will not be held by a government department (see below), the Commissioner will be able to order disclosure if she thinks the information should be released under this provision, with no possibility of a ministerial veto.

The other major class exemption in this category, under s 35, has been just as criticised. Section 35 amounts to a sweeping exemption for virtually all information relating to the formation of government policy. The duty to confirm or deny does not apply. This exemption is presumably intended to prevent government from having to decide policy in a goldfish bowl – to protect the freeness and frankness of Civil Service advice and of internal debate within government – but, once again, it appears to go far beyond what would sensibly be required to achieve this aim. Section 36 contains a harm-based exemption which covers almost exactly the same ground: it exempts government information which would, or would be likely to, inhibit (a) the free and frank provision of advice, or (b) the free and frank exchange of views for the purposes of deliberation, or (c) would otherwise prejudice, or would be likely otherwise to prejudice, the effective conduct of public affairs. Since this covers all information whose release might cause damage to the working of government – and is framed in very broad terms – it appears to be unnecessary to have a sweeping class exemption covering the same ground. Moreover, this exemption is not restricted to Civil Service advice; it covers also the background information used in preparing policy, including the underlying facts and their analysis. As the CFoI commented: 'There would be no right to know about purely descriptive reports of existing practice, research reports, evidence on health hazards, assumptions about wage or inflation levels used in calculating costs, studies of overseas practice, consultants' findings or supporting data showing whether official assertions are realistic or not.'[64]

The sole exception to this exemption appears in s 35(2); it applies only 'once a decision as to government policy has been taken' and covers 'any statistical information used to provide an informed background to the taking of the decision'. This was a concession made by the government fairly late in the Bill's passage through Parliament and is very limited. First, unlike most other freedom of information regimes, by excluding only statistical information from the exemption, s 35(2) allows the *analysis* of facts to be withheld. Secondly, it only applies once a decision has been taken. Thus, where the government gave consideration to introducing a new policy but then shelved the matter without a decision, statistics used during the consideration process would remain exempt.

The White Paper preceding the Bill proposed that there should be no class exemption for material in this area, but rather that, as under the Code, a harm test would have had to be satisfied to prevent disclosure. While information in this category is subject to a public interest test, it is important to note that, because, by definition it will generally be information held by a government department, if the Commissioner orders disclosure on public interest grounds, the ministerial veto will be available to override her.

---

63 *Ibid.*
64 *Ibid*, p 1.

Information intended for future publication where it is reasonable that information should be withheld until that future date is exempt (s 22), and the duty to confirm or deny does not apply to the extent that complying with it would itself entail disclosing such information. The problem with the class exemption under s 22 is its imprecision: it does not specify a period within which the information has to be intended for publication for this exemption to apply. The government repeatedly rejected amendments that would have provided that this exemption could only be relied upon if a date for publication within a short, specified period had already been fixed.

There are a number of further class exemptions. Information subject to legal privilege (s 42) is exempt. The duty to confirm or deny does not apply if compliance with it would itself breach legal privilege. Trade secrets (s 43(1)) are exempt, but the duty does apply. 'Communications with Her Majesty, with other members of the Royal Family or with the Royal Household', or information relating to 'the conferring by the Crown of any honour or dignity' (s 37) are exempt, and the duty to confirm or deny does not apply. It is unclear why it is necessary to bestow a class exemption relating to the royal household and honours and dignities, although this follows the voluntary Code of Practice. A separate class exemption covers information obtained for the purposes of conducting criminal proceedings and a very wide variety of investigations (specified in s 31(2)) carried out under statute or the prerogative, and which relate to the obtaining of information from confidential sources.

(c) *Harm-based exemptions not subject to the public interest test.* This third category of exemptions has only one member. There is a general, harm-based exemption under s 36 for information the disclosure of which would be likely to prejudice the effective conduct of public affairs or inhibit free and frank discussion and advice. This exemption is subject to the general public interest test with one exception: for a reason that is not readily apparent, where the information in question is held by the Commons or Lords, the public interest test cannot be considered. In order to invoke this exemption, the authority has to show that the release of the particular information concerned would cause or be likely to cause the relevant prejudice, but then need not go on to consider whether this prejudice outweighs the public interest in disclosure: once prejudice is established, that is the end of the matter.

(d) *Harm-based exemptions which are subject to the public interest test.* This category covers a vast range of exemptions. These are the exemptions under which it is hardest for the public authority concerned to resist the release of information. To do so, it must first demonstrate prejudice or likely prejudice from the release of the particular information requested and then, if prejudice is shown, go on to consider whether the public interest in forestalling that prejudice outweighs the public interest in disclosing the information under s 2.

As harm-based exemptions, these are in one respect the least controversial aspect of the Act. But it is extremely important to note that the Act departed from one of the most liberal and widely praised aspects of the White Paper, namely, the requirement that in order to make out such exemptions, the authority concerned would have to demonstrate 'substantial' harm. This has been changed to a test of simple prejudice, although government spokespersons have attempted to deny that the change would make any difference in practice. In each case, the duty to confirm or deny does not apply if, or to the extent that, compliance with it would itself cause the prejudice which the exemption seeks to prevent.

These exemptions cover information the disclosure of which would prejudice or would be likely to prejudice: defence and the armed forces (s 26), international relations (s 27), the economy (s 29), the mental or physical health or safety of any individual (s 38), auditing functions of other public authorities (s 33), the prevention, detection of crime, legal proceedings brought by a public authority arising from an investigation conducted for any of the purposes specified in s 31(2) (above) and carried out under statute or prerogative, the collection of tax, immigration controls, good order in prisons; the exercise by any public authority of its functions for any of the purposes specified in s 31(2) (above), and relations between administrations in the UK (for example, between the government and the Scottish Executive) (s 28). These exemptions are relatively straightforward, although they go beyond the information covered by the Official Secrets Act 1989.

A number of these exemptions are more contentious. Section 24 covers information the disclosure of which would prejudice or would be likely to prejudice national security. The use of the national security exemption, albeit accompanied by the harm test, may mean that sensitive matters of great political significance remain undisclosed. In particular, the breadth and uncertainty of the term 'national security' may allow matters which fall only doubtfully within it to remain secret. Had the Act been in place at the time of the change in policy regarding arms sales to Iraq, the subject of the Scott report, it is likely that information relating to it would not have been disclosed since it could have fallen within the exception clauses. The whole subject of arms sales will probably fall within the national security exception and possibly within other exceptions as well.[65]

Under s 43, information the disclosure of which would prejudice or would be likely to prejudice the commercial interests of any person (including the public authority holding it) is exempt. The CFoI commented that under this exemption, the prejudice referred to could be caused by consumers refusing to buy a dangerous product. Thus, they noted, that the fact that a company had sold dangerous products, or behaved in some other disreputable manner, could be suppressed if disclosure would lead customers to buy alternative products or shareholders to sell their shares.[66] This is clearly correct; however, in the case of unsafe products, the public interest test would surely require disclosure.

Section 36 covers information which, in the reasonable opinion of a qualified person, would prejudice or be likely to prejudice collective ministerial responsibility, or the work of the Executives of Northern Ireland and Wales, or which would be likely to inhibit the free and frank provision of advice, or the free and frank exchange of views for the purposes of deliberation, or would otherwise prejudice, or would be likely otherwise to prejudice, the effective conduct of public affairs. Two main criticisms of this exemption can be made. First, the test is not a wholly objective one, but is dependent upon 'the reasonable opinion of a qualified person'. The intention behind this provision is apparently to allow a person representing the department or body in question to make the primary determination of prejudice, with the Commissioner being able to take issue with such a finding only if it is irrational in the *Wednesbury*

---

65   See further the Minutes of Evidence before the Public Service Committee, HC 313-1 (1995–96), QQ 66 *et seq*.

66   Freedom of Information Bill, House of Lords, Committee Stage, 19 October 2000, briefing notes, p 1.

sense. The second main objection to this section is the 'catch-all' provision covering information the release of which could 'prejudice the effective conduct of public affairs', a phrase which is so vague and broad that it could mean almost anything.

12 *Expiry of certain exemptions.* As indicated above, the Act, through amendments to the Public Records Act 1958, provides that some of that Act's exemptions will cease to apply after a certain number of years (see p 620), although these limitations are hardly generous. The following exemptions will cease to apply at all after 30 years (s 63(1)): s 28 (inter-UK relations), s 30(1) (information obtained during an investigation), s 32 (documents generated in litigation), s 33 (audit functions), s 35 (information relating to internal government discussion and advice), s 36 (information which could prejudice effective conduct of public affairs), s 37(1)(a) (communications with royal household), s 42 (legal professional privilege) and s 43 (trade secrets and information which could damage commercial interests). The exemptions under s 21 (information accessible by other means) and s 22 (information intended for future publication) will cease to apply after 30 years where the relevant document is held in a public record office (s 64(1)). Still less generously, information relating to the bestowing of honours and dignities (s 37(1)(b)) only ceases to be exempt after 60 years, while we will have to wait 100 years before the expiry of the exemption for information falling within s 31, that is, information which might prejudice law enforcement, the administration of justice, etc. Additionally, one of the absolute exemptions – information provided by the security, intelligence, etc services (s 23(1)) – will cease to be absolute after 30 years, that is, the public interest in disclosure must be considered once 30 years has expired.

13 *Comparison with the Code exemptions.* The exemption under s 35(1) is much more restrictive than the equivalent exemption under the present, voluntary Code of Practice on Access to Government Information. The latter requires in para 2 that both facts and the analysis of facts underlying policy decisions, including scientific analysis and expert appraisal, be made available once decisions are announced. Material relating to policy formation can only be withheld under a harm test if disclosure would 'harm the frankness and candour of internal discussion'. In certain respects, however, the Code is, on its face, more generous, as indicated below. In particular, the total exemption under s 21 does not appear in the Code in as broad a form.[67] But in general, the exceptions under the Act will be, on the whole, less wide ranging than those under the Code, taking into account the limitations of the PCA's remit.

14 *Applying for information, time limits, practical problems.* Requests for information must be in writing (s 8) and, under s 9, a fee may be charged subject to an – as yet – unfixed maximum, which ministers indicated would probably be set initially at £10. Information requested must generally be supplied within 20 days of the request (s 10(1)). However, there is an important exception to this: where an authority finds that information is *prima facie* exempt, either because it falls within a class exemption, or the requisite prejudice is thought to be present, but then goes on to consider whether the information should nevertheless be released under the public interest test, it does not have to make a decision within the normal 20-day deadline. Instead, it must release the information only within an unspecified 'reasonable period'.

---

67 Paragraph 8 of the Code refers to information obtainable under existing statutory rights.

There may be practical problems in using the Act. The citizen may have difficulty in obtaining the document he or she requires. He or she might not be able to frame the request for information specifically enough in order to obtain the particular documents needed. The request might be met with the response that 3,000 documents are available touching on the matter in question; the citizen might lack the expert knowledge needed to identify the particular document required. If so, under s 1(3), the authority need not comply with the request and can continue to postpone its compliance until and if the requester succeeds in formulating the request more specifically. Section 1(3) does not allow the authority to postpone the request until it has had a chance to obtain further information, enabling it to deal with the request.

15 *The enforcement mechanism.* The enforcement review mechanism under the Act is far stronger than the mechanism established under the Code. The internal review of a decision to withhold information, established under the Code, was formalised under the Act and the role of the Ombudsman was, under the Act, replaced by that of the Information Commissioner (formerly the Data Protection Commissioner). The Commissioner's powers will also be much more extensive than those of the Ombudsman. As indicated below, she will have the power to order disclosure of the information and can report a failure to disclose information to the courts who can treat it in the same way as contempt of court. Under the White Paper, it was to be a criminal offence to destroy, alter or withhold records relevant to an investigation of the Information Commissioner. It was also to become a criminal offence to shred documents requested by outsiders, including the media and the public. However, the two offences are omitted from the Act. No civil liability is incurred if a public authority does not comply with any duty imposed by the Act (s 56).

The rights granted under the Act are enforceable by the Information Commissioner. Importantly, the Commissioner has security of tenure, being dismissable only by the Crown following an address by both Houses of Parliament. An appeal lies from decisions of the Commissioner to the Information Tribunal which is made up of experienced lawyers and 'persons to represent the interests' of those seeking information and of public authorities (Sched 2, Part II). See further below on the work of the Commissioner.

Under s 50, 'Any person (in this section referred to as 'the complainant') may apply to the Commissioner for a decision whether, in any specified respect, a request for information made by the complainant to a public authority has been dealt with in accordance with [the Act]'. The Commissioner must then make a decision unless the application has been made with 'undue delay', is frivolous or vexatious, or the complainant has not exhausted any complaints procedure provided by the public authority (s 50(1)). If the Commissioner decides that the authority concerned has failed to communicate information or confirm or deny when required to do so by the Act, she must serve a 'decision notice' on the authority stating what it must do to satisfy the Act. She may also serve 'Information Notices' upon authorities, requiring the authority concerned to provide her with information about a particular application or its compliance with the Act generally.

The Commissioner may ultimately force a recalcitrant authority to act by serving upon it an enforcement notice, which, *per* s 52(1), 'requir[es] the authority to take, within such time as may be specified in the notice, such steps as may be so specified for complying with those requirements'. If a public authority fails to comply with a Decision, Enforcement or Information Notice, the Commissioner can certify the failure in writing to the High Court, which, the Act provides (s 52(2)), 'may inquire into the matter and, after hearing any witness who may be produced against or on behalf of the public authority, and after hearing any statement that may be offered in defence, deal with the authority as if it had committed a contempt of court'.

In other words, the Commissioner's decisions can, in the final analysis, be enforced just as can orders of the court. These powers are buttressed by powers of entry, search and seizure to gain evidence of a failure by the authority to carry out its obligations under the Act or comply with a Notice issued by the Commissioner (detailed in Sched 3).

16 *Appeal to the Information Tribunal.* The Commissioner's decisions are themselves subject to appeal to the Tribunal, and this power of appeal is exercisable upon the broadest possible grounds. The Act provides that either party may appeal to the Tribunal (s 60) against a decision notice and a public authority against an enforcement or information notice (s 57(2) and (3)) either on the basis that the notice is 'not in accordance with the law', or 'to the extent that the notice involved an exercise of discretion by the Commissioner, that he ought to have exercised his discretion differently' (s 58(1)). The Tribunal is also empowered to review 'any finding of fact on which the notice in question was based' and, as well as being empowered to quash decisions of the Commissioner, may 'substitute such other notice as could have been served by the Commissioner'.

17 *Appeal from the Tribunal.* There is a further appeal from the Tribunal to the High Court, but on a 'point of law' only (s 59). In practice, this will probably be interpreted so as to allow review of the Tribunal's decisions, not just for error of law, but also on the other accepted heads of judicial review.

18 *The ministerial veto of the Commissioner's decisions.* The ministerial veto is viewed as a highly controversial aspect of the Act. The White Paper made no provision for such a power of veto, on the basis that to do so would undermine confidence in the regime. Such a veto clearly dilutes the basic freedom of information principle that a body independent from government should enforce the rights to information and since, in cases where the release of information could embarrass ministers, it constitutes them judge in their own cause, it is objectionable in principle.

For the veto to be exercisable, two conditions must be satisfied under s 53(1): first, the Notice which the veto will operate to quash must have been served on a government department, the Welsh Assembly or 'any public authority designated for the purposes of this section by an order made by the Secretary of State'; secondly, the Notice must order the release of information which is *prima facie* exempt but which the Commissioner has decided should nevertheless be released under the public interest test in s 2. (By *prima facie* exempt, it will be recalled, is meant information that either falls into a class exemption or, where prejudice is required to render it exempt, the Commissioner has adjudged the prejudice to be present.)

The veto is exercised by means of a certificate signed by the minister concerned stating that he has 'on reasonable grounds formed the opinion that, in respect of the request or requests concerned, there was no failure' to comply with the Act. The decision must be made at a relatively senior level. If the information is sought from a department of the Northern Irish Executive or any Northern Ireland public authority, it must be exercised by the First and Deputy Minister acting together; if a Welsh department or any Welsh public authority, the Assembly First Secretary; if from a government department or any other public authority, a Cabinet minister.

The reasons for the veto must be given to the complainant (s 56), unless doing so would reveal exempt information (s 57) and the certificate must be laid before Parliament or the Welsh/Northern Ireland Assembly as applicable.

19 *Publication schemes.* Under ss 19 and 20, public authorities must adopt 'publication schemes' relating to the publication of information by that authority. This is a significant aspect of the Act since more citizens will thereby gain access to a wider range of information. The difficulty and expense of making a request will be avoided. The scheme can be devised by the authority or, under s 20, a model scheme devised by the Information Commissioner can be used. If a tailor-made scheme is used, it must be approved by the Commissioner (s 19(1)(a)). Therefore, authorities are likely to use the model schemes, thereby avoiding the need to submit the scheme for approval. Consistency between authorities is probably desirable as promoting consistency and thereby enhancing access to information. Further information on the implementation of these schemes is provided below, in the Lord Chancellor's report.

20 *Relationship between the FoI Act 2000 and the Human Rights Act 1998.* An assertion of a right to access to information can be distinguished from an assertion of a free speech right, although the two are clearly linked.[68] This distinction receives support from the wording of Article 10 of the European Convention, which speaks in terms of the freedom to 'receive and impart information', thus appearing to exclude from its provisions the right to demand information from the unwilling speaker. Moreover, the phrase 'without interference from public authorities' does not suggest that governments should come under any duty to act in order to ensure that information is received. Information intended to be placed in the public domain may be sought when there is no speaker willing to disclose it, or where the body which 'owns' the information is unwilling that it should be disclosed. Whether such communication of confidential information should be regarded as 'speech' or not,[69] it is clearly a necessary precondition for the production of speech and therefore can be treated as deserving of the same protection as 'speech' in that the result will be that the public will be informed and debate on issues of public interest will not be stifled. The argument that such dissemination of information will render the government more readily accountable is strongly related to the justification for free speech which argues that it is indispensable to democracy, since it enables informed participation by the citizenry (see Part VI Chapter 2, pp 905–06). However, freedom of speech guarantees, including Article 10, do not tend to encompass the imposition of positive obligations and therefore, in general, are violated when a willing speaker is prevented from speaking rather than in the situation where information deriving ultimately from an unwilling speaker – usually the government – is sought, entailing the assertion of a positive right.

Further, information may be sought although it is not intended that it should be communicated to others. It is not clear that the free speech justifications considered in Part VI Chapter 2 would apply to such a situation, and therefore it would tend to be considered purely as an access to information or privacy issue. Thus, it is clear

---

68   See further E Barendt, *Freedom of Speech* (1987), pp 167–72.
69   The European Court of Human Rights takes the view that it should not. In the *Gaskin* case (1990) 12 EHRR 36 it viewed a demand for access to information which the body holding it did not wish to disclose as giving rise only to an Article 8 issue, not an Article 10 issue. The US Supreme Court has held that the First Amendment does not impose an affirmative duty on government to make information not in the public domain available to journalists (417 US 817). For discussion of this issue see Barendt, *ibid*, pp 107–13.

that many demands for access to information are not based on an assertion of free speech interests.

These remarks suggest that Article 10, scheduled in the HRA, may not have much impact on *access* to information, in the sense of using Article 10 to create an access right or in terms of interpreting the provisions of the Freedom of Information Act under s 3 of the HRA. However, the individual who wishes to receive information for his or her *private* purposes could rely on s 3 to interpret the FoI Act consistently with Article 8.[70]

21 *Conclusions.* Rodney Austin described the draft Bill as 'a denial of democracy'.[71] It is suggested that the improvements made to the Bill during its passage through Parliament, while still leaving it a far weaker and more illiberal measure than proposed by the widely praised White Paper which preceded it, render this view inapplicable to the Act itself. In particular, the public interest test has been strengthened, and applies to most of the exemptions in the Act, including, crucially, the key class exemptions relating to investigations and to the formation of government policy. However, as the CFoI points out, it is misleading to view this as converting class exemptions into 'harm-based' ones, since the very existence of a class exemption is based upon a presumption, built into the Act, that such information is, *as a class*, of a type which generally should not be released.

Despite its weaknesses, this is a constitutional development whose significance can hardly be overstated. The FoI Act, enforceable by the Information Commissioner, will be a clear improvement on the Code introduced by the Major government since it introduces a statutory right to information, its coverage is far wider and the enforcement mechanism is stronger. Ultimately, the right is enforceable if necessary through the courts The Act represents a turning point in British democracy since, for the first time in its history, the decision to release many classes of information has been removed from government departments and public authorities and placed in the hands of an independent agency, the Information Commissioner. However, as seen, the Act fences round the statutory 'right' to information with so many restrictions that, depending upon its interpretation, much information of any conceivable interest could still be withheld. Whether this turns out to be the case in practice will depend primarily upon the robustness of the stance taken by the Commissioner, particularly in applying the public interest test to the class exemptions under the Act, where it will provide the only means of obtaining disclosure.

FURTHER READING

P Birkinshaw, *Government and Information* (1990)

KD Ewing and CA Gearty, *Freedom Under Thatcher* (1990), Chapter 6

T Hartley and J Griffiths, *Government and Law* (1981), Chapter 13

D Leigh, *The Frontiers of Secrecy – Closed Government in Britain* (1980)

J Michael, *The Politics of Secrecy* (1982)

G Robertson, *Public Secrets* (1982)

S Shetreet (ed), *Free Speech and National Security* (1991)

---

70 See *ibid*.

71 R Austin, 'Freedom of information: the constitutional impact', in J Jowell and D Oliver, *The Changing Constitution* (2000), Chapter 12, p 371.

D Vincent, *The Culture of Secrecy, Britain 1832–1998* (1998)
D Wass, *Government and the Governed* (1984), p 81 *et seq*
DGT Williams, *Not in the Public Interest* (1965)
D Wilson, *The Secrets File* (1984)

For current comment, see:
R Austin, 'Freedom of information: the constitutional impact', in J Jowell and D Oliver, *The Changing Constitution* (2000), Chapter 12
SH Bailey, DJ Harris and DC Ormerod, *Civil Liberties: Cases and Materials*, 5th edn (2001), Chapter 8
J Beatson and Y Cripps, *Freedom of Expression and Freedom of Information* (2000)
P Birkinshaw, *Freedom of Information: The Law, the Practice and the Ideal*, 3rd edn (2001)
D Feldman, *Civil Liberties and Human Rights in England and Wales*, 2nd edn (2002), Chapter 14
P Gill, *Policing Politics: Security, Intelligence and the Liberal Democratic State* (1994)
L Lustgarten and I Leigh, *In From the Cold: National Security and Parliamentary Democracy* (1994)
N Whitty, T Murphy and S Livingstone, *Civil Liberties Law* (2001), Chapter 7

PART V

ADMINISTRATIVE LAW

CHAPTER I

JUDICIAL REVIEW: AVAILABILITY, APPLICABILITY, PROCEDURAL EXCLUSIVITY

INTRODUCTION

Judicial review is the procedure whereby the High Court is able, in certain cases, to review the legality of decisions made by a wide variety of bodies which affect the public, ranging from government ministers exercising prerogative[1] or statutory powers, to the actions of certain powerful self-regulating bodies. In Part V Chapter 2, the principles which the courts apply in making this assessment are considered. This chapter is concerned with the principles which determine whether review will be available or whether the complainant must rely on private law remedies; it examines the important procedural implications for the complainant which result from this public/private divide. Recent reforms to judicial review procedure represented by the new Civil Procedure Rules (CPR), Part 54 are explored. These rules came into force on 2 October 2000, the same day as the Human Rights Act 1998 (HRA). It should be noted that cases concerning applications made before this date will be governed by Order 53 of the Rules of the Supreme Court, and so will often refer to 'Ord 53'. Much of the case law decided under Ord 53 remains a reliable guide to how things will be conducted under the new CPR. As Fordham comments: 'Part 54 [CPR] is not identical to RSC Order 53 but its practical effect on key points remains the same.'[2] The issue of who may apply for review is also given thorough discussion, with particular reference to the position of campaigning groups, which are increasingly turning to legal methods as a way of attacking decisions to which they are opposed. Related matters, such as the circumstances in which review may be excluded, are also explored.

What limitations, then, are there on the availability of judicial review? Three main factors are used to decide whether aggrieved persons can challenge decisions. First, is the body which had made the decision one which it is appropriate to subject to review? Secondly, even if the body is in general terms subject to review, is the particular decision complained of reviewable? Thirdly, does the person who seeks to challenge the decision have standing (*locus standi*) to do so? Finally, what is the procedural relevance for the applicant of answers to the above questions? Does he or she have to proceed in a particular way depending on whether review is available? What will be the consequences for the applicant's case if he or she uses a procedure deemed inappropriate by the court for challenging the decision in question? These issues are examined below.

WHAT KINDS OF BODY ARE SUSCEPTIBLE TO REVIEW?

Not all decision-making bodies will be subject to review. There are clear examples of those which are. Many applications for judicial review are concerned with bodies such

---

1   For discussion specifically of the courts' ability to review the exercise of the prerogative, see Part IV Chapter 1.
2   M Fordham, 'Judicial review: the new rules' [2001] PL 4.

as local authorities carrying out statutory duties, which are quite clearly subject to public law remedies. The fact that a body derives its authority from statute will generally be conclusive. Problems tend to arise in the case of bodies which are created in some other way, such as self-regulatory bodies set up by persons with a common interest. As David Pannick notes: 'That public law does not regulate the decisions of bodies with which the applicant has voluntarily entered into a consensual relationship is well established. As Lord Parker CJ explained in 1967, "private or domestic tribunals have always been outside the scope of certiorari since their authority is derived solely from contract, that is, from the agreement of the parties concerned" [ex p Lain [1967] 2 QB 86 at 882B–C].'[3] This might appear to rule out self-regulatory bodies, since they technically depend upon voluntary submission to their findings. However, at least in some decisions, the courts have taken a more realistic view of the situation. Moreover, the advent of the CPR and the HRA, which contains a partial definition of 'public authority' for the purposes of the Act, are likely to influence the overall development of the law in this area, though it should be noted that neither bring about a clear and definite change. As will be seen below, it is doubtful whether the test used by the CPR makes any substantive change to the tests currently used by the courts, while the HRA strictly applies only to cases brought under that Act, though it may have some 'spill-over' effect on the definition used in judicial review proceedings generally.

Decisions prior to the Civil Procedure Rules and the Human Rights Act 1998

The leading case in this area is *R v City Panel on Takeovers and Mergers ex p Datafin plc* [1987] 2 WLR 699. The Court of Appeal had to consider whether the Panel on Takeovers and Mergers, a self-regulating body without statutory, prerogative or common law powers, was subject to the supervisory jurisdiction of the High Court as performing a public function. The Panel operated a Code regulating takeovers and mergers in the City.

R v City Panel on Takeovers and Mergers ex p Datafin plc [1987] 2 WLR 699, 702–05, 712–15

Sir John Donaldson MR [quoting from the Introduction to the Code]:

> The code has not, and does not seek to have, the force of law, but those who wish to take advantage of the facilities of the securities markets in the United Kingdom should conduct themselves in matters relating to take-overs according to the code. Those who do not so conduct themselves cannot expect to enjoy those facilities and may find that they are withheld . . .

The provisions of the code fall into two categories. On the one hand, the code enunciates general principles of conduct to be observed in take-over transactions: these general principles are a codification of good standards of commercial behaviour and should have an obvious and universal application. On the other hand, the code lays down a series of rules; some of which are no more than examples of the application of the general principles whilst others are rules of procedure designed to govern specific forms of take-over. Some of the general principles, based as they are upon a concept of equity between one shareholder and another, while readily understandable in the City and by those concerned with the securities markets generally, would not easily lend themselves to legislation. The code is therefore framed in non-technical language and is, primarily

---

3   D Pannick, 'Who is subject to judicial review and in respect of what?' [1992] PL 1.

as a measure of self-discipline, administered and enforced by the panel, a body representative of those using the securities markets and concerned with the observance of good business standards, rather than the enforcement of the law ...

'Self-regulation' ... can connote a system whereby a group of people, acting in concert, use their collective power to force themselves and others to comply with a code of conduct of their own devising ...

The panel is a self-regulating body in [this] sense. Lacking any authority *de jure*, it exercises immense power *de facto* by devising, promulgating, amending and interpreting the City Code on Take-overs and Mergers, by waiving or modifying the application of the code in particular circumstances, by investigating and reporting upon alleged breaches of the code and by the application or threat of sanctions. These sanctions are no less effective because they are applied indirectly and lack a legally enforceable base. Thus, to quote again from the introduction to the code:

> ... If the panel finds that there has been a breach, it may have recourse to private reprimand or public censure or, in a more flagrant case, to further action designed to deprive the offender temporarily or permanently of his ability to enjoy the facilities of the securities markets. The panel may refer certain aspects of a case to the Department of Trade and Industry, the Stock Exchange or other appropriate body. No reprimand, censure or further action will take place without the person concerned having the opportunity to appeal to the appeal committee of the panel.

The unspoken assumption, which I do not doubt is a reality, is that the Department of Trade and Industry or, as the case may be, the Stock Exchange or other appropriate body would in fact exercise statutory or contractual powers to penalise the transgressors. Thus, for example, rules 22 to 24 of the Rules of the Stock Exchange (1984) provide for the severest penalties, up to and including expulsion, for acts of misconduct and by rule 23.1:

> Acts of misconduct may consist of any of the following ... (g) Any action which has been found by the Panel on Take-overs and Mergers (including where reference has been made to it, the appeal committee of the panel) to have been in breach of the City Code on Take-overs and Mergers. The findings of the panel, subject to any modification by the appeal committee of the panel, shall not be re-opened in proceedings taken under rules 22 to 24.

The principal issue in this appeal, and only issue which may matter in the longer term, is whether this remarkable body is above the law. Its respectability is beyond question [and] ... I am content to assume for the purposes of this appeal that self-regulation is preferable in the public interest. But that said, what is to happen if the panel goes off the rails? Suppose, perish the thought, that it were to use its powers in a way which was manifestly unfair. What then? Mr Alexander submits that the panel would lose the support of public opinion in the financial markets and would be unable to continue to operate. Further or alternatively, Parliament could and would intervene. Maybe, but how long would that take and who in the meantime could or would come to the assistance of those who were being oppressed by such conduct?

... In *Criminal Injuries Compensation Board ex p Lain* [1967] 2 QB 864 ... Diplock LJ ... said, at pp 884–85:

> If new tribunals are established by acts of Government, the supervisory jurisdiction of the High Court extends to them if they possess the essential characteristics upon which the subjection of inferior tribunals to the supervisory control of the High Court is based. What are these characteristics? It is plain on the authorities that the tribunal need not be one whose determinations give rise directly to any legally enforceable right or liability. Its determination may be subject to certiorari notwithstanding that it is merely one step in a process which may have the result of altering the legal rights or liabilities of a person to whom it relates. It is not even essential that the determination must have that result, for there may be some subsequent condition to be satisfied before the determination can have any effect upon such legal rights or

liabilities. That subsequent condition may be a later determination by another tribunal (see *Postmaster-General ex p Carmichael* [1928] I KB 291; *Boycott ex p Keasley* [1939] 2 KB 651). Is there any reason in principle why certiorari should not lie in respect of a determination, where the subsequent condition which must be satisfied before it can affect any legal rights or liabilities of a person to whom it relates is the exercise in favour of that person of an executive discretion, as distinct from a discretion which is required to be exercised judicially?

... The Criminal Injuries Compensation Board, in the form which it then took, was an administrative novelty. Accordingly it would have been impossible to find a precedent for the exercise of the supervisory jurisdiction of the court which fitted the facts. Nevertheless the court not only asserted its jurisdiction, but further asserted that it was a jurisdiction which was adaptable thereafter. This process has since been taken further in *O'Reilly v Mackman* [1983] 2 AC 237, 279 *(per* Lord Diplock) by deleting any requirement that the body should have a duty to act judicially; in *Council of Civil Service Unions v Minister for the Civil Service* [1985] AC 374 by extending it to a person exercising purely prerogative power; and in *Gillick v West Norfolk and Wisbech Area Health Authority* [1986] AC 112, where Lord Fraser of Tullybelton, at p 163F and Lord Scarman, at p 178F–H expressed the view *obiter* that judicial review would extend to guidance circulars issued by a department of state without any specific authority. In all the reports it is possible to find enumerations of factors giving rise to the jurisdiction, but it is a fatal error to regard the presence of all those factors as essential or as being exclusive of other factors. Possibly the only essential elements are what can be described as a public element, which can take many different forms, and the exclusion from the jurisdiction of bodies whose sole source of power is a consensual submission to its jurisdiction.

... the panel ... is without doubt performing a public duty and an important one. This is clear from the expressed willingness of the Secretary of State for Trade and Industry to limit legislation in the field of take-overs and mergers and to use the panel as the centrepiece of his regulation of that market. The rights of citizens are indirectly affected by its decisions, some, but by no means all of whom, may in a technical sense be said to have assented to this situation, eg, the members of the Stock Exchange. At least in its determination of whether there has been a breach of the code, it has a duty to act judicially and it asserts that its *raison d'être* is to do equity between one shareholder and another. Its source of power is only partly based upon moral persuasion and the assent of institutions and their members, the bottom line being the statutory powers exercised by the Department of Trade and Industry and the Bank of England. In this context, I should be very disappointed if the courts could not recognise the realities of executive power and allow their vision to be clouded by the subtlety and sometimes complexity of the way in which it can be exerted ...

Notes

1   Sir John Donaldson also considered whether the Panel could be controlled by the use of private law remedies. Since it was clear that it could not be, he and the other members of the Court of Appeal took the view that the Panel was subject to judicial review for the reasons given. As Pannick comments:

> Since *Datafin* the issue for public lawyers is not whether one can identify a private law agreement in order to exclude judicial review, but whether the respondent body (as the Divisional Court acknowledged was the case in relation to the Jockey Club) has such a *de facto* monopoly over an important area of public life that an individual has no effective choice but to comply with their rules, regulations and decisions in order to operate in that area.[4]

However, as will become apparent, this principle has not been applied consistently in the cases.

---

4   Pannick, *op cit*.

2   It appears clear, at any rate, that the fact that the source of a body's power is non-statutory should not be decisive (a finding confirmed by *R v Royal Life Saving Society ex p Howe etc* [1990] COD 497). One crucial criterion appears to be whether, if that body did not exist, some state body would be required to regulate the area of activity in question. As Rose J remarked in *R v Football Association Ltd ex p Football League Ltd* [1993] 2 All ER 833:

> Despite its virtually monopolistic powers and the importance of its decisions to many members of the public who are not contractually bound to it, it is, in my judgment, a domestic body whose powers arise from and duties exist in private law only. I find no sign of underpinning directly or indirectly by any organ or agency of the state or any potential government interest, as Simon Brown J put it in [*R v Chief Rabbi of the United Hebrew Congregations of GB and the Commonwealth ex p Wachmann* [1993] 2 All ER 249; [1992] 1 WLR 1306], nor is there any evidence to suggest that if the FA did not exist the state would intervene to create a public body to perform its functions.

Conversely, in *R v Advertising Standards Authority ex p Insurance Services plc* (1990) 2 Admin LR 77, the ASA, a self-regulatory body which deals with complaints in relation to advertising, and has no coercive powers at all, was found to be amenable to review, on the basis that it was the practice of the Director of Fair Trading to intervene on a complaint about misleading advertising only if the ASA had not dealt satisfactorily with the complaint. This provided the 'governmental underpinning' sufficient to demonstrate a 'public element' to the ASA's functions. It has also been held that the Press Complaints Commission, a similar body, whose function is self-explanatory is probably amenable to review.[5]

3   Considering the finding in the *Datafin* decision, that to be reviewable a body needs to have 'a public element' or be under some 'public duty', Sandra Fredman and Gillian S Morris comment, 'even a cursory look at this formulation demonstrates that the dividing line between public and private remains elusive'.[6] What, after all is a 'public element' or 'public duty?' They go on to note that the test developed in later cases (and deployed by Rose J above) that the body 'should be governmental in nature so that if it did not exist the Government would be likely to step in and create a replacement' is 'singularly difficult to apply with any degree of certainty' because of the 'lack of consensus as to the proper functions of government'.[7] Fredman and Morris are arguably understating the matter here: there is not so much a 'lack of consensus' as to the proper functions of government as a heated political debate. As Lord Woolf has noted (commenting extra-judicially): 'Increasingly services which, at one time, were regarded as an essential part of Government are being performed by private bodies.'[8] This growth in the 'contracted-out state' has caused intense controversy. In the same article, Lord Woolf impliedly disapproves the 'governmental' test.[9]

4   On the other hand, Pannick[10] notes that the 'governmental' test is closely analogous with the test adopted by the European Court of Justice for deciding whether a respondent is a 'state body' with the result that directives may be directly invoked

---

5   *R v Press Complaints Commission ex p Stewart-Brady* (1997) 9 Admin LR 274.
6   S Fredman and GS Morris, 'The costs of exclusivity: public and private re-examined' [1994] PL 69. The article is quoted below, see pp 681–82, 691–92.
7   *Ibid*, p 72.
8   Lord Woolf, '*Droit public* – English style' [1995] PL 57, 63.
9   He suggests a test for determining the public/private divide which leaves the issue entirely out of the account; *ibid*, at p 64.
10 *Op cit.*

against it (see further Part II Chapter 1). The Community law principle applies to:

> ... a body, whatever its legal form, which has been made responsible, pursuant to a measure adopted by the state, for providing a public service under the control of the state and has for that purpose special powers beyond those which result from the normal rules applicable in relations between individuals ... [Foster v British Gas plc [1991] 1 QB 405 at 427G–H (ECJ)].

5   One body which has generated a great deal of litigation on this issue is the Jockey Club which regulates horse-racing in the UK. A number of inconsistent first instance decisions on the matter (Jockey Club ex p Massingberd-Mundy (1990) 2 Admin LR 609; Jockey Club ex p RAM Racecourses Ltd (1990) 3 Admin LR 265 and Jockey Club ex p the Aga Khan [1993] 2 All ER 853) led to an appeal (on the third decision) to the Court of Appeal, which was thus given the opportunity to sort out the 'confusion' left by those decisions.

R v Jockey Club ex p Aga Khan [1993] 2 All ER 853, 866–87

Lord Justice Bingham MR: ... I have little hesitation in accepting the applicant's contention that the Jockey Club effectively regulates a significant national activity, exercising powers which affect the public and are exercised in the interest of the public. I am willing to accept that if the Jockey Club did not regulate this activity the Government would probably be driven to create a public body to do so.

But the Jockey Club is not in its origin, its history, its constitution or (least of all) its membership a public body. While the grant of a royal charter was no doubt a mark of official approval, this did not in any way alter its essential nature, functions or standing. Statute provides for its representation on the Horseracing Betting Levy Board, no doubt as a body with an obvious interest in racing, but it has otherwise escaped mention in the statute book. It has not been woven into any system of governmental control of horse racing, perhaps because it has itself controlled horse racing so successfully that there has been no need for any such governmental system and such does not therefore exist. This has the result that while the Jockey Club's powers may be described as, in many ways, public they are in no sense governmental.

I would accept that those who agree to be bound by the Rules of Racing have no effective alternative to doing so if they want to take part in racing in this country. It also seems likely to me that if, instead of Rules of Racing administered by the Jockey Club, there were a statutory code administered by a public body, the rights and obligations conferred and imposed by the code would probably approximate to those conferred and imposed by the Rules of Racing. But this does not, as it seems to me, alter the fact, however anomalous it may be, that the powers which the Jockey Club exercises over those who (like the applicant) agree to be bound by the Rules of Racing derive from the agreement of the parties and give rise to private rights on which effective action for a declaration, an injunction and damages can be based without resort to judicial review. It would in my opinion be contrary to sound and long-standing principle to extend the remedy of judicial review to such a case.

Question

Lord Justice Bingham finds (a) that the Jockey Club exercises powers 'which affect the public and are exercised in the interests of the public'; (b) that it is in practice impossible to take part in racing in Britain unless one accepts the jurisdiction of the club; (c) that the government would have to do the job the Club does now if the Club did not; but that (d) whilst the Club's powers are 'public' they are not 'governmental'. He therefore concludes that it is not subject to public law. Can any coherent set of factors to determine the private/public issue be derived from these findings?

Notes

1   One clear point which appears to emerge from the decision is Bingham LJ's finding that access to private rights will preclude the availability of public law remedies. A

second crucial factor is whether persons aggrieved by the decisions of the body in question would have some other, private law remedy, for example in contract. Thus, in *R v Code of Practice etc ex p Professional Counselling Aids* (1990) *The Times*, 7 November, the fact that the Code of Practice Committee played a part in a system that operated in the public interest rendered it subject to review, while in *R v Football Association of Wales ex p Flint Town United Football Club* [1991] COD 44, the existence of a contractual relationship between the Club and the Association was decisive in the court's decision that judicial review would be inappropriate. This point has not met with universal acclaim:

The reliance on contract as the key to the availability or lack of availability of the Order 53 procedure in relation to regulatory bodies has some serious drawbacks. First, it distinguishes somewhat arbitrarily between those non-statutory bodies whose source of power is derived from contract and those whose power is not so derived. However, it is difficult to see why such bodies should be public while others with regulatory functions of similar significance should be private. Secondly, and more importantly, the equation of contract with private law is based upon the misguided belief in the voluntary, consensual nature of contract, obscuring the reality of underlying power relations ...

The second context in which contract has been deployed in order to prevent the use of the Order 53 procedure relates to bodies who, despite having an avowedly public character, have exercised their powers through the medium of contract. [This] equation of contract with private law reveals a further problem; it implies that even avowedly public bodies have 'private lives' which are beyond the scrutiny of the courts in their public-law jurisdiction.[11]

2   Lord Woolf has suggested that the existence of a private law remedy should not by itself exclude judicial review; rather the test should be whether the issue in respect of which review is sought is *'satisfactorily protected* by private law' (emphasis added).[12] This seems a more sensible test as it would take into account the cases in which a contract may be theoretically present but in which it would be either impractical or ineffective to sue on it.

The impact of the Civil Procedure Rules and the Human Rights Act 1998

Rule 54.1 of the CPR, now the governing framework, along with s 31 of the Supreme Court Act 1981, for judicial review proceedings, provides:

(2) In this Part—

  (a) a 'claim for judicial review' means a claim to review the lawfulness of—

   (i) an enactment; or

   (ii) a decision, action or failure to act in relation to the *exercise of a public function* [emphasis added].

As will appear below, it has been argued before the courts that the reference here to 'the exercise of a public function' replaces the previous, complex set of tests for determining whether a given body is amenable to judicial review with a new, single test: is it exercising a public function? This point is considered further below.

---

11 Fredman and Morris, *op cit*, at 74, 76.
12 *Op cit*, at 64.

Further, s 6(1) of the HRA states that it is 'unlawful for a public authority' to act in a way which is incompatible with a Convention right';[13] 'public authority' is not defined in the Act, but s 6(3) and (5) provides some guidance.

> (3) In this section, 'public authority' includes—
>
> (a) a court or tribunal, and
>
> (b) any person certain of whose functions are functions of a public nature ...
>
> (5) In relation to a particular act, a person is not a public authority by virtue only of subsection (3)(b) if the nature of the act is private.

This test appears to introduce a more inclusive definition of public bodies ('public authorities') for the purposes of cases brought under the HRA than is currently applied by the courts. For example, in *Aga Khan*, Bingham LJ accepted that, 'the Jockey Club effectively regulates a significant national activity, exercising powers which affect the public and are exercised in the interest of the public ... [and] that if the Jockey Club did not regulate this activity the government would probably be driven to create a public body to do so'. He then went on to add, 'But the Jockey Club is not in its origin, its history, its constitution or (least of all) its membership a public body'. This first finding, that the Jockey Club carried out a function which the government would have to perform if it did not exist, would surely be enough to make the Jockey Club a 'public authority' for the purposes of the HRA. Indeed, ministers in Parliament accepted that a wide variety of non-statutory bodies would be public authorities for the purposes of the HRA, including the Jockey Club itself,[14] the water companies,[15] the Royal National Lifeboat Institution[16] and the British Board of Film Classification.[17] The test of what is a 'public body' for the purposes of judicial review seems to be both more complex but less inclusive than that adopted under s 6(1) and (3). In *Poplar Housing and Regeneration Community Association Ltd and Secretary of State for the Environment v Donoghue* [2002] QB 48, however, the court found that:

> While HRA section 6 requires a generous interpretation of who is a public authority, it is clearly inspired by the approach developed by the courts in identifying the bodies and activities subject to judicial review. The emphasis on public functions reflects the approach adopted in judicial review by the courts and text books since the decision of the Court of Appeal (the judgment of Lloyd LJ) in ... *ex p Datafin* [1987] QB 815 at para 65(i).

Three main possibilities as to the relationship between the two tests are apparent. The first, and surely most likely, is that the courts will accept that the definition in s 6 of the HRA is more inclusive than that used in judicial review generally, but that the two tests should be harmonised in order to avert the messiness inherent in having two slightly different tests for amenability, depending upon whether the applicant is raising Convention points, or the established heads of judicial review – illegality, procedural impropriety, or irrationality. This could be done either by 'reading down' the definition of 'public authority' in s 6(3) of the HRA so that it conformed with the established case law on amenability to judicial review; alternatively the judicial review definition could be expanded to bring it into line with s 6 of the HRA. As we shall see

---

13   That is, a right under the European Convention on Human Rights, as defined by s 1 HRA 1998.
14   HC Deb col 1020 (20 May 1998).
15   *Ibid*, col 409.
16   HC Deb col 407 (7 June 1998).
17   HC Deb col 413 (17 June 1998).

in a moment, it has been argued, and accepted in at least one case, that the new CPR, Part 54, with its reference to 'public function', suggests that the test for judicial review purposes is being brought into line with that used under s 6 of the HRA. Such an approach seems to be at least encouraged by the above *dicta* from *Donoghue*.

The second possibility is that the courts will insist upon a strict distinction between the amenability of bodies to review on Convention grounds on the one hand and the (non-HRA) heads of judicial review on the other. The untidiness of such an approach has, however, already been noted, and this difficulty would become particularly acute where a single applicant raised both HRA and orthodox judicial review grounds of challenge. Would the courts really be prepared to hold that the same public body was amenable to some grounds of challenge but not others?

The third possibility is that the courts will start out with position two, but that the two lines of case law will come to influence each other, so that the two eventually become indistinguishable, an approach also seemingly encouraged by the *dicta* cited from *Donoghue*.

In fact, the first of these possibilities has already received specific judicial endorsement, at Divisional Court level.

R (on the Application of Heather, Ward and Callin) v Leonard Cheshire Foundation [2001] EWHC Admin 429

Burnton J: The Claimants submitted that the law has been changed by the Human Rights Act, which in section 6 has replaced the previous criteria for the application of judicial review with a purely functional test, and so far as jurisdiction is concerned by the similar wording of Part 54 of the CPR.

60. [Counsel's] principal submission was that the Act had replaced the former complexity and uncertainty of the law by enacting a single test: that of function. The test, he submitted, is now entirely functional, and if the nature of the function called into question is public, then irrespective of the source or nature of the power being exercised, the body exercising that function is a public body for the purposes of section 6.

65. Mr Gordon submitted that the use, in Part 54, of the identical wording as that found in section 6, in a procedural enactment which came into force on the same day as the Human Rights Act, in the same context of public law, must have the same meaning as in the Act. His submission was not disputed by [Counsel for the defendants]. It is clearly right, and is consistent with the judgment of the Court of Appeal in *Donoghue* at paragraph 65(i).

Note
It is too early to tell whether this approach will become established, still less whether the courts will in fact read s 6 of the HRA as importing a more inclusive definition of 'public authority' as suggested above. In *Cheshire* itself, Burnton J gave a relatively narrow reading to s 6(3). This point is explored further in Part VI Chapter 1 on the HRA itself, at pp 871–72 and 894–902.

WHAT KINDS OF DECISION ARE SUBJECT TO REVIEW?

Even where it is clear that the decision-making body may be described as a public body, particular decisions made by it may not be susceptible to judicial review if they are not seen to have a clear 'public' element. This issue was considered in the following case, which was concerned with an action brought, in connection with a dispute over working hours, by a prison officer against the Home Office, which then applied to strike out the action on the ground that the plaintiff ought to have proceeded by judicial review.

McClaren v Home Office [1990] ICR 824

Woolf LJ ... [his Lordship found that the plaintiff's appeal against the Divisional Court's order striking out his action should be allowed, and continued:]

In relation to his personal claims against an employer, an employee of a public body is normally in exactly the same situation as other employees. If he has a cause of action and he wishes to assert or establish his rights in relation to his employment he can bring proceedings for damages, a declaration or an injunction (except in relation to the Crown) in the High Court or the county court in the ordinary way. The fact that a person is employed by the Crown may limit his rights against the Crown but otherwise his position is very much the same as any other employee. However, he may, instead of having an ordinary master and servant relationship with the Crown, hold office under the Crown and may have been appointed to that office as a result of the Crown exercising a prerogative power or, as in this case, a statutory power. If he holds such an appointment then it will almost invariably be terminable at will and may be subject to other limitations, but whatever rights the employee has will be enforceable normally by an ordinary action. Not only will it not be necessary for him to seek relief by way of judicial review, it will normally be inappropriate for him to do so: see *Kodeeswaran v Attorney-General of Ceylon* [1970] AC 1111; *R v East Berkshire Health Authority ex p Walsh* [1984] ICR 743 and *R v Derbyshire County Council ex p Noble*.

In giving his judgment in this case, Hoffman J [1989] ICR 550, 554, was of the view that there was no 'arguable distinction between the facts of this case and those of Mr Bruce' – referring to *R v Civil Service Appeal Board ex p Bruce* [1988] ICR 649 – I disagree. In this case, unlike *ex parte Bruce*, which falls within the second category, the plaintiff is not making any complaint about disciplinary proceedings. He is seeking declarations as to the terms of his employment and a sum which he alleges is due for services rendered. If those claims have any merit they fall within the first category set out above. They are private law claims which require private rights to support them. [Counsel for the applicant] firmly disavowed any suggestion that any public law claim is being advanced by the plaintiff. Whether or not he is an employee of the Crown or has a contract of service, or holds an office under the Crown, he is entitled to bring private law proceedings if he has reasonable grounds for contending that his private law rights have been infringed. As his claim is pleaded and advanced ... it is entirely unsuited to judicial review ...

While [Counsel] accepts that the plaintiff can be dismissed at pleasure because he holds an office or is employed by the Crown, this does not mean that he cannot have a private law right in relation to matters other than his dismissal. The fact that a prison officer can be dismissed at pleasure does not mean that there do not exist other terms as to his service which are contractually enforceable and in respect of which he can have a private law remedy. There is now a considerable number of *dicta* which indicate that it is possible for a servant of the Crown to have contractual rights. In *ex parte Bruce* itself Roch J recognised that there could be terms of the appointment of a civil servant which could have legal effect. If there are such terms then they would give rise to private rights. In the case of prison officers they would result from the exercise by the Home Office of its statutory powers which are incidental to its statutory power to appoint prison officers; but even if they were derived from the prerogative, this would not alter the nature of the rights created, only the source of the authority for creating the rights. Once it is conceded, as in my view it has to be, that there is at least an arguable case for contending that the relationship between prison officers and the Home Office could have a contractual element, then (subject to it not affecting the power of the Crown to dismiss) the extent and the effect of the contractual element is a matter to be determined after evidence and full argument at the hearing.

Note

Here again, the HRA will introduce further complexity. It is generally agreed that s 6 of the HRA creates three categories of bodies, as the Home Secretary explained in Parliament:

> The effect of [s 6] is to create three categories, the first of which contains organisations which might be termed 'obvious' public authorities, all of whose functions are public. The clearest examples are Government Departments, local authorities and the police ...The second category contains organisations with a mix of public and private function.[18]

(The third category is 'organisations with no public functions [which] fall outside ... [s] 6'.)[19]

This interpretation of s 6 was accepted in *Donoghue*.[20] The significance of this is clear: bodies in Mr Straw's first category, which may be termed 'standard public authorities',[21] will be bound under s 6 of the HRA not to infringe Convention rights in respect of *all* of their activities. Thus, local and central government employees dismissed *will* be able to rely on any argument they may have under the Convention against their employer, even though, as *Walsh* illustrates, the attitude of the courts has historically been, as Lord Donaldson put it in *Walsh*, 'employment by a public authority does not per se inject any element of public law'. By contrast, bodies in the second category, which have been termed 'functional public authorities',[22] will continue to have 'private lives': their contractual and employment decisions, for example, will continue to fall outside the scope of review for breach of Convention rights under the HRA. Again, whether this will eventually influence the courts in judicial review cases outside the HRA remains to be seen.

PROCEDURAL IMPLICATIONS OF THE PUBLIC/PRIVATE DIVIDE

Applications for judicial review follow a procedure which differs in many important respects from the ordinary civil procedure.

Supreme Court Act 1981, s 31

Application for judicial review

31.—(1) An application to the High Court for one or more of the following forms of relief, namely—

(a) an order of *mandamus*, prohibition or certiorari;

(b) a declaration or injunction under subsection (2); or

(c) an injunction under section 30 restraining a person not entitled to do so from acting in an office to which that section applies,

shall be made in accordance with rules of court by a procedure to be known as an application for judicial review.

(2) A declaration may be made or an injunction granted under this subsection in any case where an application for judicial review, seeking that relief, has been made and the High Court considers that, having regard to—

---

18 HC Deb col 406 (17 June 1998).
19 *Ibid*, at col 410.
20 *Op cit*, at para 63.
21 HC Deb (17 June 1998); the terminology is taken from R Clayton and H Tomlinson, *The Law of Human Rights* (2000), at para 5.08.
22 HC Deb (17 June 1998).

(a) the nature of the matters in respect of which relief may be granted by orders of mandamus, prohibition or certiorari;

(b) the nature of the persons and bodies against whom relief may be granted by such orders; and

(c) all the circumstances of the case,

it would be just and convenient for the declaration to be made or the injunction to be granted, as the case may be.

(3) No application for judicial review shall be made unless the leave of the High Court has been obtained in accordance with rules of court; and the court shall not grant leave to make such an application unless it considers that the applicant has sufficient interest in the matter to which the application relates.

(4) On an application for judicial review the High Court may award damages to the applicant if—

(a) he has joined with his application a claim for damages arising from any matter to which the application relates; and

(b) the court is satisfied that, if the claim had been made in an action begun by the applicant at the time of making his application, he would have been awarded damages.

(5) If, on an application for judicial review seeking an order of certiorari, the High Court quashes the decision to which the application relates, the High Court may remit the matter to the court, tribunal or authority concerned, with a direction to reconsider it and reach a decision in accordance with the findings of the High Court.

(6) Where the High Court considers that there has been undue delay in making an application for judicial review, the court may refuse to grant—

(a) leave for the making of the application; or

(b) any relief sought on the application,

if it considers that the granting of the relief sought would be likely to cause substantial hardship to, or substantially prejudice the rights of, any person or would be detrimental to good administration.

(7) Subsection (6) is without prejudice to any enactment or rule of court which has the effect of limiting the time within which an application for judicial review may be made.

Note

Judicial review has now been brought within the CPR; the detailed rules which apply to judicial review proceedings are set out below. First of all, though, it should be noted that this means that judicial review proceedings are now subject to the 'overriding objective', contained in CPR, Part 1, that cases be dealt with justly. This includes:

(a) ensuring that the parties are on an equal footing;

(b) saving expense;

(c) dealing with the case in ways which are proportionate:

(i) to the amount of money involved,

(ii) to the importance of the case,

(iii) to the complexity of the issues, and

(iv) to the financial position of each party;

(d) ensuring that it is dealt with expeditiously and fairly; and

(e) allotting to it an appropriate share of the court's resources, while taking into account the need to allot resources to other cases.

Civil Procedure Rules, Part 54
PART 54 JUDICIAL REVIEW

54.1 Scope and interpretation
(1) This Part contains rules about judicial review.

(2) In this Part—

    (a) a 'claim for judicial review' means a claim to review the lawfulness of—

        (i) an enactment; or

        (ii) a decision, action or failure to act in relation to the exercise of a public function.

    (b) an order of mandamus is called a 'mandatory order';

    (c) an order of prohibition is called a 'prohibiting order';

    (d) an order of certiorari is called a 'quashing order';

    (e) 'the judicial review procedure' means the Part 8 procedure as modified by this Part;

    (f) 'interested party' means any person (other than the claimant and defendant) who is directly affected by the claim; and

    (g) 'court' means the High Court, unless otherwise stated.

. . .

54.2 When this Part must be used
The judicial review procedure must be used in a claim for judicial review where the claimant is seeking—

    (a) a mandatory order;

    (b) a prohibiting order;

    (c) a quashing order; or

    (d) an injunction under section 30 of the Supreme Court Act 1981 (restraining a person from acting in any office in which he is not entitled to act).

54.3 When this Part may be used
(1) The judicial review procedure may be used in a claim for judicial review where the claimant is seeking—

    (a) a declaration; or

    (b) an injunction.

. . .

(Where the claimant is seeking a declaration or injunction in addition to one of the remedies listed in rule 54.2, the judicial review procedure must be used)

(2) A claim for judicial review may include a claim for damages but may not seek damages alone.

. . .

54.4 Permission required
The court's permission to proceed is required in a claim for judicial review whether started under this Part or transferred to the Administrative Court.

54.5 Time limit for filing claim form
(1) The claim form must be filed—

    (a) promptly; and

    (b) in any event not later than 3 months after the grounds to make the claim first arose.

(2) The time limit in this rule may not be extended by agreement between the parties.

(3) This rule does not apply when any other enactment specifies a shorter time limit for making the claim for judicial review.

. . .

54.16 Evidence

(1) Rule 8.6 does not apply.

(2) No written evidence may be relied on unless—

    (a) it has been served in accordance with any—

        (i) rule under this Part; or

        (ii) direction of the court; or

    (b) the court gives permission.

54.17 Court's powers to hear any person

(1) Any person may apply for permission—

    (a) to file evidence; or

    (b) make representations at the hearing of the judicial review.

(2) An application under paragraph (1) should be made promptly.

54.18 Judicial review may be decided without a hearing

The court may decide the claim for judicial review without a hearing where all the parties agree.

54.19 Court's powers in respect of quashing orders

(1) This rule applies where the court makes a quashing order in respect of the decision to which the claim relates.

(2) The court may—

    (a) remit the matter to the decision-maker; and

    (b) direct it to reconsider the matter and reach a decision in accordance with the judgment of the court.

(3) Where the court considers that there is no purpose to be served in remitting the matter to the decision-maker it may, subject to any statutory provision, take the decision itself.

(Where a statutory power is given to a tribunal, person or other body it may be the case that the court cannot take the decision itself)

54.20 Transfer

The court may—

    (a) order a claim to continue as if it had not been started under this Part; and

    (b) where it does so, give directions about the future management of the claim.

(Part 30 (transfer) applies to transfers to and from the Administrative Court)

Procedural exclusivity

The most important implication of the public/private divide is the principle now known as 'procedural exclusivity': this principle governs the situation if a person brings an ordinary action when he or she should have used judicial review. CPR, rr 54.20 (above) and 30.5 give the courts broad powers to transfer cases to and from the Administrative Court, but the problem is that judicial review has an exceptionally tight time limit (three months) compared to ordinary actions in contract or tort (six years). The person mistakenly thinking that he or she can sue in tort or contract when judicial review was required is unlikely to take action within three months and is thus liable to find him- or herself out of time for a judicial review action.

The basic rule: O'Reilly v Mackman and after

The leading authority in the field is the House of Lords' decision in the following case, in which prisoners at Hull Prison, alleging that decisions made by the prison's Board of Visitors were bad for want of natural justice, attempted to proceed by way of writ or originating summons, rather than under RSC, Ord 53 (the previous rules governing applications for judicial review). Their proceedings were struck out and they appealed to the House of Lords.

O'Reilly v Mackman [1983] 2 AC 237, 283–85

Lord Diplock: ... Order 53 since 1977 has provided a procedure by which every type of remedy for infringement of the rights of individuals that are entitled to protection in public law can be obtained in one and the same proceeding by way of an application for judicial review, and whichever remedy is found to be the most appropriate in the light of what has emerged upon the hearing of the application, can be granted to him. If what should emerge is that his complaint is not of an infringement of any of his rights that are entitled to protection in public law, but may be an infringement of his rights in private law and thus not a proper subject for judicial review, the court has power under r 9(5), instead of refusing the application, to order the proceedings to continue as if they had begun by writ [see now CPR, r 54.2(a) – above]. There is no such converse power under the RSC to permit an action begun by writ to continue as if it were an application for judicial review ...

My Lords, at the outset of this speech, I drew attention to the fact that the remedy by way of declaration of nullity of the decisions of the Board was discretionary – as are all the remedies available upon judicial review. Counsel for the plaintiffs accordingly conceded that the fact that by adopting the procedure of an action begun by writ or by originating summons instead of an application for judicial review under Ord 53 (from which there have now been removed all those disadvantages to applicants that had previously led the courts to countenance actions for declarations and injunctions as an alternative procedure for obtaining a remedy for infringement of the rights of the individual that are entitled to protection in public law only) the plaintiffs had thereby been able to evade those protections against groundless, unmeritorious or tardy harassment that were afforded to statutory tribunals or decision-making public authorities by Ord 53, and which might have resulted in the summary, and would in any event have resulted in the speedy disposition of the application, is among the matters fit to be taken into consideration by the judge in deciding whether to exercise his discretion by refusing to grant a declaration; but, it was contended, this he may only do at the conclusion of the trial.

[But] to delay the judge's decision as to how to exercise his discretion would defeat the public policy that underlies the grant of those protections: *viz* the need, in the interests of good administration and of third parties who may be indirectly affected by the decision, for speedy certainty as to whether it has the effect of a decision that is valid in public law. An action for a declaration or injunction need not be commenced until the very end of the limitation period; if begun by writ, discovery and interlocutory proceedings may be prolonged and the plaintiffs are not required to support their allegations by evidence on oath until the actual trial. The period of uncertainty as to the validity of a decision that has been challenged upon allegations that may eventually turn out to be baseless and unsupported by evidence on oath, may thus be strung out for a very lengthy period, as the actions of the first three appellants in the instant appeals show. Unless such an action can be struck out summarily at the outset as an abuse of the process of the court the whole purpose of the public policy to which the change in Ord 53 was directed would be defeated.

The position of applicants for judicial review has been drastically ameliorated by the new Ord 53. It has removed all those disadvantages, particularly in relation to discovery, that were manifestly unfair to them and had, in many cases, made applications for prerogative orders an inadequate remedy if justice was to be done. This it was that justified the courts in not treating as an abuse of their powers resort to an alternative procedure by way of action for a declaration or injunction (not then obtainable on an application under Ord 53), despite the fact that this procedure had the effect of depriving the defendants of the protection to statutory tribunals and public authorities for which for public policy reasons Ord 53 provided.

Now that those disadvantages to applicants have been removed and all remedies for infringements of rights protected by public law can be obtained upon an application for judicial review, as can also remedies for infringements of rights under private law if such infringements should also be involved, it would in my view as a general rule be contrary to public policy, and as such an abuse of the process of the court, to permit a person seeking to establish that a decision of a public authority infringed rights to which he was entitled to protection under public law to proceed by way of an ordinary action and by this means to evade the provisions of Ord 53 for the protection of such authorities.

My Lords, I have described this as a general rule; for though it may normally be appropriate to apply it by the summary process of striking out the action, there may be exceptions, particularly where the invalidity of the decision arises as a collateral issue in a claim for infringement of a right of the plaintiff arising under private law, or where none of the parties objects to the adoption of the procedure by writ or originating summons. Whether there should be other exceptions should, in my view, at this stage in the development of procedural public law, be left to be decided on a case to case basis ...

In the instant cases where the only relief sought is a declaration of nullity of the decisions of a statutory tribunal, the Board of Visitors of Hull Prison, as in any other case in which a similar declaration of nullity in public law is the only relief claimed, I have no hesitation, in agreement with the Court of Appeal, in holding that to allow the actions to proceed would be an abuse of the process of the court. They are blatant attempts to avoid the protections for the defendants for which Ord 53 provides.

I would dismiss these appeals.

Notes

1   On the same day, judgment was given in *Cocks v Thanet District Council* [1983] 2 AC 286. The plaintiff had applied to the Council, which was also the local housing authority, for permanent accommodation, but was supplied only with temporary accommodation. He sued in the county court for a declaration that the Council owed him a duty to house him permanently under the Housing (Homeless Persons) Act 1977, and was in breach of that duty. The issue that eventually reached the House of Lords was whether the plaintiff was entitled to proceed in the county court or should proceed by judicial review. The judge at first instance in the High Court – to which the case was removed – had held that the plaintiff could proceed in the county court. The finding of the House of Lords on appeal was that where a person has a possible statutory right to a benefit (for example, housing), if he or she is found to satisfy the relevant criteria, he or she will have a *private* right to the benefit. However, a decision that the criteria are *not* satisfied is a matter of public law only and may be challenged only by the judicial review procedure. As Fredman and Morris put it, 'the ... decision as to whether an applicant was homeless was a public discretion, but once the discretion had been exercised in the applicant's favour it became a private right'.[23] In Lord Bridge's words:

---

23   *Op cit*, at p 80.

Once a decision has been reached by the housing authority which gives rise to the ... housing duty, rights and obligations are immediately created in the field of private law. [This] duty ... once established, is capable of being enforced by injunction and the breach of it will give rise to a liability in damages. But it is inherent in the scheme of the Act that an appropriate public law decision of the housing authority is a condition precedent to the establishment of the private law duty.[24]

2 Fredman and Morris go on to note that in *Ali v Tower Hamlets* [1992] 3 All ER 512, a 'third dimension was added': the applicant had a private law right to accommodation but, if he wished to challenge the *type* of accommodation offered, his remedy lay only in public law.

3 The doctrine of 'procedural exclusivity' established in these cases has been widely criticised, first for flawed reasoning, secondly for its tendency to lead to meritorious cases being struck out simply because the wrong procedure has been used. Fredman and Morris consider that 'the public/private barrier articulated in *O'Reilly* cannot be defended' and has produced 'deleterious consequences'. Their critique of the decision follows.

S Fredman and GS Morris, 'The costs of exclusivity: public and private re-examined' [1994] PL 69, 70–71, 80–81

In asserting that the new Ord 53 procedure was mandatory for public law cases, Lord Diplock in *O'Reilly* argued that this was necessary to prevent litigants from evading the procedural protections built into that procedure. Short time-limits, leave requirements and limitations on fact-finding facilities are, on this view, essential to protect public authorities in the exercise of their public duties. However, there are two main problems with this rationale. First, it is not clear that public authorities necessarily and invariably need such protection. There may certainly be situations in which this is the case, planning law being a good example. However, it is unclear why public authorities are thought to need this protection in relation to judicial review and not, for example, in relation to claims in tort and contract, an argument which is further strengthened by the more flexible approach to the divide articulated in *Roy v Kensington and Chelsea and Westminster Family Practitioner Committee* [[1992] 1 All ER 705] discussed below. Secondly it fails entirely to explain the many cases in which, far from evading the procedural protections, litigants have chosen to surmount the hurdles to a claim under Ord 53. In such cases, the courts have almost invariably assumed that, just as the Ord 53 procedure is mandatory for public-law issues, so, conversely, it is barred for those classified as private. Little clear justification for this symmetry has been offered, although some reasons are hinted at. Some judges have voiced their fears of opening the floodgates to applications under Ord 53. Another issue has been concern with remedies; the prerogative orders have never been applied to powers derived from contract and it has thereby been assumed, without foundation, that the Ord 53 procedure is co-extensive in its scope with these orders. In general, however, the existence of a procedural divide based on a public-private distinction has become almost axiomatic, with scant discussion as to why it should be maintained, although in some recent cases the higher judiciary has shown impatience with its constraints. A further rationale – the desire to limit judicial review to a specialist cadre of judges – seems scarcely relevant in the light of the multiplicity of judges now involved in some aspect of decision-making in relation to judicial review applications.

Recent cases demonstrate yet more strongly that the doctrine of procedural exclusivity makes it likely that meritorious claims will fail for no reason other than the wrong choice of procedure [Note that there is no provision for changing from the writ procedure to Ord 53]. One way in which this is manifested is in the fact that litigants are tempted to use the confusion for tactical advantage. The public employment cases again are a good example. The Crown has been a prime mover in this regard. In a series of cases begun by civil servants by an application for judicial review, the Crown argued that leave should not be granted on the grounds that civil servants had contracts of employment and therefore the issue was private [*R v Civil Service Appeal Board ex p Bruce* [1988] 3 All ER 686]. At the same time, the Crown has applied to strike out cases begun by civil servants under the writ procedure on the grounds that these employees did not have contracts and therefore the issue was one of public law [*McClaren v Home Office* [1990] ICR 824]. A similar point can be made in respect of the voluntary regulation cases. Thus in *Law*, the applicant was content with the writ procedure, but the Greyhound Racing Club asserted the public nature of its function in order to block the claim at the threshold. In *ex p Aga Khan*, the converse was the case: the Jockey Club asserted the private nature of its functions in order to block the Aga Khan's attempt to use public law. This phenomenon is not always deliberate: the luckless applicant in *Ali* could be forgiven for assuming that his remedy lay in private law. Yet his of all cases appears on the face of it meritorious: how could it not be unreasonable to allocate a sixth-floor flat to a disabled person?

Possibly more problematic still is the recognition in recent cases of the possibility of pursuing substantially the same argument but in a different forum. Thus, as noted above, the Court of Appeal which refused to consider the Aga Khan's claims of breach of natural justice in public law was willing to concede that the same claim could have been entertained as a private-law claim of breach of an implied term in the contract. The only difference it seems, lies in the nature of the remedies. The result is inordinate cost and expense, with case after case being struck out or refused leave for no reason other than that the incorrect procedure had been chosen. Indeed, if the courts are truly concerned at the risk of blocking up the system, this must be at least one contributing factor.

Note

By contrast, Lord Woolf comments that he 'would be loath to see the effect of [the] decision undermined'[25] and mounts a spirited defence of the principle it embodies.

Lord Woolf, 'Judicial review: a possible programme for reform' [1992] PL 221, 231–32

... It did, and still does, seem to me to be illogical to have a procedure which is designed to protect the public from unnecessary interference with administrative action, and then allow the protection which is provided to be by-passed. However, it is quite wrong to assume that the necessary price of that decision is drawn-out litigation over issues as to whether a particular action has been commenced in the wrong court. In his speech in *O'Reilly v Mackman*, Lord Diplock was careful to refer to a 'general rule'. If a litigant who has a valid claim *bona fide* but wrongly regards a case as not falling within *O'Reilly v Mackman* when it does, the principle should not be allowed to embarrass him. The court in such a situation can take the necessary steps to ensure that it can still deal with the merits of the case. Sometimes additional pleadings may be necessary. At present, Ord 53 expressly allows only for proceedings to go from judicial review (ie, public law proceedings), to proceedings begun by writ, and not vice versa. This is a matter where amendment to the rules would improve the situation. However, even without such an amendment a little judicial ingenuity can overcome the problem as long as the case is one which has merit [see, eg, *Chief Adjudication Officer v Foster* [1992] 1 QB 31 and *R v Secretary of State for the Home Department ex p Muboyayi* [1991] 3 WLR 442]. If it has no merit, then it is important for the safeguards provided by judicial review to be utilised if it is a public law case.

It is true that there is still the problem of deciding whether or not the case is a public law case and that there is a grey area where it is difficult to decide this question. However, if, as has now become the position with regard to substantive law, there are real differences between the position of a litigant in public law and his or her position in private law, this difficulty is one which

---

25 'Judicial review: a possible programme for reform' [1992] PL 221, 231.

we cannot avoid. It is, however, the responsibility of the courts to chip away at the grey area by successive decisions. That does not mean, of course, that it would not be preferable for the need for additional flexibility to be embodied in an amended Ord 53.

Note
The most important decision in this area since *O'Reilly* was that of the House of Lords in *Roy v Kensington and Chelsea and Westminster Family Practitioner Committee* [1992] 1 AC 624 in which the House of Lords appeared to show some concern to restrict the *O'Reilly* principle.

Roy v Kensington and Chelsea and Westminster Family Practitioner Committee [1992] I AC 624

Dr Roy was a general practitioner providing general medical services within the NHS. The Committee, acting under statutory powers, withheld a proportion of his basic practice allowance on the ground that he had not been devoting a substantial amount of his time to his practice. Under the relevant statutory rules, the full rate of the allowance was payable only if in the opinion of the Committee he was so devoting a substantial amount of his time. Dr Roy issued a writ claiming, *inter alia,* payment of the withheld sum, contending that he *had* devoted himself to his practice as required by the regulations. The Committee applied to have the action struck out as an abuse of the process of the court on the ground that Dr Roy should have proceeded by way of an application for judicial review under RSC, Ord 53.[26]

Lord Bridge: ... If it is important, as I believe, to maintain the [exclusivity] principle, it is certainly no less important that its application should be confined within proper limits. It is appropriate that an issue which depends exclusively on the existence of a purely public law right should be determined in judicial review proceedings and not otherwise. But where a litigant asserts his entitlement to a subsisting right in private law, whether by way of claim or defence, the circumstance that the existence and extent of the private right asserted may incidentally involve the examination of a public law issue cannot prevent the litigant from seeking to establish his right by action commenced by writ or originating summons, any more than it can prevent him from setting up his private law right in proceedings brought against him. I think this proposition necessarily follows from the decisions of this House in *Davy v Spelthorne Borough Council* [1984] AC 262 and *Wandsworth London Borough Council v Winder* [1985] AC 461. In the latter case Robert Goff LJ in the Court of Appeal, commenting on a passage from the speech of Lord Fraser of Tullybelton in the former case, said, at p **480**:

> I read this passage in Lord Fraser of Tullybelton's speech as expressing the opinion that the principle in *O'Reilly v Mackman* should not be extended to require a litigant to proceed by way of judicial review in circumstances where his claim for damages for negligence might in consequence be adversely affected. I can for my part see no reason why the same consideration should not apply in respect of any private law right which a litigant seeks to invoke, whether by way of action or by way of defence. For my part, I find it difficult to conceive of a case where a citizen's invocation of the ordinary procedure of the courts in order to enforce his private law rights, or his reliance on his private law rights by way of defence in an action brought against him, could, as such, amount to an abuse of the process of the court.

I entirely agree with this ...

Lord Lowry: ... the committee's original contention in the courts below ... was that Dr Roy should have proceeded not by action but by an application for judicial review. The authorities relied

---

26   P Cane, 'Private rights and public procedure' [1992] PL 193.

on were (and still are) *Cocks v Thanet District Council* [1983] 2 AC 286 and *O'Reilly v Mackman* [1983] 2 AC 237, two cases heard consecutively by the same appellate committee, in which the judgments were later delivered on the same day.

I have already referred to the judgment of the Court of Appeal [1990] I Med LR 328, which concluded that there was a contract for services between Dr Roy and the committee and that it was therefore in order for Dr Roy to sue the committee for a declaration of his rights and an order for payment. I cannot altogether accept the reasoning which led the members of the Court of Appeal to conclude that there was a contract ... At the same time, I would be foolish to disregard the fact that all the members of a distinguished Court of Appeal held that a contract for services existed between Dr Roy and the committee. It shows, to say the least, that there are 'contractual echoes in the relationship,' as Judge White [1989] I Med LR 10, 12, put it and makes it almost inevitable that the relationship, as was said of that which arose in Wadi's case, gave rise to 'rights and obligations' and that Dr Roy's rights were private law rights ... arising from the statute and regulations and including the very important private law right to be paid for the work that he has done. As Judge White put it, at p 12:

> The rights and duties are no less real or effective for the individual practitioner. Private law rights flow from the statutory provisions and are enforceable, as such, in the courts but no contractual relations come into existence.

The judge, however, held that, even if the doctor's rights to full payments under the scheme were contractually based, the committee's duty was a public law duty and could be challenged only on judicial review. Mr Collins admitted that, if the doctor had a *contractual* right, he could ... vindicate it by action. But, my Lords, I go further: if Dr Roy has any kind of *private law right*, even though not contractual, he can sue for its alleged breach.

In this case it has been suggested that Dr Roy could have gone by judicial review, because there is no issue of fact, but that would not always hold good in a similar type of case ... In any event, a successful application by judicial review could not lead directly, as it would in an action, to an order for payment of the full basic practice allowance. Other proceedings would be needed.

... even if one accepts the full rigour of *O'Reilly v Mackman*, there is ample room to hold that this case comes within the exceptions allowed for by Lord Diplock. It is concerned with a private law right, it involves a question which *could* in some circumstances give rise to a dispute of fact and one object of the plaintiff is to obtain an order for the payment (not by way of damages) of an ascertained or ascertainable sum of money. If it is wrong to allow such a claim to be litigated by action, what is to be said of other disputed claims for remuneration? I think it is right to consider the whole spectrum of claims which a doctor might make against the committee. The existence of any dispute as to entitlement means that he will be alleging a breach of his private law rights through a failure by the committee to perform their public duty. If the committee's argument prevails, the doctor must in all these cases go by judicial review, even when the facts are not clear. I scarcely think that this can be the right answer.

My Lords, whether Dr Roy's rights were contractual or statutory, the observations made by the Court of Appeal concerning their enforcement are important. Balcombe LJ said [1990] I Med LR 328, 331:

> Since Dr Roy's rights against the committee sound in contract, on the face of it there would appear to be no reason why he should not sue on the contract by ordinary action. Of course, as Mr Briggs accepts, the court will not substitute its opinion for that of the committee in deciding whether Dr Roy did devote a substantial amount of time to general practice. What the court can do is to decide whether the committee, in forming its opinion, did so on an incorrect view of the law and, if so, remit the question to the committee for reconsideration.

Nourse LJ said, at p 332:

> ... In order that there may be no doubt about the matter, I will add that if a practitioner wishes to question an initial decision by the committee not to accept his application to be

included on their list of doctors, he must in that case take proceedings for judicial review. At that stage no contract has come into existence and the practitioner's only right is a public law right to have his application properly considered ...

In the present case, the public law decision of the FPC to include Dr Roy's name on the medical list brought into existence private law rights and duties. These duties included a duty imposed on the FPC to consider fairly any issues which might arise for determining whether Dr Roy was eligible for the full rate of basic practice allowance. In the present case, the matter on which the FPC had to form an opinion was whether Dr Roy was devoting a substantial amount of time to general practice under the National Health Service.

The judgments to which I have referred effectively dispose of an argument pressed by the committee that Dr Roy had no right to be paid a basic practice allowance until the committee had carried out their public duty of forming an opinion under paragraph 12.1(b), with the supposed consequence that, until that had happened, the doctor had *no private law right* which he could enforce. The answer is that Dr Roy had a right to a fair and legally correct consideration of his claim. Failing that, his private law right has been infringed and he can sue the committee.

... With regard to *O'Reilly v Mackman* [1983] 2 AC 237 [Mr Lightman, for Roy] argued in the alternative. The 'broad approach' was that the rule in *O'Reilly v Mackman* did not apply generally against bringing actions to vindicate private rights in all circumstances in which those actions involved a challenge to a public law act or decision, but that it merely required the aggrieved person to proceed by judicial review only when private law rights were not at stake. The 'narrow approach' assumed that the rule applied generally to *all* proceedings in which public law acts or decisions were challenged, subject to some exceptions when private law rights were involved. There was no need in *O'Reilly v Mackman* to choose between these approaches, but it seems clear that Lord Diplock considered himself to be stating a general rule with exceptions. For my part, I much prefer the broad approach, which is both traditionally orthodox and consistent with the *Pyx Granite* principle [1960] AC 260, 286, as applied in *Davy v Spelthorne Borough Council* [1984] AC 262, 274 and in *Wandsworth London Borough Council v Winder* [1985] AC 461, 510. It would also, if adopted, have the practical merit of getting rid of a procedural minefield. I shall, however, be content for the purpose of this appeal to adopt the narrow approach, which avoids the need to discuss the proper scope of the rule ...

Whichever approach one adopts, the arguments for excluding the present case from the ambit of the rule or, in the alternative, making an exception of it are similar and to my mind convincing.

(1) Dr Roy has either a contractual or a statutory private law right to his remuneration in accordance with his statutory terms of service.

(2) Although he seeks to enforce performance of a public law duty under paragraph 12.1, his private law rights dominate the proceedings.

(3) The type of claim and other claims for remuneration (although not this particular claim) may involve disputed issues of fact.

(4) The order sought (for the payment of money due) could not be granted on judicial review.

(5) The claim is joined with another claim which is fit to be brought in an action (and has already been successfully prosecuted).

(6) When individual rights are claimed, there should not be a need for leave or a special time limit, nor should the relief be discretionary.

(7) The action should be allowed to proceed unless it is plainly an abuse of process.

(8) The cases I have cited show that the rule in *O'Reilly v Mackman* [1983] 2 AC 237, assuming it to be a rule of general application, is subject to many exceptions based on the nature of the claim and on the undesirability of erecting procedural barriers.

... In conclusion, my Lords, it seems to me that, unless the procedure adopted by the moving party is ill suited to dispose of the question at issue, there is much to be said in favour of the proposition that a court having jurisdiction ought to let a case be heard rather than entertain a debate concerning the form of the proceedings.

For the reasons already given I would dismiss this appeal.

Notes

1   Peter Cane summarises Lord Lowry's reasons why 'it was right to allow Dr Roy to bring his claim by writ rather than by application for judicial review':

> The most important of these reasons were that: (1) Dr Roy was seeking to protect private law rights (this was also the basis of Lord Bridge's speech in Dr Roy's favour); (2) those private law rights 'dominate[d] the proceedings'; (3) the remedy sought by Dr Roy, namely an order for the payment of money due, could not be granted under Ord 53; and (4) if Dr Roy's complaint against the Committee succeeded, he would be *entitled* to the payment of the money withheld, and a person should not be required to use Ord 53 to claim a non-discretionary remedy.
>
> Taking reason (4) first, it is by no means clear that the procedural limitations inherent in Ord 53 should not apply to any case in which a person seeks a non-discretionary remedy. The arguments in favour of requiring leave and imposing a short time-limit are not obviously inapplicable to all such cases; and, as Lord Lowry recognises, not all claims for non-discretionary remedies raise factual issues unsuited for resolution by Ord 53 procedure. Indeed, Dr Roy's claim raised no such issues. In fact, the distinction between discretionary and non-discretionary remedies seems to be a surrogate for the distinction between public law rights and private law rights rather than a distinction with independent force.[27]

2   Cane goes on to ask whether *Roy* helps to clarify the definition of 'private law rights', so relied on in *Roy*.

> Contractual and property rights are obviously private law rights, as are rights to obtain monetary awards for private law wrongs or to obtain restitution on some other basis than wrongful conduct (such as mistake of fact). The really difficult cases are those in which the right in question arises out of a statutory provision. Dr Roy's right was such: the Court of Appeal held that there was a contract between Dr Roy and the Committee [(1990) 1 Med LR 328] but the House of Lords declined to decide this issue and instead treated Dr Roy's right as a private law statutory one. Are all statutory 'rights' private law rights? Surely not! It is quite clear that not all statutory duties are actionable in private law. We know from *Cocks v Thanet DC* [[1983] 2 AC 286] that the statutory right of certain homeless persons to be housed by a local authority is a private law right; and we know from *Roy* that the statutory right of a registered GP, under certain circumstances, to receive a full basic practice allowance is a private law right. But just as the courts have found it impossible to provide much guidance in general terms on the question of which statutory duties are actionable in the tort of breach of statutory duty, so it seems unlikely that much general guidance will ever be available on the question of which rights are private law rights for present purposes.[28]

3   Fredman and Morris see four main advantages to the approach of the House of Lords in *Roy*:[29] first, the explicit recognition of the fact that a single claim could (as in *Roy* itself) contain a mixture of public and private law elements; secondly, the 'move away from procedural rigidity' represented by the Lords' preparedness to allow a writ action in a case concerning some public law elements, provided the private elements dominated; thirdly, the recognition that the choice of procedure should be at least partly dictated by whether it would be suitable for the type of claim in question; fourthly, the move away from contract as a key factor for locating the public/private divide. They consider the first point to be the most important in

---

27   *Ibid.*
28   *Ibid.*
29   *Op cit*, pp 82–83.

that it recognises and allows for the complexity of a mixed case to be accommodated within a single action: 'having begun his action by writ, Dr Roy's case may then depend upon invoking public law principles in order to establish his private rights and obtain a private law remedy' (p 82).

4   The third point they mention appears to have received some recognition in the House of Lords' decision in *Mercury Communications v Director General of Telecommunications* [1995] 1 All ER 575. In refusing to strike out Mercury's application challenging decisions of the Director General relating to its operational agreement with BT brought by originating summons on the grounds that Mercury should have proceeded by way of an application for judicial review, the House of Lords stated, *inter alia*, that: (a) a crucial question was whether the proceedings constituted an abuse of the procedures of the court; and (b) that in determining (a) it should be borne in mind that the procedure selected by Mercury was at least as well suited and possibly better suited for determining the issues raised than an application for judicial review. This seems to represent a move towards a pragmatic view of procedure, based on efficacy and convenience rather than some elusive public/private divide.

5   In *Steed v Secretary of State for the Home Department* [2000] 1 WLR 1169, Steed made an application to the Secretary of State for compensation under the Firearms (Amendment) Act 1997 on 29 July 1997 after handing in to the authorities various firearms. On 27 October 1997 he issued a county court summons for the sum allegedly due, claiming that there had been excessive delay in paying him the compensation due. The claims submitted under options A and B of the scheme were paid on 26 November 1997 and the Secretary of State then sought to strike out the summons as disclosing no reasonable cause of action. The application was dismissed as were two subsequent appeals. The Secretary of State appealed to the House of Lords, contending, *inter alia*, that a challenge other than by judicial review was an abuse of process at any time prior to final determination of the individual claim. It was held, dismissing the appeal, that once all conditions of the scheme had been satisfied an applicant was clearly entitled to payment under the terms of the scheme; and that since the proceedings had not sought to challenge the lawfulness of the scheme itself nor sought to take the place of a discretionary decision specifically reserved to the administration, they could not be said to constitute an abuse of process.

Collateral challenge

One exception to the general rule that public law issues should be raised only in judicial review proceedings mentioned by Lord Diplock in *O'Reilly* was collateral challenge. It was established in *Wandsworth London Borough Council v Winder* [1985] AC 461 that a tenant who was being sued in ordinary civil proceedings for arrears in rent by his local authority was entitled to use in his defence the public law plea that the increase was *ultra vires* and therefore void. In the following case, the issue arose in the criminal context: the defendant was convicted of an offence under a bylaw prohibiting smoking on trains and wished to be able to challenge the validity of the bylaw as a collateral challenge to the charges against him.

Boddington v British Transport Police [1999] 2 AC 143

Lord Irvine: . . . In every case it will be necessary to examine the particular statutory context to determine whether a court hearing a criminal or civil case has jurisdiction to rule on a defence based upon arguments of invalidity of subordinate legislation or an administrative act under it.

There are situations in which Parliament may legislate to preclude such challenges being made, in the interest, for example, of promoting certainty about the legitimacy of administrative acts on which the public may have to rely.

The recent decision of this House in *R v Wicks* [1998] AC 92 is an example of a particular context in which an administrative act triggering consequences for the purposes of the criminal law was held not to be capable of challenge in criminal proceedings, but only by other proceedings. The case concerned an enforcement notice issued by a local planning authority and served on the defendant under the then current version of section 87 of the Town and Country Planning Act 1971. The notice alleged a breach of planning control by the erection of a building and required its removal above a certain height. One month was allowed for compliance. The appellant appealed against the notice to the Secretary of State, under section 174 of the Town and Country Planning Act 1990, but the appeal was dismissed. The appellant still failed to comply with the notice and the local authority issued a summons alleging a breach of section 179(1) of the Act of 1990. In the criminal proceedings which ensued, the appellant sought to defend himself on the ground that the enforcement notice had been issued *ultra vires*, maintaining that the local planning authority had acted in bad faith and had been motivated by irrelevant considerations. The judge ruled that these contentions should have been made in proceedings for judicial review and that they could not be gone into in the criminal proceedings. The appellant then pleaded guilty and was convicted. This House upheld his conviction. Lord Hoffmann, in the leading speech, emphasised that the ability of a defendant to criminal proceedings to challenge the validity of an act done under statutory authority depended on the construction of the statute in question. This House held that the Town and Country Planning Act 1990 contained an elaborate code including provision for appeals against notices, and that on the proper construction of section 179(1) of the Act all that was required to be proved in the criminal proceedings was that the notice issued by the local planning authority was formally valid.

... However, in approaching the issue of statutory construction the courts proceed from a strong appreciation that ours is a country subject to the rule of law. This means that it is well recognised to be important for the maintenance of the rule of law and the preservation of liberty that individuals affected by legal measures promulgated by executive public bodies should have a fair opportunity to challenge these measures and to vindicate their rights in court proceedings. There is a strong presumption that Parliament will not legislate to prevent individuals from doing so: 'It is a principle not by any means to be whittled down that the subject's recourse to Her Majesty's courts for the determination of his rights is not to be excluded except by clear words.' *Pyx Granite Co Ltd v Ministry of Housing and Local Government* [1960] AC 260, 286, *per* Viscount Simonds ...

The particular statutory scheme in question in *R v Wicks* [1998] AC 92 ... did justify a construction which limited the rights of the defendant to call the legality of an administrative act into question. But in my judgment it was an important feature of [the case] that [it was] concerned with [an] administrative act specifically directed at the defendants, where there had been clear and ample opportunity provided by the scheme of the relevant legislation for those defendants to challenge the legality of those acts, before being charged with an offence.

By contrast, where subordinate legislation (eg, statutory instruments or byelaws) is promulgated which is of a general character in the sense that it is directed to the world at large, the first time an individual may be affected by that legislation is when he is charged with an offence under it: so also where a general provision is brought into effect by an administrative act, as in this case. A smoker might have made his first journey on the line on the same train as Mr Boddington; have found that there was no carriage free of no smoking signs and have chosen to exercise what he believed to be his right to smoke on the train. Such an individual would have had no sensible opportunity to challenge the validity of the posting of the no smoking signs throughout the train until he was charged, as Mr Boddington was, under byelaw 20. In my judgment in such a case the strong presumption must be that Parliament did not intend to deprive the smoker of an opportunity to defend himself in the criminal proceedings by asserting the alleged unlawfulness of the decision to post no smoking notices throughout the train. I can see nothing in [the relevant legislation,] section 67 of the Transport Act 1962 or the byelaws which could displace that presumption. It is clear from *Winder* and *Wicks* [1998] AC 92, 116 *per* Lord Hoffman that the development of a statutorily based procedure for judicial review proceedings does not of itself displace the presumption.

Accordingly, I consider that the Divisional Court was wrong in the present case in ruling that Mr Boddington was not entitled to raise the legality of the decision to post no smoking notices throughout the train, as a possible defence to the charge against him.

... In my judgment only the clear language of a statute could take away the right of a defendant in criminal proceedings to challenge the lawfulness of a byelaw or administrative decision where his prosecution is premised on its validity.

The effect of the Civil Procedure Rules

Any effect which the CPR may have on procedural exclusivity is largely untested. However, Tom Cornford provides a preliminary assessment:

[The Rules] preserve those safeguards of public authorities' interests which furnished the original justification for insisting that public law challenges be brought by means of judicial review. Thus the permission stage is retained, albeit in altered form. And as before, a claim must be commenced promptly and, in any event, not later than 3 months after the grounds to make the claim arose (r 54.5). The time limit provisions are, in fact, somewhat stricter than the old Order 53 because they provide that the time limit may not be extended by agreement between the parties (r 54.5(2)).

Furthermore, the rules setting out the remedies available on judicial review are clearly intended to preserve the arrangement adopted in 1977 – ie, the prerogative orders (or their renamed equivalents) are to be available only on judicial review, and declarations and injunctions are to be available on judicial review where a case is of the type in which one of the prerogative orders might also be sought (rr 54.2 and 54.3). [It is possible to argue that CPR, Part 54 in fact licenses the bringing of a public law challenge by means of a private law claim. This is because r 54.1(2)(a) defines a 'claim for judicial review' as 'a claim to review the lawfulness of (i) an enactment; or (ii) a decision, action or failure to act in relation to the exercise of a public function' while 54.3(1) states that '[t]he judicial review procedure *may* be used in a claim for judicial review where the claimant is seeking (a) a declaration; or (b) an injunction' (emphasis added). Taken together, these two provisions seem to suggest that one could equally well seek judicial review by claiming an injunction or declaration in private law proceedings. That this argument can be made is almost certainly an inadvertent side effect of the unprecedented attempt to give the expression 'judicial review' a substantive meaning. The reference to s 31(2) of the Supreme Court Act 1981 which succeeds the provisions of r 54.3 just quoted means that the interpretation can be definitively ruled out.] All in all, the new Rules uphold judicial review's status as a special jurisdiction, a fact which, in itself, means that some form of procedural exclusivity is likely to persist.[30]

A decision which sheds some light on the effect which CPR, Part 54 may have on the procedural exclusivity principle is *Clark v University of Lincolnshire and Humberside* [2000] 1 WLR 1988. 'The case concerned a student who had been denied the possibility of obtaining a degree of higher than third class in breach, she alleged, of university regulations. She sued on the contract between herself and the university but her claim was struck out as non-justiciable. At her appeal to the Court of Appeal, the university argued that she ought to have proceeded by way of judicial review. The Court of Appeal's judgment was given after the coming into force of the CPR but before the

---

30   T Cornford, 'The new rules of procedure for judicial review' (2000) 5 Web JCLI.

advent of Part 54.'[31] It is important to note that, as a 'new' university, the University of Hull and Lincolnshire (ULH) was not established by royal charter, and so such disputes did not, as they would with an 'old' university, fall within the exclusive jurisdiction of the University Visitor. As Sedley LJ explained: '... ULH is simply a statutory corporation with the ordinary attributes of legal personality and a capacity to enter into contracts within its powers. The arrangement between a fee-paying student and ULH is such a contract.'

Clark v University of Lincolnshire and Humberside [2000] 1 WLR 1988

Woolf MR: ... A university is a public body. This is not in issue on this appeal. Court proceedings would, therefore, normally be expected to be commenced under Order 53. If the university is subject to the supervision of a visitor there is little scope for those proceedings (*Page v Hull University Visitor* [1993] AC 682). Where a claim is brought against a university by one of its students, if because the university is a new university created by statute, it does not have a visitor, the role of the court will frequently amount to performing the reviewing role which would otherwise be performed by the visitor. The court, for reasons which have been explained, will not involve itself with issues that involve making academic judgments. Summary judgment dismissing a claim, which if it were to be entertained, would require the court to make academic judgments should be capable of being obtained in the majority of situations ...

The courts today will be flexible in their approach ... While in the past, it would not be appropriate to look at delay of a party commencing proceedings other than by judicial review within the limitation period in deciding whether the proceedings are abusive this is no longer the position. While to commence proceedings within a limitation period is not in itself an abuse, delay in commencing proceedings is a factor which can be taken into account in deciding whether the proceeding are abusive. If proceedings of a type which would normally be brought by judicial review are instead brought by bringing an ordinary claim, the court in deciding whether the commencement of the proceedings is an abuse of process can take into account whether there has been unjustified delay in initiating the proceedings.

When considering whether proceedings can continue the nature of the claim can be relevant. If the court is required to perform a reviewing role or what is being claimed is a discretionary remedy, whether it be a prerogative remedy or an injunction or a declaration the position is different from when the claim is for damages or a sum of money for breach of contract or a tort irrespective of the procedure adopted. Delay in bringing proceedings for a discretionary remedy has always been a factor which a court could take into account in deciding whether it should grant that remedy. Delay can now be taken into account on an application for summary judgment under CPR Part 24 if its effect means that the claim has no real prospect of success.

Similarly if what is being claimed could affect the public generally the approach of the court will be stricter than if the proceedings only affect the immediate parties. It must not be forgotten that a court can extend time to bring proceedings under Order 53. The intention of the CPR is to harmonise procedures as far as possible and to avoid barren procedural disputes which generate satellite litigation.

Where a student has, as here, a claim in contract, the court will not strike out a claim which could more appropriately be made under Order 53 solely because of the procedure which has been adopted. It may however do so, if it comes to the conclusion that in all the circumstances, including the delay in initiating the proceedings, there has been an abuse of the process of the court under the CPR. The same approach will be adopted on an application under Part 24.

The emphasis can therefore be said to have changed since *O'Reilly v Mackman*. What is likely to be important when proceedings are not brought by a student against a new university under Order 53, will not be whether the right procedure has been adopted but whether the protection

---

31 *Ibid.*

provided by Order 53 has been flouted in circumstances which are inconsistent with the proceedings being able to be conducted justly in accordance with the general principles contained in Part 1 ...

Note

Cornford comments:

> It was clearly Lord Woolf's purpose to emphasise the court's flexibility and minimise the importance of the choice between procedures. It is unlikely, however, that the judgment will much reduce the importance of the exclusivity principle. If the scope of the judgment is confined to litigants who have contractual rights then it breaks no new ground. As mentioned above, it is well established that holders of private rights are entitled to use private law procedure. As Sedley LJ pointed out in his judgment in *Clark* (at p 757d), the claimant's position was stronger than that of the plaintiff in the *Roy* case. At the same time, if the scope of the judgment is confined in this way, there will remain a large class of claimants who do not possess a private right or anything like it and who will continue to be obliged to use judicial review.
>
> If, on the other hand, the judgment is applied beyond the contractual context, it gives very uncertain guidance. Suppose claimants lacking anything resembling a private right were encouraged to believe that they could seek a declaration by means of private law procedure, the interests of public authorities being protected by the power of the court to strike out or give summary judgment. Such a course might be attractive given the more generous time limits and the potentially greater likelihood of documents being disclosed. The principles Lord Woolf refers to as being relevant to the decision whether to strike out or give summary judgment are those contained in the CPR's overriding objective. These say nothing about the circumstances in which public authorities need to be protected. The most relevant principles are contained in the delay provisions of s 31(6) of the Supreme Court Act 1981 which has application only to judicial review. The whole logic of having a special procedure for judicial review dictates that purely or predominantly public law cases must be decided on judicial review.
>
> To conclude ... neither the new CPR Part 54, nor Lord Woolf's application of the CPR to the problem of exclusivity are likely to do much to reduce its importance. We have probably not seen the last of fruitless litigation over procedure.[32]

2   The following discussion points out the wider difficulties caused by the procedural exclusivity principle operating within the privatised, contracted-out state.

S Fredman and GS Morris, 'The costs of exclusivity: public and private re-examined' [1994] PL 69, 81–82, 83–85

In 1986, Woolf LJ, as he then was, remarked:

> [t]he interests of the public are as capable of being adversely affected by the decision of large corporations and large associations, be they of employers or employees, and should they not be subject to challenge on *Wednesbury* grounds if their decision relates to activities which can damage the public interest? [[1986] PL 220].

This theme was echoed by Sir Gordon Borrie in 1989 in stating '[a]s power shifts from the public sector to the private sector, it seems to be desirable that the instruments of control and accountability forged to ensure that the public sector behaves itself are considered for appropriate adaptation to the private sector' [[1989] PL 552]. At a time when significant areas of public power are being re-characterised as private, such exhortations become more pressing. Privatised prisons provide a clear example of the issues raised by the re-characterisation process. Had the fact situation in *O'Reilly v Mackman* itself occurred in a private prison, would the court have held that the Ord 53 procedure was not appropriate, thus depriving the applicants of any ground of challenging their treatment? If the notion of the prisoner's 'contract' suggested by the Woolf

Inquiry [Cm 1456] were adopted, would it give rise to legitimate expectations which could be relied upon in judicial review proceedings by those held in public but not in private prisons? The courts have acknowledged that some private bodies, such as trade unions, wield power of a nature which requires supervision by the courts and the courts may exercise their private supervisory jurisdiction to extend the principles of good administration more widely. In the light of the convergence of public and private law in this respect, the maintenance of the divide does not preclude the supervision of public power in private hands. However, it still requires the proper forum for proceedings to be determined, an otiose requirement when the substantive result is the same in either. The exclusivity principle is based upon a simplistic and anachronistic model of the exercise of public power; attempts by the courts to operate the principle can only become increasingly contorted if it survives the extension of the 'contract State'.

Practical procedural differences in judicial review claims: discovery, cross-examination and third-party intervention

The procedure for judicial review, as well as the draconian three-month time limit, differs in two important respects from an ordinary civil action. Instead of discovery of documents and cross-examination of witnesses being the norm, they will be ordered only in strictly limited, exceptional circumstances, though here, too, the new CPR may have some influence. As to cross-examination, Lord Diplock had this to say in the leading case in the area.

O'Reilly v Mackman [1983] 2 AC 237, 282–83

Lord Diplock: It may well be that for the reasons given by Lord Denning MR in *George v Secretary of State for the Environment* (1979) 250 EG 339, it will only be upon rare occasions that the interests of justice will require that leave be given for cross-examination of deponents on their affidavits in applications for judicial review. This is because of the nature of the issues that normally arise upon judicial review. The facts, except where the claim that a decision was invalid on the ground that the statutory tribunal or public authority that made the decision failed to comply with the procedure prescribed by the legislation under which it was acting or failed to observe the fundamental rules of natural justice or fairness, can seldom be a matter of relevant dispute upon an application for judicial review, since the tribunal or authority's findings of fact, as distinguished from the legal consequences of the facts that they have found, are not open to review by the court in the exercise of its supervisory powers except on the principles laid down in *Edwards v Bairstow* [1956] AC 14, 36; and to allow cross-examination presents the court with a temptation, not always easily resisted, to substitute its own view of the facts for that of the decision-making body upon whom the exclusive jurisdiction to determine facts has been conferred by Parliament. Nevertheless having regard to a possible misunderstanding of what was said by Geoffrey Lane LJ in *Board of Visitors of Hull Prison ex p St Germain (No 2)* [1979] 1 WLR 1401, 1410 your Lordships may think this an appropriate occasion on which to emphasise that whatever may have been the position before the rule was altered in 1977, in all proceedings for judicial review that have been started since that date, the grant of leave to cross-examine deponents upon applications for judicial review is governed by the same principles as it is in actions begun by originating summons; it should be allowed whenever the justice of the particular case so requires.

Notes

1   As to discovery, the importance for the applicant of being able to obtain sight of certain documents was emphasised by Lord Diplock in the same case. Referring to *Anisminic Ltd v Foreign Compensation Commission* [1969] 2 AC 147, he noted that it was only through discovery that 'the minute of the Commission's decision which showed that they had asked themselves the wrong question was obtained'. It was the fact that the Commission had asked itself the wrong question which established

that it had erred in law and thus exceeded its jurisdiction.[33] Discovery therefore played a vital role in that case.

2   Nevertheless, as Cornford notes:

It soon became clear however that discovery would be ordered in only very limited circumstances. Order 24 rr 8 and 13(1) required that orders for discovery were not to be made unless the court was of the opinion that discovery was 'necessary either for disposing fairly of the cause or matter or for saving costs' and this was made the foundation of the court's restrictive approach. This approach was made clear in a series of cases in the Court of Appeal [*R v Inland Revenue Commissioners ex p J Rothschild Holdings plc* [1987] STC 163; 61 Tax Cas 178; *R v Secretary of State for Home Affairs ex p Harrison* [1997] JR 113; *R v Inland Revenue Commissioners ex p Taylor* [1989] 1 All ER 906; *R v Secretary of State for the Environment ex p London Borough of Islington and the London Lesbian and Gay Centre* [1997] JR 121; *R v Secretary of State for Health ex p Hackney London Borough Council*, 29 July 1994; *R v Secretary of State for the Home Department ex p Guardian* [1996] COD 306 ...] The applicant would bring his challenge and the respondent authority would be entitled to defend and explain its actions by means of affidavits. The court would then only accede to any application for discovery by the applicant if he could already point to evidence in his possession which cast doubt on the veracity of the affidavit. The applicant was thus in a Catch-22 situation. He could only obtain evidence to disprove the authority's version of events if he already possessed it.[34]

3   The following case is a good example of the courts' restrictive approach. The applicant was seeking discovery of the minutes of certain meetings: summaries of those minutes had been set out in affidavits filed on behalf of the respondent. The applicant argued that only disclosure of the minutes themselves would reveal fully the grounds on which the decision being challenged (to grant aid to fund the Malaysian Pergau Dam project) had been made.

R v Secretary of State for Foreign Affairs ex p the World Development Movement [1995] 1 All ER 615, 620–22

Rose LJ: As to disclosure of the two minutes of February 1991, it was common ground that in judicial review proceedings general discovery is not available as it is in a writ action under Ord 24, rr 1 and 2, that an application can be made under Ord 24, r 3, which by virtue of Ord 24, r 8 will be refused if discovery is not necessary for disposing of the case fairly, and that the judgments of the Court of Appeal in *Secretary of State for the Environment ex p Islington London BC* (1991) *The Independent*, 6 September are pertinent. In that case Dillon LJ said:

In the case of *Secretary of State for the Home Dept ex p Harrison* [1988] 3 All ER 86 ... this court ... accepted two submissions of Mr Laws, which are referred to as his 'narrower argument' and his 'wider argument'. The wider argument is stated ... to have been that an applicant is not entitled to go behind an affidavit in order to seek to ascertain whether it is correct or not unless there is some material available outside that contained in the affidavit to suggest that in some material respect the affidavit is not accurate. Without some *prima facie* case for suggesting that the affidavit is in some respects incorrect it is improper to allow discovery of documents, the only purpose of which would be to act as a challenge to the accuracy of the affidavit. With that I would, in general, agree – and indeed the decision binds us. But I would add the qualification that if the affidavit only deals partially, and not sufficiently adequately, with an issue it may be appropriate to order discovery to supplement the affidavit, rather than to challenge its accuracy. That must depend on the nature of the issue.

The narrower argument referred to in that passage is not relevant for present purposes.

---

33   For the decision itself, see Chapter 2 of this part, pp 710–11.
34   Cornford, *op cit.*

McCowan LJ said:

> The second matter which emerges from the authorities is that unless the applicant in judicial review is in a position to assert that the evidence relied on by a minister is false, or at least inaccurate, it is inappropriate to grant discovery in order to allow the applicant to check the accuracy of the evidence in question.

Mr Pleming [for the applicant] submitted that the evidence for the Foreign Secretary in the affidavit of the Foreign Secretary himself, and of Mr Manning, demonstrates, particularly when compared with the far fuller summaries of the minutes exhibited elsewhere in the evidence, that the affidavit summaries are at best incomplete, and at worst misleading. The material evidence is, in these terms, in para 4 of the Foreign Secretary's affidavit:

> The Accounting Officer of the Overseas Development Administration told me that, given its price, the project was premature by several years and that the extra cost of building it now could well exceed the value of the large sum of British taxpayers' money which the project required.

Mr Meaning's affidavit is in these terms, at para 35:

> ... Sir Tim Lancaster advised that the provision of aid funds for Pergau would not be consistent with his responsibility to ensure that aid funds were administered in a prudent and economic manner, and that he would wish to have an instruction from the Minister or from the Secretary of State if ODA were to incur expenditure on the project.

> ... In my judgment, although the affidavits of the Foreign Secretary and of Mr Manning give manifestly incomplete summaries of the minutes (to which indeed neither of them refers) and of the advice tendered to the Foreign Secretary, the Foreign Secretary's letter of 11 May 1994 provided, in the circumstances of this case, an effective answer to the claim for discovery when taken in conjunction with the summaries of the minutes exhibited elsewhere in the evidence. There appeared no basis, looking at this total picture, for questioning the accuracy of those summaries which, in the light of *ex p Islington London BC*, seems to be a necessary prerequisite for granting discovery of original documents. Furthermore, the summaries, in my view, provided the applicants with highly valuable ammunition to which it seemed unlikely that the minutes themselves would materially add. I was, therefore, wholly unpersuaded that disclosure of these minutes was necessary for the fair disposal of the issues in this case. It was for these reasons that indicated at an earlier stage that disclosure would not be ordered.

Note

Will the CPR make any difference? Michael Fordham sees the position on oral evidence and cross-examination as being even more restrictive under the CPR.

> The problem is this. Part 54 adopts and modifies Part 8. The rules regarding oral evidence and cross-examination of a witness are contained in CPR, r 8.6(2) and (3). But far from incorporating or referring to these, CPR, r 54.16(1) provides that 'Rule 8.6 does not apply'. This is most unfortunate.[35]

Cornford offers a slightly more sanguine view, taking into account the general principles set out in CPR, Part 1:

> The advent of a new procedural code naturally raises hopes that there might be some improvement in this state of affairs. In particular, features of the overriding objective suggest a more generous approach to disclosure of documents. The court's duty to ensure that the parties are on an equal footing might be interpreted, for example, as requiring it to order the defendant to support with evidence assertions made about the decision-making process in order to rebut the claimant's arguments. The parties' duty, under r 1.3, to help further the overriding objective might

---

35   M Fordham, 'Judicial review: the new rules' [2001] PL 4, 5.

be taken as requiring public authorities to give potential claimants full information about the decision in issue so that the claimant could know in advance whether it was worth proceeding with litigation.

... Arguments that the CPR have these effects can, and probably will, be made. Unfortunately, the history of Part 54 and its clear intention to preserve the features which make judicial review a special jurisdiction all point in the opposite direction. As pointed out above, in making judicial review procedure a modification of Part 8, the Rules committee has classified it as a type of proceeding 'unlikely to involve a substantial dispute of fact'. This is reflected in the fact that r 54.16 and PD 54 para 12.1 rule out disclosure of documents unless specifically ordered by the court. Furthermore, it is hardly to be expected that the CPR will encourage greater disclosure of documents in judicial review, when its basic purpose is to save court time and speed up litigation.

It thus seems unlikely that the courts will be more generous in granting disclosure, while the paragraph in the Protocols Practice Direction, quoted above, probably does no more than encourage the well-established practice of sending letters before action.

WHO MAY APPLY FOR JUDICIAL REVIEW?

Persons seeking leave – 'permission' as it is now called – to apply for judicial review will only be granted it if they can show that they have 'sufficient interest in the matter to which the application relates'.[36] This requirement has not been altered by CPR, Part 54, as Cornford notes:

Bowman recommended retention of the sufficient interest test but with the presumption in favour of the claimant: '[s]tanding should be granted when the claimant has sufficient interest in the matter to which the application relates' (*Review of the Crown Office List*, Chapter 7, paras 28–31). This was in contrast to the earlier recommendations of both the Law Commission and Lord Woolf that the possibility of granting standing on public interest grounds should be made explicit. The new Rules say nothing about standing at all. The Lord Chancellor's Department's consultation document explains, revealingly, that Bowman's proposal was rejected because 'a substantial change in wording might result in unnecessary litigation which could put an unjustified strain on the Crown Office caseload' (Lord Chancellor's Department, *Judicial Review: Proposed New Procedures and Draft Rules* (2000) CP 8/00, p 7). The course proposed, the document goes on, is not to refer to standing but to rely on developed common law.[37]

Thus, the decision below setting out the courts' interpretation of the 'sufficient interest' test will continue to govern this area. This requirement is unproblematic if the applicant is individually and directly concerned with the decision he or she disputes, for example, if it relates to his or her employment (as in *Roy*) or application for housing (as in *Ali v Tower Hamlets*). The controversial issue in this area is whether groups or individuals with no personal concern in the decision in question (for example, pressure groups, local associations, etc) have standing to question it.[38]

It was found in *R v Secretary of State for the Environment ex p Rose Theatre Trust Co* [1990] 1 All ER 754 that pressure groups whose only interest in a decision is concern about the issues involved will not in general have *locus standi* to challenge the decision. The law has moved on considerably from that position, partly as a result of an

---

36   Supreme Court Act 1981, s 31(3).
37   Cornford, *op cit*.
38   For an interesting and in-depth analysis of this issue, see C Hilson and I Cram, 'Judicial review and environmental law – is there a coherent view of standing?' (1996) 16(1) LS 3.

approach derived from *R v IRC ex p National Federation of Self Employed* [1982] AC 617. In that case, their Lordships were unanimous in stressing that the question of standing is inextricably linked with the substantive merits of the application.

R v IRC ex p National Federation of Self Employed [1982] AC 617, 649–50, 653–55

The appellants were a body of taxpayers who wished to challenge arrangements made by the Inland Revenue for the taxation of casual employees of certain Fleet Street newspapers, which, *inter alia*, involved a partial amnesty on previous tax evasion. The appellants argued that the arrangements treated the employees in question in an overly generous manner, and that they had never been given such concessions. The issue for the House of Lords was whether the appellants had standing to challenge the IRC's decision and seek an order for *mandamus* compelling the Inland Revenue to collect taxes in the usual way.

Lord Scarman: . . . I pass now to the . . . nature of the interest which the applicant has to show. It is an integral part of the Lord Advocate's argument that the existence of the duty is a significant factor in determining the sufficiency of an applicant's interest.

The sufficiency of the interest is, as I understand all your Lordships agree, a mixed question of law and fact. The legal element in the mixture is less than the matters of fact and degree: but it is important as setting the limits within which, and the principles by which, the discretion is to be exercised. At one time heresy ruled the day. The decision of the Divisional Court in *Lewisham Union Guardians* [1897] 1 QB 498 was accepted as establishing that an applicant must establish 'a legal specific right to ask for the interference of the court' by order of *mandamus*: *per* Wright J at p 500. I agree with Lord Denning MR in thinking this was a deplorable decision. It was at total variance with the view of Lord Mansfield CJ. Yet its influence has lingered on, and is evident even in the decision of the Divisional Court in this case. But the tide of the developing law has now swept beyond it, as the Court of Appeal's decision in *Greater London Council ex p Blackburn* [1976] 1 WLR 550 illustrates. In the present case the House can put down a marker buoy warning legal navigators of the danger of the decision. As Professor Wade pointed out in *Administrative Law*, 4th edn (1977), p 610, if the *Lewisham* case were correct, *mandamus* would lose its public law character, being no more than a remedy for a private wrong.

My Lords, I will not weary the House with citation of many authorities. Suffice it to refer to the judgment of Lord Parker CJ in *Thames Magistrates' Court ex p Greenbaum*, (1957) 55 LGR 129, a case of certiorari; and to words of Lord Wilberforce in *Gouriet v Union of Post Office Workers* [1978] AC 435, 482, where he stated the modern position in relation to prerogative orders: 'These are often applied for by individuals and the courts have allowed them liberal access under a generous conception of *locus standi*'. The one legal principle, which is implicit in the case law and accurately reflected in the rule of court, is that in determining the sufficiency of an applicant's interest it is necessary to consider the matter to which the application relates. It is wrong in law, as I understand the cases, for the court to attempt an assessment of the sufficiency of an applicant's interest without regard to the matter of his complaint. If he fails to show, when he applies for leave, a *prima facie* case, or reasonable grounds for believing that there has been a failure of public duty, the court would be in error if it granted leave. The curb represented by the need for an applicant to show, when he seeks leave to apply, that he has such a case is an essential protection against abuse of legal process. It enables the court to prevent abuse by busybodies, cranks, and other mischief-makers. I do not see any further purpose served by the requirement for leave.

But, that being said, the discretion belongs to the court: and, as my noble and learned friend, Lord Diplock, has already made clear, it is the function of the judges to determine the way in which it is to be exercised.

Lord Scarman then went on to find that, in fact, the appellant had failed to make out a *prima facie* case that the IRC had acted unfairly. He also noted that the Court of Appeal had been 'misled' into treating *locus standi* as an issue separate from the merits:

> The federation, having failed to show any grounds for believing that the revenue has failed to do its statutory duty, have not, in my view, shown an interest sufficient in law to justify any further proceedings by the court on its application. Had they shown reasonable grounds for believing that the failure to collect tax from the Fleet Street casuals was an abuse of the revenue's managerial discretion or that there was a case to that effect which merited investigation and examination by the court, I would have agreed with the Court of Appeal that they had shown a sufficient interest for the grant of leave to proceed further with their application. I would, therefore, allow the appeal.

Notes

1 On the question of the standing of individual tax-payers to challenge decisions of the Inland Revenue, see further *R v HM Treasury ex p Smedley* [1985] 1 All ER 589 at 594, 595, [1985] QB 657, 670, 667 *per* Slade LJ and Lord Donaldson MR.

2 The courts appeared to move beyond the position taken in *Rose Theatre* in *R v Her Majesty's Inspectorate of Pollution ex p Greenpeace Ltd (No 2)* [1994] 4 All ER 329, discussed here by Ivan Hare. Greenpeace was seeking review of the decision of Her Majesty's Inspectorate of Pollution (HMIP) to allow testing at the THORP nuclear reprocessing plant without further consultation.

> ... Greenpeace sought to impugn the substantive decision to vary BNFL's authorisation on the ground that an entirely new authorisation was required before testing at THORP could lawfully commence. This application was also dismissed but of general importance was the rejection of BNFL's claim that Greenpeace lacked sufficient standing to initiate the proceedings. In accepting that Greenpeace had *locus standi*, Otton J was influenced by a number of factors including the international reputation of the group and its significant local membership in the affected area. He also stressed that Greenpeace represented the best, and possibly the only, means by which the issues raised by the application could be addressed by a court. Two further points require some comment. First, Otton J took account of the fact that Greenpeace was seeking an order of certiorari and held that 'if *mandamus* were sought that would be a reason to decline jurisdiction'. In other words, the test of standing will vary according to the remedy sought by the applicant. This statement was purportedly based on the decision of the House of Lords in *IRC ex p National Federation of Self-Employed and Small Businesses Ltd* [1982] AC 617. In fact, Lord Wilberforce was the only member of the House to adopt a clear position in favour of this view with Lord Diplock equally clearly opposed to it and the other Lords appearing to express somewhat equivocal support for Lord Diplock's position. There is a very strong argument that the purpose of the introduction of the unified Ord 53 procedure was to remove exactly this sort of distinction between the different forms of relief. Any return to the adjectival complexity of the prerogative orders is to be regretted.
>
> Secondly, the court expressly declined to follow *Secretary of State for the Environment ex p Rose Theatre Trust Co* [1990] 1 QB 504, a case which many feared marked a rejection of the prevailing liberal attitude to *locus standi*. Some have explained the courts' occasional reluctance to grant standing to pressure groups on the basis that the function of such bodies is essentially that of the lobbyist and to allow them to litigate their concerns would risk transforming judicial review into a mode of redress for political rather than legal grievances. The judgment in the present case is an affirmation of the advantages of allowing pressure groups to contribute their expertise to the forensic process. Otton J emphasised that Greenpeace, 'with its particular experience in environmental matters, its access to experts in the relevant realms of science and technology (not to mention the law), is able to mount a carefully selected, focused, relevant and well-argued challenge'.

This aspect of the cases is to be welcomed but they also reveal that, notwithstanding that the present judicial review procedure has been in operation for almost two decades, doctrinal confusion has yet to be eliminated.[39]

3   Another issue of importance in the case was the fact that the interest Greenpeace had in the matter went clearly beyond the merely ideological. Otton J stressed the local health interest of the 2,500 supporters in the Cumbria region, whose health might be effected by emissions from the nuclear plant.[40] Thus, members of the group had a personal interest in a matter of substantial general concern – public health. Thus, although the court expressly declined to follow *Rose Theatre*, the decision was clearly distinguishable anyway: in the earlier case the group seeking to challenge the decision not to list the theatre site was only interested in the case because of its general concern about the preservation of this country's historical heritage. As Hilson and Cram remark, 'Had a substantial number of the individuals in the [Rose Theatre pressure group] lived locally, the position might well have been different'.[41]

4   A similar approach was adopted in *R v Secretary of State for the Environment ex p Friends of the Earth* [1994] CMLR 760 where the group and its director were granted leave to challenge a decision related to the quality of drinking water in certain specified areas. The fact that the director lived in one of those areas – London – gave him a personal local interest in the matter.

5   However, in other cases involving decisions of *national* importance, the courts have been prepared to move beyond this stance and allow challenges by persons whose only concern with the decision is intellectual or ideological. The rationale appears to be that, in these cases, there is no one who will be personally affected and who could therefore claim a greater interest in the matter than the applicant. The result would therefore be that if the applicant were denied leave, no one else would be able to come forward to challenge the decision so that the courts would have no opportunity to test the legality of an important decision, a position that the courts seem increasingly minded to avoid. Thus, for example, in *R v Secretary of State for Foreign and Commonwealth Affairs ex p Rees-Mogg* [1994] 1 All ER 457, it was found that the applicant had standing 'because of his sincere concern for constitutional issues'. (Compare the remarks of Lord Donaldson MR in *ex p Argyll Group plc* [1986] 2 All ER 257, 265–66.)

6   *R v Secretary of State for Employment ex p EOC* [1994] 2 WLR 409 concerned in part the standing of the Equal Opportunities Commission (EOC), a quango with the remit of curbing discrimination, to challenge statutory provisions. Certain provisions of the Employment Protection (Consolidation) Act 1978 governed the right not to be unfairly dismissed, compensation for unfair dismissal and the right to statutory redundancy pay. These rights did not apply to workers who worked less than a specified number of hours a week. The EOC considered that since the majority of those working for less than the specified number of hours were women, the provisions operated to the disadvantage or women and were therefore discriminatory. It was held, *inter alia*, that the EOC was entitled to bring judicial review proceedings in order to secure a declaration that UK law was incompatible with EC law. Declarations were made that the conditions set out in the provisions

39   I Hare (1995) 54(1) CLJ 1, 2–3.
40   Hilson and Cram, *op cit*, p 18.
41   *Ibid*, p 19.

in question were indeed incompatible with EC law. The case also illustrates the point that where both an individual *and* a group have an interest in a given decision, the courts may favour the group.[42]

7 In *R v Secretary of State for Foreign Affairs ex p the World Development Movement* [1995] 1 All ER 611, the question was whether the pressure group concerned had standing to challenge an allegedly unlawful grant of foreign aid.

R v Secretary of State for Foreign Affairs ex p the World Development Movement [1995] 1 All ER 611, 618–20

Rose LJ: Internationally, [the World Development Movement] has official consultative status with UNESCO and has promoted international conferences. It has brought together development groups within the OECD. It tends to attract citizens of the United Kingdom concerned about the role of the United Kingdom Government in relation to the development of countries abroad and the relief of poverty abroad.

Its supporters have a direct interest in ensuring that funds furnished by the United Kingdom are used for genuine purposes, and it seeks to ensure that disbursement of aid budgets is made where that aid is most needed. It seeks, by this application, to represent the interests of people in developing countries who might benefit from funds which otherwise might go elsewhere.

If the applicants have no standing, it is said that no person or body would ensure that powers under the 1980 Act are exercised lawfully. For the applicants Mr Pleming QC submitted that the Foreign Secretary himself, in a written statement of 2 March 1994, has expressly accepted that the matter is '... clearly of public and Parliamentary interest'. It cannot be said that the applicants are 'busybodies', 'cranks' or 'mischief-makers'. They are a non-partisan pressure group concerned with the misuse of aid money. If there is a public law error, it is difficult to see how else it could be challenged and corrected except by such an applicant. He referred the court to a number of authorities: *IRC v National Federation of Self-Employed and Small Businesses Ltd* [1981] 2 All ER 93, [1982] AC 617, in particular the speech of Lord Wilberforce ([1981] 2 All ER 93 at 96; [1982] AC 617 at 630) and the speech of Lord Diplock, where there appears this passage:

> It would, in my view, be a grave lacuna in our system of public law if a pressure group, like the federation, or even a single public spirited taxpayer, were prevented by outdated technical rules of *locus standi* from bringing the matter to the attention of the court to vindicate the Rule of Law and get the unlawful conduct stopped. The Attorney General, although he occasionally applies for prerogative orders against public authorities that do not form part of central Government, in practice never does so against Government departments. It is not, in my view, a sufficient answer to say that judicial review of the actions of officers or departments of central Government is unnecessary because they are accountable to Parliament for the way in which they carry out their functions. They are accountable to Parliament for what they do so far as regards efficiency and policy, and of that Parliament is the only judge; they are responsible to a court of justice for the lawfulness of what they do, and of that the court is the only judge. (See [1981] 2 All ER 93 at 107, [1982] AC 617 at 644.)

... The question of lawfulness being for the court, Mr Pleming submitted that the court in its discretion should accept the standing of the applicants. If they cannot seek relief, he said, who can? Neither a Government nor citizen of a foreign country denied aid is, in practical terms, likely to be able to bring such a challenge ...

For my part, I accept that standing (albeit decided in the exercise of the court's discretion, as Donaldson MR said) goes to jurisdiction ... But I find nothing in *IRC v National Federation of Self-Employed and Small Businesses Ltd* to deny standing to these applicants. The authorities referred to seem to me to indicate an increasingly liberal approach to standing on the part of the courts

---

42   See further on this issue, Hilson and Cram, *op cit*, pp 21–25.

during the last 12 years. It is also clear from *IRC v National Federation of Self-Employed and Small Businesses Ltd* that standing should not be treated as a preliminary issue, but must be taken in the legal and factual context of the whole case (see [1981] 2 All ER 93 at 96, 110, 113, [1982] AC 617 at 630, 649, 653 per Lord Wilberforce, Lord Fraser and Lord Scarman).

Furthermore, the merits of the challenge are an important, if not dominant, factor when considering standing. In Professor Sir William Wade's words in *Administrative Law* (7th edn, 1994), p 712:

> ... the real question is whether the applicant can show some substantial default or abuse, and not whether his personal rights or interests are involved.

Leaving merits aside for a moment, there seem to me to be a number of factors of significance in the present case: the importance of vindicating the Rule of Law, as Lord Diplock emphasised in *IRC v National Federation of Self-Employed and Small Businesses Ltd* [1981] 2 All ER 93 at 107, [1982] AC 617 at 644; the importance of the issue raised, as in *ex p Child Poverty Action Group*; the likely absence of any other responsible challenger, as in *ex p Child Poverty Action Group* and *ex p Greenpeace Ltd*; the nature of the breach of duty against which relief is sought (see *IRC v National Federation of Self-Employed and Small Businesses Ltd* [1981] 2 All ER 93 at 96, [1982] AC 617 at 630 per Lord Wilberforce); and the prominent role of these applicants in giving advice, guidance and assistance with regard to aid (see *ex p Child Poverty Action Group* [1989] 1 All ER 1047 at 1048, [1990] 2 QB 540 at 546). All, in my judgment, point, in the present case, to the conclusion that the applicants here do have a sufficient interest in the matter to which the application relates within s 31(3) of the 1981 Act and Ord 53, r 3(7).

Notes

1 On the position of pressure groups, see also *R v Secretary of State for Social Services ex p Child Poverty Action Group* [1989] 1 All ER 1047.

2 The case is clearly not a charter for the tiresomely officious: the applicants were a body whose work was of international repute and whose concern for the issue in hand was genuine.[43] Further, the fact that there was no one more closely affected by the decision in question who could have brought the case was clearly instrumental in the court's finding. The requirement that no such person or persons be available to mount a challenge will often operate to protect what Hilson and Cram term 'local autonomy';[44] the idea is that if a particular community or individual is content to acquiesce in a decision, it would show disrespect for their autonomy if other bodies, not affected by the decision, were to be allowed to challenge it. Thus, it is argued that in the case of decisions which are *only* of local significance, the courts are right to insist as they do that any challenger must have a local interest.[45] By contrast, in cases in which decisions have particular local interest but are also of national significance (for example, the *Rose Theatre* case itself), it is argued that 'the autonomy of those personally affected or locally connected ought to be overridden and standing granted to those with [only] a general interest'.[46] This does not, however, represent the current legal position.[47]

3 In *Broadmoor Special Hospital Authority v Robinson* [2000] QB 775, 787,[48] Lord Woolf MR said:

---

43 See also the finding that Rees-Mogg's concern for constitutional issues was 'sincere' and that Greenpeace was genuinely exercised about testing at THORP.
44 *Op cit*, especially pp 10–12 and 15–21.
45 *Op cit*, p 17.
46 *Ibid*, pp 15–16 and see pp 19–20.
47 *Rose Theatre*; *R v Poole Borough Council ex p Beebee* [1991] JPL 643.
48 Cf *R (Bulger) v Secretary of State for the Home Department* [2001] 3 All ER 449.

'Sufficient interest', has been approached by the courts in a generous manner so that almost invariably if an applicant can establish a case which deserves to succeed, standing will not constitute a bar to the grant of a remedy.

While this current generous view of standing is in some respects welcome, since it will allow pressure groups with particular expertise in the relevant area to raise issues of general public importance, it will tend to introduce, it is suggested, further uncertainty into the area of judicial review. Instances may tend to arise which fall on the borderlines suggested by these recent rulings; in particular it may be hard to lay down coherent and clear principles which can be used to determine whether or not an issue is sufficiently significant to fall within the rule laid down in the *World Development Movement* decision.

4   Under the HRA, applicants must show that they are 'a victim' of the action, or proposed action of the public authority (s 7(1)), clearly a more restrictive test than that considered above. The test is discussed further in Part VI Chapter 1, p 873.

5   While, as noted at the beginning of this section, the CPR do not purport to alter the law of standing, the changes they make to the obtaining of permission to bring a challenge are quite significant, in a way which may influence the courts' jurisprudence in this area. Previously, as Lord Diplock said in *ex p National Federation of Self Employed* at 644A:

> If, on a quick perusal of the material then available, the court thinks that it discloses what might on further consideration turn out to be an arguable case in favour of granting to the applicant the relief claimed, it ought, in the exercise of judicial discretion, to give him leave to apply for that relief.

As Tom Cornford and Maurice Sunkin comment:

> The single most important aspect of these reforms is the way the permission stage has been re-crafted from an essentially summary *ex parte* filter of arguability to a procedure which is both a filter of access and an *inter partes* procedure of the sort familiar in ordinary civil litigation.[49]

This may encourage the courts to scrutinise the issue of standing much more rigorously at the permission stage, rather than leaving main consideration of it to the full hearing, the present position.

CAN JUDICIAL REVIEW BE EXCLUDED?

It is a fundamental principle of English law that the courts always have a duty to ensure that a body exercising power does so within the parameters set for it in the provisions (often primary legislation) which established it or gave it power in the area under consideration. In *Anisminic Ltd v Foreign Compensation Commission* [1969] 2 AC 147, it was held that this power of the court to keep the deciding body within the remit defined in the Act which gave it its powers could not be excluded, despite apparently clear words in a statute to the contrary. To allow the court's supervisory jurisdiction to be ousted would be to accede to the proposition that the body in question had arbitrary powers, and the court was not prepared to believe that such powers are ever granted, since the granting of them would undermine the basic principle of the Rule of Law.

---

49   T Cornford and M Sunkin, 'The Bowman Report, access and the recent reforms of the judicial review procedure' [2001] PL 11, 15.

Anisminic Ltd v Foreign Compensation Commission [1969] 2 AC 147, 170

Lord Reid: ... Let me illustrate the matter by supposing a simple case. A statute provides that a certain order may be made by a person who holds a specified qualification or appointment, and it contains a provision ... that such an order made by such a person shall not be called in question in any court of law. A person aggrieved by an order alleges that it is a forgery or that the person who made the order did not hold that qualification or appointment. Does such a provision require the court to treat that order as a valid order? It is a well established principle that a provision ousting the ordinary jurisdiction of the court must be construed strictly – meaning, I think, that, if such a provision is reasonably capable of having two meanings, that meaning shall be taken which preserves the ordinary jurisdiction of the court.

Statutory provisions which seek to limit the ordinary jurisdiction of the court have a long history. No case has been cited in which any other form of words limiting the jurisdiction of the court has been held to protect a nullity. If the draftsman or Parliament had intended to introduce a new kind of ouster clause so as to prevent any inquiry even as to whether the document relied on was a forgery, I would have expected to find something much more specific than the bald statement that a determination shall not be called in question in any court of law. Undoubtedly such a provision protects every determination which is not a nullity. But I do not think that it is necessary or even reasonable to construe the word 'determination' as including everything which purports to be a determination but which is in fact no determination at all. And there are no degrees of nullity. There are a number of reasons why the law will hold a purported decision to be a nullity. I do not see how it could be said that such a provision protects some kinds of nullity but not others: if that were intended it would be easy to say so.

Notes

1 The basic idea behind the *Anisminic* decision is that by making an error in law, the body asked itself the wrong question, determined a point it was not authorised to decide and thus exceeded its *vires*. Its decision was therefore *ultra vires* and a nullity. The idea of a body being empowered to err within certain limits was rejected.

2 Section 12(1) of the Tribunals Act 1992 now provides that the supervisory functions of the superior courts will not be excluded by Acts passed prior to 1 August 1958. This or course implies that effect may be given to ouster clauses in later statutes.

Tribunals and Enquiries Act 1992

12.–(1) As respects England and Wales—

> (a) any provision in an Act passed before 1st August 1958 that any order or determination shall not be called into question in any court, or
>
> (b) any provision in such an Act which by similar words excludes any of the powers of the High Court,

shall not have effect so as to prevent the removal of the proceedings into the High Court by order of certiorari or to prejudice the powers of the High Court to make orders of *mandamus*.

Supervisory functions of superior courts not excluded by Acts passed before 1 August 1958.

Notes

1 It may be pointed out that in cases involving national security the courts have historically tended to find either that review is not available or that it is very marginal. It seems to follow from *R v Secretary of State for the Home Department ex p Cheblak* [1991] 2 All ER 329 that although the decision to exclude persons from the UK is non-justiciable, there may be some review of preconditions and procedures.[50]

---

50   See C Walker, *The Prevention of Terrorism in British Law*, 2nd edn (1992), pp 90–92.

However, if the applicant can raise a point under the ECHR, under s 6(1) of the HRA, the court will be bound to consider it, though, given a national security context, review of decisions in this area is likely to remain deferential: on deference generally see Part VI Chapter 1, pp 886–94.

2   A number of statutes governing national security concerns contain exclusion clauses, which direct complaints to specialised tribunals, often with far less satisfactory due process guarantees than the ordinary courts, and exclude the courts from reviewing the decisions of such tribunals. The Security Services Act 1989 contains such a clause in s 5(4). If a member of the public has a grievance concerning the operation of the 1989 Act, complaint to a court is not possible; under s 5 it can only be made to a tribunal and under s 5(4) the decisions of the tribunal are not questionable in any court of law. The provision of s 5(4) was criticised in 1992 by Kennedy J in refusing an application for review of the Security Service Tribunal's decision not to investigate allegations that MI5 was still holding files on Harriet Harman, the Shadow Health Minister,[51] he considered that in some circumstances the courts certainly would have jurisdiction to intervene.

FURTHER READING

SH Bailey, B Jones and A Mowbrary, *Cases and Material on Administrative Law*, 3rd edn (1997)

P Craig, *Administrative Law*, 5th edn (2003)

M Elliott, *The Constitutional Foundations of Judicial Review* (2000)

M Fordham, *Judicial Review Handbook*, 3rd edn (2001)

C Forsyth (ed), *Judicial Review and the Constitution* (2000)

S Halliday, *Judicial Review and Compliance with Administrative Law* (2003)

P Leyland and T Woods, *Textbook on Administrative Law*, 4th edn (2002)

M Taggart, *The Province of Administrative Law* (1997)

R Thomas, *Legitimate Expectations and Proportionality in Administrative Law* (2000)

HWR Wade and C Forsyth, *Administrative Law*, 8th edn (2000)

---

51   See *The Guardian*, 15 February 1992.

CHAPTER 2

GROUNDS OF JUDICIAL REVIEW

INTRODUCTION

The system of judicial review allows the judges to interfere, some would allege rather arbitrarily, in the machinery of government and administration. Using this self-made weapon, judges have struck down numerous important decisions, from the policy of the Greater London Council to reduce public transport fares in the capital by 25 per cent,[1] to a policy decision of the Home Secretary to introduce a new, non-statutory criminal injuries compensation scheme.[2] What is the justification for this interference?

One of the traditional answers to this question is the doctrine of *ultra vires*: the judges in striking down decisions on judicial review are merely upholding the will of Parliament; either in an obvious and clear way, as when they hold that a public authority's action was not permitted by the statute under which it has purported to act, or impliedly. The notion is that when the courts 'supply the omission of the legislature' and imply rules of procedural fairness into a statutory scheme that contains no such provision expressly, they are also carrying out the implicit will of Parliament, since Parliament must be taken to be aware of the developed principles of natural justice applied by the courts, and by not excluding them, has impliedly stamped them with its approval. This school of thought is referred to, broadly as the *'ultra vires'* school. An alternative justification for judicial review has been put forward by a number of scholars including Sir John Laws, as he then was.

Sir John Laws, 'Law and democracy' [1995] PL 72, 78

Lord Diplock's judicial review criterion of illegality is plain enough: no subordinate body may exceed the express bounds of its statutory power: that is, the power which on its proper construction the Act confers. But what of the other heads of review, *Wednesbury* unreasonableness and procedural unfairness? They are now as elementary as illegality. In the elaboration of these principles the courts have imposed and enforced judicially created standards of public behaviour. But the civilised imperative of their existence cannot be derived from the simple requirement that public bodies must be kept to the limits of their authority given by Parliament. Neither deductive logic nor the canons of ordinary language, which are the basic tools of statutory construction, can attribute them to that ideal, since although their application may be qualified by the words of any particular statute, in principle their roots have grown from another seed altogether. In some formulations, it is true, they have purportedly been justified by the attribution of an intention to the legislature that statutory decision-makers should act reasonably and fairly; but this is largely fictitious. In recent times, before *Ridge v Baldwin* it was not generally thought (to put it crudely) that administrative, non-judicial, bodies owed such duties as to hear the other side. Before *Padfield* it was not generally thought that it was an enforceable function of every statute conferring public power that it only justified action to promote the distinct purposes of the Act, even though the Act did not state them. Before the concept of legitimate expectation assumed the status of a substantive legal principle (whose precise date may be nicely debated), it was not generally thought that decision-makers should be prevented from departing from previous assurances as to their

---

1   *Bromley LBC v GLC* [1983] AC 768.
2   *R v Secretary of State for the Home Dept ex p Fire Brigades Union and others* [1995] 2 All ER 244, HL.

actions without giving those affected an opportunity to make representations. *Wednesbury* itself reaches back to older law; but its fruition and its maturity came 20 years and more after it was decided. It cannot be suggested that all these principles, which represent much of the bedrock of modern administrative law, were suddenly interwoven into the legislature's intentions in the 1960s and 70s and onwards, in which period they have been articulated and enforced by the courts. They are, categorically, judicial creations. They owe neither their existence nor their acceptance to the will of the legislature. They have nothing to do with the intention of Parliament, save as a fig-leaf to cover their true origins. We do not need the fig-leaf any more.

Notes

1   For criticism of Laws' view and a defence of *ultra vires* as the fundamental basis of judicial review, see Christopher Forsyth, 'Of fig-leaves and fairy tales: the *ultra vires* doctrine, the sovereignty of Parliament and judicial review' [1996] CLJ 122, esp 127–40; for further discussion of these issues see Jeffrey Jowell, 'The Rule of Law today', in J Jowell and D Oliver (eds), *The Changing Constitution*, 4th edn (2000), pp 73–75; P Craig, *Administrative Law*, 4th edn (1999), Chapter 1 and 'Competing models of judicial review' [1999] PL 428–47; HWR Wade, *Administrative Law*, 8th edn (2000), Chapters 1 and 2. A modified version of the *ultra vires* doctrine has recently been put forward by Mark Elliott, *The Constitutional Foundations of Judicial Review* (2001). For extended discussion and criticism, see P Craig and N Bamforth, 'Constitutional analysis, constitutional principle and judicial review' [2001] PL 763; for a recent rejoinder by C Forsyth and M Elliott, see 'The legitimacy of judicial review' [2003] PL 286–307.

2   Judicial review is to be distinguished from review of the merits of the decision itself. It is concerned only with the legality of the decision, which will itself depend on whether it falls within any of the three main heads of review discussed below. Sir John Laws[3] gives a clear explanation as to why constitutional principle makes the simultaneous demand that judges ensure decisions are made legally but do not assess their merits:

> [This demand] arises as a matter of definition from the very nature of the public power respectively lying in the hands of the courts and those whom they review. The paradigm of a public body subject to the public law jurisdiction is one whose power is conferred by statute. The statute is logically prior to it; and by the constitution it is for the courts to police the statute. But they do not act under the statute. They are altogether outside it. Their power is not derived from it, nor ultimately from any Act of Parliament. This state of affairs has two consequences. First, the judges have to see that the power given by the statute is not transgressed by its donee; secondly, they have no business themselves to exercise the powers conferred by it, precisely because they are not the donee. Hence the essence of the judicial review jurisdiction. It vindicates the Rule of Law not only by confining statutory power within the four corners of the Act, but also ensuring that the statute is not usurped by anyone – including the courts themselves.[4]

3   If it is found, upon review, that an authority has acted unlawfully, there are a number of remedies that can be granted. Discussion of these remedies lies outside the scope of this book;[5] a very brief summary only will be given. The following are known as the prerogative remedies. They were recently renamed, as part of the

---

3   J Laws, 'Law and democracy' [1995] PL 72.
4   *Ibid*, pp 77–78. Laws' analysis is not applicable in terms to cases in which the body which the court is reviewing does not receive its powers from statute, but it can apply by analogy; whichever source of power gave the jurisdiction to the decision-making body, it did not give a simultaneous jurisdiction to the courts.
5   Readers are referred to P Craig, *Administrative Law*, 4th edn (1999), Chapters 22–26; HWR Wade and C Forsyth, *Administrative Law*, 8th edn (2000), Chapters 16–22 for a full exposition.

Woolf reforms to judicial review. The old names, which will be found in decisions pre-dating the reforms, are given in brackets:

(a) *quashing order (certiorari)*: quashes an unlawful decision;

(b) *prohibitory order (prohibition)*: prohibits an authority from performing a proposed unlawful act;

(c) *mandatory order (mandamus)*: compels an authority to perform a particular act.

Prerogative remedies may not be granted against the Crown, though they can be granted against individual government ministers; additionally, they have not been used in relation to delegated legislation found to be unlawful.

4   In addition, the following remedies, which are non-prerogative (and thus not unique to judicial review) may be sought:

(a) *injunction*: restrains an unlawful action, and may be interim or final; for their use against the Crown and against government ministers, see *Re M* [1993] 3 WLR 433, HL and *R v Secretary of State of Transport ex p Factortame (No 2)* [1990] 1 AC 604;

(b) *declaration*: an authoritative statement by the court, for example, that a given act is unlawful; often used in relation to the Crown, or delegated legislation;

(c) *damages*: available only if the applicant has claimed one of the above remedies *and* if he or she can show that the authority has committed a breach of contract, a tort or a breach of s 6(1) of the Human Rights Act 1998 (see Part VI Chapter 1).

5   In the following decision, Lord Diplock summed up the grounds for judicial review in the following statement:

CCSU v Minister for Civil Service (the GCHQ case) [1985] AC 374, 410

Lord Diplock: Judicial review has I think developed to a stage today when without reiterating any analysis of the steps by which the development has come about, one can conveniently classify under three heads the grounds upon which administrative action is subject to control by judicial review. The first ground I would call 'illegality,' the second 'irrationality' and the third 'procedural impropriety.' That is not to say that further development on a case by case basis may not in course of time add further grounds. I have in mind particularly the possible adoption in the future of the principle of 'proportionality' which is recognised in the administrative law of several of our fellow members of the European Economic Community.

Note

To these grounds should now be added breach of rights under the European Convention on Human Rights, as defined by s 1 of the Human Rights Act 1998 (HRA). The HRA is dealt with in Part VI Chapter 1 but s 6(1) of the Act makes it 'unlawful for a public authority to act in a way which is incompatible with a Convention right'.

ILLEGALITY

As Lord Diplock explained it in the *GCHQ* case, 'By "illegality" as a ground for judicial review I mean that the decision-maker must understand correctly the law that regulates his decision-making power and must give effect to it' (at 410). The head of 'illegality' is perhaps the broadest head of judicial review; it may be summarised as including the following four types of illegality:

(a) Doing an act with no legal authority – what may be known as 'simple illegality'.

(b) *Misinterpreting* the law governing the decision.

(c) Failure to *retain* a discretion by: (i) improper delegation; or (ii) fettering of discretion through adoption of rigid policy.

(d) *Abuse* of discretion: (a) using a power for an improper purpose; (b) taking into account irrelevant considerations or failing to take account of relevant ones.

To these well established heads could tentatively be added the violation of substantive legitimate expectations, though this is a controversial area, dealt with below. Each of the above heads are now examined in turn.

Simple illegality

The first head, then, is doing an act for which the public body concerned has no legal authority. An old and clear case is *Attorney General v Fulham Corporation* [1921] Ch 440. In this case Fulham was empowered to provide facilities for local poor people to wash their own clothes. They set up a commercial washing service, whereby people could bring in their clothes and the Council would wash them for them. The Council said this would 'relieve Housewives to a great extent of this most laborious work'. The Attorney General brought an action against Fulham, and it was found that it had no power to set up commercial laundries. The following decision is another example.

Laker Airways v Dept of Trade [1977] QB 643, 704, CA

Laker Airways had been granted a licence by the Civil Aviation Authority (CAA) under statutory authority. The Secretary of State had power to issue guidance to the CAA as to its duties. As a result of a change in government, and consequent change in policy, the Secretary of State issued 'guidance' to the CAA as he was entitled to; the guidance, however, instructed the CAA to revoke Laker's licence. The result would have been to give the then state-owned British Airways a monopoly, in line with government policy. Laker sought judicial review of the decision.

Lord Denning MR: The first [question] is whether the Secretary of State was acting beyond his lawful powers when he gave the new policy guidance to the Civil Aviation Authority.

In determining this point, I have found much help from the well reasoned decisions of the Civil Aviation Authority, not only in 1972, when they granted the licence to Laker Airways, but also in 1975 when they refused to revoke it. It is plain that they applied most conscientiously and sensibly the four general objectives set out in s 3(1)(a), (b), (c) and (d) of the statute, as amplified and supplemented by the 1972 policy guidance. The new policy guidance of 1976 cuts right across those statutory objectives. It lays down a new policy altogether. Whereas the statutory objectives made it clear that the British Airways Board was not to have a monopoly, but that at least one other British airline should have an opportunity to participate, the new policy guidance says that the British Airways Board is to have a monopoly. No competition is to be allowed. And no other British airline is to be licensed unless British Airways had given its consent. This guidance was not a mere temporary measure. It was to last for a considerable period of years.

Those provisions disclose so complete a reversal of policy that to my mind the White Paper cannot be regarded as giving 'guidance' at all. In marching terms it does not say 'right incline' or 'left incline'. It says 'right about turn'. That is not guidance, but the reverse of it.

There is no doubt that the Secretary of State acted with the best of motives in formulating this new policy – and it may well have been the right policy – but I am afraid that he went about it in the wrong way. Seeing that the old policy had been laid down in an Act of Parliament, then, in order to reverse it, he should have introduced an amending Bill and got Parliament to sanction it.

He was advised, apparently, that it was not necessary, and that it could be done by 'guidance'. That, I think, was a mistake. And Laker Airways are entitled to complain of it, at any rate in its impact on them. It was in this respect *ultra vires* and the judge was right so to declare.

Notes

1 In a number of cases prior to the Human Rights Act 1998, the courts, in an attempt to provide protection for certain basic rights, including access to a court, and freedom of expression, were prepared to strike down delegated legislation that interfered with such rights on this basis of simple illegality. The argument used was that abrogation of such rights required specific authorisation in the enabling legislation, and that, absent such authorisation, the delegated legislation, in interfering with basic rights, was *ultra vires*. In other words, where basic rights were at stake, the legal authorisation required for acts that interfered with them had to be precise and specific. As Lord Hoffman put it in *ex p Simms* [2000] 2 AC 115, 131, 'fundamental rights cannot be overridden by general or ambiguous words'. See, for example, *R v Lord Chancellor ex p Witham* [1997] 2 All ER 799, an extract from which appears in Part I Chapter 4.

2 In *ex p Pierson* [1998] AC 539, 575, Lord Browne-Wilkinson summarised the principle thus:

A power conferred by Parliament in general terms is not to be taken to authorise the doing of acts by the donee of the power which adversely affect the legal rights of the citizen or the basic principles on which the law of the United Kingdom is based unless the statute conferring the power makes it clear that such was the intention of Parliament.

3 Since 2 November 2000,[6] the courts are required to read *all* legislation as not authorising interference by public authorities with rights protected under the European Convention on Human Rights (see generally Part II Chapter 2) if possible, under s 3(1) of the HRA. However, this will not preclude the courts from additionally or alternatively using and applying the presumption at common law set out by Lord Browne-Wilkinson. Indeed, in *Daly*,[7] Lord Cooke remarked:

... while this case has arisen in a jurisdiction where the European Convention for the Protection of Human Rights and Fundamental Freedoms applies, and while the case is one in which the Convention and the common law produce the same result, it is of great importance, in my opinion, that the common law by itself is being recognised as a sufficient source of the fundamental right to confidential communication with a legal adviser for the purpose of obtaining legal advice. Thus the decision may prove to be in point in common law jurisdictions not affected by the Convention. Rights similar to those in the Convention are of course to be found in constitutional documents and other formal affirmations of rights elsewhere. The truth is, I think, that some rights are inherent and fundamental to democratic civilised society. Conventions, constitutions, bills of rights and the like respond by recognising rather than creating them.

See further Part VI Chapter 1, pp 845–49.

Error of law: are *all* errors of law reviewable?

This principle is elementary: a public authority must correctly construe the legal authority under which it acts. However, an important preliminary question that has arisen is whether *any* error of law made by the decision-maker will result in it being

6   The date the Human Rights Act 1998 came into force.
7   *R v Secretary of State for the Home Department ex p Daly* [2001] 2 AC 532, at para 30.

held to have exceeded its jurisdiction and thus to have acted unlawfully. The issue is that there may be mistakes that a body is entitled to make in coming to a decision – mistakes which do not render its decision unlawful. As we shall see, if the decision-making body – a tribunal – makes a 'mistake' in the sense that it gives more weight to a particular consideration than the court would have, or if it makes a mistake as to whether a fact is proven or not, the courts will view such mistakes as being within the tribunal's jurisdiction. But are mistakes as to the law which governs a tribunal ever of this type? Or do all errors of law made by a tribunal mean that it has exceeded its rightful jurisdiction? The leading case in this area is *Anisminic Ltd v Foreign Compensation Commissioners* [1969] AC 147.

Anisminic Ltd v Foreign Compensation Commissioners [1969] AC 147, 171–75

Anisminic Ltd had had certain of its property sequestered by the Egyptian Government, and had later sold it to TEDO, an Egyptian organisation, for considerably less than its actual value. Anisminic applied for compensation to the Foreign Compensation Commission, which had the duty, under Art 4 of the Foreign Compensation etc Order 1962, of distributing compensation to businesses such as Anisminic which had suffered loss by virtue of the confiscation of their property. Article 4 stated that the Commission was to treat a claim as good if they were satisfied of the following:

(a) the applicant was the person referred to in the relevant part of Annex E of the Order as 'the owner of the property or the successor in title of such a person'; and

(b) the person referred to in that part of Annex E 'and any person who became successor in title of such person . . . were British Nationals'.

The Commission's initial finding was that Anisminic Ltd was not entitled to compensation because TEDO (its successor in title) was not a British national.

Lord Reid: It has sometimes been said that it is only where a tribunal acts without jurisdiction that its decision is a nullity. But in such cases the word 'jurisdiction' has been used in a very wide sense, and I have come to the conclusion that it is better not to use the term except in the narrow and original sense of the tribunal being entitled to enter on the inquiry in question. But there are many cases where, although the tribunal had jurisdiction to enter on the inquiry, it has done or failed to do something in the course of the inquiry which is of such a nature that its decision is a nullity. It may have given its decision in bad faith. It may have made a decision which it had no power to make. It may have failed in the course of the inquiry to comply with the requirements of natural justice. It may in perfect good faith have misconstrued the provisions giving it power to act so that it failed to deal with the question remitted to it and decided some question which was not remitted to it. It may have refused to take into account something which it was required to take into account. Or it may have based its decision on some matter which, under the provisions setting it up, it had no right to take into account. I do not intend this list to be exhaustive. But if it decides a question remitted to it for decision without committing any of these errors it is as much entitled to decide that question wrongly as it is to decide it rightly.

I can now turn to the provisions of the Order under which the commission acted, and to the way in which the commission reached their decision. The effect of the Order was to confer legal rights on persons who might previously have hoped or expected that in allocating any sums available discretion would be exercised in their favour.

The main difficulty in this case springs from the fact that the draftsman did not state separately what conditions have to be satisfied (1) where the applicant is the original owner and (2) where the applicant claims as the successor in title of the original owner. It is clear that where the applicant is the original owner he must prove that he was a British national on the dates stated. And it is equally clear that where the applicant claims as being the original owner's successor in title he must prove that both he and the original owner were British nationals on those dates, subject to later provisions in the article about persons who had died or had been born within the relevant period. What is left in obscurity is whether the provisions with regard to successors in title have any application at all in cases where the applicant is himself the original owner. If this provision had been split up as it should have been, and the conditions to be satisfied where the original owner is the applicant had been set out, there could have been no such obscurity.

This is the crucial question in this case. It appears from the commission's reasons that they construed this provision as requiring them to inquire, when the applicant is himself the original owner, whether he had a successor in title. So they made that inquiry in this case and held that TEDO was the applicant's successor in title. As TEDO was not a British national they rejected the appellants' claim. But if, on a true construction of the Order, a claimant who is an original owner does not have to prove anything about successors in title, then the commission made an inquiry which the Order did not empower them to make, and they based their decision on a matter which they had no right to take into account. If one uses the word 'jurisdiction' in its wider sense, they went beyond their jurisdiction in considering this matter. It was argued that the whole matter of construing the Order was something remitted to the commission for their decision. I cannot accept that argument. I find nothing in the Order to support it. The Order requires the commission to consider whether they are satisfied with regard to the prescribed matters. That is all they have to do. It cannot be for the commission to determine the limits of its powers. Of course if one party submits to a tribunal that its powers are wider than in fact they are, then the tribunal must deal with that submission. But if they reach a wrong conclusion as to the width of their powers, the court must be able to correct that – not because the tribunal has made an error of law, but because as a result of making an error of law they have dealt with and based their decision on a matter with which, on a true construction of their powers, they had no right to deal. If they base their decision on some matter which is not prescribed for their adjudication, they are doing something which they have no right to do and, if the view which I expressed earlier is right, their decision is a nullity. So the question is whether on a true construction of the Order the applicants did or did not have to prove anything with regard to successors in title. If the commission were entitled to enter on the inquiry whether the applicants had a successor in title, then their decision as to whether TEDO was their successor in title would I think be unassailable whether it was right or wrong: it would be a decision on a matter remitted to them for their decision. The question I have to consider is not whether they made a wrong decision but whether they inquired into and decided a matter which they had no right to consider.

[His Lordship then went on to consider whether the FCC had in fact misconstrued the Order. He found that it had, by inquiring whether TEDO was a British-owned company, something which had no relevance in this case. He concluded:] I would therefore hold that the words 'and any person who became successor in title to such person' in art 4 (1)(b)(ii) have no application to a case where the applicant is the original owner. It follows that the commission rejected the appellants' claim on a ground which they had no right to take into account and that their decision was a nullity. I would allow this appeal

Notes

1   While a number of cases subsequent to *Anisminic* appeared to cast doubt on the notion that every error of law takes a body outside its jurisdiction, two decisions of the House of Lords, *R v Lord President of the Privy Council ex p Page* [1993] 1 All ER 97, and *Boddington v British Transport Police* [1999] 2 AC 143 confirmed that all errors of law will be *prima facie* reviewable. As Lord Browne-Wilkinson said, in *Page*, it was to be assumed that 'Parliament had only conferred the decision-making power

on the basis that it was to be exercised on the correct legal basis: a misdirection in law in making the decision therefore rendered the decision *ultra vires*' (at 108).

2   The case also set out a number of exceptions to this general rule. These are, first, where the error of law is not relevant to the decision challenged; secondly, where the decision was made by an inferior court. Here, it was said that if there is legislation providing that the decision of such a court is final, then it will be allowed to err within its jurisdiction[8] though it is unclear whether this distinction survives and what the justification would be – why differentiate courts and tribunals? The third exception is specialised areas, where jurisdiction has been handed to another body, such as ecclesiastical courts, or University Visitors, as in *Page* itself.

3   A further question arises: can the body under review come to a different decision on what the law requires from what the court would have thought without having been found to have 'erred' and so to have acted unlawfully? In many cases, the answer to what the law requires will be one on which reasonable people could disagree. Will the court invariably substitute its opinion of what the law is or what it demands for the opinion of the tribunal? The answer is that the courts appear to draw a distinction between two things: (a) what is the correct interpretation of the law and (b) what is the 'right answer' when applying that legal test to the facts of the situation? It appears that courts will invariably regard a failure to reach what they regard as the correct conclusion in relation to (a) as tainting a decision with illegality. However, in relation to (b), where the legal test to be applied is inherently somewhat open-ended, the courts may not always quash the body's decision if they would have reached a different conclusion. Instead, it may find that as long as the conclusion reached is one that is within the range of conclusions open to a reasonable decision-maker applying the law in question, it can stand: *Edwards v Bairstow* [1956] AC 14.

4   A classic example is *R v Monopolies and Mergers Commission ex p South Yorkshire Transport Ltd* [1993] 1 All ER 289. Here, the Home Secretary could refer a proposed merger to the Commission if the merger would mean that the supply of over 25 per cent of the service in question 'in a substantial part of the United Kingdom' would be in the hands of only one person. The question at issue was whether the test of 'substantial part of the UK' was satisfied. The House of Lords said that it was the court's role to decide what 'substantial' meant in the context of that statute. But then having defined it, if the meaning was so imprecise that different decision-makers, applying it to the facts in front of them, might reasonably come to different conclusions, only if the conclusion reached was not within that range of reasonable responses would the court intervene. On the facts, the Home Secretary had not come to a conclusion that was aberrant. The correctness of this approach was recently reaffirmed by the House of Lords in *R v Ministry of Defence ex p Walker* [2000] 1 WLR 806.

Abuse of discretion: improper purposes

In this area, as in that of irrelevant considerations, the tests applied by the courts place under scrutiny the reasoning process used by the public body under challenge. What then is the rationale for holding that the taking into account of irrelevant considerations, or acting for a purpose not authorised by the governing statute,

---

8   *Re Racal Communications Ltd* [1981] AC 374.

renders a decision unlawful? The case of *R v Somerset County Council ex p Fewings* [1995] 1 All ER 513, QB; [1995] 3 All ER 20, CA is particularly instructive. It concerned the decision of Somerset County Council to ban stag hunting on its land and the challenge thereto. The Councillors, in making their decision, appeared to have been motivated primarily by the view that stag hunting was morally repellant; in acting for such a reason, they seemed to have assumed that they could simply act on their moral principles as if they were private citizens. The courts reminded them that as public bodies they were required to justify their acts by reference to some positive law which gave them power to do what they did. That power, the judge pointed out, would have been granted for some purpose. Parliament does not simply hand out powers which allow authorities to act because they feel like it or to serve what ever private purposes they happen to have in mind. It is a fundamental axiom of public law that power is always granted for a purpose; this is because power is granted to public authorities to serve the public interest, not to please themselves with. That basic point – the duty to serve the public interest – will rule out the use of powers for certain purposes which do not serve the particular public interests that the power in question was granted to serve. One of the basic challenges to a discretionary decision therefore is that the power was used for the wrong purpose.

To ascertain whether a public body has acted for an improper purpose, there generally must be some way of establishing authoritatively what would have been a proper purpose, though this may not always be necessary in cases of blatant misuses of power: the courts may be able to say, in effect, whatever the purpose of the statute may have been, it cannot have been to allow you to do what you did. However, in most cases, the courts need to ascertain the purpose of the statute which gave the power, if only in a broad way. These can be divided into cases where the statute states the purpose of the power granted and those where it does not. The former cases are fairly straightforward: thus, for example, in *Sydney Municipal Council v Campbell* [1925] AC 338 a statute allowed the Council to purchase land for the specific purposes of 'carrying out improvements in or remodelling any protection of the city'. It was clear that the Council had purchased the particular piece of land in question not for these purposes but simply in order to make money by benefiting from an increase in land values.

However, in most cases, there will be no clear statement of statutory purpose; but the principle that where an authority is endowed with power for one purpose, it must not use it for another applies even where the statute sets out no apparent purpose. In such cases it will be for the courts to construe such a purpose from considering the statute as a whole. They may, since *Pepper v Hart* [1993] AC 593, have regard, in certain circumstances, to what was said by the sponsor of the Bill (usually the government minister responsible) in debate in Parliament. However, as a recent decision of the House of Lords emphasises, resort to Hansard must be strictly justified by reference to the criteria laid down in that decision.

R v Secretary of State for the Environment, Transport and the Regions ex p Spath Holme Limited [2001] 2 AC 349 (extracts)

Lord Bingham: ... In *Pepper v Hart* the House (Lord Mackay of Clashfern LC dissenting) relaxed the general rule which had been understood to preclude reference in the courts of this country to statements made in Parliament for the purpose of construing a statutory provision. In his leading speech, with which all in the majority concurred, Lord Browne-Wilkinson made plain that such reference was permissible only where (a) legislation was ambiguous or obscure, or led to an absurdity; (b) the material relied on consisted of one or more statements by a minister or other promoter of the Bill together, if necessary, with such other parliamentary material as might be necessary to understand such statements and their effect; and (c) the effect of such statements was clear (see pp 640B, 631D, 634D). In my opinion, each of these conditions is critical to the majority decision:

(1) Unless the first of the conditions is strictly insisted upon, the real risk exists, feared by Lord Mackay, that the legal advisers to parties engaged in disputes on statutory construction will be required to comb through Hansard in practically every case (see pp 614G, 616A). This would clearly defeat the intention of Lord Bridge of Harwich that such cases should be rare (p 617A), and the submission of counsel that such cases should be exceptional (p 597E).

(2) It is one thing to rely on a statement by a responsible minister or promoter as to the meaning or effect of a provision in a bill thereafter accepted without amendment. It is quite another to rely on a statement made by anyone else, or even by a minister or promoter in the course of what may be lengthy and contentious parliamentary exchanges, particularly if the measure undergoes substantial amendment in the course of its passage through Parliament.

(3) Unless parliamentary statements are indeed clear and unequivocal (or, as Lord Reid put it in R v Warner [1969] 2 AC 256 at 279E, such as 'would almost certainly settle the matter immediately one way or the other'), the court is likely to be drawn into comparing one statement with another, appraising the meaning and effect of what was said and considering what was left unsaid and why. In the course of such an exercise the court would come uncomfortably close to questioning the proceedings in Parliament contrary to article 9 of the Bill of Rights 1689 and might even violate that important constitutional prohibition.

Lord Nicholls: ... Statutory interpretation is an exercise which requires the court to identify the meaning borne by the words in question in the particular context. The task of the court is often said to be to ascertain the intention of Parliament expressed in the language under consideration. This is correct and may be helpful, so long as it is remembered that the 'intention of Parliament' is an objective concept, not subjective. The phrase is a shorthand reference to the intention which the court reasonably imputes to Parliament in respect of the language used. It is not the subjective intention of the minister or other persons who promoted the legislation. Nor is it the subjective intention of the draftsman, or of individual members or even of a majority of individual members of either House. These individuals will often have widely varying intentions. Their understanding of the legislation and the words used may be impressively complete or woefully inadequate. Thus, when courts say that such-and-such a meaning 'cannot be what Parliament intended', they are saying only that the words under consideration cannot reasonably be taken as used by Parliament with that meaning. ...

In identifying the meaning of the words used, the courts employ accepted principles of interpretation as useful guides. For instance, an appropriate starting point is that language is to be taken to bear its ordinary meaning in the general context of the statute. Another, recently enacted, principle is that so far as possible legislation must be read in a way which is compatible with human rights and fundamental freedoms: see section 3 of the Human Rights Act 1998. The principles of interpretation include also certain presumptions. To take a familiar instance, the courts presume that a mental ingredient is an essential element in every statutory offence unless Parliament has indicated a contrary intention expressly or by necessary implication.

Additionally, the courts employ other recognised aids. They may be internal aids. Other provisions in the same statute may shed light on the meaning of the words under consideration. Or the aids may be external to the statute, such as its background setting and its legislative history. This extraneous material includes reports of Royal Commissions and advisory committees, reports of the Law Commission (with or without a draft Bill attached), and a statute's legislative antecedents.

... Nowadays the courts look at external aids for more than merely identifying the mischief the statute is intended to cure. In adopting a purposive approach to the interpretation of statutory language, courts seek to identify and give effect to the purpose of the legislation. To the extent that extraneous material assists in identifying the purpose of the legislation, it is a useful tool.

This is subject to an important caveat. External aids differ significantly from internal aids. Unlike internal aids, external aids are not found within the statute in which Parliament has expressed its intention in the words in question. This difference is of constitutional importance. Citizens, with the assistance of their advisers, are intended to be able to understand parliamentary enactments, so that they can regulate their conduct accordingly. They should be able to rely upon what they read in an Act of Parliament. This gives rise to a tension between the need for legal certainty, which is one of the fundamental elements of the rule of law, and the need to give effect to the intention of Parliament, from whatever source that (objectively assessed) intention can be gleaned.

... Experience has shown that the occasions on which reference to parliamentary proceedings is of assistance are rare. To be of assistance as an external aid, the parliamentary statement relied upon must be clear and unequivocal. Otherwise it is of no real use. Parliamentary statements seldom satisfy this test on the points of interpretation which come before the courts. Increasing awareness of the lack of help provided by parliamentary material will, it is to be hoped, result in counsel being more realistic and more sparing in their references to such material.

... If, however, the statements are clear, and were made by a minister or other promoter of the Bill, they qualify as an external aid. In such a case the statements are a factor the court will take into account in construing legislation which is ambiguous or obscure or productive of absurdity. They are then as much part of the background to the legislation as, say, Government white papers. They are part of the legislative background, *but they are no more than this*. This cannot be emphasised too strongly. Government statements, however they are made and however explicit they may be, cannot control the meaning of an Act of Parliament. As with other extraneous material, it is for the court, when determining what was the intention of Parliament in using the words in question, to decide how much importance, or weight, if any, should be attached to a Government statement.

Lord Hope: ... It is important to appreciate the purpose for which your Lordships have been invited to undertake the exercise [of consulting Hansard]. It is not to construe words used in the legislation which are said to be ambiguous or obscure or which, having regard to their ordinary meaning, would lead to absurdity: see *Pepper v Hart* [1993] AC 593, 640C *per* Lord Browne-Wilkinson. Its purpose is to identify the reasons of policy for which the discretionary power to make orders restricting or preventing increases in rents was sought to be obtained from Parliament by the executive. It is not the language used by the draftsman that is in issue here, but what was in the mind of the minister.

In my opinion there are sound reasons of principle for rejecting the argument that statements made by ministers in Parliament may be used to identify the policy and objects of an enactment for the purpose of identifying the scope of a discretionary power which Parliament has conferred on the executive. As Lord Reid made clear in *Padfield* ... the policy and objects of the Act must be determined by construing the Act. The underlying rule is that it is the intention of Parliament that defines the policy and objects of the Act, not the purpose or intention of the executive. The law-making function belongs to Parliament, not to the executive.

The limited exception to the general rule that resort to Hansard is inadmissible which was recognised in *Pepper v Hart* [1993] AC 593 is available to prevent the executive seeking to place a meaning on words used in legislation which is different from that which ministers attributed to those words when promoting the legislation in Parliament.

Note

It is clear, following this decision, that resort to Hansard by the courts will be relatively rare, and, as their Lordships stressed, only for the purpose of construing ambiguous provisions, *not* for determining the overall policy behind such provisions. However, even without such assistance, as the following case illustrates, the courts are prepared to infer a purpose from the general scheme of the legislation and then hold a decision *ultra vires* for failing to conform with that purpose.

Padfield v Minister of Agriculture, Fisheries and Food [1968] AC 977, 1029–32, 1034

Section 19 of the Agricultural Marketing Act 1958 provided that if persons complained to the Secretary of State about relevant matters, he could refer the complaints to a Committee of Investigation. The plaintiffs, whose complaint had not been so referred, sought judicial review of the decision not to refer their complaint.

Lord Reid: The question at issue in this appeal is the nature and extent of the minister's duty under s 19(3)(b) of the Act of 1958 in deciding whether to refer to the committee of investigation a complaint as to the operation of any scheme made by persons adversely affected by the scheme. The respondent contends that his only duty is to consider a complaint fairly and that he is given an unfettered discretion with regard to every complaint either to refer it or not to refer it to the committee as he may think fit. The appellants contend that it is his duty to refer every genuine and substantial complaint, or alternatively that his discretion is not unfettered and that in this case he failed to exercise his discretion according to law because his refusal was caused or influenced by his having misdirected himself in law or by his having taken into account extraneous or irrelevant considerations.

In my view, the appellants' first contention goes too far. There are a number of reasons which would justify the minister in refusing to refer a complaint. For example, he might consider it more suitable for arbitration, or he might consider that in an earlier case the committee of investigation had already rejected a substantially similar complaint, or he might think the complaint to be frivolous or vexatious. So he must have at least some measure of discretion. But is it unfettered?

It is implicit in the argument for the minister that there are only two possible interpretations of this provision – either he must refer every complaint or he has an unfettered discretion to refuse to refer in any case. I do not think that is right. Parliament must have conferred the discretion with the intention that it should be used to promote the policy and objects of the Act; the policy and objects of the Act must be determined by construing the Act as a whole and construction is always a matter of law for the court. In a matter of this kind it is not possible to draw a hard and fast line, but if the minister, by reason of his having misconstrued the Act or for any other reason, so uses his discretion as to thwart or run counter to the policy and objects of the Act, then our law would be very defective if persons aggrieved were not entitled to the protection of the court.

Notes

1   It was found that the minister had acted unlawfully, because his actions pursued a purpose not authorised by the statute. Wade notes that in this case the House of Lords emphasised 'in broad terms that unfettered discretion is something which the law does not admit. If it were otherwise, everyone would be helpless in the face of the unqualified powers which ministers find it so easy to obtain from Parliament'.[9]

2   Despite such approving views, the courts have been accused of using their practice of inferring a purpose as a means whereby to interfere with policy. Often the purpose inferred is uncontroversial or the courts only go so far as stating, in effect, that whatever the purpose of the body's power may be, it is not to enable it to do the act complained of (as in the well known case of *R v Barnsley MBC ex p Hook*

---

9   HWR Wade, *Constitutional Fundamentals* (1989), pp 53–54.

[1976] 1 WLR 1052 (discussed below). In other cases, however, the judiciary has been accused of inferring an unwarrantably narrow purpose from an Act which appears to grant broad discretion, and then holding a decision unlawful because it is not in conformity with this purpose. Arguably, this technique was adopted by the House of Lords in *Bromley London Borough Council v Greater London Council* [1983] 1 AC 768, discussed by Jeremy Waldron below.

Jeremy Waldron, *The Law* (1990), pp 117–19

'Within six months of winning the election, Labour will cut fares on London Transport buses and tubes by an average of 25%.' The Labour Party made that commitment in its manifesto for the 1981 elections to the Greater London Council (GLC). It won the election and within six months bus and tube fares were reduced as promised. The move necessitated an increase in the rates (*ie* property taxes) levied on the London boroughs. Bromley (a Conservative-controlled council), brought an action in the High Court to challenge the decision. The GLC did not take the challenge very seriously, and were not surprised when the High Court judge rejected the Bromley application.

A few weeks later, the Bromley council appealed, and three judges sitting in the Court of Appeal reversed the original decision and upheld the Bromley challenge. The judges condemned the fare reduction as 'a crude abuse of the poor' and they quashed the supplementary rate that the GLC had levied on the London boroughs to pay for it. The GLC appealed to the House of Lords, the highest court in the land, but to no avail.

The Law Lords held unanimously that the GLC was bound by a statute requiring it to 'promote the provision on integrated, efficient *and economic* transport facilities and services in Greater London', and they interpreted this to mean that the bus and tube system must be run according to 'ordinary business principles' of cost effectiveness. The Labour council, they said, was not entitled to lower the fares and increase the deficit of London Transport in order to promote their general social policy, and they were certainly not entitled simply to shift a large percentage of the cost of travel in London from commuters to ratepayers.

The fact that the policy had been announced in advance and had secured majority support, carried little weight with the courts. According to the Law Lords and the judges in the Court of Appeal, members of the GLC should not have treated themselves as 'irrevocably bound to carry out pre-announced policies contained in election manifestos', particularly when it became apparent that central Government would penalise the move to bodies like the GLC. So, though the voters had supported in their thousands, the fare reduction was reversed, the supplementary rate quashed, and the policy frustrated, by the order of five judges.

It is fair to say the GLC and their lawyers were taken aback by the Court of Appeal and House of Lords decisions, 'shell-shocked' was the term one lawyer used. More than anything else, the Labour councillors were flabbergasted by the Law Lords' intrusion into a decision so clearly legitimated by electoral democracy:

> For generations in local government we understood that if you put something in your manifesto and got elected, you got on and did it. We cherished the belief that people believe in democratic government. If you got a popular vote you could do it.

As they saw it, the electorate had been given a choice: to subsidise London Transport in the interest of social and environmental policy or to persist with the existing fare structure. The electorate had made their choice, and councillors couldn't understand why the judges – who knew almost nothing about the detailed policy issues involved – would want to overturn their decision. Council solicitors were at a loss to explain the vehement unanimity of the Lords' decision: 'There is always room for argument where there is discretionary power.' The only thing they could see was that the courts were indulging in a gut-level reaction to Labour policy, to the beginning of some apprehended revolutionary socialist challenge.

Note

Ambiguity as to whether a decision is tainted with illegality through the influence of 'improper purposes' can arise in the case of decisions made for a plurality of purposes – some proper, some improper – as in the following case.

R v Inner London Education Authority ex p Westminster Council [1986] I All ER 19

The Inner London Education Authority (ILEA) was opposed to government policy on rate-capping which it believed would adversely affect education provision in London. It was empowered by statute (s 142(2) of the Local Government Act 1972) to incur expenditure in the course of publicising matters within its area of information on matters relating to local government. The case arose from the decision of ILEA to retain an advertising agency in order to mount a campaign to generate 'awareness of the authority's views of the needs of the education service and to alter the basis of public debate about the effect of ... government actions'. ILEA admitted that the campaign had the dual purpose of educating the public and persuading them to share ILEA's opposition to rate-capping.

Glidewell J: If a local authority resolves to expend its ratepayers' money in order to achieve two purposes, one of which it is authorised to achieve by statute but for the other of which it has no authority, is that decision invalid?

I was referred to the following authorities: (i) *Westminster Corporation v London and North Western Railway Co* [1905] AC 426.

[Glidewell J considered the decision and concluded:]

This suggests that a test for answering the question is, if the authorised purpose is the primary purpose, the resolution is within the power. ...

(ii) More recently in *Hanks v Minister of Housing and Local Government* [1963] I QB 999, Megaw J ... quoted part of the dissenting judgment of Denning LJ in *Earl Fitzwilliam's Wentworth Estates Co Ltd v Minister of Town and Country Planning* [1951] 2 KB 284, 307:

> If Parliament grants a power to a government department to be used for an authorised purpose, then the power is only validly exercised when it is used by the department genuinely for that purpose as its dominant purpose. If that purpose is not the main purpose, but is subordinated to some other purpose which is not authorised by law, then the department exceeds its powers and the action is invalid.

It had been submitted to Megaw J that, although Denning LJ had dissented from the decision of the majority, this passage in his judgment did not differ from the view of the majority. Megaw J went on [[1963] QB 999, 1020]:

> ... In the end, it seems to me, the simplest and clearest way to state the matter is by reference to 'considerations'. A 'consideration', I apprehend, is something which one takes into account as a factor in arriving at a decision. I am prepared to assume, for the purposes of this case, that, if it be shown that an authority exercising a power has taken into account as a relevant factor something which it could not properly take into account in deciding whether or not to exercise the power, then the exercise of the power, normally at least, is bad ... I say 'normally' because I can conceive that there may be cases where the factor wrongly taken into account, or omitted, is insignificant, or where the wrong taking into account, or omission, actually operated in favour of the person who later claims to be aggrieved by the decision.

Professor Evans, in *de Smith's Judicial Review of Administrative Action*, 4th ed (1980), p 329 ... distils from the decisions of the courts five different tests upon which reliance has been placed at one time or another, including, at pp 330–2:

(1) What was the *true purpose* for which the power was exercised? If the actor has in truth used his power for the purpose for which it was conferred, it is immaterial that he was thus enabled to achieve a subsidiary object ...

(5) Was any of the purposes pursued an unauthorised purpose? If so, and if the unauthorised purpose has materially influenced the actor's conduct, the power has been invalidly exercised because irrelevant considerations have been taken into account.

... I gratefully adopt the guidance of Megaw J, and the two tests I have referred to from de *Smith's Judicial Review of Administrative Action.*

It thus becomes a question of fact for me to decide, upon the material before me, whether in reaching its decision of 23 July 1984, the staff and general sub-committee of ILEA was pursuing an unauthorised purpose, namely, that of persuasion, which has materially influenced the making of its decision. I have already said that I find that one of the sub-committee's purposes was the giving of information. But I also find that it had the purpose of seeking to persuade members of the public to a view identical with that of the authority itself, and indeed I believe that this was a, if not the, major purpose of the decision. In reaching this decision of fact, I have taken into account in particular the material to which I have referred above in AMV's 'presentation' of 18 July 1984, the passages I have quoted from the report of the Education Officer to the sub-committee, particularly the reference to 'changing the basis of public debate', and the various documents which have been published by AMV since 23 July with the approval of ILEA. I accept that some of these documents do inform, but in my view some of them contain little or no information and are designed only to persuade. This is true in particular, in my view, of the poster slogan 'Education Cuts Never Heal' (skilful though I think it is) and it is also true of the advertisement 'What do you get if you subtract £75 million from London's education budget?'

Adopting the test referred to above, I thus hold that ILEA's subcommittee did, when making its decision of 23 July 1984, take into account an irrelevant consideration, and thus that decision was not validly reached.

Notes

1 Glidewell J thus found that a decision would be unlawful if 'materially influenced' by an unauthorised purpose. Purchas LJ put forward an arguably less strict test in *Simplex GE (Holdings) Ltd v Secretary of State for the Environment* [1988] COD 160[10] where he held that, on the issue of whether an unauthorised purpose had influenced a decision, the applicant did not need to show that the decision-maker 'would or even probably would have come to a different conclusion [if he had not been influenced by the improper purpose]. He has only to exclude the ... contention ... that the [decision-maker] necessarily would still have made the same decision'. This test implies that once an unauthorised consideration can be shown to have been present, the onus of proof shifts to the decision-maker to show that he or she would clearly have made the same decision without taking account of that consideration. Glidewell J's test seemed to envisage that it was for the applicant to show 'material influence' by the consideration.

2 Recently, in *Porter v Magill* [2002] AC 357, the House of Lords had to consider a complex case on improper purposes arising from the Shirley Porter affair. It appeared that Porter, the Conservative leader of Westminster Council at the relevant time, had formulated a policy of designating certain blocks of Council houses to be sold to approved applicants, rather than being re-let, with the aim of increasing the number of likely Conservative voters in key marginal wards; the aim, in short, being electoral advantage. Capital grants of £15,000 were made

---

10 The facts of the case appear below.

available to tenants to encourage them to move. It was argued that this was an improper purpose for the Council to follow, thus rendering its actions unlawful. Porter argued that the realities of party politics were that party considerations were bound to intrude upon decisions made by elected councillors, and that provided they also had a proper purpose for any decisions they made, this in itself did not render the decision unlawful. This argument was rejected by the House of Lords.

Porter v Magill [2002] 2 AC 357, 466–67

Lord Bingham: Elected politicians of course wish to act in a manner which will commend them and their party (when, as is now usual, they belong to one) to the electorate. Such an ambition is the life-blood of democracy and a potent spur to responsible decision-taking and administration. Councillors do not act improperly or unlawfully if, exercising public powers for a public purpose for which such powers were conferred, they hope that such exercise will earn the gratitude and support of the electorate and thus strengthen their electoral position. The law would indeed part company with the realities of party politics if it were to hold otherwise. But a public power is not exercised lawfully if it is exercised not for a public purpose for which the power was conferred but in order to promote the electoral advantage of a political party. The power at issue in the present case is section 32 of the Housing Act 1985, which conferred power on local authorities to dispose of land held by them subject to conditions specified in the Act. Thus a local authority could dispose of its property, subject to the provisions of the Act, to promote any public purpose for which such power was conferred, but could not lawfully do so for the purpose of promoting the electoral advantage of any party represented on the council.

The House was referred to a number of cases in which the part which political allegiance may properly play in local government has been explored ... These cases show that while councillors may lawfully support a policy adopted by their party they must not abdicate their responsibility and duty of exercising personal judgment. There is nothing in these cases to suggest that a councillor may support a policy not for valid local government reasons but with the object of obtaining an electoral advantage.

Abuse of discretion: relevant and irrelevant considerations

This ground is very similar to that of improper purpose, but it focuses upon examining the matters taken into account by an authority in coming to its decisions (which may or may not be the same enquiry as asking what its purposes were). In *R v Somerset County Council ex p Fewings* [1995] 3 All ER 20, CA,[11] the local authority banned stag-hunting on an area of its land, which, under s 10(2)(b) of the Local Government Act 1972, they were to manage 'for the benefit of their area'. On appeal to the Court of Appeal, the decision was found to be unlawful on the grounds that, *inter alia*:

(a) the councillors, in making their decision, at no point had their attention drawn to the governing statutory provision; and

(b) that they had made their decision largely on the basis that they considered stag-hunting cruel and morally repulsive, a consideration which, though relevant, was not the only factor they should have considered under the test.

In the same case Simon Browne LJ in the Court of Appeal discussed the three kinds of considerations which logically may present themselves to a decision-maker exercising a discretion. These are: (a) factors which a decision-maker *must* take into account ('mandatory factors'); (b) factors which he or she must *not* take into account

---

11   For comment, see G Nardell [1995] PL 27.

('prohibited factors'); (c) factors which the decision-maker *may* at his or her discretion take into account. Thus, decisions which fail to take into account factors in the first category, or take into account those in the second category, will clearly be unlawful. However, the third category is there to allow for the exercise of discretion by the decision-maker: there are some factors that it is permissible, but not necessary, to have regard to, though it should be noted that courts do not always recognise this intermediate category. The leading decision in this area follows: it concerns the setting by the Home Secretary of the 'tariff' part of the sentence to be served by the notorious teenage killers of a six year old child, James Bulger. As explained in the judgment of Lord Browne-Wilkinson:

> Over the years, the Secretary of State has adopted a tariff policy in exercising his discretion whether to release adults who have been sentenced to life imprisonment ... In essence, the tariff approach is this. The life sentence is broken down into component parts, viz, retribution, deterrence and protection of the public. The trial judge and the Lord Chief Justice advise the Secretary of State as to the sentence which would be appropriate for the crime having regard to the elements of retribution and deterrence. In the light of that advice (and not being in any way bound by it) the Secretary of State makes his own decision as to the *minimum* period which the prisoner will have to serve in order to satisfy the requirements of retribution and deterrence. This is the tariff period. The policy provides that, until three years before the tariff period expires, the Secretary of State will not refer the case to the Parole Board for its advice as to whether the prisoner should or should not be released. Moreover, until the tariff period has expired the Secretary of State will not exercise his discretion to release on licence.

The challenge to the Home Secretary's decision was made on a large number of grounds; the grounds considered here were that he took into account an irrelevant consideration – public opinion – and, through his adoption of a 'tariff' policy for child offenders, ruled out consideration of relevant factors.

R v Secretary of State for the Home Department ex p Venables and others [1998] AC 407 (extracts)

Lord Goff: ... Having received this advice from the trial judge and the Lord Chief Justice, the Home Secretary, acting pursuant to his discretion under section 35 of the Criminal Justice Act 1991, and a Policy Statement dated 27 July 1993, proceeded to consider the question of the penal element in the sentence for the two boys, and decided that it should be increased to 15 years. ... In his Decision Letters, dated 22 July 1994, it was stated that the Home Secretary had regard (*inter alia*) to:

> the public concern about this case, which was evidenced by the petitions and other correspondence the substance of which were disclosed to your solicitors by our letter of 16 June 1994, and to the need to maintain confidence in the system of criminal justice.

The letter dated 16 June 1994 referred in particular to a petition, signed by some 278,300 members of the public (with some 4,400 letters in support) urging that the two boys should remain in detention for life; a petition, signed by nearly 6,000 members of the public, asking for a minimum period of detention of 25 years; and over 20,000 coupons, cut out of a popular newspaper, together with over 1,000 letters, demanding a life tariff. There were only 33 letters agreeing with the judiciary, or asking for a lower tariff.

... That there was public concern about this terrible case, there can be no doubt. But events such as this tend to provoke a desire for revenge, and calls for the infliction of the severest punishment upon the perpetrators of the crime. This elemental feeling is perhaps natural, though in today's society there is a tendency for it to be whipped up and exploited by the media. When this happens, it can degenerate into something less acceptable. Little credit can be given to favourable responses to a campaign that the two respondents should 'rot in jail' for the rest of their lives, especially when it is borne in mind that those who responded may well have been unaware that, even after the penal element in their sentences had been served, their release would not be automatic but would be the subject of very careful consideration by the responsible authorities. It was the submission of Mr Fitzgerald for Venables that material such as that which the Secretary of State had regard to in the present case was no more than public clamour, and as such worthless. It should therefore have been disregarded by the Secretary of State. In the Court of Appeal this submission was accepted by Lord Woolf MR and Hobhouse LJ, but rejected by Morritt LJ.

I approach the matter as follows. Under section 35 of the [Criminal Justice] Act 1991, the Secretary of State has a discretion regarding the release of mandatory life prisoners, including young offenders sentenced to detention during Her Majesty's pleasure. In the case of such prisoners, there is no statutory provision requiring the fixing of a penal element which must be served. That arises from the policy that there should be such an element, first established by Mr Leon Brittan in 1983, and subsequently continued by later Secretaries of State. It may therefore be said that the same considerations apply to the implementation of this policy as apply to the decision to release when taken in cases such as these ...

... when it comes to fixing the penal element, different considerations apply. In doing so, the Secretary of State is not looking at the whole picture at the material time when deciding whether in all the circumstances it is appropriate for a life prisoner to be released, when considerations of a broader character may properly be relevant. On the contrary, he is deciding what in future will be the period of time which a prisoner must serve, compassionate considerations apart, before he may be released, if it is then thought fit. It is scarcely surprising that, in *Ex parte Doody*, at p 557, Lord Mustill said of this exercise that:

> Even if the Home Secretary still retains his controlling discretion as regards the assessment of culpability the fixing of the penal element begins to look much more like an orthodox sentencing exercise, and less like a general power exercised completely at large.

Furthermore this approach derives strong support from the statutory context in which the discretion is now to be found. For in the same Part [II] of the same statute, the fixing of the penal element for discretionary life prisoners is, by section 34 of the Act of 1991, performed by the judges. They will undoubtedly act in a judicial manner when doing so; and indeed that they should do so must have been the intention of Parliament when entrusting this function to them. In so doing, they will disregard any evidence of the kind now under consideration as irrelevant and prejudicial. It follows that, if the Secretary of State was right to have regard to it, there will exist an extraordinary and anomalous conflict between neighbouring sections, sections 34 and 35, in the same statute.

It is, in my opinion, impossible to explain this conflict on the basis that a relevant distinction is to be drawn in this context between discretionary and mandatory life sentences. In my opinion the only way in which the conflict can be resolved is by recognising that, if the Secretary of State implements a policy of fixing a penal element of the sentence of a mandatory life prisoner pursuant to his discretionary power under section 35, he is to this extent exercising a function which is closely analogous to a sentencing function with the effect that, when so doing, he is under a duty to act within the same constraints as a judge will act when exercising the same function. In particular, should he take into account public clamour directed towards the decision in the particular case which he has under consideration, he will be having regard to an irrelevant consideration which will render the exercise of his discretion unlawful.

Lord Browne-Wilkinson: ... I reach the conclusion that in setting the tariff of 15 years for these two applicants the Secretary of State was applying an unlawful policy and his decisions should be quashed. The unlawfulness lies in adopting a policy which totally excludes from consideration during the tariff period factors (ie their progress and development) necessary to determine whether release from detention would be in the interests of the welfare of the applicants. Such welfare is *one* of the factors which the Secretary of State has to take into account in deciding from time to time how long the applicant should be detained. This does not mean that in relation to children detained during Her Majesty's pleasure any policy based on a tariff would be unlawful. But any such tariff policy would have to be sufficiently flexible to enable the Secretary of State to take into account the progress of the child and his development. In relation to children, the factors of retribution, deterrence and risk are not the only relevant factors: the welfare of the child is also another relevant factor.

... I would add a word on the issue whether it was procedurally improper for the Secretary of State to take into account the petitions and other material sent to him. The Court of Appeal and, I understand, the majority of your Lordships take the view that this was improper. I find it unnecessary to express any final view but I would sound a word of caution. Parliament has entrusted decisions relating to the future of these applicants to the executive, not to the judiciary. Whilst it is right for the courts to ensure that in making his decision the Secretary of State acts in accordance with natural justice, in my view the court should be careful not to impose judicial procedures and attitudes on what Parliament has decided should be an executive function. I understand it to be common ground that the Secretary of State, in setting the tariff, is entitled to have regard to 'broader considerations of a public character' including public respect for the administration of justice and public attitudes to criminal sentencing. How is the Secretary of State to discover what those attitudes are except from the media and from petitions? To seek to differentiate between the Secretary of State discovering public feeling generally (which is proper) and taking into account distasteful public reactions in a particular case (which is said to be unlawful) seems to me too narrow a distinction to be workable in practice. Public attitudes are ill-defined and are usually only expressed in relation to particular cases ...

Lord Steyn: ... may the Home Secretary take into account public clamour about the tariff to be fixed in a particular case?

... For my part the matter can be decided on a twofold basis. First, the material in fact taken into account by the Home Secretary was worthless and incapable of informing him in a meaningful way of the true state of informed public opinion in respect of the tariff to be set in the cases of Venables and Thompson ... It was therefore irrelevant. But the Home Secretary was influenced by it. He gave weight to it. On this ground his decision is unlawful. But the objection to the course adopted by the Home Secretary is more fundamental ...

In fixing a tariff the Home Secretary is carrying out, contrary to the constitutional principle of separation of powers, a classic judicial function ... Parliament entrusted the underlying statutory power, which entailed a discretion to adopt a policy of fixing a tariff, to the Home Secretary. But the power to fix a tariff is nevertheless equivalent to a judge's sentencing power. Parliament must be assumed to have acted, have entrusted the power to the Home Secretary on the supposition that, like a sentencing judge, the Home Secretary would not act contrary to fundamental principles governing the administrator of justice. Plainly a sentencing judge must ignore a newspaper campaign designed to encourage him to increase a particular sentence. It would be an abdication of the rule of law for a judge to take into account such matters. The same reasoning must apply to the Home Secretary when he is exercising a sentencing function ... I would therefore hold that public protests about the level of a tariff to be fixed in a particular case are legally irrelevant and may not be taken into account by the Home Secretary in fixing the tariff. I conclude that the Home Secretary misdirected himself in giving weight to irrelevant considerations ...

Notes

1   Lord Lloyd broadly agreed with Lord Browne-Wilkinson that the petitions were not irrelevant matters for the Home Secretary; Lord Hope agreed with Lord Woolf that setting a mandatory sentence for a child precluded the Home Secretary from taking account of relevant matters, namely 'the child's development and progress while in custody'. He also agreed with Lord Goff that 'the public clamour' was an irrelevant matter.

2   The different grounds of decision by their Lordships reveal how far judicial opinion may differ upon what are relevant and irrelevant considerations in a particular

case. Three of their Lordships considered the public clamour irrelevant; Lord Browne-Wilkinson expressed doubts as to this conclusion; while Lord Lloyd disagreed with it. Lord Browne-Wilkinson and Lord Hope thought that the fixing of a tariff period for a child, in the same way that a tariff period would be fixed for an adult murderer, was itself unlawful since it precluded the Home Secretary from taking into account, during the tariff period, relevant considerations – namely the welfare and development of the child offenders. But this was not the basis of the decision of the remainder of their Lordships.

3 In the recent House of Lords decision in *R (on the application of Mehanne) v City of Westminster Housing Benefit Review Board* [2001] 2 All ER 690, the Board was required by statute not to grant the full amount of housing benefit claimed if it considered the rent unreasonably high. The statute said that the Board should have regard 'in particular to the cost of suitable accommodation elsewhere'. It was held that the Board should have (as it had not) had regard to the particular circumstances of the applicant, including the pregnancy of his wife and his reduced level of benefits as an asylum seeker. Lord Bingham gave some general guidance on when a matter should be viewed as a relevant one under statute, saying, that absent 'very clear [statutory] language, I would be very reluctant to conclude that the . . . board were precluded from considering matters which could affect the mind of a reasonable and fair minded person'. It was also found that such an interpretation served the underlying policy objective of the legislation, namely to ensure that the housing needs of society's most disadvantaged sector were met.

4 A recurring question over the last few years has been whether local authorities in making various decisions which involve resources, for example, provision for old people and for children with special educational needs, may take into account their own limited financial resources, and if so, at what stage of the decision-making process. Local authorities have found resources increasingly tight and have often explained that in making decisions to limit or restrict services, they have been influenced by their need to preserve scarce resources. This has led to a number of challenges from those adversely affected on the grounds that the resources available were, in the context of the particular decision, not a matter to which the authority should have had regard.

The courts' response to such arguments has varied. In *R v Gloucester County Council ex p Barry* [1997] 2 WLR 459, the Council, if it considered a disabled person had certain 'needs', was under a statutory duty to make arrangements to cater for him or her. B had been previously assessed as having certain needs, which were fully catered for in 1992 and 1993. In 1994, the Council told him that, due to central government cuts in their funding, it was no longer able to provide for his full needs. The House of Lords held, by a 3:2 majority, that in assessing 'need', the Council had to consider what was an acceptable standard of living. In assessing that, the Authority could have regard to its own resources, and so had not acted unlawfully.

In *R v Sefton Metropolitan Borough Council ex p Help the Aged* [1997] 4 All ER 532, the court drew a distinction between (a) assessing a person's needs, and (b) deciding what to provide in order to meet those needs. In determining the first question, the court said that an authority could, following *Barry*, take into account resources, but once it had decided that a particular person was in need, it came under a binding duty to provide for those needs and lack of resources was not relevant. *Barry* was distinguished again in *R v East Sussex County Council ex p Tandy* [1998] 2 All ER 769, HL. Here, a local authority had a duty to provide 'suitable education' for the children in its area. T had been unable to attend school and had received tuition of five hours a week, funded by the Council. In 1996, the authority reduced this to three hours because of financial constraints. On its face, the situation seemed very similar to *Barry* – an initial provision being reduced to save money. However, the House of Lords found that the concept of 'suitable education', unlike a person's 'needs' (as in *Barry*), was objective, and did not vary according to resources. In taking account of its own resources in deciding what was 'suitable', the authority had had regard to an irrelevant consideration. Alder comments: 'In [cases other than *Barry*] the courts have interpreted the governing legislation as imposing an absolute duty, with *Barry* being confined to its statutory context.'[12]

5   It should be noted that the general attitude of the courts is that, where resources are found to be a relevant matter, it is not for the courts to substitute their judgment for that of the public authority in question as to the most efficient or desirable distribution of resources: that is a matter of policy and discretion. Some examples are given by Keith Syrett.[13]

> Neill LJ in *R v Criminal Injuries Compensation Board, ex parte P* [1995] 1 WLR 845 at 857 ... viewed the court as 'ill equipped' to deal with 'decisions involv[ing] a balance of competing claims on the public purse' ... Similar reservations have been expressed in a number of cases in which the courts have been called upon to address the clearly polycentric issue of resource allocation within the NHS, through challenges which sought to require health authorities to provide funding for particular services and treatments. These judgments exhibit a near-universal refusal to intervene on the basis that courts are not the appropriate fora for determination of such issues ...

> *R v Chief Constable of Sussex, ex p International Traders' Ferry Limited* [1999] 1 All ER 129 provides a further example, in the context of decisions by a Chief Constable as to the best allocation of policing resources. As Paul Craig and Soren Schonberg comment, '...it is not for the courts to substitute their choice as to how administrative decision ought to have been exercised for that of the administrative authority'.[14]

6   What does 'taking into account' a consideration mean? Does the authority have to satisfy the court that it has given a consideration found to be relevant at least a threshold, minimum weight.[15] In *Tesco Stores Limited v Secretary of State for the Environment* [1995] 1 WLR 759, Lord Hoffman gave a firm 'no' to this question:

> Provided that the ... authority has regard to all material considerations, it is at liberty (provided that it does not lapse into *Wednesbury* irrationality) to give them whatever weight the ... authority thinks, or indeed no weight at all. The fact that the law regards something as a material consideration therefore involves no view at all about the part, if any, which it should play in the decision-making process.[16]

Failure to retain discretion

Improper delegation

The basic principle here is that if one body is given a power to make decisions in an area, it may not delegate that power to another body. Thus, a board given power to dismiss workers at a port may not give that power to dismiss the port manager. Nor

---

12   J Alder, 'Incommensurable values and judicial review: the case of local government' [2001] PL 717, 731.
13   K Syrett, 'Of resources, rationality and rights: emerging trends in the judicial review of allocative decisions' [2001] Web JCLI.
14   P Craig and S Schonberg. 'Substantive legitimate expectations after *Coughlan*' [2000] PL 684, 694.
15   As Laws J suggested in *ex p Fewings* [1995] 1 All ER 513.
16   *Ibid*, at 780.

indeed may it lawfully ratify his or her decisions. The most it can do is to take *recommendations* from the manager and then decide *itself* whether to follow them.[17] The major exception to this provision is that ministers may delegate decisions to civil servants or other government officials, as decided by the following case.[18]

Carltona Ltd v Works Commissioners [1943] 2 All ER 560, 563

The Commissioners of Works had power under wartime regulations to requisition property, and Carltona's factory was requisitioned. A requisition notice in respect of Carltona's factory was made by a civil servant, of the rank of assistant secretary, for and on behalf of the Commissioners of Works (at the head of which was a minister).

Lord Greene MR: In the administration of Government in this county the functions which are given to ministers (and constitutionally properly given to ministers because they are constitutionally responsible) are functions so multifarious that no minister could ever personally attend to them ... It cannot be supposed that [the regulation in question] meant that, in each case, the minister in person should direct his mind to the matter. The duties imposed upon ministers and the powers given to ministers are normally exercised under the authority of the ministers by responsible officials of the department. Public business could not be carried on if that were not the case. Constitutionally, the decision of such an official is of course the decision of the minister, the minister is responsible. It is he who must answer before Parliament for anything his officials have done under his authority and if for an important matter he selected an official of such junior standing that he could not be expected competently to perform the work, the minister would have to answer for that in Parliament.

Notes

1 In some cases, the courts have indicated a readiness to scrutinise the *Carltona* principle more carefully. *R v Secretary of State for the Home Department ex p Oladehinde* [1991] 1 AC 254 concerned a challenge to the legality of the practice of the Home Secretary to delegate to immigration inspectors (officials of some seniority and considerable experience) the decision to serve notices of intention to deport. Following such a notice, deportees had a highly restricted right of appeal; the final deportation order was made by the Secretary of State. In the Court of Appeal, it was said, *per* Woolf LJ, that the *Carltona* principle was to be 'regarded as an implication which is read into a statute in the absence of [contrary] legislative intent'. Here, however, Woolf LJ noted that the whole scheme of legislation was to divide responsibilities and to assign some specific responsibilities to the Secretary of State and some to particular categories of officials. In these circumstances, it was not appropriate to allow the Secretary of State to delegate to officials powers which had in fact been conferred on him. The House of Lords agreed that the *Carltona* principle could be 'negatived or confined by clearly necessary implication' in a statute (at 278). But this, the Lords held, could only be done on *Wednesbury* grounds. In other words, the court would find the *Carltona* principle to be displaced only if the scheme of delegation was one which no reasonable minister would have put in place. The House of Lords said that the court should be slow to find further *implied* restrictions on the right to delegate where the governing statute had certain *express* prohibitions on delegation. Delegation would be appropriate provided that the decisions delegated 'were suitable to [the] grading and experience' of the official concerned and did not lead to a conflict of interest for the

---

17 *Barnard v National Dock Labour Board* [1953] 2 QB 18.
18 See generally D Lanham, 'Delegation and the alter ego principle' (1984) 100 LQR 587.

officials (at 303). So, for the House of Lords, the principle in favour of *Carltona* was difficult to displace. Thus, the mere fact that certain divisions of responsibilities are expressly laid down in a statute does not prevent further delegation from ministers to civil servants, though it might be thought that this made the efforts of the draftsman in setting out an explicit division of responsibilities in the statute somewhat futile. The Lords did emphasise, however, that the courts would be prepared to find that a particular scheme of delegation was unlawful, on the facts, though it was unclear whether it would have to be *Wednesbury* unreasonable or not.

2 It should be noted that local authorities, under s 101 of the Local Government Act 1972 may, subject to express provision in that, or any other Act, delegate functions to (a) a committee, sub-committee or officer of the authority, or (b) any other authority.

Over-rigid application of a predetermined policy

It is commonplace for public authorities to react to the granting of a broad discretion given to them by statute by adopting a fairly detailed policy, partly in order to ensure that individual decisions represent a predetermined policy which reflects that authority's priorities and partly to speed up decision-making; without such policies, each decision would have to be made on an individual, discretionary basis, and inconsistencies would be bound to arise. It is important to note that, under the principles of judicial review, there is nothing objectionable about the adoption of a policy *per se*; a problem arises only if the authority applies a given policy so rigidly that it refuses to consider whether exceptions to it should be made in atypical individual cases. The classic decision here is *British Oxygen Co Ltd v Minister of Technology* [1971] AC 610. The ministry had a discretion to make grants to those buying new plant; however, it had formed a policy of not awarding any grants in respect of items which cost less than £25 each. British Oxygen had bought a large number of cylinders over three years, at a cost of £4 million; however, the price of one individual cylinder was £20. British Oxygen did not therefore qualify for a grant and challenged the policy. Lord Reid said that, in such cases, the authority 'will almost certainly have evolved a policy so precise that it could well be called a rule. There can be no objection to that, provided the authority is always willing to listen to anyone with something new to say'. Because the Ministry had considered British Oxygen's application carefully, it had not therefore acted unlawfully.

A recent application of the doctrine by the Court of Appeal may be found in the following case, in which it was found that a health authority's policy of refusing to fund gender reassignment surgery for transsexuals was flawed. Although it acknowledged transsexualism as an illness, it failed to deal with it as such and operated what amounted to a blanket ban on the treatment.

R v North West Lancashire Health Authority ex p A and others [2000] 1 WLR 977, CA

Auld LJ: ... A, D and G suffer from an illness called 'gender identity dysphoria', commonly known as transsexualism. Each was born with male physical characteristics, but psychologically has a female sexual identity. Each has been living as a woman for some years. At the material time A and G had each been diagnosed by a specialist consultant to have a clinical need for surgery substituting female for male characteristics, a procedure known as 'gender re-assignment surgery.'

D was awaiting assessment of suitability for such surgery. They all challenge the Authority's refusal to fund their treatment, including surgery, under the National Health Service because of its policy not to do so in the absence of 'overriding clinical need' or other exceptional circumstances. They maintain that they are ill and that the Authority's policy, and refusals pursuant to it, to fund treatment for them are irrational. The Authority justifies its policy and refusals on the ground that it has a statutory obligation to care for all within its area and limited financial resources with which to do so, requiring it to give a lower priority to some medical conditions than to others and that transsexualism rightly has a low priority.

[The policy had an exception for overriding clinical need, as Auld LJ pointed out.]

... the only material illustration in the Policy of the degree of overriding clinical need that might justify an exception is serious mental illness which the treatment could be expected substantially to improve.

... It is proper for an Authority to adopt a general policy for the exercise of such an administrative discretion, to allow for exceptions from it in 'exceptional circumstances' and to leave those circumstances undefined; see In re Findlay [1985] 1 AC 318, HL, per Lord Scarman at 335H–336F. In my view, a policy to place transsexualism low in an order of priorities of illnesses for treatment and to deny it treatment save in exceptional circumstances such as overriding clinical need is not in principle irrational, provided that the policy genuinely recognises the possibility of there being an overriding clinical need and requires each request for treatment to be considered on its individual merits.

However, in establishing priorities – comparing the respective needs of patients suffering from different illnesses and determining the respective strengths of their claims to treatment – it is vital for an Authority: 1) accurately to assess the nature and seriousness of each type of illness; 2) to determine the effectiveness of various forms of treatment for it; and 3) to give proper effect to that assessment and that determination in the formulation and individual application of its policy.

Conclusions

[The] basic error, one of failure properly to evaluate such a condition as an illness suitable and appropriate for treatment, is not mitigated by the allowance in both Policies for the possibility of an exception in the case of overriding clinical need or other exceptional circumstances. As I have said, such a provision is not objectionable, but it is important that the starting point against which the exceptional circumstances have to be rated is properly evaluated and that each case is considered on its individual merits ... The Authority's relegation of what was notionally regarded as an illness to something less, in respect of which an applicant for treatment had to demonstrate an overriding clinical need for treatment, confronted each respondent with a very high and uncertain threshold.

The 1995 Policy gave no indication of what might amount to an overriding clinical need or other exceptional circumstances; nor did the 1998 Policy, save in paragraph 5.1 in which it emphasised the likely rarity and unpredictability of such circumstances, and instanced as a possibility when 'the problem' ... was the cause of serious mental illness. Expert assessment that a patient needs the treatment would not do; demonstration of the existence of some other illness was a necessary condition for consideration for treatment. The Authority gave a hint in its consideration of the case of A that epilepsy caused by her untreated transsexualism, if established, might have qualified. But, given the Authority's reluctance to accept gender reassignment as an effective treatment for transsexualism – and it would follow logically any condition caused by it – the provision for an exception in a case of 'overriding clinical need' was in practice meaningless, as Mr Blake observed. It was as objectionable as a policy which effectively excluded the exercise by the Authority of a medical judgment in the individual circumstances of each case ...

In my view, the stance of the Authority, coupled with the near uniformity of its reasons for rejecting each of the respondents' requests for funding was not a genuine application of a policy subject to individually determined exceptions of the sort considered acceptable by Lord Scarman in *Findlay*. It is similar to the over-rigid application of the near 'blanket policy' questioned by Judge J in *R v Warwickshire County Council ex p Collymore* [1995] ELR 217, at 224–226, 'which while in theory admitting of exceptions, may not, in reality result in the proper consideration of each individual case on its merits.'

... Accordingly, given the Authority's acknowledgment that transsexualism is an illness, its policy, in my view, is flawed ... the ostensible provision that it makes for exceptions in individual cases and its manner of considering them amount effectively to the operation of a 'blanket policy' against funding treatment for the condition because it does not believe in such treatment.

Note
This decision indicates that it is not enough for a public authority, in settling upon a policy, simply to *assert* that it is prepared to consider departing from it in exceptional cases: it must be able to show that such preparedness is real, not a legal fiction, designed merely to safeguard it from legal challenge. For critical analysis of the 'no-fetter' principle, see C Hilson, 'Judicial review, policies, and the fettering of discretion' [2002] PL 111.

Can decisions be reviewed for errors of fact?

In seeking to address this issue, the first question is obviously what amounts to a question of fact, as opposed to law. Clearly, certain questions, such as whether a contract exists, will require consideration of legal questions. However, it is not always clear where, for example, a word such as 'negligent' or 'reasonable' appears in a statute, whether it should be interpreted as a question of law or fact. The best approach is probably as follows: it must first be asked whether the word in the statute in question was intended to be used in its ordinary, English sense or whether it is to be understood in some technical, artificial sense. Which category it falls into is a question of law for the courts. If it is held to be the former, then it is a question of fact. Courts sometimes use the test of whether the term in question is an 'ordinary English word', for example, 'offensive' in public order legislation;[19] if so, it will be treated as a question of fact. As Jones notes, 'there are very few English cases where mistake of fact has been accepted as a ground for judicial review, and an even smaller number which appear to have been decided on this ground alone'.[20] However, it appears that there are a limited number of instances in which mistake of fact may give rise to unlawfulness.

Jurisdictional fact. A fact will be considered jurisdictional if the decision-maker is only entitled to enter upon his enquiry if the particular fact exists. In such a case, the court must itself decide whether the fact existed.[21] Wade gives the example of a tribunal having power to reduce the rent of 'a dwelling house'. If it mistakenly finds a property to be a dwelling house when in fact it is business property, it will have acted *ultra vires*, because the objective conditions that are required to be satisfied before it can enter in upon its enquiry – the property being a dwelling house – are not present.[22]

No evidence justifying a decision. Where a decision rests upon a factual basis, it may be seen as an error of law, if there is no evidence for the facts found by the decision-

---

19   See *Brutus v Cozens* [1973] AC 854.
20   T Jones, 'Mistake of fact in administration' [1990] PL 507.
21   *White and Collins v Minister of Health* [1939] 2 KB 838.
22   HWR Wade and C Forsyth, *Administrative Law* (1994), p 286.

maker.[23] In *Coleen Properties v Minister of Housing and Local Government* [1971] 1 WLR 433, a minister had disagreed with an inspector's recommendation that it was not reasonably necessary to purchase a given property in order to redevelop an area but without citing any evidence to justify his disagreement with him. Thus, making a decision with no, or insufficient, evidence may be an error of law.

Aside from these areas, the general rule is that assessment of matters of fact is not for the court to second-guess. As Lord Brightman remarked in *Puhlhofer v Hillingdon LBO* [1986] AC 484:

> Parliament intended the Local Authority to be the judge of fact ... Where the existence or non-existence of fact is left to the judgement and discretion of a public body and that fact involves a broad spectrum ranging from the obvious to the debatable to the just conceivable, it is the duty of the court to leave the decision of that fact to the [Local Authority] save where it is obvious that the public body, consciously or unconsciously, is acting perversely.

However, there is another possible way of attacking what is, in effect, an error of fact.

T Jones, 'Mistake of fact in administration' [1990] PL 507, 512–25 (extracts)

How can a mistake of fact by an administrative decision-maker fall to be regarded as the taking into account of an irrelevant consideration? An obvious point to make is that the two concepts are closely related. This can be illustrated by referring to the decision of the Court of Appeal in *Simplex GE (Holdings) Ltd v Secretary of State for the Environment and the City of St Albans District Council* [[1988] COD 160] which provides a clear example of an error of fact being treated as an irrelevant consideration. The part of this case which is relevant to the present discussion arose by way of an appeal (under s 245 of the Town and Country Planning Act 1971) whereby Simplex sought the quashing of a decision by the minister to reject its appeal against deemed refusals by the district council to grant outline planning permission in respect of a particular site. The mistake made by the minister was that he thought that a study recommended by a planning inspector relating to the question of whether the site should be retained in the green belt had formed the basis of the council's decision, when no study had been carried out by the time of the minister's decision. (In any event, this study was concerned with the narrower issue of use within the green belt designation.) The contention of Simplex was that, as a result of his mistake, the minister had taken into consideration matters which he was not entitled to take into account. The Court of Appeal agreed, concluding that the mistake had been a significant factor in the minister's decision. It was sufficient for the appellant to show, as had been done in this case, that the decision might have been different had the irrelevant consideration not been taken into account.

Notes

1   In the recent decision of *R v Criminal Injuries Compensation Board ex p A* [1999] 2 AC 330, 344–45, four members of the House of Lords were prepared to agree with Lord Slynn's *obiter* finding that there could be review of the Board's decision on a matter of fact, namely inaccurate evidence given to it by a policewoman about the findings of a medical examination aimed at ascertaining whether A had in fact suffered the injuries (rape and buggery) that she claimed. The policewoman's testimony was to the effect that the examination suggested that A's claims were probably false, whereas the report of that examination – not seen by the Board – was in fact consistent with the injuries A claimed to have suffered. This evidence was obviously of critical importance to A's claim and the Board had clearly proceeded

---

23   See, eg, *R v Secretary of State for Education ex p Tameside* [1977] AC 1014, though there has been some doubt as to the justiciability of the point.

on the basis of a mistake as to an established fact (the actual findings of the medical examination). The House of Lords in fact decided the case on the alternative basis of a breach of the rules of natural justice, so the comments made were *obiter* only. However, they are readily explicable: this is not a case where forming a view as to the 'facts' is in reality an exercise in expert, or political opinion, as, say in *Rehman* (below), with which the court would, rightly be reluctant to interfere. There was no doubt but that the evidence given to the Board was inaccurate. As such, finding an error of law on the basis of this mistake of fact could readily be analysed under traditional grounds of judicial review, as either having regard to an irrelevant matter – the inaccurate evidence given to the Board – or as failing to have regard to a relevant matter – the actual findings of the medical evidence not considered by the Board.

2   In cases that concern a grave threat to the applicant's liberty, the courts will traditionally look much more closely to see whether the decision-maker could have reasonably decided as he or she did on the evidence before him. In *R v Secretary of State for the Home Department ex p Khawaja* [1984] AC 74, immigration authorities had power to arrest and detain as a preliminary step to deporting a person thought to be an illegal immigrant. A preliminary question raised was whether the term 'illegal immigrant' could cover a person who had obtained leave to enter by deception or fraud. It was held that it could. The next question was what standard of proof the immigration officer needed to satisfy. The Home Department contended it was enough that there were some grounds on which he could reasonably have made the decision. The court found, however, that this was inadequate in the circumstances: the immigration officer's belief had to be supported by evidence which established the matter to a high probability. The court would determine whether that standard was met. In *R v Home Secretary ex p Budgaycay* [1986] AC 484, one of the issues was whether a person deported would be in danger of life or limb; the court found that it would decide for itself whether certain factual evidence that the applicant would be in such danger had been given sufficient weight by the Home Secretary.

3   A recent instance of this approach is provided by the Court of Appeal decision in *Besnik Gashi* [1999] INLR 276. In order to expel an asylum seeker to Germany, the Home Secretary had to be satisfied that Germany was a safe country, in other words, that it would not deport the applicant to a country in which he would be at risk. Buxton LJ, who gave the main judgment, accepted that statistics put forward on behalf of the applicant revealed an apparent wide disparity between German and UK acceptances of asylum applications from Kosovars over a given period and 'should have put the Secretary of State on further inquiry as to whether Germany is in fact a safe country' (304H). Buxton J concluded:

The duty of anxious consideration to enable the Secretary of State to be satisfied that there is no real risk of Mr Gashi being sent by Germany to another country otherwise than in accordance with the Convention therefore required, on the facts of this case, that the Secretary of State should consider, and almost certainly seek further explanation of, the figures as to actual recognition rates in Germany. Since he has taken no steps in that direction, his decision cannot stand [at 307].

4   However, a recent important decision of the House of Lords emphasises that findings of fact often involve an exercise of judgment, and that on the exercise of judgment, the court should be slow to interfere with the view of the original decision-maker. The House of Lords was considering an appeal from the Special Immigration Appeals Tribunal (SIAC) which had found, *inter alia*, that the Home Secretary had not satisfied it, to 'to a high civil balance of probabilities', that the

deportation of the applicant was justified on public good grounds because he had engaged in conduct that endangered the national security of the UK and, unless deported, was likely to continue to do so. SIAC, under the Special Immigration Appeals Commission Act 1997, was given power to review the findings of the Secretary of State on points of law, on matters of fact and where it considered that his discretion should have been exercised differently (see s 4 of the 1997 Act).

R v Secretary of State for the Home Department ex p Rehman [2001] 3 WLR 877 (extracts)

Lord Hoffman.

42. [SIAC] said that the appeal raised two issues. The first was whether Mr Rehman was engaged in the activities alleged by the Home Secretary. The second was whether his activities, so far as the Commission found them proved, were against the interests of the security of the United Kingdom. The view taken by the Commission was that the Home Secretary's allegations had to be established 'to a high civil balance of probabilities'. The Commission went through each of the principal allegations: (1) involvement in recruitment of British Muslims to go to Pakistan for terrorist training; (2) fund raising for LT; (3) sponsorship of individuals for militant training camps; and (4) creation of a group of returnees who had been given weapons training or been indoctrinated with extremist beliefs so as to create a threat to the security of the United Kingdom. In each case it said that it was not satisfied to the necessary standard of proof that the allegation had been made out ...

48. [The Court of Appeal found that] it was wrong to treat the Home Secretary's reasons as counts in an indictment and to ask whether each had been established to an appropriate standard of proof. The question was not simply what the appellant had done but whether the Home Secretary was entitled to consider, on the basis of the case against him as a whole, that his presence in the United Kingdom was a danger to national security. When one is concerned simply with a fact-finding exercise concerning past conduct such as might be undertaken by a jury, the notion of a standard of proof is appropriate. But the Home Secretary and the Commission do not only have to form a view about what the appellant has been doing. The final decision is evaluative, looking at the evidence as a whole, and predictive, looking to future danger. As Lord Woolf MR said, at p 1254, para 44:

> [T]he cumulative effect may establish that the individual is to be treated as a danger, although it cannot be proved to a high degree of probability that he has performed any individual act which would justify this conclusion.

49. My Lords, I will say at once that I think that on each of these points the Court of Appeal were right. In my opinion the fundamental flaw in the reasoning of the Commission was that although they correctly said that section 4(1) gave them full jurisdiction to decide questions of fact and law, they did not make sufficient allowance for certain inherent limitations, first, in the powers of the judicial branch of government and secondly, within the judicial function, in the appellate process. First, the limitations on the judicial power. These arise from the principle of the separation of powers. The Commission is a court, a member of the judicial branch of government. It was created as such to comply with article 6 of the Convention for the Protection of Human Rights and Fundamental Freedoms (1953) (Cmnd 8969). However broad the jurisdiction of a court or tribunal, whether at first instance or on appeal, it is exercising a judicial function and the exercise of that function must recognise the constitutional boundaries between judicial, executive and legislative power. Secondly, the limitations on the appellate process. They arise from the need, in matters of judgment and evaluation of evidence, to show proper deference to the primary decision-maker.

[Lord Hoffman then asked what the proper role of SIAC was, and in relation to matters of fact, said:]

... the factual basis for the executive's opinion that deportation would be in the interests of national security must be established by evidence. It is therefore open to SIAC to say that there was no factual basis for the Home Secretary's opinion that Mr Rehman was actively supporting terrorism in Kashmir.

Note
This decision nicely illustrates how even a statutory scheme, which very clearly gives a judicial body – SIAC – the power to review findings of fact made by the executive, can be read down so as to limit and curtail that power to one of merely establishing an evidentiary basis for the Secretary of State's finding of fact. In like manner, the House of Lords also read down SIAC's power in the statute to strike down the Secretary of State's finding on the basis that it would have exercised the discretion differently into an ability only to 'reject the Home Secretary's opinion on the ground that it was one which no reasonable minister advising the Crown could in the circumstances reasonably have held' (*per* Lord Hoffman, para 52).

Substantive legitimate expectations: the principle of legal certainty[24]

The concept of a legitimate or justified expectation has been used by the courts as a way of imposing on decision-makers duties to follow fair procedures, as will be seen below. In this section, however, we are concerned with a person who is claiming that he or she had been lead to believe that if he or she did x, he or she would receive a particular benefit, y, or continue to receive it, that they did not get y, or y was withdrawn from them, and should not have been.

The doctrine is usually traced to the decision in *R v Secretary of State for the Home Department ex p Khan* [1984] 1 WLR 1334. The applicant sought to adopt his brother's child from Pakistan. The Home Office had published general criteria which would be applied to decide whether to allow the child to come into the UK, including whether the applicant would be likely to be able to adopt it once it was in the UK, whether its welfare in the UK was assured and so on. The applicant appeared to satisfy all the criteria, but when the application was made, it was refused and it was evident that different criteria had been applied; in particular the Home Office appeared to have decided that because the child was living in good conditions with his mother in Pakistan, entry to the UK should not be allowed.

The court found that, this being the case, the original guidance as to the criteria was 'grossly misleading'. They found that the Home Office could not change the criteria without doing two things, one procedural and one substantive. The first was to give the applicant an opportunity to argue that the old criteria should apply to him – in effect a right to consultation on the change, which is uncontroversial. But the second and more significant finding the court made was that:

the Secretary of State ... should not in my view be allowed to resile from [the published criteria] without affording interested persons a hearing, *and then only if the overriding public interest demands it* [at 1337, emphasis added].

This head is potentially very controversial because it appears to prevent authorities from changing their policies unless the courts think the overriding public interest demands it. This is a form of fettering of discretion, which, as seen above, the courts

24   On this issue generally, see P Craig (1996) 55 CLJ 289.

normally consider to be a form of unlawfulness. Laws J sets out the arguments against such a ground of review in the following case.

R v Secretary of State for Transport ex p Richmond upon Thames London Borough Council [1994] I All ER 577, 596

Laws J: ... such a doctrine would impose an obvious and unacceptable fetter upon the power (and duty) of a responsible public authority to change its policy when it considered that that was required in fulfilment of its public responsibilities. In my judgment the law of legitimate expectation, where it is invoked in situations other that one where the expectation relied on is distinctly one of consultation, only goes so far as to say that there may arise conditions in which, if policy is to be changed, a specific person or class of persons affected must first be notified and given the right to be heard ... [to hold that a change in policy contrary to assurances that it would not be changed] must be justified by reference to 'the overriding public interest' would imply that the court is to be the judge of the public interest in such cases, and thus the judge of the merits of the proposed policy change. [This] ... must be rejected. The court is not the judge of the merits of the decision-maker's policy.

Notes

1   The views of Laws J were, however, challenged by Sedley J in *R v Ministry of Agriculture Fisheries and Food ex p Hamble Fisheries* [1995] 2 All ER 714, 723–24:

It is difficult to see why it is any less unfair to frustrate a legitimate expectation that something will or will not be done by the decision-maker than it is to frustrate a legitimate expectation that the applicant will be listened to before the decision-maker decides whether to take a particular step. Such a doctrine does not risk fettering a public body in the discharge of public duties to stand still or be distorted because of that individual's peculiar position. ... legitimacy is itself a relative concept, to be gauged proportionately to the legal and policy implications of the expectation. This, no doubt is why it has proved easier to establish a legitimate expectation that an applicant will be listened to than that a particular outcome will be arrived at by the decision-maker. But the same principle of fairness in my judgment governs both situations.

2   It is arguable that Laws J overstates the extent of the restriction that the recognition of a doctrine of substantive legitimate expectations would place upon public authorities. Such a doctrine would not, in effect, say that once a policy – such as the circumstances in which children will be allowed into the UK for adoption – has been formulated and announced, it cannot be changed unless the court considers it in the public interest. It is only saying that *in relation to those people to whom it has been announced and who have relied upon it*, a departure from it may have to be justified. That will be a limited group of people. So all that protection for legitimate expectation would mean would be that where an authority wanted to change its policy, it still could, but it might have to make special transitional arrangements for particular people who had relied upon the old policy.

3   Moreover, in many cases the applicant is not seeking to say anything about a change in general policy at all. Craig divides the cases into four categories:

(i)   A general norm or policy choice which an individual has relied on has been replaced by a different policy choice;

(ii) A general norm or policy choice [upon which an applicant has relied], is departed from in the circumstances of a particular case;

(iii) There has been an individual representation relied on by a person which the administration seeks to resile from in the light of a shift in general policy;

(iv) There has been an individual representation which has been relied upon. The administration then changes its mind and makes an individualised decision which is inconsistent with the original representation [the original representation may have been that certain criteria will be used to make a decision or simply that a particular benefit will be granted or will not be withdrawn].[25]

It is clear that it is only cases in categories (i) and (iii), in particular the former, that would impose a real restriction upon public bodies; and in fact, as appears below, restrictions based on substantive expectations are much less likely to be imposed in such cases. Conversely, it is clear that the individual will have the strongest claim in category (iv) cases. Appreciating the critical importance between these very different categories is probably the only way of making sense of a body of case law that often does not itself keep them distinct.

3   It has recently been emphasised by the House of Lords that the person seeking to rely upon an expectation that a given policy would not be changed must have been personally aware of the terms of that policy; without that, no expectation that it will not change can arise. In *R v Ministry of Defence ex p Walker* [2000] 1 WLR 806, a case concerning a change in criteria for the payment of compensation to members of the armed forces injured whilst on service, Lord Slynn observed:

> It is, however, common ground that the Ministry [of Defence] made no express representation to Sgt Walker that he would be paid compensation under the initial criteria, or at all. Although Sgt Walker said that he believed that he would be compensated, it is not established that he knew the terms of the original criteria, or what he believed to be the circumstances in which he would be compensated, or that he relied on any representation as to compensation in going to Bosnia. Accordingly, it does not seem to me that he can say that any legitimate expectation was frustrated.

4   The two points which have caused difficulty are as follows: first, in what circumstances will a person have a *legitimate* expectation as opposed to an expectation *simpliciter*? Secondly, if there is a legitimate expectation that a given benefit will be applied, what is to be the test to decide when the decision-maker may depart from it? Note that in *Kahn*, it was suggested that the test should be that an expectation found to be legitimate may only be frustrated if there was 'an overriding public interest', the judge of which was to be the court. However, later cases then moved to the position that a legitimate expectation is merely a relevant consideration for the decision-maker to consider before changing his or her policy, and that if the decision-maker decides to change the policy despite the expectation that he or she will not, only if this decision is *Wednesbury* unreasonable will the courts intervene. In other words, they will only intervene if they think that no reasonable decision-maker would have decided to frustrate the expectation. This approach moves the doctrine from being a potentially quite significant check upon decisions-makers' freedom of action to merely a particular way of falling foul of the *Wednesbury* test.

5   The first point to note then is what can the applicant *legitimately* expect. In *R v Devon County Council ex p Baker* and *ex p Curtis* [1995] 1 All ER 73, Simon Browne LJ said, 'The ... authorities show that the claimant's right will only be found established when there is a clear and unambiguous representation upon which it was reasonable for him to rely' (at 88). An expectation can, however, also be based upon a regular practice. In *R v Inland Revenue Commissioners ex p Unilever plc* [1996] STC 681, the IRC had for over 20 years allowed Unilever to claim relief for trading loss even though the relief was not properly sought, being out of time. Without warning, the IRC then revoked this practice, at a cost to Unilever running into millions of pounds. It was held that Unilever was entitled to rely upon the well-established practice of the Revenue and it was unlawful, as an abuse of power, to withdraw the policy without notice. Note, however, that this was a category (iv)

25   Craig (1999), *op cit*, p 613.

case – of an individual promise (in effect) being altered to a new individualised decision – something that probably explains the applicant's success.

6   However, in other cases, particularly those falling in categories (i) and (iii), it may not be reasonable for a person to expect that a given policy will not be changed. In such cases, the courts may use the fact that the expectation has to be *legitimate* – that is justified in their eyes – to deny it almost any content at all. As Sedley J said in *R v Ministry of Agriculture, Fisheries and Foods ex p Hamble Fisheries* [1995] 2 All ER 714, 731, legitimacy is 'not an absolute. It is a function of expectations induced by Government and of policy considerations which militate against their fulfilment'. Therefore, if the applicant is demanding that the old policy be applied to them, his or her expectation that policy will remain the same must be balanced both against the general desirability of allowing policy to be freely changed and also any particular factors in favour of change which apply in the particular case. In *R v Department for Education and Employment ex p Begbie* [2001] 1 WLR 1115 it was held that promises made by prominent members of the Labour Party, both while in Opposition and in power, that children already benefiting from the assisted places scheme[26] would continue to receive this until they finished their schooling, could not then be imposed upon the (Labour) Secretary of State, as this would fetter his discretion under the relevant statute.[27] In particular, it was said that it was clear that a party in opposition would not know all the facts and ramifications of a promise until it achieved office and to hold that a pre-election promise bound a new government could be inimical to good government. In other words, once again, the applicants failed at the first stage: they could not show that their expectation was *legitimate*. This was not surprising, given that this case fell into category (iii): the applicants were seeking to object to a shift in general policy, albeit one contrary to a representation made to them.

7   Thus, if there are powerful public interests at stake – as there often will be where a general change in policy has been made – it may be very difficult for the applicant to convince the court that he or she had any *legitimate* expectation that the policy in question would remain unchanged. In other words, an expectation will not be regarded as legitimate if the applicant could have foreseen that the policy or promise was likely to change. An important case is *Findlay v Secretary of State for the Home Department* [1985] AC 318, HL, in which the minister announced changes to parole policy, motivated by public concern about prisoners obtaining parole seemingly too soon into their sentences and also about prisoners committing offences while on parole. The changes meant that, amongst other things, life prisoners would have to serve much longer sentences than they had been lead to believe under the old policy. They claimed a legitimate expectation that the old policy would be applied to them. The House of Lords rejected their claim and Lord Scarman said:

> ... but what was [the prisoners'] *legitimate* expectation? Given the substance and purpose of the legislative provisions governing parole, the most that a convicted prisoner can legitimately expect is that this case will be examined individually in the light of whatever policy the Secretary of State sees fit to adopt [provided the new policy] is a lawful exercise of ... discretion ... Bearing in mind the complexity of the issues which the [Minister has to consider and the importance of the public interest in the administration of parole I cannot think that Parliament intended the discretion to be restricted in this way [at 388].

---

26   Whereby members of poor families are given subsidised places at private schools.
27   Education (Schools) Act 1997, s 2(2)(b).

The reasoning was presumably that because public safety was in issue, the public interest must be overriding. Note that in this case, therefore, the concept of public interest in unfettered discretion was deployed not to overcome the expectation and allow change but to deny that any 'legitimate', that is, reasonable, expectation that no change would be made arose in the first place.

8   The second issue, logically, after deciding whether there is any legitimate expectation at all, is the circumstances in which a decision-maker is allowed to frustrate the expectation by departing from the policy, and in particular who is to be the judge of that question. Since it is a legally recognised interest, there must be some public interest justification for overriding it. Without such a justification, therefore, the authority will be held to have acted unlawfully.[28] But suppose it claims that there *was* such a justification? As noted above, in *Khan*, the court thought that the standard was that departure was only allowed where the 'overriding public interest' demanded it and that the court was to be the judge of whether that overriding interest was present. This view was also supported by Sedley LJ in *ex p Hamble*. There he said that the matter of when a decision-maker could override a legitimate expectation was a matter for the court. However, this approach was then expressly condemned by the Court of Appeal in *R v Secretary of State for the Home Department ex p Hargreaves* [1997] 1 WLR 906.[29] Hirst LJ said:

Mr Beloff characterised Sedley J's approach as heresy and in my judgement he was right to do so. On matters of substance (as contrasted with procedure), *Wednesbury* provides the correct test.

Pill LJ agreed, saying:

The courts can quash the decision only if, in relation to the expectation and in all the circumstances, the decision to apply the new policy in the particular case was unreasonable in the *Wednesbury* sense.

In other words, the court will only intervene if it thinks that no reasonable decision-maker would have decided to frustrate the expectation in question, an approach which leaves the doctrine of substantive legitimate expectations as merely one means of falling foul of the *Wednesbury* test and thus robs it of any independent bite.[30] This, however, was a case involving a generalised change of policy (category (i)) and so the decision was not surprising. The above *dicta*, however, sought to exclude any protection, save *Wednesbury* unreasonableness, in *all* cases of substantive expectations. However, such a blanket exclusion of proper protection for such expectations was rejected in the more recent decision in the following case.

R v North and East Devon Health Authority ex p Coughlan [2000] 2 WLR 622 (extracts)

The applicant was a woman severely disabled as a result of a road accident, some years earlier. In 1993 she and seven comparably disabled patients were moved with their agreement from Newcourt Hospital, which it was desired to close, to a purpose-built facility, Mardon House, on the clear understanding that Mardon House would be their home for life. The patients were consulted over the facilities and layout of

---

28   As, eg, in *R v IRC ex p Unilever plc* [1996] STC 681; *R v Inland Revenue Commissioners ex p MFK* [1990] 1 WLR 1545, 1577.

29   For comment, see C Forsyth, '*Wednesbury* protection of substantive legitimate expectations' [1997] PL 375.

30   For critical comment on this case see P Craig, 'Substantive legitimate expectations and the principles of judicial review', in M Andenas, *English Public Law and the Common Law of Europe* (1998); TRS Allan, 'Procedure and substance in judicial review' [1997] CLJ 246; S Foster, 'Legitimate expectations and prisoners' rights' (1997) 60 MLR 727.

Mardon House and individual flatlets were specifically tailored to their needs; they were assured by the then General Manager of the Health Authority, as follows: 'I confirm ... that the Health Authority has made it clear to the Community Trust that it expects the Trust to continue to provide good quality care for you at Mardon House for as long as you choose to live there.' The case concerned a challenge to the subsequent decision of the Health Authority to close Mardon House. A number of issues were raised by the case; the extracts below concern only the argument of the applicant that the decision to close Mardon House represented a violation of her (substantive) legitimate expectation that it would be a home for life and that the Health Authority had advanced no overriding public interest to justify such a violation. A crucial issue was whether it was for the Authority itself or for the court to determine whether any public interest in closure amounted to a sufficiently overriding interest to justify the frustration of the applicant's expectation.

Lord Woolf MR, Mummery and Sedley LJJ: ... It has been common ground throughout these proceedings that in public law the Health Authority could break its promise to Miss Coughlan that Mardon House would be her home for life if, and only if, an overriding public interest required it. Both Mr Goudie and Mr Gordon adopted the position that, while the initial judgment on this question has to be made by the Health Authority, it can be impugned if improperly reached. We consider that it is for the court to decide in an arguable case whether such a judgment, albeit properly arrived at, strikes a proper balance between the public and the private interest.

[The Court went on to find that the evidence showed that the Health Authority had taken into account – and given weight to – its own previous promise to the applicant and others in now deciding whether to close Mardon House.]

It is necessary to begin by examining the court's role where what is in issue is a promise as to how it would behave in the future made by a public body when exercising a statutory function. ...

There are at least three possible outcomes. (a) The court may decide that the public authority is only required to bear in mind its previous policy or other representation, giving it the weight it thinks right, but no more, before deciding whether to change course. Here the court is confined to reviewing the decision on *Wednesbury* grounds. This has been held to be the effect of changes of policy in cases involving the early release of prisoners (see *Re Findlay* [1985] AC 318; *R v Home Secretary ex parte Hargreaves* [1997] 1 WLR 906). (b) [The court then noted that in other instances 'the court may decide that the promise or practice induces a legitimate expectation of, for example, being consulted before a particular decision is taken'.] (c) Where the court considers that a lawful promise or practice has induced a legitimate expectation of a *benefit which is substantive*, not simply procedural, authority now establishes that here too the court will in a proper case decide whether to frustrate the expectation is so unfair that to take a new and different course will amount to an abuse of power. Here, once the legitimacy of the expectation is established, the court will have the task of weighing the requirements of fairness against any overriding interest relied upon for the change of policy.

The court having decided which of the categories is appropriate, the court's role in the case of the second and third categories is different from that in the first. In the case of the first, the court is restricted to reviewing the decision on conventional grounds. The test will be rationality and whether the public body has given proper weight to the implications of not fulfilling the promise. In the case of the second category the court's task is the conventional one of determining whether the decision was procedurally fair. In the case of the third, the court has when necessary to determine whether there is a sufficient overriding interest to justify a departure from what has been previously promised.

In many cases the difficult task will be to decide into which category the decision should be allotted. In what is still a developing field of law, attention will have to be given to what it is in the first category of case which limits the applicant's legitimate expectation (in Lord Scarman's words in *Re Findlay*) to an expectation that whatever policy is in force at the time will be applied to him. ... most cases of an enforceable expectation of a substantive benefit (the third category) are likely in the nature of things to be cases where the expectation is confined to one person or a few people, giving the promise or representation the character of a contract. We recognise that the courts' role in relation to the third category is still controversial; but, as we hope to show, it is now clarified by authority.

We consider that [both Counsel] are correct, as was the judge, in regarding the facts of this case as coming into the third category ... Our reasons are as follows. First, the importance of what was promised to Miss Coughlan, (as we will explain later, this is a matter underlined by the Human Rights Act 1998); second, the fact that promise was limited to a few individuals, and the fact that the consequences to the Health Authority of requiring it to honour its promise are likely to be financial only.

The court's task in all these cases is not to impede executive activity but to reconcile its continuing need to initiate or respond to change with the legitimate interests or expectations of citizens or strangers who have relied, and have been justified in relying, on a current policy or an extant promise. The critical question is by what standard the court is to resolve such conflicts. It is when one examines the implications for a case like the present of the proposition that so long as the decision-making process has been lawful, the court's only ground of intervention is the intrinsic rationality of the decision, that the problem becomes apparent. Rationality, as it has developed in modern public law, has two faces: one is the barely known decision which simply defies comprehension; the other is a decision which can be seen to have proceeded by flawed logic (though this can often be equally well allocated to the intrusion of an irrelevant factor). The present decision may well pass a rationality test; the Health Authority knew of the promise and its seriousness; it was aware of its new policies and the reasons for them; it knew that one had to yield, and it made a choice which, whatever else can be said of it, may not easily be challenged as irrational. As Lord Diplock said in *Secretary of State for Education and Science v Tameside MBC*:

> The very concept of administrative discretion involves a right to choose between more than one possible course of action upon which there is room for reasonable people to hold differing opinions as to which is to be preferred.

But to limit the court's power of supervision to this is to exclude from consideration another aspect of the decision which is equally the concern of the law.

In the ordinary case there is no space for intervention on grounds of abuse of power once a rational decision directed to a proper purpose has been reached by lawful process. The present class of case is visibly different. It involves not one but two lawful exercises of power (the promise and the policy change) by the same public authority, with consequences for individuals trapped between the two. The policy decision may well, and often does, make as many exceptions as are proper and feasible to protect individual expectations ... If it does not, as in the *Unilever* case, the court is there to ensure that the power to make and alter policy has not been abused by unfairly frustrating legitimate individual expectations. In such a situation a bare rationality test would constitute the public authority judge in its own cause, for a decision to prioritise a policy change over legitimate expectations will almost always be rational from where the authority stands, even if objectively it is arbitrary or unfair. It is in response to this dilemma that two distinct but related approaches have developed in the modern cases.

One approach is to ask not whether the decision is *ultra vires* in the restricted *Wednesbury* sense but whether, for example through unfairness or arbitrariness, it amounts to an abuse of power.

[The court then reviewed various authorities exemplifying this approach, including *Re Preston, Preston Group* [1985] AC 835, HL, para 69 and continued:]

Abuses of power may take many forms. One, not considered in the *Wednesbury* case (even though it was arguably what the case was about), was the use of a power for a collateral purpose. Another, as cases like *Preston* now make clear, is reneging without adequate justification, by an otherwise lawful decision, on a lawful promise or practice adopted towards a limited number of individuals. There is no suggestion in *Preston* or elsewhere that the final arbiter of justification, rationality apart, is the decision-maker rather than the court ...

Fairness in such a situation, if it is to mean anything, must for the reasons we have considered include fairness of outcome. This in turn is why the doctrine of legitimate expectation has emerged as a distinct application of the concept of abuse of power in relation to substantive as well as procedural benefits, representing a second approach to the same problem. If this is the position in the case of the third category, why is it not also the position in relation to the first category? May it be (though this was not considered in *Findlay* or *Hargreaves*) that, when a promise is made to a category of individuals who have the same interest it is more likely to be considered to have binding effect than a promise which is made generally or to a diverse class, when the interests of those to whom the promise is made may differ or, indeed, may be in conflict? Legitimate expectation may play different parts in different aspects of public law. The limits to its role have yet to be finally determined by the courts. Its application is still being developed on a case by case basis. Even where it reflects procedural expectations, for example concerning consultation, it may be affected by an overriding public interest. It may operate as an aspect of good administration, qualifying the intrinsic rationality of policy choices. And without injury to the *Wednesbury* doctrine it may furnish a proper basis for the application of the now established concept of abuse of power.

[The court then reviewed further decisions and went on:]

Nowhere in this body of authority, nor in *Preston,* nor in *Findlay,* is there any suggestion that judicial review of a decision which frustrates a substantive legitimate expectation is confined to the rationality of the decision. But in *R v Home Secretary ex parte Hargreaves* [1997] 1 WLR 906 Hirst LJ (with whom Peter Gibson LJ agreed) was persuaded to reject the notion of scrutiny for fairness as heretical, and Pill LJ to reject it as 'wrong in principle'.

Hargreaves concerned prisoners whose expectations of home leave and early release were not to be fulfilled by reason of a change of policy. Following *Re Findlay* [1985] AC 318, this court held that such prisoners' only legitimate expectation was that their applications would be considered individually in the light of whatever policy was in force at the time: in other words the case came into the first category. This conclusion was dispositive of the case. What Hirst LJ went on to say under the head of [the approach of the court in balancing the public interest against the expectation] was therefore *obiter.* However Hirst LJ accepted in terms the submission of leading counsel for the Home Secretary that, beyond review on *Wednesbury* grounds, the law recognised no enforceable legitimate expectation of a substantive benefit.

Hargreaves can, in any event, be distinguished from the present case ... In this case it is contended that fairness in the statutory context required more of the decision maker than in *Hargreaves* where the sole legitimate expectation possessed by the prisoners had been met. It required the Health Authority, as a matter of fairness, not to resile from their promise unless there was an overriding justification for doing so. Another way of expressing the same thing is to talk of the unwarranted frustration of a legitimate expectation and thus an abuse of power or a failure of substantive fairness. Again the labels are not important except that they all distinguish the issue here from that in *Hargreaves.* They identify a different task for the court from that where what is in issue is a conventional application of policy or exercise of discretion. Here the decision can only be justified if there is an overriding public interest. Whether there is an overriding public interest is a question for the court.

[The court cited further authority in support of this conclusion, including *R v Home Secretary ex parte Ruddock* [1987] 1 WLR 1482 and *R v Home Secretary ex parte Khan* [1984] 1 WLR 1337; *dicta* of Lord Diplock in *CCSU v Minister for Civil Service* [1985] 374, 408 referring to 'benefits or advantages which the applicant can legitimately expect to be permitted to continue to enjoy' and went on:]

For our part, in relation to this category of legitimate expectation, we do not consider it necessary to explain the modern doctrine in *Wednesbury* terms, helpful though this is in terms of received jurisprudence. We would prefer to regard the *Wednesbury* categories themselves as the major instances (not necessarily the sole ones: see *GCHQ* [1985] AC 374, 410, per Lord Diplock) of how public power may be misused. Once it is recognised that conduct which is an abuse of power is contrary to law its existence must be for the court to determine.

The fact that the court will only give effect to a legitimate expectation within the statutory context in which it has arisen should avoid jeopardising the important principle that the executive's policy-making powers should not be trammelled by the courts (see *Hughes v DHSS* [1985] AC 766, 788, per Lord Diplock). Policy being (within the law) for the public authority alone, both it and the reasons for adopting or changing it will be accepted by the courts as part of the factual data – in other words, as not ordinarily open to judicial review. The court's task – and this is not always understood – is then limited to asking whether the application of the policy to an individual who has been led to expect something different is a just exercise of power. In many cases the authority will already have considered this and made appropriate exceptions (as was envisaged in *British Oxygen v Board of Trade* [1971] AC 610 and as had happened in *Hamble Fisheries*), or resolved to pay compensation where money alone will suffice. But where no such accommodation is made, it is for the court to say whether the consequent frustration of the individual's expectation is so unfair as to be a misuse of the authority's power.

Fairness and the Decision to Close

How are fairness and the overriding public interest in this particular context to be judged? ... What matters is that, having taken [all factors] into account, the Health Authority voted for closure in spite of the promise. The propriety of such an exercise of power should be tested by asking whether the need which the Health Authority judged to exist to move Miss Coughlan to a local authority facility was such as to outweigh its promise that Mardon House would be her home for life.

... This was an express promise or representation made on a number of occasions in precise terms. It was made to a small group of severely disabled individuals who had been housed and cared for over a substantial period in the Health Authority's predecessor's premises at Newcourt. It specifically related to identified premises which it was represented would be their home for as long as they chose. It was in unqualified terms. It was repeated and confirmed to reassure the residents. It was made by the Health Authority's predecessor for its own purposes, namely to encourage Miss Coughlan and her fellow residents to move out of Newcourt and into Mardon House, a specially built substitute home in which they would continue to receive nursing care. The promise was relied on by Miss Coughlan. Strong reasons are required to justify resiling from a promise given in those circumstances. This is not a case where the Health Authority would, in keeping the promise, be acting inconsistently with its statutory or other public law duties. A decision not to honour it would be equivalent to a breach of contract in private law.

The Health Authority treated the promise as the 'starting point' from which the consultation process and the deliberations proceeded. It was a factor which should be given 'considerable weight', but it could be outweighed by 'compelling reasons which indicated overwhelmingly that closure was the reasonable and the right course to take'. The Health Authority, though 'mindful of the history behind the residents' move to Mardon House and their understandable expectation that it would be their permanent home', formed the view that there were 'overriding reasons' why closure should nonetheless proceed. The Health Authority wanted to improve the provision of reablement services and considered that the mix of a long stay residential service and a reablement service at Mardon House was inappropriate and detrimental to the interests of both users of the service. The acute reablement service could not be supported there without an uneconomic investment which would have produced a second class reablement service. It was argued that there was a compelling public interest which justified the Health Authority's prioritisation of the reablement service.

It is, however, clear from the Health Authority's evidence and submissions that it did not consider that it had a legal responsibility or commitment to provide a *home*, as distinct from care or funding of care, for the Applicant and her fellow residents. It considered that ... the provision of care services to the current residents had become 'excessively expensive', having regard to the needs of the majority of disabled people in the Authority's area and the 'insuperable problems' involved in the mix of long term residential care and reablement services at Mardon House. Mardon House had, contrary to earlier expectations, become:

> a prohibitively expensive white elephant.... Its continued operation was dependent upon the Authority supporting it at an excessively high cost. This did not represent value for money and left fewer resources for other services.

... But the cheaper option favoured by the Health Authority misses the essential point of the promise which had been given. The fact is that the Health Authority has not offered to the Applicant an equivalent facility to replace what was promised to her. The Health Authority's undertaking to fund her care for the remainder of her life is substantially different in nature and effect from the earlier promise that care for her would be provided *at Mardon House*. That place would be her home for as long as she chose to live there.

We have no hesitation in concluding that the decision to move Miss Coughlan against her will and in breach of the Health Authority's own promise was in the circumstances unfair. It was unfair because it frustrated her legitimate expectation of having a home for life in Mardon House. There was no overriding public interest which justified it. In drawing the balance of conflicting interests the court will not only accept the policy change without demur but will pay the closest attention to the assessment made by the public body itself. Here, however, as we have already indicated, the Health Authority failed to weigh the conflicting interests correctly ... There was unfairness amounting to an abuse of power by the Health Authority.

Notes

1 It should be noted that this decision only comes into play if it has already been determined that there is a *legitimate* expectation (that is, the applicant has satisfied the criteria of the representation being clear and unequivocal, that is was reasonable for him or her to rely upon it, etc). This is likely to happen only in cases falling within category (iv), and (a weaker claim) category (ii). But if the legitimacy of that expectation can be established, and a public authority asserts that an overriding public interest justifies frustrating it, the decision lays down a radically different test from *Hargreave*. In *Hargreave*, it was suggested that it was for the *public authority* to decide whether the public interest justified overriding the legitimate expectation and the court should only intervene if it considers its decision is wholly unreasonable. *Coughlan*, having found that this suggestion was *obiter*, provides that the *Hargreave* approach should be applied only in some cases. In others, the court should decide itself whether the public interest should have properly overridden the legitimate expectation.

2 The court said that in order to decide which approach to take, courts should use the following criteria:

   (a) whether 'the expectation is confined to one person or a few people, giving the promise or representation the character of a contract' (that is, category (iv) cases);

   (b) the importance of the promise to the individual;

(c) the level of detriment to the public authority of being forced to honour promise.[31] This detriment will clearly be greater if the authority is seeking to resile from the promise because of a generalised change in policy (category (iii) cases).

3   Laws LJ in *ex p Begbie* [2001] 1 WLR 1115[32] took the opportunity to make some cautionary remarks about the application of the principles enunciated in *Coughlan*. As Elliott puts it,[33] he argued that 'substantive review operates on a sliding scale' between the deferential *Wednesbury* approach on the one hand and high intensity proportionality review on the other, and that this scale:

> embraces many different levels of judicial intervention with the standard of review being determined by the specific features of the case. Thus, if the matter in question lies in the 'macro-political' field, raises 'wide-ranging issues of general policy' or is likely to have 'multi-layered effects' which substantially reduce the government's freedom to formulate policy, a less intrusive form of review is called for.[34]

4   *Coughlan* was clearly a controversial decision, since it allowed judges, albeit in a limited category of case, to make the primary judgment as to whether a legitimate expectation was outweighed by the public interest, precisely the approach that had been described not just as mistaken but as 'heresy' in *Hargreaves*. However, it has been cited in a couple of House of Lords' decisions[35] with no hint of disapproval, indeed with apparent endorsement.

PROCEDURAL IMPROPRIETY

Procedural impropriety is one of the three main grounds of review identified by Lord Diplock in *Council of Civil Service Unions v Minister for the Civil Service* [1985] AC 374; [1984] 3 All ER 935; it can denote both a failure to observe express procedural requirements (most commonly consultation) and a breach of the common law rules of natural justice, also known as the 'duty to act fairly'. When dealing with the effects of failure to undertake statutory consultation, the courts have tended to classify such requirements as either mandatory or directory. Breach of a mandatory requirement will render the decision or act in question invalid, in contrast to breach of a directory requirement which will not.[36] The terminology was recast in *Wang v Commissioner of Inland Revenue* [1994] 1 WLR 1286, in which the court said that it was preferable to approach the issue by asking two questions: (a) did the legislature intend the person to comply with the requirement; (b) did the legislature intend that a failure to comply with the requirement would render the decision void? The problem here is that the statute generally gives little guidance as to whether the requirement should be

---

31   For general comment, see Craig and Schonberg, *op cit*.
32   See M Elliott, 'The Human Rights Act 1998 and the standard of substantive review' [2001] CLJ 301, 315–22.
33   M Elliott, 'Legitimate expectation: the substantive dimension' [2000] CLJ 421, at p 424.
34   *Ibid*.
35   See *R v MOD ex p Walker* [2000] 1 WLR 806, *per* Lord Hoffmann: 'This is not a case like *R v North and East Devon Health Authority ex p Coughlan* [1999] Lloyd's Rep (Medical) 306, in which a public authority made a specific promise and then withdrew it.' *Dicta* in *R v Secretary of State for the Home Department ex p Hindley* [2001] 1 AC 410 left the status of *Coughlan* carefully open, while not explicitly endorsing it (*ibid*, at 419, *per* Lord Steyn and at 421, *per* Lord Hobhouse).
36   For a recent application of this approach, see *R v Sekhon* [2003] 1 Cr App R 34.

complied with and absolutely none as to the consequences if it is not. So finding Parliament's intention becomes, in reality, a question of the courts asking whether it is fair or desirable in all the circumstances to quash the decision.

A more helpful approach entails examination of the *impact* of the alleged procedural breach on the person who should have been consulted and on the public at large. Courts following this approach will first ask what was the *purpose* of the consultation requirement in question? Having established this, they will then go on to consider whether the failure to take the step in question substantially detracted from the expressed purpose. In *R v Lambeth London Borough Council ex p Sharp* (1986) 55 P & CR 232, a Council was obliged by statute to give people living in its area the opportunity to comment on plans for a new development. The notice it put up in purported compliance with this obligation was defective as first, it did not say the time period during which representations had to be received to be considered, and secondly, it did not state that representations, to be considered, had to be in writing. The court found that the purpose of the provision was to enable local people to have a say in the question of planning permission; the deficiencies in the notice made it likely that this purpose would be hindered. It therefore quashed the eventual decision to grant planning permission.[37]

What, though, will be the position if there are no statutory requirements about consultation or other types of procedures or if there are provisions but these do not state what kinds of procedures are required? In other words, when must a person affected by a decision be consulted about it (and allowed to make representations, in whatever form) and what kind of consultation must take place? These questions will be addressed in turn.

When is a duty to act fairly required?

The courts will have to decide this question in two cases: first, where there is no statute governing the area (for example, where dealing with a non-statutory body) or where there *is* a relevant statute but it makes no provision for procedural fairness. For much of the first half of this century, the courts drew a distinction between administrative decisions and 'judicial' type decisions, allowing the right to a hearing, or consultation, only in the latter type of case. This distinction led to many cases being decided on this rather unhelpful and artificial distinction. It was artificial because, with the complexities of modern government and the way it makes decisions, it was often exceedingly difficult to classify a particular decision confidently as one or the other. It was unhelpful as a tool for deciding when fair procedures should be followed because it appeared to ignore what was surely the key point, namely the importance of the decision concerned for the individual affected by it. As one judge has remarked, it is not much comfort for someone who attends a court case on a parking offence where, because the proceedings were judicial, a rigidly fair and careful procedure was followed, to come home and find a letter from the Council to say that his house is going to be demolished because of a planning decision and be told by this lawyer that he has no right to fair procedure because it is an administrative decision. This distinction was largely swept away by the decision in *Ridge v Baldwin* [1964] AC 40,

---

37 For a similar approach, see *R v Immigration Appeal Tribunal ex p Jeyeanthan* [1999] 3 All ER 231.

described by Wade as 'the turning point of judicial policy'.[38] *Ridge* made it clear that it was not so much the type of decision being made, or the status of the person making it, that was important, so much as whether fairness demanded consultation. In what circumstances, then, will consultation be required? In determining this issue, the primary matter to look at is the impact of the decision on the person affected and, in particular, what rights or interests of the person are affected by the decision.

If the decision affects a person's legal rights, then the decision-maker will generally be required to follow a high standard of fairness.[39] More difficult are those cases where the decision will affect an interest, for example, a person's business, but will not infringe his or her rights. A classic example would be a case where the decision in question was whether to grant a licence to someone to run a business, or whether to revoke it. In general, the individual interest will have to be balanced against the cost and inconvenience to the decision-maker of holding hearings and following lengthy procedures. But sometimes in cases of this sort, a person affected by a decision may also be able to claim a right to a hearing or consultation simply by virtue of the importance of the decision for his or her livelihood, reputation or some other vital interest. The following well known case illustrates the principle well:

R v Barnsley Metropolitan Borough Council ex p Hook [1976] 1 WLR 1052, 1055–57

Lord Denning MR: [The plaintiff] is a street trader in the Barnsley market. He has been trading there for some six years without any complaint being made against him; but, nevertheless, he has now been banned from trading in the market for life. All because of a trifling incident. On Wednesday, 16 October 1974, the market closed at 5.30. So were all the lavatories, or 'toilets' as they are now called. They were locked up. Three-quarters of an hour later, at 6.20, Harry Hook had an urgent call of nature. No one was about except one or two employees of the council, who were cleaning up. They rebuked him. He said: 'I can do it here if I like'. They reported him to a security officer who came up. The security officer reprimanded Harry Hook ... Harry Hook made an appropriate reply ... the security officer described them as words of abuse.

On the Thursday morning the security officer reported the incident. The market manager thought it was a serious matter. So he saw Mr Hook the next day, Friday 18 October. Mr Hook admitted it and said he was sorry for what had happened. The market manager was not satisfied to leave it there. He reported the incident to the chairman of the amenity services committee of the council. He says the chairman agreed 'that staff should be protected from such abuse'. That very day the market manager wrote a letter to Mr Hook, banning him from trading in the market.

So there he was on Friday, 18 October, dismissed as from the next Wednesday, banned for life.

He was, however, granted a further hearing. On the next Thursday, 24 October, he was allowed to state his case before the chairman of the amenity services committee, the vice-chairman, the amenities officer and the market manager himself. He went there accompanied by the president of the Barnsley Market Traders' Union. The matter was discussed. The council people saw no reason to alter the decision, but told Mr Hook that he could be heard further by the indoor services subcommittee. This met on the following Wednesday, 30 October. Mr Hook went there with a young articled clerk from his solicitors and the trade union representative. The committee met at 10 am but Mr Hook and his representatives had to wait for an hour before they were allowed in. Then the articled clerk and the union representative went in. But Mr Hook himself did not go in.

---

38 *Op cit*, p 79.
39 Though note that this is not invariable. In cases of urgency, for example, arrest, the courts have not found that the police have any duty to allow the person concerned to make any statement in their defence.

He stayed outside in the corridor. The articled clerk and the union representative were allowed to address the committee, but they were not given particulars of the charge or of the evidence against Mr Hook. At that meeting the market manager was present and was in a position to tell the committee his view of the evidence. After Mr Hook's representatives has been heard, that subcommittee discussed the case (with the market manager still present) and decided to adhere to the original decision ...

I do not think that the right of a stallholder arises merely under a contact or licence determinable at will. It is a right conferred on him by the common law under which, so long as he pays the stallage, he is entitled to have his stall there; and that right cannot be determined without just cause. I agree that he has to have the permission of the market-holder to start with. But once he has it and has set up his stall there, then so long as he pays the stallage, he has a right to keep it there. It is not to be taken away except for just cause and then only in accordance with the provisions of natural justice. I do not mind whether the market-holder is exercising a judicial or an administrative function. A stallholder counts on this right in order to enable him to earn his living.

Note

A crucial aspect of the decision was the simple fact that it deprived Mr Hook of his livelihood. Where someone complains of a decision not to give them a licence in the first place, he or she is far less likely to be able to attack the procedure surrounding such a decision successfully. This is because he or she is seen not as having been deprived of any benefit he or she previously had, but merely as not having a benefit granted to him or her. Furthermore, as compared with cases where people have been deprived of a pre-existing benefit as a result of wrong-doing of some sort, there generally is no question of a 'case against them' which it appears fair to allow them to reply. In many cases, it will simply be the case that there were more deserving applicants for the benefit. In *McInnes v Onslow Fane* [1974] 1 WLR 1520, Megarry VC said that in mere application cases the standard was far lower than in revocation cases. In his view, in application cases, all that the applicant could reasonably demand was that the decision-maker should reach an 'honest conclusion without bias and not in pursuance of any capricious policy', that is any wrongful or fanciful policy. But he or she could demand nothing in the way of any particular procedure. However, it is not now a matter of clear law that in so-called application cases there can never be some duty to follow a fair procedure. Where an application being made results in evidence being put in by third parties against the application, or, particularly the applicant, the courts have found that fairness requires that the applicant be given the substance of the objections and a chance to reply to them: *R v Huntingdon District Council ex p Cowan* [1984] 1 WLR 501. Thus, if a body charged with deciding upon an application receives submissions from one side, it may have to disclose them to the other, in accordance with the classic principle, *audi alteram partem*.[40] *R v Secretary of State for the Home Department ex p Al Fayed* [1997] 1 All ER 228, discussed below, illustrates the same principle.

In cases involving interests rather than rights, an important concept often used to determine whether a hearing is required is the concept of legitimate expectation. This is especially helpful where the case does not involve a clear right. These decisions tend to lie somewhere between simply being refused a benefit at one extreme and having one's rights infringed on the other.[41] This notion was first formulated by Lord Denning MR in *Schmidt v Home Secretary* [1969] 2 Ch 149 and its principles clarified in the *GCHQ*

---

40 Literally, 'hear the other side'.
41 See generally on legitimate expectation, the very useful analysis by P Craig (1992) 108 LQR 79.

case, in which the Civil Service unions sought review of the decision, made by the Prime Minister without consultation, to ban trade unions at GCHQ.

Council of Civil Service Unions v Minister for the Civil Service (the GCHQ case) [1985] AC 374, 400–01, 412–13

Lord Fraser: Mr Blom-Cooper [for the applicants] submitted that the minister had a duty to consult the CCSU, on behalf of employees at GCHQ, before giving instruction on 22 December 1983 for making an important change in their conditions of service. His main reason for so submitting was that the employees had a legitimate, or reasonable, expectation that there would be such prior consultation before any important change was made in their conditions.

It is clear that the employees did not have a legal right to prior consultation.

[Lord Fraser explained why, and went on:]

But even where a person claiming some benefit of privilege has no legal right to it, as a matter of private law, he may have a legitimate expectation of receiving the benefit or privilege, and, if so, the courts will protect his expectation by judicial review as a matter of public law.

[Such] expectation may arise either from an express promise given on behalf of a public authority or from the existence of a regular practice which the claimant can reasonably expect to continue ...The submission on behalf of the appellants is that the present case is of the latter type. The test of that is whether the practice of prior consultation of the staff on significant changes in their conditions of service was so well established by 1983 that it would be unfair or inconsistent with good administration for the Government to depart from the practice in this case. Legitimate expectations such as are now under consideration will always relate to a benefit or privilege to which the claimant has no right in private law, and it may even be to one which conflicts with his private law rights. In the present case the evidence shows that, ever since GCHQ began in 1947, prior consultation has been the invariable rule when conditions of service were to be significantly altered. Accordingly in my opinion if there had been no question of national security involved, the appellants would have had a legitimate expectation that the minister would consult them before issuing the instruction of 22 December 1983 ...

Lord Diplock: ... *Prima facie* ... civil servants employed at GCHQ who were members of national trade unions had, at best in December 1983, a legitimate expectation that they would continue to enjoy the benefits of such membership and of representation by those trade unions in any consultations and negotiations with representatives of the management of that Government department as to changes in any term of their employment. So, but again *prima facie* only, they were entitled, as a matter of public law under the head of 'procedural propriety', before administrative action was taken on a decision to withdraw that benefit, to have communicated to the national trade unions by which they had therefore been represented the reason for such withdrawal, and for such unions to be given an opportunity to comment on it.

Notes

1　Their Lordships went on to find that, though the failure to consult had been unfair, the decision was justified on national security grounds.

2　The requirement that if a practice is to give rise to legitimate expectation, the fact that it must be regular was stressed in the case. As R Baldwin and D Horne note: 'It is to be anticipated, therefore, that where a body is engaged in irregular, non-recurring forms of decision-making it will be deemed less likely to create expectations than where it deals with a series of similar decisions.'[42]

3　In the *GCHQ* case, the legitimate expectation arose from a regular practice but it was acknowledged of course that an express undertaking could also give rise to the

---

42　'Expectations in a joyless landscape' (1986) 49 MLR 685, 700.

expectation. One such case, described by Baldwin and Horne[43] is *R v Liverpool Corporation ex p Liverpool Taxi Fleet Operator's Association* [1972] 2 WLR 1262:

> The corporation had limited the number of taxi-cab licences in Liverpool to 300 and had assured the owners that they would not change the policy without hearing representations. When the corporation resolved to increase the number, the Court of Appeal said that this could not be done without hearing the owners. The basis of the decision was fairness rather than either estoppel or a general duty to consult when rule-making. An expectation (and, it seems, one that had been relied upon) could not be dashed with impunity, especially one accompanied by an undertaking to pursue a particular course of action or procedure.

4   A useful attempt at setting out the law in this area in a systematic way can be found in the cases of *R v Devon County Council ex p Baker; R v Durham County Council ex p Curtis* [1995] 1 All ER 73 heard together in the Court of Appeal. The cases concerned decisions by the two councils to shut down certain residential homes for the elderly. Devon had engaged in fairly extensive consultation with the residents; Durham only specifically made the residents aware of the plan five days before the final decision was made to go ahead with it. Residents from both homes claimed that they had had a legitimate expectation of proper consultation, which had been frustrated by the Councils' actions. Simon Browne LJ found that cases of legitimate expectation could be broken down in four different categories. The first was substantive expectation (dealt with above). He then went on to consider the others.

R v Devon County Council ex p Baker; R v Durham County Council ex p Curtis [1995] 1 All ER 73, 88–91

(2) The concept of legitimate expectation is used to refer to the claimant's interest in some ultimate benefit which he hopes to retain (or, some would argue, attain). Here, therefore, it is the interest itself rather than the benefit that is the substance of the expectation. In other words the expectation arises not because the claimant asserts any specific right to a benefit but rather because his interest in it is one that the law holds protected by the requirements of procedural fairness; the law recognises that the interest cannot properly be withdrawn (or denied) without the claimant being given an opportunity to comment and without the authority communicating rational grounds for any adverse decision. Of the various authorities drawn to our attention, *Schmidt v Secretary of State for Home Affairs* [1969] 1 All ER 904, [1969] 2 Ch 149, *O'Reilly v Mackman* [1982] 3 All ER 1124, [1983] 2 AC 237 and the recent decision of Roch J in *R v Rochdale Metropolitan BC, ex p Schemet* (1993) 1 FCR 306 are clear examples of this head of legitimate expectation.

(3) Frequently, however, the concept of legitimate expectation is used to refer to the fair procedure itself. In other words it is contended that the claimant has a legitimate expectation that the public body will act fairly towards him. As was pointed out by Dawson in *A-G for New South Wales v Quin* (1990) 93 ALR at 39 this use of the term is superfluous and unhelpful: it confuses the interest which is the basis of the requirement of procedural fairness with the requirement itself:

> No doubt people expect fairness in their dealings with those who make decisions affecting their interests, but it is to my mind quite artificial to say that this is the reason why, if the expectation is legitimate in the sense of well founded, the law imposes a duty to observe procedural fairness. Such a duty arises, if at all, because the circumstances call for a fair procedure and it adds nothing to say that they also are such as to lead to a legitimate expectation that a fair procedure will be adopted.

---

43   *Ibid*, at 699.

(4) The final category of legitimate expectation encompasses those cases in which it is held that a particular procedure, not otherwise required by law in the protection of an interest, must be followed consequent upon some specific promise or practice. Fairness requires that the public authority be held to it. The authority is bound by its assurance, whether expressly given by way of a promise or implied by way of established practice. *Re Liverpool Taxi Owners' Association,* [1972] 2 QB 299 and *A-G of Hong Kong v Ng Yuen Shiu* [1983] 2 All ER 346, [1983] 2 AC 629 are illustrations of the court giving effect to legitimate expectations based upon express promises; *Council of Civil Service Unions v Minister for the Civil Service* an illustration of a legitimate expectation founded upon practice albeit one denied on the facts by virtue of the national security implications.

[The judge went on to find that the appellants in the *Devon* case had had full opportunity to make representations in favour of their case.]

It is when one turns to the *Durham* case that the issue of consultation arises in its sharpest form, no promises or practice of consultation here being asserted by the appellants, no actual process of consultation being in fact afforded by the council. The *Durham* case, in short, on the facts, could hardly be more unlike the *Devon* case.

The legitimate expectation argument in the *Durham* case is advanced in these terms:

> The County Council's decision deprived the appellants of a benefit or advantage which they had hitherto been permitted by the County Council to enjoy and which they could legitimately expect either to continue indefinitely, or at least to continue unless and until the County Council communicated to them some rational ground for withdrawing the benefit on which they were given an opportunity to comment.

This, of course, is asserting a legitimate expectation in category 2 ...

As stated, the second category of legitimate expectation comprises those interests which the law recognises are of a character which require the protection of procedural fairness. What then is the touchstone by which such interests can be identified? It cannot be merely that the law insists they be not unfairly denied else there would be no point in introducing the concept of legitimate expectation in the first place; one would simply look at the decision in question and ask whether the administrator acted fairly in taking it.

[His Lordship then cited Lord Diplock's speech in the *GCHQ* case [1985] AC 374 at 408 where he spoke of a situation in which a decision affects someone:]

> by depriving him of some benefit or advantage which ... he has in the past been permitted by the decision-maker to enjoy and which he can legitimately expect to be permitted to continue to do until there has been communicated to him some rational grounds for withdrawing it on which he has been given an opportunity to comment ...

Thus the only touchstone of a category 2 interest emerging from Lord Diplock's speech is that the claimant has in the past been permitted to enjoy some benefit or advantage. Whether or not he can then legitimately expect procedural fairness, and if so to what extent, will depend upon the court's view of what fairness demands in all the circumstances of the case. That, frankly, is as much help as one can get from the authorities.

In short, the concept of legitimate expectation when used, as in the *Durham* case, in the category 2 sense seems to me no more than a recognition and embodiment of the unsurprising principle that the demands of fairness are likely to be somewhat higher when an authority contemplates depriving someone of an existing benefit or advantage than when the claimant is a bare applicant for a future benefit. That is not to say that a bare applicant will himself be without any entitlement to fair play. On the contrary, the developing jurisprudence suggests that he too must be fairly dealt with, not least in the field of licensing.

With these thoughts in mind I return to the *Durham* case. That the appellants have hitherto been enjoying some benefit or advantage of which the county council now proposes to deprive them cannot be doubted. On the authorities they accordingly get to first base in terms of asserting a legitimate expectation of some procedural fairness in the decision-making process. But it is no good pretending that the authorities carry them or the courts a single step further than that. The fact is that it still remains for the court to say, unassisted by authority save only in so far as there may exist other cases analogous on their facts, whether that legitimate expectation ought to be recognised and, if so, precisely what are the demands of fairness in the way of an opportunity to comment and so forth.

As stated, I share Dillon LJ's view on the facts of this case that five days' notice of the proposed closure of Ridgeway House gave the residents wholly insufficient opportunity to make such representations as they would have wished to make in favour of their home being kept open in preference to others.

Note
It is interesting to note Simon Browne LJ's frankness as to the limited amount of precise guidance which can be gained from the authorities. His judgment amounts to an assertion that the courts can merely apply common sense and reasonableness, unencumbered – and unassisted – by any more detailed guidance.

What is required for a fair hearing?

Two points will be in issue here. The first is the manner in which a person affected by a decision must be permitted to make his case; to put it another way, what, in different circumstances will be the *content* of the duty to act fairly. The second is the rule against bias in the decision-maker. These will be dealt with in turn.

Jowell, in the extract below, gives an indication of the kinds of factors that may weigh with the court in determining what level of procedural protection should be afforded in a particular case.

J Jowell, 'The Rule of Law today', in J Jowell and D Oliver (eds), *The Changing Constitution*, 4th edn (2000), pp 14–15

This kind of procedural protection through adjudication, whether established by statute or the common law, is a concrete Rule of Law. Its content is variable ... As with rules, adjudication is not appropriate in all situations. Where speed and administrative despatch are required, it may be excluded: could one really allow a pavement hearing before a police officer is able to tow away an illegally parked car? In some situations it is felt that an authoritative judgment without the opportunity of challenge is required (the marking of examination scripts may serve as an example here, or admission to a university). Sometimes parties who have to live with each other after the dispute prefer techniques of mediation or conciliation to negotiate an acceptable solution. These forms of resolving disputes differ from adjudication where the final decision is taken by the independent 'judge' and is imposed rather than agreed, a feature not acceptable in all situations and which also partially explains the move to negotiated solutions noted above. Finally, it should be borne in mind that the opportunity for a hearing may not easily be taken: hearings take time, may need expertise, and are often costly (legal aid is generally not provided to parties before administrative tribunals or inquiries).

In ascending order of seriousness, the different procedural safeguards which the courts may find required are as follows: notice of the charge or case against a person; the right to a hearing; the right to call witnesses and cross-examine the other party's witnesses; the right to legal representation.

Notice of the case against

The first of these safeguards then is notice of the case against a person, or of the decision that a person may wish to object to. This is the lowest level of procedural protection; if a person has no notice of the case against him/her, then clearly he or she cannot make any effective representations on his or her own behalf. In *R v Governing Body of Dunraven School and Another ex p B (by his Mother and Next Friend)* (2000) *The Times,* 3 February, a 15-year-old boy was excluded from his school. He applied for judicial review on the basis that he had not been informed of the main evidence against him (provided by another boy). His parents had a right to make representations about the decision. It was held that the duty to act fairly required him to have been informed of the allegations against him, since otherwise it would be impossible for his parents to argue effectively against the decision to exclude. Because this right is so basic, it is only likely to be denied either for very pressing reasons of public policy (for example, national security) or where the applicant is a mere applicant for a benefit, for example, the applicants in *McInnes* (above). This is for two reasons. First, in these cases, no wrong-doing has usually been alleged against the applicant. The case is therefore radically different from one in which someone is facing a sanction of some sort – disciplinary proceedings for example, or expulsion from a school – and needs notice of the case against him or her in order to be able to defend him or herself. Secondly, if the applicant is asking why his or her application has been turned down, in the hope of being able to persuade the decision-maker to change his or her mind, the courts may treat his or her request as one for reasons for a final decision – and as noted below, there is no general duty to give reasons for decisions. As Craig notes, in these kinds of cases, 'there has been a tension between two principles operating within this area, the right to notice, and the absence of any general duty to give reasons'.[44]

However, in cases where it becomes evident that the reason a benefit is being withheld is because of allegations or evidence given by a third party, then this brings the case into the position where there is a 'case against' someone. In such cases, there may be a duty to disclose at least the substance of the allegations or case against that person, or his or her application, as in *R v Huntingon District Council ex p Cowan,* discussed above.

The only other circumstance in which the right to notice may be excluded is if the court takes the view that even if notice been given, it would have been pointless as nothing the applicant could have said in response would have made a difference. *R v Chief Constable of North Wales Police ex p Thorpe* [1998] 3 WLR 57, CA is an example. The applicants were paedophiles, recently released from prison after serving long sentences for sexual offences against children and having difficulties in finding anywhere to live. They eventually hired a caravan on a site in North Wales. Unfortunately, there were numerous children in the caravan park from time to time. The police therefore asked them to move; when they refused, the police showed the site owner press cuttings revealing the applicants' past; the owner then made them leave site. In the Court of Appeal, the applicants argued that they had been treated unfairly as they had not been shown the police information and given opportunity to comment. It was held that while the gist of the police case should have been disclosed,

---

44 (1999) *op cit,* p 307.

nothing the applicants could have said would have made any difference to the police decision: therefore there had been no substantial injustice.

The right to make representations

The next question which arises is whether a person must be allowed to make representations in response to the case against him or her, and if so whether he or she must be allowed to do so at an oral hearing or whether it will be sufficient to allow a person to make his or her representations in writing only.

As with notice, the situations in which a person is likely not to be granted such a right is in the bare application cases; this follows logically from the refusal to grant him or her notice of the case against him or her. However, again, if the refusal of a benefit amounts to an implied slur on his or her character, it may be held that representations should have been allowed. A good example is *R v Secretary of State for the Home Department ex p Al Fayed* [1997] 1 All ER 228. The Fayed brothers applied to the Home Secretary to be naturalised (awarded British citizenship). They clearly satisfied all the conditions laid down under the relevant statute except for one which was nebulous: the requirement that they be of good character. The Home Secretary refused citizenship and gave no reasons. Section 44(2) of the British Nationality Act stated that the Home Secretary 'shall not be required to assign any reason' for such a decision. It was held that the Home Secretary ought to have identified to the Al Fayeds the areas which were causing him difficulty in granting nationality and given them a chance to respond, since the decision clearly amounted to an implied slur upon their good name. The decision was clearly based on the principle that reputation is something the applicant has already and if the net result of his or her application is to lower that reputation then he or she is in danger of being *deprived* of something; therefore, the standards of fairness ought to be higher.

Clearly, as with other areas of procedural fairness, such as reasons, if vital rights or interests are at stake, the right to make representations will generally be upheld. So in *R v Secretary of State for the Home Dept ex p Harry* [1998] 1 WLR 1737, the applicant was a mental patient detained under conditions of security which would mean minimal liberty. Following a review of his case, the Home Secretary was advised by an advisory board that a recommendation by a mental health review tribunal that he be transferred to a lower security hospital, with considerably more freedom, be refused, with the result that Harry would stay at a maximum security classification. The Home Secretary did not disclose the advice to the detainee, or allow him to make representations. It was found that he should have done both in the circumstances. A similar decision is *R (Hirst) v Secretary of State for the Home Department* (2001) *The Times,* 22 March, CA in which a prisoner was moved from a Category C to a Category B prison, a decision which significantly affected his chances of being released on licence. It was held that he should have been given the opportunity to make representations before the final decision to move him was taken.

In other cases, where the nature of the interest of the applicant would not be enough by itself to give him or her a right to be heard, the concept of legitimate expectation may require this, as in *GCHQ* (above).

Another strand of thinking the courts have employed is to look to the *purpose* any oral hearing will serve. In some cases, this brings the courts perilously close to admitting into consideration the argument that giving a hearing would have made no difference. In such cases (*Thorpe*, above, is an example) the courts do not seem to have fully worked out whether they are concerned with upholding substantive fairness (that is, a fair outcome) or procedural fairness (that is, a fair procedure, regardless of the likely outcome of the case). Thus, they sometimes seem to use the test of 'fairness' to mean, was the result 'fair'? The reasoning will be that if the court thinks that in fact allowing the applicants to make representations, or call witnesses, as the case may be, could have made no difference to the applicant, then he or she has suffered no real unfairness.

Such tendencies can be seen in the following, leading case.

Lloyd and Others v McMahon [1987] I AC 625 (extracts)

Liverpool City Council had been late in setting a rate and, as a result, the Council had lost income – the rates it would have collected had the rate been set at the proper time. The district auditor (DA) wrote to the councillors warning them that due to their wilful misconduct they were in danger of being held personally liable – surcharged – to make up this loss. The individual councillors were informed that they could make written representations to the DA before he reached his decision. They did so. He then found them jointly and severally liable for the sum lost, namely £106,103. The case was an appeal against the DA's decision under the Local Government Act 1982, s 20. The main issue was whether the DA's decision should be struck down because he had not allowed the councillors to make representations in their defence at an oral hearing.

Lord Keith of Kinkel: ... My Lords, if the district auditor had reached a decision adverse to the appellants without giving them any opportunity at all of making representations to him, there can be no doubt that his procedure would have been contrary to the rules of natural justice and that ... the decision would fall to be quashed. In the event, written representations alone were asked for. These were duly furnished, in very considerable detail, and an oral hearing was not requested, though that could very easily have been done, and there is no reason to suppose that the request would not have been granted ... The true question is whether the district auditor acted fairly in all the circumstances. It is easy to envisage cases where an oral hearing would clearly be essential in the interests of fairness, for example where an objector states that he has personal knowledge of some facts indicative of wilful misconduct on the part of a councillor. In that situation justice would demand that the councillor be given an opportunity to depone to his own version of the facts. In the present case the district auditor had arrived at his provisional view upon the basis of the contents of documents, minutes of meetings and reports submitted to the council from the auditor's department and their own officers. All these documents were appended to or referred to in the notice of 26 June sent by the district auditor to the appellants. Their response referred to other documents, which were duly considered by the district auditor, as is shown by his statement of reasons dated 6 September 1985. No facts contradictory of or supplementary to the contents of the documents were or are relied on by either side. If the appellants had attended an oral hearing they would no doubt have reiterated the sincerity of their motives from the point of view of advancing the interests of the inhabitants of Liverpool. [But] ... the sincerity of the appellants' motives is not something capable of justifying or excusing failure to carry out a statutory duty, or of making reasonable what is otherwise an unreasonable delay in carrying out such a duty. In all the circumstances I am of opinion that the district auditor did not act unfairly, and that the procedure which he followed did not involve any prejudice to the appellants

Lord Browne-Wilkinson: ... My Lords the so-called rules of natural justice are not engraved on tablets of stone. To use the phrase which better expresses the underlying concept, what the requirements of fairness demand when any body, domestic, administrative or judicial, has to make a decision which will affect the rights of individuals depends on the character of the decision-making body, the kind of decision it has to make and the statutory or other framework in which it operates. In particular, it is well-established that when a statute has conferred on any body the power to make decisions affecting individuals, the courts will not only require the procedure prescribed by the statute to be followed, but will readily imply so much and no more to be introduced by way of additional procedural safeguards as will ensure the attainment of fairness ...

Note
The decision at first sight seems open to criticism: the councillors' reputations were at stake and they were also in danger of suffering the equivalent of a criminal sanction – a fine, indeed a heavy one. These factors would generally point to a high level of procedural fairness. The real basis of the decision seemed to be that the applicants had lost nothing by not having an oral hearing; partly because they were given a full opportunity to make written representations with full knowledge of the case against them.

Failure to give reasons for decisions as a ground of challenge

It is important to distinguish this head of review from the allegation that the applicant was not given notice of the case against him or her, dealt with above. In the latter head, the applicant is arguing that there was a stage in the decision-making process in which he or she should have been given the opportunity to hear the case against him or her, so that he or she could make representations against it, prior to any final decision being made. In the former, with which we are concerned here, the applicant is arguing that the *final decision eventually made* should be quashed, regardless of the fairness of the procedure leading up to its being made, simply because he or she was not given any reasons for it. The leading case follows.

R v Secretary of State for the Home Department ex p Doody and Others [1994] I AC 531, 560–65 (extracts)
The four applicants had each received mandatory life sentences for murder. The Home Secretary, after consulting with the Lord Chief Justice and the trial judge (referred to in the judgment as 'the judges'), had set the 'penal element'[45] in the sentence, which reflected the demands of retribution and deterrence. Once the penal part of the sentence had been served, the case would then go to the Parole Board which could then recommend whether it was safe to release the prisoner on licence or whether further imprisonment was needed to protect the public from the prisoner (referred to as 'the risk element'). In this case, the Home Secretary determined the penal period without consulting the prisoners; he then informed them of his decision, but did not give them any reason for it, or tell them whether he had fixed a period which differed from that recommended by the judges. The applicants sought, *inter alia*, declarations that (a) they were entitled to make representations to the Home Secretary on the matter; (b) the Home Secretary was required to inform them what period had been recommended by the judges and their reasons; (3) he was also required to inform them, if he had differed from the judges, of his reasons for so doing. On appeal, the first two declarations were granted by the Court of Appeal. The Home Secretary appealed to the House of Lords and the applicants cross-appealed. The extract below is concerned only with issue (c) – reasons.

Lord Mustill: ... The only issue is whether the way in which the scheme is administered falls below the minimum standard of fairness.

---

45 Also referred to as the 'tariff sentence'.

I begin by inquiring what requirements of fairness, germane to the present appeal, attach to the Home Secretary's fixing of the penal element. As general background to this task, I find in the more recent cases on judicial review a perceptible trend towards an insistence on greater openness, or if one prefers the contemporary jargon 'transparency', in the making of administrative decisions. This tendency has been accompanied by an increasing recognition, both in the requirements of statute (cf s 1(4) of the [Criminal Justice Act 1991]) and in the decisions of the Criminal Division of the Court of Appeal, that a convicted offender should be aware what the court has in mind for his disposal. Whilst the current law and practice concerning discretionary life sentences conform entirely with this trend the regime for mandatory life prisoners conspicuously does not. Should this distinction be maintained in its entirety?

... I accept without hesitation, and mention it only to avoid misunderstanding, that the law does not at present recognise a general duty to give reasons for an administrative decision. Nevertheless, it is equally beyond question that such a duty may in appropriate circumstances be implied, and I agree with the analyses by the Court of Appeal in *Civil Service Appeal Board, ex p Cunningham* [1991] 4 All ER 310 of the factors which will often be material to such an implication.

Turning to the present dispute ... I prefer simply to assert that within the inevitable constraints imposed by the statutory framework, the general shape of the administrative regime which ministers have lawfully built around it, and the imperatives of the public interest, the Secretary of State ought to implement the scheme as fairly as he can. The giving of reasons may be inconvenient, but I can see no ground at all why it should be against the public interest: indeed, rather the reverse. This being so, I would ask simply: Is refusal to give reasons fair? I would answer without hesitation that it is not. As soon as the jury returns its verdict the offender knows that he will be locked up for a very long time. For just how long immediately becomes the most important thing in the prisoner's life ... Where a defendant is convicted of, say, several armed robberies he knows that he faces a stiff sentence: he can be advised by reference to a public tariff of the range of sentences he must expect; he hears counsel address the judge on the relationship between his offences and the tariff; he will often hear the judge give an indication during exchanges with counsel of how his mind is working; and when sentence is pronounced he will always be told the reasons for it. So also when a discretionary life sentence is imposed ... Contrast this with the position of the prisoner sentenced for murder. He never sees the Home Secretary; he has no dialogue with him: he cannot fathom how his mind is working. There is no true tariff, or at least no tariff exposed to public view which might give the prisoner an idea of what to expect. The announcement of his first review date arrives out of thin air, wholly without explanation. The distant oracle has spoken, and that is that.

My Lords, I am not aware that there still exists anywhere else in the penal system a procedure remotely resembling this. I ... simply ask, is it fair that the mandatory life prisoner should be wholly deprived of the information which all other prisoners receive as a matter of course. I am clearly of the opinion that it is

... My Lords, I can moreover arrive at the same conclusion by a different and more familiar route, of which *ex p Cunningham* provides a recent example. It is not, as I understand it, questioned that the decision of the Home Secretary on the penal element is susceptible to judicial review. To mount an effective attack on the decision, given no more material than the facts of the offence and the length of the penal element, the prisoner has virtually no means of ascertaining whether this is an instance where the decision-making process has gone astray. I think it important that there should be an effective means of detecting the kind of error which would entitle the court to intervene, and in practice I regard it as necessary for this purpose that the reasoning of the Home Secretary should be disclosed. If there is any difference between the penal element recommended by the judges and actually imposed by the Home Secretary, this reasoning is bound to include, either explicitly or implicitly, a reason why the Home Secretary has taken a different view.

Notes

1 As NR Campbell observes,[46] with Craig,[47] this last 'justification [for requiring reasons] could apply to all administrative decisions potentially susceptible to … judicial review'. Campbell continues:

> It must be compared with the House of Lords' previous view on this issue, expressed by Lord Keith in *Lonrho plc v Secretary of State for Trade and Industry* [[1989] 2 All ER 609 at 620]:
>
>> The only significance of the absence of reasons is that if all other known facts and circumstances appear to point overwhelmingly in favour of a different decision, the decision-maker, who has given no reasons cannot complain if the court draws the inference that he had no rational reason for his decision.
>
> On this previous view, the absence of reasons was irrelevant unless the decision was *prima facie* unreasonable.[48]

2 Campbell goes on to propose tentatively that *Doody* may now be taken to require reasons to be given in all cases by the authorities when making decisions which directly affect the liberty of the applicant, instancing *R v Secretary of State for the Home Department ex p Duggan* [1993] 3 All ER 277 in which it was held that a category A prisoner was entitled to be given reasons for the decision that he should remain in this category and therefore remain very unlikely to be released on licence. In decisions lacking such implications for personal liberty 'it is suggested that the duty to provide reasons may arise only where, because of the circumstance of the decision [it] is in particular need of explanation'.[49]

3 Campbell also gives three such exceptional instances:[50]

> First, a decision is in particular need of explanation where, by itself, it is *prima facie* unreasonable. This may arise because all the known facts point to a decision different from that reached by the decision-maker [as] in *Sinclair* [(1992) *The Times*, 5 February].
>
> *Prima facie* unreasonableness may also arise where a decision is substantially different from that which the applicant reasonably or legitimately expected [as in] *Cunningham*.
>
> Secondly, a decision may be in particular need of explanation where, by itself, it is *prima facie* unlawful [as in] *R v Northavon District Council, ex p Smith* [[1993] 3 WLR 776, CA].
>
> Thirdly, a decision may be in particular need of explanation where there is some conflict of evidence, and it is unclear what view of the evidence the decision-maker has taken in reaching its conclusion. Without knowledge of those factual conclusions a person adversely affected by the decision may be unable to determine whether the decision-maker has acted lawfully or reasonably, and thus whether there are grounds for review. So much seems implicit in *R v Criminal Injuries Compensation Board, ex p Cummins* [(1992) *The Times*, 21 January].

4 *Doody* certainly moved English law a little closer to imposing a general duty to give reasons for administrative decisions. However, the following case, in which the duty was found not to be present, demonstrates that much will depend on the particular circumstances of the case.

---

46 NR Campbell, 'The duty to give reasons in administrative law' [1994] PL 184.
47 (1994) 110 LQR 12.
48 Campbell, *op cit*, 186.
49 *Ibid*, 188.
50 Only the skeleton of Campbell's argument is given here; *op cit*, at 188–89.

R v Higher Education Funding Council ex p Institute of Dental Surgery [1994] 1 All ER 651, 667–70

The applicant institution wished to challenge the decision of the HEFC to award it a lower-than-hoped-for rating for its research, likely to result in a £270,000 cut in its funding.

Sedley J: ... In the present state of the law there are two classes of case now emerging: those cases, such as *Doody's* case, where the nature of the process itself calls in fairness for reasons to be given; and those, such as *Cunningham's* case, where (in the majority view) it is something peculiar to the decision which in fairness calls for reasons to be given. This does not mean that differing tests of fairness are to be applied; only that, as always, the requirements of fairness will vary with the process to which they are being applied. In this context we unhesitatingly reject Mr Beloff's submission that the judicial character of the Civil Service Appeal Board and the quasi-judicial function of the Home Secretary in relation to life sentence prisoners distinguish the cases requiring reasons from cases of purely administrative decisions such as the present one. In the modem state the decisions of administrative bodies can have a more immediate and profound impact on people's lives than the decisions of courts, and public law has since *Ridge v Baldwin* [1963] 2 All ER 66, [1964] AC 40 been alive to that fact. While the judicial character of a function may elevate the practical requirements of fairness above what they would otherwise be, for example by requiring contentious evidence to be given and tested orally, what makes it 'judicial' in this sense is principally the nature of the issue it has to determine, not the formal status of the deciding body.

The first limb of [counsel for the applicant's] submission is accordingly that the decision of the respondent was of a kind for which fairness requires that reasons be given. His written contention is that this will be the case –

> when the relevant decision has important consequences for the individual or body concerned, especially if the absence of reasons makes it very difficult for the applicant and the court to know whether the respondent has acted by reference to irrelevant factors, and especially if there is no justification for withholding reasons.

In our view this formula will not do. The absence of reasons *always* makes it difficult to know whether there has been an error of approach. The question of justification for withholding reasons logically comes after the establishment of a *prima facie* duty to give them. Neither can therefore add to the principal ground advanced, which is of such width that it would make a duty to give reasons a universal rule to which the only exception would be cases of no importance to anybody. There are certainly good arguments of public law and of public administration in favour of such a rule, but it is axiomatically not, or not yet, part of our law.

The chief benchmark of significance which we have at present in this setting is *Doody's* case. There the applicant knew the evidence on which he had been convicted but little else, while a considerable body of highly relevant matter had accumulated in the hands of the decision-maker and was going to affect many years of his liberty. If the Home Secretary were then to depart from the judicial view of tariff, it is not easy to think of a stronger case for the disclosure of reasons not merely to the applicant but to all mandatory life sentence prisoners, to each of whom the result of the case will necessarily apply. Equally here the argument, it seems to us, must be good for all applicants, not just disappointed ones, if they want to know why they have been rated as they have been. One would like to be able to hold that for all such applicants, disappointed or not, the importance of the decision alone was enough. But to do so would generalise the duty to give reasons to a point to which this court, at least, cannot go.

We must therefore look also at the other indicia: the openness of the procedure, widely canvassed in advance and published in circular form, the voluntary submission of self-selected examples of work; the judgment of academic peers. These, it seems to us, shift the process substantially away from the pole represented by *Doody's* case, not on mere grounds of dissimilarity (there will be many dissimilar cases in which reasons are nevertheless now required) but because the nature of the exercise was that it was open in all but its critical phase, and its critical phase was one in which, as Professor Davies deposes, 'the grade awarded to a particular institution was not determined by a score against specific features' ... In the result, the combination of openness in the run-up with the proscriptively oracular character of the critical decision makes the respondent's allocation of grades inapt, in our judgment, for the giving of reasons, notwithstanding the undoubted importance of the outcome to the institutions concerned.

... Purely academic judgments, in our view, will as a rule not be in the class of case, exemplified (though by no means exhausted) by *Doody's* case, where the nature and impact of the decision itself call for reasons as a routine aspect of procedural fairness. They will be in the *Cunningham* case class, where some trigger factor is required to show that, in the circumstances of the particular decision, fairness calls for reasons to be given.

Is there then such a trigger factor here? The second limb of Mr Pannick's submission is that the applicant institute has been confronted with a decision which, on the evidence, is inexplicable: the institute's excellence is widely acknowledged and attested. We lack precisely the expertise which would permit us to judge whether it is extraordinary or not. It may be a misfortune for the applicant that the court, which in *Cunningham's* case could readily evaluate the contrast between what the board awarded and what an industrial tribunal would have awarded, cannot begin to evaluate the comparative worth of research in clinical dentistry; but it is a fact of life. The applicant's previous grading, the volume and frequency of citation of its research and the high level of peer-reviewed outside funding which it has attracted, to all of which Mr Pannick points, may well demonstrate that the applicant has been unfortunate in the grading it has received, but such a misfortune can well occur within the four corners of a lawfully conducted evaluation.

Notes

1 TRS Allan has criticised this decision; he notes that 'the court rejected the council's stated objections to giving reasons' – that it would undermine the assessment exercise – as 'casuistic and disingenuous'.[51] The judge could not see why distinguished academics were unable to give reasons for their individual and collective judgments. The judge also found the procedure for assessment to be somewhat defective. Noting this, and the fact that 'the importance of the rating to the Institute's standing and morale could scarcely be exaggerated', Allan concludes that 'the court's refusal to require the council to explain its decision seems hard to justify'.[52]

2 Article 6 of the European Convention on Human Rights (ECHR), now binding on UK courts under s 6 of the Human Rights Act 1998 (HRA) provides:

In the determination of his civil rights and obligations, or of any criminal charge against him, everyone is entitled to a fair and public hearing within a reasonable time by an independent and impartial tribunal established by law.

Article 6 may have a significant impact on this area of judicial review, as the following two cases reveal. Both concern appeals from the General Medical Council to the Privy Council.

Stefan v General Medical Council [1999] 1 WLR 1293, PC

The appellant, a medical practitioner, had been before the Health Committee of the General Medical Council on several occasions. Initially medical reports had been obtained and thereafter a number of decisions were made holding that the appellant's fitness to practice was seriously impaired ... Finally the Committee decided to suspend her registration indefinitely pursuant to

51 (1994) 52(2) CLJ 207, 209.
52 *Ibid.*

section 37(1) of the Medical Act 1983, having determined that on consideration of all the information presented to them, they continued to be deeply concerned about the appellant's medical condition which led them to judge that her fitness to practice was seriously impaired. No reason was given to support the conclusion that there was still a serious impairment of fitness due to the appellant's medical condition nor why an indefinite suspension was appropriate. The appellant appealed to Her Majesty in Council under section 40 of the Medical Act 1983. On appeal a question arose as to whether there was any duty on the Committee to state their reasons and whether, if there was an obligation under common law, it was one which arose in the special circumstances of the particular case or whether it was of application to all decisions made by the Health Committee.[53] [There was no provision in the governing statutory rules[54] for the Health Committee of the GMC to give reasons for its decisions.]

Judgment

... It was pointed out that in two sections of the Act an express provision was made for the giving of reasons, sections 29(1) and 44(4), but the context of those provisions is very different from that in the present case. In the case of each of the two sections in question the provision appears in relation to what appears to be a procedure for administrative redress, with no evident provision for a hearing and nothing comparable with the elaborate procedure set out in the rules relative to proceedings before the Health Committee which have something of a judicial character about them. In any event their Lordships adopt the observation of Lord Donaldson of Lymington MR in *R v Civil Service Appeal Board, ex p Cunningham* [1992] ICR 816 at 826 that

> I do not accept that, just because Parliament has ruled that some tribunals should be required to give reasons for their decisions, it follows that the common law is unable to impose a similar requirement upon other tribunals, if justice so requires.

Their Lordships now turn to the alternative approach, that of the common law. In its most general form the argument proposes that there should be a general obligation on all decision-makers to give reasons for their decisions ...

The trend of the law has been towards an increased recognition of the duty upon decision-makers of many kinds to give reasons. This trend is consistent with current developments towards an increased openness in matters of government and administration. But the trend is proceeding on a case by case basis ... and has not lost sight of the established position of the common law that there is no general duty, universally imposed on all decision-makers. But it is well established that there are exceptions where the giving of reasons will be required as a matter of fairness and openness. These may occur through the particular circumstances of a particular case. Or, as was recognised in *ex. p. Institute of Dental Surgery* [1994] 1 WLR 242 at 263, there may be classes of cases where the duty to give reasons may exist in all cases of that class ... There is certainly a strong argument for the view that what were once seen as exceptions to a rule may now be becoming examples of the norm, and the cases where reasons are not required may be taking on the appearance of exceptions. But the general rule has not been departed from and their Lordships do not consider that the present case provides an appropriate opportunity to explore the possibility of such a departure. They are conscious of the possible re-appraisal of the whole position which the passing of the Human Rights Act 1998 may bring about. The provisions of Article 6(1) of the Convention on Human Rights, which are now about to become directly accessible in national courts, will require closer attention to be paid to the duty to give reasons, at least in relation to those cases where a person's civil rights and obligations are being determined. But it is in the context of the application of that Act that any wide-reaching review of the position at common law should take place.

Turning to the particular circumstances of the present case their Lordships are persuaded that there was a duty at common law upon the Committee in the present case to state the reasons for

---

53 This account of facts is taken from the headnote.
54 The General Medical Council Health Committee (Procedure) Rules Order of Council 1987–97 (SI 1987/2174, as amended by SI 1996/1219 and SI 1997/1529).

their decision. In the first place there is the consideration that the decision was one which was open to appeal under the statute. The appeal was only on a ground of law but, as has already been mentioned, the existence of such a provision points to the view that as matter of fairness in deciding whether there are grounds for appeal, and as matter of assistance in the presentation and determination of any appeal, the reasons for the decision should be given. Secondly, a consideration of the whole procedure and function of the Committee prompts the conclusion that the procedures which it follows and the function which it performs are akin to those of a court where the giving of reasons would be expected. The distinction between administrative and judicial decisions as a factor in the susceptibility of a decision to review was destroyed by *Ridge v Baldwin* [1964] AC 40. Thus the fact that an administrative function is being performed does not exclude the possibility that reasons may require to be given for a decision ... But the carrying out of a judicial function remains, as was recognised by McCowan LJ in *R v Civil Service Appeal Board, ex p Cunningham* [1991] 4 All ER 310 and accepted by Hooper J in *R v Ministry of Defence, ex p Murray* [1998] COD 134 at 136, 'a consideration in favour of a requirement to give reasons'.

Thirdly, the issue was one of considerable importance for the practitioner ... the suspension causes Dr Stefan considerable hardship, not only in financial terms through her inability to work as a registered practitioner, but also in respect of her own natural desire to spend the remaining years of her professional career in some fulfilling and satisfying capacity in the medical service. The importance of the issue may not closely equate with the importance of personal liberty, but the matter is of very real significance in her own eyes and deserves to be respected. In *R v City of London Corporation, ex p Matson* (1995) 94 LGR 443 at 457 the effect on the reputation of the complainer of a rejection from office without the disclosure of reasons was one factor in requiring an explanation to be given. It is not obvious why it was considered that Dr Stefan's fitness for the work which she sought to do was not only impaired but seriously impaired.

Fourthly, Dr Stefan has repeatedly asked for an explanation of the Committee's view and for the diagnosis which they have reached of her condition. ... The Committee stated that they were deeply concerned about her mental condition, but they do not explain precisely what the nature of that concern was, nor how it impaired her fitness to practise.

Fifthly, the only expert witness who had examined Dr Stefan and appeared to give evidence before the Committee, Dr Adams, stated in his written report that she was now well able to control the expression of her attitudes to race and gender, which had been matter of earlier concern, and that the passage of time had reduced the intensity of her distress and anger. He stated that her 'paranoid ideas have less emotional drive behind them and are less expressed' and that she 'is at present fit to practice on a limited basis as a Clinical Assistant in Ophthalmology or in the pharmaceutical industry'. In cross-examination and in response to questions from members of the Committee he modified his view, but still appeared to be saying that she was fit to practise albeit under stringent conditions of supervision. The risk appeared to be one of paranoid behaviour under stress. But it is not evident that he was retracting his view that her condition had improved and it is not clear why in the light of his evidence the Committee reached the decision which they did.

Sixthly, this was the first time that an indefinite suspension was decided upon. The departure from the periodic suspensions which had been imposed before was certainly a legitimate course under the amended legislation but, particularly in light of an apparently less serious condition, the selection of it called for an explanation. Rule 33A provides in mandatory terms that the Committee 'shall' direct an indefinite suspension, but for that mandatory provision to apply two conditions are set out, of which the second is that the Committee shall have determined that it is not sufficient to direct a further extension of the suspension for a period of up to 12 months. Presumably, although it is not so stated, the Committee did make such a determination. If they did not consider that question they were in error. If they did, then in the circumstances of this case some explanation of the departure from a limited period of suspension was required. It may be that they conceived that the mental condition from which they believed Dr Stefan to be suffering was a permanent one, but in light of her own request for the diagnosis that quality of the condition should have been explained. Furthermore at the hearing Dr Stefan made it clear that she was prepared to see Dr Adams regularly and accept his advice, if that was required as a condition of employment. It is not clear why that was rejected by the Committee, as presumably it was.

Their Lordships should also mention one other matter of concern. Certain questions were put to Dr Stefan by the Committee about her qualifications to undertake ophthalmic work. Consideration of her qualifications was irrelevant to the issue before the Committee. That issue was whether her fitness to practise was seriously impaired by reason of her physical or mental condition. It may be that these questions and the answers were not regarded as of any moment by the Committee, but the anxiety arises that they may have played a part in the decision, and without any reasons being given it is not possible to lay that anxiety at rest.

In addition, however, to that narrow approach their Lordships are also persuaded that in all cases heard by the Health Committee there will be a common law obligation to give at least some brief statement of the reasons which form the basis for the decision. Plainly the Health Committee are bound to carry out their functions with due regard to fairness. The first two of the grounds already mentioned will apply to any case coming before the Committee: the provision of a right of appeal and the judicial character of the body point to an obligation to give reasons. Furthermore in every case the subject matter will be the future right of the doctor to work as a registered practitioner, and while there may be differences between individual cases as to the significance of that from the point of view of the particular practitioner, the general consideration will remain that the Committee are adjudicating upon the right of a person to work as a registered practitioner.

There is nothing in the Act nor the Rules requiring reasons not to be given and no grounds of policy or public interest justifying such restraint. In the light of the character of the Committee and the framework in which they operate, it seem to their Lordships that there is an obligation on the Committee to give at least a short statement of the reasons for their decisions.

While the decision involves the application of some medical expertise in the assessment of fitness, the articulation of the reasons for a value judgment should not give rise to difficulty (ex p *Matson* (1995) 94 LGR 443 at 465). Their Lordships have observed that in certain other appeals from the Health Committee which have come before them succinct but adequate reasons have been stated in the decision. Unfortunately such a course was not adopted in the present case.

Notes

1   Clearly, the most significant passage in this judgment for general purposes is as follows:

> There is certainly a strong argument for the view that what were once seen as exceptions to a rule may now be becoming examples of the norm, and the cases where reasons are not required may be taking on the appearance of exceptions [at 1301].

However, it should be noted that the Privy Council also expresses the view that the possibility of any shift in the general rule should be considered in the context of Article 6 of the ECHR and the HRA.

2   The recent Privy Council decision in *Gupta v GMC* [2002] 1 WLR 1691 appears to lay to rest any hopes of an immediate shift in the courts' basic approach to lack of reason-giving as a head of review. This decision also involved an appeal to the Privy Council from a decision of the GMC on the ground, *inter alia*, that no reasons had been given from the decision. However, in this case, the decision in question was one of the Professional Conduct Committee, not, as in the *Stefan* decision, of the Medical Committee. It involved not an assessment that the doctor in question was medically unfit to practise, but a finding that the doctor had been guilty of serious professional misconduct. The appellant contended that:

Except in ... very straightforward cases, however, the Committee should now give reasons not of the sophisticated nature that could be demanded of a professional judge but sufficient to inform the parties in broad terms as to why the Committee had reached its decision.

The Privy Council first found that Article 6 of the ECHR now required that 'either the Committee itself had to be an independent and impartial tribunal or, if not, that its processes had to be subject to control by an appellate body with full jurisdiction to reverse its decision' (at para 8). That appellate body was the Privy Council. The argument essentially was that any body which, like the GMC, determined a person's 'civil rights and obligations', if it could not itself satisfy the requirement of being 'an independent and impartial tribunal established by law' it had to be subject to review by a body which did, and was of full jurisdiction, that is, able to overturn the decisions of the subordinate body on questions of fact as well as law. To be able to exercise this function, the Privy Council needed to know the reasons for the Committee's decision and therefore it should be required to give them. This argument, as one of general principle, was not rejected; rather it was found that in the particular circumstances of the case, the manner in which the Committee made its findings sufficiently revealed its reasons for them for the Privy Council to carry out its review function, particularly bearing in mind the deference that it would inevitably extend to the findings of the Committee on the facts, the credibility of witnesses, etc.

3   What is important about the decision, then, is the seeming acceptance of the basic argument, outlined above. The appellant lost, simply because it was found that, on the facts, she knew enough of the reasons for the Committee's decision to be able to mount an effective challenge to it. But in cases where this was not so, the argument from Article 6 of the ECHR now amounts to a powerful one in the applicant's favour, but only of course where the applicant's 'civil rights and obligations' are engaged.

4   In the following case, the court provided a useful summary as to the principles governing the giving of reasons (these exclude the Article 6 argument).

R v Ministry of Defence ex p Murray [1998] COD 134 (extract)

The applicant relied on three cases all concerned with a failure or refusal to give reasons: R v Civil Service Appeal Board, ex p Cunningham [1991] 4 All ER 310; R v Secretary of State for the Home Department, ex p Doody [1994] 1 AC 531; and R v Higher Education Funding Council, ex p Institute of Dental Surgery [1994] 1 WLR 241. The following principles may be deduced from those cases.

(a) The law does not at present recognise a general duty to give reasons (Doody at 564E).

(b) When a statute has conferred on any body the power to make decisions affecting individuals, the court will not only require the procedure prescribed by statute to be followed, but will readily imply so much and no more to be introduced by way of additional procedural standards as will ensure the attainment of fairness (Cunningham, per Donaldson LJ at 318, quoting Lloyd v McMahon [1987] 1 AC 625 at 702–703 and Doody at 564F).

(c) In the absence of a requirement to give reasons, the person seeking to argue that reasons should have been given must show that the procedure adopted of not giving reasons is unfair (Doody at 561A).

(d) There is a perceptible trend towards an insistence on greater openness ... or transparency in the making of administrative decisions (Doody at 561E).

(e) In deciding whether fairness requires a tribunal to give reasons regard will be had not only to the first instance hearing but also to the availability and the nature of any appellate remedy or remedy by way of judicial review:

(i) the absence of any right of appeal may be a factor in deciding that reasons should be given (*Cunningham* at 322j); and

(ii) if it is important that there should be an effective means of detecting the kind of error [by way of judicial review] which would entitle the court to intervene, then the reasoning may have to be disclosed (*Doody* at 565H and also *Cunningham* at 323a).

(f) The fact that a tribunal is carrying out a judicial function is a consideration in favour of a requirement to give reasons (*Cunningham* at 323a) and particularly where personal liberty is concerned (*Institute of Dental Surgery* at 263A).

(g) If the giving of a decision without reasons is insufficient to achieve justice then reasons should be required (*Cunningham* at 323a) as also where the decision appears aberrant (*Institute of Dental Surgery* at 263a, cited with approval in R v Mayor, Commonalty and Citizens of the City of London, ex p Matson (1996) 8 Admin LR 49 at 62).

(h) In favour of giving reasons are the following factors: the giving of reasons may among other things concentrate the decision-maker's mind on the right questions; demonstrate to the recipient that this is so; show the issues have been conscientiously addressed and how the result has been reached; or alternatively alert the recipient to a justiciable flaw in the process (*Institute of Dental Surgery* at 256H, cited with approval in ex p Matson at 71).

(i) In favour of not requiring reasons are the following factors: it may place an undue burden on decision-makers; demand an appearance of unanimity where there is diversity; call for articulation of sometimes inexpressible value judgments; and offer an invitation to the captious to comb the reasons for previously unsuspected grounds of challenge (*Institute of Dental Surgery* at 257A).

(j) Although fairness may favour a requirement for reasons, there may be considerations of public interest which would outweigh the advantages of requiring reasons (*Cunningham* at 323b).

(k) The giving of reasons will not be required if the procedures of the particular decision-maker would be frustrated by a requirement to give reasons, even short reasons (*Cunningham* at 323b).

Note

For further comments see Andrew Le Sueur, 'Legal duties to give reasons' (1999) 52 CLP 150.

The right to call witnesses and to cross-examine opposing witnesses

The essential test here will be whether the calling of witnesses, and allowing their cross-examination by the applicant, are necessary to ensure a fair hearing of the applicant's case. The reason witnesses are required is where there are disputed matters of fact, and the only way of establishing which side is telling the truth is to try and get some impression of the sincerity of those supporting either side's version of events. So in a case which involves merely the interpretation of rules, or the law, or an examination of one person's isolated conduct, a public authority will not generally be required to permit their use. In *R v Board of Visitors of Hull Prison ex p St Germain (No 2)* [1979] 3 All ER 545 it was held that a Board of Visitors must be able to exercise a discretion to refuse a prisoner's request for witnesses if it is felt that he or she is purposely trying to obstruct or subvert the proceedings by calling large numbers of witnesses or if, where the request is made in good faith, it is felt that the calling of large numbers of witnesses is unnecessary. However, mere administrative inconvenience would not support a decision to refuse such a request and so, if the only reason for the refusal was, for example, the inconvenience involved in recalling the witnesses from other prisons, that would be insufficient. The principles established in the above case were confirmed in *R v Board of Visitors for Nottingham Prison ex p Moseley* (1981) *The Times*, 23 January; it was held that if it were established that a prisoner had asked for and been refused permission to call witnesses that would, *prima facie*, be unfair.

In many instances it would seem essential that a prisoner should be able to call witnesses in order to challenge the evidence against him or her. Moreover, it may be unlikely that a case will often be so straightforward as to require only one witness for the defence. Therefore, if a prisoner can demonstrate that calling more than one witness was necessary due to the nature of his or her defence, it would follow that he or she should have been allowed to call them. In *St Germain (No 2)*, Lane LJ also considered whether the prisoners must be allowed to cross-examine those who had given evidence against them, or whether such evidence could be given by way of written statements only.

R v Board of Visitors of Hull Prison ex p St Germain (No 2) [1979] 3 All ER 545, 552–53

... It is clear that the entitlement of the board to admit hearsay evidence is subject to the overriding obligation to provide the accused with a fair hearing. Depending upon the facts of the particular case and the nature of the hearsay evidence provided to the board, the obligation to give the accused a fair chance to exculpate himself, or a fair opportunity to controvert the charge ... or a ... of full opportunity of presenting his case – to quote the language of s 47 or r 49 – may oblige the board not only to inform the accused of the hearsay evidence but also to give the accused a sufficient opportunity to deal with that evidence. Again, depending upon the nature of that evidence and the particular circumstances of the case, a sufficient opportunity to deal with the hearsay evidence may well involve the cross-examination of the witness whose evidence is initially before the board in the form of hearsay.

We again take by way of example the case in which the defence is an alibi. The prisoner contends that he was not the man identified on the roof. He, the prisoner, was at the material time elsewhere. In short the prisoner has been mistakenly identified. The evidence of identification given by way of hearsay may be of the 'fleeting glance' type as exemplified by the well-known case of *Turnbull* [1977] QB 224. The prisoner may well wish to elicit by way of question all manner of detail, eg the poorness of the light, the state of the confusion, the brevity of the observation, the absence of any contemporaneous record, etc, all designed to show the unreliability of the witness. To deprive him of the opportunity of cross-examination would be tantamount to depriving him of a fair hearing.

We appreciate that there may well be occasions when the burden of calling the witness whose hearsay evidence is readily available may impose a near impossible burden upon the board. However, it has not been suggested that hearsay evidence should be resorted to in the total absence of any first-hand evidence and this is the usual practice. Accordingly where a prisoner desires to dispute the hearsay evidence and for this purpose to question the witness, and where there are insuperable or very grave difficulties in arranging for his attendance the board should refuse to admit that evidence, or, if it has already come to their notice, should expressly dismiss if from their consideration....

Notes

1 The refusal of witnesses and of cross-examination led to the quashing of six findings of guilt by way of *certiorari*. In *R v Deputy Governor of Long Lartin Prison ex p Prevot* [1988] 1 All ER 485, HL, Prevot, a prisoner was punished after a visit by his wife. It was alleged that his wife had masturbated him under the table during her visit. At the hearing to determine the facts and award the appropriate penalty,

he was given no opportunity to call his wife as a witness or any of the prisoners in the room at the time. He was awarded 21 days loss of remission – that is effectively three extra weeks in prison. It was found that he should have been allowed to call the witnesses he needed.

2   It should be noted that disciplinary hearings in prisons are basically adversarial procedures where the purpose of the procedures in question is the determination of a person's guilt or innocence. In this respect, they are very similar to court proceedings. In cases involving more polycentric disputes, where an adjudicator is attempting to reach a conclusion on an administrative matter, after hearing evidence from numerous sources, and weighing up the conflicting priorities bearing upon his decision, the courts are much more reluctant to impose formal, judicial style practices, such as cross-examination. See, for example, on witnesses, *R v City Panel on Mergers and Takeovers ex p Guinness plc* [1990] 1 QB 46.

3   The leading case here is *Bushell v Secretary of State for the Environment* [1981] AC 75. The procedure in question was a public enquiry, the purpose of which was to allow an inspector holding the enquiry to hear local objections to the plan to build a new motorway which he would then take account of in advising the minister whether the scheme should go ahead. One of the key factors in the decision by the Department of Environment (DoE) whether to build new motorways, and if so where, was their projections of what the increase in traffic on existing roads would be over the next 15 years. The method of making these projections, which was highly complicated, was set out in a publication called the Red Book. Some of those who were objecting to the plan to build the motorway believed that the method set out in the Red Book of predicting increases in traffic flow was flawed and overestimated the probable growth. At the enquiry, they were allowed by the inspector holding it to call witnesses who attacked the methodology set out in the Red Book. These criticisms were set out by the inspector in his eventual report to the minister. However, the inspector did not allow the objectors to cross-examine representatives from the DoE on the Red Book methodology. Some of the objectors, including those whose property values would be affected by the motorway, applied for an order quashing the road-building schemes on the ground that they had been wrongfully deprived of the opportunity to cross-examine the experts. The judgment contains valuable comment on the issue of procedural fairness generally.

Bushell and Another v Secretary of State for the Environment **[1981] AC 75** (extracts)

Lord Diplock: ... Proceedings at a local inquiry at which many parties wish to make representations without incurring the expense of legal representation and cannot attend the inquiry throughout its length ought to be as informal as is consistent with achieving those objectives. To 'over-judicialise' the inquiry by insisting on observance of the procedures of a court of justice which professional lawyers alone are competent to operate effectively in the interests of their clients would not be fair. It would, in my view, be quite fallacious to suppose that at an inquiry of this kind the only fair way of ascertaining matters of fact and expert opinion is by the oral testimony of witnesses who are subjected to cross-examination on behalf of parties who disagree with what they have said. Such procedure is peculiar to litigation conducted in courts that follow the common law system of procedure, it plays no part in the procedure of courts of justice under legal systems based upon the civil law, including the majority of our fellow member states of the European Community ... So refusal by an inspector to allow a party to cross-examine orally at a local inquiry a person who has made statements of facts or has expressed expert opinions is not unfair *per se*.

Whether fairness requires an inspector to permit a person who has made statements on matters of fact or opinion, whether expert or otherwise, to be cross-examined by a party to the inquiry who wishes to dispute a particular statement must depend on all the circumstances. In the instant case, the question arises in connection with expert opinion upon a technical matter. Here the relevant circumstances in considering whether fairness requires that cross-examination should be allowed include the nature of the topic upon which the opinion is expressed, the qualifications of the maker of the statement to deal with that topic, the forensic competence of the proposed cross-examiner, and, most important, the inspector's own views as to whether the likelihood that cross-examination will enable him to make a report which will be more useful to the minister in reaching his decision than it otherwise would be is sufficient to justify any expense and inconvenience to other parties to the inquiry which would be caused by any resulting prolongation of it.

The circumstances in which the question of cross-examination arose in the instant case were the following. Before the inquiry opened each objector had received a document containing a statement of the minister's reasons for proposing the draft scheme ... The second paragraph of the minister's statement of reasons said: 'The government's policy to build these new motorways [sc for which the two schemes provided] will not be open to debate at the forthcoming inquiries [sic]: the Secretary of State is answerable to Parliament for this policy.'

'Policy' as descriptive of departmental decisions to pursue a particular course of conduct is a protean word and much confusion in the instant case has, in my view, been caused by a failure to define the sense in which it can properly be used to describe a topic which is unsuitable to be the subject of an investigation as to its merits at an inquiry at which only persons with local interests affected by the scheme are entitled to be represented. A decision to construct a nationwide network of motorways is clearly one of government policy in the widest sense of the term. Any proposal to alter it is appropriate to be the subject of debate in Parliament, not of separate investigations in each of scores of local inquiries before individual inspectors up and down the country upon whatever material happens to be presented to them at the particular inquiry over which they preside. So much the respondents readily concede.

At the other extreme the selection of the exact line to be followed through a particular locality by a motorway designed to carry traffic between the destinations that it is intended to serve would not be described as involving government policy in the ordinary sense of that term. It is an appropriate subject for full investigation at a local inquiry ...

Between the black and white of these two extremes, however, there is what my noble and learned friend, Lord Lane, in the course of the hearing described as a 'grey area.' Because of the time that must elapse between the preparation of any scheme and the completion of the stretch of motorway that it authorises, the department, in deciding in what order new stretches of the national network ought to be constructed, has adopted a uniform practice throughout the country of making a major factor in its decision the likelihood that there will be a traffic need for that particular stretch of motorway in 15 years from the date when the scheme was prepared ... The propriety of adopting it is clearly a matter fit to be debated in a wider forum [than a local inquiry] and with the assistance of a wider range of relevant material than any investigation at an individual local inquiry is likely to provide; and in that sense at least, which is the relevant sense for present purposes, its adoption forms part of government policy ...

But whether the uniform adoption of particular methods of assessment is described as policy or methodology, the merits of the methods adopted are, in my view, clearly not appropriate for investigation at individual local inquiries by an inspector whose consideration of the matter is necessarily limited by the material which happens to be presented to him at the particular inquiry which he is holding. It would be a rash inspector who based on that kind of material a positive recommendation to the minister that the method of predicting traffic needs throughout the country should be changed and it would be an unwise minister who acted in reliance on it.

At the local inquiry into the M42 Bromsgrove and the M40 Warwick ... the objectors were allowed to voice their criticisms of the methods used to predict traffic needs for the purposes of the two schemes and to call such expert evidence as they wanted to in support of their criticisms. What they were not allowed to do was to cross-examine the department's representatives upon the reliability and statistical validity of the methods of traffic prediction described in the Red Book and applied by the department for the purpose of calculating and comparing traffic needs in all localities throughout the country. This is the only matter in relation to the conduct of the inquiry by the inspector of which complaint is made.

Was this unfair to the objectors? For the reasons I have already given ... I do not think it was. I think that the inspector was right in saying that the use of the concept of traffic needs in the design year *assessed by a particular method* as the yardstick by which to determine the order in which particular stretches of the national network of motorways should be constructed was government policy in the relevant sense of being a topic unsuitable for investigation by individual inspectors upon whatever material happens to be presented to them at local inquiries held throughout the country ...

Viscount Dilhorne: ... It is clear that the objectors at this inquiry had every opportunity of putting forward their case. An inspector at an inquiry has a wide discretion as to its conduct. He may, in my view, properly disallow a particular line of cross-examination if it is not likely to serve any useful purpose. An admission or expression of view in the course of cross-examination at a trial may well affect the result, but the views of departmental witnesses as to the comparative merits of different methods of forecasting traffic elicited in the course of cross-examination are not likely to affect the ultimate outcome.

Lord Edmund-Davies (dissenting): ... The general law may, I think, be summarised in this way: (a) In holding an administrative inquiry (such as that presently being considered), the inspector was performing quasi-judicial duties. (b) He must therefore discharge them in accordance with the rules of natural justice. (c) Natural justice requires that objectors (no less than departmental representatives) be allowed to cross-examine witnesses called for the other side on all relevant matters, be they matters of fact or matters of expert opinion. (d) In the exercise of jurisdiction outside the field of criminal law, the only restrictions on cross-examination are those general and well-defined exclusionary rules which govern the admissibility of relevant evidence; beyond those restrictions there is *no* discretion on the civil side to exclude cross-examination on relevant matters.

There is ample authority for the view that, as Professor HWR Wade QC puts it (*Administrative Law*, 4th ed (1977), p 418): '... it is once again quite clear that the principles of natural justice apply to administrative acts generally.' and there is a massive body of accepted decisions establishing that natural justice requires that a party be given an opportunity of challenging by cross-examination witnesses called by another party on relevant issues ...

Then is there any reason why those general rules should have been departed from in the present case? We have already seen that the parameters of the inquiry, as agreed to by the department representatives, embraced need as a topic relevant to be canvassed and reported upon. We have already considered the unacceptable submission that the Red Book was 'government policy.' And, while I am alive to the inconvenience of different inspectors arriving at different conclusions regarding different sections of a proposed trunk road, the risk of that happening cannot, in my judgment, have any bearing upon the question whether justice was done at this particular inquiry, which I have already explained was, in an important respect, unique of its kind.

There remains to be considered the wholly novel suggestion, which has found favour with your Lordships, that there is a 'grey area' — existing, as I understand, somewhere between government policy (which admittedly may not be subjected to cross-examination) and the exact 'line' of a section of a motorway (which may be) — and that in relation to topics falling within the 'grey area' cross-examination is a matter of discretion. I find that suggestion to be too nebulous to be grasped. Furthermore, why such an area should exist has not been demonstrated – certainly not to my satisfaction – nor have its boundaries been defined, unlike those existing restrictions on cross-examination to which I have already referred and I confess to abhorrence of the notion that any such area exists. For the present case demonstrates that its adoption is capable of resulting in an individual citizen denied justice nevertheless finding himself with no remedy to right the wrong done to him.

My Lords, it is for the foregoing reasons that I find myself driven to the conclusion that the refusal in the instant case to permit cross-examination on what, by common agreement, was evidence of cardinal importance was indefensible and unfair and, as such, a denial of natural justice. But, even so, can it be said that no prejudice to the respondents resulted? [His Lordship found that there was a 'very real possibility' that cross-examination of the department witnesses on the lines projected might have created serious doubts in his mind regarding their traffic forecasts and therefore as to whether need for the motorways had been established and those doubts ... could well have led him to different conclusions and findings.] That the objectors were in truth prejudiced is, in my judgment, clear. Professor Wade has warned (*Administrative Law*, 4th ed, p 454): '... in principle it is vital that the procedure and the merits should be kept strictly apart, since otherwise the merits may be prejudged unfairly' and Lord Wright said in *General Medical Council v Spackman* [1943] AC 627, 644–645:

> If the principles of natural justice are violated in respect of any decision, it is, indeed, immaterial whether the same decision would have been arrived at in the absence of the departure from the essential principles of justice. The decision must be declared to be no decision.

[His Lordship found that the decision should have been quashed.]

Notes

1　The reasoning of the majority is clearly open to criticism. First, no reason was given as to why it was thought that informality of procedure, which it is plausible to suppose, encourages people to participate would be undermined by allowing representatives from the DoE to be questioned. Secondly, the reasoning is arguably contradictory: if the use of the Red Book with its assumptions was not a subject on which criticism should be allowed at all because it was government policy, then on what basis did the inspector allow witnesses to be called to attack that policy, but not allow cross-examination of witnesses defending it? No basis is given for the drawing of such a distinction.

2　This decision, then, seems to leave law in a fairly confused state. Do those arguing that they should have been permitted cross-examination have to prove that they would have derived positive advantage from it? Will a plea of 'policy' always defeat a claim for cross-examination? Do applicants have to prove it was likely that the decision in question would have been different had cross-examination been permitted?

Legal representation

The approach here has been very much to deny any clear 'right' to legal representation except in courts and in certain tribunals (in statutory tribunals, the position is that legal representation should normally be permitted, in the absence of statutory provision to the contrary). This has been so even in cases where the nature of the proceedings in question is virtually identical, for example, the trying of prisoners for disciplinary offences by Boards of Visitors. In *R v Board of Visitors of HM Prison, the Maze ex p Hone* [1988] 1 AC 379, the applicant had been convicted of assaulting prisoner officers at a hearing in which he had had no legal representation. He appealed to the House of

Lords on the question whether legal representation should be available as of right due to the requirements of natural justice. The House of Lords found that in some cases legal representation ought to be allowed but that there was no general right to it. The House of Lords took into account the delay and cost of obtaining legal advice which the House thought would be prejudicial to the administration of discipline in the prison, and also that, once granted, it would be difficult to deny the right in governors' hearings. If legal advice were imported into governors' hearings it was thought that difficulties would arise as such hearings would not be sufficiently expeditious.

In another prisoners' rights case, *R v Secretary of State for the Home Dept ex p Tarrant* [1984] 2 WLR 613; [1985] QB 251, the court put forward a number of factors which it said the Board of Visitors ought to consider in deciding in its discretion whether to grant permission for legal advice. These were (a) the seriousness of the charge and of the penalty, (b) the likelihood that points of law might be likely to arise, (c) the ability of the prisoner to conduct his own case, and (d) the need for speed in making the adjudication. In less serious cases, clearly it will be very difficult to claim a right to legal advice. Thus, for example, in *Pett v Greyhound Racing Association Ltd (No 2)* [1970] 1 QB 46, a greyhound owner was facing a serious disciplinary charge after traces of drugs had been found in his dog's urine. It was found that he had not been entitled to legal representation despite the clear threat to his livelihood and reputation.

The rule against bias

One of the two rules of natural justice, *nemo judex in causa sua*, is commonly expressed to forbid bias on the part of the decision-maker. It is now clear that there are two basic classes of bias: direct and indirect interests on the part of the decision-maker in the case in question, though the dividing line between the two will not always be clear. In the former type of case, once it is shown that the direct interest was present, the judge is automatically disqualified from hearing the case; in the second kind of case, it is not enough to show that the interest was there. It must be shown that the presence of the interest was such as to cause a fair-minded observer to conclude that there was a real danger that the decision-maker was biased.

Direct interest

The simplest cases are those in which the decision-maker has some financial interest in the outcome. If the decision-maker has such an interest – that is, he stands to profit if the case is decided one way but not another – there is no need for the challenger to show that there was any actual risk of the financial interest influencing the outcome of the decision; he or she simply has to show that the decision-maker has a financial interest in the outcome of the decision. If he or she can show this, this will automatically invalidate the decision. In the leading case, *Dimes v Grand Junction Canal Co Proprietors* [1852] 3 HLC 759, a decision of the Lord Chancellor was set aside because he owned shares in one of the parties. The House of Lords made a point of stressing that they did not believe that the Lord Chancellor had in fact been influenced by his ownership of shares, but that this was not the point.

As Lord Goff commented in *R v Gough* [1993] AC 646:

In such a case therefore, not only is it irrelevant that there was in fact no bias on the part of the tribunal, but there is no question of investigating, from an objective point of view, whether there was any real likelihood of bias, or any reasonable suspicion of bias, on the facts of the particular case. The nature of the interest is such that public confidence in the administrating of justice requires that the decision should not stand.

This principle still remains. The same rule will apply if it is a close relative of the decision-maker who has the interest. However, as the Court of Appeal stressed in the recent case of *Locabail (UK) Ltd v Bayfield Properties Ltd* [2000] QB 451, 'the link had to be so close and direct as to render the interest of that other person for all practical purposes indistinguishable from an interest of the judge'. The rule is also subject to a *de minimis* exception: if the financial interest is so small or slight that it could not reasonably be thought to have any chance of affecting the judge's mind, it will be ignored (at 473).[55]

Until recently, it was considered that it was only financial interests that gave rise to automatic disqualification. However, the case of *R v Bow Street Metropolitan Stipendiary Magistrate and Others ex p Pinochet Ugarte (No 2)* [2000] 1 AC 119 has added another category. The background to the case was the arrest in the UK of Senator Pinochet, after Spain had requested that he be extradited to Spain to face charges of torture, extra-judicial killings, kidnapping and 'disappearances'. The House of Lords heard an appeal from a challenge by Pinochet against his continuing detention. Pinochet argued that, as a former head of state, he was immune from prosecution and extradition. During the hearing of this case, Amnesty International was given leave to intervene and argued that no immunity should be granted to Pinochet. The House of Lords decided 3:2 that he was not immune, meaning that the extradition process could proceed. One of the judges who voted against immunity was Lord Hoffman. It then transpired that Lord Hoffman was a Director and Chairperson of Amnesty International Charity Limited (AICL), a registered charity incorporated to undertake those aspects of the work of Amnesty International Limited (AI) which are charitable under UK law. In other words, he was a director of an organisation which was, as Lord Browne-Wilkinson found in *Pinochet*, 'a constituent part' of Amnesty International, one of the actual parties to the appeal. Pinochet then petitioned the House of Lords to set aside its own earlier judgment on the grounds of an appearance of bias on the part of Lord Hoffman.

R v Bow Street Metropolitan Stipendiary Magistrate and Others ex p Pinochet Ugarte (No 2) [2000] I AC I 19 (extracts)

Lord Browne-Wilkinson: ... In my judgment, this case falls within the first category of case, viz where the judge is disqualified because he is a judge in his own cause. In such a case, once it is shown that the judge is himself a party to the cause, or has a relevant interest in its subject matter, he is disqualified without any investigation into whether there was a likelihood or suspicion of bias. The mere fact of his interest is sufficient to disqualify him unless he has made sufficient disclosure ... I will call this 'automatic disqualification.'

... By seeking to intervene in this appeal and being allowed so to intervene, in practice AI became a party to the appeal. Therefore if, in the circumstances, it is right to treat Lord Hoffmann as being the alter ego of AI and therefore a judge in his own cause, then he must have been automatically

---

55 The cases cited in support of this are *BTR Industries South Africa (Pty) Ltd v Metal and Allied Workers' Union* 3 SA 673, 694 (1992); *R v Inner West London Coroner ex p Dallaglio* [1994] 4 All ER 139, 162; *Auckland Casino Ltd v Casino Control Authority* [1995] 1 NZLR 142, 148.

disqualified on the grounds that he was a party to the appeal. Alternatively, even if it be not right to say that Lord Hoffmann was a party to the appeal as such, the question then arises whether, in non-financial litigation, anything other than a financial or proprietary interest in the outcome is sufficient automatically to disqualify a man from sitting as judge in the cause.

Are the facts such as to require Lord Hoffmann to be treated as being himself a party to this appeal? [His Lordship found that Lord Hoffman himself could not be treated as personally being a party to the appeal and went on:]

Then is this a case in which it can be said that Lord Hoffmann had an 'interest' which must lead to his automatic disqualification? Hitherto only pecuniary and proprietary interests have led to automatic disqualification. But, as I have indicated, this litigation is most unusual. It is not civil litigation but criminal litigation. Most unusually, by allowing AI to intervene, there is a party to a criminal cause or matter who is neither prosecutor nor accused. That party, AI, shares with the government of Spain and the CPS, not a financial interest but an interest to establish that there is no immunity for ex-heads of state in relation to crimes against humanity. The interest of these parties is to procure Senator Pinochet's extradition and trial, a non-pecuniary interest. So far as AICL is concerned, clause 3(c) of its memorandum provides that one of its objects is 'to procure the abolition of torture, extra-judicial execution and disappearance.' AI has, amongst other objects, the same objects. Although AICL, as a charity, cannot campaign to change the law, it is concerned by other means to procure the abolition of these crimes against humanity. In my opinion, therefore, AICL plainly had a non-pecuniary interest, to establish that Senator Pinochet was not immune.

That being the case, the question is whether in the very unusual circumstances of this case a non-pecuniary interest to achieve a particular result is sufficient to give rise to automatic disqualification and, if so, whether the fact that AICL had such an interest necessarily leads to the conclusion that Lord Hoffmann, as a director of AICL, was automatically disqualified from sitting on the appeal? My Lords, in my judgment, although the cases have all dealt with automatic disqualification on the grounds of pecuniary interest, there is no good reason in principle for so limiting automatic disqualification. The rationale of the whole rule is that a man cannot be a judge in his own cause. In civil litigation the matters in issue will normally have an economic impact; therefore a judge is automatically disqualified if he stands to make a financial gain as a consequence of his own decision of the case. But if, as in the present case, the matter at issue does not relate to money or economic advantage but is concerned with the promotion of the cause, the rationale disqualifying a judge applies just as much if the judge's decision will lead to the promotion of a cause in which the judge is involved together with one of the parties. Thus in my opinion if Lord Hoffmann had been a member of AI he would have been automatically disqualified because of his non-pecuniary interest in establishing that Senator Pinochet was not entitled to immunity ...

Can it make any difference that, instead of being a direct member of AI, Lord Hoffmann is a director of AICL, that is of a company which is wholly controlled by AI and is carrying on much of its work? Surely not. The substance of the matter is that AI, AIL and AICL are all various parts of an entity or movement working in different fields towards the same goals. If the absolute impartiality of the judiciary is to be maintained, there must be a rule which automatically disqualifies a judge who is involved, whether personally or as a director of a company, in promoting the same causes in the same organisation as is a party to the suit. There is no room for fine distinctions if Lord Hewart CJ's famous dictum is to be observed: it is 'of fundamental importance that justice should not only be done, but should manifestly and undoubtedly be seen to be done:' see R v Sussex Justices, Ex parte McCarthy [1924] 1 KB 256, 259.

... It is important not to overstate what is being decided. It was suggested in argument that a decision setting aside the order of 25 November 1998 would lead to a position where judges would be unable to sit on cases involving charities in whose work they are involved. It is suggested that, because of such involvement, a judge would be disqualified. That is not correct. The facts of this present case are exceptional. The critical elements are (1) that AI was a party to the appeal; (2)

that AI was joined in order to argue for a particular result; (3) the judge was a director of a charity closely allied to AI and sharing, in this respect, AI's objects. Only in cases where a judge is taking an active role as trustee or director of a charity which is closely allied to and acting with a party to the litigation should a judge normally be concerned either to recuse himself or disclose the position to the parties. However, there may well be other exceptional cases in which the judge would be well advised to disclose a possible interest.

Lord Goff of Chieveley: ... Your Lordships are concerned with a case in which a judge is closely connected with a party to the proceedings ... The question which arises is whether his connection with that party will (subject to waiver) itself disqualify him from sitting as a judge in the proceedings, in the same way as a significant shareholding in a party will do, and so require that the order made upon the outcome of the proceedings must be set aside. Such a question could in theory arise, for example, in relation to a senior executive of a body which is a party to the proceedings, who holds no shares in that body; but it is, I believe, only conceivable that it will do so where the body in question is a charitable organisation. He will by reason of his position be committed to the well-being of the charity, and to the fulfilment by the charity of its charitable objects. He may for that reason properly be said to have an interest in the outcome of the litigation, though he has no financial interest, and so to be disqualified from sitting as a judge in the proceedings. The cause is 'a cause in which he has an interest,' in the words of Lord Campbell in the *Dimes* case, at p 793. It follows that in this context the relevant interest need not be a financial interest.

... AI, AIL and AICL can together be described as being, in practical terms, one organisation, of which AICL forms part. The effect for present purposes is that Lord Hoffmann, as chairperson of one member of that organisation, AICL, is so closely associated with another member of that organisation, AI, that he can properly be said to have an interest in the outcome of proceedings to which AI has become party ... It follows that Lord Hoffmann had an interest in the outcome of the present proceedings and so was disqualified from sitting as a judge in those proceedings.

Lord Hope: ... It seems to me that the conclusion is inescapable that Amnesty International has associated itself in these proceedings with the position of the prosecutor. The prosecution is not being brought in its name, but its interest in the case is to achieve the same result because it also seeks to bring Senator Pinochet to justice. This distinguishes its position fundamentally from that of other bodies which seek to uphold human rights without extending their objects to issues concerning personal responsibility. It has for many years conducted an international campaign against those individuals whom it has identified as having been responsible for torture, extra-judicial executions and disappearances. Its aim is that they should be made to suffer criminal penalties for such gross violations of human rights. It has chosen, by its intervention in these proceedings, to bring itself face to face with one of those individuals against whom it has for so long campaigned.

... I think that the connections which existed between Lord Hoffmann and Amnesty International were of such a character, in view of their duration and proximity, as to disqualify him on this ground. In view of his links with Amnesty International as the chairman and a director of Amnesty International Charity Ltd. he could not be seen to be impartial. There has been no suggestion that he was actually biased. He had no financial or pecuniary interest in the outcome. But his relationship with Amnesty International was such that he was, in effect, acting as a judge in his own cause. I consider that his failure to disclose these connections leads inevitably to the conclusion that the decision to which he was a party must be set aside.

Notes

1   The principle laid down in this case is not as clear as it could be, partly because four different speeches were given. However, it appears that there is a clear narrow *ratio* from the case. The narrow rule established is that:

If the absolute impartiality of the judiciary is to be maintained, there must be a rule which automatically disqualifies a judge who is involved, whether personally or as a Director of a company, in promoting the same causes in the same organisation as is a party to the suit ([2000] 1 AC 119, 135, per Lord Browne-Wilkinson).

In other words, Lord Hoffman was a director of an organisation that was a constituent part of one of the parties to the appeal. That party to the appeal clearly had an interest in the outcome, that is, it wanted it to be established that Pinochet was not immune from prosecution. Since Lord Hoffman was the director of an organisation which in effect was a party to the appeal and had an interest in a particular outcome, he must be automatically disqualified. So the narrow, clear rule is confined to cases where a judge belongs to and has the same interest as an organisation *which is a party to the hearing*. That is clear.

2   But is there a wider principle established? Suppose a judge had an interest in the outcome of a hearing because he belonged to an organisation which campaigned on the matter: would he still be treated as automatically disqualified? On the whole, the case suggests that it is only where the organisation concerned is actually a party to the hearing that the automatic disqualification rule should apply. Indeed, Lord Browne-Wilkinson seemed concerned to make it clear that the principle in the *Pinochet* case should not be extended too widely. He said that some were voicing fears that judges could not hear cases involving charities for whom they work. In response, he said quite clearly:

Only in cases where a judge is taking an active role as trustee or Director of a charity which is closely allied to *and acting with a party to the litigation* should a judge normally be concerned either to recuse himself or disclose the position to the parties [at 136].

However, in the Court of Appeal decision in *Locabail*, which heard a number of appeals on bias grounds, the Court said:

The automatic disqualification rule until recently, had widely, if wrongly, been thought to apply only in cases of a judge's pecuniary or proprietary interest in the outcome of the litigation. [*Pinochet*] made it plain that the rule extended to a limited class of non-financial interests, such as an interest in the subject matter in issue arising from the judge's promotion of some particular cause.

This does not add the vital qualification that the automatic rule applies only where the judge has the same interest as one of the parties to the case. So the matter has not been left absolutely free of doubt, but of course, *Pinochet* is a House of Lords' decision and there are numerous passages in the case which suggest that the fact that AI was a party to the case was crucial to the automatic rule.

3   For comment and criticism of the *Pinochet* decision, see K Malleson, 'Judicial bias and disqualification after *Pinochet (No 2)*' (2000) 63 MLR 119 and A Olowofoyeku, 'The *nemo judex* rule: the case against automatic disqualification' [2000] PL 456.

Rule against bias: indirect interests

In contrast to the position with 'direct interests' where the automatic disqualification rule applies, where the interest is 'indirect', it had always been the position that it must be shown that there was, objectively, some risk, or danger of bias, or that there could be a reasonable apprehension of such a danger. Until recently, the leading case on this was *R v Gough* [1993] AC 646. The approach it set out has since been modified (below) but it is important to appreciate the reasoning behind it. The case arose from the discovery (after the trial) by a member of the jury in the trial of the appellant that she lived next door to the appellant's brother. Lord Goff considered whether the authorities established that there were two rival and alternative tests for bias, which could be termed the reasonable suspicion test and the real likelihood test.

R v Gough [1993] AC 646, 668 (extract)

Lord Goff: In conclusion, I wish to express my understanding of the law as follows. I think it possible, and desirable, that the same test should be applicable in all cases of apparent bias, whether concerned with justices or members of other inferior tribunals, or with jurors, or with arbitrators. Likewise I consider that, in cases concerned with jurors, the same test should be applied by a judge to whose attention the possibility of bias on the part of a juror has been drawn in the course of a trial, and by the Court of Appeal when it considers such a question on appeal. Furthermore, I think it unnecessary, in formulating the appropriate test, to require that the court should look at the matter through the eyes of a reasonable man, because the court in cases such as these personifies the reasonable man; and in any event the court has first to ascertain the relevant circumstances from the available evidence, knowledge of which would not necessarily be available to an observer in court at the relevant time. Finally, for the avoidance of doubt I prefer to state the test in terms of real danger rather than real likelihood, to ensure that the court is thinking in terms of possibility rather than probability of bias. Accordingly, having ascertained the relevant circumstances, the court should ask itself whether, having regard to those circumstances, there was a real danger of bias on the part of the relevant member of the tribunal in question, in the sense that he might unfairly regard (or have unfairly regarded) with favour, or disfavour, the case of a party to the issue under consideration by him; though, in a case concerned with bias on the part of a justices' clerk, the court should go on to consider whether the clerk has been invited to give the justices advice and, if so, whether it should infer that there was a real danger of the clerk's bias having infected the views of the justices adversely to the applicant.

Note

Although the following case has been superseded by *Porter v Magill* [2002] 2 AC 357 as a definitive statement of the law, it contains very useful general guidance on the circumstances in which the courts are likely to find a reasonable apprehension of bias, as well as some practical examples, in the five cases considered. It is also valuable for its guidance on when the *Dimes/Pinochet* automatic disqualification test should apply, and when the reasonable apprehension of bias test is applicable. The decision gave judgments in five cases; for reasons of space, the extract below considers those given in the first three only.

Locabail (UK) Ltd v Bayfield Properties Ltd [2000] 2 WLR 870, CA (extracts)

In the first two cases [*Locabail (UK) Ltd v Bayfield Properties Ltd and Another; Locabail (UK) Ltd and Another v Waldorf Investment Corporation and Others*] [the actions were heard by] a solicitor, the senior partner in a large firm of solicitors [Herbert Smith], sitting as a deputy judge of the High Court. During the hearing E produced material relating to her matrimonial proceedings which included a press cutting from which the judge learnt that his firm was acting for clients in litigation for the enforcement of financial claims and of bankruptcy against E's former husband [Sudoexport and Howard Holdings Inc]. The judge immediately disclosed that connection, stating that he knew no more of that litigation than had appeared from the cutting. Neither party sought an adjournment, no objection was raised and the hearing continued. The judge gave judgment for the plaintiffs and thereafter E applied to the judge to disqualify himself from further involvement in the cases and to set aside his judgment on the ground of bias. The judge concluded that his firm's engagement to clients involved in litigation against E's former husband had not created a conflict of interest such as to disqualify him from dealing with the cases and he accordingly refused her application.

In the third case [*Timmins v Gormley*] the defendant admitted liability for personal injuries sustained by the claimant but disputed the quantum of damage. Trial of that issue was heard by a member of the Bar, sitting as a recorder, who was a specialist practitioner in personal injury cases and had, by regular contributions to specialist literature, shown consistent support for claimants in obtaining damages from defendants and their insurers ... Following judgment in the claimant's favour the defendant learnt of an article written by the recorder and published shortly after trial in which he had expressed views in trenchant terms in favour of claimants and critical of defendants and their insurers.

Lord Woolf MR and Sir Richard Scott V-C [giving the judgment of the court:]

... It would be dangerous and futile to attempt to define or list the factors which may or may not give rise to a real danger of bias. Everything will depend on the facts, which may include the nature of the issue to be decided. We cannot, however, conceive of circumstances in which an objection could be soundly based on the religion, ethnic or national origin, gender, age, class, means or sexual orientation of the judge. Nor, at any rate ordinarily, could an objection be soundly based on the judge's social or educational or service or employment background or history, nor that of any member of the judge's family; or previous political associations; or membership of social or sporting or charitable bodies; or Masonic associations; or previous judicial decisions; or extra-curricular utterances (whether in textbooks, lectures, speeches, articles, interviews, reports or responses to consultation papers); or previous receipt of instructions to act for or against any party, solicitor or advocate engaged in a case before him; or membership of the same Inn, circuit, local Law Society or chambers ... By contrast, a real danger of bias might well be thought to arise if there were personal friendship or animosity between the judge and any member of the public involved in the case; or if the judge were closely acquainted with any member of the public involved in the case, particularly if the credibility of that individual could be significant in the decision of the case; or if, in a case where the credibility of any individual were an issue to be decided by the judge, he had in a previous case rejected the evidence of that person in such outspoken terms as to throw doubt on his ability to approach such person's evidence with an open mind on any later occasion; or if on any question at issue in the proceedings before him the judge had expressed views, particularly in the course of the hearing, in such extreme and unbalanced terms as to throw doubt on his ability to try the issue with an objective judicial mind (see *Vakauta v Kelly* (1989) 167 CLR 568); or if, for any other reason, there were real ground for doubting the ability of the judge to ignore extraneous considerations, prejudices and predilections and bring an objective judgment to bear on the issues before him. The mere fact that a judge, earlier in the same case or in a previous case, had commented adversely on a party or witness, or found the evidence of a party or witness to be unreliable, would not without more found a sustainable objection. In most cases, we think, the answer, one way or the other, will be obvious. But if in any case there is real ground for doubt, that doubt should be resolved in favour of recusal. We repeat: every application must be decided on the facts and circumstances of the individual case. The greater the passage of time between the event relied on as showing a danger of bias and the case in which the objection is raised, the weaker (other things being equal) the objection will be.

We do not consider that waiver, in this context, raises special problems ... If, appropriate disclosure having been made by the judge, a party raises no objection to the judge hearing or continuing to hear a case, that party cannot thereafter complain of the matter disclosed as giving rise to a real danger of bias. It would be unjust to the other party and undermine both the reality and the appearance of justice to allow him to do so.

[Their Lordships then moved to give judgments in the cases before them:]

Locabail (UK) Ltd v Bayfield Properties Ltd and Another; Locabail (UK) Ltd and Another v Waldorf Investment Corporation and Others

This is not a case in which actual bias on the part of the deputy judge is alleged. Is it a case in which the judge has a sufficient pecuniary or proprietary interest in the outcome of the trial so as to attract the automatic disqualification principle expressed in the *Dimes* case, 3 HL Cas 759? It was suggested by Miss Williamson [for the applicants] that this was a case to which the Dimes case applied. Her argument went like this. The deputy judge is a partner in Herbert Smith. Herbert Smith was acting for Sudoexport and Howard Holdings Inc in litigation against Mr Emmanuel. Success in achieving the maximum possible recovery from Mr Emmanuel would enhance the goodwill of Herbert Smith and thereby tend to increase its profits. The deputy judge would share in the firm's profits ... In our judgment this is not a case to which the *Dimes* principle of automatic disqualification applies. The *Gough* test must be applied and the court must ask itself whether 'in the circumstances of the case ... it appears that there was a real likelihood, in the sense of a real possibility, of bias' on the part of the deputy judge: see [1993] AC 646, 668, *per* Lord Goff.

In answering this question, the court must take into account the actual facts as disclosed by the evidence and, in particular, what it was that the judge knew at the time the case was being heard ...

In the present case, the deputy judge told the parties, when he made the disclosure on 28 October 1998, that he knew no more of the litigation in which Herbert Smith were acting than was disclosed by the article. No one then or since has suggested that that was not true ... In our view, once the hypothesis that the judge 'did not know of the connection' is accepted, the answer, unless the case is one to which the *Dimes* case applies, becomes obvious. How can there be any real danger of bias, or any real apprehension or likelihood of bias, if the judge does not know of the facts that, in argument, are relied on as giving rise to the conflict of interest?

Timmins v Gormley

The defendant's case on bias ... turns on the statements that the recorder made in the articles to which we have referred. It is not inappropriate for a judge to write in publications of the class to which the recorder contributed. The publications are of value to the profession and for a lawyer of the recorder's experience to contribute to those publications can further rather than hinder the administration of justice. There is a long established tradition that the writing of books and articles or the editing of legal textbooks is not incompatible with holding judicial office and the discharge of judicial functions. There is nothing improper in the recorder being engaged in his writing activities. It is the tone of the recorder's opinions and the trenchancy with which they were expressed which is challenged here. Anyone writing in an area in which he sits judicially has to exercise considerable care not to express himself in terms which indicate that he has preconceived views which are so firmly held that it may not be possible for him to try a case with an open mind. This is the position notwithstanding the fact that, as Mr Edis submits, there can be very real advantages in having a judge adjudicate in the area of law in which he specialises. But if this is to happen it must be recognised that his opinions as to particular features of the subject will become known. The specialist judge must therefore be circumspect in the language he uses and the tone in which he expresses himself. It is always inappropriate for a judge to use intemperate language about subjects on which he has adjudicated or will have to adjudicate.

... We have found this a difficult and anxious application to resolve. There is no suggestion of actual bias on the part of the recorder. Nor, quite rightly, is any imputation made as to his good faith. His voluntary disclosure of the matters already referred to show that he was conscious of his judicial duty. The views he expressed in the articles relied on are no doubt shared by other experienced commentators. We have, however, to ask, taking a broad common sense approach, whether a person holding the pronounced pro-claimant anti-insurer views expressed by the recorder in the articles might not unconsciously have leaned in favour of the claimant and against the defendant in resolving the factual issues between them. Not without misgiving, we conclude that there was on the facts here a real danger of such a result. We do not think a lay observer with knowledge of the facts could have excluded that possibility, and nor can we. We accordingly grant permission to appeal on this ground, allow the defendant's appeal and order a retrial.

Note

The test for indirect bias established in *Gough* and applied in *Locabail* fell to be reassessed in the light of the coming into force of the Human Rights Act 1998, which makes Article 6 of the ECHR – the right to a fair trial – binding upon all UK public authorities who are determining a person's 'civil rights and obligations'. The recent Court of Appeal decision in *Director General of Fair Trading v Proprietary Association of*

Great Britain and Proprietary Articles Trade Association [2001] 1 WLR 700, also known as *Medicaments and Related Classes of Goods (No 2)*, contains an exhaustive analysis of Strasbourg case law on bias, under Article 6(1).

> ... **83** We would summarise the principles to be derived from the [Strasbourg] line of cases as follows:
>
> (1) If a judge is shown to have been influenced by actual bias, his decision must be set aside.
>
> (2) Where actual bias has not been established the personal impartiality of the judge is to be presumed.
>
> (3) The court then has to decide whether, on an objective appraisal, the material facts give rise to a legitimate fear that the judge might not have been impartial. If they do the decision of the judge must be set aside.
>
> (4) The material facts are not limited to those which were apparent to the applicant. They are those which are ascertained upon investigation by the court.
>
> (5) An important consideration in making an objective appraisal of the facts is the desirability that the public should remain confident in the administration of justice.
>
> **84** This approach comes close to that in *Gough*. The difference is that when the Strasbourg court considers whether the material circumstances give rise to a reasonable apprehension of bias, it makes it plain that it is applying an objective test to the circumstances, not passing judgment on the likelihood that the particular tribunal under review was in fact biased.

Note

The leading case on this issue is now the House of Lords' decision in *Porter v Magill* [2002] 2 AC 357. The background facts appear above, at pp 719–20. The issue of bias arose because of the role of the district auditor, Magill, in investigating the 'home for votes' scandal in Westminster City Council, and in particular the statutory liability for wilful misconduct of Porter and others personally to make good the losses sustained by the Council as a result of the unlawful sale of Council houses, a liability of several million pounds. In particular, the auditor was said, in effect, to combine the roles of investigator, prosecutor and judge. Moreover, in the press conference he gave in which he announced his preliminary findings, he was said to have effectively prejudged the issue and made it clear that, although he had not yet reached a final conclusion, his mind was effectively made up. This was argued to raise issues both under the common law of bias and to preclude the auditor from being an independent and impartial tribunal under Article 6(1) of the ECHR (above). It was found that the issue under Article 6(1) was satisfactorily answered by there being a full statutory right of appeal against the district auditor's findings to the High Court, which clearly did satisfy the requirements of Article 6(1). Lord Hope dealt with the issue of common law bias, taking the opportunity to lay down a general modification of the *Gough* test.

Porter v Magill [2002] 2 AC 357, 493–95 (extracts)

Lord Hope: ... The 'reasonable likelihood' and 'real danger' tests which Lord Goff described in *R v Gough* have been criticised by the High Court of Australia on the ground that they tend to emphasise the court's view of the facts and to place inadequate emphasis on the public perception of the irregular incident: *Webb v The Queen* (1994) 181 CLR 41, 50, per Mason CJ and McHugh J. [The Scottish court's] approach, which has been described as 'the reasonable apprehension of bias' test, is in line with that adopted in most common law jurisdictions. It is also in line with that which the Strasbourg court has adopted, which looks at the question whether there was a risk of bias objectively in the light of the circumstances which the court has identified.

The English courts have been reluctant, for obvious reasons, to depart from the test which Lord Goff of Chieveley so carefully formulated in *R v Gough*. ... [But] in my opinion however it is now possible to set this debate to rest. [His Lordship considered the findings of the Court of Appeal in *Re Medicaments* (quoted above) ending with the following quote from that decision:]

85. When the Strasbourg jurisprudence is taken into account, we believe that a modest adjustment of the test in *Gough* is called for, which makes it plain that it is, in effect, no different from the test applied in most of the Commonwealth and in Scotland. The court must first ascertain all the circumstances which have a bearing on the suggestion that the judge was biased. It must then ask whether those circumstances would lead a fair-minded and informed observer to conclude that there was a real possibility, or a real danger, the two being the same, that the tribunal was biased.

I respectfully suggest that your Lordships should now approve the modest adjustment of the test in *R v Gough* set out in that paragraph. It expresses in clear and simple language a test which is in harmony with the objective test which the Strasbourg court applies when it is considering whether the circumstances give rise to a reasonable apprehension of bias. It removes any possible conflict with the test which is now applied in most Commonwealth countries and in Scotland. I would however delete from it the reference to 'a real danger'. Those words no longer serve a useful purpose here, and they are not used in the jurisprudence of the Strasbourg court. The question is whether the fair-minded and informed observer, having considered the facts, would conclude that there was a real possibility that the tribunal was biased.

Turning to the facts ... I think that it is plain, as the Divisional Court observed, at p 174b, that the auditor made an error of judgment when he decided to make his statement in public at a press conference. The main impression which this would have conveyed to the fair-minded observer was that the purpose of this exercise was to attract publicity to himself, and perhaps also to his firm. It was an exercise in self-promotion in which he should not have indulged. But it is quite another matter to conclude from this that there was a real possibility that he was biased. Schiemann LJ said, at p 1457d–e, that there was room for a casual observer to form the view after the press conference that the auditor might be biased. Nevertheless he concluded, at p 1457h, having examined the facts more closely, that there was no real danger that this was so. I would take the same view. The question is what the fair-minded and informed observer would have thought, and whether his conclusion would have been that there was real possibility of bias. The auditor's conduct must be seen in the context of the investigation which he was carrying out, which had generated a great deal of public interest. A statement as to his progress would not have been inappropriate. His error was to make it at a press conference. This created the risk of unfair reporting, but there was nothing in the words he used to indicate that there was a real possibility that he was biased. He was at pains to point out to the press that his findings were provisional. There is no reason to doubt his word on this point, as his subsequent conduct demonstrates. I would hold, looking at the matter objectively, that a real possibility that he was biased has not been demonstrated.

IRRATIONALITY

The conceptual basis of the doctrine

It must be stated at the outset that some confusion exists as to whether this is a kind of mixed-bag category, which encompasses a number of diverse matters such as improper considerations, basing a decision on no evidence, etc or properly speaking refers only to 'pure unreasonableness'. Indeed, this may be because, in fact, unreasonableness or irrationality as a wholly separate head arguably has no independent conceptual life, and, unless made more substantive in its scope, may as well be subsumed into 'illegality', a point returned to below. Lord Diplock's formulation of this head in the *GCHQ* case [1985] AC 374, 410 (in which he referred to it as 'irrationality') was as follows:

By 'irrationality' I mean what can by now be succinctly referred to as '*Wednesbury* unreasonableness ...' It applies to a decision which is so outrageous in its defiance of logic or of accepted moral standards that no sensible person who had applied his mind to the question to be decided could have arrived at it.

The notion of unreasonableness, as indicated, found its genesis in the following decision.

Associated Provincial Picture Houses v Wednesbury Corporation [1948] 1 KB 223, 228–29, 231, CA

The Wednesbury Corporation had power to grant licences for the opening of cinemas on Sundays 'subject to such conditions as the authority think fit to impose'. The Corporation imposed a condition in a Sunday licence that no children under 15 should be admitted to the cinema.

Lord Greene MR: When discretion of this kind is granted, the law recognises certain principles upon which that discretion must be exercised, but within the four corners of those principles the discretion, in my opinion, is an absolute one and cannot be questioned in any court of law.

It is true the discretion must be exercised reasonably. Now what does that mean? Lawyers familiar with the phraseology commonly used in relation to exercise of statutory discretions often use the word 'unreasonable' in a rather comprehensive sense. It has frequently been used and is frequently used as a general description of the things that must not be done. For instance, a person entrusted with a discretion must, so to speak, direct himself properly in law. He must call his own attention to the matters which he is bound to consider. He must exclude from his consideration matters which are irrelevant to what he has to consider. If he does not obey those rules, he may truly be said, and often is said, to be acting 'unreasonably'. Similarly, there may be something so absurd that no sensible person could ever dream that it lay within the powers of the authority.

It appears to me quite clear that the matter dealt with by this condition was a matter which a reasonable authority would be justified in considering when they were making up their mind what condition should be attached to the grant of this licence. Nobody, at this time of day, could say that the well-being and the physical and moral health of children is not a matter which a local authority, in exercising theirs powers, can properly have in mind when those questions are germane to what they have to consider. Here Mr Gallop [for the plaintiff] did not, I think, suggest that the council were directing their mind to a purely extraneous and irrelevant matter, but he based his argument on the word 'unreasonable', which he treated as an independent ground for attacking the decision of the authority; but once it is conceded, as it must be conceded in this case, that the particular subject-matter dealt with by this condition was one which it was competent for the authority to consider, there, in my opinion, is an end of the case. Once that is granted, Mr Gallop is bound to say that the decision of the authority is wrong because it is unreasonable, and in saying that he is really saying that the ultimate arbiter of what is and is not reasonable is the court and not the local authority. It is just there, it seems to me, that the argument breaks down. It is clear that the local authority are entrusted by Parliament with the decision on a matter which the knowledge and experience of that authority can best be trusted to deal with. The subject-matter with which the condition deals is one relevant for its consideration. They have considered it and come to a decision upon it. It is true to say that, if a decision on a competent matter is so unreasonable that no reasonable authority could ever have come to it, then the courts can interfere. That, I think, is quite right; but to prove a case of that kind would require something overwhelming, and in this case, the facts do not come anywhere near anything of that kind. I think Mr Gallop in the end agreed that his proposition that the decision of the local authority can be upset if it is proved to be unreasonable, really meant that it must be proved to be unreasonable in the sense that the court considers it to be a decision that no reasonable body could have come to. It is not what the court considers unreasonable, a different thing altogether. If it is what the court considers unreasonable, the court may very well have different views than that of a local authority on matters of high public policy of this kind. Some courts might think that no children ought to be admitted on Sundays at all, some courts might think the reverse, and all over the country I have no doubt on a thing of that sort honest and sincere people hold different views. The effect of the legislation is not to set up the court as an arbiter of the correctness of one view over another. It is the local authority that are set in that position.

The court is entitled to investigate the action of the local authority with a view to seeing whether they have taken into account matters which they ought not to take into account, or, conversely, have refused to take into account or neglected to take into account matters which they ought to take into account. Once that question is answered in favour of the local authority, it may be still possible to say that, although the local authority have kept within the four corners of the matters which they ought to consider, they have nevertheless come to a conclusion so unreasonable that no reasonable authority could ever have come to it. In such a case, again, I think the court can interfere. [His Lordship reiterated that this was not such a case.]

Notes

1   *Wednesbury* is sometimes seen as implying a test of bare rationality. However, it clearly has a substantive dimension, at least in Diplock's reformulation in *GCHQ* (above). As J Jowell and A Lester point out:

Lord Diplock's third ground of review, 'irrationality', identifies a way in which the substance of official decisions may be challenged by the courts. By separating irrationality from illegality, he made the point that even though a decision may be legal (in the sense of being within the scope of the legislative scheme), it may nevertheless be substantively unlawful. In other words, he recognised that the courts may strike down a decision because it offends substantive principles, independent of those provided for by the statute in question. Lord Diplock said as much, defining irrationality as applying to 'a decision which is so outrageous in its defiance of logic or of accepted moral standards that no sensible person who had applied his mind to the question to be decided could have arrived at it.'[56]

An important case in this area is *Wheeler v Leicester City Council* [1985] AC 1054, which concerned the decision of Leicester City Council to withdraw certain facilities from Leicester City Football Club on the ground that it had failed to condemn the 1984 Rugby Tour of South Africa or to discourage its members from playing. The Council had asked the club four questions: does the club support the Government's opposition to the tour; does the Club agree that the tour is an insult to a large proportion of the Leicester population; will the Club press the RFU to call off the tour; will the Club press the players to pull out of the tour? The Council made it clear that only an affirmative answer to all four questions would be acceptable. The stance of the club was that it was a matter of opinion whether a sporting boycott assisted in breaking down apartheid, and that it was a matter of individual conscience for its members whether they took part in the tour.

Wheeler v Leicester City Council [1985] AC 1054, 1077–79, HL

Lord Roskill: The council's main defence rested on s 71 of the Race Relations Act 1976. That section appears as the first section in Part X of the Act under the cross-heading 'Supplemental'. For ease of reference I will set out the section in full:

Without prejudice to their obligation to comply with any other provision of this Act, it shall be the duty of every local authority to make appropriate arrangements with a view to securing that their various functions are carried out with due regard to the need—

(a) to eliminate unlawful racial discrimination; and

---

56 J Jowell and A Lester, 'Beyond *Wednesbury*: substantive principles of administrative law' [1987] PL 368, 369–70.

(b) to promote equality of opportunity, and good relations, between persons of different racial groups.

[His Lordship considered argument on the construction of the statute and concluded:]

I do not doubt that the council were fully entitled in exercising their statutory discretion under, for example, the Open Spaces Act 1906 and the various Public Health Acts, which are all referred to in the judgments below, to pay regard to what they thought was in the best interests of race relations.

The only question is, therefore, whether the action of the council of which the club complains is susceptible of attack by way of judicial review. It was forcibly argued by Mr Sullivan QC for the council, that once it was accepted, as I do accept, that s 71 bears the construction for which the council contended, the matter became one of political judgment only, and that by interfering the courts would be trespassing across that line which divides a proper exercise of a statutory discretion based on a political judgment, in relation to which the courts must not and will not interfere, from an improper exercise of such a discretion in relation to which the courts will interfere.

To my mind the crucial question is whether the conduct of the council in trying by their four questions, whether taken individually or collectively, to force acceptance by the club of their own policy (however proper that policy may be) on their own terms, as for example, by forcing them to lend their considerable prestige to a public condemnation of the tour, can be said either to be so 'unreasonable' as to give rise to 'Wednesbury unreasonableness' or to be so fundamental a breach of the duty to act fairly which rests upon every local authority in matters of this kind and thus justify interference by the courts.

I do not for one moment doubt the great importance which the council attach to the presence in their midst of a 25% population of persons who are either Asian or of Afro-Caribbean origin. Nor do I doubt for one moment the sincerity of the view expressed in Mr Soulsby's affidavit regarding the need for the council to distance itself from bodies who hold important positions and who do not actively discourage sporting contacts with South Africa. Persuasion, even powerful persuasion, is always a permissible way of seeking to obtain an objective. But in a field where other views can equally legitimately be held, persuasion, however powerful, must not be allowed to cross that line where it moves into the field of illegitimate pressure coupled with the threat of sanctions. The four questions, coupled with the insistence that only affirmative answers to all four would be acceptable, are suggestive of more than powerful persuasion. The second question is to my mind open to particular criticism. What, in the context, is meant by 'the club?' The committee? 90 playing members? 4,300 non-playing members? It by no means follows that the committee would all have agreed on an affirmative answer to the question and still less that a majority of their members, playing or non-playing, would have done so. Nor would any of these groups of members necessarily have known whether 'the large proportion', whatever that phrase may mean in the context, of the Leicester population would have regarded the tour as 'an insult' to them.

I greatly hesitate to differ from four learned judges on the Wednesbury issue but for myself I would have been disposed respectfully to do this and say that the actions of the club were unreasonable in the Wednesbury sense.

Note

The following case concerned a challenge by Nottinghamshire County Council to a decision of the Secretary of State for the Environment relating to the rate support grant for the authority. One ground of challenge was that the decision was unreasonable because it was disproportionately disadvantageous to a small group of authorities.

Nottinghamshire County Council v Secretary of State for the Environment
[1986] 2 AC 240, 246–50

Lord Scarman: My Lords, in December 1984 the Secretary of State for the Environment laid before the House of Commons the Rate Support Grant Report (England) for the year 1985–86. In due course the report was approved by resolution of the House. The Secretary of State included in the report (additionally to the matters which he was required by law to specify therein) expenditure guidance to local authorities for that year.

[His Lordship considered the *Wednesbury* submission of the applicants which was] that, even if the guidance complies with the words of the statute, it offends a principle of public law in that the burden which the guidance imposes on some authorities, including Nottingham and Bradford, is so disproportionately disadvantageous when compared with its effect upon others that it is a perversely unreasonable exercise of the power conferred by the statute upon the Secretary of State. The respondents rely on what has become known to lawyers as the 'Wednesbury principles'.

The submission raises an important question as to the limits of judicial review. We are in the field of public financial administration and we are being asked to review the exercise by the Secretary of State of an administrative discretion which inevitably requires a political judgment on his part and which cannot lead to action by him against a local authority unless that action is first approved by the House of Commons.

The Secretary of State's guidance which is challenged was included in the Rate Support Grant Report for 1985–86 which was laid before and approved by the House of Commons [as required by statute].

My Lords, I think that the courts below were absolutely right to decline the invitation to intervene ... I cannot accept that it is constitutionally appropriate, save in very exceptional circumstances, for the courts to intervene on the ground of 'unreasonableness' to quash guidance framed by the Secretary of State and by necessary implication approved by the House of Commons, the guidance being concerned with the limits of public expenditure by local authorities and the incidence of the tax burden as between taxpayers and ratepayers. Unless and until a statute provides otherwise, or it is established that the Secretary of State has abused his power, these are matters of political judgment for him and for the House of Commons. They are not for the judges or your Lordships' House in its judicial capacity.

For myself, I refuse in this case to examine the detail of the guidance or its consequences. My reasons are these. Such an examination by a court would be justified only if a *prima facie* case were to be shown for holding that the Secretary of State had acted in bad faith, or for an improper motive, or that the consequences of his guidance were so absurd that he must have taken leave of his senses. The evidence comes nowhere near establishing any of these propositions. ... It is recognised that the Secretary of State and his advisers were well aware that there would be inequalities in the distribution of the burden between local authorities but believed that the guidance upon which he decided would by discouraging the high spending and encouraging the low spending authorities be the best course of action in the circumstances. And, as my noble and learned friend, Lord Bridge of Harwich, demonstrates, it was guidance which complied with the terms of the statute. This view of the language of the statute has inevitably a significant bearing upon the conclusion of 'unreasonableness' in the *Wednesbury* sense. If, as your Lordships are holding, the guidance was based on principles applicable to all authorities, the principles would have to be either a pattern of perversity or an absurdity of such proportions that the guidance could not have been framed by a *bona fide* exercise of political judgment on the part of the Secretary of State. And it would be necessary to find as a fact that the House of Commons had been misled: for their approval was necessary and was obtained to the action that he proposed to take to implement the guidance.

In my judgment, therefore, the courts below acted with constitutional propriety in rejecting the so-called 'Wednesbury unreasonableness' argument in this case.

Notes

1   In *R (Asif Javed) v Secretary of State for the Home Department* [2001] 3 WLR 323, CA the Court of Appeal held that the House of Lords in *Nottinghamshire* had not laid down any general rule that review of any order approved by Parliament by affirmative resolution would only be proper where there was bad faith or manifest absurdity; they had merely applied the test appropriate for the subject matter before them.

2   The approach of Lord Templeman in the case clearly seems to indicate that in cases such as the one before him, the court should apply a higher threshold of unreasonableness, making it harder for the decision to be found unlawful. Indeed, reading his judgment carefully, it sounds as if even an outrageously immoral or illogical decision would not be subject to review, provided that Parliament had properly approved it and the decision was made in good faith. In *R v Secretary of State for the Environment ex p Hammersmith LBC* [1991] 1 AC 521, another case on economic policy, Lord Bridge held that the decision 'was not open to challenge on grounds of irrationality short of the extremes of bad faith, improper motive or manifest absurdity'. Have these cases laid down that in certain areas of decision-making – for example, matters of economic policy which had been approved by Parliament – a 'super *Wednesbury*' test should be applied? In *R v Ministry of Defence ex p Smith and others* [1995] 4 All ER 427, HL; [1996] 1 All ER 257, CA,[57] which concerned a challenge by homosexual servicemen and women to the ban on homosexuals serving in the armed forces, Simon Browne LJ, without commenting on whether 'super *Wednesbury*' was a legitimate development, considered that it would not in any event apply in a case where like the instant, human rights were at stake; he appeared to believe that national economic policy issues could raise the reasonableness threshold but that the mere fact that the policy in question had been debated by Parliament would not. When the case came to the Court of Appeal, Sir Thomas Bingham MR took a clear stance on the matter.

R v Ministry of Defence ex p Smith and others [1996] 1 All ER 257, 264, CA

Sir Thomas Bingham MR: ... It was argued for the ministry, in reliance on [the *Nottinghamshire* and *Hammersmith*] decisions, above, that a test more exacting than *Wednesbury* was appropriate in this case. The Divisional Court rejected this argument and so do I. The greater the policy content of a decision, and the more remote the subject matter of a decision from ordinary judicial experience, the more hesitant the court must necessarily be in holding a decision to be irrational. That is good law and, like most good law, common sense. Where decisions of a policy-laden, esoteric or security-based nature are in issue, even greater caution than normal must be shown in applying the test, but the test itself is sufficiently flexible to cover all situations.

Notes

1   Aside from doubt over 'super *Wednesbury*', this head of review is, it is submitted, in an unsatisfactory state. Both ways of expressing it appear to reveal muddled judicial thinking. Lord Diplock's definition of irrationality in *Council of Civil Service Unions v Minister for Civil Service* [1985] AC 374 (above) is arguably essentially redundant; it is hard to visualise circumstances in which a decision which is outrageously immoral or illogical would not in any event be seen by the judiciary as being outside the purposes of the Act, and therefore *ultra vires*. The head of irrationality is alternatively expressed as referring to decisions that are so unreasonable that no reasonable man could come to them. Three comments can be made about this definition. First, such decisions would again surely be outside the

---

57   The phrase 'super-*Wednesbury*' originated in this case.

purpose of the parent Act; secondly, as Jowell and Lester argue, the definition is tautologous (a decision is unreasonable if a reasonable man could not have made it).[58] Thirdly, the definition seems to be merely another way of saying that the decision has fallen foul of the test in *Edwards v Bairstow* (above); in other words the decision-maker has come to a conclusion which is not *capable* of being considered correct. It therefore seems arguable that the doctrine of unreasonableness as presently understood adds nothing to the law of judicial review.

2   Recent significant *dicta* of Lord Cooke in a House of Lords' decision[59] indicate the beginnings of open judicial dissatisfaction with the *Wednesbury* test *per se*, though it should be noted that his remarks were not supported by his brethren in the case. They are quoted below in the context of the discussion of proportionality as a possible future head of judicial review.

THE FUTURE DEVELOPMENT OF JUDICIAL REVIEW

One of the main areas in which judicial review has been developing rapidly has been in applying the new head of review introduced by s 6(1) of the Human Rights Act: 'it is unlawful for a public authority to act in way that is incompatible with a Convention right' (that is, a right guaranteed under the European Convention on Human Rights, as defined in s 1 of and Sched 1 to the HRA). This issue is considered in Part VI Chapter 1 but for critical discussion of the application of the proportionality principle in Convention cases under the HRA, see I Leigh, 'Taking rights proportionately: judicial review, the Human Rights Act and Strasbourg' [2002] PL 73.

Aside from the further possible development of protection for substantive legitimate expectations, discussed above, the other main development lying on the horizon is a possible move away from the relatively blunt tool of *Wednesbury* unreasonableness towards the more structured notion of proportionality. This is a very large and complex topic, and only a brief discussion can be essayed here.[60] It should first of all be noted that when the courts are within the scope of application of EU law, they must apply the proportionality principle, which is one of the general principles of EU law.[61] Proportionality is also an established principle within the law of the European Convention on Human Rights;[62] therefore when applying Convention law under the Human Rights Act, the courts will have to deploy the proportionality doctrine here also.[63] The issue therefore is whether proportionality may come to 'spill over' into judicial review in cases not involving either of these areas of law. In other words, may it come to function as a free-standing general head of English judicial review? In *Council of Service Unions v Minister for the Civil Service* [1985] AC 374 (the GCHQ case), Lord Diplock, after his seminal summary of the current heads of judicial

---

58   *Op cit.*

59   *R v Secretary of State for the Home Department ex p Daly* [2001] 2 AC 532, at 549.

60   For further guidance, see J Jowell, 'Beyond the Rule of Law: towards constitutional judicial review' [2000] PL 671; Craig (1999), *op cit*; D Feldman, 'Proportionality and the Human Rights Act 1998', in *The Principle of Proportionality in the Laws of Europe* (1999), pp 117, 127 *et seq*; G Wong, 'Towards the Nutcracker principle: reconsidering the objections to proportionality' [2000] PL 92.

61   For a brief overview, See Craig, *ibid*, pp 595–98; for more extensive discussion, see T Tridimas, *The General Principles of EU Law* (1999), Chapters 3 and 4.

62   See further Part II Chapter 2, pp 245–47.

63   See further Part VI Chapter 1, pp 889–94 and Craig, *ibid*, pp 558–63.

review as illegality, procedural impropriety and irrationality, added, in a well-known passage (at 410):

> That is not to say that further development on a case by case bias may not in course of time add further grounds. I have in mind particularly the possible adoption of future of the principle of proportionality, which is recognised in the administrative law of several of our fellow members of the [EEC].

However, in *Brind and another v Secretary of State for the Home Department* [1991] 1 All ER 720, HL, this possibility appeared to recede. Lord Bridge and Lord Roskill were prepared to leave the possibility open for the future (at 724 and 725), but Lord Ackner thought it should be ruled out, in the absence of its introduction in legislation by Parliament (at 735) and it was also disapproved by Lord Lowry, who observed:

> ... there can be very little room for judges to operate an independent judicial review proportionality doctrine in the space which is left between the conventional judicial review doctrine and the admittedly forbidden appellate approach [ie review on the merits].

These *dicta* appeared to misunderstand the principled basis for the proportionality doctrine, which is *not* the equivalent of 'merits' review. Paul Craig provides a very clear explanation:

P Craig, *Administrative Law*, 4th edn (1999), pp 590–91

It is important at the outset to ascertain the *place* of proportionality within the general scheme of review, and its relationship with other existing methods of control. It is clear, as a matter of principle, that to talk of proportionality at all assumes that the public body was entitled to pursue its desired objective. The presumption is, therefore, that the general objective was a legitimate one, and that the public body was not seeking to achieve an improper purpose. If the purpose was improper then the exercise of discretion should be struck down upon this ground, without any investigation as to whether it was disproportionate. Proportionality should then only be considered once the controls [represented by the existing heads of 'Illegality' review] ... have been satisfied.

Let us turn now to the *meaning* of the concept itself. It is obvious that at a general level proportionality involves some idea of balance between competing interests or objectives, and that it embodies some sense of an appropriate relationship between means and ends. We can, however, go beyond this. There are six steps in any application of proportionality:

(i) The relevant interests must be identified.

(ii) There must be some ascription of weight or value to those interests, since this is a necessary condition precedent to any balancing since this operation.

(iii) Some view must be taken as to whether certain interests can be traded off to achieve other goals at all. Should we, for example, trade off a fundamental right in order to enhance the general economic good? Certain respected theories would answer no [eg modern theories of liberalism espoused by writers such as Rawls and Dworkin].

(iv) A decision must be made as to whether the public body's decision was indeed proportionate or not on the facts of the case in the light of the above considerations. Differing criteria can be used when answering this question. The test could be formulated in a number of ways: is the disputed measure the least restrictive which could be adopted in the circumstances; is the challenged act suitable and necessary for the achievement of its objective, and one which does not impose excessive burdens on the individual; what are the relative costs and benefits of the disputed measure? It will be seen that different formulations tend to be used in different types of case. For example, the first version will commonly be used in cases where the disputed measure is in conflict with a fundamental right. The most common version of the test is, however, the second. This requires the court to go through three stages and ask whether the measure was necessary to achieve the desired objective, whether it was suitable for this end, and whether it none the less imposed excessive burdens on the individual. The last part of this inquiry is often termed proportionality *stricto sensu* [in a strict sense]

(vi) The court will have to decide how intensively it is going to apply any one of the tests mentioned above. It is important to realise that the tests can be applied more or less intensively ...

Note

The most important recent judicial observations on this matter appear in the following case. Lord Steyn's comments are mainly directed towards the approach required under the Human Rights Act 1998, but are of wider interest; Lord Cooke's plainly are of general application.

R v Secretary of State for the Home Department ex p Daly [2001] 2 AC 532, 547, 549

Lord Steyn: ... The contours of the principle of proportionality are familiar. In *de Freitas v Permanent Secretary of Ministry of Agriculture, Fisheries, Lands and Housing* [1999] 1 AC 69 the Privy Council adopted a three stage test. Lord Clyde observed, at p 80, that in determining whether a limitation (by an act, rule or decision) is arbitrary or excessive the court should ask itself:

whether: (i) the legislative objective is sufficiently important to justify limiting a fundamental right; (ii) the measures designed to meet the legislative objective are rationally connected to it; and (iii) the means used to impair the right or freedom are no more than is necessary to accomplish the objective.

Clearly, these criteria are more precise and more sophisticated than the traditional grounds of review. What is the difference for the disposal of concrete cases? The starting point is that there is an overlap between the traditional grounds of review and the approach of proportionality. Most cases would be decided in the same way whichever approach is adopted. But the intensity of review is somewhat greater under the proportionality approach. Making due allowance for important structural differences between various convention rights, which I do not propose to discuss, a few generalisations are perhaps permissible. I would mention three concrete differences without suggesting that my statement is exhaustive. First, the doctrine of proportionality may require the reviewing court to assess the balance which the decision maker has struck, not merely whether it is within the range of rational or reasonable decisions. Secondly, the proportionality test may go further than the traditional grounds of review inasmuch as it may require attention to be directed to the relative weight accorded to interests and considerations. Thirdly, even the heightened scrutiny test developed in *R v Ministry of Defence, Ex p Smith* [1996] QB 517, 554 is not necessarily appropriate to the protection of human rights. It will be recalled that in *Smith* the Court of Appeal reluctantly felt compelled to reject a limitation on homosexuals in the army. The challenge based on article 8 of the Convention for the Protection of Human Rights and Fundamental Freedoms (the right to respect for private and family life) foundered on the threshold required even by the anxious scrutiny test. The European Court of Human Rights came to the opposite conclusion: *Smith and Grady v United Kingdom* (1999) 29 EHRR 493. The court concluded, at p 543, para 138:

the threshold at which the High Court and the Court of Appeal could find the Ministry of Defence policy irrational was placed so high that it effectively excluded any consideration by the domestic courts of the question of whether the interference with the applicants' rights answered a pressing social need or was proportionate to the national security and public order aims pursued, principles which lie at the heart of the court's analysis of complaints under article 8 of the Convention.

In other words, the intensity of the review, in similar cases, is guaranteed by the twin requirements that the limitation of the right was necessary in a democratic society, in the sense of meeting a pressing social need, and the question whether the interference was really proportionate to the legitimate aim being pursued.

The differences in approach between the traditional grounds of review and the proportionality approach may therefore sometimes yield different results. It is therefore important that cases involving convention rights must be analysed in the correct way. This does not mean that there has been a shift to merits review. On the contrary, as Professor Jowell [2000] PL 671, 681 has pointed out the respective roles of judges and administrators are fundamentally distinct and will remain so. To this extent the general tenor of the observations in *Mahmood* [2001] 1 WLR 840 are correct. And Laws LJ rightly emphasised in *Mahmood*, at p 847, para 18, 'that the intensity of review in a public law case will depend on the subject matter in hand'. That is so even in cases involving Convention rights. In law context is everything.

Lord Cooke: ... I think that the day will come when it will be more widely recognised that *Associated Provincial Picture Houses Ltd v Wednesbury Corporation* was an unfortunately retrogressive decision in English administrative law, insofar as it suggested that there are degrees of unreasonableness and that only a very extreme degree can bring an administrative decision within the legitimate scope of judicial invalidation. The depth of judicial review and the deference due to administrative discretion vary with the subject matter. It may well be, however, that the law can never be satisfied in any administrative field merely by a finding that the decision under review is not capricious or absurd.

Notes

1 In *R (on the application of Alconbury Developments) v Secretary of State for the Environment* [2001] 2 WLR 1389; [2001] 2 All ER 929, Lord Slynn observed that 'even without reference to the [HRA] the time has come to recognise that [proportionality] is part of English Administrative law, not only when judges are dealing with [EU law] but also when they are dealing with acts subject to domestic law' (at 976). If *Wednesbury's* days are numbered, as Lord Cooke suggests (it should be noted that his remarks were not endorsed by any of the other Law Lords deciding the case), then the obvious replacement would be some form of proportionality. In *R v Secretary of State for the Home Department ex p Hindley* [2001] 1 AC 410, one of the arguments advanced by the applicant was that the imposition upon her by the Secretary of State of a 'whole life tariff', that is, a sentence that she spend the rest of her natural life in custody was unlawful because it was disproportionate. It is worthy of note that the response of their Lordships to this argument was not simply to observe that proportionality is not a recognised head of review in English law, outside the context of EU and ECHR law; rather it was found merely that, on the facts, the sentence could not be considered disproportionate.[64] Similarly, in *R v Secretary of State for the Environment, Transport and the Regions ex p Spath Holme Limited* [2001] 2 AC 349, one of the arguments advanced was that ministers had acted 'unreasonably, unfairly and disproportionately'; again the argument was not rejected on grounds of principle by their Lordships but simply dealt with on the facts of the case (see at 396, *per* Lord Bingham). While clearly not a positive endorsement of the use of proportionality as a free-standing ground of review, these decisions appear to indicate a much greater readiness to countenance it than was apparent 10 years ago in *Brind* [1991] 1 All ER 720, HL.

2 In a recent article,[65] Mark Elliott has discussed, *inter alia*, the relationship between the *Wednesbury* and proportionality tests. He argues that the two are not, 'as often

---

64 See the speech of Lord Steyn, at 412, and of Lord Hobhouse, at 421: 'I agree with your Lordships that this aspect of the appellant's case fails on the facts.'
65 M Elliott, 'The Human Rights Act 1998 and the standard of substantive review' [2001] CLJ 301.

presented ... radically different types of review', though 'postulating such a clear distinction between the tests is perhaps justifiable when the *Wednesbury* doctrine is considered in its traditional, unreconstructed form'.[66] But when the doctrine appears in the more sophisticated form approved in *Smith* (above)[67] it is apparent that the difference between the two tests is 'one of degree' – the degree of latitude afforded to the decision-maker – not 'of type'.[68] He goes on to identify the ways in which the two doctrines actually necessitate the same stages of enquiry.

M Elliott, 'The Human Rights Act 1998 and the standard of substantive review' [2001] 60(2) CLJ 301, 311–313 (extracts)

[Under *Wednesbury*], as with a proportionality analysis, the court identifies the substantive value which the administrative process appears to have compromised, and requires a competing policy objective to be advanced as justification for the infraction of the identified value. Thus in *Brind*, Lord Bridge said that the court is:

> perfectly entitled to start from the premise that any restriction of the right to freedom of expression requires to be justified and that nothing less than any important competing public interest will be sufficient to justify it [[1991] 1 AC 696, at 748–49].

The distinction between *Wednesbury*, viewed thus, and proportionality only becomes evident at the final stage of the analysis when the court balances the two competing claims against each other.... *Wednesbury* accords to the executive a substantial margin of freedom, thereby permitting judicial intervention only if the lack of balance is so great as to be manifestly unreasonable. In contrast, the proportionality doctrine requires much closer scrutiny of the balance; in turn a much lower level of imbalance is needed in order to trigger intervention by the reviewing court. Although this does not collapse the distinction between appeal and review, it significantly attenuates the administration's capacity to make policy choices which affect those substantive values whose infraction attracts strict scrutiny review.

[The author earlier argues that *Wednesbury* should continue to stand alongside proportionality, for cases other than those raising human rights or EU law points:]

If as the courts evidently believed, it was formerly constitutionally inappropriate for substantive intervention to transcend *Wednesbury* review and if the Human Rights Act cloaks such judicial scrutiny with legitimacy in relation to human rights cases, it is arguable that the ... Act – and, hence, the human rights context – demarcates the legitimate limits within which the proportionality doctrine may be applied. Moreover, it is possible to argue that conceptualising the matter in this way reveals an intelligible legislative policy, according to which Parliament has ordained that a stricter form of substantive review is appropriate within the specific context of fundamental rights ...'

Note

This argument, for the survival of *Wednesbury* in non-HRA or EU law cases, seems sound enough. However, the argument above, that *Wednesbury* and proportionality represent but different degrees of scrutiny on a continuum with each other is more problematic. Elliott argues the point using the version of *Wednesbury* which, precisely, had been marked out by the courts as suitable for use in human rights cases. But since such cases will now be decided under the HRA instead,[69] it is to be presumed that for

---

66 *Ibid*, at 312.
67 *R v Secretary of State for the Home Department ex p Smith* [1996] QB 517 at 554, *per* Lord Bingham; quoted above, p 783.
68 Elliott, *op cit*, at 308.
69 The exception will arise, as Elliott himself points out, where persons wishing to bring a challenge under the HRA cannot satisfy its standing test – in s 7 – which is stricter than that applied in judicial review proceedings generally (see Chapter 1 of this part, pp 695–701, and on s 7 of the HRA, Part VI Chapter 1, at p 873).

cases which do not raise such fundamental rights, the courts will continue to use the traditional *Wednesbury* test, which, Elliott concedes, is 'highly unsatisfactory, because it fails to expose the structure and underlying values of the judicial reasoning process which necessarily precedes a finding of unreasonableness'.[70] In other words, Elliott's argument for the partial equivalence of the two tests rests upon arguments based on a version of *Wednesbury* that is probably now otiose.

FURTHER READING

See Part V Chapter 1.

---

70 Elliott, *op cit*, at 312. Elliott here expressly adopts the criticism of the doctrine made by Jowell and Lester, *op cit*.

INTRODUCTION

The following description of the concept of ombudsmen is taken from a leading international reference work on the subject:

> The ombudsman is an independent and non-partisan officer ... often provided for in the Constitution, who supervises the administration. He deals with specific complaints from the public against administrative injustice and maladministration. He has the power to investigate, report upon, and make recommendations about individual cases and administrative procedures. He is not a judge or tribunal, and he has no power to make orders or to reverse administrative action. He seeks solutions to problems by a process of investigation and conciliation. His authority and influence derive from the fact that he is appointed by and reports to one of the principal organs of state, usually either the parliament or the chief executive.[1]

The first UK ombudsman was the Parliamentary Commissioner for Administration (PCA); that office was set up under the Parliamentary Commissioner Act 1967. Since then the system has been extended to other areas (see below), suggesting that it has shown itself to be of value. It is important to bear in mind the role the PCA was set up to fulfil. Pre-existing judicial and parliamentary remedies did not, it appeared, provide adequate redress for members of the public who had suffered as a result of maladministration in central government. The Crichel Down Affair in 1954 had provided a particularly prominent example of such conduct. Defective administrative action was going unremedied either because it fell outside the jurisdiction of the courts or because MPs did not have sufficient powers to investigate it satisfactorily.

There will be some overlap between the range of administrative actions the ombudsman can consider and those which can be considered where there is a statutory right of appeal or in judicial review proceedings. A court can intervene in judicial review proceedings only where a decision is *ultra vires*, where it is considered *Wednesbury* unreasonable, where there has been a breach of natural justice or where the decision violates one of the rights under the European Convention on Human Rights protected by the Human Rights Act 1998 (see Chapter 2 of this part). In a number of respects the ombudsman system may be more effective as a means of providing redress for the citizen mistreated by government authorities than judicial and Parliamentary remedies, principally, perhaps, because use of the PCA is free to the complainant. However, it should be borne in mind that the ombudsman system was not set up as a *replacement* for other remedies, but in order to fill gaps they created.

A note on abbreviations and terminology: this chapter, as well as referring to the Parliamentary Commissioner for Administration, will also mention the Commissioner for Local Administration – the ombudsman who oversees local government, known either as the CLA or, sometimes, the Local Government Ombudsman (LGO). The Health Service Commissioner (HSC) will also be mentioned. Where 'the ombudsman' is mentioned, the reference is to the PCA unless the context indicates otherwise. Note that all PCA reports are available online at www.ombudsman.org.uk/publications. html#england.

---

1   GE Caiden (ed), *International Handbook of the Ombudsman* (1983), p 13.

Evidence submitted to the Select Committee on the PCA[2] demonstrates the growth of the ombudsman system. In the public sector, the PCA has been joined by the following: the Health Service Commissioner for England, Scotland, Wales; the Commission for Local Administration in England; the Commission for Local Administration in Wales; the Commissioner for Local Administration in Scotland; the Northern Ireland Parliamentary Commissioner for Administration and Commissioner for Complaints; the Prisons Ombudsman for England and Wales (from end of 1993). Of these, the PCA, LGO, HSC and Northern Ireland Ombudsman have been given a statutory footing. In the private sector, ombudsmen include the following: the Banking Ombudsman; the Building Societies Ombudsman; the Ombudsman for Corporate Estate Agents; the Insurance Ombudsman; the Investment Ombudsman; the Legal Services Ombudsman; the Legal Services Ombudsman for Scotland; the Pensions Ombudsman.

To the above should now be added the new ombudsman established to investigate complaints relating to the devolved institutions set up for Wales, Scotland and Northern Ireland.

A wide-ranging and radical review of the work of the PCA and other public sector ombudsmen has recently been carried out by the Cabinet Office.[3] The principal recommendations for reform of this important report are considered in the final section of this chapter. However, where earlier sections deal with issues on which the report made a recommendation (for example, on access to the PCA), that recommendation is considered at that point.

THE POSITION, ROLE AND WORK OF THE PCA

The position and role of the PCA

Parliamentary Commissioner Act 1967, as amended

Appointment and tenure of office

1.–(1) For the purpose of conducting investigations in accordance with the following provisions of this Act there shall be appointed a Commissioner, to be known as the Parliamentary Commissioner for Administration.

(2) Her Majesty may by Letters Patent from time to time appoint a person to be the Commissioner, and any person so appointed shall (subject to subsections (3) and (3A) of this section) hold office during good behaviour.

(3) A person appointed to be the Commissioner may be relieved of office by Her Majesty at his own request, or may be removed from office by Her Majesty in consequence of Addresses from both Houses of Parliament, and shall in any case vacate office on completing the year of service in which he attains the age of sixty-five years.

(3A) Her Majesty may declare the office of Commissioner to have been vacated if satisfied that the person appointed to be the Commissioner is incapable for medical reasons—

(a) of performing the duties of his office; and

(b) of requesting to be relieved of it.

. . .

---

2   HC 42 (1993–94), Vol II.
3   *Review of the Public Sector Ombudsmen in England*, Cabinet Office, April 2000.

Matters subject to investigation

5.–(1) Subject to the provisions of this section, the commissioner may investigate any action taken by or on behalf of a Government department or other authority to which this Act applies, being action taken in the exercise of administrative functions of that department or authority, in any case where—

(a) a written complaint is duly made to a member of the House of Commons by a member of the public who claims to have sustained injustice in consequence of maladministration in connection with the action so taken; and

(b) the complaint is referred to the commissioner, with the consent of the person who made it, by a member of that House with a request to conduct an investigation thereon.

[For s 5(2)–(3), see below, p 799.]

(5) In determining whether to initiate, continue or discontinue an investigation under this Act, the commissioner shall, subject to the foregoing provisions of this section, act in accordance with his own discretion; and any question whether a complaint is duly made under this Act shall be determined by the commissioner.

Provisions relating to complaints

6.–(1) A complaint under this Act may be made by any individual, or by any body of persons whether incorporated or not, not being—

(a) a local authority or other authority or body constituted for purposes of the public service or of local government or for the purposes of carrying on under national ownership any industry or undertaking or part of an industry or undertaking;

(b) any other authority or body whose members are appointed by Her Majesty or any minister of the Crown or Government department, or whose revenues consist wholly or mainly of moneys provided by Parliament.

. . .

(3) A complaint shall not be entertained under this Act unless it is made to a member of the House of Commons not later than 12 months from the day on which the person aggrieved first had notice of the matters alleged in the complaint; but the commissioner may conduct an investigation pursuant to a complaint not made within that period if he considers that there are special circumstances which make it proper to do so.

Obstruction and contempt

9.–(1) If any person without lawful excuse obstructs the commissioner or any officer of the commissioner in the performance of his functions under this Act, or is guilty of any act or omission in relation to an investigation under this Act which, if that investigation were a proceeding in the Court, would constitute contempt of court, the commissioner may certify the offence to the Court. . . .

Reports by Commission

10. . . . .

(3) If, after conducting an investigation under this Act, it appears to the commissioner that injustice has been caused to the person aggrieved in consequence of maladministration and that the injustice has not been, or will not be, remedied, he may, if he thinks fit, lay before each House of Parliament a special report upon the case.

(4) The commissioner shall annually lay before each House of Parliament a general report on the performance of his functions under this Act and may from time to time lay before each House of Parliament such other reports with respect to those actions as he thinks fit.

(5) For the purposes of the law of defamation, any such publication as is hereinafter mentioned shall be absolutely privileged, that is to say—

(a) the publication of any matter by the commissioner in making a report to either House of Parliament for the purposes of this Act;

(b) the publication of any matter by a member of the House of Commons in communicating with the commissioner or his officers for those purposes or by the commissioner or his officers in communicating with such a member for those purposes;

(c) the publication by such a member to the person by whom a complaint was made under this Act of a report or statement sent to the member in respect of the complaint in pursuance of subsection (1) of this section;

(d) the publication by the commissioner to such a person as is mentioned in subsection (2) of this section of a report sent to that person in pursuance of that subsection.

. . .

The Criminal Injuries Compensation Scheme

11B.–(1) For the purposes of this Act, administrative functions exercisable by an administrator of the Criminal Injuries Compensation Scheme ('Scheme functions') shall be taken to be administrative functions of a government department to which this Act applies.

. . .

Interpretation

12.–(1) In this Act the following expressions have the meanings hereby respectively assigned to them, that is to say—

'action' includes failure to act, and other expressions connoting action shall be construed accordingly;

'the Commissioner' means the Parliamentary Commissioner for Administration;

'the Court' means, in relation to England and Wales the High Court, in relation to Scotland the Court of Session, and in relation to Northern Ireland the High Court of Northern Ireland;

'enactment' includes an enactment of the Parliament of Northern Ireland, and any instrument made by virtue of an enactment . . .

. . .

(3) It is hereby declared that nothing in this Act authorises or requires the Commissioner to question the merits of a decision taken without maladministration by a government department or other authority in the exercise of a discretion vested in that department or authority.

Notes

1   The Scotland Act 1998 requires the Scottish Parliament to legislate for the creation of an ombudsman to investigate actions of the Scottish Executive (s 91). That legislation duplicates the excluded areas set out in the PCA 1967 but does not require the system established to include the criticised MP filter (see below, pp 804 *et seq*). Legislation was duly forthcoming, in the form of the Scottish Public Services Ombudsman Act 2002. In relation to Northern Ireland, an Assembly Ombudsman was established under the Northern Ireland Act 1998 (see SI 1996/1298 (N18)). Under s 111 of the Government of Wales Act 1998, the Crown appoints a Welsh Administrative Ombudsman with power to investigate and make reports on complaints of maladministration on the part of the Welsh Assembly, its members, officers and a number of other Welsh public bodies (see Sched 9).

2   As provided in s 1, the PCA has security of tenure. She is appointed by the government, but, by convention, following consultation with the chair of the Select

Committee on the PCA (now the Public Administration Committee) and the Leader of the Opposition. Shee appoints her own staff, around 100 in number.[4]

3   There are clear advantages for the aggrieved citizen in using the ombudsman rather than relying on an MP to resolve the problem. Although MPs are of course able to hear a wide range of complaints, their powers of investigation are limited. The PCA in contrast has broad powers of investigation. Under s 7 of the Act, she may examine all documents relevant to the investigation, and the duty to assist her overrides the duty to maintain secrecy under the Official Secrets Act 1989. The PCA does not, however, have access to Cabinet papers.

4   Parliamentary procedures such as Questions and Select Committees operate within the doctrine of ministerial responsibility; in other words the expectation is that the minister in question will remedy matters. As Harlow points out, the doctrine may actually shelter more administrative blunders than it exposes.[5] The PCA can be more effective in practice as she on the other hand looks behind that expectation and considers the workings of the administrative body itself.

5   The PCA was given the ability to investigate a wider range of complaints than could be investigated in a court and given greater investigative powers than those available to MPs. In some instances of maladministration there may be a statutory right of appeal to a tribunal. Where a court or tribunal could consider such defective administration, the PCA will not investigate the matter unless it would be unreasonable to expect the complainant to seek redress in litigation. She is empowered to consider maladministration under s 10(3) of the Act as opposed to illegality. Maladministration has been described by Richard Crossman in the debate on the Parliamentary Commissioner Bill 1967 as including 'bias, neglect, inattention, delay, incompetence, ineptitude, perversity, turpitude, arbitrariness'.[6]

6   It must not be forgotten that once maladministration is found, it must be shown that it caused 'injustice'. It was recently clarified in the case of *ex p Balchin (No 2)*, 24 May 1999 that 'injustice' is specifically *not* limited to identifiable loss or damage, but includes 'a sense of outrage caused by unfair or incompetent administration'. See further below, at pp 821–24.

7   Although maladministration is a wide concept it does mean that the PCA is generally concerned with procedural defects rather than with the merits of a decision. This distinction is contained in s 12(3) of the Act which provides that the PCA may not investigate the merits of a decision taken without maladministration. However, the distinction between substance and procedure is not always easy to draw (as appears from the contrast between the judgment of Nolan J at first instance and that of Lord Donaldson in the Court of Appeal in *R v Local Commissioner ex p Eastleigh Borough Council* [1988] 3 WLR 116, below), and the PCA has complied with the demand from the Select Committee on the PCA to interpret his role widely. Therefore, this apparent limitation on the PCA's remit is less significant than may at first appear.

8   The third report from the Select Committee on the PCA for the Session 1993–94 noted that the PCA has produced an expanded list of forms of maladministration.

---

4   See G Drewry, 'The ombudsman: parochial stopgap or global panacea?', in P Leyland and T Woods (eds), *Administrative Law: Facing the Future* (1997), p 98.

5   'Ombudsmen in search of a role' (1978) 41 MLR 452.

6   HC Deb vol 754 col 51 (1966).

Third Report from the Select Committee on the Parliamentary Commissioner for Administration, HC 345 (1993–94)

Maladministration

10 ... The commissioner has always made clear his preference for the term maladministration, included in the statute without definition, in that it gives him considerable freedom and flexibility in interpretation. ... At paragraph 7 of his annual report Mr Reid produced an expanded list in the language of the 1990s [PCA Annual Report for 1993, para 7]:

- rudeness (though that is a matter of degree);

- unwillingness to treat the complainant as a person with rights;

- refusal to answer reasonable questions;

- neglecting to inform a complainant on request of his or her rights or entitlement;

- knowingly giving advice which is misleading or inadequate;

- ignoring valid advice or overruling considerations which would produce an uncomfortable result for the overruler;

- offering no redress or manifestly disproportionate redress;

- showing bias whether because of colour, sex, or any other grounds;

- omission to notify those who thereby lose a right of appeal;

- refusal to inform adequately of the right of appeal;

- faulty procedures;

- failure by management to monitor compliance with adequate procedures;

- cavalier disregard of guidance which is intended to be followed in the interest of equitable treatment of those who use a service;

- partiality;

- failure to mitigate the effects of rigid adherence to the letter of the law where that produces manifestly inequitable treatment.

11 Mr Reid [then Ombudsman] emphasised that he was not seeking to define maladministration, seeing strength in the fact that there is no statutory definition of the word.

Notes

1 In investigating maladministration, the ombudsman system may have some advantages over a court hearing. Its informality in investigation may be more effective at times in discovering the truth than the adversarial system in the courts. Moreover, in court, the Crown may plead public interest immunity to avoid disclosing documents (see Part IV Chapter 3, pp 598–616) whereas the PCA can look at all departmental files. Such flexibility is also reflected in the fact that the ombudsman procedure is not circumscribed by rules as regards time limits and therefore may provide a remedy in instances which cannot be considered by a court. The *Ostler* case [1977] QB 122 illustrates the advantage of such flexibility in comparison with judicial agreement between the department concerned and a third party. The court also introduced changes in its procedures in order to deal with his court costs.

2 Whilst the jurisdiction of the PCA is, strictly speaking, limited to investigating specific cases of maladministration, he can and does make general findings and recommendations to improve the administration of a given department. In a recent annual report, the PCA appeared to be widening his remit still further, to include

criticisms of actual government policies. The report claimed that the policy of slimming down the Civil Service (reduced to under 500,000 in 1996 for the first time in over 50 years) had resulted in an upsurge in complaints, up 28 per cent from the previous year in 1995. It went on, quoting with approval the warning of a previous PCA, 'There is a risk that fewer staff will lead to slower service and more mistakes, because civil servants will have less time for thought to enable them to pursue considered and prudent action. I doubt whether automation and technology will compensate fully for cuts in human resources. I foresee more, not less, maladministration, despite the references to efficiency savings.'[7] Acknowledging that 'The underlying policy issues are, of course, matters for government and Parliament; and it is not for me to express a view on them', he went on:

But ... greater complexity, with fewer resources to administer it, will lead to more maladministration occasioning more injustice ... this is a matter of legitimate concern to me. The injustice will be visited on a random selection of those within the scope of the scheme or the system, without regard to circumstances or desert. It is inequitable that they alone should suffer detriment while the generality of taxpayers enjoy the benefits of savings on administrative costs. ... In a number of cases which have raised these issues, departments or agencies have argued, in effect, that they have done the best that they could with the resources available to them; that they are therefore not guilty of maladministration; and that any losses resulting from shortcomings in the running of the scheme or system must lie where they fall. Even if I accepted the premise – which not infrequently is open to debate – I could not accept the conclusion. The decisions of the department may not have been maladministrative in the sense that they were taken without due thought and care. But they were maladministrative because they were bound to lead to inequity; and fairness requires that their consequences must be redressed.[8]

3   The most recent PCA to hold the post, Ms Ann Abrahams, has made it clear that she is firmly of the view that her remit does *not* include making recommendations on specific policy issues not arising from complaints made to her. In oral evidence to a Select Committee, she was asked about a particular problem in relation to drug prescription and the so called 'post-code lottery'.

Oral Evidence before the Public Administration Select Committee, 11 March 2003, HC 506-I

[Question] ... there is a huge controversy about the Department of Health guidance on beta interferon for people who suffer from MS, and there was a postcode lottery [regarding access to the drug] notwithstanding the fact that there was Department of Health guidance on who should and who should not receive this particular drug? Is that something that you would want to look at ...?

(Ms Abraham) No, I do not want to get involved in the policy areas, that is not my job. I feel very much that an Ombudsman is not doing a complete job if they do not ensure that the evidence which emerges from casework is not fed back to service providers and public service generally; that does not mean that I am going to be looking for areas of concern that do not emerge from the casework, so I think that is different. I am very much of the view that what drives our work are the complainants who come to us, the problems that they bring to us, and therefore that will always be the foundation for anything we do in terms of improving public services.

---

7   Annual Report for 1999–2000, para 1.23.
8   *Ibid*, para 1.24.

JURISDICTION: EXCLUDED AREAS

Although the jurisdiction of the PCA has recently been extended to cover a much wider range of governmental bodies, much of the ongoing debate surrounding the PCA continues to concern the areas of governmental activity that are excluded from her remit. Schedules 2 and 3 to the Act, as amended, list, respectively, the bodies generally subject to her jurisdiction and the areas of work within those bodies that are specifically excluded.

Parliamentary Commissioner Act 1967, ss 4, 5 and Scheds 2 and 3

Departments etc subject to investigation

4.–(1) Subject to the provisions of this section and to the notes contained in Schedule 2 to this Act, this Act applies to the government departments, corporations and unincorporated bodies listed in that Schedule; and references in this Act to an authority to which this Act applies are references to any such corporation or body.

(2) Her Majesty may by Order in Council amend Schedule 2 to this Act by the alteration of any entry or note, the removal of any entry or note or the insertion of any additional entry or note.

(3) An Order in Council may only insert an entry if—

(a) it relates—

(i) to a government department; or

(ii) to a corporation or body whose functions are exercised on behalf of the Crown; or

(b) it relates to a corporation or body—

(i) which is established by virtue of Her Majesty's prerogative or by an Act of Parliament or an Order in Council or order made under an Act of Parliament or which is established in any other way by a Minister of the Crown in his capacity as a Minister or by a government department;

(ii) at least half of whose revenues derive directly from money provided by Parliament, a levy authorised by an enactment, a fee or charge of any other description so authorised or more than one of those sources; and

(iii) which is wholly or partly constituted by appointment made by Her Majesty or a Minister of the Crown or government department.

[Section 4(3A) and (3B) preclude bodies being acted that are covered by the Welsh Administration Ombudsman and the Scottish Administration and 'any Scottish public authority with mixed functions or no reserved functions within the meaning of the Scotland Act 1998'.]

(4) No entry shall be made in respect of a corporation or body whose sole activity is, or whose main activities are, included among the activities specified in subsection (5) below.

(5) The activities mentioned in subsection (4) above are—

(a) the provision of education, or the provision of training otherwise than under the Industrial Training Act 1982;

(b) the development of curricula, the conduct of examinations or the validation of educational courses;

(c) the control of entry to any profession or the regulation of the conduct of members of any profession;

    (d) the investigation of complaints by members of the public regarding the actions of any person or body, or the supervision or review of such investigations or of steps taken following them.

(6) No entry shall be made in respect of a corporation or body operating in an exclusively or predominantly commercial manner or a corporation carrying on under national ownership an industry or undertaking or part of an industry or undertaking.

(7) Any statutory instrument made by virtue of this section shall be subject to annulment in pursuance of a resolution of either House of Parliament. . . .

5.–(2) Except as hereinafter provided, the commissioner shall not conduct an investigation under this Act in respect of any of the following matters, that is to say

    (a) any action in respect of which the person aggrieved has or had a right of appeal, reference or review to or before a tribunal constituted by or under any enactment or by virtue of Her Majesty's prerogative;

    (b) any action in respect of which the person aggrieved has or had a remedy by way of proceedings in any court of law;

provided that the commissioner may conduct an investigation notwithstanding that the person aggrieved has or had such a right or remedy if satisfied that in the particular circumstances it is not reasonable to expect him to resort or have resorted to it.

    (3) Without prejudice to subsection (2) of this section, the commissioner shall not conduct an investigation under this Act in respect of any such action or matter as is described in Schedule 3 to this Act.

. . .

Schedule 3

Matters not subject to investigation

1. Action taken in matters certified by a Secretary of State or other Minister of the Crown to affect relations or dealings between the Government of the United Kingdom and any other Government or any international organisation of States or Governments.

2. Action taken, in any country or territory outside the United Kingdom, by or on behalf of any officer representing or acting under the authority of Her Majesty in respect of the United Kingdom, or any other officer of the Government of the United Kingdom other than action which is taken by an officer (not being an honorary consular officer) in the exercise of a consular function on behalf of the government of the United Kingdom

3. Action taken in connection with the administration of the Government of any country or territory outside the United Kingdom which forms part of Her Majesty's dominions or in which Her Majesty has jurisdiction.

4. Action taken by the Secretary of State under the Extradition Act 1870, the Fugitive Offenders Act 1881 or the Extradition Act 1989.

5. Action taken by or with the authority of the Secretary of State for the purposes of investigating crime or of protecting the security of the state, including action so taken with respect to passports.

6. The commencement or conduct of civil or criminal proceedings before any court of law in the United Kingdom, of proceedings at any place under the Naval Discipline Act 1957, the Army Act 1955 or the Air Force Act 1955, or of proceedings before any international court or tribunal.

6A. Action taken by any person appointed by the Lord Chancellor as a member of the administrative staff of any court or tribunal, so far as that action is taken at the direction, or on the authority (whether express or implied), of any person acting in a judicial capacity or in his capacity as a member of the tribunal.

6B.(1) Action taken by any member of the administrative staff of a relevant tribunal, so far as that action is taken at the direction, or on the authority (whether express or implied), of any person acting in his capacity as a member of the tribunal.

6B.(2) In this paragraph, 'relevant tribunal' has the meaning given by section 5(8) of this Act.

6C. Action taken by any person appointed under section 5(3)(c) of the Criminal Injuries Compensation Act 1995, so far as that action is taken at the direction, or on the authority (whether express or implied), of any person acting in his capacity as an adjudicator appointed under section 5 of that Act to determine appeals.

7. Any exercise of the prerogative of mercy or of the power of a Secretary of State to make a reference in respect of any person to ... the High Court of Justiciary or the Courts-Martial Appeal Court

8.(1) Action taken on behalf of the Minister of Health or the Secretary of State by [various health bodies].

. . .

9. Action taken in matters relating to contractual or other commercial transactions, whether within the United Kingdom or elsewhere, being transactions of a government department or authority to which this Act applies or of any such authority or body as is mentioned in paragraph (a) or (b) of subsection (1) of section 6 of this Act and not being transactions for or relating to—

(a) the acquisition of land compulsorily or in circumstances in which it could be acquired compulsorily;

(b) the disposal as surplus of land acquired compulsorily or in such circumstances as aforesaid.

10.(1) Action taken in respect of appointments or removals, pay, discipline, superannuation or other personnel matters, in relation to—

(a) service in any of the armed forces of the Crown, including reserve and auxiliary and cadet forces;

(b) this Act applies; or

(c) service in any office or employment, or under any contract for services, in respect of which power to take action, or to determine or approve the action to be taken, in such matters is vested in Her Majesty, any Minister of the Crown or any such authority as aforesaid.

. . .

11. The grant of honours, awards or privileges within the gift of the Crown, including the grant of Royal Charters.

Notes

1 Some of the departments listed in Sched 2 contract out certain of their functions to private companies and these are covered by the PCA.[9] Prior to 1987, the PCA's jurisdiction was limited to central government departments and agencies, but the Parliamentary and Health Service Commissioners Act 1987 amended the 1967 Act in order to add about 50 non-departmental public bodies such as the Arts Council and the Equal Opportunities Commission to its remit.

2 Below, a report from the Select Committee on the PCA gives the reasons for various exclusions.

---

9 Deregulation and Contracting Out Act 1994, s 72.

Evidence Taken Before the Select Committee on the PCA, HC 64 (1993–94), Vol II, Annexes A and B

Annex A

PCA: subject areas outside jurisdiction

Means of referring a complaint (s 5(1))

Implications of s 5(1) are that it excludes from jurisdiction (a) bodies which are distinct entities from those in Schedule 2 and which are exercising functions of their own, and (b) legislative, judicial and quasi-judicial functions.

Right of appeal to tribunal (s 5(2)(a))

Any action in which a right of appeal to a tribunal exists is excluded. A tribunal is not defined in the Act. They were considered outside the scope of PCA at the outset, because (a) their functions are quasi-judicial, not administrative, and (b) they are distinct from departments listed in Schedule 2 and exercise functions of their own. This was seen to conform with the underlying policy of the Act, that PCA was not to replace existing institutions or safeguards, but to supplement them by providing protection for the citizen in his/her dealings with the executive where otherwise they do not exist.

Legal remedy (s 5(2)(b))

Actions where a legal remedy exists are excluded, again reflecting the principle that PCA should not usurp the functions of existing institutions which provide protection for the citizen. (The proviso to the clause recognised the fact that there are few situations where there is ground for complaint of maladministration and where legal proceedings in some form or another cannot be instituted.)

Contractual or commercial transactions (Schedule 3, para 9)

The original reason for this exclusion was that PCA was intended to operate in the field of relationships between the Government and the governed. Commercial judgments are by nature discriminatory, so the justification ran, and so allowing the commercial judgments of departments to be open to examination by private interests while leaving those interests themselves free from investigation would amount to putting departments, and with them the taxpayer, at a disadvantage.

In its response to the fourth report of the select committee 1979–80, the Government repeated this argument in rejecting the Committee's conclusion that the continued exclusion of these matters would not be justified, and stated more generally that only these activities unique to Government should be subject to PCA. (The committee felt that all Government activities should be examinable unless there was a compelling argument otherwise.) . . .

Exercise of extradition orders (Schedule 3, para 4)

In the exercise of extradition orders, the Secretary of State is acting in a quasi-judicial capacity as a final appellate authority. Adding, in effect, a further appeal an investigation by PCA would, the argument ran, be inappropriate and inconsistent with the Government's responsibility for compliance with international obligations.

Power of Secretary of State to intercept communications and withhold or withdraw passports when investigating crime (Schedule 3, para 5)

The exclusion of complaints relating to the above was justified because (a) the use of the power ought to be kept secret, and (b) its use must form part of criminal investigations which are not, in other respects, a matter for central government and thus outside the PCA's scope.

Note

Most controversial has been the exclusion from the PCA's remit of contractual and commercial matters although, despite this criticism, the same matters have been excluded in the Scottish Public Services Ombudsman Act 2002 (Sched 4, para 7). Drewry comments that, 'Looking at other ombudsman systems, such exclusions are rare – and the Northern Ireland PCA (whose office is modelled closely on that of the mainland PCA) does exercise jurisdiction in this area, without this causing any apparent difficulties'.[10] The government's justification for the exclusion, as appears above, is based both on a theoretical contention that such matters are not in themselves governing activities, but only incidental to them, and also on the more practical ground that such scrutiny would place government departments at a commercial disadvantage, compared to the private interests which would not be open to scrutiny in the same way. The exemption clearly excludes a potentially wide range of decisions from the ambit of the PCA, though as Mary Seneviratne notes, it has in practice ... accounted for few rejections, perhaps because its scope has been limited by successive PCAs, who have decided that a service does not become commercial [merely] because a charge is made for it.[11] The Fourth Report from the Select Committee on the PCA 1979 considered, *inter alia*, that the exclusion of commercial matters was unjustified.

Fourth Report from the Select Committee on the PCA, HC 593 (1979–80)

4 In his evidence the commissioner placed much emphasis on a point made by the Select Committee in 1978, namely that s 5 of the Parliamentary Commissioner Act provided that the commissioner would not take up a case where a legal remedy was available, save in exceptional circumstances, and so if [the commercial exclusion were abolished] there would still be no danger of the commissioner being involved in disputes about the performance of contracts. He believed, as his predecessors had, that paragraph 9 was unnecessary and undesirable in addition to s 5, and by its sweeping scope has had the effect of excluding many complaints which may have been found on investigation to be entirely justifiable. What he was concerned about was the way in which a department conducted the administrative side of Government buying and selling, where there was considerable scope for maladministration that could not be brought before the courts. He cited the case of a small office cleaning company, which had as the mainstay of its business a contract with a Government department; when the contract came up for renewal the company was not invited to tender, and on making enquiries it was told that another Government department had communicated confidential information of a damaging nature about the company to the department with which it had held the contract. The commissioner told us that he could investigate a complaint about the communication of confidential information because that was an administrative matter, but he would not be able to look into whether the information was used to remove the company from the list of tenderers for the contract because that was a commercial matter excluded by paragraph 9 of the Schedule.

...

8 We do not accept the Government's contention that only those activities, which are unique to the function of government, should be subject to review by the Parliamentary Commissioner; rather we believe that in principle all areas of government administration should be investigable by him unless in particular cases a compelling argument can be made out for their exclusion. Accordingly the claim that the Government's commercial activities should be exempt from examination because private contractors are exempt is in our view beside the point. The Government has a duty to administer its purchasing policies fairly and equitably, and if those policies are the subject of complaint then the complaints should be investigated; this is particularly important if any future Government were again to use the award of contracts as a political weapon. Section 12(3) of the Act would prevent the commissioner from questioning a *bona fide* commercial decision to purchase goods or services from one firm rather than another, or the legitimate exercise of a department's discretion to give selective assistance to one firm or one industry rather than another, but if decisions of this kind are taken with maladministration then it

10   *Op cit*, p 99.
11   M Seneviratne, *Ombudsman in the Public Sector* (1994), p 23.

is right that they should be reviewed ... We are satisfied that ss 5 and 12(3) of the Parliamentary Commissioner Act are sufficient on their own and that the further exemption from investigation conferred by paragraph 9 of Schedule 3 is not justified.

Notes

1 It is apparent that one of the main fears of the Committee in relation to the commercial exclusion was that the government's immense public purchasing power could be used as a political weapon; for example, it could reward businesses which were pursuing policies in line with government recommendations (for example, on wage levels) with lucrative contracts. The reassurance offered by the government witnesses on this point seems weak: Nigel Lawson simply said that the present government had no intention of using its purchasing power in this way. This does not even amount to an undertaking; it also leaves wholly unanswered the question of how a change of government intention could be detected, still less remedied, if the PCA cannot investigate.

2 Witnesses giving evidence to the Public Administration Committee in 2000 took a strong view on removal of the contractual exemption:

[This is] a real problem because in this country public contracts are not subjected to any legal scrutiny through the courts, as there was hardly any litigation until very recent years. ... Public money should be followed wherever it is spent and however it is spent and through whatever form it is spent. The problem with a contractual exemption is, if you say that a contractor is performing with maladministration then you can go for that and criticise it. If the contractor turns around and says, 'This relates to the terms of our contract and this is a contractual dispute that I have with the public authority contractor', then it may well be able to get itself out of the framework.

The reason why the contract exemption was put there in the first place was for the Ministry of Defence, as I understand it, who are very sensitive about defence procurement. [But the exemption] ... covers a whole range of public expenditure of money and the delivery of public services and public goods ... I would prefer to have [the exemption] out altogether and to leave something along the lines, 'If there is a legal remedy then you pursue that. [But] the Ombudsman might be asked by third parties to investigate matters where there is no contractual nexus, so there is no legal remedy'.[12]

The point being made here is that while an actual contractor with the government, who had a complaint about the government's performance of that contract, should be required to pursue any complaint through the courts, where it had the prospect of a remedy, such an option would not be available to a third party, complaining about abuse of the government's contractual power, since the third party would have no contract upon which to sue.

3 The Committee also complained about the exclusion of public personnel matters, which, as Seneviratne notes[13] are within the remit of both MPs in their individual capacity and of ombudsmen in other countries (though not the new Scottish Ombudsman: Scottish Public Services Ombudsman Act 2002 (Sched 4, para 8). The government did have a clear argument of principle here, namely that it would be unfair to give public servants special protection which is denied to other employees. The PCA's reply, that the government, as the country's largest employer, should set a good example may seem unpersuasive: it could be argued that the government could set its example simply by being a scrupulously fair and

---

12 Third Report of the Select Committee on Public Administration, HC 612 (1999–2000), Evidence, 28 June 2000, QQ 56–59 (Professor Patrick Birkinshaw).

13 *Ibid.*

thoughtful employer, not by giving its employees special protection which is unavailable to others.

ACCESS TO THE PCA: THE 'MP FILTER'

Complaints cannot be made directly to the PCA by a Member of Parliament. Under s 5(1) of the PCA 1967, the PCA may investigate a written complaint made by a member of the public to a Member of Parliament if the complaint is referred by the MP and both he and the complainant agree to investigation by the PCA. This filter role played by MPs has been the subject of much controversy. It was intended initially as a experimental measure, to be reviewed after five years, but it is still in place at the time of writing. The filter system is virtually unique amongst the other countries in the world which have created ombudsmen; only the French ombudsman is subject to a similar filter. A summary of the problems with the present system, appears below.

First Report from the Select Committee on the PCA, HC 33 II (1993–94)

Summary of objections to the MP filter

65 Objections to the MP filter can be summarised as follows:

(1) The public should have direct access to the commissioner as a matter of right.

(2) The filter is an anomaly, almost unknown in other ombudsman systems. No such requirement exists, for instance, in the case of the Health Service Commissioner.

(3) Individuals with complaints may be unwilling to approach an MP, while desiring the ombudsman's assistance.

(4) The filter means that the likelihood of individuals cases being referred to the commissioner will largely depend on the views and practice of the particular constituency MP. Some look with more favour on the Office of the commissioner than others.

(5) The filter acts as an obstacle to the commissioner effectively promoting his services.

(6) The filter creates an unnecessary bureaucratic barrier between the complainant and the commissioner involving considerable paperwork for MPs and their offices.

Notes

1 Evidence that the MP filter may reduce the number of complaints received by the PCA came in a paper submitted to the above Select Committee:

The number of complaints received by the Parliamentary Ombudsman is far lower than envisaged when the Parliamentary Ombudsman was introduced. The level is still more surprising when compared with the number of complaints received by ombudsmen in other countries. For example figures for 1991 show:

Danish ombudsman	5 million population:	2,000 complaints
Swedish ombudsman	8 million population:	4,000 complaints
British ombudsman	55 million population:	766 complaints

The jurisdiction and constitutional position of the Scandinavian ombudsmen is very different from the Parliamentary Ombudsman. Even so, the number of complaints received by the ombudsmen in this country still appears low.[14]

---

14 Appendix to the Minutes of Evidence Taken before the Select Committee on the PCA, HC 64 (1993–94), vol II, para 3.7.

2   The following extract indicates the chief objections MPs have to the removal of the
    MP filter.

First Report from the Select Committee on the PCA, HC 33 II (1993–94)

74 We believe that the abolition of the MP filter would result not only in unheard complaints being
heard for the first time but in some complaints reaching the ombudsman's office which would
previously have been more appropriately resolved by a Member. The effect of this will be either to
increase unnecessarily the resources allocated to the ombudsman's office or to cause a decline in
the thoroughness of the ombudsman's investigations as his office struggles to cope with the
increased volume of work. . . .

75 The most important issue in deciding the fate of the MP filter remains a constitutional one. Will
direct access undermine the constitutional role of Members in taking up the grievances of their
constituents? Should the Parliamentary Ombudsman remain an instrument of MPs or should
access to his services now be seen as a right of the citizen? It is clear that the majority of
Members appreciate the filter. We continue to believe that the Member of Parliament has an
irreplaceable role in pursuing complaints of the public against the executive, notwithstanding the
development within public bodies of an array of direct access complaint and redress mechanisms
for the citizen. We note that since the introduction of direct access in the case of the Local
Government Ombudsman the proportion of cases referred by Councillors has declined from 28%
in the first year of direct access to 8% by the end of 1992–93. Moreover only approximately 5% of
cases are referred by MPs to the Health Service Ombudsman where direct access applies. Direct
access, it appears, may well result in fewer MPs being involved in the ombudsman's work.

76 The work of the Parliamentary Ombudsman, acting at the behest of MPs and reporting to them
the details of his investigations, has a vital role in equipping the Member for the tasks of
Parliament. The knowledge of the details of and problems in administration has an important part
in any effective scrutiny of the executive. The publication of anonymised reports can never be a
genuine substitute for direct involvement in the case which the Member has referred. Direct
access will result in the denial to Members of expertise in the problems facing their constituents
as they come into contact with the executive. This is to impoverish parliamentary, and thus
political, life.

Notes[15]

1   As appears from the above, the primary concern of MPs about removing their
    screening function is the fear that allowing direct access would undermine their
    constitutional role as defenders of the citizen against the executive. Apart from any
    symbolic undermining, the concrete threat, according to the Select Committee,
    appears to boil down to the fear that, 'Direct access will result in the denial to
    Members of expertise in the problems facing their constituents ... This is to
    impoverish parliamentary, and thus, political life'. A number of points may be
    made in response to this. First of all, the argument, even if sound, seems rather self-
    serving. One may fairly predict that most constituents would consider that gaining
    a more efficient system for remedying their grievances easily outweighed this
    rather speculative harm. Secondly, the argument seems flawed in its own terms: it
    fails to recognise that direct access by the public to the PCA need not necessarily
    cause any decrease at all in either the involvement of MPs in the matters raised or
    in the flow of information to them, the second of which is certainly vital to their
    role as scrutinisers of the executive. The Committee says that the publication of
    anonymised reports can never be a genuine substitute for direct involvement in the

---

15   For general discussion of the relationship between the PCA and MPs, see G Drewry and
     C Harlow, 'A cutting edge? The Parliamentary Commissioner and MPs' (1990) 53 MLR 745.

case which the Member has referred. But this is not the only alternative to the present system. If direct access were introduced, the continued involvement and knowledgability of MPs could be ensured very simply; the PCA would simply copy the appropriate MP into any complaint received, and with news of the investigation of the complaint (if he or she decided to take it up) as it proceeded.[16] It does not seem clear that MPs' constitutional role necessarily demands that they should have to make the *decision* as to whether a complaint should be investigated, particularly as it may reasonably be feared that their political allegiance could distort their judgment in sensitive cases. Thirdly, MPs would, of course, continue to receive numerous complaints on a variety of matters, many of which would be outside the PCA's jurisdiction. A former PCA, Mr Buckley, expressed similar views when he told the Public Administration Committee:

There is possibly a misplaced fear among Members that if there were not that filter this new Commission would go off and wander away from Parliament. I would hate that to happen. I think it is absolutely essential that the new Commission should work very closely with Parliament. I think it should do so, not by handling individual cases for referring Members but much more by being under parliamentary scrutiny, the way it works, the way it gets its finances, its efficiency, and drawing to the attention of Parliament what we find in terms of general problems or general features of public administrations.[17]

2   The Cabinet Office Review set out a reasoned position on a number of similar arguments surrounding the MP filter.

Review of the Public Sector Ombudsmen in England, April 2000

3.47 A further point made in favour of retaining the MP filter is that the MP has a wider range of 'tools' available to assist the citizen seeking redress. Research (for example, Gregory and Alexander in 1973) has looked at different Parliamentary techniques for seeking redress of grievances including through the PCA. The evidence we have seen shows that a letter to a Minister is the most likely 'tool' to be used. Annual surveys by the Cabinet Office show that Ministers receive around 200,000 letters each year, mainly from MPs. In contrast, the PCA receives about 1,500 new complaints each year. Gregory and Alexander also looked at perceptions of effectiveness – over 70% of MPs judged a letter to a minister as 'effective or highly effective' against 22% judging the PCA accordingly. Although the research was carried out some time ago the volume of letters to Ministers and replies to our survey suggests that letters to ministers may still be regarded as more effective ...

3.48 The PCA was originally introduced to add a further powerful tool for MPs, to be used when other means such as a letter to a minister were found or thought likely to be ineffective ... The key issue is whether removing the MP filter would mean that complainants were sent to the PCA when an MP could have got speedier redress more easily by use of another tool.

3.49 Removing the MP filter does not necessarily remove the MP. Constituents could still be referred to the PCA and the PCA's office might advise many enquirers that going to their MP was a good way forward. Removing the filter would simply remove going to the MP as a mandatory step in complaining to the PCA ...

Notes

1   The Review went on to note that one of the main problems with the MP filter system is simple ignorance amongst MPs of the jurisdiction of the PCA:

---

16   The Cabinet Office Review, see below, made a similar recommendation: see para 3.51.
17   Third Report of the Select Committee on Public Administration, HC 612 (1999–2000), Evidence, 21 June 2000, Q 7.

In 1998/99 nearly half the cases put to the PCA by Members of Parliament were outside jurisdiction, or were not about administrative actions or were cases in which the PCA thought it reasonable that the complainant go to a court or tribunal ... In these cases particularly, the time wasted by the complainant, the MP and the PCA is considerable and, for the complainant, the experience must often have been frustrating or distressing.

2 The Review went on to point out the practical reason for such relative ignorance amongst MPs of the work of the PCA:

The PCA receives about 1,500 new cases each year. Therefore, typically an MP will refer 2 or 3 cases each year but levels of use varies – from the survey, 6% of MPs sent at least 10 cases, 24% between 5 and 10, 62% between 1 and 5, and 7% sent none (para 3.27).

3 This relative ignorance by MPs of the Ombudsman and the possibility that some are reluctant to refer complaints to the PCA was the subject of scathing criticism in evidence submitted to the Select Committee on the PCA.

Appendix to the Minutes of Evidence Taken before the Select Committee on the PCA, HC 64 (1993–94), Vol II, para 3.7

From available data it appears that MPs very rarely take the initiative of suggesting to a complainant that his or her complaint be referred to the Parliamentary Ombudsman. There is evidence that some MPs have actually discouraged complainants from seeking to have their complaints referred to the ombudsman ...

These figures demonstrate that it is extremely difficult for consumers to gain access to the Parliamentary Ombudsman. Complainants must know of the existence of the office. Secondly, they must know the process for persuading the MP to refer the complaint letter to an MP requesting that he or she refers the complaint to the ombudsman. Thirdly, they must persuade the MP that the complaint should be investigated by the Parliamentary Ombudsman.

Very little research or information is publicly available about how the MP filter works. The limited information which is available indicates that, from the consumer's perspective, the MP filter operates inequitably. A complainant's chance of having a grievance dealt with by the Parliamentary Ombudsman seems to depend on the approach of individual MPs.

3.8 MPs referrals to the Parliamentary Ombudsman (1986 figures):

263 MPs	(40.5%)	referred no complaints
200 MPs	(51.7%)	referred one complaint
102 MPs	(26.4%)	referred two complaints
43 MPs	(11.1%)	referred three complaints
30 MPs	(7.8%)	referred four complaints
7 MPs	(1.8%)	referred five complaints
4 MPs		referred six complaints
1 MP		referred seven complaints

These figures show that in one year, as many as four out of 10 MPs refer a single complaint to the Parliamentary Ombudsman; 85 MPs were responsible for 315 (44%) of referrals.

The existing system puts the interest of MPs above the interests of individual consumers with a grievance. If the MP filter does serve the interests of MPs, it does so at the expense of individual consumers and citizens for whom it constitutes a barrier to accessing a very important system of redress.

Notes

1   As the Cabinet Office Review pointed out, the problem here is the unaccountable and unreviewable[18] discretion of MPs as to whether to refer a complaint to the PCA:

> ... how MPs use the PCA is up to them – they can bar all access, refer complaints mechanically or operate strictly as a filter. They can filter out the frivolous but they do not have to. They can take an active interest in the investigation and any report, or simply act as a post box for the complainant. What happens depends on the MP – each sets his or her own policy for the gatekeeper role (para 3.46).

Some amelioration of this system of making complaints has occurred. Since 1978, when the PCA receives a complaint directly from a member of the public, the complainant's MP will be contacted and, if he or she is in agreement, the PCA will investigate. This system does not, however, encourage citizens to complain directly to the PCA and due to his low profile, many will in any event be unaware that complaint is possible. In New South Wales, where complaints can come directly from the public or from MPs, the vast majority of complaints come directly from the public. The British system, as JUSTICE pointed out in 1979,[19] weakens the PCA because he is unable to publicise himself as available directly to receive complaints when he is not so available. It may be noted that the authors of a comparative study of ombudsmen consider that 'direct access ... is an essential requirement of the office'.[20]

2   It appears that the above arguments have eventually won the day and that the days of the MP filter are probably numbered. The Cabinet Office Review, the PCA himself and the Public Administration (PA) Committee agreed that it had outlived its usefulness and should be removed. It is particularly significant that the PA Committee, whose predecessor Committees, as seen above, had consistently argued for the retention of the filter, has now changed its view, and expressed it in such firm terms:

> We believe that the idea of an MP filter, which was inserted at the genesis of the ombudsman scheme to assuage the sensibilities of MPs about a new form of redress, is now inconsistent with the world of public service charters and ought to be replaced by direct public access to the public sector ombudsmen.[21]

3   At the time of writing, a Private Member's Bill abolishing the MP filter is before Parliament and will be considered by Parliament in 2003.

4   Before and after the expected removal of the filter, it is evident that increasing knowledge by both MPs and consumers of the existence and worth of the PCA is the key to increasing his practical accessibility to the public. It appears that the PCA and government departments covered by his work are making much greater efforts in this respect: see, for example, the First Report of the Select Committee on the PCA, HC 112 (1994–95), paras 8–9. A booklet called *The Ombudsman in Your Files*, which explains the role and procedures of the PCA, was published in December 1995 by the Cabinet Office. In his subsequent annual report,[22] the PCA

---

18   The decision of an MP as to whether or not to refer a case to the PCA would be regarded as non-justiciable and so not amenable to judicial review.
19   JUSTICE report, HC 593 (1979–80).
20   See G Drewry, 'The ombudsman: parochial stopgap or global panacea', in P Leyland and T Woods (eds), *Administrative Law: Facing the Future* (1997), p 96.
21   Third Report, *op cit*, para 12.
22   Annual Report for 1995, Cm 296, p 2, para 5.

welcomed this measure, though Mr Reid notes that the Cabinet Office did not publicise the booklet.

5 In spite of these measures, relatively low public awareness of the PCA has remained a problem. As the Cabinet Office Review noted:

> A survey by MORI for the Citizen's Charter Unit in 1997 showed that less than half the population were aware of the PCA or the CLA. A similar figure was found by MORI in a survey for the CLA in 1995. In 1996 a survey by the Consumers' Association found that 41% of all respondents in a sample of 1000 adults had no awareness of the PCA, HSC or CLA. The figure rose to 51% in social group C2DE [para 3.6].

THE WORK OF THE PCA: PROCESS, REMEDIES AND SOME EXAMPLES

Number of cases investigated

The most recent figures show that the steady upsurge in complaints is accelerating, peaking at 2,139 complaints, an increase of 24 per cent on the previous year and the highest figure on record. As the PCA's Annual Report for 2001–02 indicates:

> The Ombudsman received 2,139 new complaints from Members of Parliament, compared with 1,721 in 2000–01 – an increase of 24% and the highest intake ever. He settled 1,988 complaints, including concluding 195 statutory investigations – (1,787 last year including 247 statutory investigations). There are now fewer concluded statutory investigations because other – often simpler and faster – means of resolving complaints short of concluding a statutory investigation are increasingly being used. In a growing number of cases this enables the Ombudsman to achieve the same outcome for a complainant more quickly and cheaply than using the statutory process.[23]

Investigations: process and procedure

Parliamentary Commissioner Act 1967, as amended

Procedure in respect of investigations

7.–(1) Where the commissioner proposes to conduct an investigation pursuant to a complaint under this Act, he shall afford to the principal officer of the department or authority concerned, and to any other person who is alleged in the complaint to have taken or authorised the action complained of, an opportunity to comment on any allegations contained in the complaint.

(2) Every such investigation shall be conducted in private, but except as aforesaid the procedure for conducting an investigation shall be such as the commissioner considers appropriate in the circumstances of the case; and without prejudice to the generality of the foregoing provision the commissioner may obtain information from such persons and in such manner, and make such inquiries, as he thinks fit, and may determine whether any person may be represented, by counsel or solicitor or otherwise, in the investigation.

...

---

23 HC 897 (2001–02).

Evidence

8.–(1) For the purposes of an investigation under this Act the commissioner may require any minister, officer or member of the department or authority concerned or any other person who in his opinion is able to furnish information or produce documents relevant to the investigation to furnish any such information or produce any such document.

(2) For the purposes of any such investigation the commissioner shall have the same powers as the Court in respect of the attendance and examination of witnesses (including the administration of oaths or affirmations and the examination of witnesses abroad) and in respect of the production of documents.

(3) No obligation to maintain secrecy or other restriction upon the disclosure of information obtained by or furnished to persons in Her Majesty's service, whether imposed by any enactment or by any rule of law, shall apply to the disclosure of information for the purposes of an investigation under this Act; and the Crown shall not be entitled in relation to any such investigation to any such privilege in respect of the production of documents or the giving of evidence as is allowed by law in legal proceedings.

(4) No person shall be required or authorised by virtue of this Act to furnish any information or answer any question relating to proceedings of the Cabinet or of any committee of the Cabinet or to produce so much of any document as relates to such proceedings; and for the purposes of this subsection a certificate issued by the Secretary of the Cabinet with the approval of the Prime Minister and certifying that any information, question, document or part of a document so relates shall be conclusive.

(5) Subject to subsection (3) of this section, no person shall be compelled for the purposes of an investigation under this Act to give any evidence or produce any document which he could not be compelled to give or produce in proceedings before the Court.

10.–(1) In any case where the commissioner conducts an investigation under this Act or decides not to conduct such an investigation, he shall send to the member of the House of Commons by whom the request for investigation was made (or if he is no longer a member of that House, to such member of that House as the commissioner thinks appropriate) a report of the results of the investigation or, as the case may be, a statement of his reasons for not conducting an investigation.

(2) In any case where the commissioner conducts an investigation under this Act, he shall also send a report of the results of the investigation to the principal officer of the department or authority concerned and to any other person who is alleged in the relevant complaint to have taken or authorised the action complained of.

Notes

1   It is important to appreciate that, for the complainant, the PCA is not the beginning of his or her complaint process but probably the end. Some government departments have set up arrangements for independent review – these might be independent review panels as is the case with the Benefits Agency or independent complaints examiners such as the Adjudicator for the Inland Revenue, Customs and Excise and Contributions Agency and the Independent Complaints Examiner for the Child Support Agency. Generally, complainants must exhaust an internal complaints system before being referred to its independent review tier.

2   The first stage of the PCA's work is deciding whether or not to investigate a complaint referred to him, a process succinctly described in the Cabinet Office Review.

The staff of the PCA screen all new complaints to decide if they are within jurisdiction. They must be satisfied that there is *prima facie* evidence of maladministration leading to injustice and (usually) that the complaint is not about matters which gave rise to a complaint more than twelve months before it was referred to the MP and is not a matter for the courts. The PCA's staff then use his discretion, which is delegated to them, to decide how to deal with the case. A proportion go forward to full investigation and the production of a detailed report in which some form of redress can be recommended (but not enforced) if maladministration leading to injustice is found (para 1.24).

3 This leads to the problem of delay. The Cabinet Office Review found that 'the very long throughput time of cases investigated' was 'the principal criticism' of the PCA (para 2.8).

4 Throughout the 1990s, the comparative slowness of the PCA investigative procedure had allowed a large backlog of cases to build up, causing the throughput time for a full investigation to rise to 87 weeks by 1996. In the Annual Report for 1997–98, the PCA describes new working practices adopted to cut down the backlog, and thus the time taken to deal with new cases. These include both different working methods and a change in overall approach – as described in paras 2.5–2.8 below, the PCA now attempts to dispose of some cases through more informal, and thus more rapid methods.

Annual Report for 1997–98, paras 2.5–2.8

2.5 If it appears from a complaint that something has gone wrong we may first contact the body concerned to ask them informally whether they agree that they have made a mistake. If they do, we ask them to provide a suitable remedy to the complainant. Such informal enquiries can help avoid the time-consuming process of putting a complaint formally to the department, receiving their comments, and then starting a full investigation. In 1997/98 we made informal enquiries in 541 cases, and 519 in 1997 (compared to 294 in 1996). In some cases, though, it takes a formal investigation to resolve a complaint, either because the body in question denies fault or because the issues are too complex, or the picture too unclear, to be resolved informally. Such formal investigations, where the Ombudsman uses his powers to call for a body's papers and may interview its staff and the complainant, are still central to the work of the Office, but are now supplemented by more flexible informal methods of complaint resolution.

2.6 Sometimes our informal enquiries indicate that whatever the complainant believed (and he or she may not have been in possession of all the facts, or have fully understood complex legislation or administrative procedures) there has not been maladministration. In other cases, our enquiries may suggest that, although there have been mistakes, they have not caused injustice to the complainant, or such injustice as has been caused has been put right. In those instances, our explanation why a formal investigation is not warranted is intended, by explaining the situation, to reassure the complainant. Some complainants, however, are not pleased to be told that their grievances are unfounded, or that they have already received due redress. Inevitably, a few question the independence of the Ombudsman, and of his staff, and accuse the Office of accepting 'excuses' from departments.

2.7 Categorically, that is not the case. Staff do not accept unquestioningly whatever they are told, but test it against the documents and other information presented to them by the complainant, and their experience from many other cases.

2.8 If it is evident that a failure in administration has caused some injustice which has not been put right, we consider, on the facts of each case, whether the outcome of an informal approach is sufficient to put the matter right ... Thanks to the willing cooperation of departments and agencies in dealing with, in some cases, numerous informal enquiries, often by telephone, those informal methods have proved their worth. Such work can be time-consuming for the department or agency concerned; but it is worthwhile if it achieves a satisfactory resolution to the complaint without a costly full investigation. In 1997/98 our screening staff obtained through informal enquiries what the Ombudsman regarded as due redress in 110 cases, (89 in 1997) ranging from apologies, the provision of information or the carrying out of correct procedures, to the payment of quite large sums of money.

Notes

1 As appears below, the new approach of the PCA's office resulted in a considerable reduction in investigation times, 'from 91 weeks in 1998/99 to 44 weeks in 1999/00 [as] . . . a natural consequence of having cleared the backlog'.[24]

2 The new, more flexible range of procedures that the PCA has introduced are summarised in his report for 2000–01.

Annual Report for 2000–01, HC 5 (2001–2002)

2.7 We have introduced a wider range of responses to complaints, matching outcomes to the individual circumstances of cases. The range of possible outcomes that can flow from a complaint to the Ombudsman is:

2.8 **Outcome 1:** If the body complained against or the subject matter of a complaint is outside the Ombudsman's jurisdiction the matter cannot be considered further.

The Ombudsman continues to receive significant numbers of complaints about areas which are clearly outside his jurisdiction, such as personnel or contractual matters, or decisions which carry a right of appeal. He also receives considerable numbers of complaints about planning matters, where the complainants are unhappy with a planning decision, and essentially want him to criticise a Planning Inspector's professional judgement. In such cases, the most the Ombudsman can do is satisfy himself that the correct procedures have been followed.

Outcome 2: After further consideration within the office the complaint is not taken further, for example if there is no evidence of maladministration resulting in an unremedied personal injustice, or no worthwhile outcome is likely.

Outcome 3A: As an alternative to starting an investigation enquires are made of the department which result in an appropriate outcome to the complaint. Many complaints can be settled quickly and efficiently in this way without a statutory investigation. It is evident from the reaction of complainants and the bodies complained against alike that many appreciate the benefits of this approach.

Outcome 3B: Enquiries of the department or agency concerned result in the complaint not being taken further, eg because no injustice has been suffered or no worthwhile outcome is likely.

2.9 When a statutory investigation is initiated, we issue a statement of the complaint to the body concerned; this is copied to the referring Member.

Outcome 4: The investigation process is initiated, but ended when an appropriate outcome has been achieved or no remedy is available.

Outcome 5: A statutory investigation report is sent to the referring Member.

It is also copied to the body complained against (which has previously had the opportunity to comment on the facts to be reported and their presentation).

2.10 In an increasing proportion of cases it is possible to resolve complaints without completing a statutory report; in those cases, the investigator sends to the referring Member and the body complained against a brief account setting out the main points agreed (2000–01).

Notes

1 As indicated above, the screening process requires the PCA both to take a *prima facie* view of the merits of the complaint and also to decide, in an exercise of his

---

24 Annual Report for 1999–2000, para 1.2.

discretion under the 1967 Act, whether it would be an appropriate use of resources to investigate the complaint. However, late in the 1990s, the PCA came to the view that his office had perhaps been requiring too much in the way of evidence from complainants to satisfy his office that there was a *prima facie* case. As the Cabinet Office Review found:

> ... There is much emphasis on establishing whether there is a *prima facie* case before the ombudsman is prepared to investigate – this puts pressure on complainants to (in effect) prove their case ... A complex complaint can involve considerable investigation during screening, and result in rejection if it fails to leap all the hurdles or acceptance for investigation of only part of the complaint (para 6.53).

2 The PCA had already concluded that 'there is a risk that the evidential burden can be set too high', as reported in his Annual Report for 1998–99 (paras 1.6–1.8). In his Annual Report for 1999–2000, the PCA explained:

> It will still be right to refuse to investigate complaints when it is clear that they express nothing more than discontent with the substance of a discretionary decision. Otherwise, my Office will exercise a clear bias in favour of starting an investigation. The Office began to give this modified approach effect from November 1999: since then, the proportion of complaints accepted for investigation has risen by 6% (para 1.14).

Remedies[25]

Findings and recommendations made by the PCA are not enforceable in law. Thus the adverse publicity generated by a refusal to comply with a recommendation is the only sanction for non-compliance. However, it appears that the influence of the PCA is far greater in practice than his formal powers. Government in practice accepts that the PCA's findings should be complied with as the following Treasury Guidance indicates:

> The PCA's recommendations on remedies are not legally binding on departments and could be rejected. However, the Financial Secretary to the Treasury in giving evidence to the Select Committee on the PCA on 18 December 1991 said, 'I am not aware of any circumstances in which the (the PCA's) recommendations have been ignored. This is the basis on which the Government has tended to work – and has, as far as I am aware always worked – in that we do accept and implement the recommendations that are made'.[26]

This is borne out by the testimony of the PCA himself:

Annual Report for 1998–99, HC 572, para 1.4.

Redress of itself is not a measure of achievement. Redress should be given only when justified. Nevertheless, the subsequent chapters in this report record many examples of redress achieved, sometimes tens of thousands of pounds when the facts of a case justified it. Such redress is not always easily achieved. I am concerned at the numbers of cases in which, even after a full investigation by my Office and a carefully scrutiny of the relevant facts, departments continue to resist for a time the provision of redress which is clearly due. I do not take 'no' for an answer on such occasions. It is pleasing to report that, despite large individual compensation payments sometimes being involved, there were no cases in which eventually departments failed to concede redress if my staff and I were clear that it was due. Nevertheless, in some cases that process took far longer than it should.

---

25 For a recent survey of the PCA's success in securing *ex gratia* payments for complainants, see M Amos [2000] PL 21.

26 Official Guidance to Departments and Agencies concerning *ex gratia* financial compensation, DAO (GEN) 15/92, para 8.

Notes

1   Although the PCA's lack of formal powers might appear to weaken the institution, it has been argued that the need for such a limitation is inherent in his role as suggested in the definition above in the introduction to this chapter. If the PCA could award compulsory remedies, it would be necessary to give the department complained about a full and formal opportunity to answer the allegations made. Probably some of the procedures would have to be conducted in public. The fact that the PCA operates informally and privately has been thought to enhance his powers of persuasion. Where a particular complaint seems to be merely symptomatic of a deep-seated problem in a department, the PCA can sometimes persuade it to change its general procedure. This occurred in the *Ostler* case [1977] QB 122: the Department of the Environment was persuaded to introduce new procedures in order to prevent a repetition of the situation that led to Ostler's complaint. Thus, this apparent weakness in the PCA's powers may underlie one of his main strengths. On the other hand, the lack of a power to award a remedy may in some situations appear to amount to a weakness in the PCA system. In *Congreve v Home Office* [1976] 2 QB 629, the applicant succeeded in showing that the Home Office had acted unlawfully as regards television licence fees and a refund was awarded. The situation had already been investigated by the PCA which had found inefficiency on the part of the Home Office but had not recommended a remedy for licence holders.

2   However, as the Cabinet Office Review noted at para 6.76,

> Resolution in favour of the complainant will almost always involve some form of redress. This might be an action following intervention to solve a problem (for example, providing the service which has not been delivered or the benefit which has been delayed) or retrospective redress such as an explanation, apology or compensation. Sometimes both may be involved – both restoration of benefit including arrears and perhaps interest and consolatory payments.

> *Ex gratia* payments to individuals adversely affected by maladministration appear to be made in roughly half of the cases in which the PCA makes a finding of maladministration (in 92 out of 177 cases in 1992 and in 108 out of 236 cases in 1995). Apologies, reconsideration of an individual case and/or changes to administrative rules and procedures may also result. Remedies may also be offered to other members of the public known to have been affected by a problem similar to that of the complainant.

3   However, as Austin has noted, compliance with the PCA's recommendations usually involves the payment of *ex gratia* compensation, an apology or the reconsideration of a prior decision by the correct process. Rarely does it involve reversal on merits of an important policy decision.[27] Indeed, in certain cases the government will explicitly state that it does not accept the PCA's finding of maladministration but is prepared to offer payment or an apology as a gesture of goodwill or out of respect for the PCA. This occurred in relation to the notorious Barlow Clowes affair: the PCA found five areas of serious maladministration by the Department of Trade and Industry in relation to the affair, in which many investors lost their life savings when Barlow Clowes – a brokerage business – collapsed. The government rejected the findings, but nevertheless, 'out of respect for the office of Parliamentary Commissioner'[28] offered very considerable *ex gratia* payments to the victims totalling £150 million, an outcome which Wade and Forsyth describe as 'his

---

27 'Freedom of information: the constitutional impact', in J Jowell and D Oliver (eds), *The Changing Constitution*, 3rd edn (1994), p 443.
28 HC Deb 164 cols 201–11 (19 December 1989).

most spectacular single achievement thus far'.[29] (There was a similar outcome in the Channel Tunnel rail link case (below p 819).)

4   The compensation procured by the PCA may not always satisfy the complainant. As the Cabinet Office Review noted at para 6.77:

> One difficulty at present is that the ombudsman cannot necessarily provide all the redress which a complainant may feel entitled to. The principle which the ombudsmen adhere to is that as far as possible a complainant should be put back in the position they would have been in if the action complained of had not occurred. This may not be achievable and can raise expectations in complainants ... Complainants may be dissatisfied with compensation payments because they feel the compensation does not put them back in the position they would have been in (for example, compensation for the loss of highly speculative future profit claimed by a business) or that they are inadequate for the stress and inconvenience suffered. There can also be a gap between what a respondent body can be held responsible for and the impact felt by a complainant.

5   A further problem with the remedial system operated by the PCA is that of delay: whilst departments nearly always accept the PCA's recommendations in the end, considerable time may be spent in haggling over the compensation suggested. The Public Administration Committee's report on the PCA's Annual Report for 1998–99 commented:

> We are particularly concerned that the delays mentioned above can still be attributed in part to 'prolonged delays before departments accepted our recommendations for redress in cases in which we had found complaints of maladministration to be justified'.[30]

From the latest commentary of the Select Committee on the PCA, it appears that this situation has, if anything, got worse.

Third Report of the Public Administration Select Committee, *Ombudsman Issues*, HC 448 (26 February 2003)

15. When he published his annual report last year, Sir Michael said 'We have noticed a tendency for departments to take a harder line and be less co-operative' adding that investigations into mismanagement by departments were 'uphill work'. He also accused officials of double standards in 'imposing strict deadlines for public complaints while taking too long to sort things out when complaints were upheld'. We find it unacceptable that departments should be so casual about meeting their responsibilities.

16. The Ombudsman made the point that the length of time taken by the bodies with which his office is in contact, will inevitably impact upon the ability of his office to meet its own targets and improve performance ... In his annual report last year Sir Michael commented 'I remain concerned at the length of time that it takes departments and agencies both to respond to the statement of complaint which is the precursor of an investigation and to agree to redress when investigation by my office has disclosed injustice resulting from maladministration'.

. . .

33. The evidence we received from these organisations suggests that the Ombudsman is quite right to be concerned about their administrative capacities. The failure of organisations to respond to the deadlines given to them by the Ombudsman is for instance a real concern. Whether the request relates to an initial investigation or comments on the Ombudsman's draft findings, prompt replies will enhance public administration. Failure to meet these deadlines will affect the capacity of the Ombudsman's office to provide a speedy and effective service to the public. As the then minister, Mr Leslie made clear in his evidence: 'The Prime Minister talks of the four pillars of public service reform, and the first of those is higher standards of inspection and accountability'. The

---

29   HWR Wade and C Forsyth, *Administrative Law*, 8th edn (2000), p 100.
30   HC 106, para 9.

Ombudsman is a key component of the mechanisms which hold government to account. If the Government wishes to make public services responsive to citizens, as it claims, it must ensure that public service agencies take their obligations to the Ombudsman more seriously. One practical step in this direction would be for each department or agency to have a designated unit which liaises directly with the Ombudsman. We understand that some agencies already operate such a system, but we would like to see this improved and expanded.

Note

The PCA will often enter into extended consultation with a department over the compensation it proposes to offer, especially in complex cases. The following, which involved the disastrous advice and mismanagement by the preceding administration over the State Earnings Repayment Scheme, is an example:

Annual Report for 2000–01, HC 5 (2001–02), para 12

In my Annual Report for 1999/2000 I described my investigations into complaints about incomplete and inaccurate guidance from the Department of Social Security (DSS) concerning changes in SERPS; and I said that when details of the government's proposals on a scheme for redress were available I intended to offer Parliament my advice on whether the proposals were in principle capable of providing appropriate redress. During the year DSS consulted me as they developed their proposals, although I was mindful that my primary responsibility is to advise Parliament, not the government. Partly as a result of those discussions DSS substantially revised their original plan for a protected rights scheme for those who could demonstrate that they had been misled … I laid a further report before Parliament on 26 February (HC 271) in which I broadly welcomed the government's proposals as providing a global solution to the problem of making good the effects of past maladministration. Regulations to give effect to the proposals were approved by Parliament in March.

Examples of the PCA's work

The following extracts from PCA Annual Reports give a flavour of the kinds of cases investigated by the PCA, and the outcomes his office can procure.

[C.373/00]
Benefits Agency

Mr W complained that the Benefits Agency had refused to pay him invalid care allowance backdated to May 1995 when his wife had claimed disability living allowance. *After our informal enquiry, the Agency said that they recognised that the claim pack for invalid care allowance in circulation between April 1991 and April 1995 had misdirected customers by telling them not to make a claim until the person they looked after had been awarded disability living allowance at the middle or highest rate. On this basis the Agency made an ex gratia payment to Mr W of £6,496.20 for the period May 1995 to September 1998 to compensate him for the invalid care allowance he should have received.*

[C.1571/00]
Benefits Agency

The Benefits Agency mishandled a claim to disability living allowance on behalf of D (a child), who sadly died six months later. There had been confusion over whether the claim, which had been made under normal rules, could be considered under special rules for those terminally ill. The claim was disallowed and the confusion caused a loss of opportunity to appeal. *As a result of our informal enquiry, the Agency reviewed the case under their new decision making and appeals system, and were able to decide to award D the higher rate of care and mobility components of disability living allowance for the six months in question, amounting to £2,467.*

[C.1276/99]
Employment Service
Ms G lost her job on 5 August 1997; and jobcentre staff told her incorrectly on 8 August 1997 that she would not qualify for jobseeker's allowance as she was attending a part-time course. After completing her course, Ms G applied successfully for jobseeker's allowance on 10 March 1998 and was then told that the advice she had been given in August had been incorrect. Ms G was awarded jobseeker's allowance backdated for three months (the maximum allowed under the regulations) on the grounds that she had been misdirected in August 1997. On 11 August 1998 Ms G applied for backdated jobseeker's allowance for the period 8 August 1997 to 3 December 1997. This application was disallowed, and her subsequent appeal to a social security appeal tribunal was dismissed. *As a result of our informal enquiry, the Employment Service concluded that Ms G had lost an opportunity to claim income-based jobseeker's allowance as a result of having been given incorrect information about the effect of training she was undertaking on her eligibility for jobseeker's allowance. They awarded her an ex gratia payment of £820 for that loss and £20 as compensation for late payment.*

[C.334/99]
Legal Aid Board
The Legal Aid Board (as it then was) delayed making amendments to reduce the statutory charge owed then by Mrs L and sending her a recalculated statement as they had promised to do. *Our informal enquiry showed that the Board had delayed taking corrective action and had sent the promised recalculation late. They offered apologies for that. The information, however, was not clearly presented; and a second informal enquiry resulted in a fuller breakdown of Mrs L's account and clarification of earlier statements. There had been no financial loss to Mrs L.*

[C.852/00]
Court Service
The Court Service mishandled requests for copy papers, particularly those for copies of a witness summons, and also Mrs R's attempts to complain about that mishandling. *Following our informal enquiry, the Court Service acknowledged their mishandling, explained what papers the court held, and what had gone wrong with their dealings with Mrs R on the issue, advised the court manager responsible for the court how things might have been better handled, and apologised for their failings.*

[C.551/99]
Child Support Agency: loss of entitlement to child support maintenance
The Ombudsman upheld Mrs X's complaint that she had no enforceable right to child support maintenance for a period of more than a year because an interim maintenance assessment which CSA had imposed was defective. Subsequently the non-resident parent had told CSA that he had become employed and had provided the details of his employer; but CSA had taken no action to make a full maintenance assessment or to obtain payment from him during the period of 13 months while he was employed. Following a report on the case by the Independent Case Examiner, CSA agreed to make Mrs X a payment of £160 for the trouble she had been caused and for her out-of-pocket expenses, but they refused to compensate her for loss of entitlement to child support maintenance on the grounds that the non-resident parent had not established a regular pattern of payments. *Following the Ombudsman's intervention, CSA accepted that a regular payment pattern would have been established but for their maladministration. CSA agreed to make Mrs X an advance payment of £9,447.91 in respect of arrears owed by the non-resident parent, and compensatory payments totalling £3,745.41 for her lost entitlement to child support maintenance and interest.*

[C.543/00]
Child Support Agency: mishandling a claim to child support maintenance
The Ombudsman found that CSA had made a number of serious mistakes in their handling of Mrs H's case. Mrs H applied for child support maintenance in January 1994. CSA imposed an interim

maintenance assessment on the non-resident parent in May 1994, but took no action to collect child support maintenance until September 1996. They discovered in November 1997 that the interim maintenance assessment was invalid, but did not issue a new one until January 1999. When the qualifying child reached the age of 19 CSA closed the case and mistakenly informed the non-resident parent that he owed nothing. CSA had made Mrs H a consolatory payment of £150. *Following the Ombudsman's intervention, CSA made Mrs H a further payment of £20 to cover postage and telephone calls. They also decided that they had had sufficient information to make full maintenance assessments from the outset and made Mrs H a lump sum advance payment of arrears of £13,289.34, plus £2,137.42 as interest for loss of use of that money, and agreed to consider compensation for her*

Note

One of the most important recent investigations by the PCA concerned a number of complaints by those whose property has been affected by the Channel Tunnel rail link.[31] The investigation was notable in being the largest ever undertaken by the PCA;[32] it also involved the PCA in the unusual step of examining the department's[33] handling of the project as a whole, albeit in the context of five individual complaints. The problems generated concerned peoples' homes, the value of which had been blighted by the prospect that the rail link would run past or near them. The PCA's report[34] found that there had been maladministration, causing widespread blight for which the government had not, in line with existing policy, made any provision; however, it also found that there were a number of cases of exceptional hardship, in respect of which it recommended that compensation should be offered. The Select Committee on the PCA backed the PCA's findings and recommendations.[35] The department denied that there had been any maladministration, and, unusually, refused to implement the PCA's recommendations. Neither the PCA nor the Select Committee were impressed by the department's arguments; in particular, both denied strongly that in asking the department to look again at exceptional cases, they were criticising the general government policy of not offering compensation for generalised blight. On this point, the Select Committee said:

> At the heart of this debate is a definition of maladministration found in the [PCA's 1993 Annual Report] failure to mitigate the effects of rigid adherence to the letter of the law where that produces manifestly inequitable treatment ... The definition, which we fully support, implies an expectation that, when an individual citizen is faced with extraordinary hardship as a result of strict application of law or policy, the executive must be prepared to look again and consider whether help can be given.[36]

The department faced with the embarrassing prospect of a debate in the Commons on the matter, in which it would have been opposed by a unanimous, cross-party Select Committee, eventually agreed to look again at the possibility of a compensation scheme for those affected to an exceptional or extreme degree by the generalised blight. However, the government made it clear that it agreed to this only out of respect for the PCA Select Committee and the office of Parliamentary Commissioner, and without admission of fault of liability, a concession described by Diane Longley and Rhoda James as grudging.[37] Nevertheless, in terms of winning compensation, the PCA had prevailed again.

---

31 See generally on this, *ibid*. We are indebted to the authors for the discussion that follows.
32 Annual Report of the PCA for 1995, Cm 296, p 3, para 7.
33 The department concerned was Transport.
34 Fifth Report of the PCA, HC 193 (1994–95).
35 Sixth Report of the Select Committee on the PCA, HC 270 (1994–95).
36 *Ibid*, para 20; quoted in D Longley and R James, *Administrative Justice: Central Issues in UK and European Administrative Law* (1999), p 42.
37 *Op cit*, p 44.

ACCOUNTABILITY OF THE PCA

Parliamentary accountability

Appendix to the Minutes of Evidence Taken before the Select Committee on the PCA, HC 64 (1993–94), Vol II

3.9 Accountability of the ombudsmen

One advantage of the present schemes is that the ombudsmen are accountable to the Select Committee for their working practices. This is clearly a powerful tool. However, much of the public accountability of the ombudsmen depends on how far the Select Committee will raise issues with the ombudsmen which affect consumers. While the number of cases investigated and the time taken to complete investigations is assessed, these are throughput measures. Such efficiency measures have little meaning for consumers unless effectiveness is also included in the equation.

Therefore the accountability of the ombudsman services would be improved if more information about service-targets and standards were made publicly available. The Parliamentary Ombudsman and the Health Services Ombudsman should set service targets or standards and report their performance against them. In addition to the information they already provide, they each should account for their performance in the following areas:

(i) Consumer satisfaction: how satisfied are complainants with the way the ombudsman handled their complaint?

(ii) Efficiency: how long it takes the ombudsmen to get Government departments and agencies to respond to requests for information and how long does it take for the ombudsman to complete an investigation?

(iii) Effectiveness: to what extent Government departments and agencies comply with the ombudsmen's recommendations?

(iv) Complaints not investigated: details about the number and types of complaints which are not investigated, why they were not investigated, and what alternative dispute resolution process was available to the complainant, if any?

The ombudsmen should consider producing a Citizens Charter style document or Standards Statement, which would contain many of the above features.

Note

The PCA's Annual Reports and his reports on special and on selected cases are laid before Parliament and provide a means of explaining the PCA's role and work. As part of the Cabinet Office Review, MPs were asked how often they read these reports: 12 per cent of those replying to the survey never read them, 35 per cent hardly ever, 47 per cent occasionally, and only 5 per cent frequently reading the reports.[38]

Judicial control

The decision in *R v Parliamentary Commissioner for Administration ex p Dyer* [1994] 1 WLR 621 had indicated that, in principle, the decisions of the PCA were subject to judicial review, though Simon Brown LJ 'emphasised that the court was not readily to be persuaded to interfere with the exercise of the Commissioner's discretion. Indeed he went so far as to wonder whether in reality the end result is much different from that arrived at by Lord Bridge of Harwich in *ex p Hammersmith and Fulham* [[1994] 1

---

38 Cabinet Office Review, para 3.24.

WLR 621, 626]',[39] in other words that review would lie only to correct the extremes of bad faith, improper motive or manifest absurdity (see Chapter 2 of this part, pp 780–83). Subsequent case law has indicated a somewhat less deferential approach to review of the PCA. The two *ex p Balchin* decisions have pushed forward the extent and depth of judicial scrutiny of decisions of the PCA.

R v Parliamentary Commissioner for Administration ex p Balchin [1998] PLR I

A proposed new bypass, approved by the Department of Transport (DOT), caused serious blight to the Balchins' £400,000 home, rendering it worthless, and thus causing the Balchins to become bankrupt when banks called in the loans secured on the house and Mr Balchin's business failed as a consequence. Norfolk local authority did not compulsorily purchase the property, deciding instead to follow a scheme whereby compensation would be paid to the Balchins only once the road was completed. In fact, the road scheme was abandoned.

The Balchins complained to the PCA on the basis that the minister responsible had been guilty of maladministration in approving the scheme without seeking assurances from the local authority that it would compensate the Balchins. The PCA's finding was that the DOT had not been guilty of maladministration because the minister was under no obligation to seek such assurances, and even though his officials could have pointed out to the Council its statutory discretionary power to purchase the property under s 246(2A) of the Highways Act, it was evident that the Council would not have acted under it (it had rejected an invitation from the Balchins' bank to exercise its powers under this provision). The Balchins sought judicial review of the PCA's decision, arguing, *inter alia*, that he had misdirected himself in relation to the DOT's failure to point out to the Council its powers under s 246(2A).

> **Sedley J:** I have hesitated long before concluding that, notwithstanding the very wide area of judgment and discretion given to the Commissioner by the Act, he has been led by a scrupulous regard for his jurisdictional remit, excluding as it does local government, into a failure to consider the relevant fact of Norfolk's attitude – not with a view to deciding whether it was unlawful or even (to use his own neologism) maladministrative but in order to decide, as his own findings made it necessary for him to do, whether the Department of Transport ought in response to have drawn the council's attention to its new power to acquire blighted property [s 246(2A)] and perhaps also to its obligation to consider exercising it. In other words, once Norfolk's apparent disregard of its obligations was established by him, the Commissioner could not properly avoid the question whether correct advice with the imprimatur of central government might have made a difference.
>
> Whether the Department's undoubted failure to tender such advice amounted to a maladministration and whether, if it did, it caused injustice to the Balchins remains entirely a question for the Commissioner. My decision is limited to holding that in declining to consider the ostensible propriety of Norfolk County Council's negative attitude to its compensatory powers and its amenability to correction by the Department, the Commissioner omitted a potentially decisive element from his consideration of whether the Department of Transport had caused injustice to the Balchins by maladministration in its dealings with the county council.

Notes

1   The ruling was thus that the PCA should reconsider the Balchins' complaint, taking into account this time the failure of the DOT to draw the attention of the Council to

---

39   N Marsh, 'The extent and depth of judicial review of the decisions of the Parliamentary Commissioner for Administration' [1994] PL 347.

their power under s 246(2A). It was careful not to give any indication as to whether, had the PCA taken this into account, he would be bound to have made a finding of maladministration, as that would have been to invade the PCA's discretionary area of judgment. Nevertheless, as Giddings points out, 'This ruling was the first time a finding by the Parliamentary Ombudsman had been overturned in the courts.'[40]

2   In the light of this decision, the case was then reconsidered by the PCA;[41] his fresh report indicated that he had explicitly considered whether the Secretary of State had been at fault in not specifically drawing the Council's attention to the new power, and whether it would have made any difference if he had. The PCA's new report, at para 22, cited the evidence of the Permanent Secretary of the DOT:

> He said in DOT's view it had been reasonable and proper for them to have assumed that the council were aware of the extension to their previous powers. DOE had informed local authorities of the new legislative provision through DOE Circular No 15/91, issued on 4 September 1991, which had included an annex drawing specific attention to the extended powers. In addition, DOT had issued a press notice in January 1992, signalling their own intention to consider using the new powers on merit by reference to published guidelines. That press notice had been widely reported at the time. DOT saw it as the duty of the council to ensure that they were aware of statutory powers available to them.

The PCA concluded that the minister had not acted maladministratively, principally because the Council had been informed of the new power by a standard government circular, and the minister was entitled to assume that the Council were therefore aware of their new powers. This decision was once again challenged by way of judicial review. One of the arguments relied upon was that the PCA had given no reason for finding, as he had, that the DOT had in fact borne in mind the s 246(2A) power in relation to the Balchins' home.

R v Parliamentary Commissioner for Administration ex p Balchin (No 2), 24 May 1999, QBD[42]

Dyson J: The words attributed to the Permanent Secretary in paragraph 22 of the decision seem to me to have been carefully chosen. Nowhere does he say expressly that those who were handling the Balchins' case were aware of the existence of section 246(2A). But he clearly implies that the DOT was aware of the section, since otherwise he could hardly have said that it was reasonable 'in DOT's view' to have assumed that the Council was aware of the power. It would appear that the Commissioner did not explore with the Permanent Secretary the state of knowledge of those in the DOT who were actually dealing with the Balchins' case. But, in my view, if he had thought about the picture that was disclosed by the contemporaneous documents that were before him, he would surely have pressed the Permanent Secretary on this point. This is because the documents pointed very strongly to the conclusion that those involved with the case had indeed overlooked the existence of the power.

... As we have seen, the first Commissioner did raise with the DOT the question of why section 246(2A) was not mentioned in these documents, and was given the explanation of 'overstepping the mark', which he found 'unconvincing'. The second Commissioner did not raise this question. But it was a critical question, since the answer to it would cast shafts of light on the issue of whether those in the Department who were handling the Balchins' case were aware of section 246(2A).

---

40   P Giddings [2000] PL 201.
41   In fact it was considered by a new PCA, Mr Buckley.
42   Reported at (2000) LGLR 87.

In the result, the Commissioner made no finding as to whether any, and if so which, of the officials in the Department who were handling the Balchins' case were aware of section 246(2A). In my judgment, this is a crucial omission. It was immaterial that there were some officials within the Department who were aware of the section at the material time. What mattered, for the purpose of an inquiry into whether there had been maladministration in failing to seek to persuade the Council to exercise its power under section 246(2A), was whether those who were dealing with this case were aware of it. The reason why this omission is so important is that the documents make it overwhelmingly likely that all of those persons overlooked the existence of the power at the material time.

In short, the finding that the DOT did not overlook section 246(2A) was at the heart of the Commissioner's conclusion that there was no maladministration. It was this finding that enabled him to conclude that the decision reached by the DOT was 'within the reasonable range of responses open to them given their knowledge' and 'one they were entitled to take' (paragraph 29). It is not possible to say what conclusion he would have reached on the issue of maladministration if he had found that those handling the Balchins' case had overlooked section 246(2A). I think that the Commissioner was unwittingly led into error by the rather unspecific evidence of the Permanent Secretary. It is possible that, as Mr Elvin suggests, there were persons in the DOT handling the Balchins' case who had not overlooked section 246(2A). But if that is so, there is no trace of them in any of the material that has been placed before me. Moreover, given the close interest shown by the Minister, and the terms in which his various letters were expressed, the hypothesis suggested by Mr Elvin is inherently unlikely. This emphasises the shortcomings in the reasoning of the Commissioner's decision.

In reaching the conclusion that the decision on maladministration is flawed, I am very conscious of what Sedley J referred to as 'the very wide areas of judgment and discretion given to the Commissioner by the Act' (page 929). I have had regard to the warning as to the limited scope for interference by the courts in these cases given by the Divisional Court in ex parte Dyer [1994] 1 WLR 621. But that was a case in which the ground of challenge was about the manner in which the Commissioner handled the complaint. Simon Brown LJ said that the Act gave the Commissioner a broad discretion as to the scope of any investigation, and the way in which he conducted it. It is not, however, disputed by Mr Elvin that a decision of the Commissioner is susceptible to a reasons challenge, where there is real doubt in relation to the principal controversial issues as to what was decided and why: see Clarke Homes Limited v The Secretary of State 66 P&CR 263, 271–2.

Mr Elvin also relies on the passage in the judgment of Sir Thomas Bingham MR in ex parte Smith [1996] QB 517, 554–556 that 'the greater the policy content of a decision, and the more remote the subject matter of a decision from ordinary judicial experience, the more hesitant the Court must necessarily be in holding a decision to be irrational'. He submits that the court should be particularly reluctant to interfere with decisions of the Commissioner, since they are 'policy laden'. I would not quarrel with this as a general rule. But where the court finds that there is a real shortcoming in the reasoning of the Commissioner, it seems to me that it is not passing judgment on the substance of a policy decision. It is criticising the reasoning on grounds which do not depend in any way on the policy element of the decision.

[Dyson J went on to consider a further ground of challenge, based on the argument that the PCA had impliedly concluded that no injustice, within the meaning of the 1967 Act had been caused to the Balchins because, even had the DOT specifically drawn the attention of the Council to the s 246(2A) power, the Council would not have exercised it.]

At page 926 of his judgment, Sedley J said this of injustice:

> Less judicial attention had been devoted so far to the meaning of 'injustice' in the legislation, but de Smith, Woolf and Jowell, Judicial Review of Administrative Action (5th ed) write at paragraph 1–102: 'Injustice' has been widely interpreted so as to cover not merely injury redressible in a court of law, but also 'the sense of outrage aroused by unfair or incompetent

administration, even where the complainant has suffered no actual loss' (citing Mr RHS Crossman, speaking as Leader of the House of Commons). It follows that the defence familiar in legal proceedings, that because the outcome would have been the same in any event there has been no redressible wrong, does not run in an investigation by the Commissioner.

... regard can be had to what Mr Crossman said in Parliament when promoting the 1967 Act. What he said was: 'We have not tried to define injustice by using such terms as "loss or damage". These may have legal overtones which could be held to exclude one thing which I am particularly anxious shall remain – the sense of outrage aroused by unfair or incompetent administration, even where the complainant has suffered no actual loss ... or damage in the legal sense of those terms ...'

[Dyson J then considered, but rejected, an argument that the PCA must be found to have misdirected himself as to the meaning of the word 'injustice', but went on:]

... the Balchins had a very strong case on outrage. They had been financially ruined by the proposed scheme, and the Minister had made it clear to his officials that he wanted to ensure that the Council helped them. And yet, *ex hypothesi*, in its dealings with the Council over the Balchins' case, the DOT overlooked the existence of the only power which, if invoked, could have helped them. It is not possible to know what view the Commissioner had as to how bad a case of maladministration this would have been, and how intense a sense of outrage it would have aroused, on the assumption (contrary to his findings) that the DOT did overlook the power and was guilty of maladministration.

This leads me straight to the question of the adequacy of the Commissioner's reasons. He could have simply refused to deal with the issue of injustice on the grounds that his findings of maladministration were sufficient to dispose of the matter. But I have rejected Mr Elvin's argument that this is what he did ... It is clear that the issue of injustice was one of the principal controversial issues, and the Commissioner was required to give reasons in relation to it, which were sufficient to enable the parties to know what he decided, and why. In my judgment, since the case on outrage was so strong, the Commissioner should have made it clear that he had considered it, and why he had decided that it did not involve injustice in this case. The failure to mention it leads to the reasonable suspicion that he failed to have regard to it at all, or that, if he did, his reasons for concluding that there was no injustice would not bear scrutiny. In my view, this reasons challenge is justified. I would rest this part of my decision on the simple fact that the Commissioner should have dealt expressly with the outrage point.

Notes

1   Giddings comments that the first finding of unlawfulness – the failure of the PCA to give proper reasons as to his finding that the DOT *did* bear in mind the s 246(2A) power when dealing with the Council – amounts to:

a further move towards setting a standard of reasoning on the record for the Ombudsman which could put at risk the essential informality and accessibility of the institution. If judges require the Ombudsman to meet the decision-making standards set for courts, then what was an informal, non-judicial mechanism for complaints-handling will become a formal, judicial one ...[43]

2   Giddings concludes that the case:

clarifies in two important respects the reach of judicial review of the [PCA] ... and those two aspects lie at the heart of the Ombudsman's statutory remit: to determine whether the complainant has suffered injustice in consequence of maladministration. First, the Ombudsman's process for finding maladministration has been held to be amenable to judicial review – and in this case was found wanting by the court in two respects: investigative failure and shortcomings in

---

43   [2000] PL 201, 203.

subsequent reasoning. Secondly, the meaning of 'injustice has been clarified to include not only loss but also a sense of outrage and indignation'.[44]

3   The extent of the amenability of decision-making by the PCA to judicial review is now such that in the 2000 Cabinet Office Review,[45] the authors said simply: 'The Ombudsman's entire process is subject to judicial review.'

THE LOCAL OMBUDSMEN

The ombudsman system has proved very popular: it was extended to the Health Service with the establishment of three Health Service Commissioners in 1972 and 1973, to Northern Ireland under the Commissioner for Complaints Act (Northern Ireland) 1969, and to local government (the LGO) under the Local Government Act 1974. In 1990, a Legal Services Ombudsman was set up. There is also a non-statutory Prison Services Ombudsman, established in 1993. A number of ombudsmen have also been established in the private sector (see p 792 above). Consideration of most of the other ombudsmen is outside the remit of this book, but brief consideration will be given to the work of the LGO.

Review of the Public Sector Ombudsmen in England, April 2000

1.32 The Commission for Local Administration administers the Local Government Ombudsmen who deal with complaints about local authorities. The CLA includes on its board the three Local Government Ombudsmen and the Parliamentary Commissioner in an ex officio capacity, and it supervises the organisation, finance and accommodation of the Ombudsmen who otherwise operate independently covering different parts of England from offices in York, Coventry and London. Complainants can approach the ombudsmen direct with requests to investigate their complaints. Although the general principles of the PCA and HSC schemes apply in respect of jurisdictional and timeliness issues there are some exceptions to the jurisdiction which were introduced into the Local Government Act 1974, for example there are considerable restrictions on the ombudsman's ability to examine education problems.

1.33 The Local Government Ombudsmen tend to intervene rather earlier in cases and seek rather more frequently the pragmatic solutions or mediation which lead to what are known as 'local settlements'. Out of 15,653 decided cases in 1998/99, local settlement accounted for 2,251. Including cases fully investigated (subject to formal report), redress was obtained or recommended in 2,624 cases. The number of cases received is rising considerably after several years of stability and may reach 18,000 by the end of 1999/2000. The reasons for this are unclear.

1.34 As with the PCA/HSC, only a small proportion (about 5%) of cases are fully investigated. But local settlement provides many complainants with the redress which they were denied by the local authority's own complaints process. As a result of different working methods the CLA tends to have shorter throughput times than the PCA/HSC. In 1999, the LGOs decided 54.9% of cases within 13 weeks, and 81.1% within 26 weeks.

Notes

1   Seneviratne notes that the following bodies are subject to investigation by the Local Government Ombudsmen (LGO): district, borough, city, or county councils (not town or parish councils); the Commission for New Towns or new town development corporations (housing matters only); housing action trusts; police

---

44   *Ibid*, at 204.
45   *Review of the Public Sector Ombudsmen in England*, April 2000, para 1.24.

authorities; fire authorities; any joint board of local authorities, including the National Park Boards; the National Rivers Authority (flood defence and land drainage matters only); and the Broads Authority. In practice, the vast majority of investigations involve local councils.[46]

2   Although the distinction between policy (which the LGO may not question) and administration is generally maintainable, it has on occasion caused disagreement. The distinction is clearly of the greatest importance in terms of defining the proper ambit of the LGO's investigations; it arose for consideration in *R v Local Commissioner ex p Eastleigh Borough Council* [1988] 3 WLR 116. Michael Jones comments:[47]

Eastleigh's first importance, perhaps, is that it helps to clarify the impact which s 34(3) of the 1974 Act has upon the scope of the commissioner's jurisdiction [s 34(3) is in the same terms as s 12(3) PCA 1967, above p 794] ... In *Eastleigh*, the court's interpretation of s 34(3) affirms the orthodox view, and the legislatures intent, that the commissioners ought not to usurp the policy-making discretions of democratically elected authorities; by s 26(1) of the 1974 Act, they are directed to investigate action taken in the exercise of [the] administrative functions of [an] authority. The justification for the exclusion of policy-oriented complaints is clear:

Legislators, local as well as national, regard policy as the area where they alone are sovereign, where their decisions of principle must not be constitutionally questioned except by themselves in their own chamber. To allow an ombudsman to enter would be to diminish that prerogative of rulership [Glasser, *Town Hall* (1984), p 159].

But how far does the prohibition in s 34(3) extend? Parker LJ ... recognised that the immunity conferred by s 34(3) is not absolute: the terms of s 34(3) do not preclude the ombudsman from questioning the merits of all discretionary policy decisions, but only those taken without maladministration [*ibid*, at 123]. In other words, the local ombudsmen (and their parliamentary colleague) may continue to find maladministration in the processes by which discretionary decisions are made upon grounds which closely resemble the *Wednesbury* principles of review employed by the courts: relevancy, proper purposes and so on. And there may still be room for a finding of maladministration where a commissioner considers that the terms of an authority's policy transcend the bounds of reasonableness, and step into perversity, capriciousness, or what the courts now term irrationality. After all, the Parliamentary Commissioner, prompted by his Select Committee, has developed the analogous concept of the bad rule.

2   The LGO has a dual role: the redress of individual grievances and the achievement of better administration. However the great bulk of the work centres on individual grievance handling;[48] one role is clearly subordinate to the other.[49]

3   The LGO has responded to its (subordinate) role as general advice-giver in a number of ways. One is the preparation of guidance notes for local authorities on a wide variety of topics, including disposal of land, declaration of interests, and repair and improvement of council houses.[50] Another lies in its practice of making general recommendations on good administrative practice when dealing with an individual complaint, with the aim of preventing such complaints recurring. Seneviratne notes how, in a recent case (CLA case report 89/A/939), the LGO felt that the council had failed to conform to some basic standards of good administration in dealing with an application for housing, and it took the trouble to

46 Seneviratne, *op cit*, p 85.
47 M Jones [1988] PL 608.
48 *Ibid*, p 86.
49 For discussion of the potentiality of the LGO to improve administration generally, see C Crawford, 'Complaints, codes, and ombudsmen in local government' [1988] PL 246.
50 Seneviratne, *op cit*, p 117.

itemise in the annual report four basic axioms of good administration. These are, first, that although it is not wrong in itself for a council to discriminate for or against certain classes of applicants, such discrimination must be made for proper reasons and be seen to be fair. Secondly, that when allocating housing, and when making many other decisions, proper criteria should be used. Thirdly, that reasons should be given for administrative decisions; and last, that such reasons should be noted in writing (CLA annual report 1990–91, 14).[51]

4   The LGO, like the PCA, has no powers to enforce his findings. This, however, has proved somewhat more controversial in relation to the LGO, as the following discussion indicates.

DCM Yardley, 'Local ombudsmen in England: recent trends and developments' [1983] PL 522, 525–27, 529–31

The great majority of local authorities respond promptly, willingly and positively to reports issued by the Local Ombudsman, and it is not often necessary to issue further reports. ... But there remains a hard core of resistance in some local authorities which for various reasons take the view that in the cases concerned they have acted rightly, and that the Local Ombudsman's findings do not persuade them to the contrary....

... Some writers have drawn attention to the provisions in the Commissioner for Complaints Act (Northern Ireland) 1969 whereby the person aggrieved may, on a finding by the commissioner of injustice caused by maladministration, apply to the county court for damages or a mandatory or other injunction if the authority have not complied with the report. Little use has been made of this provision in practice, but some think that it would act powerfully upon the will of local authorities to comply with reports which are adverse to them.

[However,] the fact remains that ombudsmen normally work entirely by persuasion, backed by the force of publicity and parliamentary criticism. It is my view and that of my colleagues that this is how we should continue to work, and for the present we are agreed that our practice of talking to authorities and their leaders and chief executives, and of seeking to persuade them, is preferable to a relationship of policeman and potential offender and we hope that we shall be able to keep our functions truly extra-judicial. But we recognise that if the number of failures increases, or if the recalcitrant authorities become more determined in their rejection of adverse criticism from Local Ombudsmen, Parliament may well find the movement for the introduction of more teeth into the powers of the Commission becomes irresistible. This would be one more nail in the coffin of local government independence, and we should regret it. Independence can only be maintained if it is enjoyed and exercised responsibly, and with a suitably sensitive reaction to the constructive criticisms made from time to time by the statutory ombudsmen who are charged with the duty to offer it.

Notes

1   Seneviratne notes that, by 1992, the total number of cases in which the local authority had not provided a satisfactory remedy after a finding of maladministration and injustice amounted to 186, about six per cent of all cases of maladministration and injustice. She concludes that 'Non-compliance is therefore a serious problem ... [as] recognised by JUSTICE, which felt that it was bringing the LGO into disrepute'.[52] Dr Yardley rejects the proposal of giving the LGO power to enforce his findings in the county court and states that he sees the need to reconsider the possibility only if the number of failures increases. As Jones notes

---

51   Quoted *ibid*.
52   Seneviratne, *op cit*, pp 98–99.

(writing in 1994),[53] the Commissions have now abandoned attempts at moral persuasion supported by JUSTICE, and the Widdecombe Committee has called for the 1974 Act to be amended along the lines of the legislation in force in Northern Ireland (mentioned by Yardley above). Yardley's grounds for opposing the proposal to give the LGO more teeth seem curiously weak; nowhere does he say that he thinks that using the courts would not work or explain how it would harm local authorities, apart from saying that it would be another nail in the coffin of [their] independence, a fear which it is hard to understand. It is not readily apparent how the ability of local authorities to flout the findings of an independent investigator that they have been guilty of maladministration is necessary for their independence.

2   A more persuasive argument in this respect is put forward by Patrick Birkinshaw and Norman Lewis in *When Citizens Complain* (1993). They considered that giving the LGO such powers would imperil their relationship with local authorities, which, they feared, would become defensive and minimalist in their responses to LGO recommendations. The current practice of negotiating the response of the authorities in a consensual and informal way would be placed in jeopardy (p 39). This view can, of course, be challenged; it could be argued that, even if the LGO was given enforcement powers, consensual methods would still be used; that they would still be, and would be presented as being, very much the norm; that court action would be kept very much out of mind, seen as an exceptional and rarely resorted-to last resort. It must be borne in mind that arguments as to the harm which might be caused by the introduction of enforcement powers are in the end speculative hypotheses which must be weighed against a concrete harm, the 6 per cent of LGO findings that are currently going unenforced.[54]

3   Overall, however, the Cabinet Office Review drew favourable conclusions as to the work of the LGO. Stage II of the Financial Management and Policy Review of the CLA in 1996, which drew on polls by MORI in 1995, concluded that the work of the LGO was generally well respected by complainants, their advisers and local authorities; although there was widespread concern about delays. A survey by MORI of complainants to the LGO in 1999 reported 'a broadly encouraging improvement from the 1995 survey [para 1.5]'.

REFORM OF THE PUBLIC SECTOR OMBUDSMEN: THE CABINET OFFICE REVIEW 2000

The problems of the present system

In its overall review of the ombudsmen, which examined the PCA, the LGO and the Health Service Commissioner, the Cabinet Office concluded:

> the broad concept of the public sector ombudsmen is widely regarded as successful. As JUSTICE, in its submission to this review, noted:
>
> a) their independence is unquestioned;
>
> b) whilst following the rules of natural justice, the procedures of the ombudsmen are informal, inquisitorial and non-adversarial;
>
> c) legal representation is not necessary;

---

53   'The local ombudsman and judicial review' [1994] PL 608.
54   For a full discussion of this issue see, C Himsworth (ed), *Judicial Teeth for Local Ombudsman?* (1985).

d) the service provided is free and (unlike the court system) there is no risk to the complainant of having to pay the others party's costs if the complaint is not upheld.

These important characteristics have been widely acknowledged by contributors to this review as valuable features of the public sector ombudsmen [paras 2.3 and 2.4].

Why then, is there a perceived need for radical reform? In what follows, the Cabinet Office Review explores the problems of the current system, starting with the views of the ombudsmen themselves, in their paper submitted to the Review.

Review of the Public Sector Ombudsmen in England, April 2000

[from appendix A – paper submitted by Ombudsmen]

11. The present arrangements are unhelpful to complainants. Complaints do not necessarily relate only to the actions of a body within one ombudsman's jurisdiction.

For example:

a. an elderly or mentally ill person may have a complaint about the way a hospital and a social services authority dealt with his or her discharge from hospital; or

b. parents may be aggrieved by the delay in issuing a Statement of their child's Special Educational Needs partly because of tardiness by the education authority and partly because of dilatoriness by the health authority in providing reports for the child's assessment or may be aggrieved by the subsequent failure of both types of authority to secure the provision of the speech therapy specified in the Statement;

c. a claimant of Housing Benefit may have been caused injustice because of faults not only by the council but also by the DSS or the Rent Officer Service.

12. Increasingly, partnerships are being forged between, for example, NHS bodies and local authorities so as to achieve better assessment of the client's needs and the delivery of services to meet them. It is clear from, for example, the White Paper on modernising local government that the Government wishes to see partnerships going further and wider. This is welcome but the present jurisdictions of the English Ombudsmen do not sit easily with this trend.

13. Complainants find it difficult to know to which Ombudsman to complain and rarely complain to more than one at the same time even though they would have good grounds to do so. . . .

14. At present, far from having only 'one door' to knock on, the complainant (often vulnerable, inarticulate and poor) is faced with at least three. Indeed, complainants cannot even knock on the PCA's door themselves but have to find an MP who will refer them to the PCA.

15. Information and publicity about getting redress is fragmented because the PCA, HSC and LGOs produce separate brochures, complaint forms and press notices. It seems likely, therefore, that awareness and understanding about what the English Ombudsmen can do is impaired . . .

20. Responsibility is fragmented for considering how the lessons of investigations could be applied across the public sector. So it is more difficult to identify good and bad practice and make proposals for improvements to public administration across the broad.

21. One of the findings of the Citizen's Charter Unit is that complaints systems should be easy for complainants to understand and use. The present organisation of the English Ombudsmen flies in the fact of that finding. The proliferation of other bodies . . . adds to the confusion and complexity.

[extract from the Review]

2.29 The effect of this complex environment can be to lead to a sense of confusion. The public on the whole do not understand how it all fits together. If they have a problem, it is often not clear where to go and frequently only part of their problem can be dealt with by any single body. A complaint which crosses boundaries between agencies (for example, a discharge from a hospital to local authority social services which goes wrong) may need to be pursued through two or more complaints processes, eventually to two or more ombudsmen. Complainants in these circumstances are often vulnerable and may have disadvantages such as language or literacy difficulties which make it difficult to pursue their complaints to a satisfactory conclusion.

All of the public sector ombudsmen and perhaps the Independent Housing Ombudsman might find themselves involved in such a complaint, dealing with them as four separate complaints each of which might have been pursued through separate internal complaints processes before arriving on each ombudsman's desk.

. . .

2.31 We were surprised when a number of the ombudsmen's staff told us that they rarely handled boundary-crossing complaints. Our impression in looking at a number of cases, which included direct contact with complainants, was that problems arising because of boundaries between agencies are very common. In one group of 6 cases, 3 involved multiple agencies and the words 'being pushed from pillar to post' were used frequently. Because each agency feels itself responsible for its own transactions but not for an entire activity slip-ups occur and arrangements for resolving the problems are lacking. If a complaint does reach an ombudsman he or she can deal only with the element involving bodies within jurisdiction. When the problem giving rise to the complaint has arisen because of the boundary (for example, a communication failure) it may be difficult to resolve the matter satisfactorily and obtain redress – particularly if the major fault lies with the body out of jurisdiction on the other side of the boundary.

Note

In order to combat these problems, the Review recommended a radical solution – the restructuring of the PCA, LCA and HSC into one, collegiate structure of public sector ombudsmen, able to take complaints about any matter within jurisdiction regardless of whether it concerned a local authority, the NHS or a government department.

Restructuring the ombudsmen: a single new Commission for the public sector

Review of the Public Sector Ombudsmen in England, April 2000

At present, the ombudsmen are defined by function – central government, health service and local government – and each is confined in his or her jurisdiction to that particular function. This will be too rigid in future. All ombudsmen should be able to cover the complete jurisdiction, any functional divides being purely an administrative arrangement in the same way as areas of the country are at present with the CLA. Structural arrangements within the new organization will need to allow for new partnerships cutting across functions but we envisage that a functional focus will predominate. This would provide advantages by maintaining expertise and engagement with the various areas of government. We see advantages in retaining specific Local Government and Health Service Ombudsman roles to underpin this focus but neither they nor their colleagues should be confined by law to particular areas of the jurisdiction. By building in this flexibility from the start we believe that the new Commission could be easily reshaped to accommodate changing government structures and it would allow other functional allocations to be made (eg an Education Ombudsman) if appropriate. We recommend that a collegiate structure (the new Commission) is put in place . . .

As long as the external requirements of accountability, service to the public, value for money and transparency are met we recommend that the ombudsmen should be able to manage the internal arrangements of the new Commission, including the location of offices, to adapt it to the changing external environment over time. . . . We recommend that the following framework is adopted in planning the legislation for, and organisation of, the new Commission:

- The organisation must be resilient in its ability to respond to developments in the delivery of public services by central and local government. If it is 'government shaped' it may be too inflexible when the shape of government changes.

- The internal organisation must operate as a single entity for the management of work and generally for accountability, policy-making, funding and resource management.

- The individual ombudsmen must be appointed as office-holders with a personal jurisdiction across the entire work of the new Commission. They should not be appointed to have particular functional or geographical responsibilities. However by agreement within the new Commission they would each be identified with a particular group of the bodies under jurisdiction. Thus, for example, local authorities will know which member of the new Commission will deal with them individually or corporately on questions of policy and practice.

- The staff of the new Commission should specialise in aspects of the functions of bodies under jurisdiction and as necessary form teams to deal with partnership working by those bodies. Such partnerships may involve bodies not under jurisdiction, or under the jurisdiction of another complaints investigation scheme, and innovative collaborative arrangements will be needed.

- The new Commission must work closely with central and local government authorities and the National Health Service, as appropriate through the central unit (which we recommend later in this chapter) to address the jurisdictional issues raised by partnerships, franchises, contracted out services or other developing mechanisms for the delivery of public services.

- Each ombudsman will be responsible for his own cases and will not be subject to any other ombudsman. No ombudsman should be superior to another in making decisions and recommendations about matters under jurisdiction nor should any ombudsman act in any appellate capacity if a complainant disagrees with another ombudsman's decision.

- The new Commission will be answerable to Parliament.

- The new Commission should be chaired by one of the ombudsmen for the purposes of representing it externally, for management purposes and when there is a requirement to answer to Parliament. We envisage that this ombudsman would be responsible for matters relating to the UK as a whole and for reserved matters in Scotland, Wales and Northern Ireland.

- The responsibilities of the ombudsmen for bodies under jurisdiction or for the geographical division of work should be agreed within the new Commission.

- The chairman of the new Commission should lay a report annually to Parliament on the work of the Commission which should include an account of the management of the casework of each ombudsman. The chairman should be able to present to Parliament and publish under absolute privilege [ie immunity from suit in defamation – ed] such other reports as may be necessary on individual or systemic investigation into complaints. Separate arrangements should be made for publishing widely under absolute privilege reports about individual or systemic complaints.

5.4 In suggesting a new Commission we are proposing two major changes: a new Act to replace three separate pieces of legislation, and a new organisation formed from three separate though related organisations. This will be a substantial task though made easier by commonality between the different legislation and existing close working relationships between the three ombudsmen.

The jurisdiction and powers of the new Commission will in the first instance be derived from those of the existing ombudsmen:

- The bodies within jurisdiction will include central government including executive agencies, certain non-departmental public bodies, the NHS and local authorities, and any other bodies currently within jurisdiction.

- The matters within jurisdiction and powers will be those which currently exist for each functional area.

Notes

1   What was being aimed at is indicated by the comments of witnesses to the Select Committee:

Presumably in the public sector you could just invite complainants, 'If you have a complaint against virtually any public body, just write to the Ombudsman, London.' Maybe you would not even need the 'London' (QQ 1, Prof Gregory).

When we went to Sweden we went into the public end of the Ombudsman's office and there was a desk with somebody at the back of it taking complaints off the street and he was there for all the Ombudsmen, local government, this one and the other ... that would be the ideal situation, taking the MPs away from it, taking the councillors away from it and letting members of the public come into a National Ombudsman's shop to make their complaint there and then.

Mr Osmotherly (the LGO): ... I very much sympathise with that ... [55]

2   As to jurisdiction, the Review was relatively cautious, merely recommending that there should be no overall reduction in the jurisdiction of the new Commission and that any changes to jurisdiction should not be made in piecemeal way, but as part of a higher level review of the overall role and powers of the public sector ombudsmen (para 5.9).

3   By contrast the Public Administration Committee, in its report on the Review, took a more radical line: in answering the question, *'Should the legislation specify the bodies which are not within the ombudsmen's jurisdiction, rather than those which are'*, it answered, firmly, 'This change has been consistently recommended by our predecessor committees[56] and it should be seen as a basic principle of any new system'.[57] One of their witnesses put it thus: 'The onus of jurisdiction needs to be shifted in favour of the complainant. All state agencies and their activities should be in jurisdiction unless otherwise specifically excluded. That is the complainant's citizen-friendly way of addressing the question.'[58]

4   Another important issue for the Review was whether the new Commission should, unlike the present ombudsmen, be allowed to conduct investigations off his own bat, so called 'own initiative investigations'. On this, the Review was again conservative, observing, 'An ombudsman's function must remain grounded in addressing injustice caused to an individual and own-initiative investigation appears inconsistent with impartiality' (para 6.15); it may be noted that two witnesses giving evidence to the Public Administration Committee took a different line. Professor Birkinshaw observed that 'The great majority of ombudsmen in other countries do have this power [and] I have never heard it said that this has undermined the sense of confidence in them as being independent.'[59] Professor Seneviratne agreed: 'I think that is essential if an Ombudsman is going to have an over-arching searching out of systemic problems.'[60]

5   The Review also considered the relationship of the new Commission, which would have jurisdiction only in England, with the ombudsmen for Scotland and Wales. It

---

55   Third Report of the Select Committee on Public Administration, HC 612 (1999–2000), Evidence, 21 June 1999, Q 10 (Mr Campbell).
56   That is, previous Select Committees on the PCA.
57   Third Report *op cit*, para 15.
58   *Ibid*, Evidence, 28 June 2000, Q 48 (Prof Giddings).
59   *Ibid*, Q 77.
60   *Ibid*, Evidence, 9 November 1999, QQ 26–27.

noted that 'cases sometimes cross borders (for example, a complaint by a person living in Wales using medical services in England or concerning a child moving countries involving two sets of social services)' and concluded that ' "associate" arrangements for public sector ombudsmen in the other three countries [should be] put in place' (para 7.11) to allow one body to investigate, by agreement with the other, such cross-border cases. It further pointed out that, 'There may ... occasionally, be instances of serious maladministration, which apply beyond England and where the new Commission may wish to address the matter on a United Kingdom basis, perhaps making a special report to Parliament. We recommend that the new Commission remains able to report to Parliament on a United Kingdom basis.' (para 7.12).

Access to the new Commission: the 'gateway'

As discussed above, the Review was clear that the MP filter was an outdated, obstructive anomaly that should be removed, a view now backed by the Public Administration Committee (see above, at pp 804–08). The public should have direct access to the new Commission, whatever the subject matter of their complaint, via a single entry point, to be known as 'the gateway'.

Review of the Public Sector Ombudsmen in England, April 2000
6.47 **We recommend that a single point of access to the new Commission is created which we term 'the gateway'.** All complaints whether about central or local government, health services, other public bodies within jurisdiction or partnerships will be submitted through the gateway. The gateway will also provide information and advice to enquirers, taking over the current ombudsmen's advice line functions ...

6.49 In many cases the complaint may be within jurisdiction but 'premature', that is, it will have been insufficiently considered or not considered within the respondent body's complaints process. The gateway will provide oversight of such complaints particularly where a complainant is vulnerable. Where jurisdiction over the complaint overlaps with that of another ombudsman or commissioner the gateway will liaise to agree who should take forward the complaint and how.

6.50 The gateway will belong to the new Commission as a whole and will act in an informal manner, with customer service principles at the heart of its operation. The aim will be to route a complaint to the right place as quickly as possible. The gateway will operate on the telephone or electronically as well as by written correspondence ...

6.78A function of the new gateway should be to provide information and if necessary refer complainants elsewhere for appropriate advice so that as far as possible complainants have reasonable expectations about what can be achieved and are more likely to set out on the path which is right for them.

Working method and focus of the new Commission

How far the new Commission should be permitted, even encouraged to move away from the relatively formal, thorough, but time-consuming method of the PCA is a question intimately related to a broader question – its overall role. A tension lies at the heart of the PCA between two competing conceptions of his role: on the one hand, the imperative to provide a rapid, cheap and satisfactory remedy *to the particular complainant*. This aspect of his role is often served best by informality, by flexibility in dealing with complaints and a non-confrontational approach to the respondent of the complaint. On the other hand, the PCA can carry out major investigations into serious policy failures, acting as a tool of parliamentary accountability, and as primarily an *investigative* and *critical* agency, rather than a remedy providing one. As the Review noted, such a role requires fidelity to the formal, thorough – but time-consuming procedure – laid down in the PCA 1967 itself.

Review of the Public Sector Ombudsmen in England, April 2000

The fundamental nature of the approach adopted by the PCA to his work was laid down at the inception of the office. The PCA was to be an investigator of maladministration, an instrument of MPs to assist them in their role in seeking redress for complainants. The result of the PCA's investigation would be a report sent to an MP and, in certain circumstances, a report to Parliament. The emphasis was therefore on process (an investigation) and output (a report) rather than outcome (resolution of the complaint). The 1967 Act was designed around this conception of the PCA's role, and subsequent ombudsmen legislation has to a large extent been modelled on the 1967 Act.

6.3 An audit approach is natural if the focus is to root out maladministration. An investigation will aim to establish what happened, whether a body was at fault and if so what is needed to provide a remedy for the complainant. The investigation may unearth grounds for criticism and concerns about conduct – it therefore needs to be thorough and fair. The investigation may identify systemic problems so that remedies need to be provided to people other than the complainant, serious faults corrected and greater publicity given to the problem found. On the other hand, resolution of a complaint may not depend on establishing what happened or why. Modern complaints management often tries to take a positive stance, avoiding a blame culture, valuing the chance to put things right and learn lessons.

6.9 A criticism which has been expressed about non-investigation approaches is that it turns the ombudsmen into a 'small-claims court' (many local settlements are compensation cases) and goes against an important justification for the role of the ombudsman – to identify and publicise systemic problems. Any future arrangements must safeguard this aspect of the ombudsmen's role.

Investigations are the 'big-stick' which keeps Parliament engaged and ultimately underpins the ombudsman's ability to ensure redress for complainants. MPs and organisations like Citizens Advice Bureaux can assist complainants with interventions and settlements but the ombudsman has unique powers to investigate complaints.

6.10 Formal investigations are likely to be required in three circumstances: where the investigation is the resolution (this is particularly likely with health cases), where a respondent body has not co-operated in trying to achieve resolution and where the wider public interest means that full details of what happened need to be exposed.

Notes

1   Professor Giddings, in evidence to the Public Administration Committee expressed the view that ombudsmen could be seen to have as many as four different roles:

Is the Ombudsman primarily a complaint handling facility, a way of enabling individuals who have a problem to get that problem resolved, or is the Ombudsman there not to do that, as you have other complaint handling mechanisms internally, but as a way of using complaints to identify and remedy systemic faults in an organisation that is being made accountable? Is the Ombudsman there to in a sense stand aside, monitor and review other complaint handling procedures? For example, to use a generic term, the adjudicators are dealing with the mass business of all the complaints which have not been successfully resolved by the internal mechanisms and then the Ombudsman would be seen as monitoring the adjudicators, ensuring that they are acting effectively or, fourthly, is the Ombudsman there as a sort of super advocate for the individual citizen, in international terms, the citizen's protector concept? Those four roles are not mutually exclusive but they do have different implications for the way you organise and deliver the service.[61]

2   Interestingly, the National Association of Citizens Advice Bureaux, when giving evidence to the Public Administration Committee, was very clear that it was the audit, rather than the individual complaint resolution aspect of the PCA's work, that to them was the most important:

> For us, what is far more important, is that as well as the individual complaint which is investigated in private, that the work is put into the public domain: namely, that it has influence in terms of standards of practice and setting benchmarks on what is acceptable and unacceptable. So we would be looking, therefore, very much at what we call a wider public good. Seeking out systemic problems and dealing with systemic problems.[62]

The Review was concerned that the working methods of the new body should be suitably flexible to allow all these aspects of the ombudsmen's roles to be continued (see paras 6.16 and 6.71).

3   It was not proposed that the new Commissioner should have the power to award compulsory remedies. Aside from the other issues, canvassed above (at pp 813–16 and esp 826–27), it was feared that, if the Commissioner had such a power, it could become subject to Article 6 of the European Convention on Human Rights, thus imposing a more formal, court-like procedure.[63]

4   In essence, then, the proposals recognise the value of the new, informal approach taken by the PCA in some cases to complaints resolution, but advocate a revised statutory framework which would give explicit recognition and sanction to such an approach, whilst preserving the legal ability of the PCA to insist upon the formal, heavyweight, investigative process where that seemed appropriate to the complaint or to the problems it *prima facie* revealed.

5   Some commentary on the Review has criticised its conservative nature – '... the Review ... essentially accepts the ombudsman's role and function as they are at present.'[64] However, while academics might always wish for more radical reappraisals of underlying issues when such reviews are undertaken, it should be recalled that the purpose of this review was ultimately to make a series of workable proposals for practical reform of the current system. Had it gone into the fundamental issues explored above, which would also have had to have been considered by its witnesses and the Public Administration Committee, there would have been a danger that the Review would have become so bogged down in relatively theoretical argument as to the role of ombudsmen within the wider context of administrative justice and public law generally that the chances of it also being able to produce a set of concrete proposals for reform would have been greatly diminished.

6   At the time of writing, considerable concern is being expressed both by the Public Administration Committee and by the PCA in relation to the failure of government to introduce concrete legislative proposals to give effect to the reforms

---

61   *Ibid*, Q 2.
62   *Ibid*, Evidence, 28 June 2000, Q 79 (Mrs Edwards).
63   *Ibid*, (answer to consultation Q 11).
64   M Seneviratne, '"Joining up" the ombudsmen – the review of the public sector ombudsmen in England' [2000] PL 582, 590; for further discussion, see M Thompson (2001) 64 MLR 459.

recommended by the Cabinet Office Review. In his Annual Review of 2000–01,[65] the PCA said:

> if anything, matters are going backwards rather than forwards. The government has, for example, canvassed the possibility of setting up yet another public sector complaints body – a 'Victims' Ombudsman'. But one of the main concerns which led to the setting up of the Review was the growing complexity and multiplicity of complaints mechanisms in the public sector ...
>
> I find this lack of progress deeply disappointing. The conclusions of the Cabinet Office Review were welcomed by a wide range of interests ... It is now over two and a half years since the English Public Sector Ombudsmen proposed the Review; but there is still no indication of the government's intentions, even in general terms.

7   The Select Committee agreed, saying in a recent report: 'We reiterate our concerns [about delay] and once again recommend that the Government produce a draft bill to implement the review of the Ombudsmen.'[66]

FURTHER READING

JUSTICE, *Our Fettered Ombudsman: A Report* (1977)

S Geoffrey, *Ombudsmen* (1968)

S Nyagah, *The Ombudsman: Constitutional and Legal Processes for the Protection of the Citizen from Administrative Abuses* (1970)

DC Rowat, *The Ombudsman: Citizen's Defender* (1968)

M Seneviratne, *Ombudsmen: Public Services and Administrative Justice* (2002)

65   HC 5 (2001–02), paras 6 and 7.
66   HC 897 (2001–02), para 11.

PART VI

THE PROTECTION OF CIVIL LIBERTIES IN THE UK

THE TRADITIONAL PROTECTION OF CIVIL LIBERTIES IN BRITAIN AND THE IMPACT OF THE HUMAN RIGHTS ACT 1998

INTRODUCTION

In many Western democracies, the rights of citizens are enshrined in a constitutional document sometimes known as a Bill or Charter of Rights. Until the inception of the Human Rights Act 1998 (HRA), the UK had no similar charter of rights. In 2000, when it came fully into force, the HRA afforded further effect to the European Convention on Human Rights (see Part II Chapter 2) in domestic law. Thus, UK citizens could rely for the first time on an instrument resembling a Bill of Rights. This chapter will contrast the current methods of protecting human rights and freedoms under the HRA with the methods used pre-HRA. It will try to show that although the HRA has brought about significant changes, it can be viewed as forming part of a process as opposed to creating abrupt and radical change in that protection. Further, its inception was not intended to entail fundamental constitutional change.

Traditionally, in order to discover which freedoms were protected and the extent of that protection, it was necessary to examine the common law, statutes and the influence of treaties to which the UK is a party, especially the European Convention on Human Rights. Certain characteristics of the UK constitution determined the means of protecting fundamental freedoms in the UK. The doctrine of the supremacy of Parliament meant that constitutional law could be changed in the ordinary way – by Act of Parliament. As every student of constitutional law knows, Parliament has the power to abridge freedoms that in other countries are seen as fundamental rights. It follows from this that all parts of the law are equal – there is no hierarchy of laws and therefore constitutional law cannot constrain other laws. This fundamental characteristic of the UK constitution has been preserved in the HRA in ss 3(2) and 6(2), as explained below.

Further, there was (and is) no judicial review of Acts of Parliament. If, for example, a statute was passed containing a provision which in some way limited freedom of speech, a judge merely had to apply it, whereas in a country with an 'entrenched' Bill of Rights (one given special constitutional protection – a protection greater than that afforded to 'ordinary' law), the statutory provision might be struck down as unconstitutional. However, there were, prior to the inception of the HRA, two possible constraints on this process. If the judge considered that the provision in question was at all ambiguous, he or she could interpret it in such a way that freedom of speech was maintained, by relying on Article 10 of the Convention. Further, if the domestic provision came into conflict with an EU provision, the judge could decide to 'disapply' it, unless the conflict could be resolved. Thus, parliamentary sovereignty had suffered some limitation in the pre-HRA era. Where the EU had (and has) an impact, it could provide a protection which could broadly be said to have removed certain fundamental freedoms, or aspects of them, from the reach of Parliament.

Civil liberties thus were traditionally defined as residual, not entrenched as in other countries: they were seen as the residue of freedom left behind after the legal restrictions had been defined. Thus, it was often said that civil liberties in the UK were in a more precarious position than they were in other democracies, although this did not necessarily mean that they were inevitably less well protected: some Bills of Rights offered only a theoretical protection to freedoms which was not reflected in practice. These constitutional arrangements have not been fundamentally changed under the HRA; a judge will not be able to declare a statutory provision invalid because it conflicts with a Convention right protected by the Act. It might appear then that the HRA has not affected the traditional methods of protecting liberties. However, as will become apparent below, this is not the case: under s 3 of the HRA, judges have a greater obligation than they had previously to seek to ensure that statutory provisions are consistent with the Convention rights.

That is the constitutional background to the HRA. It is still of great significance since it was crucial in the development of civil liberties in this country and because the HRA has been greatly influenced by the domestic constitutional traditions: its main provisions represent a compromise between maintaining those traditions and giving greater protection to human rights. This chapter begins by considering the nature and adequacy of the traditional domestic arrangements which protected fundamental freedoms only as liberties, and will go on to consider the extent to which the Convention influenced the domestic protection of civil liberties in the pre-HRA era. It will then examine the instrument that has afforded the Convention further effect in domestic law – the HRA.

The HRA was introduced by the Labour government in 1998 on the basis that rights were, finally, to be 'brought home'.[1] There were expectations at that time that the HRA would revive the civil liberties tradition – there was a sense of a break with the erosions of liberty associated with the Conservative governments of 1979–97.[2] But the legislation passed after the HRA, which is considered in this Part, including the Terrorism Act 2000 and the Criminal Justice and Police Act 2001, is in some respects more authoritarian than much of the legislation passed in the recent pre-HRA years. Thus, the fact that we now have a document that looks something like a Bill of Rights, in the tradition of other democracies, should not blind us to the traditional concerns of the executive which are especially pressing at the present time.

THE TRADITIONAL PROTECTION OF CIVIL LIBERTIES UNDER THE BRITISH CONSTITUTION

The Diceyan tradition

AV Dicey, *The Law of the Constitution* (1959), pp 197–98

The Rule of Law: Its Nature and General Applications

There is in the English constitution an absence of those declarations or definitions of rights so dear to foreign constitutionalists. Such principles, moreover, as you can discover in the English constitution are, like all maxims established by judicial legislation, mere generalisations drawn either from the decisions or *dicta* of judges, or from statutes which, being passed to meet special

---

1 See *Bringing Rights Home: Labour's plans to incorporate the ECHR into UK Law: A Consultation Paper*, December 1996 (1997) and the White Paper, *Rights Brought Home*, Cm 3782, October 1997; see also J Straw and P Boateng (1997) 1 EHRR 71.
2 See Cooke, 'The British embracement of human rights' (1999) EHRLR 243; D Feldman, 'The Human Rights Act and constitutional principles' (1999) 19(2) LS 165.

grievances, bear a close resemblance to judicial decisions, and are in effect judgments pronounced by the High Court of Parliament. To put what is really the same thing in a somewhat different shape, the relation of the rights of individuals to the principles of the constitution is not quite the same in countries like Belgium, where the constitution is the result of a legislative act, as it is in England, where the constitution itself is based upon legal decisions. In Belgium, which may be taken as a type of countries possessing a constitution formed by a deliberate act of legislation, you may say with truth that the rights of individuals to personal liberty flow from or are secured by the constitution. In England the right to individual liberty is part of the constitution, because it is secured by the decisions of the courts, extended or confirmed as they are by the Habeas Corpus Acts. If it be allowable to apply the formulas of logic to questions of law, the difference in this matter between the constitution of Belgium and the English constitution may be described by the statement that in Belgium individual rights are deductions drawn from the principles of the constitution, whilst in England the so called principles of the constitution are inductions or generalisations based upon particular decisions pronounced by the courts as to the rights of given individuals.

This is of course a merely formal difference. Liberty is as well secured in Belgium as in England, and as long as this is so it matters nothing whether we say that individuals are free from all risk of arbitrary arrest, because liberty of person is guaranteed by the constitution, or that the right to personal freedom, or in other words to protection from arbitrary arrest, forms part of the constitution because it is secured by the ordinary law of the land. But though this merely formal distinction is in itself of no moment, provided always that the rights of individuals are really secure, the question whether the right to personal freedom or the right to freedom of worship is likely to be secure does depend a good deal upon the answer to the inquiry whether the persons who consciously or unconsciously build up the constitution of their country begin with definitions or declarations of rights, or with the contrivance of remedies by which rights may be enforced or secured. Now, most foreign constitution-makers have begun with declarations of rights. For this they have often been in no wise to blame. Their course of action has more often than not been forced upon them by the stress of circumstances, and by the consideration that to lay down general principles of law is the proper and natural function of legislators. But any knowledge of history suffices to show that foreign constitutionalists have, while occupied in defining rights, given insufficient attention to the absolute necessity for the provision of adequate remedies by which the rights they proclaimed might be enforced.

TRS Allan, 'Constitutional rights and common law' (1991) 2 OJLS 453, pp 456–60

Rights and Liberties at Common Law

Contemporary reluctance to view the common law as a source of constitutional rights may be partly the consequence of defective legal analysis. At the root of common misunderstanding lies a confusion about the residual nature of liberty.

If common law liberty is merely residual, it is argued, it may be eaten away by ever-encroaching restrictions and restraints until deprived of all substance. The argument benefits here from the failure to distinguish between liberty and liberties.

It is important to make the distinction between liberty and liberties in understanding the common law. The common law does, of course, recognise a general right to liberty – in the sense that every encroachment by the state (or by another) on one's freedom must be justified. There need not be special moral justification of the kind which permits restriction of a basic liberty, such as freedom of speech. But there must be lawful *authority* for coercive action, and legislative restrictions on individual freedom must be duly enacted in the appropriate constitutional manner. If, then, liberty is residual, in the sense that everything which is not expressly forbidden the individual is permitted, the *foundation* of constitutional rights is laid. The burden is on the government or public authority to justify coercion. This is the aspect of the Rule of Law illuminated by *Entick v Carrington* [(1765)

19 St Tr 1029]: every coercive act of government which is not shown to be authorised is automatically illegal.

But the common law is also solicitous of liberties: it acknowledges the importance of freedoms of speech and assembly, as well as of liberties of the person and rights of property. The case-law is replete with references to the significance of freedom of expression and freedom of conscience as public interests which deserve judicial protection [see Alan Boyle, 'Freedom of expression as a public interest in English law' [1982] PL 574]. A constitutional right at common law is a product of these two interacting faces of the Rule of Law. My right to freedom of speech is the outcome, first, of my undifferentiated residual liberty – whose restriction needs lawful authority and thereby moral (albeit utilitarian) justification – and secondly, of the court's attachment to the value of free speech, which is anti-utilitarian in character (in Dworkin's sense) and is of critical importance in determining the scope and effect of purported restrictions on my liberty.

In his dissenting judgment in the Court of Appeal in *Wheeler v Leicester City Council* [[1985] AC 1054 (see further my notes at (1985) 48 Mod LR 448; (1986) 49 Mod LR 121], Browne-Wilkinson LJ recognised that freedoms of speech and conscience were fundamental – and so immune from interference without express parliamentary sanction – despite the absence of a written constitution. He noted that modern polarisation of political attitudes had diminished the effectiveness of conventions which protected individuals from discriminatory action by the majority. But he did not suggest that, with the erosion of convention, the common law was helpless. Citing *Verrall v Great Yarmouth Borough Council* [[1981] 1 QB 202] to illustrate the importance accorded to freedom of speech, he concluded that 'it is undoubtedly part of the constitution of this country that, in the absence of express legislative provisions to the contrary, each individual has the right to hold and express his own views'.

Browne-Wilkinson LJ's approach demonstrates the basic dynamic of constitutional rights at common law. The positive value accorded to freedoms of speech and conscience was harnessed to the general principle of residual liberty to protect the applicant from oppressive treatment by the local authority. The authority had required the applicant's rugby club to endorse its views on sporting links with South Africa, as a condition of permission to use a local recreation ground for practice. It had thereby unlawfully interfered with the 'fundamental right of the club and its members to freedom of speech and conscience'. The intrinsic importance of the freedom justified a jealous and critical scrutiny of a claim to statutory support for encroachment on residual liberty. It could not assist the local authority that their stance in respect of apartheid was part of their policy of promoting good race relations; and that the Race Relations Act 1976, s 71 imposed a duty to ensure that their functions were exercised with due regard for such an objective. Although the Act made racially discriminatory actions unlawful, it conferred no power to penalise individuals for holding particular views:

> Basic constitutional rights in this country such as freedom of the person and freedom of speech are based not on any express provisions conferring such a right but on freedom of an individual to do what he will save to the extent that he is prevented from so doing by the law. Thus, freedom of the person depends on the fact that no one has the right lawfully to arrest the individual save in defined circumstances. The right to freedom of speech depends on the fact that no one has the right to stop the individual expressing his views, save to the extent that those views are libellous or seditious. These fundamental freedoms therefore are not positive rights but an immunity from interference by others. Accordingly, I do not consider that general words in an Act of Parliament can be taken as authorising interference with these basic immunities which are the foundation of our freedom. Parliament (being sovereign) can legislate so as to do so; but it cannot be taken to have conferred such a right on others save by express words [[1985] AC 1054 at 1065].

The speeches in the House of Lords, which affirmed Browne-Wilkinson LJ's conclusions, were less convincing because more loosely argued. Lord Roskill chose to frame his objection to the authority's conduct in terms of 'procedural impropriety' or unfairness; and his refusal to endorse

Browne-Wilkinson LJ's 'somewhat wider ground' surely betrayed a weaker grasp of constitutional doctrine. Lord Templeman, though his speech failed to address the level of principle demanded by the freedoms in issue, gave at least general support to the correct approach. 'A private individual or a private organisation cannot be obliged to display zeal in the pursuit of an object sought by a public authority and cannot be obliged to publish views dictated by a public authority [*ibid* at 1080].'

The case is a good illustration of the dispiriting but notorious tendency of British judges to prefer pragmatism over principle [see further my 'Pragmatism and theory in public law' (1988) 104 LQR 422]. Browne-Wilkinson LJ's principled judgment is conspicuous for its contrasting approach, but that hardly denies its value as an example. The broadly stated grounds of judicial review of administrative action sometimes conceal as much as they reveal. If a case involves questions of constitutional rights – or basic constitutional values – they should be openly confronted. And we should not mistake the deficiencies of particular judgments – even in the House of Lords – or the inadequacy of their reasoning, for inherent defects of 'constitutional' adjudication at common law.

If the speeches of the House of Lords in the '*Spycatcher*' litigation were also somewhat disappointing, its result also shows that analysis of the right to freedom of expression as purely residual is incomplete. In some circumstances, at least, protection of the freedom is perceived as a public interest or value entitled to independent weight in a balance of argument to be struck between disclosure and secrecy. The House of Lords refused to grant a final injunction restraining the *Sunday Times*, *The Guardian* and *The Observer* newspapers from publishing extracts from *Spycatcher*, the book of memoirs of a retired intelligence officer published abroad in breach of his duty of confidentiality owed to the Crown [*AG v Guardian Newspapers* (No 2) [1990] AC 109]. Affirming that the 'general rule is that anyone is entitled to communicate anything he pleases to anyone else, by speech or in writing or in any other way', Lord Keith rejected the Crown's submission that whenever a Crown servant had made a wrongful disclosure, anyone to whom knowledge of the information came and who was aware of the breach of confidence came under a duty not to communicate it to anyone else [*ibid* at 256–57]. He cited the decision of the High Court of Australia in *Commonwealth of Australia v John Fairfax*, in which Mason J emphasised the court's duty to determine the Government's claim to confidentiality in the light of the public interest in open discussion of public affairs. Confidentiality would be upheld only where disclosure would be inimical to the public interest because national security, relations with foreign countries or the ordinary business of government would be prejudiced [(1980) 147 CLR 39, 51–52].

Admittedly, Lord Keith chose to ground his decision on the view that all possible damage to the interest of the Crown had already been done by publication of the book abroad: he was unwilling to engage in any balancing of public interests or to base his decision on any considerations of freedom of the press. Nonetheless, it is clear that the intrinsic importance of freedom of political speech – concerning matters of government and public affairs – played an important role in limiting the principle protecting confidentiality. Moreover, Lord Goff envisaged a balancing operation, in which the court would weigh the public interest in maintaining the confidence against a countervailing public interest favouring disclosure. In order to restrain disclosure of government secrets, the Crown must show that restraint was in the public interest. Confidentiality alone was not sufficient justification 'because in a free society there is a continuing public interest that the workings of government should be open to scrutiny and criticism' [[1990] AC 109, p 283. See also Scott J's judgment at first instance, especially 144–56, 169–72].

Notes

1   The Diceyan tradition holds that the absence of a written constitution in Britain is not a weakness but a source of strength. This is because the protection of the citizen's liberties is not dependent on vaguely worded constitutional documents but, rather, flow from specific judicial decisions which give the citizen specific

remedies for infringement of his or her liberties.³ Dicey regarded one of the great strengths of the British constitution as lying in the lack of broad discretionary powers vested in the executive. Citizens could only be criminalised for clear breaches of clearly established laws. Where there was no relevant law, they could know with absolute confidence that they could exercise their liberty as they pleased without fear of incurring any sanction. The Diceyan thesis finds support in the seminal decision of *Derbyshire County Council v Times Newspapers* [1993] AC 534. The House of Lords found, without referring to Article 10 of the European Convention, that the importance the common law attached to free speech was such that defamation could not be available as an action to local (or central) government.

2   Harry Street, in *Freedom, the Individual and the Law* (1982), argues that 'our judges may be relied on to defend strenuously some kinds of freedom. Their emotions will be aroused where personal freedom is menaced by some politically unimportant area of the executive'.⁴ The reluctance of judges to intervene in the politically important areas such as national security or deportation is evidenced by the decisions in *Council of Civil Service Unions v Minister for the Civil Service* [1985] AC 374 and *R v Secretary of State for the Home Department ex p Hosenball* [1977] 1 WLR 766.

3   Contrary to the Diceyan view, it may be found that where an attempt has been made in a statute (perhaps due to decisions of the European Court of Human Rights or the European Court of Justice) to give the law some coherence with a view to ensuring that a particular freedom is protected, as is the case with freedom of speech in the Contempt of Court Act 1981, the common law may begin to take on a role which undermines the statutory provisions.⁵ Or the common law provisions may in some respects curtail liberty more than the statutory ones; this has been said of the common law doctrines of breach of the peace,⁶ contempt and conspiracy to corrupt public morals. Keith Ewing and CA Gearty have argued that for this reason a Bill of Rights may be undesirable as the people need Parliament to protect them from the judges, not merely the judges to protect them from Parliament.⁷

Judicial review and civil liberties

In one area – judicial review – the judges have shown a general determination to develop the common law with the basic aim of preventing the exercise of arbitrary power. However, in the pre-HRA era, the doctrine was fundamentally limited in that as long as a minister appeared to have followed a correct and fair procedure, to have acted within his or her powers and to have made a decision which was not clearly unreasonable, the decision had to stand regardless of its potentially harmful impact on civil liberties. Thus, the fact that basic liberties were curtailed in the *GCHQ*⁸ and *Brind*⁹ cases did not in itself provide a ground for review. In other words, the courts were confined to looking back at the method of arriving at the decision rather than forward to its likely effects. In cases which touch particularly directly on national security, so

3   *Op cit*, p 190.
4   At p 318. Reference is to 5th edn.
5   See Part VI Chapter 3, at pp 933–35.
6   See Part VI Chapter 3, at pp 974–78.
7   KD Ewing and CA Gearty, *Freedom under Thatcher: Civil Liberties in Modern Britain* (1989), pp 270–71.
8   *Council of Civil Service Unions v Minister for Civil Service* [1984] 3 All ER 935 (the Prime Minister's decision struck directly at freedom of association).
9   [1991] 1 All ER 720, HL (political speech was directly curtailed).

sensitive were the judges to the executives' duty to uphold the safety of the realm, that they might define their powers even to look back on the decision as almost non-existent (see *R v Secretary of State for Home Department, ex p Stitt* (1987) *The Times*, 3 February). Sir John Laws considered, however, that judicial review might develop in such a way that it would provide greater protection for civil liberties.[10]

Sir John Laws, 'Is the High Court the guardian of fundamental constitutional rights?' [1993] PL 59, pp 71–75

Now there has been much reference in the recent public law learning to [the concept of proportionality], but the courts have in fact only flirted with it. If it is to play the part which I believe it can, it is particularly important to analyse it properly. The first stage is to see why it has not taken root so far.

What has happened is that the courts have only recognised proportionality as a facet or species of *Wednesbury*, often at the invitation or upon the concession of counsel [see *Pegasus Holdings* [1988] I WLR 990 at 1001F and *R v Secretary of State for Health ex p United States Tobacco* [1992] I QB 353 at 366G].

The difficulty is that if proportionality is merely a facet of irrationality, it adds nothing to *Wednesbury* and lacks all utility as a category of judicial review: indeed it is *not* itself a category of judicial review at all. But if it is to take its place as a distinct concept, then there must be cases where it may succeed as a ground of substantive challenge, where *Wednesbury* would not; and this means that the court must be willing to strike down a decision on substantive and not merely procedural grounds where *ex hypothesi* the decision is not an irrational one. The reason why so far the courts have been unwilling to take this step is surely the received wisdom that to do so would be to turn the public law court into a court of merits, and so to usurp the primary function of the decision-maker under review.

The truth is that the most interesting, and important, types of challenge to discretionary decisions – certainly those involving fundamental rights – are not usually about simple irrationality, or a failure to call attention to relevant matters. They are much more likely to be concerned with the way in which the decision-maker has ordered his priorities; the very essence of discretionary decision-making consists, surely, in the attribution of relative importance to the factors in the case. And here is my point: this is precisely what proportionality is about. ... if we are to entertain a form of review in which fundamental rights are to enjoy the court's distinct protection, the very exercise consists in an insistence that the decision-maker is not free to order his priorities as he chooses ... an insistence that he accord the first priority to the right in question unless he can show a substantial, objective, public justification for overriding it. Proportionality is surely the means of doing this. It is a ready-made tool in our hands.

It will be said that this approach falls foul of one of the received nostrums in our public law, ... the rule that the relative weight to be accorded to the factors in play is always and only for the decision-maker to decide. ... But if the issue is freedom of speech, or person, or the like, the application of this principle would mean that the decision-maker is at liberty to accord a high or low importance to the right in question, as he chooses. This cannot be right.

What is therefore needed is a preparedness to hold that a decision which overrides a fundamental right without sufficient objective justification will, as a matter of law, necessarily be disproportionate to the aim in view. It will be misleading and unhelpful, not to say something of an affront to the decision-maker, to categorise these cases in conventional *Wednesbury* terms. ... If the courts do go down this road, many problems will remain and will have to be worked through case by case. In particular, the judges will have to grapple with the need to build principles for the

---

10 See also Part V Chapter 2, pp 784–89 in relation to developments in judicial review.

ascertainment of what is to count as a permissible justification for the abrogation of a fundamental right. For the reasons I have given, there is nothing to prevent their looking to the Strasbourg jurisprudence if it is felt to offer assistance.

Notes

1   In the years immediately preceding the inception of the HRA, the judiciary showed a determination to use judicial review to protect fundamental rights in a large number of instances. In *R v Secretary of State for the Home Department and Another ex p Norney and Others* (1995), the Secretary of State had made a determination that he would not refer the cases of the applicants, IRA life sentence prisoners, to the parole board until after the expiry of the tariff period of the sentences. Given the timetable of the parole board, this meant that in effect every tariff period was increased by 23 weeks. The applicants sought judicial review of the decision of the Secretary of State. It was found that the practice flouted the principles of common law and Article 5(4) of the European Convention. A declaration was therefore granted that the Home Secretary should have referred the applicants' cases to the parole board at such a time as would have ensured as far as possible that they would be heard immediately after expiry of the tariff period.

2   In *R v Ministry of Defence ex p Smith and Others* [1996] 1 All ER 257,[11] the argument used by the Master of the Rolls in reaching the decision has some apparent affinity with that advanced by Sir John Laws above. The applicants had sought judicial review of the policy of the Ministry of Defence in maintaining a ban on homosexuals in the armed forces. The applicants had been dismissed due to the existence of the ban. In conducting such review the court applied the usual *Wednesbury* principles of reasonableness. This meant that the court could not interfere with the exercise of an administrative discretion on substantive grounds save where it was satisfied that the decision was unreasonable in the sense that it was beyond the range of responses open to a reasonable decision-maker; but it was found that in judging whether the decision-maker had exceeded that margin, the human rights context was important; the more substantial the interference with human rights, the more the court would require by way of justification before it was satisfied that the decision was reasonable. Applying such principles and taking into account the support of the policy in both Houses of Parliament, it was not found that the policy crossed the threshold of irrationality. Thus, the appeal was dismissed.

Question

Does the *Smith* case suggest that the judges were prepared to take fundamental rights into account in judicial review proceedings in the manner suggested by Laws?

The influence of the European Convention on Human Rights and of European Union law

The influence of the European Convention on Human Rights increasingly provided further protection for civil liberties, domestically, even *prior* to the inception of the HRA.[12] The European Union also had such an influence, an influence that is currently

---

11   See also *R v Cambridge Health Authority ex p B* [1995] TLR 159, CA; [1995] 1 WLR 898.
12   As pointed out in Part II Chapter 2, the Treaty on European Union, Article 6 provides that the EU will respect fundamental rights as recognised by the Convention. For further discussion of the recognition in the Union of fundamental rights as guaranteed under the Convention, see pp 253–59.

increasing. It is clear that membership of the European Union and the influence of the Convention have had an enormous impact on civil liberties in the UK in the last three decades. European Union law has already had an important impact in the areas of sex discrimination,[13] data protection[14] and freedom of movement.[15]

The rulings of the European Court of Human Rights have led to better protection of human rights in such areas as prisoners' rights,[16] freedom of expression[17] and privacy.[18] Its influence as an *external* force is, however, inherently limited. The effect of a ruling of the European Court of Human Rights is dependent on the government in question making a change in the law. The British government may be able to minimise the impact of an adverse judgment by interpreting defeat narrowly,[19] by avoiding implementation of a ruling[20] or by obeying the letter of the Article in question but ignoring its spirit.[21] The impact of the Convention is also lessened because the process of invoking it remains cumbersome, lengthy and expensive, as discussed in Part II Chapter 2.[22]

The Convention has probably had a more significant influence within domestic law since the judges are increasingly prepared to take it into account in reaching a decision. Each state decides on the status the Convention enjoys in national law; there is no obligation under Article 1 to allow individuals to rely on it in *national* courts. In some states it has the status of constitutional law;[23] in others ordinary law.[24] However, in Britain, until the inception of the HRA, it had no binding force. Successive UK governments considered that it was not necessary for the Convention to be part of British law; they maintained that the UK's unwritten constitution was in conformity with it. Thus, until the HRA came into force, a UK citizen could not go before a UK court and simply argue that a Convention right had been violated. Nevertheless, the influence of the Convention was rapidly becoming more significant in domestic law through rulings in UK courts in the immediate pre-HRA period.

Brind v Secretary of State for the Home Department [1991] 1 All ER 720, pp 722–23, 733–35

Lord Bridge of Harwich: .... It is accepted, of course, by the applicants that, like any other treaty obligations which have not been embodied in the law by statute, the Convention is not part of the domestic law, that the courts accordingly have no power to enforce Convention rights directly and that, if domestic legislation conflicts with the Convention, the courts must nevertheless enforce it. But it is already well settled that, in construing any provision in domestic

---

13 See, eg, *Marshall v Southampton and South West Hampshire Area Health Authority (No 2)* (Case 271/91) [1993] 4 All ER 586.
14 The Data Protection Act 1984 derived from the European Convention for the Protection of Individuals with regard to the Automatic Protection of Data, 17 September 1980.
15 Article 39 of the EC Treaty, which is directly enforceable.
16 *Golder v United Kingdom*, Series A No 18, (1975) 1 EHRR 524.
17 *Sunday Times v United Kingdom* (1979) 2 EHRR 245.
18 *Gaskin v United Kingdom* (1989) 12 EHRR 36.
19 *Golder v United Kingdom*, Series A No 18, (1975) 1 EHRR 524.
20 *Brogan, Coyle, McFadden and Tracey v United Kingdom* (1989) 13 EHRR 439. The government refused to implement the ruling, entering a derogation under Article 15.
21 *Abdulaziz, Cabales and Balkandali v United Kingdom* (1985) 7 EHRR 471. To implement the ruling, the UK 'equalised down'.
22 In Part II Chapter 2, pp 248–49.
23 Eg, Austria.
24 This includes Belgium, France, Italy, Luxembourg and Germany.

legislation which is ambiguous in the sense that it is capable of a meaning which either conforms to or conflicts with the Convention, the courts will presume that Parliament intended to legislate in conformity with the Convention, not in conflict with it. Hence, it is submitted, when a statute confers upon an administrative authority a discretion capable of being exercised in a way which infringes any basic human right protected by the Convention, it may similarly be presumed that the legislative intention was that the discretion should be exercised within the limitations which the Convention imposes. I confess that I found considerable persuasive force in this submission. But in the end I have been convinced that the logic of it is flawed.

But I do not accept that this conclusion means that the courts are powerless to prevent the exercise by the executive of administrative discretions, even when conferred, as in the instant case, in terms which are on their face unlimited, in a way which infringes fundamental human rights. Thus, Article 10(2) of the Convention spells out and categorises the competing public interests by reference to which the right to freedom of expression may have to be curtailed. In exercising the power of judicial review we have neither the advantages nor the disadvantages of any comparable code to which we may refer or by which we are bound. But again, this surely does not mean that in deciding whether the Secretary of State, in the exercise of his discretion, could reasonably impose the restriction he has imposed on the broadcasting organisations, we are not perfectly entitled to start from the premise that any restriction of the right to freedom of expression requires to be justified and that nothing less than an important competing public interest will be sufficient to justify it.

Derbyshire County Council v Times Newspapers Ltd [1992] 3 WLR 28, 60–61, CA

Butler-Sloss LJ: In *Attorney-General v Guardian Newspapers Ltd (No 2)* [1990] 1 AC 109, Lord Goff of Chieveley said (in relation to breach of confidential information), at p 283:

> ... I wish to observe that I can see no inconsistency between English law on this subject and Article 10 of the European Convention on Human Rights. This is scarcely surprising, since we may pride ourselves on the fact that freedom of speech has existed in this country perhaps as long as, if not longer than, it has existed in any other country in the world. The only difference is that, whereas Article 10 of the Convention, in accordance with its avowed purpose, proceeds to state a fundamental right and then to qualify it, we in this country (where everybody is free to do anything, subject only to the provisions of the law) proceed rather upon an assumption of freedom of speech, and turn to our law to discover the established exceptions to it. In any event I conceive it to be my duty, when I am free to do so, to interpret the law in accordance with the obligations of the Crown under this treaty.

Adopting, as I respectfully do, that approach to the Convention, the principles governing the duty of the English court to take account of Article 10 appear to be as follows: where the law is clear and unambiguous, either stated as the common law or enacted by Parliament, recourse to Article 10 is unnecessary and inappropriate. ... But where there is an ambiguity, or the law is otherwise unclear or so far undeclared by an appellate court, the English court is not only entitled but, in my judgment, obliged to consider the implications of Article 10.

... In the present case there is no binding authority upon this court, and I do not consider the law to be clear. Accordingly, it is for this court to consider the application of Article 10 to the question whether a local authority may sue for libel ...

Notes

1   The decision in *Brind* reaffirmed the accepted principle in the pre-HRA era that the Convention should be taken into account where domestic legislation is ambiguous. It also determined that state officials are *not* bound by the Convention in exercising discretionary power. The ruling in *Brind* relied on the general principle of construction that statutes will be interpreted if possible so as to conform with

international treaties to which Britain is a party on the basis that the government is aware of its international obligations and would not intend to legislate contrary to them. The position as regards the Convention was reiterated in *Re M and H (Minors)* [1988] 3 WLR 485 by Lord Brandon of Oakbrook: '... while English courts may strive where they can to interpret statutes as conforming with the obligations of Britain under the Convention, they are nevertheless bound to give effect to statutes which are free from ambiguity ... even if those statutes may be in conflict with the Convention.' Thus, if a statute unambiguously violated fundamental rights the courts had to apply it in the pre-HRA era, unless the statute implemented EU law (see note 5 below).

2　Applying Article 10, the Court of Appeal found in the *Derbyshire* case that a local authority cannot sue for libel. The House of Lords considered that in the particular instance, the common law could determine the issues in favour of freedom of speech.[25]

3　Lord Scarman in *Attorney-General v BBC* [1981] AC 303, 354 considered the influence of the Convention on the common law. He said that where there was some leeway to do so, a court which must adjudicate on the relative weight to be given to different public interests under the common law should try to strike a balance in a manner consistent with the treaty obligations accepted by the government. 'If the issue should ultimately be ... a question of legal policy, we must have regard to the country's international obligation to observe the Convention as interpreted by the Court of Human Rights.' Lord Scarman's approach was endorsed by the House of Lords in *Attorney-General v Guardian Newspapers (No 2)* [1990] 1 AC 109.

4　In the immediate pre-HRA era a number of decisions recognised certain common law rights which, it was found, cannot be abrogated except by express words or necessary implication – where there is only one way of reading the legislation in question. These included the rights of access to the courts,[26] to free speech,[27] and to basic subsistence.[28] The rule of construction in these instances was described in one of the most significant of these decisions, *R v Secretary of State for the Home Department ex p Simms* [1999] 3 All ER 400, by Lord Hoffman, as follows at 412:

> Parliamentary sovereignty means that Parliament can if it chooses legislate contrary to fundamental principles of human rights ... But the principle of legality means that Parliament must squarely confront what it is doing and count the political cost. Fundamental rights cannot be overridden by general or ambiguous words ... because there is too great a risk that the full implications of their unqualified meaning may have passed unnoticed in the democratic process ... In this way the courts of the UK, though acknowledging the sovereignty of Parliament, apply principles of constitutionality little different from those which exist in countries where the power of the legislature is expressly limited by a constitutional document.

> In *R v Lord Chancellor ex p Witham* [1998] QB 575, Laws J found that the power of the Lord Chancellor to prescribe court fees was not based on sufficiently precise words to allow him to deny the right of access to a court by preventing an applicant on income support from issuing proceedings for defamation.

25　[1993] AC 534, esp at 551.

26　*R v Lord Chancellor ex p Witham* [1998] QB 575. But cf *R v Lord Chancellor ex p Lightfoot* [2000] 2 WLR 318. For comment on the first instance decision [1998] 4 All ER 764, see M Elliott, 'Lightfoot: tracing the perimeter of constitutional rights' [1998] JR 217.

27　*R v Secretary of State for the Home Dept ex p Simms* [1999] 3 All ER 400, CA; [1999] 3 WLR 328, HL.

28　*R v Secretary of State for Social Security ex p Joint Council of Welfare of Immigrants* [1996] 4 All ER 835; Lord Saville in *Criminal Injuries Compensation Board ex p A* [1999] 2 AC 300; [1999] 4 All ER 860.

5   Article 6(1) of the Treaty of Maastricht which created the European Union
provides that Member States will respect fundamental rights as guaranteed by
the Convention as general principles of Community law. Under the Treaty of
Amsterdam, voting rights of Member States who fail to observe the principle
embodied by Article 6 can be suspended. The EU Charter of Fundamental Rights,
although not of binding force, will aid in the interpretation of EU law (see Part
II Chapter 2, pp 255). Thus, in domestic law, implementation of Community
measures is clearly subject to respect for the Convention rights. In *R v Secretary
of State for Transport ex p Factortame (No 2)* [1991] 1 AC 603 and *Secretary of State
for Employment v Equal Opportunities Commission* [1995] 1 AC 1 the House of Lords
determined that a domestic statute could be disapplied if it conflicted with EU
law. Thus, if a British citizen believes that one of his or her Convention rights
has been violated by a domestic statute, and the violation arises in an area
affected by a European Union measure, it would seem that he or she could seek
judicial review of the statutory provision in question (assuming that no private
law remedy was available), relying on the incompatibility found between
domestic and EU law once the EU measure had been interpreted in accordance
with the Convention.[29]

Questions

1   How does Laws' thesis, above, fit with the decision in *Brind v Secretary of State for
the Home Department*?

2   Simon Lee in *Judging Judges* (1989), p 160 stated, 'We already have a Bill of Rights in
the European Convention', as part of an argument that the whole Bill of Rights
debate is misguided. Do you agree?

3   Is the decision in the *Smith* case, above, as regards the relevance of the Convention
to the exercise of administrative discretion, distinguishable from Lord Bridge's
findings on this point in *Brind*?

THE BILL OF RIGHTS QUESTION

In the latter half of the 20th century, support grew for the notion that there was a need
for some constitutional change to safeguard civil liberties and that that change should
take the form of a Bill of Rights. In 1968, Anthony Lester QC proposed the
incorporation of the European Convention on Human Rights into national law[30] and
since then a number of Private Members' Bills have made the same proposal.[31] Support
for a Bill of Rights grew among lawyers,[32] academics[33] and politicians during the 1980s
and early 1990s.

---

29   See further Part II Chapter 2, pp 253 *et seq*, as to rulings of the European Court of Justice taking
the Convention into account, in particular *P v S and Cornwall County Council* (Case C-13/94)
(1996) *The Times*, 7 May.

30   A Lester, *Democracy and Individual Rights* (1968), pp 13–15.

31   Not all Bills proposing the introduction of a Bill of Rights have advocated incorporating the
Convention. The Charter 88 Group advocated enshrining civil liberties by means of a Bill of
Rights but it did not put forward a text. See N Stanger (1990) 8 Index on Censorship 14.

32   In particular Lord Scarman: see *English Law – The New Dimension* (1974), Parts II and VII; see
also G Robertson, *Freedom, the Individual and the Law*, 7th edn (1993), Chapter 12; A Lester,
'Fundamental rights: the United Kingdom isolated' [1984] PL 46.

33   See M Zander, *A Bill of Rights?* (1985), p 90; E Barendt, *Freedom of Speech* (1987), pp 329–32.

But some judges[34] and academic writers[35] remained opposed to or uneasy as to the adoption of a Bill of Rights. It was argued that the whole notion of endowing an unelected group with a considerable area of power removed from the reach of the legislature was incompatible with democratic theory. This issue is discussed by Dworkin and Waldron below.

Ronald Dworkin, *A Bill of Rights for Britain* (1990), pp 32–38

Is Incorporation Undemocratic?

The argument for parliamentary supremacy is often thought to rest on a more important and fundamental argument, however, according to which Britain should not have subscribed to the European Convention in the first place. This is the argument: that it is undemocratic for appointed judges rather than an elected Parliament to have the last word about what the law is. People who take that view will resist incorporation, because incorporation enlarges the practical consequences of what they regard as the mistake of accepting the Convention. They will certainly resist the idea that domestic judges should have the power to read the Convention more liberally and so provide more protection than Strasbourg requires.

Their argument misunderstands what democracy is, however. In the first place, it confuses democracy with the power of elected officials. There is no genuine democracy, even though officials have been elected in otherwise fair elections, unless voters have had access to the information they need so that their votes can be knowledgeable choices rather than only manipulated responses to advertising campaigns. Citizens of a democracy must be able to participate in government not just spasmodically, in elections from time to time, but constantly through informed and free debate about their Government's performance between elections. Those evident requirements suggest what other nations have long ago realised: that Parliament *must* be constrained in certain ways in order that democracy be genuine rather than sham. The argument that a Bill of Rights would be undemocratic is therefore not just wrong but the opposite of the truth.

The depressing story of the Thatcher Government's concentrated assault on free speech is more than enough to prove that point. In the *Harman*, *Ponting* and *Spycatcher* cases, in denying a public interest exception in the new Official Secrets Act, in the broadcasting bans, in the *Death on the Rock* matter, government tried to censor information of the type citizens need in order to vote intelligently or criticise officials effectively. The officials who took these decisions acted out of various motives: out of concern for confidentiality, or to discourage views they thought dangerous, or to improve the morale of the police and security services, or sometimes just to protect themselves from political damage. But none of these reasons is good enough: in a democracy officials have no right to dictate what the voters should know or think. The politicians would very likely have acted differently in every one of these cases if Article 10 of the European Convention had been part of British law, and the prospect of judicial intervention had been immediate and certain rather than delayed and in doubt. British democracy would obviously have been strengthened not weakened as a result.

It is true, however, that the European Convention forbids Governments to adopt or retain some laws that a majority of their citizens do want, and would continue to want even if they had all the information anyone might wish. The European Court struck down Northern Ireland's homosexuality law, for example, not because the Court doubted that a majority of the voters of

---

34 Eg, Lord McCluskey in his 1986 Reith Lectures, Lord Browne-Wilkinson [1992] PL 397, 409.
35 See, eg, Ewing and Gearty, *op cit*, pp 273 *et seq*; Waldron (below, pp 853–54); M Loughlin, *Public Law and Political Theory* (1992), esp pp 220–27.

Northern Ireland wanted that law, but because the Convention prohibits that form of discrimination whether the majority wishes it or not. If the European Convention were incorporated, British judges might strike down Britain's blasphemy law, which prohibits books or art deeply offensive to orthodox Christianity, even if a majority favoured retaining that law. The blasphemy law violates Articles 9 and 10 of the Convention, which protect freedom of conscience and free speech. In my view (although British courts have rejected the suggestion) the blasphemy law also violates Articles 9 and 14, which taken together prohibit religious discrimination, because that law discriminates in favour of Christianity. (Moslems said it was unjust that Salman Rushdie's book, The Satanic Verses, could not be prosecuted as blasphemous of their religion.) Of course the blasphemy law should not be extended to other religions, as they argued it should. It should instead be repealed, because it would violate the Convention even if it applied to religion in general.

Would it offend democracy if a British court had the power to strike down the blasphemy law as inconsistent with the Convention? No, because true democracy is not just *statistical* democracy, in which anything a majority or plurality wants is legitimate for that reason, but *communal* democracy, in which majority decision is legitimate only if it is a majority within a community of equals. That means not only that everyone must be allowed to participate in politics as an equal, through the vote and through freedom of speech and protest, but that political decisions must treat everyone with equal concern and respect, that each individual person must be guaranteed fundamental civil and political rights no combination of other citizens can take away, no matter how numerous they are or how much they despise his or her race or morals or way of life.

That view of what democracy means is at the heart of all the charters of human rights, including the European Convention. It is now the settled concept of democracy in Europe, the mature, principled concept that has now triumphed throughout Western Europe as well as in North America. It dominates the powerful movement towards democracy in Eastern Europe and Russia, and it was suppressed only with the most horrible tyranny in China. The rival, pure statistical concept of democracy, according to which democracy is consistent with oppressing minorities, was the concept proclaimed as justification by the Communist tyrannies after the Second World War: they said democracy meant government in the interests of the masses. The civilised world has recoiled from the totalitarian view, and it would be an appalling irony if Britain now embraced it as a reason for denying minorities constitutional rights.

This seems to me a decisive answer to the argument that incorporation would be undemocratic. I hope and believe that a different but equally decisive answer can also be made in Britain now: that the argument is self-defeating because the great majority of British people themselves rejects the crude statistical view of democracy on which the argument is based. Even people who do not think of themselves as belonging to any minority have good reasons for insisting that a majority's power to rule should be limited. Something crucially important to them – their religious freedom or professional independence or liberty of conscience, for example – might one day prove inconvenient to the Government of the day. Even people who cannot imagine being isolated in that way might prefer to live in a genuine political community, in which everyone's dignity as an equal is protected, rather than just in a state they control.

A public opinion poll in Britain in 1986, taken before a parliamentary debate about incorporation, reported that twice as many of those questioned favoured incorporation as opposed it, and that 71% thought a constitutional Bill of Rights would improve democracy. Britain will not have a Bill of Rights, even in the relatively weak form we have been discussing, unless it turns out, after an intense period of public debate, that the preference is genuine, that the British people do share a constitutional sense of justice. If so, and if we assume that this sense of justice will be shared by their descendants, then the argument that incorporation is undemocratic will have been defeated on its own terms.

Jeremy Waldron, 'A right-based critique of constitutional rights' (1993) 13 OJLS 18, pp 46–47, 50–51

Democratic Self-Restraint

If a Bill of Rights is incorporated into British law it will be because Parliament (or perhaps the people in a referendum) will have voted for incorporation. Ronald Dworkin has argued that this fact alone is sufficient to dispose of the democratic objections we have been considering. The objections, in his view, are self-defeating because polls reveal that more than 71% of people believe that British democracy would be improved by the incorporation of a Bill of Rights [Dworkin, *A Bill of Rights for Britain*, pp 36–37].

However, the matter cannot be disposed of so easily. For one thing, the fact that there is popular support, even overwhelming popular support, for an alteration in constitutional procedures does not show that such alteration therefore makes things more democratic. Certainly, my arguments entail that if the people want a regime of constitutional rights, then that is what they should have: democracy requires *that*. But we must not confuse the reason for carrying out a proposal with the character of the proposal itself. If the people wanted to experiment with dictatorship, principles of democracy might give us a reason to allow them to do so. But it would not follow that dictatorship is democratic. Everyone agrees that it is possible for a democracy to vote itself out of existence; that, for the proponents of constitutional reform, is one of their great fears. My worry is that popular support for the constitutional reforms envisaged by Dworkin and other members of Charter 88 amounts to exactly that: voting democracy out of existence, at least so far as a wide range of issues of political principle is concerned.

Dworkin also suggests that the democratic argument against a Bill of Rights is self-defeating in a British context, 'because a majority of British people themselves rejects the crude statistical view of democracy on which the argument is based' [*ibid*, p 36]. But although democracy connotes the idea of popular voting, it is not part of the concept of democracy that its own content be fixed by popular voting. If a majority of the British people thought a military dictatorship was democratic (because more in tune with the 'true spirit of the people' or whatever), that would not show that it was, nor would it provide grounds for saying that democratic arguments against the dictatorship were 'self-defeating'. If Dworkin wants to make a case against 'the crude statistical view' as a conception of democracy, he must argue for it ... In the end, I think, the matter comes down to this. If a process is democratic and comes up with the correct result, it does no injustice to anyone. But if the process is non-democratic, it inherently and necessarily does an injustice, in its operation, to the participatory aspirations of the ordinary citizen. And it does this injustice, tyrannises in *this* way, whether it comes up with the correct result or not.

If we are going to defend the idea of an entrenched Bill of Rights put effectively beyond revision by anyone other than the judges, we should try and think what we might say to some public-spirited citizen who wishes to launch a campaign or lobby her MP on some issue of rights about which she feels strongly and on which she has done her best to arrive at a considered and impartial view. She is not asking to be a dictator; she perfectly accepts that her voice should have no more power than that of anyone else who is prepared to participate in politics. But – like her suffragette forebears – she wants a vote; she wants her voice and her activity to count on matters of high political importance.

In defending a Bill of Rights, we have to imagine ourselves saying to her: 'You may write to the newspaper and get up a petition and organise a pressure group to lobby Parliament. But even if you succeed, beyond your wildest dreams, and orchestrate the support of a large number of like-minded men and women, and manage to prevail in the legislature, your measure may be challenged and struck down because your view of what rights we have does not accord with the judges' view. When their votes differ from yours, theirs are the votes that will prevail.' It is my submission that saying this does not comport with the respect and honour normally accorded to ordinary men and women in the context of a theory of rights.

Notes

1 Dworkin argues that the implications of Waldron's thesis are themselves contrary to true democracy.[36] Further, the refusal to disable the majority by entrenchment of rights includes a refusal to entrench democracy itself. This refusal in effect means that Waldron will not deny the right of the majority of the day to destroy democracy by disenfranchising a group such as all non-whites, or even by voting itself out of existence, thereby denying democracy to future generations.

2 Dworkin's main argument is that a Bill of Rights is ultimately concerned with *preserving* a worthwhile democracy for the future, and therefore that entrenched basic rights show *more* respect for democratic principles than do the advocates of retaining the untrammelled power of the majority of the day.[37]

Protection for a Bill of Rights

In the pre-HRA era, it was generally accepted that if a 'Bill of Rights' were introduced, it would rely on the guarantees of the European Convention on Human Rights. A number of commentators considered possible methods of protecting the rights. The extent to which democracy might seem to be infringed if unelected judges had to apply the Bill of Rights was clearly partly dependent on its authority and on the availability of review of legislation. The most contentious possibility was the adoption of the American model. It would have meant that judges would be empowered to strike down prior and subsequent legislation in conflict with the Bill of Rights. It would also have meant giving the Bill of Rights higher authority than other Acts of Parliament by entrenching it, so that no possibility of correction of judicial decisions by subsequent legislation arose, except in so far as provided for by the method of entrenchment.

A much less contentious possibility, in democratic terms, which was considered was that of allowing the Bill of Rights to prevail only over prior inconsistent legislation. A 'middle way', which was also the most likely possibility, would have been to protect the Convention rights only by a so-called 'notwithstanding clause' on the Canadian model – on that model subsequent legislation would only have been able to override the rights if the intention of doing so was clearly stated in the legislation; that is, a statutory provision would be included in such legislation stating, for example, 'the provisions of s 6 are to take effect notwithstanding the requirements of Article 6 of Schedule 1 to the Bill of Rights'. This 'middle way' undermines the argument against a Bill of Rights as undemocratic since under it the legislative body, at least in theory, remains free to pass legislation that is contrary to one of the rights; since the Bill of Rights is not entrenched, it also retains the power to amend or repeal part or all of it.

Ronald Dworkin, *A Bill of Rights for Britain* (1990), pp 28–30

How Could the Convention be Incorporated?

Several influential supporters of a Bill of Rights (including Lord Scarman, a former member of the House of Lords, who has been a pioneer in the argument for incorporation) have proposed that in

36 A further paradox in Waldron's argument, the existence of which he concedes (at p 46), is that if the majority vote in a referendum for an entrenched Bill of Rights they must, on his argument, be allowed to have one. Clearly, the only way to prevent the majority from entrenching a Bill of Rights would be to have an entrenched law forbidding the entrenchment of laws. This would obviously be impossible on its own terms. Since, as Dworkin notes, opinion polls reveal that more than 71 per cent of the population favour an entrenched Bill of Rights, Waldron's argument appears to be self-defeating.

37 See further R Dworkin, 'Liberalism', in *A Matter of Principle* (1985). See also HLA Hart, *Law Liberty and Morality* (1963), and Lord Lester, *Democracy and Individual Rights* (1968).

the first instance incorporation should take what is technically a weaker form: the incorporating statute should provide that an inconsistent statute is null and void unless Parliament has expressly stated that it *intends* the statute to override the Convention. In practice this technically weaker version of incorporation would probably provide almost as much protection as the stronger one. If a Government conceded that its statute violated the Convention, it would have no defence before the Commission or Court in Strasbourg. In any case, quite apart from that practical point, no respectable Government would wish to announce that it did not care whether its legislation or decisions violated the country's domestic promises and international obligations. If a Government felt itself able to make such an announcement, except in the most extraordinary circumstances, the spirit of liberty would be dead anyway, beyond the power of any constitution to revive.

Should Parliament be Supreme?

The politicians say that the very idea of a Bill of Rights restricting the power of Parliament is hostile to the British tradition that Parliament and Parliament alone should be sovereign. That supposed tradition seems less appealing now, when a very powerful executive and well-disciplined political parties mean less effective power for back-bench MPs than it did before these developments. The tradition has already been compromised in recent decades, moreover. It was altered by the European Communities Act, for example, under which judges have the power to override parliamentary decisions in order to enforce directly effective Community rules.

In any case, quite apart from these considerations, incorporating the European Convention would not diminish Parliament's present power in any way that could reasonably be thought objectionable. Parliament is already bound by international law to observe the terms of that Convention ... It is hard to argue that this further limitation would be wrong in principle, however. Britain agreed when it accepted the European Convention and the jurisdiction of the European Court of Human Rights, that it would be bound by the principles laid down in the Convention as these principles were interpreted not by Parliament but by a group of judges. If that limitation on the power of Parliament is acceptable, how can it be unacceptable that the principles be interpreted not by mainly foreign judges but by British judges trained in the common law and in the legal and political traditions of their own country?

The argument for parliamentary supremacy would be irrelevant, moreover, if the Convention were incorporated in the weaker form I suggested should be the initial goal. For then Parliament could override the Convention by mere majority vote, provided it was willing expressly to concede its indifference about doing so. No doubt that condition would, in practice, prevent a Government from introducing legislation it might otherwise enact. That is the point of incorporation, even in the weak form. But forcing Parliament to make the choice between obeying its international obligations and admitting that it is violating them does not limit Parliament's supremacy, but only its capacity for duplicity. Candour is hardly inconsistent with sovereignty.

THE HUMAN RIGHTS ACT 1998

Introduction[38]

After the 1997 General Election, the Labour government committed itself in the Queen's Speech to introducing a Bill incorporating the 'main provisions' of the Convention. The Human Rights Bill, receiving the 'main provisions' of the

---

38 See generally on the Human Rights Act: J Wadham and H Mountfield, *Blackstone's Guide to the Human Rights Act* 1998 (1999) (a useful guide); D Pannick and Lord Lester of Herne Hill QC, *Human Rights Law and Practice* (1999); R Clayton and H Tomlinson, *The Law of Human Rights* (2000); H Fenwick, *Civil Rights: New Labour, Freedom and the Human Rights Act* (2000), Chapter 2; F Klug and K Starmer [2001] PL 654; D McGoldrick, 'The HRA in theory and practice' (2001) 50(4) ICLQ 901.

Convention into domestic law, was introduced into Parliament in October 1997. The previous discussion has indicated that the Human Rights Act 1998 came onto the constitutional scene at a point when there was already an acceptance of the notion that fundamental rights must be strongly protected, a notion which to an extent was dependent on the influence of the Convention in domestic law. The HRA also had to find a place within a strongly established, if unwritten, constitution. The following section considers and analyses the HRA and certain early, very significant decisions taken under it. It is intended to provide a framework for the discussion of the impact of the Act, which pervades Part VI. The discussion seeks to show that the HRA represents a compromise between parliamentary supremacy and protection for human rights, but that flaws in the idea of seeking to create such a compromise are already becoming apparent (see Part I Chapter 4, pp 163–67). Further, the discussion suggests that more attention should have been paid in the pre-HRA era to the *content* of the Convention rights rather than to the mechanics of the HRA. The early decisions discussed below and in the rest of this Part suggest that the interpretation of the Articles of the Convention, sometimes in a minimal or even hostile fashion, is one of the main preoccupations of the courts, rather than the mechanics of the HRA itself. The minimalist or hostile approach arises, it is argued, partly from a degree of intellectual laziness on the part of the judiciary and partly from patriotic pride in established common law traditions.

The Green Paper, *Bringing Rights Home*,[39] concluded: 'We aim to change the relationship between the State and the citizen, and to redress the dilution of individual rights by an over-centralising government that has taken place over the past two decades.' This aim was to be achieved by means of the European Convention on Human Rights as afforded further effect in domestic law under the HRA. The Act came fully into force on 2 October 2000. The Convention thus received into domestic law creates a transformation in constitutional terms in the sense that it provides positive rights in place of negative liberties. Since, traditionally, the Constitution recognised only negative liberties as opposed to positive rights, the judicial focus of concern always tended to be on the content and nature of the restrictions in question rather than on the value and extent of the right. In other words, despite proud traditions of upholding certain fundamental rights, constitutional inadequacy became, inevitably, apparent.

This was a bold, imaginative constitutional change. However, such boldness had limits, which are reflected in the HRA. A seminal constitutional decision involving a choice between judicial and parliamentary checks on executive power, and therefore as to the allocation of power, had to be taken regarding the choice of model for the enforcement of the Convention. The choice made was, as indicated below, to leave parliamentary power formally unchecked: judicial rulings remain (at least theoretically) subject to primary legislation (see further Part I Chapter 4). The HRA therefore seeks to reconcile a transfer of power to the judiciary with parliamentary supremacy. It is readily apparent, then, that there is a contradiction between the liberal aim of affording the Convention rights efficacy in domestic law in order to aid in reversing the effects of the over-centralisation of power, and the aim of preserving the key feature of the constitution which gave rein to that power – parliamentary supremacy (see further, pp 163–67, above).

---

39 J Straw and P Boateng, *Bringing Rights Home: Labour's Plans to Incorporate the ECHR into UK Law*: A Consultation Paper, December 1996 (1997).

It is important to point out that although the Convention contains a list of rights that look very similar to those contained in a number of Bills or Charters of Rights, the HRA does not create a Bill or Charter of Rights in the way that the Canadian Charter or the US Amendments to the Constitution can be said to constitute a Bill of Rights, since those rights have the force of 'ordinary' law and also, in very different respects, have a higher status than such law. Further, unlike the German Basic Law or the US Amendments, the HRA can simply be repealed or amended like any ordinary statute and it is, therefore, in a far more precarious position. The HRA is modelled on the New Zealand Bill of Rights which uses a rule of construction under s 6 to the effect that a court is obliged, wherever an enactment can be given a meaning that is consistent with the rights and freedoms contained in the Bill of Rights, to prefer that meaning to any other meaning.[40] In so far as one expects a Bill of Rights to demonstrate a strong commitment to human rights, demanding, if necessary, constitutional changes to provide such protection, the HRA, like the New Zealand Bill of Rights, does not have the characteristics of a Bill of Rights. The HRA does *not* 'incorporate' the Convention rights into substantive domestic law, since it does not provide that they are to have the 'force of law', the usual form of words used when international treaties are incorporated into domestic law.[41] Instead, under s 1(2) of the HRA, certain of the rights discussed in Chapter 2 of this Part are to 'have effect for the purposes of this Act'.

Below, extracts from the text of the HRA are set out and this is followed by notes on the provisions. After the notes, extracts from a number of the early and most significant cases on the key HRA provisions are provided. These cases are grouped under certain headings, but they should also be read as indicating in a more general way the approaches that the courts are taking to the HRA.

Human Rights Act 1998
Chapter 42

Introduction

The
Convention
Rights.

1.–(1) In this Act 'the Convention rights' means the rights and fundamental freedoms set out in—
    (a) Articles 2 to 12 and 14 of the Convention;
    (b) Articles 1 to 3 of the First Protocol; and
    (c) Articles 1 and 2 of the Sixth Protocol,
as read with Articles 16 to 18 of the Convention.
(2) Those Articles are to have effect for the purposes of this Act subject to any designated derogation or reservation (as to which see sections 14 and 15).

. . .

(4) The Secretary of State may by order make such amendments to this Act as he considers appropriate to reflect the effect, in relation to the United Kingdom, of a protocol.

. . .

Interpretation
of Convention.

2.–(1) A court or tribunal determining a question which has arisen in connection with a Convention right must take into account any rights—

---

40 For discussion as to the use of this model, see M Taggart, 'Tugging on Superman's cape: lessons from the experience with the New Zealand Bill of Rights' [1998] PL 266; A Butler, 'Why the New Zealand Bill of Rights is a bad model for Britain' [1997] OJLS 332; H Schwartz, 'The short and happy life and tragic death of the New Zealand Bill of Rights' [1998] NZLR 259.
41 See, eg, the Carriage of Goods by Sea Act 1971, s 1(2).

(a) judgment, decision, declaration or advisory opinion of the European Court of Human Rights;

(b) opinion of the Commission given in a report adopted under Article 31 of the Convention;

(c) decision of the Commission in connection with Article 26 or 27(2) of the Convention; or

(d) decision of the Committee of Ministers taken under Article 46 of the Convention,

whenever made or given, so far as, in the opinion of the court or tribunal, it is relevant to the proceedings in which that question has arisen.

Legislation

Interpretation of legislation.
3.–(1) So far as it is possible to do so, primary legislation and subordinate legislation must be read and given effect in a way which is compatible with the Convention rights.

(2) This section —

(a) applies to primary legislation and subordinate legislation whenever enacted;

(b) does not affect the validity, continuing operation or enforcement of any incompatible primary legislation; and

(c) does not affect the validity, continuing operation or enforcement of any incompatible subordinate legislation if (disregarding any possibility of revocation) primary legislation prevents removal of the incompatibility.

Declaration of incompatibility.
4.–(1) Subsection (2) applies in any proceedings in which a court determines whether a provision of primary legislation is compatible with a Convention right.

(2) If the court is satisfied that the provision is incompatible with a Convention right, it may make a declaration of that incompatibility.

(3) Subsection (4) applies in any proceedings in which a court determines whether a provision of subordinate legislation, made in the exercise of a power conferred by primary legislation, is compatible with a Convention right.

(4) If the court is satisfied —

(a) that the provision is incompatible with a Convention right; and

(b) that (disregarding any possibility of revocation) the primary legislation concerned prevents removal of the incompatibility,

it may make a declaration of that incompatibility.

(5) In this section 'court' means—

(a) the House of Lords;

(b) the Judicial Committee of the Privy Council;

(c) the Courts-Martial Appeal Court;

(d) in Scotland, the High Court of Justiciary sitting otherwise than as a trial court or the Court of Session;

(e) in England and Wales or Northern Ireland, the High Court or the Court of Appeal.

(6) A declaration under this section ('a declaration of incompatibility')—

(a) does not affect the validity, continuing operation or enforcement of the provision in respect of which it is given; and

(b) is not binding on the parties to the proceedings in which it is made.

Right of Crown to intervene.
5.–(1) Where a court is considering whether to make a declaration of incompatibility, the Crown is entitled to notice in accordance with rules of court.

(2) In any case to which subsection (1) applies —

(a) a Minister of the Crown (or a person nominated by him);
(b) a member of the Scottish Executive;
(c) a Northern Ireland Minister;
(d) a Northern Ireland department,

is entitled, on giving notice in accordance with rules of court, to be joined as a party to the proceedings.

(3) Notice under subsection (2) may be given at any time during the proceedings.

(4) A person who has been made a party to criminal proceedings (other than in Scotland) as the result of a notice under subsection (2) may, with leave, appeal to the House of Lords against any declaration of incompatibility made in the proceedings.

...

Public authorities

Acts of public authorities.
6.–(1) It is unlawful for a public authority to act in a way which is incompatible with a Convention right.

(2) Subsection (1) does not apply to an act if—

(a) as the result of one or more provisions of primary legislation, the authority could not have acted differently; or

(b) in the case of one or more provisions of, or made under, primary legislation which cannot be read or given effect in a way which is compatible with the Convention rights, the authority was acting so as to give effect to or enforce those provisions.

(3) In this section 'public authority' includes —

(a) a court or tribunal; and

(b) any person certain of whose functions are functions of a public nature,

but does not include either House of Parliament or a person exercising functions in connection with proceedings in Parliament.

(4) In subsection (3) 'Parliament' does not include the House of Lords in its judicial capacity.

(5) In relation to a particular act, a person is not a public authority by virtue only of subsection (3)(b) if the nature of the act is private.

(6) 'An act' includes a failure to act but does not include a failure to —

(a) introduce in, or lay before, Parliament a proposal for legislation;
or
(b) make any primary legislation or remedial order.

Proceedings.
7.–(1) A person who claims that a public authority has acted (or proposes to act) in a way which is made unlawful by section 6(1) may —

(a) bring proceedings against the authority under this Act in the appropriate court or tribunal; or

(b) rely on the Convention right or rights concerned in any legal proceedings,

but only if he is (or would be) a victim of the unlawful act.

(2) In subsection (1)(a) 'appropriate court or tribunal' means such court or tribunal as may be determined in accordance with rules; and proceedings against an authority include a counterclaim or similar proceeding.

(3) If the proceedings are brought on an application for judicial review, the applicant is to be taken to have a sufficient interest in relation to the unlawful act only if he is, or would be, a victim of that act.

(4) If the proceedings are made by way of a petition for judicial review in Scotland, the applicant shall be taken to have title and interest to sue in relation to the unlawful act only if he is, or would be, a victim of that act.

(5) Proceedings under subsection (1)(a) must be brought before the end of—

    (a) the period of one year beginning with the date on which the act complained of took place; or

    (b) such longer period as the court or tribunal considers equitable having regard to all the circumstances,

but that is subject to any rule imposing a stricter time limit in relation to the procedure in question.

(6) In subsection (1)(b) 'legal proceedings' includes—

    (a) proceedings brought by or at the instigation of a public authority; and

    (b) an appeal against the decision of a court or tribunal.

(7) For the purposes of this section, a person is a victim of an unlawful act only if he would be a victim for the purposes of Article 34 of the Convention if proceedings were brought in the European Court of Human Rights in respect of that act.

(8) Nothing in this Act creates a criminal offence.

(9) In this section 'rules' means—

    (a) in relation to proceedings before a court or tribunal outside Scotland, rules made by the Lord Chancellor or the Secretary of State for the purposes of this section or rules of court;

    (b) in relation to proceedings before a court or tribunal in Scotland, rules made by the Secretary of State for those purposes;

    (c) in relation to proceedings before a tribunal in Northern Ireland—

        (i) which deals with transferred matters; and

        (ii) for which no rules made under paragraph (a) are in force,

    rules made by a Northern Ireland department for those purposes,

and includes provision made by order under section 1 of the Courts and Legal Services Act 1990.

(10) In making rules, regard must be had to section 9.

(11) The Minister who has power to make rules in relation to a particular tribunal may, to the extent he considers it necessary to ensure that the tribunal can provide an appropriate remedy in relation to an act (or proposed act) of a public authority which is (or would be) unlawful as a result of section 6(1), by order add to—

    (a) the relief or remedies which the tribunal may grant; or

    (b) the grounds on which it may grant any of them.

(12) An order made under subsection (11) may contain such incidental, supplemental, consequential or transitional provision as the Minister making it considers appropriate.

(13) 'The Minister' includes the Northern Ireland department concerned.

Judicial remedies.

8.–(1) In relation to any act (or proposed act) of a public authority which the court finds is (or would be) unlawful, it may grant such relief or remedy, or make such order, within its powers as it considers just and appropriate.

(2) But damages may be awarded only by a court which has power to award damages, or to order the payment of compensation, in civil proceedings.

(3) No award of damages is to be made unless, taking account of all the circumstances of the case, including —

    (a) any other relief or remedy granted, or order made, in relation to the act in question (by that or any other court); and

    (b) the consequences of any decision (of that or any other court) in respect of that act,

the court is satisfied that the award is necessary to afford just satisfaction to the person in whose favour it is made.

(4) In determining—
    (a) whether to award damages; or
    (b) the amount of an award,
the court must take into account the principles applied by the European Court of Human Rights in relation to the award of compensation under Article 41 of the Convention.

(5) A public authority against which damages are awarded is to be treated—
    (a) in Scotland, for the purposes of section 3 of the Law Reform (Miscellaneous Provisions) (Scotland) Act 1940 as if the award were made in an action of damages in which the authority has been found liable in respect of loss or damage to the person to whom the award is made;
    (b) for the purposes of the Civil Liability (Contribution) Act 1978 as liable in respect of damage suffered by the person to whom the award is made.

(6) In this section—
'court' includes a tribunal;
'damages' means damages for an unlawful act of a public authority; and
'unlawful' means unlawful under section 6(1).

Judicial acts.   **9.**–(1) Proceedings under section 7(1)(a) in respect of a judicial act may be brought only—
    (a) by exercising a right of appeal;
    (b) on an application (in Scotland a petition) for judicial review; or
    (c) in such other forum as may be prescribed by rules.

(2) That does not affect any rule of law which prevents a court from being the subject of judicial review.

(3) In proceedings under this Act in respect of a judicial act done in good faith, damages may not be awarded otherwise than to compensate a person to the extent required by Article 5(5) of the Convention.

(4) An award of damages permitted by subsection (3) is to be made against the Crown; but no award may be made unless the appropriate person, if not a party to the proceedings, is joined.

(5) In this section—
'appropriate person' means the Minister responsible for the court concerned, or a person or government department nominated by him;
'court' includes a tribunal;
'judge' includes a member of a tribunal, a justice of the peace and a clerk or other officer entitled to exercise the jurisdiction of a court;
'judicial act' means a judicial act of a court and includes an act done on the instructions, or on behalf, of a judge; and
'rules' has the same meaning as in section 7(9).

Remedial action

Power to take   **10.**–(1) This section applies if—
remedial action.   (a) a provision of legislation has been declared under section 4 to be incompatible with a Convention right and, if an appeal lies —
        (i) all persons who may appeal have stated in writing that they do not intend to do so;
        (ii) the time for bringing an appeal has expired and no appeal has been brought within that time; or
        (iii) an appeal brought within that time has been determined or abandoned; or

(b) it appears to a Minister of the Crown or Her Majesty in Council that, having regard to a finding of the European Court of Human Rights made after the coming into force of this section in proceedings against the United Kingdom, a provision of legislation is incompatible with an obligation of the United Kingdom arising from the Convention.

(2) If a Minister of the Crown considers that there are compelling reasons for proceeding under this section, he may by order make such amendments to the legislation as he considers necessary to remove the incompatibility.

(3) If, in the case of subordinate legislation, a Minister of the Crown considers—

(a) that it is necessary to amend the primary legislation under which the subordinate legislation in question was made, in order to enable the incompatibility to be removed; and

(b) that there are compelling reasons for proceeding under this section,

he may by order make such amendments to the primary legislation as he considers necessary.

(4) This section also applies where the provision in question is in subordinate legislation and has been quashed, or declared invalid, by reason of incompatibility with a Convention right and the Minister proposes to proceed under paragraph 2(b) of Schedule 2.

(5) If the legislation is an Order in Council, the power conferred by subsection (2) or (3) is exercisable by Her Majesty in Council.

(6) In this section 'legislation' does not include a Measure of the Church Assembly or of the General Synod of the Church of England.

(7) Schedule 2 makes further provision about remedial orders.

Other rights and proceedings

Safeguard for existing human rights.

11. A person's reliance on a Convention right does not restrict—

(a) any other right or freedom conferred on him by or under any law having effect in any part of the United Kingdom; or

(b) his right to make any claim or bring any proceedings which he could make or bring apart from sections 7 to 9.

Freedom of expression.

12.–(1) This section applies if a court is considering whether to grant any relief which, if granted, might affect the exercise of the Convention right to freedom of expression.

(2) If the person against whom the application for relief is made ('the respondent') is neither present nor represented, no such relief is to be granted unless the court is satisfied—

(a) that the applicant has taken all practicable steps to notify the respondent; or

(b) that there are compelling reasons why the respondent should not be notified.

(3) No such relief is to be granted so as to restrain publication before trial unless the court is satisfied that the applicant is likely to establish that publication should not be allowed.

(4) The court must have particular regard to the importance of the Convention right to freedom of expression and, where the proceedings relate to material which the respondent claims, or which appears to the court, to be journalistic, literary or artistic material (or to conduct connected with such material), to —

(a) the extent to which—

(i) the material has, or is about to, become available to the public; or

(ii) it is, or would be, in the public interest for the material to be published;

(b) any relevant privacy code.

(5) In this section—

'court' includes a tribunal; and

'relief includes any remedy or order (other than in criminal proceedings).

Freedom of thought, conscience and religion.

13.–(1) If a court's determination of any question arising under this Act might affect the exercise by a religious organisation (itself or its members collectively) of the Convention right to freedom of thought, conscience and religion, it must have particular regard to the importance of that right.

(2) In this section 'court' includes a tribunal.

Derogations and reservations

Derogations.

14.–(1) In this Act 'designated derogation' means—

(a) the United Kingdom's derogation from Article 5(3) of the Convention; and

(b) any derogation by the United Kingdom from an Article of the Convention, or of any protocol to the Convention, which is designated for the purposes of this Act in an order made by the Secretary of State.

(2) . . .

(3) If a designated derogation is amended or replaced it ceases to be a designated derogation.

(4) But subsection (3) does not prevent the Secretary of State from exercising his power under subsection (1)(b) to make a fresh designation order in respect of the Article concerned.

(5) The Secretary of State must by order make such amendments to Schedule 3 as he considers appropriate to reflect —

(a) any designation order; or

(b) the effect of subsection (3).

(6) A designation order may be made in anticipation of the making by the United Kingdom of a proposed derogation.[42]

Reservations.

15.—(1) In this Act 'designated reservation' means—

(a) the United Kingdom's reservation to Article 2 of the First Protocol to the Convention; and

(b) any other reservation by the United Kingdom to an Article of the Convention, or of any protocol to the Convention, which is designated for the purposes of this Act in an order made by the Secretary of State.

(2) The text of the reservation referred to in subsection (1)(a) is set out in Part II of Schedule 3.

(3) If a designated reservation is withdrawn wholly or in part it ceases to be a designated reservation.

(4) But subsection (3) does not prevent the Secretary of State from exercising his power under subsection (1)(b) to make a fresh designation order in respect of the Article concerned.

(5) The Secretary of State must by order make such amendments to this Act as he considers appropriate to reflect —

(a) any designation order; or

(b) the effect of subsection (3).

---

42 Sections 14 and 16 and Sched 3, Part I were amended by the Human Rights Act (Amendment) Order (No 1) SI 2001/1216. The amendment reflected the withdrawal of the derogation to Art 5(3) which had been necessary as a result of the decision of the European Court of Human Rights in *Brogan v UK* (1988) 11 EHRR 117. Changes effected under the Terrorism Act 2000 allowed for the withdrawal of the derogation; see Part VI Chapter 4, pp 1027–28.

Period for which designated derogations have effect

16.–(1) If it has not already been withdrawn by the United Kingdom, a designated derogation ceases to have effect for the purposes of this Act ... at the end of the period of five years ... beginning with the date on which the order designating it was made.

(2) At any time before the period—

     (a) fixed by subsection (1) ...; or

     (b) extended by an order under this subsection,

comes to an end, the Secretary of State may by order extend it by a further period of five years.

(3) An order under section 14(1) ... ceases to have effect at the end of the period for consideration, unless a resolution has been passed by each House approving the order.

(4) Subsection (3) does not affect—

     (a) anything done in reliance on the order; or

     (b) the power to make a fresh order under section 14(1).

(5) In subsection (3) 'period for consideration' means the period of 40 days beginning with the day on which the order was made.

(6) In calculating the period for consideration, no account is to be taken of any time during which—

     (a) Parliament is dissolved or prorogued; or

     (b) both Houses are adjourned for more than four days.

(7) If a designated derogation is withdrawn by the United Kingdom, the Secretary of State must by order make such amendments to this Act as he considers are required to reflect that withdrawal.

Periodic review of designated reservations.

17.–(1) The appropriate Minister must review the designated reservation referred to in section 15(1)(a)—

     ...

(3) The Minister conducting a review under this section must prepare a report on the result of the review and lay a copy of it before each House of Parliament.

     ...

Parliamentary procedure

Statements of compatibility.

19.–(1) A Minister of the Crown in charge of a Bill in either House of Parliament must, before Second Reading of the Bill —

     (a) make a statement to the effect that in his view the provisions of the Bill are compatible with the Convention rights ('a statement of compatibility'); or

     (b) make a statement to the effect that although he is unable to make a statement of compatibility the government nevertheless wishes the House to proceed with the Bill.

(2) The statement must be in writing and be published in such manner as the Minister making it considers appropriate.

     ...

Interpretation, etc.

21.–(1) In this Act—

     ...

'primary legislation' means any —

     (a) public general Act;

     (b) local and personal Act;

     (c) private Act;

     (d) Measure of the Church Assembly;

     (e) Measure of the General Synod of the Church of England;

     (f) Order in Council—

     (i)   made in exercise of Her Majesty's Royal Prerogative;

    (ii) made under section 38(1)(a) of the Northern Ireland Constitution Act 1973 or the corresponding provision of the Northern Ireland Act 1998; or

   (iii) amending an Act of a kind mentioned in paragraph (a), (b) or (c);

and includes an order or other instrument made under primary legislation (otherwise than by the National Assembly for Wales, a member of the Scottish Executive, a Northern Ireland Minister or a Northern Ireland department) to the extent to which it operates to bring one or more provisions of that legislation into force or amends any primary legislation;

. . .

'subordinate legislation' means any —

  (a) Order in Council other than one—

     (i)   made in exercise of Her Majesty's Royal Prerogative;

    (ii) made under section 38(1)(a) of the Northern Ireland Constitution Act 1973 or the corresponding provision of the Northern Ireland Act 1998; or

   (iii) amending an Act of a kind mentioned in the definition of primary legislation;

  (b) Act of the Scottish Parliament;

  (c) Act of the Parliament of Northern Ireland;

  (d) Measure of the Assembly established under section 1 of the Northern Ireland Assembly Act 1973;

  (e) Act of the Northern Ireland Assembly;

  (f) order, rules, regulations, scheme, warrant, byelaw or other instrument made under primary legislation (except to the extent to which it operates to bring one or more provisions of that legislation into force or amends any primary legislation);

  (g) order, rules, regulations, scheme, warrant, byelaw or other instrument made under legislation mentioned in paragraph (b), (c), (d) or (e) or made under an Order in Council applying only to Northern Ireland;

  (h) order, rules, regulations, scheme, warrant, byelaw or other instrument made by a member of the Scottish Executive, a Northern Ireland Minister or a Northern Ireland department in exercise of prerogative or other executive functions of Her Majesty which are exercisable by such a person on behalf of Her Majesty;

'transferred matters' has the same meaning as in the Northern Ireland Act 1998; and

'tribunal' means any tribunal in which legal proceedings may be brought.

(2) The references in paragraphs (b) and (c) of section 2(1) to Articles are to Articles of the Convention as they had effect immediately before the coming into force of the Eleventh Protocol.

(3) The reference in paragraph (d) of section 2(1) to Article 46 includes a reference to Articles 32 and 54 of the Convention as they had effect immediately before the coming into force of the Eleventh Protocol.

(4) The references in section 2(1) to a report or decision of the Commission or a decision of the Committee of Ministers include references to a report or decision made as provided by paragraphs 3, 4 and 6 of Article 5 of the Eleventh Protocol (transitional provisions).

(5) Any liability under the Army Act 1955, the Air Force Act 1955 or the Naval

Discipline Act 1957 to suffer death for an offence is replaced by a liability to imprisonment for life or any less punishment authorised by those Acts; and those Acts shall accordingly have effect with the necessary modifications.

Short title, commencement, application and extent.

22.–(1) This Act may be cited as the Human Rights Act 1998.

(2) Sections 18, 20 and 21(5) and this section come into force on the passing of this Act.

(3) The other provisions of this Act come into force on such day as the Secretary of State may by order appoint; and different days may be appointed for different purposes.

(4) Paragraph (b) of subsection (1) of section 7 applies to proceedings brought by or at the instigation of a public authority whenever the act in question took place; but otherwise that subsection does not apply to an act taking place before the coming into force of that section.

(5) This Act binds the Crown.

(6) This Act extends to Northern Ireland.

(7) Section 21(5), so far as it relates to any provision contained in the Army Act 1955, the Air Force Act 1955 or the Naval Discipline Act 1957, extends to any place to which that provision extends.

SCHEDULES

Schedule 1

THE ARTICLES

PART I

THE CONVENTION

RIGHTS AND FREEDOMS

Schedule 1 includes Articles 2–12 and 14–18 of the Convention and the Sixth Protocol (the Articles and the Sixth Protocol are set out in Part II Chapter 3 (pp 00–000).

Schedule 2

REMEDIAL ORDERS

Orders

1.–(1) A remedial order may—

    (a) contain such incidental, supplemental, consequential or transitional provision as the person making it considers appropriate;

    (b) be made so as to have effect from a date earlier than that on which it is made;

    (c) make provision for the delegation of specific functions;

    (d) make different provision for different cases.

(2) The power conferred by sub-paragraph (1)(a) includes —

    (a) power to amend primary legislation (including primary legislation other than that which contains the incompatible provision); and

    (b) power to amend or revoke subordinate legislation (including subordinate legislation other than that which contains the incompatible provision).

(3) A remedial order may be made so as to have the same extent as the legislation which it affects.

(4) No person is to be guilty of an offence solely as a result of the retrospective effect of a remedial order.

Procedure

2. No remedial order may be made unless —

    (a) a draft of the order has been approved by a resolution of each House of Parliament made after the end of the period of 60 days beginning with the day on which the draft was laid; or

    (b) it is declared in the order that it appears to the person making it that, because of the urgency of the matter, it is necessary to make the order without a draft being so approved.

. . .

Urgent cases

4.–(1) If a remedial order ('the original order') is made without being approved in draft, the person making it must lay it before Parliament, accompanied by the required information, after it is made.

(2) If representations have been made during the period of 60 days beginning with the day on which the original order was made, the person making it must (after the end of that period) lay before Parliament a statement containing —

    (a) a summary of the representations; and

    (b) if, as a result of the representations, he considers it appropriate to make changes to the original order, details of the changes.

(3) If sub-paragraph (2)(b) applies, the person making the statement must—

    (a) make a further remedial order replacing the original order; and

    (b) lay the replacement order before Parliament.

(4) If, at the end of the period of 120 days beginning with the day on which the original order was made, a resolution has not been passed by each House approving the original or replacement order, the order ceases to have effect (but without that affecting anything previously done under either order or the power to make a fresh remedial order).

. . .

Schedule 3

DEROGATION AND
RESERVATION

PART I

DEROGATION[43]

PART II
RESERVATION

At the time of signing the present (First) Protocol, I declare that, in view of certain provisions of the Education Acts in the United Kingdom, the principle affirmed in the second sentence of Article 2 is accepted by the United Kingdom only so far as it is compatible with the provision of efficient instruction and training, and the avoidance of unreasonable public expenditure.

Dated 20 March 1952

Made by the United Kingdom Permanent Representative to the Council of Europe.

. . .

---

43   Amended by the Human Rights Act 1998 (Amendment) Order (No 2) SI 2001/4032, Art 2 in order to reflect the Human Rights Act 1998 (Designated Derogation) Order 2001 SI 2001/3644. See further below, pp 875–76.

Notes

1 As indicated above, the form of protection for the Convention most favoured by a number of commentators was by means of a so-called 'notwithstanding clause'. However, this model was not used for the HRA, although the constitutional protection it has received bears some similarities to the use of a 'notwithstanding clause'. Of course, there is nothing in the HRA to prevent Parliament from including a 'notwithstanding' clause in legislation which contains provisions incompatible with one or more of the Convention rights.

2 *The interpretative obligation under s 3.*[44] Under s 3 of the HRA, the Convention[45] receives a subtle form of constitutional protection since under s 3(1) primary and subordinate legislation must be read and given effect in a way which is compatible with the Convention rights 'so far as it is possible to do so'. Significantly, s 3(2)(a) makes it clear that the obligation imposed by s 3 arises in relation to both previous and subsequent enactments. It is clear from s 3 that the Convention will have, in one sense, a lower status than ordinary statutes in that it will not automatically override pre-existing law. But, most significantly, s 3(1) demands that *all* statutes should be rendered, if possible, compatible with the Convention rights. Therefore, by imposing this interpretative obligation on courts, the rights become capable of affecting subsequent legislation in a way that is not normally possible.[46] The requirement to construe legislation 'so far as it is possible to do so' consistently with the Convention makes it clear that a very determined stance under s 3 best reflects the intention of Parliament, although it may also be pointed out that since Parliament has enacted s 4, it clearly contemplated some limits on what could be achieved by means of s 3. There is also the question whether using very bold techniques such as reading words into statutes has democratic legitimacy. If judges depart from interpretative techniques and, in effect, rewrite the legislation, they will usurp the function of Parliament and marginalise the role of s 4. This point is returned to below. Below, certain early decisions on s 3(1) indicate the approaches that the courts are taking to this strong interpretative obligation.

3 Section 21(1) defines 'primary legislation' to include Orders in Council made under the royal prerogative. Thus, executive power as well as parliamentary sovereignty is preserved under the HRA.[47] This is clearly an anomalous provision, since it renders individual rights subordinate to powers which may be used to infringe them and which cannot claim legitimacy derived from the democratic process.

4 Subordinate legislation covers Orders in Council not made under the royal prerogative, orders, rules, regulations, bylaws or other instruments made under primary legislation unless the rule etc 'operates to bring one or more provisions of that legislation into force or amends any primary legislation'. The last provision is significant, since it means that where provision is made under primary legislation for amendment by executive order, subject to the negative, or even the affirmative resolution procedure, the amendment, which will almost certainly have received virtually no parliamentary attention, will still be able to override Convention provisions.

---

44 For further discussion see M Elliott, 'Fundamental rights as interpretative constructs: the constitutional logic of the HRA', in C Forsyth (ed), *Judicial Review and the Constitution* (2001).

45 The term 'the Convention' will be used to refer to the Convention rights currently included in Sched 1 to the HRA 1998.

46 For extensive consideration of this point, see R Clayton and H Tomlinson, *The Law of Human Rights* (2000), Chapter 4.

47 For discussion of the effect of treating this exercise of prerogative powers as primary legislation, see N Squires, 'Judicial review of the prerogative after the HRA' (2000) 116 LQR 572–75.

5   If legislation cannot be rendered compatible with the rights, its validity is unaffected (s 3(2)(b) and (c)), but a declaration of the incompatibility can be made by a higher court under s 4. Parliament may then modify the offending provisions under s 10. The incompatible legislation must continue to be enforced. The declaration of incompatibility also does not affect the validity of the legislation. This subtle form of protection avoids formal entrenchment and therefore creates a compromise between leaving the protection of rights to the democratic process and entrusting them fully to the judiciary.[48]

6   *The position of the Scottish Parliament, the Northern Ireland Assembly and the Welsh Assembly.* The devolution legislation places the Scottish Parliament, the Northern Ireland Assembly and the Welsh Assembly in a different position from that of the Westminster Parliament as regards the legal status of the Convention rights. The Welsh Assembly is not able to pass primary legislation and it is bound by the Convention under s 107(1) of the Government of Wales Act 1998. The Scottish Parliament cannot act incompatibly with the Convention under s 29(2)(d) of the Scotland Act 1998. The Executive and law officers in Scotland are also bound.[49] Under s 21 of the HRA, legislation passed by the Scottish Parliament and by the Northern Ireland Assembly is regarded as secondary legislation. Under s 3 of the HRA, any primary legislation[50] passed by the Westminster Parliament and applicable to Scotland, Northern Ireland and Wales will be binding, even if it is not compatible with the Convention. These arrangements mean that Scotland has, in effect, a Bill of Rights in the traditional sense since the Scottish Parliament is bound by the Convention and therefore cannot pass primary legislation which conflicts with it.[51] The references to 'legislation', so far and below, are to legislation emanating from the Westminster Parliament.

7   *The 'declaration of incompatibility' and the remedial process.*[52] Section 4(2) applies under s 4(1) when a court is determining in any proceedings whether a provision of primary legislation is incompatible with a Convention right. If a court is satisfied that the provision is incompatible with the right, 'it may make a declaration of that incompatibility' – a declaration that it is not possible to construe the legislation in question to harmonise with the Convention. Section 4(4) applies to incompatible secondary legislation where incompatible primary legislation prevents the removal of the incompatibility. Again, the incompatibility can be declared.

8   But only certain courts can make the declaration (s 4(5)). A court falling within s 4(5) has a discretion to make a declaration of incompatibility. Section 4(2) clearly leaves open the possibility that such a court, having found an incompatibility, might nevertheless decide not to make a declaration of it. In *Wilson v First County Trust Ltd* [2001] 3 All ER 229, the Court of Appeal found that s 127(3) of the Consumer Credit Act 1974 was incompatible with Article 6 and with Article 1 of the First Protocol to the Convention. The Court considered that, having found an incompatibility, it should make a declaration of it for three reasons (at para 47).

---

48   It is argued in Part I Chapter 4, pp 163–67 that the HRA may be *de facto* entrenched as a result of the interrelationship between ss 3 and 19.

49   See the Scotland Act, s 57. Thus, in Scotland and Wales, the Convention became binding from 1 July 1999, when the devolution legislation came into force, over a year before the HRA came fully into force.

50   The Scotland Act 1988, s 29(2)(b) and Sched 5, and the Government of Wales Act 1998, Sched 2.

51   See further S Tierney, 'Devolution issues and s 2(1) of the HRA' (2000) 4 EHRLR 380–92.

52   For further discussion of the significance of the ministerial power to make remedial orders, see Part I Chapter 3, pp 107–09.

First, the question of the incompatibility had been fully argued at a hearing appointed for that purpose. Secondly, the order required by s 127(3) could not lawfully be made on the appeal unless the court was satisfied that the section could not be read in such a way as to give effect to the Convention rights, and that fact should be formally recorded by a declaration that 'gives legitimacy to that order'. Thirdly, a declaration provides a basis for a minister to consider whether the section should be amended under s 10(1) (see below). The Court duly went on to make the declaration. The declaration can be overturned on appeal to a higher court, as occurred in *R (on the application of Alconbury Developments) v Secretary of State for the Environment and Other Cases* [2001] 2 WLR 1389. The Divisional Court made a declaration of incompatibility which was overturned on appeal to the House of Lords.

9   Once a declaration of incompatibility has been made, the legislative provision in question remains valid (s 4(6)). As indicated above, s 3 provides that the interpretative obligation does not affect the validity, continuing operation or enforcement of any incompatible primary legislation, and this is equally the case under s 4(6) if a declaration of incompatibility is made. The Convention guarantee in question will be disapplied by the court in relation to that incompatible provision.

10 If a declaration of incompatibility is made, s 10 will apply which allows a minister to make amendments to the offending legislation by means of the 'fast track' procedure. Section 10 may also be used where a decision of the European Court of Human Rights suggests that a provision of legislation is incompatible with the Convention. However, as indicated above, the minister is under no obligation to make the amendment(s), either after any such decision or after a declaration of incompatibility under s 4, and may only do so if he or she considers that there are 'compelling reasons for proceeding under this section'. In other words, the fact that a declaration of incompatibility has been made will not necessarily in itself provide a compelling reason, although the circumstances in which it is made may do so. Schedule 2, set out above, provides two procedures for making a 'remedial order' which must, under s 20, be in the form of a statutory instrument. In *R (on the Application of H) v London North and East Mental Health Review Tribunal* [2001] QB 1, a declaration of incompatibility was made between s 73 of the Mental Health Act 1983 and Article 5. Once the declaration had been made, the Secretary of State for Health, acting under s 10 of the HRA, made a remedial order amending s 73 in order to achieve compatibility.

11 *Declarations as to the compatibility of new Bills with the Convention rights.* Under s 19(a) of the HRA, a minister must state that any future Bill is compatible with the Convention or that while unable to make such a declaration, the government nevertheless wishes to proceed with the Bill. When the relevant minister has made a declaration of compatibility under s 19(a), its effects may be viewed as additional to the duty the courts are already under, arising from s 3(1), to ensure that the legislation is rendered compatible with the guarantees if at all possible. The Lord Chancellor has said: 'Ministerial statements of compatibility will inevitably be a strong spur to the courts to find the means of construing statutes compatibly with the Convention.'[53] All legislation passed since the obligation to make a statement regarding compatibility came into force[54] has been accompanied by a declaration of

53   Lord Irvine [1998] PL 221. See further, on s 19, pp 166–67, above
54   The obligation to make a statement of compatibility came into force on 24 November 1998, under the Human Rights Act 1998 (Commencement) Order 1998 SI 1998/2882.

its compatibility with the Convention rights, under s 19. But this need not mean that all such legislation is in fact compatible: the mere fact that a declaration is made does not mean that it can be assumed that compatibility was in fact achieved.

12 *The position of public authorities under the HRA.* Section 6 is the central provision of the HRA. Section 6(1) provides: 'It is unlawful for a public authority to act in a way which is incompatible with a Convention right.' This is the main provision giving effect to the Convention rights: rather than incorporation of the Convention, it is made binding against public authorities. Under s 6(6), 'an act' includes an omission, but does not include a failure to introduce in or lay before Parliament a proposal for legislation or a failure to make any primary legislation or remedial order. Section 6(6) was included in order to preserve parliamentary sovereignty and prerogative power: in this case, the power of the executive to introduce legislation. Thus, apart from its impact on legislation, the HRA also creates obligations under s 6 which bear upon 'public authorities'. Such obligations have a number of implications. Independently of litigation, public authorities must put procedures in place in order to ensure that they do not breach their duty under s 6.

13 An exception had to be made under s 6 in order to bring it into harmony with s 3 and to realise the objective of preserving parliamentary sovereignty. This is accomplished in section 6(2)(a) and (b). Thus, s 6(2)(a) creates a strong obligation requiring public authorities to do their utmost to act compatibly. It may be noted that s 6(2)(a) applies to primary legislation only, whereas s 6(2)(b) applies also to subordinate legislation made under incompatible primary legislation. This is implicit in the use of the words 'or made under' used in the latter sub-section, but not the former. The exception under s 6 applies to legislation only (which, as indicated above, includes Orders in Council made under the royal prerogative, under s 21(1)). If a common law provision conflicts with the duty of a public body under s 6, the duty will prevail. Therefore, certain common law reforms under s 6 may occur more readily than statutory reform; as indicated above, no provision has been included in the Act allowing the common law to override the Convention or creating restrictions as to those courts which can find incompatibility between the two.

14 *'Standard' and 'functional' public authorities and private bodies.* Under s 6, Convention guarantees are binding only against 'public authorities'. Under s 6(3)(a), the term 'public authority' includes a court or under s 6(3)(b), a tribunal, and under s 6(3)(c), 'any person certain of whose functions are functions of a public nature'. Parliament 'or a person exercising functions in connection with proceedings in Parliament' is expressly excluded from the definition. This refers to the Westminster Parliament; the Scottish Parliament, the Northern Ireland Assembly and the Welsh Assembly will be public authorities. Not only is the definition under s 6(3) non-exhaustive, it also leaves open room for much debate on the meaning of 'functions of a public nature'.[55] The interaction between the terms 'public authorities' and 'public functions' was explained in the Notes on Clauses accompanying the Bill as indicating that where a body is clearly recognisable as a public authority, there is no need to look at the detailed provisions of s 6(3)(a)–(c). Thus, the term 'public authority' includes bodies which are self-evidently of a public nature, such as the police, government departments, the Probation Service, local authorities, the security and intelligence services, and the BBC. They are referred to as 'standard

---

55 For discussion as to the way that this test interacts with the existing test for amenability to judicial review, see Part V Chapter 1, pp 665–73.

public bodies'. Below, certain early decisions on the terms 'public authority' and 'public function' indicate the approach that the courts are taking to these terms.

15 Under s 6(5), 'in relation to a particular act, a person is not a public authority by virtue only of s 6(3)(c) if the nature of the act is private'. Since, in relation to standard public authorities, there is no need to consider s 6(3)(c), this provision refers to functional public authorities and has the effect of excluding the private acts of functional public authorities from the scope of the HRA (but see the discussion of 'horizontal effect', below). This is a very significant matter, since the private acts of standard public authorities are not excluded. Therefore, for example, assuming that acts relating to employment are private acts, an employee of a standard public authority could use the HRA directly against the authority, as explained below, while the employee of a functional public authority could not.

16 Under the generally accepted view of s 6(3) and (5), the provisions can be said to create three categories of body in relation to the Convention rights: first, standard ('pure') public authorities which can never act privately, even in respect of matters governed by private law, such as employment relations; secondly, functional (quasi-public) authorities which have a dual function and which can act privately; and thirdly, purely private bodies which have no public function at all. It was accepted in Parliament in debate on the Human Rights Bill that this was the correct reading of s 6.[56]

17 'Horizontal effect'. What is the position if a private body or person wishes to sue another private body relying on a Convention right? If the citizen could take the newspaper to court relying on s 6, the HRA would create direct 'horizontal' effect. But s 6 appears to prevent the creation of full direct 'horizontal' effect since it only applies to public authorities. Thus, legal effects between private parties (for example, citizens, newspapers) may be limited to the creation of indirect horizontal effect, that is, the use of the Convention in relation to existing proceedings. Statutes which affect the legal relations between private parties are affected by s 3 of the HRA and therefore, in this sense, the Act clearly creates indirect horizontal effects.[57] The position is less clear in relation to the common law. As regards the effect of s 6, this is the area of greatest uncertainty under the Act and it has therefore proved to be a focus for academic debate.[58] The academic debate became polarised, Professor Wade perceiving no distinction between the obligations of private and public bodies[59] and Buxton LJ taking the stance that no

---

56 See Straw, HC Official Report cols 409–10 (1998).
57 It could be argued that as private individuals do not have Convention rights against each other, there is no need to construe the statute in question compatibly with the rights under s 3. The courts have not taken this stance: Wilson v the First County Trust Ltd [2001] 3 All ER 229 is authority for the proposition that where a statute is being interpreted and applied in a dispute between two private parties, the obligation in s 3(1) applies as it would if one of them was a public authority. On this point see N Bamforth, 'The true "horizontal effect" of the HRA' (2001) 117 LQR 34.
58 See, eg, M Hunt, 'The 'horizontal' effect of the Human Rights Act' [1998] PL 423; I Leigh, 'Horizontal rights, the Human Rights Act and privacy: lessons from the Commonwealth' (1999) 48 ICLQ 57; W Wade, 'The United Kingdom's Bill of Rights', 1998, pp 62–64, and on the Convention generally: A Clapham, Human Rights in the Private Sphere (1993); A Clapham, 'The privatisation of human rights' [1995] EHRLR 20; G Phillipson, 'The Human Rights Act, 'horizontal effect' and the common law: a bang or a whimper' (1999) 62 MLR 824; Buxton LJ, 'The Human Rights Act and private law' (2000) 116 LQR 48. Clayton and Tomlinson, op cit, provide a very full discussion of the various aspects of 'horizontal effect' that also considers the position in a variety of jurisdictions (pp 204–38). See also I Hare (2001) 5 EHRLR 526.
59 'The United Kingdom's Bill of Rights', 1998, pp 62–63.

horizontal effects are created.[60] Wade has argued that a citizen claiming that a private body had breached his or her Convention rights could claim that the court as a public authority under s 6 must afford a remedy itself for the breach.[61] This book takes the middle ground in perceiving the creation of indirect horizontal effect. This position has been endorsed in certain early decisions under the HRA[62] and by the majority of commentators.[63] At present, then, it is possible to say with some confidence that private bodies cannot sue other private bodies relying directly on the Convention rights – they must find an existing cause of action which can then be interpreted compatibly with the Convention rights by the court in reliance on its duty under s 6.

18 *Victims.* Section 7(1)(a) of the Act allows a person who claims that a public authority has acted or proposes to act in breach of a Convention right to bring proceedings against the public authority. Section 7(1)(b) allows a person to rely on the Convention in any legal proceedings. But in either case, the person must be (or would be) a 'victim' of the unlawful act. Section 7(7) provides: '... a person is a victim of an unlawful act only if he would be a victim for the purposes of Article 34 of the Convention if proceedings were brought in the European Court of Human Rights in respect of that act.' It was accepted in Parliament that the Strasbourg interpretation of 'victim' would be used, rather than the wider test for standing under the UK judicial review doctrine which allows pressure groups to bring actions so long as they satisfy the 'sufficient interest' test.[64] The Strasbourg test was considered in Part II Chapter 2.[65] As Joanna Miles points out, it cannot be said that the concept of 'victim' has been interpreted consistently at Strasbourg, although it is clear that those indirectly affected may be covered.[66] There will, therefore, be substantial room for domestic litigation on this issue.

19 *Actions under s 7(1)(a).* Section 7(1)(a) allows a victim of a breach or threatened breach of a Convention right to bring an action against a standard public authority or a functional body acting in its public capacity[67] on that basis. The action must be brought in 'the appropriate court or tribunal' which will be determined 'by rules' (s 7(2)). Under s 7(9), the term 'rules' means: '... in relation to proceedings in a court or tribunal outside Scotland rules made by the Lord Chancellor or the

---

60 'The Human Rights Act and private law' (2000) 116 LQR 48. Wade, having set out his position in favour of full direct horizontal effect, as indicated above, then returned to the attack, replying to Buxton LJ in 'Horizons of horizontality' (2000) 116 LQR 217.

61 There is a strong consensus that the courts' inclusion within the definition of those bodies bound not to infringe Convention rights is the key to the horizontal effect of the Act upon the common law (above). See also Hunt, *op cit.*

62 *Douglas, Catherine Zeta-Jones, Northern and Shell plc v Hello! Ltd* [2001] 2 WLR 992, CA; *Thompson and Venables v Associated Newspapers and Others* [2001] 1 All ER 908; *A v B* [2002] 2 All ER 545.

63 Phillipson, *op cit;* Hunt, *op cit.* Hunt's and Phillipson's positions differ as to the scope of the duty under s 6, but the concept of indirect horizontal effect as argued for by both has been accepted by Lester and Pannick, *op cit*, p 32 and by Clayton and Tomlinson, *op cit*, pp 236–38.

64 See the ruling of Rose LJ in *R v Secretary of State for Foreign Affairs ex p the World Development Movement* [1995] 1 All ER 611, pp 618–20. See also Part V Chapter 1, pp 695–701, above.

65 For extensive discussion, see Clayton and Tomlinson, *op cit*, pp 1484–98.

66 J Miles, 'Standing under the Human Rights Act: theories of rights enforcement and the nature of public law adjudication' (2000) 59(1) CLJ 133–67, p 137. She further points out that while pressure groups cannot bring actions in their own name, there are other public interest enforcement mechanisms at Strasbourg including the possibility, exceptionally, of third party intervention which can be used to seek to ensure that the rights are secured.

67 The term 'public authority' will be used to encompass both types of body for the purposes of the rest of the discussion.

Secretary of State for the purpose of this section or rules of court . . .' Thus, the HRA creates a new form of action based on a liability of public authorities to provide a remedy for breaching the Convention rights – a new public law wrong. The claim may take the *form* of a complaint such as to a specialised tribunal, an appeal, that of judicial review.

20 *Invoking the Convention under s 7(1)(b).* Unlike s 7(1)(a), which provides for a new cause of action against public authorities, s 7(1)(b) allows for Convention points to be raised once an action has begun under an existing cause of action, where the other party is a public authority. Therefore, s 7(1)(b) is likely to be invoked far more frequently. Under s 7(1)(b), there are a number of possible instances in which a victim can raise Convention arguments in proceedings in which a public authority is involved. In the contexts covered by this book, the Convention would frequently be invoked in criminal proceedings.

21 *Remedies.* Under s 8(1), a court which has found that an act or proposed act of a public authority is unlawful is authorised to grant 'such relief or remedy or . . . order within its powers as [the court] considers just and appropriate'. The term 'unlawful' clearly does not mean 'breach of a Convention guarantee' where such a breach is 'lawful' due to incompatible primary legislation or secondary legislation made under such legislation. In such circumstances, no remedy is available other than a declaration of incompatibility and the ability to make such a declaration is, as indicated, confined to certain higher courts. A litigant in a lower court or tribunal, in such circumstances, appears to be completely remediless, since even the empty remedy of a declaration is unavailable. In criminal proceedings, however, the courts may take the view that to convict a defendant in breach of the Convention would be an abuse of process.[68] Assuming that a breach of the Convention is found which is not the result of incompatible legislation, all the familiar remedies including certiorari (now a quashing order), a declaration or mandamus (a mandatory order) and a prohibiting order (now a prohibition) are available so long as they are within the jurisdiction of the relevant court or tribunal. Under s 8(2), damages cannot be awarded in criminal proceedings, but this obviously leaves open the possibility that they could be awarded in judicial review as well as other civil proceedings. Traditionally, the courts have been reluctant to award damages in public law cases and s 8(3) of the HRA encourages the continuance of this tradition in requiring consideration to be given first to any 'other relief or remedy granted or order made', the consequences of the court's decisions and the necessity of making the award.

22 Under s 8(4), the court, in deciding to award damages, must take into account the principles applied by the European Court of Human Rights. This suggests that awards are likely to be low. The Court can award compensation under what is now Article 41 (previously Article 50). The purpose of the reparation is to place the applicant in the position he would have been in had the violation not taken place. Compensation will include costs unless the applicant has received legal aid, although where only part of a claim is upheld, the costs may be diminished accordingly.[69] It can also include loss of earnings, travel costs, fines and costs unjustly awarded against the applicant.[70] Compensation is also available for

---

68 See the views of Lord Steyn in *R v DPP ex p Kebilene and Others* [1999] 4 All ER 801.
69 *Steel v UK* (1999) 28 EHRR 603, para 125.
70 See, as to heads of loss, N Burns (2001) 151 NLJ 164.

intangible or non-pecuniary losses such as loss of future earnings[71] or opportunities,[72] unjust imprisonment,[73] stress or loss of personal integrity.[74] A claim for damages can be brought in the county court or the High Court.[75]

23 *Protecting the media under s 12.* Press lobbying on the Human Rights Bill focused overwhelmingly upon the fear that the Act would introduce a right to privacy against the media 'through the back door', due to judicial development of the common law in the post-HRA era. The media received special protection under s 12. Section 12(2) provides special provision against the grant of *ex parte* injunctions, which is discussed further in Part IV, Chapter 3. Section 12(3) affects the grant of interim injunctions generally and is also discussed further in Part IV, Chapter 3.

24 *Protecting religious organisations under s 13.* The Church of England also lobbied fiercely during the passage of the Human Rights Bill to be given special protection for religious freedom. Section 13 does not allow the Church, and other religious organisations, to disregard human rights, but it does appear to give Article 9 some special status.

25 *Derogations and reservations under s 14.* Section 14 preserves the possibility of escaping from the effects of the Convention rights, within limits. Reservations are normally made at the time of ratification and therefore are very unlikely to be made to the existing rights. Also, as indicated above, a derogation from Article 5(3) which originally formed part of Sched 3 has been withdrawn, but another derogation has been entered. The Anti-Terrorism, Crime and Security Act 2001 contains provisions in Part 4, s 23 allowing for the indefinite detention without trial of non-British citizens suspected of international terrorism, with an initial appeal to the Special Immigration Appeals Tribunal (SIAC) set up under the Special Immigration Appeals Commission Act 1997. The government considered that the new provisions would be incompatible with Article 5(1) of the Convention, which protects the right to liberty and security of the person, and therefore entered a derogation to Article 5(1), under s 14 of the HRA,[76] within the terms of Article 15 of the Convention. Although there is an exception under Article 5(1)(f) allowing for detention of 'a person against whom action is being taken with a view to deportation or extradition', it would not cover the lengthy detentions envisaged during which deportation proceedings would not be in being and attempts to find a safe third country had manifestly failed.[77]

---

71 Eg, in *Young, James and Webster v UK*, Series A No 44; (1982) 5 EHRR 201, pecuniary and non-pecuniary costs, taking such loss into account, were awarded: the Court ordered £65,000 to be paid.

72 *Weekes v UK* (1988) 13 EHRR 435.

73 In *Steel and Others v UK* (1999) 28 EHRR 603, para 122, the three successful applicants were each imprisoned for seven hours. The Court, without giving reasons, awarded them £500 each in compensation for non-pecuniary damage.

74 See further A Mowbray, 'The European Court of Human Rights' approach to just satisfaction' [1997] PL 647; D Feldman, 'Remedies for violation of Convention rights under the HRA' [1998] EHRLR 691; M Amos, 'Damages for breach of the Human Rights Act' [1999] EHRLR 178; I Leigh and L Lustgarten 'Making Rights Real: the courts, remedies and the HRA' (1999) 58(3) CLJ 509.

75 HRA 1998: Rules CP5/00, March 2000, para 12.

76 Sections 14(1)(b), (4) and (6) provide power for the Secretary of State to make a 'designation order', designating any derogation from an Article or Protocol to the Convention; it can be made in anticipation of the making of the proposed derogation.

77 See *Chahal v UK* (1996) 23 EHRR 413, para 113. Deportation proceedings should be in being and it should be clear that they are being prosecuted with due diligence.

The government made an Order under s 14 of the HRA, the Human Rights Act (Designated Derogation) Order 2001.[78] The Schedule to the Order, which takes the form of a draft letter to the Secretary General, points out that the UN Security Council recognised the September 11 attacks as a threat to international security and required states in Resolution 1373 to take measures to prevent terrorist attacks, which include denying a safe haven to those who plan, support or commit such acts. The Schedule argues that on this basis, there is a domestic public emergency, which is especially present since there are foreign nationals in the UK who threaten its national security. On this basis, therefore, it argues, the measures in Part 4 are clearly and strictly required by the very grave nature of the situation. Schedule 3 to the HRA was also amended to include the derogation under the Human Rights Act 1998 (Amendment) (No 2) Order 2001.[79] It may be noted that the government has also derogated from Article 9 of the International Covenant on Civil and Political Rights[80] as a further method of safeguarding the derogation from challenge.

Early decisions on ss 3 and 4 of the HRA

The following case is one of the leading decisions on the meaning of s 3 of the HRA.

R v A (No 2) [2002] I AC 45[81]

(Note that the key words of Lord Steyn's speech regarding s 3 of the HRA are in bold.)

The case concerned a form of 'rape shield' law, under s 41 of the Youth Justice and Criminal Evidence Act 1999, that prevented a woman being questioned as to an alleged previous sexual relationship with the defendant. The defendant (respondent) was charged with rape. He claimed that the intercourse was consensual. He also claimed that this was part of a continuing sexual relationship and that the consensual sexual relationship covered a period of approximately three weeks prior to 14 June 2000; and in particular, that he had had consensual sexual relations with her, including sexual intercourse, at his flat on occasions between 26 May 2000 and 14 June 2000.

At a preparatory hearing, the defendant sought leave under s 41 of the Youth Justice and Criminal Evidence Act 1999 to adduce evidence and to ask questions relating to the alleged consensual sexual relationship between himself and the complainant over the preceding three weeks, the most recent act of sexual intercourse having occurred one week before the alleged offence. The judge ruled that the complainant could be cross-examined with regard to sexual behaviour that had allegedly occurred 'at or about the same time as the event which is the subject matter of the charge' within the meaning of s 41(3)(b) of the 1999 Act, but that evidence as to any prior consensual sexual relationship with the defendant would not be admissible under s 41(3)(b) or at all. In giving leave to appeal, the judge observed that his ruling would *prima facie* result in a breach of Article 6 of the European Convention on Human Rights as scheduled to the HRA. The defendant indicated that on the prospective

---

78 SI 2001/3644. It was laid before Parliament on 12 November 2001, coming into effect on the following day. It designates the proposed derogation as one that is to have immediate effect.
79 SI 2001/4032. 2. 'Before Part II of Schedule 3 to the Human Rights Act 1998 there is inserted, as Part I, the text of the derogation set out in the Schedule to this Order.' The Order came into force on 20 December 2001.
80 Under Article 4(1) of the Covenant: see UK Derogation under the ICCPR of 18 December 2001.
81 This decision is also discussed in Part I Chapter 4, at pp 164–66.

appeal, he would invite the House to construe s 41 in accordance with its interpretative duty under s 3 of the HRA so as to achieve compatibility with Article 6 and that he would in the alternative seek a declaration of incompatibility under s 4 of the HRA. Accordingly, under s 5 of the HRA on the petition of the Secretary of State, the House of Lords joined him as a party to the appeal.

On the petition of the Rape Crisis Federation of England and Wales, the Campaign to End Rape, the Child and Woman Abuse Studies Unit and Justice for Women, to be heard or otherwise intervene in the appeal, the House of Lords ordered that they might lodge written submissions only. Pursuant to that order, such submissions were lodged with the House.

Lord Steyn: ... the blanket exclusion of prior sexual history between the complainant and an accused in section 41(1), subject to narrow categories of exception in the remainder of section 41, poses an acute problem of proportionality.

As a matter of common sense, a prior sexual relationship between the complainant and the accused may, depending on the circumstances, be relevant to the issue of consent. ... a prior relationship between a complainant and an accused may sometimes be relevant to what decision was made on a particular occasion.

... good sense suggests that it may be relevant to an issue of consent whether the complainant and the accused were ongoing lovers or strangers. To exclude such material creates the risk of disembodying the case before the jury. It also increases the danger of miscarriages of justice. These considerations raise the spectre of the possible need for a declaration of incompatibility in respect of section 41 under section 4 of the Human Rights Act 1998.

In order to assess whether section 41 is incompatible with the Convention right to a fair trial, it is necessary to consider what evidence it excludes. The mere fact that it excludes some relevant evidence would not by itself amount to a breach of the fair trial guarantee. On the other hand, if the impact of section 41 is to deny the right to accused in a significant range of cases from putting forward full and complete defences it may amount to a breach.

Counsel for the Secretary of State has argued that unfairness to an accused will rarely arise because evidence of sexual experience between a complainant and an accused will almost always be admissible on the basis of the defence that the accused thought that the complainant consented. His argument has assumed that in practice, an accused will almost invariably be able to put forward both defences. Counsel for the defendant has persuaded me that the defence of belief in consent would often have no air of reality and would in practice not be available, eg, in cases where there are diametrically opposite accounts of the circumstances of the alleged rape, with the complainant insisting that it was perpetrated with great violence and the accused saying that the complainant took the initiative in an act of consensual intercourse. In any event, it does not meet the difficulty that the judge's direction to the jury would always have to be to the effect that the past experience between the complainant and the accused is irrelevant to the issue of consent. ... Counsel for the Secretary of State further relied on the principle that, in certain contexts, the legislature and the executive retain a discretionary area of judgment within which policy choices may legitimately be made: see *Brown v Stott* [2001] 2 WLR 817. Clearly the House must give weight to the decision of Parliament that the mischief encapsulated in the twin myths must be corrected. On the other hand, when the question arises whether in the criminal statute in question Parliament adopted a legislative scheme which makes an excessive inroad into the right to a fair trial, the court is qualified to make its own judgment and must do so. The methodology to be adopted is important. ... It is well established that the guarantee of a fair trial under Article 6 is absolute: a conviction obtained in breach of it cannot stand. *R v Forbes* [2001] 1 AC 473, 487, para 24. The only balancing permitted is in respect of what the concept of a fair trial entails: here account may be taken of the familiar triangulation of interests of the accused, the victim and society. In this context proportionality has a role to play. The criteria for determining the test of proportionality have been analysed in similar terms in the case law of the European Court of Justice and the European Court of Human Rights. It is not necessary for us to re-invent the wheel. In *de Freitas v Permanent Secretary of Ministry of Agriculture, Fisheries, Lands and Housing* [1999] 1 AC 69, Lord Clyde adopted a precise and concrete analysis of the criteria. In determining whether a limitation is arbitrary or excessive a court should ask itself:

> ... whether: (i) the legislative objective is sufficiently important to justify limiting a fundamental right; (ii) the measures designed to meet the legislative objective are rationally connected to it; and (iii) the means used to impair the right or freedom are no more than is necessary to accomplish the objective.

The critical matter is the third criterion. Given the centrality of the right of a fair trial in the scheme of the Convention, and giving due weight to the important legislative goal of countering the twin myths, the question is whether section 41 makes an excessive inroad into the guarantee of a fair trial. Subject to narrow exceptions section 41 is a blanket exclusion of potentially relevant evidence. Section 41 must however be construed in order to determine its precise exclusionary impact on alleged previous sexual experience between the complainant and the accused. Two processes of interpretation must be distinguished. First, ordinary methods of purposive and contextual interpretation may yield ways of minimising the prima facie exorbitant breadth of the section. Secondly, the interpretative obligation in section 3(1) of the 1998 Act may come into play. It provides that 'So far as it is *possible* to do so, primary legislation ... *must* be read and given effect in a way which is compatible with the Convention rights'. It is a key feature of the 1998 Act.

> ... section 41(3)(c) permits evidence where: '(c) it is an issue of consent and the sexual behaviour of the complainant to which the evidence or question relates is alleged to have been, in any respect, so similar – (i) to any sexual behaviour of the complainant which (according to evidence adduced or to be adduced by or on behalf of the accused) took place as part of the event which is the subject matter of the charge against the accused ... that the similarity cannot reasonably be explained as a coincidence.' This gateway is only available where the issue is whether the complainant consented and the evidence or questioning relates to behaviour that is so similar to the defence's version of the complainant's behaviour at the time of the alleged offence that it cannot reasonably be explained as a coincidence. ... In my view, ordinary methods of purposive construction of section 41(3)(c) cannot cure the problem of the excessive breadth of the section 41, read as a whole, so far as it relates to previous sexual experience between a complainant and the accused. Whilst the statute pursued desirable goals, the methods adopted amounted to legislative overkill.

On the other hand, the interpretative obligation under section 3 of the 1998 Act is a strong one. It applies even if there is no ambiguity in the language in the sense of the language being capable of two different meanings. It is an emphatic adjuration by the legislature: *R v Director of Public Prosecutions ex p Kebilene* [2000] 2 AC 326, *per* Lord Cooke of Thorndon, at p 373f; and my judgment, at p 366b. The White Paper made clear that the obligation goes far beyond the rule which enabled the courts to take the Convention into account in resolving any ambiguity in a legislative provision: see *Rights Brought Home: The Human Rights Bill* (1997) (Cm 3782), para 2.7. The draftsman of the Act had before him the slightly weaker model in section 6 of the New Zealand Bill of Rights Act 1990 but preferred stronger language. Parliament specifically rejected the legislative model of requiring a reasonable interpretation. Section 3 places a duty on the court to strive to find a possible interpretation compatible with Convention rights. Under ordinary methods of interpretation a court may depart from the language of the statute to avoid absurd consequences: section 3 goes much further. Undoubtedly, a court must always look for a contextual and purposive interpretation: section 3 is more radical in its effect. It is a general principle of the interpretation of legal instruments that the text is the primary source of interpretation: other sources are subordinate to it: compare, for example, Articles 31 to 33 of the Vienna Convention on the Law of Treaties (1980) (Cmnd 7964). Section 3 qualifies this general principle because it requires a court to find an interpretation compatible with Convention rights if it is possible to do so. In the progress of the Bill through Parliament the Lord Chancellor observed that 'in 99% of the cases that will arise, there will be no need for judicial declarations of incompatibility' and the Home Secretary said 'We expect that, in almost all cases, the courts will be able to interpret the legislation compatibility with the Convention': *Hansard* (HL Debates), 5 February 1998, col 840 (3rd Reading) and *Hansard* (HC Debates), 16 February 1998, col 778 (2nd Reading). In accordance with the will of Parliament as reflected in section 3 it will sometimes be necessary to adopt an interpretation which linguistically may appear strained. The techniques to be used will not only involve the reading down of express language in a statute but also the implication of provisions. A declaration of incompatibility is a measure of last resort. It must be avoided unless it is plainly impossible to do so. If a *clear* limitation on Convention rights is stated in terms, such an impossibility will arise: *R v Secretary of State for the Home Department ex p Simms* [2000] 2 AC 115, 132a–b, *per* Lord Hoffmann. There is, however, no limitation of such a nature in the present case.

In my view, section 3 requires the court to subordinate the niceties of the language of section 41(3)(c), and in particular the touchstone of coincidence, to broader considerations of relevance judged by logical and common sense criteria of time and circumstances. After all, it is realistic to proceed on the basis that the legislature would not, if alerted to the problem, have wished to deny the right to an accused to put forward a full and complete defence by advancing truly probative material. **It is therefore possible under section 3 to read section 41, and in particular section 41(3)(c), as subject to the implied provision that evidence or questioning which is required to ensure a fair trial under Article 6 of the Convention should not be treated as inadmissible.** The result of such a reading would be that sometimes logically relevant sexual experiences between a complainant and an accused may be admitted under section 41(3)(c). On the other hand, there will be cases where previous sexual experience between a complainant and an accused will be irrelevant, eg, an isolated episode distant in time and circumstances. Where the line is to be drawn must be left to the judgment of trial judges. On this basis a declaration of incompatibility can be avoided. If this approach is adopted, section 41 will have achieved a major part of its objective but its excessive reach will have been attenuated in accordance with the will of Parliament as reflected in section 3 of the 1998 Act. That is the approach which I would adopt.

The appeal before the House concerns a concrete case. It involves the permissibility of questioning a complainant about an alleged recent sexual relationship between her and the defendant, and the admissibility of evidence on that point. These are matters for the trial judge to rule on at the resumed trial. But in my view he must do so on the broader interpretation of section 41(3)(c) required by section 3 of the 1998 Act.

Lord Hope of Craighead: I would take, as my starting point for examining section 41, the proposition that there are areas of law which lie within the discretionary area of judgment which the court ought to accord to the legislature. As I said in *R v Director of Public Prosecutions ex p Kebilene* [2000] 2 AC 326, 380–81e, it is appropriate in some circumstances for the judiciary to defer, on democratic grounds, to the considered opinion of the elected body as to where the balance is to be struck between the rights of the individual and the needs of society: see also *Brown v Stott* [2001] 2 WLR 817, *per* Lord Bingham of Cornhill, at p 835a–b, and Lord Steyn, at p 842f–g. I would hold that *prima facie* the circumstances in which section 41 was enacted bring this case into that category. As I shall explain in more detail later (see paragraph 90, *post*), the right to lead evidence and the right to put questions with which that section deals are not among the rights which are set out in unqualified terms in Article 6 of the Convention. They are open to modification or restriction so long as this is not incompatible with the right to a fair trial. The essential question for your Lordships, as I see it, is whether Parliament acted within its discretionary area of judgment when it was choosing the point of balance that is indicated by the ordinary meaning of the words used in section 41. If it did not, questions will arise as to whether the incompatibility that results can be avoided by making use of the rule of interpretation in section 3 of the Human Rights Act 1998, failing which whether a declaration of incompatibility should be made. But I think that the question which I have described as the essential question must be addressed first. As Lord Woolf CJ said in *Poplar Housing and Regeneration Community*

Association Ltd v Donaghue [[2002] QB 48], para 75, unless the legislation would otherwise be in breach of the Convention section 3 of the 1998 Act can be ignored. So the courts should always ascertain first whether, absent section 3, there would be any breach of the Convention.

... the facts which the respondent wishes to elicit by cross-examination and to adduce in evidence in support of the defence of consent bring into sharp focus the following questions: (a) whether the questions and evidence will be admissible under section 41 when that section is construed according to ordinary common law principles and (b) if not, whether to exclude them would be compatible with his Convention right to a fair trial. If both of these questions are answered in the negative, two further questions will arise. The first is whether the critical parts of section 41 can be given a different meaning by using the techniques of statutory interpretation indicated by section 3 of the Human Rights Act 1998, which requires that the legislation must be read and given effect to, so far as it is possible to do so, in a way which is compatible with the respondent's Convention right. If that cannot be done, consideration will have to be given to the question whether to make a declaration of incompatibility under section 4 of the 1998 Act.

It may be noted in passing that a statement of compatibility was attached to the Bill before second reading that its provisions were compatible with the Human Rights Act 1998. [Such statements] are based on the best advice that is available. But they are no more than expressions of opinion by the minister. They are not binding on the court, nor do they have any persuasive authority.

... Article 6 does not give the accused an absolute and unqualified right to put whatever questions he chooses to the witnesses. As this is not one of the rights which are set out in absolute terms in the Article, it is open, in principle, to modification or restriction so long as this is not incompatible with the absolute right to a fair trial in Article 6(1). The test of compatibility which is to be applied where it is contended that those rights which are not absolute should be restricted or modified will not be satisfied if the modification or limitation 'does not pursue a legitimate aim and if there is not reasonable proportionality between the means employed and the aim sought to be achieved': *Ashingdane v United Kingdom* (1985) 7 EHRR 528, 547, para 57. A fair balance must be struck 'between the demands of the general interest of the community and the requirements of the protection of the individual's fundamental rights': *Sporrong and Lönnroth v Sweden* (1982) 5 EHRR 35, 52, para 69. ... The question whether a legitimate aim is being pursued enables account to be taken of the public interest in the rule of law. The principle of proportionality directs attention to the question whether a fair balance has been struck between the general interest of the community and the protection of the individual.

In my opinion the placing of restrictions on evidence or questions about the sexual behaviour of complainants in proceedings for sexual offences serves a legitimate aim. The prevalence of sexual offences, especially those involving rape, which are not reported to the prosecuting authorities indicates a marked reluctance on the part of complainants to submit to the process of giving evidence at any trial. The rule of law requires that those who commit criminal acts should be brought to justice. Its enforcement is impaired if the system which the law provides for bringing such cases to trial does not protect the essential witnesses from unnecessary humiliation or distress.

It seems to me that the critical question, so far as the accused's right to a fair trial is concerned, is that of proportionality. The impact of [s 41] on the right to a fair trial is highlighted by the fact that they are binding on the trial judge. They are mandatory. He has no discretion to admit the evidence or to allow the questioning if he thinks that it is in the interests of justice to do so.

The question is whether these provisions have achieved a fair balance. This will be achieved if they do not go beyond what is necessary to accomplish their objective. That is the essence, in this context, of the principle of proportionality.

... It is plain that the question is in the end one of balance. Has the balance between the protection of the complainant and the accused's right to a fair trial been struck in the right place? As I indicated earlier in this judgment (see paragraph 58, *ante*), I think that, if any doubt remains on this matter, it raises the further question whether Parliament acted within its discretionary area of judgment when it was choosing the point of balance indicated by section 41. The area is one where Parliament was better equipped than the judges are to decide where the balance lay. There are choices to be made. There are indications from the wording and structure of section 41 that close attention was paid to the more recent Canadian and Scottish models. But in significant ways it has departed from both of them. The element of judicial discretion has been reduced to the minimum. There are risks involved in that choice. It has deprived the judge of the opportunity, in the last resort, of preventing unfairness to the defendant in circumstances where to do this would not significantly prejudice the proper administration of justice.

But two important factors seem to me to indicate that *prima facie* the solution that was chosen was a proportionate one. The first is the need to restore and maintain public confidence in the system for the protection of vulnerable witnesses. Systems which relied on the exercise of a discretion by the trial judge have been called into question. Doubts have been raised as to whether they have achieved their object. I think that it was within the discretionary area of judgment for Parliament to decide not to follow these systems. The second is to be found in a detailed reading of the section as a whole. As I have tried to show in my analysis of the various subsections, it contains important provisions which preserve the defendant's right to ask questions about and adduce evidence of other sexual behaviour by the complainant where this is clearly relevant. While section 41(3) imposes very considerable restrictions, it needs to be seen in its context. I would hold that the required level of unfairness to show that in *every case* where previous sexual behaviour between the complainant and the accused is alleged the solution adopted is not proportionate has not been demonstrated.

I emphasise the words 'every case', because I believe that it would only be if there was a material risk of incompatibility with the Article 6 right in *all* such cases that it would be appropriate to lay down a rule of *general* application as to how, applying section 3 of the Human Rights Act 1998, section 41(3) ought to be read in a way that is compatible with the Convention right or, if that were not possible, to make a declaration of general incompatibility. I do not accept that there is such a risk. This is because I do not regard the mere fact that the complainant had consensual sexual intercourse with the accused on previous occasions as relevant to the issue whether she consented to intercourse on the occasion of the alleged rape.

For these reasons I consider that it has not been shown that, if the ordinary principles of statutory construction are applied to them, the provisions of section 41 which are relevant to the respondent's case are incompatible with his Convention right to a fair trial. I would hold that the question whether they are incompatible cannot be finally determined at this stage, as no attempt has been made to investigate the facts to the required level of detail to show that section 41 has made excessive inroads into the Convention right. It seems to me that it is neither necessary nor appropriate at this stage to resort to the interpretative obligation which is described in section 3 of the Human Rights Act 1998 in order to modify, alter or supplement the words used by Parliament. I think that it would only be appropriate to resort to surgery of that kind in this case if the words used by Parliament were unable, when they were given their ordinary meaning, to stand up to the test of compatibility. ... I should like to add however that I would find it very difficult to accept that it was permissible under section 3 of the Human Rights Act 1998 to read in to section 41(3)(c) a provision to the effect that evidence or questioning which was required to ensure a fair trial under Article 6 of the Convention should not be treated as inadmissible. ... the rule [under s 3] is only a rule of interpretation. It does not entitle the judges to act as legislators. As Lord Woolf CJ said in *Poplar Housing and Regeneration Community Association Ltd v Donoghue* [2001] QB 48, section 3 does not entitle the court to legislate; its task is still one of interpretation. The compatibility is to be achieved only so far as this is possible. ... In the present case it seems to me that the entire structure of section 41 contradicts the idea that it is possible to read into it a new provision which would entitle the court to give leave whenever it was of the opinion that this was required to ensure a fair trial. The whole point of the section, as was made clear during the debates in Parliament, was to address the mischief which was thought to have arisen due to the width of the discretion which had previously been given to the trial judge. .... Section 41(2) *forbids* the exercise of such a discretion *unless* the court is satisfied as to the matters which that subsection identifies. It seems to me that it would not be possible, without contradicting the plain intention of Parliament, to read in a provision which would enable the court to exercise a wider discretion than that permitted by section 41(2).

The appeal was dismissed. Lord Clyde, Lord Slynn and Lord Hutton concurred with Lord Steyn as to the reasons for so doing.

S (Children) and Re W (Care Orders) [2002] 2 AC 291; [2002] UKHL 10, HL (referred to below as 'Re S and Re W')

This is a very important decision on the use of s 3 of the HRA. It concerned a very radical re-interpretation – or, more accurately, a rewriting – of provisions of the Children Act 1989 by the Court of Appeal relying on s 3, to introduce a system referred to below as 'the new starring system' with a view to satisfying the demands of Articles 6 and 8 of the Convention. The decision provides very useful guidance as to the proper use of s 3.

Lord Nicholls of Birkenhead:

My Lords,

I These appeals concern the impact of the Human Rights Act 1998 on Parts III and IV of the Children Act 1989. The Court of Appeal (Thorpe, Sedley and Hale LJJ) made, in the words of Thorpe LJ, two major adjustments and innovations in the construction and application of the Children Act. The principal issue before your Lordships' House concerns the soundness of this judicial initiative. ....

Section 3 of the Human Rights Act

35 It is entirely understandable that the Court of Appeal should seek some means ... by which the courts may assist children where care orders have been made but subsequently, for whatever reason, care plans have not been implemented as envisaged and, as a result, the welfare of the children is being prejudiced. .... The question is whether the courts have power to introduce into the working of the Children Act a range of rights and liabilities not sanctioned by Parliament.

36 On this I have to say at once, respectfully but emphatically, that I part company with the Court of Appeal. I am unable to agree that the court's introduction of a 'starring system' can be justified as a legitimate exercise in interpretation of the Children Act in accordance with section 3 of the Human Rights Act. Even if the Children Act is inconsistent with Articles 6 or 8 of the Convention, which is a question I will consider later, section 3 does not in this case have the effect suggested by the Court of Appeal.

37 Section 3(1) is a powerful tool whose use is obligatory. It is not an optional canon of construction. Nor is its use dependent on the existence of ambiguity.

38 But the reach of this tool is not unlimited. Section 3 is concerned with interpretation. This is apparent from the opening words of section 3(1): 'so far as it is possible to do so.' The side heading of the section is 'Interpretation of legislation'. Section 4 (power to make a declaration of incompatibility) and, indeed, section 3(2)(b) presupposes that not all provisions in primary legislation can be rendered Convention compliant by the application of section 3(1). The existence of this limit on the scope of section 3(1) has already been the subject of judicial confirmation, more than once: see, for instance, Lord Woolf CJ in *Poplar Housing and Regeneration Community Association Ltd v Donoghue* [2001] 3 WLR 183, 204, para 75 and Lord Hope of Craighead in *R v Lambert* [2001] 3 WLR 206, 233–35, paras 79–81.

39 In applying section 3 courts must be ever mindful of this outer limit. The Human Rights Act reserves the amendment of primary legislation to Parliament. By this means the Act seeks to preserve parliamentary sovereignty. The Act maintains the constitutional boundary. Interpretation

of statutes is a matter for the courts; the enactment of statutes, and the amendment of statutes, are matters for Parliament.

40 Up to this point there is no difficulty. The area of real difficulty lies in identifying the limits of interpretation in a particular case. This is not a novel problem. If anything, the problem is more acute today than in past times. Nowadays courts are more 'liberal' in the interpretation of all manner of documents. The greater the latitude with which courts construe documents, the less readily defined is the boundary. What one person regards as sensible, if robust, interpretation, another regards as impermissibly creative. For present purposes it is sufficient to say that a meaning which departs substantially from a fundamental feature of an Act of Parliament is likely to have crossed the boundary between interpretation and amendment. This is especially so where the departure has important practical repercussions which the court is not equipped to evaluate. In such a case the overall contextual setting may leave no scope for rendering the statutory provision Convention compliant by legitimate use of the process of interpretation. The boundary line may be crossed even though a limitation on Convention rights is not stated in express terms. Lord Steyn's observations in *R v A (No 2)* [2002] 2 AC 45, 68D–E, para 44 are not to be read as meaning that a clear limitation on Convention rights in terms is the only circumstance in which an interpretation incompatible with Convention rights may arise.

...

42 I return to the Children Act. . . . the starring system is inconsistent in an important respect with the scheme of the Children Act. It would constitute amendment of the Children Act, not its interpretation. It would have far-reaching practical ramifications for local authorities and their care of children. The starring system would not come free from additional administrative work and expense. It would be likely to have a material effect on authorities' allocation of scarce financial and other resources. This in turn would affect authorities' discharge of their responsibilities to other children.

...

44 These are matters for decision by Parliament, not the courts. It is impossible for a court to attempt to evaluate these ramifications or assess what would be the views of Parliament if changes are needed.

In my view, in the present case the Court of Appeal exceeded the bounds of its judicial jurisdiction under section 3 in introducing this new scheme.

Notes

1   *The rule of construction under s 3. Re S and Re W* does not have the same authority as *R v A* in stating the current position regarding the use of s 3. Lord Nicholls found that there was in any event no incompatibility between Articles 6 and 8 and the relevant provisions of the Children Act, necessitating a re-interpretation of those provisions. His remarks are therefore strictly speaking *obiter* since reliance on s 3, demanding consideration of its effects, was not determinative of the outcome in this instance. In contrast, in *R v A* the findings on s 3 must be viewed as part of the *ratio* of the case since they led to a change to the statutory provision in question.

In *R v A*, Lord Clyde, Lord Slynn and Lord Hutton concurred with Lord Steyn in considering that s 41 Youth Justice and Criminal Evidence Act could be rendered compatible with Article 6 by reading s 41(3) as 'subject to the implied provision that evidence or questioning which is required to ensure a fair trial under Article 6 of the Convention should not be treated as inadmissible'. Lord Hope considered that s 41 could be found to be compatible with Article 6 using ordinary principles of statutory interpretation and therefore, there was no need to invoke s 3 of the HRA. It is clear that the other Law Lords used an extremely bold interpretative technique. In so doing, they in fact went beyond using interpretative techniques and – in effect – rewrote the legislation. The stance of the Lords – apart from Lord Hope – in that instance suggests that the judiciary are prepared to take an extremely vigorous stance when interpreting existing law in the light of Convention provisions: they are prepared to ensure that the outcome which allows the Convention to prevail is achieved even if this involves a significant disregard for statutory language. In *R v A*, the House of Lords very clearly accepted that a declaration of incompatibility was a last resort and that s 3 could be used in an extremely creative fashion in order to avoid having to make one.

It is suggested that this approach tends to marginalise the democratic process: if s 3 is used, even if it emasculates a legislative provision, as in *R v A*, Parliament has not been asked – under the s 4 procedure – to amend the provision. The whole process remains in the hands of the judiciary. In this sense, *R v A* has, it is contended, placed the whole carefully crafted scheme of the HRA in jeopardy. Even in these early days, the tensions inherent in the scheme have been explored and heightened, since it appears possible that s 3 will frequently be used to outflank s 4 and s 10, where incompatibility appears to arise. The idea, which seemed to be inherent in s 4, that declarations of incompatibility would be made, even in criminal cases, seems to have been shown to be misconceived.

In response to *R v A*, it would seem on the face of it possible for Parliament merely to reinstate the offending provision, using words that left no leeway at all for the bold 'interpretation' placed upon s 41(3)(c) of the Youth Justice and Criminal Evidence Act 1999. It should be noted that the House of Lords considered that the provision had provided a 'gateway' for the very creative interpretation adopted.[82] However, so doing might invite a declaration of incompatibility; if no amendment was forthcoming under s 10 of the HRA, a defendant affected by the legislation would be likely to apply to Strasbourg. If at some point the European Court of Human Rights in response found a breach of Article 6, the government would probably view itself as obliged to amend the legislation. Thus, s 3 of the HRA, combined with the UK's international obligations, does appear to have made an inroad into the principle of parliamentary supremacy.

2 A more cautionary note was sounded regarding the application of s 3 in *Poplar Housing and Regeneration Community Association Ltd and Secretary of State for the Environment v Donoghue* [2001] 3 WLR 183. Lord Woolf said that s 3 'does not entitle the court to legislate; its task is still one of interpretation but interpretation in accordance with the direction contained in s 3' (paras 75 and 76). He went on to say that the most difficult task facing the courts is that of distinguishing between interpretation and legislation. This approach was confirmed by Lord Nicholls in *Re S and Re W (Care Orders)*, above. Clearly, 'the precise limits of the s 3 rule of construction remain controversial'.[83] But those limits are now beginning to become apparent. Deference will be shown to Parliament except in areas that the judges regard as peculiarly their own domain, such as admission of evidence. The question of deference is addressed in a number of cases, below.

3 The approach in *R v A* can also be contrasted with the decision of the Privy Council in *Brown v Stott* [2001] 2 WLR 817,[84] below, the first decision of the Law Lords on the Convention rights under the HRA. The decision illustrates, it is suggested, the problems that may arise due to the adoption of a form of 'purposive' approach and of 'reading down' Convention rights by reference to the purpose in question. Lord Steyn found: '. . . national courts may accord to the decisions of national legislatures

---

82 *R v A (No 2)* [2002] 1 AC 45, *per* Lord Steyn, para 42.
83 Clayton and Tomlinson, *op cit*, p 169.
84 See, for the Scottish decision, *Stott v Brown* 2000 SLT 379. See also, for discussion, K Kerrigan [2000] Journal of Civil Liberties 193.

some deference where the context justifies it ... the subject [road safety] invites special regulation ... some infringements [of Article 6] may be justified.' Lord Hope said: '... the jurisprudence of the Court of Human Rights tells us ... that [in the case of a non-absolute right] the ... restriction contended for has to have a legitimate aim in the public interest. If so is there a reasonable relationship of proportionality between the means employed and the aim sought to be realised?' He found that, in relation to s 172 of the Road Traffic Act, which requires that drivers identify themselves, on pain of a fine, as driving a car at the material time, the answer to both questions, in terms of limiting the right not to incriminate oneself under Article 6(1), was in the affirmative. This decision exemplifies, it is suggested, the possibilities of undermining the Convention rights by taking a particular view as to the general purposes of the Convention and then by 'reading down' a particular right in order to further that purpose.

4 *Use of declarations of incompatibility.* A declaration of incompatibility was made by the Divisional Court in respect of four planning cases: *R (on the application of Alconbury Developments) v Secretary of State for the Environment and Other Cases* [2001] HRLR 2, but the declaration was then reversed by the House of Lords [2001] 2 WLR 1389, on the basis that a close reading of the Convention jurisprudence revealed that no incompatibility arose. A further early declaration was made by the Court of Appeal in relation to the system of appeals for prisoners detained on mental health grounds in *R(H) v London North and East Region Mental Health Review Tribunal* [2002] QB 1. The Court found that s 73 of the Mental Health Act was incompatible with Article 5 since it in effect reversed the burden of proof against the detained person. The declaration was surprising in the sense that s 3 could have been used more strenuously to find that the system of appeals in such mental health cases could be viewed as compliant with the Convention.

5 In *Wilson v First County Trust Ltd* [2001] 3 All ER 229, the Court of Appeal found that s 127(3) of the Consumer Credit Act 1974 was incompatible with Article 6 and with Article 1 of the First Protocol to the Convention since it imposed an inflexible prohibition against the making of an enforcement order in an instance where a loan agreement did not contain the terms prescribed for the purposes of s 61(1) of the Act. The effect of s 127(3) was therefore to prevent the creditor from obtaining a judicial remedy where the loan agreement did not contain all the prescribed terms. The Court considered the possibility of finding 'some other legitimate interpretation' of the words of the section which would avoid the finding of incompatibility (para 41). It said that a court is 'required [by s 3] to go as far as but not beyond what is legally possible ... the court is not required or entitled to give to words a meaning which they cannot bear' (para 42). In the instance in question, the court did not think that the words would bear a Convention-friendly interpretation. Clearly, it is possible that this declaration will also be reversed in the House of Lords on the basis that Article 6 and Article 1 of the first Protocol can be interpreted differently. It would not seem possible for the Lords to accept their interpretation as indicated by the Court of Appeal but then go on to find that the words of s 127(3) can be forced to take a Convention-friendly meaning. Clearly, the Court of Appeal considered that there are limits to what can be achieved even under s 3, a finding that is hardly consonant with that of the House of Lords in *R v A.*

6 *Stages in the use of ss 3 and 4.* Following the lead of the judges in the five key decisions mentioned, *R v A, Brown v Stott, Donoghue, Alconbury* and *Re S and Re W (Care Orders)*, it is suggested that a three-stage approach is being adopted when Convention rights are invoked in relation to a legislative provision. First, whether

or not a declaration of incompatibility has already been made in a lower court (or, if in a court unable to make a formal declaration, an informal finding of incompatibility), the Strasbourg jurisprudence will be considered afresh under ordinary principles of interpretation in order to determine whether there is, on close scrutiny, a problem regarding compatibility. It may be found when considering the applicability of s 3 of the HRA that it is unnecessary to strive to re-interpret the statutory provision in question since when the demands of the Convention guarantee are considered afresh incompatibility does not arise. That may be the end of the matter, as in *Alconbury* and *Brown v Stott*.[85] But if it appears that *prima facie* a declaration of incompatibility may have to be made, the court may consider using s 3 in a very creative fashion, as indicated by Lord Steyn in *R v A*, in order to avoid a finding of incompatibility unless, according to *Donoghue* and *Re S and Re W*, so doing would mean crossing the boundary between interpreting and legislating. This second stage is the difficult one since a line has to be drawn between legislating and interpreting. Finally, if the words used are so clear that the use of s 3 cannot provide a method of finding compatibility, a declaration of the incompatibility will have to be made, as a last resort, when and if the matter reaches a court able to make such a declaration, under s 4 as in *Wilson v First County Trust Ltd*[86] and in *R (on the Application of H) v London North and East Region Mental Health Review Tribunal*.

Deference and the 'discretionary area of judgment'

Brown v Stott [2001] 2 All ER 97, PC

(This case is also extracted and discussed in Part VI Chapter 4, pp 1046–47.)

The case arose from a charge of drink-driving. It concerned the compatibility of a statutory provision with a Convention right – Article 6. Under the Scotland Act 1998, acts of members of the Scottish Executive on devolution issues are invalid if they are incompatible with Convention rights (s 57(2)). No declaration of incompatibility is available. On 3 June 1999, a vehicle belonging to Miss Brown was parked in a car park of a supermarket in Dunfermline. In reliance on s 172 (2) of the Road Traffic Act 1988, a police officer asked Miss Brown who had been the driver of her vehicle when it entered the car park. She answered: 'It was me.' The issue arose whether the procurator fiscal could lead evidence of the admission which Miss Brown had been compelled by law to make under s 172(2). The High Court of Justiciary found that he could not since s 172(2) is incompatible with the implied right against self-incrimination under Article 6 of the European Convention on Human Rights and is therefore unlawful: 2000 SLT 379. The procurator fiscal appealed to the Privy Council.

Lord Steyn:

In the first real test of the Human Rights Act 1998 it is opportune to stand back and consider what the basic aims of the Convention are. One finds the explanation in the very words of the preambles of the Convention. There were two principal objectives. The first was to maintain and further realise human rights and fundamental freedoms. The second aim was to foster effective

---

85 This approach receives support from *Poplar Housing and Regeneration Community Association Ltd and the Secretary of State for the Environment v Donoghue* [2001] 3 WLR 183; [2001] 4 All ER 604 (below p 894). The Lord Chief Justice said that 'unless legislation would otherwise be in breach of the Convention s 3 can be ignored; so courts should always ascertain whether, absent s 3, there would be any breach of the Convention' (at para 75).

86 Although, arguably, it is unclear that the Convention absolutely demanded this result.

political democracy. The inspirers of the European Convention, among whom Winston Churchill played an important role, and the framers of the European Convention ... realised only too well that a single minded concentration on the pursuit of fundamental rights of individuals to the exclusion of the interests of the wider public might be subversive of the ideal of tolerant European liberal democracies. The European Convention requires that where difficult questions arise, a balance must be struck. Subject to a limited number of absolute guarantees, the scheme and structure of the Convention reflects this balanced approach. ... And it is a basic premise of the Convention system that only an entirely neutral, impartial, and independent judiciary can carry out the primary task of securing and enforcing Convention rights. This contextual scene is not only directly relevant to the issues arising on the present appeal but may be a matrix in which many challenges under the Human Rights Act 1998 should be considered.

The present case is concerned with Article 6 of the Convention which guarantees to every individual a fair trial in civil and criminal cases. The centrality of this principle in the Convention system has repeatedly been emphasised by the European Court. But even in respect of this basic guarantee, there is a balance to be observed. First, it is well settled that the public interest may be taken into account in deciding what the right to a fair trial requires in a particular context. Thus in *Doorson v The Netherlands*, it was held that 'principles of fair trial also require that in appropriate cases the interests of the defence are balanced against those of witnesses or victims called upon to testify': at (1996) 22 EHRR, p 358, para 70.

It is well settled, although not expressed in the Convention, that there is an implied privilege against self-incrimination under Article 6. Moreover, s 172(2) undoubtedly makes an inroad on this privilege. On the other hand, it is also clear that the privilege against self-incrimination is not an absolute right. ... In these circumstances it would be strange if a right not expressed in the Convention or any of its Protocols, but implied into Article 6 of the Convention, had an absolute character. In my view the right in question is plainly not absolute. From this premise it follows that an interference with the right may be justified if the particular legislative provision was enacted in pursuance of a legitimate aim and if the scope of the legislative provision is necessary and proportionate to the achievement of the aim.

In considering whether an inroad on the privilege against self-incrimination can be justified, it is necessary to concentrate on the particular context. An intense focus on s 172 (2) is required. It reads as follows [his Lordship quoted its terms and continued:]

The subject of s 172 (2) is the driving of vehicles. It is a notorious fact that vehicles are potentially instruments of death and injury. The statistics placed before the board show a high rate of fatal and other serious accidents involving vehicles in Great Britain. ... The effective prosecution of drivers causing serious offences is a matter of public interest. But such prosecutions are often hampered by the difficulty of identifying the drivers of the vehicles at the time of, say, an accident causing loss of life or serious injury or potential danger to others. The tackling of this social problem seems in principle a legitimate aim for a legislature to pursue.

The real question is whether the legislative remedy in fact adopted is necessary and proportionate to the aim sought to be achieved. There were legislative choices to be made. The legislature could have introduced a reverse burden of proof clause which placed the burden on the registered owner to prove that he was not the driver of the vehicle at a given time when it is alleged that an offence was committed. ... there was [also] the possibility of requiring information about the identity of the driver to be revealed by the registered owner and others. ... It is also important to keep in mind the narrowness of the interference. Section 172(2) is directed at obtaining information in one category, namely the identity of the driver at the time when an offence was allegedly committed. The most important part of s 172(2) is para (a) since the relevant information is usually peculiarly within the knowledge of the owner ... Section 172(2) does not authorise general questioning by the police to secure a confession of an offence. On the other hand, s 172(2) does, depending on the circumstances, in effect authorise the police officer to invite the owner to make an admission of one element in a driving offence ... It is therefore a relatively narrow interference with the privilege in one area which poses widespread and serious law enforcement problems.

Under the Convention system the primary duty is placed on domestic courts to secure and protect Convention rights. The function of the ECHR is essential but supervisory. In that capacity it accords to domestic courts a margin of appreciation, which recognises that national institutions are in principle better placed than an international court to evaluate local needs and conditions. That principle is logically not applicable to domestic courts. On the other hand, national courts may accord to the decisions of national legislatures some deference where the context justifies it: see *R v DPP ex p Kebilene,* per Lord Hope of Craighead at pp 993–94. . . . This point is well explained in Lester and Pannick (*Human Rights Law and Practice,* 1999, p 74): 'Just as there are circumstances in which an international court will recognise that national institutions are better placed to assess the needs of society, and to make difficult choices between competing considerations, so national courts will accept that there are some circumstances in which the legislature and the executive are better placed to perform those functions.'

In my view this factor is of some relevance in the present case. Here s 172(2) addresses a pressing social problem, namely the difficulty of law enforcement in the face of statistics revealing a high accident rate resulting in death and serious injuries. The legislature was entitled to regard the figures of serious accidents as unacceptably high. It would also have been entitled to take into account that it was necessary to protect other Convention rights, viz the right to life of members of the public exposed to the danger of accidents: see Article 2.1. On this aspect the legislature was in as good a position as a court to assess the gravity of the problem and the public interest in addressing it. It really then boils down to the question whether in adopting the procedure enshrined in s 172(2), rather than a reverse burden technique, it took more drastic action than was justified. While this is ultimately a question for the court, it is not unreasonable to regard both techniques as permissible in the field of the driving of vehicles. After all, the subject invites special regulation; objectively the interference is narrowly circumscribed; and it is qualitatively not very different from requiring, for example, a breath specimen from a driver. Moreover, it is less invasive than an essential modern tool of crime detection such as the taking of samples from a suspect for DNA profiling. If the matter was not covered by authority, I would have concluded that s 172(2) is compatible with Article 6.

The decision of the European Court in *Saunders* gave some support to the view of the High Court of Justiciary. With due respect I have to say that the reasoning in *Saunders* is unsatisfactory and less than clear. . . . The European Court did not rule that the privilege against self-incrimination is absolute. Surprisingly in view of its decision in *Murray* that the linked right of silence is not absolute, it left the point open in respect of the privilege against self-incrimination: para 74. On the other hand, the substance of its reasoning treats both privileges as not absolute. The court observed (at para 68): 'The Court recalls that, although not specifically mentioned in Article 6 of the Convention, the right to silence and the right not to incriminate oneself are generally recognised international standards which lie at the heart of the notion of a fair procedure under Article 6. Their rationale lies, *inter alia*, in the protection of the accused from improper compulsion by the authorities thereby contributing to the avoidance of miscarriages of justice and to the fulfilment of the aims of Article 6.'

In my view the observations in *Saunders* do not support an absolutist view of the privilege against self-incrimination. It may be that the observations in *Saunders* will have to be clarified in a further case by the European Court. As things stand, however, I consider that the High Court of Justiciary put too great weight on these observations. In my view they were never intended to apply to a case such as the present.

That brings me back to the decision of the High Court of Justiciary. It treated the privilege against self-incrimination as virtually absolute. That conclusion fits uneasily into the balanced Convention system, and cannot be reconciled with Article 6 in all its constituent parts and the spectrum of jurisprudence of the European Court on the various facets of Article 6.

I would hold that the decision of the High Court of Justiciary on the merits was wrong. The procurator fiscal is entitled to lead the evidence of Miss Brown's admission under s 172 (2).

For these reasons, as well as the reasons given by Lord Bingham of Cornhill, I would allow the appeal and quash the declaration made by the High Court.

The appeal was allowed unanimously.

In the following case, deference was not accorded to the decision-maker. The reasons why this was the case are considered below.

R (on the Application of Daly) v Secretary of State for the Home Department [2001] 2 WLR 1622, HL

The applicant, who was serving a sentence of imprisonment in a closed prison, stored in his cell correspondence with his solicitor about his security categorisation reviews and parole. Like all prisoners in the closed prison system in England and Wales, he was subject to a standard cell searching policy set out in paras 17.69 to 17.74 of a security manual issued as an instruction to prison governors by the Secretary of State, who had power to make rules for, *inter alia*, the regulation and control of prisoners under s 47(1) of the Prison Act 1952. The policy required that prisoners be excluded during cell searches to prevent intimidation and to prevent prisoners acquiring a detailed knowledge of search techniques, and provided that officers were to examine, but not read, any legal correspondence in the cell to check that nothing had been written on it by the prisoner, or stored between its leaves, which was likely to endanger prison security. The applicant sought leave to apply for judicial review of the decision to require examination of prisoners' legally privileged correspondence in their absence.

Lord Bingham:

23 Article 8(1) gives Mr Daly a right to respect for his correspondence. While interference with that right by a public authority may be permitted if in accordance with the law and necessary in a democratic society in the interests of national security, public safety, the prevention of disorder or crime or for protection of the rights and freedoms of others, the policy interferes with Mr Daly's exercise of his right under Article 8(1) to an extent much greater than necessity requires. In this instance, therefore, the common law and the Convention yield the same result. But this need not always be so. In *Smith and Grady v United Kingdom* (1999) 29 EHRR 493, the European Court held that the orthodox domestic approach of the English courts had not given the applicants an effective remedy for the breach of their rights under Article 8 of the Convention because the threshold of review had been set too high. Now, following the incorporation of the Convention by the Human Rights Act 1998 and the bringing of that Act fully into force, domestic courts must themselves form a judgment whether a Convention right has been breached (conducting such inquiry as is necessary to form that judgment) and, so far as permissible under the Act, grant an effective remedy.

I would allow the appeal

Lord Steyn:

25 There was written and oral argument on the question whether certain observations of Lord Phillips of Worth Matravers MR in *R (Mahmood) v Secretary of State for the Home Department* [2001] 1 WLR 840 were correct. He explained the new approach to be adopted. The Master of the Rolls concluded, at p 857, para 40:

> When anxiously scrutinising an executive decision that interferes with human rights, the court will ask the question, applying an objective test, whether the decision-maker could reasonably have concluded that the interference was necessary to achieve one or more of the legitimate

aims recognised by the Convention. When considering the test of necessity in the relevant context, the court must take into account the European jurisprudence in accordance with section 2 of the 1998 Act.

26 The explanation of the Master of the Rolls in the first sentence of the cited passage requires clarification. It is couched in language reminiscent of the traditional *Wednesbury* ground of review (*Associated Provincial Picture Houses Ltd v Wednesbury Corpn* [1948] 1 KB 223), and in particular the adaptation of that test in terms of heightened scrutiny in cases involving fundamental rights as formulated in *R v Ministry of Defence ex p Smith* [1996] QB 517, 554e–g per Sir Thomas Bingham MR. There is a material difference between the *Wednesbury* and *Smith* grounds of review and the approach of proportionality applicable in respect of review where Convention rights are at stake.

27 The starting point is that there is an overlap between the traditional grounds of review and the approach of proportionality. . . . the intensity of review is somewhat greater under the proportionality approach. . . . even the heightened scrutiny test developed in *R v Ministry of Defence ex p Smith* [1996] QB 517, 554 is not necessarily appropriate to the protection of human rights. It will be recalled that in *Smith* the Court of Appeal reluctantly felt compelled to reject a limitation on homosexuals in the army. The challenge based on Article 8 of the Convention for the Protection of Human Rights and Fundamental Freedoms (the right to respect for private and family life) foundered on the threshold required even by the anxious scrutiny test. The European Court of Human Rights came to the opposite conclusion: *Smith and Grady v United Kingdom* (1999) 29 EHRR 493. The court concluded, at p 543, para 138:

> . . . the threshold at which the High Court and the Court of Appeal could find the Ministry of Defence policy irrational was placed so high that it effectively excluded any consideration by the domestic courts of the question of whether the interference with the applicants' rights answered a pressing social need or was proportionate to the national security and public order aims pursued, principles which lie at the heart of the court's analysis of complaints under Article 8 of the Convention.

In other words, the intensity of the review, in similar cases, is guaranteed by the twin requirements that the limitation of the right was necessary in a democratic society, in the sense of meeting a pressing social need, and the question whether the interference was really proportionate to the legitimate aim being pursued.

28 The differences in approach between the traditional grounds of review and the proportionality approach may therefore sometimes yield different results. It is therefore important that cases involving Convention rights must be analysed in the correct way. This does not mean that there has been a shift to merits review. On the contrary, as Professor Jowell [2000] PL 671, 681 has pointed out, the respective roles of judges and administrators are fundamentally distinct and will remain so. To this extent the general tenor of the observations in *Mahmood* [2001] 1 WLR 840 are correct. And Laws LJ rightly emphasised in *Mahmood*, at p 847, para 18, 'that the intensity of review in a public law case will depend on the subject matter in hand'. That is so even in cases involving Convention rights. In law context is everything.

Lord Cooke of Thorndon:

30 First, while this case has arisen in a jurisdiction where the European Convention for the Protection of Human Rights and Fundamental Freedoms applies, and while the case is one in which the Convention and the common law produce the same result, it is of great importance, in my opinion, that the common law by itself is being recognised as a sufficient source of the fundamental right to confidential communication with a legal adviser for the purpose of obtaining legal advice. Thus, the decision may prove to be in point in common law jurisdictions not affected by the Convention. Rights similar to those in the Convention are of course to be found in constitutional documents and other formal affirmations of rights elsewhere. The truth is, I think, that some rights are inherent and fundamental to democratic civilised society. Conventions, constitutions, bills of rights and the like respond by recognising rather than creating them.

31 To essay any list of these fundamental, perhaps ultimately universal, rights is far beyond anything required for the purpose of deciding the present case. It is enough to take the three identified by Lord Bingham: in his words, access to a court; access to legal advice; and the right to communicate confidentially with a legal adviser under the seal of legal professional privilege. As he says authoritatively from the woolsack, such rights may be curtailed only by clear and express words, and then only to the extent reasonably necessary to meet the ends which justify the curtailment. The point that I am emphasising is that the common law goes so deep.

32 The other matter concerns degrees of judicial review. Lord Steyn illuminates the distinctions between 'traditional' (that is to say in terms of English case law, *Wednesbury*) standards of judicial review and higher standards under the European Convention or the common law of human rights. As he indicates, often the results are the same. But the view that the standards are substantially the same appears to have received its quietus in *Smith and Grady v United Kingdom* (1999) 29 EHRR 493 and *Lustig-Prean and Beckett v United Kingdom* (1999) 29 EHRR 548 . . .[87]

I, too, would therefore allow the present appeal.

Notes

1   *The margin of appreciation doctrine.* A central issue under the HRA concerns the part to be played, domestically, by the margin of appreciation doctrine. Since it has probably been the key dilutant of Convention standards, as Part II Chapter 2 indicated (see p 246), it is essential that UK judges and other public authorities reject it as a relevant factor in their own decision-making under the Convention, although there will be some instances, as indicated below, when it will be appropriate to recognise a 'discretionary area of judgment'. As indicated in Part II Chapter 2, the margin of appreciation doctrine is a distinctively international law doctrine, based on the need to respect the decision-making of nation states within defined limits. Therefore, it has no application in national law.

2   *The discretionary area of judgment.* In *R v DPP ex p Kebilene* [1999] 3 WLR 972, Lord Hope said: 'This technique [the margin of appreciation] is not available to the national courts when they are considering Convention issues arising within their own countries [but] . . . In some circumstances it will be appropriate for the courts to recognise that there is an area of judgement within which the judiciary will defer, on democratic grounds, to the considered opinion of [the democratic body or person] whose act or decision is said to be incompatible with the Convention.' In the context of the case, which concerned the compatibility of primary terrorist legislation with the Convention, these findings were used to justify a deferential approach. The approach was one which sought to introduce qualifications into a guarantee which on its face was unqualified. The term used by Lord Hope to describe the area in which choices between individual rights and societal interests might arise was 'the discretionary area of judgment'; he found that it would be easier for such an area of judgment to be recognised 'where the Convention itself requires a balance to be struck, much less so where the right [as in Article 6(2)] is stated in terms which are unqualified . . . But even where the right is stated in [such] terms . . . the courts will need to bear in mind the jurisprudence of the European Court which recognises that due account should be taken of the special nature of terrorist crime and the threat which it poses to a democratic society'.[88] In support of his balancing approach, Lord Hope referred to Lord Woolf's findings in

---

87   For further extracts and discussion of proportionality generally, see Part V Chapter 2, pp 784–87.

88   He gave the example of the ruling of the Court in *Murray v UK* (1994) 19 EHRR 193, p 222, para 47.

Attorney-General of Hong Kong v Lee Kwong-kut [1993] AC 951, at 966. Lord Woolf considered the Canadian approach when applying the Canadian Charter of Rights and Freedoms, Article 1 of which states that the rights and freedoms which it guarantees are: '... subject only to such reasonable limits prescribed by law as can be demonstrably justified in a free and democratic society.' He said: 'In a case where there is real difficulty, where the case is close to the borderline, regard can be had to the approach now developed by the Canadian courts in respect of section 1 of their Charter.'

3   In *Brown v Stott*, as seen above, the Lords adopted an approach of according an area of discretion to the legislature in coming to its decision. Bearing that doctrine in mind, it was argued that Article 6 itself does not expressly require that coerced statements should be excluded from evidence and that although a right to freedom from self-incrimination could be implied into it, the right had not been treated at Strasbourg as an absolute right. The Lords relied on decisions to that effect at Strasbourg that had been influenced by the margin of appreciation doctrine. Lord Bingham found: 'Limited qualification of [Article 6] rights is acceptable if reasonably directed by national authorities towards a clear and proper public objective and if representing no greater qualification than the situation calls for.' The objective in question was the laudable one of curbing traffic accidents. On that basis, by importing a form of balancing test into Article 6, it was found that answers given under s 172 could be adduced in evidence at trial. The decision, it is suggested, exemplifies a minimalist approach in the sense that it required a 'reading down' of the Convention right in question.

4   The decision in *Brown* may have the effect of undermining the implied right not to incriminate oneself in Article 6(1), in a range of circumstances. The combination of the uses of the doctrine of deference to the legislature, combined with the use of Strasbourg decisions affected by the margin of appreciation doctrine, has led, it is argued, to a decision that affords the right a lesser significance than Strasbourg has accorded it. If the intention had been to balance the rights in Article 6 against a range of societal interests, a paragraph could have been included, as in Articles 8–11, setting out the exceptions and the tests to be applied in using them. Alternatively, a general exception could have been included, as in Article 1 of the Canadian Charter. The decision not to adopt either of these courses implies that there is little or no room for the use of implied exceptions. In so far as Strasbourg has suggested that the Article 6 rights are qualified, the Lords should have considered whether adoption of that stance was due to the use of the doctrine of the margin of appreciation.

5   The approach of Lord Hope in *ex p Kebilene* towards the development of a broad domestic doctrine of deference was therefore based on a watering down of the Convention rights since a provision equivalent to s 1 of the Charter was omitted from the basic Convention rights under Articles 2–7. Thus, a minimalist approach to the rights, aided by interpretations of the European Court or Commission of Human Rights influenced by the margin of appreciation doctrine, allows the courts, in certain circumstances, to adopt a deferential stance. This stance was evident in *Brown v Stott*. But the deference was accorded to the democratically elected legislature. In contrast, in *Daly*, the possibility of deference to the executive was implicitly rejected.

6   *Daly* indicates the approach that would be followed under the HRA, although in the particular instance their Lordships found that the case could be disposed of using common law principles (see the speeches of Lord Bingham and Lord Cooke above). As para 27 of Lord Steyn's judgment shows, greater protection for human

rights may in some instances be available than would be provided under judicial review principles, since the domestic courts have to consider proportionality: an interference will be disproportionate where it goes beyond satisfying the legitimate aim in question and, further, or therefore, cannot answer to a pressing social need. In other words, the intensity of the review flows from the requirement, first, that the limitation of the right is necessary in a democratic society, in the sense of meeting a pressing social need, and secondly, that the interference is proportionate to the legitimate aim being pursued. It might be concluded that therefore activism would be especially apparent in the field of judicial review under the HRA. However, even in this field, a minimalist approach is available, even absent a deferential stance. Where the Strasbourg jurisprudence allows different views to be taken of the need for a particular restriction, a domestic court fully applying it, including its margin of appreciation aspects, would tend – in the outcome – to defer to the judgment of the executive. Clearly, this approach is distinguishable from that of heightened *Wednesbury* unreasonableness,[89] but it would often lead to the same outcome.[90]

7 *Minimalism*. A minimalist approach may be adopted to the Convention rights even though a deferential stance is inappropriate. Under such an approach, a court might ostensibly refuse to apply the margin of appreciation doctrine and yet would adopt a restrained stance in some circumstances. The court, following notions of common law restraint expressed in a manner similar to the *Kebilene* 'area of discretionary judgment' doctrine, might find that it could afford a limited interpretation to Strasbourg decisions if to do so would be in accordance with common law tradition. Obvious examples in which this stance might be taken are in respect of the exclusion of improperly or illegally obtained non-confession evidence, where the common law tradition may be termed 'amoral',[91] or in public protest decisions where the common law approach has not fully reflected the Convention since the focus of concern has been, broadly, on proprietorial rather than protest rights.[92]

8 *Activism*. A further approach, which takes a more generous stance towards the Convention rights, may be termed activist. Such an approach might be viewed as a development from the activism shown in developing a common law of human rights in the pre-HRA era, as discussed above (see p 849). Such an approach assumes that the common law recognises and upholds fundamental human rights and that, therefore, an approach which takes an activist stance towards such rights is in accordance with UK legal tradition. It is suggested that the approach taken in *ex p Daly* exemplifies such a stance.

9 An activist approach would recognise the existence of a discretionary area of judgment, but it would do so on carefully scrutinised grounds. Thus, the democratic quality of the rights-infringing rule would be considered: in a stance contrary to that taken in *R v A*, legislation would be treated with greater deference than executive decisions. This approach might take a more rights-affirming stance

---

89 See *R v Ministry of Defence ex p Smith and Others* [1996] 1 All ER 257, 263.

90 It might collapse into it if, in effect, a general test of 'reasonableness' rather than necessity and proportionality is adopted as D Beatty suggests it has been in Canada under the Canadian Charter: (1997) 60(4) MLR 487, at p 493.

91 M Zander, *The Police and Criminal Evidence Act 1984* (1995), p 236. See further Part VI Chapter 4, pp 1051–52.

92 See Gray and Gray, 'Civil rights, civil wrongs and quasi-public places' (1999) 1 EHRLR 46, and see further Part VI Chapter 3.

than Strasbourg in certain selected contexts, since common law traditions of deference were particularly apparent only in certain areas of executive decision-making, areas which do not fully coincide with areas covered by the margin of appreciation doctrine.[93] Where Strasbourg activism coincided with common law activism, this approach would lead to greater protection for rights, not least because the judiciary would derive reassurance from the Convention underpinning provided for the preferred approach.

Early decisions on ss 6,7 and 8 of the Human Rights Act

One of the key issues as to the interpretation of the Human Rights Act is the meaning given to the terms 'public authority' and 'public function' in s 6. The decision below is the leading decision on that issue.[94] The decision is also of interest since further indications as to the proper interpretation of s 3 are given.

Poplar Housing and Regeneration Community Association Ltd and Secretary of State for the Environment v Donoghue [2001] 4 All ER 604, CA

In February 1998, the defendant was granted a weekly, non-secure tenancy of a property by the local housing authority, pending a decision as to whether she was intentionally homeless. In December 1998, the property was transferred to the claimant housing association, a registered social landlord for the purposes of the Housing Act 1996, which had been created by the local authority in order to transfer to it a substantial proportion of the authority's housing stock. In June 2000, the defendant was informed that she was a tenant of the housing association and that she was subject to an assured shorthold tenancy. The housing association then notified her that possession of the property was required and, subsequently, it issued a summons for possession under s 21(4) of the Housing Act 1988, as amended by s 98 of the 1996 Act. The defendant applied for an adjournment to enable her to place before the court evidence that the housing association was a public authority, or performing a public function, for the purposes of s 6 of the HRA and that, therefore, it was unlawful for it to act in a way which was incompatible with the European Convention on Human Rights, as scheduled to the HRA, and that in seeking an order for possession under s 21(4) of the 1988 Act, it was contravening her right to respect for her private and family life and her home under Article 8(1) of the Convention. The application for an adjournment was refused.

The defendant appealed.

Lord Woolf CJ:

Public bodies and public functions

The importance of whether Poplar was at the material times a public body or performing public functions is this: the Human Rights Act 1998 will only apply to Poplar if it is deemed to be a public body or performing public functions. Section 6(1) of the Human Rights Act 1998 makes it unlawful for a public authority to act in a way which is incompatible with a Convention right. Section 6(3) states that a 'public authority' includes '(b) any person certain of whose functions are functions of a public nature'. Section 6(3) means that hybrid bodies, which have functions of a public and private nature, are public authorities, but *not* in relation to acts which are of a private nature. The renting

---

93 Eg, the decision of *R v Samuel* [1988] QB 615 on exclusion of evidence may be viewed as more 'activist' than the decision in the same context at Strasbourg in *Schenk v Switzerland* Series A No 140; (1988) 13 EHRR 242.

94 This decision is also discussed in Part V Chapter 1, at p 672.

out of accommodation can certainly be of a private nature. The fact that through the act of renting by a private body a public authority may be fulfilling its public duty, does not automatically change into a public act what would otherwise be a private act. The purpose of section 6(3)(b) is to deal with hybrid bodies which have both public and private functions. It is not to make a body, which does not have responsibilities to the public, a public body merely because it performs acts on behalf of a public body which would constitute public functions were such acts to be performed by the public body itself. An act can remain of a private nature even though it is performed because another body is under a public duty to ensure that that act is performed.

In coming to our conclusion as to whether Poplar is a public authority within the Human Rights Act 1998 meaning of that term, we regard it of particular importance in this case that:

(i)   While section 6 of the Human Rights Act 1998 requires a generous interpretation of who is a public authority, it is clearly inspired by the approach developed by the courts in identifying the bodies and activities subject to judicial review. The emphasis on public functions reflects the approach adopted in judicial review by the courts and textbooks since the decision of the Court of Appeal (the judgment of Lloyd LJ) in R v Panel on Take-overs and Mergers ex p Datafin plc [1987] QB 815.

(ii) Tower Hamlets, in transferring its housing stock to Poplar, does not transfer its primary public duties to Poplar. Poplar is no more than the means by which it seeks to perform those duties.

(iii) The act of providing accommodation to rent is not, without more, a public function for the purposes of section 6 of the Human Rights Act 1998. Furthermore, that is true irrespective of the section of society for whom the accommodation is provided.

(iv) The fact that a body is a charity or is conducted not for profit means that it is likely to be motivated in performing its activities by what it perceives to be the public interest. However, this does not point to the body being a public authority. In addition, even if such a body performs functions, that would be considered to be of a public nature if performed by a public body, nevertheless such acts may remain of a private nature for the purpose of sections 6(3)(b) and 6(5).

(v)   What can make an act, which would otherwise be private, public is a feature or a combination of features which impose a public character or stamp on the act. Statutory authority for what is done can at least help to mark the act as being public; so can the extent of control over the function exercised by another body which is a public authority. The more closely the acts that could be of a private nature are enmeshed in the activities of a public body, the more likely they are to be public. However, the fact that the acts are supervised by a public regulatory body does not necessarily indicate that they are of a public nature. This is analogous to the position in judicial review, where a regulatory body may be deemed public but the activities of the body, which is regulated, may be categorised private.

(vi) The closeness of the relationship which exists between Tower Hamlets and Poplar. Poplar was created by Tower Hamlets to take a transfer of local authority housing stock; five of its board members are also members of Tower Hamlets; Poplar is subject to the guidance of Tower Hamlets as to the manner in which it acts towards the defendant.

(vii) The defendant, at the time of transfer, was a sitting tenant of Poplar and it was intended that she would be treated no better and no worse than if she remained a tenant of Tower Hamlets. While she remained a tenant, Poplar therefore stood in relation to her in very much the position previously occupied by Tower Hamlets.

While these are the most important factors in coming to our conclusion, it is desirable to step back and look at the situation as a whole. As is the position on applications for judicial review, there is no clear demarcation line which can be drawn between public and private bodies and functions. In a borderline case, such as this, the decision is very much one of fact and degree. Taking into account all the circumstances, we have come to the conclusion that while activities of housing associations need not involve the performance of public functions, in this case, in providing accommodation for the defendant and then seeking possession, the role of Poplar is so closely assimilated to that of Tower Hamlets that it was performing public and not private functions. Poplar therefore is a functional public authority, at least to that extent. We emphasise that this does not mean that all Poplar's functions are public.

To evict the defendant from her home would impact on her family life. The effect of Article 8(2) is therefore critical.

... in considering whether Poplar can rely on Article 8(2), the court has to pay considerable attention to the fact that Parliament intended when enacting section 21(4) of the 1988 Act to give preference to the needs of those dependent on social housing as a whole over those in the position of the defendant. The economic and other implications of any policy in this area are extremely complex and far-reaching. This is an area where, in our judgment, the courts must treat the decisions of Parliament as to what is in the public interest with particular deference. ... We are satisfied that notwithstanding its mandatory terms, section 21(4) of the 1988 Act does not conflict with the defendant's right to family life. Section 21(4) is certainly necessary in a democratic society in so far as there must be a procedure for recovering possession of property at the end of a tenancy. The question is whether the restricted power of the court is legitimate and proportionate. This is the area of policy where the court should defer to the decision of Parliament. We have come to the conclusion that there was no contravention of Article 8 or of Article 6.

As we have decided that there is no contravention of Articles 6 and 8, strictly, there is no need for us to speculate as to whether, if there had been a contravention, this would have created a situation of incompatibility. We note that if we decided that there was a contravention of Article 8, the Department would prefer us not to interpret section 21(4) 'constructively' but instead to grant a declaration of incompatibility. However, so far, the sections of the Human Rights Act 1998 dealing with interpretation and incompatibility have been subject to limited guidance and for that reason we hope it will be helpful if we set out our views even though they are strictly *obiter*.

... It is difficult to overestimate the importance of section 3 ... the following points, which are probably self- evident, should be noted:

(a) Unless the legislation would otherwise be in breach of the Convention, section 3 can be ignored (so courts should always first ascertain whether, absent section 3, there would be any breach of the Convention).

...

(c) Section 3 does not entitle the court to *legislate* (its task is still one of *interpretation*, but interpretation in accordance with the direction contained in section 3).

The most difficult task which courts face is distinguishing between legislation and interpretation. Here practical experience of seeking to apply section 3 will provide the best guide. However, if it is necessary in order to obtain compliance to radically alter the effect of the legislation this will be an indication that more than interpretation is involved.

In this case Mr Luba contends that all that is required is to insert the words 'if it is reasonable to do so' into the opening words of section 21(4) of the 1988 Act. The amendment may appear modest but its effect would be very wide indeed. It would significantly reduce the ability of landlords to recover possession and would defeat Parliament's original objective of providing certainty. It would involve legislating.

The appeal is dismissed.

The following decision gives further indications as to the meaning of 'public function' in s 6(3)(b) of the HRA, and makes it clear that the amenability of bodies to judicial review and to duties under the HRA may not be based on the same tests.

R (on the Application of Heather) v Leonard Cheshire Foundation; R (on the Application of Ward) v Leonard Cheshire Foundation [2002] 2 All ER 936, CA

H and W, residents of a home for the disabled, owned and run by Leonard Cheshire Foundation (LCF), a charity, appealed against the dismissal of their application for judicial review of L's decision to redevelop the home. As a consequence of the redevelopment, H would no longer be accommodated at the home. The local authority had exercised its statutory powers in placing H at the home and funding the placements pursuant to ss 21(1) and 26(1) of the National Assistance Act 1948, as amended by s 19 of the Local Government Act 1972. The appeal is against the dismissal of their application for judicial review of LCF's decision to close the home in the way in which it is run at present. The application was dismissed after a preliminary hearing as a result of which Stanley Burnton J held that LCF was not a 'public authority' within the meaning of that term in s 6 of the HRA. It is the correctness of this conclusion which is the subject of this appeal.

4 LCF is the United Kingdom's leading voluntary sector provider of care and support services for the disabled. The majority of the residents at the home, including the appellants, had been placed there by the social services departments of their local authority or by their health authority. In making the placements and providing the funding which the placements required, the authorities were exercising statutory powers.

. . .

6 In the proceedings for judicial review the claimants contended that in making these decisions LCF was exercising functions of a public nature within the meaning of s 6(3)(b) of the HRA and so, as a public authority, was required not to act in a way which was incompatible with Article 8 of the European Convention on Human Rights. It was argued that instead the trustees had contravened Article 8 by not respecting the claimants' right to a home and failing to take into account, *inter alia*, promises made to them that Le Court would be their 'home for life'.

In our judgment the role that LCF was performing manifestly did not involve the performance of public functions. The fact that LCF is a large and flourishing organisation does not change the nature of its activities from private to public.

(i) It is not in issue that it is possible for LCF to perform some public functions and some private functions. In this case it is contended that this was what has been happening in regard to those residents who are privately funded and those residents who are publicly funded. But in this case except for the resources needed to fund the residents of the different occupants of Le Court, there is no material distinction between the nature of the services LCF has provided for residents funded by a local authority and those provided to residents funded privately.

(ii) There is no other evidence of there being a public flavour to the functions of LCF or LCF itself. LCF is not standing in the shoes of the local authorities. Section 26 of the NAA provides statutory authority for the actions of the local authorities, but it provides LCF with no powers. LCF is not exercising statutory powers in performing functions for the appellants.

LCF is clearly not performing any public function.

. . . we dismiss this appeal.

The facts of the next case are as set out above in the previous extract. The following comprises the second part of Lord Nicholls' speech. This part of his speech is of interest in that it indicates what can be done under ss 6, 7 and 8 in relation to the duties of public authorities where those duties are already determined by statute and it is argued that no effective remedy has been provided for a breach by the authority of a Convention right.

**Re S (Children) and Re W (Care Orders) [2002] 2 AC 291; [2002] UKHL 10,
HL (referred to below as 'Re S and Re W')**

Lord Nicholls:

45 Sections 7 and 8 of the Human Rights Act have conferred extended powers on the courts. Section 6 makes it unlawful for a public authority to act in a way which is incompatible with a Convention right. Section 7 enables victims of conduct made unlawful by section 6 to bring court proceedings against the public authority in question. Section 8 spells out, in wide terms, the relief a court may grant in those proceedings. The court may grant such relief or remedy, or make such order, within its powers as it considers just and appropriate. Thus, if a local authority conducts itself in a manner which infringes the Article 8 rights of a parent or child, the court may grant appropriate relief on the application of a victim of the unlawful act.

. . .

47 In the present case the Court of Appeal seems to have placed some reliance on sections 7 and 8 for the extension of the court's powers envisaged by the starring system. Thorpe LJ said, in paragraph 32 of his judgment:

> The responsibility on the courts in the exercise of extended or additional powers is of course to ensure that they are used only to avoid or prevent the breach of an Article 6 or Article 8 right of one of the parties. If no actual or prospective breach of right is demonstrated the power does not arise.

48 I do not think sections 7 and 8 can be pressed as far as would be necessary if they were to bring the introduction of the starring system within their embrace. Sections 7 and 8 are to be given a generous interpretation, as befits their human rights purpose. But, despite the cautionary words of both Thorpe and Hale LJJ, the starring system goes much further than provide a judicial remedy to victims of actual or proposed unlawful conduct by local authorities entrusted with the care of children.

49 Section 7 envisages proceedings, brought by a person who is or would be a victim, against a public authority which has acted or is proposing to act unlawfully. The question whether the authority has acted unlawfully, or is proposing to do so, is a matter to be decided in the proceedings. Relief can be given against the authority only in respect of an act, or a proposed act, of the authority which the court finds is or would be unlawful. For this purpose an act includes a failure to act. But the starring system would impose obligations on local authorities in circumstances when there has been no such finding and when, indeed, the authority has committed no breach of a Convention right and is not proposing to do so. Unless an authority is acting in bad faith, the possibility or prospect of non-fulfilment, for example, of a placement for a child cannot by itself be evidence that the authority is 'proposing' to act unlawfully contrary to section 6. Nor can the non-fulfilment of a starred event, when the obligation to report arises, necessarily be equated with a breach or threatened breach of a Convention right. Failure to adhere to a care plan may be due to a change in circumstances which, in the best interests of the child, calls for a variation from the care plan which was approved by the court.

Statutory incompatibility

50 Thus far I have concluded that, even if there is incompatibility between the Children Act and Articles 6 or 8 of the Convention, the introduction of the starring system is beyond the powers of the court under section 3 of the Human Rights Act. Moreover, sections 7 and 8 of the Human Rights Act do not provide a legal basis for the introduction of this new system.

51 The mother of the children in the Torbay case contended that if the Children Act does not permit the introduction of the starring system, the Act is incompatible with Articles 6 and 8. She claims to be a victim of an infringement of her rights under these two articles. Save for the intervention of the Court of Appeal matters might well have gone even more seriously wrong.

. . .

Compatibility and Article 8

53 The essential purpose of this article is to protect individuals against arbitrary interference by public authorities.

54 Clearly, if matters go seriously awry, the manner in which a local authority discharges its parental responsibilities to a child in its care may violate the rights of the child or his parents under this article. The local authority's intervention in the life of the child, justified at the outset when the care order was made, may cease to be justifiable under Article 8(2). Sedley LJ pointed out that a care order from which no good is coming cannot sensibly be said to be pursuing a legitimate aim. A care order which keeps a child away from his family for purposes which, as time goes by, are not being realised will sooner or later become a disproportionate interference with the child's primary Article 8 rights: see paragraph 45 of his judgment.

55 Further, the local authority's decision-making process must be conducted fairly and so as to afford due respect to the interests protected by Article 8. For instance, the parents should be involved to a degree which is sufficient to provide adequate protection for their interests: *W v United Kingdom* (1987) 10 EHRR 29, 49–50, paragraphs 62–64.

56 However, the possibility that something may go wrong with the local authority's discharge of its parental responsibilities or its decision-making processes, and that this would be a violation of Article 8 so far as the child or parent is concerned, does not mean that the legislation itself is incompatible, or inconsistent, with Article 8. The Children Act imposes on a local authority looking after a child the duty to safeguard and promote the child's welfare.

57 If an authority duly carries out these statutory duties, in the ordinary course there should be no question of infringement by the local authority of the Article 8 rights of the child or his parents. Questions of infringement are only likely to arise if a local authority fails properly to discharge its statutory responsibilities. Infringement which then occurs is not brought about, in any meaningful sense, by the Children Act. Quite the reverse. Far from the infringement being compelled, or even countenanced, by the provisions of the Children Act, the infringement flows from the local authority's failure to comply with its obligations under the Act. True, it is the Children Act which entrusts responsibility for the child's care to the local authority. But that is not inconsistent with Article 8. Local authorities are responsible public authorities, with considerable experience in this field. Entrusting a local authority with the sole responsibility for a child's care, once the 'significant harm' threshold has been established, is not of itself an infringement of Article 8. There is no suggestion in the Strasbourg jurisprudence that absence of court supervision of a local authority's discharge of its parental responsibilities is itself an infringement of Article 8.

58 Where, then, is the inconsistency which is alleged to exist? As I understand it, the principal contention is that the incompatibility lies in the absence from the Children Act of an adequate remedy if a local authority fails to discharge its parental responsibilities properly and, as a direct result, the rights of the child or his parents under Article 8 are violated. The Children Act authorises the state to interfere with family life. The Act empowers courts to make care orders whose effect is to entrust the care of children to a public authority. ... Failure by the state to provide an effective remedy for a violation of Article 8 is not itself a violation of Article 8. This is self-evident. So, even if the Children Act does fail to provide an adequate remedy, the Act is not for that reason incompatible with Article 8. This is the short and conclusive answer to this point.

. . .

60 However, I should elaborate a little further. In Convention terms, failure to provide an effective remedy for infringement of a right set out in the Convention is an infringement of Article 13. But Article 13 is not a Convention right as defined in section 1(1) of the Human Rights Act. So legislation which fails to provide an effective remedy for infringement of Article 8 is not, for that reason, incompatible with a Convention right within the meaning of the Human Rights Act.

61 Where, then, does that leave the matter so far as English law is concerned? The domestic counterpart to Article 13 is sections 7 and 8 of the Human Rights Act, read in conjunction with

section 6. This domestic counterpart to Article 13 takes a different form from Article 13 itself. Unlike Article 13, which declares a right ('Everyone whose rights ... are violated shall have an effective remedy'), sections 7 and 8 provide a remedy. Article 13 guarantees the availability at the national level of an effective remedy to enforce the substance of Convention rights. Sections 7 and 8 seek to provide that remedy in this country. The object of these sections is to provide in English law the very remedy Article 13 declares is the entitlement of everyone whose rights are violated.

62 Thus, if a local authority fails to discharge its parental responsibilities properly, and in consequence the rights of the parents under Article 8 are violated, the parents may, as a longstop, bring proceedings against the authority under section 7. I have already drawn attention to a case where this has happened. I say 'as a longstop', because other remedies, both of an administrative nature and by way of court proceedings, may also be available in the particular case. For instance, Bedfordshire council has an independent visitor, a children's complaints officer and a children's rights officer. Sometimes court proceedings by way of judicial review of a decision of a local authority may be the appropriate way to proceed. In a suitable case an application for discharge of the care order is available. One would not expect proceedings to be launched under section 7 until any other appropriate remedial routes have first been explored.

63 In the ordinary course a parent ought to be able to obtain effective relief, by one or other of these means, against an authority whose mishandling of a child in its care has violated a parent's Article 8 rights. More difficult is the case, to which Thorpe LJ drew attention in paragraph 34, where there is no parent able and willing to become involved. In this type of case the Article 8 rights of a young child may be violated by a local authority without anyone outside the local authority becoming aware of the violation. In practice, such a child may not always have an effective remedy.

64 I shall return to this problem at a later stage. For present purposes it is sufficient to say that, for the reason I have given, the failure to provide a young child with an effective remedy in this situation does not mean that the Children Act is incompatible with Article 8: failure to provide a remedy for a breach of Article 8 is not itself a breach of Article 8.

Notes

1   *Public authorities and public functions.* As indicated above, there are three categories of body for HRA purposes – standard or functional public authorities and private bodies. The latter are not within s 6 of the HRA and therefore are not directly bound by the Convention rights. Determinations as to which bodies fall within the group generally referred to as 'functional public authorities', the terminology used in the Notes on Clauses accompanying the Bill, can be problematic, as *Donaghue* indicates. Functional public authorities (or 'hybrid bodies') are bodies which have a public and a private function and, under s 6(5), are bound by the Convention rights in respect of the former function only. A hospital, for example, exercises a public function in relation to NHS patients, a private one in relation to private patients. But there will clearly be room for debate as to those bodies that should be classified as standard rather than functional.[95] Classic functional bodies are likely to include Railtrack, privatised water companies and certain other contracted-out services,[96] although this is ultimately a matter for the courts. Those bodies that are public authorities, listed in Sched 1 to the Freedom of Information Act 2000, are likely to be standard or functional public authorities for HRA purposes, although for this purpose the list must be viewed as non-exhaustive. At present, the point at which it is possible to draw a line between functional and private bodies is unclear,[97] but

95   See S Grosz, J Beatson and P Duffy, *Human Rights: The 1998 Act and the European Convention* (1999), on this point: para 4-10 *et seq.*
96   583 HL Deb col 758 (24 November 1997).
97   See further D Oliver, 'The frontiers of the State: public authorities and public functions under the HRA' [2000] PL 476. See also for extensive discussion of the definition of public authorities, Clayton and Tomlinson, *op cit*, pp 186–204.

Donaghue and *Cheshire Homes* give some indications as to the dividing line. Clearly, the distinctions between standard and functional bodies and between functional and private bodies are going to give rise to a great deal of further litigation. *Donaghue* makes it clear that certain registered social landlords (RSL) are functional public bodies if they are in a very close relationship with a public authority and are therefore bound by the Convention rights under s 6 in respect of their public functions. It is also now established that a National Health Service Trust is a functional public authority,[98] but care homes in the voluntary sector are unlikely to be (from *Cheshire Homes*); the RSPCA[99] is not a functional public authority.

2   A variety of approaches are possible in order to determine whether a body has a public function, but the most significant one will be, following *Donaghue*, consideration of the principles deriving from judicial review case law on the question whether the decision-maker is a public body.[100] As Lord Woolf puts it: 'The emphasis on public functions in s 6 reflects the approach adopted in judicial review.' Most commentators have accepted that this will be the primary, or at least a very significant method of answering this question,[101] although it has been argued that the judicial review cases will not be definitive, partly because the Strasbourg jurisprudence takes an autonomous approach to the nature of public bodies that differs from the judicial review approach.[102] The Court in *Donaghue* found that the definition of who is a public authority, and what is a public function, for the purposes of s 6, should be given a generous interpretation. It further said that the fact that a body performs an activity which otherwise a public body would be under a duty to perform cannot mean that such performance is necessarily a public function.[103]

3   The starting point used in judicial review cases is the finding that the body is statutory or is acting under prerogative powers. But the source of a body's power is now viewed as far less significant than the public element in its functions.[104] Where a body is non-statutory, a further determining factor concerns the question whether there is evidence of government support or control for the body,[105] while a relevant, although not conclusive, factor will be whether it has monopoly power.[106] A further significant but, after *Donaghue*, possibly non-determinative factor concerns the question whether, had the body not existed, the government would have set up an equivalent body.[107] The courts now have the task of resolving differences between

---

98   *Re A (children) (conjoined twins)* [2000] 4 All ER 961, at 1017.

99   [2001] All ER (D) 188.

100 See Straw, HC Deb cols 408, 409 (17 June 1998).

101 See Clayton and Tomlinson, *op cit*, p 194, Lester and Pannick, *op cit*, para 2.6.3.

102 See Grosz, Beatson and Duffy, *op cit*, para 4-04; they rely on the decision in *Chassagnou v France* (1999) 7 BHRC 151, in which it was found that the classification of a body as public or private in national law is only a starting point. See further N Bamforth, 'The application of the HRA to public authorities and private bodies' [1999] 58 CLJ 159. Bamforth argues that the definition under s 6(1) is out of kilter with the criteria used in judicial review for determining whether a body is a public one.

103 See further, eg, Lord Woolf and J Jowell, in SA de Smith, Lord Woolf and J Jowell, *Judicial Review of Administrative Action*, 5th edn (1995); see also D Pannick, 'Who is subject to judicial review and in respect of what?' [1992] PL 1.

104 This can now be said due to the influence of the finding to this effect in *R v Panel of Take-overs and Mergers ex p Datafin* [1987] QB 815, 838. See further N Bamforth, 'The scope of judicial review: still uncertain' [1993] PL 239.

105 *R v Disciplinary Committee of the Jockey Club ex p Aga Khan* [1993] 1 WLR 909.

106 *R v Football Association ex p Football League* [1993] 2 All ER 833.

107 *R v Disciplinary Committee of the Jockey Club ex p Aga Khan* [1993] 1 WLR 909.

these tests, if any, and the test of public function under s 6(1). This is a matter that is considered further in Part V Chapter 1, pp 666–73.

4 Under s 6(3) hybrid bodies, who have functions of a public and private nature are public authorities, but *not* in relation to acts which are of a private nature. As pointed out in *Donaghue*, the renting out of accommodation can be of a private nature and:

> The fact that through the act of renting by a private body a public authority may be fulfilling its public duty, does not automatically change into a public act what would otherwise be a private act. An act can remain of a private nature even though it is performed because another body is under a public duty to ensure that that act is performed ... What can make an act, which would otherwise be private, public is a feature or a combination of features which impose a public character or stamp on the act. Statutory authority for what is done can at least help to mark the act as being public; so can the extent of control over the function exercised by another body which is a public authority. The more closely the acts that could be of a private nature are enmeshed in the activities of a public body, the more likely they are to be public.

The Court went on to find that a very close relationship existed between Tower Hamlets and Poplar. 'The role of Poplar is so closely assimilated to that of Tower Hamlets that Poplar should be viewed as performing public functions.' However, the Court emphasised that as in applications for judicial review, 'there is no clear demarcation line which can be drawn between public and private bodies and functions' and that in a borderline case, such as the instant one, 'the decision is very much one of fact and degree'. On these grounds the court found that Poplar was a functional public authority which of course did not mean that all Poplar's functions would be public.

5 Since the s 6(3) test seems to be more generous than the test of amenability, then if a body is amenable to judicial review, it will be likely to be a functional public authority. Standard public authorities will usually be subject to judicial review,[108] although not necessarily in relation to all their functions.[109] The test in Part 54 of the Civil Procedure Rules referring to public functions and the test under s 6(3)(b) of the HRA suggest that the same test will determine the amenability of bodies to judicial review and to duties under the HRA (see further pp 671–73). However, *R (on the Application of Heather) v Leonard Cheshire Foundation* makes it clear that although this is a starting point, amenability to judicial review and to HRA duties may not necessarily and in all instances be based on the same tests. Therefore, the fact that a body has been found to be a functional public authority does not necessarily mean (as the law stands at present) that it will be amenable to judicial review.

6 *Use of ss 7 and 8 of the HRA.* Sections 7 and 8 HRA allow for proceedings to be brought by a person who is or would be a victim, against a public authority which has acted or is proposing to act unlawfully by breaching the Convention rights and provide a remedy if the proceedings are successful in the sense of finding such a breach. In *Re S and Re W (Care Orders)* [2002] UKHL 10, Lord Nicholl had to consider whether ss 7 and 8 of the HRA provide a statutory basis for demanding that the authority should put in place procedures designed to avoid a breach of the rights where no such finding has been made. He said 'sections 7 and 8 [cannot] be pressed as far as would be necessary if they were to bring the introduction of the

---

108 See Clayton and Tomlinson, *op cit*, pp 197–98, for an extensive list.
109 See *McClaren v Home Office* [1990] ICR 824; *R v Jockey Club ex p RAM Racecourses Ltd* [1993] 2 All ER 225, 246. See further Part V Chapter 1, pp 673–75.

starring system within their embrace'. He found that the question whether the authority has acted unlawfully, or is proposing to do so, is a matter to be decided in the proceedings under s 7. 'Relief can be given against the authority only in respect of an act, or a proposed act, of the authority which the court finds is or would be unlawful. For this purpose, an act includes a failure to act. But the starring system would impose obligations on local authorities in circumstances when there has been no such finding.' He considered that the non-fulfilment of a 'starred event' could not necessarily be equated with a breach or threatened breach of a Convention right. Assuming that the failure to introduce a system such as the starring system would constitute a breach of Article 8 (Lord Nicholl did not consider that this was the case), then the authority in question would be failing in its duty under s 6 of the HRA if it did not introduce such a system, unless it was unable to do so due to the operation of primary legislation (s 6(2)).

Questions

1   Assume that the government wishes to reinstate the 'rape shield' provisions affected by the ruling of the Lords in *R v A*; it intends to introduce legislation in Parliament with this object in mind. What could be done to safeguard such legislation from further judicial intervention?

2   A statute is passed in 2006 which contains the following provision: 'Section 3 of the Human Rights Act is hereby repealed.' How might the courts react to the provision when deciding cases raising Convention points and how might they react to subsequent legislation which appeared to be inconsistent with one or more of the Convention rights?

3   Indications are now emerging as to those bodies which are bound by the Convention rights and as to those which are not. Do you find the bases for distinguishing between these bodies convincing and coherent? Is there a convincing rationale underlying this distinction between private and public bodies?

4   How much force, if any, is there in Waldron's argument (above) in relation to the protection for the Convention rights under the Human Rights Act as opposed to making provision for their formal entrenchment?

5   Do you consider that the rights of minority groups who tend to be unpopular with the majority of voters (such as suspected criminals, prisoners, suspected terrorists, new age travellers) are likely to be better protected through the operation of the democratic process or by affording the European Convention on Human Rights further effect in domestic law under the HRA?

FURTHER READING

SJ Bailey, DJ Harris and D Ormerod, *Bailey, Harris and Jones, Civil Liberties: Cases and Materials* 5th edn (2002), Chapter 1

R Clayton and H Tomlinson *The Law of Human Rights* (2000) esp Chapters 3, 4, 5

D Feldman, *Civil Liberties and Human Rights* (2002), Chapter 2

H Fenwick, *Civil Liberties and Human Rights* (2002), Chapter 3

CHAPTER 2

FREEDOM OF EXPRESSION

INTRODUCTION

Freedom of expression is widely regarded as one of the most significant human rights. For example, in the US the first amendment to the constitution provides: 'Congress shall make no law ... abridging the freedom of speech or of the press.' The justifications for according this particular freedom such significance have been much debated. One of the most significant is that citizens cannot participate fully in a democracy unless they have a reasonable understanding of political issues; therefore, open debate on such matters is essential. In *Derbyshire County Council v Times Newspapers* [1993] AC 534, Lord Keith, in holding that neither local nor central government could sustain an action in defamation, said: 'It is of the highest importance that a democratically elected governmental body ... should be open to uninhibited public criticism.' Barendt considers that this theory is 'probably the most attractive ... of the free speech theories in modern Western democracies', and concludes that 'it has been the most influential theory in the development of 20th century free speech law'.[1] Eric Barendt also accepts the validity of the thesis that freedom of speech is necessary to enable individual self-fulfilment.[2] It is argued that individuals will not be able to develop morally and intellectually unless they are free to air views and ideas in debate with each other.

These justifications have received recognition within the Strasbourg and UK expression of jurisprudence. The European Court of Human Rights has repeatedly asserted that freedom of expression 'constitutes one of the essential foundations of a democratic society',[3] and that it is applicable not only to 'information' or 'ideas' that are favourably received or regarded as inoffensive or as a matter of indifference, but also to those that 'offend, shock or disturb'.[4] Particular stress has been laid upon the pre-eminent role of the press in a state governed by the Rule of Law which, in 'its vital role of public watchdog' has a duty 'to impart information and ideas on matters of public interest' which the public 'has a right to receive'.[5] It is a marked feature of the Strasbourg jurisprudence that clearly political speech receives a much more robust degree of protection than other types of expression. Thus the 'political' speech cases of *Sunday Times v UK* (1979) 2 EHRR 245, *Jersild v Denmark* (1994) 19 EHRR 1,[6] *Lingens v Austria* (1986) 8 EHRR 103,[7] and *Thorgeirson v Iceland* (1992) 14 EHRR 843[8] all resulted in findings that Article 10 had been violated and all were marked by an intensive

---

1   E Barendt, *Freedom of Speech* (1987), pp 20 and 23 respectively.
2   *Op cit*, p 15.
3   *Observer and Guardian v UK*, Series A No 216; (1991) 14 EHRR 153, para 59.
4   See, eg, *Thorgeirson v Iceland* (1992) 14 EHRR 843, para 63.
5   *Castells v Spain*, Series A No 236, (1992) 14 EHRR 445, para 43.
6   *Jersild v Denmark* concerned an application by a Danish journalist who had been convicted of an offence of racially offensive behaviour after preparing and broadcasting a programme about racism which included overtly racist speech by the subjects of the documentary.
7   *Lingens v Austria* concerned the defamation of a political figure.
8   *Thorgeirson v Iceland* concerned newspaper articles reporting allegations of brutality against the Reykjavik police.

review of the restriction in question in which the margin of appreciation was narrowed almost to vanishing point.[9]

A similar pattern may be found in the domestic free speech jurisprudence. Earlier pronouncements to the effect that 'The media ... are an essential foundation of any democracy'[10] have recently been emphatically reinforced by pronouncements in the House of Lords' decision in *Reynolds v Times Newspapers* (1999), which afforded an explicit recognition to their duty to inform the people on matters of legitimate public interest. Press freedom in relation to political expression has clearly been recognised as having a particularly high value in UK law and Convention jurisprudence. The argument from self-development – that the freedom to engage in the free expression and reception of ideas and opinions in various media is essential to human development – has received some recognition at Strasbourg[11] and recently in the House of Lords.[12]

However, freedom of expression is not absolute in any jurisdiction; other interests can overcome it, including the interests in protecting morals, the reputation of others, national security, fair trials and public order. In fact, freedom of expression comes into conflict with a greater variety of interests than any other liberty and is therefore in more danger of being curtailed. Most Bills of Rights list these interests as exceptions to the primary right of freedom of expression, as does the European Convention on Human Rights (ECHR), Article 10. This does not mean that the mere invocation of the other interest will lead to displacement of freedom of expression; there must be strong reasons for allowing the other interest to prevail. Under Article 10 of the Convention it is necessary to show that there is a pressing social need to allow the other interest to prevail (see below at p 926).

Prior to the inception of the Human Rights Act 1998 (HRA), Article 10 of the ECHR was taken into account by the courts in construing ambiguous legislation on the basis, as Chapter 1 of this part indicated, that as Parliament must have intended to comply with its treaty obligations, an interpretation should be adopted which would allow it to do so (see pp 848–49). Article 10 has also, on occasion, been taken into account where there is ambiguity in the common law. Combined with the effects of certain very significant decisions at Strasbourg, Article 10 has had a greater impact on UK law than its fellow Article, Article 11. However, its impact has been variable. It has not had as much impact as might perhaps have been expected as far as the laws of obscenity and decency are concerned. As Chapter 3 of this Part explains, it has also had little effect on expression in the form of public protest. As Part IV Chapter 3 indicates, access to information does not appear to be covered by Article 10, although such access may be viewed as associated with expression.

Under s 3 of the HRA, the obligation to interpret legislation compatibly with Article 10, and the related Articles 9 and 11 (see Part II Chapter 2), is much stronger than it was in the pre-HRA era, while the courts and other public authorities, including the police, are bound by the Convention under s 6 to uphold freedom of expression. As

---

9   See the discussion of the doctrine in Part II Chapter 1, pp 246–47.
10   *Francome v MGN* [1984] 2 All ER 408, 898, *per* Sir John Donaldson.
11   The European Court of Human Rights has frequently asserted that freedom of expression is one of the essential foundations for the 'development of everyone' (in, eg, *Otto-Preminger v Austria* (1994) 19 EHRR 34, para 49).
12   *Per* Lord Steyn in *Secretary of State for the Home Department ex p Simms* [2000] AC 115; [1999] 3 WLR 328, at 498.

Chapter 1 of this Part indicated, s 12 of the HRA has an impact when a court is considering granting a remedy in civil proceedings which affects freedom of expression. Article 10 provides a strong safeguard for freedom of expression in relation to competing interests, since it takes the primary right as its starting point. The content of speech will rarely exclude it from the protection of Article 10, although not all speech is included.[13] Article 10(2) demands that interferences with the primary right should be both necessary and proportionate to the legitimate aim pursued. But, as indicated, interferences with expression have not all been subject to the same intensity of scrutiny at Strasbourg.

This chapter will indicate that there are two methods of protecting those interests which compete with freedom of expression: prior and subsequent restraints. Prior restraints, including censorship, are generally seen as more pernicious. Subsequent restraints operate after publication of the article in question: the persons responsible may face civil or criminal liability. The trial may then generate publicity and the defendants may have an opportunity of demonstrating why they published the article in question. However, the distinction between the two kinds of restraint may not be as stark as this implies. Subsequent restraints may have a chilling effect on publications; editors and others may well not wish to risk the possibility of incurring liability.

A judicial willingness to respect the values of freedom of expression became apparent in the 1990s.[14] This chapter considers the judges' concern, in the context of both prior and subsequent restraints, to strike a balance between free expression and a variety of other interests in the pre-HRA era, and then goes on to indicate the impact of Article 10 as given further effect under the HRA in this area. The main concern of this chapter and the next one is to evaluate the change in this 'balance' which is occurring under the HRA.

RESTRAINING FREEDOM OF EXPRESSION TO PROTECT THE STATE OR GOVERNMENT

Introduction

Broadly speaking, speech criticising or attacking the government or purporting to reveal state abuse of power will not attract criminal or civil liability.[15] However, there are a number of qualifications to this general rule. Journalists revealing material covered by the Official Secrets Act 1989 risk prosecution. Information on which such criticism or attacks might be based may not be available either because, as discussed in Part IV Chapter 3, it is covered by the Official Secrets Act 1989 or because, although the Act does not apply, it is unavailable under the Government Code on Access to Information or, in future, the Freedom of Information Act 2000.

Some forms of the speech in question may amount to sedition if accompanied by an intention to bring into hatred or contempt or to excite disaffection against the sovereign or the government, or to attempt otherwise than by lawful means to alter the

---

13 In *Jersild v Denmark* (1994) 19 EHRR 1 it was assumed that the actual racist utterances of racists in a broadcast were not protected.
14 See the House of Lords' decision in the *Derbyshire* case [1993] AC 534 and *ex p Simms* [1999] QB 349.
15 See Lord Keith's comments in the *Derbyshire* case [1993] AC 534.

law or promote feelings of ill will between different classes of subjects.[16] In *R v Chief Metropolitan Magistrate ex p Choudhury* [1991] 1 QB 429,[17] a case which arose out of the publication of Salman Rushdie's *The Satanic Verses*, the applicants argued that the crime of seditious libel would extend to the image of Islam which the book presented. This offence at one time seemed to cover any attack on the institutions of the state, but in modern times it has been interpreted to require an intention to incite to violence, and the words used must have a tendency to incite to violence against such institutions.[18] It was not therefore apt to cover the offence caused to Muslims by the book which could be said to be intended to arouse general hostility and ill will between sections of the community but not against the public authorities. This finding as regards the ambit of seditious libel means that it is likely to be infrequently invoked.

However, apart from the methods of controlling the release of state information discussed in Part IV Chapter 3, there are certain other disparate means available to the government in order to suppress or constrain speech which may be viewed as undermining the state, emanations of the state or government. Two such means are discussed in this section and the regulation of political broadcasting is also considered.

Breach of confidence

Introduction[19]

Breach of confidence is a civil remedy affording protection against the disclosure or use of information which is not generally known, and which has been entrusted in circumstances imposing an obligation not to disclose it without authorisation from the person who originally imparted it. This area of law developed as a means of protecting secret information belonging to individuals and organisations. However, it can also be used by the government to prevent disclosure of sensitive information and is in that sense a substitute for or complementary to the other measures available, including the Official Secrets Act 1989.[20] It is clear that governments are prepared to use actions for breach of confidence against civil servants and others in instances falling outside the categories of information covered by that Act – or within them. In some respects, breach of confidence actions may be more valuable than the criminal sanction provided by the 1989 Act. Their use may attract less publicity than a criminal trial, no jury will be involved and they offer the possibility of quickly obtaining an interim injunction.

However, where the government, as opposed to a private individual, is concerned, the courts will not merely accept that it is in the public interest that the information should be kept confidential. It will have to be shown that the public interest in keeping the information confidential due to the harm its disclosure would cause is not

---

16 *Burns* (1886) 16 Cox 355.
17 For comment, see M Tregilgas-Davey (1991) 54 MLR 294–99.
18 *Burns* (1886) 16 Cox CC 333; *Aldred* (1909) 22 Cox CC 1; cf *Caunt* (1947) unreported, but see (1948) 64 LQR 203; for comment see Barendt, *op cit*, pp 152–60.
19 General reading: SJ Bailey, DJ Harris and D Ormerod; *Bailey, Harris and Jones: Civil Liberties: Cases and Materials* (2001), pp 848–89; D Feldman, *Civil Liberties and Human Rights*, 2nd edn (2002), pp 872–89.
20 See Part IV Chapter 3, pp 576 *et seq*. For comment on the role of breach of confidence in this respect, see Bailey, Harris and Ormerod, *op cit*, pp 858–68.

outweighed by the public interest in disclosure. This issue is considered in *Attorney-General v Jonathan Cape* [1976] QB 752, below. The nature of the public interest defence – the interest in disclosure – was clarified in *Lion Laboratories v Evans and Express Newspapers* [1985] QB 526. The Court of Appeal held that the defence extended beyond situations in which there had been serious wrongdoing by the plaintiff. Even where the plaintiff was blameless, publication would be excusable where it was possible to show a serious and legitimate interest in the revelation. Thus, the *Daily Express* was allowed to publish information extracted from the manufacturer of the intoximeter (a method of conducting breathalyser tests), even though it did not reveal iniquity on the part of the manufacturer. It did, however, reveal a matter of genuine public interest: that wrongful convictions might have been obtained in drink-driving cases due to possible deficiencies of the intoximeter.

Just as the Official Secrets Act 1989 creates a direct interference with political speech, the doctrine of confidence as employed by the government can do so too. Therefore, the use of the doctrine in such instances will require careful scrutiny, with Article 10 in mind. Since this is a common law doctrine, s 3 HRA will not apply. But the courts have a duty under s 6 HRA to develop the doctrine compatibly with Article 10. The duty of the courts in relation to the doctrine of confidence under the HRA was considered by Sedley LJ in *Douglas and Others v Hello! Ltd* [2001] QB 967. The case concerned private individuals, not the state, but the findings are relevant since principles from such private cases have been relied upon by the state, as indicated below, in seeking to use the doctrine to prevent the disclosure of governmental information. Sedley LJ found that the jurisprudence of the Strasbourg Court and the common law 'now run in a single channel because, by virtue of s 2 and s 6 of the HRA, the courts of this country must not only take into account jurisprudence of both the Commission and the European Court of Human Rights ... they must themselves act compatibly with that and the other Convention rights'.

Thus a court, as itself a public authority under s 6, is obliged to give effect to Article 10, among other provisions of the Convention when considering the application of this doctrine. Section 12 of the HRA is also applicable where interference with the right to freedom of expression is in issue as it inevitably will be in this context. Section 12(4) requires the court to have particular regard to the right to freedom of expression under Article 10. Thus, s 12(4) provides added weight to the argument that in the instance in which the state seeks to suppress the expression of an individual using this doctrine, the court must consider the pressing social need to do so and the requirements of proportionality under Article 10(2) very carefully, interpreting those requirements strictly. In considering Article 10 the court should, under s 12(4)(a), take into account the extent to which the material is or is about to become available to the public and the public interest in publication. These two matters are central in breach of confidence actions. As *Attorney-General v Times Newspapers* [2001] 1 WLR 885 (below) demonstrates, s 12(4) has made it more difficult for the state to obtain an injunction where a small amount of prior publication has taken place.

In breach of confidence actions the Attorney-General, as indicated below, typically seeks an interim injunction and then, if it is obtained, the case may proceed to the trial of the permanent injunction. This possibility was very valuable to the government because, in many instances, the other party (usually a newspaper) did not pursue the case to a trial of the permanent injunction since the secret was often no longer newsworthy by that time. However, s 12(3) of the HRA provides that prior restraint on expression should not be granted except where the court considers that the claimant is 'likely' to establish at trial that publication should not be allowed. Moreover, *ex parte* injunctions cannot be granted under s 12(2) unless there are compelling reasons why the respondent should not be notified or the applicant has taken all reasonable steps to notify the respondent. All these requirements under the HRA must now be taken into account in applying the doctrine of confidence. The result is that the doctrine appears to be undergoing quite a significant change from the interpretation afforded to it in the *Spycatcher* litigation (below). This is indicated by *Attorney-General v Times*, below.

Attorney-General v Jonathan Cape [1976] QB 752; [1975] 3 All ER 484, 491, 494, 495, 496

The Attorney-General invoked the law of confidence to try to stop publication of Richard Crossman's memoirs on the ground that they concerned Cabinet discussions. The diaries of Mr Crossman, a Cabinet minister in the Wilson government, included detailed accounts of Cabinet and Cabinet Committee meetings, including the attribution to members of views which they expressed there. The Lord Chief Justice accepted that such public secrets could be restrained but only on the basis that the balance of the public interest came down in favour of suppression. As the discussions had taken place 10 years previously it was not possible to show that harm would flow from their disclosure; the public interest in publication therefore prevailed.

Lord Widgery CJ: The Attorney General contends that all cabinet papers and discussions are *prima facie* confidential, and that the court should restrain any disclosure thereof if the public interest in concealment outweighs the public interest in a right to free publication.

... in *Coco v AN Clarke Ltd* [1969] RPC 41 at 47 Megarry J, reviewing the authorities, set out the requirements necessary for an action based on breach of confidence to succeed:

> In my judgment three elements are normally required if, apart from contract, a case of breach of confidence is to succeed. First, the information itself ... must 'have the necessary quality of confidence about it'. Secondly, that information must have been imparted in circumstances importing an obligation of confidence. Thirdly, there must be an unauthorised use of that information to the detriment of the party communicating it. ...

In my judgment, the Attorney General has made out his claim that the expression of individual opinions by Cabinet ministers in the course of Cabinet discussion are matters of confidence, the publication of which can be restrained by the court when this is clearly necessary in the public interest.

The maintenance of the doctrine of joint responsibility within the Cabinet is in the public interest, and the application of that doctrine might be prejudiced by premature disclosure of the views of individual ministers. There must, however, be a limit in time after which the confidential character of the information, and the duty of the court to restrain publication, will lapse. Since the conclusion of the hearing in this case I have had the opportunity to read the whole of volume I of the diaries, and my considered view is that I cannot believe that the publication at this interval of anything in volume I would inhibit free discussion in the Cabinet of today, even though the individuals involved are the same, and the national problems have a distressing similarity with those of a decade ago. It is unnecessary to elaborate the evils which might flow if, at the close of a cabinet meeting, a minister proceeded to give the press an analysis of the voting, but we are dealing in this case with a disclosure of information nearly 10 years later.

It may, of course, be intensely difficult in a particular case, to say at what point the material loses its confidential character, on the ground that publication will no longer undermine the doctrine of joint cabinet responsibility. It is this difficulty which prompts some to argue that cabinet discussions should retain their confidential character for a longer and arbitrary period such as 30 years, or even for all time, but this seems to me to be excessively restrictive. The court should intervene only in the clearest of cases where the continuing confidentiality of the material can be demonstrated. In less clear cases – and this, in my view, is certainly one – reliance must be placed on the good sense and good taste of the minister or ex-minister concerned.

For these reasons I do not think that the court should interfere with the publication of volume I of the diaries and I propose, therefore, to refuse the injunctions sought ...

Attorney-General v Guardian Newspapers Ltd [1987] 3 All ER 316, 319, 321, 322

In 1985 the Attorney-General commenced proceedings in New South Wales[21] in an attempt (which was ultimately unsuccessful)[22] to restrain publication of *Spycatcher* by Peter Wright. The book included allegations of illegal activity engaged in by MI5 and alleged that some MI5 officers had conspired to destabilise the Labour government under Harold Wilson. In the UK on 22 and 23 June 1986, *The Guardian* and *The Observer* published reports of the forthcoming hearing which included some *Spycatcher* material, and on 27 June the Attorney-General obtained temporary *ex parte* injunctions preventing them from further disclosure of such material. *Inter partes* injunctions were granted against the newspapers on 11 July 1986 by Millet J. On 12 July 1987, the *Sunday Times* began publishing extracts from *Spycatcher* and the Attorney-General obtained an injunction restraining publication on 16 July. On 14 July 1987 the book was published in the United States and many copies were brought into the UK. *The Guardian* and *The Observer* applied to the Vice-Chancellor for discharge of the injunctions.

Sir Nicolas Browne-Wilkinson VC: There are three applications. The first two are made by *The Guardian* and *The Observer* newspapers to discharge interlocutory junctions made against them in two orders made by Millett J on 11 July 1986 and confirmed (subject to minor modifications) by the Court of Appeal on 25 July 1986. ...

In my judgment, there has been a most substantial change in circumstances. In 1986, as I have said, the publication in *The Guardian* and *The Observer* was, so far as that court was aware and so far as I am aware, the only breach in the security walls. Otherwise the matter had not hit the press in any way, save that the action was pending in Australia. Of the allegations made by Mr Wright in the book there had been no other indication.

Due to the change in circumstances, the Vice-Chancellor discharged the Millet injunctions, but they were restored by the Court of Appeal ([1987] 3 All ER 316) in modified form. The newspapers appealed to the House of Lords ([1987] 3 All ER 316, 346–47).

Lord Bridge: Having no written constitution, we have no equivalent in our law to the First Amendment to the constitution of the United States of America. Some think that puts freedom of speech on too lofty a pedestal. Perhaps they are right. We have not adopted as part of our law the European Convention on Human Rights ... to which this country is a signatory. Many think that we should. I have hitherto not been of that persuasion, in large part because I have had confidence in the capacity of the common law to safeguard the fundamental freedoms essential to a free society including the right to freedom of speech which is specifically safeguarded by Article 10 of the Convention. My confidence is seriously undermined by your Lordships' decision. ...

Freedom of speech is always the first casualty under a totalitarian regime. Such a regime cannot afford to allow the free circulation of information and ideas among its citizens. Censorship is the indispensable tool to regulate what the public may and what they may not know. The present

21 (1987) 8 NSWLR 341.
22 High Court of Australia (1988) 165 CLR 30; for comment, see M Turnbull (1989) 105 LQR 382.

attempt to insulate the public in this country from information which is freely available elsewhere is a significant step down that very dangerous road. The maintenance of the ban, as more and more copies of the book *Spycatcher* enter this country and circulate here, will seem more and more ridiculous. If the Government are determined to fight to maintain the ban to the end, they will face inevitable condemnation and humiliation by the European Court of Human Rights in Strasbourg. Long before that they will have been condemned at the bar of public opinion in the free world.

Lord Brandon of Oakbrook: I was a party to the majority decision of this House given on 30 July 1987 that the injunctions in issue should not be discharged but should be continued until trial. My reasons for being a party to that decision can be summarised in nine propositions as follows.

(1) The action brought by the Attorney General against *The Guardian* and *The Observer* has as its object the protection of an important public interest, namely the maintenance so far as possible of the secrecy of the British security service.

(2) The injunctions in issue are interlocutory, that is to say temporary injunctions, having effect until the trial of the action only.

(3) Before the publication of *Spycatcher* in America the Attorney General had a strong arguable case for obtaining at trial final injunctions in terms similar to those of the temporary injunctions.

(4) While the publication of *Spycatcher* in America has much weakened that case, it remains an arguable one.

(5) The only way in which it can justly be decided whether the Attorney General's case, being still arguable, should succeed or fail is by having the action tried.

(6) On the hypothesis that the Attorney General's claim, if tried, will succeed, the effect of discharging the temporary injunctions now will be to deprive him, summarily and without a trial, of all opportunity of achieving that success.

(7) On the alternative hypothesis that the Attorney General's claim, if tried, will fail, the effect of continuing the temporary injunctions until trial will be only to postpone, not to prevent, the exercise by *The Guardian* and *The Observer* of the rights to publish which it will in that event have been established that they have.

(8) Having regard to (6) and (7) above, the discharge of the temporary injunctions now is capable of causing much greater injustice to the Attorney General than the continuation of them until trial is capable of causing to *The Guardian* and *The Observer*.

(9) Continuation of the injunctions until trial is therefore preferable to their discharge.

By a 3:2 majority the House of Lords upheld the interim injunctions.

Attorney-General v Guardian (No 2) [1990] 1 AC 109; [1988] 3 All ER 545, 639, 640, 641–46

On 21 December 1987 in the trial of the permanent injunctions, Scott J discharged the interlocutory injunctions. The Court of Appeal upheld this decision. The Attorney-General appealed to the House of Lords.

Lord Keith of Kinkel: In so far as the Crown acts to prevent [disclosure of confidential information] or to seek redress for it on confidentiality grounds, it must necessarily, in my opinion, be in a position to show that the disclosure is likely to damage or has damaged the public interest. How far the Crown has to go in order to show this must depend on the circumstances of each case. In a question with a Crown servant himself, or others acting as his agents, the general public interest in the preservation of confidentiality, and in encouraging other Crown servants to preserve it, may suffice. But where the publication is proposed to be made by third parties unconnected with the particular confidant, the position may be different. The Crown's argument in the present case would go the length that, in all circumstances where the original disclosure has been made by a Crown servant in breach of his obligation of confidence, any person to whose knowledge the information comes and who is aware of the breach comes under an equitable duty binding his conscience not to communicate the information to anyone else irrespective of the circumstances under which he acquired the knowledge. In my opinion that general proposition is untenable and impracticable, in addition to being unsupported by any authority. ... it can scarcely be a relevant detriment to the Government that publication of material concerning its actions will merely expose it to public discussion and criticism. It is unacceptable in our democratic society that there should be a restraint on the publication of information relating to Government when the only vice of that information is that it enables the public to discuss, review and criticise Government action.

Accordingly, the court will determine the Government's claim to confidentiality by reference to the public interest. Unless disclosure is likely to injure the public interest, it will not be protected.

...

I am of the opinion that the reports and comments proposed by *The Guardian* and *The Observer* would not be harmful to the public interest, nor would the continued serialisation by the *Sunday Times*. I would therefore refuse an injunction against any of the newspapers. I would stress that I do not base this upon any balancing of public interest nor upon any considerations of freedom of the press, nor upon any possible defences of prior publication or just cause or excuse, but simply upon the view that all possible damage to the interest of the Crown has already been done by the publication of *Spycatcher* abroad and the ready availability of copies in this country.

The majority in the House of Lords concurred in dismissing the appeal of the Attorney-General.

The Observer and The Guardian v United Kingdom (1991) 14 EHRR 153, 190–95

The Guardian and *The Observer* applied to the European Commission on Human Rights alleging, *inter alia*, a breach of Article 10 in respect of the temporary injunctions. The Commission referred the case to the Court, having given its unanimous opinion that the injunctions constituted a breach of Article 10.

56 The Court is satisfied that the injunctions had the direct or primary aim of 'maintaining' the authority of the judiciary, which phrase includes the protection of the rights of litigants [see *Sunday Times v United Kingdom*, para 56].

It is also incontrovertible that a further purpose of the restrictions complained of was the protection of national security.

57 The interference complained of thus had aims that were legitimate under paragraph (2) of Article 10.

...

Was the interference 'necessary in a democratic society'?

59 The Court's judgments relating to Article 10, starting with *Handyside v United Kingdom* (1976) 1 EHRR 737, concluding most recently, with *Oberschlick v Austria*, Series A No 204 ... announce the following major principles.

(a) Freedom of expression constitutes one of the essential foundations of a democratic society

    ...

(b) These principles are of particular importance as far as the press is concerned. Whilst it must not overstep the bounds set, *inter alia*, in the 'interests of national security' or for 'maintaining the authority of the judiciary', it is nevertheless incumbent on it to impart information and ideas on matters of public interest. Not only does the press have the task of imparting such information and ideas: the public also has a right to receive them. ...

60 ... the court would only add to the foregoing that Article 10 of the Convention does not in terms prohibit the imposition of prior restraints on publication, as such. This is evidenced ... by the *Sunday Times* judgment of 26 April 1979 and its *Markt Intern Verlag GmbH and Klaus Beerman* judgment of 20 November 1988 [(1990) 12 EHRR 161]. On the other hand, the dangers inherent in prior restraints are such that they call for the most careful scrutiny on the part of the court. This is especially so as far as the press is concerned, for news is a perishable commodity and to delay its publication, even for a short period, may well deprive it of all its value and interest.

2 The period from 11 July 1986 to 30 July 1987

In forming its own opinion, the Court has borne in mind its observations concerning the nature and contents of *Spycatcher* and the interests of national security involved; it has also had regard to the potential prejudice to the Attorney General's breach of confidence actions, this being a point that has to be seen in the context of the central position occupied by Article 6 of the Convention and its guarantee of the right to a fair trial [see *Sunday Times v United Kingdom*, para 55]. Particularly in the light of these factors, the court takes the view that, having regard to their margin of appreciation, the English courts were entitled to consider the grant of injunctive relief to be necessary and that their reasons for so concluding were 'sufficient' for the purposes of paragraph (2) of Article 10.

...

64 It has nevertheless to be examined whether the actual restraints imposed were 'proportionate' to the legitimate aims pursued.

In this connection, it is to be noted that the injunctions did not erect a blanket prohibition. Whilst they forbade the publication of information derived from or attributed to Mr Wright in his capacity as a member of the security service, they did not prevent *The Observer* and *The Guardian* from pursuing their campaign for an independent inquiry into the operation of that service.

65 Having regard to the foregoing, the court concludes that, as regards the period from 11 July 1986 to 30 July 1987, the national authorities were entitled to think that the interference complained of was 'necessary in a democratic society'.

3 The period from 30 July to 13 October 1988

66 On 14 July 1987 *Spycatcher* was published in the USA. This changed the situation that had obtained since 11 July 1986. In the first place, the contents of the book ceased to be a matter of speculation and their confidentiality was destroyed. Furthermore, Mr Wright's memoirs were obtainable from abroad by residents of the UK. ...

68 The fact that the further publication of *Spycatcher* material could have been prejudicial to the trial of the Attorney General's claims for permanent injunctions was certainly in terms of the aim of maintaining the authority of the judiciary, a 'relevant' reason for continuing the restraints in question. The court finds, however, that in the circumstances it does not constitute a 'sufficient' reason for the purposes of Article 10.

It is true that the House of Lords had regard to the requirements of the Convention even though it is not incorporated into domestic law. It is also true that there is some difference between the casual importation of copies of *Spycatcher* into the UK and mass publication of its contents in the press. On the other hand, even if the Attorney General had succeeded in obtaining permanent injunctions at the substantive trial, they would have borne on material the confidentiality of which had been destroyed in any event – and irrespective of whether any further disclosures were made by *The Observer* and *The Guardian* – as a result of the publication in the US. Seen in terms of the protection of the Attorney General's rights as a litigant, the interest in maintaining the confidentiality of that material had, for the purposes of the Convention, ceased to exist by 30 July 1987 [see, *mutatis mutandis, Weber v Switzerland* (1990) 12 EHRR 508, at para 51].

69 As regards the interests of national security relied on, the Court observes that, in this respect, the Attorney General's case underwent, to adopt the words of Scott J, 'a curious metamorphosis'

[*Attorney-General v Guardian Newspapers (No 2)* [1990] AC 109]. As emerges from Sir Robert Armstrong's evidence [see para 16 above], injunctions were sought at the outset, *inter alia*, to preserve the secret character of information that ought to be kept secret. By 30 July 1987, however, the information had lost that character and, as was observed by Lord Brandon of Oakbrook [see para 36(a)(iv), above], the major part of the potential damage adverted to by Sir Robert Armstrong had already been done. By then, the purpose of the injunctions had thus become confined to the promotion of the efficiency and reputation of the security service, notably by: preserving confidence in that service on the part of third parties; making it clear that the unauthorised publication of memoirs by its former members would not be countenanced; and deterring others who might be tempted to follow in Mr Wright's footsteps.

The Court of Human Rights concluded unanimously that the objectives considered were insufficient to justify continuing the restriction after July 1987 since it prevented newspapers exercising their right to purvey information which was already available on a matter of legitimate public interest. Thus, a breach of Article 10 was found in respect of the maintenance of the injunctions after, but not before, 30 July 1987.[23]

Attorney-General v Times Newspapers [2001] 1 WLR 885, CA

The findings in this case suggest that Article 10 is having a greater impact in breach of confidence actions than it had at Strasbourg in relation to the *Spycatcher* material. Tomlinson, a former MI6 officer, wrote a book, *The Big Breach*, about his experiences in MI6,[24] which the *Sunday Times* intended to serialise. There had been a small amount of publication of the material in Russia. The Attorney-General sought an injunction to restrain publication. The key issue concerned the duty of a newspaper to demonstrate that a degree of prior publication had occurred whereby it could be said that the material had lost its quality of confidentiality.

[The *Sunday Times* and the Attorney General agreed on a formula regarding the undertaking relating to publication] that was satisfactory to both parties, subject to one important matter. The agreed variation altered the disputed terms of the undertaking so as to read as follows:

'Nothing in this undertaking prevents the defendants or any of them from republishing anything which at the date of publication or intended publication by the defendant or defendants: ...

(ii) has previously been published in any other newspaper, magazine or other publication, whether within or outside the jurisdiction of the Court, to such an extent that the information is in the public domain (other than in a case where the only such publication was made by or was caused by the defendants or any of them);

(iii) has previously been published by or through the internet or other electronic media to such an extent that the information is in the public domain (other than in a case where the only such publication was made by or was caused by the defendants or any of them).'

There remains, however, a bone of contention, which is quite a big bone. That is the submission by the Attorney General that the relevant formula in the proviso should be preceded by the phrase:

... where the defendants can demonstrate that ...

[It was] submitted that the proposed variation should, in effect, require TNL to get clearance from the Attorney General or the court that anything they wished to publish was indeed in the public domain before they would be entitled to publish it. This had the effect of rendering the proposed variation nugatory. TNL would be little, if any, better off if they remained under an obligation to get

23 *Sunday Times v United Kingdom (No 2)* (1991) 14 EHRR 229. For comment, see I Leigh [1992] PL 200–08.
24 Tomlinson was charged with an offence under s 1 of the Official Secrets Act 1989, pleaded guilty and was imprisoned for six months.

clearance from the Attorney General or the court before publishing. [On behalf of the TNL, publishers of the *Sunday Times*] counsel invoked Article 10 of the European Convention on Human Rights. He submitted that the clause proposed by the Attorney General would constitute an unjustified fetter on the right to freedom of expression to the detriment both of the newspaper, which had the right to impart information, and the public which had the right to receive it. He also relied upon section 12 of the Human Rights Act 1998,

[Counsel for TNL, Mr Tugendhat] referred to the decision of the European Court of Human Rights in the case of *Bladet Tromso and Stensaas v Norway* (20 May 1999) and in particular to this passage from paragraph 62 of the judgment of the court: 'whilst the mass media must not overstep the bounds imposed in the interests of the protection of private individuals, it is incumbent on them to impart information and ideas concerning matters of public interest. Not only does the press have the task of imparting such information and ideas: the public also has a right to receive them. Consequently, in order to determine whether the interference was based on sufficient reasons which rendered it "necessary", regard must be had to the public-interest aspect of the case.'

Eady J found:

> It is in practical terms for the Attorney General to demonstrate, particularly perhaps in the light of the European Convention, that any restriction on freedom of expression sought to be imposed, or continued, can itself be justified by some countervailing and substantial public interest. In the light of what is today going to be readily available in the public domain in Russia, the United States and elsewhere in the world, I am afraid I am not persuaded that the public interest requires the *Sunday Times* to be restricted, for reasons based on a duty of confidence, to any greater extent than any other organ of the media. . . . all that is in issue here before me today, important though it is, is the question of whether or not the *Sunday Times* should be placed on the same footing as other media organisations or continue in the somewhat artificial position in which they now find themselves for purely historical reasons. . . . it is necessary for me to bear in mind, as was mentioned in argument, that an important part of freedom of expression is not only the freedom to publish what one wishes but the ability to publish it when one wishes to do so.

I think it is desirable that there should usually be consultation between a newspaper and representatives of the SIS before the newspaper publishes information that may include matters capable of damaging the Service or endangering those who serve in it. I understand from Mr Tugendhat that such consultation takes place. I do not, however, think it right to impose on TNL the requirement that they should seek confirmation from the Attorney General or the court that facts that they intend to republish have been sufficiently brought into the public domain by prior publication so as to remove from them the cloak of confidentiality. That is a matter on which an editor will be in a position to form his own judgment and he should be left responsible for exercising that judgment. That is consonant with Article 10 of the European Convention on Human Rights and section 12 of the Act.

Appeal dismissed.

Notes

1   The European Court of Human Rights in *The Observer and The Guardian v United Kingdom* concluded that once publication of *Spycatcher* had occurred in the US the objectives considered were insufficient to justify continuing the restriction since it prevented the newspapers exercising their right to purvey information which was already available on a matter of legitimate public interest. The test put forward by the House of Lords at the interlocutory stage thus breached Article 10: it allowed an injunction to be granted, even where disclosure would not cause clear damage to the public interest, on the basis that confidentiality had to be preserved until the case could be fully looked into. This test left open the possibility that the other

party would not pursue the case to the permanent stage and therefore that freedom of speech could be suppressed on grounds which were not well founded.

2 The facts of *Attorney-General v Blake (Jonathan Cape Ltd, Third Party)* [2001] 1 AC 268 bear some resemblance to those in *Attorney-General v Guardian (No 2)*, although the Attorney-General's claim of breach of confidence was rejected in the *Blake* case (the information was no longer confidential). George Blake, a former member of the Secret Intelligence Service, became a double agent working for the Soviet Union. In Moscow he wrote a book, *No Other Choice*, drawing on information acquired during his term as an intelligence officer. The Crown, suing by the Attorney-General, sought to extract from Blake any financial benefit he might gain from publishing the book. The Attorney-General argued that Blake owed the Crown a fiduciary duty not to use his position as a member of the SIS to make a profit for himself. The House of Lords found that Blake's actions were in breach of contract and that, in the exceptional circumstances, the Attorney-General was entitled to restitutionary damages for the breach. This was a significant judgment since it found what appeared to be a novel basis for the decision. It creates a deterrent discouraging members of the intelligence and security services from making disclosures even in instances in which the disclosure of confidential information is not in question.

3 The existence of the D notice system[25] may tend to deter or dissuade the press and others from the publication of confidential or sensitive government information. The 'D' Notice Committee was set up with the object of letting the press know which information could be printed and at what point. Press representatives sit on the Committee as well as civil servants and officers of the armed forces. In the Third Report from the Defence Committee,[26] the 'D' notice system was examined and it was concluded that it was failing to fulfil its role. It was found that major newspapers did not consult their 'D' notices to see what was covered by them and that the wording of 'D' notices was so wide as to render them meaningless. The system conveyed an appearance of censorship which had provoked strong criticism. The review which followed this report reduced the number of notices and confined them to specific areas. The system was reviewed again in 1992 (*The Defence Advisory Notices: A Review of the D Notice System*, MOD Open Government Document No 93/06), leading to a reduction in the number of notices to six.

4 After the decision in *Attorney-General v Times*, which took into account the requirements of the HRA, an injunction is unlikely to be granted where prior publication has already taken place, even if only a small amount of publication has occurred. Further, a newspaper need not demonstrate that prior publication has occurred. The decision does not, however, decide the question of granting an injunction restraining publication where *no* prior publication has taken place, but the material is of public interest (which could clearly have been said of the Wright material). Following *Bladet-Tromso v Norway*, RJD 1999-III, it is suggested that an injunction should not be granted where such material is likely, imminently, to come into the public domain, a position consistent with the demands of s 12(4) of the HRA which refers to such a likelihood. Even where this cannot be said to be the case, it would be consonant with the requirements of Article 10 and s 12 to refuse to grant an interim injunction on the basis of the duty of newspapers to report on such material. The burden would be placed on the state to seek to establish that a

25 On the system generally, see J Jaconelli, 'The "D" notice system' [1982] PL 39.
26 HC 773 (1979–80), para 640 i–v, *The 'D' Notice System.*

countervailing pressing social need was present and that the injunction did not go further than necessary in order to serve the end in view.

Questions

1   Is it fair to conclude that the decisions in the *Spycatcher* case undermine the Diceyan claim that the judges are the guardians of freedom of speech?

2   Does the decision of the European Court of Human Rights in relation to the temporary injunctions in the *Spycatcher* case suggest that the Convention may be confidently relied upon to maintain a high standard of free speech protection?

3   Is it safe to conclude that the HRA has already had quite a radical impact on the doctrine of breach of confidence?

Controls over political broadcasting

Government influence over broadcasting is of enormous significance due to the importance of broadcasting as the main means of informing the public as to matters of public interest. The openly partisan nature of the popular press means that broadcasting provides the only impartial source of information for most people.

Independent broadcasting is governed by the Broadcasting Acts 1990 and 1996. Prior to the introduction of the Broadcasting Act 1990, the Independent Broadcasting Authority (IBA) was charged with the regulation of independent television. As part of the policy of deregulation of television, the 1990 Act set up the Independent Television Commission (ITC) to replace the IBA as a public body charged with licensing and regulating non-BBC television services. The function of the ITC in this respect is similar to that of the Radio Authority (RA), which has the statutory function, under Part III of the 1990 Act, of licensing and monitoring the independent radio stations. Public broadcasting is governed by the royal charter of the BBC which partly comprises a Licence Agreement (Cmnd 8233). The BBC operates under this Agreement and also under the terms of its Charter (Cmnd 8313). Under these instruments the board of governors of the BBC has the responsibility for maintaining standards of impartiality. The current (1996) Charter and Agreement set out in more detail the obligations of the BBC as a public broadcaster operating by means of the licence fee, in particular its obligation to maintain independence.

Control over political broadcasting is exerted via the current statutory regimes. Exceptionally, the government can also exert direct control by the use of its censorship powers in relation to independent television under s 10(3) of the Broadcasting Act 1990 and in relation to the BBC via clause 13(4) of the BBC's Licence Agreement. It can also do so through more subtle means, such as the criteria used to determine appointments to the BBC governors.

The power of the Secretary of State to control broadcasting under s 10(3) of the Broadcasting Act 1990 previously arose under s 29(3) of the Broadcasting Act 1981. This power was invoked by the Secretary of State in 1988 in order to issue directives requiring the Independent Broadcasting Authority (IBA) to refrain from broadcasting words spoken by persons representing certain extremist groups or words spoken supporting or inviting support for those groups. The very similar power under clause 13(4) of the 1981 licence and agreement between the Home Secretary and the BBC was invoked in order to apply the same ban to the BBC. The ban covered organisations proscribed under the Northern Ireland (Emergency Provisions) legislation as well as

Sinn Fein, Republican Sinn Fein and the Ulster Defence Association. The ban was challenged by the National Union of Journalists and others, but not by the broadcasting organisations themselves.

Brind and Others v Secretary of State for the Home Department [1991] I All ER 720, 722–24[27]

Lord Bridge of Harwich: My Lords, this appeal has been argued primarily on the basis that the power of the Secretary of State, under s 29(3) of the Broadcasting Act 1981 and under clause 13(4) of the licence and agreement which governs the operations of the British Broadcasting Corpn (BBC) (Cmnd 8233), to impose restrictions on the matters which the Independent Broadcasting Authority (IBA) and the BBC respectively may broadcast may only be lawfully exercised in accordance with Article 10 of the European Convention on Human Rights.

[Lord Bridge considered, but did not accept the submission that:]

... when a statute confers upon an administrative authority a discretion capable of being exercised in a way which infringes any basic human right protected by the Convention, it may similarly be presumed that the legislative intention was that the discretion should be exercised within the limitations which the Convention imposes ...

... I find it impossible to say that the Secretary of State exceeded the limits of his discretion. In any civilised and law-abiding society the defeat of the terrorist is a public interest of the first importance. That some restriction on the freedom of the terrorist and his supporters to propagate his cause may well be justified in support of that public interest is a proposition which I apprehend the appellants hardly dispute. The Secretary of State, for the reasons he made so clear in Parliament, decided that it was necessary to deny to the terrorist and his supporters the opportunity to speak directly to the public through the most influential of all the media of communication and that this justified some interference with editorial freedom. I do not see how this judgment can be categorised as unreasonable. What is perhaps surprising is that the restriction imposed is of such limited scope ... The viewer may see the terrorist's face and hear his words provided only that they are not spoken in his own voice.

... [the complaints of the journalists] fall very far short of demonstrating that a reasonable Secretary of State could not reasonably conclude that the restriction was justified by the important public interest of combating terrorism.

The House of Lords unanimously dismissed the appeal.

Notes

1   As Chapter 1 of this Part explained, the inception of the HRA has had the effect of reversing the decision in *Brind*. If the power of censorship is invoked again, it will have to be used within Convention limits. This would not necessarily mean that such a ban would breach Article 10: it may be noted that a challenge to the ban failed at Strasbourg: *Brind and McLaughlin v UK* (1994) 77-A DR 42. The ban remained in place until September 1994 when it was lifted after the IRA declared the cessation of violence. When the ceasefire broke down in 1996, the ban was not re-imposed.

2   In general, BBC censorship operates by a process of 'reference up' the corporation management hierarchy: producers refer to middle management, who may seek direction from departmental heads, who may then consult the managing director or even the director general. Thus, censorship is largely self-imposed, but the board of governors of the BBC is appointed by the government, and although they usually leave editorial matters to the director general they may occasionally

---

27   For comment see J Jowell [1990] PL 149 (on the Court of Appeal ruling).

intervene. They did so in 1985 in relation to a programme about an IRA sympathiser in Belfast, 'Real Lives', after condemnation by the Prime Minister of an incident perceived as damaging to the BBC's reputation for independence from the government.[28]

3 Expressions of concern from the then Conservative government regarding the independent stance of the IBA appear to have played a part in the inclusion in the Broadcasting Act 1990 of provisions designed to preserve political neutrality in broadcasting. When the 1990 Act set up the ITC and the Radio Authority to replace the IBA, it imposed a detailed impartiality requirement on the ITC,[29] a controversial requirement that is clearly an infringement of the freedom of expression of broadcasters. The ITC was required, under the impartiality clause introduced by s 6(1)(c) of the 1990 Act, to set up a Code to require that politically sensitive programmes must be balanced in order to ensure due impartiality. Such programmes can be balanced by means of a series of programmes (s 6(2)); it is not necessary that any one programme should be followed by another specific balancing programme.

4 The ITC Programme Code (last revised Autumn 1998) clause 3.3(i) makes it clear that a company cannot be heard to argue that a programme which might be said to have an anti-government bias may be balanced by programmes broadcast by other companies: the company has to achieve impartiality in its own programming. The Code also indicates in clause 3.3 that it may sometimes be appropriate to ensure that opposing views are indicated in a single programme, where it is unlikely that the subject will be considered again in the near future or where the issues are of 'current or active controversy'. The impartiality clause only affects non-BBC broadcasting, although the BBC has undertaken to comply generally with the statutory duties placed on the IBA (replaced by the ITC).[30]

5 Under the current statutory scheme, political advertising, which includes advertising by a body whose objects are wholly or mainly of a political nature, must not be broadcast by a licensed service (ss 8(1)(a) and 92 of the Broadcasting Act 1990). The challenge of a sub-group of Amnesty International (a group campaigning on human rights abuses) to this ban was unsuccessful on the basis that a material proportion of its objects were political (see *R v Radio Authority ex p Bull and Another* (1997)).

6 The Office of Communications Act 2002 provides powers to create one super-regulator, OFCOM, who will replace the BSC and the ITC. Once the Communications Bill 2002 comes into force, it will determine OFCOM's functions in relation to the regulation of communications. OFCOM will have the responsibility for maintaining standards of impartiality. The BBC will retain its current role, but the public service element of the ITV companies will be subject to less prescriptive regulation.

7 The HRA may have some significant impact in this context. In particular, journalists, film-makers and groups such as Amnesty, whose advertising has been rejected,[31] can challenge media regulators, including, in future, OFCOM, directly, by invoking s 7(1)(a) of the HRA (above, pp 859 and 873–74). Decisions as to licensing,

---

28 G Robertson and A Nichol, *Media Law* (1999), p 484.
29 The function of the Radio Authority is similar in this respect to that of the ITC.
30 This undertaking is annexed to the corporation's licence agreement. The BBC operates under this agreement and also under the terms of its royal charter (see Cmnd 8233 and 8313 respectively).

political advertising, and adjudications regarding impartiality may be subjected thereby to a more intensive scrutiny. Assuming that the independent television companies are not public authorities, they can also bring such proceedings, as 'victims' under the HRA. Proceedings under s 7(1)(a) cannot be brought *against* the independent companies, but decisions of the public service broadcasters – the BBC and Channel 4[32] – as to programming policy etc can be challenged directly by invoking s 7(1)(a) of the HRA, so long as the person bringing the action satisfies the victim requirement under s 7(3) of the HRA. The use of s 7(1)(a) would mean that such decisions would be tested more directly against Convention standards than they have been by means of judicial review. Section 12 of the HRA is applicable. The application of the various Codes of Practice could also be challenged in such proceedings, including the new ones which will be promulgated by OFCOM. Provisions of such Codes could be struck down by the courts unless primary legislation prevented the removal of the incompatibility. Given that the detailed provisions are commonly contained in the Codes, this is a significant possibility. The principle of non-interference with political expression, except in exceptional circumstances, is well established under the Convention. The Strasbourg standard as regards political expression is very strict, as the Introduction to this chapter indicated. Thus reliance on Article 10 in these instances might well prove fruitful.

8   The decision in the Court of Appeal in *R (on the application of Pro-life Alliance) v British Broadcasting Corporation* [2002] 2 All ER 756, below, demonstrates that the courts are prepared to take a far more interventionist stance towards the decisions of broadcasters or media regulators than they were in the pre-HRA era. Not only are such decisions tested more directly against Convention standards than they could be by means of judicial review, the courts, depending on the context, are prepared to accord almost no deference to the media bodies as decision-makers. The degree of deference to be accorded will be determined by the nature of the expression in question: a higher degree will be accorded to the media bodies in respect of entertainment, while virtually no deference will be accorded in respect of political expression at election times. Note: the decision was overturned by the House of Lords (*R (on the Application of the Pro-life Alliance) v BBC* [2003] 2 All ER 977) on the basis that the court should not substitute its decision for that of the broadcaster, and the broadcaster had decided that the broadcast offended against the regulations on taste and decency. The application of such regulations was not found in itself to breach Article 10.)

The Pro-life Alliance v The British Broadcasting Corporation [2002] 2 All ER 756, CA

The Pro-life Alliance, the applicant, is a registered political party which opposes abortion. At the 1997 general election the applicant put up enough parliamentary candidates to qualify for a party election broadcast (PEB). The applicant submitted a video showing, *inter alia*, an abortion being carried out. The broadcasters refused to broadcast the video on the grounds that it offended against good taste and decency and would cause widespread offence. The applicant's application for permission to

---

31   In this instance the group – or a representative sub-group directly concerned with advertising – could be viewed as a 'victim' under s 7(3), HRA: see Chapter 1 of this part, p 873 for discussion of the term.

32   The BBC is clearly a public authority, while Channel 4 probably is: both bodies have a public function in respect of their public service remit which is especially significant in the case of the BBC. Channel 4's role is governed by statute – s 25 of the 1990 Act. See above, pp 871–72, on the meaning of 'public function' in s 6(3)(b) HRA.

seek judicial review was refused by Dyson J and by the Court of Appeal and its application to the European Court of Human Rights was declared inadmissible. At the 2001 General Election the applicant put up enough parliamentary candidates to qualify for a PEB in Wales. The applicant submitted a modified form of the video which it had submitted in 1997, which had been edited to remove the most distressing images but still showed aborted foetuses in a mutilated state. The broadcasters again refused to broadcast the video. The applicant applied for permission to seek judicial review. The application was dismissed by Scott-Baker J. Like Dyson J, Scott-Baker J held that the broadcasters' decision was not irrational. The applicant appealed.

Laws LJ:

I This case is about the censorship of political speech. . . .

29 This issue was framed by the appellant in such a way as to ask the question, whether the prohibition was 'necessary in a democratic society' (for the protection of the rights of others), which is, of course, the language of ECHR, Art. 10(2) . . . the term 'necessary in a democratic society' imports a test of proportionality into the court's judgment whether the interference complained of may be justified in light of any of the particular considerations set out in Article 10(2). It is also well recognised that where a public authority seeks to justify an interference with the right of free expression, its restriction of the right will not be regarded as proportionate unless it fulfils a 'pressing social need'. The English court is not a Strasbourg surrogate. The very difference between the international margin of appreciation and the municipal margin of discretion illustrates the confusion that would arise if the court so regarded itself. Our duty is to develop, by the common law's incremental method, a coherent and principled domestic law of human rights. In doing it, we are directed by the HRA (s 6) to insist on compliance by public authorities with the standards of the Convention, and to comply with them ourselves. We are given new powers and duties (HRA, ss 3 and 4) to see that that is done. In all this we are to take account of the Strasbourg cases (s 2, to which I have already referred).

34 . . . We are concerned with the protection of free expression in the context of political debate. In the rancour and asperity of a general election this duty, owed to the people, is surely at its highest.

35 This position is in my judgment wholly consistent with the domestic learning on freedom of expression. It has often been said that the core rights enshrined in the ECHR by and large reflect principles which the common law itself espouses. In R. v Central Independent Television plc [1994] 3 All ER 641 Hoffmann LJ, as he then was, said this at 651j–652b:

> The motives which impel judges to assume a power to balance freedom of speech against other interests are almost always understandable and humane on the facts of the particular case before them. . . . [P]ublication may cause needless pain, distress and damage to individuals or harm to other aspects of the public interest. But a freedom which is restricted to what judges think to be responsible or in the public interest is no freedom. Freedom means the right to publish things which government and judges, however well motivated, think should not be published. It means the right to say things which 'right-thinking people' regard as dangerous or irresponsible.

In ex p Simms [2000] AC 115 these observations of Lord Steyn at 126 are especially pertinent for the importance of political speech:

> Freedom of speech is the lifeblood of democracy. The free flow of information and ideas informs political debate. It is a safety valve: people are more ready to accept decisions that go against them if they can in principle seek to influence them. It acts as a brake on the abuse of power by public officials . . .

36 Supported by such authority as this I would assert that as a matter of domestic law the courts owe a special responsibility to the public as the constitutional guardian of the freedom of political debate. This responsibility is most acute at the time and in the context of a public election,

especially a general election. It has its origin in a deeper truth, which is that the courts are ultimately the trustees of our democracy's framework. I consider that this view is consonant with the common law's general recognition, apparent in recent years, of a category of fundamental or constitutional rights: see for example *Derbyshire County Council v Times Newspapers Ltd* [1993] AC 534, *Leech* [1994] QB 198, *Witham* [1998] QB 575, *Pierson v Secretary of State* [1998] AC 539, *Reynolds* [1999] 3 WLR 1010, and with respect perhaps especially *Simms* [2000] 2 AC 115 *per* Lord Hoffmann at 131. Freedom of expression is plainly such a constitutional right, and its enjoyment by an accredited political party in an election contest must call, if anything, for especially heightened protection. We are in any case long past the point when interference with fundamental rights by public authorities can be justified by a bare demonstration of rationality or reasonableness: see *Ex p Daly* [2001] 2 WLR 1622.

37 These considerations, with respect, give the lie to Mr Pannick's plea for deference to the decision-makers. If a producer were so insensitive as to authorise the inclusion of what is to be seen in the appellant's PEB video in an episode of a TV soap, the broadcasters would of course forbid its being shown and the courts would of course uphold them. That is at the extreme. There might be other more marginal situations, in which the courts would incline to defer to the broadcasters' judgment. Where the context is broadcast entertainment, I would accept without cavil that in the event of a legal challenge to a prohibition the courts should pay a very high degree of respect to the broadcasters' judgment, given the background of BA 1990, BA 1996, the BBC Agreement, the codes of guidance and the BSC adjudications. Where the context is day-to-day news reporting the broadcasters' margin of discretion may be somewhat more constrained but will remain very considerable. But the *milieu* we are concerned with in this case, the cockpit of a general election, is inside the veins and arteries of the democratic process. The broadcasters' views are entitled to be respected, but their force and weight are modest at best. But in this context the court's constitutional responsibility to protect political speech is over-arching. It amounts to a duty which lies on the court's shoulders to decide for itself whether this censorship was justified.

44 There may be instances, even in the context of a general election, in which political speech may justifiably be censored on grounds of taste or offensiveness. But in my judgment it would take a very extreme case, most likely involving factors, to which I have already referred, such as gratuitous sensationalism and dishonesty ... On the facts of this case the broadcasters have in my judgment failed altogether to give sufficient weight to the pressing imperative of free political expression. ... There is no recognition of the critical truth, the legal principle, that considerations of taste and decency cannot prevail over free speech by a political party at election time save wholly exceptionally.

The appeal was allowed.

RESTRAINING FREEDOM OF EXPRESSION TO PROTECT THE ADMINISTRATION OF JUSTICE

Introduction[33]

This section considers two interests which are frequently perceived as being in conflict: the interest in protecting the administration of justice and the interest in media freedom. Domestically, the interest in the administration of justice has been protected by the law of contempt. A number of aspects of contempt law are discussed below, including its use in curbing discussions and publicity in the media which might

---

33 General reading: G Robertson and A Nichol, *Media Law* (1999), Chapter 6; *Arlidge, Eady and Smith on Contempt*, 2nd edn (1999).

influence those involved in forthcoming proceedings, specific reporting restrictions, and requirements to disclose journalistic sources.

It should be pointed out that within UK law the protection of the administration of justice is viewed as a general societal concern rather than as a means of protecting an individual's right to a fair trial, although it may have that effect. Nevertheless, the fact that many aspects of the law of contempt can be seen as having as their *ultimate* rationale the protection of the right to fair trial leads to the conclusion that in so far as this other individual right is clearly at stake, free speech may be compromised to a certain extent. Such a conclusion would be in accord with the European Convention on Human Rights (ECHR), which guarantees both the right to free speech (Article 10) and the right to a fair trial (Article 6). Interferences with the guarantee of free speech under Article 10, as afforded further effect in domestic law under the HRA, may be justified where they have the legitimate aim of 'maintaining the authority and impartiality of the judiciary' under para 2. This phrase may be taken to cover the preservation of the integrity of the administration of justice, including the rights of litigants. Since contempt law has a role to play in preventing prejudice to proceedings or deterring the media from causing such prejudice, it may be viewed as a means of protecting Article 6 rights (see Part II Chapter 2, p 242), although the main responsibility for providing such protection falls on the trial judge.[34] Viewed as exceptions to Article 10, such rights fall within the rubric 'the rights of others' in para 2, as well as that of 'maintaining the authority of the judiciary'. Contempt law therefore comes into conflict with free expression, either on the basis of protecting general societal interests and/or other individual rights.

Publications prejudicing particular criminal or civil proceedings

Contempt of court at common law curtailed the freedom of the media to discuss and report on issues arising from criminal or civil proceedings on the basis that those proceedings might suffer prejudice. The elements of common law contempt consisted of the creation of a real risk of prejudice (the *actus reus*) and an intention to publish. The period during which the risk in question might arise was known as the *sub judice* period. In *R v Savundranayagan and Walker* [1968] 1 WLR 1761, it was found that the starting point of this period occurred when the proceedings were 'imminent'.

Attorney-General v Times Newspapers Ltd [1973] 3 All ER 54, 65, 73, 74

The decision concerned an article discussing the Thalidomide tragedy, and in particular the legal conflict between Distillers and the parents of the Thalidomide children. The House of Lords considered that the article prejudged the legal issues and placed pressure on Distillers to forego their legal rights and settle the dispute by paying full compensation to the children.

Lord Reid: ... There is ample authority for the proposition that issues must not be prejudged in a manner likely to affect the minds of those who may later be witnesses or jurors. But very little has been said about the wider proposition that trial by newspaper is intrinsically objectionable. ... I think that anything in the nature of prejudgment of a case or of specific issues in it is objectionable not only because of its possible effect on that particular case but also because of its side effects which may be far reaching. Responsible 'mass media' will do their best to be fair, but there will also

---

34 See the comments of Simon Brown LJ regarding the differing roles of the judge in contempt proceedings and at trial: *Attorney-General v Birmingham Post and Mail Ltd* [1998] 4 All ER 49. But cf the findings in *Attorney-General v Guardian Newspapers* [1999] EMLR 904.

be ill-informed, slapdash or prejudiced attempts to influence the public. If people are led to think that it is easy to find the truth, disrespect for the processes of the law could follow and, if mass media are allowed to judge, unpopular people and unpopular causes will fare very badly. ... I do not think that the freedom of the press would suffer, and I think that the law would be clearer and easier to apply in practice if it is made a general rule that it is not permissible to prejudge issues in pending cases ...

My Lords, to hold a party up to public obloquy for exercising his constitutional right to have recourse to a court of law for the ascertainment and enforcement of his legal rights and obligations is calculated to prejudice the first requirement for the due administration of justice: the unhindered access of all citizens to the established courts of law. Similarly, 'trial by newspaper', ie, public discussion or comment on the merits of a dispute which has been submitted to a court of law or on the alleged facts of the dispute before they have been found by the court on the evidence adduced before it, is calculated to prejudice the third requirement: that parties to litigation should be able to rely on there being no usurpation by any other person of the function of that court to decide their dispute according to law. ...

I agree with all your lordships that the publication of the article proposed to be published by the *Sunday Times* in respect of which an injunction is sought by the Attorney General would fall within this latter category of conduct. As has already been sufficiently pointed out, it discussed prejudicially the facts and merits of Distillers' defence to the charge of negligence brought against them in the actions before these have been determined by the court or the actions disposed of by settlement.

Notes

1   This ruling created the prejudgment test, which seemed to be wider than the test of real risk of prejudice, in that little risk to proceedings might be shown, but it might still be possible to assert that they had been prejudged. This test had a potentially grave effect on freedom of speech because it was very difficult to draw the line between legitimate discussion in the media of issues of possible relevance in civil or criminal actions and prejudgment.

2   The decision of the House of Lords was found to breach Article 10 of the ECHR.

Sunday Times v United Kingdom Series A, No 30; (1980) 2 EHRR 245, 275–81

The European Court of Human Rights found that the injunction clearly infringed freedom of speech under Article 10(1); the question was whether one of the exceptions within Article 10(2) could be invoked.

[The article in question subjects] Distillers to public and prejudicial discussion of the merits of their case, such exposure being objectionable as it inhibits suitors generally from having recourse to the courts;

- it would subject Distillers to pressure and to the prejudices of prejudgment of the issues in the litigation, and the law of contempt was designed to prevent interference with recourse to the courts;

- prejudgment by the press would have led inevitably in this case to replies by the parties, thereby creating the danger of a 'trial by newspaper' incompatible with the proper administration of justice;

- the courts owe it to the parties to protect them from the prejudices of prejudgment which involves their having to participate in the flurries of pre-trial publicity.

The Court regards all these various reasons as falling within the aim of maintaining the 'authority ... of the judiciary' as interpreted by the court in the second paragraph of Article 10.

Accordingly, the interference with the applicants' freedom of expression had an aim that is legitimate under Article 10(2).

Was the interference 'necessary in a democratic society' for maintaining the authority of the judiciary?

The Court has noted that, whilst the adjective 'necessary', within the meaning of Article 10(2), is not synonymous with 'indispensable', neither has it the flexibility of such expressions as 'admissible', 'ordinary', 'useful', 'reasonable' or 'desirable' and that it implies the existence of a 'pressing social need' [Handyside v UK Series A No 24; (1976) 1 EHRR 737, para 48].

... the Court has underlined that the initial responsibility for securing the rights and freedoms enshrined in the Convention lies with the individual contracting States. Accordingly, 'Article 10(2) leaves to the contracting states a margin of appreciation. This margin is given both to the domestic legislator ... and to the bodies, judicial amongst others, that are called upon to interpret and apply the laws in force' [ibid].

Nevertheless, Article 10(2) does not give the contracting states an unlimited power of appreciation. 'The Court ... is empowered to give the final ruling on whether a 'restriction'... is reconcilable with freedom of expression as protected by Article 10. The domestic margin of appreciation thus goes hand in hand with a European supervision' which 'covers not only the basic legislation but also the decision applying it, even one given by an independent court' [ibid, at p 23, para 49].

Again, the scope of the domestic power of appreciation is not identical as regards each of the aims listed in Article 10(2). The Handyside case concerned the 'protection of morals'. The view taken by the contracting states of the 'requirements of morals', observed the Court, 'varies from time to time and from place to place, especially in our era', and 'state authorities are in principle in a better position than the international judge to give an opinion on the exact content of these requirements' [ibid, p 22, para 48]. Precisely the same cannot be said of the far more objective notion of the 'authority' of the judiciary. The domestic law and practice of the contracting states reveal a fairly substantial measure of common ground in this area. This is reflected in a number of provisions of the Convention, including Article 6, which have no equivalent as far as 'morals' are concerned. Accordingly, here a more extensive European supervision corresponds to a less discretionary power of appreciation.

The draft article was nonetheless the principal subject-matter of the injunction. It must therefore be ascertained in the first place whether the domestic courts' views as to the article's potential effects were relevant in terms of the maintenance of the 'authority of the judiciary'.

One of the reasons relied on was the pressure which the article would have brought to bear on Distillers to settle the actions out of court on better terms. However, even in 1972, publication of the article would probably not have added much to the pressure already on Distillers. ... The speeches in the House of Lords emphasised above all the concern that the processes of the law may be brought into disrespect and the functions of the courts usurped either if the public is led to form an opinion on the subject-matter of litigation before adjudication by the courts or if the parties to litigation have to undergo 'trial by newspaper'. Such concern is in itself 'relevant' to the maintenance of the 'authority of the judiciary'...

Nevertheless, the proposed Sunday Times article was couched in moderate terms and did not present just one side of the evidence or claim that there was only one possible result at which a court could arrive ... Accordingly, even to the extent that the article might have led some readers to form an opinion on the negligence issue, this would not have had adverse consequences for the 'authority of the judiciary', especially since, as noted above, there had been a nationwide campaign in the meantime.

64 At the time when the injunction was originally granted and at the time of its restoration, the Thalidomide case was at the stage of settlement negotiations. The applicants concur with the

Court of Appeal's view that the case was 'dormant' and the majority of the Commission considers it unlikely that there would have been a trial of the issue of negligence.

As the Court remarked in its *Handyside* judgment, freedom of expression constitutes one of the essential foundations of a democratic society; subject to paragraph 2 of Article 10, it is applicable not only to information or ideas that are favourably received or regarded as inoffensive or as a matter of indifference, but also to those that offend, shock or disturb the state or any sector of the population [*ibid*, at p 23, para 49]. As the Court has already observed, Article 10 guarantees not only the freedom of the press to inform the public but also the right of the public to be properly informed (see para 65 above). In the present case, the families of numerous victims of the tragedy, who were unaware of the legal difficulties involved, had a vital interest in knowing all the underlying facts and the various possible solutions. They could be deprived of this information, which was crucially important for them, only if it appeared absolutely certain that its diffusion would have presented a threat to the 'authority of the judiciary'.

Notes

1 In the light of these findings, the court ruled that the injunction was not 'necessary in a democratic society'. Thus, the exception under Article 10(2) could not apply: Article 10 had been breached.

2 The UK government responded to this decision in the enactment of the Contempt of Court Act 1981,[35] which was supposed to take account of the ruling of the European Court of Human Rights and was also influenced to an extent by the proposals of the Phillimore Committee.[36]

Contempt of Court Act 1981

Strict liability

1. In this Act 'the strict liability rule' means the rule of law whereby conduct may be treated as a contempt of court as tending to interfere with the course of justice in particular legal proceedings regardless of intent to do so.

2.–(1) The strict liability rule applies only in relation to publications ...

   (2) The strict liability rule applies only to a publication which creates a substantial risk that the course of justice in the proceedings in question will be seriously impeded or prejudiced.

   (3) The strict liability rule applies to a publication only if the proceedings in question are active within the meaning of this section at the time of the publication.

   (4) Schedule 1 applies for determining the times at which proceedings are to be treated as active within the meaning of this section.

3.–(1) A person is not guilty of contempt of court under the strict liability rule as the publisher of any matter to which that rule applies if at the time of publication (having taken all reasonable care) he does not know and has to reason to suspect that relevant proceedings are active.

   (2) A person is not guilty of contempt of court under the strict liability rule as the distributor of a publication containing any such matter if at the time of distribution (having taken all reasonable care) he does not know that it contains such matter and has no reason to suspect that it is likely to do so.

   (3) The burden of proof of any fact tending to establish a defence afforded by this section to any person lies upon that person ...

---

35 See the Green Paper, Cmnd 7145 (1978).
36 See Report of the Committee on Contempt of Court, Cmnd 5794 (1974).

4.–(1) Subject to this section a person is not guilty of contempt of court under the strict liability rule in respect of a fair and accurate report of legal proceedings held in public, published contemporaneously and in good faith.

(2) In any such proceedings the court may, where it appears to be necessary for avoiding a substantial risk of prejudice to the administration of justice in those proceedings, or in any other proceedings pending or imminent, order that the publication of any report of the proceedings, or any part of the proceedings, be postponed for such period as the court thinks necessary for that purpose. . . .

5. A publication made as or as part of a discussion in good faith of public affairs or other matters of general public interest is not to be treated as a contempt of court under the strict liability rule if the risk of impediment or prejudice to particular legal proceedings is merely incidental to the discussion.

6. Nothing in the foregoing provisions of this Act—

. . . (c) restricts liability for contempt of court in respect of conduct intended to impede or prejudice the administration of justice.

Schedule 1
Times when proceedings are active for purposes of section 2

Criminal proceedings

3. Subject to the following provisions of this Schedule, criminal proceedings are active from the relevant initial step specified in paragraph 4 until concluded as described in paragraph 5.

4. The initial steps of criminal proceedings are—

(a) arrest without warrant;

(b) the issue, or in Scotland the grant, of a warrant for arrest;

(c) the issue of a summons to appear, or in Scotland the grant of a warrant to cite;

(d) the service of an indictment or other document specifying the charge . . .

5. Criminal proceedings are concluded–

(a) by acquittal or, as the case may be, by sentence;

(b) by any other verdict, finding, order or decision which puts an end to the proceedings;

(c) by discontinuance or by operation of law.

. . .

Other proceedings at first instance

12. Proceedings other than criminal proceedings and appellate proceedings are active from the time when arrangements for the hearing are made or, if no such arrangements are previously made, from the time the bearing begins, until the proceedings are disposed of or discontinued or withdrawn. . . .

Appellate proceedings

15. Appellate proceedings are active from the time when they are commenced–

(a) by application for leave to appeal or apply for review, or by notice of such an application;

(b) by notice of appeal or of application for review;

(c) by other originating process, until disposed of or abandoned, discontinued or withdrawn.

Attorney-General v English **[1983] 1 AC 116; [1982] 2 All ER 903, 914, 919–20, HL**

This judgment is the leading case on a number of aspects of the use of the 1981 Act.

Lord Diplock: My Lords, this is an appeal brought by the editor and publishers of the *Daily Mail* ..., holding them to be guilty of contempt of court by publishing an article entitled 'The vision of life that wins my vote' on 15 October 1980, which was published the morning of the third day of the trial in the Crown Court at Leicester of a well-known paediatrician, Dr Arthur, on a charge of murdering a three-day-old mongoloid baby boy.

... Next for consideration is the concatenation in the subsection [s 2(2)] of the adjective 'substantial' and the adverb 'seriously', the former to describe the degree of risk, the latter to describe the degree of impediment or prejudice to the course of justice. ... In combination I take the two words to be intended to exclude a risk that is only remote.

My Lords, that Mr Malcolm Muggeridge's article was capable of prejudicing the jury against Dr Arthur at the early stage of his trial when it was published seems to me to be clear. It suggested that it was a common practice among paediatricians to do that which Dr Arthur was charged with having done, because they thought that it was justifiable in the interests of humanity even though it was against the law. ... The judge thought at that stage of the trial that the risk was substantial, not remote. So, too, looking at the matter in retrospect, did the Divisional Court despite the fact that the risk had not turned into an actuality since Dr Arthur had by then been acquitted. For my part I am not prepared to dissent from this evaluation. I consider that the publication of the article on the third day of what was to prove a lengthy trial satisfied the criterion for which s 2(2) of the 1981 Act provides.

Having found that s 2(2) was satisfied Lord Diplock went on to consider s 5.

The article, however, fell also within the category dealt with in s 5. It was made, in undisputed good faith, as a discussion in itself of public affairs, viz Mrs Carr's candidature as an independent 'pro-life' candidate in the North West Croydon by-election ... It was also part of a wider discussion on a matter of general public interest that had been proceeding intermittently over the last three months, on the moral justification of mercy killing and in particular of allowing newly born hopelessly handicapped babies to die. So it was for the Attorney General to show that the risk of prejudice to the fair trial of Dr Arthur, which I agree was created by the publication of the article at the stage the trial had reached when it was published, was not 'merely incidental' to the discussion of the matter with which the article dealt.

My lords, the article that is the subject of the instant case appears to me to be in nearly all respects the antithesis of the article which this House (pace a majority of the judges of the European Court of Human Rights) held to be a contempt of court in *A-G v Times Newspapers Ltd* [1973] 3 All ER 54, [1974] AC 273. There the whole subject of the article was the pending civil actions against the Distillers Co arising out of their having placed on the market the new drug Thalidomide, and the whole purpose of it was to put pressure on that company in the lawful conduct of their defence in those actions. In the instant case, in contrast, there is in the article no mention at all of Dr Arthur's trial. It may well be that many readers of the *Daily Mail* who saw the article and had read also the previous day's report of Dr Arthur's trial, and certainly if they were members of the jury at that trial, would think 'That is the sort of thing that Dr Arthur is being tried for; it appears to be something that quite a lot of doctors do'. But the risk of their thinking that and allowing it to prejudice their minds in favour of finding him guilty on evidence that did not justify such a finding seems to me to be properly described in ordinary English language as 'merely incidental' to any meaningful discussion of Mrs Carr's election policy as a pro-life candidate in the by-election due to be held before Dr Arthur's trial was likely to be concluded, or to any meaningful discussion of the wider matters of general public interest involved in the current controversy as to the justification of mercy killing. To hold otherwise would have prevented Mrs Carr from putting forward and obtaining publicity for what was a main plank in her election programme and would have stifled all discussion in the press on the wider controversy about mercy killing from the time that Dr Arthur was charged in the magistrates' court in February 1981 until the date of his acquittal at the beginning of November of that year; for those are the dates between which under s 2(3) and Schedule 1, the legal proceedings against Dr Arthur would be 'active' and so attract the strict liability rule.

Such gagging of *bona fide* public discussion in the press of controversial matters of general public interest, merely because there are in existence contemporaneous legal proceedings in which some particular instance of those controversial matters may be in issue, is what s 5 of the Contempt of Court Act 1981 was in my view intended to prevent. I would allow this appeal.

The other four Law Lords agreed.

Attorney-General v News Group Newspapers [1986] 3 WLR 365, 375, CA

This judgment gives helpful guidance as to the meaning of s 2(2) of the 1981 Act.

Sir John Donaldson MR: ... [T]here has to be some risk that the proceedings in question will be affected at all. Second, there has to be a prospect that, if affected, the effect will be serious. The two limbs of the test can overlap, but they can be quite separate. I accept Mr Laws' submission that 'substantial' as a qualification of 'risk' does not have the meaning of 'weighty,' but rather means 'not insubstantial' or 'not minimal.' The 'risk' part of the test will usually be of importance in the context of the width of the publication. To declare in a speech at a public meeting in Cornwall that a man about to be tried in Durham is guilty of the offence charged and has many previous convictions for the same offence may well carry no substantial risk of affecting his trial, but, if it occurred, the prejudice would be most serious. By contrast, a nationwide television broadcast at peak viewing time of some far more innocuous statement would certainly involve a substantial risk of having some effect on a trial anywhere in the country and the sole effective question would arise under the 'seriousness' limb of the test. Proximity in time between the publication and the proceedings would probably have a greater bearing on the risk limb than on the seriousness limb, but could go to both.

Notes

1   The 1981 Act modified the common law without bringing about radical change. It introduced various liberalising elements but it was intended, as a number of commentators observed, to maintain the stance of the ultimate supremacy of the administration of justice over freedom of speech, while moving the balance further towards freedom of speech.[37] In particular it introduced stricter time limits, a more precise test for the *actus reus*, as proposed by the Phillimore Committee, and under s 5 allowed some publications dealing with matters of public interest to escape liability, even though a risk of prejudice to proceedings had been created.

2   The test under s 2(2) has also been considered in quite a large number of cases. The ruling in *Attorney-General v News Group Newspapers* made it clear that the proximity of the article to the trial will be relevant to the question of risk. The Court of Appeal held that a gap of 10 months between the two could not create the substantial risk in question because the jury would be likely to have forgotten the article by the time the trial came on. Even if the article were faintly recollected at the time of the trial it might be likely to have little impact. In *Attorney-General v Independent TV News and Others* [1995] 2 All ER 370, TV news and certain newspapers published the fact that a defendant in a forthcoming murder trial was a convicted IRA terrorist who had escaped from jail where he was serving a life sentence for murder. It was found that s 2(2) was not satisfied since the trial was not expected to take place for nine months, there had only been one offending news item and there had been limited circulation of only one edition of the offending newspaper items. The risk of prejudice was found to be too small to be termed substantial. A

---

37   For comment on the 1981 Act, see CJ Miller [1982] Crim LR 71; JC Smith [1982] Crim LR 744.

publication during the trial is clearly most likely to create a risk. If the case will be very much in the public eye due to the persons or issues involved (as was the case in respect of the article in *Hislop and Pressdram* concerning Sonia Sutcliffe, wife of the Yorkshire Ripper) the article is more likely to make an impact, although the mere fact that the issue attracts a great deal of media coverage will not mean that jurors will be unable to put it from their minds.

3   Serious prejudice can arise in various ways. In *Attorney-General v Morgan* [1998] EMLR 294, an article in *The News of the World* referred to the criminal record of one of the defendants and to the criminal background of both defendants. These references were given great prominence and were repeated throughout the article. Despite the lapse of time before the trial – eight months – a substantial risk of serious prejudice was found to have been created. However, in *Attorney-General v Guardian Newspapers* [1992] 3 All ER 38, the publication of the fact that one unidentified defendant out of six in a Manchester trial was also awaiting trial elsewhere was not found to satisfy s 2(2) since it was thought that it would not cause a juror of ordinary good sense to be biased against the defendant.

4   *Attorney-General v English*, above, is the leading case on s 5 and is generally considered to provide a good example of the kind of case for which s 5 was framed.[38] Lord Diplock's ruling was seen as giving a liberal interpretation to s 5. As he points out, a narrower interpretation of s 5 would have meant that all debate in the media on the topic of mercy killing would have been prevented for almost a year – the time during which the proceedings in Dr Arthur's case were active from charge to acquittal. (It may be noted that Dr Arthur was acquitted; therefore the article presumably did not influence the jurors against him. That fact, however, did not preclude a finding that there was a substantial risk of serious prejudice to his trial.) The proper interpretation of s 5 has also been considered in the following cases: *Attorney-General v Times Newspaper* (1983) *The Times*, 12 February; *Attorney-General v Hislop* [1991] 1 QB 514; *Daily Express* case (1981) *The Times*, 19 December. In *Attorney-General v TVS Television; Attorney-General v HW Southey and Sons* (1989) *The Times*, 7 July, it was determined that a TVS programme concerned with the possibility that Rachmanism had arisen in the south of England but focused on landlords in Reading, which coincided with the charging of a Reading landlord with conspiring to defraud the DHSS, could not create a merely incidental risk.

5   It is arguable that strict liability contempt does not fully meet the requirements of Article 10, afforded further effect in domestic law under the HRA, since matters of great public interest cannot be published where they create a non-incidental risk of serious prejudice to proceedings. In other words, despite the fact that the 1981 Act was introduced to meet Convention requirements, it may fail to do so when tested against those requirements under the HRA. One possible reform would be to interpret s 5 broadly under s 3 of the HRA so as to allow for discussion of matters of great public interest, including those focusing mainly or partly on the particular case, even where the risk of prejudice can hardly be described as 'incidental'.

Questions
1   Is the boundary between creation of a risk of prejudice which is merely incidental to a discussion and creation of a risk which is not so incidental (that is, it is crucial or fairly crucial to the discussion) reasonably clear?

---

38   See, eg, G Zellick [1982] PL 343.

2   Bearing in mind the interpretation of s 5 favoured in *Attorney-General v English*, would an article similar to that at issue in the *Sunday Times* case fall within s 5 if published today (within the active period)?

Orders restricting reporting of court proceedings

There are a large number of specific statutory restrictions on reporting of trials. This section deals only with two of them. Section 4(2) of the 1981 Act provides that during any legal proceeding held in public a judge may make an order postponing reporting of the proceedings if such action 'appears necessary for avoiding a substantial risk of prejudice to the administration of justice in those proceedings', thus creating an exception to s 4(1).[39] This might typically involve the reporting of matters which the defence wished to argue should be ruled inadmissible. A right of appeal against such orders in relation to trials on indictment was created by s 159 of the Criminal Justice Act 1988 in order to take account of a challenge under Article 10 at Strasbourg.[40] The position of the media when a s 4(2) order is made in respect of reporting a summary trial is less clear. However, it was established in *R v Clerkenwell Metropolitan Stipendiary Magistrate ex p The Telegraph and Others* (1993) that in such circumstances the media have a right to be heard and must be allowed to put forward the case for discharging the order.

Section 11 of the 1981 Act allows a court, which has power to do so, to make an order prohibiting publication of names or other matters if this appears necessary 'for the purpose for which it was so withheld'. Thus, s 11 does not itself confer such a power and therefore refers to other statutes[41] and to the imprecise common law powers. The leading authority is the House of Lords' decision in *Attorney-General v Leveller Magazine Ltd* [1979] AC 440; [1979] 2 WLR 247.[42]

Attorney-General v Leveller Magazine Ltd [1979] AC 440; [1979] 2 WLR 247, 272–73, HL

Three newspapers published the name of a witness who had been allowed to give evidence as Colonel B for security reasons. The newspapers were convicted of contempt but the House of Lords allowed their appeal.

Lord Scarman: ... the nature of the criminal offence of contempt ... is interference, with knowledge of the court's proceedings, with the course of administration of justice ... It was for this reason, no doubt, that Lord Widgery CJ in this case stressed the element of 'flouting' the authority of the court. ... In the present case the examining justices took a course which was a substitute for sitting in private ... But since the common law power to sit in private arises only if the administration of justice be threatened, the third question becomes one of fact. What was the reason for the justices' ruling? If it was to avert an interference with the administration of justice, was there material upon which the ruling could reasonably be based? The third question cannot therefore be answered without considering the facts. Here I find myself in a state of doubt.

---

39 For comment on s 4 of the 1981 Act, see C Walker, I Cram and D Brogarth (1992) 55 MLR 647.
40 The journalist, Crook, attempted to challenge a s 11 anonymity order: *R v Central Criminal Court ex p Crook* (1984) *The Times*, 8 November. When the challenge failed, Crook took the case to Strasbourg.
41 A number of statutory provisions impose restrictions such as allowing certain persons concerned in a case to remain anonymous. This is provided for in relation to complainants in rape cases under s 4 of the Sexual Offences (Amendment) Act 1976, as amended, and for children under s 39(1) of the Children and Young Persons Act 1933.
42 For comment on s 11 of the 1981 Act, see Walker, Cram and Brogarth, *op cit*.

I do not think that the Attorney General has discharged the burden of proof upon him. . . . The justices clearly had regard to national security, but did they understand that, in exercising their common law power, the national security risk must be shown also to be a risk to the administration of justice and assess the degree of the latter risk? Did they address themselves to that question at all? It cannot be said with any certainty that they did, or that the Crown adduced any material, by way of evidence or otherwise, to show that the national security issue was such that publication of the colonel's name would endanger the due administration of justice.

Notes
1 Section 11 of the 1981 Act allows a departure from the principles of free speech and of open justice since it allows a court to prohibit reporting of certain matters. However, as the *Leveller* decision makes clear, the fundamental importance of open justice will be outweighed only if very clear detriment to the general public interest would be likely to flow from publication of the matters in question.[43]

2 The interest in open justice is recognised under s 4(1) of the 1981 Act, which creates an exception to the strict liability rule, although under s 4(2) a judge may make an order postponing reporting of the proceedings in order to protect the administration of justice. The following rulings have suggested that s 4(2) should be used sparingly: *R v Horsham Magistrates ex p Farquharson and Another* [1982] QB 762; *R v Clerkenwell Metropolitan Stipendiary Magistrate ex p the Telegraph and Others* (1993); *Re Central Independent Television plc and Others* [1991] 1 All ER 347.

Intentionally prejudicing proceedings: common law contempt

Section 6(c) of the 1981 Act preserves liability for contempt at common law if intention to prejudice the administration of justice can be shown. 'Prejudice (to) the administration of justice' clearly includes prejudice to particular proceedings. Once the requirement of intent is satisfied it is easier to establish contempt at common law rather than under the Act, as it is only necessary to show at common law 'a real risk of prejudice', proceedings need only be 'imminent', not 'active', and there is no provision protecting free speech equivalent to that under s 5.

Attorney-General v Times Newspapers and Another [1992] 1 AC 191; [1991] 2 WLR 994, 1000, 1003 and 1004[44]

As indicated above, in 1986 *The Guardian* and *The Observer* published reports which included some *Spycatcher* material and the Attorney-General obtained temporary *ex parte* injunctions preventing them from further disclosure of such material.[45] While the temporary injunctions were in force the *Independent* and two other papers published material covered by them. The question arose whether such actions could amount to common law contempt. In *Attorney-General v Newspaper Publishing plc* (1990) *The Times*, 28 February, the Court of Appeal found that the respondents' publications could amount to a contempt of court and remitted the case for trial. Just before that ruling the *Sunday Times* had published extracts from *Spycatcher*. The Attorney-General brought proceedings for contempt against the publishers and editors of the *Sunday Times*. At first instance it was found that the publishers and editors of the *Independent* and the *Sunday Times* had been guilty of contempt, and that finding was confirmed by the

---

43 See also *R v Dover Justices ex p Dover District Council and Wells* [1992] Crim LR 371.
44 For comment, see J Laws (1990) 43 CLP 99.
45 For discussion of this branch of the litigation, see pp 911–18, above.

Court of Appeal. Times Newspapers appealed to the House of Lords. The only matter still at issue was whether the appellants had committed the *actus reus* of common law contempt.

Lord Brandon of Oakbrook: It is, in my opinion, of the utmost importance to formulate with precision the question which falls to be decided in this appeal. For the purpose of such formulation it is necessary to assume a situation in which one person, B, is a party to an action brought against him by another person, A, and the court grants A an injunction restraining B from doing certain acts. ... The question for decision is whether, in the situation assumed, it is a contempt of court for C, with the intention of impeding or prejudicing the administration of justice by the court in the action between A and B, himself to do the acts which the injunction restrains B from committing ...

It remains to consider in what circumstances conduct by C, in knowingly doing acts which would, if done by B, be a breach of an injunction against him, is such as to impede or interfere with the administration of justice by the court in the action between A and B.

I do not think that it would be wise, even if it were possible, to try to give an exhaustive answer to that question. A principal example, however, of circumstances which will have that effect is where the subject matter of the action is such that, if it is destroyed in whole or in part before the trial of the action, the purpose of the trial will be wholly or partly nullified.

The present case presents a similar situation. The claims of the Attorney General in the confidentiality actions were for permanent injunctions restraining the defendants from publishing what may conveniently be called *Spycatcher* material. The purpose of the Millett injunctions was to prevent the publication of any such material pending the trial of the confidentiality actions. The consequence of the publication of *Spycatcher* material by the publishers and editor of the *Sunday Times* before the trial of the confidentiality actions was to nullify, in part at least, the purpose of such trial, because it put into the public domain part of the material which it was claimed by the Attorney General in the confidentiality actions ought to remain confidential. It follows that the conduct of the publishers and editor of the *Sunday Times* constituted the *actus reus* of impeding or interfering with the administration of justice by the court in the confidentiality actions. *Mens rea* in respect of such conduct having been conceded by Mr Lester, both the necessary ingredients of contempt of court were present ... In the result I would affirm the judgment of the Court of Appeal and dismiss the appeal. [The other four Law Lords concurred.]

Notes

1   Liability can be established at common law in instances when it might also be established under the 1981 Act as occurred in *Attorney-General v Hislop* [1991] 1 QB 514, and in instances in which the Act will not apply because proceedings are inactive. The *actus reus* of common law contempt will be satisfied by a publication which creates a real risk of prejudice to the administration of justice (*Thompson Newspapers* (1968)). There may be a number of different methods of fulfilling this test as *Hislop* demonstrated. In *Attorney-General v Times Newspapers*, extracted above, the House of Lords found that the test may be fulfilled in certain circumstances if part of the media frustrates a court order against another part. This decision affirmed the principle that, once an interlocutory injunction has been obtained restraining one organ of the media from publication of allegedly confidential material, the rest of the media may be in contempt if they publish that material, even if their intention in doing so is to bring alleged iniquity to public attention. The decision thus created an inroad into the general principle that a court order should only affect the party to which it is directed, as only that party will have a chance to argue that the making of the order would be wrong.

2   From the Court of Appeal ruling in the *Spycatcher* case, it is clear that the *mens rea* for common law contempt is specific intent and therefore it cannot include

recklessness. The test may be summed up as follows: did the defendant either wish to prejudice proceedings or foresee that such prejudice was a virtually inevitable consequence of publishing the material in question? This test is based on the meaning of intent arising from rulings on the *mens rea* for murder from *R v Hancock and Shankland* [1986] AC 455, *R v Nedrick* [1986] 1 WLR 1025 and *R v Woollin* [1999] AC 82.

3   At common law the *sub judice* period began when proceedings could be said to be imminent (*R v Savundranayagan*). However, it may not always be necessary to establish imminence. In *Attorney-General v Newsgroup Newspapers plc* [1988] 2 All ER 906, it was held *obiter* that, where it is established that the defendant intended to prejudice proceedings, it is not necessary to show that proceedings are imminent. This was endorsed, *obiter*, in one of the rulings on imminence in *Attorney-General v Sport* [1992] 1 All ER 503.

4   The HRA may have a much greater effect on this form of contempt than on strict liability contempt. Development of a form of 'public interest defence' at common law is possible through the application of the Article 10(2) test under the HRA, assuming that the common law continues to have a role. The imprecision of the common law as regards the *sub judice* period may mean that it cannot be viewed as being 'prescribed by law'. If the current test was replaced by the 'active' test, the role of common law contempt, such as it is, might almost disappear. It should be noted that the use of the imminence test could allow the s 3 'ignorance' test to be circumvented.

Protection for journalistic sources

The protection of sources is clearly vital to the role of journalists. If sources do not believe that their identity will be protected they will not normally contact journalists and therefore the most potent source of information, that of a person who is in some sense an 'insider', will be denied to them. If sources are afraid to come forward the result will be that the public will not be informed on matters which are frequently of grave public interest.

Section 10 of the 1981 Act provides: '... no court may require a person to disclose ... the source of information contained in a publication for which he is responsible, unless it be established to the satisfaction of the court that disclosure is necessary in the interests of justice or national security or for the prevention of disorder or crime.'[46]

Section 10 creates a presumption in favour of journalists who wish to protect their sources which is, however, subject to four wide exceptions. The courts' interpretation of the exceptions has, it is argued, undermined the protection s 10 could have afforded to journalistic sources. It was found in *Secretary of State for Defence v Guardian Newspapers* [1985] AC 339 that disclosure of the identity of the source would only be ordered where this was necessary in order to identify him or her; if other means of identification were reasonably readily available they should be used. On the other hand, this did not mean that all other means of enquiry which might reveal the identity of the source must be exhausted before disclosure would be ordered. A civil servant who considered that Parliament was being misled as regards the arrival of cruise missiles in Britain, sent a photocopy of a memorandum regarding the timing to *The Guardian*. The Secretary of State wished to discover the identity of the

---

46   For comment on s 10, see T Allan [1991] CLJ 131.

civil servant and sought the return of the photocopy since it would reveal the identity. The Secretary of State, the plaintiff, claimed that the national security exception under s 10 applied on the basis that the fact that a secret document with restricted circulation relating to defence had come into the hands of a national newspaper was of great significance in relation to the maintenance of national security. The majority in the House of Lords accepted this, Lord Bridge stating that any threat to national security ought to be eliminated by the most effective and speedy means possible. The identity of the source was duly discovered when the photocopy was returned and she was prosecuted. The majority therefore took the traditional stance of failing to afford a full scrutiny to imprecise claims of a threat to national security made by the executive.

X Ltd v Morgan-Grampian Ltd [1990] 2 All ER 1, 6–10

A confidential plan was stolen from the plaintiffs, a company named Tetra; information apparently from the plan was given by an unidentified source by telephone to William Goodwin, a journalist. The plaintiffs applied for an order requiring Goodwin to disclose the source and sought discovery of his notes of the phone conversation in order to discover his or her identity. The House of Lords had to consider the application of s 10 to these facts. Lord Bridge, with whom the other Law Lords unanimously agreed, found that the interest of the plaintiffs in identifying the source outweighed the interests of the journalist in protecting it. Goodwin refused to reveal the identity of the source and was fined £5,000 for refusing to obey the court's order.

Lord Bridge: The courts have always recognised an important public interest in the free flow of information.

It has been accepted in this case at all levels that [s 10 of the 1981 Act] applies to the circumstances of the instant case ... It is also now clearly established that the section is to be given a wide, rather than a narrow, construction in the sense that the restriction on disclosure applies not only to direct orders to disclose the identity of a source but also to any order for disclosure of material which will indirectly identify the source, and applies, notwithstanding that the enforcement of the restriction may operate to defeat rights of property vested in the party who seeks to obtain that material: see *Secretary of State for Defence v Guardian Newspapers Ltd* [1984] 1 All ER 453 at 459, [1984] Ch 156 at 166–67 per Griffiths LJ; [1984] 3 All ER 601 at 607, [1985] AC 339 at 349–50 per Lord Diplock. As a statement of the rationale underlying this wide construction I cannot do better than quote from the passage in the judgment of Griffiths LJ to which I have referred, where he said:

> The press have always attached the greatest importance to their ability to protect their sources of information. If they are not able to do so, they believe that many of their sources would dry up and this would seriously interfere with their effectiveness. It is in the interests of us all that we should have a truly effective press, and it seems to me that Parliament by enacting s 10 has clearly recognised the importance that attaches to the ability of the press to protect their sources ... I can see no harm in giving a wide construction to the opening words of the section because by the latter part of the section the court is given ample powers to order the source to be revealed where in the circumstances of a particular case the wider public interest makes it necessary to do so.

It follows then that, whenever disclosure is sought, as here, of a document which will disclose the identity of a source within the ambit of s 10, the statutory restriction operates unless the party seeking disclosure can satisfy the court that 'disclosure is necessary' in the interests of one of the four matters of public concern that are listed in the section ... [A judge] starts with the assumptions, first, that the protection of sources is itself a matter of high public importance, second, that nothing less than necessity will suffice to override it, third, that the necessity can only arise out of concern for another matter of high public importance, being one of the four interests listed in the section ...

In discussing the section generally Lord Diplock said in *Secretary of State for Defence v Guardian Newspapers Ltd* [1984] 3 All ER 601 at 607, [1985] AC 339 at 350:

> The exceptions include no reference to 'the public interest' generally and I would add that in my view the expression 'justice', the interests of which are entitled to protection, is not used in a general sense as the antonym of 'injustice' but in the technical sense of the administration of justice in the course of legal proceedings in a court of law ...

I agree entirely with the first half of this *dictum*. To construe 'justice' as the antonym of 'injustice' in s 10 would be far too wide. But to confine it to 'the technical sense of the administration of justice in the course of legal proceedings in a court of law' seems to me, with all respect due to any dictum of Lord Diplock, to be too narrow. It is, in my opinion, 'in the interests of justice', in the sense in which this phrase is used in s 10, that persons should be enabled to exercise important legal rights and to protect themselves from serious legal wrongs whether or not resort to legal proceedings in a court of law will be necessary to attain these objectives.

Construing the phrase 'in the interests of justice' in this sense immediately emphasises the importance of the balancing exercise ... The judge's task will always be to weigh in the scales the importance of enabling the ends of justice to be attained in the circumstances of the particular case on the one hand against the importance of protecting the source on the other hand. In this balancing exercise it is only if the judge is satisfied that disclosure in the interests of justice is of such preponderating importance as to override the statutory privilege against disclosure that the threshold of necessity will be reached ...

In estimating the importance to be given to the case in favour of disclosure there will be a wide spectrum within which the particular case must be located. If the party seeking disclosure shows, for example, that his very livelihood depends on it, this will put the case near one end of the spectrum. If he shows no more than that what he seeks to protect is a minor interest in property, this will put the case at or near the other end....

In the circumstances of the instant case, I have no doubt that Hoffmann J and the Court of Appeal were right in finding that the necessity for disclosure of Mr Goodwin's notes in the interests of justice was established. The importance to the plaintiffs of obtaining disclosure lies in the threat of severe damage to their business, and consequentially to the livelihood of their employees, which would arise from disclosure of the information contained in their corporate plan while their refinancing negotiations are still continuing. This threat, accurately described by Lord Donaldson MR ([1990] 1 All ER 616 at 630, [1990] 2 WLR 421 at 439) as 'ticking away beneath them like a time bomb', can only be defused if they can identify the source either as himself, the thief of the stolen copy of the plan, or as a means to lead to the identification of the thief and thus put themselves in a position to institute proceedings for the recovery of the missing document. The importance of protecting the source on the other hand is much diminished by the source's complicity, at the very least, in a gross breach of confidentiality which is not counterbalanced by any legitimate interest which publication of the information was calculated to serve. Disclosure in the interests of justice is, on this view of the balance, clearly of preponderating importance so as to override the policy underlying the statutory protection of sources and the test of necessity for disclosure is satisfied.

The appeal was accordingly dismissed.

Ashworth Hospital Authority v MGN Ltd **[2001] 1 WLR 515**

In this case there was a risk of further leaks of the information in question and the source had revealed confidential medical records. Disclosure was ordered, taking the interest in the preservation of the confidentiality of such records into account. The Court of Appeal considered the approach that should be taken to s 10, taking into account the requirements of the HRA.

Lord Phillips MR: In *Camelot Group Plc v Centaur Communications Ltd* [1999] QB 124 at 132 Schiemann LJ remarked that the 1981 Act was enacted to bring domestic law into line with the requirements of the ECHR. . . . [Counsel for the defendants] contends, however, that the decisions of the English Court do not properly reflect the importance that the Strasbourg Court has attached to the freedom of the press . . .

What light does the lengthy catalogue in Article 10 throw on the meaning of the phrase 'the interests of justice' in section 10? This question is of some importance, for a stark difference of view has been expressed in the House of Lords which must now, I believe, be resolved by reference to the Strasbourg jurisprudence rather than according to the doctrine of precedent, should the two be in conflict.

In *Defence Secretary v Guardian Newspapers* [1985] AC 339 at 350 Lord Diplock stated:

. . . in my view the expression 'justice', the interests of which are entitled to protection, is not used in a general sense as the antonym of 'injustice' but in the technical sense of the administration of justice in the course of legal proceedings in a court of law . . .

These views did not form part of the reason for the decision. In *X Ltd v Morgan-Grampian (Publishers) Ltd* [1991] 1 AC 1 at 43 Lord Bridge advanced a wider interpretation:

It is, in my opinion, 'in the interests of justice' that persons should be enabled to exercise important legal rights and to protect themselves from serious legal wrongs whether or not resort to legal proceedings in a court of law will be necessary to attain these objectives.

Ashworth rely on Lord Bridge's interpretation, for they have made it plain that if the source is identified their intention is to dismiss rather than implead him or her.

In *Goodwin v UK* (1996) 22 EHRR 123 at 140 the European Court recorded the fact that Lord Diplock's interpretation had been replaced by that of Lord Bridge without adverse comment. It seems to me that both interpretations are consistent with Article 10, but that the interpretation of Lord Bridge accords more happily with the scheme of Article 10. Thus 'interests of justice' in section 10 mean interests that are justiciable.

It seems to me that the approach of the European Court to the question of whether disclosure of a source is 'necessary' involves a single exercise in which the Court considers not merely whether, on the facts of the particular case, disclosure of the source is necessary to achieve the legitimate aim but, more significantly, whether the achievement of the legitimate aim on the facts of the instant case is so important that it overrides the public interest in protecting journalistic sources in order to ensure free communication of information to and through the press.

The argument that *Goodwin* established a stricter standard than *X Ltd v Morgan-Grampian* was advanced in *Camelot Group plc v Centaur Communications* [1999] QB 124. Schiemann LJ rejected this submission, holding at page 135 that the different result merely reflected the fact that different courts can reach different conclusions although applying the same principles to the same facts. Mr Browne submitted that this explanation would not wash, because the margin of appreciation applied by the European Court would have prevented such a result.

I consider that Schiemann LJ correctly identified that the European Court differed from the English courts in its view of the implications that non-disclosure of the source would have for the plaintiff company. At the same time I am inclined to accept [the] submission that the decisions of the European Court demonstrate that the freedom of the press has in the past carried greater weight in Strasbourg than it has in the courts of this country.

Notwithstanding this conclusion, I have decided that the judgment of Rougier J should be upheld. In *Goodwin*, at page 137, the Commission expressed the view that only in 'exceptional circumstances where vital public or individual interests are at stake' can an order requiring journalists to disclose their sources be justified.

The disclosure of confidential medical records to the press is misconduct which is not merely of concern to the individual establishment in which it occurs. It is an attack on an area of confidentiality which should be safeguarded in any democratic society. The protection of patent information is of vital concern to the National Health Service and, I suspect, to health services throughout Europe. This is an exceptional case. If the order made by Rougier J discourages press sources from disclosing similar information in the future, this will be no bad thing I would dismiss the appeal.

The appeal was dismissed and the decision was affirmed by the House of Lords [2002] 4 All ER 193. Was the use of the disclosure order necessary and proportionate to the aim in view – to protect the interests of justice, under s 10 and Article 10?

Lord Woolf: The situation here is exceptional, as it was in *Financial Times Ltd v Interbrew SA* [2002] EWCA Civ 274 and as it has to be, if disclosure of sources is to be justified. The care of patients at Ashworth is fraught with difficulty and danger. The disclosure of the patients' records increases that difficulty and danger and to deter the same or similar wrongdoing in the future it was essential that the source should be identified and punished. This was what made the orders to disclose necessary and proportionate and justified. The fact that Ian Brady had himself disclosed his medical history did not detract from the need to prevent staff from revealing medical records of patients.

The other Law Lords agreed with his findings. The order of disclosure was upheld.

Notes

1   The decision in *Morgan-Grampian* seems to give the phrase 'necessary in the interests of justice' a broad meaning. However, it also made it clear that the fact that such interests would be served would not always provide a basis for making an order of disclosure. Disclosure will only be deemed to be 'necessary' if the interests of justice are so strong as to override the interest in protecting sources which s 10 recognises. Thus, it will be harder to establish a basis for obtaining a disclosure order under this exception than under the 'prevention of crime' and 'protection of national security' heads.

2   In *Goodwin v UK* (1996) 22 EHRR 123,[47] the European Court of Human Rights found that the order against Goodwin violated his right to freedom of expression under Article 10 of the ECHR. The Court found that the protection of sources is an aspect of Article 10(1) and that the UK courts had failed to give sufficient weight to the public interest in protecting sources in order to facilitate investigative journalism. The disclosure order was disproportionate to the purpose in question and therefore could not be said to be necessary. Tetra's interest in disclosure, including its interest in unmasking a disloyal employee, did not outweigh the vital public interest in the protection of journalistic sources.

3   The approach of the UK courts changed to an extent in order to take the *Goodwin* decision into account, even prior to the inception of the HRA. Given that the European Court of Human Rights allowed the domestic authorities a margin of appreciation (albeit circumscribed) in determining the issue of proportionality in *Goodwin*, one would have expected the domestic authorities to take an even stricter view of the issue. Such a change of approach was not, however, evident in *Camelot Group Ltd v Centaur Communications* [1999] QB 124. The company,

---

47   See also *Fressoz and Roire v France* (1999) 5 BHRC 654.

Camelot, runs the UK national lottery. An anonymous source sent Camelot's draft accounts to the newspaper, which published them. Camelot sought return of the documents in order to identify the source and the paper relied on s 10. The Court of Appeal found that the public interest in finding and dismissing a disloyal employee should outweigh the public importance attached to the protection of sources. The Court considered that in reaching this finding it was applying the same test as was applied by the European Court of Human Rights in *Goodwin*. Clearly, the terms used in s 10 leave room for varying interpretations. Nevertheless, the determinations as to proportionality in *Camelot* and *Goodwin* differ, it is suggested, in the weight they afford to the role of the media in informing the public.

4	In the pre-HRA decision in *Saunders v Punch Ltd* [1998] 1 WLR 986, in which an injunction had been granted to restrain use of the information in question, it was found that the interests of justice were not so pressing as to require the statutory privilege against disclosure to be overridden. In *John v Express Newspapers* [2000] 1 WLR 1931, this approach was followed by the Court of Appeal. As similar cases arise under the HRA it may be expected, bearing in mind the importance accorded at Strasbourg to the protection of sources under Article 10 as a vital part of the media's role, that the question of proportionality will be resolved by taking account of the effect of the use of an injunction and of attempts to obtain the information by other means. Nevertheless, in exceptional cases disclosure is likely to be ordered, as it was in the *Ashworth* case. That case provides important guidance as to the approach that is likely to prevail in the post-HRA era.

RESTRAINING FREEDOM OF EXPRESSION ON MORAL GROUNDS

Introduction

The Williams Committee,[48] convened in 1979 to report on obscenity (see *Pornography and Politics: The Williams Committee in Retrospect* (1983)), found that interference with the free flow of ideas and artistic endeavour was unacceptable since it amounted to ruling out in advance possible modes of human development, before it was known whether or not they would be desirable or necessary. Since they also reached the conclusion that 'no one has invented, or in our opinion could invent, an instrument that would suppress only [worthless pornography] and could not be turned against something ... of [possibly] a more creative kind',[49] they concluded that the risk of suppressing worthwhile creative art ruled out censorship of the written word. (They regarded standard photographic pornography as not expressing anything that could be regarded as an 'idea' and so as susceptible to regulation.) This liberal position is not reflected in UK law or in Article 10 of the ECHR which allows restraint of freedom of speech on the ground of protection of morality. The development of UK law has been based on the suppression of speech to avoid the corruption of persons, particularly the more vulnerable.

48	*Report of the Committee on Obscenity and Film Censorship* (Williams Committee), Cmnd 7772 (1979).
49	*Op cit*, para 5.24.

Obscenity[50]

Obscene Publications Act 1959, as amended by the Obscene Publications Act 1964

Test of obscenity

1.–(1) For the purposes of this Act an article shall be deemed to be obscene if its effect or (where the article comprises two or more distinct items) the effect of any one of its items is, if taken as a whole, such as to tend to deprave and corrupt persons who are likely, having regard to all relevant circumstances, to read, see or hear the matter contained or embodied in it.

  (2) In this Act 'article' means any description of article containing or embodying matter to be read or looked at or both, any sound record, and any film or other record of a picture or pictures.

Prohibition of publication of obscene matter

2.–(1) Subject as hereinafter provided, any person who, whether for gain or not, publishes an obscene article [or who has an obscene article for gain (whether gain to himself or gain to another)] shall be liable—

  (a) on summary conviction to a fine not exceeding [£5,000] or to imprisonment for a term not exceeding six months;

  (b) on conviction on indictment to a fine or to imprisonment for a term not exceeding three years or both.

...

3.–(1) If a justice of the peace is satisfied by information on oath that there is reasonable ground for suspecting that ... obscene articles are ... kept for publication for gain ... the justice may issue a warrant ... empowering any constable ... to seize and remove any article.

  (2) ... any articles seized under s (1) of this section shall be brought before a justice of the peace acting for the same petty sessions area as the justice who issued the warrant ... if the court is satisfied ... that at the time when they were sized they were obscene articles kept for publication for gain the court shall order the articles to be forfeited ...

Defence of public good

4.–(1) A person shall not be convicted of an offence against section 2 of this Act, and an order for forfeiture shall not be made under the foregoing section, if it is proved that publication of the article in question is justified as being for the public good on the ground that it is in the interests of science, literature, art or learning, or of other objects of general concern.

  (2) It is hereby declared that the opinion of experts as to the literary, artistic, scientific or other merits of an article may be admitted in any proceedings under this Act either to establish or to negative the said ground.

R v Anderson [1972] 1 QB 304, 313, 314

At first instance it was found that a certain magazine, *Oz: 'School Kids' Issue*, was obscene.

Lord Widgery CJ: In the ordinary run of the mill cases ... the issue 'obscene or no' must be tried by the jury without assistance of expert evidence on that issue, and we draw attention to the failure to observe that rule in this case in order that that failure may not occur again.

---

50 See generally Robertson and Nichol, *op cit*, Chapter 3.

We are not oblivious of the fact that some people, perhaps many people, will think a jury, unassisted by experts, a very unsatisfactory tribunal to decide such a matter. ...

I turn now to criticisms which have been made ... of the directions given by the judge in this case ... It is said that in directing the jury as to the meaning of 'obscenity' under the Obscene Publications Act 1959, the judge did not make it clear that for the purpose of that Act 'obscene' means, and means only, a tendency to deprave or corrupt.

... we feel ... that at least there is grave danger that the jury from that passage in the direction to them, took the view, or might have taken the view, that 'obscene' for all purposes including the purposes of the Obscene Publications Act 1959 included 'repulsive', 'filthy', 'loathsome' or 'lewd'.

The appeal was allowed, partly on this ground.

DPP v Whyte [1973] AC 849; [1972] 3 All ER 12, 23

This decision concerned a book shop which sold pornographic material. The proprietors were prosecuted under s 1 of the 1959 Act.

Lord Pearson: ... in my opinion, the words 'deprave and corrupt' in the statutory definition, as in the judgment of Cockburn CJ in *Hicklin* [(1868) LR 3 QB 360], refer to the effect of pornographic articles on the mind, including the emotions, and it is not essential that any physical sexual activity (or any 'overt sexual activity', if that phrase has a different meaning) should result. According to the findings the articles did not leave the regular customers unmoved. On the contrary, they fascinated them and enabled them to engage in fantasies. Fantasies in this context must, I think, mean fantasies of normal or abnormal sexual activities. In the words of Cockburn CJ, the pornographic books in the respondents' shop suggested to the minds of the regular customers 'thoughts of a most impure and libidinous character'.

The majority in the House of Lords found that the respondents should have been convicted.

Knuller (Publishing, etc) Ltd v DPP [1973] AC 435; [1972] 3 WLR 143, 148, 149

In *Shaw v DPP* [1962] AC 220,[51] the House of Lords found that a common law offence known as conspiracy to corrupt public morals existed. This was reconsidered in *Knuller v DPP* which concerned homosexual contact advertisements.

Lord Reid: Section 1(1) [of the 1959 Act] provides: 'For the purposes of this Act an article shall be deemed to be obscene if its effect ... is ... such as to tend to deprave and corrupt persons' likely to read it. The obvious purpose of s 2(4) is to make available, where the essence of the offence is tending to deprave and corrupt, the defences which are set out in the Act ...

This matter was raised in the House of Commons on 3 June 1964, when the Solicitor-General gave an assurance, repeating an earlier assurance 'that a conspiracy to corrupt public morals would not be charged so as to circumvent the statutory defence in subsection (4)' (*Hansard,* vol 695, col 1212).

That does at least show that Parliament has not been entirely satisfied with *Shaw's* case. It is not for me to comment on the undesirability of seeking to alter the law by undertakings or otherwise than by legislation ...

I think that the meaning of the word 'corrupt' requires some clarification. One of my objections to the *Shaw* decision is that it leaves too much to the jury. I recognise that in the end it must be for the jury to say whether the matter published is likely to lead to corruption. ..... 'Corrupt' is a strong word and the jury ought to be reminded of that, as they were in the present case. I find

---

51 See also *R v Gibson* [1990] 2 QB 619.

nothing in the Act to indicate that Parliament thought or intended to lay down that indulgence in [homosexual acts between adult males in private] is not corrupting. I read the Act as saying that, even though it may be corrupting, if people choose to corrupt themselves in this way that is their affair and the law will not interfere. But no licence is given to others to encourage the practice. So if one accepts *Shaw's* case as rightly decided it must be left to each jury to decide in the circumstances of each case whether people were likely to be corrupted. In this case the jury were properly directed and it is impossible to say that they reached a wrong conclusion. It is not for us to say whether or not we agree with it. So I would dismiss the appeal as regards the first count.

The House of Lords upheld the conviction for conspiracy to corrupt public morals.

Handyside v United Kingdom Series A No 24; (1976) 1 EHRR 737, 753–56

A book called *The Little Red Schoolbook*, which contained chapters on masturbation, sexual intercourse and abortion, was prosecuted under the 1959 Act on the basis that it appeared to encourage early sexual intercourse. The publisher applied for a ruling under Article 10 to the European Commission on Human Rights. The Commission referred the case to the Court.

European Court of Human Rights – judgment

The Court points out that the machinery of protection established by the Convention is subsidiary to the national systems safeguarding human rights [*Belgian Linguistic case (No 2)* (1968) 1 EHRR 252, 296, para 10 *in fine*]. The Convention leaves to each contracting state, in the first place, the task of securing the rights and freedoms it enshrines. The institutions created by it make their own contribution to this task, but they become involved only through contentious proceedings and once all domestic remedies have been exhausted (Article 26).

These observations apply, notably, to Article 10(2). In particular, it is not possible to find in the domestic law of the various contracting states a uniform European conception of morals. The view taken by their respective laws of the requirements of morals varies from time to time and from place to place, especially in our era which is characterised by a rapid and far-reaching evolution of opinions on the subject. By reason of their direct and continuous contact with the vital forces of their countries, state authorities are in principle in a better position than the international judge to give an opinion on the exact content of these requirements as well as on the 'necessity' of a 'restriction' or 'penalty' intended to meet them. . . . it is for the national authorities to make the initial assessment of the reality of the pressing social need implied by the notion of 'necessity' in this context.

Consequently, Article 10(2) leaves to the contracting states a margin of appreciation. This margin is given both to the domestic legislator ('prescribed by law') and to the bodies, judicial amongst others, that are called upon to interpret and apply the laws in force [*Engel v The Netherlands* (1976) EHRR 684, para 100] . . . The Court's supervisory functions oblige it to pay the utmost attention to the principles characterising a 'democratic society'. Freedom of expression constitutes one of the essential foundations of such a society, one of the basic conditions for its progress and for the development of every man. Subject to Article 10(2), it is applicable not only to 'information' or 'ideas' that are favourably received or regarded as inoffensive or as a matter of indifference, but also to those that offend, shock or disturb the state or any sector of the population. Such are the demands of that pluralism, tolerance and broadmindedness without which there is no 'democratic society'. This means, amongst other things, that every 'formality', 'condition', 'restriction' or 'penalty' imposed in this sphere must be proportionate to the legitimate aim pursued.

From another standpoint, whoever exercises his freedom of expression undertakes 'duties and responsibilities' the scope of which depends on his situation and the technical means he uses. The Court cannot overlook such a person's 'duties' and 'responsibilities' when it enquires, as in this case; whether 'restrictions' or 'penalties' were conducive to the 'protection of morals' which made them 'necessary' in a 'democratic society'.

50 It follows from this that it is in no way the Court's task to take the place of the competent national courts but rather to review under Article 10 the decisions they delivered in the exercise of their power of appreciation.

52 The Court attaches particular importance to a factor to which the judgment of 29 October 1971 did not fail to draw attention, that is the intended readership of the *Schoolbook*. It was aimed above all at children and adolescents aged from 12 to 18 ...The applicant had made it clear that he planned a wide-spread circulation. ... the book included, above all in the section on sex and in the passage headed 'Be yourself' in the chapter on pupils, sentences or paragraphs that young people at a critical stage of their development could have interpreted as an encouragement to indulge in precocious activities harmful for them or even to commit certain criminal offences. In these circumstances, despite the variety and the constant evolution in the UK of views on ethics and education, the competent English judges were entitled, in the exercise of their discretion, to think at the relevant time that the *Schoolbook* would have pernicious effects on the morals of many of the children and adolescents who would read it.

Paragraph 2 of Article 10 therefore applied; no breach of the Article was found.

Notes

1   The 'deprave and corrupt' test can be applied to any material which might corrupt; it is clear from the ruling in *Calder, John (Publications) Ltd v Powell* [1965] 1 QB 509 that it is not confined to descriptions or representations of sexual matters, and it could therefore be applied to a disturbing book on the drug-taking life of a junkie. This ruling was followed in *R v Skirving* [1985] QB 819, which concerned a pamphlet on the means of taking cocaine in order to obtain maximum effect. In all instances the test for obscenity should not be applied to the type of behaviour advocated or described in the article in question but to the article itself. Thus, in *Skirving* the question to be asked was not whether taking cocaine would deprave and corrupt but whether the pamphlet itself would.

2   The jury has to consider whether the article would be likely to deprave and corrupt a significant proportion of those likely to encounter it. It was determined in *R v Calder and Boyars Ltd* [1969] 1 QB 151 that the jury must determine what is meant by a significant proportion, and this was approved in *DPP v Whyte* [1973] AC 849, Lord Cross explaining that 'a significant proportion of a class means a part which is not numerically negligible but which may be much less than half'. This formulation was adopted in order to prevent sellers of pornographic material claiming that most of their customers would be unlikely to be corrupted by it.

3   The defence of public good, which arises under the 1959 Act, s 4, was intended to afford recognition to artistic merit and thus may be seen as a significant step in the direction of protecting freedom of speech. In *R v Penguin Books* [1961] Crim LR 176, it appeared that the jury found *Lady Chatterley's Lover* to be obscene but considered that the s 4 defence applied. The defence will not be available if, as in *Knuller*, conspiracy to corrupt public morals is charged, thus circumventing the statutory protection for free speech.

4   Under s 3 of the Act, magazines and other material, such as videos, can be seized in forfeiture proceedings if they are obscene and have been kept for gain. No conviction is obtained; the material is merely destroyed and no other punishment is imposed, and therefore s 3 may operate at a low level of visibility. These proceedings may mean that the safeguards provided by the Act can be bypassed; in particular, consideration may not be given to the possible literary merits of such material because the public good defence need not be taken into account when the seizure warrant is issued. However, s 3 can be used only in respect of material which may be obscene rather than in relation to any form of pornography; it was

held in *Darbo v DPP* [1992] Crim LR 56 that a warrant issued under s 3 allowing officers to search for 'sexually explicit material' was bad on its face as such articles would fall within a much wider category of articles than those which could be called obscene.

5   At Strasbourg it is fair to say that artistic expression appears to have a lower place in the hierarchy of expression than political expression (see p 905). Nevertheless, no decisions defending restrictions on the freedom of expression of *adults* can be found, except in respect of 'hard core' pornography with no pretensions at all to artistic merit, or where a risk to children is also present, or in the context of offending religious sensibilities. In the *Handyside* case (extracted above), the European Court of Human Rights found that domestic law on obscenity was in harmony with Article 10 of the ECHR. In finding that para 2 applied, the judgment accepted that domestic legislators would be allowed a wide margin of appreciation in attempting to secure the freedoms guaranteed under the Convention in this area. This stance was again taken in *Müller v Switzerland* (1991) 13 EHRR 212 in respect of a conviction arising from the exhibition of explicit paintings; the fact that the paintings had been exhibited in other parts of Switzerland and abroad did not mean that their suppression could not amount to a pressing social need. In contrast, in *Scherer v Switzerland* Series A No 287; (1994) 18 EHRR 276[52] it was found that the conviction of the proprietor of a sex shop for showing obscene and explicit videos had not breached Article 10 since access was restricted to adults and no one was likely to confront them unwittingly.

6   Any prosecutions under the 1959 Act or forfeiture actions constitute interferences with freedom of expression under the HRA, although subject to justification. In relation to any particular decision, the public authorities involved are bound by s 6 of the HRA to ensure that the tests under Article 10 are satisfied, while the provisions of the 1959 Act must be interpreted consistently with Article 10. As Chapter 1 of this Part indicated, s 12 of the HRA does not apply to criminal proceedings. Forfeiture proceedings have the hallmarks of criminal proceedings in a number of respects, although a conviction is not obtained, and therefore they may be outside the ambit of s 12. Given the wide margin of appreciation afforded to the domestic authorities in the relevant decisions, little guidance as to the requirements of Article 10 in this context is available, especially where the material is directed at a willing adult audience. The domestic judiciary is therefore theoretically free to take a different stance. The decisions considered above at Strasbourg on the 1959 Act indicate that the statutory regime relating to publication of an obscene article under s 2 is broadly in harmony with Article 10 of the ECHR. Nevertheless, a specific decision might not meet the proportionality requirements, scrutinised more intensively than at Strasbourg.

7   The UK forfeiture regime has not been tested at Strasbourg. The HRA requirements may be especially pertinent in relation to forfeiture: the magistrates conducting the proceedings are, of course, bound by Article 10 and therefore would be expected to approach the task with greater rigour. In particular, it is arguably necessary to examine each item even where a large scale seizure has occurred, rather than considering a sample of items only.[53] But since, in practice, a vast amount of material is condemned as obscene in legal actions for forfeiture, the practical difficulties facing magistrates make it possible, especially initially, that the impact

---

52   The case was discontinued in the Court due to the death of the applicant.
53   It was found that such sampling was acceptable in *R v Snaresbrook Crown Court ex p Commissioner of the Metropolis* (1984) 79 Cr App R 184.

of the HRA will be more theoretical than real. It seems probable that, in practice, magistrates will not examine each item and will give only cursory attention, if any, to considering the application of the somewhat elusive Strasbourg case law. However, if on occasion publishers seek to contest s 3 orders before a jury, the proportionality of the measures adopted may receive more attention. Moreover, it is arguable that Article 6 might be breached by the procedure since it could be said to lack impartiality, given that the same magistrate may sign the seizure order and determine forfeiture.

FURTHER READING

E Barendt, *Freedom of Speech* (1987)
R Clayton and H Tomlinson, *The Law of Human Rights* (2000), Chapter 15
D Feldman, *Civil Liberties and Human Rights*, 2nd edn (2002), Part IV

CHAPTER 3

FREEDOM OF ASSEMBLY, PUBLIC PROTEST AND PUBLIC ORDER

INTRODUCTION

Freedom of assembly, which is guaranteed under the Universal Declaration of Human Rights, Article 20 and in the European Convention on Human Rights (ECHR), Article 11, is a fundamental freedom which in part derives its legitimacy from its close association with freedom of speech. The exercise of freedom of assembly allows individuals to make their views known publicly and obtain public support. Free societies recognise the need to allow citizens to express views at variance with government views or 'mainstream' views, and to allow the public expression of such views. Allowing citizens to engage in public protest is seen as being one of the main distinctions between a totalitarian society and a democracy. Protest is valuable partly as demonstrating to the government that it has strayed too far from the path of acceptability in policy making and partly in deterring it from doing so.

This chapter is concerned with the conflict between the legitimate interest of the state in maintaining order and the protection of freedom of protest and assembly. Therefore, it will focus on those provisions of the criminal law most applicable in the context of demonstrations, marches or meetings. Many of these restraints are not aimed specifically at assemblies but generally at keeping the peace. The legal regime aimed at preserving public order relies on the use of both prior and subsequent restraints. Prior restraint on assemblies may mean that an assembly cannot take place at all or that it can take place only under various limitations. Subsequent restraints, usually arrests and prosecutions for public order offences, may be used after the assembly is in being. Although the availability of subsequent restraints may have a 'chilling' effect, they are used publicly and may receive publicity. If an assembly takes place and subsequently some of its members are prosecuted for public order offences, it will have achieved its end in gaining publicity and may in fact have gained greater publicity due to the prosecutions. If the assembly never takes place, its object will probably be completely defeated.

Prior and subsequent restraints arise from a large number of wide-ranging and sometimes archaic powers which spring partly from a mix of statutory provisions, partly from the common law and partly from the royal prerogative.[1] To an extent the number of restraints available is unsurprising because the range of state interests involved is wider than any other expressive activity would warrant: they include the possibilities of disorder, violence to citizens and damage to property. Clearly, the state has a duty to protect citizens from the attentions of the mob.

Most of these restraints are not aimed specifically at assemblies and protesters, but generally at keeping the peace. Nevertheless, they severely affect the freedoms of protest and assembly. Therefore, those seeking to exercise the freedoms of protest and

---

1   For discussion of the various offences, see JC Smith, *Smith and Hogan Criminal Law*, 8th edn (1996) (the standard criminal law text), Chapter 21; P Thornton, *Public Order Law* (1987); ATH Smith, *Offences Against Public Order* (1987).

assembly have historically been in a vulnerable position[2] and currently they are in an especially precarious legal position, since a web of overlapping and imprecise public order provisions now exists and is constantly increasing.[3] Clearly, some restraint on public protest is needed in order to protect the interests which are at stake due to the possibilities of disorder, violence to citizens and damage to property.[4] The difficulty is that, in furtherance of the interest in public order (which in itself protects freedom of assembly), the constitutional need to allow freedom of assembly in a democracy may be obscured. Prior to the inception of the Human Rights Act 1998 (HRA) there was some very limited recognition of a right to freedom of assembly in UK law. Under the Representation of the People Act 1983, local authorities are placed under a very limited positive obligation to allow election meetings to take place. The Education (No 2) Act 1986, s 43 provided protection for meetings in universities. Also a liberty to assemble appeared to exist. The Public Order Act 1986, ss 12 and 14 (see below) impliedly recognise the freedom to assemble so long as the statutory requirements are complied with. There are certain specific statutory prohibitions on meetings in certain places or at certain times, such as the Seditious Meetings Act 1817, s 3 which prohibits meetings of 50 or more in the vicinity of Westminster during a parliamentary session. Such restrictions impliedly supported the existence of a general negative freedom to meet or march which would exist if not specifically prohibited.[5]

However, for the first time in UK law, citizens can rely on an express recognition in domestic law of rights to protest and assemble within Articles 10 and 11 of the ECHR as afforded further effect in UK law under the HRA. This constitutes a potentially climactic break with the traditional UK constitutional position. That position was that citizens might do anything which the law did not forbid, whereas under the HRA they are able to exercise rights to protest and assembly, circumscribed, as Chapter 1 of this Part explains, only in a manner compatible with specified Convention exceptions or, exceptionally, by incompatible domestic legislation.[6]

The focus of this chapter is on the mass of common law and statutory public order provisions, in the light of the new rights to the freedoms of assembly and protest. Having considered the justifications underpinning such rights, it will evaluate possible responses of the judiciary to the acceptance of the values underlying public expression under Articles 10 and 11 in UK public order law. It will be argued that the common law has failed to provide the recognition for the value of public protest as a form of political expression which is evident in respect of media expression. This is due, it will be contended, to the desire to protect countervailing interests, particularly proprietorial rights, but the judiciary have not made this explicit: the express balancing act which may be carried out at Strasbourg between political expression and other societal interests has not occurred in the judgments of domestic courts, often because the former value is merely afforded no recognition at all. Moreover, the guarantees of

---

2   See KD Ewing and CA Gearty, *The Struggle for Civil Liberties* (1999).
3   The latest provision is contained in the Criminal Justice and Police Act 2001, s 42; see p 973, below.
4   See the leading US case, *Hague v Committee for Industrial Organisation* 307 US 496 (1938).
5   See DG Barnum [1977] PL 310 and (1981) 29 AJCL 59; LA Stein [1971] PL 115 for discussion of the constitutional status of public protest.
6   HRA 1998, s 3(2).

freedom of expression and peaceful assembly under Articles 10 and 11 of the ECHR have hardly been adverted to in the domestic courts as aids to statutory interpretation or to resolve common law policy issues in public protest cases, as the decisions discussed below reveal. The close relationship between assembly and expression has failed to receive recognition when low level public order offences, committed in the course of, or directly through, the exercise of political protest, are adjudicated upon.

The 1980s witnessed a series of disturbances beginning with the Brixton riots in 1981[7] and continuing with the disorder associated with the miners' strike in 1984–85. Such disorder formed the background to the Public Order Act 1986, but it is unclear that further police powers to control disorder were needed. It did not appear that the police had lacked powers to deal with these disturbances; on the contrary, a number of different common law and statutory powers were invoked, including breach of the peace, obstruction of a constable and watching and besetting under s 7 of the Conspiracy and Protection of Property Act 1875.[8] The 1986 Act itself, however, came to be seen as inadequate as a means of controlling certain forms of protest. The late 1980s and the early 1990s witnessed a range of protest, notably the anti-poll tax demonstrations, protest against *The Satanic Verses* and against the Criminal Justice and Public Order Act 1994 itself ('Kill the Bill' protests). Mass protest was not a hallmark of the 1990s, but the period did see an enormous growth in the use of direct action by a variety of groups, usually protesting about environmental and animal rights issues. The rise in direct action suggested that the traditional aim of protest – to persuade – was being abandoned. The response of the Major government was to introduce more draconian measures under the Criminal Justice and Public Order Act 1994, aimed largely at direct action in order to suppress it.[9]

The coming into power of the Labour Party in 1997 did not herald any diminution of the direct action form of protest, on the government's own analysis of its predicted prevalence.[10] The concerns of protesters against motorway development, abuse of human rights and on environmental matters, including the introduction of genetically modified crops, continued to be expressed in this form.[11] The response of the New Labour government to the likelihood that the direct action form of protest would continue in evidence during its period of office resembled that of the Major government in terms of its authoritarian stance. It passed the Criminal Justice and Police Act 2001, s 42, which was aimed at this form of protest.

The central theme of this chapter will concern the impact of the HRA on the mass of restrictions on freedom of assembly.

---

7   See the inquiry by Lord Scarman, *The Brixton Disorders*, Cmnd 8427 (1981).
8   See S McCabe and P Wallington, *The Police, Public Order and Civil Liberties: Legacies of the Miners' Strike* (1988), esp appendix 1; P Wallington, 'Policing the miners' strike' (1985) 14 ILJ 145. During the miners' strike, over 10,000 offences were charged; see P Wallington (1985) 14 ILJ 145.
9   For the background to the 1994 Act, see the introduction in M Wasik and RD Taylor's *Guide to the Criminal Justice and Public Order Act 1994* (1995), p 1. For discussion of the public order offences, see ATH Smith [1995] Crim LR 19.
10 *Legislation Against Terrorism: A Consultation Paper*, Cm 4178 (1998).
11 See the Newbury Bypass website – www.geocities.com/newburybypass/index.html; Reports of protests at Newbury, *The Daily Telegraph*, 11 January 1999 and 30 April 1999; the Greenpeace website – www.greenpeace.org.uk.

THE RIGHTS OF FREEDOM OF ASSEMBLY AND PROTEST UNDER THE HUMAN RIGHTS ACT 1998

Under s 6 of the HRA, those seeking to exercise rights of protest and assembly can rely on Articles 10 and 11 of the ECHR, and any other relevant right,[12] against public authorities, in particular the police. All the legislation already mentioned and discussed below must be interpreted compatibly with those rights, under s 3 of the HRA, taking the Strasbourg jurisprudence into account under s 2. But, in order to evaluate the impact of the Convention, it is necessary to consider the scope and content of the Article 10 and 11 rights of protest and assembly.

Article 11 of the ECHR, received into UK law under the HRA, is specifically aimed at freedom of assembly. Forms of public protest as examples of both assembly and expression will fall within Article 10 also. Article 11 leaves a great deal of discretion to the judiciary. It is not a far-reaching provision since, as explained in Part II Chapter 2, it protects only freedom of *peaceful* assembly and since, in common with Articles 8–10, it contains a long list of exceptions in para 2.[13] In interpreting it, the UK judiciary is obliged, under s 2 of the HRA, to take the relevant Strasbourg jurisprudence into account. That jurisprudence is not, on the whole, of a radical nature, although the Court has found that the right to organise public meetings is 'fundamental'[14] and includes the right to organise marches, demonstrations and other forms of public protest. Article 11 may impose limited positive duties on the state to ensure that an assembly or protest can occur even though it is likely to provoke others to violence; the responsibility for any harm caused appears to remain with the counter-demonstrators.[15] The acceptance of further positive duties, including a duty to require owners of private land to allow some peaceful assemblies on their property, has not yet been accepted under the Convention but remains a possibility,[16] especially, as David Harris, Michael O'Boyle and Chris Warbrick point out,[17] in view of the growth of quasi-public places such as large, enclosed shopping centres and the privatisation of previously public places.

'Direct action' used in a symbolic sense has been found to fall within Article 11.[18] The key factor in determining whether a protest counts as a peaceful assembly appears to be whether it is violent in itself or whether any violence arises incidentally.[19] The Court has only found an infringement of freedom of assembly under Article 11 in one judgment, *Ezelin v France* Series A No 202-A; (1991) 14 EHRR 362, discussed below. In two further instances, *Steel and Others v UK* and *Hashman and Harrup v UK*, a violation

---

12 Article 5 may have particular applicability. See Part II Chapter 2, p 241.

13 See Part II Chapter 2, p 243.

14 *Rassemblement Jurassien Unite Jurassienne v Switzerland* Application No 819/78, (1979) 17 DR 93, 119.

15 *Plattform 'Ärtze für das Leben' v Austria* Series A No 139; (1988) 13 EHRR 204.

16 See *De Geillustreede Pers v Netherlands*, Application No 5178/71, (1976) 8 DR 5 Com Rep; the Commission accepted that States may have positive obligations to uphold freedom of expression in the context of media ownership. In the US, the 'access' issue was initially resolved in favour of the property right, but now seems to be moving towards acceptance of exceptions favouring expressive rights; see G Nardell, 'The Quantock hounds and the Trojan horse' [1995] PL 27 on *R v Somerset CC ex p Fewings* [1995] 1 All ER 513 for discussion of the shopping mall/'constitutional fora' cases.

17 DJ Harris, M O'Boyle and C Warbrick, *Law of the European Convention on Human Rights* (1995), p 419.

18 *G v Federal Republic of Germany* Application No 13079/87, (1989) 60 DR 256, 263. Currently, the Court views such protest as falling most readily within Article 10; see below, p 981.

19 *Christians against Racism and Fascism v UK* Application No 8440/78, (1980) 21 DR 138, 148.

of Article 10 was found in respect of public protest and the Court therefore did not find it necessary to consider Article 11 (see below, at p 981). It has been a feature of the practice that applications do not reach the Court since the Commission has readily found them to be manifestly ill founded.[20] This cautious stance largely arises from the wide margin of appreciation that has been afforded to national authorities in determining what is needed to preserve public order at local level.

The Article 10 jurisprudence relating specifically to public protest is meagre, as this chapter will indicate. However, the extensive jurisprudence on expression generally, especially political expression, is clearly applicable to public protest.[21] The *content* of speech will rarely exclude it from Article 10 protection: thus, speech as part of a protest likely to cause such low level harm as alarm or distress may be protected according to the *dicta* of the Court in *Müller v Switzerland* (1991) 13 EHRR 212 to the effect that the protection of free speech extends equally to ideas which 'offend, shock or disturb'. The Court has repeatedly asserted that freedom of expression 'constitutes one of the essential foundations of a democratic society', that exceptions to it 'must be narrowly interpreted and the necessity for any restrictions ... convincingly established'.[22] As Chapter 2 of this Part indicates, it is a marked feature of the Strasbourg jurisprudence that political expression receives a high degree of protection. One of the leading works on the Convention concludes, 'It is clear that the Court ascribes a hierarchy of value' to different classes of speech, attaching 'the highest importance to the protection of political expression ... widely understood'.[23]

Prima facie all forms of protest that can be viewed as the expression of an opinion fall within Article 10 according to the findings of the Court in *Steel and Others v UK* (1999) 28 EHRR 603. Thus, the direct action form of protest, such as symbolic or actual physical obstruction, does fall within the scope of Article 10,[24] a finding that was reiterated in *Hashman and Harrup v UK* (2000) 30 EHRR 241.[25] In *Steel*, protesters who were physically impeding grouse shooters and road builders and had been arrested for breach of the peace, were found to be engaging in 'expression' within the meaning of Article 10. The findings in *Steel* suggest that while actual obstruction falls within Article 10, it may have a lower status than protest in the form of pure speech.

Owing to the likelihood that, as indicated, most forms of protest will fall within Article 10, and probably also Article 11, the emphasis of Strasbourg findings is on the para 2 exceptions which include 'in the interests of national security ... public safety

---

20 *Friedl v Austria* Application No 15225/89, (1992) unreported; *Christians Against Racism and Fascism v UK* Application No 8440/78, (1980) 21 DR 138.

21 *Steel and Others v UK* (1999) 28 EHRR 603.

22 *The Observer and The Guardian v UK* Series A No 216; (1991) 14 EHRR 153, para 59.

23 Harris, O'Boyle and Warbrick, *op cit*, pp 397 and 414. The second rank is artistic speech, the third commercial speech, eg, advertising. They acknowledge that these terms may be too narrow (at fn 14 and associated text). In particular, the term 'artistic' is too restrictive since it does not cover all speech, including some forms of protest, which may be said to be supported by the free speech arguments.

24 See *Steel and Others v UK* (1999) 28 EHRR 603, para 92: 'It is true that the protests took the form of physically impeding the activities of which the applicants disapproved, but the Court considers nonetheless that they constituted expressions of opinion with the meaning of Article 10.'

25 *Hashman and Harrup v UK* (2000) 30 EHRR 241; (2000) BHRC 104 does not offer much guidance as to the scope of protection for direct action since, having found that a sanction applied to the applicants for blowing a horn with the intention of disrupting a hunt was a form of expression within Article 10, the Court went on to find that the interference was not 'prescribed by law': the domestic law – the *contra bonos mores* doctrine – was found to be insufficiently precise.

... for the prevention of disorder or crime ... for the protection of the ... rights of others'. In order to be justified, state interference with Article 10 and 11 guarantees must be prescribed by law, have a legitimate aim, be necessary in a democratic society and be applied in a non-discriminatory fashion (Article 14). In carrying out this assessment, the domestic courts are obliged to take the Strasbourg public protest jurisprudence into account although they are not bound by it.[26]

In freedom of expression cases, Strasbourg's main concern has been with the 'necessary in a democratic society' requirement; the notion of 'prescribed by law' has been focused upon to some extent but almost always with the result that it has been found to be satisfied. It was not satisfied by the *contra bonos mores* (contrary to a good way of life) power arising under the Justices of the Peace Act 1361, due to its imprecision.[27] The 'legitimate aim' requirement will normally be readily satisfied; as Harris, O'Boyle and Warbrick point out, the grounds for interference are so wide that 'the State can usually make a plausible case that it did have a good reason for interfering with the right'.[28] The provision against non-discrimination arising under Article 14 is potentially very significant, especially in relation to minority public protests, but so far it has not been a significant issue in the relevant freedom of expression jurisprudence.

The Court tends to afford a wide margin of appreciation when reviewing the necessity of interferences with expression in the form of protest, viewing measures taken to prevent disorder or protect the rights of others as peculiarly within the purview of the domestic authorities, in contrast to its stance in respect of 'pure' speech. In finding that applications are manifestly ill founded, the Commission has been readily satisfied that decisions of the national authorities to adopt quite far reaching measures, including complete bans, in order to prevent disorder are within their margin of appreciation.[29] The Court has also found 'the margin of appreciation extends in particular to the choice of the reasonable and appropriate mean to be used by the authority to ensure that lawful manifestations can take place peacefully'.[30] Thus, states are typically *not* required to demonstrate that lesser measures than those actually taken would have been inadequate to deal with the threats posed by demonstrations – disorder, interferences with the rights of others and so on.

However, in *Ezelin v France* the Court took a 'hard look' at the issue of proportionality. The applicant, an advocate, took part in a demonstration against the judicial system generally and against particular judges, involving the daubing of slogans attacking the judiciary on court walls, and eventual violence. Ezelin did not himself take part in any illegal acts, but did not disassociate himself from the march, even when it became violent. He was disciplined by the Bar Association and eventually given a formal reprimand, which did not impair his ability to practice. No fine was imposed. The French government's argument was that '[b]y not disavowing the unruly incidents that had occurred during the demonstration, the applicant had ipso facto approved them [and that] it was essential for judicial institutions to react to

---

26   HRA 1998, s 2(1).
27   See *Hashman and Harrup v UK* (2000) 30 EHRR 241; (2000) 8 BHRC 104.
28   *Op cit*, p 290.
29   See *Christians against Racism and Fascism v UK* Application No 8440/78, (1980) 21 DR 138; and *Friedl v Austria* Application No 15225/89, (1992) unreported.
30   *Chorherr v Austria* Series A No 266-B; (1993) 17 EHRR 358, para 31.

behaviour which, on the part of an 'officer of the court ... seriously impaired the authority of the judiciary and respect or court decisions'.[31] The argument was rejected; Article 11 was found to have been violated. In an emphatic judgment, the Court found: '... the freedom to take part in a peaceful assembly – in this instance a demonstration that had not been prohibited – is of such importance that it cannot be restricted in any way, even for an advocate, so long as the person concerned does not himself commit any reprehensible act on such an occasion.'[32]

The broad phrasing of Articles 10 and 11[33] inevitably leaves a great deal of interpretative discretion to the UK judiciary in considering their application to existing law under the HRA. But certain conclusions can be drawn: the European Court of Human Rights will not tolerate the arrest and detention of purely peaceful protesters, even if the protest degenerates into violence, so long as the protesters in question have not themselves committed 'reprehensible acts'. The finding of the Court in *Steel v UK*, reiterated in *Hashman v UK*, that direct action protest such as physical obstruction does fall within the scope of Article 10,[34] is of great significance, as is the finding of the Commission that protesters engaged in a 'sit-in' blocking a road are covered by Article 11.[35] It appears to be the case that Strasbourg views such expression as having a lower status than 'purely' expressive and speech-based protest activities, but a distinction has not been drawn between actual and symbolic obstruction, although it may be inferred that actual obstruction might be viewed as reprehensible. Thus, apart from violent or threatening protest, most forms of protest and assembly are within the scope of both Articles 10 and 11, although ceremonious processions and assemblies will probably be considered only within Article 11,[36] while the recent tendency is to consider forms of direct action within Article 10. Thus, forms of protest including those far removed from the classic peaceful assembly holding up banners or handing out leaflets engage these Articles, but interference with direct action protest can be readily justified, even where it is primarily of a symbolic nature.

THE LEGAL CONTROL OF MEETINGS, MARCHES, DEMONSTRATIONS, PROTESTS

Prior restraints in domestic law

Controlling marches and assemblies

Public Order Act 1986, Part II
Processions and assemblies

Advance notice of public processions
11.–(1) Written notice shall be given in accordance with this section of any proposal to hold a public procession intended—

---

31 *Ezelin v France* (1991) 14 EHRR 362, para 49.
32 *Ibid*, para 53.
33 Articles 5 and 6 may also be relevant in some circumstances.
34 In *Steel and Others v UK* (1999) 28 EHRR 603, para 92: 'It is true that the protests took the form of physically impeding the activities of which the applicants disapproved, but the Court considers nonetheless that they constituted expressions of opinion with the meaning of Article 10.'
35 *G v FRG* Application No 13079/87, (1980) 21 DR 138.
36 See *Chorherr v Austria* (1993) 17 EHRR 358; see below, p 981.

(a) to demonstrate support for or opposition to the views or actions of any person or body of persons,

(b) to publicise a cause or campaign, or

(c) to mark or commemorate an event,

unless it is not reasonably practicable to give any advance notice of the procession.

(2) Subsection (1) does not apply where the procession is one commonly or customarily held in the police area . . .

(3) The notice must specify the date when it is intended to hold the procession, the time when it is intended to start it, its proposed route, and the name and address of the person (or of one of the persons) proposing to organise it.

(4) Notice must be delivered to a police station—

(a) in the police area in which it is proposed the procession will start . . .

(5) If delivered not less than six clear days before the date when the procession is intended to be held, the notice may be delivered by post . . .

(6) If not delivered in accordance with subsection (5), the notice must be delivered by hand. . . .

(7) Where a public procession is held, each of the persons organising it is guilty of an offence if—

(a) the requirements of this section as to notice have not been satisfied, or

(b) the date when it is held, the time when it starts, or its route, differs from the date, time or route specified in the notice.

(8) It is an offence for the accused to prove that he did not know of, and neither suspected nor had reason to suspect, the failure to satisfy the requirements or (as the case may be) the difference of day, time or route.

(9) To the extent that an alleged offence turns on a difference of date, time or route, it is a defence for the accused to prove that the difference arose from circumstances beyond his control or from something done with the agreement of a police officer or by his direction.

Imposing conditions on public processions

12.–(1) If the senior police officer, having regard to the time or place at which and the circumstances in which any public procession is being held or is intended to be held and to its route or proposed route, reasonably believes that—

(a) it may result in serious public disorder, serious damage to property or serious disruption to the life of the community, or

(b) the purpose of the persons organising it is the intimidation of others with a view to compelling them not to do an act they have a right to do, or to do an act they have a right not to do,

he may give directions imposing on the persons organising or taking part in the procession such conditions as appear to him necessary to prevent such disorder, damage, disruption or intimidation, including conditions as to the route of the procession or prohibit it from entering any public place specified in the directions.

(2) In subsection (1) 'the senior police officer' means—

(a) in relation to a procession being held, or to a procession intended to be held in a case where persons are assembling with a view to taking part in it, the most senior in rank of the police officers present at the scene, and

(b) in relation to a procession intended to be held in a case where paragraph (1) does not apply, the chief officer of police.

(4) A person who organises a public procession and knowingly fails to comply with a condition imposed under this section is guilty of an offence, but it is a defence for him to prove that the failure arose from circumstances beyond his control.

(5) A person who takes part in a public procession and knowingly fails to comply with a condition imposed under this section is guilty of an offence, but it is a defence for him to prove that the failure arose from circumstances beyond his control.

(6) A person who incites another to commit an offence under subsection (5) is guilty of an offence.

(7) A constable in uniform may arrest without warrant anyone he reasonably suspects is committing an offence under subsection (4), (5) or (6).

Prohibiting public processions

13.–(1) If at any time the chief officer of police reasonably believes that, because of particular circumstances existing in any district or part of a district, the powers under section 12 will not be sufficient to prevent the holding of public processions in that district or part from resulting in serious public disorder, he shall apply to the council of the district for an order prohibiting for such period not exceeding three months as may be specified in the application the holding of all public processions (or of any class of public procession so specified) in the district or part concerned.

(2) On receiving such an application, a council may with the consent of the Secretary of State make an order either in the terms of the application or with such modifications as may be approved by the Secretary of State. . . .

(7) A person who organises a public procession the holding of which he knows is prohibited by virtue of an order under this section is guilty of an offence.

(8) A person who takes part in a public procession the holding of which he knows is prohibited by virtue of an order under this section is guilty of an offence.

(9) A person who incites another to commit an offence under subsection (8) is guilty of an offence.

(10) A constable in uniform may arrest without warrant anyone he reasonably suspects is committing an offence under subsection (7), (8) or (9).

Imposing conditions on public assemblies

14.–(1) If the senior police officer, having regard to the time or place at which and the circumstances in which any public assembly is being held or is intended to be held, reasonably believes that—

(a) it may result in serious public disorder, serious damage to property or serious disruption to the life of the community, or

(b) the purpose of the persons organising it is the intimidation of others with a view to compelling them not to do an act they have a right to do, or to do an act they have a right not to do,

he may give directions imposing on the persons organising or taking part in the assembly such conditions as to the place at which the assembly may be (or continue to be) held, its maximum duration, or the maximum number of persons who may constitute it, as appear to him necessary to prevent such disorder, damage, disruption or intimidation.

(2) In subsection (1) 'the senior police officer' means—

(a) in relation to an assembly being held, the most senior in rank of the police officers present at the scene, and

(b) in relation to an assembly intended to be held, the chief officer of police.

(4) A person who organises a public assembly and knowingly fails to comply with a condition imposed under this section is guilty of an offence, but it is a defence for him to prove that the failure arose from circumstances beyond his control.

(5) A person who takes part in a public assembly and knowingly fails to comply with a condition imposed under this section is guilty of an offence, but it is a defence for him to prove that the failure arose from circumstances beyond his control.

(6) A person who incites another to commit an offence under subsection (5) is guilty of an offence.

(7) A constable in uniform may arrest without warrant anyone he reasonably suspects is committing an offence under subsection (4), (5) or (6).

Prohibiting trespassory assemblies[37]

14A.–(1) If at any time the chief officer of police reasonably believes that an assembly is intended to be held in any district at a place on land to which the public has no right of access or only a limited right of access and that the assembly—

(a) is likely to be held without the permission of the occupier of the land or to conduct itself in such a way as to exceed the limits of any permission of his or the limits of the public's right of access, and

(b) may result—

(i) in serious disruption to the life of the community, or

(ii) where the land, or a building or monument on it, is of historical, architectural, archaeological or scientific importance, in significant damage to the land, building or monument,

he may apply to the council of the district for an order prohibiting for a specified period the holding of all trespassory assemblies in the district or a part of it, as specified.

(2) On receiving such an application, a council may—

(a) in England and Wales, with the consent of the Secretary of State make an order either in the terms of the application or with such modifications as may be approved by the Secretary of State; or

(b) in Scotland, make an order in the terms of the application.

(5) An order prohibiting the holding of trespassory assemblies operates to prohibit any assembly which—

(a) is held on land to which the public has no right of access or only a limited right of access, and

(b) takes place in the prohibited circumstances, that is to say, without the permission of the occupier of the land or so as to exceed the limits of any permission of his or the limits of the public's right of access.

(6) No order under this section shall prohibit the holding of assemblies for a period exceeding 4 days or in an area exceeding an area represented by a circle with a radius of 5 miles from a specified centre.

(9) In this section and ss 14B and 14C—

'assembly' means an assembly of 20 or more persons;

'land', means land in the open air;

---

37   Inserted by the Criminal Justice and Public Order Act 1994, s 70.

'limited', in relation to a right of access by the public to land, means that their use of it is restricted to use for a particular purpose (as in the case of a highway or road) or is subject to other restrictions;

Offences in connection with trespassory assemblies and arrest therefor

14B.–(1) A person who organises an assembly the holding of which he knows is prohibited by an order under section 14A is guilty of an offence.

(2) A person who takes part in an assembly which he knows is prohibited by an order under section 14A is guilty of an offence.

(3) In England and Wales, a person who incites another to commit an offence under subsection (2) is guilty of an offence.

(4) A constable in uniform may arrest without a warrant anyone he reasonably suspects to be committing an offence under this section.

Stopping persons from proceeding to trespassory assemblies

14C.–(1) If a constable in uniform reasonably believes that a person is on his way to an assembly within the area to which an order under section 14A applies which the constable reasonably believes is likely to be an assembly which is prohibited by that order, he may, subject to subsection (2) below—

(a) stop that person, and

(b) direct him not to proceed in the direction of the assembly.

(2) The power conferred by subsection (1) may only be exercised within the area to which the order applies.

(3) A person who fails to comply with a direction under subsection (1) which he knows has been given to him is guilty of an offence.

(4) A constable in uniform may arrest without a warrant anyone he reasonably suspects to be committing an offence under this section.

Notes

1   The notice requirement under s 11 may have some inhibiting effect on organisers of marches, but except in that sense, it cannot readily be characterised 'an interference' with freedom of expression or assembly under the HRA since it is not a request for *permission* to hold the march. Once notice is correctly given, the march can take place, although conditions may be imposed on it, the matter considered in the next section. As indicated above, prior restraints on marches, including complete bans, have been upheld at Strasbourg, although the margin of appreciation doctrine was influential.[38] Owing to its relatively minimal impact on marches, which means that it is probably – depending on the circumstances of a particular case – proportionate to the aims pursued, the notice requirement, assuming that it exempts spontaneous marches, appears to be compatible with Articles 10 and 11.

2   The phrase 'serious disruption to the life of the community', used in ss 12(1)(a), 14(1)(a) and now 14A(1)(b), is very broad and clearly offers police officers wide scope for interpretation. This 'trigger' has attracted particular criticism from commentators. It has been said that 'some inconvenience is the inevitable consequence of a successful protest. The Act ... threatens to permit only those demonstrations that are so convenient that they become invisible'.[39] Bonner and

---

38   Eg, *Christians Against Racism and Fascism v UK* (1980) 21 DR 138.
39   Ewing and Gearty, *op cit*, p 121.

Stone have warned of 'the dangers that lie in the vague line between serious disruption and a measure of inconvenience'.[40] It has been noted that the term 'the community' used in ss 12, 14 and 14A is ambiguous. In the case of London, it is unclear whether the term could be applied to Oxford Street or inner London or the whole Metropolitan area.[41] The more narrowly the term is defined, the more readily a given march or assembly could be said to cause serious disruption.

3   The conditions that can be imposed if one of the 'triggers' under s 12(1) or 14(1) is thought be present are limited in scope under s 14, but very wide in the case of marches under s 12. In *Director of Public Prosecutors v Jones* [2002] EWHC Admin 110 (below) it is made clear that the possible conditions under s 12 cannot be imported into s 14. The use of such broad wording does not oust the jurisdiction of the courts to assess the legality of the decision made.[42] Thus, at least in theory, it is not the case that any decision which appears necessary to an officer will in fact be lawful. However, it must be noted that in dealing with police action to maintain public order, the courts have been very unwilling to find police decisions to have been unlawful.[43] Also, unless the conditions were imposed some time before the assembly, a challenge to them by way of judicial review would be pointless.

4   The power to prohibit public processions under s 13 is open to criticism in that once a banning order has been imposed it prevents all marches in the area it covered for its duration. Thus, a projected march likely to be of an entirely peaceful character would be caught by a ban aimed at a violent march. The Campaign for Nuclear Disarmament attempted unsuccessfully to challenge such a ban (under the predecessor of s 13 – s 3 of the 1936 Act) after it had had to cancel a number of its marches: *Kent v Metropolitan Police Commissioner* (1981) *The Times*, 15 May.

5   It might seem that the s 13 banning power would be in breach of Article 11 of the ECHR, in that the banning of a march expected to be peaceful would not appear to be justified under Article 11, para 2 in respect of the need to prevent disorder. However, in *Christians Against Racism and Fascism v UK* (1984) 24 Yearbook 178, the applicants' argument that a ban imposed under s 3(3) of the Public Order Act 1936 infringed, *inter alia*, Article 11 was rejected by the Commission as manifestly ill founded, on the ground that the ban was justified under the exceptions to Article 11 contained in para 2, since there was a real danger of disorder which it was thought could not be 'prevented by other less stringent measures'. Thus, it may be irrelevant that a particular march affected by the ban was unlikely in itself to give rise to disorder. Nevertheless, the s 13 power may be open to amelioration under the HRA in order to achieve compatibility with Articles 10 and 11. A court confronted with the kind of situation that arose in *Christians Against Racism and Fascism* under the HRA could take a hard look at the question of proportionality. The court could take the view that the geographical or temporal scope of the ban had been greater than was needed to obviate the risk of serious disorder. Or it could find that the ban need not have been imposed at all since the imposition of conditions under s 12 would have been sufficient.

Police v Lorna Reid [1987] Crim LR 702 (Commentary: Professor D Birch)

The defendant, with about 20 others, demonstrated outside South Africa House in Trafalgar Square on the occasion of a reception there. She shouted slogans through a megaphone and the others

40   'The Public Order Act 1986: steps in the wrong direction?' [1987] PL 202.
41   Ewing and Gearty, *op cit*.
42   See, eg, *Secretary of State for Education and Science v Tameside* [1977] AC 1014.
43   See *Kent v Metropolitan Police Commission* (1981) *The Times*, 15 May.

joined in. All raised their arms and waved their fingers at the arriving guests as they did so. The slogans included 'Apartheid murderers, get out of Britain' and 'You are a dying breed'. One visitor turned to remonstrate with the demonstrators.

The chief inspector in charge decided that this was intimidatory and purported to impose a condition on the assembly, relying on s 14(1) of the Public Order Act 1986. He used a police megaphone to say, 'This is a police message. You are required to go to the mouth of Duncannon Street, north of the tree'. The defendant made a speech over her megaphone, saying that they would not move.

When the group reached the tree, the defendant refused to go further and her arresting officer said that she pushed against him saying 'I am going back to where I came from'. She was arrested and charged with knowingly failing to comply with a condition imposed on a public assembly, contrary to s 14(5) of the 1986 Act.

In cross-examination, the chief inspector said that he defined intimidation as 'putting people in fear or discomfort'.

Held, the question was whether these demonstrators acted with a view to compelling visitors not to go into South Africa House or merely with the intention of causing them discomfort so as to make them look again at what was going on in South Africa. The chief inspector had equated intimidation with discomfort. That was the wrong test. Causing someone to feel uncomfortable would not be intimidation. The officer needed to go further and reasonably believe that the organisers acted with a view to compelling. Since he had not said that he had done so in this case, there was no ground for imposing a condition on the assembly and the defendant had therefore not committed the offence.

Director of Public Prosecutions v Jones [2002] EWHC Admin 110, QBD

. . .

2. The respondent was charged with an offence contrary to section 14(5) and (9) of the Public Order Act 1986, in that she ... took part in a public assembly and knowingly failed to comply with a condition imposed by a senior police officer under section 14 of the Public Order Act 1986, that is she failed to remain in the designated demonstration area.

3. The charge arose out of the respondent's alleged participation in a demonstration outside Huntingdon Life Services premises at Woolley, near Huntingdon ...

4. On 26th October 2000 the Assistant Chief Constable for Cambridgeshire issued a notice under section 14 of the Public Order Act 1986 imposing certain conditions upon the assembly to be held on 4th November 2000. The conditions prescribed and defined in writing (by reference to a map) the area within which the assembly could take place. The assembly was to be permitted to take place between seven in the morning and seven in the evening. The respondent was arrested at about 4 o'clock on 4th November 2000 outside the area in which the demonstration was permitted. When interviewed she admitted that she had been given a copy of the section 14 notice upon her arrival at the demonstration, and that she had been warned before her arrest that she was outside the area designated in the notice within which the assembly was permitted. She said at interview that she had no sense of direction and had got lost when trying to find her way back to the road and had fallen into a ditch.

5. At the trial before the magistrates on 23rd March of last year, the appellant led evidence relating to the existence and terms of the section 14 notice. Submissions were then made on behalf of the respondent that certain of the terms of the notice were *ultra vires* because they were not related to the place of an assembly, therefore terms which could not properly be included in the section 14 notice.

6. The justices at that stage held that the particular terms of the notice did not relate to the place and that the defect in terms rendered the whole notice unlawful. Thus, at that stage, before the close of the Crown's evidence, they dismissed the charge. The case, therefore, at that stage turned on the legality of the notice of 26th October 2000 ...

10. It is three of the five conditions of the notice in this case which are said to be *ultra vires* the senior police officer's powers under section 14, and to render the notice unlawful in its entirety, as was found by the magistrates ... it is contended by the respondent that the three conditions said to be *ultra vires* are permitted by section 12 of the 1986 Act but not section 14 ...

16. The contention for the respondent before the justices was set out at paragraph 5 of the case, which states: 'It was contended by the Respondent that the document was unlawful in that it exceeded the powers of the Assistant Chief Constable under section 14 of the Public Order Act 1986. The substance of the order went too far and invoked powers under section 12 of the Public Order Act 1986 namely, the route, rendering the order unlawful. The order whilst using conditions relevant to a notice under section 14 Public Order Act 1968 also used conditions relevant to a notice under section 12 of the Public Order Act 1968 thereby rendering the notice *ultra vires*.'...

20 ... the question [for us] should be considered in two parts, namely are conditions [relating to the route] *ultra vires* of the Deputy Chief Constable's powers under section 14 of the Public Order Act? Secondly, if so, are they severable?

24. In my judgment, the magistrates were correct in concluding in this case that conditions [regarding the route], fell outside the Deputy Chief Constable's power under section 14 ...

29. I turn now to the second part of the question. In my judgment, any decision on the question of severability will, as my Lord, Auld LJ, posed in argument, necessarily take place in retrospect as a judicial exercise. If a person taking part in an assembly breaches a condition which is clear and properly severable from conditions which are not valid, for my part I can see nothing unfair in him or her being prosecuted for their breach ...

32. In my judgment the test to be applied in this case is that explained by Lord Bridge in *Director of Public Prosecutions v Hutchinson*. ... 'A legislative instrument is texturally severable if a clause, a sentence, a phrase or a single word may be disregarded, as exceeding the lawmaker's power, and what remains of the text is still grammatical and coherent. A legislative instrument is substantially severable if the substance of what remains after severance is essentially unchanged in its legislative purpose, operation and effect ...'

36. In any event, in my judgment, the test for a notice under section 14 cannot be more restrictive than for legislative provisions. For my part, I am content in this case to adopt the test of the legislative provisions as explained by Lord Bridge. On the basis of that test, I conclude that the [*ultra vires*] conditions of the section 14 notice can be severed without invalidating the whole notice. Textually there is no difficulty in severing the conditions. Conditions 1 and 2 go together and deal with disembarkation and movement to the permitted area. Condition 5 deals with the movement away from the permitted area. Neither is textually connected with conditions 3 and 4, which define the permitted area.

37. Similarly, in my judgment, to sever those conditions passes the test for substantial severance. What remains on severance are the conditions dealing with the permitted area for assembly. This, in my judgment, is exactly what section 14 permits.

Auld LJ: For the reasons given, and in accordance with the answers given by my Lord to the questions formulated by him, I agree that the appeal should be allowed.

Director of Public Prosecutions v Jones (Margaret) and Another [1999] 2 AC 240, HL

The defendants took part in a peaceful, non-obstructive assembly on a highway in respect of which there was in force an order under s 14A of the Public Order Act 1986 prohibiting the holding of trespassory assemblies. They were convicted before justices of taking part in a trespassory assembly knowing it to be prohibited, contrary to section 14B(2) of the 1986 Act, as inserted. On appeal, the Crown Court held that there was no case for them to answer on the basis that the holding of a peaceful, non-obstructive assembly was part of the public's limited rights of access to the highway and so was not prohibited by the order. The Divisional Court allowed an appeal by the Director of Public Prosecutions.

Lord Irvine of Lairg LC: My Lords, this appeal raises an issue of fundamental constitutional importance: what are the limits of the public's rights of access to the public highway? Are these rights so restricted that they preclude in all circumstances any right of peaceful assembly on the public highway? On 1 June 1995 at about 6.40 pm Police Inspector Mackie counted 21 people on the roadside verge of the southern side of the A344, adjacent to the perimeter fence of the monument at Stonehenge. Some were bearing banners with the legends, 'Never Again', 'Stonehenge Campaign 10 years of Criminal Injustice' and 'Free Stonehenge'. He concluded that they constituted a 'trespassory assembly' and told them so. When asked to move off, many did, but some, including the defendants, Mr Lloyd and Dr Jones, were determined to remain and put their rights to the test. They were arrested for taking part in a 'trespassory assembly' and convicted by the Salisbury justices on 3 October 1995. Their appeals to the Salisbury Crown Court, however, succeeded. The court held that neither of the defendants, nor any member of their group, was 'being destructive, violent, disorderly, threatening a breach of the peace or, on the evidence, doing anything other than reasonably using the highway'. About an hour before, a different group of people had scaled the fence of the monument and entered it. They had been successfully escorted away by police officers without any violence or arrests; but there were no grounds for apprehension that any of the group of which Mr Lloyd and Dr Jones were members proposed an incursion into the area of the monument. An appeal by way of case stated to the Divisional Court [1998] QB 563 followed. It was assumed for the purposes of that appeal (per McCowan LJ, at p 568c) that (a) the grass verge constituted part of the public highway; and (b) the group was peaceful, did not create an obstruction and did not constitute or cause a public nuisance. The defendants had been charged with 'trespassory assembly' under section 14B(2) of the Public Order Act 1986; s 14A (as inserted) of the Act of 1986 permits a chief officer of police to apply, in certain circumstances, to the local council for an order prohibiting for a specified period 'trespassory assemblies' within a specified area. An order of that kind may be obtained only in respect of land 'to which the public has no right of access or only a limited right of access'; had been obtained in this case; and covered the area in which the defendants, with others, had assembled.

The Divisional Court reinstated the defendants' convictions. It held that a peaceful assembly on the public highway exceeds the limits of the public's right of access (within the meaning of section 14A(5)). The 'particular purpose' mentioned in the definition of 'limited' in section 14A(9) was held not to include the use of the highway for peaceful assembly. The central issue in the case thus turns on two interrelated questions: (i) what are the 'limits' of the public's right of access to the public highway at common law? and (ii) what is the 'particular purpose' for which the public has a right to use the public highway?

... in broad terms the basis of the Divisional Court's decision is the proposition that the public's right of access to the public highway is limited to the right to pass and repass, and to do anything incidental or ancillary to that right. Peaceful assembly is not incidental to the right to pass and repass. Thus peaceful assembly exceeds the limits of the public's right of access and so is conduct which fulfils the *actus reus* of the offence of 'trespassory assembly'.

The Divisional Court's decision is founded principally on three authorities. In *ex parte Lewis* (1888) 21 QBD 191 the Divisional Court held *obiter* that there was no public right to occupy Trafalgar Square for the purpose of holding public meetings. However, Wills J, giving the judgment of the court, had in mind, at p 197, an assembly 'to the detriment of others having equal rights ... in its nature irreconcilable with the right of free passage ...'. Such an assembly would probably also amount to a public nuisance, and, today, involve the commission of the offence of obstruction of the public highway contrary to section 137(1) of the Highways Act 1980. Such an assembly would probably also amount to unreasonable user of the highway. It by no means follows that this same reasoning should apply to a peaceful assembly which causes no obstruction nor any public nuisance.

Harrison v Duke of Rutland [1893] 1 QB 142 ... [established that using the highway], not for the purpose of using it in order to pass and repass, or for any reasonable or usual mode of using the highway as a highway, [is trespass]

...The question to which this appeal gives rise is whether the law today should recognise that the public highway is a public place, on which all manner of reasonable activities may go on. For the reasons I set out below in my judgment it should. Provided these activities are reasonable, do not involve the commission of a public or private nuisance, and do not amount to an obstruction of the highway unreasonably impeding the primary right of the general public to pass and repass, they should not constitute a trespass. Subject to these qualifications, therefore, there would be a public right of peaceful assembly on the public highway ... Nor can I attribute any hard core of meaning to a test which would limit lawful use of the highway to what is incidental or ancillary to the right of passage. In truth very little activity could accurately be described as 'ancillary' to passing along the highway: perhaps stopping to tie one's shoe lace, consulting a street-map, or pausing to catch one's breath. But I do not think that such ordinary and usual activities as making a sketch, taking a photograph, handing out leaflets, collecting money for charity, singing carols, playing in a Salvation Army band, children playing a game on the pavement, having a picnic, or reading a book, would qualify. These examples illustrate that to limit lawful use of the highway to that which is literally 'incidental or ancillary' to the right of passage would be to place an unrealistic and unwarranted restriction on commonplace day-to-day activities. The law should not make unlawful what is commonplace and well accepted.

... If the right to use the highway extends to reasonable user not inconsistent with the public's right of passage, then the law does recognise (and has at least since Lord Esher MR's judgment in *Harrison v Duke of Rutland* [1893] 1 QB 142 recognised) that the right to use the highway, goes beyond the minimal right to pass and repass. That user may in fact extend, to a limited extent, to roaming about on the highway, or remaining on the highway. But that is not of the essence of the right.

I conclude therefore the law to be that the public highway is a public place which the public may enjoy for any reasonable purpose, provided the activity in question does not amount to a public or private nuisance and does not obstruct the highway by unreasonably impeding the primary right of the public to pass and repass: within these qualifications there is a public right of peaceful assembly on the highway. Since the law confers this public right, I deprecate any attempt artificially to restrict its scope. It must be for the magistrates in every case to decide whether the user of the highway under consideration is both reasonable in the sense defined and not inconsistent with the primary right of the public to pass and repass. In particular, there can be no principled basis for limiting the scope of the right by reference to the subjective intentions of the persons assembling.

... If, contrary to my judgment, the common law of trespass is not as clear as I have held it to be, then at least it is uncertain and developing, so that regard should be had to the Convention for the Protection of Human Rights and Fundamental Freedoms in resolving the uncertainty and in determining how it should develop: *Derbyshire County Council v Times Newspapers Ltd* [1992] QB 770, *per* Balcombe LJ, at p 812b–c, and Butler-Sloss LJ, at p 830a–b; and see *Attorney-General v Guardian Newspapers Ltd (No 2)* [1990] 1 AC 109, 283, *per* Lord Goff of Chieveley. Article 11 confers a 'right to freedom of peaceful assembly' and then entitles the state to impose restrictions on that right. The effect of the Divisional Court's decision in this case would be that any peaceful assembly on the public highway, no matter how minor or harmless, would involve the commission of the tort of trespass.

Unless the common law recognises that assembly on the public highway *may* be lawful, the right contained in Article 11(1) of the Convention is denied. Of course the right may be subject to restrictions (for example, the requirements that user of the highway for purposes of assembly must be reasonable and non-obstructive, and must not contravene the criminal law of wilful obstruction of the highway). But in my judgment our law will not comply with the Convention unless its *starting point* is that assembly on the highway will not necessarily be unlawful ... Thus, if necessary, I would invoke Article 11 to clarify or develop the common law in the terms which I have held it to be; but for the reasons I have given I do not find it necessary to do so. I would therefore allow the appeal.

Lord Slynn of Hadley: It cannot, of course, be said that the public has no right of access to the highway; it is not suggested that the public's right of access is absolute. The question is what are the limits to the right (not, it should be noted, the practice) of the public to use or be on the highway. For this purpose it is not necessary to distinguish between 'highway' and 'road' since the definition of 'limited' includes both, though no issue has been raised that the place where the defendants were was not a highway. I assume that it was and that as such the public had some right of access to it ... As I see it the essential feature of the public's right was explained in the judgment of Lopes LJ, with whom in substance Kay LJ agreed, in *Harrison v Duke of Rutland* [1893] 1 QB 142. Lopes LJ said, at p 152: 'The interest of the public in a highway consists solely in the right of passage ...'

He quotes, at p 153, Crompton J in *Reg v Pratt* (1855) 4 E & B 860, 868–69 who said: '... I take it to be clear law that, if a man use the land over which there is a right of way for any purpose, lawful or unlawful, other than that of passing and repassing, he is a trespasser.' ... Thus the core right is to pass and to repass although ... [as regards] uses incidental to passing and repassing – stopping to adjust a bridle or to repair a carriage wheel – would have constituted a trespass.

The right of assembly, of demonstration, is of great importance but in English law it is not an absolute right which requires all limitations on other rights to be set aside or ignored. These cases, in limiting or linking rights of user by the public of the highway to passage or repassage, in themselves exclude a right to stay on the highway other than for purposes connected with such passage ...

The right is restricted to passage and reasonable incidental uses associated with passage. I am willing to assume that more people are now more conscious of the importance of assembly and demonstration than they were in previous centuries, but I do not see that this in itself is enough to justify changing the nature and scope of the public's right to use the highway. That it cannot in itself justify as of right assemblies or demonstrations on private land is obvious. The defendants' argument in effect involves giving to members of the public the right to wander over or to stay on land for such a period and in such numbers as they choose so long as they are peaceable, not obstructive, and not committing a nuisance. It is a contention which goes far beyond anything which can be described as incidental or ancillary to the use of a highway as such for the purposes of passage; nor does such an extensive use in my view constitute a reasonable, normal or usual use of the highway as a highway.

... the fact that an assembly is peaceful or unlikely to result in violence, or that it is not causing an obstruction at the particular time when the police intervene, [does not] in itself change what is otherwise a trespass into a legal right of access ... Reference was also made to the European Convention for the Protection of Human Rights and Fundamental Freedoms, not, of course, as in itself governing the legal position in the United Kingdom, but as indicating what our law should now be. It is desirable to look at the Convention for guidance even at the present time, but this is not a case in my opinion where there is any statutory ambiguity to be resolved or any doubt as to what the common law is: see *per* Butler-Sloss LJ in *Derbyshire County Council v Times Newspapers Ltd* [1992] QB 770, 830. In any event, I am not satisfied that the existing law on highways is necessarily in conflict with article 11 of the Convention providing for a right of assembly, or of article 10 relating to freedom of expression. Both provide for exceptions to the rights created. I accept that it is arguable that a restriction on assembly even on the highway may interfere with the right of assembly in some situations, as the decisions of the European Court of Human Rights, which have been referred to, show, but I am not satisfied that there was here such a violation either by the law relating to access to the highway as it stands, or in its application to the facts of this case, which should compel us to change the law as I believe it to be.

It follows in my view that the Crown Court deciding essentially that what happened was a reasonable use of the highway erred in law and that the Divisional Court was right in the result to reverse their decision. The justices who heard the case through were entitled to find that there had been a trespassory assembly. The question certified in essence asks whether the lack of obstruction prevents an assembly of 20 or more persons on the highway from being a trespassory assembly. I would answer that in the negative. Put in the way in which the question is framed, ie whether such an assembly where there is no obstruction does exceed the public right of access to the highway so as to constitute a trespassory assembly contrary to section 14A of the Act of 1986, I would answer in the affirmative. I would accordingly dismiss the appeal.

In the event the Lords allowed the appeal by a majority of 3:2.

Notes

1 The fourth 'trigger' arising under ss 12(1)(b) and 14(1)(b) requires a reasonable belief in the presence of two elements: intimidation and coercion. Courts tend to take the stance that behaviour of a fairly threatening nature must be present in order to cross the boundary between discomfort and intimidation.[44] This stance was evident in *Reid*, above.

2 The decision of the House of Lords in *Jones*, above, is disappointing in that one would have expected a greater reliance on the Convention, given the imminent inception of the HRA. All the Lords in the majority delivered substantial and quite different speeches; therefore, it is a matter of some difficulty to identify the *ratio*, but the key finding in common was that since *the particular assembly in question* had been found by the tribunal of fact to be a reasonable user of the highway, it was therefore not trespassory and so not caught by the s 14A order. The conduct of the protesters, according to the majority, thus had the classic character of an English negative liberty: since it was not unlawful, it was permitted, and the police had 'no right' to remove the protesters. This was the basis of the judgment, not any finding that the protesters had a positive right to peaceful protest which the police were under a corresponding duty to respect.[45] The majority, therefore, apparently found a liberty to peaceful assembly on the highway. A liberty generally is precarious for two reasons: there is no duty upon the state (or anyone else) to respect it or facilitate its exercise, and the legislature (or the judiciary through the common law) may encroach upon it at any time. Not one of their Lordships was prepared to find that assemblies on the highway which were both peaceful and non-obstructive were invariably lawful.

3 Are there grounds for expecting a radical change in approach to ss 12–14A under the HRA? The findings of the House of Lords in *Jones* strongly suggest that the traditionally blinkered and deferential judicial approach to public protest prevails. Therefore, challenges to ss 12–14A under the HRA present the judiciary with a dilemma, since they are expected to construe existing law so that it complies with the Convention, 'in so far as it is possible to do so' under s 3 of the HRA. In an instance such as *Jones*, or in respect of ss 12–14, the courts' approach to the problem can be expected to undergo a radical change, at least in methodology. Rather than focusing primarily upon the limitations upon otherwise lawful conduct that these sections create, the starting point ought to be the Convention

---

44 See *News Group Newspapers Ltd v SOGAT 1982* [1986] ICR 716.
45 Lord Hutton did appear to assert this ([1999] 2 WLR 625, 660), but his conclusion (at 666) upholds only the narrow and precarious liberty formulated by Lords Irvine and Clyde.

rights in issue. Courts should find that a protest which is wholly peaceful falls within Article 11 and, following *Steel*, it should also find Article 10 applicable. *Prima facie* interference with the right(s) would clearly have occurred, including the arrests of the defendants and any convictions sustained.[46] Having made this determination, a court would then be expected to consider the exceptions within para 2 of those Articles. It is bound under s 3 of the HRA to find an interpretation of ss 12–14A which is compatible with the Convention if at all possible, but the question of what is required in order to achieve compatibility is open to interpretation, depending on the view of the Strasbourg jurisprudence adopted. It may be noted that although this is the approach one would *expect* the courts to follow in the post- HRA era, it was very clearly absent from the discussion in *Jones*, above, on s 14 of the 1986 Act.

4   In *Steel and Others v UK* (1999) 28 EHRR 603,[47] the Court found that the interference with an entirely peaceful protest which had occurred was disproportionate to the aim of preventing disorder, and in *Ezelin v France* (1991) 14 EHRR 362, para 53 the Court found: '... that the freedom to take part in a peaceful assembly ... is of such importance that it cannot be restricted in any way ... so long as the person concerned *does not himself* commit any reprehensible act on such an occasion.' On its face,[48] this finding would prohibit the application of criminal sanctions to peaceful protesters[49] as a result of the use of blanket bans, a possibility which, as noted above, is left open by *Jones*.

It would also prohibit the imposition of conditions which can, depending on the circumstances, have an effect on an assembly almost as severe as that created by a ban. As indicated above, conditions can be imposed on peaceful assemblies where it is thought that a risk of disruption to the life of the community may arise. Following *Steel* and *Ezelin* the courts could impose a narrow interpretation on ss 12–14A, under s 3 of the HRA.

Subsequent restraints

Subsequent restraints arising from a variety of sources can be used as an alternative, or in addition, to the powers arising under the 1986 and 1994 Acts and, as will be seen, many of the powers overlap. It should be noted that the powers arising under ss 12 and 14 of the 1986 Act may be used during the assembly, not merely prior to it. The senior police officer present, who may of course be a constable, can impose the conditions mentioned if, after the assembly has begun, it is apparent that one of the 'triggers' is in being or is about to come into being.

---

46   Where an arrest and police detention took place but no charges were laid, or no conviction sustained, there would still be a *prima facie* violation of Articles 10 and 11, following *Steel and Others v UK* (1999) 28 EHRR 603: violations were found in relation to the third, fourth and fifth applicants who were arrested and detained but not tried (the prosecution adduced no evidence).

47   The applicants had been holding a banner and giving out leaflets outside an arms exhibition.

48   The Crown might argue that it is inapplicable beyond its particular facts: it concerned professional disciplinary sanctions applied to a lawyer who took part in a march that became violent and disorderly, but who conducted himself peacefully.

49   It might be argued that a distinction should be drawn between protesters who take part in a peaceful demonstration which they know to be banned, arguably thereby committing a 'reprehensible act', and those who obey the ban by abandoning their proposed demonstrations, but bring proceedings to test its legality.

Violence, threats, abuse, insults

Public Order Act 1986

Fear or provocation of violence

4.–(1) A person is guilty of an offence if he—

(a) uses towards another person threatening, abusive or insulting words or behaviour, or

(b) distributes or displays to another person any writing, sign or other visible representation which is threatening, abusive or insulting,

with intent to cause that person to believe that immediate unlawful violence will be used against him or another by any person, or to provoke the immediate use of unlawful violence by that person or another, or whereby that person is likely to believe that such violence will be used, or it is likely that such violence will be provoked. . . .

(3) A constable may arrest without warrant anyone he reasonably suspects is committing an offence under this section.

Intentional harassment, alarm or distress[50]

4A.–(1) A person is guilty of an offence if, with intent to cause a person harassment, alarm or distress, he—

(a) uses threatening, abusive or insulting words or behaviour, or disorderly behaviour, or

(b) displays any writing, sign or other visible representation which is threatening, abusive or insulting,

thereby causing that or another person harassment, alarm or distress. . . .

(3) It is a defence for the accused to prove—

(a) that he was inside a dwelling and had no reason to believe that the words or behaviour used, or the writing, sign or other visible representation displayed, would be heard or seen by a person outside that or any other dwelling, or

(b) that his conduct was reasonable.

(4) A constable may arrest without warrant anyone he reasonably suspects is committing an offence under this section.

Harassment, alarm or distress

5.–(1) A person is guilty of an offence if he—

(a) uses threatening, abusive or insulting words or behaviour, or disorderly behaviour, or

(b) displays any writing, sign or other visible representation which is threatening, abusive or insulting within the hearing or sight of a person likely to be caused harassment alarm or distress thereby.

(2) An offence under this section may be committed in a public or a private place, except that no offence is committed where the words or behaviour are used, or the writing, sign or other visible representation is displayed, by a person inside a dwelling and the other person is also inside that or another dwelling.

(3) It is a defence for the accused to prove—

(a) that he had no reason to believe that there was any person within hearing or sight who was likely to be caused harassment, alarm or distress, or

---

50   Inserted by the Criminal Justice and Public Order Act 1994, s 154.

(b) that he was inside a dwelling and had no reason to believe that the words or behaviour used, or the writing, sign or other visible representation displayed, would be heard or seen by a person outside that or any other dwelling, or

(c) that his conduct was reasonable.

(4) A constable may arrest a person without warrant if—

(a) he engages in offensive conduct which the constable warns him to stop, and

(b) he engages in further offensive conduct immediately or shortly after the warning.

(5) In subsection (4) 'offensive conduct' means conduct the constable reasonably suspects to constitute an offence under this section, and the conduct mentioned in paragraph (a) and the further conduct need not be of the same nature.

Mental element: miscellaneous

6.–(3) A person is guilty of an offence under section 4 only if he intends his words or behaviour, or the writing, sign or other visible representation to be threatening, abusive or insulting, or is aware that it may be threatening, abusive or insulting.

(4) A person is guilty of an offence under section 5 only if he intends his words or behaviour, or the writing, sign or other visible representation to be threatening, abusive or insulting, or is aware that it may be threatening, abusive or insulting or (as the case may be) he intends his behaviour to be or is aware that it may be disorderly.

Note

The words/behaviour must be 'threatening, abusive or insulting'. The term 'insulting' was considered in *Brutus v Cozens* [1973] AC 854 in respect of disruption of a tennis match involving a South African player by an anti-apartheid demonstrator.

Brutus v Cozens **[1973] AC 854, 860–63**

Lord Reid: My Lords, the charge against the appellant is that on 28 June 1971, during the annual tournament at the All England Lawn Tennis Club, Wimbledon, he used insulting behaviour whereby a breach of the peace was likely to be occasioned, contrary to s 5 of the Public Order Act 1936, as amended.

While a match was in progress on No 2 Court he went on to the court, blew a whistle and threw leaflets around. On the whistle being blown nine or ten others invaded the court with banners and placards. I shall assume that they did this at the instigation of the appellant though that is not made very clear in the case stated by the magistrates. Then the appellant sat down and had to be forcibly removed by the police. The incident lasted for two or three minutes. This is said to have been insulting behaviour.

It appears that the object of this demonstration was to protest against the apartheid policy of the Government of South Africa. But it is not said that that Government was insulted. The insult is said to have been offered to or directed at the spectators. The spectators at No 2 Court were upset; they made loud shouts, gesticulated and shook their fists and, while the appellant was being removed, some showed hostility and attempted to strike him.

... the question of law in this case must be whether it was unreasonable to hold that the appellant's behaviour was not insulting. To that question there could in my view be only one answer – no.

But as the divisional court [[1972] 1 WLR 484] have expressed their view as to the meaning of 'insulting' I must, I think, consider it. It was said, at p 487:

> It is, as I think, quite sufficient for the purpose of this case to say that behaviour which affronts other people, and evidences a disrespect or contempt for their rights, behaviour which reasonable persons would foresee is likely to cause resentment or protest such as was

aroused in this case, and I rely particularly on the reaction of the crowd as set out in the case stated, is insulting for the purpose of this section.

I cannot agree with that. Parliament had to solve the difficult question of how far freedom of speech or behaviour must be limited in the general public interest. It would have been going much too far to prohibit all speech or conduct likely to occasion a breach of the peace because determined opponents may not shrink from organising or at least threatening a breach of the peace in order to silence a speaker whose views they detest. Therefore vigorous and it may be distasteful or unmannerly speech or behaviour is permitted so long as it does not go beyond any one of three limits. It must not be threatening. It must not be abusive. It must not be insulting. I see no reason why any of these should be construed as having a specially wide or a specially narrow meaning. They are all limits easily recognisable by the ordinary man. Free speech is not impaired by ruling them out. But before a man can be convicted it must be clearly shown that one or more of them has been disregarded.

The spectators may have been very angry and justly so. The appellant's conduct was deplorable. Probably it ought to be punishable. But I cannot see how it insulted the spectators.

I would allow the appeal with costs.

Notes

1 The conviction of the defendant under the predecessor of s 4 of the 1986 Act was therefore overturned.

2 The test for 'insulting' appears to be whether an ordinary sensible person at whom the words in question are directed would find them insulting. The fact that the persons in question who hear the words are particularly likely to find them insulting may not preclude a finding that they are insulting, although whether or not the speaker knows that such persons will hear the words appears to be immaterial as far as this ingredient of ss 5, 4 and 4A is concerned (*Jordan v Burgoyne* [1963] 2 QB 744).

3 Section 5 is the lowest level public order offence contained in the 1986 Act and the most contentious, since it brings behaviour within the scope of the criminal law which was previously thought of as too trivial to justify the imposition of criminal liability.[51] In Northern Ireland, s 5 was used against a poster depicting youths stoning a British Saracen with a caption proclaiming 'Ireland: 20 years of resistance'.[52] In the so-called *Madame M* case, four students were prosecuted for putting up a satirical poster depicting Margaret Thatcher as a 'sadistic dominatrix';[53] the students were acquitted but it was disturbing that such a case was brought in a democracy.

DPP v Clarke, Lewis, O'Connell and O'Keefe [1992] Crim LR 60

It was alleged against the respondents that they 'on 16 December 1989 ... did display writing, a sign or visible representation which was threatening, abusive or insulting, within the hearing or sight of a person likely to be caused harassment, alarm or distress thereby contrary to ss 5(1)(b) and 6 of the Public Order Act 1986'.

The events which gave rise to these charges took place outside a licensed abortion clinic. On 16 December the respondents, who were opposed to the procuring of abortions, assembled on the pavement outside the clinic, each carrying a picture of an aborted foetus which they displayed to

---

51 For background to s 5, see Law Commission Report No 123, *Offences Relating to Public Order* (1983); for comment see D Williams [1984] PL 12.
52 Reported in the *Independent*, 12 September 1988; mentioned in Ewing and Gearty, *op cit*, p 123.
53 P Thornton, *Decade of Decline: Civil Liberties in the Thatcher Years* (1990), p 37.

police officers who were on uniform patrol duty and, in one case, to passers-by. The respondents refused to comply with police requests not to display the pictures. The magistrates concluded that the pictures were abusive and insulting giving the words their ordinary everyday meaning and that they were displayed in the sight of a person likely to be caused harassment alarm or distress, and did in fact cause alarm and distress to the police officer concerned. Applying an objective test to s 5(3)(c) they found that, in all the circumstances, the respondents' conduct was not reasonable; applying s 6 and using a subjective test they concluded that, on the balance of probabilities, none of the respondents intended the pictures to be threatening, abusive or insulting, nor was any of them aware that they might be. The respondents were therefore acquitted by the magistrates.

Held, dismissing the appeal;

(i) The two limbs of s 5(1) must be distinguished. First, the thing displayed must be threatening, abusive or insulting; secondly, the display must be within the sight of a person likely to be caused harassment, alarm or distress thereby. However, s 6(4) provided that a person was only guilty under s 5 if he intended the writing, sign or other visible representation to be threatening, abusive or insulting or was aware that it might be. It did not, therefore, avail the appellant to argue that the respondents must have intended the pictures to cause harassment, alarm or distress or been aware that they might do so; a picture might cause harassment, alarm or distress without being threatening, abusive or insulting and vice versa. The magistrates' conclusion that, although the pictures were abusive and insulting and the police officer found them so, the respondents lacked the necessary intention or awareness, was unassailable. The question whether the pictures were abusive or insulting was essentially one for the magistrates; *Brutus v Cozens* [1973] AC 854.

(ii) The magistrates were correct in applying an objective test to the defence of reasonable conduct in s 5(3)(c) of the Act.

(iii) The magistrates correctly imputed a subjective awareness to the words 'is aware that it may be threatening, abusive or insulting' in s 6(4) of the Act.

R v Horseferry Road Magistrate ex p Siadatan [1991] 1 All ER 324, 325–29

Watkins LJ: On 26 September 1988 Viking Penguin Books Ltd (Viking Penguin) published a book entitled *The Satanic Verses,* the author of which is Mr Salman Rushdie. It is clear that many devout Muslims have found the book offensive.

[The applicant's] solicitors, acting on the applicant's instructions, laid before the Horseferry Road Magistrates' Court an information in these terms:

> Penguin Books Limited on or before the 19th of June 1989 at 157 Kings Road, Chelsea SW3 and other places unknown distributed books entitled *The Satanic Verses* by Salman Rushdie containing abusive and insulting writing whereby it was likely that unlawful violence would be provoked contrary to s 4(1) of the Public Order Act, 1986.

... The issue is whether the words 'such violence', where they appear in that subsection, mean 'unlawful violence' or 'immediate unlawful violence' ...

A consequence of construing the words 'such violence' in s 4(1) as meaning 'immediate unlawful violence' will be that leaders of an extremist movement who prepare pamphlets or banners to be distributed or carried in public places by adherents to that movement will not be committing any offence under s 4(1) albeit that they intend the words in the pamphlet or on the banners to be threatening, abusive and insulting, and it is likely that unlawful violence will be provoked by the words in the pamphlet or on the banners.

The context in which s 4(1) appears in the 1986 Act is the first matter which leads us to our conclusion. Section 4 appears in the first part of the Act together with the creation of new offences, namely riot by s 1, violent disorder by s 2, affray by s 3, harassment, alarm or distress by s 5. The provisions of those sections are such that the conduct of the defendants must produce, in an actual or notional person of reasonable firmness, fear in relation to ss 1, 2 and 3 which is contemporaneous with the unlawful violence being used by the defendants, or harassment, alarm or distress which is contemporaneous with the threatening, abusive or insulting conduct under s 5. We consider it most unlikely that Parliament could have intended to include, among sections which undoubtedly deal with conduct having an immediate impact on bystanders, a section creating an offence for conduct which is likely to lead to violence at some unspecified time in the future.

A ... very compelling reason for our conclusion on the correct construction of this subsection is that here we are construing a penal statute, of which there are, or may be, two possible readings. It is an elementary rule of statutory construction that, in a penal statute where there are two possible readings, the meaning which limits the scope of the offence thus created is that which the court should adopt.

For these reasons we hold that the magistrate was right to refuse to issue a summons.

Finally, we consider it advisable to indicate our provisional view on the meaning of the word 'immediate'.

It seems to us that the word 'immediate' does not mean 'instantaneous', that a relatively short time interval may elapse between the act which is threatening, abusive or insulting and the unlawful violence. 'Immediate' connotes proximity in time and proximity in causation, that it is likely that violence will result within a relatively short period of time and without any other intervening occurrence.

Application dismissed.

Percy v Director of Public Prosecutions (2002) 166 JP 93

The appellant was convicted of using threatening, abusive and insulting words or behaviour likely to cause harassment, alarm or distress contrary to s 5 of the Public Order Act 1986. The convictions arose from her behaviour at an American air base at RAF Feltwell. She had experience over many years of protesting against the use of weapons of mass destruction and against American military policy, including the Star Wars National Missile Defence System. She defaced the American flag by putting a stripe across the stars and by writing the words 'Stop Star Wars' across the stripes. She stepped in front of a vehicle and she placed the flag down in front of it and stood upon it. Those affected by her behaviour were mostly American service personnel or their families, five of whom gave evidence of their distress to varying degrees. They regarded her acts as a desecration of their national flag to which they attach considerable importance. The district judge found that the appellant's behaviour with the flag was insulting to American citizens at whom it was directed.

3. The appellant did, however, satisfy the court that her behaviour was motivated by strongly held beliefs that the 'Star Wars' project was misguided, posed a danger to international stability and was not in the best interests of the United Kingdom. She failed to persuade the court that her conduct on the balance of probabilities was reasonable. Having made his findings of fact ... the District Judge then turned to the impact of Article 10 of the European Convention on Human Rights on section 5 of the Public Order Act. He highlighted ... that under Article 10(2) the right is not unqualified. The exercise of the right to freedom of expression carries attendant duties and responsibilities and so may be restricted and made subject to penalties, provided they there are prescribed by law and are necessary in a democratic society (for example, for the prevention of disorder, or for the protection of the rights of others). The court considered in this case the risk of disorder and criminal offences by others to be slight. His only concern, therefore, was as to the protection of the rights of others.

4. He ... went on to consider, however: 'The need to protect the rights of American service personnel and their families occupying the base to be free from gratuitously insulting behaviour in the ordinary course of their professional and private lives and their right to have their national flag, of significant symbolic importance to them, protected from disrespectful treatment.'

5. He concluded: 'The court found two aspects of this balancing exercise to be of particular significance. First, it was satisfied that there is a pressing social need in a multi-cultural society to prevent the denigration of objects of veneration and symbolic importance for one cultural group. Secondly, it was quite clear that the defendant's conduct which offended against section 5 was not the unavoidable consequence of a peaceful protest against the 'Star Wars' project, which was the defendant's stated intention, but arose from the particular manner in which the defendant chose to make her protest. The court finds the restrictions and penalties attached by section 5 to the defendant's article 10 right to freedom of expression to be necessary in a democratic society for the protection of the rights of others and proportionate to the need to protect such rights.'

. . .

27. [The court found on appeal] Where the right to freedom of expression under Article 10 is engaged, as in my view is undoubtedly the case here, it is clear from the European authorities put before us that the justification for any interference with that right must be convincingly established. Article 10(1) protects in substance and in form a right to freedom of expression which others may find insulting. Restrictions under Article 10(2) must be narrowly construed. In this case, therefore, the court had to presume that the appellant's conduct in relation to the American flag was protected by Article 10 unless and until it was established that a restriction on her freedom of expression was strictly necessary.

28. I have no difficulty in principle with the concept that there will be circumstances in which citizens of this country and visiting foreign nationals should be protected from intentionally and gratuitously insulting behaviour, causing them alarm or distress. There may well be a pressing social need to protect people from such behaviour. It is, therefore, in my view, a legitimate aim, provided of course that any restrictions on the rights of peaceful protesters are proportionate to the mischief at which they are aimed . . . A civilised society must strike an appropriate balance between the competing rights of those who may be insulted by a particular course of conduct and those who wish to register their protest on an important matter of public interest. The problem comes in striking that balance, giving due weight to the presumption in the accused's favour of the right to freedom of expression.

29. . . . The message [Ms Percy] wished to convey, namely 'Stop Star Wars' was a perfectly lawful, political message. It only became insulting because of the manner in which she chose to convey the message. That manner was only insulting because she chose to use a national flag of symbolic importance to some of her target audience . . .

31. The fact that the appellant could have demonstrated her message in a way which did not involve the use of a national flag of symbolic significance to her target audience was undoubtedly a factor to be taken into account when determining the overall reasonableness and proportionality of her behaviour and the state's response to it. But, in my view, it was only one factor.

32. Relevant factors in a case such as this, depending on the court's findings, might include the fact that the accused's behaviour went beyond legitimate protest; that the behaviour had not formed part of an open expression of opinion on a matter of public interest, but had become disproportionate and unreasonable; that an accused knew full well the likely effect of their conduct upon witnesses; that the accused deliberately chose to desecrate the national flag of those witnesses, a symbol of very considerable importance to many, particularly those who are in the armed forces; the fact that an accused targeted such people, for whom it became a very personal matter; the fact that an accused was well aware of the likely effect of their conduct; the fact that an accused's use of a flag had nothing, in effect, to do with conveying a message or the expression of opinion; that it amounted to a gratuitous and calculated insult, which a number people at whom it was directed found deeply distressing.

33. In my judgment, at the crucial stage of a balancing exercise under Article 10 the learned District Judge appears to have placed either sole or too much reliance on just the one factor, namely that the appellant's insulting behaviour could have been avoided. This seems to me to give insufficient weight to the presumption in the appellant's favour, to which I have already referred. On the face of it, this approach fails to address adequately the question of proportionality which should have been, and may well have been, uppermost in the District Judge's mind. Merely stating that interference is proportionate is not sufficient. It is not clear to me from the District Judge's reasons, given in relation to his findings under Article 10, that he has in fact applied the appropriate test. Accordingly, in my view, it appears that the learned judge inadvertently, in the course of a very careful and thorough examination of the facts and the law, has fallen into error. I am driven to the conclusion, therefore, that this conviction is incompatible with the appellant's rights under the European Convention on Human Rights and I would answer the first question posed in the case stated [Was the appellant's conviction under s 5 of the Public Order Act 1986 compatible with Article 10 of the European Convention on Human Rights and Fundamental Freedoms?] 'No'.

34. I am satisfied that, in all the circumstances, the appropriate course, therefore, is simply to quash the convictions.

Notes

1   In *DPP v Fidler and Moran* [1992] 1 WLR 91[54] the respondents were part of a group shouting at and talking to persons attending the clinic, displaying plastic models of human foetuses, photographs of dead foetuses and placards. On the basis of these findings, it was accepted on appeal that s 5 of the Public Order Act 1986 was satisfied.

2   In *DPP v Orum* [1988] 3 All ER 449 the Divisional Court found that a police officer may be a person who is caused harassment, alarm or distress by the various kinds of words or conduct to which s 5(1) applies.

3   The criminalisation of speech which causes the low level of harm connoted by the terms 'alarm' or 'distress' may be contrary to *dicta* of the European Court of Human Rights in *Müller v Switzerland* (1991) 13 EHRR 212, to the effect that the protection of free speech extends equally to ideas which 'offend, shock or disturb'.[55]

4   The number of prosecutions being brought under s 5 suggests that the police may not be showing restraint in using this area of the Act. The old s 5 offence under the 1936 Public Order Act, an offence with a higher harm threshold,[56] accounted for the majority of the 8,194 charges brought in connection with the miners' strike of 1984. In a survey of 470 1988 public order cases, conducted in two police force areas, it was found that 56 per cent of the sample led to charges under s 5. Research has also shown that during the period 1986–88 the number of charges brought for public order offences doubled, and this is thought to be due not to increased unrest, but to the existence of new offences, particularly s 5 with its low level of harm.[57]

5   Section 4A of the 1986 Act (as amended) provides an area of liability which to some extent overlaps with s 5. The *actus reus* under s 4A is the same as that under s 5, with the proviso that the harm in question must actually be caused. The *mens rea* differs somewhat from that under s 5 since the defendant must intend the person in

---

54 For comment see JC Smith [1992] Crim LR 63.
55 It should be noted that in *Brutus v Cozens* [1973] AC 854, Lord Reid said that s 5 of the previous 1936 Public Order Act was 'not designed to penalise the expressions of opinion that happen to be disagreeable, distasteful or even offensive, annoying or distressing'.
56 It was similar to the offence which replaced it, s 4 of the 1986 Act.
57 T Newburn *et al*, 'Policing the streets' (1990) 29 HORB 10 and 'Increasing public order' (1991) 7 Policing 22; quoted in SH Bailey, DJ Harris and BL Jones, *Civil Liberties: Cases and Materials*, 4th edn (1995), pp 229–30.

question to suffer harassment, alarm or distress. Section 4A provides another possible level of liability with the result that using offensive words is now imprisonable, without any requirement (as under s 4) to show that violence was intended or likely to be caused. It may also therefore offend against the protection for freedom of speech under Article 10 of the ECHR, which clearly includes protection for forms of forceful or offensive speech.

6   Section 4 of the Act overlaps with s 5 or s 4A in terms of the words or behaviour it covers (aside from disorderly behaviour which is not included in s 4) but it requires certain additional ingredients in terms of the intention of the defendant or in terms of the consequences which may flow from the words or behaviour used. Its applicability only in the public order context is confirmed by *R v Horseferry Road Metropolitan Stipendiary Magistrate ex p Siadatan* [1991] 1 QB 260.

7   Section 42 of the Criminal Justice and Police Act 2001 clearly draws on the ingredients of ss 5 and 4, although there are also significant differences. There are also similarities with the offences under s 14C of the 1986 Act and s 69 of the 1994 Act (see below). Section 42 allows a constable to give any direction to persons, including a direction to leave the scene where they are outside or in the vicinity of a dwelling, if the constable reasonably believes (a) that they are seeking to persuade a person living at the dwelling not to do something that he or she has a right to do or to do something she or he is not under any obligation to do, and (b) that the presence of the persons (normally protesters) is likely to cause harassment, alarm or distress to the person living at the residence. Disobedience to a direction is an arrestable offence.

Section 42 is an offence with a minimal *actus reus*, as is apparent when it is compared with the requirements of s 5 of the 1986 Act or ss 69 and 68 of the 1994 Act. The requirement that the words or conduct should be abusive, etc, in s 5 is missing; the requirements of s 69 or 68 that the persons in question should be trespassing and must do something intended to be obstructive or intimidatory or disruptive are also absent. But s 42 is similar to s 69 and a number of the other recent offences discussed in this chapter in that it conflates the exercise of police powers with the substantive offence. The key limiting requirement is that the persons must be outside or in the vicinity of a dwelling, although the term 'the vicinity' is open to quite a wide interpretation. The need for the introduction of this new offence must be questioned, bearing in mind that s 5 or s 4A could be used against intimidation by protesters gathered outside the home of the person targeted.

8   Suggestions as to the effect of the HRA on ss 5, 4A and 4 have already been made. Section 5 is the most problematic provision, as indicated. The similar offence under s 42 of the 2001 Act is also problematic in the sense that it hits directly at peaceful protest – protest that need not be abusive, etc, but is aimed only at persuading. The protesters need have no intention of causing harassment, alarm or distress so long as a constable reasonably believes that the target of the protest might experience those feelings. In catching peaceful protest, this offence comes directly into conflict with Articles 10 and 11. However, s 41 can also be viewed as protecting Article 8 rights but a court would be expected to consider the extent to which those rights could be said to be at stake and the proportionality of the police response, in using s 41 as opposed to a lesser measure. The use of ss 5, 4A and 4 should be carefully limited in order to answer to the strict requirements of proportionality under Articles 10 and 11. *Percy v DPP*, above, illustrates an approach which affords weight to Article 10(1) and takes a careful approach to such requirements. It is notable that in reaching its conclusion, the court relied upon s 6 of the HRA rather

than s 3, an approach which may be expected to change after the decision of the House of Lords in *S (Children) and Re W (Care Orders)* [2002] 2 AC 291; [2002] UKHL 10 (see Chapter 1 of this part, p 882).

Questions
1   Had the decision in *Siadatan* found that s 4 carries with it no requirement of immediacy, a very wide curb on freedom of speech would have been created. The decision affirms that s 4 creates a very clear demarcation between 'pure' speech and speech as an aspect of freedom of assembly. This is also clearly true of ss 5 and 4A. Is such demarcation wholly warranted, or can it be argued that forceful and insulting language used as part of a public protest should not be suppressed?
2   Within the context of freedom of assembly (as opposed to the general public order context) in the post-HRA era, is the existence of s 5 of the 1986 Act both necessary and warranted, bearing in mind the existence of the more serious public order offences under ss 1, 2 and 3, the doctrine of breach of the peace (below) and the provisions of ss 12, 13, 14A, 14B and 14C?

Breach of the peace[58]

The common law power to prevent a breach of the peace[59] overlaps with a number of the powers arising under the 1986 Act and is, in one sense, more useful to the police than the 1986 Act powers as its definition is so broad and uncertain. This means that it can be used in such a way as to undermine attempts in statutory provisions to carve out more clearly defined areas of liability. Power to prevent a breach of the peace may be used to disperse or prevent a peaceful protest or meeting which may provoke others to violence or disorder. *Beatty v Gillbanks* (1882) 9 QBD 308 established the important principle that organisers of assemblies could not be held responsible for the actions of those opposed to them whose actions in expressing their opposition created a breach of the peace. However, in *Duncan v Jones* [1936] 1 KB 218 it was found that speakers could be held responsible when persons in agreement with them might be induced to breach the peace.

Duncan v Jones [1936] I KB 218, 221–23[60]

Lord Hewart CJ: There have been moments during the argument in this case when it appeared to be suggested that the Court had to do with a grave case involving what is called the right of public meeting. I say 'called', because English law does not recognise any special right of public meeting for political or other purposes. The right of assembly, as Professor Dicey puts it [Dicey's *Law of the Constitution*, 8th edn, p 499], is nothing more than a view taken by the court of the individual liberty of the subject. If I thought that the present case raised a question which has been held in suspense by more than one writer on constitutional law – namely, whether an assembly can properly be held to be unlawful merely because the holding of it is expected to give rise to a breach of the peace on the part of persons opposed to those who are holding the meeting – I should wish to hear much more argument before I expressed an opinion. This case, however, does not even touch that important question.

Our attention has been directed to the somewhat unsatisfactory case of *Beatty v Gillbanks*. The circumstances of that case and the charge must be remembered, as also must the important

---

58   For further explanation of what may amount to a breach of the peace see Chapter 4 of this part, p 1013. For comment see 'Breaching the peace and disturbing the quiet' [1982] PL 212; DGT Williams, *Keeping the Peace: The Police and Public Order* (1967).
59   It should be noted that breach of the peace, although arrestable, is not a criminal offence.
60   For comment see T Daintith [1966] PL 248.

passage in the judgment of Field J, in which Cave J concurred. Field J said: 'I entirely concede that every one must be taken to intend the natural consequences of his own acts, and it is clear to me that, if this disturbance of the peace was the natural consequence of acts of the appellants, they would be liable, and the justices would have been right in binding them over. But the evidence set forth in the case does not support this contention; on the contrary, it shows that the disturbances were caused by other people antagonistic to the appellants, and that no acts of violence were committed by them'. Our attention has also been directed to other authorities where the judgments in *Beatty v Gillbanks* have been referred to, but they do not carry the matter any further, although they more than once express a doubt about the exact meaning of the decision. In my view, *Beatty v Gillbanks* is apart from the present case. No such question as that which arose there is even mooted here.

The present case reminds one rather of the observations of Bramwell B in *Prebble* [1 F & F 325, 326], where, in holding that a constable, in clearing certain licensed premises of the persons thereon, was not acting in the execution of his duty, he said: 'It would have been otherwise had there been a nuisance or disturbance of the public peace, or any danger of a breach of the peace.' The case stated which we have before us indicates clearly a causal connection between the meeting of May 1933 and the disturbance which occurred after it – that the disturbance was not only post the meeting but was also prior to the meeting. In my view, the deputy-chairman was entitled to come to the conclusion to which he came on the facts which he found, and to hold that the conviction of the appellant for wilfully obstructing the respondent when in the execution of his duty was right. This appeal should, therefore, be dismissed.

Redmond-Bate v DPP (1999) 163 JP 789

The Human Rights Act 1998 was not fully in force at the time. The appellant was one of three women Christian fundamentalists who had agreed with the police to preach from the steps of a cathedral. A police officer on uniformed foot patrol received a complaint about the women's activities. He went to investigate. No crowd had gathered, but he warned the women not to stop people. He returned later to find that a crowd of more than one hundred had gathered. Some members of that crowd were showing hostility. Fearing a breach of the peace, the police officer asked the women to stop preaching, and when they refused to do so, he arrested them all for wilfully obstructing him in the execution of his duty under s 89(2) of the Police Act 1996. The appellant was convicted and appealed. The issue which arose on appeal was whether it was reasonable for the police officer, in the light of what he perceived, to believe that the appellant was about to cause a breach of the peace.

Sedley LJ: Among the duties of a constable was the prevention of breaches of the peace. A member of the public who failed to comply with a reasonable request properly made to this end was guilty of obstructing the constable in the execution of his duty. The test of the reasonableness of a police officer's action was objective in the sense that it was for the court to decide not whether the view taken by the officer fell within the broad band of rational decisions, but whether, in the light of what the officer knew and perceived at the time, the court was satisfied that it was reasonable to fear an imminent breach of the peace ... A judgment as to the imminence of a breach of the peace did not conclude the police officer's task. The next critical question for the officer, and in turn for the court, was where the threat was coming from, because it was to there that the preventive action had to be directed; the common law should seek compatibility with the values of the European Convention on Human Rights in so far it did not already share them; executive action which breached the Convention ran the risk, if uncorrected by law, of putting the United Kingdom in breach of the Convention and rendering it liable to proceedings before the European Court of Human Rights. There was, therefore, a good reason for the police and the law in the present field to respect the Convention ... It was only if otherwise lawful conduct gave rise to a reasonable apprehension that it would, by interfering with the rights or liberties of others, provoke violence which, though unlawful, would not be entirely unreasonable that a police officer was empowered to take steps to prevent it; regard had to be had also to the fact that free speech included not only the inoffensive, but the irritating, the contentious, the eccentric, the heretical, the unwelcome and the provocative provided it did not tend to provoke violence. Freedom only to speak inoffensively was not worth having. The world had seen too many examples of State control of unofficial ideas, a central purpose of the Convention had been to set close limits to any such assumed power; police officers in a situation like that in the present case had difficult on the spot judgments to make. As they were judgments which impinged directly on important civil liberties and human rights, the courts had in their turn to scrutinise them with care. There was, however, nothing particularly obscure in the law as it now stood and as the Human Rights Act would shortly reinforce it. The question for the police officer was whether there was a real threat of violence and if so, from whom it was coming. If there was no real threat, no question of breach of the peace arose. If the appellant and her companions were being so provocative that someone in the crowd, without behaving wholly unreasonably, might be moved to violence, he was entitled to ask them to stop and to arrest them if they would not. If the threat of disorder or violence was coming from passers-by who were taking the opportunity to react so as to cause trouble, then it was they and not the preachers who would be asked to desist and arrested if they would not; the court had to be alert to the fact that ours was a society of many faiths and none, and many opinions. If the public promotion of faith or opinion was conducted in such a way as to insult or provoke others in breach of statute or common law, then the fact that it was done in the name of religious manifestations or freedom of speech would not necessarily save it. It might forfeit the protection of Articles 9 and 10 by reason of the limitations permitted in both Articles, provided they were necessary and proportionate, in the interests of public order and the protection of the rights of others; the situation perceived and recounted by the police officer in the present case had not justified him in apprehending a breach of the peace, much less a breach of the peace for which the appellant would be responsible, accordingly he had not been acting in the execution of his duty when he required the women to stop preaching, and the appellant was therefore not guilty of obstructing him in the execution of his duty when she refused to comply; it would not do to say that blame could not attach for breach of the peace to a speaker so long as what she said was inoffensive. Free speech includes not only the inoffensive but the irritating, the contentious, the eccentric, the heretical, the unwelcome and the provocative provided it does not tend to provoke violence. Freedom to speak only inoffensively was not worth having.

The appeal was allowed.

Notes

1   The leading pre-HRA case on breach of the peace is *R v Howell* [1981] 3 All ER 383 in which it was determined that breach of the peace will arise if an act is done or threatened to be done which either harms a person or, in his presence, his property, or is likely to cause such harm, or which puts a person in fear of such harm. Threatening words are not in themselves a breach of the peace but they may lead a police officer to apprehend a breach. In a later case, *R v Chief Constable for Devon and Cornwall ex p CEGB* [1982] QB 458, Lord Denning, dissenting, offered a rather different definition of the offence. His view was that violence is unnecessary; he considered that 'if anyone unlawfully and physically obstructs a worker – by lying down or chaining himself to a rig or the like – he is guilty of a breach of the peace'.

2   Despite Lord Hewart's comments, above, in *Duncan v Jones*, it is arguable that *Beatty v Gillbanks* (1882) 15 Cox CC 138 applies to instances in which a peaceful assembly triggers off a violent response, even where such a response was foreseen by members of the peaceful assembly. If the decision in *Beatty v Gillbanks* is interpreted in this way the decision in *Duncan v Jones* is not in accord with it, in that the freedom of the speaker was infringed, not because of her conduct but because of police fears about the possible response of the audience. Similarly, in *Jordan v*

Burgoyne [1963] 2 QB 744[61] it was found that a public speaker could be guilty of breach of the peace if he spoke words which were likely to cause disorder amongst the particular audience present, even where the audience had come with the express intent of causing trouble.

3   The decision in *Nicol v DPP* (1996) 1 Journal of Civil Liberties 75, which concerned the behaviour of fishing protesters, has not brought much clarity into this area. The protesters' behaviour in blowing horns and in attempting to dissuade the anglers from fishing provoked the anglers so that they were on the verge of using force to remove the protesters. It was found that the protesters were guilty of conduct whereby a breach of the peace was likely to be caused since their conduct, although lawful, was unreasonable and was likely to provoke the anglers to violence. This finding places a curb on the use of breach of the peace in this context since it means that behaviour which has as its natural consequence the provoking of others to violence will not amount to a breach of the peace unless it is also unreasonable. However, the decision also affirms that this area of law is subject to a wide and uncertain test of reasonableness. The judiciary may be disinclined to find that the behaviour of groups such as hunt saboteurs or tree protesters, while lawful, is reasonable.

4   The HRA may have quite a significant impact on the doctrine of breach of the peace as applied in this context, although it is not incompatible with the demands of Articles 10 and 11. In *Steel and Others v UK* (1999) 28 EHRR 603, The European Court of Human Rights found that the breach of the peace doctrine provided sufficient guidance and was formulated with sufficient precision to satisfy the requirement of Article 5(1)(c) that arrest and detention should be in accordance with a procedure prescribed by law, and that the 'prescribed by law' requirement of Article 10 was also satisfied. In *McLeod v UK* (1998) 27 EHRR 493, the Court found that the breach of the peace doctrine was 'in accordance with the law' under Article 8. Thus, in respect of the key elements of 'prescribed by law' – legal basis, certainty and accessibility – the breach of the peace doctrine meets Strasbourg standards.

5   Reappraisal and reform of the doctrine of breach of the peace is more likely to occur by reference to the notion of what is 'necessary in a democratic society' within Articles 10 and 11, para 2. This issue was extensively considered by the Court in *Steel*, but the findings were quite strongly influenced by the doctrine of the margin of appreciation.[62] The first applicant had taken part in a protest against a grouse shoot and had stood in the way of participants to prevent them taking shots. Since this behaviour was likely to be provocative, the Court found that her arrest and detention, although constituting serious interferences with her freedom of expression, could be viewed as proportionate to the aim of preventing disorder and of maintaining the authority of the judiciary[63] and this could also be said of her subsequent detention in the police station for 44 hours,[64] bearing in mind the findings of the police or magistrates that disorder might have occurred. The Court made little attempt to evaluate the real risk of disorder, taking into account the margin of appreciation afforded to the domestic authorities in determining what is

---

61   It should be noted that the case was concerned with breach of the peace under the Public Order Act 1936, s 5.

62   This was acknowledged by the Court, *Steel and Others v UK* (1999) 28 EHRR 603, para 101.

63   *Ibid*, para 104 and 107.

64   *Ibid*, para 105. The Commission acknowledged (para 156) 'some disquiet as to the proportionality of a detention of this length' which continued long after the grouse shoot was over.

necessary to avoid disorder in the particular domestic situation (para 101). The second applicant had taken part in a protest against the building of a motorway, placing herself in front of the earth-moving machinery in order to impede it. The Court found unanimously that her arrest also could be viewed as proportionate to the aim of preventing disorder, even though it accepted that the risk of immediate disorder was not so high as in the case of the first applicant (para 109). The Court accepted the finding of the magistrates' court that there had been such a risk.

The third, fourth and fifth applicants were peacefully holding banners and handing out leaflets outside a fighter helicopter conference when they were arrested for breach of the peace. The Court found that there was no justification for their arrests at all since there was no suggestion of any threat of disorder (para 110). A violation of Article 10 was therefore found in respect of those applicants. These findings suggest that interferences with protest as direct action may frequently fall within the national authorities' margin of appreciation. But, significantly, the findings also make it clear that such protest constitutes expressions of opinion and therefore fall within Articles 10 and 11. This was re-affirmed in *Hashman and Harrup v UK* (2000) 30 EHRR 241. Thus, the findings of the Court in *Steel* require a re-structuring of the domestic scrutiny of interference with such expression, which takes the primary right as the starting point. *Steel* clearly affords the domestic judiciary a wide discretion in interpreting the requirements of the Convention in an analogous case. Following an activist approach, the domestic judiciary, faced with similar facts, but disapplying the margin of appreciation aspects of *Steel*, would find that the interference was unjustified since their review of the decisions of the police or of magistrates would be less restrained. Within this model, some interferences with freedom of expression would be allowed, where direct action was likely to provoke immediate disorder due to the degree of provocation offered, but the measures taken in response, such as the length of detention, would be much more strictly scrutinised for their proportionality with the aims pursued.

6   Under this approach, greater protection would be afforded to insulting or offensive persuasion or symbolic direct action, following *Steel*, and this approach would also receive some endorsement from *Plattform 'Ärtze für das Leben' v Austria* (1988) 13 EHRR 204 which adopted a version of the *Beatty v Gillbanks* approach. Such an approach to the decision in *Steel* was, in some respects, taken by Sedley LJ in *Redmond-Bate v DPP*, above, in the period before the HRA was fully in force. Applying *Steel*, the Divisional Court found that there were no sufficient grounds on which to determine that a breach of the peace was about to be caused or, moreover, on which to determine that the threat was coming from Ms Redmond-Bate, bearing in mind the tolerance one would expect to be extended to offensive speech. This decision simplified the tests from *Nicol* of determining which party was acting reasonably where one was provoked to violence and as to which was exercising rights. The key test put forward was one of reasonableness: a breach of the peace will occur where violence was threatened or provoked, in the sense of infringing rights or liberties, unless the provoked party acts wholly – not partly – unreasonably.

Criminal trespass

Criminal Justice and Public Order Act 1994

Offence of aggravated trespass

68.–(1) A person commits the offence of aggravated trespass if he trespasses on land in the open air and, in relation to any lawful activity which persons are engaging in or are about to engage in on that or adjoining land in the open air, does there anything which is intended by him to have the effect—

    (a) of intimidating those persons or any of them so as to deter them or any of them from engaging in that activity,

    (b) of obstructing that activity, or

    (c) of disrupting that activity.

(2) Activity on any occasion on the part of a person or persons on land is 'lawful' for the purposes of this section if he or they may engage in the activity on the land on that occasion without committing an offence or trespassing on the land.

(3) A person guilty of an offence under this section is liable on summary conviction to imprisonment for a term not exceeding three months or a fine not exceeding level four on the standard scale, or both.

(4) A constable in uniform who reasonably suspects that a person is committing an offence under this section may arrest him without a warrant.

(5) In this section 'land' does not include—

    (a) the highways and roads excluded from the application of section 61 by paragraph (b) of the definition of 'land' in subsection (9) of that section; or

    (b) a road within the meaning of the Roads (Northern Ireland) Order 1993.

Powers to remove persons committing or participating in aggravated trespass

69.–(1) If the senior police officer present at the scene reasonably believes—

    (a) that a person is committing, has committed or intends to commit the offence of aggravated trespass on land in the open air; or

    (b) that two or more persons are trespassing on land in the open air and are present there with the common purpose of intimidating persons so as to deter them from engaging in a lawful activity or of obstructing or disrupting a lawful activity,

he may direct that person or (as the case may be) those persons (or any of them) to leave the land.

(2) A direction under subsection (1) above, if not communicated to the persons referred to in subsection (1) by the police officer giving the direction, may be communicated to them by any constable at the scene.

(3) If a person knowing that a direction under subsection (1) above has been given which applies to him–

    (a) fails to leave the land as soon as practicable, or

    (b) having left again enters the land as a trespasser within the period of three months beginning with the day on which the direction was given, he commits an offence and is liable on summary conviction to imprisonment for a term not exceeding three months or a fine not exceeding level 4 on the standard scale, or both.

(4) In proceedings for an offence under subsection (3) it is a defence for the accused to show—

    (a) that he was not trespassing on the land, or

    (b) that he had a reasonable excuse for failing to leave the land as soon as practicable or, as the case may be, for again entering the land as a trespasser.

(5) A constable in uniform who reasonably suspects that a person is committing an offence under this section may arrest him without a warrant.

(6) In this section 'lawful activity' and 'land' have the same meaning as in section 68.

Notes

1   The offence of aggravated trespass under s 68 was aimed at certain groups such as hunt saboteurs or motorway protesters, animal rights activists and the 'peace convoys' which gather for the summer solstice festival at Stonehenge. No defence is provided and it is not necessary to show that the lawful activity was affected. This is a very broad power since a great many peaceful demonstrations are intended to have some impact of an obstructive nature on lawful activities (for example, export of veal calves or closure of schools or hospitals).

2   'Land' is defined in s 61(9); it does not include metalled highway or buildings apart from certain agricultural buildings and scheduled monuments; common land and non-metalled roads are included. Thus, s 68 does not apply to demonstrations on a metalled highway or in most, but not all, buildings. It does apply to public paths, such as bridleways.

3   Where a person is in receipt of the direction under s 69, even though it was erroneously given (since in fact the person did not have the purpose of committing the s 68 offence), it would seem that he or she will still commit an offence if thereafter he or she re-enters the land in question during the specified time.

4   Section 68 has been used against hunt saboteurs and other protesters on a number of occasions and some of the decisions on the section have had the effect of widening the area of liability created still further. In *Winder v DPP* (1996) *The Times*, 14 August the appellants had been running after the hunt. It was accepted that they did not intend to disrupt it by running but it was found that running after it was more than a preparatory act and that it was close enough to the contemplated action to incur liability. The willingness of the court to extend the boundaries of s 68 to catch such activities was all the more disturbing given that s 69 allows a direction to be given where it is suspected that the s 68 offence will be committed, a provision surely intended to cover precisely this set of circumstances.

5   Although s 68 may not lead to the criminalisation of persons who simply walk on to land as trespassers, s 69 has the potential to do so, depending on the interpretation given by the courts to the 'reasonable excuse' defence. *Capon v DPP* (1998) *The Times*, 23 March[65] made it clear that the offence under s 69 could be committed even though the offence under s 68 was not established. The defendants were videoing the digging out of a fox when they were threatened with arrest under s 68 by a police officer if they did not leave and were asked whether they were leaving the land. This exchange and question was found to be sufficient, in the circumstances, to constitute the direction necessary under s 69. Their intention in undertaking the videoing was not found to be to disrupt, intimidate or interfere with the activity in question. Despite the fact that the protesters had been peaceful and non-obstructive throughout, and it was very doubtful whether the officer had directed his mind towards all the elements of the offence, including the *mens rea*,[66] it was found that there was sufficient evidence. It was further found that there was no defence of 'reasonable excuse' in the circumstances,[67] even though the protesters were still in the process of trying to find out what offence they were being arrested for when they were, in fact, arrested, and genuinely believed that no direction under s 69(1) had been made against them.

---

65   Considered by D Mead, 'Will peaceful protesters be foxed by the Divisional Court decision in *Capon v DPP*?' [1998] Crim LR 870.
66   As Mead notes, *ibid*.
67   'The fact that the appellants were not . . . committing an offence under s 68 plainly . . . does not provide a reasonable excuse for not leaving the land. So to hold would emasculate the obvious intention of the section' (*per* Lord Bingham).

H Fenwick and G Phillipson, 'Direct action, Convention values and the Human Rights Act' (2001) 21(4) LS 535–68

The effect of the Convention under the HRA on prosecutions brought under ss 68 and 69 will be, at least superficially, quite dramatic, whether a minimalist or an activist approach is followed. As indicated above, judicial consideration of these provisions pre-HRA gave no recognition to the Convention rights at stake. By contrast, as discussed above,[68] the European Court made a clear finding in *Steel* [(1999) 28 EHRR 603], confirmed in *Hashman* [(2000) 30 EHRR 241], that protest which takes the form of physical obstruction nevertheless falls within the protection of Article 10 – and presumably Article 11.[69] Unless the courts simply refuse to follow this aspect of the *Steel* and *Hashman* judgments – as they could do[70] – they will be bound to find that the actions of similar protesters engage Articles 10 and 11.[71] Acceptance of such engagement would – at least in formal terms – entirely change the approach to the determination of such cases. Instead of merely undertaking a standard exercise in statutory interpretation, the courts will have to decide whether the interference with the protesters' Convention rights is justifiable under the second paragraphs of those Articles.

In the absence of further direct guidance, it is necessary both to resort to inference from the *outcomes* of direct action and other cases, and to attempt to draw conclusions from the more general Convention principles enunciated at Strasbourg. As indicated above, it appears that while there is no express statement to the effect that 'expression' in the form of direct action has a lower status than 'pure' expression, such a finding can be inferred from the case law. In *Steel* itself, the Court appeared to be readily convinced of the necessity and proportionality of the interferences with the two direct action protests complained of by the first two applicants.[72] In contrast, as discussed above, the Court in *Ezelin* [(1991) 14 EHRR 362] found that it was impossible to justify interferences with the freedom of peaceful assembly unless the person exercising the freedom himself committed a 'reprehensible act'. The first two applicants in *Steel* were both acting 'peacefully' in the sense that they were not themselves offering violence. In order to reconcile the two decisions, therefore, it must be assumed either that *obstructive* protest, while it does fall within at least Article 10, does not constitute that class of purely 'peaceful' protest which, according to *Ezelin*, 'cannot be restricted in any way' or that any restriction is more readily justifiable.

It seems clear from the findings in *Steel* as to the first and second applicants, and from the Commission decision in *G v FRG* [(1980) 21 DR 138], that where a protester is engaged in obstructive, albeit non-violent activity, arrest and imprisonment are in principle justifiable under

---

68 See p 953, above. The findings were that protesters who were arrested and detained after, respectively, obstructing a grouse shoot and sitting in the path of road-making equipment had suffered a *prima facie* violation of Article 10.

69 The Court in *Steel* found that there was no need to consider the applications under Article 11, implying that since the matter had been resolved under Article 10, consideration of Article 11 would be otiose, as raising the same issues. It may be noted that Article 11 protects only freedom of 'peaceful' assembly; it is arguable that this restriction should also be read into Article 10, although since the words were not expressly included, it might be interpreted more broadly in relation to that Article since it potentially reduces the scope of the primary right.

70 Under the HRA 1998, s 2.

71 Even where an arrest and detention had occurred, but no further action had been taken, an interference might be viewed as subsisting on the basis that protesters would not be able to exercise their Convention rights free from the fear of arrest and charges: see *Dudgeon v UK* (1982) 4 EHRR 149.

72 The case also concerned third, fourth and fifth applicants, who had engaged in purely peaceful protests with no element of obstruction or other 'action'. The first applicant, who had been impeding grouse shooters, was detained for 44 hours and sentenced to 28 days' imprisonment upon refusing to be bound over; the second, who had been lying down in front of digging equipment, suffered a 17-hour detention and seven days' imprisonment. The Court found that these were 'serious interference[s]' with the applicants' Article 10 rights. However, it had little difficulty in going on to find them to be both necessary and proportionate.

the Convention. Such an acceptance does not, however, entail a finding that s 68 is Convention-compliant. Section 68 is aimed only at disruptive protesters, not at those engaged purely in verbal persuasion, and therefore the powers it provides may, depending on their interpretation, be compatible with Article 10 as interpreted in *Steel*. However, it must be recalled that in *Steel*, *actual disruption* had been caused by the protesters: by contrast, s 68 makes clear on its face that it is necessary only that 'acts' additional to trespass, committed with the *intention* of causing disruption, obstruction or intimidation are required to make out the offence. Thus, in cases where the protesters have engaged in action intended to be disruptive, etc, but no such disruption has actually been caused, it is doubtful whether the imposition of criminal liability could be seen as 'necessary' under the Convention. Its imposition would arguably be incompatible with *Steel* and would amount to a clear departure from the principle set out in *Ezelin*, that peaceful protest cannot be interfered with, unless the particular protesters arrested commit 'reprehensible acts'.[73]

If this argument is accepted, a significant narrowing of the area of liability generated by s 68 will be required: the offence will have to be re-interpreted under s 3(1) of the HRA so that it catches only 'acts' that actually have some disruptive, etc, effect. This would entail a clear departure from the literal meaning of the section, but it is presumably a 'possible' interpretation under s 3. On this basis, *Winder*, which allows the criminalisation of protest at a stage even further away from actual obstruction, would also have to be reconsidered and, it is suggested, overruled.

Section 69, as interpreted by *Capon*, is similarly problematic. As *Capon* made clear, s 69 allows peaceful protesters to be arrested even though in fact there was no obstruction, intimidation or disruption of others and no risk of disorder, as long as a police officer reasonably believed that such factors were present. This belief is supposed to be 'reasonable',[74] but as *Capon* vividly demonstrates, the inhibiting effect of this requirement in practice can all but disappear due to the courts' marked disinclination to take issue with the judgments of police officers on the spot.[75] Therefore, it may be argued, depending on the particular circumstances, that certain s 69 'bans' may be unjustifiable under para 2 of Articles 10 and 11, bearing in mind the extent of the discretion to interfere with peaceful protest which this section vests in the police without any independent check, and the extent of the interference – in effect, a complete ban on entering the land in question, potentially lasting for three months. Since s 69 can operate as a prior restraint, Article 10 would demand that any direction given should be strictly scrutinized.

Such protesters have clearly committed no 'reprehensible' acts, as *Ezelin* requires. One possible response, therefore, would be to reinterpret s 69 under s 3(1) HRA so as to allow for a lawful direction to be given only where in fact one of the above elements is actually present. Reasonable belief will have to be taken to mean reasonable and true belief.[76] While such a reading renders s 69 largely otiose (since s 68 would cover such a situation) it is again a 'possible' reading under s 3(1). A further, more likely, possibility would be to find by reference to Articles 10 and 11 that the erroneousness of the senior police officer's original 'reasonable belief' should amount to a reasonable excuse. It would also be possible to find that purely peaceful protesters have a 'reasonable excuse' for not obeying a s 69 direction under s 69(4)(b). Moreover, under this view, courts will surely find that the Convention requires officers to use the clearest possible words when ordering persons to leave the land, precisely what the court failed to do in *Capon*.

That decision also raises the possibility that a direction under s 69, if it can be given in such an imprecise form, might be found in future to fail to satisfy the test denoted by the term 'prescribed

---

73   Reading *Steel* and *Ezelin* together, it must be assumed that the 'reprehensible acts' mentioned in *Ezelin* included obstructive behaviour.

74   Section 69(1).

75   (1999) 28 EHRR 603, pp 609–10, 638–39 and 647: the arrest of purely peaceful protesters (the third, fourth and fifth applicants) was found to create breaches of Articles 5(1) and 10.

76   It should be noted that s 69 raises an issue distinct from that of arresting under s 68(4) on the basis of reasonable suspicion of committing the offence under s 68. Since s 68(4) requires reasonable suspicion as to the commission of an offence, it is in principle compatible with Article 5 under the exception of para (1)(c).

by law' under Articles 10 and 11, assuming that the activity in question could be viewed as constituting the expression of an opinion so as to engage those Articles. It might well be argued that if a direction can be given in the form of a question, as in *Capon*, the term is too imprecise to satisfy that test. But, equally, the domestic court would be free to apply a doctrine of deference to the executive, whereby the nature of the direction should not be scrutinised too closely since the circumstances could be best assessed by the police officer on the ground. In the words of Lord Slynn, in the *International Ferry Traders* case [[1999] 1 All ER 129], the courts might show respect to 'the margin of appreciation or discretion' of the police officers in question in refusing to undertake a rigorous review of the wording of a direction. But since the courts will be forced to recognise that they are dealing with the exercise of a fundamental right under the Convention, it would be problematic to allow for its abrogation on the exceptionally flimsy grounds upheld in that case.

Questions

1 In debate on the Criminal Justice and Public Order Bill in the House of Lords, it was said that these provisions 'act as an open invitation to the police to interfere in the legitimate activities of people'. Do you agree? Is this also true of the 1986 Act?

2 The Criminal Justice and Public Order Act 1994 has undoubtedly increased the power of the authorities to prevent protest. Do you consider that eventually a declaration of incompatibility may have to be made between any of its public order provisions and Article 10 or 11 of the ECHR, under s 4 of the HRA?

3 'Taking all these provisions together and bearing in mind particularly the decision in *Nicol v DPP* (1996) it may be argued that public protest may now take place only on the basis that it is so anodyne and emasculated that it can hardly be termed protest at all.' Is this a fair evaluation of the current scheme or might it be argued that the restrictions placed on the use of some of these provisions, such as the defence of reasonableness under s 5(3)(c) of the 1986 Act or under s 69(4)(b) of the 1994 Act, provide sufficient protection for peaceful protest, taking into account the need to interpret the defences compatibly with Articles 10 and 11 under s 3 of the HRA?

FURTHER READING

For discussion and criticism of the Public Order Act 1986, see:

D Bonner and R Stone, 'The Public Order Act 1986: steps in the wrong direction?' [1987] PL 202

E Card, *Public Order: the New Law* (1987)

C Gearty, 'Freedom of assembly and public order', in C McCrudden and G Chambers (eds), *Individual Rights and the Law in Britain* (1994)

ATH Smith, 'The Public Order Act 1986 Part I' [1987] Crim LR 156

For current criticism, see:

S Bailey, D Harris, B Jones and D Ormerod, *Civil Liberties: Cases and Materials*, 5th edn (2001), Chapter 4

R Clayton and H Tomlinson, *The Law of Human Rights* (2000), Chapter 16

D Feldman, *Civil Liberties and Human Rights*, 2nd edn (2002), Chapter 18

H Fenwick and G Phillipson, 'Public protest, the HRA and judicial responses to political expression' [2000] PL 627–50

H Fenwick, *Civil Liberties and Human Rights* (2002), Chapter 9

PAJ Waddington, *Liberty and Order* (1994)
N Whitty, T Murphy and S Livingstone, *Civil Liberties Law* (2001), Part V

On this topic, see generally:
VT Bevan, 'Protest and public disorder' [1979] PL 163
I Brownlie and M Supperstone, *Law Relating to Public Order and National Security*, 2nd edn (1981)
K Ewing and C Gearty, *Freedom under Thatcher* (1990), Chapter 4
K Ewing and C Gearty, *The Struggle for Civil Liberties* (1999)
G Marshall, 'Freedom of speech and assembly' ,in *Constitutional Theory* (1971), p 154
ATH Smith, *Offences Against Public Order* (1997)
A Sherr, *Freedom of Protest, Public Order and the Law* (1989)
S Uglow, *Policing Liberal Society* (1988)
DGT Williams, *Keeping the Peace* (1967) (an excellent historical account)

CHAPTER 4

POLICE POWERS

INTRODUCTION

The exercise of police powers, such as arrest and detention, represents an invasion of personal liberty which is tolerated in the interests of the prevention and detection of crime. However, in accepting the need to allow such invasion, the interest in personal liberty requires that it should be strictly regulated. The rules governing the exercise of police powers are still largely contained in the scheme created under the Police and Criminal Evidence Act 1984 (PACE), which is made up of rules deriving from the Act itself, from the Codes of Practice made under it, and from the notes for guidance contained in the Codes. The exercise of police powers is also influenced by Home Office circulars.

Before the inception of PACE, the police had no general and clear powers of arrest, stop and search or entry to premises. They wanted such powers put on a clear statutory basis so that they could exercise them where they felt it was their duty to do so without laying themselves open to the possibility of a civil action. PACE was introduced in order to provide clear and broad police powers, but these were supposed to be balanced by greater safeguards for suspects. Such safeguards were in part adopted due to the need to ensure that miscarriages of justice, such as that which occurred in the *Confait* case,[1] would not recur. The Royal Commission on Criminal Procedure,[2] whose report influenced PACE, was set up largely in response to the inadequacies of safeguards for suspects which were exposed in the *Confait* report.[3] The result was a scheme in which the broad discretionary powers granted were to be balanced by two central structuring constraints. First, there were general precedent conditions for the exercise of such powers, the most common and significant being the requirement of reasonable suspicion or belief. Secondly, there was the provision of specific countervailing due process rights, in particular a general right of custodial access to legal advice, in most cases laid down in, or underpinned by, quasi- and non-legal rules – the Codes of Practice and Notes for Guidance made under PACE.[4] Redress for breaches of the due process safeguards was largely to be within the disciplinary rather than the judicial sphere: breach of the Codes constituted automatically a breach of the police disciplinary Code.[5]

Post-PACE, the discovery of a number of miscarriages of justice – the cases of the *Birmingham Six*,[6] the *Guildford Four*,[7] *Judith Ward*,[8] *Stefan Kiszko*,[9] the *Tottenham Three*,[10]

---

1   See report of the inquiry by the hon Sir Henry Fisher, HC 90 (1977–78).
2   Royal Commission on Criminal Procedure Report, Cmnd 8092 (1981) (RCCP Report).
3   HC 90 (1977–78).
4   PACE 1984, s 66, Codes of Practice.
5   *Ibid*, s 67(8). For the current position, see p 993, fn 23.
6   See *R v McIlkenny and Others* [1992] 2 All ER 417.
7   See *Report*, HC 449 (1993–94), Chapter 17.
8   *R v Ward* (1992) 96 Cr App R 1.
9   *R v Kiseka* (1992) *The Times*, 18 February.
10 *R v Silcott* (1991) *The Times*, 9 December.

the *Maguire Seven*[11] – raised due process concerns again. After the Birmingham Six were freed in 1992, another Royal Commission under Lord Runciman[12] was set up in order to consider further measures which could be introduced, but although there appeared to be a link between the announcement of the Royal Commission and the *Birmingham Six* case owing to proximity in time, the Commission interpreted its remit as not requiring an analysis of the miscarriage of justice in that case. The remit was to examine the efficacy of the criminal justice system in terms of securing the conviction of the guilty and the acquittal of the innocent.[13] Once again, a Royal Commission was seeking to reconcile potentially conflicting aims – concern to protect due process, but also to further crime control. After the Commission reported, the Major government introduced legislation, most notably the Criminal Justice and Public Order Act 1994 (CJPOA), which increased police powers significantly while removing a number of safeguards for suspects. In particular, the 1994 Act curtailed the right of silence, although the Runciman Royal Commission had recommended that the right should be retained since its curtailment might lead to further miscarriages of justice. Thus, there were significant developments in police powers during the Major years and the balance PACE was supposed to strike between such powers and due process was, it will be argued, undermined.

The legislation passed under the Labour government since 1997, most notably the Terrorism Act 2000 and the Criminal Justice and Police Act 2001, continues this trend. One especially evident tendency has been the movement away from the need to show reasonable suspicion as a necessary condition for the exercise for police powers. However, the Labour government was also responsible for the introduction of the Human Rights Act 1998 (HRA). Thus, the UK now has a benchmark by which to measure standards of procedural justice. Given the current trend away from protecting suspects' rights which this chapter will outline, the HRA could be perceived as providing a means of re-infusing due process into criminal procedure. It will be argued, however, that the impact of the HRA is likely to be diluted and unpredictable due to the weakness of the Strasbourg jurisprudence in certain key areas, areas in which the common law has traditionally failed to protect due process. Early decisions under the HRA indicate that the inception of the HRA is likely to have little impact in such areas. More generally, judicial intervention and formal rules have always had an uncertain impact on the institutional culture of the criminal justice system, and it would probably be unduly optimistic to predict a clear change of stance under the HRA.

In this chapter, the powers of the police and the accompanying safeguards are evaluated with a view to considering how far the suspects' rights granted by PACE have had an impact on police working practice and how far, if at all, change may occur in the light of the HRA. This is followed by a consideration of the value of the means of redress available, as affected by the inception of the HRA, if the police fail to comply with the rules.

---

11   See *R v Maguire* [1992] 2 All ER 433.
12   Runciman Report, Cm 2263 (1993).
13   Effectiveness in securing 'the conviction of those guilty of criminal offences and the acquittal of those who are innocent', *ibid*, Chapter 1, para 5.

STOP AND SEARCH POWERS

Current statutory stop and search powers are meant to maintain a balance between the interest of society as represented by the police in crime control and the interest of the citizen in personal liberty. The use of such powers may be a necessary part of effective policing and represents less of an infringement of liberty than an arrest, but on the other hand their exercise may create a sense of grievance and of violation of personal privacy. There was no general power at common law to detain without the subject's consent in the absence of specific statutory authority. Instead there were a miscellany of such powers, the majority of which were superseded under PACE.

The grant of further powers post-PACE has not been accompanied by a strengthening of the protection for the due process rights of suspects. One of the key structuring constraints, identified above as intended to protect due process under the Police and Criminal Evidence Act 1984, was the requirement of reasonable suspicion. This requirement has been eroded in the post-PACE developments; it has been dropped from the more recently introduced special powers, and under the Terrorism Act 2000 it continues to be unnecessary in respect of terrorist suspects.

The use of stop and search powers remains a contentious matter that continues to attract public attention, especially as it has frequently been suggested that they may be used in a discriminatory fashion. This issue was raised in relation to the *Stephen Lawrence* case in the MacPherson Report in 1999.[14] Their recorded use has more than trebled since PACE came into force in 1986[15] and, as indicated below, a large number of further powers have been introduced in the post-PACE period. The efficacy of such powers is debatable. Only around 10–14 per cent of stops lead to an arrest and only around three per cent to a charge.[16] There are, of course, other methods of measuring the crime control value of stop and search powers; in particular, they have some value in terms of information-gathering and, more controversially, as a means of asserting police authority on the streets.

Police and Criminal Evidence Act 1984 (as amended by the Criminal Justice Act 1988, s 140)

Part I – Powers to stop and search

Power of constable to stop and search persons, vehicles etc

1.–(1) A constable may exercise any power conferred in this section—

   (a) in any place to which ... the public or any section of the public has access ... or

   (b) in any other place to which people have ready access at the time when he proposes to exercise the power but which is not a dwelling.

(2) Subject to subsections (3) to (5) below, a constable—

   (a) may search—

      (i) any person or vehicle;

      (ii) anything which is in or on a vehicle, for stolen or prohibited articles [or any article to which subsection 8A below applies]; and

   (b) may detain a person or vehicle for the purpose of such a search.

---

14 Cm 4262-I (1999).

15 Home Office Statistical Bulletin 21/93; Statistical Bulletin 27/97.

16 Home Office Statistical Bulletin 21/93.

(3)   This section does not give a constable power to search a person or vehicle or anything in or on a vehicle unless he has reasonable grounds for suspecting that he will find stolen or prohibited articles [or any article to which subsection 8A below applies] ...

(6)   If in the course of such a search a constable discovers an article which he has reasonable grounds for suspecting to be a stolen or prohibited article, he may seize it.

(7)   An article is prohibited for the purposes of this part of this Act if it is—

     (a)   an offensive weapon; or

     (b)   an article—

        (i)   made or adapted for use in the course of or in connection with an offence to which this sub-paragraph applies; or

        (ii)   intended by the person having it with him for such use by him or by some other person.

(8)   The offences to which subsection (7)(b)(i) above applies are—

     (a)   burglary;

     (b)   theft;

     (c)   offences under section 12 of the Theft Act 1968 (taking motor vehicle or other conveyance without authority); and

     (d)   offences under section 15 of that Act (obtaining property by deception).

[(8A) This subsection applies to any article in relation to which a person has committed, or is committing, or is going to commit an offence under section 139 of the Criminal Justice Act 1988].

(9)   In this part of this Act 'offensive weapon' means any article—

     (a)   made or adapted for use for causing injury to persons, or

     (b)   intended by the person having it with him for such use by him or by some other person; ...

Provisions relating to search under s1 and other powers

...

2.–(2)   If a constable contemplates a search, other than a search of an unattended vehicle, in the exercise—

     (a)   of the power conferred by section 1 above; or

     (b)   of any other power...

        (i)   to search a person without first arresting him; or

        (ii)   to search a vehicle without making an arrest,

     it shall be his duty, subject to subsection (4) below, to take reasonable steps before he commences the search to bring to the attention of the appropriate person—

        (i)   if the constable is not in uniform, documentary evidence that he is a constable; and

        (ii)   whether he is in uniform or not, the matters specified in subsection (3) below,

     and the constable shall not commence the search until he has performed that duty.

(3)   The matters referred to in subsection (2)(ii) above are—

     (a)   the constable's name and the name of the police station to which he is attached;

     (b)   the object of the proposed search;

     (c)   the constable's grounds for proposing to make it; and

     (d)   the effect of section 3(7) or (8) below, as may be appropriate. ...

Duty to make records concerning searches

3.–(1) Where a constable has carried out a search ...

he shall make a record of it in writing unless it is not practicable to do so. ...

(7) If a constable who conducted a search of a person made a record of it, the person who was searched shall be entitled to a copy of the record if he asks for one. ...

Criminal Justice and Public Order Act 1994

Powers to stop and search in anticipation of violence

60.–(1) Where a police officer of or above the rank of superintendent reasonably believes that –

(a) incidents involving serious violence may take place in any locality in his area; and

(b) it is expedient to do so to prevent their occurrence,

he may give an authorisation that the powers to stop and search persons and vehicles conferred by this section shall be exercisable at any place within that locality for a period not exceeding 24 hours.

(2) The power conferred by subsection (1) above may be exercised by a chief inspector or an inspector. ...

(3) If it appears to the officer who gave the authorisation or to a superintendent that it is expedient to do so, having regard to offences which have, or are reasonably suspected to have, been committed in connection with any incident falling within the authorisation, he may direct that the authorisation shall continue in being for a further six hours.

(4) This section confers on any constable in uniform power—

(a) to stop any pedestrian and search him or anything carried by him for offensive weapons or dangerous instruments;

(b) to stop any vehicle and search the vehicle, its driver and any passenger for offensive weapons or dangerous instruments.

(5) A constable may, in the exercise of those powers, stop any person or vehicle and make any search he thinks fit whether or not he has any grounds for suspecting that the person or vehicle is carrying weapons or articles of that kind.

(6) If in the course of a search under this section a constable discovers a dangerous instrument or an article which he has reasonable grounds for suspecting to be an offensive weapon, he may seize it. ...

(8) A person who fails

[(a) to stop or (as the case may be) to stop a vehicle; or

(b) to remove any item worn by him][17]

when required to do so by a constable in the exercise of his powers under this section shall be liable on summary conviction to imprisonment for a term not exceeding one month or to a fine not exceeding level 3 on the standard scale or both.

Terrorism Act 2000

44.–(1) An authorisation under this subsection authorises any constable in uniform to stop a vehicle in an area or at a place specified in the authorisation and to search—

(a) the vehicle;

(b) the driver of the vehicle;

---

17   As amended by the Crime and Disorder Act 1998, s 25(3).

(c) a passenger in the vehicle;

(d) anything in or on the vehicle or carried by the driver or a passenger.

(2) An authorisation under this subsection authorises any constable in uniform to stop a pedestrian in an area or at a place specified in the authorisation and to search—

(a) the pedestrian;

(b) anything carried by him.

(3) An authorisation under subsection (1) or (2) may be given only if the person giving it considers it expedient for the prevention of acts of terrorism....

Exercise of power

45.–(1) The power conferred by an authorisation under section 44(1) or (2)—

(a) may be exercised only for the purpose of searching for articles of a kind which could be used in connection with terrorism, and

(b) may be exercised whether or not the constable has grounds for suspecting the presence of articles of that kind.

(2) A constable may seize and retain an article which he discovers in the course of a search by virtue of section 44(1) or (2) and which he reasonably suspects is intended to be used in connection with terrorism.

Duration of authorisation

46.–(1) An authorisation under section 44 has effect, subject to subsections (2) to (7), during the period—

(a) beginning at the time when the authorisation is given, and

(b) ending with a date or at a time specified in the authorisation.

(2) The date or time specified under subsection (1)(b) must not occur after the end of the period of 28 days beginning with the day on which the authorisation is given.

(3) The person who gives an authorisation shall inform the Secretary of State as soon as is reasonably practicable. ...

(6) The Secretary of State may cancel an authorisation with effect from a specified time.

(7) An authorisation may be renewed in writing by the person who gave it or by a person who could have given it; and subsections (1) to (6) shall apply as if a new authorisation were given on each occasion on which the authorisation is renewed.

Offences

47.–(1) A person commits an offence if he—

(a) fails to stop a vehicle when required to do so by a constable in the exercise of the power conferred by an authorisation under section 44(1);

(b) fails to stop when required to do so by a constable in the exercise of the power conferred by an authorisation under section 44(2); ...

Additional powers of seizure

Criminal Justice and Police Act 2001, s 51

Additional powers of seizure from the person

51.–(1) Where—

(a) a person carrying out a lawful search of any person finds something that he has reasonable grounds for believing may be or may contain something for which he is authorised to search,

(b) a power of seizure to which this section applies or the power conferred by subsection (2) would entitle him, if he found it, to seize whatever it is that he has grounds for believing that thing to be or to contain, and

(c) in all the circumstances it is not reasonably practicable for it to be determined, at the time and place of the search—

(i) whether what he has found is something that he is entitled to seize, or

(ii) the extent to which what he has found contains something that he is entitled to seize,

that person's powers of seizure shall include power under this section to seize so much of what he has found as it is necessary to remove from that place to enable that to be determined.

(2) Where—

(a) a person carrying out a lawful search of any person finds something ('the seizable property') which he would be entitled to seize but for its being comprised in something else that he has (apart from this subsection) no power to seize,

(b) the power under which that person would have power to seize the seizable property is a power to which this section applies, and

(c) in all the circumstances it is not reasonably practicable for the seizable property to be separated, at the time and place of the search, from that in which it is comprised,

that person's powers of seizure shall include power under this section to seize both the seizable property and that from which it is not reasonably practicable to separate it.

Notes

1 The concept of reasonable suspicion as the basis for the exercise of certain stop and search powers, including the PACE powers, is set out briefly in Code of Practice A on 'stop and search', paras 1.6 and 1.7 (below). There must be a concrete basis for this suspicion which relates to the particular person in question and could be evaluated by an objective observer. However, research in the area suggests that there is a tendency to view reasonable suspicion as a flexible concept which may denote quite a low level of suspicion.[18] The case law is meagre, but suggests that an imprecise and inconsistent standard is maintained. In *Slade* LEXIS CO/1678/96 (1996), the suspect was close to the house of a well known drug dealer; on noticing the officer, he put his hand in his pocket and smiled. This was found to give rise to reasonable suspicion. However, in *Black v DPP* (1995) unreported, 11 May, the fact of visiting a well known drug dealer was found in itself to be insufficient as a basis for reasonable suspicion. In *Samuels v Commissioner of Police for the Metropolis* (1999) unreported, 3 March S was ambling along, in a high crime area, with his hands in his pockets and did not tell the officer where he was going when asked. It was found that these facts could not give rise to reasonable suspicion.

2 Section 23 of the Misuse of Drugs Act 1971 provides a stop and search power which is frequently invoked. Under s 23, a constable may stop and search a person whom the constable has reasonable grounds to suspect is in possession of a controlled drug. Code A and ss 2 and 3 of PACE apply to this as they do to other statutory stop and search powers unless specific exceptions are made (see below).

---

18 D Dixon (1989) 17 Int J Soc Law 185–206.

3   A very broad power to stop vehicles arises under s 163 of the Road Traffic Act 1988 (RTA). Its ambit remains unclear. Section 163 provides a constable in uniform with power to stop vehicles, which may be unqualified as to purpose[19] and does not depend upon reasonable suspicion.

4   Section 60 of the 1994 Act, as amended by s 8 of the Knives Act 1997, provides police officers with a further stop and search power which does not depend on showing reasonable suspicion of particular wrongdoing on the part of an individual. The powers under s 60 of the 1994 Act and ss 44–47 of the Terrorism Act 2000 (TA) arise in addition to the general PACE power to stop and search.

5   Previous stop and search powers relating to terrorism under the Prevention of Terrorism (Temporary Provisions) Act 1989, as amended, (PTA) and the Northern Ireland (Emergency Provisions) Act 1996, as amended (EPA), are reproduced, but broadened, under the TA, since they depend on suspicion that a person is a terrorist (s 43) and the stop is to discover whether he has in his possession anything which may constitute evidence that he is a terrorist. 'Being a terrorist' is not in itself an offence under the TA (unless the 'terrorist' group in question is also proscribed), although some, but not all, actions falling within the definition of terrorism in s 1 of the TA are coterminous with existing offences; therefore, this power is not dependent on suspicion of commission of an offence or of carrying prohibited articles.

6   There were also powers in s 16 and para 4(2) of Sched 5 to the PTA, which empowered the police and others to stop, question and search people about to enter or leave Great Britain or Northern Ireland, to determine whether they had been concerned in acts of terrorism. These powers are reproduced in Sched 7 to the TA and, again, they are not dependent on showing reasonable suspicion.

7   Since all these powers on their face allow for stop and search on subjective grounds, they may tend to be used disproportionately against the black community. Post-PACE research has consistently suggested that stop and search powers are used in a discriminatory fashion.[20] However, the amendments made to the Race Relations Act 1976 in 2000 by the Race Relations (Amendment) Act 2000 may have an impact on police practice since discrimination on grounds of race in police operational decisions is now covered by the 1976 Act.

8   The Criminal Justice and Police Act 2001 (CJPA) introduced certain new seizure powers. The new powers are significant since, *inter alia*, they allow the police officers to remove items from persons even where they are not certain that – apart from s 51 – they have the power to do so. This new power is 'balanced' by the provisions of ss 52–61 which provide a number of safeguards. They are discussed below in relation to seizures from property since the same safeguards apply.

Code of Practice A (revised 2003)

The Code applies to all statutory powers to search a person or vehicle without first making an arrest. It does not apply to the powers under the Aviation Security Act 1982, s 27(2), PACE, s 6(1) and the Terrorism Act 2000, Sched 7.

1.5 An officer must not search a person, even with his consent, where no power to search is applicable. Even where a person is prepared to submit to a search voluntarily, the person must not

---

19   See HC Standing Committee E col 339 (13 December 1983).
20   See Skogan, HO Research Study No 117, 1990, p 34; *Entry into the Criminal Justice System*, August 1998 and Statistics on Race and the Criminal Justice System, December 1998; MacPherson Report (1999), Cm 4262-I.

be searched unless the necessary legal power exists and the search must be in accordance with the relevant power and the provisions of this Code. The only exception, where an officer does not require a specific power, applies to searches of persons entering sports grounds or other premises carried out with their consent given as a condition of entry.

Searches requiring reasonable grounds for suspicion

2.2 Reasonable grounds for suspicion depend on the circumstances in each case. There must be an objective basis for that suspicion based on facts, information, and/or intelligence which are relevant to the likelihood of finding an article of a certain kind, or in the case of searches under s 43 Terrorism Act 2000, to the likelihood that the person is a terrorist. Reasonable suspicion can never be supported on the basis of personal factors alone without reliable supporting intelligence or information or some specific behaviour by the person concerned. For example, a person's race, age, appearance, or the fact that the person is known to have a previous conviction, cannot be used alone or in combination with each other as the reason for searching that person.

2.3 Reasonable suspicion can sometimes exist without specific information or intelligence and on the basis of some level of generalisation stemming from the behaviour of a person. ...

2.6 Where there is reliable information or intelligence that members of a particular group or gang habitually carry knives unlawfully or weapons or controlled drugs and wear a distinctive item of clothing or other means of identification to indicate their membership of the group or gang that distinctive item of clothing or other means of identification may provide reasonable grounds to stop and search a person.

Notes

1   All the stop and search powers mentioned are subject to the same procedural requirements under ss 2 and 3 of PACE and Code A (para 3.8 and para 4) as those relating to the powers under s 1 of PACE. Information giving and record keeping is intended to ensure that officers do not overuse the stop and search power, partly because it means that the citizen can make a complaint later and partly because the police station will have a record of the number of stops being carried out.

2   The 2003 version of Code A (para 1.5) forbids consensual searches: officers can no longer ask members of the public to consent to a search where no power to search exists. Paragraph 1.5 represents a very significant change from the previous position. It reflects the concern that voluntary contacts can have a sinister side: some people might 'consent' to a search in the sense of offering no resistance to it due to uncertainty as to the basis or extent of the police power in question.[21] Once a search was so classified, none of the statutory or Code A safeguards needed to be observed.

3   Failures to follow the procedural requirements under ss 2 and 3 of PACE may affect the legality of the search. There is no provision under the TA, PACE or Code A to the effect that if the procedural requirements are not complied with, the search will be unlawful, but if it is unlawful, tortious liability will be incurred. A number of due process requirements are contained only in Code A[22] and therefore their breach cannot give rise to civil liability.[23] But breach of certain of the *statutory* procedural

21   See D Dixon, 'Consent and the legal regulation of policing' (1990) Int J Soc Law 245–362.

22   Code A made under PACE 1984, s 66 and the TA Code made under the TA, ss 96 and 98 in respect of Northern Ireland and the new Code introduced under Sched 14 in respect of the UK.

23   Under PACE 1984, s 67(10). The TA Codes will have the same status as the PACE Codes; under Sched 14, para 6(2) 'The failure by an officer to observe a provision of a code shall not of itself make him liable to criminal or civil proceedings', but under para 6(3) 'A code (a) shall be admissible in evidence in criminal and civil proceedings, and (b) shall be taken into account by a court or tribunal in any case in which it appears to the court or tribunal to be relevant'.

requirements will render searches unlawful, as will breach of the statutory powers. It has been held that a failure to make a written record of the search in breach of s 3 will not render it unlawful,[24] whereas a failure to give the grounds for it will do so, following *R v Fenelley* [1989] Crim LR 142 and *Samuel v Commissioner of Police for the Metropolis* (1999) unreported, 3 March, as will a failure to comply with the duties to provide identification under s 2(3), following *Osman v Director of Public Prosecutions* (1999) *The Times*, 29 September.

4 The PACE and TA Codes are admissible in evidence.[25] It is possible for a defendant who claims that a search was conducted improperly or unlawfully to seek the limited form of redress represented by exclusion of evidence which has been obtained as a result of a breach of PACE or Code A. This possibility is discussed below (at pp 1049–52).

5 *Relevance and impact of the Human Rights Act.* Article 5 of the European Convention on Human Rights (ECHR), set out in Part II Chapter 2 (at p 247) provides a guarantee of 'liberty and security of person'. It appears that the short period of detention represented by a stop and search is sufficient to constitute a deprivation of liberty.[26] Deprivation of liberty can occur only on a basis of law (see p 1028 below) and in certain specified circumstances, including, under Article 5(1)(b), the detention of a person in order to secure the fulfilment of any obligation prescribed by law and, under Article 5(1)(c), the 'lawful detention of a person effected for the purpose of bringing him before the competent legal authority on reasonable suspicion of having committed an offence'. Both these provisions may cover temporary detention for the purposes of a search. Article 5(1)(b) has received a restrictive interpretation at Strasbourg. In *Lawless* (1961) 1 EHRR 15, it was found that a specific and concrete obligation must be identified; once it has been, detention can in principle be used to secure its fulfilment. It is unclear whether the term 'obligation' could apply to the current statutory provisions. The requirements are to submit to a search, and, apart from the power under s 163 of the Road Traffic Act 1988, to remain under police detention for the period of time necessary to allow it to be carried out.[27]

6 Under the interpretation in *Lawless*, the PACE, Misuse of Drugs Act, CJPOA and TA stop and search provisions are of doubtful compatibility with Article 5(1)(b). In *McVeigh, O'Neill and Evans v UK* (1981) 5 EHRR 71 a requirement to submit to an examination on arrival in the UK was found not to violate Article 5(1)(b) since it was sufficiently specific and concrete, but it was emphasised that this was found on the basis that the obligation in question only arose in limited circumstances and had a limited purpose – to combat terrorism. The PACE powers, the Misuse of Drugs Act power and, arguably, the power arising under s 43 of the TA, which is a permanent power, not one adopted temporarily to meet an emergency as in *McVeigh*, could not readily be said to arise in limited circumstances. The CJPOA and other TA powers have more limited purposes in the sense that the place in which they can be exercised is circumscribed either by its nature (as in port or border controls) or by the authorisation given, which is based on the need for special powers. Whether any particular authorisation would be viewed as

---

24 *Basher v DPP* (1993) unreported, 2 March.
25 PACE 1984, s 67(11); TA 2000, Sched 14, para 6(3).
26 *X v Austria* (1979) 18 DR 154.
27 See *McVeigh, O'Neill and Evans v UK* (1981) 5 EHRR 71; the obligation imposed was a requirement to 'submit to examination'.

rendering the obligation in question sufficiently specific will be open to question, depending on the factual situation.

7   The powers considered may fall within Article 5(1)(c), which requires reasonable suspicion of the commission of an *offence*. This immediately calls into question s 43 of the TA, since no such suspicion is required. It also means that the exercise of the powers under PACE may, depending on the circumstances of a search, be of doubtful compatibility. Section 1 requires suspicion as to carriage of an article, not as to an offence; it is clearly aimed at gathering evidence of offences and its requirements are not fully coterminous with the relevant range of offences. Carrying certain of the articles which fall within s 1 of PACE is not an offence[28] even if the carrier can be said to 'possess' them, although the officer may also require suspicion as to *mens rea*, while carriage of prohibited articles without sufficient 'possession' will clearly not constitute an offence.

8   The use of force in order to carry out a stop and search is permitted under s 117 of PACE, which provides: 'the officer may use reasonable force, if necessary, in the exercise of the [PACE] power.' The TA provides an equivalent provision in s 114(2). But, under Article 3, the use of force must be strictly in proportion to the conduct of the detainee.

Questions
1   If, despite para 1.5, police officers stop and search a person on a consensual basis, without following the PACE procedure under ss 2 and 3, and find an article for which they would have been empowered to search under s 1 of PACE, what redress would the subject of the search have?

2   Are the Code A safeguards for suspects likely to maintain, in practice, a balance between suspects' rights and the increased police powers under the CJPOA and TA?

POWER TO ENTER AND SEARCH PREMISES[29]

In America, the Fourth Amendment to the Constitution guarantees freedom from unreasonable search and seizure, thus recognising the invasion of privacy which a search of premises represents. A search without a warrant will normally[30] be unreasonable; therefore an independent check is usually available on the search power. In contrast, the common law in Britain, despite some rulings asserting the importance of protecting the citizen from the invasion of private property,[31] allowed search and seizure on wide grounds, going beyond those authorised by statute.[32] Thus, the common law did not provide full protection for the citizen and PACE goes some way towards remedying this by placing powers of entry and seizure on a clearer basis and

---

28   Under s 1(7)(b), such articles could include credit cards or keys.
29   See generally RTH Stone, *Entry, Search and Seizure* (1989); R Clayton and H Tomlinson, *Civil Actions Against the Police*, 2nd edn (1999), Chapter 7; SJ Bailey, DJ Harris and D Ormerod, *Bailey, Harris and Jones: Civil Liberties: Cases and Materials*, 5th edn (2002), pp 225–56.
30   *Coolidge v New Hampshire* 403 US 443 (1973); exception accepted where evidence might otherwise be destroyed.
31   See, eg, rulings in *Entick v Carrington* (1765) 19 St Tr 1029; *Morris v Beardmore* [1981] AC 446.
32   The ruling in *Ghani v Jones* [1970] 1 QB 693 authorised seizure of a wide range of material once officers were lawfully on premises. The ruling in *Thomas v Sawkins* [1935] 2 KB 249 allowed a wide power to enter premises to prevent crime.

ensuring that the person whose premises are searched understands the basis of the search and can complain as to its conduct if necessary.

Entry without warrant

Police and Criminal Evidence Act 1984 (as amended)
Entry and search after arrest

18.–(1) Subject to the following provisions of this section, a constable may enter and search any premises occupied or controlled by a person who is under arrest for an arrestable offence, if he has reasonable grounds for suspecting that there is on the premises evidence other than items subject to legal privilege, that relates—

    (a) to that offence; or

    (b) to some other arrestable offence which is connected with or similar to that offence.

(2) A constable may seize and retain anything for which he may search under subsection (1) above. . . .

(4) Subject to subsection (5) below, the powers conferred by this section may not be exercised unless an officer of the rank of inspector or above has authorised them in writing.

(5) A constable may conduct a search under subsection (1) above—

    (a) before taking the person to a police station; and

    (b) without obtaining an authorisation under subsection (4) above, if the presence of that person at a place other than a police station is necessary for the effective investigation of the offence.

Search upon arrest

. . .

32.–(2) Subject to subsections (3) to (5) below, a constable shall also have power in any such case—

. . .

    (b) to enter and search any premises in which he was when arrested or immediately before he was arrested for evidence relating to the offence for which he has been arrested. . . .

(6) A constable may not search premises in the exercise of the power conferred by subsection (2)(b) above unless he has reasonable grounds for believing that there is evidence for which a search is permitted under that paragraph on the premises.

Note

The s 18 power to enter and search without a warrant is subject to a significant limitation since it does not arise in respect of an arrest under s 25 of PACE. If a search was considered necessary in respect of a s 25 arrest, a search warrant would have to be obtained unless the provisions of s 32 applied.

Entry to premises under a search warrant or written authority

Police and Criminal Evidence Act 1984
Part II – Powers of entry, search and seizure

8.–(1) If on an application made by a constable a justice of the peace is satisfied that there are reasonable grounds for believing—

(a) that a serious arrestable offence has been committed; and

(b) that there is material on premises specified in the application which is likely to be of substantial value ... to the investigation of the offence; and

(c) that the material is likely to be relevant evidence; and

(d) that it does not consist of or include items subject to legal privilege, excluded material or special procedure material; and

(e) that any of the conditions specified in subsection (3) below applies,

he may issue a warrant authorising a constable to enter and search the premises.

(2) A constable may seize and retain anything for which a search has been authorised under subsection (I) above.

(3) The conditions mentioned in subsection (1)(e) above are—

(a) that it is not practicable to communicate with any person entitled to grant entry to the premises;

(b) ... it is not practicable to communicate with any person entitled to grant access to the evidence;

(c) that entry to the premises will not be granted unless a warrant is produced;

(d) that the purpose of a search may be frustrated or seriously prejudiced unless a constable arriving at the premises can secure immediate entry to them.

Special provisions as to access

9.–(1) A constable may obtain access to excluded material or special procedure material for the purposes of a criminal investigation by making an application under Schedule 1 below....

Meaning of 'items subject to legal privilege'

11.–(1) ... in this Act 'excluded material' means—

(a) personal records which a person has acquired or created in the course of any trade, business, profession ... and which he holds in confidence ...

(c) journalistic material which a person holds in confidence.

12.   ... 'personal records' means documentary and other records concerning an individual ... relating—

(a) to his physical or mental health;

(b) to spiritual counselling or assistance given or to be given to him; or

(c) to counselling or assistance given or to be given to him....

14.   In this Act 'special procedure material' means—

(a) material to which subsection (2) below applies; and

(b) journalistic material, other than excluded material.

(2) This subsection applies to material ... in the possession of a person who—

(a) acquired or created it in the course of any trade.... or for the purpose of any paid or unpaid office; and

(b) holds it subject—

(i) to an express or implied undertaking to hold it in confidence ...

Search warrants – safeguards

15.   (2) Where a constable applies for any such warrant, it shall be his duty—

(a) to state—

  (i) the ground on which he makes the application; and

  (ii) the enactment under which the warrant would be issued;

(b) to specify the premises which it is desired to enter and search; and

(c) to identify, so far as is practicable, the articles or persons to be sought ...

(5) A warrant shall authorise an entry on one occasion only.

(6) A warrant—

  (a) shall specify—

    (i) the name of the person who applies for it;

    (ii) the date on which it is issued;

    (iii) the enactment under which it is issued; and

    (iv) the premises to be searched; and

  (b) shall identify, so far as is practicable, the articles or persons to be sought.

Execution of warrants

16.–(5) ... the constable—

  (a) shall identify himself to the occupier and, if not in uniform, shall produce to him documentary evidence that he is a constable;

  (b) shall produce the warrant to him; and

  (c) shall supply him with a copy of it.

[Note: Part II extended by the Criminal Justice (International Co-operation) Act 1990, s 7(1).]

Schedule 1

1. If on an application made by a constable a Circuit Judge is satisfied that one or other of the sets of access conditions is fulfilled, he may make an order. ... That order is for the production of material to a constable or the provision of access to it.

2. The first set of access conditions is fulfilled if—

  (a) there are reasonable grounds for believing—

    (i) that a serious arrestable offence has been committed;

    (ii) that there is material which consists of special procedure material or includes special procedure material and does not also include excluded material on premises specified in the application;

    (iii) that the material is likely to be of substantial value (whether by itself or together with other material) to the investigation in connection with which the application is made; and

    (iv) that the material is likely to be relevant evidence (which by the application of s 8(4) means anything that would be admissible in evidence at a trial for the offence);

  (b) other methods of obtaining the material—

    (i) have been tried without success; or

    (ii) have not been tried because it appears that they were bound to fail; and

  (c) it is in the public interest, having regard—

(i) to the benefit likely to accrue to the investigation if the material is obtained; and

(ii) to the circumstances under which the person in possession of the material holds,

that the material should be produced or that access to it should be given.

Terrorism Act 2000
Schedule 5
Terrorist Investigations: Information

Searches

1.–(1) A constable may apply to a justice of the peace for the issue of a warrant under this paragraph for the purposes of a terrorist investigation.

(2) A warrant under this paragraph shall authorise any constable—

(a) to enter the premises specified in the warrant,

(b) to search the premises and any person found there, and

(c) to seize and retain any relevant material which is found on a search under paragraph (b).

(3) For the purpose of sub-paragraph (2)(c) material is relevant if the constable has reasonable grounds for believing that—

(a) it is likely to be of substantial value, whether by itself or together with other material, to a terrorist investigation, and

(b) it must be seized in order to prevent it from being concealed, lost, damaged, altered or destroyed.

(4) A warrant under this paragraph shall not authorise—

(a) the seizure and retention of items subject to legal privilege ...

(5) Subject to paragraph 2, a justice may grant an application under this paragraph if satisfied—

(a) that the warrant is sought for the purposes of a terrorist investigation,

(b) that there are reasonable grounds for believing that there is material on premises specified in the application which is likely to be of substantial value, whether by itself or together with other material, to a terrorist investigation and which does not consist of or include excepted material (within the meaning of paragraph 4 below), and

...

(5) An authorisation under this paragraph shall not authorise—

(a) the seizure and retention of items subject to legal privilege ...

(6) An authorisation under this paragraph shall not be given unless the person giving it has reasonable grounds for believing that there is material to be found on the premises which—

(a) is likely to be of substantial value, whether by itself or together with other material, to a terrorist investigation, and

(b) does not consist of or include excepted material.

(7) A person commits an offence if he wilfully obstructs a search under this paragraph.

Excepted material

Excluded and special procedure material: production & access

5.–(1) A constable may apply to a Circuit judge for an order under this paragraph for the purposes of a terrorist investigation.

...

(3) An order under this paragraph may require a specified person—

    (a) to produce to a constable within a specified period for seizure and retention any material which he has in his possession, custody or power and to which the application relates;

    (b) to give a constable access to any material of the kind mentioned in paragraph (a) within a specified period;

    (c) to state to the best of his knowledge and belief the location of material to which the application relates if it is not in, and it will not come into, his possession, custody or power within the period specified under paragraph (a) or (b).

(1) A circuit judge may grant an application under paragraph 5 if satisfied—

    (a) that the material to which the application relates consists of or includes excluded material or special procedure material,

    (b) that it does not include items subject to legal privilege, and

    (c) that the conditions in sub-paragraphs (2) and (3) are satisfied in respect of that material.

(2) The first condition is that—

    (a) the order is sought for the purposes of a terrorist investigation, and

    (b) there are reasonable grounds for believing that the material is likely to be of substantial value, whether by itself or together with other material, to a terrorist investigation.

(3) The second condition is that there are reasonable grounds for believing that it is in the public interest that the material should be produced or that access to it should be given having regard—

    ... to the benefit likely to accrue to a terrorist investigation if the material is obtained ...

Excluded or special procedure material: search

11.–(1) A constable may apply to a Circuit judge for the issue of a warrant under this paragraph for the purposes of a terrorist investigation.

(2) A warrant under this paragraph shall authorise any constable—

    (a) to enter the premises specified in the warrant,

    (b) to search the premises and any person found there, and

    (c) to seize and retain any relevant material which is found on a search under paragraph (b).

(3) A warrant under this paragraph shall not authorise—

    (a) the seizure and retention of items subject to legal privilege;

(4) For the purpose of sub-paragraph (2)(c) material is relevant if the constable has reasonable grounds for believing that it is likely to be of substantial value, whether by itself or together with other material, to a terrorist investigation.

(2) A Circuit judge may also grant an application under paragraph 11 if satisfied that there are reasonable grounds for believing that—

    (a) there is material on premises specified in the application which consists of or includes excluded material or special procedure material but does not include items subject to legal privilege, and

    (b) the conditions in sub-paragraphs (3) and (4) are satisfied.

(3) The first condition is that—

(a) the warrant is sought for the purposes of a terrorist investigation, and

(b) the material is likely to be of substantial value, whether by itself or together with other material, to a terrorist investigation.

(4) The second condition is that it is not appropriate to make an order under paragraph 5 in relation to the material because—

(a) it is not practicable to communicate with any person entitled to produce the material,

(b) it is not practicable to communicate with any person entitled to grant access to the material or entitled to grant entry to the premises on which the material is situated, or

(c) a terrorist investigation may be seriously prejudiced unless a constable can secure immediate access to the material.

Notes

1 The PACE search warrant provisions provide a scheme which is dependent on magistrates observing its requirements. Research suggests that in practice some magistrates make little or no attempt to ascertain whether the information a warrant contains may be relied upon, while magistrates who do take a rigorous approach to the procedure and refuse to grant warrants may not be approached again.[33]

2 Searching of premises other than under ss 17 and 18 of PACE or under the TA can, in general, only occur if a search warrant is issued under s 8 PACE by a magistrate. However, there are also special provisions arising under the Drug Trafficking Offences Act 1986, s 27 and the Criminal Justice Act 1987, s 2(4).

3 As revised, Code of Practice B made under PACE provides for an increase in the amount of information to be conveyed to owners of property to be searched by use of a standard form, the Notice of Powers and Rights (para 5.7). It covers certain information including specification of the type of search in question, a summary of the powers of search and seizure arising under PACE and the rights of the subjects of searches. This notice must normally be given to the subject of the search before it begins, but under para 5.8 need not be if to do so would lead to frustration of the object of the search or danger to the police officers concerned or to others.

Powers of seizure and retention

Police and Criminal Evidence Act 1984

General power of seizure

19.–(1) The powers conferred by subsections (2), (3) and (4) below are exercisable by a constable who is lawfully on any premises.

(2) The constable may seize anything which is on the premises if he has reasonable grounds for believing—

(a) that it has been obtained in consequence of the commission of an offence; and

(b) that it is necessary to seize it in order to prevent it being concealed, lost, damaged, altered or destroyed.

(3) The constable may seize anything which is on the premises if he has reasonable grounds for believing—

---

33 See D Dixon (1991) 141 NLJ 1586.

(a) that it is evidence in relation to an offence which he is investigating or any other offence; and

(b) that it is necessary to seize it in order to prevent the evidence being concealed, lost, altered or destroyed. ...

(6) No power of seizure conferred on a constable under any enactment (including an enactment contained in an Act passed after this Act) is to be taken to authorise the seizure of an item which the constable exercising the power has reasonable grounds for believing to be subject to legal privilege.

Criminal Justice and Police Act 2001

Additional powers of seizure from premises

50.–(1) Where—

(a) a person who is lawfully on any premises finds anything on those premises that he has reasonable grounds for believing may be or may contain something for which he is authorised to search on those premises,

(b) a power of seizure to which this section applies or the power conferred by subsection would entitle him, if he found it, to seize whatever it is that he has grounds for believing that thing to be or to contain, and

(c) in all the circumstances, it is not reasonably practicable for it to be determined, on those premises—

(i) whether what he has found is something that he is entitled to seize, or

(ii) the extent to which what he has found contains something that he is entitled to seize,

that person's powers of seizure shall include power under this section to seize so much of what he has found as it is necessary to remove from the premises to enable that to be determined.

(2) Where—

(a) a person who is lawfully on any premises finds anything on those premises ('the seizable property') which he would be entitled to seize but for its being comprised in something else that he has (apart from this subsection) no power to seize,

(b) the power under which that person would have power to seize the seizable property is a power to which this section applies, and

(c) in all the circumstances it is not reasonably practicable for the seizable property to be separated, on those premises, from that in which it is comprised,

that person's powers of seizure shall include power under this section to seize both the seizable property and that from which it is not reasonably practicable to separate it.

Notice of exercise of power under s. 50 or 51

52.–(1) Where a person exercises a power of seizure conferred by section 50, it shall (subject to subsections (2) and (3)) be his duty, on doing so, to give to the occupier of the premises a written notice—

... specifying what has been seized ...

the grounds on which those powers have been exercised;

... specifying the name and address of the person to whom notice of an application ... must be given.

Obligation to return items subject to legal privilege

54.–(1) If ...

(a) it appears to the person for the time being having possession of the seized property in consequence of the seizure that the property—

   (i) is an item subject to legal privilege, or

   (ii) has such an item comprised in it,

and

(b) in a case where the item is comprised in something else which has been lawfully seized, it is not comprised in property falling within subsection (2),

it shall be the duty of that person to secure that the item is returned as soon as reasonably practicable after the seizure.

Obligation to return excluded and special procedure material

. . .

55.–(2) Property in which any excluded material or special procedure material is comprised falls within this subsection if—

(a) the whole or a part of the rest of the property is property for which the person seizing it had power to search when he made the seizure but is not property the return of which is required by this section or section 54; and

(b) in all the circumstances, it is not reasonably practicable for that material to be separated from the rest of that property (or, as the case may be, from that part of it) without prejudicing the use of the rest of that property, or that part of it, for purposes for which (disregarding that material) its use, if retained, would be lawful.

Property seized by constables etc.

56.–(1) The retention of [seized property]—

   . . . is authorised by this section if the property falls within subsection (2) or (3).

(2) Property falls within this subsection to the extent that there are reasonable grounds for believing—

(a) that it is property obtained in consequence of the commission of an offence; and

(b) that it is necessary for it to be retained in order to prevent its being concealed, lost, damaged, altered or destroyed.

(3) Property falls within this subsection to the extent that there are reasonable grounds for believing—

(a) that it is evidence in relation to any offence; and

(b) that it is necessary for it to be retained in order to prevent its being concealed, lost, altered or destroyed.

Notes

1   Under s 22(1) of PACE, anything which has been so seized may be retained 'so long as is necessary in all the circumstances'. It was made clear in *R v Chief Constable of Lancashire ex p Parker and McGrath* [1993] 2 WLR 428 that the above provisions assume that the search itself is lawful; in other words, material seized during an unlawful search cannot be retained and if it is, an action for trespass to goods may arise.

2   Under s 9 of PACE, excluded or special procedure material or material covered by legal privilege cannot be seized during a search not under warrant and it is exempt from the s 8 search warrant procedure under s 8(1). However, the police may gain access to excluded or special procedure material (not legally privileged material) by making an application to a circuit judge in accordance with Sched 1 or, in the case of special procedure material only, to a magistrate for a search warrant. Access to

excluded material may only be granted where it could have been obtained under the previous law relating to such material.

3 Personal records include records held by schools, universities, probation officers and social workers. 'Special procedure material' defined under s 14 operates as a catch-all category which is, it seems, frequently used[34] to cover confidential material which does not qualify as personal records or journalistic material.[35] A production order will not be made unless there is reasonable suspicion that a serious arrestable offence has been committed, the material is likely to be of substantial value to the investigation and admissible at trial. It should be noted that when enquiries relating to terrorist offences are made, Sched 7, para 3 of the Prevention of Terrorism Act 1989 allowed access to both special procedure and excluded material. This power is reproduced in Sched 5 of the Terrorism Act 2000. The judge only needs to be satisfied that there is a terrorist investigation in being, that the material would substantially assist it and that it is in the public interest that it should be produced. It may well be that once the first two requirements are satisfied, it will be rare to find that the third is not.

4 The ruling in *R v Guildhall Magistrates' Court ex p Primlaks Holdings Co (Panama) Limited* [1989] 2 WLR 841 made it clear that a magistrate must satisfy him or herself that there were reasonable grounds for believing that the items covered by the warrant did not include material subject to the special protection. The magistrates had issued search warrants authorising the search of two solicitors' firms. Judicial review of the magistrates' decision to issue a warrant was successfully sought; it was found that the magistrate had merely accepted the police officer's view that s 8(1) was satisfied rather than independently considering the matter.

5 The strongest protection extends to items subject to legal privilege, since they cannot be searched for or seized by police officers and, therefore, the meaning of 'legal privilege' is crucial. Under s 10, it will cover communications between client and solicitor connected with giving advice or with legal proceedings. However, if items are held with the intention of furthering a criminal purpose they will not, under s 10(2), attract legal privilege. The House of Lords in *R v Central Criminal Court ex p Francis and Francis* [1989] AC 346[36] found that material which figures in the criminal intentions of persons other than solicitor or client will not be privileged. A judge must give full consideration to the question whether particular documents have lost legal privilege.[37] This interpretation of s 10(2) was adopted on the basis that, otherwise, the efforts of the police in detecting crime might be hampered, but it may be argued that it gives insufficient weight to the need to protect the special relationship between solicitor and client and, as argued below, may be vulnerable to challenge under the HRA.

6 The Criminal Justice and Police Act 2001 (CJPA), s 50(2) extends the power of seizure very significantly. This provision is significant since, *inter alia*, it allows police officers to remove items from premises even where they are not certain that – apart from s 50 – they have the power to do so. Thus, a number of items can now be seized from premises although no power of seizure – apart from that now arising under s 50 – in fact arises.

34 See K Lidstone (1989) NILQ 333, p 342.
35 For comment on these provisions see Stone [1988] Crim LR 498.
36 For comment see Stevenson (1989) Law Soc Gazette, 1 February, p 26.
37 *R v Southampton Crown Court ex p J and P* [1993] Crim LR 962.

7   As indicated above, the seizure of excluded or special procedure material is restricted, while material covered by legal privilege could not previously be seized. Most significantly, s 50 may serve to undermine these protections for certain material since where such material is part of other material and cannot practicably be separated, it can be seized. It can also be seized where a police officer takes the view on reasonable grounds that it is something that he has the power to seize, although it turns out later that it falls within one of the special categories.

8   Special provisions are made under the 2001 Act for the return of excluded or special procedure material or material covered by legal privilege. For obvious reasons, these provisions are most significant in relation to material covered by legal privilege since they could aid in undermining the privilege. Under s 54, such material must be returned unless it falls within s 54(2). Section 54(2) covers a legally privileged item comprised in other material. Such an item will fall within that sub-section if the retention of the rest of the property would be lawful and it is not reasonably practicable to separate the legally privileged item from the rest of the property without prejudicing the use of the rest of that property. Section 57(3) provides that ss 53–56 do not authorise the retention of property where its retention would not be authorised apart from the provisions of Part 2 of the CJPA. Under s 62, inextricably linked property cannot be examined or copied but under s 62(4) can be used to the extent that its use facilitates the use of property in which the inextricably linked property is comprised.

9   Sections 50, 54 and 55 of the CJPA taken together do provide avenues to the seizure and non-return of the specially protected material. The new provisions thus circumvent the limitations placed on the seizure of excluded or special procedure material and, most importantly of all, provide an avenue to the seizure and use of legally privileged material. It can be said that for the first time legally privileged material has lost part of the protection it was accorded under the common law and under PACE.

10 These wide CJPA powers are 'balanced' by the provisions of ss 52–61 which provide a number of safeguards. But despite these safeguards, it is unclear that the new powers, especially to seize and use legally privileged material, are fully compatible with the requirements of the Convention under the HRA.

Impact of the Human Rights Act

In the following two cases, the European Court of Human Rights considers the compatibility of searches of property with the Convention rights.

Camenzind v Switzerland (1999) 28 EHRR 458

A Whether there was an interference with the right to respect for the home under Article 8(1)

It suffices for the Court to find that in any event (and this was common ground) the search of the room occupied by the applicant amounted to an interference, within the meaning of Article 8, with his right to respect for his home.

It accordingly has to be determined whether the interference was justified under paragraph 2 of Article 8, in other words whether it was 'in accordance with the law', pursued one or more of the legitimate aims set out in that paragraph and was 'necessary in a democratic society' to achieve the aim or aims in question.

B Whether the interference was justified

I 'In accordance with the law'

The Court reiterates that the expression 'in accordance with the law', within the meaning of Article 8(2) of the Convention, requires that the impugned measure should have some basis in domestic law and that the law in question should be accessible to the person concerned – who must moreover be able to foresee its consequences for him – and compatible with the rule of law. [FN35] In the instant case it notes, [the relevant offence under section 42 of the Federal Act of 1922] ... The Court further notes ... that the Act contains safeguards against arbitrary interference by the authorities with the right to respect for the home. ... the Court accepts that the measure complained of was 'in accordance with the law'.

2 *Legitimate aim*

the search ... pursued ... the 'prevention of disorder or crime'.

3 *'Necessary in a democratic society'*

Under the Court's settled case law, the notion of 'necessity' implies that the interference corresponds to a pressing social need and, in particular, that it is proportionate to the legitimate aim pursued; in determining whether an interference is 'necessary in a democratic society', the Court will take into account that a margin of appreciation is left to the Contracting States.

The Court will assess whether the reasons adduced to justify [the search] were relevant and sufficient and whether the aforementioned proportionality principle has been adhered to. As regards the latter point, the Court must first ensure that the relevant legislation and practice afford individuals 'adequate and effective safeguards against abuse' notwithstanding the margin of appreciation which the Court recognises the Contracting States have in this sphere, it must be particularly vigilant where, as in the present case, the authorities are empowered under national law to order and effect searches without a judicial warrant. If individuals are to be protected from arbitrary interference by the authorities with the rights guaranteed under Article 8, a legal framework and very strict limits on such powers are called for. Secondly, the Court must consider the particular circumstances of each case in order to determine whether, in the concrete case, the interference in question was proportionate to the aim pursued.

With regard to the safeguards provided by Swiss law, the Court notes that ... a search may, subject to exceptions, only be effected under a written warrant ... Searches can only be carried out in 'dwellings and other premises ... if objects or valuables liable to seizure or evidence of the commission of an offence are to be found there'; they cannot be conducted on Sundays, public holidays or at night 'except in important cases or where there is imminent danger'. At the beginning of a search the investigating official must produce evidence of identity and inform the occupier of the premises of the purpose of the search. ... In principle, there will also be a public officer present to ensure that '[the search] does not deviate from its purpose'. A record of the search is drawn up immediately. ... Furthermore, searches for documents are subject to special restrictions. In addition, suspects are entitled, whatever the circumstances, to representation; anyone affected by an 'investigative measure' who has 'an interest worthy of protection in having the measure ... quashed or varied' may complain to the Indictment Division of the Federal Court.

Having regard to the safeguards provided by Swiss legislation and especially to the limited scope of the search, the Court accepts that the interference with the applicant's right to respect for his home can be considered to have been proportionate to the aim pursued and thus 'necessary in a democratic society' within the meaning of Article 8. Consequently, there has not been a violation of that provision.

Özgür Gündem v Turkey (2001) 31 EHRR 49

This part of the ruling concerned the police operation at the Özgür Gündem (a newspaper) premises in Istanbul on 10 December 1993.

The Court finds that the operation, which resulted in newspaper production being disrupted for two days, constituted a serious interference with the applicants' freedom of expression. It accepts that the operation was conducted according to a procedure 'prescribed by law' for the purpose of preventing crime and disorder within the meaning of the second paragraph of Article 10. It does not, however, find that a measure of such dimension was proportionate to this aim. No justification has been provided for the seizure of the newspaper's archives, documentation and library. Nor has the Court received an explanation for the blanket apprehension of every person found on the newspaper's premises. . . .

As stated in the Commission's report, the necessity for any restriction in the exercise of freedom of expression must be convincingly established. The Court concludes that the search operation, as conducted by the authorities, has not been shown to be necessary, in a democratic society, for the implementation of any legitimate aim.

In the following two domestic cases, powers of search and seizure are considered in relation to common law principle and the Convention rights.

R v Central Criminal Court ex p Bright [2001] 2 All ER 244, DC

Judicial review was sought of production orders under s 9 of PACE. The orders concerned material relating to David Shayler, a former employee of MI5, who had made allegations about the involvement of MI6 in a plot to assassinate Colonel Gadafy. *The Guardian* had published an emailed letter from Shayler; *The Observer* had published an article about his allegations; production orders had sought material from both newspapers regarding Shayler. The Court had to consider the principles to be applied including the question whether the order infringed the privilege against self-incrimination. The orders were quashed.

Judge LJ: In my judgment ... it is clear that the judge personally must be satisfied that the statutory requirements have been established. ... This follows from the express wording of the statute, 'if . . . a Circuit Judge is satisfied that one ... of the sets of access conditions is fulfilled'. The purpose of this provision is to interpose between the opinion of the police officer seeking the order and the consequences to the individual or organisation to whom the order is addressed, the safeguard of a judgment and decision of a circuit judge. ... In my judgment it is equally clear that the constable making the application must satisfy the judge that the relevant set of conditions is established. ... Another feature of the rules arises from the clear language that if the relevant set of access conditions is fulfilled then the judge is empowered, but not bound, to make the order. Assuming that access conditions are established to his satisfaction, he has a discretion or power to refuse the application. ... If he is so satisfied, how, putting the matter rhetorically, can he refuse the order?

The answer appears to arise from the somewhat limited conditions which are said expressly to be relevant to the 'public interest'. They are restricted to the potential benefit to the investigation and the circumstances in which the person against whom the order is sought 'holds' the material. So, for example, nothing is said about open discussion in the media of questions of public importance or the consequences to which the person against whom the order is made may be exposed. . . .

This provision, as it seems to me, is the final safeguard against an oppressive order, and in an appropriate case, provides the judge with the opportunity to reflect on and take account of matters which are not expressly referred to in the set of relevant access conditions and, where they arise, to reflect on all the circumstances, including where appropriate, what can, without exaggeration, be described as fundamental principles. ... Our attention was drawn to a number of decisions of the European Court of Human Rights. ... by now, we surely fully appreciate that the principles to be found in Articles 6 and 10 of the European Convention are bred in the bone of the common law. ... generally ... citations ... of the decisions of the European Court, simply repeat ... long standing and well understood principles of the common law ...

The common law principle was expressed nearly two hundred and fifty years ago in the famous case of *Entick v Carrington* (1765) 19 ST 1029.

Entick was a clerk whose home in Stepney was broken into ... by [officials] acting under the authority of a warrant issued by the Earl of Halifax ... which authorised and requested them to make strict and diligent search for the plaintiff and to bring him with his books and papers in safe custody ... to be examined. The issue was whether the Secretary of State had jurisdiction to seize the papers ... The judgment of Lord Camden, CJ, at 1066, includes statements of fundamental principle.

No man can set his foot upon my ground without my licence, but he is liable to an action, though the damage is nothing ... If he admits the fact, he is bound to show by way of justification, that some positive law has empowered or excused him. The justification is submitted to the judges, who are to look into the books and if such a justification can be maintained by the text of the statute law, or by the principles of common law. ... He continued: Papers are the owner's goods and chattels ... and so far from enduring a seizure, ... they will hardly bear an inspection ... Where is the written law that gives any magistrate such a power? I can safely answer, there is none; and therefore it is too much for us without such authority to pronounce a practice legal, which would be subversive of all the comforts of society.

William Pitt, Earl of Chatham (1708–1778) was expounding the same principle, when he said:

> The poorest man may in his cottage bid defiance to all the forces of the Crown. It may be frail – its roof may shake – the wind may blow through it – the storm may enter – the rain may enter – but the King of England cannot enter – all his force dares not cross the threshold of the ruined tenement.

These principles are interlinked. Premises are not to be entered by the forces of authority or the State to deter or diminish, inhibit or stifle the exercise of an individual's right to free speech or the press of its freedom to investigate and inform, and orders should not be made which might have that effect unless a circuit judge is personally satisfied that the statutory preconditions to the making of an order are established, and, as the final safeguard of basic freedoms, that in the particular circumstances it is indeed appropriate for an order to be made.

... Legal proceedings directed towards the seizure of the working papers of an individual journalist, or the premises of the newspaper or television programme publishing his or her reports, or the threat of such proceedings, tends to inhibit discussion. ... The judge, alert to the need to safeguard basic freedoms, must simultaneously acknowledge the public interest which underpins the relevant legislation, and section 9 and Schedule 1 in particular, that crime should be discouraged and those responsible for crime should be detected and brought to justice. Balancing these interests where they appear to be in conflict is a decision to be made in each individual case where apparent conflict arises.

These principles, which I derive from the common law, are interlinked. They are encapsulated and reflected in the European Convention. ...

The next matter for consideration is Mr Emmerson's contention that a successful application against Mr Bright would infringe his privilege against self-incrimination. ... attention was drawn to the decisions of the European Court of Justice in *Saunders v UK* (1997) 23 EHRR 313, *Funke v France* (1993) 16 EHRR 297, and *Serves v France* (1999) 28 EHRR 265.

In *R v Hertfordshire County Council, ex p Green Environmental Industries Limited* [2000] 1 All ER 773, the impact of Article 6(1) and 6(2) of the European Convention, and the relevant decisions of the European Court on these provisions were analysed by Lord Hoffmann in the context of domestic legislation. ... Lord Hoffmann explained ... [that the] question of whether a statute which confers a power to ask questions or obtain documents or information excludes the privilege against self incrimination in one or other of its forms is therefore one of construction.

With these principles in mind I turn to sections 8 and 9 of the 1984 Act which are directed to the proper investigation of a serious crime, after its commission, or more accurately, when there are reasonable grounds for believing that it has been committed, and involve the search for likely relevant and admissible evidence. These sections are directly concerned with the criminal process and the search for incriminating material in serious arrestable offences. That indeed is their exclusive purpose. ...

Under section 8 a warrant to enter premises owned or occupied either by a suspect or someone against whom no hint of suspicion arises may be granted. If necessary, force may be deployed. During the course of the search incriminating material may be seized, and if so, used at a subsequent trial. The privilege against self-incrimination is untouched. Of itself the warrant does not permit a suspect to be questioned, ... He is entitled to remain entirely passive.

By contrast, an order under section 9 imposes a specific obligation, enforceable by a penal sanction, to produce or grant access to material which is likely to be relevant and admissible at a subsequent trial. It would be an odd and surprising development if the special procedure rules excluded the privilege against self-incrimination, when the same privilege is maintained in section 8. ... this permits the search of the premises, but does not require a suspect to produce incriminating material to the police, or to give them access to it ...

The objective of section 9 is to enable the police to obtain journalistic material in the possession of a journalist, which is relevant to the criminal activities of others, including the individual who provided him with the material.

... the requirements in paragraph 4(a) and 4(b) should be read together. Read in this way they represent the process by which access may be gained by the police to journalistic material. It may be impossible, or highly inconvenient, for material to be physically produced by the journalist to the investigating officers. .... So, as an alternative to handing the material over to the police officer he must provide access to it.

In any event, even if it were right to treat the obligation under paragraph 4(b) as a distinct provision, the question of self-incrimination would still arise. ... in such circumstances, if the suspect journalist were obliged to take any positive step to comply with the demand, he would be providing or helping to provide material which could be used at his trial. Passive giving of access in such circumstances is improbable: unlike 'allow' or 'permit','give' implies more than mere passivity.

... section 9 and Schedule 1 do not provide sufficient authority for the proposition that Mr Bright, and *The Observer,* must produce documents or give access to material which may incriminate them.

Finally, I must add, that as a matter of fundamental principle, and for the reasons analysed earlier in this judgment, if I am wrong, I have no doubt that in exercising his discretion, the judge should take account of the fact that a possible consequence of his order would be the danger of self-incrimination. This factor does not, in my judgment, become irrelevant because of the undoubted discretion provided in section 78 of the Act for the trial judge to exclude evidence.

In the application concerning *The Guardian,* I have considerable doubts whether there is any sufficient evidence to justify the conclusion that there were reasonable grounds for believing that a serious arrestable offence had been committed. .... I further doubt whether the evidence being sought, that is, Shayler's email address, would provide relevant and admissible evidence against him. ... Given the scarcity of information about Shayler's alleged offences it is also difficult to examine whether the material sought by D.S. Flynn was likely to be of 'substantial' value to the investigation. In all the circumstances I am not impressed with the proposition that ability of the Crown unequivocally to prove that Shayler actually wrote the letter published under his name in *The Guardian* is of substantial importance. ....

In my judgment the necessary access conditions were not established. No question of the exercise of the judge's discretion arose. The order should not have been made. The appeal should be allowed.

In the wide terms sought in the original application, I believe that it would have had a devastating and stifling effect on the proper investigation of the Shayler story. Virtually any journalist who made contact with him, and any newspaper publishing an article based on discussions with Shayler, would be at risk of a similar application to the present. To my mind that would be an unhealthy development, quite disproportionate to any practical advantages to the prosecution process.

R (Rottman) v Commissioner of Police of the Metropolis [2002] 2 WLR 1315

In 2000, a provisional warrant for the claimant's arrest was issued under s 8(1)(b) of the Extradition Act 1989. The claimant was arrested; thereafter the arresting officers entered and searched his house and removed items belonging to the claimant which they suspected might hold evidence of the alleged offences or proceeds of the offences, having acted in purported reliance on s 18 in Part II of PACE and in the belief that they had in any event power under the common law to search the premises of a suspect following his arrest on an extradition warrant. The claimant applied to the Divisional Court for an order directed to the Commissioner of Police of the Metropolis requiring the delivery up of all items seized and a declaration that the entry and search had been unlawful and in breach of the claimant's rights under Article 8 of the European Convention on Human Rights as scheduled to the Human Rights Act 1998. The Divisional Court held that the statutory powers of entry, search and seizure without a warrant in Part II of PACE did not extend to extradition cases, that any powers of search under the common law had been extinguished when the 1984 Act came into force and that accordingly the search and seizure had been unlawful and in violation of the claimant's rights under Article 8.

> **Lord Hutton:** [having referred to and approved *Ghani v Jones* [1970] 1 QB 693] ... if the police have power at common law to search the person of the individual whom they have arrested under a warrant issued pursuant to section 8(1)(b) PACE, it seems contrary to common sense to hold that they do not have power to seize material evidence present in the room where he is arrested and also to search other rooms in his house and seize material evidence found in them. Accordingly I would hold that the common law power of search and seizure after the execution of a warrant of arrest issued pursuant to section 8(1)(b) was not extinguished by PACE and that the police officers were entitled to exercise that power after the arrest of the respondent.
>
> **80** I am unable to accept the respondent's submission that the common law power of search and seizure after arrest constitutes a violation of his rights under article 8. The search and seizure was in accordance with the law which was clearly stated by Lloyd LJ in *Osman* [1990] 1 WLR 277. ... The power has the legitimate aim in a democratic society of preventing crime, and is necessary in order to prevent the disappearance of material evidence after the arrest of a suspect. The power is proportionate to that aim because it is subject to the safeguards that it can only be exercised after a warrant of arrest has been issued by a magistrate or a justice of the peace in respect of an extradition crime and where the evidence placed before him would, in his opinion, justify the issue of a warrant for the arrest of a person accused of a similar domestic offence.
>
> **81** Accordingly I would answer the certified question 'Yes, a police officer who has arrested a person in or on his premises pursuant to a warrant of arrest issued under section 8 of the Extradition Act 1989 has power to search those premises for, and to seize, any goods or documents which he reasonably believes to be material evidence in relation to the extradition crime in respect of which the warrant was issued.' I would allow the appeal and would set aside the order of the Divisional Court.

The Lords agreed to allow the appeal, Lord Hope dissenting.

Notes

1 *Impact of the HRA.* Article 8(1) of the ECHR provides a right to respect for private and family life, the home and correspondence, subject to a number of exceptions enumerated in para 2. (See Part II Chapter 2, p 243.) The European Court of Human Rights has found that entry, search and seizure can create interferences with all the Article 8 guarantees apart from that of the right to respect for family

life.[38] Search for and seizure of documents is covered by the term 'correspondence' and the documents do not have to be personal in nature.[39] Such interferences can be justified only if they are in accordance with the law (Article 8(2)). This requirement covers not only the existence of national law, but its quality.[40] The statutory and common law powers probably meet this requirement[41] and have the legitimate aim of preventing crime or protecting national security.

2   Any interference with the Article 8(1) guarantees must 'correspond to a pressing social need and, in particular, [must be] proportionate to the legitimate aim pursued'.[42] It was found in the context of intercept warrants in *Klass v FRG* (1978) 2 EHRR 214 that judicial or administrative authority for warrants would provide a degree of independent oversight: sufficient safeguards against abuse were available. It could be argued that the arrangements whereby magistrates issue search warrants might fail to meet this requirement since, although in appearance an independent judicial check is available before the event, the 'check' may be almost a formality in reality.[43] Research suggests that in practice, some magistrates make little or no attempt to ascertain whether the information a warrant contains may be relied upon, while it seems possible that magistrates who do take a rigorous approach to the procedure and refuse to grant warrants are not approached again.[44] Therefore, a breach of Article 8 might be established in respect of the practice of certain magistrates. It may be noted, however, that this argument failed in the Scottish case of *Birse v HM Advocate* (2000) unreported, 13 April.

3   A search of premises that is authorised but goes beyond the authorisation is likely to be viewed as disproportionate to the legitimate aim pursued. As indicated above, in *Camenzind v Switzerland* (1997) 28 EHRR 458, there were specific procedures in place and the search was of a limited scope: it was found, therefore, to be proportionate to the aim pursued.

4   The decision of the House of Lords in *R v Central Criminal Court ex p Francis and Francis* [1989] AC 346 regarding material subject to legal professional privilege may require reconsideration in relation to Article 8. As indicated above, the House of Lords found that privilege is lost when the material is innocently held, but is for a third party's criminal purpose. The approach in *Niemietz v Germany*, Series A No 251-B, (1992) 16 EHRR 97 was to the effect that a search of a lawyer's office had led to a breach of Article 8 since it was disproportionate to the aims of preventing crime and of protecting the rights of others. That decision also raises questions about the provisions of Part 2 of the CJPA. Since the CJPA was accompanied by a declaration of its compatibility with the Convention rights, legal advice to the government must have been to the effect that Part 2 was compatible with Article 8. Clearly, this advice could subsequently be found to be flawed; the judiciary remains entirely free (in the higher courts, as Chapter 1 of this part explained) to make a declaration of incompatibility between one or more of the Part 2 provisions and Article 8.

---

38   See *Funke v France* (1993) 16 EHRR 297; *Mialhe v France* (1993) 16 EHRR 332.
39   See *Niemietz v Germany* Series A No 251-B; (1992) 16 EHRR 97.
40   *Kopp v Switzerland* (1999) 27 EHRR 91, paras 70–71.
41   In *McLeod v UK* (1998) 27 EHRR 493 powers to enter to prevent a breach of the peace were found to meet this requirement (paras 38–45).
42   *Olsson v Sweden*, Series A No 130, (1988) 11 EHRR 259, para 67.
43   See R Clayton and H Tomlinson, *The Law of Human Rights* (2000), p 863.
44   This point is made by Dixon (1991), *op cit*.

5 Article 8 values might come to influence this search and seizure scheme due to the use of arguments under s 7(1)(b) of the HRA, either raised in criminal proceedings, in civil actions against the police for trespass, trespass to goods or for conversion, or as freestanding actions under s 7(1)(a) of the HRA. The PACE and CJPA schemes are subject to an Article 8-friendly interpretation, taking the Convention jurisprudence above into account, under s 3 of the HRA.

6 Special procedure material and journalistic material are not afforded as much protection as legally privileged material. Where the search and seizure takes place on the premises of a media organisation, Article 10 as well as Article 8 is relevant, as *Özgür Gündem v Turkey* demonstrates. It has been argued that the judiciary have not provided sufficient protection for journalistic material.[45] Both Articles 8 and 10 could be relied upon in arguing that a production order under s 9 of and Sched 1 to PACE should not have been issued on grounds of disproportionality. Article 6(1), which encapsulates the privilege against self-incrimination, may also be relevant; the result of the *Bright* case is that s 9 does not allow for a production order where infringement of that principle might occur. The findings in that case were made just before the HRA came fully into force. The comments of Judge J as to the relationship between the ECHR jurisprudence and common law principle provide some encouragement to argument that under the HRA such orders should not be made where a breach of Article 6(1) would be likely to arise thereby. The judge making the order would be bound by s 6 of the HRA and therefore would have to comply with Article 6(1), unless it was argued that s 6(2) of the HRA applies. Moreover, according to Judge J's comments, a result consistent with that required under the Convention might be arrived at following common law principles.

7 *R (Rottman) v Commissioner of Police of the Metropolis* confirms that broad common law powers can continue to supplement the statutory ones and that domestic judges consider such a position to be entirely compatible with Article 8.

Question
What does the *Bright* case tell us about the attitude that some judges take to the European Convention on Human Rights and what do we learn about the relationship some judges perceive as existing between the Convention and common law principle?

POWERS OF ARREST AND DETENTION

Any arrest represents a serious curtailment of liberty; therefore, use of the arrest power requires careful regulation. An arrest is seen as *prima facie* illegal necessitating justification under a specific legal power. If an arrest is effected where no arrest power arises, a civil action for false imprisonment will lie. Despite the need for clarity and precision, such powers were, until relatively recently, granted piecemeal with the result that, prior to PACE, they were contained in a mass of common law and statutory provisions. The powers are now contained largely in PACE but common law powers remain, while some statutes create a specific power of arrest which may overlap with the PACE powers. All the powers must now be exercised within the constraints created by Article 5.

The due process and crime control views of arrest and detention are diametrically opposed. Under the due process model, arrest should be based on strong suspicion

---

45 R Costigan [1996] Crim LR 231.

that the individual has committed a specific offence, since arrest and subsequent detention represent a severe infringement of individual rights. Under the crime control model, arrest and detention need not be sanctioned merely in relation to specific offences, but should be both an investigative tool and a means of asserting police authority over persons with a criminal record or of doubtful character, with a view to creating a general deterrent effect. Under this model, reasonable suspicion is viewed as a needless irrelevancy, an inhibitory rule standing in the way of an important police function.

At common law – power to arrest for breach of peace[46]

PACE has not affected the power to arrest which arises at common law for breach of the peace. Factors present in a situation in which breach of the peace occurs may also give rise to arrest powers under PACE, but may extend further than they do due to the wide definition of breach of the peace. The leading case is *R v Howell* [1981] 3 All ER 383.[47]

R v Howell [1981] 3 All ER 383

Watkins LJ: We hold that there is power of arrest for breach of the peace where:

(1) a breach of the peace is committed in the presence of the person making the arrest; or

(2) the arrestor reasonably believes that such a breach will be committed in the immediate future by the person arrested although he has not yet committed any breach; or

(3) where a breach has been committed and it is reasonably believed that a renewal of it is threatened.

The public expects a policeman not only to apprehend the criminal but to do his best to prevent the commission of crime, to keep the peace in other words. To deny him, therefore, the right to arrest a person who he reasonably believes is about to breach the peace would be to disable him from preventing that which might cause serious injury to someone or even to many people or to property. The common law, we believe, whilst recognising that a wrongful arrest is a serious invasion of a person's liberty, provides the police with this power in the public interest. In those instances of the exercise of this power which depend on a belief that a breach of the peace is imminent it must, we think we should emphasise, be established that it is not only an honest, albeit mistaken, belief but a belief which is founded on reasonable grounds.

Power of arrest with warrant

Magistrates' Courts Act 1980
Part I

Issue of summons to accused or warrant for his arrest

1.–(1) Upon an information being laid before a justice of the peace for an area to which this section applies that any person has, or is suspected of having, committed an offence, the justice may. ...

    (a) issue a summons directed to that person requiring him to appear before a magistrates' court for the area to answer to the information, or

---

46 For commentary on breach of the peace generally see Glanville Williams [1954] Crim LR 578. See Part VI Chapter 3 for further discussion of the use of breach of the peace.

47 For comment see Glanville Williams (1982) 146 JPN 199–200, 217–19.

(b)	issue a warrant to arrest that person and bring him before a magistrates' court for the area or such magistrates' court as is provided in subsection (5) below.

(4)	No warrant shall be issued under this section for the arrest of any person who has attained the age of 18 years unless—

(a)	the offence to which the warrant relates is an indictable offence or is punishable with imprisonment, or

(b)	the person's address is not sufficiently established for a summons to be served on him.

Powers of arrest without warrant

Police and Criminal Evidence Act 1984

Part III – Arrest

Arrest without warrant for arrestable and other offences

24.–(1) The powers of summary arrest conferred by the following subsections shall apply—

(a)	to offences for which the sentence is fixed by law;

(b)	to offences for which a person of 21 years of age or over (not previously convicted) may be sentenced to imprisonment for a term of five years (or might be so sentenced but for the restrictions imposed by s 33 of the Magistrates' Courts Act 1980); and

(c)	to the offences to which subsection (2) below applies, and in this Act 'arrestable offence' means any such offence.

(2) The offences to which this subsection applies are—

(a)	offences for which a person may be arrested under the customs and excise Acts ...

(b)	offences under the Official Secrets Act 1920. ...

(bb)	offences under any provision of the Official Secrets Act 1989 except section 8(1), (4) or (5)....

(c)	offences under section ... 22 (causing prostitution of women) or 23 (procuration of girl under 21) of the Sexual Offences Act 1956;

(d)	offences under section 12(1) (taking motor vehicle or other conveyance without authority, etc) or 25(1) (going equipped for stealing, etc) of the Theft Act 1968; ...

(e)	any offence under the Football (Offences) Act 1991 ...

(k)	an offence under s 1(1) of the Prevention of Crime Act 1953 ...

(l)	an offence under s 139(1) of the Criminal Justice Act 1988 ...

(n)	an offence under the Protection from Harassment Act 1997 ...

(o)	an offence under s 60(8)(b) of the Criminal Justice and Public Order Act 1994

(p)	an offence falling within s 32(1)(a) of the Crime and Disorder Act 1998 ...

(r)	an offence under s 12(4) of the Criminal Justice and Police Act 2001 ...

(4) Any person may arrest without a warrant—

(a)	anyone who is in the act of committing an arrestable offence;

(b)	anyone whom he has reasonable grounds for suspecting to be committing such an offence.

(5) Where an arrestable offence has been committed, any person may arrest without a warrant—

(a)	anyone who is guilty of the offence;

(b)	anyone whom he has reasonable grounds for suspecting to be guilty of it.

(6) Where a constable has reasonable grounds for suspecting that an arrestable offence has been committed, he may arrest without a warrant anyone whom he has reasonable grounds for suspecting to be guilty of the offence.

(7) A constable may arrest without a warrant—

(a) anyone who is about to commit an arrestable offence;

(b) anyone whom he has reasonable grounds for suspecting to be about to commit an arrestable offence.

General arrest conditions

25.–(1) Where a constable has reasonable grounds for suspecting that any offence which is not an arrestable offence has been committed or attempted, or is being committed or attempted, he may arrest the relevant person if it appears to him that service of a summons is impracticable or inappropriate because any of the general arrest conditions is satisfied.

(2) In this section, 'the relevant person' means any person whom the constable has reasonable grounds to suspect of having committed or having attempted to commit the offence or of being in the course of committing or attempting to commit it.

(3) The general arrest conditions are—

(a) that the name of the relevant person is unknown to, and cannot be readily ascertained by, the constable;

(b) that the constable has reasonable grounds for doubting whether a name furnished by the relevant person as his name is his real name;

(c) that—

(i) the relevant person has failed to furnish a satisfactory address for service; or

(ii) the constable has reasonable grounds for doubting whether an address furnished by the relevant person is a satisfactory address for service;

(d) that the constable has reasonable grounds for believing that arrest is necessary to prevent the relevant person—

(i) causing physical harm to himself or any other person;

(ii) suffering physical injury;

(iii) causing loss of or damage to property;

(iv) committing an offence against public decency; or

(v) causing an unlawful obstruction of the highway;

(e) that the constable has reasonable grounds for believing that arrest is necessary to protect a child or other vulnerable person from the relevant person....

(5) Nothing in subsection (3)(d) above authorises the arrest of a person under sub-paragraph (iv) of that paragraph except where members of the public going about their normal business cannot reasonably be expected to avoid the person to be arrested.

(6) This section shall not prejudice any power of arrest conferred apart from this section.

Arrest under the Terrorism Act 2000

Terrorism Act 2000

Terrorist: interpretation

40.–(1) In this Part 'terrorist' means a person who—

(a) has committed an offence under any of sections 11, 12, 15 to 18, 54 and 56 to 63, or

(b) is or has been concerned in the commission, preparation or instigation of acts of terrorism.

Arrest without warrant

41.–(1) A constable may arrest without a warrant a person whom he reasonably suspects to be a terrorist.

(2) Where a person is arrested under this section the provisions of Schedule 8 (detention: treatment, review and extension) shall apply.

(3) Subject to subsections (4) to (7), a person detained under this section shall (unless detained under any other power) be released not later than the end of the period of 48 hours beginning—

(a) with the time of his arrest under this section, or

(b) if he was being detained under Schedule 7 when he was arrested under this section, with the time when his examination under that Schedule began....

Notes

1 There are a large number of statutory provisions allowing an arrest warrant to be issued of which the most significant is that arising under s 1 of the Magistrates' Courts Act 1980. This provision limits the circumstances under which a warrant can be sought as an alternative to using the non-warrant powers under PACE.

2 In broad terms, s 24 of PACE provides a power of arrest in respect of more serious offences while s 25 covers all offences however trivial (including, for example, dropping litter) if certain conditions are satisfied apart from suspicion that the offence in question has been committed. The difference between s 24 and s 25 is significant since, once a person has been arrested under s 24, he or she is said to have been arrested for 'an arrestable offence' and this may have an effect on his or her treatment later on. An 'arrestable offence' is therefore one for which a person can be arrested, if the necessary reasonable suspicion is present, without need to show any other ingredients in the situation at the time of arrest. Offences for which a person can be arrested under s 25 may also be classified as 'serious arrestable offences' under s 116. This does not affect the power of arrest, but does affect various safeguards and powers which may be exercised during detention.

3 In order to arrest under s 25 two steps must be taken: first, there must be reasonable suspicion relating to the offence in question; second, one of the arrest conditions must be fulfilled. The need for one of the general arrest conditions to be satisfied and for the officer to have reasonable suspicion relating to the offence in question was emphasised in *Edwards v DPP* (1993) 97 Cr App R 301.

4 The terrorist offences under the Terrorism Act 2000 (formerly contained in the Prevention of Terrorism (Temporary Provisions) Act 1989) are arrestable offences under s 24 of PACE. Section 14(1)(a) of the PTA also empowered a constable to arrest for certain specified offences under the PTA. As these offences were arrestable offences in any event, this power overlapped with that under s 24 of PACE. That power is reproduced in s 41 read with s 40(1)(a) of the TA, which covers arrest in respect of certain TA offences. If an arrest is effected under s 41 of the TA, as opposed to s 24 of PACE, this has an effect on the length of detention, as will be seen below.

5 Police discretion is particularly wide where no reasonable suspicion of any particular offence is necessary in order to arrest. Such a power is provided by s 41 of the TA read with s 40(1)(b), which largely reproduces s 14(1)(b) of the PTA. The continuation of this power is controversial, since it was adopted in the face of an

emergency situation which is no longer in being and the arrest power is now applicable to a far wider range of groups under s 1 of the TA. Under s 14(1)(b) of the PTA, a constable had to have reasonable grounds for suspecting that a person was concerned in the preparation or instigation of acts of terrorism connected with the affairs of Northern Ireland or 'any other act of terrorism except those connected solely with the affairs of the UK or a part of the UK' in order to arrest. Under s 41 of the TA read with s 40(1)(b), the qualifying words are omitted. This power provides a completely separate power from the PACE power; it allows arrest without needing to show suspicion relating to a particular offence. This arrest is not for an offence but in practice for investigation, questioning and general intelligence gathering. Thus, this power represents a departure from the principle that liberty should be curtailed only on clear and specific grounds which connect the actions of the suspect with a specific offence under criminal law.[48]

6   For an arrest to be valid an arrest warrant must have been issued or there must be a power of arrest without warrant. Also, the requirements of the power must be satisfied; usually this is the requirement of reasonable suspicion. Sections 24 and 25 of PACE and s 41 of the TA depend on the concept of reasonable suspicion; the idea behind it is that an arrest should take place at quite a late stage in the investigation. This limits the number of arrests and makes it less likely that a person will be wrongfully arrested. It is interpreted objectively and the provisions as to reasonable suspicion under Code A could be taken into account. Certain matters, such as an individual's racial group, could never be factors which could support a finding of reasonable suspicion unless the racial group was an identifying factor.

7   The objective nature of suspicion required is echoed in various decisions on the suspicion needed for an arrest.[49] In *Dallison v Caffrey* [1965] 1 QB 348, 371 Lord Diplock said the test was whether 'a reasonable man assumed to know the law and possessed of the information which in fact was possessed by the defendant would believe there were [reasonable grounds]'. Thus, it is not enough for a police officer to have a hunch that a person has committed or is about to commit an offence; there must be a concrete basis for this suspicion which relates to the particular person in question and could be evaluated by an objective observer.

8   The decisions on arrest seem to endorse a fairly low level of suspicion; *Ward v Chief Constable of Somerset and Avon Constabulary* (1986) *The Times*, 26 June[50] suggested that a high level of suspicion was not required, and this might also be said of *Castorina v Chief Constable of Surrey* (1988) 138 NLJ 180. Detectives were investigating a burglary of a company's premises and on reasonable grounds came to the conclusion that it was an 'inside job'. The managing director told them that a certain employee had recently been dismissed and that the documents taken would be useful to someone with a grudge. However, she also said that she would not have expected the particular employee to commit a burglary. The detectives then arrested the employee, having found that she had no previous criminal record. She was detained for nearly four hours and then released without charge. She claimed damages for false imprisonment. The Court of Appeal found that the question was whether there was reasonable cause to suspect the plaintiff of burglary. Given that

---

48   For discussion of this arrest power under the PTA 1984, see C Walker (1984) 47 MLR 704–08; D Bonner, *Emergency Powers in Peace Time* (1985), pp 170–81.

49   Eg, *Nakkuda Ali v Jayaratne* [1951] AC 66, 77; *Allen v Wright* (1835) 8 C & P 522.

50   Cf *Monaghan v Corbett* (1983) 147 JP 545, DC (however, although this demonstrated a different approach the restriction it imposed may not be warranted: see *DPP v Wilson* [1991] Crim LR 441, DC).

certain factors could be identified, including inside knowledge of the company's affairs and the motive of the plaintiff, the Court found that there was sufficient basis for the detectives to have reasonable grounds for suspicion.

9   The reasonableness of the suspicion is to be judged by what the arresting officer had in mind at the time: *Redmond-Bate v DPP* [1999] Crim LR 998 (see pp 975–76, above). In *O'Hara v Chief Constable of the RUC* [1997] 2 WLR 1, a decision on s 12(1) of the PTA, the House of Lords found that a constable could form a suspicion based on what he had been informed of previously as part of a briefing by a superior officer, or otherwise. The question to be asked was whether a reasonable man would personally have formed the suspicion after receiving the relevant information.

10 Research into the use of arrest suggests that, in practice, the concept of reasonable suspicion is interpreted very flexibly by the police, as it is in respect of stop and search powers. A wealth of academic research and analysis has established that the need for reasonable suspicion provides uncertain protection against wrongful arrest. Somewhat doubtful grounds sometimes appear to be sufficient to provide reasonable grounds to justify deprivation of liberty. Further, only in exceptional instances will an officer's use of this power be found to have been wrongful; the courts are quite ready to find that these somewhat hazy tests have been satisfied.[51]

11 There is nothing to prevent a police officer asking any person to come to the police station to answer questions, even where there is no legal power to do so. This creates something of a grey area as the citizen may not realise that he or she does not need to comply with the request.[52] The government refused to include a provision in PACE requiring the police to inform citizens of the fact that they are not under arrest at the point when the request is made.

Procedural elements of arrest

Police and Criminal Evidence Act 1984

Information to be given on arrest

28.–(1) Subject to subsection (5) below, when a person is arrested otherwise than by being informed that he is under arrest, the arrest is not lawful unless the person arrested is informed that he is under arrest as soon as is practicable after his arrest. ...

(3) Subject to subsection (5) below, no arrest is lawful unless the person arrested is informed of the ground for the arrest at the time of, or as soon as is practicable after, the arrest.

Notes

1   For an arrest to be made validly, not only must the power of arrest exist, whatever its source, and its requirements be satisfied, but the procedural elements must be complied with. The fact that a power of arrest arises will not alone make the arrest lawful.

2   The procedural elements are of crucial importance due to the consequences which may flow from a lawful arrest which will not flow from an unlawful one.[53] Such consequences include the right of the officer to use force in making an arrest if

---

51 See C Ryan and K Williams, 'Police discretion' [1986] PL 285, and D Brown, *PACE Ten Years On: A Review of the Research* (1997).

52 See I McKenzie, R Morgan and R Reiner, 'Helping the police with their enquiries' [1990] Crim LR 22.

53 The question as to the difference between a valid and invalid arrest has been much debated; see KW Lidstone [1978] Crim LR 332; D Clark and D Feldman [1979] Crim LR 702; M Zander (1977) 127 NLJ 352; JC Smith [1977] Crim LR 293.

necessary and the loss of liberty inherent in an arrest. If an arrest has not occurred, the citizen is free to go wherever he or she will and any attempt to prevent him or her doing so will be unlawful.[54] It is therefore important to convey the fact of the arrest to the arrestee and to mark the point at which the arrest comes into being and general liberty ceases.

3 Where the arrest is under s 25 of PACE, the offence the defendant is suspected of committing should be made known and so should the general arrest condition which has been breached. The arrest cannot be said to be for breach of the condition. In *Ghafar v Chief Constable of West Midland Police* (2000) unreported, 21 May, CA, the defendant was stopped for driving a car without wearing a seatbelt and failed to provide a name and address; he was arrested on that basis. It was found that both the relevant matters should have been communicated to him. Where there are grounds for the arrest, but the ulterior motive is to investigate the involvement of the suspect in a more serious offence, it is sufficient to inform the defendant of the apparent ground so long as it is a valid reason for the arrest: *R v Chalkley and Jeffries* [1998] QB 848, CA. But where it seems that the defendant is deliberately being misled into thinking he or she is in custody on a less serious charge (which may mean that he or she will not seek access to legal advice) the police should, having made the arrest, ensure, before questioning him or her about the more serious offence, that he or she is aware of the true nature of the investigation.[55] In general the private view of an officer as to the probability that a charge will result from an arrest is not relevant so long as he or she is acting in good faith.[56]

4 Conveying the fact of the arrest under s 28 does not involve using a particular form of words,[57] but sufficient detail must be given so that the arrestee will be in a position to give a convincing denial and therefore be more speedily released from detention.[58]

5 The reason for the arrest need only be made known as soon as practicable. The meaning and implications of this provision were considered in the following case.

DPP v Hawkins [1988] 3 All ER 673, 675, 676

A police officer took hold of the defendant to arrest him but did not give the reason. The youth struggled and was therefore later charged with assaulting an officer in the execution of his duty. The question which arose was whether the officer was in the execution of his duty as he had failed to give the reason for the arrest. If the arrest was thereby rendered invalid he could not be in the execution of his duty as it could not include effecting an unlawful arrest.

Simon Brown J: ... is a police officer acting in the execution of his duty during the period of time between his arresting a person and it first thereafter becoming practicable for him to inform that person of the ground of arrest, given that, at this later time, he in fact gives the wrong ground or no ground at all? If so, then clearly an assault on him by the person arrested during that period of time would constitute a criminal offence. Otherwise not.

---

54 *Rice v Connolly* [1966] 2 QB 414; *Kenlin v Gardner* [1967] 2 QB 510.
55 *R v Kirk* [1999] 4 All ER 698, CA.
56 *Martin v Metropolitan Police Commissioner* (2001) unreported, 18 June, CA.
57 The Court of Appeal confirmed this in *R v Brosch* [1988] Crim LR 743. In *Abassy and Others v Newman and Others* (1989), *The Times,* 18 August, it was found that there was no need for precise or technical language in conveying the reason for the arrest; the question whether the reason had been given was a matter for the jury.
58 *Murphy v Oxford* (1988) unreported, 15 February, CA.

... by virtue of s 28(3) the arrest ultimately proved to be unlawful. But that is not to say that all the earlier steps taken during the course of events leading to that ultimate position must themselves be regarded as unlawful. Still less does it follow that conduct on the part of the police officer, which at the time was not only permitted but positively required of him in the execution of his duty, can become retrospectively invalidated by reference to some later failure (a failure which, I may add, could well have been that of some officer other than himself).

Section 28(3) plainly dictates the circumstances in which an arrest may be found to have been unlawful and it determines decisively the consequences following the time at which that becomes apparent. In my judgment, however, it says nothing in respect of the intermediate period during which it is not practicable to inform the person arrested of the ground for his arrest. Least of all does it supply the answer to the question, hitherto unconsidered by the authorities, whether a police officer is acting in the execution of his duty during that intermediate period. That is a question which I regard as logically separate and apart from the eventual lawfulness or otherwise of the arrest on which he is engaged. ...

Notes

1   The Court of Appeal found that the arrest became unlawful when the time came at which it was practicable to inform the defendant of the reason but he was not so informed. This occurred at the police station or perhaps in the police car, but did not occur earlier due to the defendant's behaviour. Thus, the officer in question was acting in the course of his duty during the period until informing of the reason for arrest became practicable, despite the fact that when so informing became practicable the officer failed to do so.

2   The police, therefore, have a certain leeway as to informing the arrestee; the lawfulness of the arrest will not be affected, and nor will other acts arising from it, until the time when it would be practicable to inform of the reason for it has come and gone. Following *Hawkins*, what can be said as to the status of the suspect before the time came and passed at which the requisite words should have been spoken? Was he or was he not under arrest at that time?

3   In *Murray v Ministry of Defence* [1988] 2 All ER 521, HL,[59] soldiers occupied a woman's house, thus clearly taking her into detention, but did not inform her of the fact of arrest for half an hour. The question arose whether she was falsely imprisoned during that half hour. The House of Lords found that delay in giving the requisite information was acceptable due to the alarm which the fact of arrest, if known, might have aroused in the particular circumstances – the unsettled situation in Northern Ireland. The European Court of Human Rights found (*Murray v United Kingdom* (1994) 19 EHRR 193) that no breach of Article 5(1) (which requires, *inter alia*, that deprivation of liberty can occur only if arising from a lawful arrest founded on reasonable suspicion) had occurred even though the relevant legislation (s 14 of the Northern Ireland (Emergency Provisions) Act 1987) required only suspicion, not reasonable suspicion, since there was some evidence which would provide a basis for the suspicion in question. No breach was found of Article 5(2), which provides that a person must be informed promptly of the reason for arrest. Mrs Murray was eventually informed during interrogation of the reason for the arrest, and allowing an interval of a few hours between arrest and informing of the reason for it could still be termed prompt. The violation of privacy fell within the exception under Article 8(2) in respect of the prevention of crime. No violation of the Convention was therefore found.

---

59   For comment see Williams (1991) 54 MLR 408.

It seems that, under UK law and under Article 5 of the Convention, an arrest which does not comply with all the procedural requirements can still be an arrest as far as all the consequences arising from it are concerned, for a period of time. It is therefore in a more precarious position than an arrest which from its inception complies with all the requirements, because it will cease to be an arrest at an uncertain point. It is clear that some departure has occurred from the principle that there should be a clear demarcation between the point at which the citizen is at liberty and the point at which his or her liberty is restrained.

Questions

1 At what point after the police had detained him, if at all, could a suspect in the position of the suspect in *DPP v Hawkins* attempt lawfully to regain his liberty?

2 Does the decision in *DPP v Hawkins* accept the existence of a concept of lawful detention as distinct from the concept of an arrest?

Use of force[60]

Criminal Law Act 1967

Use of force in making arrest, etc

3.–(1) A person may use such force as is reasonable in the circumstances in the prevention of crime, or in effecting or assisting in the lawful arrest of offenders or suspected offenders or of persons unlawfully at large.

Police and Criminal Evidence Act 1984

Power of constable to use reasonable force

117. Where any provision of this Act—

(a) confers a power on a constable, and

(b) does not provide that the power may only be exercised with the consent of some person, other than a police officer,

the officer may use reasonable force, if necessary, in the exercise of the power.

Notes

1 Force may include, as a last resort, the use of firearms; such use is governed by Home Office guidelines and the most recent version is the Association of Chief Officers of Police (ACPO), *Manual of Guidance on Police Use of Firearms* (2001).[61] It states that firearms should be used only where absolutely necessary, where conventional methods have been tried and have failed or would be likely to fail if tried, for example, if there is reason to suppose that a person to be apprehended is so dangerous that he or she could not be safely restrained otherwise.

2 Section 3 is in one sense wider than s 117, since it authorises the use of force by any person, although only in relation to making an arrest or preventing crime. The prevention of crime would include resistance to an unlawful arrest. Section 117 only applies to police officers and then only in relation to provisions under PACE which do not provide that the consent of someone other than a constable is required. Under the 1967 Act, the force can only be used if it is 'necessary' and the

---

60 For comment see: [1982] Crim LR 475; *Report of Commissioner of Police of the Metropolis for 1983*, Cmnd 9268.

61 Available from www.acpo.police.uk.

amount of force used must be 'reasonable'. 'Reasonable' is taken to mean 'reasonable in the circumstances'[62] and, therefore, allows extreme force if the suspect is also using or appears to be about to use extreme force.

DETENTION IN POLICE CUSTODY

Detention after arrest under the Police and Criminal Evidence Act 1984

Police and Criminal Evidence Act 1984, Part IV

Review of police detention[63]

40.–(1) Reviews of the detention of each person in police detention in connection with the investigation of an offence shall be carried out periodically in accordance with the following provisions of this section—

    (a) in the case of a person who has been arrested and charged, by the custody officer; and

    (b) in the case of a person who has been arrested but not charged, by an officer of at least the rank of inspector who has not been directly involved in the investigation. . . .

    (3) Subject to subsection (4) below—

        (a) the first review shall be not later than six hours after the detention was first authorised;

        (b) the second review shall be not later than nine hours after the first;

        (c) subsequent reviews shall be at intervals of not more than nine hours.

    (4) A review may be postponed—

        (a) if, having regard to all the circumstances prevailing at the latest time for it specified in subsection (3) above, it is not practicable to carry out the review at that time; . . .

    (7) The review officer shall record the reasons for any postponement of a review in the custody record. . . .

    (12) Before determining whether to authorise a person's continued detention the review officer shall give—

        (a) that person (unless he is asleep); or

        (b) any solicitor representing him who is available at the time of the review,

an opportunity to make representations to him about the detention.

Use of video and telephone links for decisions about detention[64]

Use of telephone for review under s 40

40A. (1) This section applies . . . where in the case of a person who has been arrested but not charge—

    (a) it is not reasonably practicable for an officer of at least the rank of inspector to be present in the police station where that person is held . . .

---

62 See the ruling in *Farrell v Secretary of State for Defence* [1980] 1 All ER 166, HL.

63 Section 40 applied with modifications by Police and Criminal Evidence Act 1984 (Application to Customs and Excise) Order 1985 (SI 1985/1800), Arts 3–11, Scheds 1, 2.

64 Section 40A was inserted by s 73 of the Criminal Justice and Police Act 2001.

(2) The review may be carried out by an officer of at least the rank of inspector who has access to a means of communication by telephone to persons in the police station where the arrested person is held.

(3) Where any review is carried out under this section by an officer who is not present at the station where the arrested person is held—

. . .

 (c) the requirements under section 40(12) and (13) above for—

  (i) the arrested person, or

  (ii) a solicitor representing him,

to be given any opportunity to make representations (whether in writing or orally) to that officer shall have effect . . .

Limits on period of detention without charge

41.–(1) Subject to the following provisions of this section and to sections 42 and 43 below, a person shall not be kept in police detention for more than 24 hours without being charged.

 (2) The time from which the period of detention of a person is to be calculated (in this Act referred to as 'the relevant time')—

  (a) in the case of a person to whom this section applies, shall be—

   (i) the time at which that person arrives at the relevant police station, or

   (ii) the time 24 hours after the time of that person's arrest, whichever is the earlier. . . .

Authorisation of continued detention

42.–(1) Where a police officer of the rank of superintendent or above who is responsible for the police station at which a person is detained has reasonable grounds for believing that—

  (a) the detention of that person without charge is necessary to secure or preserve evidence relating to an offence for which he is under arrest or to obtain such evidence by questioning him;

  (b) an offence for which he is under arrest is a serious arrestable offence; and

  (c) the investigation is being conducted diligently and expeditiously, he may authorise the keeping of that person in police detention for a period expiring at or before 36 hours after the relevant time.

 (2) Where an officer such as is mentioned in subsection (1) above has authorised the keeping of a person in police detention for a period expiring less than 36 hours after the relevant time, such an officer may authorise the keeping of that person in police detention for a further period expiring not more than 36 hours after that time if the conditions specified in subsection (1) above are still satisfied when he gives the authorisation.

Warrants of further detention

43.–(1) Where, on an application on oath made by a constable and supported by an information, a magistrates' court is satisfied that there are reasonable grounds for believing that the further detention of the person to whom the application relates is justified, it may issue a warrant of further detention authorising the keeping of that person in police detention.

 (2) A court may not hear an application for a warrant of further detention unless the person to whom the application relates—

  (a) has been furnished with a copy of the information; and

  (b) has been brought before the court for the hearing.

(3) The person to whom the application relates shall be entitled to be legally represented at the hearing and, if he is not so represented, but wishes to be so represented—

   (a) the court shall adjourn the hearing to enable him to obtain representation; and

   (b) he may be kept in police detention during the adjournment.

(4) A person's further detention is only justified for the purposes of this section or section 44 below if—

   (a) his detention without charge is necessary to secure or preserve evidence relating to an offence for which he is under arrest or to obtain such evidence by questioning him;

   (b) an offence for which he is under arrest is a serious arrestable offence; and

   (c) the investigation is being conducted diligently and expeditiously.

Extension of warrants of further detention

44.–(1) On an application on oath made by a constable and supported by information, a magistrates' court may extend a warrant of further detention issued under section 43 above if it is satisfied that there are reasonable grounds for believing that the further detention of the person to whom the application relates is justified.

(2) Subject to subsection (3) below, the period for which a warrant of further detention may be extended shall be such period as the court thinks fit, having regard to the evidence before it.

(3) The period shall not—

   (a) be longer than 36 hours; or

   (b) end later then 96 hours after the relevant time.

(4) Where a warrant of further detention has been extended under subsection (1) above, or further extended under this subsection, for a period ending before 96 hours after the relevant time, on an application such as is mentioned in that subsection, a magistrates' court may further extend the warrant if it is satisfied as there mentioned; and subsections (2) and (3) above apply to such further extensions as they apply to extensions under subsection (1) above. . . .

(7) Where an application under this section is refused, the person to whom the application relates shall forthwith be charged or, subject to subsection (g) below, released, either on bail or without bail.

Use of video-conferencing facilities for decisions about detention[65]

45A.–(1) Subject to the following provisions of this section, the Secretary of State may by regulations provide that, in the case of an arrested person who is held in a police station, . . . the functions in subsection (2) may be performed . . . by an officer who—

   (b) has access to the use of video-conferencing facilities that enable him to communicate with persons in that station.

(2) Those functions are—

   (a) the functions . . . [which would be] functions of a custody officer under section 37, 38 or 40 above; and

   (b) the function of carrying out a review under section 40(1)(b) . . .

---

65   Section 45A was inserted by s 73(3) of the Criminal Justice and Police Act 2001.

Notes

1   The position under the law prior to the 1984 Act with regard to detention before charge and committal before a magistrate was vague and the police had no clearly defined power to hold a person for questioning. It was governed by the Magistrates' Courts Act 1980, s 43 which allowed the police to detain a person in custody until such time as it was 'practicable' to bring him before a magistrate, in the case of a 'serious' offence. However, the common law had developed to the point when it could be said that detention for the purpose of questioning was recognised.[66] The detention scheme governed by Part IV of PACE put the power to hold for questioning on a clear basis and it is made clear under s 37(2) that the purpose of the detention is to obtain a confession.

2   Under s 41, the detention can be for up to 24 hours, but in the case of a person in police custody for a serious arrestable offence (defined in s 116) it can extend to 96 hours. Part IV of PACE does not apply to detention under the Terrorism Act 2000 (below) or to detention by immigration officers.[67] Under s 42(1), a police officer of the rank of superintendent or above can sanction detention for up to 36 hours if the three conditions specified apply. After 36 hours, detention can no longer be authorised by the police alone. Under s 43(1), the application for authorisation must be supported by information and brought before a magistrates' court, which can authorise detention under s 44 for up to 96 hours if the conditions are met as set out above.

3   It may be noted that a person unlawfully detained can apply for a writ of habeas corpus in order to secure release from detention, and this remedy is preserved in s 51(d). Its usefulness in practice is, however, very limited since the courts have developed a practice of adjourning applications for 24 hours in order to allow the police to present their case. Thus, detention can continue for that time allowing the police to carry out questioning or other procedures in the meantime.

4   The safeguards surrounding the powers to detain under ss 41–44 can be called into question. D Dixon in 'Safeguarding the rights of suspects in police custody' (1990) 1 Policing and Society 130–31 suggests that the periodic review of detention and the right to make representations tend to be treated not as genuine investigations into the grounds for continuing the detention, but as formalities. Perhaps in recognition of the need for rigour in relation to reviews, a proposal made in 1999 by the Chief Constable of Kent Police that detention review should be by video link in the majority of cases was rejected in judicial review proceedings on the ground, discussed below, that it might undermine the protection for liberty they are intended to offer, taking Article 5 into account.[68] However, the government then brought forward legislation – s 73 of the Criminal Justice and Police Act 2001 (CJPA) – to reverse the effect of this decision. As set out above, s 73 inserts new ss 40A and 45A into PACE to allow for the use of telephone and video links for reviews of detention. Clearly, these new provisions in relation to review of detention detract from the face-to-face confrontation that was originally envisaged.

Terrorism Act 2000

41.–(2) Where a person is arrested under this section the provisions of Schedule 8 (detention: treatment, review and extension) shall apply.

---

66   *Mohammed-Holgate v Duke* [1984] QB 209, HL.
67   PACE 1984, s 51.
68   *R v Chief Constable of Kent Constabulary ex p Kent Police Federation Joint Branch Board and Another* (1999) *The Times*, 1 December.

(3) Subject to subsections (4) to (7), a person detained under this section shall (unless detained under any other power) be released not later than the end of the period of 48 hours beginning—

(a) with the time of his arrest under this section, or

(b) if he was being detained under Schedule 7 when he was arrested under this section, with the time when his examination under that Schedule began.

Schedule 8
Detention
Part II
Review of Detention under Section 41

Requirement

21.–(1) A person's detention shall be periodically reviewed by a review officer.

(2) The first review shall be carried out as soon as is reasonably practicable after the time of the person's arrest.

(3) Subsequent reviews shall, subject to paragraph 22, be carried out at intervals of not more than 12 hours.

(4) No review of a person's detention shall be carried out after a warrant extending his detention has been issued under Part III. . . .

Grounds for continued detention

23.–(1) A review officer may authorise a person's continued detention only if satisfied that it is necessary—

(a) to obtain relevant evidence whether by questioning him or otherwise,

(b) to preserve relevant evidence, . . .

(3) The review officer shall not authorise continued detention by virtue of sub-paragraph (1)(c) to (f) unless he is satisfied that the process pending the completion of which detention is necessary is being conducted diligently and expeditiously. . . .

Review officer

24.–(1) The review officer shall be an officer who has not been directly involved in the investigation in connection with which the person is detained.

(2) In the case of a review carried out within the period of 24 hours beginning with the time of arrest, the review officer shall be an officer of at least the rank of inspector.

. . .

Representations

26.–(1) Before determining whether to authorise a person's continued detention, a review officer shall give either of the following persons an opportunity to make representations about the detention—

(a) the detained person, or

(b) a solicitor representing him who is available at the time of the review.

. . .

Extension of detention under section 41

29.–(2) A warrant of further detention—

(a) shall authorise the further detention under section 41 of a specified person for a specified period, and

(b) shall state the time at which it is issued.

(3) The specified period in relation to a person shall end not later than the end of the period of seven days beginning–

(a) with the time of his arrest under section 41, or

(b) if he was being detained under Schedule 7 when he was arrested under section 41, with the time when his examination under that Schedule began. . . .

Time limit

30.–(1) An application for a warrant shall be made—

(a) during the period mentioned in section 41(3), or

(b) within six hours of the end of that period ...

(3) For the purposes of this Schedule, an application for a warrant is made when written or oral notice of an intention to make the application is given to a judicial authority. . . .

Grounds for extension

32.–(1) A judicial authority may issue a warrant of further detention only if satisfied that—

(a) there are reasonable grounds for believing that the further detention of the person to whom the application relates is necessary to obtain relevant evidence whether by questioning him or otherwise or to preserve relevant evidence, and

(b) the investigation in connection with which the person is detained is being conducted diligently and expeditiously. . . .

Representation

33.–(1) The person to whom an application relates shall—

(a) be given an opportunity to make oral or written representations to the judicial authority about the application, and

(b) subject to sub-paragraph (3), be entitled to be legally represented at the hearing.

(3) A judicial authority may exclude any of the following persons from any part of the hearing—

(a) the person to whom the application relates;

(b) anyone representing him. . . .

Notes

1 The detention scheme adopted in respect of terrorist suspects allows for the suspect to be detained for longer periods than PACE allows. If a person was arrested under s 14 of the PTA as opposed to s 24 of PACE, whether the arrest was for an offence or on suspicion of being a terrorist, the detention provisions under PACE did not apply. The arrestee could be detained for up to 48 hours following arrest (s 14(4)) of the PTA) but this period could be extended by the Secretary of State by further periods not exceeding five days in all (s 14(5) of the PTA). Thus, the whole detention could be for seven days and, in contrast to the PACE provisions, the courts were not involved in the authorising process; it occurred at a low level of visibility as an administrative decision. The similar provision under the PTA 1984 was found to be in breach of Article 5(3) (see Part II Chapter 2, p 247) in *Brogan v UK* (1989) 11 EHRR 117 on the ground that holding a person for longer than four days without judicial authorisation was a violation of the requirement that persons should be brought promptly before a judicial officer.

2 The *Brogan* decision presented the government with a difficulty in formulating the Terrorism Act 2000 (TA). The government's solution, in the TA, was to make provision for judicial authorisation of detention, rather than to decrease the length of time during which terrorist suspects could be detained, harmonising it with the PACE period.

3　The maximum period of detention, applicable to a person arrested under s 41 of the TA, continues to be seven days, but para 29, Sched 8 provides that it must be under a warrant issued by a 'judicial authority'. The conditions under para 32 must be satisfied and the detainee or his solicitor has the right to make written or oral representations under para 33(1). Thus, authorisation may not be merely 'on the papers'. Such a possibility might not have satisfied the aim of achieving compliance with Article 5(3), despite the involvement of a judicial figure.

4　The police can detain a person on its own authority for 48 hours under s 41(3) and s 41(4)–(7) of the TA provide three possibilities of continuing the detention beyond 48 hours, over and above the possibility of extension under judicial authorisation.

5　As part of the port and border controls regime, Sched 5 of the PTA provided a further power of detention in allowing a person to be detained for 12 hours before examination at ports of entry into Britain or Northern Ireland. The period could be extended to 24 hours if the person was suspected of involvement in the commission, preparation or instigation of acts of terrorism. These provisions are partially reproduced in Sched 7 to the TA; they are modified to take account of the abolition of the exclusion power.

6　*Duties imposed on public authorities under the HRA regarding arrest and detention of terrorist and non-terrorist suspects.* Article 5(1) of the ECHR provides a right to liberty subject to certain exceptions which must have a basis in law. Not only must an exception apply, the requirements under Article 5(2), (3) and (4) must also be met. All the public authorities involved, including the police, are bound under s 6 of the HRA to abide by the Article 5 requirements.

7　The first and most essential requirement of Article 5 is that a person's detention is in accordance with a procedure prescribed by law. This means that the procedure should be in accordance with national law and with recognised Convention standards, including Convention principles, and is not arbitrary.[69] Thus, where one of the Article 5(1) exceptions applies to a person's detention, this requirement will also have to be satisfied. The procedure covers the arrest provisions[70] and the procedure adopted by a court in authorisations of detention.[71] The requirement that the detention should be in accordance with the law was given a robust interpretation in one of the first domestic decisions in the pre-HRA period to place a heavy reliance on Article 5: *R v Chief Constable of Kent Constabulary ex p Kent Police Federation Joint Branch Board and Another* (1999) *The Times*, 1 December. The court had to consider an application that the conduct of reviews of police detention under s 40(1)(b) of the 1984 Act should be, in the majority of cases, by video link. Lord Bingham concluded that Parliament had provided for a face-to-face confrontation between the review officer and the suspect and, if important rights enacted to protect the subject were to be modified, it was for Parliament after appropriate consultation so to rule and not for the courts. This decision indicated a determination to give real efficacy to Article 5.

8　In considering the exceptional circumstances in which liberty can be taken away, the requirements connoted by the general provision that they must have a basis in law under Article 5(1) are also implied into the 'prescribed by law' rubric of each sub-paragraph.[72] Article 5(1)(c) of the Convention sets out one of the circumstances

69　*Winterwerp v Netherlands*, Series A No 33, (1979) 2 EHRR 387, para 39.
70　*Fox, Campbell and Hartley v UK*, Series A No 182, (1990) 13 EHRR 157.
71　*Weston v UK* (1981) 3 EHRR 402 (also known as *H v UK*); *Van der Leer v Netherlands* Series A No 170-A; (1990) 12 EHRR 567.
72　*Winterwerp v Netherlands* (1980) Series A No 33, (1979) 2 EHRR 387, para 39.

in which an individual can be detained. It permits the lawful arrest or detention of a person effected for the purpose of bringing him before the competent legal authority on reasonable suspicion of having committed an offence, or where it is reasonably considered that an arrest is necessary to prevent the person in question from committing an offence or fleeing after having done so. In requiring arrest only for specific offences and not for general crime control purposes, Article 5(1)(c) adheres closely to the due process model of arrest indicated above. Sections 24 and 25 of PACE and s 41 of the TA (in so far as it relates to certain specific terrorist offences under s 40(1)(a)) may *prima facie* comply with these provisions owing to their requirements of reasonable suspicion.

9   In *Fox, Campbell and Hartley v UK* Series A No 182; (1990) 13 EHRR 157, the applicants had been arrested in accordance with s 11 of the Northern Ireland (Emergency Provisions) Act 1978 which required only suspicion, not reasonable suspicion. The only evidence put forward by the government for the presence of reasonable suspicion was that the applicants had convictions for terrorist offences and that when arrested, they were asked about particular terrorist acts. The European Court of Human Rights found that although allowance could be made for the difficulties of evidence gathering in an emergency situation, reasonable suspicion which 'arises from facts or information which would satisfy an objective observer' that the person concerned may have committed the offence'[73] had not been established. Moreover, 'the exigencies of dealing with terrorist crime cannot justify stretching the notion of reasonableness to the point where the essence of the safeguard secured by Article 5(1)(c) is impaired'.[74] The arrests in question could not, therefore, be justified. In *Murray v UK* (1994) 19 EHRR 193, it was again emphasised that an objective standard of reasonable suspicion was required,[75] although the information grounding the suspicion might acceptably remain confidential in the exigencies of a situation such as that pertaining at the time of the arrest in question, in Northern Ireland.[76]

9   The *purpose* of the arrest should also be in compliance with Article 5(1)(c), even where reasonable suspicion is established, in that it should be effected in order to 'bring [the suspect] before the competent legal authority', although this does not mean that every arrest must lead to a charge.[77] It was found in *Chalkley and Jeffries* [1998] 2 All ER 155 that the existence of a collateral motive for an arrest would not necessarily render it unlawful. Under the HRA, a domestic court would have to consider whether Article 5 would be satisfied by an arrest with a 'mixed' purpose.

10 The test under Article 5(1)(c) relies on reasonable suspicion regarding an offence and therefore calls into question s 41 of the TA, in so far as it relates to suspicion that a person is a terrorist in the sense of (under s 40(1)(b)) being concerned in the commission, preparation, or instigation of an act of terrorism. Section 41 therefore allows for arrest without reasonable suspicion that a particular offence has been committed. The compatibility of s 41 and Article 5(1)(c) depends on the interpretation afforded to *Brogan and Others v UK* (1989) 11 EHRR 117. The case concerned the EPA provision which was largely reproduced in s 41, read with s 40(1)(b). The Court applied two tests to the basis for the arrests in finding that the

---

73   *Fox, Campbell and Hartley v UK* Series A No 182; (1990) 13 EHRR 157, para 32.
74   *Ibid*, para 32.
75   *Ibid*, para 50.
76   *Ibid*, para 58–59.
77   *K-F v Germany* (1997) 26 EHRR 390.

power of arrest was justified within Article 5(1)(c). First, the definition of acts of terrorism was 'well in keeping with the idea of an offence'.[78] Secondly, after arrest, the applicants were asked about specific offences. Thus, 'the Court decided the point on the basis that involvement in "acts of terrorism" indirectly meant the commission of specific criminal offences under Northern Irish law, which would appear to be the better approach on the facts'.[79] On either test, arrests under s 41 read with s 40(1)(b) might be in a more doubtful position given the breadth of the definition of terrorism under s 1 of the TA. The application of the second test would partly depend in practice on the particular instance which arose before a domestic court. If a person was arrested under s 41 as part of an investigation and was not asked about specific offences on arrest, the connection with the basis of the arrest, bearing in mind the width of the s 1, TA definition, might be viewed as too tenuous to be termed an arrest on reasonable suspicion of an offence.

11 Article 5(2), which provides that a person must be informed promptly of the reason for arrest, corresponds to s 28 of PACE. In *Fox, Campbell and Hartley v UK*, Series A No 182, (1990) 13 EHRR 157, the applicants, who were arrested on suspicion of terrorist offences, were not informed of the reason for the arrest at the time of it, but were told that they were being arrested under a particular statutory provision. Clearly, this could not convey the reason to them at that time. At a later point, during interrogation, they were asked about specific criminal offences. The European Court of Human Rights found that Article 5(2) was not satisfied at the time of the arrest, but that this breach was healed by the later indications made during interrogation of the offences for which they had been arrested. Under s 28 of PACE, the police also have a certain leeway as to informing the arrestee. A domestic court in the post-HRA era might be prepared to take a strict approach to the interpretation of s 28 in a non-terrorist case, under s 3 of the HRA, bearing Article 5(2) in mind.

12 Article 5(3) confers a right to be brought promptly before the judicial authorities; in other words, not to be held for long periods without a hearing. It covers both arrest and detention. There will be some allowable delay in both situations; the question is therefore what is meant by 'promptly'. In requiring judicial authorisation for detention for up to seven days under s 41 of and Sched 7 to the TA, the government has sought to ensure, as indicated above, that the new detention provisions comply with Article 5(3) as interpreted in *Brogan*. One question which will probably be raised eventually in the domestic courts under the HRA or at Strasbourg will be whether allowing a detention for seven days, even with judicial authorisation, is in accordance with Article 5. Further, it appears that the new arrangements could allow for detention for longer than 48 hours with authorisation only by the police itself.

POLICE INTERVIEWING AND ACCESS TO LEGAL ADVICE[80]

This section does not concentrate only on interviews or exchanges inside the police station because contact between police and suspect may take place a long time before the police station is reached. This has been recognised in the provisions of Part V of

---

78 *Ibid*, para 51.
79 D Harris, K O'Boyle and C Warbrick, *Law of The European Convention on Human Rights* (1995), p 116.
80 For further reading see: Brown, *op cit*; A Sanders and R Young, *Criminal Justice*, 2nd edn (2000); T Bucke and D Brown, *In Custody* (1997) .

PACE and Code of Practice C which govern treatment of suspects and interviewing, but have some application outside as well as inside the police station. The most crucial events during a person's contact with police will probably be the interviews, and therefore this section will concentrate on the safeguards available for the suspect which are intended to ensure that interviews are fair and that admissions made can be relied upon, if necessary, in court. The safeguards for terrorist suspects are not as extensive as for non-terrorist suspects.

Access to legal advice, discussed below, is generally viewed as the most important safeguard for the suspect.[81] The main safeguards available currently for interviews include contemporaneous recording or tape recording,[82] the ability to read over, verify and sign the notes of the interview as a correct record, notification of legal advice,[83] the right to have advice before and during questioning and, where appropriate, the presence of an adult.[84] One of the most important issues in relation to these safeguards is the question when they come into play. There may be a number of stages in a particular investigation, beginning with first contact between police and suspect, and perhaps ending with the charge. Two factors can be identified which decide which safeguards should be in place at a particular time. First, it must be asked whether an exchange between police and suspect can be called 'an interview' and secondly whether it took place inside or outside the police station.

Interviews and exchanges with suspects

Code of Practice C (revised 2003)

11. Interviews: general

(a) Action

11.1A   An interview is the questioning of a person regarding his involvement or suspected involvement in a criminal offence or offences which, by virtue of paragraph 10.1 of Code C, is required to be carried out under caution. Whenever a person is interviewed they must be informed of the nature of the offence or further offence concerned. ....

11.1   Following a decision to arrest a suspect they must not be interviewed about the relevant offence except at a police station or other authorised place of detention unless the consequent delay is likely—

(a) to lead to interference with or harm to evidence connected with an offence or interference with or physical harm to other persons; or

(b) to lead to the alerting of other persons suspected of having committed an offence but not yet arrested for it; or

(c) to hinder the recovery of property obtained in consequence of the commission of an offence.

Interviewing in any of these circumstances should cease once the relevant risk has been averted or the necessary questions have been put in order to attempt to avert that risk.

11.2   Immediately prior to the commencement or re-commencement of any interview at a

---

81   See D Dixon in C Walker and K Starmer (eds), *Miscarriages of Justice* (1999), p 67.
82   Under Code E, para 3.
83   Under Code C, para 3.1.
84   Under Code C, para 11.14.

police station or other authorised place of detention, the interviewing officer shall remind the suspect of his entitlement to free legal advice. ...

11.4　At the beginning of an interview carried out in a police station, the interviewer, after cautioning the suspect, shall put to them any significant statement or silence which occurred before the start of the interview ... The interviewer shall ask the suspect whether they confirm or deny that earlier statement or silence and whether they wish to add anything. A 'significant' statement is one which appears capable of being used in evidence against the suspect, in particular a direct admission of guilt. A significant silence is a failure or refusal to answer a question or to answer it satisfactorily which might, allowing for the restriction on drawing adverse inferences from silence, give rise to an inference under Part III of the Criminal Justice and Public Order Act 1994.

11.5　No police officer may try to obtain answers to questions or to elicit a statement by the use of oppression or shall indicate, except in answer to a direct question, what action will be taken on the part of the police if the person being interviewed answers questions, makes a statement or refuses to do either. ...

(b) Interview records

11.7　(a)　An accurate record must be made of each interview with a person ...

(a)　An accurate record must be made of each interview with a person suspected of an offence, whether or not the interview takes place at a police station.

(b)　The record must state the place of the interview, the time it begins and ends, the time the record is made (if different), any breaks in the interview and the names of all those present ...

(c)　The record must be made during the course of the interview, unless in the investigating officer's view this would not be practicable or would interfere with the conduct of the interview, and must constitute either a verbatim record of what has been said or, failing this, an account of the interview which adequately and accurately summarises it.

...

11.13　A written record shall also be made of any comments made by a suspected person, including unsolicited comments, which are outside the context of an interview but which might be relevant to the offence. Any such record must be timed and signed by the maker.

Notes for guidance

11C　It is important to bear in mind that, although juveniles or persons who are mentally disordered or mentally handicapped are often capable of providing reliable evidence, they may, without knowing or wishing to do so, be particularly prone in certain circumstances to provide information which is unreliable, misleading or self-discriminating. Special care should therefore always be exercised in questioning such a person, and the appropriate adult should be involved, if there is any doubt about a person's age, mental state or capacity. ...

11.18　*Vulnerable suspects: Urgent interviews at police stations*

An interview of the following persons may not take place in a police station or other authorized place of detention unless an officer of the rank of superintendent or above considers that delay will lead to the consequences set out in paragraph 11.1(a)–(c):

(a)　anyone other than in (b) below who ... appears unable to appreciate the significance of questions put to them ... due to the influence of drink or drugs or any illness. ...

(b)　a juvenile or a person who is mentally disordered or otherwise mentally vulnerable if at the time of the interview the appropriate adult is not present;

(c) a person who has difficulty in understanding English or who has a hearing disability if at the time of the interview an interpreter is not present.

Notes

1   The term 'interview' is now defined in para 11.1.A. The term 'grounds to suspect' in para 10.1 (below), which is crucial in determining when an 'interview' as opposed to a general enquiry has begun, is significant: there must be grounds for suspicion that an offence has been committed by the person in question, not a mere hunch or suspicion that somebody has committed the offence.[85]

2   Paragraph 11.1 allows for some interviewing outside the police station due to its requirement of a higher level of suspicion than that denoted by para 11.1A. The suspect interviewed outside the police station may be unaware of the right to legal advice[86] and it is also at present unlikely that the interview would be tape recorded; Code E does not envisage tape recording taking place anywhere but inside the police station.[87]

4   Once the suspect is inside the police station under arrest or under caution,[88] any interview[89] should be tape recorded unless an exception under the tape recording code, Code E, applies. Interviews with certain groups of terrorist suspects need not be taped.

5   PACE does not attempt to regulate the conduct of the interview except in so far as such regulation can be implied from the provision of s 76 that confessions obtained by oppression or in circumstances likely to render them unreliable will be inadmissible (see also Code C, para 11.5). It seems that use of a degree of intimidation, haranguing, and indirect threats is still quite common, especially in interviews with juveniles.[90]

Questions

1   Does the definition of an interview under para 11.1A cover all exchanges between police and suspect when there are grounds to suspect him or her of an offence? Can an 'interview' be distinguished clearly from 'relevant' comments (para 11.13)?

2   Is the point at which the suspect must be taken to the police station for further questioning clearly demarcated? Why is this a matter of significance?

Access to legal advice

Police and Criminal Evidence Act 1984

Access to legal advice

58.–(1) A person arrested and held in custody in a police station or other premises shall be entitled, if he so requests, to consult a solicitor privately at any time.

---

85   *R v Shah* [1994] Crim LR 125; *R v James* (1996) unreported, 8 March; *R v Blackford* (2000) WL 362561.

86   Notification of the right to legal advice is governed by Code C, para 3.1 which is expressed to apply only within the police station.

87   Code E, para 3.1. Some police forces have experimented with hand-held tape recorders used outside the police station, but at present this is by no means common practice.

88   Under Code E, para 3.4, once a volunteer becomes a suspect (ie, at the point when he should be cautioned) the rest of the interview should be tape recorded.

89   Under Code E, para 3.1(a), an interview with a person suspected of an offence triable only summarily need not be taped.

90   See R Evans, *The Conduct of Police Interviews with Juveniles*, Home Office Research Study No 8 (1993).

. . .

(4) If a person makes such a request, he must be permitted to consult a solicitor as soon as is practicable except to the extent that delay is permitted by this section.

(5) In any case he must be permitted to consult a solicitor within 36 hours from the relevant time, as defined in section 41(2) above.

(6) Delay in compliance with a request is only permitted—

(a) in the case of a person who is in police detention for a serious arrestable offence; and

(b) if an officer of at least the rank of superintendent authorises it.

. . .

(8) Subject to sub-section (8A) below an officer may only authorise delay where he has reasonable grounds for believing that the exercise of the right conferred by subsection (1) above at the time when the person detained desires to exercise it—

(a) will lead to interference with or harm to evidence connected with a serious arrestable offence or interference with or physical injury to other persons; or

(b) will lead to the alerting of other persons suspected of having committed such an offence but not yet arrested for it; or

(c) will hinder the recovery of any property obtained as a result of such an offence.

(8A) An officer may also authorise delay where the serious arrestable offence is a drug trafficking offence or an offence to which Part VI of the Criminal Justice Act 1988 applies and the officer has reasonable grounds for believing—

(a) ... that the recovery of the value of that person's proceeds of drug trafficking will be hindered by the exercise of the right conferred by *subsection (1)* above; and

(b) ... the recovery of the value of the property obtained by that person from or in connection with the offence or of the pecuniary advantage derived by him from or in connection with it will be hindered by the exercise of the right conferred by *subsection (1)* above.

(9) If delay is authorised—

(a) the detained person shall be told the reason for it; and

(b) the reason shall be noted on his custody record.

(10) The duties imposed by subsection (9) above shall be performed as soon as is practicable.

(11) There may be no further delay in permitting the exercise of the right conferred by subsection (1) above once the reason for authorising delay ceases to subsist.

(12) Nothing in this section applies to a person arrested or detained under the terrorism provisions.[91]

Terrorism Act 2000

Schedule 8

Rights: England, Wales and Northern Ireland

7.–(1) Subject to paragraphs 8 and 9, a person detained under Schedule 7 or section 41 at a police station in England, Wales or Northern Ireland shall be entitled, if he so requests, to consult a solicitor as soon as is reasonably practicable, privately and at any time . . .

8.–(1) ... an officer of at least the rank of superintendent may authorise a delay—

. . .

---

91 Substituted by the TA 2000, Sched 15, para 5(6).

(b) in permitting a detained person to consult a solicitor under paragraph 7.

...

(3) Subject to sub-paragraph (5), an officer may give an authorisation under sub-paragraph (1) only if he has reasonable grounds for believing—

(a) in the case of an authorisation under sub-paragraph (1)(a), that informing the named person of the detained person's detention will have any of the consequences specified in sub-paragraph (4), or

(b) in the case of an authorisation under sub-paragraph (1)(b), that the exercise of the right under paragraph 7 at the time when the detained person desires to exercise it will have any of the consequences specified in sub-paragraph (4).

(4) Those consequences are—

(a) interference with or harm to evidence of a serious arrestable offence,

(b) interference with or physical injury to any person,

(c) the alerting of persons who are suspected of having committed a serious arrestable offence but who have not been arrested for it,

(d) the hindering of the recovery of property obtained as a result of a serious arrestable offence or in respect of which a forfeiture order could be made under section 23,

(e) interference with the gathering of information about the commission, preparation or instigation of acts of terrorism,

(f) the alerting of a person and thereby making it more difficult to prevent an act of terrorism, and

(g) the alerting of a person and thereby making it more difficult to secure a person's apprehension, prosecution or conviction in connection with the commission, preparation or instigation of an act of terrorism. ...

Rights: Scotland

...

16.–(6) A person detained shall be entitled to consult a solicitor at any time, without delay.

(7) A police officer not below the rank of superintendent may authorise a delay in holding the consultation where, in his view, the delay is necessary on one of the grounds mentioned in paragraph 17(3) ...

17.–(3) The grounds mentioned in paragraph 16(4) and (7) and in sub-paragraph (1) are—

(a) that it is in the interests of the investigation or prevention of crime;

(b) that it is in the interests of the apprehension, prosecution or conviction of offenders;

(c) that it will further the recovery of property obtained as a result of the commission of an offence or in respect of which a forfeiture order could be made under section 23;

(d) that it will further the operation of Part VI of the Criminal Justice Act 1988, Part I of the Proceeds of Crime (Scotland) Act 1995 or the Proceeds of Crime (Northern Ireland) Order 1996 (confiscation of the proceeds of an offence).

Code of Practice C

6. Right to legal advice

(a) Action

6.1 Subject to the provisos in Annex B all people in police detention must be informed that they may at any time consult and communicate privately, whether in person, in writing or by telephone with a solicitor [see para 3.1, note 6B and note 6J]. ...

6.4 No police officer shall do or say anything with the intention of dissuading a person in detention from obtaining legal advice.

6.5 The exercise of the right of access to legal advice may be delayed only in accordance with Annex B to this code. Whenever legal advice is requested (and unless Annex B applies) the custody officer must act without delay to secure the provision of such advice to the person concerned. If, on being informed or reminded of the right to legal advice, the person declines to speak to a solicitor in person, the officer shall point out that the right to free legal advice includes the right to speak with a solicitor on the telephone and ask him if he wishes to do so. If the suspect continues to waive his right to legal advice the officer should ask him the reasons for doing so and any reasons shall be recorded on the custody record....

6.6 A person who wants legal advice may not be interviewed or continue to be interviewed until he has received such advice unless—

(a) Annex B applies in which case the restriction on drawing adverse inferences from silence (para 10.4) will apply because the person is not allowed an opportunity to consult a solicitor; or

(b) an officer of the rank of superintendent or above has reasonable grounds for believing that—

(i) the consequent delay would be likely to lead to interference with or harm to evidence connected with an offence or physical harm to other people or serious loss of, or damage to, property; or lead to the alerting of other people suspected of having committed an offence ... or hinder the recovery of property obtained in consequence of the commission of an offence;

(ii) where a solicitor, including a duty solicitor, has been contacted and has agreed to attend, awaiting his arrival would cause unreasonable delay to the process of investigation;

and in these cases the restriction on drawing adverse inferences from silence (para 10.4) will apply ...

(c) The solicitor nominated by the person, or selected by him from a list—

(i) cannot be contacted; or

(ii) has previously indicated that they do not wish to be contacted; or

(iii) having been contacted, has declined to attend;

and the person has been advised of the Duty Solicitor Scheme but has declined to ask for the duty solicitor. In these circumstances the interview may be started or continued without further delay provided that an officer of the rank of Inspector or above has given agreement for the interview to proceed. In these circumstances the restriction on drawing adverse inferences from silence (para 10.4) will not apply because the person is allowed an opportunity to consult a solicitor.

(d) The person who wanted legal advice changes his mind, in which case the restriction on drawing adverse inferences from silence (para 10.4) will not apply because the person is allowed an opportunity to consult a solicitor.

In these circumstances the interview may be started or continued without further delay provided that the person has given his agreement in writing or on tape to being interviewed without receiving legal advice and that an officer of the rank of Inspector or above, having inquired into the suspect's reasons for his change of mind, has given agreement for the interview to proceed in those circumstances. The name of the authorising officer and the reason for the suspect's change of mind should be recorded and repeated on tape at the beginning or re-commencement of interview.

R v Samuel [1988] 2 All ER 135; [1988] 2 WLR 920, 930, 931, 932 CA

The leading case determining the scope of the s 58 exceptions is *Samuel*. The appellant was arrested on suspicion of armed robbery and, after questioning at the police station, asked to see a solicitor. The request was refused, apparently on the grounds that other suspects might be warned[92] and that recovery of the outstanding stolen money might thereby be hindered;[93] the appellant subsequently confessed to the robbery and was later convicted. On appeal the defence argued that the refusal of access was not justifiable under s 58(8) and that therefore the confession obtained should not have been admitted into evidence as it had been obtained due to impropriety.

Hodgson J: ...The right denied is a right 'to consult a solicitor privately'. The person denied that right is in police detention. In practice, the only way that the person can make any of [s 58(8)] (a) to (c) happen is by some communication from him to the solicitor. For (a) to (c) to be made to happen the solicitor must do something. If he does something knowing that it will result in anything in (a) to (c) happening he will, almost inevitably, commit a serious criminal offence. Therefore, inadvertent or unwitting conduct apart, the officer must believe that a solicitor will, if allowed to consult with a detained person, thereafter commit a criminal offence. Solicitors are officers of the court. We think that the number of times that a police officer could genuinely be in that state of belief will be rare. ...

Mr Jones was unable to point to any inadvertent conduct by Mr Warner which could have led to any of the results in (a)–(c) save his transmission to someone of some sort of coded message. We do not know who made the decision at 4.45pm but we find it impossible to believe that whoever did had reasonable grounds for the belief required by s 58(8).

The more sinister side to the decision is, of course, this. The police had, over a period exceeding 24 hours, interviewed this young man four times without obtaining any confession from him in respect of the robbery. Time was running out for them. ... Thirty-six hours from the relevant time would expire in the early hours of the morning; then access to a solicitor would have to be permitted. On the following day the appellant would have to be taken before the magistrates' court: s 46. As he had already been interviewed four times and been in police custody for over 24 hours, the expectation would be that a solicitor might well consider that, at least for that evening, enough was enough and that he ought to advise his client not to answer further questions. There were, therefore, very few hours left for the police to interview the appellant without his having legal advice. And, as events showed, that was something the police very much wanted to do; this one knows because, within 37 minutes, he was in fact interviewed. ... The interview at 5.20pm was conducted by a detective inspector, the sergeant and detective being present, so that the appellant now faced a different questioner and a total of three police officers. At that interview he made the confession to the robbery. Regrettably we have come to the conclusion that whoever made the decision to refuse Mr Warner access at 4.45pm was very probably motivated by a desire to have one last chance of interviewing the appellant in the absence of a solicitor.

... we find that the refusal of access to Mr Warner at 4.45pm was unjustified. That being so the interview, without a solicitor being present, should not have taken place: Code 6.3.

Notes

1   The consequence of the finding in *Samuel* that s 58 had been breached is considered below.

---

92   See s 58(8)(b).
93   See s 58(8)(c).

2   As indicated, both PACE and the TA entitle a suspect to consult an advisor privately under a publicly funded scheme;[94] to be informed of this right;[95] and to be permitted to have the solicitor present during questioning.[96] In cases involving 'serious arrestable offences', however, there are, as set out above, certain saving provisions allowing an officer of at least the rank of superintendent to authorise delay, and a further power to delay access arises under Code C (above). The exceptions are, however, narrowly drawn and received a narrow interpretation in *Samuel*.

3   The factor which previously motivated the police to delay access to legal advice remains unchanged: the suspect still has the right to remain silent (see below) and the legal advisor may advise him or her to exercise it in the particular circumstances of the case, despite the risk that adverse inferences may be drawn later at court. Quite a large body of research suggests that the police continue to prefer to interview suspects who have not had advice and without an advisor present.[97] Research confirms that the possibility of formally delaying access to legal advice is not as significant as the more informal police influence on the notification and delivery of advice and on securing the presence of the advisor.[98] This may be due in part to the determination shown by the Court of Appeal to protect this due process right by restrictive interpretation of the formal exceptions under s 58(8) of PACE in a key decision.[99] Apart from the statutory exceptions and exceptions under Code C, there are a number of less formal means of evading access to legal advice such as subverting the notification of advice and encouraging the suspect to defer it.[100]

4   *Impact of the HRA.* Provision of access to legal advice is in accordance with the demands of Article 6 and may go beyond them, but the flaws and loopholes in the scheme mean that Article 6 may be breached where the suspect does not receive advice. Thus, the HRA may have an impact on the legal advice scheme since the police and the courts have a duty to abide by Article 6 under s 6 of the HRA and the legal advice provisions should be interpreted compatibly with the demands of Article 6 under s 3 of the HRA. Section 34(2A) of the CJPOA (see below), which was introduced to meet Article 6 demands, now caters for some situations in which the suspect has not had access to legal advice, but not all of them.

5   Article 6(3)(c) provides that everyone charged with a criminal offence has the right to defend himself through legal assistance of his own choosing (see Part II Chapter 2, p 242). Access to legal advice in pre-trial questioning, as opposed to such access for the purposes of the trial, is not expressly provided for in Article 6. However, some protection for such access can be implied into Article 6(1) and 6(3)(c). In *Murray (John) v UK* (1996) 22 EHRR 29 the Court found that Article 6(1) and (3)(c) had been breached by the denial of custodial access to a lawyer for 48 hours, since such access was essential where there was a likelihood that adverse inferences would be drawn from silence. It found that Article 6 would normally require that the accused should be allowed to benefit from the assistance of a lawyer in the

---

94   See the Legal Aid Act 1988, Sched 6.
95   Code C, para 3.1(ii).
96   Code C, para 6.8.
97   The research undertaken by Sanders *et al*, *Advice and Assistance at Police Stations*, November 1989; Brown, *op cit*, p 77.
98   Brown, *ibid*, found that approximately 35 per cent of suspects may have been influenced against advice by the police.
99   *R v Samuel* [1988] 2 All ER 135; [1988] 2 WLR 920.
100 See A Sanders, 'Access to legal advice and police malpractice' [1990] Crim LR 494.

initial stages of police interrogation, although that right might be subject to restrictions for good cause. In *Averill v UK* (2001) 31 EHRR 36; (2000) *The Times*, 20 June,[101] the Court found a breach of Article 6(3)(c) read with Article 6(1) on the basis – which it noted in *Murray* – that, bearing in mind the possibility of drawing adverse inferences from silence it was of 'paramount importance for the rights of the defence that an accused has access to a lawyer at the initial stages of police interrogation'.[102] Bearing in mind the scheme under ss 34, 36 and 37 of the CJPOA, which is similar to the Northern Ireland scheme under equivalent legislation, the findings in *Murray* and *Averill* cover most or all police interviews under caution, since once the caution has been given, it is clear that adverse inferences may be drawn from silence. Thus, a right of access to legal advice in custodial questioning may be implied into Article 6(3)(c) when read with Article 6(1) where adverse inferences may be drawn from silence.

6   Where access to legal advice has formally been delayed, and the suspect has stayed silent, s 34(2A) of the CJPOA will not allow the drawing of adverse inferences. In such an instance, there would be no need to rely on Article 6 arguments raised under s 7(1)(b) of the HRA. But where access to legal advice has formally been delayed, particularly in the case of terrorist suspects, who can be denied access for up to 48 hours, and the suspect has *not* stayed silent, the grounds for denial will have to be subjected to strict scrutiny in the light of the requirements of Article 6. There seems to be no reason in principle to confine the findings in *Murray* and *Averill* to a circumstance where the defendant in fact stayed silent. Rather, as the Court implied, it may be that the suspect who fails to remain silent is most in need of legal advice.[103]

7   Article 6 might be breached where legal advice is not *formally* denied to the defendant for a period of time, as in *Murray*, although he or she has not in fact received advice before being interviewed. This argument might be raised where a suspect has been influenced by police ploys in failing to obtain advice (whether due to inadequacies in the informing procedure or to direct or more subtle persuasion). The admission of a subsequent interview might be viewed as affecting the fairness of the trial, following *Murray*.

8   It is clear that the courts have the opportunity, if they are prepared to take an activist line in giving a wide interpretation to *Murray*, to curb the formally allowed and informally developed police discretion in affording access to legal advice which this chapter has discussed. Eventually, Code C may have to be revised to allow for notification of advice on caution, to clarify the provisions allowing for delays in access and to require a positive decision to refuse advice. Further moves towards improving the quality of advice may have to be undertaken.

The right to silence

The large body of writing on the right to silence generally came down on the side of its retention.[104] The 1993 Royal Commission on Criminal Justice favoured retention[105] but

---

101 See also *Magee v UK* (2001) 31 EHRR 35; (2000) *The Times*, 20 June.

102 *Averill v UK* (2001) 31 EHRR 36, para 59.

103 See further on this point, T Bucke *et al*, *The Right to Silence* (2000).

104 See Philips Commission Report Cmnd 8092 (1981); Report of the Home Office Working Group on the Right to Silence 1989 (in favour of modification of the right). For criticism of the report, see Zuckermann [1989] Crim LR 855. For review of the debate, see S Greer (1990) 53 MLR 709.

105 Cm 2263, Proposal 82.

considered that, once the prosecution case was fully disclosed, defendants should be required to offer an answer to the charges made against them at the risk of adverse comment at trial on any new defence they then disclose. However, despite the proposals of the Royal Commission, the right to silence was curtailed under the Criminal Justice and Public Order Act 1994 and this was reflected in the cautioning provisions introduced under the 1995 revision of Code C. Those provisions were modified in 2003 in order to ensure that the scheme meets Article 6 standards.

Criminal Justice and Public Order Act 1994[106]

Effect of accused's failure to mention facts when questioned or charged.[107]

34.–(1) Where, in any proceedings against a person for an offence, evidence is given that the accused—

(a) at any time before he was charged with the offence, on being questioned under caution by a constable trying to discover whether or by whom the offence had been committed, failed to mention any fact relied on in his defence in those proceedings; or

(b) on being charged with the offence or officially informed that he might be prosecuted for it, failed to mention any such fact,

being a fact which in the circumstances existing at the time the accused could reasonably have been expected to mention when so questioned, charged or informed, as the case may be,

(2) Where this subsection applies—

(a) a magistrates' court inquiring into the offence as examining justices;

(b) a judge, in deciding whether to grant an application made by the accused under—

(i) section 6 of the Criminal Justice Act 1987 ...

(ii) paragraph 5 of Schedule 6 to the Criminal Justice Act 1991 ...

(c) the court, in determining whether there is a case to answer; and

(d) the court, in determining whether the accused is guilty of the offence charged,

may draw such inferences from the failure as appear proper.

(2A) Where the accused was at an authorised place of detention at the time of the failure, subsections (1) and (2) above do not apply if he had not been allowed an opportunity to consult a solicitor prior to being questioned, charged or informed as mentioned in subsection (1) above.[108]

(3) In section 36 (effect of accused's failure or refusal to account for objects, substances or marks), after subsection (4) there shall be inserted—

'(4A) Where the accused was at an authorised place of detention at the time of the failure or refusal, subsections (1) and (2) above do not apply if he had not been allowed an opportunity to consult a solicitor prior to the request being made.'

(4) In section 37 (effect of accused's failure or refusal to account for presence at a particular place), after subsection (3) there shall be inserted—

---

106 Sections 34–38 applied, with modifications to armed forces by Criminal Justice and Public Order Act 1994 (Application to the Armed Forces) Order 1997 (SI 1997/16), Sched 1, para 1.
107 In force, 1 February 1997.
108 Added by s 58 of the Youth Justice and Criminal Evidence Act 1999 in order to seek to ensure compliance with Article 6(1) of the ECHR.

'(3A) Where the accused was at an authorised place of detention at the time of the failure or refusal, subsections (1) and (2) do not apply if he had not been allowed an opportunity to consult a solicitor prior to the request being made.'

...

36.–(1) Where—

    (a) a person is arrested by a constable and there is—

        (i)   on his person; or

        (ii) in or on his clothing or footwear; or

        (iii) otherwise in his possession; or

        (iv) in any place in which he is at the time of his arrest,

    any object, substance or mark, or there is any mark on any such object; and

    (b) that or another constable investigating the case reasonably believes that the presence of the object, substance or mark may be attributable to the participation of the person arrested in the commission of an offence specified by the constable; and

    (c) the constable informs the person arrested that he so believes, and requests him to account for the presence of the object, substance or mark; and

    (d) the person fails or refuses to do so, then if, in any proceedings against the person for the offence so specified, evidence of those matters is given, subsection (2) below applies.

Effect of accused's failure or refusal to account for presence at a particular place

37.–(1) Where—

    (a) a person arrested by a constable was found by him at a place at or about the time the offence for which he was arrested is alleged to have been committed; and

    (b) that or another constable investigating the offence reasonably believes that the presence of the person at that place and at that time may be attributable to his participation in the commission of the offence; and

    (c) the constable informs the person that he so believes, and requests him to account for that presence; and

    (d) the person fails or refuses to do so,

    then if, in any proceedings against the person for the offence, evidence of those matters is given, subsection (2) below applies.

[Subsection (2) of ss 36 and 37 echoes s 34(2).]

Code of Practice C

(a) When a caution must be given

10.1   A person whom there are grounds to suspect of an offence must be cautioned before any questions about it (or further questions if it is his answers to previous questions that provide grounds for suspicion) are put to them if either his answers or his silence (ie failure to answer a question or failure to answer satisfactorily) may be given in evidence to a court in a prosecution. He therefore need not be cautioned if questions are put for other purposes ...

10.2   Whenever a person who is not under arrest is initially cautioned or reminded that they are under caution they must at the same time be told that they are not under arrest and are free to leave if they wish to do so ...

(b) Inferences from silence

10.4 Sections 34, 36 and 37 of the Criminal Justice and Public Order Act 1994 as amended by section 58 of the Youth Justice and Criminal Evidence Act 1999 describe the conditions under which adverse inferences may be drawn from [silence]. These provisions are however subject to an overriding restriction which means that a court or jury is not allowed to draw adverse inferences from a person's silence. This restriction applies:

(a) to a person detained at a police station who, before being interviewed ...

(i) has asked for legal advice

(ii) has not been allowed to consult a solicitor ... and

(iii) has not changed their mind about wanting legal advice. ...

10.5 The caution ... shall be in the following terms—

'You do not have to say anything. But it may harm your defence if you do not mention when questioned something which you later rely on in court. Anything you do say may be given in evidence.'

10.6 Whenever a requirement to administer a caution arises and at the time it is given the restriction on drawing adverse inferences from silence applies, the caution shall be in the following terms:

'You do not have to say anything. But anything you do say may be given in evidence.'

Special warnings under sections 36 and 37 of the Criminal Justice and Public Order Act 1994

10.11 When a suspect who is interviewed at a police station or other authorized place of detention after arrest fails or refuses to answer certain questions ... after due warning, a court or jury may draw such inferences as appear proper under sections 36 and 37 of the Criminal Justice and Public Order Act 1994. This applies only when the restriction on drawing adverse inferences from silence does not apply and—

(a) a suspect is arrested by a constable and there is found on his person or in or on his clothing or footwear or otherwise in his possession or in the place where he was arrested, any objects, marks or substances, or marks on such objects, and the person fails or refuses to account for the objects, marks or substances found; or

(b) an arrested person was found by a constable at a place at or about the time the offence for which he was arrested, is alleged to have been committed, and the person or fails or refuses to account for his presence at that place.

10.12 For an inference to be drawn ... the interviewing officer must first tell the suspect in ordinary language—

(a) what offence is being investigated;

(b) what fact the suspect is being asked to account for;

(c) that this fact may be due to the suspect's taking part in the commission of the offence in question;

(d) that a court may draw a proper inference if the suspect fails or refuses to account for the fact about which he is being questioned.

(e) that a record is being made of the interview and that it may be given in evidence if the suspect is brought to trial.

(c) Juveniles, the mentally disordered and the mentally handicapped

10.13 If a juvenile or a person who is mentally disordered or mentally handicapped is cautioned in the absence of the appropriate adult, the caution must be repeated in the adult's presence.

Notes

1   Curtailment of the right to silence had already been foreshadowed. It was abolished in Northern Ireland in 1988 and curtailed in Britain in cases involving serious fraud.

2   *R v Saunders* (1966) 1 Cr App R 464 concerned the existence of the right to silence in serious fraud investigations. Inspectors of the Department of Trade and Industry interviewed Saunders, regarding allegations of fraud. They acted under s 437 of the Companies Act 1985 which provides for a sanction against the person being investigated if he refuses to answer questions. Thus, Saunders lost his privilege against self-incrimination, which he argued was unfair and amounted to an abuse of process. Saunders took his case to Strasbourg; see below for the findings of the European Court of Human Rights.

3   The value of the right to silence is discussed below by S Greer and this is followed by consideration of the likely impact of the provisions, by I Dennis

S Greer, 'The right to silence: a review of the current debate' (1990) 53 MLR 709, 726–28

Innocent suspects in England and Wales must currently balance two risks which police interviews pose for any subsequent trial: the risk that if they stay silent this may be taken as an indication of guilt even if no adverse comment is made about it in court, and the risk that if they talk they may inadvertently make a remark which is misinterpreted at the trial, thus damaging their defence. The abolition of the right to silence would tend to oblige them to take the latter option even if there were good reasons for staying silent. One of the key considerations in balancing these risks is that the suspect is likely to be at least partially ignorant of the police case against him and is thus open to manipulation. ... This is not necessarily to imply bad faith on the part of the police, although the Guildford Four, Birmingham Six and West Midlands Serious Crime Squad scandals show that it can clearly no longer be ruled out. Police officers acting in good faith are likely to see themselves as being capable of skilfully manoeuvring a guilty offender into giving the game away. The problem is that police assumptions about the guilt or innocence of any given suspect can be fundamentally mistaken. Instead of winkling a crook out of his shell they may instead inadvertently trick an innocent suspect into compromising his position by making remarks which are open to misrepresentation at trial. It is now widely recognised that under pressure people are capable of confessing to offences which it would have been impossible for them to have committed.

The right to silence also provides an incentive for other evidence to be sought by the police and subsequently adduced at trial. Its removal might create a risk of a decline in policing standards. It also ensures that anything which the suspect does say will have added credibility because it was offered without fear of the consequences of staying silent.

Innocent reasons for silence

There are a number of legitimate reasons why an entirely innocent suspect may be well advised not to answer at least certain police questions. They may be in an emotional and highly suggestible state of mind. They may feel guilty when in fact they have not committed an offence. They may be ignorant of some vital fact which explains away otherwise suspicious circumstances. They may be confused and liable to make mistakes which could be interpreted as deliberate lies at the trial. ... They may use loose expressions unaware of the possible adverse interpretations which could be placed upon them at trial ... They may have already given an explanation in the police car on the way to the police station which was not believed and thus prove reluctant to repeat it in the formal interview. Their silence may be an attempt to protect others or a reluctance to admit to having done something discreditable but not illegal. Some suspects may not want to be tricked into giving information about others because this could result in being stigmatised as an informer with all the dangers which this label carries, particularly in Northern Ireland.

Ian Dennis, 'The evidence provisions' [1995] Crim LR 4, 11–12, 15–16

... the court or jury may draw such inferences as appear proper from the failure to mention facts relied on subsequently. However, the Act gives no further guidance on what inferences might be proper ... The most obvious inference is that the previously undisclosed fact is untrue, a conclusion based on an argument that the accused did not mention the fact to the police because he knew that they would expose its falsity. Whether this inference can form part of a chain of reasoning leading to a conclusion that the accused is guilty rather depends on the issue in the case, the nature of the fact in question and the state of the other evidence. If the 'fact' is in the nature of a 'confession and avoidance' defence, whereby the accused admits the *actus reus* and *mens rea* of the offence but sets up some independent ground of justification or excuse such as self-defence, then the rejection of that defence is almost certain to lead to the conclusion that the accused has no defence at all and is guilty. On the other hand, if the issue is identity, and the other evidence against the accused is circumstantial, the rejection of one fact offered as an innocent explanation of one piece of circumstantial evidence may not necessarily yield a further inference of guilt. This suggests that it would be wrong for a court to conclude simply because an accused fails to mention a fact relied on subsequently that he is therefore guilty. Accordingly trial judges will have to direct juries carefully on the inferences which may fairly be drawn from such failures.

R v Argent [1997] 2 Cr App R 27

Lord Bingham CJ: What then are the formal conditions to be met before the jury may draw such an inference? ... the alleged failure must occur during questioning under caution by a constable. ... the constable's questioning must be directed to trying to discover whether or by whom the alleged offence had been committed. Here ... [t]he Detective Constable was trying to discover who inflicted the fatal wound ... the alleged failure by the defendant must be to mention any fact relied on in his defence in those proceedings. That raises two questions of fact: first, is there some fact which the defendant has relied on in his defence; and secondly, did the defendant fail to mention it to the constable when he was being questioned in accordance with the section? Being questions of fact these questions are for the jury as the tribunal of fact to resolve. Here it would seem fairly clear that there were matters which the appellant relied on in his defence which he had not mentioned. ... The sixth condition is that the appellant failed to mention a fact which in the circumstances existing at the time the accused could reasonably have been expected to mention when so questioned. The time referred to is the time of questioning, and account must be taken of all the relevant circumstances existing at that time. The courts should not construe the expression 'in the circumstances' restrictively: matters such as time of day, the defendant's age, experience, mental capacity, state of health, sobriety, tiredness, knowledge, personality and legal advice are all part of the relevant circumstances ... When reference is made to 'the accused' attention is directed not to some hypothetical, reasonable accused of ordinary phlegm and fortitude but to the actual accused with such qualities, apprehensions, knowledge and advice as he is shown to have had at the time. Like so many other questions in criminal trials this is a question to be resolved by the jury in the exercise of their collective common-sense, experience and understanding of human nature. Sometimes they may conclude that it was reasonable for the defendant to have held his peace for a host of reasons ...

In other cases the jury may conclude ... that he could reasonably have been expected to [answer].

Notes

1   *The curtailed right to silence: impact of the HRA.* The presumption of innocence under Article 6(2) is closely linked to the right to freedom from self-incrimination which the Court has found to be covered by the right to a fair hearing under Article 6(1).[109] Article 6(2) further impliedly requires that when carrying out their duties,

---

109 *Funke v France* (1993) 16 EHRR 297.

members of a court should not start with the preconceived idea that the accused has committed the offence charged; the burden of proof is on the prosecution, and any doubt should benefit the accused. These matters are at issue when silence under interrogation by law enforcement bodies is penalised by a formal penalty or by drawing adverse inferences from it. The Court has drawn a distinction between these matters, although it recognised in *Murray (John) v UK* (1996) 22 EHRR 29[110] that they were not entirely distinct, since adverse inference-drawing is clearly a form of penalty; it was termed 'indirect compulsion'.

2   It is possible that curtailment of the right to silence under ss 34, 36 or 37 of the CJPOA may, depending on the particular circumstances of a case, lead to a breach of Article 6, received into domestic law under the HRA, on the basis that it infringes the presumption of innocence under Article 6(2) and the right to freedom from self-incrimination.[111] Consideration of the judgments in *Saunders v UK* (1997) 23 EHRR 313, paras 69–75 and *Murray (John) v UK* reveals that it is only where a penalty formally attaches to silence, and the interview may then be used in evidence, that a breach of Article 6 is almost bound to be established, but that where adverse inferences can be drawn from the silence at trial, a breach may be established, taking into account the question whether the suspect has had access to legal advice.

3   The decision in *Murray (John) v UK* may be contrasted with that in *Saunders* since it suggests that, depending on the circumstances of a case, Article 6 takes a different stance towards imposing a formal penalty on silence and drawing adverse inferences from it. Murray was arrested. A detective superintendent, pursuant to the Northern Ireland (Emergency Provisions) Act 1987, decided to delay access to a solicitor for 48 hours. While being interviewed, Murray repeatedly stated that he had 'nothing to say'. After he had seen his solicitor, he stated that he had been advised not to answer the questions. The Criminal Evidence (Northern Ireland) Order 1988 enables a court in any criminal trial to exercise discretion to draw adverse inferences from an accused's failure to mention a fact during police questioning. Such inferences were drawn from Murray's silence in the police interviews once the prosecution had established a *prima facie* case against him, and he was convicted. The Strasbourg Court emphasised that its decision was confined to the particular facts of the case in finding that no breach of Article 6(1) or (2) had occurred where adverse inferences had been drawn. The Court placed emphasis on the fact that he had been able to remain silent; also, given the strength of the evidence against him, the matter of drawing inferences was one of common sense which could not be regarded as unfair.[112] But, crucially, the Court did find that Article 6(1) and (3)(c) had been breached by the denial of custodial access to a lawyer for 48 hours since it found that such access was essential where there was a likelihood that adverse inferences would be drawn from silence.

4   The regime under the 1988 Order is, in essence, the same as that under s 34 of the CJPOA, which may therefore be vulnerable to challenge under the HRA. Drawing adverse inferences from silence in police interviewing does not necessarily breach Article 6(1) or (2), but the greater the reliance placed on such inferences at the trial, the greater the likelihood that a breach will occur. Under s 38(3) of the CJPOA, a

---

110 For comment, see Munday [1996] Crim LR 370.
111 See the comments of the Court of Appeal in *Birchall* [1999] Crim LR 311; see also Bucke, *op cit*.
112 *Murray (John) v UK* (1996) 22 EHRR 29, para 54.

conviction cannot be based 'solely' on silence. Article 6(1) and (2) might therefore be found to be breached in circumstances differing from those applicable in *Murray*, including those in which the evidence against the defendant was less overwhelming. *Murray* made it clear that drawing adverse inferences from silence when the defendant had not had access to legal advice prior to the failure to reply to questioning will breach Article 6. As indicated above, s 58 of the Youth Justice and Criminal Evidence Act 1999 addressed that finding by inserting s 34(2A) into the CJPOA. At present, the circumstances in which adverse inference drawing will amount to a breach of Article 6 remain uncertain,[113] except in the instance in which access to legal advice is also denied. In that instance, under s 34(2A) of the CJPOA, no inferences may be drawn from silence and this is now recognised in Code C, para 6 as indicated above. There is a restriction on drawing adverse inferences where no opportunity to have legal advice has arisen. But s 34(2A) of the CJPOA does not cover the defendant who has not had legal advice but makes *admissions* in response to the new caution or (*prima facie*) the defendant who wishes to obtain advice but fails to do so, although no formal denial occurs. In such an instance a breach of Article 6 but arguably not of s 34(2A) might occur if adverse inferences were drawn.

5   It need not be assumed that Article 6 will necessarily be satisfied where a defendant has had access to legal advice prior to the point at which he remains silent. In *Condron* [1997] 1 Cr App R 185 the defendants acted on legal advice in refusing to answer questions. It was found on appeal that adverse inferences could nevertheless be drawn from their silence. It was found at Strasbourg that the applicants in *Condron v UK* (2001) 31 EHRR 1; [2000] Crim LR 679 had failed to receive a fair trial under Article 6 on the basis that the appeal court should not have found that the conviction was safe, despite the erroneous direction of the judge to the jury. Since the Court could not know what part the drawing of adverse inferences played in the jury's decision, it should have allowed the appeal. That decision impliedly confirms that juries should be directed that they should not draw adverse inferences where they consider that there was a sound reason for advising silence. The decision affects the role of the Court of Appeal; it does not give guidance on, *inter alia*, the question when a no comment interview, based on legal advice, should be excluded from evidence, or as to the reasons which might be viewed as sound for advising a suspect to remain silent.

6   *Saunders v UK* (1997) 23 EHRR 313, paras 69–75 establishes that the use of direct coercion to obtain statements from persons will clearly be incompatible with Article 6(1) if the statement is then used against him or her in criminal proceedings. It was found at Strasbourg that the applicant's right to freedom from self-incrimination had been infringed in that he had been forced to answer questions put to him by inspectors investigating a company take-over or risk the imposition of a criminal sanction. Section 172 of the Road Traffic Act 1988 (RTA) makes it an offence for motorists not to tell police who was driving their vehicle at the time of an alleged offence. The coerced statement can then be used in evidence at trial for the RTA offence in question. The provision clearly contravenes the right against self-incrimination, and this was found to be the case in Scotland in *Stott v Brown* 2000 SLT 379[114] during the period of time when the Convention was in force in

---

113 See further D Birch, 'Suffering in silence: a cost-benefit analysis of s 34 of the CJPOA' [1999] Crim LR 769.
114 See [2000] J Civ Lib 193.

Scotland, but not in England.[115] The defendant encountered the police officers after parking her car and was suspected of driving while intoxicated; she was asked under s 172 to reveal the name of the person driving the car at the relevant time. On pain of the penalty under s 172 she did so, revealing that she had been driving, and was convicted of driving while intoxicated, after the coerced statement was admitted into evidence. The Privy Council found (*Brown v Stott* [2001] 2 WLR 817 – see Part VI Chapter 1, pp 886–89) that it was not necessary to declare that s 172 is incompatible with Article 6(1) or (2). They reached the decision that the two were compatible, despite the findings in *Saunders v UK*, on the basis that the requirements of Article 6 admit of implied restriction. The restriction, Lord Hope said, must have a legitimate aim in the public interest. It was found that this was the case, bearing in mind the need to promote road safety. If so, he went on to ask, 'is there a reasonable relationship of proportionality between the means employed and the aim sought to be realised'? He found that the answer to the question, in terms of limiting the right not to incriminate oneself under Article 6(1), was in the affirmative since the section demands a response to a single question, and does not allow prolonged questioning, as in *Saunders*. The decision in *Brown* rested on the finding that coercing a statement from the defendant was not a disproportionate response to the legitimate aim of seeking to address the problem of road safety.

Questions

1 Are ss 34, 36 and 37 of the CJPOA confined to formal interviews within the police station? Why is this a matter of significance?

2 Are there grounds for fearing that curtailment of the right to silence may lead to further miscarriages of justice?

3 Is the curtailment of the right to silence under ss 34, 36 and 37 of the CJPOA in breach of Article 6 of the ECHR, as afforded further effect in domestic law under the HRA?

REDRESS FOR POLICE IMPROPRIETY

Introduction

This chapter has been concerned so far with the question of the balance to be struck between the exercise of powers by the police in conducting an investigation on the one hand, and safeguards for the suspect against abuse of power on the other. As we have seen, PACE sets out to maintain this balance by declaring certain standards for the conduct of criminal investigations. However, it may be that an investigation does not, at certain points, reach those standards. In such circumstances certain means of redress are available,[116] and these are considered below.

Exclusion of evidence

PACE provides four separate tests which can be applied to a confession to determine whether it is admissible in evidence.[117] In theory, all four tests could be applied to a

---

115 The Convention rights were brought into force in Scotland under the Scotland Act 1998, s 57(2).

116 See generally D Birch, 'Confessions and Confusions under the 1984 Act' [1989] Crim LR 95; D Feldman [1990] Crim LR 452.

117 See Birch, *ibid*.

particular confession, although in practice it may not be necessary to consider all of them. They are the 'oppression' test (s 76(2)(a)), the 'reliability' test (s 76(2)(b)), and the 'fairness' test (s 78). PACE also preserves the residual common law discretion to exclude evidence, under s 82(3). The scheme in respect of non-confession evidence is less complex: only ss 78 and 82(3) need be considered. Physical evidence which is discovered as a result of an inadmissible confession will be admissible under s 76(4)(a).

Police and Criminal Evidence Act 1984

Confessions

76.–(2) If, in any proceedings where the prosecution proposes to give in evidence a confession made by an accused person, it is represented to the court that the confession was or may have been obtained—

(a) by oppression of the person who made it; or

(b) in consequence of anything said or done which was likely, in the circumstances existing at the time, to render unreliable any confession which might be made by him in consequence thereof,

the court shall not allow the confession to be given in evidence against him except in so far as the prosecution proves to the court beyond reasonable doubt that the confession (notwithstanding that it may be true) was not obtained as aforesaid.

...

(4) The fact that a confession is wholly or partly excluded in pursuance of this section shall not affect the admissibility in evidence—

(a) of any facts discovered as a result of the confession; or

(b) where the confession is relevant as showing that the accused speaks, writes or expresses himself in a particular way, of so much of the confession as is necessary to show that he does so. ...

(8) In this section 'oppression' includes torture, inhuman or degrading treatment, and the use or threat of violence (whether or not amounting to torture). ...

Exclusion of unfair evidence

78.–(1) In any proceedings the court may refuse to allow evidence on which the prosecution proposes to rely to be given if it appears to the court that, having regard to all the circumstances, including the circumstances in which the evidence was obtained, the admission of the evidence would have such an adverse effect on the fairness of the proceedings that the court ought not to admit it.

(2) Nothing in this section shall prejudice any rule of law requiring a court to exclude evidence.

R v Fulling [1987] QB 426; [1987] 2 All ER 65, 67, 69, 70, CA

Lord Lane CJ: '... oppression' in s 76(2)(a) should be given its ordinary dictionary meaning. The *Oxford English Dictionary* as its third definition of the word runs as follows: 'Exercise of authority or power in a burdensome, harsh, or wrongful manner; unjust or cruel treatment of subjects, inferiors, etc; the imposition of unreasonable or unjust burdens.' One of the quotations given under that paragraph runs as follows: 'There is not a word in our language which expresses more detestable wickedness than oppression.'

We find it hard to envisage any circumstances in which such oppression would not entail some impropriety on the part of the interrogator. We do not think that the judge was wrong in using that test. What however is abundantly clear is that a confession may be invalidated under s76(2)(b) where there is no suspicion of impropriety.

Appeal dismissed.

R v Keenan [1990] 2 QB 54

Hodgson J: ... We think that in cases where there have been 'significant and substantial' breaches of the 'verballing' provisions of the code, the evidence so obtained will frequently be excluded. We do not think that any injustice will be caused by this. It is clear that not every breach or combination of breaches of the code will justify the exclusion of interview evidence under s 76 or s 78. They must be significant and substantial. If this were not the case, the courts would be undertaking a task which is no part of their duty; as Lord Lane CJ said in *Delaney* (at 341):'It is no part of the duty of the court to rule a statement inadmissible simply in order to punish the police for failure to observe the codes of practice.'

R v Samuel [1988] 2 WLR 920, 933, 934

The Court of Appeal found that the appellant had been unlawfully denied access to a solicitor and that, if the right to such access is denied, this can lead to the exclusion of evidence obtained at unlawful interviews conducted after the denial by the exercise of the judge's power under s 78(1).

Hodgson J: [The solicitor in question] gave evidence ... on this occasion, knowing that his client had already been interviewed on four occasions and at each had strenuously denied complicity in the robbery and had already been charged with two serious offences, he would probably, after consultation, have advised his client, for the time being at any rate, to refuse to answer further questioning.

In this case this appellant was denied Improperly one of the most important and fundamental rights of a citizen. The trial judge fell into error in not so holding. If he had arrived at correct decisions on the two points argued before him he might well have concluded that the refusal of access and consequent unlawful interview compelled him to find that the admission of evidence as to the final interview would have 'such an adverse effect on the fairness of the proceedings' that he ought not to admit it. Such a decision would, of course, have very significantly weakened the prosecution case (the failure to charge earlier ineluctably shows this). In those circumstances this court feels that it has no alternative but to quash the appellant's conviction on count 1 in the indictment, the charge of robbery.

Attorney-General's Reference (No 3 of 1999) [2001] 2 AC 91, HL

In this case the police had retained a DNA sample (arguably in breach of Article 8) in breach of s 64 of PACE; the question was whether such evidence should be admissible in the instant case – a very serious rape case. Lord Steyn in the House of Lords treated the possible breach of both Article 8 and PACE as *not* engaging Article 6(1); he looked only at the requirements of s 78 of PACE. The general conclusion was that regardless of the inception of the HRA, invocation of Article 6 did not aid the argument since the question of admissibility is a matter of national law

Lord Steyn: Article 6 provides, *inter alia*, that in the determination of any criminal charge against him everyone is entitled to a fair and public hearing within a reasonable time by an independent and impartial tribunal established by law. Under the general law the trial judge has adequate powers to ensure fairness: (1) he has jurisdiction to stay the proceedings as an abuse of the process and (2) he has a discretion to exclude evidence under section 78 if it would be unfair to admit the evidence 'having regard to all the circumstances, including the circumstances in which the evidence was obtained'. If trial is allowed to proceed, and the evidence is not excluded, the accused will have a full opportunity to contest the reliability and accuracy of the DNA evidence. In any event, the question of admissibility is a matter for regulation under national law. There is no principle of Convention law that unlawfully obtained evidence is not admissible: *Schenk v Switzerland* (1988) 13 EHRR 242, 265–266, para 46; *R v Khan (Sultan)* [1997] AC 558.

Notes

1   The principle underlying the oppression test under s 76(2)(a), which derives from the rule as it was at common law, is that threats of violence or other oppressive behaviour are so abhorrent that no further question as to the reliability of a confession obtained by such methods should be asked. Under this head, once the defence has advanced a reasonable argument (*R v Liverpool Juvenile Court ex p* [1987] 2 All ER 688) that the confession was obtained by oppression, it will not be admitted in evidence unless the prosecution can prove that it was not so obtained. The reliability of a confession obtained by oppression is irrelevant; it matters not whether the effect of the oppression is to frighten the detainee into telling the truth or alternatively into lying in order to get out of the situation.

2   In *R v Paris* [1994] Crim LR 361, the case of the 'Cardiff Three', confessions made by one of the defendants after some 13 hours of high-pressured and hostile questioning were excluded on the ground of oppression. He was a man of limited intelligence but the Court of Appeal thought that the questioning would have been oppressive even with a suspect of normal intelligence. It does not appear that a breach of the Act or Codes can constitute oppression unless accompanied by bad faith. The Court of Appeal in *R v Hughes* [1988] Crim LR 545 held that a denial of legal advice due, not to bad faith on the part of the police, but to a misunderstanding, could not amount to oppression. Bad faith appears to be a necessary but not sufficient condition for the operation of s 76(2)(a), whereas it will be highly likely to render a confession inadmissible under s 78. If bad faith is shown, it would seem that it should be accompanied by improper behaviour which reaches a certain level of seriousness.[118]

3   The 'reliability' test under s 76(2)(b) is concerned with objective reliability; the judge must consider the situation at the time the confession was made and ask whether the confession would be likely to be unreliable, not whether it is unreliable.

4   In many instances the 'something said or done' under s 76(2)(b) will consist of some impropriety on the part of the police, and in such instances a court will go on to consider whether any circumstances existed which rendered the impropriety particularly significant. The 'circumstances' could include the particularly vulnerable state of the detainee. The vulnerability may relate to a physical or mental state. In *R v Delaney* (1988) 88 Cr App R 339 the defendant was 17, had an IQ of 80 and, according to an educational psychologist, was subject to emotional arousal which would lead him to wish to bring a police interview to an end as quickly as possible. These were circumstances in which it was important to ensure that the interrogation was conducted with all propriety. In fact, the officers offered some inducement to the defendant to confess by playing down the gravity of the offence and by suggesting that if he confessed he would get the psychiatric help he needed. They also failed to make an accurate, contemporaneous record of the interview in breach of Code C, para 11.3. Failing to make the proper record was of indirect relevance to the question of reliability as it meant that the court could not assess the full extent of the suggestions held out to the defendant. The confession was excluded under s 76(2)(b).

5   Under s 78, it has been found that a 'substantial and significant' breach of PACE and/or a Code provision may affect any confession made after it, and admission of the confession may render the trial unfair (*R v Walsh* (1990) 91 Cr App R 161).

---

118 See *R v L* [1994] Crim LR 839.

6   In *R v Samuel* (1988) 87 Cr App R 380, the Court of Appeal found that the confession should have been excluded under s 78 because it was causally linked to the police impropriety – a failure to allow the appellant access to legal advice. The Court of Appeal in *R v Alladice* (1988) 87 Cr App R 380,[119] also faced with a breach of s 58, accepted that the key factor in exercising discretion under s 78 after a breach of the interrogation procedure was the causal relationship between breach and confession, and, by implication, between breach and fairness at the trial. However, since the appellant stated that he did not need a solicitor to advise on the right to silence but only in order to see fair play, the causal relationship between breach and confession could not be established, and therefore the Court found that admitting the confession had not had an adverse effect on the fairness of the proceedings.

7   If a substantial breach of a recording provision has been identified, a court will be likely to react by excluding the confession on the basis that it is impossible to be sure of its reliability,[120] and therefore its prejudicial quality may outweigh its probative value. In other words, a jury may place reliance on an inaccurate record or believe a fabricated confession which clearly has no evidential value at all.

8   Non-confession evidence can in theory be excluded under s 78. Identification evidence is seen as particularly vulnerable; if some doubt is raised as to the reliability of the identification due to delay[121] or to a failure to hold an identification parade where one was practicable,[122] the identification evidence is likely to be excluded. It would be possible to apply the test from *Samuel* to a silence, although the courts have shown little inclination to do so. For example, if no notification as to the availability of legal advice was given before an interview occurred in which the suspect may have needed advice in order to appreciate the import of the caution, it could be argued that the failure to notify of the right to advice was causally linked to the silence.

9   Illegally obtained physical evidence, such as fingerprints, was admissible at common law unless the evidence had been tricked out of the detainee,[123] in which case there would be a discretion to exclude it. At the present time *Attorney-General's Reference (No 3 of 1999)* (above) and *R v Khan (Sultan)* [1997] AC 558 make it clear that there is only a very narrow discretion under s 78 to exclude physical evidence and probably all non-confession evidence.

10 *Impact of the HRA.* What does Article 6 demand in relation to the admissibility of improperly obtained evidence? It was found in an early decision, *Austria v Italy* Application No 788/60, (1961) 4 Yearbook 112, that maltreatment with the aim of extracting a confession had created a breach of Article 6(2). The question of pressure on the applicant in the interview was taken into account by the European Court of Human Rights in reaching its conclusion that Article 6 had been breached in *Saunders v UK* (1997) 23 EHRR 313 by the admission in evidence of the coerced admissions. This approach to *confession* evidence accords, broadly, with the pre-HRA domestic approach which may therefore continue to prevail, post-HRA.

11 Under current domestic practice, non-confession evidence gained through a very serious impropriety, possibly including a breach of a Convention right, is

---

119 The Court of Appeal appeared to have a similar test in mind in relation to a failure to caution in *R v Weerdesteyn* [1995] Crim LR 239.
120 See, eg, *R v Keenan* [1990] 2 QB 54.
121 *R v Quinn* [1990] Crim LR 581.
122 *R v Ladlow* [1989] Crim LR 219.
123 *Callis v Gunn* [1964] 1 QB 495.

nevertheless admissible. The discretion to exclude non-confession evidence is very narrow and the impact which s 78 has had in encouraging adherence to due process may be diminishing at the present time. As L-T Choo observes: 'recent decisions of the Court of Appeal signal a movement away from focusing on the nature of the breach [of PACE or the Codes] and towards an approach which takes the nature of the evidence as its central consideration.'[124] In other words, the movement is away from due process values and towards acceptance of the crime control norm that the end – a conviction – justifies the means.

12 The requirements placed on the domestic courts by the HRA depend on the view taken of the meaning of fairness under Article 6. Strasbourg and the domestic courts have united in finding that a breach of another Convention right, perpetrated pre-trial, does not automatically render the trial unfair.[125] Therefore, the fact that such a breach has occurred is part of the history of the case which can be taken into account in considering the proceedings as a whole, but which, except in the case of a breach of Article 3 in order to obtain a confession,[126] is not conclusive of the issue regarding fairness under s 78. The same argument applies to findings that flaws in the custodial and investigative procedures, including breaches of the PACE or TA Codes of Practice, not amounting in themselves to breaches of Convention rights, have occurred.

13 The current narrow interpretation of s 78 of PACE,[127] indicated above, means that improperly obtained non-confession evidence is unlikely to be excluded, in accordance with the demands of the HRA, whether or not the impropriety also amounted to a breach of a Convention right. In other words, the admission of evidence in such circumstances need not amount to a breach of Article 6. The findings in *Attorney-General's Reference (No 3 of 1999)*[128] suggest that, at present, there is a tendency to reject the possibility of using exclusion of evidence to uphold fundamental rights. This seems to be the case even where such rights are recognised within a statutory scheme; and possibly also where the breach is of a Convention right. The case of *Khan v UK* (2001) 31 EHRR 45 can be utilised by the courts to support this probability, despite the inception of the HRA. It was found in *Khan* that the admission of evidence obtained in breach of Article 8 did not create a breach of Article 6.[129]

Questions

1 The confession made in *Samuel* may have been truthful. Why was it excluded from evidence?

2 What principles may underlie determinations as to the admissibility of physical evidence?

3 Assume that s 34 of the CJPOA 1994 was in force when Samuel was detained and interviewed. What effect, if any, would it have had on the decision of the Court of Appeal that Samuel's confession should have been excluded from evidence?

---

124 Choo and Nash.
125 *R v Khan* [1997] AC 558 and *Khan v UK* (2001) 31 EHRR 45.
126 Under s 76(2)(a).
127 See *R v Chalkley* [1998] 2 All ER 155; *R v Khan* [1997] AC 558 and *R v Shannon* [2001] 1 WLR 51.
128 [2001] 2 WLR 56, *per* Lord Steyn at 64 and *per* Lord Cook of Thorndon, at 65.
129 But see the decision of the Court of Appeal in *R v Radak and Others* [1999] 1 Cr App R 187 in which it was found that a witness statement should not have been admitted in evidence since its admission breached Article 6(3)(d).

4   Is it probable that the domestic courts will decide to rely on Article 6 under s 3 or s 6 of the HRA to exclude improperly obtained non-confession evidence? Would this be a desirable development?

Tortious remedies[130]

Tort damages will be available in respect of some breaches of PACE. For example, if a police officer arrests a citizen where no reasonable suspicion arises under s 24 or 25 of PACE, an action for false imprisonment will be available. Equally, such a remedy would be available if the Part IV provisions governing time limits on detention were breached.[131] Trespass to land or to goods will occur if the statutory provisions governing search of premises or seizure of goods are not followed. Malicious prosecution will be available where police have abused their powers in recommending prosecution to the Crown Prosecution Service. Actions for malicious prosecution are quite common but the claimant carries quite a heavy burden in the need to prove that there was no reasonable or probable cause for the prosecution.[132] It may be that if the prosecution is brought on competent legal advice, this action will fail, but this is unclear.[133]

Almost the whole of the interviewing scheme which is contained mainly in Codes C and E, rather than in PACE itself, is unaffected by tortious remedies. Section 67(10) of PACE provides that no civil or criminal liability arises from breaches of the Codes of Practice. This lack of a remedy also extends to some statutory provisions, in particular the most significant statutory interviewing provision, the entitlement to legal advice. There is no tort of denial of access to legal advice; the only possible tortious action would be for breach of statutory duty.

Examples of the use of civil actions are given below (obviously the sums awarded must be considered in the light of inflation).

R Clayton and H Tomlinson, *Civil Actions Against the Police*, 2nd edn (1992), pp 413, 420
Ballard, Stewart-Park, Findlay v Metropolitan Police Commissioner (1983) 133 NLJ 1133; *Legal Action*, 10 January 1984
Westminster County Court, judge.

Facts: P1 and P2 had been hit over the head by police officers with truncheons in the course of a demonstration, P2 carried spread-eagled and dumped on ground from a height of four feet. P3 was lawfully arrested and was prodded in stomach, hit over eye with truncheon and, as a result suffered migrainous attacks.

Damages: P1 – compensatory £400 including small sum for aggravated damages (1992 value: £660). P2 – compensatory £600 including aggravated damages (1992 value: £990). P3 – compensatory £3,000 including aggravated damages (1992 value: £4,950).

---

130 See generally, R Clayton and H Tomlinson, *Civil Actions Against the Police*, 3rd edn (1999).
131 Eg, *Edwards v Chief Constable of Avon and Somerset* (1992) unreported, 9 March: the plaintiff was detained for eight hours, 47 minutes following a lawful arrest. The detention was wrongful because it was 'unnecessary'; compensation was awarded.
132 See *Glinskie v McIver* [1962] AC 726.
133 *Abbott v Refuge Assurance Co Ltd* [1962] 1 QB 632.

Lewis v Chief Constable of South Wales, 5 October 1989; unreported

Bridgend County Court, jury.

Facts: Ps' arrest unlawful as a result of their not being given reasons. The unlawfulness of these arrests was cured by subsequent giving of reasons, to P1 after 10 minutes and P2 after 23 minutes (Court of Appeal upheld judge's ruling on law [1991] 1 All ER 206).

Damages: £200 for each P (1992 value: £232).

Leigh-Williams v Chief Constable of Essex, The Guardian, 18 October 1990

High Court, Michael Davies J and a jury.

Facts: P, a former vicar, was unlawfully arrested and detained for 40 hours for breach of the peace. He had previously been lawfully arrested for assault on a 13-year old boy and was unlawfully arrested near the boy's home.

Damages: £4,000 (1992 value: £4,184).

Notes

1   One of the highest awards was made in *White v Metropolitan Police Commissioner* (1982) *The Times*, 24 April. Police officers unlawfully entered a house and, it was alleged, attacked one of the plaintiffs, an elderly man. The police then charged both plaintiffs with various offences in order to cover up their own conduct. The plaintiffs were awarded £20,000 exemplary damages each plus, respectively, £6,500 and £4,500 aggravated damages.

2   In 1996, a number of very high awards were made against the Metropolitan Police. In *Goswell v Commissioner of Metropolitan Police* (1996) *The Guardian*, 27 April, Goswell was awarded £120,000 damages for assault, £12,000 for false imprisonment and £170,000 exemplary damages for arbitrary and oppressive behaviour. In *Hsu v Commissioner of Metropolitan Police* (1996) unreported, the plaintiff won £220,000 damages for assault and wrongful arrest at his home.

3   The decision in *Hsu* was appealed together with that in another case in *Thompson v Commissioner of Police for the Metropolis* [1997] 2 All ER 762. The court laid down guidelines for the award of damages which took as a starting point a basic award of £500 for the first hour of unlawful detention, with decreasing amounts for subsequent hours. It was found that aggravated damages could be awarded where there were special features of the case, such as oppressive or humiliating conduct at the time of arrest. Such damages would start at around £1,000 but would not normally be more than twice the level of the basic damages. Exemplary damages should only be awarded where aggravated and basic damages together would not appear to provide a sufficient punishment. Exemplary damages would be not less than £5,000, but the total figure awarded as exemplary damages would not be expected to amount to more than the basic damages multiplied by three. The overall award should not exceed £50,000. In accordance with these guidelines, the award made in *Hsu* was reduced to £50,000.

4   In *Gerald v MPC* (1998) *The Times*, 26 June, the Court of Appeal found that the guidelines in *Thompson* should not be applied in a rigid fashion. In *Rutherford v Chief Constable of Kent* (2001) unreported, 15 May, an award of £50,000 was made where officers had falsified records and assaulted the claimant.

5   If a civil action against a police officer is successful, he or she will not be personally liable; s 48 of the Police Act 1964 provides that a chief constable will be vicariously liable in respect of torts committed by constables under his direction or control in the performance or purported performance of their functions.

6   If a civil action is brought against an officer on the basis that he or she has acted *ultra vires* and the officer shows that the statutory conditions for the exercise of power were present, the onus lies on the claimant to establish the relevant facts (*Greene v Home Secretary* [1942] AC 284, HL).

7   Sections 6 and 8 of the HRA require the courts to offer a remedy where a public authority violates the Convention rights,[134] unless in so doing it is acting in accordance with incompatible legislation.[135] Articles 3, 5, 8 and 14 of the ECHR potentially cover certain pre-trial rights of suspects. Tortious liability would arise and damages could be awarded under s 8 of the HRA if one or more of these Articles were found to have been breached in respect of police treatment of suspects. As indicated, some custodial treatment in breach of these Articles is already tortious under domestic law, and civil actions against the police have provided an increasingly significant means of creating some police accountability,[136] but this possibility would clearly be of particular significance where domestic law currently fails to provide a tortious remedy in respect of the maltreatment of detainees.

Police complaints and disciplinary proceedings[137]

Police Act 1996, Chapter 16

Part IV Complaints, Disciplinary Proceedings etc

Preliminary

67.–(1) Where a complaint is submitted to the chief officer of police for a police area, he shall taken any steps that appear to him to be desirable for the purpose of obtaining or preserving evidence relating to the conduct complained of.

(2) After complying with subsection (1), the chief officer shall determine whether he is the appropriate authority in relation to the member of a police force whose conduct is the subject of the complaint.

(3) If the chief officer determines that he is not the appropriate authority, he shall—

(a) send the complaint or, if it was submitted orally, particulars of it, to the appropriate authority . . .

(4) Nothing in this Chapter shall have effect in relation to a complaint in so far as it relates to the direction or control of a police force by the chief officer of police . . .

(5) If any conduct to which a complaint wholly or partly relates is or has been the subject of criminal or disciplinary proceedings, none of the provisions of this Chapter which relate to the recording and investigation of complaints shall have effect in relation to the complaint in so far as it relates to that conduct. . . .

---

134 Sections 6(1), 7 and 8. For discussion, see Part VI Chapter 1, pp 871 *et seq.*

135 Section 6(2). Section 3 requires that the legislation should be rendered compatible with the Convention rights 'so far as it is possible to do so'.

136 See the Home Affairs Committee, First Report 1997–98, Police Disciplinary and Complaints Procedures, printed 16 December 1997, which noted (para 32) the 'striking' rise in the cost of civil settlements for the Metropolitan Police, from £0.47m in 1991 to £2.69m in 1996. (This figure may decline owing to the decision in *Thompson* [1997] 2 All ER 762.) The Police Action Lawyers Group and the Commission for Racial Equality attributed the rise to disillusionment with the complaints process.

137 See A Sanders and R Young, *Criminal Justice*, 2nd edn (2000), Chapter 11, Part 4, pp 400–15; House of Commons Home Affairs Select Committee, Police Disciplinary and Complaints Procedure, First Report, HC 258-1 (1998).

References of complaints to Authority.

70.–(1) The appropriate authority—

    (a) shall refer to the Authority—

        (i) any complaint alleging that the conduct complained of resulted in the death of, or serious injury to, some other person, and

        (ii) any complaint of a description specific for the purposes of this section in regulations made by the Secretary of State, and

    (b) may refer to the Authority any complaint which is not required to be referred to them.

    (2) The Authority may require the submission to them for consideration of any complaint not referred to them by the appropriate authority; and the appropriate authority shall comply with any such requirement. . . .

Police and Magistrates' Courts Act 1994
Part I, Chapter 2

37.– The following provisions of the Police and Criminal Evidence Act 1984 shall cease to have effect —

    (a) section 67(8) (failure to comply with a code of practice is a disciplinary offence) . . .

Notes

1 PACE set up the Police Complaints Authority (PCA) as an independent body with an involvement in the complaints and disciplinary system. The idea was to afford an appearance of independence to the system. The scheme set up by PACE for dealing with complaints, contained in ss 83–106, was repealed and re-enacted in the Police Act 1996.[138]

2 Commentators tend to view the police complaints mechanism as ineffective as a means of redress.[139] It does not allow for compensation to the victim or for the victim to attend any disciplinary proceedings. In any event, most complaints do not result in disciplinary proceedings; as many as 30 per cent of complaints are dealt with by informal resolution[140] and commentators have suggested that unreasonable pressure may be put on complainants to adopt the informal resolution process. Maguire and Corbett conducted a review of the operation of the complaints system from 1968–88,[141] which found that the majority of complainants were dissatisfied and that the public did not have confidence in the system. The PCA Report of 1998 stated that 141 complaints concerned serious assaults; eight per cent of those fully investigated led to disciplinary action. A total of 16,550 complaints were received in 1998–99; 317 were fully investigated, a figure of approximately two per cent.[142] In 1997, the Home Affairs Committee considered the figures for the outcome of complaints and found that over the previous two years, two per cent of all recorded complaints were substantiated following a formal

---

138 Which came into force on 1 April 1999, replacing PACE 1984, Part IX.
139 See, eg, comment from J Harrison and S Cragg (1993) 143 NLJ 591.
140 *PCA Triennial Review*, HC 466 (1985–88), para 1.14, p 8.
141 *A Study of the Police Complaints System* (HMSO, 1991).
142 The 1998–99 Annual Report of the PCA, Table 5: 2,415 complaints concerned assaults; 81 disciplinary charges were preferred. 203 complaints concerned racially discriminatory behaviour; three charges were preferred. The report does not give the figure for disciplinary action as a percentage of fully investigated complaints.

investigation and less than half of one per cent of complaints led to disciplinary or criminal charges.[143]

3   New procedures intended to reform the disciplinary process were introduced in April 1999,[144] including, in particular, abolition of the criminal standard of proof in disciplinary proceedings.[145] Under the new procedure, the hearing will be private, but the complainant can attend the proceedings, although not before his evidence is given,[146] and he may be allowed to cross-examine witnesses.[147] A number of provisions, however, allow for the exclusion of the complainant.[148] Racist language and behaviour is now a breach of the police code of conduct, but it is not yet possible to determine how far-reaching such change might be.

4   There is quite a strong consensus that the independent element in the complaints and disciplinary process is too weak and is the key factor in the inefficacy of the system. The MacPherson Report recommended that there should be an independent tribunal for serious complaints.[149] In 2000, the government commissioned a feasibility study into the practicality of using independent investigators for police complaints.[150] The government issued a Consultation Paper in 2000 which proposed importing greater independence into the system, by means of a new body, the Independent Police Complaints Commission,[151] but made it clear that in the vast majority of cases, a full independent investigation would not occur, owing to cost. Once the system contains this independent element, a number of problems may remain even in relation to those exceptional cases in which independent investigation by civilian investigators occurs. Institutional factors, including obstruction of the system by the police and the possibility that civilian investigators will be affected by police culture, may continue to hamper the system; the success rate may remain low.

FURTHER READING

SH Bailey, DJ Harris, D Ormerod, *Bailey, Harris and Jones: Civil Liberties: Cases and Materials*, 5th edn (2002), Chapter 3

D Feldman, *Civil Liberties and Human Rights in England and Wales*, 2nd edn (2002), Chapters 6 and 10

H Fenwick, *Civil Liberties and Human Rights*, 3rd edn (2002), Chapters 13 and 14

A Sanders and R Young, *Criminal Justice*, 2nd edn (2000)

M Zander, *The Police and Criminal Evidence Act 1984* (1995)

---

143 Home Affairs Committee First Report (1997–98), Police Disciplinary and Complaints Procedures, printed 16 December 1997, para 27.

144 The Police (Conduct) Regulations 1999 (SI 1999/730). The new procedures operated alongside the 1995 Regulations until March 2000, when the transitional arrangements ended; all cases are now being dealt with under the new procedures.

145 *Ibid*, reg 23(3).

146 *Ibid*, reg 25(3).

147 *Ibid*, reg 25(4).

148 Under reg 25(5) the complainant can be removed if he interrupts. Under reg 27, he can be excluded if matters arise which it would not be in the public interest to disclose to him.

149 Cm 4262-I (1999), Recommendation 58.

150 *Feasibility of an Independent System for Investigating Complaints Against the Police*, HO PRS Paper No 124 (2000).

151 *Complaints against the Police: Framework for a New System* (2001). See proposals: HL Deb vol 620 col WA45 (19 December 2000).